ENCYCLOPEDIA OF
COMMUNICATION
THEORY

Editorial Board

ENCYCLOPEDIA OF
COMMUNICATION THEORY

1

Stephen W. Littlejohn ∘ Karen A. Foss

University of New Mexico

EDITORS

Los Angeles | London | New Delhi
Singapore | Washington DC

A SAGE Reference Publication

For information:

 SAGE Publications, Inc.
2455 Teller Road
Thousand Oaks, California 91320
E-mail: order@sagepub.com

SAGE Publications Ltd.
1 Oliver's Yard
55 City Road
London, EC1Y 1SP
United Kingdom

SAGE Publications India Pvt. Ltd.
B 1/I 1 Mohan Cooperative Industrial Area
Mathura Road, New Delhi 110 044
India

SAGE Publications Asia-Pacific Pte. Ltd.
33 Pekin Street #02–01
Far East Square
Singapore 048763

Printed in the United States of America.

Library of Congress Cataloging-in-Publication Data
Encyclopedia of communication theory / Stephen W. Littlejohn, Karen A. Foss, editors.
    p. cm.
Includes bibliographical references and index.
ISBN 978-1-4129-5937-7 (cloth)

   1. Communication—Encyclopedias. 2. Information theory—Encyclopedias. 3. Linguistics—Encyclopedias. I. Littlejohn, Stephen W. II. Foss, Karen A.
P87.5.E496 2009
302.203—dc22   2009002948

This book is printed on acid-free paper.

10 11 12 13 10 9 8 7 6 5 4 3 2

Publisher:	Rolf A. Janke
Acquisitions Editor:	Jim Brace-Thompson
Editorial Assistant:	Michele Thompson
Developmental Editor:	Yvette Pollastrini
Reference Systems Manager:	Leticia Gutierrez
Reference Systems Coordinator:	Laura Notton
Production Editor:	Kate Schroeder
Copyeditors:	Bonnie Freeman, Renee Willers
Typesetter:	C&M Digitals (P) Ltd.
Proofreaders:	Kevin Gleason, Sandy Zilka Livingston
Indexer:	Joan Shapiro
Cover Designer:	Candice Harman
Marketing Manager:	Amberlyn McKay

Contents

List of Entries

Reader's Guide

The Reader's Guide is provided to assist readers in locating articles on related topics. It classifies entries into 17 general topical categories:

- Applications and Contexts
- Critical Orientations
- Cultural Orientations
- Cybernetic and Systems Orientations
- Feminist Orientations
- Group and Organizational Concepts
- Information, Media, and Communication Technology
- International and Global Concepts
- Interpersonal Concepts
- Non-Western Orientations
- Paradigms, Traditions, and Schools
- Philosophical Orientations
- Psycho-Cognitive Orientations
- Rhetorical Orientations
- Semiotic, Linguistic, and Discursive Orientations
- Social-Interactional Orientations
- Theory, Metatheory, Methodology, and Inquiry

Entries may be listed under more than one topic.

Applications and Contexts

Advertising Theories
Argumentation Theories
Broadcasting Theories
Campaign Communication Theories
Communication Across the Life Span
Communication in Later Life
Communication Skills Theories
Community
Competence Theories
Computer-Mediated Communication
Conflict Communication Theories
Corporate Campaign Theories
Cultivation Theory
Cultural Theories of Health Communication
Deliberative Democratic Theories
Entertainment–Education

Environmental Communication Theories
Ethics Theories
Family and Marital Schemas and Types
Family Communication Theories
Film Theories
Gay, Lesbian, Bisexual, and Transgender Theories
Globalization Theories
Group Communication Theories
Groupthink
Health Communication Theories
Humorous Communication Theory
Informatization
Intercultural Communication Theories
International Communication Theories
International Development Theories
Journalism and Theories of the Press
Learning and Communication

Legal Communication Theories
Media and Mass Communication Theories
Medium Theory
Negotiation Theory
Ordinary Democracy
Organizational Communication Theories
Political Communication Theories
Religious Communication Theories
Visual Communication Theories

Critical Orientations

Action-Implicative Discourse Analysis
Activity Theory
Americanization of Media
Archeology and Genealogy
Autoethnography
Black Feminist Epistemology
Chicana Feminism
Citizenship
Co-Cultural Theory
Complexity and Communication
Critical Communication Pedagogy
Critical Constructivism
Critical Discourse Analysis
Critical Ethnography
Critical Organizational Communication
Critical Race Theory
Critical Rhetoric
Critical Theory
Cultural Studies
Deconstruction
Diaspora
Digital Divide
Discourse Theory and Analysis
Existentialism
Feminist Communication Theories
Feminist Rhetorical Criticism
Feminist Standpoint Theory
Flow and Contra-Flow
Frankfurt School
French Feminism
Gay, Lesbian, Bisexual, and Transgender Theories
Gender and Media
Genderlect Theory
Hermeneutics
Hybridity
Identity Theories
Ideological Rhetoric
Ideology

Interracial Communication
Intersectionality
Marxist Theory
Materiality of Discourse
Media Sovereignty
Medium Theory
Muted Group Theory
Neocolonialism
New Media Theory
Positioning Theory
Postcolonial Feminism
Postcolonial Theory
Postmodern Theory
Poststructuralism
Power and Power Relations
Privilege
Propaganda Theory
Public Sphere
Queer Theory
Racial Formation Theory
Silence, Silences, and Silencing
Social Justice
Spectatorship
Structuration Theory
Transculturation
Vernacular Discourse
Whiteness Theory
Womanism

Cultural Orientations

Afrocentricity
Asian Communication Theory
Black Feminist Epistemology
Buddhist Communication Theory
Chicana Feminism
Chinese Harmony Theory
Chronemics
Co-Cultural Theory
Community
Community of Practice
Confucian Communication Theory
Contextual Theory of Interethnic
    Communication
Critical Ethnography
Critical Race Theory
Cross-Cultural Adaptation Theory
Cultivation Theory
Cultural Contracts Theory
Cultural Performance Theory

Cultural Studies
Cultural Theories of Health Communication
Cultural Types Theories
Culture and Communication
Diaspora
Effective Intercultural Workgroup
    Communication Theory
Ethnography of Communication
Ethnomethodology
Face Negotiation Theory
Fans, Fandom, and Fan Studies
Feminist Standpoint Theory
Gay, Lesbian, Bisexual, and Transgender Theories
Genderlect Theory
Gender Role Theory
Hindu Communication Theory
Hybridity
Identity Theories
Indian *Rasa* Theory
Informatization
Intercultural Communication Competence
Intercultural Communication Theories
Interpretive Theory
Interracial Communication
Intersectionality
Japanese *Kuuki* Theory
Latino Perspectives
Linguistic Relativity
Medium Theory
Membership Categorization Analysis (MCA)
Myth and Mythic Criticism
Neocolonialism
Organizational Culture
Performance Ethnography
Performance Theories
Popular Culture Theories
Postcolonial Theory
Privilege
Proxemics
Racial Formation Theory
Religious Communication Theories
Silence, Silences, and Silencing
Social Identity Theory
Social Justice
Speech Codes Theory
Taoist Communication Theory
Transculturation
Values Theory: Sociocultural Dimensions and
    Frameworks
Vernacular Discourse

Whiteness Theory
Womanism

Cybernetic and Systems Orientations

Actor–Network Theory
Autoethnography
Complexity and Communication
Convergence Theory
Coordinated Management of Meaning
Co-Orientation Theory
Cybernetics
Dual-Level Connectionist Models of Group
    Cognition and Social Influence
Functional Group
    Communication Theory
Information Theory
Mathematical Theory of
    Communication
Metacommunication
Organizational Co-Orientation Theory
Organizing, Process of
Palo Alto Group
Pragmatics
Relational Control Theory
Relational Dialectics
Stakeholder Theory
Structuration Theory
System Theory

Feminist Orientations

Black Feminist Epistemology
Chicana Feminism
Feminist Communication Theories
Feminist Rhetorical Criticism
Feminist Standpoint Theory
French Feminism
Gender and Media
Genderlect Theory
Gender Role Theory
Gender Schema Theory
Intersectionality
Invitational Rhetoric
Muted Group Theory
Postcolonial Feminism
Power and Power Relations
Queer Theory
Womanism

Group and Organizational Concepts

Actor–Network Theory
Bona Fide Group Theory
Campaign Communication Theories
Collective Information Sampling
Community
Community of Practice
Co-Orientation Theory
Corporate Campaign Theories
Creativity in Groups
Critical Organizational Communication
Cross-Cultural Decision Making
Dual-Level Connectionist Models of Group
    Cognition and Social Influence
Effective Intercultural Workgroup
    Communication Theory
Field Theory of Conflict
Functional Group Communication Theory
Group Communication Theories
Groupthink
Health Communication Theories
Institutional Theories of Organizational
    Communication
Interaction Process Analysis
Leadership Theories
Media Richness Theory
Membership Categorization Analysis (MCA)
Organizational Communication Theories
Organizational Control Theory
Organizational Co-Orientation Theory
Organizational Culture
Organizational Identity Theory
Organizational Socialization and Assimilation
Organizing, Process of
Sense-Making
Social Identity Theory
Stakeholder Theory
Symbolic-Interpretive Perspective on Groups

Information, Media, and Communication Technology

Activation Theory of Information Exposure
Advertising Theories
Affect-Dependent Theory of Stimulus
    Arrangements
Agenda-Setting Theory
Americanization of Media
Audience Theories
Broadcasting Theories

Campaign Communication Theories
Communication in Later Life
Computer-Mediated Communication
Corporate Campaign Theories
Critical Theory
Cultivation Theory
Cultural Studies
Diaspora
Diffusion of Innovations
Digital Divide
Discourse Theory and Analysis
Documentary Film Theories
Entertainment–Education
Environmental Communication Theories
Expectancy Violations Theory
Fans, Fandom, and Fan Studies
Film Theories
Flow and Contra-Flow
Framing Theory
Frankfurt School
Gender and Media
Globalization Theories
Health Communication Theories
Information Theory
Informatization
International Development Theories
Interpretive Communities Theory
Journalism and Theories of the Press
Marxist Theory
Materiality of Discourse
Media and Mass Communication Theories
Media Democracy
Media Diplomacy
Media Effects Theories
Media Equation Theory
Media Ethics Theories
Media Richness Theory
Media Sovereignty
Medium Theory
Membership Categorization Analysis (MCA)
Motivated Information Management Theory
Neocolonialism
Network Society
New Media Theory
New World Information and Communication
    Order (NWICO)
Political Communication Theories
Popular Culture Theories
Postcolonial Theory
Presence Theory

Non-Western Orientations

Paradigms, Traditions, and Schools

Philosophical Orientations

Psycho-Cognitive Orientations

Rhetorical Orientations

Metaphor
Myth and Mythic Criticism
Narrative and Narratology
Organizational Control Theory
Political Communication Theories
Religious Communication Theories
Rhetorical Sensitivity
Symbolic Convergence Theory
Visual Communication Theories

Semiotic, Linguistic, and Discursive Orientations

Accounts and Account Giving
Action-Implicative Discourse Analysis
Activity Theory
Actor–Network Theory
Archeology and Genealogy
Argumentation Theories
Autoethnography
Chronemics
Classical Rhetorical Theory
Constitutive View of Communication
Conversational Constraints Theory
Conversation Analysis
Critical Discourse Analysis
Cultural Studies
Deconstruction
Ethnomethodology
Feminist Rhetorical Criticism
Genderlect Theory
General Semantics
Genre Theory
Hermeneutics
Identification
Ideological Rhetoric
Interpretive Theory
Intrapersonal Communication Theories
Kinesics
Language and Communication
Linguistic Relativity
Materiality of Discourse
Meaning Theories
Metacommunication
Metaphor
Narrative and Narratology
Neocolonialism

Nonverbal Communication Theories
Paralanguage
Politeness Theory
Popular Culture Theories
Positioning Theory
Poststructuralism
Proxemics
Semiotics and Semiology
Silence, Silences, and Silencing
Speech Act Theory
Speech Codes Theory
Stories and Storytelling
Symbolic Convergence Theory
Symbolic Interactionism
Visual Communication Theories

Social-Interactional Orientations

Accounts and Account Giving
Action-Implicative Discourse Analysis
Activity Theory
Actor–Network Theory
Agency
Agenda-Setting Theory
Audience Theories
Autoethnography
Bona Fide Group Theory
Communication and Language Acquisition and
    Development
Communication Theory of Identity
Community
Community of Practice
Consequentiality of Communication
Constitutive View of Communication
Conversational Constraints Theory
Conversation Analysis
Coordinated Management of Meaning
Co-Orientation Theory
Cultural Performance Theory
Dialogue Theories
Diffusion of Innovations
Discourse Theory and Analysis
Dramatism and Dramatistic Pentad
Ethnomethodology
Facework Theories
Framing Theory
Functional Group Communication Theory

Theory, Metatheory, Methodology, and Inquiry

Theorists

(Continued)

Theorists	Entry Titles
Bem, Sandra	Gender Schema Theory Power, Interpersonal Rules Theories
Benjamin, Walter	Critical Theory Frankfurt School
Bennett, Lance	Legal Communication Theories
Bentham, Jeremy	Ethics Theories
Berger, Charles	Cognitive Theories Communication Goal Theories Intercultural Communication Theories Interpersonal Communication Theories Relational Uncertainty Uncertainty Management Theories Uncertainty Reduction Theory
Berger, Peter	Ethnomethodology Language and Communication Institutional Theories of Organizational Communication Social Construction of Reality
Berlo, David	Empathy Process of Communication
Bernstein, Basil	Elaborated and Restricted Codes
Bertalanffy, Ludwig	System Theory
Bhabha, Homi K.	Hybridity Postcolonial Theory
Bharata	Indian *Rasa* Theory
Bhartrhari	Asian Communication Theory Hindu Communication Theory
Billig, Michael	Discourse Theory and Analysis
Biocca, Frank	Presence Theory
Birdsell, David	Interpersonal Communication Theories Legal Communication Theories Nonverbal Communication Theories

Theorists	Entry Titles
Birdwhistell, Ray	Kinesics Rules Theories Social Interaction Theories
Bitzer, Lloyd	Rhetorical Theory
Blake, Robert	Conflict Communication Theories
Blumer, Herbert	Grounded Theory Interpersonal Communication Theories Learning and Communication Symbolic Interactionism
Blumler, Jay	Audience Theories Uses, Gratifications, and Dependency
Bohm, David	Dialogue Theories
Borel, Marie-Jeanne	Constructivism
Bormann, Ernest G.	Group Communication Theories Symbolic Convergence Theory
Bosmajian, Haig	Legal Communication Theories
Boulding, Elise	Peace Theories
Boulding, Kenneth	Peace Theories
Bourdieu, Pierre	Learning and Communication Popular Culture Theories
Bowlby, John	Attachment Theory
Boyd-Barrett, Oliver	Flow and Contra-Flow
Brashers, Dale	Motivated Information Management Theory Uncertainty Management Theories
Brown, Penelope	Accounts and Account Giving Compliance-Gaining Strategies Facework Theories Impression Management Interpersonal Communication Theories Politeness Theory

Theorists	Entry Titles	Theorists	Entry Titles
Cheney, George	Critical Organizational Communication Organizational Control Theory Organizational Culture Organizational Identity Theory	Cooley, Charles	Interpretive Theory Learning and Communication Symbolic Interactionism Traditions of Communication Theory

Chomsky, Noam	Communication and Language
	   Acquisition and Development
	Consequentiality of Communication
	Critical Discourse Analysis
	Language and Communication
	Propaganda Theory
	Rules Theories
		Cooren, François	Actor–Network Theory
			Constitutive View of Communication
			Organizational Communication
			   Theories

		Craig, Robert T.	Constitutive View of Communication Practical Theory
Christians, Clifford	Media Ethics Theories	Crenshaw, Kimberlé	Critical Race Theory Intersectionality
Cialdini, Robert	Compliance Gaining Strategies	Cronen, Vernon	Coordinated Management of Meaning Interpersonal Communication Theories Practical Theory Rules Theories
Cicero	Classical Rhetorical Theory Legal Communication Theories Metaphor Rhetorical Theory		
		Crystal, David	Paralanguage
Cixous, Hèléne	Feminist Communication Theories French Feminism	Cua, Antonio	Asian Communication Theory
Cloud, Dana L.	Ideology Materiality of Discourse	Cupach, William	Communication Skills Theories Competence Theories Identity Theories
Cohen, Bernard	Media Effects Theories	Daft, Richard	Media Richness Theory

Collier, Mary
  Jane
	Cultural Identity Theory
	Culture and Communication
	Identity Theories
		Dance,
		  Frank E. X.
			Communication and Language
			   Acquisition and Development

Collins, Patricia
  Hill
	Black Feminist Epistemology
	Womanism
		Darwin, Charles	Cultural Types Theories
			Nonverbal Communication
			   Theories
			Realism and the Received View
			System Theory

Condit, Celeste	Feminist Communication Theories		
Coney, Russell	Advertising Theories		

Confucius	Confucian Communication Theory
	Ethics Theories
	Taoist Communication Theory
	Values Studies: History and Concepts
		Deetz, Stanley A.	Corporate Colonization Theory
			Critical Organizational
			   Communication
			Organizational Communication
			   Theories

Conquergood,
  Dwight
	Critical Ethnography
	Cultural Performance Theory
	Performance Ethnography
	Performance Theories
		DeFleur, Marvin	Uses, Gratifications, and
			   Dependency

		De la Garza, Sarah Amira	Chicana Feminism Latino Perspectives
		Deleuze, Gilles	Film Theories

(Continued)

Theorists	Entry Titles	Theorists	Entry Titles
Fishbein, Martin	Persuasion and Social Influence Theories Reasoned Action Theory Uses, Gratifications, and Dependency	Frentz, Thomas	Myth and Mythic Criticism Rules Theories
Fisher, Roger	Negotiation Theory	Freud, Sigmund	Agency Critical Theory Humorous Communication Theory Spectatorship
Fisher, Walter	Narrative and Narratology		
Fiske, John	Popular Culture Theories	Friesen, Wallace	Kinesics Nonverbal Communication Theories
Fitzpatrick, Mary Anne	Conflict Communication Theories Family and Marital Schemas and Types Family Communication Theories Relational Communication Theory	Gadamer, Hans Georg.	Dialogue Theories Ethnomethodology Hermeneutics Interpretive Theory Modernism Stories and Storytelling Traditions of Communication Theory
Foerster, Heinz von	Cybernetics System Theory		
Foss, Sonja K.	Feminist Communication Theories		
Foss, Sonja	Feminist Communication Theories Invitational Rhetoric	Galtung, Johan	Peace Theories
Foucault, Michel	Archeology and Genealogy Critical Constructivism Critical Discourse Analysis Critical Rhetoric Critical Theory Discourse Theory and Analysis Ethics Theories Ideology Materiality of Discourse Neocolonialism Popular Culture Theories Postmodern Theory Poststructuralism Practical Theory Queer Theory Rhetorical Theory	Gardner, Howard	Learning and Communication
		Garfinkel, Herbert	Conversation Analysis Ethnomethodology Rules Theories
		Gearhart, Sally Miller	Feminist Communication Theories Invitational Rhetoric
		Geertz, Clifford	Dramatism and Dramatistic Pentad Intercultural Communication Theories Interpretive Theory Organizational Culture Stories and Storytelling
		Gerbner, George	Broadcasting Theories Cultivation Theory Cultural Indicators Gender and Media Media Effects Theories Violence and Nonviolence in Media Studies
Freire, Paulo	Critical Communication Pedagogy Dialogue Theories Learning and Communication		
French, John R. P.	Compliance Gaining Strategies Dyadic Power Theory Power, Interpersonal	Ghandi, Mohandas	Violence and Nonviolence in Media Studies

(Continued)

Theorists	Entry Titles	Theorists	Entry Titles
Habermas, Jürgen	Asian Communication Theory Communicative Action Theory Competence Theories Corporate Colonization Theory Critical Constructivism Critical Discourse Analysis Critical Organizational Communication Critical Theory Culture and Communication Deliberative Democratic Theories Ethics Theories Frankfurt School Globalization Theories Hermeneutics Media Ethics Theories Medium Theory Metatheory Modernism in Communication Theory Political Communication Theories Power and Power Relations Public Opinion Theories Public Sphere Rhetorical Theory Social Interaction Theories Traditions of Communication Theory	Hall, Stuart	Audience Theories Broadcasting Theories Critical Discourse Analysis Cultural Studies Culture and Communication Fans, Fandom, and Fan Studies Language and Communication Power and Power Relations Visual Communication Theories
		Halliday, Michael A. K.	Critical Discourse Analysis
		Hamelink, Cees	International Communication Theories
		Harraway, Donna	Feminist Standpoint Theory
		Harré, Rom	Positioning Theory
		Harris, Tina M.	Interracial Communication
		Harris, Zelig	Discourse Theory and Analysis
		Hart, Roderick	Theory Rhetorical Sensitivity
Hall, Edward T.	Chronemics Cultural Types Theories Culture and Communication Intercultural Communication Theories Interpersonal Communication Theories Nonverbal Communication Theories Popular Culture Theories Proxemics Rules Theories Values Theory: Sociocultural Dimensions and Frameworks	Harwood, Jake	Communication in Later Life
		Hasain, Marouf	Legal Communication Theories
		Hebdidge, Dick	Fans, Fandom, and Fan Studies
		Hecht, Michael	Communication Theory of Identity Cultural Identity Theory Identity Theories Interracial Communication
		Hegde, Radha	Feminist Communication Theories Postcolonial Feminism Postcolonial Theory
		Hegel, Georg	System Theory
		Heidegger, Martin	Critical Theory Hermeneutics Phenomenology Traditions of Communication Theory

(Continued)

Theorists	Entry Titles	Theorists	Entry Titles
Jackson, Ronald L., II	Cultural Contracts Theory Identity Theories Interracial Communication	Katz, Elihu	Audience Theories Media Effects Theories Two-Step and Multi-Step Flow Uses, Gratifications, and Dependency
Jackson, Sally	Language and Communication Practical Theory	Keane, John	Media Democracy
Jacobs, Scott	Language and Communication	Kelley, Harold	Attribution Theory Interpersonal Communication Theories
James, William	Interpretive Theory		
Jakobson, Roman	Poststructuralism Pragmatics	Kelly, George	Constructivism
Jamieson, Kathleen	Feminist Communication Theories Genre Theory	Kelman, Herbert	Attitude Theory
		Key, Valdimer O.	Public Opinion Theories
Janis, Irving	Functional Group Communication Theory Group Communication Theories Groupthink	Kilmann, Ralph	Conflict Communication Theories
		Kim, Min-Sun	Conversational Constraints Theory
Jefferson, Gail	Conversation Analysis Language and Communication	Kim, Young Yun	Contextual Theory of Interethnic Communication Cross-Cultural Adaptation Theory Cross-Cultural Communication Identity Theories
Jenkins, Henry	Fans, Fandom, and Fan Studies New Media Theory		
Jenkins, Steven	Ideological Rhetoric	Kincaid, D. Lawrence	Convergence Theory
Jensen, Klaus Bruhn	Interpretive Communities Theory		
		Kintsch, Walter	Cognitive Theories
Johannesen, Richard	Dialogue Theories	Klapper, Joseph	Media Effects Theories Spiral Models of Media Effects
Jones, Edward	Impression Management	Klein, Gary	Sense-Making
Jourard, Sydney	Self-Disclosure	Kluckhohn, Clyde	Values Studies: History and Concepts Values Theory: Sociocultural Dimensions and Frameworks
Jung, Carl	Myth and Mythic Criticism		
Kahneman, Daniel	Cognitive Theories	Knapp, Mark	Interpersonal Communication Theories Relational Communication Theory Relational Development
Kant, Immanuel	Agency Ethics Theories Media Ethics Theories Modernism in Communication Theory		
		Knobloch, Leanne K.	Relational Uncertainty
Karatani, Kojin	Popular Culture Theories	Koerner, Ascan F.	Conflict Communication Theories Family and Marital Schemas and Types Family Communication Theories Relational Communication Theory
Katz, Daniel	Attitude Theory		

(Continued)

Theorists	Entry Titles	Theorists	Entry Titles
Lindlof, Thomas R.	Interpretive Communities Theory	Marwell, Gerald	Compliance Gaining Strategies
Lippmann, Walter	Corporate Campaign Theories Framing Theory Learning and Communication Public Opinion Theories	Marx, Karl	Agency Critical Discourse Analysis Frankfurt School Ideology Marxist Theory Power and Power Relations System Theory Traditions of Communication Theory
Littlejohn, Stephen W.	Conflict Communication Theories		
Lombard, Matthew	Presence Theory	Maslow, Abraham	Humanistic Perspective
Luckmann, Thomas	Ethnomethodology Language and Communication Social Construction of Reality	Matson, Floyd	Dialogue Theories
		Mattelart, Armand	International Communication Theories
Luhmann, Niklas	Cybernetics	Maturana, Humberto	Constructivism Cybernetics
Lull, James	Social Action Media Studies	McCombs, Maxwell	Agenda-Setting Theory Broadcasting Theories Framing Theory Media Effects Theories Political Communication Theories Public Opinion Theories
Lundsford, Andrea	Feminist Communication Theories		
Lyman, Stanford	Accounts and Account Giving		
Lyotard, Francois	Narrative and Narratology Popular Culture Theories Poststructuralism	McCornack, Steven	Deception Detection
Madison, Soyini	Performance Ethnography Performance Theories	McCroskey, James C.	Communibiology Social and Communicative Anxiety Trait Theory
Manalansan, Martin	Queer Theory	McGee, Michael	Critical Rhetoric Critical Theory Ideological Rhetoric Myth and Mythic Criticism
Marcuse, Herbert	Broadcasting Theories Critical Constructivism Critical Theory Frankfurt School Popular Culture Theories Power and Power Relations		
		McGrew, Anthony	Globalization Theories
Marshall, T. H.	Citizenship	McGuire, William	Attitude Theory Inoculation Theory Persuasion and Social Influence Theories
Martin, Judith	Identity Theories		
Martinez, Jacqueline	Latino Perspectives	McIntosh, Peggy	Privilege

(Continued)

Theorists	Entry Titles	Theorists	Entry Titles
Newcomb, Theodore	Co-Orientation Theory	Osborn, Michael M.	Metaphor Myth and Mythic Criticism
Nietzsche, Friedrich	Agency Ethics Theories Interpretive Theory	Osgood, Charles	Cross-Cultural Communication Persuasion and Social Influence Theories
Noddings, Nel	Ethics Theories	Pacanowsky, Michael	Organizational Communication Theories Organizational Culture
Noelle-Neumann, Elisabeth	Broadcasting Theories Japanese *Kuuki* Theory Media Effects Theories Public Opinion Theories Spiral Models of Media Effects Spiral of Silence	Palmgreen, Phillip	Activation Theory of Information Exposure Uses, Gratifications, and Dependency
Norton, Robert	Style, Communicator Trait Theories	Panini	Asian Communication Theory
Nussbaum, Jon	Communication Across the Life Span	Parameswaran, Radhika	Cultural Studies Postcolonial Feminism
O'Donnell-Trujillo, Nick	Organizational Communication Theories Organizational Culture	Paramitas	Ethics Theories
		Paredes, Américo	Latino Perspectives
Oetzel, John G.	Conflict Communication Theories Effective Intercultural Workgroup Communication Theory	Parsons, Talcott	Values Studies: History and Concepts Values Theory: Sociocultural Dimensions and Frameworks
Ogawa, Dennis	Interracial Communication	Pearce, W. Barnett	Conflict Communication Theories Coordinated Management of Meaning Interpersonal Communication Theories Rules Theories
Ogden, C. K.	Meaning Theories		
Olien, Clarice	Public Opinion Theories		
Olson, David	Family Communication Theories		
Olson, Scot Robert	International Communication Theories	Peirce, Charles S.	Interpretive Communities Theory Interpretive Theory Meaning Theories Semiotics and Semiology Traditions of Communication Theory
Omi, Michael	Racial Formation Theory		
Ong, Walter	Meaning Theories Medium Theory		
Ono, Kent	Vernacular Discourse	Perelman, Chaïm	Argumentation Theories Rhetorical Theory
Oravec, Christine	Environmental Communication Theories	Peterson, Eric	Performance Theories
Orbe, Mark P.	Co-Cultural Theory Identity Theories Interracial Communication	Peterson, Theodore	Journalism and Theories of the Press
Ortiz, Fernando	Transculturation	Petronio, Sandra	Self-Disclosure Privacy Management Theory

(Continued)

Theorists	Entry Titles	Theorists	Entry Titles
Ricoeur, Paul	Critical Organizational Communication Hermeneutics	Saussure, Ferdinand de	Consequentiality of Communication Cultural Studies Documentary Film Theories Film Theories Language and Communication Meaning Theories Poststructuralism Rules Theories Semiotics and Semiology Traditions of Communication Theory
Robinson, John	Two-Step and Multi-Step Flow		
Rogers, Carl	Dialogue Theories Empathy Humanistic Perspective Rogerian Dialogue Theory Traditions of Communication Theory		
Rogers, Everett M.	Culture and Communication Diffusion of Innovations Entertainment–Education Two-Step and Multi-Step Flow	Schank, Roger	Cognitive Theories
		Schechner, Richard	Cultural Performance Theory Performance Ethnography Performance Theories
Rogers, L. Edna	Relational Communication Theory Relational Control Theory	Schegloff, Emmanuel	Conversation Analysis Language and Communication Rules Theories
Rollins, Boyd C.	Dyadic Power Theory	Schein, Edgar	Organizational Socialization and Assimilation
Roskos-Ewoldsen, David	Cognitive Theories		
Rowe, Aimee Carrillo	Privilege	Schenk-Hamlin, William	Compliance Gaining Strategies
Ruesch, Jürgen	Pragmatics	Schiller, Herbert	Flow and Contra-Flow Free Flow Doctrine Globalization Theories International Communication Theories Power and Power Relations
Russell, Daniel	Sense-Making		
Rust, Paula	Gay, Lesbian, Bisexual, and Transgender Theories		
Sacks, Harvey	Conversation Analysis Ethnomethodology Language and Communication Membership Categorization Analysis (MCA) Rules Theories	Schleiermacher, Friedrich	Hermeneutics Interpretive Theory
		Schmidt, David	Compliance Gaining Strategies
		Schramm, Wilbur	Constitutive View of Communication Journalism and Theories of the Press Media and Mass Communication Theories Propaganda Theory
Said, Edward	Culture and Communication Dramatism and Dramatistic Pentad Postcolonial Theory		
Sanchez, George	Latino Perspectives	Schutz, Alfred	Ethnomethodology Social Action Media Studies
Śankara, Adi	Hindu Communication Theory	Schutz, William	Interpersonal Communication Theories
Sapir, Edward	Cultural Types Theories Linguistic Relativity	Schwartz, Shalom	Values Theory: Sociocultural Dimensions and Frameworks

(Continued)

Theorists	Entry Titles	Theorists	Entry Titles
Sudnow, David	Conversation Analysis	Tölölyan, Khachig	Diaspora
Sunzi	Asian Communication Theory	Tompkins, Philip	Critical Organizational Communication Organizational Control Theory Organizational Culture Organizational Identity Theory
Swales, John	Community		
Tajfel, Henri	Identity Theories		
Tannen, Deborah	Genderlect Theory Gender Role Theory Rules Theories Social Interaction Theories		
		Toulmin, Stephen	Argumentation Theories Constructivism Critical Constructivism
Tarde, Gabriel	Diffusion of Innovations	Tracy, Karen	Action-Implicative Discourse Analysis Ordinary Democracy
Taussig, Michael	Silence, Silences, and Silencing		
Taylor, Dalmas	Interpersonal Communication Theories Relational Communication Theory Self-Disclosure	Trager, George	Paralanguage
		Triandis, Harry	Cross-Cultural Communication Values Theory: Sociocultural Dimensions and Frameworks
Taylor, James	Actor–Network Theory Constitutive View of Communication Organizational Communication Theories Organizational Co-Orientation Theory	Tuchman, Gaye	Gender and Media
		Tunstall, Jeremy	Flow and Contra-Flow
		Turkle, Sherry	New Media Theory
		Turner, John C.	Identity Theories
te Molder, Hedwig	Discourse Theory and Analysis	Turner, Victor	Cultural Performance Theory Performance Ethnography Performance Theories
Tenayuca, Emma	Latino Perspectives		
		Ury, William	Negotiation Theory
Thibault, John	Interpersonal Communication Theories	Van Dijk, Jan	Network Society
		Van Dijk, Teun	Cognitive Theories Critical Discourse Analysis Discourse Theory and Analysis
Thomas, Kenneth	Conflict Communication Theories		
Thomas, William	Attitude Theory Interpretive Theory Symbolic Interactionism Values Studies: History and Concepts	Van Eemeren, Frans	Argumentation Theories
		Van Elteren, Mel	Americanization of Media
Tichenor, Phillip	Public Opinion Theories	Van Langenhove	Positioning Theory
Ting-Toomey, Stella	Conflict Communication Theories Cross-Cultural Communication Face Negotiation Theory Facework Theories Identity Theories Intercultural Communication Theories	Van Maanen, John	Organizational Socialization and Assimilation
		Varela, Francisco	Constructivism Cybernetics
		von Neumann, John	Cybernetics Organizational Co-Orientation Theory

(Continued)

About the Editors and Editorial Board

General Editors

Stephen W. Littlejohn is an adjunct professor of communication and journalism at the University of New Mexico. He is also a communication consultant and mediator. He has a long-standing interest in communication theory, having coauthored *Theories of Human Communication*, currently going into its 10th edition. In addition to numerous papers and articles, Littlejohn has also coauthored several books, including *Moral Conflict: When Social Worlds Collide*, *Elements of Speech Communication*, *Persuasive Transactions*, *Engaging Communication in Conflict: Systemic Practice*, *Mediation: Empowerment in Conflict Management*, *Facework: Bridging Theory and Practice*, and *Communication, Conflict, and the Management of Difference*. He received his PhD in communication at the University of Utah.

Karen A. Foss is a regents professor and a professor of communication and journalism at the University of New Mexico. She earned a PhD in communication from the University of Iowa and an MA in communication from the University of Oregon, and she has been at the forefront of bringing issues of gender and feminist perspectives into the communication discipline. She was named Scholar of the Year at Humboldt State University, a Presidential Teaching Fellow at the University of New Mexico, and Gender Scholar of the Year for 2005 by the Southern Communication Association. She also was awarded the Francine Merritt Award, given by the National Communication Association, for contributions to the lives of women in communication. She is the coauthor of *Contemporary Perspectives on Rhetoric*, *Women Speak: The Eloquence of Women's Lives*, *Inviting Transformation: Presentational Speaking for a Changing World*, *Feminist Rhetorical Theories*, and *Theories of Human Communication*, which have consistently defined and challenged the communication discipline.

Editorial Board

Brenda J. Allen is an associate dean in the College of Liberal Arts and Sciences and a professor in the Department of Communication at the University of Colorado Denver. Her research and teaching areas are organizational communication, social identity, social construction, critical pedagogy, and computer-mediated communication. Among her numerous publications is a groundbreaking book titled *Difference Matters: Communicating Social Identity*. She is a coeditor of the *International and Intercultural Communication Annual*, and she recently received a Master Teacher Award from the Western States Communication Association.

J. Kevin Barge is a professor of communication at Texas A&M University. He received his MA and PhD degrees from the University of Kansas. His research interests center on developing a social constructionist approach to management and leadership, exploring the role of appreciative forms of communication to transform organizations and articulating the relationship between dialogue and organizing in organizational and community contexts. His research has been published in the *Academy of Management Review*, *Management Communication Quarterly*, *Journal of Applied Communication Research*, *The OD Practitioner*, *Communication Theory*, and *Communication Monographs*.

Roger de la Garde is a retired professor of sociology, Department of Communication, Laval University (Quebec, Canada). Still active in the academic field, he continues to supervise doctoral theses and remains is editor of the scientific journal *Communication*, which he cofounded in 1975. Past president of the Canadian Communication Association, his research interests and publications cover popular culture, mass communication, ideology, public discourse, and identity. He has contributed to the *Canadian Journal of Communication; Media, Culture & Society;* and the *Encyclopedia of Television.* He is a member of the editorial board of *Communication Theory* and *Cyberlegenda.*

Lisa A. Flores is an associate professor of communication at the University of Colorado Boulder. Her research explores rhetorical dynamics of domination and subordination, principally as linked to race and gender. Current projects include a rhetorical history of Mexican immigrants and Mexican Americans and a rhetorical analysis of contemporary representations of masculinity. Her work has appeared in such places as the *Quarterly Journal of Speech, Critical Studies in Media Communication,* and *Text and Performance Quarterly.*

Vijai N. Giri is an associate professor in the Department of Humanities & Social Sciences, Indian Institute of Technology, Kharagpur, India. He received his PhD in *Interpersonal Communication* from Indian Institute of Technology Kharagpur in January 2002. He has been teaching undergraduate, postgraduate, and MBA students since 1984. His excellent academic record is evidenced by his many awards and distinctions. To mention a few, he was awarded the National Merit Scholarship and the *German Academic Exchange Service* (DAAD) Fellowship, and he has visited Germany several times to conduct his research in the area of organizational-intercultural communication. He has published a book, six book chapters, and about 30 research articles in refereed journals. He is a member of the editorial board of *Communication Theory.* He worked as the guest editor of *International Journal of Communication* and ad hoc reviewer of *Social Behaviour and Personality: An International Journal.* He organizes short-term training programs on *Interpersonal Communication* for college teachers and middle-level managers. His current research interests include interpersonal, intercultural, and organizational communication.

Charlotte Krøłøkke holds a PhD and serves as an associate professor of communication and cultural studies at the Institute of Literature, Culture and Media at the University of Southern Denmark. She is the coauthor of *Gender Communication Theories and Analyses: From Silence to Performance* and the author of several articles within the areas of computer-mediated communication, gender and technology, and reproductive technology. She is currently working on a project on three-dimensional fetal ultrasound imaging in which focus rests on the ways in which participants assign personhood, gender, and nationality to the fetus. Krøłøkke is also board member of the Danish National Gender Association and vice-chair of the board of the Danish National Gender Library, Kvinfo.

Mark P. Orbe received his PhD from Ohio University and is a professor of communication and diversity in the School of Communication at Western Michigan University where he holds a joint appointment in the Gender and Women's Program. His teaching and research interests center on the inextricable relationship between culture and communication as played out in a number of contexts (intrapersonal, interpersonal, intergroup, mass media). He has presented over 80 papers at regional, national, and international academic conferences, published close to 75 articles in scholarly journals or chapters in edited books. He has also published seven books to date, including the seminal work, *Constructing Co-Cultural Theory: An Explication of Culture, Power, and Communication.* Orbe is the immediate past editor of *The Journal of Intergroup Relations,* current coeditor of *The International and Intercultural Communication Annual,* as well as the guest editor of a *Critical Studies in Media Communication* special issue on race and reality TV.

James Taylor is a professor emeritus of communication science at the Université de Montréal, a department that he initiated as its first chair in 1970. His role in developing communication studies in Canada was recognized by the university at the time of its hundredth anniversary, by naming him one of its pioneers. Author or coauthor of eight books and nearly a hundred published papers, he was honored by being named Fellow of the International Communication Association in 2007. His role in breaking new ground in the development of a theory of communication as the basis of organization has recently been recognized by the holding of a major international conference that addresses this theme in May of 2008. He is now preparing a new book aimed at publication in 2009.

Ingrid Volkmer is an associate professor of media and communication, University of Melbourne, Australia. She has held visiting appointments at Harvard and MIT. Her main field of interest is the influence of globalization on public cultures of vari-ous societies. She has published widely in this area. Among her latest publications are *News in Public Memory* and an article, "Governing the Spatial Reach: Sphere of Influence and Challenges to Global Media Policy." Volkmer is an associate editor of the *Encyclopedia Globalization* and serves as chair of the Philosophy of Communication Division of the International Communication Association and on the advisory board of various journals, such as *Global Media & Communication.*

Contributors

Walid Afifi
*University of California,
Santa Barbara*

Brenda J. Allen
University of Colorado Denver

Mark DaCosta Alleyne
Georgia State University

Hector Amaya
Southwestern University

Peter A. Andersen
San Diego State University

Rob Anderson
Saint Louis University

Pat Arneson
Duquesne University

John Arthos
Denison University

Molefi Kete Asante
Temple University

Austin S. Babrow
Purdue University

J. Kevin Barge
Texas A&M University

Leslie A. Baxter
University of Iowa

Michael J. Beatty
University of Miami

Tim Berard
Kent State University

Teresa Bergman
University of the Pacific

Joseph A. Bonito
University of Arizona

Robert Bostrom
University of Kentucky

Jonathan M. Bowman
University of San Diego

Oliver Boyd-Barrett
Bowling Green State University

Janet A. Bridges
Sam Houston State University

Benjamin J. Broome
Arizona State University

Larry Browning
University of Texas at Austin

Tom Bruneau
Radford University

Judee K. Burgoon
University of Arizona

Rhiannon Bury
Athabasca University

Kristina Busse
University of South Alabama

Milton N. Campos
Université de Montréal

Robert E. Carlson
*University of Nebraska
at Omaha*

John Carr
University of New Mexico

Donald J. Cegala
Ohio State University

Briankle G. Chang
*University of Massachusetts
Amherst*

Karma R. Chávez
University of New Mexico

Guo-Ming Chen
University of Rhode Island

Young Cheon Cho
*California State University,
Chico*

Kenneth N. Cissna
University of South Florida

Dana L. Cloud
University of Texas at Austin

Joelle Collier
College of Santa Fe

Mary Jane Collier
University of New Mexico

François Cooren
Université de Montréal

Steven Corman
Arizona State University

Patricia Olivia Covarrubias
Baillet
University of New Mexico

Bryan Crable
Villanova University

Robert T. Craig
University of Colorado Boulder

Janet M. Cramer
University of New Mexico

Stuart Cunningham
Queensland University of Technology

Fabienne Darling-Wolf
Temple University

John J. Davies
Brigham Young University

Dennis K. Davis
Penn State University

Olga Idriss Davis
Arizona State University

Roger de la Garde
Laval University

Sarah Amira De la Garza
Arizona State University

Stanley A. Deetz
University of Colorado Boulder

Sarah E. Dempsey
University of North Carolina at Chapel Hill

Alan R. Dennis
Indiana University

Brenda Dervin
Ohio State University

Elizabeth A. Dickinson
University of New Mexico

Wimal Dissanayake
University of Hawai'i

Lewis Donohew
University of Kentucky

Norah E. Dunbar
University of Oklahoma

Deborah Dunn
Westmont College

Mohan J. Dutta
Purdue University

Amy Ebesu Hubbard
University of Hawai'i at Manoa

Eric M. Eisenberg
University of South Florida

Donald Ellis
University of Hartford

Valentín Escudero
University of La Coruña

Lisa A. Flores
University of Colorado Boulder

Karen A. Foss
University of New Mexico

Sonja K. Foss
University of Colorado Denver

Lawrence R. Frey
University of Colorado Boulder

Shiv Ganesh
Waikato Management School

Robert H. Gass
California State University, Fullerton

John Gastil
University of Washington

Kathleen M. German
Miami University

Howard Giles
University of California, Santa Barbara

Vijai N. Giri
Indian Institute of Technology Kharagpur, India

Daena J. Goldsmith
Lewis & Clark College

Loril M. Gossett
University of North Carolina at Charlotte

John O. Greene
Purdue University

Kathryn Greene
Rutgers University

Ronald Walter Greene
University of Minnesota

Cindy L. Griffin
Colorado State University

Shelton A. Gunaratne
Minnesota State University Moorhead

Joshua Gunn
University of Texas at Austin

Eddie Harmon-Jones
Texas A&M University

Robert Hassan
University of Melbourne

Michael L. Hecht
Pennsylvania State University

Dean E. Hewes
University of Minnesota

Charles A. Hill
University of Wisconsin–Oshkosh

David Holmes
Monash University

Youichi Ito
Akita International University

Ronald L. Jackson II
University of Illinois at Urbana-Champaign

Fern L. Johnson
Clark University

Vamsee Juluri
University of San Francisco

Min-Sun Kim
University of Hawai'i at Manoa

Young Yun Kim
University of Oklahoma

D. Lawrence Kincaid
*Johns Hopkins Bloomberg
School of Public Health*

Leanne K. Knobloch
University of Illinois

Ascan F. Koerner
University of Minnesota

Cheris Kramarae
University of Oregon

Gary L. Kreps
George Mason University

Klaus Krippendorff
University of Pennsylvania

Charlotte Kroløkke
*University of Southern
Denmark*

Steve J. Kulich
*Shanghai International Studies
University*

Teruyuki Kume
Rikkyo University

John C. Lammers
University of Illinois

James P. Lantolf
Penn State University

Kwan Min Lee
*University of Southern
California*

Wendy Leeds-Hurwitz
*University of Wisconsin–
Parkside*

Thomas R. Lindlof
University of Kentucky

Lisbeth Lipari
Denison University

Stephen W. Littlejohn
University of New Mexico

Owen Hanley Lynch
*Southern Methodist
University*

Susan Mackey-Kallis
Villanova University

Virginia McDermott
University of New Mexico

Raymie E. McKerrow
Ohio University

Sara L. McKinnon
University of New Mexico

Ed McLuskie
Boise State University

Mark Lawrence McPhail
*Western College Program at
Miami University*

Robert D. McPhee
Arizona State University

Sandra Metts
Illinois State University

Alan C. Mikkelson
Whitworth University

Tema Milstein
University of New Mexico

Steven Y. Miura
University of Hawai'i at Hilo

Dreama G. Moon
*California State University, San
Marcos*

Karen K. Myers
*University of California,
Santa Barbara*

Scott A. Myers
West Virginia University

Charles M. Naumer
University of Washington

Anne Maydan Nicotera
George Mason University

Janice M Odom
Valdosta State University

John G. Oetzel
University of New Mexico

Mark P. Orbe
Western Michigan University

Michael M. Osborn
University of Memphis

Alessandra Padula
*Università degli Studi di
L'Aquila*

Saumya Pant
University of New Mexico

Charles Pavitt
University of Delaware

Kevin J. Pearce
Bryant University

Sandra Petronio
*Indiana University Purdue
University Indianapolis*

Patrick Lee Plaisance
Colorado State University

Marshall Scott Poole
University of Illinois

Michael H. Prosser
*Shanghai International Studies
University*

Artemio Ramirez
Arizona State University

Andrew S. Rancer
University of Akron

Scott Reid
*University of California,
Santa Barbara*

Jessica S. Robles
University of Colorado Boulder

L. Edna Rogers
University of Utah

Richard A. Rogers
Northern Arizona University

Michael Roloff
Northwestern University

Abran J. Salazar
University of Rhode Island

Jennifer A. Samp
University of Georgia

Kim Christian Schrøder
Roskilde University

Janice Schuetz
University of New Mexico

Cliff Scott
*University of North Carolina
at Charlotte*

John S. Seiter
Utah State University, Logan

James Shanahan
Fairfield University

Susan B. Shimanoff
San Francisco State University

Stuart J. Sigman
Naropa University

Kami J. Silk
Michigan State University

Arvind Singhal
University of Texas El Paso

Michael D. Slater
Ohio State University

Rachel A. Smith
Pennsylvania State University

Thomas M. Steinfatt
University of Miami

Cynthia Stohl
*University of California,
Santa Barbara*

Scott R. Stroud
*University of Texas-
Pan American*

Robert C. Swieringa
*Grand Valley State
University*

James Taylor
Université de Montréal

Hedwig te Molder
Wageningen University

Jennifer A. Theiss
Rutgers University

Pradip Thomas
University of Queensland

Stella Ting-Toomey
*California State University
at Fullerton*

Karen Tracy
University of Colorado Boulder

Sarah J. Tracy
Arizona State University

April Vannini
European Graduate School

Don Rodney Vaughan
*East Mississippi Community
College*

Ingrid Volkmer
University of Melbourne

John T. Warren
Southern Illinois University

David Weiss
*Montana State University
Billings*

Olaf H. Werder
University of New Mexico

Christopher Joseph Westgate
Texas A&M University

Bryan B. Whaley
University of San Francisco

Michele White
Tulane University

Julia T. Wood
*University of North Carolina
at Chapel Hill*

Xiaosui Xiao
Hong Kong Baptist University

Gust A. Yep
San Francisco State University

Jing Yin
University of Hawai'i at Hilo

Julie Yingling
Humboldt State University

Introduction

Communication students frequently approach librarians seeking a source that will provide a ready summary of a particular theory or tradition. Communication scholars also occasionally need a good central reference for their teaching and research. This encyclopedia provides a one-stop source for theories and theoretical concepts and a relatively comprehensive overview of the entire field of communication theory. It is a significant resource because it summarizes in one place the diversity of theory in the communication field. Yet unlike larger topical encyclopedias that try to cover all topics in many volumes, this is a relatively small set focused just on theory. It will provide an excellent starting place for individuals seeking information on the various topics covered. Furthermore, readers will be able to see how topics relate to one another, get a sense of larger traditions and histories, and find a variety of bibliographical sources with which they can begin to expand their reading lists.

About This Encyclopedia

This encyclopedia is a two-volume set that, in more than 300 entries, offers current descriptions of the theories that explain numerous aspects of communication and present the background issues and concepts that comprise these theories. These entries have been written by nearly 200 contributors from 10 countries, including Australia, Canada, China, Denmark, India, Italy, Japan, Spain, the United Kingdom, and the United States. Entries range in length—from 1,000 to 3,000 words, depending upon the scope and detail required. To ensure adequate coverage, an editorial board of 10 members—also of diverse cultures and countries of origin—was formed to review the entries. All are recognized experts in several areas within communication theory and have contributed

significantly to its development. All reviewers are also contributors.

The entries are written for the introductory reader—students who have little or no background in the topic. For the most part, contributors have avoided unnecessary jargon and defined terms as needed. Although many of the entries require attentive reading, serious readers will find them accessible and informative, and those who want more advanced treatment can pursue further readings or entries in the bibliography. Readers who may have trouble understanding an entry can move to related topics identified in the "See also" sections and then return to the more difficult one.

We made the decision to feature elements, concepts, dimensions, and traditions of theory, as well as to feature individual theories, as entries. Individual theorists are listed separately with reference to the entries in which their work is discussed. Entries do not include citations, but each lists a few key sources as Further Readings. Cross-references are provided in the "See also" section at the end of each entry. A single classified bibliography of major theoretical works is also included. Readers can access the information in a number of ways:

- The alphabetical list of entries at the beginning of each volume provides the easiest way for a reader to identify topics of interest. Readers may want to start here by scanning the list of topics to identify those most relevant to their research.
- The Reader's Guide at the beginning of the set provides a classified list of topics organized around 17 themes. With this guide readers can begin with a broad theme and see which entries relate to it. This guide is also of value for showing connections among theories and for developing a sense of the field as a whole.

- The alphabetical list of theorists adjacent to the Reader's Guide will be an important index for readers who wish to learn more about individual scholars and their work. This list identifies the entries that cover each theorist's work.
- The Selected Bibliography of Major Works by Topic, located at the back of Volume 2, will be a vital resource for readers seeking original works. Readers can scan the alphabetical listing of topics to find major works of interest. This tool comes with instructions on how best to use it.
- The Chronology, located immediately after this introduction, lists major events in the history of communication theory. This tool facilitates an understanding of the various developments in the field of communication as a whole.
- The index is an obvious method of accessing information. It is a detailed list of topics with page references.

A Brief History

Communication as a concept always has been with us, but the origins of the discipline are more recent. In the United States, the humanistic roots of the discipline can be found in the study of rhetoric in ancient Greece and Rome, while the social scientific side typically dates its origins to the rise of studies of mass media, public opinion, propaganda, and persuasion early in the 20th century and especially during World War II. Both strands had a decidedly pragmatic bent: The five canons of rhetoric—invention, organization, style, delivery, and memory—were designed to help a speaker better prepare for and argue a position in the court, the assembly, or at a ceremonial event. Social scientists had a similarly pragmatic concern in understanding the functions and possibilities for communication in advertising, media, and technology as well as in face-to-face contexts.

Communication theory, then, followed from the pragmatic concerns about the study of communication. At first, communication scholars turned to existing disciplines for theories—not surprising since virtually every discipline concerned with the human being must study communication to some degree. The recognition of social sciences as legitimate disciplines after World War II gave even more credence to the contributions of psychology and sociology for understanding human communicative behavior. European scholars began to influence communication theory in the United States after World War II as well; heavily influenced by Marxist theories, European scholars from a variety of disciplines have been responsible for the introduction of critical–cultural theories and methods into the study of communication.

Gradually, however, separate communication departments began to form. At first often referred to as departments of speech communication to reflect both the rhetorical and social scientific roots, most departments today are simply called departments of communication or communication studies. In contrast to scholars in related disciplines who tend to consider communication a secondary process for transmitting information about the world, communication scholars see communication as the organizing principle of human social life: Communication constructs the social world rather than simply providing the means for describing that world.

Of course, theories of communication are not distinctive to the Western tradition and the United States. Virtually every culture has been concerned with the nature and functions of communication, and communication scholars are beginning to integrate theories from a variety of countries and cultures. Feminist scholars have sought to describe ways feminine worldviews might foster different modes of communication since the 1970s. Afrocentric and Asiacentric communication are perhaps the best articulated bodies of work to date that describe the communication assumptions and practices of African Americans and Asians, respectively. Increasingly, then, communication scholars are seeking to understand similarities and differences across cultures and to articulate more nuanced theories to reflect these more comprehensive understandings of how communication works.

Although the communication field now has the legitimacy and coherence that comes from disciplinary status, it remains a continually evolving and changing discipline. This encyclopedia will offer the student of communication a sense of the history, development, and current status of the discipline with an emphasis on the theories that comprise it. We hope readers in communication will engage these theories in a spirit of ongoing inquiry that is crucial to the continued development of the field. And we hope those in related fields will gain a better understanding of what the communication discipline is all about.

Acknowledgments

We are indebted to our editorial board and to all of our contributors, listed by name at the beginning of the encyclopedia. Their expertise, effort, and commitment contributed to the excellence of this project. We are especially indebted to our colleagues in the Communication and Journalism Department at the University of New Mexico who provided guidance and wrote contributions to this work. This work is the product not only of authors and managing editors, but also of a team of professionals at Sage Publications who made the successful completion of the project possible by their many hours of work from its inception to final publication. We want to express particular appreciation to these individuals: Jim Brace-Thompson, Yvette Pollastrini, Laura Notton, Bonnie Freeman, Renee Willers, Kevin Gleason, Sandy Zilka Livingston, Joan Shapiro, and Kate Schroeder. Because of the efforts of all involved, we are confident that this encyclopedia will be an important resource about and reference for communication theories.

Chronology

This chronology contains major themes and developments in each period and is not intended to be exhaustive.

Classical Period

Foundations of Western thought are established in ancient Greece and Rome.

- Western debates on epistemology, ontology, ethics, and axiology form the bases of Western philosophy, prefiguring debates about knowledge, being, and values that continue to the present day within communication.
- Plato and Aristotle lay foundations for classical rhetorical theory.
- Forensics is established as the field of legal communication.
- Ancient Greek rhetoricians grapple with what constitutes persuasive technique and skill.
- Cicero codifies the classical canons of rhetoric—invention (invention), disposition (organization), elocution (style), memoria (memory), and pronunciation (delivery).
- Cicero and other Romans develop speaking standards consistent with the Roman legal code and delineated legal issues that must be argued.
- Greeks and Romans such as Theophrastus, Cicero, and Quintilian study gestures as persuasive accompaniment to rhetorical discourses, setting the stage for contemporary studies of nonverbal communication.
- Augustine writes *On Christian Doctrine,* which sets out a guide for interpreting scriptures, later to be taken as one of the foundational works in hermeneutics.
- Eastern religions and philosophies emerge with future implications for how non-Western cultures will come to think about and practice communication. Laozi and Zhuangzi found

Taoism, which remains influential in Eastern thought regarding communication, human relationships, and values.

- The creation of the *Vedas* through an oral tradition in India provides a basis for religious rituals in the Hindu tradition.
- The creation of the texts known as *Upaniśads* in ancient India form the core of modern Hinduism.
- Confucius's teaching begins to influence many strands of religion and philosophy, including modern-day ideas about communication.
- Buddha and his disciplines travel in what is now northern India and Nepal and spread teachings that were later written by disciples and became the foundation of Buddhism.
- Bhartfhari and Śankara analyze language and speech, providing a foundation for Hindu communication theory.
- The concept of *rasa* is developed in the writings of Bharata and Abhinavagupta in India.

The role of African civilizations in human life, communication, rhetoric, and world history is established.

- Egyptian and Nubian thought emerge.
- Imhotep, Ptahhotep, Kagemni, Merikare, and Duauf establish a classical set of philosophies that contribute to Afrocentric ideas about communication.

1600 to 1700

The age of rationalism and the Enlightenment begin, as major issues in epistemology are set by philosophers of this period.

- René Descartes develops ideas about the cognitive and rational basis of human experience, becoming a major influence in Western thought in many branches of science and humanities.

- Jean-Jacques Rousseau writes about the social contract as a means of establishing order in society, greatly influencing Western concepts of the person and social life.
- Immanuel Kant extends Western rationalism by integrating ideas about empirical experience and human knowing.
- John Milton writes *Areopagitica,* which sets the stage for freedom of speech, leading to much work in public communication in the centuries to come.

The Reformation, begun a century earlier, contributes to the broadening of reading and the need for textual interpretation.

- Matthias Flacius, a follower of Luther, develops principles for scriptural interpretation.

1800s

Scholars intensify an interest in gesture and various forms of expression.

- Charles Darwin writes *The Expression of Emotions in Man and Animals.*
- Garrick Mallery compares North American Plains sign language with other languages, including that of the deaf.
- The elocution movement, focusing on the art of expression in public address, anticipates an intense interest in communication as performance in the next century.

Dialectical thinking emerges, influencing social critiques.

- Georg Hegel proposes a philosophy of change based on dialectic, which influences Karl Marx and later dialectical and critical schools of thought in communication.
- Following the ideas of Hegel, Marx publishes social and economic critiques that form the foundation for 20th-century communist and critical thought.
- Friedrich Nietzsche creates a philosophy of power and self-interest that has influenced social scientific thinking to the present day, including theories of communication.

Interest in collective action and public communication becomes a topic of scholarly interest.

- Crowd theories and theories of mass society set the stage for media effects work in the following century.

- Gabriel Tarde introduces the concept of diffusion of innovations, later to inspire a whole tradition of work in the following century.
- British utilitarian thinkers such as John Stuart Mill and Jeremy Bentham set the stage for intense interest in public communication and democratic processes.

Major work centers on the relationship among signs and between signs and signified objects.

- Charles Sanders Peirce founds the field of semiotics, which continues to influence the study of signs, language, and logic to this day.

Early persuasion work begins.

- St. Elmo Lewis proposes a stair-step hierarchical framework for sales.

1900 to 1910

Interest in collective action continues.

- The term *fandom* comes to be used for sports-club fans and later science fiction fans as well, setting the stage for more recent studies of fans and fandom.
- Walter Dill Scott begins historic research on advertising.

Psychoanalysis captures intellectual interest, later to become a major factor in behavioral and social theory.

- Sigmund Freud publishes landmark works on psychoanalysis, setting a counterpoint to rationalist empiricist philosophies of human agency.

1910 to 1920

Interest in nonlinguistic expression continues.

- Wilhelm Wundt conceives of gestural communication as a universal language.

Phenomenology becomes a branch of philosophy.

- Edmund Husserl publishes his philosophy of phenomenology, which later impacts thinking throughout the social sciences and humanities, including communication.

Psychoanalysis continues with intense interest in hidden processes of human thought and action.

- Carl Jung's ideas on the collective unconscious open interest in the study of mythology across several fields, including communication.

Structural theories of language develop.

- Ferdinand Saussure publishes *Course in General Linguistics,* providing a foundation for the study of signs and language that remains alive and influential to the present day.

Studies of collective action turn toward the formal study of organizations.

- Max Weber publishes *The Theory of Social and Economic Organization,* a landmark work giving rise to much 20th century thought on institutions and organizations.

American pragmatism shifts philosophical attention toward practical action.

- John Dewey introduces the reflecting thinking process in his classic treatise *How We Think,* which will later have a huge effect on communication, especially group process.

Attitudes become an object of study, leading the way to serious research and theory development later in the century.

- William Thomas and Florian Znanicki define attitude as a mental and neural state of readiness.

1920 to 1930

Studies of mass media rise.

- Science fiction fandom becomes apparent.
- Early media research, based in large part on stimulus-response psychology, assumes powerful media effects leading to the hypodermic needle theory or magic bullet approach.
- French writers identified film as an art form, referring to it as the "sixth art."
- Journalist Walter Lippmann asserted that media develop simplistic "pictures" in the public of a complex social world.

Phenomenology and existentialism advance.

- Martin Heidegger publishes major philosophical works in the phenomenological tradition, including his classic *Being and Time.*

Scholars begin to develop interest in human social behavior and relationships.

- Early impression formation studies in psychology provide an impetus for ongoing research on how people make attributions and evaluations of others through communication.
- Martin Buber publishes *I and Thou,* which is widely translated and influences studies of communication and dialogue throughout the century and beyond.
- The now famous studies at the Hawthorne Works outside Chicago led to the discovery of the Hawthorne effect, which sparked intense interest in employee-centered approaches to organizational communication.

Language studies become popular.

- I. A. Richards publishes foundational work in literary criticism, semiotics, and meaning, influencing theories of communication to the current day.

Psychologists become intensely interested in how humans think and how cognition relates to behavior.

- Jean Piaget begins a 50-year investigation into the stages of human cognitive development, influencing cognitive theory in many fields, including communication.
- B. F. Skinner develops the radical behaviorism project, which will come to have immense influence in the social sciences.

The critical turn in social theory intensifies.

- Felix Weil founds the Institute for Social Research at the University of Frankfurt am Main in Germany, providing a home for the well-known Frankfurt School, which led the way in Marxist thinking in the 20th century.

1930 to 1940

The first serious work on individual traits begins.

- Psychologist Gordon Allport advances the concepts of personality and attitudes, which sets the stage for work on communication traits and persuasion.

Studies on signs, language, and meaning continue.

- Kenneth Burke begins a career of study and writing on human symbol use and its relationship to identification between persons and groups, later to heavily influence thinking in contemporary rhetoric.
- Russian psychologist Lev Vygotsky publishes highly influential works on human development and language and thought, later to have an impact on critical and linguistic theory.
- Aleksei Leontiev, a close colleague of Vygotsky, begins work on activity theory, the idea that meanings are created in concrete social-interaction activities.
- Charles Morris establishes an influential model for dividing semiotics into semantics, syntactics, and pragmatics, which gives rise to interest in studying the pragmatics of language, or how language is used in actual talk.
- Roman Jakobson defines six functions of language, functions which help further the new pragmatic approach to language and communication.
- *Mind, Self, and Society,* based on the lectures of George Herbert Mead, provides the basis of symbolic interactionism, which will have a tremendous impact on social interaction theories of communication.
- Benjamin Lee Whorf and Edward Sapir develop the ideas now known as linguistic relativity theory.

Marxist critical theory continues to advance.

- Antonio Gramsci writes prison notebooks, substantially elaborating and extending Marxist thought, especially the idea of hegemony.
- Emma Tenayuca put forward an American perspective on Marxism by applying it to peoples in the United States bound culturally to Mexico.

Studies of media communication grow.

- The growing popularity of radio raises important research questions about media effects and leads to such studies as Hadley Cantril's famous study of H. G. Wells's *War of the Worlds.*

1940 to 1950

Social scientists look more closely at the influence of culture and situation.

- David Efron investigates the influence of race and environment on use of gesture.
- Fernando Ortiz introduces the concept of transculturation, later to influence both cultural and critical studies.

New major works in phenomenology appear.

- Maurice Merleau-Ponty begins to publish his ideas about phenomenology.

Social psychology begins to influence thinking about behavior, social action, and communication.

- Kurt Lewin, commonly acknowledged as the father of social psychology, develops a field theory of conflict and also explores group influence.

The power and role of the media are explored.

- In landmark media-effects studies, Paul Lazarsfeld, Bernard Berelson, and Hazel Gaudet shift the view of media from powerful to limited effects, granting much influence to interpersonal rather than mass channels and leading the way to the two-step and multi-step flow models.
- Harold Lasswell and Charles Wright identify major functions of the press.
- The Hutchins Commission publishes *A Free and Responsible Press,* outlining the normative obligations of journalism to society.

As the technical challenges of communication increase, mathematical and engineering approaches emerge.

- Claude Shannon and Warren Weaver publish their classic *A Mathematical Theory of Communication,* which builds an information theory model of communication.
- The Macy Conferences on Cybernetics bring together important intellectuals of the era.
- John von Neumann and Oskar Morgenstern publish *Theory of Games and Economic Behavior,* which launches an entire field of investigation on rational behavior, interdependency, and negotiation.

Applications of dialectical thinking to critical theory become clearer.

- Max Horkheimer and Theodor Adorno publish *The Dialectic of Enlightenment,* giving rise to the theory of the culture industry.
- Roland Barthes begins to publish critical works related to literature, semiotics, and society, his influence felt throughout the humanities and social sciences today.

Organizational studies continue.

- Philip Selznick's studies of leadership and administration bring attention to the relationship between institutions and communities.

Serious clinical studies of relational communication begin.

- Jürgen Ruesch and Gregory Bateson introduce the concept of metacommunication, or communication about communication, moving the study of communication beyond superficial ideas about simple message transmission.

The crucial distinction between sex and gender calls attention to the place and role of women in society.

- Simone de Beauvoir publishes her landmark treatise, *The Second Sex.*

1950 to 1954

Studies of nonverbal communication develop in earnest.

- Ray Birdwhistell explores social interaction and becomes known especially for kinesics, the study of symbolic bodily movements.
- George Trager begins pioneering work into paralanguage and voice quality.

Attitude change research, particularly in social psychology, becomes a major field of study.

- Theodore Newcomb publishes a co-orientational model, one of the first relationally oriented approaches, which stimulated much thinking in attitude theory and organizational communication.
- Carl Hovland and his colleagues begin landmark persuasion studies at Yale University, highly influencing the study of attitude change and persuasion in several disciplines, including communication.
- Foundational values studies are produced by Talcott Parsons, Clyde Kluchkhohn, Alex Inkeles, Daniel Levinson, and others.

Studies of media influence intensify.

- International communication flow studies begin to show a predominant one-way influence of more powerful nations to less powerful ones.
- Harold Adams Innis publishes landmark works on the biasing effects of the predominant media of an era.
- Fred Siebert, Theodore Peterson, and Wilbur Schramm publish their classic *Four Theories of the Press,* outlining various roles media can take in society.

Rhetorical and language studies broaden to include new forms of discourse and new ways of looking at discourse.

- Kenneth Burke introduces the concept of dramatism from literary theory, which sparks a long-term multidisciplinary interest in this topic as a way of understanding communication.
- Ludwig Wittgenstein publishes *Philosophical Investigations,* leading the way to the study of meaning as intentional communication.

Cybernetics emerges as an important field.

- Norbert Wiener publishes highly influential books on cybernetics and society.

Citizenship is explored.

- Thomas Humphrey Marshall conceptualizes citizenship, giving rise to ongoing research in this area.

Group communication studies advance.

- Robert Bales first develops interaction process analysis, stimulating much research and theory-building in group communication.

1955 to 1959

Interpersonal communication studies broaden significantly with the introduction of fresh new approaches.

- Carl Rogers begins to publish ideas about client-centered therapy, which launches decades of study of person-centered communication and dialogue.
- Erving Goffman begins publishing a well-known series of books on human interaction and self-presentation that heavily influenced research and theory building in interpersonal communication.
- George Kelly presents his personal construct theory, which provides the basis for constructivism in the United States.
- John French and Bertram Raven publish their highly popular model of interpersonal power, positing five sources of power frequently cited in the communication literature.
- George Homans publishes a foundational article titled "Social Behavior as Exchange," opening a scholarly movement throughout the social sciences on social exchange theory, which has had a major influence on studies of interpersonal communication.
- Fritz Heider publishes his acclaimed book *The Psychology of Interpersonal Relations*.
- George Trager advances paralinguistics by creating a voice classification system.
- Edward T. Hall proposes the study of proxemics, or the study of space in communication, in his landmark book *The Silent Language*.

Powerful media effects models wane.

- Joseph Klapper publishes *The Effects of Mass Communication*, giving credence to the limited-effects theory.
- Elihu Katz, Jay Blumler, and Michael Gurevitch introduce the uses and gratifications approach to media, leading to a movement of studies on how people choose and use media and the ways in which they become dependent on media.

Social psychological approaches to attitude and attitude change continue to develop and now begin to have a major impact on the study of persuasion.

- Leon Festinger begins a visible program of research on cognitive dissonance, which is to have a major impact on persuasion and attitude studies.

Profound shifts occur in our understanding of language and discourse.

- Noam Chomsky proposes a new way of thinking about language and thought based in transformational grammar.

- Stephen Toulmin publishes *The Uses of Argument*, which is to impact the study of argumentation by directing attention toward informal and away from formal logic.

1960 to 1964

Research on persuasion dominates the empirical research agenda.

- Muzafer Sherif and his colleagues publish their landmark work on social judgment theory.
- William McGuire proposes inoculation theory to explain resistance to persuasion.

Alternative approaches to the study of language broaden the study of symbols and communication.

- Michael M. Osborn, Douglas Ehninger, and others begin a decades-long inquiry into the role of metaphor in language, rhetoric, and communication.
- Murray Edelman takes a communication perspective in his classic treatise *The Symbolic Uses of Politics*.
- Jacques Lacan, already a practicing and controversial psychotherapist, begins a 2-decade series of public seminars in which he connects human subjectivity and the unconscious to language, furthering the poststructuralist move in the study of language and society.
- Hans-Georg Gadamer completes the first edition of his magnum opus *Truth and Method*, which would propel hermeneutics into social science and humanities scholarship in the coming decades.
- J. L. Austin publishes *How to Do Things with Words*, widely considered the beginning of speech act theory.
- Basil Bernstein produces his theory-breaking article on elaborated and restricted codes.

Critical theory begins a significant foray into communication studies.

- Jürgen Habermas writes his first book, *The Structural Transformations of the Public Sphere*, published in English in 1989, which creates intense interest in public democratic communication. Habermas's publications, spanning nearly 40 years, make him one of the most influential communication theorists in the critical and pragmatic traditions.
- Richard Hoggart founds the Centre for Contemporary Cultural Studies at the Birmingham

University in United Kingdom, which will become a base for much influential work on power and cultural production.

- Scholars begin developing postmodern theory as a counterpoint to modernism and in the process open new questions about truth claims and traditional values.

Diffusion theory is published.

- Everett Rogers publishes the first edition of his classic book *Diffusion of Innovations*.

The second wave of feminism begins.

- Betty Friedan publishes *The Feminine Mystique*.
- Effects of media on society and human thought are explored.
- Marshall McLuhan publishes landmark works on the biasing effects of media.

1965 to 1969

Qualitative approaches involving careful attention to the details of social life begin to develop.

- Harold Garfinkel introduces ethnomethodology.
- Influenced by ethnomethodology, Harvey Sacks lays the foundation for work in conversation analysis.
- Marvin Scott and Stanford Lyman publish their landmark work on accounts.
- Dell Hymes proposes an ethnography of speaking, which sparks later interest in the study of cultures in the communication field.
- Bernie Glaser and Anselm Strauss introduce grounded theory.

Alternative critical theories challenge traditional views of language and discourse in society.

- Michel Foucault begins a career of writing and study about the relationship of discourse, language, and knowledge to power relations in society.
- Jacques Derrida first publishes *Of Grammatology* in French, introducing the idea of deconstruction, which greatly influenced poststructuralist thinking.

Nonverbal communication studies continue apace.

- Paul Ekman and Wallace Friesen begin research on types of nonverbal communication, with emphasis on the face and hands.
- George Trager and others continue work relating paralanguage to animal vocalization.
- Albert Mehrabian introduces his concept of immediacy, which will have a great effect on the study of nonverbal communication.

Considerable new thinking about human relationships begins.

- The pragmatic work of the Palo Alto Group becomes widely known when Paul Watzlawick, Janet Beavin, and Don Jackson write their landmark treatise *Pragmatics of Human Communication: A Study of Interactional Patterns, Pathologies, and Paradoxes*, which influenced theories of relationships, interpersonal communication, and systems.
- John Bowlby publishes pioneering work on human relational attachment.
- With the concept of transparency, Sidney Jourard begins a tradition of research and theory on self-disclosure.

Cybernetics and system theory gain attention.

- Ludwig von Bertalanffy popularizes system theory and starts a movement around General System Theory (GST), later inspiring advances in systems theory and complexity theory.

Rhetorical and discourse studies broaden from traditional concepts to an increasingly wide range of phenomena.

- Lloyd Bitzer codifies the rhetorical situation, providing a major conceptual center for rhetorical theory.
- Chaim Perelman and Lucie Olbrechts-Tyteca publish their book, *The New Rhetoric*.
- John Searle publishes *Speech Acts: An Essay on the Philosophy of Language*.

Major new proposals in media theory develop.

- Gerbner introduces cultivation theory, which grants heavy television viewing great power to affect individuals' perceptions of the world around them.
- After studying the 1968 presidential campaign, Maxwell McCombs and Donald Shaw propose an agenda-setting theory of media, which begins a

decades-long project to weigh agenda-setting effects.

- The term *johoka* is coined in Japan to refer to the use of information technologies and dissemination of information through media to the public, leading to the development of informatization policies in Japan.

Traditional epistemologies are challenged by social approaches.

- Peter Berger and Thomas Luckmann publish their highly influential work on the social construction of reality, catalyzing a movement in communication and throughout the social sciences.

Gender and cultural perspectives start to gain attention.

- The Combahee River collective begins a womanist movement, later theorized by Patricia Hill Collins, to express the perspectives and experiences of Black women.

Cognitive studies in communication are born.

- Jean-Blaise Grize begins a career-long project on the logic of everyday communication, developing the concept of schemes, which will later come to be commonplace in cognitive theories of communication.

Communication strategy studies gain popularity.

- Gerald Marwell and David Schmidt identify 16 compliance-gaining strategies, sparking a whole tradition of research on this subject.
- Richard E. Walton and Robert B. McKersie publish their classic book, *A Behavioral Theory of Labor Negotiations,* introducing the concepts of distributive and integrative bargaining.

1970 to 1974

Major new developments in philosophy and epistemology occur.

- Thomas Kuhn publishes landmark work, *The Structure of Scientific Revolutions.*
- Richard Lanigan introduces the field to important philosophical concepts, particularly

phenomenology, later to evolve into the field of philosophy of communication.

- Umberto Maturana and Francisco Verela publish first works on autopoiesis, or self-defining systems, later to impact the study of the cybernetics of knowing.

Interest in nonverbal communication increases.

- Canadian linguist Fernando Poyatos shows the relationship between written punctuation marks and paralinguistic characteristics.
- Fernando Poyatos also coins the term *chronemics* to capture the role of time in communication.

Critical theory focuses on language, discourse, and media.

- The rise of the Birmingham school opens avenues for increased fan studies.
- Herbert Schiller publishes sharp critiques of U.S. media and cultural hegemony, calling attention of critical scholars to this form of imperialism.
- Jeremy Tunstall chronicles the global influence of U.S. media.
- Michael Halliday introduces critical linguistics, greatly influencing critical approaches to discourse analysis.
- Louis Althusser publishes his highly influential ideas about ideology and state apparatuses.
- Paulo Freire publishes *Pedagogy of the Oppressed* in English, giving rise to a more critical approach to communication education and critical theory.

Interpersonal communication becomes a major emphasis in the field.

- Irwin Altman and Dalmas Taylor present social penetration theory, which influenced much thinking about relational development and disclosure.
- Roderick Hart and Don Burks describe rhetorical sensitivity as an ideal approach to framing messages in communication, later to be elaborated by a team of colleagues.
- Gregory Bateson publishes his landmark treatise *Steps to an Ecology of Mind,* providing a basis for decades of research on systemic and social approaches to relationships.
- Harold Kelley stimulates a huge line of work throughout the social sciences on attribution theory, which will come to influence the study of

interpersonal communication in the following decades.

- Michael Argyle and his colleagues explore skilled interaction behavior.
- Milton Rokeach publishes *The Nature of Human Values.*

Gender and feminist studies rise in the communication field.

- Cheris Kramer (later Kramarae) introduces the idea that women's and men's language may be different, leading the way to genderlect theory.
- Karlyn Kohrs Campbell publishes her highly influential article on the rhetoric of women's liberation, setting in motion a tradition of feminist rhetorical criticism.
- French feminism, later to influence U.S. feminist communication thought, begins to develop.

New methods of discourse and conversation analysis are developed.

- H. Paul Grice produces his principle of cooperation and identifies conversational maxims, which provide a foundation for the ongoing tradition of conversation analysis.

Media theory expands.

- Elisabeth Noelle-Neumann proposes a fresh approach to understanding public opinion known as the spiral of silence.
- Maxwell McCombs and Donald Shaw's agenda-setting theory elicits a decades-long interest in ways that the media and audiences shape the public agenda of important issues.
- George Gerbner begins research on cultural indicators, leading to fruitful investigations of media impacts on culture and the development of cultivation theory.
- The U.S. Surgeon General's 1972 report on television violence stimulates much research interest in the effects of media violence.

Culture studies enter the picture.

- Mary Pukui revives interest in *ho'oponopono*, the traditional form of Native Hawaiian conflict resolution, increasing interest and inquiry into this thoroughly alternative form.

- Clifford Geertz publishes influential works on the interpretation of cultures, impacting studies in communication and culture.
- Scholars such as Victor Turner and Richard Schechner highlight performance as integral to human experience, influencing the study of communication and culture.
- Andrea Rich and Arthur Smith (later Molefi Kete Asante) publish ground-breaking books on interracial communication.

New rhetorical methods continue to be developed.

- Ernest Bormann builds on ideas from Robert Bales's work on group communication and popularizes fantasy theme analysis, later to develop this into symbolic convergence theory.
- Phillip Wander and Steven Jenkins publish the foundational article on ideological rhetoric titled "Rhetoric, Society, and the Critical Response."

Group influence is studied.

- Irving Janis introduces the groupthink hypothesis.

The field of communication begins to look at human developmental issues.

- Frank Dance and Carl Larson propose a speech theory of human communication.

1975 to 1979

Rules theory is introduced to the communication field.

- W. Barnett Pearce, Vernon Cronen, and colleagues first propose coordinated management of meaning, a highly published and popular theory that will later go through several extensions.
- A doctoral honors seminar sponsored by the Speech Communication Association provides a springboard for a tradition of work on rules theory.

Empirical research and theory building on interpersonal processes rise markedly.

- Charles Berger and colleagues publish first works on uncertainty reduction theory, which will influence several generations of interpersonal communication scholars and stimulate a whole tradition of related theory.

- Frank Millar and L. Edna Rogers begin a long tradition of research on relational control patterns.
- Jesse Delia and his colleagues begin developing the theory of constructivism and person-centered communication, which is to become a mainstay in the study of interpersonal communication.
- Howard Giles begins a program on speech accommodation, which leads to a fruitful 3-decade project and the development of communication accommodation theory.
- Penelope Brown and Stephen Levinson introduce politeness theory, which will become highly heuristic in stimulating much research in conversation, culture, and interpersonal relations.
- Nancy Rollins and Kathleen Bahr explore power in interpersonal relations.
- John Wiemann begins to theorize communication competence.

Attitude theory and persuasion research remain popular and influential.

- Martin Fishbein and Icek Ajzen propose the theory of reasoned action to explain how attitudes are formed and how they in turn predict behavior.

Rhetorical methods continue to expand.

- Karlyn Kohrs Campbell and Kathleen Hall Jamieson elaborate a contemporary version of genre theory in rhetorical studies.

Concerns for media culture and power relations continue.

- Oliver Boyd-Barrett defines media imperialism in terms of the international flow of information and influence.
- James Lull, James Anderson, and others introduce ideas leading to social action media studies.

Investigations of the discourse of cultural communities, including marginalized groups, receive increasing attention.

- Michael Omi and Howard Winant introduce racial formation theory.

- Anthropologists Edwin Ardener and Shirley Ardener propose muted group theory, which will have a major influence on feminist analyses of communication.
- Gerry Philipsen publishes "Speaking like a Man in Teamsterville," sparking a tradition of communication ethnographies and leading to a cultural speech codes movement in communication theory.
- Derrick Bell introduces the first formal statement of critical race theory based on the influential writings of W. E. B. DuBois, Martin Luther King, Jr., César Chávez, and others.

Poststructuralism and the challenge to stable meaning emerge.

- Jacques Derrida introduces deconstruction, questioning the stable meaning of words and texts and thereby no stability in being or self.

Organizational communication becomes an increasingly popular subject of theory.

- John Van Maanen and Ed Schein introduce a model of organizational socialization.
- Karl Weick publishes his influential book, *The Social Psychology of Organizing*, which forwards the idea that organizing is an interactional process.

Work on communication apprehension begins.

- James McCroskey and his colleagues begin a decades-long research program on social and communicative anxiety.

Postcolonialism is introduced.

- Edward Said publishes *Orientalism*.

1980 to 1984

Nonverbal communication studies continue.

- Adam Kendon studies relationship of gesture and speech.

Communication trait research explodes.

- Dominic A. Infante and his colleagues publish initial work on argumentativeness, later expanding this work to include verbal aggressiveness and assertiveness.

- Donald J. Cegala and his colleagues begin to operationalize the concept of interaction involvement, based on ideas from Erving Goffman.
- Robert Norton summarizes his research and theory on communicator style in his monograph of the same name, identifying a major thematic area of interest in interpersonal communication.

European communication theory is "discovered" by North American communication scholars and begins to make a huge impact.

- Translations of Mikhail Bakhtin's works make his ideas, published during the 20th century, accessible in the English-speaking world.
- Habermas publishes *The Theory of Communicative Action*, which greatly influences critical communication theory.
- Scholars affiliated with science and technology studies, particularly Michel Callon, Bruno Latour, and John Law, begin to study science as symbolic production, leading to a line of work now known as actor–network theory.
- Stuart Hall broadens the popularity of British Cultural Studies among critical scholars.

Cognitive theory becomes a serious focus within communication.

- John O. Greene first proposes action assembly theory, which will later influence thinking about cognitive processes in communication.
- Sandra Bem first proposes gender schema theory, paving the way for much research in gender and communication.
- George Lakoff and Mark Johnson publish their highly influential text *Metaphors We Live By*.

Media response theories continue to develop.

- Lewis Donohew and Philip Palmgreen introduce their activation theory of communication exposure.
- Stanley Fish introduces the idea of interpretive communities in his classic *Is There a Text in This Class*, later to be applied to media communities by Janice Radway in *Reading the Romance*.

Organizational and group communication studies emerge as a major theoretical voice.

- George Cheney and Philip Tompkins begin to explore rhetorical dimensions of organizational communication, particularly control and identification.
- Michael Pacanowsky and Nick O'Donnell Trujillo introduce studies of organizational culture, opening great interest in this subject within the field of organizational communication.
- Dennis Gouran and Randy Hirokawa introduce functional group communication theory.

System theory exerts serious influence on the study of communication.

- D. Lawrence Kincaid first proposes convergence theory, an application of cybernetics and information theory to meaning and human understanding.

A new era of electronic communication stimulates a flood of research and theory on new media.

- William Gibson coins the term *cyberspace* in his novel *Neuromancer*, and the term stuck.
- Marvin Minsky introduces the term *presence* to capture the feeling of being transported to another location through telecommunications, a term later to be applied to all virtual environments.

Rules theory, popularized in the 1970s, becomes codified and well known in the field.

- Susan B. Shimanoff publishes an influential book on rules theory, codifying the work done in this area to date.

Interpersonal communication studies intensify.

- Sandra Petronio begins to develop and later to publish privacy management theory.
- Edward Jones and colleagues publish their influential theory of self-presentation.
- Brian Spitzberg, William Cupach, and others present theories of interpersonal communication competence.

New forms of public and media communication are explored.

- Jane Mansbridge inspires a tradition of research on local nonadversarial democracy in her classic study of a Vermont town hall meeting.
- United Nations Educational, Scientific and Cultural Organization's MacBride Commission first explores

issues of media sovereignty, opening increased scholarship on media and globalization.

The study of environmental communication emerges.

- Christine Oravec publishes a now-classic study of conservationism and preservationism in the Hetch-Hetchy controversy.

Feminist studies produce increasing insights about women and communication.

- Janice Radway conducts ethnographic studies of women's engagement with media.

1985 to 1989

Communication scholars first begin to explore the life span perspective.

- Jon Nussbaum is the first communication scholar to articulate a life span perspective.

Critical communication theory intensifies its focus on oppressive arrangements, with special attention to particular groups.

- Fan studies see a shift from a descriptive approach to emphasize the resistive and subversive status of fan communities.
- Donna Haraway applies Marxist standpoint theory to feminist thought leading to work in communication on feminist standpoint theory.
- Norman Fairclough introduces critical discourse analysis as a way of uncovering power and ideology in social relations.
- Tuen Van Dijk expands work on discourse analysis to expose the development of oppressive systems of meaning.
- Chicana feminist Gloria Anzaldúa creates the theory of borderlands about the Chicana experience, sparking scholarly interest about Mexican American women within the communication field.
- Peggy McIntosh forwards ideas about how privilege works, adding additional substance to feminist and critical thought.
- Gayatri Spivak, Chandra Talpade Mohanty, Trinh T. Minh-ha, and others address postcolonial feminism.
- Teresa de Lauretis introduces queer theory.

- The concept of diaspora, originally used in regard to the Jewish people, is revived and applied to all peoples who are dispersed from their original lands.
- Raymie E. McKerrow codifies critical rhetoric in his well-known article "Critical Rhetoric: Theory and Praxis."

Dual-processing models of cognition and persuasive communication are developed.

- Richard Petty and John Cacioppo publish elaboration likelihood theory, which will have a major influence on persuasion research and theory.
- Shelly Chaiken introduces the heuristic-systematic model of information processing.

Media choice and use continue as a popular theme in media theory.

- Dolf Zillman and Jennings Bryant explain media choice in terms of maximizing pleasure and minimizing unpleasant stimuli, leading to the affect-dependent stimulus arrangement theory.

Culture studies and intercultural communication theory continue to mature.

- Mary Jane Collier, Michael L. Hecht, and others begin to explore cultural identity formation, leading to a line of research and theory in this area.
- Guo-Ming Chen and his colleagues begin research and theory building on intercultural communication competence.
- Stella Ting-Toomey introduces face negotiation theory.
- Young Yun Kim first presents cross-cultural adaptation theory.

Serious theoretical attention is given to gender differences in communication.

- Alice Eagly publishes gender role theory.

Behavioral-cognitive theories of interpersonal communication continue.

- Judee K. Burgoon and her colleagues introduce expectancy violations theory.

Increasing attention is given to global communication.

- Ulrich Beck proposes a critical paradigm on globalization.

1990 to 1994

Performance studies emerges as an important development in communication theory.

- Dwight Conquergood takes a critical turn in the development of performance ethnography.

Studies of culture and community expand.

- Min-Sun Kim and her colleagues introduce culture as an important factor in conversational constraints.
- Michael L. Hecht relates identity and culture.
- Jean Lave and Etienne Wenger introduce the concept of communities of practice.
- Mark Lawrence McPhail introduces complicity theory.

Discourse theory advances.

- Margaret Wetherall and Jonathan Potter introduce positioning theory.
- Larry D. Browning raises awareness of lists as a legitimate and important form of discourse that can be researched and theorized.
- Frans van Eemeren, Rian Grootendorst, and their colleagues develop the pragma-dialectical approach to argument and argumentative conversation.

Modern-Postmodern debates dominate critical communication theory.

- Kimberl Crenshaw introduces the idea of intersectionality, claiming that categories like race and gender cannot be homogenized and challenging essentialist notions of identity.
- Dana L. Cloud publishes her well-known critique of the materiality of discourse, sparking a lively debate on the nature of discourse and the material world.

Cognitive approaches to interpersonal communication advance.

- Austin S. Babrow introduces problematic integration theory.
- William Gudykunst introduces anxiety/uncertainty management theory.

Relational communication theory intensifies.

- Daniel Canary and his colleagues publish initial works on relational maintenance.

New communications technologies give rise to the study of virtual relationships.

- Howard Rheingold publishes his book *Virtual Community,* expanding the discussion of new technologies to digital cultures created in cyberspace.
- Joseph Walther introduces social information processing theory.
- Jan Van Dijk publishes *The Network Society* in Dutch, which would be translated into English later in the decade.
- Mark Poster announces the arrival of the second media age.

Group and organizational communication theory explores new directions.

- Linda Putnam and Cynthia Stohl first articulate bona fide group theory.
- Stanley A. Deetz publishes his landmark book *Democracy and Corporate Colonization of America,* opening intense interest in power, domination, and resistance in organizations.

1995 to 1999

Traditional definitions of rhetoric are questioned.

- Sonja Foss and Cindy L. Griffin introduce invitational rhetoric as an alternative to traditional notions of persuasion.

New developments in media bring about shifts in theoretical attention.

- Byron Reeves and Clifford Nass introduce media equation theory, suggesting that people treat media as persons.
- Frank Biocca, Matthew Lombard, and others explore communication in virtual environments.

Interest in relationships and small groups continues.

- Leslie A. Baxter and Barbara Montgomery first articulate the relational dialectics theory.
- John G. Oetzel introduces culture as a variable into group task work.
- Peter A. Andersen advances thinking on intimacy in his cognitive valence theory.
- In a well-known monograph, Charles Berger relates planning to ideas about communication goals.

- Judee K. Burgoon, Lesa Stern, and Leesa Dillman introduce interaction adaptation theory.
- David Buller and Judee K. Burgoon introduce interpersonal deception theory.

Critical attention to discourse continues.

- Luk Van Lanagenhove and Rom Harré publish their foundational work on positioning theory.
- Kent Ono and John Sloop identify vernacular discourse as the object of critical rhetorical study.
- Raka Shome introduces postcolonialism to the communication field with the publication of her germinal essay on this subject.
- Thomas Nakayama and Robert Krizek introduce Whiteness theory.

2000 to 2008

- Julie Yingling extends the relational-dialogical perspective to communication development across the life span.
- Norah E. Dunbar introduces advances in dyadic power theory.
- Fan studies moves toward a spectacle–performance paradigm that emphasized the everyday nature of fandom.
- James Taylor and associates develop a co-orientational approach to organizational communication, bringing a constitutive view of organizational communication to the fore and founding that theoretical perspective known as the Montréal School.
- James Price Dillard proposes a model of communication goals featuring goals, plans, and action.

- Patricia Hill Collins integrates and publishes ideas about Black feminist epistemology.
- Guo-Ming Chen introduces Chinese harmony theory.
- Andrea Feenberg and Maria Bakardijeva, in separate studies, propose a constructivist critique of technology.
- Wallid Affifi and Judith Weiner first publish motivated information management theory.
- Leanne K. Knobloch and Denise Solomon begin to publish work on relational uncertainty.
- Michael J. Beatty, James McCroskey, and their colleagues put forward a biological approach to communication, which stands in opposition to many social theories in the field.
- Kwan Min Lee explains how people come to feel presence in virtual environments.
- Victoria DeGrazia, Jeremy Tunstall, and Mel van Elteren raise awareness of the Americanization of media.
- Jon Nussbaum and colleagues set forth a broad life span theory that integrates much work in this area and provides a possible umbrella for all communication theory.
- Karen Tracy advocates the study of ordinary communication practices through action-implicated discourse analysis.
- Deanna Fassett and John T. Warren bring together critical approaches to communication education and introduce the term *critical communication pedagogy*.
- Combining critical and constructivist ideas, Milton N. Campos proposes a theory of the ecology of meanings.
- Michael D. Slater summarizes work done to refocus media effects theory on reinforcing spirals.

ACCOMMODATION THEORY

Sociolinguistic research in the 1950s and 1960s had shown how people change the degree of formality of their language as a function of the social contexts in which they find themselves. This was explained in terms of social norms dictating language use. In other words, we should speak very softly and respectfully here, but we can be more boisterous and casual there. *Communication* (or speech) *accommodation theory* (CAT), while acknowledging such normative demands, was an attempt to move beyond these and toward a more dynamic framework underscoring the more complex sociopsychological dynamics involved in language use. More specifically, the theory provides a framework for understanding how and why people adapt their communication *toward and away from others* and the social consequences of doing so.

Spawning a robust literature over the past 40 years, CAT has been elaborated many times. Importantly, it has been revised regularly as a formal propositional structure that indicates the conditions likely to trigger certain accommodative moves, as well as the social effects that can ensue from these moves. In what follows, forms of accommodation—as well as the motives attending them—are introduced, as are some of the satellite models that sprang from the theory.

Accommodative Moves

CAT first emerged as a consequence of observing people shifting their dialects—and bilingual speakers switching their languages—toward others they address on an everyday basis. Many times, these shifts, called *convergences,* come about so as to reduce significant social distances between the speakers. For example, speakers can shift their accents toward higher, as well as sometimes lower, prestige-sounding speakers, shifts called *upward* and *downward convergence,* respectively. In response, recipients might, or might not, reciprocate, thereby resulting in *symmetrical* or *asymmetrical* patterns. Although these shifts could be strategic and consciously performed, other times participants may not have been consciously aware that such convergent activities had even occurred.

The driving force behind these convergent adjustments was initially construed in positive reinforcement terms. In other words, increasing one's similarity with another's communicative style would promote mutual liking—which research in fact confirmed. In this vein, CAT proposed that the more you admire or wish to gain the respect of an influential person, the more likely you are to converge toward that individual, assuming you have the communicative repertoire to enable this. While an abundance of accommodative moves is good for greasing the wheels of interactional success, there can be limits to this. Hence, CAT addresses notions of optimal magnitudes and rates of convergence in that social costs could be incurred by completely converging toward the communicative style of another (e.g., deliberately mimicking them in a potentially patronizing manner), and also doing so too swiftly.

As this discussion would suggest, relative social power became integral to the theory in the sense that it was people of lower status who converged more to people of higher status than vice versa as people of higher status controlled more social capital. Similarly, the process of immigrant acculturation is, in large part, a communicative one: Immigrants converge to the dominant language of their new culture whereas members of the host community typically feel little need to accommodate the various subordinate ethnic groups around them. Indeed, near nativelike proficiency in the host language can often be one of the strongest symbols that immigrants have assimilated to the new culture's values, practices, and ideologies.

Nonaccommodative Moves

Not converging toward another individual or other group can signal that the speaker does not value the approval or respect of the other. Predictably, nonconvergence would be unfavorably evaluated by recipients. After all, most of us do not appreciate it when we are not taken seriously or when we are not considered a worthy ally. That said, the attributions we make about why accommodations and nonaccommodations occur can be critical in mediating our evaluative reactions to them. For instance, an American sojourner's inability to speak or even pronounce the Welsh language could assuage any negative reactions associated with nonconvergence by most open-minded Welsh people.

The other side of the accommodative coin of convergence is, of course, *divergence,* and its ability to explain these contrastive shifts provides CAT much of its theoretical bite. Hence, depending on circumstances, speakers may diverge upwardly by sounding more sophisticated than their partner, for instance, while on other occasions, they may diverge downwardly and emphasize their contrastive cultural roots, regional origins, and so forth. Either way, these forms of divergence can increase perceived social distance as well as dissimilarities and are often consciously crafted for such purposes.

On the basis of social identity theory, divergence can often be conceived of as a strategy of social differentiation. In interethnic situations, diverging speakers are those who accentuate their in-group language style and do so when their ethnicities are salient within the situation and when they feel their group is accorded an illegitimately low status by others. An example would be an African American adopting more Black Vernacular English when encountering an aloof (and possibly prejudiced) White speaker. Although in-group peers might applaud such divergent moves, recipients of it might not view it quite so positively. Indeed, sometimes recipients can interpret divergences as personally directed when in fact they are actually intended to diverge from the group and not the individual.

Divergences can, however, fulfill other social and cognitive functions, as in the case of a speaker really slowing down in reaction to another talking way too quickly, and agitatedly so, about a topic he or she knows little about. Such a divergent reaction would be enacted in an attempt to calm the person down, thereby getting them to pace their utterances in a more measured fashion. Interestingly, CAT acknowledges the feasibility of blending convergences and divergences simultaneously, but at different communicative levels, in order to fulfill complementary identity and social needs. For instance, a communicator might wish to be respectful to a workplace superior and hence converge on some linguistic and nonverbal levels (such as politeness and deference), yet also wish to emphasize his or her own cultural allegiance by diverging on others (e.g., in-group slang, pronunciations, and posture).

Elaborations on the Theory

CAT really began to blossom as a more general theory of language and communication when it stepped beyond the adaptive use of accents and languages to embracing different discourse styles and nonverbal practices (e.g., gait, smiling, and dress). In addition, the theory has been invoked beyond face-to-face interactions into the domain of electronic communications, such as e-mail, text messages, and voice mail, and has also been used to explain interpersonal and intergroup encounters within the family. Furthermore, convergence and divergence, called in the theory *approximation strategies,* have been conceived of as but two of the many ways in which people do or do not accommodate. Attention now is also being paid to *interpretability strategies, discourse management,* and *interpersonal control* by taking into account the knowledge shared by the communicators and their communicative needs and relative social statuses. Once again, though, speakers can be more or less accommodative. Underaccommodative individuals— that is, those who may talk more from their own idiosyncratic agendas and feelings—may be viewed as egotistic, insensitive, and uncaring.

Subsequently, CAT took on more of a *subjectivist twist*. The insight here was that communicators accommodate not to where others are in any objectively measurable sense but rather to where they are believed to be. An example would be slowing down one's speech rate for an older person who is stereotyped as somewhat incompetent (and erroneously so), simply because of advanced age. This tactic, sometimes intended to nurture, could also be conceived of as overaccommodation. In parallel fashion, and drawing on self-categorization theory, people sometimes diverge from a contrastive out-group member and toward the linguistic *prototype* of what they believe is a typical-sounding in-group member. Speakers have, of course, widely different prototypes of what, say, an American should sound like, and hence divergences can manifest in very different forms. Indeed, miscarried convergences and divergences—albeit with positive intent—can be very potent forms of miscommunication. Put another way, effective accommodation is really an integral component of communicative competence.

The larger-scale social conditions necessary to trigger communicative differentiations (e.g., high group vitality) led to the development of *ethnolinguistic identity theory*, which in turn inspired the intergroup model of second language acquisition. The theoretical position holds that immigrants' inability to master, or failure to accommodate, their host country's dominant language could often be due to their desire to retain a strong and healthy vitality for their heritage language. Hence, what is typically attributed to learners' cognitive incapacities or to inadequacies of teacher or material could be more successfully defined as rugged cultural maintenance.

Satellite models emerged in other intergroup contexts as well, such as between people of different genders, physical abilities, and institutional roles and status (including medical specialties and in police–civilian interactions). Of prominence here was the development of the *communication predicament of aging model*. This theoretical position

has fueled a large amount of work in communication and aging and examined the ways in which accommodative acts, mediated by age stereotypes, can negatively impact older people's somatic processes to the extent that they actually accelerate physical demise. In addition, the model implies that a highly accommodative family or network climate can contribute to life satisfaction and maybe even longevity.

Concluding Remarks

Gratifyingly, CAT has achieved some stature in influential communication theory texts as well as in other disciplines, and many of its propositions have received empirical support across an array of diverse languages, cultures, and applied settings. The theory, like most others, can still be developed and applied to new situations without falling prey to the temptation of moving beyond its explanatory boundaries. Hence important issues still face CAT: (a) Which kinds of linguistic and communicated features are, more precisely, accommodated? (b) What constitutes optimal levels of accommodation? (c) Why do those who have not accommodated to their new linguistic communities for years continue not to do so, despite manifold rewards for being heard to be vocally a part of this group? (d) Finally, a future challenge will be to theorize about, not only how sociopsychological processes mediate accommodative communications, but how accommodation mediates sociopsychological processes.

Howard Giles

See also Action Assembly Theory; Attribution Theory; Interaction Adaptation Theory; Intercultural Communication Theories; Interpersonal Communication Theories; Power, Interpersonal; Social Exchange Theory; Social Identity Theory

Further Readings

Gallois, C., Ogay, T., & Giles, H. (2005). Communication accommodation theory: A look back and a look ahead. In W. Gudykunst (Ed.), *Theorizing about intercultural communication* (pp. 121–148). Thousand Oaks, CA: Sage.

Giles, H. (2008). Accommodating translational research. *Journal of Applied Communication Research, 36,* 121–127.

Giles, H., Coupland, N., & Coupland, J. (Eds.). (1991). *The contexts of accommodation.* New York: Cambridge University Press.

Giles, H., & Ogay, T. (2006). Communication accommodation theory. In B. Whaley & W. Samter (Eds.), *Explaining communication: Contemporary theories and exemplars* (pp. 293–310). Mahwah, NJ: Lawrence Erlbaum.

ACCOUNTS AND ACCOUNT GIVING

Accounts help people explain or make sense of events when something out of the ordinary occurs. An account can range from a speech to a story to a single word or nonverbal expression. Much of the research in this area focuses on accounts as linguistic devices employed in response to evaluations by self or others; accounts are communicated following troublesome conduct in order to transform what might otherwise be viewed as offensive into something acceptable. Accounts perform what is called *remedial work* and are linked to theories of politeness, face, attribution, conflict escalation, and impression management.

Accounts are of particular relevance to communication researchers, not only because they are firmly grounded in spoken and written discourse, but because the entire accounting process both enables and constrains present and future communication possibilities. Accounts create and maintain social order, they are used by people to influence one another, and they help people make sense of communication situations in particular and life in general. We account for our own failure events, but we also spend a great deal of time collaboratively constructing events and meanings based on the accounts of others. Speculating as to why someone did something is a ubiquitous conversation activity, whether in romantic relationships, in work settings, or around the family dinner table. In a very applied sense, the study of accounts may help individuals actively create better relationships in personal and professional contexts and be both better understood and more understanding. In their 1968 work, Marvin Scott and Stanford Lyman noted that the giving and receiving of accounts can potentially repair what is perceived to be broken and restore a relationship in the face of estrangement. Finally, people often focus on the construction of coherent identities and life stories in their narrative accounts when faced with traumatic losses and relational endings.

To fully appreciate the research on accounts, it is helpful to understand the background and history of research in accounts, to examine some of the empirical findings and typologies, and to look toward some of the promising new trends and directions in this line of inquiry.

Accounts in Conversation

The Account Episode

The interactional nature of accounts is clearly seen in the *account episode.* The account episode is initiated when someone recognizes a *failure event* (a violation of expectations or norms) that needs to be explained. The communication sequence is initiated by a verbal or nonverbal *reproach,* followed by the communication of an account and ultimately the *evaluation of the account.* Various researchers have focused on the types of accounts and their varying levels of politeness and preferability, the interactivity between the nature and severity of the reproach and the type of account given, and the subsequent attributions of the account giver after the account episode.

Types of Accounts

Early research on accounts focused on neutralizing offenses or performing remedial work, especially in interpersonal contexts. Scott and Lyman originally proposed two forms of accounts: e*xcuses* and *justifications.* Excuses acknowledge the failure event, but the account giver claims that she or he is not responsible for the failure event. The excuse maker may appeal to an accident, a biological drive, or a scapegoat. *Justifications* acknowledge the failure event, and the account giver accepts some responsibility for his or her actions but claims that the actions were not harmful or that the actions actually resulted in positive outcomes. The justification may deny the injury or victim altogether, may minimize the harm that came from the action, may appeal to a higher loyalty, may condemn the condemner, or may rely on a sad tale to justify current behaviors. Some forms of justifications are more credible and influential if they appeal to the values shared by the hearer, fostering a loyalty to the organization or cause rather than the individual.

Later researchers added *refusals* and *apologies* to the typology, noting that account givers have more options than excuses and justifications. Refusals may rely on logical argument or physical evidence, as seen in Michael Cody and Margaret McLaughlin's research on accounts used in traffic court, or refusals may challenge the authority of the person seeking the account or the fundamental labeling of the behavior as a failure event. Further, a person may offer a refusal in the form of a *denial.*

Apologies or *concessions* acknowledge one's responsibility for the failure event. The five elements of a *full apology* most likely to result in successful remedial work in a relationship are (1) an expression of guilt or remorse; (2) clarification that one recognizes what the appropriate conduct would have been and acknowledges that negative sanctions apply for having committed the failure event; (3) rejection of the inappropriate conduct and disparagement of the bad self that misbehaved; (4) acknowledgment of the appropriate conduct and a promise to behave accordingly in the future; and (5) penance, restitution, or an offer to compensate the victim(s).

Politeness Theory

Early research on accounts suggested that apologies were preferred speech acts for receivers, while justifications and denials were not. Apologies were seen as more polite and served to maintain positive face for hearers. Penelope Brown and Stephen Levinson note that politeness is expected and predicated on the notion of the "mutual vulnerability of face." That is, both individuals must cooperate to maintain face. People are generally more polite with powerful others who control resources or rewards, when the offense or goal is relatively serious, and when interacting with others who are socially distant. For example, people are often more polite with strangers and coworkers than with their own family members. In general, politeness theory predicted that concessions and full apologies would be received well because they communicate respect for the hearer and pose little or no threat to the hearer's face. An excuse is considered the second-most-polite form because

face is maintained for the hearer (an acknowledgment is made that the failure event occurred) as well as the speaker (he or she did not intend for the action to take place or had no control over the causes leading to the failure event). Justifications rank third in politeness since the account giver must fundamentally disagree with the hearer's perception of the situation, thereby failing to maintain the hearer's face. Denials and refusals are considered the least polite and are least preferred interpersonally since the hearer is challenged or proven wrong, threatening the hearer's positive face, or feelings of worth, and negative face, or freedom from intrusion.

Politeness theory is further relevant because empirical research indicates that how one asks for an account influences the kind of account provided. Initially, research indicated a matching of reproach–account–evaluation sequences. Polite reproaches elicit polite accounts. Polite accounts, or mitigating accounts such as apologies and excuses, often conclude with a positive evaluation by the hearer. Less polite reproaches, also called *aggravating reproaches,* threaten one's negative face and therefore elicit more aggravating accounts:

> You're late again! Don't tell me you couldn't leave work at a reasonable time again!

> I'm not late! You said you needed me here at 8:00 and here I am! *(denial)* Besides, who else is going to pay for your new garage if I don't bring home that bonus! *(justification)*

While not all the empirical research supports the notion that polite reproaches elicit polite accounts, we do know that with few exceptions, aggravating reproaches lead to aggravating accounts. Aggravating reproaches tend to predict aggravating accounts, which tend to be rejected, which tends to result in conflict escalation.

The second application of politeness theory focuses on the way that accounts operate in performing *remedial work* in relationships. Apologies are generally thought to be more effective (followed by excuses, justifications, and last, denials) in neutralizing negative evaluations, reducing penalties, reducing the perceived seriousness of the offense, reducing anger and aggression, and helping resolve disputes. A substantial body of literature supports this notion of mitigating or polite accounts in contrast with aggravating or less polite accounts, but much of this research involves a single-offense scenario in which severity is low and there are no legal ramifications. For long-term or stable, reoccurring offenses that harm others, such as ethnic prejudice and sexual harassment, or for situations such as accounting for infidelity, many excuses are far more aggravating than mitigating. For example, relying on an appeal to a biological drive, as in "boys will be boys," or denying intent ("Yes, I did proposition her, but I didn't mean to offend her—she should take it as a compliment!") is received with incredulity or anger.

It is also important to point out that expectations and forms of politeness may vary by culture. For example, while both Japanese and Americans generally prefer apologies, the second-most-preferred strategy for Japanese may be to say nothing. Other differences may include how elaborate, spontaneous, sincere, or relational apologies are in different cultural contexts. There are also differences in reproach, account, and evaluation based on status and power.

Attributions and Credibility

When hearing a reproach, when hearing an account, when evaluating an account, or when evaluating the entire account episode, communicators are making a whole series of judgments about the other. Hearers are judging whether the causes of behavior are stable or unstable, internal or external, personal or impersonal, controllable or uncontrollable, and intentional or unintentional. Empirical research suggests that excuses citing causes that are unintentional, unstable, uncontrollable, and external are more effective in achieving interpersonal goals than excuses that cite intentional, stable, controllable, and internal causes. We would rather hear that our date is late because of traffic than because of a lack of regard for us.

Related to attribution theory is *impression management,* or how individuals project a desirable and believable image and achieve particular goals through either *assertive* or *defensive* behaviors. Research indicates that accounts are most credible when they acknowledge both the gravity and the beliefs people hold about the situation at hand. Other research suggests that excuses may serve

account givers well in the short term, but at least in the workplace, excuses may lead to long-term attributions of being less competent and in control of one's life. While excuses may initially get someone "off the hook," an overreliance on them may prove detrimental to long-term impressions of competence. Some early studies found that workers employing justifications (accepting responsibility for one's actions) and refusals were more likely to be judged as competent leaders than were workers relying on excuses.

In addition to the above findings regarding the correlation between an account giver and his or her public image, Deborah Dunn and Michael Cody demonstrated that an account giver also impacts the public image of others. In a study of sexual harassment accounts, the accused was able to significantly impact the public image of the accuser, relative to the account provided. Several projects have linked the communication of accounts to self-presentations, showing that account givers were perceived as more likable if they fully apologized or used the "higher involvement" justification, or used a justification that showed a higher level of involvement, followed by excuses and justifications that minimized harm. Those using denials or challenges to authority were considered unlikable. Account givers were rated as both "competent" workers and "dedicated" workers if they used a full apology, justified their actions, or used a "logical proof," demonstrating their innocence. On the other hand, excuse givers (and individuals communicating only a perfunctory apology) were perceived as weak or indecisive, especially if using the "appeal to accident" claim, and people employing excuses were generally rated as less dedicated and competent (compared with those using a full apology or a justification). Attributions of strength, power, and intimidation followed from challenging a reproacher's authority or from using a denial.

New Directions

Most of the research done on accounts has focused on conversational events or hypothetical interpersonal scenarios. Some of the new directions in accounts research include crisis communication, organizational communication, and narrative therapy. Research conducted in crisis communication and organizational contexts highlights the challenge of communicating accounts to multiple audiences or stakeholders, which could also prove relevant in small groups and relational networks. New trends in narrative therapy indicate the power of accounts in narrating a coherent and healthy self.

Deborah Dunn

See also Attribution Theory; Conversation Analysis; Discourse Theory and Analysis; Impression Management; Interpersonal Communication Theories; Politeness Theory

Further Readings

Braaten, D. O., Cody, M. J., & Bell DeTienne, K. (1993). Account episodes in organizations: Remedial work and impression management. *Management Communication Quarterly, 6,* 219–250.

Brown, P., & Levinson, S. C. (1987). *Politeness: Some universals in language usage.* Cambridge, UK: Cambridge University Press.

Dunn, D., & Cody, M. J. (2000). Account credibility and public image: Excuses, justifications, denials, and sexual harassment. *Communication Monographs, 67,* 372–391.

Goffman, E. (1971). *Relations in public: Microstudies of the public order.* New York: Harper & Row.

McLaughlin, M. L., Cody, M. J., & Read, S. J. (Eds.). (1992). *Explaining one's self to others: Reason giving in a social context.* Hillsdale, NJ: Lawrence Erlbaum.

Schonbach, P. (1990). *Account episodes: The management or escalation of conflict.* Cambridge, UK: Cambridge University Press.

Scott, M. B., & Lyman, S. M. (1968). Accounts. *American Sociological Review, 33,* 46–62.

Sheer, V. C., & Weigold, M. F. (1995). Managing threats to identity: The accountability triangle and strategic accounting. *Communication Research, 22,* 592–611.

ACTION ASSEMBLY THEORY

Action assembly theory (AAT) is an approach to explicating the processes by which people produce verbal and nonverbal messages. The domain encompassed by verbal and nonverbal message production is obviously quite broad, and thus AAT addresses issues such as the nature of consciousness, the processes that give rise to creativity in what people think and do, the link between thoughts and overt actions, the relationship between verbal and nonverbal components of behavior, and how people plan and edit what they say. AAT has been applied in investigating a range of phenomena, including the nature of the self-concept, the behavioral cues that accompany deception, communication skill and skill acquisition, communication apprehension, and conditions that affect speech fluency. The theory is most closely associated with John Greene, his colleagues, and his students.

Every theory is developed within a matrix of assumptions, methods, research findings, and even other theories. It is useful, then, to examine key elements of the intellectual matrix in which a theory is embedded. In the case of AAT, four hierarchically ordered, foundational influences are particularly noteworthy. At the most basic level, AAT reflects the commitments of *science* as a way of knowing (i.e., an emphasis on empiricism, intersubjectivity, and rigor). Moving up one level, the particular branch of science reflected in the theory is that of *cognitivism*—explanation of behavior by recourse to descriptions of the mental states and processes that give rise to that behavior. Cognitive science itself encompasses a number of distinct philosophical and methodological approaches. The cognitive approach exemplified in AAT is primarily that of *functionalism* (i.e., inferring the nature of the mind from observed input–output regularities). At the fourth level of the hierarchy, the theory reflects the commitments of *generative realism:* the idea that people are simultaneously social, psychological, and physical beings and that theories of human behavior need to incorporate all three of these elements.

Just as one's grasp of a theory is enhanced by understanding the assumptions and scholarly traditions that it reflects, it is similarly useful to be able to locate a theory along a timeline of pertinent intellectual developments. Relevant to AAT, cognitive science emerged as the dominant approach in experimental psychology in the mid-1950s, partly as a result of growing recognition of the inadequacies of behaviorism. The assumptions and techniques of cognitivism were quickly assimilated by scholars studying linguistics and speech production, but cognitive science was rather slow to gain a foothold in the field of communication proper. Not until the mid-1970s did scholars in the field begin to adopt a cognitive perspective in exploring communication processes. By the early 1980s, cognitivism had become an important force in the field, but, with a few notable exceptions, this work was focused almost exclusively on input processing (e.g., message comprehension) rather than output processes (e.g., message production). In this context, in 1984, the first article on AAT appeared—a publication that subsequently received the National Communication Association's Woolbert Award for seminal contributions to communication research. In 1997, "A Second Generation Action Assembly Theory" (AAT2) was published, and research and conceptual refinements in the AAT framework continue to the present.

Key Aspects of the Theory

Pattern and Creativity

The particular form and substance of AAT was shaped by the intellectual traditions and assumptions described in the introduction above, but the single most important idea from which the theory sprang is a very simple observation that had been around long before AAT was developed. This fundamental idea is that all human behavior is both patterned and creative. In other words, a person's behavior exhibits his or her characteristic ways of doing things—the topics the person talks about, what he or she has to say about them, the vocabulary used to say those things, ways of pronouncing those words, facial expressions and gestures that accompany his or her speech, and so on. At the same time that speech and nonverbal behavior reflect each person's patterned ways of doing things, they are also always novel or creative: It turns out that we never exactly repeat ourselves, and even more importantly, we can use our patterned ways of thinking, speaking, and moving to create ideas, utterances, and actions that we have never produced before. In that simple observation lies the seed from which AAT grew: If behavior is both patterned and creative, then how can we understand where the patterned aspect of action comes from, and how can we understand how patterns give rise to novelty?

Mental Structures and Processes

As noted above, in keeping with a cognitive *functionalist* perspective, AAT attempts to explain behavior by specifying the nature of the mental structures and processes that give rise to that behavior. In the case of AAT, the fundamental question, again, is how to understand the patterned and creative property of human behavior. According to the theory, the patterned aspect of action arises from structures in long-term memory that have been acquired over the course of one's lifetime. These memory structures, termed *procedural records,* are like tiny packets of information about *what to do* (i.e., *action features*) in particular *situations* in order to accomplish specific *objectives*. So a person might have learned, for example, to say "I'm sorry" in an effort to undo the damage in a situation in which he or she hurt another's feelings.

Three things about procedural records are important to note. First, the memory codes in which they are represented reflect a hierarchy of levels of abstraction. Some codes, such as the example of saying "I'm sorry," are abstract (conceptual, languagelike). But other procedural records are expressed in codes that are far more basic than that. Some records, for example, consist of the motor-code memories that a person has acquired for walking, reaching and grasping, pronouncing the sound units of his or her native language, and swinging a golf club. An extension of the first point, the second is that a single procedural record does not represent all the information used to produce a behavior. People do not, for example, have one record that holds all the information they use to flick on a light switch or raise a glass of water to their lips; rather, even simple movements such as these reflect the combination of multiple action features. And in the same way, a person may have an abstract record that indicates the need to say "I'm sorry," but to actually produce that utterance, the person will have to rely on lower-level records for pronouncing those words. The third point is that people possess a very large number of procedural records. A conservative estimate might be that an adult possesses perhaps tens to hundreds of thousands of them.

In simplest terms, then, AAT holds that the patterned properties of behavior reflect the contents of procedural records held in long-term memory: Our behavior tends to reflect our own repertoire of ways of doing things. The creative character of behavior arises as a result of two processes by which the contents of procedural records are actually used in producing action. The first of these, *activation,* is basically a selection process that serves to retrieve those records that are relevant to one's goals and the situation, and the second, *assembly,* then integrates or combines activated action features to produce one's unfolding behavior. In essence, we think and do new things when we assemble new configurations of action features. Just as a child might construct an endless variety of forts, towers, and walls out of the same small set of building blocks, communicators constantly are assembling new thoughts, utterances, and nonverbal behaviors by combining novel configurations of action features.

The linchpin of AAT is the nature of the assembly process, which is described as *coalition formation*—combining action features that "fit" together, as, for example, when a high-level feature like the abstract notion to turn left meshes with motor-level features for turning the steering wheel and pressing the brake pedal. Activated action features that do not find their way into coalitions quickly decay and are not manifested in overt behavior. In contrast, those features that do mesh with others (a) stay activated longer, (b) are more likely to actually emerge in what a person says and does, and (c) are more likely to enter conscious awareness. The property of conscious awareness, in turn, brings to bear self-regulatory processes such as rehearsing, planning, problem solving, and editing.

The Nature of Message Behavior

From the perspective of AAT, human behavior is a complex, dynamic constellation of action features reflecting various hierarchically ordered representational codes. At any moment, only some coalitions will recruit motor-level features that permit them to be manifested in overt action; as a result, verbal and nonverbal behaviors reveal less than a person "means" (i.e., his or her momentary collection of coalitions). Conversely, because only a subset of coalitions is available to consciousness at any time, those same message behaviors will reveal more than the person "knows" (i.e., the

contents of phenomenal awareness). In contrast to standard goals–plans–action models of message behavior, AAT presents a picture of a much more rapid, chaotic, and disjointed system underlying message production. AAT is also distinguished from models of social skill that suggest that skilled behavior is the product of motivation and ability. AAT holds that people may be motivated to behave in socially appropriate and effective ways, and also possess requisite knowledge for doing so, and yet fail to act in an optimal way because of the nature of the activation and assembly processes.

Assembly Difficulties and Failures

A key point of emphasis in the various empirical and theoretical applications of AAT has been on situations in which people encounter difficulties in assembling action features. As might be expected, one effect of assembly problems is to slow message production. As a result, studies of the time course of message behavior have been an important part of the AAT research program. For example, several experiments have focused on the production of messages designed to accomplish multiple social goals. The general finding of these studies is that when one's social goals are incompatible (e.g., conveying a negative performance appraisal while showing support for the other), speech fluency is reduced. Another program of research, focused on skill acquisition, has examined patterns of improvement in speech fluency as a result of practice. An ongoing research program examines *creative facility*—individual differences in people's ability to produce novel messages—in an effort to understand why some seem to be better than others at "thinking on their feet."

John O. Greene

See also Cognitive Theories; Intrapersonal Communication Theories; Nonverbal Communication Theories; Scientific Approach

Further Readings

Greene, J. O. (1984). A cognitive approach to human communication: An action assembly theory. *Communication Monographs, 51,* 289–306.

Greene, J. O. (1997). A second generation action assembly theory. In J. O. Greene (Ed.), *Message* production: *Advances in communication theory* (pp. 151–170). Hillsdale, NJ: Lawrence Erlbaum.

Greene, J. O. (2007). Formulating and producing verbal and nonverbal messages: An action assembly theory. In B. B. Whaley & W. Samter (Eds.), *Explaining communication: Contemporary theories and exemplars* (pp. 165–180). Mahwah, NJ: Lawrence Erlbaum.

Greene, J. O. (2008). Action assembly theory: Forces of creation. In L. A. Baxter & D. O. Braithwaite (Eds.), *Engaging theories in interpersonal communication: Multiple perspectives* (pp. 23–35). Thousand Oaks, CA: Sage.

Greene, J. O., & Graves, A. R. (2007). Cognitive models of message production. In D. R. Roskos-Ewoldsen & J. L. Monahan (Eds.), *Communication and social cognition: Theories and methods* (pp. 17–45). Mahwah, NJ: Lawrence Erlbaum.

ACTION-IMPLICATIVE DISCOURSE ANALYSIS

Action-implicative discourse analysis (AIDA), developed by Karen Tracy, is the methodological arm of *grounded practical theory,* an approach that sees the cultivating of communicative practices as the desired end goal for research. Grounded practical theory, growing out of Robert Craig's work on communication as a practical discipline, is similar to Glaser and Strauss's *grounded theory.* Like grounded theory, grounded practical theory begins on the ground, studying existing communicative practices. Unlike grounded theory, which builds explanatory social science theory, AIDA, with its grounded practical theory roots, works to reconstruct the problems, interaction strategies, and normative ideals of a practice so that participants will be able to reflect in sophisticated ways about how to act.

AIDA is a theory–method hybrid that melds the analytic moves of discourse analysis—attending to situated talk and texts—with the goal of understanding a practice. AIDA takes a rhetorical point of view, presuming that people can make reflective decisions about how to communicate in order to achieve or avoid certain outcomes. It is also a normative approach, or one that has potential usefulness as a guide for acting wisely.

AIDA focuses on communicative practices in institutional sites. At its core, *practice* can be thought of as a way of referring to activities that occur in specific places among specific kinds of people; practice is another way to refer to a speech event that participants take to frame a situation. Ordinary names given to practices often call up a constellation of site–people–purpose connections. School board meetings, departmental colloquia, and classroom discussions are examples of easily recognized practices related to educational settings. A practice can be taken as a unit of the social world for purposes of analysis. Communicative practices that AIDA has studied have included physician–patient consultations, school board meetings, law enforcement crisis negotiations, and routine business meetings. Since institutional practices involve multiple categories of people who are positioned differently within any practice, the problems of a practice will differ with participants' positions.

As a kind of discourse analysis, AIDA begins by taping interaction and making a transcript of the talk involved in the practice. These two moves are the hallmark of any discourse analysis. In contrast to conversation analysis, another discourse approach, AIDA has a strong ethnographic thread, which means that the researcher must have extensive knowledge about the routine actions and variation in the practice. This requires observation of the practice, including how participants talk with each other in the practice (the focal discourse) and how the practice is discussed or written about in relevant institutional documents.

A basic assumption of AIDA is that most communicative practices are shaped by interactional dilemmas. In academic discussions, for instance, graduate students and faculty members want to appear intelligent but do not want to be seen as self-aggrandized and out to show off. In school boards, the meeting chair wants to move the meeting along so that decisions can get made but wants to do so in a way that ensures citizens feel they have had a fair chance to be heard. As a result of the dilemmas that are part of all practices, a normative proposal about how participants ought to act needs to weigh the multiple goods to which a practice is committed.

At the level of discourse moves and strategies, AIDA seeks to name and describe the site-specific interaction techniques that reveal a practice's problems and that participants use to manage these problems. In a public meeting, for instance, in which a school district was working on its policy regarding how gay, lesbian, bisexual, and transgendered students were to be treated, the elected board members and citizen speakers spent several months arguing over whether the school district's policy should state that it *respected* or *valued* diversity. The activity of arguing over words—usually characterized negatively—was found to be essential; it was deeply intermeshed with the activity of managing the sensitive value differences that the policy needed to address. In seeking to address this dilemma, people in the public meetings repeatedly found themselves advocating that certain wording changes were more than technical editing and were necessary to resolve value differences in the policy itself.

At the normative level of a practice, similar to critical discourse analytic approaches, AIDA is interested in addressing the question of how communicative conduct ought to be done. A difference between the two approaches is that critical discourse analyses tend to focus on critique, exposing invisible practices of power and domination rooted in macrosocial inequities, whereas AIDA is interested in positive reconstructions of practices that propose how a practice ought to be conducted in ways that recognize the multiple, competing purposes that are part of most communicative practices.

A study of academic brown-bag occasions, for instance, forwarded a normative proposal about the importance of a dilemma faced by participants: to see intellectual discussion as a communicative activity that needed to take ideas seriously, which would include criticizing bad ideas, and at the same time to see the importance of honoring people, their relationships, and their feelings, keeping in mind the consequences if people felt humiliated. "Ideas matter and people count" was the proposed conduct norm for academic discussion. In addition, the AIDA studies made visible the array of novel discourse strategies participants used to pursue this two-headed goal.

Karen Tracy

See also Conversation Analysis; Critical Discourse Analysis; Discourse Theory and Analysis; Ethnography of Communication; Facework Theories; Grounded Theory; Pragmatics

Further Readings

Craig, R. T., & Tracy, K. (1995). Grounded practical theory: The case of intellectual discussion. *Communication Theory, 5,* 248–272.

Tracy, K. (2005). Reconstructing communicative practices: Action-implicative discourse analysis. In K. Fitch & R. Sanders (Eds.), *Handbook of language and social interaction* (pp. 301–319). Mahwah, NJ: Lawrence Erlbaum.

Tracy, K. (2008). Action-implicative discourse analysis: Theorizing communicative practices. In L. A. Baxter & D. O. Braithwaite (Eds.), *Engaging theories in interpersonal communication* (pp. 149–160). Thousand Oaks, CA: Sage.

Tracy, K., & Ashcraft, C. (2001). Crafting policies about controversial values: How wording disputes manage a group dilemma. *Journal of Applied Communication Research, 29,* 297–316.

ACTIVATION THEORY OF INFORMATION EXPOSURE

The activation theory of information exposure, developed by Lewis Donohew and Philip Palmgreen, explains individual differences in attention and continued exposure to mass and interpersonal messages. The theory treats messages as sources of stimulation and holds that their success or failure to attract and hold listeners, viewers, or readers is a function of both cognitive and biologically based individual needs. Successful messages are those possessing enough novelty, movement, color, intensity, and other such formal features to generate a level of activation that will maintain attention but not so high as to cause distraction. Persons with lower stimulation needs may turn away from stronger messages and be attracted instead to messages with lower levels of stimulation. Messages may possess enhanced persuasive power when they are able to attract and hold attention long enough for the content to be processed.

In its early form, the theory relied primarily on the cognitive attraction experienced by message receivers and their conscious decisions about what information to view or read. It has evolved to include more emphasis on formal, nonverbal features of message stimuli and out-of-awareness decisions to turn away from or stay exposed to certain information.

The theory has gone through a number of iterations since it was originally published in the 1980s. In one, Nancy Harrington, Derek Lane, and associates expanded the model to include need for cognition or thought, with John Cacioppo and Richard Petty's need-for-cognition scale as the measure. In another, Rick Zimmerman and associates broadened the studies to include other measures of appetitive and inhibitory systems and impulsive decision making. Some of the most recent research involves pilot functional magnetic resonance imaging (fMRI) studies of brain responses to messages, which support the expectation that messages meeting novelty and sensation-generating criteria would generate arousal among higher risk takers in the more primal areas of the brain.

The activation theory of information exposure is deductive and nomological in nature. It is *deductive* in that it moves logically from general propositions to more specific ones. The theory is *nomological* in that it provides explanations of what causes the predicted responses across cases. The theory was developed in the tradition of *use-inspired basic research,* described as *Pasteur's quadrant,* which begins with a real-life problem and development of a general theory to account for underlying causes. On the basis of this explanation, a remedy is developed. In this instance, the problem was how to get people to expose themselves to information that could motivate them to accomplish a socially desirable goal such as becoming more competent citizens of a society. This entry explains the theory and provides a summary of supporting research.

Sensation Seeking and Message Exposure

A primary influence on the evolution of the theory has been the body of research on *sensation seeking* by Marvin Zuckerman and colleagues. Sensation seeking is a biologically based personality trait defined by Zuckerman as the tendency to seek varied, novel, complex, and intense sensations and experiences and the willingness to take physical, social, legal, and financial risks for the sake of such experiences. Sensation seeking and sensation avoidance are thought to have developed as fundamental survival behaviors for adaptation to dangerous

environments. Novel stimuli tend to alert the system for fight or flight, and the absence of such stimuli means safety, permitting relaxation and a turn to other activities. According to the developers of the activation theory of information exposure, the stimuli may appear in the form of messages, which are more likely to be attended to by *high-sensation seekers* if they possess one or more of the unsafe, risky characteristics mentioned above.

In research, sensation seeking was treated as a correlate of underlying social, genetic, and neurobiological forces that generate risky behavior. These forces involve the same neural substrate that mediates the rewarding effects of often-abused drugs, for example. These forces also mediate other individual differences possibly related to differences in the mesolimbic dopamine system of the brain. At this point, it is not known whether individuals can accurately assess either their level of need or how well the source of stimulation satisfies that need. In fact, many of these actions may be carried out without the individual's being consciously aware of them. Recent fMRI research described later in this entry indicates a possible role for more primitive areas of the brain.

The activation theory of information exposure holds that individuals have differing needs that determine how comfortable they are with activation or stimulation, and these needs become a major force in exposure to messages. The theory posits that attention to a stimulus source—in this situation, a message—is in large part a function of how well the need for stimulation is met by the amount of stimulation provided by the message. In research on messages likely to reach high-sensation seekers, Donohew, Palmgreen, and associates found that these messages contained higher levels of one or more of the characteristics indicating a need for alertness. These were (a) novel, creative, or unusual; (b) complex; (c) intense, emotionally powerful, or physically arousing; (d) graphic or explicit; (e) somewhat ambiguous; (f) unconventional; (g) fast paced; or (h) suspenseful. Other messages possessing lower levels of these attributes are classified as having low sensation value. High-sensation-value messages have been found in later research to appeal to individuals who are greater risk takers, whereas the risk takers were not attracted to messages possessing only moderate levels of the characteristics. Lower risk takers paid greater attention to the more moderate messages.

A primary proposition deduced from the above is that if the level of arousal generated is too high or too low, individuals will not achieve or maintain the sought-after state and will seek another source of stimulation, which could be another message. This could be accomplished with a click—or possibly many clicks—of the channel changer, which often appear to be made more or less automatically. A student listening to a lecture or a person reading a book might merely drift off into daydreaming. For high-sensation seekers in particular, messages are likely to be too boring if they do not provide considerable novelty, action, or other characteristics. This may also be true for *low-sensation seekers* but would occur at a lower level of sensation value. Certain very stimulating messages are far more likely to attract and hold the attention of high-sensation seekers but may be too threatening or otherwise repelling for lows. This is illustrated by the fact that high-sensation seekers tend to prefer scary movies far more than low-sensation seekers do. A second deduced proposition is that if activation remains within an individual's accepted range, that person is more likely to continue exposure to the message.

Research

Research involving the theory has been carried out by scholars in communication, psychology, and sociology, largely in the United States and Europe, studying prevention of drug abuse, risky sex, alcohol abuse, and other health-threatening behaviors. Given the tendency of the high-sensation seekers to engage in risky behaviors such as starting to have sex at an early age, having more sex partners, having sex without protection, and engaging in greater drug use, these individuals have become primary targets in health campaigns. Research involving predictions from the activation theory has established that with messages and other interventions designed to meet higher needs for novelty and sensation, attention to health information can be increased and desired behavioral responses can be brought about. Indeed, intervention programs using media and interpersonal communication and guided by this theory in combination with an applied model known as Sensation Seeking

Targeting, developed by Donohew and Palmgreen, have been highly successful in altering such risky behavior. One of the applications for *health campaigns* that emerged from this finding was that campaigns did not need to include both types of messages. High-sensation-value campaigns could be designed to persuade the prime target audiences, and these same messages could serve to reinforce the low-sensation seekers as well.

However, early research on the model did not involve either sensation seeking or health behaviors but rather responses to *political information* according to individual differences in cognitive and affective styles of information processing. Early on, however, the biological basis of the differences was suspected, and the sensation-seeking concept was adopted. Then came studies of message stimuli, leading to identification of characteristics of messages more attractive to high-sensation seekers and those more attractive to low-sensation seekers, as described earlier. This was followed by laboratory experiments in which messages possessing high- or low-sensation-value characteristics were shown on a television screen to high- and low-sensation seekers, and the amount of time spent with eyes on the screen was measured. It was discovered that high-sensation seekers tended to turn away from low-sensation-value messages, but low-sensation seekers tended to watch not only the latter but also almost as much of the high-sensation-value messages as high-sensation seekers did.

Although multiple studies were conducted with increasing levels of success, three in particular, carried out in two matched communities (Lexington, Kentucky, and Knoxville, Tennessee) and using controlled interrupted time series analysis, have offered the most convincing evidence in support of the activation theory in the service of persuasion campaigns. In the first, two televised antimarijuana campaigns were conducted in one city (Lexington) and, coinciding with the second campaign, in a comparison city (Knoxville). One hundred adolescents were interviewed each month in each city for 32 months—before, during, and after each campaign. All the campaigns significantly reversed upward developmental trends in marijuana use among high-sensation seekers. Several months after the first Lexington campaign, there was a "wear-out" effect for the persuasive message: Marijuana use had again begun to rise.

However, its use dropped again after the second campaign. Low-sensation seekers had low marijuana use across the period of measurement, and no campaign effects were observed.

In the second campaign study, the antimarijuana component of the Office of National Drug Control Policy's national media campaign was evaluated in the two cities by means of the same methodology as in the first two cities' study. Much of the campaign was declared a failure by the new drug czar, who called for more "hard-hitting" public service announcements (PSAs). The new PSAs came much closer to meeting criteria set out for high-sensation-value messages. These PSAs arrived in time for the final 6 months of the campaign and led to a dramatic reversal of use among high-sensation-seeking participants. Low-sensation seekers performed the same as in the previous study.

The third campaign was also conducted in Lexington and Knoxville but this time had as its goal a reduction of a number of specific risky sexual behaviors and the practice of specific safe-sex behaviors. Again, the approach was highly successful, even regarding a behavior that has been especially difficult to achieve: increased condom use among young adults, particularly those identified as high in sensation seeking.

Study of differential brain responses to messages drawing on the activation theory is in an early stage. An illustration of this work is a pilot study in which it was hypothesized that high-sensation seekers might attend more to the messages because they are biologically predisposed to show a greater response to visually presented arousal stimuli. In this instance, the messages were in the form of photographs. Researchers conducted fMRI with signals enhanced in the measurement of subcortical regions of the brain, including the hippocampus, nucleus accumbens, and amygdala. Research participants classified as high- or low-sensation seekers according to established criteria were given an emotional induction task, and brain images were collected while the participants viewed photographs, with half of the pictures classified as high arousal and half as low arousal in an established psychophysiological stimulus set known as the International Affective Picture Set. The most important finding was that limbic structures were more extensively activated in high-sensation seekers than in low-sensation seekers, with the *left*

medial orbitofrontal cortex (in the front or more advanced part of the brain) activated for both highs and lows and the *right amygdala* and *right insula* (in the rear or more primitive part of the brain) more extensively activated in the highs. This finding lends tentative support to the proposition that differences in exposure to information stimuli have a biological basis and have as yet unstudied implications for the human attention process.

Lewis Donohew

See also Communibiology; Health Communication Theories; Media Effects Theories; Trait Theory

Further Readings

Donohew, L. (2006). Media, sensation seeking, and prevention. In M. Vollrath (Ed.), *Handbook of personality and health* (pp. 299–314). London: Wiley.

Donohew, L., Lorch, E. P., & Palmgreen, P. (1998). Applications of a theoretic model of information exposure to health interventions. *Human Communication Research, 24,* 454–468.

Donohew, L., Zimmerman, R., Cupp, P., Novak, S., Colon, S., & Abell, R. (2000). Sensation seeking, impulsive decision-making, and risky sex: Implications for risk-taking and design of interventions. *Personality and Individual Differences, 28,* 1079–1091.

Palmgreen, P., Donohew, L., Lorch, E. P., Hoyle, R. H., & Stephenson, M. T. (2001). Television campaigns and adolescent marijuana use: Tests of sensation seeking targeting. *American Journal of Public Health, 91,* 292–296.

Stephenson, M. T. (2003). Examining adolescents' responses to antimarijuana PSAs. *Human Communication Research, 29,* 343–369.

Zuckerman, M. (1994). *Behavioral expressions and biosocial bases of sensation seeking.* New York: Cambridge University Press.

ACTIVITY THEORY

Activity theory is a psychological theory whose foundation was laid down by the Russian psychologist Lev S. Vygotsky. It has its roots in the Marxist concept of praxis—the dialectical connection of ideal and practical material activity.

Humans generally carry out activities ideally (symbolically) before they carry them out materially (concretely). Planning thus avoids, or at least mitigates, the dangers and pitfalls that inhere in straightforward trial-and-error activity. The symbolic activity, as one pole of praxis, can occur completely on the internal plane, as when a speaker plans what to say in a conversation, or it can take place externally, as when an architect uses a computer to develop plans for a skyscraper. An important aspect of the ideal pole of praxis is that it takes account of the conditions of practical material activity. Speakers are sensitive to the constraints of language, and the architect considers physical forces of nature (e.g., gravity and load-bearing properties of building materials).

Vygotsky proposed that the basic unit of analysis of mind is *word meaning*. This entails far more than simple reference, whereby a word such as *apple* references a particular object. It also reflects an abstract concept that allows us to reference linguistically (i.e., symbolically) such objects regardless of their specific features (e.g., size, color, content) and to link these to other concepts (e.g., orange, fruit, nutrition). In addition, words create categories that mediate our thoughts and actions even though the categories themselves may not actually exist in the material world. The English word *fruit,* for example, is a generalization that references no single concrete object that exists in the absence of the word itself. Things called apples, oranges, and pears exist, but not fruit. The fact that English, and other, though certainly not all, languages, use the category fruit means that speakers of these languages think and therefore act through the generalized category—for instance, when medical experts extol the health merits of eating fruit. What is consumed, however, is not fruit per se, but apples, oranges, or pears.

The explanatory principle that Vygotsky proposed to account for the origin and function of mind is *activity*. Although he laid the foundation for the theory, he did not fully flesh it out. This task was taken up by Vygotsky's colleague, A. N. Leontiev. (Some contemporary scholars have moved the theory in directions that diverge from Vygotsky's original and Leontiev's expanded notion of the concept and that background its psychological implications.) *Mind,* or more appropriately *consciousness* in Vygotsky's theory, is the ideal representation of activity interacting with an external object. The object can be a thing, a person, or an event. Importantly, included in the individual's representation of the activity is the attitude of others that emerges through social interaction. This is because individual consciousness results from the internalization of the meanings made available as the individual participates in socially organized and goal-directed collective activity aimed at transforming the natural world into a cultural, or humanized, world (e.g., transforming a piece of wood into a chair). The activity is mediated primarily through spoken (and written) communication. To communicate is to take account of not only one's own point of view but also that of others, including the objects they attend to and how they attend to and what they do in relation to these objects. In this way, our consciousness is imbued with representations of the needs, interests, and positions of others who participate in our social activity. In essence, we are first and foremost social individuals, but through social activity, we become psychological individuals. In other words, the inner plane of consciousness is created as we internalize the meanings that arise in and through social activity.

Leontiev proposed a unified theory of activity comprised of three distinct, though integrated, components: activity, action, and operation. Although the general theory is referred to as activity theory, one of its three components is characterized as activity, which, on the ideal plane, corresponds to the motive or driving force of activity. The motive arises from crystallization of a (biological or social) need (e.g., hunger, shelter, learning, labor, accumulation of wealth). Action corresponds to the material goal toward which an activity is directed. Operation refers to the concrete conditions under which an activity is carried out.

Consider first the case of a working-class family of four with an annual income of $50,000 whose members wish to satisfy the basic human need for shelter. They have a few options for meeting the need, including renting an apartment or purchasing a house. If they decide on the latter option, their need then coalesces into a motive, which drives their search for an appropriate abode. However, the motive is impacted by such conditions as the range of houses they have access to, given their income. The factors that come into play are size, amenities, location, taxes, insurance costs, and mortgage rate. Consequently, the goal of their search then becomes a concrete object constrained by the motive.

Next, consider the case of a family whose annual income exceeds $1 million and whose members also wish to satisfy the need for shelter. They are not constrained by the same conditions as the previous family, although nothing in principle would prevent them from purchasing the same type of house. As a result, their motive is likely shaped not only by their need for shelter but also by the socially influenced need to display their wealth. Thus, factors such as size, amenities, location, taxes, and the like will play out very differently in this case. For one thing, on the American scene, location and taxes play a major role in determining the quality of schools that children attend, which in turn impacts the odds of the children attending university. Even though both families are searching for a house, they are engaged in different activities, given that the search is driven by different motives and conditions. The ideal concept *house* that guides the concrete search action is quite different in each case. For one family, it is constrained by low cost, modest size, and lack of upscale amenities, and it most likely does not include concern for the quality of schools the children will attend. For the other, the concept entails high price, upscale amenities, ostentatious size, and concern over school quality. Thus, the families have divergent concepts of house, which means they talk, think, and act accordingly with regard to the object. Activity theory explains the difference.

James P. Lantolf

See also Cognitive Theories; Language and Communication; Marxist Theory; Reasoned Action Theory; Social Construction of Reality; Social Interaction Theories

Further Readings

Leontiev, A. N. (1978). *Activity, consciousness, and personality*. Englewood Cliffs, NJ: Prentice Hall.

Leontiev, A. N. (1981). *Problems of the development of the mind*. Moscow: Progress.

Rieber, R. W., & Carton, A. S. (Eds.). (1987). *The collected works of L. S. Vygotsky: Vol. 1. Problems of general psychology* (including thinking and speech). New York: Plenum Press.

ACTOR–NETWORK THEORY

Actor–network theory (ANT), also known as *sociology of translation*, is a theory initially developed by *science and technology studies* scholars—notably Michel Callon, Bruno Latour, and John Law—to account for the hybrid and plural nature of scientific work. Instead of starting from culture and society or, conversely, from nature and technology to explain the production of scientific knowledge, ANT scholars proposed from the 1980s to develop what they call a *performative* view of the production of science, a view that takes into account not only what scientists accomplish in their laboratory or fieldwork but also what nonhumans do, whether they be machines, texts, or even objects of study.

Accounting for the logic of scientific work is impossible, ANT scholars contend, if we do not acknowledge the difference that sensors, graphs, or samples make, for instance in the development of scientific practices. Symmetrically, they contend that political agendas and strategic alliances also make a difference in the unfolding of such practices. As scholars, we therefore do not have to choose between two starting points—nature or technology versus society or culture—to explain given practices; we have, on the contrary, to start from these practices themselves to explain the production of nature, technology, culture, and society.

Although this perspective could have remained limited to science and technology studies, it quickly became quite influential in many different disciplines, such as geography, philosophy, anthropology, organizational studies, and communication, to name just a few. In communication studies, this approach was especially introduced through the work of representatives of the Montreal School of Organizational Communication, constituted around the work of James R. Taylor. According to this perspective, an organization, as any collective, should never be considered the starting point of our studies and reflection but should rather be understood as the product of communication activities. This bottom-up approach thus proposes to study the organizing properties of communication by analyzing various interactional and textual activities that literally constitute what we call an organization. An organization, according to this approach, should be considered as literally filled with agencies in interaction, whether these agencies are procedures, managers, computers, architectural elements, workers, or machines.

Several key concepts have been developed over the years to account for the constitution of the hybrid and plural world we live in. One of the most important is *spokesperson,* or *macroactor,* in that it shows how a given (human or nonhuman) actor can become a network (and vice versa); hence the expression *actor–network.* Acting and/or speaking in the name of, on behalf of, and/or in the stead of something or someone else, that is, *macroacting,* is indeed the main way by which collectives or networks are constituted. Once an agent is recognized and acknowledged as acting or speaking in the name of others, whether they are a collection of individuals (a *we*) or a collective (an *it*), these others can be said not only to have an identity—they start to exist as a we or as an entity, an it—but also to act from a distance, that is, to tele-act or telecommunicate.

For instance, when French diplomats meet their U.S. counterparts in official settings, it is not only they who talk to each other but also the respective countries they each represent and even, to a certain extent, the citizens of these two countries. If these representatives are recognized as speaking and acting on behalf of their respective countries and constituents, their voices become France's and the United States' voices, as well as the voices of the French and of the Americans. As can be seen in this example, and it is another distinguishing feature of ANT, we do not need to choose between so-called macro- and microperspectives, given that this illustration shows how one country can talk to another without leaving the terra firma of interaction. What France and the United States are and do can be defined only through who and what their spokespersons and "spokesobjects" are and do in their name. In other words, both are performed into being each time representatives are interactively acknowledged as acting and speaking for them.

Another key concept developed by ANT is *translation.* Using the same illustration, one could notice that these diplomats are supposed to not only incarnate or represent—that is, make present—their respective country's interests but also translate them. Translation implies transformation, which means that translating requires, by

definition, that the result of this operation be sanctioned (positively or negatively). Do the constituents or president recognize themselves in these talks? Are the diplomats faithfully translating their interests? This is a question that any activity of representation and/or translation implies. Interestingly enough, translation can be used to account not only for political representation but also for any kind of activity or practice (whether scientific, technological, or cultural).

For instance, a traffic light installed in a busy intersection is supposed to technically translate an injunction to stop or go at regular intervals of time. From the administrative body that authorized this device through the engineers who designed it to the workers who actually installed the lights, a series of translations took place that made this traffic regulation possible. ANT is precisely interested in all these activities of translation that involve the filling in of forms, the designing of plans, the mobilization of machines, all partaking in the unfolding and tracing of an organized and collective activity.

What makes this approach especially interesting to communication scholars is that any act of communication can be understood as an activity of translation. Whenever people talk or write to each other, what is said is supposed to translate what is meant by the interlocutors, but what is meant always implies a form of implicit or explicit sanction that is displayed physically in the turns of talk (especially through the presence or absence of conversational repairs, or corrections, as shown by conversation analysts). Through the detailed study of interaction, one can also retrace what or who is made present in a given discussion, whether under the form of collectives, ideologies, passions, principles, attitudes, or emotions. Thanks to this approach, one can show how our world is literally performed into being through interaction.

François Cooren

See also Conversation Analysis; Ethnomethodology; Organizational Communication Theories; Organizational Co-Orientation Theory; Performance Theories; Semiotics and Semiology

Further Readings

Cooren, F. (2006). The organizational world as a plenum of agencies. In F. Cooren, J. R. Taylor, & E. J. Van

Every (Eds.), *Communication as organizing: Empirical and theoretical explorations in the dynamic of text and conversation* (pp. 81–100). Mahwah, NJ: Lawrence Erlbaum.

Latour, B. (2005). *Reassembling the social: An introduction to actor-network theory.* London: Oxford University Press.

Taylor, J. R., & Van Every, E. J. (2000). *The emergent organization: Communication as site and surface.* Mahwah, NJ: Lawrence Erlbaum.

ADVERTISING THEORIES

Since the early 1900s, scholars have attempted to discern whether advertising has its own distinctive theories because it seemed that any serious profession should draw from a systematic analysis of its trade rather than from chance or instinct. With U.S. advertising expenditures at about $149 billion in 2007 (about 1.1% of the total U.S. gross domestic product), there is no doubt that advertising can be looked at as a serious industry. Yet when Walter Dill Scott, director of the Psychological Laboratory of Northwestern University, conducted his research in 1903 for his work on advertising theories, he could not find any reference to a theory other than psychological approaches. Even more contemporary works, such as the well-known title *How Advertising Works*, still describe the advertising process as a strategic communication procedure whose function is to create a psychological (and subsequently behavioral) change in a potential consumer of a product, service, or idea. Thus, when we talk about advertising theories, we basically talk about theories of consumer psychology.

Lacking its own theories but operating at the intersection of business and social sciences, advertising has not only borrowed from these disciplines but often attracted these disciplines to engage with it and explain the advertising process and its success with their own models and theories. In general, the major influence of advertising seems to occur in the area of consumer perception of a brand. To that extent, advertising must understand the meaning an object has over the life of a consumer, as well as the limits of these cultural definitions, before trying to amplify this object into a brand. Irving White provided a fitting example with the social values implied by the concept of perfume. Given that this concept invokes ideas of femininity for many individuals in the U.S. culture, advertising of male cosmetics has to carefully sidestep beliefs about femininity and narcissism. At the same time, this example illustrates how conceptual valuations of an object or idea—ideas, beliefs, feelings, and actions expressed by members of a culture—can shift over time. Today's brand advertising of male-oriented cosmetic products is different from that of just 20 or 30 years ago for the very reason that perceptions of men using perfume have changed.

The idea of how people come to understand and relate to artifacts is of interest to social psychology and anthropology. As thinkers such as George Herbert Mead and Jean Piaget have indicated, the relationship between objects and users is dynamic; as individuals acculturate into the larger society, they redefine their relationship to an object in accordance with the values frame of their environment. Culture, in other words, fills a product with meaning based on biological, social, and psychic needs the product fulfills. In other words, consumers purchase not just the plain product but also the multitude of meanings associated with the product. The function of advertising is to create subcategories of values and needs within the social structure and to connect these with the product. Consumers then select those brands whose sets of implied experiences fit into the subgroup with which they identify.

With the growing globalization of brands in an emerging global marketplace, advertising increasingly takes (sub)cultural differences into account. The different social histories of Europe, Asia, and other parts of the world produce consumers who exhibit unique cultural characteristics that influence their needs and wants, their methods of satisfying them, and the messages to which they are most likely to respond. Failure to understand the cultural environment can lead to miscommunication. Beginning to understand that words and symbols have specific meanings for consumers in a given culture, scholars in international advertising turned to the idea of cultural distance. Advertising studies now include the analyses of the meaning of verbal and nonverbal language, concepts of time and space, and cultural-values indicators such as individualism–collectivism, masculinity–femininity, uncertainty avoidance, and long-term versus short-term orientation.

It is difficult to succinctly group theoretical approaches to advertising into neat categories since the literature on advertising is varied and is rooted in different premises. For instance, works focusing on the functional areas of advertising would group it by campaign creation, media placement, budgeting, and testing and measurement. Literature focusing on advertising processes would highlight rational and emotional theories of persuasion such as the *elaboration likelihood model* and *conditioning* theories. Literature focusing on advertising outcomes would categorize along persuasive components such as *argument strategies, arousal strategies,* and *endorser strategies.* Psychological process analyses would regard persuasion as one component of effects, along with *attitude change* and *involvement.* Finally, popular culture studies would analyze advertisements themselves as an *expression of symbolic structures* that give significance and importance via subjective constructions and decoding procedures (e.g., presentation of minorities and women, commercialism, group dynamics). In addition, the different approaches are highly interrelated and overlapping. For instance, affective and cognitive models populate all but one approach. Therefore, the most prevalent theories will be discussed here, acknowledging that many others exist.

Hierarchy-of-Effects Models

Originally developed in the personal-selling literature, the *hierarchy-of-effects model* has undergone various modifications in its historical development such that today we use it in the plural form, indicating that competing models exist.

In 1898, St. Elmo Lewis proposed a stair-step hierarchical framework that theorized the necessity for salespeople to attract attention, interest, and desire in a logical sequence. By the later addition of action as a final step, this original model came to be known as action-implicative discourse analysis, which is still one of the most referred-to models in the advertising and sales literature. In the 1960s, Robert Lavidge and Gary Steiner challenged the immediate-sales argument of advertising effectiveness, arguing instead that advertising effects are

often long-term in nature and do not necessarily translate into sales (e.g., brand image building). They proposed seven steps consumers go through en route to the purchasing point: unawareness, awareness, knowledge, favorable attitude toward the product, favorable attitude toward the brand, desire and conviction, and actual purchase. At the same time, Russell Coney developed his model, known as *defining advertising goals for measured advertising results,* which stressed an awareness, comprehension, conviction, and action hierarchy. Coney reasoned that most advertising objectives were too vague for their effectiveness to be measured with sales data and hence should be measured with communication objectives.

While these models loosely touched on the cognition, affect, and conviction stages, psychological and sociological research addressing the consistency between attitudes and beliefs incorporated the described hierarchy of persuasive communication into consumer behavior models. For example, William McGuire's information processing model suggested that information first has to be presented, then attended to, then comprehended, then yielded to, then retained, and finally acted on.

A serious challenge to the traditional hierarchy came in the 1970s from Michael Ray and his colleagues, who argued that there are actually three different models that can explain audience responses. The first, the so-called learning model, puts cognitive understanding (thinking) first, before attitude development (feeling) and later action (behaving). This model most closely resembles the original models discussed above. A second model, known as dissonance-attribution hierarchy, suggests a reversal of the previous model, that is, consumers first behave or act, then develop feelings toward the brand as a result of their actions, and finally create cognitive arguments to support their behavior. Finally, as the result of research on repetition and slow learning processes in advertising, the third model, known as the low-involvement hierarchy, contends that consumers act, then learn as a result, and finally develop feelings and attitudes from the combined results of the behavior and learning.

Despite the ongoing modification attempts to its structure, the persistent attention given to the hierarchy of effects in advertising research attests to its continuing importance. Nevertheless, questions about the direction of research tied to this concept remain. For instance, a result of challenges and subsequent debates about the "right" hierarchy has been a growing perception that advertising might be less powerful than originally thought and that its main contribution lies more in its reinforcement of an idea than in its original persuasive force. Moreover, hierarchy-of-effects models are theoretically weak as they are missing the motivational mechanisms necessary to explain how to move individuals to the various stages in the models. Finally, given the many influence factors present, advertising's impact on sales seems to be less immediate and direct than originally assumed. One factor, for instance, is the concept of involvement, which has been considered by many as a crucial mediating variable in the sequential nature of the three main phases of the hierarchy of effects.

Audience Involvement

In response to the accepted position that persuasive communication depends on active message processing, Herbert Krugman, in 1965, offered a thesis that linked message effectiveness with the audience's degree or lack of personal involvement with the message. More specifically, Krugman understood involvement not as attention or interest but as connections that an audience member makes between the message stimuli and the member's own life; Krugman distinguished between two types of involvement (high and low), both of which can lead to effective advertising. The argument goes that a decrease in involvement does not increase resistance to the message but rather lowers processing; that is, learning is passive as consumers do not connect the message with a personal want or need and hence learn information randomly as a result of repetitive message encounter. In high involvement, a message acts directly on modifying beliefs; in low involvement, the impact is rather on exposure to sensory appeals (e.g., brand logos). As the latter occurs more gradually, effectiveness requires repeated exposure. According to Krugman, there are only three levels of exposure in psychological terms: curiosity, recognition, and decision. Since many advertisers misunderstood his arguments as ideas about effective media planning and placement, his thesis of a *frequency of three* subsequently became ensnared in debates about message repetition and recency effects.

Involvement also plays a pivotal role in Carolyn and Muzafer Sherif and colleagues' work in *social judgment theory*. According to the theory, the level of ego involvement depends on whether the issue arouses an intense attitude. It further argues that individuals who are highly involved in an issue are more likely to evaluate all possible positions, therefore increasing their standpoint of unacceptability regarding the issue. Because discrepant positions are less tolerable when a person is highly involved, highly involved individuals will be harder to persuade than will uninvolved individuals. Uninvolved consumers are willing to consider more brands but less willing to evaluate brands. In short, lack of involvement leads to perception with little or no cognitive activity.

A third theory connected with involvement is the *elaboration likelihood model*, a framework developed by psychologists Richard Petty and John Cacioppo in 1981. This cognitive-process model derives its name from the likelihood that a person thinks deeply (elaborates) about an advertisement when exposed to it and is primarily concerned with changing the direction of attitudes through persuasion. The basic premise of this model is that the route by which a message persuades consumers depends on their involvement with the message. Two routes exist: the *central route* and the *peripheral route*. In the former, people have both the motivation and the ability to evaluate the message and will hence diligently process the message; that is, they will look for and respond to strong arguments in favor of the message and counter what they perceive as weak arguments. In the latter, people may lack the motivation or ability to evaluate the message and thus are more likely to respond to cues associated with the message, such as entertainment value or a celebrity spokesperson, rather than to cognitive arguments. In short, high involvement leads to central processing resembling traditional hierarchy models, whereas low involvement leads to peripheral processing.

Important to note is that attitude change in terms of central processing is the result of thoughtful reflection on information. As such, change does not occur just as an outward compliance (behavior change) but indicates a change in beliefs (personal acceptance or a shift in values or opinion). This kind of change, then, is seen as fairly stable and resistant to counterarguments that may be encountered later. Attitude change in the peripheral route of processing, on the other hand, emanates from affective cues or social compliance. While it seems plausible to assume that this would lead to an unstable change process, this is not necessarily so. Empirical work based on the model has shown that people can internalize a message solely on the fact that it is socially and emotionally satisfying; that is, persuasion relies not necessarily on information and logic alone but also on social and affective factors.

Theories of Personality and Motivation

In the discussion of advertising strategy and consumer targeting, one central topic is the factors within the recipient of a message that render an advertising appeal successful; that is, how can messages use an individual's personality or motivation to create favorable brand attitudes and images? Individual factors include the reasonably stable patterns of emotions, motives, and behavior that distinguish one person from another. Personality is the key to adjustment. Similarly, most motivation theorists assume that motivation is involved in the performance of all learned responses; that is, a learned behavior will not occur unless it is energized. The major question among psychologists, in general, is whether motivation is a primary or secondary influence on behavior. That is, are changes in behavior better explained by principles of environmental influences, perception, memory, cognitive development, and emotion, or are concepts unique to motivation more pertinent?

Association Theories

Associationism in philosophy refers to the idea that mental processes operate by the association of one state with its successor states. The idea was first recorded in Plato and Aristotle, especially with regard to the succession of memories. Four principles define the core of the theory: (1) All ideas are associated together in the mind through experience; (2) all ideas can be reduced to a basic stock of simple ideas; (3) these simple ideas are elementary, unstructured sensations; and (4) simple, additive rules are sufficient to predict the properties of complex ideas from the properties of the underlying simple ideas.

Association theory was advanced primarily by a succession of 18th- and 19th-century British philosophers, such as John Locke, David Hume, and John Stuart Mill. Many principles have been proposed to explain how ideas become associated with each other. These include contiguity (ideas formed close together in time), repetition (ideas that occur together repeatedly), recency (associations formed recently are the easiest to remember), and vividness (the most vivid experiences form the strongest associative bonds). A closely related concept to associationism is behaviorism, whose principles of conditioning are based on the association of responses to stimuli.

The relevance of the above principles for advertising becomes evident when we consider that humans are able to associate with each other via symbolic bonds and thus have collective existences built on symbols that encapsulate shared memories. Therefore, the aim of consumer advertising is to associate products with symbols that exemplify values, group identity, pleasure, achievement, and the like. Since brand names themselves carry associations, the idea of *brand image* is entirely based on association concepts as anything associated with a brand has the potential to affect its image.

Furthermore, brand image is often used as a heuristic for brand choice. On one hand, it saves cognitive energy (consumer as *cognitive miser* concept); on the other hand, it relieves or avoids inner tension or doubt about the choice (*cognitive dissonance* and *loyalty* concept). Since this choice is consequently purely one of likability and trust, advertising has to make sure of two things. First, it must create a likable and trustworthy association cue, such as a likable spokesperson, a positive emotional state (nostalgia, fun), or effective symbolism (patriotic signs, desirable lifestyles). Second, it must monitor consumers' impression of these cues over time. The effect that, for instance, a celebrity spokesperson's tarnished image can have on a brand (Martha Stewart and Kmart, Kobe Bryant and Nike) is an example of the close connection that is built in people's minds.

Reversal Theory

Reversal theory is a theory of motivation and emotion. Unlike conventional trait theories, which measure the amount and consistency of one's behavior, reversal theory focuses on flexibility and what spurs reversals from one psychological state to another. The theory is organized into four domains of focus (means–end, rules, transactions, and relationships). Each has two opposing motivational states. An individual reverses between states as situations—and the meaning one attributes to them—change. A person's emotions result from whether one's motives are being fulfilled or not. If they are, good emotions result; if they are not, negative emotions emerge. The theory's name comes from the idea that there is a frequent switching between the two modes. If we are bored, we seek excitement; if we are anxious, we seek relaxation.

Advertising applies these ideas in two ways: (1) It aims to understand the mental state that is conducive to positive brand associations in order to create targeted strategies (e.g., destination marketing), and (2) it attempts to switch someone's motivation in order to be able to reduce the number of valid arguments that need to be brought forth to influence someone (e.g., when in a positive, playful mood, people create fewer counterarguments).

Summary

Advertising is a complex and diverse field, and often even those involved with it have difficulty discerning what works and why. In 1976, Charles Ramond argued that advertising has no general theory that is widely accepted but forms a discipline in which a collection of pseudotheories exist whose reason for existence is introspection. While advertising typically uses information, the emphasis in a persuasive advertising message is on influencing the receiver. Moreover, since the advent of the Internet and online marketing, the long-held notion of the mass market has given way to that of a more individualized consumer as digital consumers are no longer "passive" receivers of the advertiser's message but will actively select the advertising message or completely disregard it. New theoretical models are emerging to explain the many-to-many communication processes evolving.

Olaf H. Werder

See also Attitude Theory; Cognitive Theories; Elaboration Likelihood Theory; Emotion and Communication; Persuasion and Social Influence Theories; Social Judgment Theory

Further Readings

Barry, T. E. (1987). The development of the hierarchy of effects: An historical perspective. In J. H. Leigh & C. R. Martin Jr. (Eds.), *Current issues and research in advertising* (pp. 251–295). Ann Arbor: University of Michigan Press.

Jones, J. P. (Ed.). (1998). *How advertising works: The role of research.* Thousand Oaks, CA: Sage.

Mehta, R., & Sivadas, E. (1995). Direct marketing on the Internet: An empirical assessment of consumer attitudes. *Journal of Direct Marketing, 9*(3), 21–32.

O'Shaughnessy, J., & O'Shaughnessy, N. J. (2004). *Persuasion in advertising.* New York: Routledge.

Ramond, C. (1976). *Advertising research: The state of the art.* New York: Association of National Advertisers.

Ray, M. L. (1973). Marketing communication and the hierarchy of effects. In P. Clarke (Ed.), *New models for communication research* (pp. 146–175). Beverly Hills, CA: Sage.

Sandage, C. H., & Fryburger, V. (Ed.). (1960). *The role of advertising: A book of readings.* Homewood, IL: Irwin.

Scott, W. D. (1903). *The theory of advertising.* Boston: Small, Maynard.

Tellis, G. J. (2004). *Effective advertising: Understanding when, how, and why advertising works.* Thousand Oaks, CA: Sage.

AFFECT-DEPENDENT THEORY OF STIMULUS ARRANGEMENTS

Based on the core assumption that individuals are motivated to seek pleasure and avoid pain, the affect-dependent theory of stimulus arrangements of Dolf Zillmann and Jennings Bryant can be applied to many communication contexts. However, in practice, applications of the theory have been used to explain how and why individuals choose particular media content when faced with numerous alternatives. In our world of abundant, if not excessive, media options, the theory provides a parsimonious account of media choice based on individuals' moods and emotional states. This entry describes fundamental assumptions, identifies four key predictor variables, and briefly notes recent theoretical developments.

The idea that individuals are hedonists forms the foundation of the affect-dependent theory of stimulus arrangements. This means that individuals will actively arrange their surroundings in such a way that minimizes exposure to unpleasant stimuli while maximizing exposure to positive stimuli. The theory further assumes that individuals learn through a process of operant conditioning the types of environmental stimuli that best aid in accomplishing this hedonistic objective. In other words, people come to associate exposure to mediated communication, particularly entertainment media, with positive outcomes—either relief from negative moods and other unpleasant stimuli or the enhancement of pleasurable experiences. The theory is broad enough, however, to allow that nonmediated experiences can also serve the hedonistic objective.

Research evidence in support of the theory relies mainly on preferences for entertainment media as the dependent variable and the initial emotional state of individuals as the crucial independent variable. These investigations have identified three message-related characteristics and one psychophysiological factor that predict media choice: excitatory homeostasis, message–behavioral affinity, intervention potential, and hedonic valence.

Excitatory homeostasis refers to the notion that individuals prefer to experience a state of arousal that is neither over- nor understimulating. Thus, in the context of the theory, it is assumed that overstimulated individuals will arrange their environments so as to decrease their level of arousal, whereas individuals who are understimulated will do the opposite. By unobtrusively recording the television programs preferred by bored or stressed study participants, Jennings Bryant and Dolf Zillmann observed this tendency to seek out excitatory homeostasis in a carefully controlled experiment. In that study, they found that bored participants selected arousing media content and avoided relaxing fare when given the opportunity to do so. Conversely, participants who were manipulated to feel stressed opted to view relaxing programs for longer periods of time than bored individuals did.

The second key predictor of selective exposure to entertainment media is *message–behavioral affinity*. This variable refers to the degree of similarity between communication content and affective state. A seminal study by Dolf Zillmann, Richard Hezel, and Norman Medoff tested the hypothesis that mood would dictate preferences for situation comedies, game shows, and action dramas on television. To a large degree their

predictions were supported, with one notable exception. Unexpectedly, participants who were placed in a bad mood did not opt for situation comedies, as predicted; they avoided such content. Subsequent analyses and follow-up studies showed that this behavior can be attributed to a motivation to avoid media content that is similar or related to a person's negative emotional state. Thus, study participants who were insulted tended to avoid situation comedies that featured put-downs and other insults. Therefore, the theory assumes that individuals experiencing negative mood states will prefer messages with little behavioral affinity, whereas individuals in positive moods will tend to prefer messages with high behavioral affinity.

Researchers have also observed that media content has varying ability to alter emotional states, primarily due to its capacity to disrupt mental rehearsal of thoughts related to specific moods. Thus, media essentially functions as a distracter by preventing individuals from dwelling on their current mood or feelings. This ability of media content to engage cognitive processing resources is referred to as its *intervention potential* (some literature also uses the term *absorption potential* or *capacity*). Messages with a high intervention potential have the greatest potential to diminish the intensity of a mood, so long as the content in that message is not related to an individual's emotional state. For example, in one study, viewing a game show effectively reduced anger in provoked individuals whereas viewing an aggression-filled ice hockey match failed to do so. However, a nature film demonstrated little intervention potential for either provoked or nonprovoked participants.

The fourth key predictor is *hedonic valence,* which refers to the positive or negative quality of a media message. Media content that can be described as noxious, threatening, and distressing has a negative hedonic valence, but uplifting, amusing, happy, and reassuring media content has a positive hedonic valence. In general, individuals in negative moods prefer hedonically opposite media content, whereas positive moods will tend to motivate preferences for hedonically similar content.

Theoretically, these four factors are conceptually distinct and can be experimentally manipulated to ascertain their effects on media selections, but in practice it is not always possible to isolate each variable. For example, messages that are highly negative or positive also tend to be inherently involving. Despite these difficulties, a large body of literature supports the basic assumptions of the affect-dependent theory of stimulus arrangements.

Recently, the theory has been expanded to include other concepts, namely, spontaneous and telic hedonism and informational utility. To date, the bulk of the research supporting the theory has investigated situations that explore the effects of prevailing moods on immediate selection of media—so-called *spontaneous hedonism*. However, at times individuals may opt to delay the immediate management of mood states in favor of other goals or needs. In such cases, their behavior may appear to be counterhedonistic in the short run but may conform to theoretical expectations at a later time. *Telic hedonism* refers to this type of behavior. The concept of *information utility* refers to situations in which individuals seek out information in order to reduce uncertainty. At present, only a handful of studies have explicitly incorporated these new concepts in experimental research.

John J. Davies

See also Cognitive Dissonance Theory; Emotion and Communication; Uses, Gratifications, and Dependency

Further Readings

Zillmann, D. (1988). Mood management: Using entertainment to full advantage. In L. Donohew, H. E. Sypher, & E. T. Higgins (Eds.), *Communication, social cognition and affect* (pp. 147–171). Hillsdale, NJ: Lawrence Erlbaum.

Zillmann, D. (2000). Mood management in the context of selective exposure theory. In M. E. Roloff (Ed.), *Communication yearbook 23* (pp. 103–123). Thousand Oaks, CA: Sage.

Zillmann, D., & Bryant, J. (1985). Affect, mood, and emotion as determinants of selective exposure. In D. Zillmann & J. Bryant (Eds.), *Selective exposure to communication* (pp. 157–190). Hillsdale, NJ: Lawrence Erlbaum.

AFROCENTRICITY

Afrocentricity is a philosophical paradigm that emphasizes the centrality and agency of the African person within a historical and cultural context. As such it is a rejection of the historic marginality and racial otherness often present in the ordinary paradigm of European racial domination. What is more, Afrocentrists articulate a counterhegemonic or domination-resisting view that questions the application of epistemological ideas rooted in the cultural experiences of Europe to Africans or others as if these ideas were universal principles. In this sense, Afrocentricity is a critique of domination that aggressively establishes the agency of Africans in their own communication sphere. This critique may be discovered in the type of language, art forms, expressive styles, arguments, economics, or social ideas within an interactive situation. Thus, the Afrocentric idea is critical to any behavioral activity that involves Africans or people of African descent. One cannot very easily engage in communication study of Africans without some appreciation of the authentic voices of Africans. This implies, of course, a serious study of the deep structure of African philosophical thought.

Necessitated by the conditions of history that have removed Africans from their traditional cultural, expressive, philosophical, and religious base, the Afrocentric idea in communication seeks to reposition Africans in the center of their own historical experiences rather than on the margins of European experiences. In essence, two political situations removed Africans from their own terms. First, the enslavement of African people brought about a massive physical and cultural dislocation of millions of Africans. Such a large-scale movement did not have mere displacement implications but more profound implications for how Africans would communicate out of the new reality and what Africans would say about their new reality. Thus, it was both *how* and *what* that mattered in the process of communication among Africans in the Americas. The second political situation was the colonizing of the continent of Africa itself, which left people on the continent but already endangered in their cultural, psychological, and cognitive selves. Thus, the disassembly of African ideas, ideals, standards, and methods was fundamental to the making of both enslaved Africans and colonized Africans.

The Afrocentrist's claim that Africans were removed from their own terms in expressive and religious ways is an existential claim based on the reality of the European slave trade and the imperial colonization of Africa. When Africans were forbidden to speak their own languages, to dress in their own clothes, and in some cases, to use their own names, they were in the midst of the turmoil of dislocation. Those who were also separated from their familiar physical and environmental contexts were further alienated from their own cultural terms.

The quest for Afrocentric location, that is, a place from which the African can view reality and phenomena associated with reality from the standpoint of Africans, is a liberating journey. One experiences the quest in the language of the best orators in the African American community. They are forever on the road to bringing into the arena of now the language and color of the African reality. Their voices, words, and cadences are those of Africans who are discovering their way back to the center of their own histories. Marginality is a place, but it is not a stable place from which to seek redefinition, relocation, and centering of one's perspective.

This is a philosophical turn that is essential for conceptualizing Africans as subjects or agents within the communication process. If Africans are not subjects—empowered actors—in the situation, then the old patterns of marginality and peripherality are maintained; the interaction takes the form of one party taking an active role against another, more passive party, rather than subject-to-subject communication, in which both parties are agents who speak from the position of self-activation, of being in charge of one's self. Consequently, if the subject-to-subject pattern does not adhere, then the communication cannot be authentic.

In its attempt to shift discourse about African phenomena from ideas founded in European constructs to a more centered perspective, Afrocentricity announces itself as a form of antiracist, antipatriarchal, and antisexist ideology that is innovative, challenging, and capable of creating exciting ways to acquire and express knowledge. The denial of the exploitative expression of race, gender, and class often found in older ideas about knowledge is at once controversial and a part of the evolving process of developing a new way of thinking about knowledge. Afrocentricity confronts the marginality of Africans and critiques European patriarchy and sexism as a part of the baggage of the hegemonic tendencies frequently found in Western communication. Like the double ax of the African god Shango, Afrocentricity strikes going and coming. On one hand, it challenges African communicators to come from the margins of European reality and to claim their own centered space. On the other hand, in its emphasis on each person's assuming agency and not being trampled on or victimized, Afrocentricity offers a liberating space for the struggle against all forms of oppression.

Origins

The origin of Afrocentricity as a concept is traced to a quartet of books written by Molefi Kete Asante between 1979 and 2008: *Afrocentricity; The Afrocentric Idea; Kemet, Afrocentricity, and Knowledge;* and *An Afrocentric Manifesto.* Ama Mazama's *The Afrocentric Paradigm* and *L'Imperatif Afrocentrique,* which appeared in 2003 and 2005, respectively, added immensely to the theoretical and intellectual development of the theory. Afrocentricity became a discourse that thrust the concept of agency into the intellectual arena as a perspective whose core was the interpretation and explanation of phenomena from the standpoint of Africans as subjects rather than victims or objects.

In order to return to an authentic consciousness rooted in self-respect, affirmation, and dignity, it was necessary for African people to see themselves in the midst of their own history and not as in the margins of Europe. Viewing oneself as an agent means also knowing one's history. Someone who does not know his or her own history will speak with the wrong metaphors and appeal to inauthentic events and phenomena to make a communication case.

The Afrocentrist believes that it is essential to return to the classical civilizations of Africa for necessary models of argument, construction, encounter, and ethics, in much the same way as Westerners had harkened back to the likes of the ancient Greeks and Romans. Thus, the return to a discussion of the ancient African civilizations of Egypt (2900 BCE to 330 BCE) and Nubia (750 BCE to 340 CE) during the classical periods was essential for an appreciation of the role that Africans and Africa played in human behavior, communication, rhetoric, and world history.

Afrocentrists were the first to see the overthrow in the African's mind of European domination by a return to classical Africa. Besides its acceptance of classical Africa, Afrocentricity was grounded in the historical reality of African people through the presentation of key intellectual ideas. The point is that the Afrocentric idea in communication was not merely stuck in the fertile ground of ancient philosophies of Imhotep (2700 BCE), Ptahhotep (2414 BCE), Kagemni (2300 BCE), Merikare (1990 BCE), or Duauf (1340 BCE); rather the theorists saw these philosophers as departure positions, not destinations. They wrote on themes such as aging, books, the value of speaking well, and protocol. For example, it was important for the Afrocentrist to contend that the Eurocentric view had become an ethnocentric view, which elevated the European experience as universal and downgraded all others. For the Afrocentrist, it was clear that Afrocentricity was not the counterpoint to Eurocentricity but a particular perspective for analysis that did not seek to occupy all space and time, as Eurocentrism has often done. All human cultures must be centered, in fact, the subject of their own realities.

Key Points

In the Afrocentric view, the problem of location takes precedence over the topic or the data under consideration. Two methodological devices have emerged to assist in the construction of a new body of knowledge: *reasonable plausibility,* or believability based on careful consideration, and *intelligent conclusion,* or logical inference. Both are common terms used in a definite and precise sense to deal with the issue of historical, social, and cultural lacunae, or gaps, in many discourses on African people.

Afrocentrists contend that human beings cannot divest themselves of culture, whether participating in their own historical culture or that of some other group. A contradiction between history and perspective produces a kind of incongruity that is called *decenteredness.* Thus, when an African American speaks from the viewpoint of Europeans who came to the Americas on the Mayflower when Africans really came on slave ships, or when literary critics write of Africans as the Other, Afrocentrists claim that Africans are being peripheralized within their own narrative.

Metaphor of Location

Metaphors of location and dislocation—being centered or decentered from events, situations, texts, buildings, dreams, and literary works—are the principal tools of analysis. To be centered is to be located as an agent instead of as the Other. Such a critical shift in thinking has involved the explanation of psychological misorientation and disorientation, attitudes that affect Africans who consider themselves to be Europeans or who believe that it is impossible to be African and human. Severe forms of this psychological attitude have been labeled extreme misorientation by some Afrocentrists. Additional issues have been the influence of a centered approach to education, particularly as it relates to the revision of the American educational curriculum. Hundreds of dissertations and numerous books and articles have been written extending the idea of Afrocentricity in communication, architecture, social work, religion, politics, historical and cultural analysis, criminology, and philosophy.

Afrocentricity creates, among other things, a critique of human communication and social history in the search for a unique standing place for agency. Such an action is at once a liberalizing and a liberating event, marking both the expansion of consciousness and the freeing of the mind from hegemonic thinking. Therefore, Afrocentric communication theory raises the bar for an authentic relationship of equals in which African people are no longer viewed in the traditional Western manner as victims and objects.

Molefi Kete Asante

See also Black Feminist Epistemology; Critical Race Theory; Critical Rhetoric; Critical Theory; Interracial Communication; Neocolonialism; Postcolonial Theory; Power and Power Relations; Privilege; Racial Formation Theory; Whiteness Theory

Further Readings

Asante, M. K. (1990). *Kemet, Afrocentricity, and knowledge.* Trenton, NJ: Africa World Press.

Asante, M. K. (1998). *The Afrocentric idea.* Philadelphia: Temple University.

Asante, M. K. (2003). *Afrocentricity.* Chicago: AAI Press. (Original work published 1980 by Amulefi Publishing, Buffalo, NY)

Asante, M. K. (2008). *An Afrocentric manifesto.* Cambridge, UK: Polity.

Conyers, J. L., Jr. (2003). *Afrocentricity and the academy: Essays on theory and practice.* Jefferson, NC: McFarland.

Mazama, A. (Ed.). (2003). *The Afrocentric paradigm.* Trenton, NJ: Africa World Press.

Mazama, A. (2004). *L'imperatif afrocentrique.* Paris: Editions Menaibuc.

Ziegler, D. (1995). *Molefi Kete Asante and Afrocentricity: In praise and in criticism.* Nashville, TN: Winston-Derek.

AGENCY

Agency is a concept that is generally understood as a capacity to act or cause change. The person who—or thing which—acts or causes change is termed an *agent.* In communication theory, agency is most commonly associated with people, as opposed to animals or things. To communicate, an agent must have the capacity, or *agency,* to do so. Consequently, most communication theories assume the existence of agency. Not all communication theories, however, require agency to be human in origin. Until the late 20th century, agency was a relatively straightforward concept in communication studies. In light of human irrationality and evil in the past century, however, a number of scholars have called many assumptions about human agency into question.

Terminological Confusion

The notion of an agent and the capacity of agency are often confused or conflated with closely related, but nevertheless distinct, concepts. Chief among them are the *subject,* a philosophical concept that refers to a typical, or paradigm, self-conscious human being, and *subjectivity,* a concept that refers to the conscious awareness of oneself as a subject. Originally, being a subject meant that one was ruled by, or under the legal control of, a king or prince, but gradually the term came to denote one's status as a citizen beholden to the laws of a given government or nation-state (e.g., "Josh is a subject of the United States").

In philosophical circles, the subject has come to denote a perceiving human being who is conscious of himself or herself as a human being. In this philosophical sense, the subject is discussed in relation to the *object,* which refers to that which is perceived by the subject or that which the subject knows he or she is not. The philosophical distinction between the subject and object as categories, however, is not stable, and the meaning can change from one context to the next. In psychoanalysis, for example, the subject denotes a self-conscious person, but the object denotes another person whom the subject loves, hates, is ambivalent about, and so on (e.g., the infant subject loves the maternal object, mother).

A subject who self-consciously acts or causes change is said to possess agency. Hence, a subject with agency is an agent. An agent does not necessarily need to be a subject, however, nor does a subject necessarily possess agency. To complicate matters, agency is often confused with the term *subjectivity* as well. Whereas the subject denotes a self-conscious person, subjectivity refers to consciousness of one's perceptions as an individual or discrete subject. Consciousness of oneself as a discrete individual (subjectivity) does not mean that one has agency or is an agent. Only an awareness of one's ability or capacity to act (subjectivity) imbues the subject with agency.

In sum, agency is the capacity to act; the agent is the source or location of agency; the subject is a self-conscious human being; and subjectivity is consciousness as a subject. All these concepts are implicated in the idea of communication.

Agency and Modern Philosophy

Contemporary understandings of agency can be linked to 18th-century Western thought, often termed the *Enlightenment.* Although Enlightenment thought is not easily summarized, key among its goals was the use of reason to improve society and understand the natural world. In Enlightenment thought, we find agency and the subject tied together in complex ways. For example, just prior to the Enlightenment, the philosopher René Descartes reasoned that absent any knowledge or sensory perception whatsoever, an individual could know one thing: It thinks, therefore it exists (this argument is known as the *cogito*). Insofar as thinking is a type of action, this "it" that thinks is an agent, but it is not necessarily a subject. The it or agent that thinks is not a subject until it is conscious of itself as an agent who thinks (subjectivity). The Enlightenment thinker Immanuel Kant extended Descartes' argument about this most basic kernel of knowledge—something exists that is thinking or acting, and therefore agency and an agent exist. Yet self-conscious knowledge, he suggested, depends on exposure to the world outside our minds, or the empirical world. In other words, to be subjects, we have to have sensory experience. Subjectivity, consequently, is wholly "in our heads" but requires a confrontation with the external world. The resulting concept of the *transcendental subject* advanced by Kant consisted in both the necessity of a thinking thing independent of the outside world and the necessity of that outside world to make the thinking thing conscious of itself (subjectivity). For Kant, all knowledge subsequent to fact of self-existence is impossible without sensory experience. The meaning of the external world, however, is entirely dependent on the way in which the human mind works. This view implies that the paradigm self-conscious human being, or subject, is destined to become an agent and thus harbors an incipient agency at birth.

After Kant, the concept of the subject emerged as the relatively stable notion of a self-conscious agent. Consequently, in the mature subject, agency was understood as the ability to cause change or act by making *choices*. In other words, the subject was believed to have agency because he or she could cause change by choosing among alternative actions. Insofar as choosing was a key characteristic of the agency of the modern subject, Enlightenment thinkers associated agency with freedom and, by extension, individual autonomy: One became an autonomous subject by understanding and accepting his or her freedom, using reason to make choices.

Because of the influence of modern philosophy, agency became associated with self-transparency, self-knowledge, and rational choice making. Because choice making was understood as a component of human agency, today agency is often associated with matters of epistemology (how we come to knowledge), ethics (how we discern right from wrong), and politics (how we act collectively in the face of uncertain outcomes). In the social sciences, agency is also understood as a component of one's self-perception as autonomous. Owing to these associations, in educational settings *giving agency* to students is often expressed as a goal of teaching: By working with students on their communication stills, it is thought, communication educators can help students to better realize their agency and become social, moral, and political actors in the public sphere and in private life.

The Posthumanist Critique of Agency

The Enlightenment view of agency and subjectivity is classically *humanist,* meaning that it is party to a larger perspective on the world termed *humanism.* In general, humanism is the view that human beings have a special status in the universe, a status that is superior to the supernatural or divine, on one hand, and a status that cannot be resigned to scientific naturalism or biologism, on the other. It is commonly assumed the humanist subject is an autonomous, self-transparent, fully conscious agent who acts rationally by making choices. In the 19th century, this view of the subject and agency was challenged by a number of thinkers. For example, Friedrich Wilhelm Nietzsche argued that humans were motivated by the "will to power" and made choices that were typically self-interested. Karl Marx argued that human choices were constrained by material circumstances and frequently animated by the interests of those in power (*ideology*). Sigmund Freud argued that the choices of human subjects were often irrational and motivated by unconscious desires. Together, the critiques of the Enlightenment agency advanced by Nietzsche, Marx, and Freud laid the groundwork for what would come to be known as *posthumanism,* a view that would rigorously dispute human subjectivity as the seat of agency.

Although difficult to define, posthumanism is the idea that the human being is only one of many types of beings in the universe and, as such, has no special status or value (other than, of course, what human beings assign to themselves). More specifically, in the theoretical humanities, posthumanism mounts a critique of the subject as self-transparent, autonomous, choice making, and rational. Understandably, if the human subject is not characterized by these qualities, then the Enlightenment notion of human agency as rational choice making is also questioned by posthumanism. Many 20th-century thinkers associated with posthumanism, such as Judith Butler, Jacques Derrida, Michel Foucault, and Jacques Lacan, for example, would not deny that human agency consists of choices; they would question, however, the extent to which such choices were conscious or reasoned, arguing that they are constrained by larger forces such as language, ideology, social norms, the threat of imminent death, and so on.

The frequent rationale for questioning the fully conscious, rational, choice-making capacity of human subjects concerns world wars, torture, genocide, and other atrocities caused by human beings. For example, although it is unquestionably the case that many Nazi war criminals made conscious decisions to do evil, it is also the case that many Nazi sympathizers aided and abetted such evil without consciously doing so. In the latter instance, the status of agency in the conduct of evil is unclear. Furthermore, insofar as human reason can be used toward evil ends (e.g., the rationally calculated extermination of millions of Jewish people during World War II), posthumanism questions the value once afforded to reason by Enlightenment thinkers.

Because the problem of evil poses complex questions about the character of agency without any clear answers, posthumanist thinkers prefer to leave the status of the human subject open, as if the concept of the subject is a question itself, never to be fully answered. Agency after the posthumanist critique in the theoretical humanities is thus disassociated from full consciousness, choice making, freedom, and autonomy, becoming a term for the capacity to act. The agent, in turn, can be anything that causes change or action.

Agency in Rhetorical Studies

Owing to the Enlightenment legacy of agency, scholars who study persuasive speaking and writing (*rhetoric*) have traditionally taken the Enlightenment subject for granted. Since the days of Plato, Aristotle, and the ancient Greeks, rhetoricians understood the persuasive process to involve speakers or writers who consciously developed their rhetoric by making conscious choices. A persuader, or *rhetor,* would select a topic, then proceed to outline an essay or speech, selecting some arguments and ignoring others. The rhetor would choose the appropriate language and tone of the

address, analyze the intended audience to help adapt to its expectations, and so on. These assumptions about the persuader tend to assume a self-transparent, autonomous subject.

In the 20th century, however, the influence of Nietzsche, Marx, and Freud on rhetorical studies began to shift focus from the agency of the rhetor to the active understanding of audiences (a psychological move). The work of Kenneth Burke was particularly influential in this regard. Burke argued that persuasion was not the result of arguments offered by a rhetor but rather the result of *identification,* or the ability of persuader and "persuadee" to understand each other as sharing a common identity in some fundamental way (*consubstantiality*). Diane Davis has even suggested that Burke's redefinition of persuasion leads us to the domain of the unconscious and the possibility that persuasion is akin to hypnosis. If this is the case, then agency in persuasive encounter is difficult to locate in any one individual as it is a shared, unconscious, and dynamic relation between two or more people.

Because of the posthumanist critique of human subjectivity, one finds a variety of positions on the concept of agency among rhetorical scholars at present. There is no consensus among them about what agency means; some would even dispute this summary. Very generally, these positions can be reduced to three: (1) rhetoricians who continue to defend the Enlightenment subject and agency as conscious choice making (humanistic agency), (2) rhetoricians who understand agency as a complex negotiation of conscious intent and structural limitation (dialectical agency), and (3) rhetoricians who narrowly define agency as a capacity to act and the subject as an open question (posthumanist agency).

Agency in Social Science

Among social-scientific scholars in communication studies, the concept of agency has been less controversial, and the literature is decidedly larger in volume and scope. In various theories of communication from a scientific standpoint, agency is assumed to be the capacity to act and is usually associated with human subjects, as the preponderance of studies of communication concerns humans. Owing to centuries-old discussions in modern philosophy discussed above, much of the work in social-scientific communication theory associates agency with autonomy. More specifically, agency in communication theory can be traced to social-scientific studies that investigate individuals' self-perceptions of autonomy, control, and free choice in respect to a number of cognate concepts, including Piaget's investigations of agency, Albert Bandura's studies on the *locus of control,* and various explorations of *attributional* or *explanatory style.* These and similar studies, in turn, are indebted to classical investigations by Jack Brehm on *reactance* and Erving Goffman's theory of *facework:* Brehm's work investigated how subjects reacted to perceptions of constraint, and Goffman's focused on the ways in which subjects tend to work to preserve perceptions of autonomy and respect for others.

Closely related to common understandings of agency in social science is the concept of power, and a number of studies in the area of social and management psychology have focused on how various power structures (social, cultural, economic, relational, etc.) influence one's perception of agency and autonomy in interpersonal dynamics. This research overlaps with scholarship conducted in organizational communication studies. Because organizational environments often foreground a tension between the human subject and the housing institution, agency has been a fertile topic of discussion and debate: To what degree do organizational norms constrain the agency of the individual? To what degree do organizational structures empower an employee? Actor–network theory has been particularly influential among organizational scholars in answering these and related questions.

Finally, owing to the powerful role of nonhuman structures on organizations, it stands to reason that the agency of nonhuman things is an important dynamic worthy of study. Although the idea of nonhuman agency has been operative of the fields of linguistics and sociology for decades, it has become a topic of concern in organizational communication studies only in the 21st century. In this respect, François Cooren and others have argued that nonhuman agencies, especially what Cooren terms *textual agencies,* are crucial for understanding organizational cultures.

Joshua Gunn

See also Actor–Network Theory; Axiology; Empiricism; Facework Theories; Ideology; Ontology; Postmodern Theory; Poststructuralism; Power and Power Relations; Pragmatics; Spectatorship

Further Readings

Bandura, A. (1997). *Self-efficacy: The exercise of control.* New York: W. H. Freeman.

Brehm, J. W. (1966). *A theory of psychological reactance.* New York: Academic Press.

Buchanan, G. M., & Seligman, M. E. P. (1997). *Explanatory style.* Mahwah, NJ: Lawrence Erlbaum.

Burke, K. (1969). *A rhetoric of motives.* Berkeley: University of California Press.

Butler, J. (1999). *Gender trouble: Feminism and the subversion of identity* (2nd ed.). New York: Routledge.

Campbell, K. K. (2005). Agency: Promiscuous and protean. *Communication and Critical/Cultural Studies, 2,* 1–19.

Castor, T., & Cooren, F. (2006). Organizations as hybrid forms of life: The implications of the selection of human and non-human agents in problem-formulation. *Management Communication Quarterly, 19,* 570–600.

Davis, D. (2008). Identification: Burke and Freud on who you are. *Rhetoric Society Quarterly, 38,* 132–147.

Geisler, C. (2004). How ought we to understand the concept of rhetorical agency? Report from the ARS. *Rhetoric Society Quarterly, 34,* 9–17.

Gruenfeld, D. H., Inesi, M. E., Magee, J. C., & Galinsky, A. D. (2008). Power and objectification of social targets. *Journal of Personality & Social Psychology, 95,* 111–127.

Law, J., & Hassard, J. (Eds.). (1999). *Actor network theory and after.* Malden, MA: Oxford.

Lundberg, C., & Gunn, J. (2005). "Ouija board, are there any communications?" Agency, ontotheology, and the death of the humanist subject, or, continuing the ARS conversation. *Rhetoric Society Quarterly, 35,* 83–105.

Rotter, J. (1966). Generalized expectancies for internal versus external control of reinforcement. *Psychological Monographs, 80,* 1–28.

Thibault, P. J. (2006). *Agency and consciousness in discourse: Self-other dynamics as a complex system.* New York: Continuum.

Weick, M., & Guinote, A. (2008). When subjective experiences matter: Power increases reliance on the ease of retrieval. *Journal of Personality & Social Psychology, 94,* 956–970.

Williams, C. (2001). *Contemporary French philosophy: Modernity and the persistence of the subject.* New York: Continuum.

AGENDA-SETTING THEORY

Agenda-setting theory, as originally formulated in 1972 by Maxwell McCombs and Donald Shaw, explains the relationships between the emphasis that the mass media place on issues and the importance that media audiences attribute to those issues. While agenda-setting theory started out as an explanation of media impact on political behavior and attitudes during election years—specifically, the ways that news media coverage can prioritize issues, or *set the agenda*, for the public—in the decades since McCombs and Shaw's initial study was published, the theory has inspired hundreds of subsequent explorations into the ways that media and other institutions prime and frame issues and events for their audiences and therefore influence and shape public opinion, either intentionally or unintentionally. As a result, agenda-setting theory has had a profound influence, not only on mass communication and political communication research, but also on the development of various organizational communication, persuasion, and diffusion-of-innovations theories. At the same time, the original theory has been revised by Maxwell McCombs, one of its codevelopers, in ways that expand and even contradict one of its key tenets.

Early Days of Agenda-Setting Research

Although McCombs and Shaw were the first scholars to speak of an *agenda-setting function* of the mass media, the idea that media contribute to audience perceptions, values, and priorities predates their study. Indeed, McCombs and Shaw used a famous quotation by political scientist Bernard Cohen as a way of encapsulating their own early conception of agenda setting. As Cohen had observed in 1963, the press "may not be successful much of the time in telling people what to think, but it is stunningly successful in telling its readers what to think *about*." In other words, the idea behind McCombs and Shaw's original notion of agenda-setting theory is that while the media do not tell us what attitudes or opinions we should have (what to think) and do not set out to deliberately or purposely engineer public opinion, they do tell us which issues we should be focusing on

(what to think about)—that is, which issues are most important and therefore most worthy of inclusion on our mental agendas.

What was groundbreaking about their 1972 article, "The Agenda-Setting Function of Mass Media," was that McCombs and Shaw provided empirical support for the claim that the news media priorities become public priorities. Their article detailed the results of a study they conducted during the 1968 presidential campaign in which they asked 100 registered yet uncommitted voters in Chapel Hill, North Carolina, a set of fairly simple questions: "What are you *most* concerned about these days? That is, regardless of what politicians say, what are the two or three main things which you think the government *should* concentrate on doing something about?" At the same time, McCombs and Shaw analyzed the political news contents of the mass media used by Chapel Hill voters during the campaign (four local newspapers, *The New York Times*, the newsmagazines *Time* and *Newsweek,* and the NBC and CBS evening news broadcasts). McCombs and Shaw found an almost perfect correlation between the issues listed by the voters as most important and the topics that were given the most space, time, and prominence in the news media. Additionally, the priority order given by voters to the issues almost perfectly matched the relative amounts of time or space given by the media to coverage of those issues.

McCombs and Shaw concluded that there is a strong relationship between the emphasis placed on issues by the media (that is, the *media agenda*) and voters' own judgments about the salience and importance of campaign issues (that is, the *public agenda*). The researchers suggested that this was a straightforward, one-way, causal relationship, meaning that we learn from the media not only about an issue but also how much importance to attach to it. More broadly, by seeing an issue covered in the news media—and seeing it covered repeatedly and with great emphasis—we come to share with the media the view that the issue has legitimacy and thus place it on our own agendas.

Evolutions and Revolutions

The original McCombs and Shaw study inspired a variety of questions and challenges by other communication researchers (and ultimately, even by McCombs himself). The studies in which these questions and challenges were investigated resulted in numerous revisions and extensions to the theory's initial formulation. Among the more important issues raised in the years since the first agenda-setting research was published are the following:

Who Sets the Media's Agenda?

Many researchers raised what might appear to be an obvious question: If the news media set the agenda for the public, then who (or what) sets the media agenda? Indeed, several scholars have suggested that the public agenda has an effect on the media agenda: audiences make clear to the media (through ratings, audience studies, market research, and consumption patterns) what they want to watch and read about, and the media simply respond. In other words, the media are market driven and thus give their audiences what they know will sell. Other scholars have argued that politicians and public relations practitioners contribute to the setting of the media agenda. In any case, news organization executives do not construct the media agenda in a vacuum.

How Many Agendas?

Everett Rogers and James Dearing believed that agenda-setting theory should acknowledge the coexistence and interrelationships among three agendas: In addition to the *public agenda* and the *media agenda*, Rogers and Dearing argued, scholars should also attend to the *policy agenda*—the hierarchy of issues that governments and other policy makers act on. In some cases, no one group sets the agendas for the others; rather, the real-world importance of an issue or event (e.g., a major earthquake or an act of war) will equally affect all three, and therefore all three groups will agree on its importance without one group's influencing the others. *Agenda building* was offered by Rogers and Dearing as a more appropriate term than *agenda setting* to characterize this collective, reciprocal process.

Do the Media (Also) Tell Us What to Think?

The most important challenges to the original claims of agenda-setting research directly rebut Bernard Cohen's claim that the media tell us only what to think about but not what to think. Indeed, since the mid-1980s, communication scholars have published hundreds of studies showing that the media do tell us both what to think about (which issues to focus on) and what to think (which attitudes and judgments to have about them). Moreover, these scholars argue, there is a connection between the two: The perceived *salience* of an issue (the relative prominence given to an issue by the media and, presumably, agreed on by audiences) is related to the *evaluations* that audience members have about the political actors associated with the issue. Thus, agenda-setting scholarship—and agenda-setting theory—has expanded to encompass both the cognitive aspects of the agenda-setting function (the setting or structuring of the agenda by the mass media) and its affective or emotional aspects (influences on how audiences feel about the items on the agenda).

Central to this expansion have been the concepts of *priming* and *framing,* which McCombs and other theorists now claim to be natural extensions of agenda setting. Just as priming a pump prepares the device to work quickly and readily, the repetition and prominence given to a media message about a topic is said to prime our thoughts about that topic: The topic is brought to the forefront of our active cognition, becomes more immediately available to memory, and is thus made more salient (more quickly and readily remembered). As certain issues are primed, so are our attitudes about those issues and their attributes—attitudes that are formed in part by their media framing.

When applied to news coverage, the term *framing* describes the process of organizing, defining, and structuring a story. Many media theorists argue that even when journalists intend to be objective or balanced in their coverage, they necessarily report on issues in ways that give audiences cues as to how to understand the issues, including which aspects of the issues to focus on and which to ignore. Indeed, the core task of all media gate-keepers—to determine which stories to include or exclude from a given day's newspaper or broadcast and what to emphasize within those stories that are included—itself frames the issues covered in their publications and programs. Beyond inclusion–exclusion decisions, news producers present or represent issues and political actors in specific ways; how a story is told contributes to its framing and therefore to the communication of how the issues and actors comprising the story should be evaluated by the audience. (Even a seemingly straightforward headline about an election result inevitably involves a framing choice: An editor must decide whether the result should be framed as "Smith beats Jones" or, alternatively, as "Jones loses to Smith.")

Limitations to Agenda Setting's Power

Although agenda-setting theory and research now encompass both the what-to-think-about and the what-to-think components of Cohen's formulation, debate still swirls around the core questions of media influence, namely, how directly and to what degree the media set the public agenda. Recent studies suggest that personal variables can mitigate the effects of media agenda setting on individual audience members. Those viewers who do not find the media (or a particular media outlet or source) credible are less likely to have their agendas set by the media. Similarly, viewers who actively disagree with the news values of the sources they use ("How could CNN possibly consider *that* to be an important story?") will be less susceptible to the agenda-setting function of the media. Still, the findings of nearly four decades of agenda-setting, -priming, and -framing research provide a great deal of support for the claims first made in the 1960s and 1970s by Cohen and by McCombs and Shaw.

David Weiss

See also Diffusion of Innovations; Framing Theory; Media and Mass Communication Theories; Media Effects Theories; Political Communication Theories; Public Opinion Theories

Further Readings

Cohen, B. C. (1963). *The press and foreign policy.* Princeton, NJ: Princeton University Press.

Iyengar, S., & Kinder, D. R. (1987). *News that matters: Television and American opinion.* Chicago: University of Chicago Press.

McCombs, M. E. (1997). New frontiers in agenda setting: Agendas of attributes and frames. *Mass Communication Review, 24,* 4–24.

McCombs, M. E., & Shaw, D. L. (1972). The agenda-setting function of mass media. *Public Opinion Quarterly, 36,* 176–187.

Reese, S. D. (1991). Setting the media's agenda: A power balance perspective. *Communication Yearbook, 14,* 309–340.

Rogers, E. M., & Dearing, J. W. (1988). Agenda-setting research: Where has it been, where is it going? *Communication Yearbook, 11,* 555–594.

Scheufele, D. A., & Tewksbury, D. (2007). Framing, agenda setting, and priming: The evolution of three media effects models. *Journal of Communication, 57,* 9–20.

Sheafer, T. (2007). How to evaluate it: The role of story-evaluative tone in agenda setting and priming. *Journal of Communication, 57,* 21–39.

AGGRESSIVENESS

See Argumentativeness, Assertiveness, and Verbal Aggressiveness Theory

AMERICANIZATION OF MEDIA

At a time when economic, political, environmental, cultural, social, and even religious issues are raised on a global scale, communication research is faced with the question of the media's power to influence these issues and their outcome. This question is usually phrased in terms of the overwhelming presence of U.S. media and their contents around the globe. Increasingly this power to influence has come to be recognized as the impact that the U.S. model of media production and distribution has on non-U.S. media and their reception—a process known as the Americanization of the media.

The debate over Americanization began around the 1800s within the context of cultural, technological, and economic exchanges between the United States and Europe, particularly Britain, France, and Germany. The United States embodied the essentials of modernity, democracy, progress, and freedom as it experimented with new and powerful ideas, values, knowledge, technology, and symbols. From both inside and outside its borders, questions were raised as to how to exercise control over these new and powerful social forces and to whom this control could be (or not be) entrusted.

While much of the pioneering work in developing modern mass media was done in Europe during the early 19th century (for example, the penny press in France), it was, as Jeremy Tunstall argues, in the United States and especially in and around New York City that most new media were first successfully industrialized and sold to the bulk of the population. While a developing mass-market economy and urbanization were contributing factors, the need to integrate and acculturate the surge of immigrants from countries other than those of western Europe between the end of the 19th and the beginning of the 20th centuries also acted as an agent for the pulling together of scientific, technological, financial, entrepreneurial, and even moral forces to create what was to become the foundation of the U.S. cultural industries—contemporary mass media. These were set up to Americanize the incoming mass of immigrants and to Americanize the population within the United States, whose divisive wounds of the Civil War had not completely healed. Even today the Americanization of the media is carried on within the United States when foreign contents are acculturated, either through narrative posturing or through editing, to better fit a preconceived and homogenizing U.S. worldview.

Over the decades and centuries, then, ideas, values, knowledge, and artifacts from the United States have traveled across time and space through the words and deeds of men and women in every walk of life: entrepreneurs, teachers, artists, missionaries, journalists, humanitarians, athletes, military personnel, tourists, intellectuals, politicians, ambassadors, students, scientists, and consultants. Each served as a representative of what the United States stood for and, more globally, what America stood for. The United States became identified with America, the American dream, and the American way of life, thus co-opting all the Americas (North, Central, and South) and all that they contain.

This spreading of things "made in America"—first into Europe, then into the other Americas and parts of Asia, and finally touching every region of the planet—was sometimes imposed, sometimes solicited, sometimes welcomed, sometimes resisted.

Depending on the host country's economic, political, cultural, religious, social, and historical context and power structures, at times the elites would resist and the popular would welcome, or the contrary would occur. In many cases, the representatives of the United States would side, outwardly or through intermediaries, with those whose power to influence the outcome was decisive.

The Americanization of the media is characterized by a push–pull dynamic. Media technology and content, as well as distribution and marketing strategies and practices, are pushed on importing-country buyers, raising issues and accusations of U.S. media imperialism. When someone speaks of Americanization, the image of an invasion of media products "made in America" in the local/national markets immediately comes to mind. But Americanization also refers to the apprehended menace of losing one's cultural identity by "acting American," by adopting from the United States "ways of doing things"—whether in the realms of politics, economics, or social and cultural practices. This means adopting the market economy of media ownership, production, distribution, and merchandization; the popularization of media contents; the ethics of news journalism (as opposed to opinion journalism); and the overt and covert alliances between culture and supply economy (as opposed to publicly funded culture) and between journalists and decision centers (as opposed to social critics).

However, there is also a "pull" factor based on high-quality technology and innovations, content attractiveness, and effective distribution. As a result, the importing countries are pressured to emulate and redefine their policies, modes of production, and canons of culture (especially those of popular culture) along the lines of those prevalent in the United States. The pull factor, then, can be interpreted as the political and cultural will to compete with the United States in the lucrative global market and also to safeguard national and regional cultures and identities by aggressively promoting their own highly attractive, professional, popular cultural productions. For some this is seen as beating the Americans at their own games; for others it is nothing more than a sellout to the United States.

There is no doubt that the media in the United States still influence media organization and content in other countries (press, music, television, cinema); the counterinfluence, however, is rarely acknowledged. Waxing over such key components as intellectual property and national identities often fosters Americanization within the United States. Case in point: Disney made Cinderella and other figures from the writings of German academics Jacob and Wilhelm Grimm as American as Huckleberry Finn. In promoting *The Brothers Grimm,* Hollywood portrayed the brothers as "Will and Jake, traveling con-artists."

Another case in point is the popular televised show *Deal or No Deal,* which is not U.S.-American but U.S.-Americanized. Because it is broadcast on a U.S. network with local participants, audiences assume that it, and its Canadian-born host Howie Mandel, are American. However the concept was developed and is owned by Endemol, a Netherlands-based production company known for creating such shows as *Big Brother* and *Fear Factor.* The first version of the show was broadcast in the Netherlands as *Miljoenenjacht* (The Hunt for Millions), followed by Australia, which was the first to broadcast it under the title *Deal or No Deal.* Versions of this show are now broadcast in 45 countries across the continents.

The combined weight of history, technology, and financial entrepreneurship has given the U.S. media such an overwhelming, self-centered, dominant position that even when the U.S. media import contents and formats from other countries, these are Americanized for the audiences within the United States and assumed as such by other countries. In this sense, the first successful industrialized mass media are the Americanized U.S. media. For other countries that underwent the same process of urbanization, industrialization, and nation building, this first social experiment in creating a contemporary, popular, urban, industrialized culture became a benchmark to be either emulated, adapted, or resisted.

For every argument that the media outside the United States are becoming more and more Americanized, there can be found a counterargument. The financial capacity to mass-produce and, more importantly, to effectively distribute U.S.-American media products, particularly film and television, across the globe is still impressive. Also impressive, as investigated by Jeremy Tunstall, are the large foreign revenues earned by Hollywood movies and television series through exports to other countries. Screens everywhere, in airports, hotel rooms, theaters, private homes, bars, and waiting rooms, seem to offer an endless array of films, news reports, sitcoms, reality shows, talk shows, and sports events "made in the USA." Such a massive presence is made possible because, through technology, financial investments, marketing, and merchandising, U.S. operators have obtained arrangements that favor the cornering of key distribution outlets and because they can over-produce and undersell many of the media products in countries outside the United States. In Canada, for example, as in many other countries around the world, the screens of film and television are overwhelmingly filled with U.S.-American content simply because the need to fill them is there (the attractiveness and aggressiveness of the market) and because it is cheaper to buy American than to produce and distribute national products.

While the issues at the heart of Americanization of media have shifted, the importance of the issue remains. During the decades of the 1960s and 1970s, the concepts and ideologies of cultural and media imperialism and the question of the hegemonic power of the U.S.-American media were an integral part of the battle between capitalism and Communism over the establishment of a new world order. At the same time, documented research has shown that, with the possible notable exception of music, national popular culture, while less favored in terms of exposition and financing, regularly wins the favor of the reading, listening, and viewing audiences. National media products reflect and may differentiate and reinforce cultural identities and even shore up resistance to Americanization. This does not mean that U.S. media will not impinge on values, norms, belief systems, mentalities, habits, rules, technologies, practices, institutions, and behaviors of non-U.S. Americans. Evidence to support this is quite strong, and those who argue that cultural resistance and adaptation can not only successfully counter Americanization but, in fact, de-Americanize national media underestimate the ties between U.S. cultural industries and the economic, military, and political interests of the United States and its power to influence change on a global scale. These ties are powerful in the sense that they allow cultural industries, in their own right, to wield power, defined as the ability to bring forth the results one wants and, if necessary, to change the behavior of others to make this happen.

While this power to bring about desired change can no longer be expressed in terms of imperialism, of a forceful imposition on passive recipients reduced to a state of colonized people, it can be expressed in the Gramscian vocabulary of hegemony, particularly when a country's economy is founded, more and more, on mass consumption and on lifestyles for which the media are the major promoters and working agents. Adapting national standards, policies, and habits to accessible, popularized, and (relatively) low-cost imported U.S.-American media practices (genres, modes of production, programming, marketing, distribution, and merchandizing) is really adopting a politicoeconomical model that gears cultural products to fuel an economy based on a lifestyle of consumption. In this sense, the Americanization of the media is occurring not necessarily through their content but through the ties that interlock cultural industries with economic, political, and even military power interests within and outside the United States.

The United States' cultural influence is put to the test, and attested, when non-American and non-Western countries that have adopted the industrialized U.S. mass media system actively seek to acquire, either outright or through international coproduction, the hardware and software to foster and strengthen their own cultural identity and to better resist Americanization. Ironically, the way to counter and resist the influence of U.S. media is to accelerate the process of cultural exchange and diversity by using the very technology and practices that gave and still are giving dominance to the U.S. media.

Today the debate over Americanization of the media has moved from the spotlight of the international political arena to the more tempered circles of academia and international bodies such as the United Nations Educational, Scientific, and Cultural Organization and the World Trade Organization, under the repeated and sustained critiques from fields of inquiry as diverse as political economy, cultural studies, postmodernism, and postcolonialism. But because this issue is now absent from the political, economic, and cultural public agendas of governments does not mean it does not have economic, political, and cultural implications; in fact, given the globalization of media, the issue remains pressing. The United States was the first country to shape a media-based, modern, industrial, urban popular culture. The early capability to mass-produce, to attract hardworking, mobile, skilled migrants, and to expand trade certainly helped spread U.S.-American cultural products, entrepreneurship, and commercial practices abroad. Today the tendency toward Americanization of global media remains strong chiefly because the history of media production and urban culture is interlocked with the history of U.S. economic, political, and military power, which, in turn, has created an uneven playing field for the many newly competing national and regional cultural industries and their specific audiences.

To study the Americanization of the media, one needs to take into consideration two interconnected historical questions: First, what are the economic, technological, political, military, and social interests that Americanization best serves, and second, what are the social, economic, and political constraints countries must overcome to best appropriate the U.S. cultural industries' power to influence?

Roger de la Garde

See also Critical Theory; Popular Culture Theories

Further Readings

De Grazia, V. (2005). *Irresistible empire: America's advance through twentieth-century Europe.* Cambridge, MA: Belknap Press.

Tunstall, J. (2008). *The media were American: U.S. mass media in decline.* New York: Oxford University Press.

van Elteren, M. (2006). *Americanism and Americanization: A critical history of domestic and global influence.* Jefferson, NC: McFarland.

van Elteren, M. (2006). Rethinking Americanization abroad: Toward a critical alternative to prevailing paradigms. *Journal of American Culture, 29,* 345–367.

ANXIETY/UNCERTAINTY MANAGEMENT THEORY

The anxiety/uncertainty management (AUM) theory, developed by William B. Gudykunst, explains how strangers can practice communication effectiveness via the mindful management of anxiety and uncertainty levels of interaction. The root of the AUM theory was based on an integration of the *uncertainty reduction theory* of Charles Berger and the *social identity theory* of Henri Tajfel. AUM theory is one of the major intercultural communication theories that explains the antecedent, process, and outcome dimensions of intergroup (intercultural) and interpersonal communication effectiveness.

The fermentation stage of the AUM theory first appeared in 1985 with a strong emphasis on effective intergroup communication process. Several versions later, the first "official" version of the theory—labeled clearly as the AUM theory—appeared in 1993. The theory was intended to be a practical theory to improve the quality of intergroup and interpersonal relations. In a later rendition, in 1998, the AUM theory was extended to explain effective intercultural adjustment processes. The building-block concepts of the theory include strangers, anxiety, uncertainty, thresholds, mindfulness, cross-cultural variability, effective communication, and intercultural adjustment.

According to the basic premise of the AUM theory, when individuals encounter strangers or culturally dissimilar others, they often experience both anxiety and uncertainty. The concept of *stranger* is drawn from the sociological work of Georg Simmel, which held that a stranger can reflect both *near* and *far* qualities; nearness connotes physical closeness, and remoteness refers to dissimilar values, outlooks, or behaviors. From this stranger–in-group, figure–ground context, AUM theory emphasizes the notion that almost all initial interactions are both intergroup and interpersonal in nature and characterized by anxiety and uncertainty.

Anxiety refers to affective feelings such as uneasiness, awkwardness, confusion, stress, or apprehensiveness about what might occur in the encounter. *Uncertainty,* on the other hand, is a cognitive phenomenon and involves both *predictive uncertainty* and *explanatory uncertainty*. While predictive uncertainty refers to our inability to predict strangers' attitudes or behaviors, explanatory uncertainty refers to our inability to come up with a coherent explanation for strangers' unfamiliar behaviors. In addition, as individuals navigate across cultural boundaries, they have minimum and maximum thresholds for tolerating anxiety and uncertainty. Too much or too little anxiety or uncertainty hampers intercultural communication effectiveness.

For example, when emotional anxiety is too high, cultural strangers would tend to communicate on automatic pilot and interpret dissimilar others' behaviors using their own cultural frame of reference. However, when emotional anxiety is too low, they might act in a very indifferent or ethnocentric manner. Likewise, when cognitive uncertainty is too high, cultural strangers would not be able to accurately interpret each other's incoming verbal and nonverbal messages. When cognitive uncertainty is too low, cultural strangers might overrely on stereotypes to decode the intercultural interaction episode and make overgeneralized attributions.

The final version of the AUM-based effective communication theory has 47 axioms that deal with relationships among self-concept, motivation to interact, reaction to strangers, social categorization of strangers, situational processes, connections with strangers, ethical interactions, uncertainty management, anxiety management, mindfulness, and communication effectiveness. Two of the AUM axioms provide an illustration:

Axiom 5: An increase in perceived threats to our social identities when interacting with strangers will produce an increase in our anxiety and a decrease in our confidence in predicting their behavior.

Axiom 37: An increase in our mindfulness of the process of our communication with strangers will produce an increase in our ability to manage anxiety and an increase in our ability to manage our uncertainty.

According to the core thrust of the AUM theory, intercultural or intergroup communication is effective when individuals are able to maximize understandings and minimize misunderstandings. In order to achieve this meaning coordination process, individuals have to learn to be *mindful*. The characteristics of mindfulness are derived from the social psychology research work of Ellen Langer in 1989. To be mindful means being open to new information and multiple cultural perspectives, creating more differentiated categories to understand cultural strangers' viewpoints, and being sensitive to the complex process of meaning negotiation between different identity groups. Mindfulness serves as the key moderating process between the two underlying causes (anxiety management and uncertainty management) and communication effectiveness.

For example, in applying the AUM theory to the intercultural adjustment process, strangers or sojourners need to keep their anxiety and uncertainty levels within the threshold ranges so that they can activate mindfulness. Mindfulness, in the stranger–host cultural context, can mean increasing cultural knowledge about and language skills of the unfamiliar culture or increasing the tendency to describe rather than evaluate negatively the host nationals' "bizarre" behaviors. In addition, members of the host culture can be mindful of such conditions as receptivity levels to strangers and how perceptions of discrimination can decrease or increase anxiety or stress in a new cultural milieu. Finally, cross-cultural value dimensions such as individualism–collectivism and weak–strong uncertainty avoidance are incorporated in the AUM theory to predict the influence of cultural values on strangers' cultural adjustment process. Based on the core tenets of the AUM theory, an intercultural adjustment training blueprint has been developed with the overall goal of helping sojourners to adjust effectively to a new and unfamiliar cultural landscape.

Stella Ting-Toomey

See also Cross-Cultural Adaptation Theory; Intercultural Communication Theories; Social and Communicative Anxiety; Social Identity Theory; Uncertainty Management Theories; Uncertainty Reduction Theory

Further Readings

Gudykunst, W. B. (1995). Anxiety/uncertainty management (AUM) theory: Current status. In R. L. Wiseman (Ed.), *Intercultural communication theory* (pp. 8–58). Thousand Oaks, CA: Sage.

Gudykunst, W. B. (2004). *Bridging differences: Effective intergroup communication* (4th ed.). Thousand Oaks, CA: Sage.

Gudykunst, W. B. (2005). An anxiety/uncertainty management (AUM) theory of effective communication: Making the mesh of the net finer. In W. B. Gudykunst (Ed.), *Theorizing about intercultural communication* (pp. 281–322). Thousand Oaks, CA: Sage.

Gudykunst, W. B. (2005). An anxiety/uncertainty management (AUM) theory of strangers' intercultural adjustment. In W. B. Gudykunst (Ed.), *Theorizing about intercultural communication* (pp. 419–458). Thousand Oaks, CA: Sage.

Langer, E. J. (1998). *The power of mindful learning.* Cambridge, MA: Da Capo Press.

Simmel, G., and Levine, D. N. (Eds.). (1972). *Georg Simmel on individuality and social forms.* Chicago: University of Chicago Press.

ARCHEOLOGY AND GENEALOGY

Although the terms *archeology* and *genealogy* have established meanings in other disciplines, in the context of communication theory they are most often associated with methods for researching the past proposed by French theorist Michel Foucault. The goal of both archeological and genealogical approaches to history is to uncover how it is that certain ways of thinking and approaches to knowledge have become "common sense." Archeologies of history tend to be directed toward uncovering the moments at which various ways of knowing come to be dominant and institutionalized, thus demonstrating how contingent the "taken for granted" has always been. Genealogies of history seek to tie these archeological shifts in knowledge and consciousness to broader historical transformations and the exercise of power behind those transformations. Both archeology and genealogy provide research approaches that question whether the development of communication theory and practice is the result of continual refinement and evolution or the result of historically contingent shifts in power.

Both of these methodologies spring from a fundamental skepticism about the nature of traditional histories. Foucault argues that most historical accounts suffer from a variety of interlinked but functional shortcomings. Stated simply, conventional accounts of the evolution of thought and historic events vastly oversimplify both those events and their causes. While this is an inherent quality of all histories, Foucault believed that the creation of knowledge about the past serves as part of a broader project by which people and institutions determine what range of truths will be widely accepted. Thus, rather than simply reflecting what "really" happened in the past, histories document those ideas, institutions, and political actors who emerged victorious from highly contested struggles over truth, meaning, and power while excluding or marginalizing other ideas, institutions, and people. In the case of histories of knowledge and technology, presenting the past as an orderly unfolding of ever increasingly rational and accurate ideas about science, government, education, and society is not only an oversimplification but a distortion. Rather than simply tracing major refinements in ways of thinking, such histories conceal struggles over truth and meaning whose outcomes were never inherently more superior, accurate, or inevitable than other potential outcomes. Equally important, they silence those individuals, ideas, experiences, and ways of living that did not prevail, erasing their existence from the historical record. Similarly, Foucault argued that political, economic, and social histories similarly serve to legitimate the power and authority of the victors of past power struggles, while overlooking the real power relationships that impact people on a day-to-day basis.

The problem with traditional histories is not simply that they are dishonest or incomplete but that they establish a "commonsense" or "taken for granted" understanding of the past that serves to continue and reinforce the power of the winners of those distant struggles into the present. By defining the range of ideas and outcomes that are conceivable under our commonly held understandings of what truth is; what ideas, institutions, and technologies are legitimate; and what ways of living are healthy and moral, histories shape and foreclose possibilities in the present. Thus, Foucault saw the creation of knowledge—and especially historical knowledge—as inseparable from the exercise of power. And histories constitute a particularly effective and problematic form of "*knowledge/ power*" in that they simultaneously reproduce the exercises of power that underlie our stories about the past, while cloaking those exercises of power by presenting contemporary understandings as largely uncontested and inevitable.

The first research approach Foucault developed in an effort to simultaneously expose and remedy these tendencies was what he termed *archeology.* As with all his approaches to research methodology, archeology is premised on the belief that the exercise of mundane, localized, and bureaucratic authority and ideas is more important in shaping peoples' lives than are the traditional big-picture events covered by conventional histories, such as the procession of governmental leaders or the conduct of wars. This premise has several important methodological ramifications. First, archeologies tend to focus on specific bodies of scientific or bureaucratic practice and knowledge in order to determine how they inform contemporary taken-for-granted understandings about such generally uncontested areas of "truth" as medicine, psychiatry, and the human sciences in general. Second, archeologies focus on what Foucault described as *discourses*—interrelated sets of statements that serve to convey, embody, and reinforce a range of valid claims about what is true and knowable by a given group of people at a given time. Foucault argued that these systems of truth claims by which certain knowledges are possible, or *discursive formations,* largely work below the consciousness of authors and actors but may be ascertained by examining the documents and statements by which knowledge is practiced and promulgated. Thus, while the term *archeology* suggests an effort to dig beneath the surface of conventional accounts of the past to uncover the "truth," Foucault actually believed that the ideas, stories, experiences, and struggles that are otherwise excluded or marginalized by traditional histories are readily ascertainable by looking at the surface of texts and artifacts from the past, which then allow the researcher to dig beneath the consciousness of those who created those texts and artifacts. By focusing on the ways that contemporary understandings of such issues as mental illness and medical knowledge gained the status of common sense, archeology involves exploring discourses by which those systems of knowledge achieved dominance. In so doing, archeologies seek to demonstrate how such taken-for-granted truths are actually contingent and contestable products of specific exercises of power at specific times and in specific places.

Foucault's subsequent *genealogies* were intended to build on the method of archeology while tracing the processes by which one set of discursive formations yields to another. Actively disputing histories of thought that present the evolution of knowledge as the manifestation of increasingly rational or efficient ways of thinking, genealogies seek to expose the ways that transformations in knowledge are both driven by and inseparable from shifts in power. This involves a study, not only of such archeological sources as texts and artifacts for the discourses they reveal, but also of broader social power relations that actually help animate the emergence of certain discourses and the disappearance of others. Thus, genealogy involves the simultaneous analysis of discourses and of the ways those discourses are integrated into and reproduced by personal habits, social norms, institutional rules, governmental agencies, and the like. For example, Foucault's genealogies trace the ways that knowledge about sexual and criminal deviance is both reflected in and reproduced by individuals and institutions as part of broader projects to extend social control over bodies. In seeking to expose both the ways that knowledge and power are linked (as with archeologies) and the ways that shifts in commonsense knowledge result from specific power struggles and historical contingencies, genealogies seek to challenge simultaneously the grand narratives of traditional histories and the "taken for grantedness" of contemporary systems of knowledge and belief.

John Carr

See also Critical Discourse Analysis; Critical Rhetoric; Critical Theory; Discourse Theory and Analysis; Poststructuralism; Power and Power Relations

Further Readings

Foucault, M. (1975). *Discipline & punish: The birth of the prison.* New York: Vintage.

Foucault, M. (1982). *The archaeology of knowledge and the discourse on language.* New York: Pantheon.

Foucault, M. (1990). *The history of sexuality: Vol. 1. An introduction.* New York: Vintage.

Foucault, M. (2003). *Society must be defended* (D. Macy, Trans.). New York: Picador.

ARGUMENTATION THEORIES

No single theory of argumentation exists. Instead, a constellation of features and concepts drawn from philosophy, rhetoric, and social theories infuses different concepts and explanations of argumentation. Since ancient times, an emphasis on rationality and reasonable communication distinguished argumentation from other kinds of communication. Argumentation is a cooperative process in which communicators make inferences from various grounds and evidence; provide justifications for their conclusions or claims based on those starting points; choose among disputed options in controversies; and promote, defend, and amend positions and standpoints in response to other participants in the argumentative processes.

In contrast to formal logic, argumentation emphasizes *practical reasoning*, the everyday arguments that people use to solve disputes in interpersonal and public contexts. Examining products, processes, and procedures provides general perspectives for theorizing argumentation. Pragmadialectics, the new rhetoric, and narrative paradigms explain and offer prominent frameworks for theorizing about argumentation.

General Perspectives for Theorizing Argumentation

Joseph Wenzel conceptualized three perspectives for studying argumentation theory: *products* derived from logic, *processes* associated with rhetoric, and *procedures* connected with dialectic. These perspectives have been reconfigured by some theorists to take into account the different fields or *spheres* in which they occur.

Products From Logic

Argument *products* extend the concepts of *formal logic*, a correct form of reasoning based on the linguistic progression that moves from a certitude stated in a major premise to an assertion of conditions in the minor premise and ends with a claim solely derived from both premises. *Informal logic* emphasizes everyday reasoning in which people make inferences, draw conclusions, and reason from one set of options to another in order to resolve disagreements or solve public problems. A long tradition of pedagogy based on informal logic theorized about argument products as different types of evidence, reasoning, and methods for creating and evaluating arguments.

Evidence, the primary feature of argument products, consists of one or more grounds that arguers put forth as the basis for believing their claims. Naming and identifying adequate evidence is a common approach for teaching argumentation theory. Evidence consists of definitions, testimony, examples, personal experiences, history, and statistics located in complicated chains of reasoning found in speeches, essays, literary works, proposals, and other discourses. Pedagogical approaches to argumentation establish explicit norms and standards for evaluating a particular type of evidence. For example, a norm for assessing the quality of statistical evidence depends on the extent to which numerical measures derive from reliable and valid methods that are up-to-date and generalizable to populations other than those from which the statistical evidence originated.

Of equal importance are the *types of logical connections* that supply the *implicative structure* in arguments, including signs, examples, cause–effect, analogy, authority, and definition. Argumentation pedagogy explicates the different types of reasoning and the relevant implicative structure that links evidence to claims. If an argument fails to meet these standards, a *fallacy* may result. Fallacies are errors in reasoning that deceive an audience by seeming to prove a claim based on a faulty inference. A cause–effect argument, for example, should establish a relationship between two events so that the first brings about the second; that is, the high price of oil is the cause of inflation. A type of fallacy, *false cause (post hoc)*, results when two events or actions occur at the same time and the arguer infers that one event is the cause of the other without considering other possible causes. Errant logical connections lead to a variety of other fallacies resulting from appeals to authority, pity, fear, the majority, or tradition. Because fallacies are both common and interesting, teachers often engage students in diagnosing the errors in argument products and explaining how flawed arguments can be avoided.

Wayne Brockriede and Douglas Ehninger adapted a model developed by philosopher Stephen Toulmin for teaching argumentation that describes and evaluates a unit of proof as an argument product by creating a visual construction of its parts. Diagramming begins with a *claim:* the judgment or conclusion that the arguer wants someone to accept. The diagram identifies the *evidence* (grounds or data) that serves as the basis for the claim and the *warrants* that make the connection between the evidence and claim. A *reservation* placed under the claim states the conditions under which the claim does not hold, and a *qualifier* acknowledges a limitation on the generalizability of the claim, using words like *most, many,* or *some. Backing* provides additional evidence to support the warrant. Although Toulmin diagrams proved to be a useful tool for teaching students about logical products, they have limited potential as a method for analyzing and evaluating complex argumentative processes.

Processes From Rhetoric

The conception of argument *processes* derives from rhetorical theory and concentrates on the ways people argue in interpersonal and public interactions. Processes of *practical reasoning* concentrate on reasoned and purposeful rhetorical interactions that seek to resolve disagreements and disputes.

One simple concept of practical reasoning is the *enthymeme,* a truncated syllogism in which one or more of the premises or the conclusion is unstated but supplied by the audience to complete the argument. Examples of condensed arguments of this type are abundant. Many advertisements use enthymemes that present a conclusion—buy this brand of cola or vote for this candidate—that rely on audiences to fill in the missing premise and thereby supply the logical principles on which the conclusion is based. Enthymemes appear in many argumentative processes because audiences commonly contribute to the meaning of the reasons.

Argumentation *processes* take into account the rhetorical resources used by arguers in interpersonal and public disputes. For example, theories about argumentation processes consider the uses and effects of multiple chains of reasoning of complex arguments and counterarguments that involve rhetorical concepts, such as arguers' character, stylistic features of the discourses and interactions, and exigencies of the situation that generated the argument. Other relational, ideological, or ideational concepts impact argumentation processes in substantive ways. Examining the intricacies of argumentation processes reveals how arguers find and construe issues; what choices they make regarding evidence; what strategies they use to assert, modify, and refute arguments of others; and how arguments are first assembled and then altered in the process of resolving disagreements and making decisions. This process perspective applies to analyses of the development, use, and outcomes of argumentation in marital disputes, children's playground disagreements, and roommate conflicts and investigations of complex public policy disputes such as those involving women's rights, immigration, global warming, and stem cell research.

Procedures From Dialectic

Argument *procedures* include explicit and implicit rules and interactional protocols that influence disputes and reveal the situational constraints and cultural norms affecting argumentative processes. *Dialectic,* the art of arguing for or against an issue from a particular standpoint, proceeds according to rules and norms agreed on by disputants, such as searching for probable truths, avoiding fallacies, and resolving controversial issues. *Strategic dialectical processes* are planned interactions that arguers employ to test ideas by asserting and defending standpoints and by refining and reformulating evidence, claims, and inferential patterns in response to the reasoning of other disputants. Dialectic is a cooperative means of arriving at a reasoned decision according to specific procedures.

Dialectical procedures help to promote ethical argumentation and enable disputants to reason in a civil manner. Several features characterize dialectical procedures: (a) Arguers cooperate in obeying rules in order to achieve a common purpose; (b) arguers present complete and accurate content; (c) arguers are open about their positions and standpoints and clear about the ideas they offer to support them; (d) arguers apply rigorous standards for presenting their own arguments and evaluating those of other disputants; (e) arguers respect other disputants; and (f) arguers act as restrained partisans who retain a standpoint at the same time they show a willingness to accept the amendments and judgments of others toward that standpoint. Parliamentary procedure is an example of a procedure that regulates the structure, content, and ethical interaction during decision-making processes.

Spheres

Some theorists reconfigure products, processes, and procedures of arguments according to the different fields or spheres in which they occur. Thomas Goodnight and others elaborated this construct by examining contextual similarities among *spheres*—collections of people or groups, organizations, and professions—that interact with one another to make decisions or resolve disputes. The reasonableness of argumentation in a particular sphere depends on how arguers construct reasons; engage with others; and support, defend, and amend issues and standpoints according to the norms and rules of a sphere. For example, differences exist between personal, technical, and public spheres because arguers emphasize different procedures and processes in constructing and evaluating evidence, providing justifications, using language, and pursuing specific goals of a sphere. In *personal spheres,* arguers seek to resolve interpersonal disputes by identifying issues and negotiating outcomes according to mutually agreed-on rules. Friends and coworkers tend to resolve their disputes in personal spheres. Argumentation in *technical spheres,* however, adheres to explicit rules of evidence and modes of justification that direct reasoning processes toward specific goals and outcomes. The scientific and legal professions are exemplars of technical spheres. *Public spheres* are discursive arenas in which arguers take into account customs, traditions, and requirements of a polity and deal with the public business in deliberative forums, such as town meetings, legislative arenas, or the Internet. In *counterpublic spheres,* minority groups argue in ways that challenge and resist the standpoints defended by those holding positions of public power. Sphere theories construe argument products, processes, and procedures in innovative ways that bring attention to the importance of various contexts, goals, and procedures of argumentation theories.

Sample Theories

Various frameworks have been developed to theorize the argumentation process. Three sample theories will be discussed here: pragma-dialectics, the new rhetoric, and the narrative paradigm.

Pragma-Dialectics

Pragma-dialectics, an argumentation theory introduced and refined by theorists at the University of Amsterdam, relies on reasoned and orderly dialectical procedures and practical reasoning processes for resolving differences of opinion. This perspective emphasizes how particular speech acts used in social-reasoning processes increase or decrease the acceptability of arguers' controversial standpoints in disputes. This perspective stresses both the dialectical procedures and the instrumental and pragmatic goals that arguers pursue. One key procedural rule is that proponents of a *standpoint* must defend their positions when requested to do so, and another is that arguers must defend standpoints using correct *argumentative schemes* that address the patterns of inference underlying an argument. A scheme consists of types of arguments, such as appeal to authority, cause–effect reasoning, or analogy. Explicit standards exist for judging a particular scheme, such as determining whether an analogy shows sufficient similarity to another idea that it establishes a reasonable connection.

Argument analysis is the primary goal of pragma-dialectics. After categorizing a dispute according to sequential stages of confrontation, opening, argumentation, and conclusion, analysts then describe the disputed issues, identify standpoints of the arguers in relation to those issues, state the explicit and implicit arguments associated with disputants' standpoints, and explain the complex structures and standards that apply to the arguments. Specifically, analysts utilize pragma-dialectics to explain disputes according to the interplay of argumentative speech acts, instrumental goals, and dialectical procedures. *Speech acts* take the form of arguers' verbal claims—assertives, declaratives, and expressives—offered to support, defend, and amend specific standpoints. Instrumental actions consist of the *strategic maneuvers* that arguers employ to achieve their goals by accommodating their ideas to others. Strategic maneuvers demand consideration of the sufficiency of evidence, the commitments implicated in the speech acts, and the schemes utilized in relation to arguers' standpoints. Resolving disagreements also depends on how arguers meet their dialogical obligations of cooperation, thoroughness, and the presentation of appropriate evidence. Pragma-dialectic analysis can be applied to resolutions of simple disagreements between a tenant and an apartment manager, for example, as well as complex disputes in legal forums and international negotiations.

The New Rhetoric

The new rhetoric emphasizes appeals to values as the primary means that arguers use to persuade others. Audiences consist of ensembles of people from whom arguers seek adherence to their claims. In order to make their claims acceptable to audiences, arguers construct reasons based on *premises* that come from facts (ideas that are of general knowledge and are verifiable), *presumptions* (shared and generally believed ideas about reality), and *values* (judgments about what is good or moral in society). Gaining audiences' adherence to arguments depends on how arguers make connections between their own values and those of their audiences. The particular audience consists of real and definable groups of people that arguers seek to persuade in a specific situation. Voters in a city election, for example, are the particular audience addressed by a city council candidate. The *universal audience* is not the real ensemble of people addressed but is instead an ideal of competent and reasonable people holding universal values of justice, fairness, and equality. In order for arguers to gain the adherence of audiences to the reasons they put forth, the arguers must explicitly address the values of their particular audience and implicitly invoke the values of the universal audience.

Argument types depend on values. The *quasilogical argument,* for example, creates illusions about the connection between claims and the audience values on which those claims are based. These arguments are partially logical because they contain the structure of arguments, value associations, and connections, but not the logical content. For example, when legislators claim that new taxes hurt the middle class more than the upper class, they give the impression that the tax code is unfair although the taxes may in fact reduce the income of the upper class by a higher percentage than they do the income of the middle class. The persuasiveness of arguments about taxation policy depends on arguers' and audiences' sharing values of fairness rather than on causal logic based on facts. Another type, *arguments based on the structure of reality,* justifies arguers' positions by linking them to audiences' opinions and experiences of reality. For example, when arguers claim that global warming is a threat to the future of the planet, arguers rely more on their audiences' opinions and experiences related to climate change than on their own ideas. This type of argumentation assumes that audiences already hold a view of reality, and so arguers create reasons directly aligned with audiences' preexisting knowledge of reality. In contrast, *arguments establishing the structure of reality* promote a view at odds with the reality familiar to audiences. In this type of reasoning, arguers utilize examples, analogies, and models to construct a reasonable view of reality that is not part of the audiences' knowledge. For example, to create a structure of reality for a criminal trial, defense attorneys may try to construe a criminal action as accidental rather than intentional based on the supposed reality in which it occurred. Although the jurors have no direct knowledge of the circumstances surrounding the crime, the defense attorney creates a reality (a description of circumstances) based on analogies of events familiar to jurors. The attorney's descriptions serve as the basis for arguments showing that an action was accidental, not intentional.

The new rhetoric explains arguers' strategic uses of reasoning based on associations and dissociations of ideas and issues in ways that gain audiences' adherence. The reasonableness of argumentation process is influenced, not by external rules or norms, but by arguers' explicit and implicit connections of their reasoning to the values of the particular and universal audience.

Narrative Paradigm

Narrative paradigm theory also conceptualizes rhetorical processes of argumentation influenced by values. Although stories are not the most common form for expressing arguments, they are a prominent kind of practical reasoning used by arguers to influence their audiences. Narratives convey specialized social knowledge that evokes reasoned responses from audiences but does not rely on the same kinds of evidence, modes of inference, and justifications typical of other products and processes of argumentation. Instead, narrative reasoning depends on how audiences make meaning from the values embedded in narratives

and how these values inform their judgments and actions. Narratives contain both a logic and a rationality derived from how audiences attribute coherence and fidelity, along with probability, or the likelihood that the events described could have happened, to the stories they hear, read, and see. *Coherence* refers to the internal fit of the narrative parts, that is, the consistency of characters, action, dialogue, and setting. *Fidelity* relates to the truth value of the story, whether the narrative fits with the experiences of the audiences and their notions about sound reasoning. Taken together, both create *narrative rationality,* a quality that enables people to understand the actions of others and judge narrative accounts as reasoned explanations of human choice and action. Values are the core of narratives because they supply good reasons that authorize, sanction, or justify certain kinds of beliefs and actions for audiences. Good narrative reasoning embodies characteristics similar to other argumentation processes; it includes facts, assumes relevance, contains inferential patterns, embodies coherence and consistency, and addresses transcendent issues.

Narrative paradigm theory de-emphasizes informal logical products and stresses argument processes as social constructions of values. Narrative rationality applies to argumentation in fictional literature, television and stage dramas, and biographies and autobiographies, as well as to processes of jury decision making, organizational advocacy, and many kinds of political discourse. Some communication theorists apply narrative paradigm theory so generally that they lose sight of the centrality of practical reasoning processes and values and instead concentrate on narrative as a general idea related to communication practices.

Conclusion

Argument theories examine practical reasoning products, processes, and procedures. Theorists are indebted to traditions of logic, rhetoric, and dialectic for the concepts they have appropriated, modified, and constructed to explain argumentation. Early theories of argumentation developed in response to pedagogical goals. Later theories of pragma-dialectics, the new rhetoric, and narrative paradigm responded to pragmatic, analytical, and interpretive goals pertinent to the use of reasoning as a means of settling disagreements or disputes, making critical decisions, and socially constructing knowledge. In this way, argumentation theories are constellations of concepts that explain the centrality of reasoning to theories of communication.

Janice Schuetz

See also Conversation Analysis; Discourse Theory and Analysis; Narrative and Narratology; Public Sphere; Rhetorical Theory; Speech Act Theory

Further Readings

Asen, R., & Brouwer, D. C. (2001). *Counterpublics and the state.* Albany: State University of New York.

Ehninger, D., & Brockriede, W. (1978). *Decision by debate.* New York: Harper & Row.

Freely, A. J. (1993). *Argumentation and debate.* Belmont, CA: Wadsworth.

Goodnight, G. T. (1982). The personal, technical, and public spheres of argument: A speculative inquiry into the art of public deliberation. *Journal of the American Forensic Association, 18,* 1–27.

Perelman, C., & Olbrechts-Tyteca, L. (1969). *The new rhetoric: A treatise on argumentation* (J. Wilkinson & P. Weaver, Trans.). Notre Dame, IN: University of Notre Dame.

Toulmin, S. (2003). *The uses of argument.* Cambridge, UK: Cambridge University. (Original work published 1958)

Trapp, R., & Schuetz, J. (Eds.). (2007). *Perspectives on argumentation.* New York: IDEA. (Original work published 1990)

van Eemeren, F. H., Grootendorst, R., & Henkemans, F. S. (1996). *Fundamentals of argumentation theory.* Mahwah, NJ: Lawrence Erlbaum.

Wenzel, J. W. (1990). Three perspectives on argument: Rhetoric, dialectic, logic. In J. Schuetz & R. Trapp (Eds.), *Perspectives on argumentation: Essays in honor of Wayne Brockriede* (pp. 9–26). Prospect Heights, IL: Waveland.

ARGUMENTATIVENESS, ASSERTIVENESS, AND VERBAL AGGRESSIVENESS THEORY

Predispositions toward aggressive communication have been found to explain much of a person's message-sending and message-receiving behavior. Understanding the role of aggressive communication in conflict provides valuable insight into communication behaviors people exhibit when disagreement exists. Individuals engaged in aggressive communication often adopt "attack" and "defend" modes of thinking and behavior. These behaviors can be employed destructively as well as constructively. This entry defines aggressive communication, distinguishes constructive from destructive symbolic aggressive communication, describes assertiveness, argumentativeness, hostility, and verbal aggressiveness, and explores consequences of constructive and destructive aggressiveness in relationships.

Symbolic Aggressive Communication

The first distinction made in categorizing aggression is physical versus symbolic. Aggression can take both physical and symbolic forms. Physical aggression involves the aggressor's forceful use of his or her body (roughly handling or striking objects or others). *Symbolic aggression* involves the aggressor's forceful use of his or her communication (words, gestures, facial expressions, vocal tone, etc.). It is this latter set of behaviors with which aggressive communication is concerned.

Symbolic aggression can be divided into two types: *constructive* and *destructive*. Aggressive communication is composed of not one, but several traits, including assertiveness, argumentativeness, hostility, and verbal aggressiveness. Each of these traits interacts with environmental factors to produce message behavior.

Constructive Aggressive Communication

Assertiveness is considered a constructive trait because it involves verbal and nonverbal symbols to exert control, obtain justified rewards, and stand up for one's rights. Individuals who are assertive can use symbols aggressively but tend to do so in socially acceptable ways. One facet of assertiveness is *argumentativeness,* defined as a stable trait that predisposes individuals involved in a conflict to defend positions on controversial issues and to verbally attack the positions of others. Argumentativeness is considered a subset of assertiveness as all arguing is assertive communication, but not all assertiveness involves arguing.

Individuals differ in their levels of trait argumentativeness and can be classified into three groups: high, low, and moderate. A person *high in argumentativeness* enjoys arguing and will eagerly and readily use arguments to attack others' positions and defend their own positions on issues. Highly argumentative individuals view arguing as an intellectual challenge and as an exciting competitive situation that allows them to display to others how communicatively skillful they are.

People *low in argumentativeness* often feel uncomfortable about arguing before, during, and after the event that calls for argument. They frequently lack the motivation, desire, and skill to argue across most situations and generally avoid talking about controversial issues because it makes them uncomfortable. Those low in argumentativeness can even hold negative beliefs about arguing. Individuals can also be *moderate in argumentativeness*. There are three types: conflicted, apathetic, and neutral.

Conflicted feelings often cause moderates to be highly emotional when it comes to arguing; they can feel compelled to argue due to their level of competitiveness yet be highly anxious about arguing due to their fear of failure. *Apathetic-moderate argumentatives* tend to be low in emotion when it comes to arguing yet feel little to no anxiety about engaging in an argument. *Neutral-moderate argumentatives* normally argue only when they see some good coming out of it and feel that they have a good chance of winning.

Destructive Aggressive Communication

There are two destructive forms of symbolic aggressive communication: hostility and verbal aggressiveness. *Hostility* is exhibited in interpersonal communication when people use messages to express irritability, negativity, resentment, and suspicion. *Irritable communicators* usually have quick tempers, show little patience, are moody, and appear exasperated when things go wrong for them. *Negative communicators* typically express a great deal of pessimism, display little cooperative effort, and often are antagonistic toward authority, rules, and social conventions. *Resentment* is expressed through jealousy and brooding about perceived slights, either real or imagined. *Suspicion* is communicated by distrust of others.

Verbal aggressiveness is defined as the tendency to attack the self-concept of individuals instead of, or in addition to, their positions on topics of communication. These attacks most commonly take the form of character attacks (e.g., "You're a liar and a cheater!"), competence attacks (e.g., "You can't do anything right" or "You're a lousy lover"), teasing, ridicule, profanity, maledictions (i.e., wishing someone harm, as when we say to someone, "Drop dead"), background attacks, attacks on physical appearance ("Your nose looks like a pig's nose"), threats, and nonverbal behaviors (e.g., raising the middle finger in the "up yours" gesture, sticking out the tongue, rolling the eyes).

The essential difference between argumentativeness and verbal aggressiveness is in the locus of the attack. In argumentativeness, the attack is on the adversary's *position* on the controversial issue; in verbal aggressiveness, the attack is on the adversary's *self-concept*. For example, one spouse suggests purchasing a vehicle made by an American manufacturer. The other disagrees, stating "American cars depreciate much more quickly than Japanese vehicles." This constitutes an example of an argumentative response. Stating, "American cars stink, and you're an idiot for wanting to waste our money buying one" would constitute a verbally aggressive response and one that is potentially destructive to the relationship. Verbally aggressive behavior is more common in exchanges in which the consequences are very meaningful to those involved.

Causes of Verbal Aggressiveness

Several reasons have been offered for the development of the verbal aggressiveness trait: psychopathology (repressed hostility or neuroticism), disdain for the other person, social learning of aggression, and argumentative skill deficiency (i.e., not possessing the skill and ability to generate constructive arguments during a conflict). Communication scholars have suggested a fifth cause of verbal aggressiveness—the inherited trait explanation. This explanation suggests that verbal aggressiveness can be an expression of temperament. That is, some people are born with a set of biologically determined temperaments that are relatively consistent throughout their lives, of which verbal aggressiveness is one.

Individuals high in verbal aggressiveness have been found to view competence attacks, character attacks, maledictions, nonverbal emblems (i.e., gestures which take the place of words), ridicule, and threats as less hurtful than do those who are low in verbal aggressiveness. Many individuals high in verbal aggressiveness reported several reasons for being verbally aggressive, such as trying to appear tough, rational discussions' degenerating into verbal fights, wanting to be mean to the other person, and wanting to express disdain for the other. In another study, it was observed that highly verbally aggressive individuals often perceive that their verbal aggression is justified.

Consequences of Constructive and Destructive Aggressive Communication

The most fundamental conclusion that has been reached by the vast amount of research conducted on aggressive communication over the past quarter of a century is that most outcomes of argumentativeness are constructive, while most outcomes of verbal aggressiveness are destructive. Several benefits have been associated with argumentativeness. First, argumentativeness can enhance perceived credibility. Argumentativeness has been related to credibility because of the assumption that higher levels of the trait may indicate more skill in arguing and reasoning. Research has revealed that more skillful advocacy, refutation, and rebuttal behaviors frequently indicate greater competence in communication. High argumentatives are more likely than low argumentatives to be seen as leaders in groups. Argumentativeness has also been associated with higher levels of self-esteem, especially perceptions of personal power and competence.

Recall that a skill deficiency in argument has been suggested as one explanation for verbal aggressiveness. That is, when individuals are low in motivation to argue and lack the skill to generate arguments during conflict, these deficiencies can lead to verbal attacks being directed to another person's self-concept instead of his or her position on controversial issues. Verbal aggression has been suggested as a catalyst for physical aggression. Thus, being high in motivation and skill in argument may reduce the likelihood that this cycle will result because skilled and motivated arguers are better able to direct a verbal attack

toward their adversary's position, and not their self-concept.

Andrew S. Rancer

See also Conflict Communication Theories

Further Readings

Beatty, M. J., & McCroskey, J. C. (1997). It's in our nature: Verbal aggressiveness as temperamental expression. *Communication Quarterly, 45,* 446–460.

Infante, D. A. (1995). Teaching students to understand and control verbal aggression. *Communication Education, 44,* 51–63.

Infante, D. A., & Rancer, A. S. (1982). A conceptualization and measure of argumentativeness. *Journal of Personality Assessment, 46,* 72–80.

Infante, D. A., Riddle, B. L., Horvath, C. L., & Tumlin, S. A. (1992). Verbal aggressiveness: Messages and reasons. *Communication Quarterly, 40,* 116–126.

Infante, D. A., & Wigley, C. J. (1986). Verbal aggressiveness: An interpersonal model and measure. *Communication Monographs, 53,* 61–69.

Martin, M. M., Anderson, C. M., & Horvath, C. L. (1996). Feelings about verbal aggression: Justifications for sending and hurt from receiving verbally aggressive messages. *Communication Research Reports, 13,* 19–26.

Rancer, A. S. (1998). Argumentativeness. In J. C. McCroskey, J. A. Daly, M. M. Martin, & M. J. Beatty (Eds.), *Communication and personality: Trait perspectives* (pp. 149–170). Cresskill, NJ: Hampton Press.

Rancer, A. S., & Avtgis, T. A. (2006). *Argumentative and aggressive communication.* Thousand Oaks, CA: Sage.

Rancer, A. S., & Nicotera, A. M. (2007). Aggressive communication. In B. B. Whaley & W. Samter (Eds.), *Explaining communication* (pp. 129–147). Mahwah, NJ: Lawrence Erlbaum.

ASIAN COMMUNICATION THEORY

Asian communication theory refers to the body of literature covering concepts and theories derived from the rereading of Asian classical treatises, non-Eurocentric comparisons, East–West theoretical syntheses, explorations into Asian cultural concepts, and critical reflections on Western theory. This entry will begin with a definition of

Asian communication theory and then will examine Asian communication theory in relation to the seven communication traditions that Robert Craig elucidated in 1999: rhetorical, semiotic, phenomenological, cybernetic, sociopsychological, sociocultural, and critical.

Definition

The three words constituting *Asian communication theory* need clarification because each word contains multiple meanings. Although geographically Asia includes the Middle East, Central Asia, and eastern Russia, *Asian* theory focuses primarily on the great philosophies of India and China and the cultures of the region between them. Asian communication theory adds to the different meanings of *communication,* and it conflicts with the positivist view of *theory,* which is an artifact of Western science. Asian theory emphasizes systems, groups, networks, and the macro approach and is therefore more akin to philosophy, which cannot be easily tested in the Western scientific manner.

These different approaches to communication and theory result in an Asian worldview that differs from the West's in its premises about self, nature, space and time, knowledge, and the transpersonal. Johan Galtung summarizes these differences as follows:

- The West emphasizes *individualism;* the East emphasizes the reciprocal responsibility between individual and society.
- The West emphasizes *control* of nature; the East emphasizes *harmony* with nature.
- The West looks at a world *divided* into center (West), periphery (West's allies), and outer periphery (all the rest); the East looks at the world and universe as a single unit (an interconnected and interdependent *whole*).
- The West sees *bounded time;* the East sees *infinite time.*
- The West sees knowledge in terms of atomism and deductivism (and uses these fragments to engender contradiction-free theoretical frameworks following Newtonian science); the East sees knowledge in terms akin to systems theory such that axiology (values), epistemology (knowledge), and ontology (metaphysics) all become essential parts of theorizing.

- The West subordinates humans to a supreme being; the East places faith in following the path of righteousness—*dharma* in Buddhism and Hinduism, *yi* in Confucianism, and the nondivine Supreme Reality in Daoism.

Asian Theories Within Western Traditions

Robert Craig divided the field of communication into seven traditions on the basis of underlying conceptions of communicative practice. Although designed to organize Western theories, these traditions can reflect East–West differences and are used in the following discussion to classify various Asian theories.

The Rhetorical Tradition

Rhetoric (study of principles and rules of composition formulated by ancient critics and of writing or speaking as a means of communication or persuasion) has a long history traceable to Greek sophists (c. 600 BCE). Communication scholar Robert T. Oliver failed to see any paradigmatic examples of Asian rhetoric that are compact enough to be subjected to a thorough analysis. However, Steven Combs was able to derive a unique model of Chinese rhetoric from a rereading of the ancient Daoist texts.

Chinese Rhetoric

Antonio S. Cua attempted to formulate a Confucian rhetoric on the lines of the Aristotelian model. Cua concluded that a society that values harmony and tolerance could not be expected to embrace the values of debate and persuasion. In his study of Xunzi's moral epistemology, Cua asserted that the ethics of a Confucian rhetoric arose from the background notions of *li* (propriety), *yi* (righteousness), and *jen* (benevolence).

Combs, however, contends that Daoism—as explicated in the classics *Dao de jing* (attributed to Laozi), *Zhuangzi* (by Zhuangzi), and *Art of War* (attributed to Sunzi)—offers no explicit definition of rhetoric or an inventory of rhetorical canons inasmuch as Daoists do not think of rhetoric as a distinct subject although their overall philosophy on language and communication (rhetoric) shows spontaneity and creativity. The concepts Dao (Way/Path/Supreme Reality), *de* (efficacy/virtuality), yin–yang (passive energy–active energy) polarity, *ziran* (natural way), harmony, and *wu–wei* (actionless action) are key components of Daoist rhetoric.

Laozi thematizes the need to avoid contentiousness and unnatural verbosity. Laozi uses two negative methods (negation and paradox) and two positive methods (analogy/metaphor and vague expressions) for communicating Daoism. The outstanding rhetorical strategy that Zhuangzi uses is *evocativeness*, intended to draw others into interactive communication aimed at engendering self-persuasion. Evocativeness differs from Aristotle's *enthymeme* and Kenneth Burke's *identification* and adds a vital element to Western rhetorical theory. Zhuangzi uses parables creatively to go beyond the limitations of language; he introduces the readers to the essential unity of the Dao, the errors of making distinctions or passing judgments, wu–wei, and the natural way of things. Sunzi's underlying strategic principle in *Art of War*, when applied to persuasion, is the *rhetoric of parsimony*, which has three key attendant principles: *knowledge, strategy,* and *responsiveness.* Sunzi, who upholds the Daoist principle of avoiding conflict, says that justification for war must be made on the basis of harmony. Sunzi's rhetoric is also comparable at times with Western rhetorical concepts such as *presumption* and *identification.* Combs asserted that the genre of Daoist rhetoric has the potential to provide a lens for viewing the limitations of current Western rhetorical theorizing.

Indian Rhetoric

Western scholars have often used the term *Asian rhetoric* in a pejorative sense because of the alleged Indian preference for form (e.g., exaggeration, embellishment) over substance. However, communication scholars have yet to reread the 550 *Jataka* (*Rebecoming*) stories of the Buddha or the hymns of the four *Vedas* (sacred knowledge), the 108 *Upanishads* (philosophical commentaries on the Vedas), or even the *Bhagavadgita* (the Song of God extracted from the *Mahabharata* epic) to derive a genre of Indian rhetoric.

The rhetoric of India, in both its Hindu and its Buddhist forms, has an ethical basis. The Hindu rhetorician seeks *aretaic* qualities (virtues)—those by which the individual may fully represent the traditions of family, community, and caste—while the Buddhist rhetorician values truthfulness, compassion, and conciliation.

Reasoning is an aspect of rhetoric. Bimal K. Matilal claims that India's *dharma* tradition evolved through an attempt of a rational criticism of itself. Stories in the epics and the *puranas* mention Carvaka's use of *tarka* or *hetusastra*, the science of reasoning, to ask questions and challenge the validity of Vedic rituals.

Nagarjuna, the 2nd-century Buddhist philosopher, used logic to show that nothing in the phenomenal world had full being and all was ultimately unreal. Therefore, every rational theory about the world would be a theory about something unreal evolved by an unreal thinker with unreal thoughts. Western communication theory has failed to examine communication through the critical lens of Nagarjuna because of the undercurrents of Orientalism and Eurocentrism.

The Semiotic Tradition

John Locke's language theory, explicated in *An Essay on Human Understanding*, published in 1690, is credited with setting off *semiotics* as a distinct tradition of communication theory. *Pragmaticism* and *linguistics*, reflected in the current theories of language, discourse, interpretation, nonverbal communication, culture, and media, are contemporary areas of study that rely on the semiotic tradition. Semiotics defines communication as intersubjective mediation by signs.

Chinese Semiotics

Asian communication scholars have yet to develop comparable semiotic theories. However, elements of a distinct theory of Chinese semiotics are reflected in the communication pattern of those who make use of the Chinese ideographic system of writing, which entails the interpretation of symbols—itself a semiotic exercise. Despite the mutual unintelligibility of the spoken language systems and the very different language stocks in Korea, Japan, and Vietnam, all of East Asia during the Tang dynasty adopted the Chinese ideographic system that the Japanese called *kanji* (*hanja* in Korean and *hanzi* in Chinese). Because kanji are inextricably tied to a particular set of ideas, unlike the letters of an alphabet, the use of kanji throughout East Asia created an "empire of ideas"—a powerful glue that bound the region together.

Moreover, the *Yijing* (Book of Changes) system— with the basic yin and yang signs that make up bigrams, trigrams, and hexagrams (various word combinations)—could be considered a semiotic masterpiece. It dates back to the 12th century BCE. The Ten Commentaries for the understanding of the *Yijing* were written in the 3rd or 4th century BCE. The philosophy of Chinese semiotics is an explicit manifestation of the metaphysics implicit in the signs or forms (*xiang*). Chung-Ying Cheng points out that the *Yijing* incorporates four functions—interpretative, integrative, practical, and ingraining— that define a system of communication.

Indian Semiotics

Rhetoric can be looked at as the branch of semiotics that studies the structures of language and argument mediating between communicators and audiences. The Indian theories of syntax and semantics are clear Asian contributions to this tradition.

Panini, the author of *Astadhyayi* (probably written in the 5th century BCE), explicated the structure of a natural language (Sanskrit), which enabled the Nyaya-Vaisesika school of Indian philosophy to work out the theory that puts meanings closest to the syntactic form of words. Bhartrhari, the 5th-century Indian philosopher of language who wrote the treatise *Vakyapadiya*, described thought as a unitary thing that fractured and altered form as it passed into words, interacting with other factors in the mind and the speaker's environment to produce intricate displays of sound and fragmented meaning.

The Phenomenological Tradition

Phenomenology is the study of consciousness from first-person perspective. It views communication as dialogue or experience of otherness. Martin Buber explicates that dialogue is based on the experience of authentic, direct, and unmediated contact with others. The description of the phenomenon of consciousness is the objective of phenomenology as evident in the three main categories of phenomenological thinking—*essentialist* (Edmund Husserl), *ontological* (Martin Heidegger), and *existentialist* (Jean-Paul Sartre and Maurice Merleau-Ponty).

The phenomenological tradition has a degree of consonance with Asian communication philosophy. Buddha often adopted the dialogic form to experience otherness, as testified in *Jataka* stories. The phenomenologists' focus on the centrality of language in human interaction, not as a mere means for conveying thought, but as constituting thought itself, resonates with Indian philosophy. The concepts of the structure of consciousness and the communicative environment are central to Asian verbal or nonverbal communication (e.g., Japanese *kuuki* [atmosphere requiring compliance] and *ishin-denshin* [communication without language]).

In a reader edited by Alexander Macfie, Reinhard May has documented the East Asian influences on Martin Heidegger's work, and Irene Eber has documented dialogist Martin Buber's considerable interest in Daoism. Heidegger's concept of *Dasein* is believed to have been inspired by the Daoist concept of *das-in-dem-Welt-sein* (to be in the being of the world), used in *The Book of Tea* by Okakura Kakuzo to describe Zhuangzi's philosophy. Heidegger himself had contacts with some leading Japanese intellectuals of the Kyoto School. Moreover, convergent phenomenology has combined Husserl's phenomenological concept of *transcendental ego* with 8th-century Indian philosopher Sankara's concept of the primacy of self-consciousness. Thus, major aspects of phenomenology show links to Asian communication theory.

The Cybernetic Tradition

Modern communication theory emerged with the cybernetic tradition in the mid-20th century featuring the works of scholars like Claude Shannon, Norbert Wiener, John von Neumann, and Alan Turing. This tradition includes current theories as diverse as systems and information science, cognitive science and artificial intelligence, functionalist social theory, network analysis, and the Batesonian school of interpersonal communication.

Asian communication theory is remarkably congruent with the systems approach of the cybernetic tradition. First, both systems theory and Asian philosophy emphasize the whole because the whole has the attribute called *emergence*, which the parts lack (although sociologists and economists differ on this point). Second, both accept the epistemological/ontological phenomenon of part–whole interconnection and interdependence, although postmodern systems theorists prefer to emphasize the system–environment interdependence. Third, both tend to agree on the inevitability of change in the light of the arrow of time, its direction toward infinity. Because of the dynamic behavior of every phenomenon, no predictions are possible; only probabilities can be worked out.

The Buddhist paradigm of *dependent co-arising* (*paticca samuppāda*) and the Chinese *Yijing* paradigm reflect these characteristics. The first illustrates the dynamic operation of all dependent co-arising factors to produce any given phenomenon. It rejects the linear independent–dependent dichotomy inherent in the Newtonian paradigm, which tends to imply the existence of permanent factors. The second illustrates how unity gives rise to a multiplicity of co-arising positive (yang) and negative (yin), interconnected and interdependent factors (bigrams, trigrams, and hexagrams) that evolve within the bounds of unity (system). It affirms the Chinese philosophical thesis that everything consists of the unity of opposites.

The Sociopsychological Tradition

This is the tradition dependent on social psychology, a development of the past century, that theorizes communication as a process of expression, interaction, and influence that may occur through face-to-face or through technological mediation from one to one, one to many, or many to many. Most of *communication science* falls into this tradition, as exemplified by the experimental persuasion studies of Carl Hovland, as well as the voting studies of Paul Lazarsfeld and Bernard Berelson.

Although much of Buddhist philosophy relates to psychological phenomena, endogenous Asian communication theories befitting this tradition are scarce except as appendages to Western theories, mainly because of the testability requirement of science as conceived by the West. However, principles of persuasion (discovered and synthesized through the Yale experimental studies) were used in China by lobbyists (e.g., Su Qin and Zhang Yi) during the chaotic half millennium from the 8th to the 3rd century BCE. The Asian contribution to the sociopsychological tradition needs more systematic investigation to enable East–West synthesis. This tradition in the West has come under criticism for excessive individualism, inattention to macro social forces, and insensitivity to cultural differences.

The Sociocultural Tradition

This tradition, which owes its intellectual inheritance to sociology and anthropology, theorizes communication as a symbolic process that produces and reproduces shared sociocultural patterns. Media are explicated as environments. Although this tradition views the existing sociocultural order as largely a reproduction of our everyday interactions, it also recognizes the creative process that adds to those interactions. Two poles have emerged within this tradition: structural theories that explicate relative stability of macrolevel patterns and interactionist–interpretive theories that explicate microlevel patterns of social-order creation.

The sociocultural tradition agrees with the Asian and Buddhist view that individuals are products of their social environments; the Confucian view that groups develop particular norms, rituals, and worldviews and the idea that that social change can be difficult and disruptive; and the Daoist view that attempts to intervene actively in social processes often have unintended consequences. The Buddhist and Daoist philosophies also emphasize the inevitability of change. However, because this tradition is another Western creation, the endogenous Asian contribution has yet to be documented.

The Critical Tradition

Although this tradition has ancient historical roots, the modern Western tradition of critical social theory is claimed to run from Karl Marx through the Frankfurt School to Jürgen Habermas. Alternatively, one could also include other strands of late Marxism and post-Marxism, current theories of political economy, critical cultural studies, feminist theory, and related schools of theory associated with new social movements (such as postcolonial theory and queer theory).

Normative media theories, which facilitate the critique of existing media systems, can also fall within this tradition. Cultural and media imperialism theory, dependency theory, and world-systems analysis are exemplars of the contemporary critical tradition.

Daoism anticipates a great deal of the contemporary critical tradition, particularly postmodernism as reflected in the views of Jean Baudrillard, Jean-Francois Lyotard, and Michel Foucault, as well as of Jacques Derrida and other poststructuralists. Daoism, like postmodernism, denies objective foundations for knowledge, essential meanings of identities, and universal truths and deprivileges reason and rationality. For example, Daoist sage Laozi contends that universal statements are impossible because words, which are finite and temporal, cannot express what is infinite. Therefore, communicators must resign themselves to the conditionality of their discourse or try to express themselves by using means other than words.

Asian communication theory includes a substantial contribution to this tradition, as exemplified by the works of scholars such as, among others, Guo-ming Chen, Wimal Dissanayake, Shelton Gunaratne, Satoshi Ishii, and Yoshitaka Miike. They reflect the influence of critical metatheories of Edward Said (Orientalism), Samir Amin (Eurocentrism), Farid Alatas (academic dependency), and others.

Shelton A. Gunaratne

See also Buddhist Communication Theory; Chinese Harmony Theory; Confucian Communication Theory; Hindu Communication Theory; Indian *Rasa* Theory; Informatization; Japanese *Kuuki* Theory; Taoist Communication Theory; Traditions of Communication Theory

Further Readings

Cheng, C.-Y. (1988). The *I Ching* as a symbolic system of integrated communication. In W. Dissanayake (Ed.), *Communication theory: The Asian perspective* (pp. 79–104). Singapore: Amic.

Combs, S. C. (2005). *The Dao of rhetoric*. Albany: State University of New York Press.

Craig, R. T. (1999). Communication theory as a field. *Communication Theory, 9,* 119–161.

Cua, A. S. (1985). *Ethical argumentation: A study in Hsun Tzu's moral philosophy*. Honolulu: University of Hawai'i Press.

Davis, L. (1988). Deep structure and communication. In W. Dissanayake (Ed.), *Communication theory: The Asian perspective* (pp. 20–38). Singapore: Amic.

Galtung, J., & Vincent, R. C. (1992). *Global glasnost: Toward a new world information and communication order?* (pp. 30–38). Cresskill, NJ: Hampton Press.

Gunaratne, S. A. (2005). *The Dao of the press: A humanocentric theory*. Cresskill, NJ: Hampton Press.

Gunaratne, S. A. (2008). Falsifying two Asian paradigms and de-Westernizing science. *Communication, Culture & Critique, 1,* 72–85.

Kincaid, D. L. (Ed.). (1987). *Communication theory: Eastern and Western perspectives*. San Diego, CA: Academic Press.

Macfie, A. L. (Ed.). (2003). *Eastern influences on Western philosophy: A reader*. Edinburgh, UK: Edinburgh University Press.

Miike, Y., & Chen, G.-M. (Eds.). (2007). Special issue: Asian contributions to communication theory. *China Media Research, 3*(4), 1–111.

Oliver, R. T. (1971). *Communication and culture in ancient India and China*. Syracuse, NY: Syracuse University Press.

ATTACHMENT THEORY

Early notions of attachment in close relationships were first proposed in 1969 and again throughout the 1970s in an attempt to give insight into the development of intimacy and closeness among humans across early stages of the life span. John Bowlby can be said to have initiated this area of study when he broadened his conceptualization of the bonding and attachment processes to extend beyond just those experiences of infants; his book, *Attachment Theory*, became one of the more widely used theories of intimacy in relationships. With Cindy Hazan and Phillip Shaver's 1987 extrapolation of Bowlby's original ideas to include romantic dyads, attachment is now one of the most often used variables in adult romantic relationship research. The major tenets of this theory include not only the explication of attachment across the life span but also the development of specific *attachment styles* with predictive and explanatory power. These attachment styles are seen as having specific utility in both relationship processes and outcomes.

Infant Attachment

Early attachment research focused on one's earliest interpersonal experiences. During infancy, humans begin to develop what may eventually become lifelong patterns of interdependence with one another. This *interdependence* (typically described as an intertwining of lives, leading to mutual influence and reliance) is often seen as an interpersonal response that has evolved through natural selection processes. Indeed, the earliest attachments are enacted through proximity-seeking behaviors; the cries or grasping of infants are an adaptive response to an otherwise uncertain world, ensuring protection from a caregiver and the resulting survival that such security affords. Over time, the responsive caregiver becomes the object of the infant's primary *attachment bond* as the child relies on that person as a source of comfort or security. As a result of this attachment, infants will typically turn to the primary caregiver in times of distress or uncertainty. The amount of reliance on a caregiver is moderated by the individual experiences of the infant; a child who has experienced sensitive, warm, responsive, and/or consistent caregivers tends to have stronger attachment bonds with those caregivers. A child experiencing a distant, cold, unavailable, or inconsistent caregiver is believed to have weaker or unhealthier attachment bonds with that caregiver.

Adolescent and Adult Attachment

While early attachment figures are typically caregivers providing for the physical and/or safety needs of an infant or young child, attachment bonds are also formed throughout adolescence and adulthood. Just as infants turn to caregivers in times of distress or uncertainty, adolescents and adults tend to turn to a specific individual when they need affirmation related to security, closeness, or intimacy. This attachment bond is typically characterized by an enduring affiliation with an attachment figure through both good and bad episodes in the relationship; the bond is often so enduring that perceptions of grief and loss often occur if the affiliation is somehow severed. Obviously, adolescent and adult attachment bonds are not limited to caregivers, since those relationships likely occur with decreasing frequency throughout adolescence and early adulthood. Adult attachment bonds have been found to occur in close relationships such as close friendships, sibling relationships, parent–child relationships, and even the occasional patient–therapist relationship.

The strongest attachment bond that adults may experience, however, is the pairing between romantic partners. Much like other attachment pairings, one's pattern of relating within adult romantic relationships is heavily influenced by one's early relational experiences. Scholars have long argued that the manner in which one forms an attachment bond with one's early caregivers sets up a style of interacting and relating within romantic relationships that continues over the course of the life span. These composite styles of interacting and relating comprise an attachment pattern that often predicts and explains one's relational style.

Attachment Patterns

While the study of attachment formation across the life span offers broad generalizations about the creation and maintenance of close relationships, there are many individual differences that may lead to a wide range of attachment-related behaviors. Scholars have distilled the broad range of individual attachment behaviors into four distinct patterns; while these four categories have great conceptual utility, it must be understood that attachment-related behaviors are not inherently categorical in nature.

Secure Attachment

The *secure* pattern of attachment is characterized by a strong sense of self-worth. Individuals displaying a *secure* pattern of attachment typically view others as worthy of trust, and these individuals are typically quite comfortable with both closeness and intimacy in their significant relationships. Because they often attribute positive character traits to attachment figures, *secure* individuals are confident in their relational status and are typically found to rate quite high on the four key relational characteristics of commitment, trust, interdependence, and satisfaction. The romantic experiences of a secure individual are generally characterized by positive emotional affect and mutual friendship. The secure pattern of attachment can be characterized by the useful memory tool that I am OK and you are OK too.

Preoccupied Attachment

As compared with the secure pattern of attachment, individuals displaying the *preoccupied* pattern of attachment (occasionally referred to as the *anxious–ambivalent* pattern of attachment) are often characterized by a weak sense of self-worth. While preoccupied individuals do exhibit a comfort with closeness and intimacy in their significant relationships, an underlying theme of feeling unworthy of love or affection causes an excessive dependence on closeness or intimacy that can be taken to an often uncomfortable extreme. These preoccupied individuals fear abandonment from their attachment figures and typically overmonitor their relationships with these figures. The romantic experiences of a preoccupied individual are generally characterized by emotional extremes and have low levels of trust and satisfaction as a result of the fear of abandonment from their relational partner. The preoccupied pattern of attachment can be boiled down to the useful memory tool that I am not OK but you are OK.

Dismissive Attachment

The *dismissive* pattern of attachment is characterized by individuals with not only a high level of self-worth, but also an equally low level of trust for other individuals. While these individuals are not fearful of intimacy-related behaviors, they do tend to avoid making the significant attachments in which these intimacy-related behaviors are most likely to occur. Dismissive individuals often denigrate the importance of attachment and downplay their previous rejections or negative experiences with attachment figures. As a result, the preoccupation with avoiding intimacy often leads to romantic experiences characterized by a discomfort with closeness, minimal intimacy and intimacy-related behaviors, and displays of distancing behaviors toward their romantic partner. The dismissive pattern of attachment can be boiled down to the useful memory tool that I am OK but you are not.

Fearful Avoidant Attachment

The *fearful avoidant* pattern of attachment is characterized by both avoidance of intimacy and anxiety about forming attachments. Fearful avoidant individuals have the same weak sense of self-worth as do preoccupied individuals; the difference is that they avoid, rather than cling to, those individuals who serve as attachment figures. While

fearful avoidant individuals may actually crave intimacy and attachment, the overwhelming fear of rejection negates their willingness to form those bonds in which closeness may occur. As such, they have an aversion to behaviors associated with intimacy (e.g., disclosure, touch, and affection) except in those situations where rejection is unlikely to occur (e.g., in caring for older people). The fearful avoidant pattern of attachment can be described by the useful memory tool that I am not OK and you are not OK.

The bulk of attachment research focuses on the similarities and differences between the affective, cognitive, behavioral, and social attributes of individuals displaying each of the aforementioned four attachment patterns. Because one's attachment pattern is often determined through survey methods or observation techniques at a single point in time, or at multiple times during a particular stage of one's life, it must be noted that some scholars argue that the stability of one's particular attachment pattern over the course of the life span has not been sufficiently empirically demonstrated. As relationship experiences influence one's attachment behaviors, it is entirely possible that attachment patterns may shift in subtle ways throughout the course of one's life.

Attachment Patterns and Relational Attributes

Much research has been done on the relationship between one's attachment pattern and the relational attributes that one experiences in one's social world. While scholars often describe attachment patterns as causing many of the following specific relational outcomes, it must be noted that attachment patterns are typically studied using quasi-experimental methods and cannot empirically demonstrate causality with full confidence. Additionally, the attachment patterns of one's relational partner likely influence the expression of one's own attachment pattern; also, partner choice may be influenced by the intimacy-related behaviors of that partner and therefore depend on the partner's attachment pattern.

Relationship Quality

Much research has demonstrated the robust finding that secure individuals are generally more likely to report higher quality relationships, with elements of trust and positive affect. For relationships that are not securely attached, men are often most dissatisfied with their relationships because of low comfort with closeness (dismissive and fearful avoidant men), while women are most dissatisfied with their relationships because of high anxiety (preoccupied and fearful avoidant women).

Relationship Stability

While individuals with a secure pattern of attachment often report the highest relationship quality, a secure pattern of attachment is not the only predictor of relationship stability. As expected, research tends to report relatively stable relationships for secure individuals; unexpectedly, the relationships of preoccupied women and fearful avoidant men have also been found to be quite enduring, despite ratings of low relationship quality and negative affect.

Disclosure

In research scrutinizing how personal communication within relationships is affected by one's attachment pattern, secure individuals are found to exhibit the most skilled communicative abilities; secure individuals report a high amount of disclosure and a wide variety of disclosure topics for both relational partners and relative strangers, a finding reified using observational research techniques. Dismissive and fearful avoidant individuals, however, have a low level of disclosure amount and demonstrate less flexibility of disclosure in similar situations. Preoccupied individuals exhibit a slightly more complex pattern of communication within their relationships; while typically disclosing at a high level, preoccupied individuals are relatively inflexible in disclosure topic across a wide range of situations. Both secure and preoccupied individuals consider themselves capable of eliciting disclosure from others within a conversation, while dismissive and fearful avoidant individuals are relatively unlikely to report that same ability to elicit disclosure from others.

In summary, attachment theory argues that one's early relational experiences have a significant impact on one's manner of navigating one's social world. Infant caregivers provide one of the earliest forms of social interaction in the human experience and may help socialize individuals about how to manage their social and interpersonal relationships. Building on their early experiences, individuals develop their own relatively stable manner of interacting with significant others, including the development of conceptualizations about trust, affection, closeness, and other intimacy-related behaviors. The expressions of these individual differences often group into one of four general attachment patterns, which in turn may influence both process and outcome variables related to how one acts within many close or romantic relationships.

Jonathan M. Bowman

See also Communication Across the Life Span; Interpersonal Communication Theories; Relational Development

Further Readings

Bowlby, J. (1982). *Attachment and loss: Vol. 1. Attachment.* New York: Basic Books. (Original work published 1969)

Cassidy, J., & Shaver, P. R. (1999). *Handbook of attachment: Theory, research, and clinical applications.* New York: Guilford.

Collins, N. L., & Feeney, B. C. (2004). An attachment theory perspective on closeness and intimacy. In D. J. Mashek & A. Aron (Eds.), *Handbook of closeness and intimacy* (pp. 163–187). Mahwah, NJ: Lawrence Erlbaum.

Feeney, J. A., Noller, P., & Roberts, N. (2000). Attachment and close relationships. In C. Hendrick & S. S. Hendrick (Eds.), *Close relationships: A sourcebook* (pp. 185–201). Thousand Oaks, CA: Sage.

ATTITUDE ACCESSIBILITY THEORY

See Cognitive Theories

ATTITUDE THEORY

Attitude has been a difficult concept to define adequately, primarily because it has been defined by so many, but also because of the word's differing lay uses and connotations. Since the early 1900s, a number of theories have been developed to provide a framework for the attitude–behavior relationship that would provide explanatory and predictive information. Research on attitudes has been consequently popular in many disciplines. A key historic root for the fascination with the term is found in psychology's interest in individual differences and the need for scientists to find a concept that could name and explain a consistency in individual behavior across a variety of situations.

More specifically, throughout the history of social psychology, the concept of attitude has played a major role in explaining human action, viewing attitudes as behavioral disposition. In fact, Gordon Allport, one of the founding figures of personality psychology, claimed 60 years ago that *attitude* probably is the most distinctive and indispensable concept in contemporary American social psychology. One of the earliest definitions of attitude was proposed in 1918 by William Thomas and Florian Znaniecki, who defined it as a mental and neural state of readiness, organized through experience, exerting a directive or dynamic influence on the individual's response to all objects and situations with which it is related. A more recent definition by Philip Zimbardo and Michael Leippe proclaims attitude as an evaluative disposition toward some object, based on cognitions, affective reactions, behavioral intentions, and past behaviors, that can influence cognitions, affective responses, and future intentions and behaviors. In short, attitudes are learned predispositions to respond—they serve to provide direction to subsequent actions.

The key issue for theories and explanatory models is the notion of the origin of attitudes. In other words, why do people have attitudes? By and large, research has proposed four main reasons. First, attitudes help organize and simplify a complex environment and thus facilitate understanding of the world around us. Second, attitudes protect our self-esteem by helping us to avoid unpleasant truths because they direct us to comingle with those who share our own worldviews. Third, attitudes make our environment more predictable as they trigger an existing repertoire of reactions toward a set of attitude objects. This saves us from having to decide each time what the proper reaction or behavior should be. Finally, attitudes allow us to express some aspects of our individual personality or fundamental values.

Early studies seemed to confirm the validity of unidimensional effects of attitudes on behavior. Findings, however, such as the one by the social scientist Richard LaPiere's classic study, raised doubts about this assumption as it provided some evidence that people's verbal reports of their attitudes might not be very good predictors of their actual behavior. By the late 1950s, a multicomponent view was adopted, and attitudes were viewed as a complex system comprising a person's beliefs about an object, feelings toward the object, and action tendencies with respect to the object.

Modern cognitive psychology maintains that attitudes are the result of four components: (1) affective responses, (2) cognitive responses, (3) experiences of past behavior, and (4) behavioral intentions. The latter two are sometimes combined into a single component called behavior. The first component consists of a person's emotional response to a situation, object, or person (e.g., pleasure, anxiety). The second one is conceptualized as a person's factual knowledge of a situation, object, or person. The third component is related to how often a person had engaged in a certain behavior or been exposed to a certain situation or person in the past; that is, what kind of experience the person had collected about a situation, object, or person. The fourth component involves a person's plans to behave in a certain way when faced with a particular situation, even if these ideas are never acted on. These four components of attitude produce an organizing framework of the attitude construct known as *cognitive schemata*, which guide the information processes related to attention, interpretation, and recreation of a stimulus.

Given that attitudes are composed from various forms of judgments, unlike personality, attitudes are expected to change as a function of experience. While the concept of attitudes played a central role in the development of attitude measurement and scaling techniques before World War II, postwar research was dedicated primarily to theoretical and empirical issues in attitude change as a result of army-sponsored research to study the persuasive effects of propaganda during the war. As a result of the celebrated work at Yale University in the 1950s and 1960s by Carl Hovland, who found that attitudes can be changed through persuasion, a host of theories of attitude formation and attitude change emerged.

The most common classification of attitude theories into (a) behavioristic/learning theories, (b) consistency theories, (c) social judgment theory, and (d) functional theories will be used as an organizing framework here.

Behavioristic/Learning Theories

These theories were developed during the 1950s and 1960s, a time when learning theories reflected behavioral psychology. A major commonality of these theories was their emphasis on the stimulus characteristics of the communication situation. Leonard Doob, for instance, saw attitudes as an implicit, mediating process, an intervening variable between an objective stimulus and an overt response. As such, laws of attitude formation can be looked on in a parallel fashion to laws of classical conditioning. Furthermore, attitudes are learned through reinforcement or congruity. If an action has been highly regarded in the past, attitude toward it will likely be strengthened. Carl Hovland and his associates in the Yale Communication Research Program were a major driving force behind the emphasis on learning theories of attitude change. They proposed that opinions tend to persist unless an individual undergoes some new learning experience. The Yale researchers emphasized the role of incentives for change to occur. Incentives were broadly defined as ranging from direct financial or physical benefits to more abstract forms such as knowledge gain, social acceptance by respected others, or self-approval from the feeling that one is right.

Following the radical behaviorism ideas of B. F. Skinner, Daryl Bem developed a self-perception theory that attributed attitude change to an observation of one's own behaviors and conclusions about what attitudes must have caused them. The theory's main assumptions reflect the viewpoint that attitudes are learned as a result of previous experience with the environment since a person depends on outside cues to tell him or her how to feel internally.

Finally, Arthur Staat's work on attitude formation has the most immediate connection to behaviorist thinking, especially the ideas of classical conditioning. According to his arguments, emotional responses in an individual are created by events in the environment. As new stimuli are consistently paired with old stimuli (events), the new stimuli develop the power to create an emotional response in the individual. For instance, since words and objects are often paired with particular events, those words and objects evoke affective responses.

Consistency Theories

The basic assumption of cognitive theories is the need of the individual for consistency. There must be consistency between one's various attitudes, one's various behaviors, and one's attitudes and behaviors. A lack of consistency causes discomfort, so an individual attempts to ease the tension by adjusting attitudes or behaviors in order to maintain homeostasis, that is, achieve balance or consistency again.

One of the earliest consistency theories was the *balance theory,* developed by the Austrian psychologist Fritz Heider, whose work has been related to the Gestalt school. This theory looks at the relationship among three things: the perceiver, another person, and an object. Relationships are either positive or negative, based on the cognitive perceptions of the perceiver; these result in four balanced and four unbalanced configurations. Since unbalanced states are recognized as being unstable, perceivers attempt to restore balance by changing their attitudes toward either the object or the other person. There have been a variety of extensions to Heider's balance theory.

One important extension was the *theory of cognitive consistency,* developed by Robert Abelson and colleagues. Cognitive consistency suggests that people will try to maintain consistency among their beliefs and make changes (i.e., accept or reject ideas) when this does not occur. In other words, if a liked object helps attain other liked objects, attitudes are consistent. However, if a liked object hinders attainment of other liked objects, there is inconsistency. When inconsistency exceeds a certain level of tolerance, attitudes will change to achieve consistency. For example, if a person who adheres to certain social values and also wants to vote for a particular candidate is presented with the fact that people who usually vote for this candidate have opposite social values, the person will either reject this proposition or change his or her attitudes about voting for the candidate or about holding on to the social values. As such, the theory suggests four additional modes of restoring balance besides changing one's attitudes: (1) denial, (2) bolstering, (3) differentiation, and (4) transcendence.

In 1957, Leon Festinger developed his *cognitive dissonance theory*. This theory focuses on consequences of incompatibility between two related cognitions. Since dissonance occurs when elements are logically or psychologically inconsistent, it motivates the individual to reduce the dissonance and return to consonance by avoiding situations or information that may increase dissonance.

One of the major criticisms of consistency theories is that there are too many of them. Today, interest in consistency theories has diminished significantly as a result of the progress made in social psychology to better understand the processes that consistency theorists investigated, namely, the interactions between attitudes, beliefs, actions, and behavioral intentions.

Social Judgment Theory

Social judgment theory, developed by Muzafer Sherif and colleagues, is different from other consistency theories for two reasons: First, it argues that a receiver interprets or judges how much a message agrees or disagrees with his or her own attitude. In other words, it is an attempt to apply the principles of judgment to the study of attitude change. Second, the theory maintains that a message receiver's involvement in the topic of the persuasive message, that is, how important a topic is to a listener, is an important factor in attitude change.

Social judgment theory has been called by some more of an approach to studying attitudes, not a complete theory. Overall, it is based on the use of analogy, whereby an individual's initial attitude serves as an anchor for the judgment of related attitude communications. An advocated position is evaluated against this point of reference and is placed on an attitudinal continuum from acceptance via noncommitment to rejection. The amount of attitude change or whether change occurs at all depends on the discrepancy within the self—only

after a communicated opinion falls within the limits of the range of acceptance will it affect attitude change. Thus, the greater the difference between the initial opinion and the communicated opinion, the greater the attitude change will be. This theory further argues that the level of ego involvement in a topic depends on whether the issue arouses an intense attitude; that is, individuals who are highly involved in an issue are more likely to evaluate all possible positions, therefore increasing the anchoring property of their initial attitudes and broadening their range of rejection of a communicated opinion. Thus, a persuader facing a highly involved receiver may be able to advocate safely only a small change.

Since most other approaches deal only marginally with previous attitudes, social judgment theory has obtained an important place in the research literature. Recently, however, researchers have questioned the basic principles of social judgment theory and how the theory's principles relate to one another.

Functional Theories

Functional theories of attitude entered the literature in the 1950s when researchers developed the idea that attitudes served varying psychological needs and thus had variable motivational bases. A common and central theme of these early efforts was the listing of the specific personality functions that attitudes served for individuals. The idea is that people strive for goals and will adjust their attitudes to meet those goals. By and large, these theories are expanded argumentations of the original question about why individuals hold attitudes, discussed above. The most basic assumption of functional theories is that the key factors for attitude change are the relationships between events and information in the environment, on one hand, and the individual's values pattern and motives, on the other. It is the match or mismatch of those two forces that leads either to assimilation of the incoming information (i.e., attitude change) or to rejection of it.

The American psychologist Daniel Katz discussed four functions that attitudes perform for the personality: instrumental/utilitarian (the maximization of rewards and minimization of penalty from the environment), ego defensive (a protection from uncomplimentary truths about the self), value expressive (the expression of pleasure derived from basic values), and knowledge function (a need to understand and predict the environment). He argued that in order for attitude change to occur, there must be an inconsistency between the need being met by the attitude and the attitude itself. Changing an attitude, then, requires knowledge of what function an attitude performs for a person since the function that attitudes perform provides a frame of reference for comprehending and categorizing objects, persons, and events.

A related theory—Herbert Kelman's *functional analysis*—looked at social relationships that occur in social influence situations. He looked at three processes of opinion change: compliance, identification, and internalization. Those processes are closely related to the three roles or relational reasons of attitude change: power, attractiveness, and credibility of the source. *Compliance* results in only a surface-level attitude change in order to receive a favorable reaction from another powerful person or group. This attitude is usually expressed only when the other person is present. For instance, members of a group headed by a strong leader usually openly agree with that leader's choices regardless of whether they hold the same attitude toward a topic. The attitude change resulting from *identification* occurs both publicly and privately but does not become part of the person's value system. The change is dependent on the relationship with the source but not with the source's presence. An example would be the asserted identification with an attractive celebrity that can wane quickly once more important events overshadow this relationship. Attitudes that are *internalized* become part of an individual's value system. This usually occurs when a believable sender of a message convinces a receiver of the legitimacy of an idea to the extent that it becomes the receiver's idea henceforth.

Inoculation theory, developed by social psychologist William McGuire in 1961, is primarily concerned with the function of resistance to change; that is, it aims to explain how to keep original attitudes and beliefs consistent in the face of persuasion attempts. The main argument of the theory is that most attitudes are established in an environment that does not expose the individual to counterarguments and attack on the new attitude.

Therefore, the individual has little chance to develop resistance to possible future attacks. The theory argues that to prevent attitude change from occurring, it is necessary to strengthen preexisting attitudes. There are two key components to successful inoculation. The first is *threat*, which provides motivation to protect one's attitudes. The second component is known as *refutational preemption*, which is the cognitive part of the process. It is the ability to activate one's own argument for future defense and strengthen existing attitudes through counterarguing. This theory is loosely related to conflict theories, in which new information also presents a challenge to existing attitudes, and individuals are forced to seek alternative actions.

Many assessments of attitude theories argue that functional theories are in the mainstream of attitude research, and their theoretical approaches remain conceptually relevant to investigators because of their breadth and unique focus on the functional bases for attitudes. Functional theories are uniquely qualified to provide a link between the behavioral theories proposed during the 1950s (consistency theories, behavioral/learning theories, and social judgment theories) and the processing and cognitive themes of more recent theorizing (e.g., theory of reasoned action, social learning theory, transtheoretical model).

Summary

Attitude research is a major area in which theory building has been characteristic of the research. These theories, especially the functional theories discussed last, have provided guidance for many applied areas in communication. As an example, these theories have been invaluable for research on media effects and strategic communication as they led to the development of recommendations for the design of persuasive messages delivered by media and commercial advertisers.

Olaf H. Werder

See also Advertising Theories; Cognitive Dissonance Theory; Cognitive Theories; Co-Orientation Theory; Inoculation Theory; Learning and Communication; Media and Mass Communication Theories; Persuasion and Social Influence Theories; Reasoned Action Theory; Social Judgment Theory

Further Readings

Allport, G. (1935). Attitudes. In C. Murchison (Ed.), *Handbook of social psychology* (pp. 798–844). Worcester, MA: Clark University Press.

Eagly, A., & Chaiken, S. (1993). *The psychology of attitudes.* Fort Worth, TX: Harcourt.

Fishbein, M., & Ajzen, I. (1975). *Belief, attitude, intention, and behavior: An introduction to theory and research.* Reading, MA: Addison-Wesley.

Heider, F. (1958). *The psychology of interpersonal relations.* New York: Wiley.

Hovland, C., Janis, I., & Kelley, H. (1953). *Communication and persuasion.* New Haven, CT: Yale University Press.

Katz, D. (1960). The functional approach to the study of attitudes. *Public Opinion Quarterly, 24,* 163–204.

Kelman, H. (1958). Compliance, identification, and internalization: The process of attitude change. *Journal of Conflict Resolution, 2,* 51–60.

Kiesler, C., Collins, B., & Miller, N. (1969). *Attitude change: A critical analysis of theoretical approaches.* New York: Wiley.

Rajecki, D. W. (1990). *Attitudes* (2nd ed.). Sunderland, MA: Sinauer.

Sherif, M., & Hovland, C. (1961). *Social judgment, assimilation and contrast effects in communication and attitude change.* New Haven, CT: Yale University Press.

Thomas, W. I., & Znaniecki, F. (1918). *The Polish peasant in Europe and America.* Boston: Badger.

Triandis, H. C. (1971). *Attitude and attitude change.* New York: Wiley.

Zimbardo, P., & Leippe, M. (1991). *The psychology of attitude change and social influence.* Philadelphia: Temple University Press.

ATTRIBUTION THEORY

To make sense of the world, people develop explanations about what is happening and why people are acting certain ways. When people are interacting with others, communication decisions are influenced by the implicit theories, or attributions, of the participants. Ineffective communication may be partly a consequence of the parties' idiosyncratic inferences and incompatible interpretations. Attribution theory provides a framework for understanding how people explain their own and others' behavior. This entry reviews the attribution process and examines the importance of attributions for determining success or failure, for managing conflict in interpersonal relationships, and for determining people's stigmatizing attitudes and discriminatory behaviors. It ends with information about the fundamental attribution error and the self-perception theory.

An important basis of attribution theory is that people behave the way they do for a reason. In other words, people have reasons for developing their impressions of others. Fritz Heider, one of the first researchers to write about the attribution process, was interested in how one person develops an impression of another. These impressions, he argued, are developed through a three-step process: (1) observation of behavior, (2) determination of whether the behavior is deliberate, and (3) categorization of the behavior as internally or externally motivated.

Attribution Process

When a person encounters someone, how he or she interacts with that person is, in part, determined by his or her interpretation of the other person's behavior. Internal attributions, which are also called *dispositional* attributions, occur when an observer infers that another's behavior was caused by something about the person, such as personality, attitude, or upbringing. External attributions, or *situational* attributions, occur when the observer ascribes the cause of the behavior to the situation or outside circumstances. For example, Daniel's roommate Tom rushes into the house, slams the door, throws his books on the table, and runs upstairs. Tom does not say a word to Daniel, and Daniel wonders about what is happening. Daniel can develop different explanations for Tom's behavior. If he attributes Tom's behavior to an internal factor, he might think that Tom is rude and inconsiderate. If he attributes Tom's behavior to external factors, he might conclude that Tom is late for an appointment and rushing to get things done. Daniel's attributions will affect how he interacts with Tom when they next encounter each other. Based on Daniel's internal attribution, he may ignore Tom when Tom comes down the stairs. However, if Daniel selects an external attribution, then when Tom walks down the stairs, Daniel may ask whether Tom needs anything. Daniel's attribution affects his actions, and his actions can affect how the roommates manage their interaction and relationship.

Before Daniel decides whether to attribute Tom's behavior to dispositional or to situational factors, he needs to examine a few other factors. Harold Kelley, a social psychologist specializing in personal relationships, proposed that there are three general guidelines that influence people's attributions: consensus, consistency, and distinctiveness.

Consensus describes how other people, in the same circumstances, would behave. If all Daniel's roommates tend to rush into the house and run upstairs, then Tom's behavior is likely determined by the situation, leading Daniel to make an external attribution. If Tom is the only one who behaves this way, Daniel is more likely to make an internal attribution.

Consistency refers to whether the person being observed behaves the same way, in the same situation, over time. If every time Tom entered the house he behaved this way, Daniel would likely make an internal attribution. However, if this was an unusual way for Tom to behave, Daniel would likely look for an external explanation.

Distinctiveness refers to the variations in the observed person's behavior across situations. If, for example, Tom rushed through the door at work and ran through the hallways at school, his behavior on entering his house would not be distinct from his normal behavior. In that case, Daniel would likely attribute it to internal, dispositional causes. Conversely, if in most situations, Tom was mellow and slow moving, Daniel might attribute his rushing behavior to external, situational causes.

Although each of these three factors is important for attributing cause to either internal or external factors, when an observer can combine these factors, patterns can emerge. For example, when a person behaves a certain way over time and across situations, but others do not behave the same way, people tend to make dispositional attributions (That's just the way she is). However, when someone's behavior is not typical of that person or expected in the situation, observers have a difficult time attributing cause to the person or the situation. In these cases, the observer tends to assume that something peculiar is happening (I don't know what's going on; something must be wrong).

In addition to the three factors Kelley originally identified, two more guidelines influence whether

an observer makes an internal or external attribution. If a person violates a *social norm,* behavior that is typical or expected for a situation, others tend to make internal attributions. Additionally, in the absence of situational cues, observers tend to make dispositional attributions.

Attribution theory provides a framework for understanding both our own and others' behaviors. It provides guidelines for interpreting actions, so it is useful for examining motivations for achievement and conflict in interpersonal relationships. This theory has also been used to examine stigmatizing behavior and discrimination.

Attribution and Achievement

Bernard Weiner extended attribution theory to how people explain their own and others' success and failure. He contends that interpretations of achievement can be explained with three dimensions of behavior: *locus of control* (Whose fault is it?), *stability* (Is it ongoing?), and *controllability* (Can I change it?). First, a person's success or failure is attributable to either internal factors (I am a smart person) or to external factors (My computer crashed). Second, the cause of the success or failure can be either stable (It's always going to be like this) or unstable (This is a one-time event). Finally, the event may be perceived as controllable (I can change this if I want to) or uncontrollable (Nothing I do can change this situation).

These three dimensions, together, create eight scenarios that people use to explain their own achievements and disappointments:

1. Internal-stable-uncontrollable (I'm not very smart)
2. Internal-stable-controllable (I always wait until the last minute)
3. Internal-unstable-uncontrollable (I felt ill)
4. Internal-unstable-controllable (I forgot about the assignment)
5. External-stable-uncontrollable (The teacher's expectations are unrealistic)
6. External-stable-controllable (The teacher hates me)
7. External-unstable-uncontrollable (I was in a car accident)
8. External-unstable-controllable (The dog ate my homework)

Understanding how to motivate students to achieve academically requires an understanding of their attributions. People's explanations for their own success or failure will help determine how hard they work in similar situations. Students who perceive that their successes and failures are controllable are more likely to continue to work hard academically. When people perceive that they have no control over a situation, believe that the situation is permanent, and think that the outcomes are due to their own characteristics, they are likely to stop working and may exhibit signs of *learned helplessness*.

Attributions and Interpersonal Conflict

People tend to choose conflict styles based on their attributions about their partner's intent to cooperate, the locus of responsibility for the conflict, and the stability of the conflict. Their attributions about these issues influence the strategies they adopt; specifically, they tend to adopt *conflict management strategies* they believe are congruent with their partner's projected responses. The attribution process causes people to see others as more competitive, more responsible for the conflict, and more stable and traitlike than they perceive themselves to be. They underestimate the role of unstable situation factors and overestimate the extent to which behavior is caused by stable personality traits. The bias in this process often discourages *integrative* modes of conflict resolution. The choice of conflict strategies affects the likelihood of conflict resolution and the degree of satisfaction in the relationship.

Attributions and Stigmatizing Behavior

Attribution theory is an important framework for understanding why people endorse *stigmatizing* attitudes and engage in discriminatory behaviors. A person's attributions about the cause and controllability of another's illness or situation can lead to emotional reactions that affect their willingness to help and their likelihood of punishing the other. If you assume that another person's difficult situation is that person's fault and could have been prevented, you may be less likely to offer assistance and more likely to react with anger. For example, Sue is an office manager and Terry is a new employee. If Sue thinks that Terry's unorthodox and unpredictable behavior is caused by injuries he suffered when he was a child, she may be tolerant and understanding. If, however, Sue thinks Terry's unorthodox behavior is the result of years of illegal drug use, she may be more likely to get angry with him and take punitive actions. People's attributions about the causes of another's illness can lead to prejudice and discrimination.

Fundamental Attribution Error

The *fundamental attribution error* is a common attribution error in which people overemphasize personality or dispositional (internal) causes of others' negative behavior or bad outcomes and underestimate the situational (external) factors. When interpreting another's positive actions or outcomes, however, people overemphasize the situational causes and underestimate the dispositional causes. For example, Alicia is a server in a restaurant, and one of her coworkers, Julia, just got a really big tip. Alicia thinks to herself, "Wow, Julia keeps getting lucky because the hostess keeps giving her the good customers." An hour later, another coworker complains that he got a bad tip, and Alicia thinks, "Well, if you weren't such a crappy server, you would get good tips." Alicia just committed the fundamental attribution error. She assumed that when something bad happened to one coworker, it was the coworker's fault and that when something good happened to another coworker, it was the situation that brought about the positive result.

Conversely, the *self-serving bias* (or *actor–observer bias*) is an error in which individuals attribute their own success and failure to different factors. One's own success and positive outcomes are attributed to internal, dispositional characteristics whereas one's failures or negative outcomes are ascribed to external, situational causes. To continue the restaurant example, Alicia gets a really big tip and thinks, "I worked really hard for that group and gave great service," but when another group leaves a bad tip, she thinks, "They are cheapskates."

In sum, attribution errors work in the following ways:

- When good things happen to me, I deserve it (*I worked hard* or *I am a special person*).

- When good things happen to you, you don't deserve it (*the teacher likes you* or *you just got lucky*).
- When bad things happen to me, it's not my fault (*the teacher doesn't like me* or *he started it*).
- When bad things happen to you, it's your fault (*you should work harder* or *you should be more careful*).

Self-Perception Theory

Daryl Bem's self-perception theory, like attribution theory, relies on internal and external attributions to explain behavior. However, instead of observing others, we use the same process to interpret our own behavior. Bem argues that we come to know our own thoughts and beliefs by observing our actions and interpreting what caused our behaviors. Our explanation for our behavior is determined by the presence or absence of situational cues. For example, if Debbie earns $100 campaigning for 3 hours for a politician, she can attribute her behavior to external causes ("I did it for the money"). If, however, Debbie earns only $5 for her 3 hours of campaigning, she will likely attribute her behavior to internal causes ("I did it because I like the candidate"). Self-perception theory is important in persuasion research because people who are internally motivated are more likely to maintain behaviors.

Virginia M. McDermott

See also Cognitive Theories; Conflict Communication Theories; Interpersonal Communication Theories; Learning and Communication; Persuasion and Social Influence Theories

Further Readings

Bem, D. J. (1972). Self-perception theory. In L. Berkowitz (Ed.), *Advances in experimental social psychology* (Vol. 6, pp. 1–6). New York: Academic Press.

Corrigan, P., Markowitz, F., Watson, A., Rowan, D., & Kubiak, M. A. (2003). An attribution model of public discrimination towards person with mental illness. *Journal of Health and Social Behavior, 44,* 162–179.

Graham, S., & Folkes, V. S. (1990). *Attribution theory: Applications to achievement, mental health, and interpersonal conflict.* Hillsdale, NJ: Lawrence Erlbaum.

Heider, F. (1958). *The psychology of interpersonal relations.* New York: Wiley.

Jones, E. E., Kanouse, D. E., Kelley, H. H., Nisbett, R. E., Valins, S., & Weiner, B. (1972). *Attribution: Perceiving the causes of behavior.* Morristown, NJ: General Learning Press.

Kelley, H. H. (1971). *Attributions in social interaction.* Morristown, NJ: General Learning Press.

Manusov, V., & Harvey, J. H. (2001). *Attribution, communication behavior, and close relationships.* Cambridge, UK: Cambridge University Press.

Sillars, A. L. (1981) Attributions and interpersonal conflict resolution. In J. H. Harvey, W. Ickes, & R. Kidd (Eds.), *New directions in attribution research* (Vol. 3, pp. 281–306). Hillsdale, NJ: Lawrence Erlbaum.

Weiner, B. (1974). *Achievement motivation and attribution theory.* Morristown, NJ: General Learning Press.

AUDIENCE THEORIES

Audience theories have been of crucial importance for the way mediated communication has been understood since the first modern communication theories were formulated almost a century ago. They have followed the changing scientific climates and successive intellectual fashions in the social sciences and humanities, affecting both the different ways in which communication processes have been conceptualized and the ways in which succeeding scholarly traditions have researched them. In recent years, the concept of audience has been put into question as the emerging digital, interactive media appear to be blurring the deep-rooted distinction between media production and media consumption that has characterized the era of mass media.

The main theoretical difficulty with the concept of *audience* is that it is a single term applied to an increasingly diverse and complex reality. The term has thus come to comprise many shades of meaning gathered around a common core. This core denotes a group of people being addressed by and paying attention to a communication message that someone is producing and intending for them to perceive, experience, and respond to in one way or another.

The range of meanings for *audience* includes, on one hand, the idea of a group of spectators gathered in the same physical location for a performance of some kind on which their attention is focused. On the other hand, an audience can be the dispersed, anonymous individuals who in the privacy of their home attend simultaneously or with a time delay to the content offered by a particular mass medium.

Another distinction within the concept of audience has to do with the power distribution between the content producers and the users of mediated content. Media can be divided into three types, according to Jan Bordewijk and Ben Van Kaam. Until the 1980s, the audiences of classic *transmission media* such as radio and television had control over neither content production nor reception: They could be reached only when the broadcasters chose to transmit centrally produced messages to them, which they then passively consumed. The audiences of *consultation media* such as print, on the other hand, actively choose when to access the centrally provided content and what content to access. Finally, *conversational media* rely on a communicative relationship characterized by the genuine, dialogical coproduction of meaning in which the roles of sender and recipient alternate.

Another definitional question is whether audiences are a politically active public or a more passive and private group. A *public* in this connection has been defined as a collectivity mobilized by independently existing cultural or political forces (such as a political party or a cultural interest group) and being served by media provided by this public for itself. More traditionally, audiences have been regarded as a domestic, passive, and politically impotent collectivity, totally defined by and dependent on media provisions, often of an entertainment-oriented nature. However, as a consequence of the increasing "mediatization" of all aspects of modern life and the undeniable participatory qualities of the culture of media convergence, the American scholar Henry Jenkins and many others have proposed that the binary opposition of audiences and publics should give way to a conceptualization that recognizes their potential interdependence.

These identifiable audience definitions have been identified with various successive scientific paradigms in the social sciences and humanities. This entry summarizes several of the most important of these.

The Hypodermic Needle Theory

The first audience theory that gained large-scale importance was metaphorically labeled the theory of media as a *hypodermic needle*. It not only was a product of the ruling behaviorist scientific climate in the 1920s and 1930s but also sprang from contemporary political and cultural concerns. According to the hypodermic theory, a mediated message could be seen as something injected under the skin of the recipient. Media effects were thus seen as direct, immediate, and strong. The emergence of this theory was a direct consequence of the emergence of the new broadcasting technology of radio, which made it possible for the first time to simultaneously reach the ears of all consumers and citizens in a nation. The Nazi leaders' use of radio for blatant propaganda purposes, as well as the more democratically motivated use by U.S. president Franklin D. Roosevelt of radio addresses to the nation, gave rise to widespread concern that it would become possible for those in power to transform the citizens into mere puppets.

At the same time, the hypodermic needle theory was inspired by influential sociological theories that the modern mass-society individual was lonely, vulnerable, and easily manipulated. The critical/cultural theories of the Frankfurt School were also influential; these scholars argued that the new cultural industries were functioning under a capitalist logic that would ideologically seduce and deceive the subordinate classes, through fascinating but mindless entertainment, into accepting conditions that would impoverish their life opportunities.

This notion of *defenseless audiences* has continued, though in less crude form, to influence the understanding of processes of mediated persuasion as many advertising and public information campaigns are still based on a strategy that seeks to change the knowledge, attitudes, and behaviors of individuals by exposing them repeatedly to mass-communicated stimuli. Similarly, this understanding of audiences also continues to frame widespread concerns over the effects of violent visual representations in television and computer game fictions on the vulnerable minds of children and young people. While the label *hypodermic needle* is extremely evocative, Everett Rogers and Roger Storey have admonished us that it is actually a label applied after the fact to capture the widely shared understanding of audience processes to which scholars were constructing an alternative. This alternative has become known as the two-step model of communication.

The Two-Step Flow Theory

The *two-step flow theory* arose out of some large-scale empirical studies in the United States in the 1940s, conducted by a team of researchers directed by the exiled Austrian scholar Paul Lazarsfeld, who found that both consumers' choice of products and voters' choice of politicians depended more on their interpersonal relations to significant others in their networks of family and friends than on their direct exposure to mass-mediated commercial or political messages. A campaign was thus found to influence its audiences as a result of the complex interrelations between a mass-mediated endeavor and the subsequent interpersonal process in which the campaign message got talked about in human networks. The label *two-step flow* was adopted because the studies found that the mass-mediated message would, as a first step, reach individuals with above-average prominence in their community—so-called *opinion leaders*. If the message succeeded in passing these *gatekeepers*' filters of relevance and importance, they would then spread the message to more dependent individuals in their immediate surroundings (second step). This theory was supported by the fact that mass-mediated campaigns often were found to have minimal and indirect effects.

The two-step flow theory, while encapsulating a fundamental truth about the communicative conditions of processes of social change, has been criticized for conceptualizing these processes in a much too mechanistic manner. Sven Windahl and Benno Signitzer have argued that we should rather see mediated processes of influence in terms of a *multistep model* of communication. It is possible to see Everett Rogers's immensely influential theory of the diffusion of innovations to different groups of audiences (divided into innovators, early adopters, early majority, late majority, and laggards, depending on the speed with which they are likely to adopt innovations, both in the form of new products and in the form of new ideas) as such a more developed theory.

Another alternative suggests the emergence of *viral communication,* in which the overly mechanistic idea of steps is abandoned altogether. Here, the channels through which communication spreads will have to be represented in a sophisticated model of intersecting personal networks, existing in the sea of discourses of the "mediatized" society.

Uses-and-Gratifications Theory

The next milestone theory of audiences, *uses-and-gratifications theory*, takes audience empowerment one step further by exploring what people do with the media. The key idea of uses-and-gratifications theory is that the *uses* that audiences make of the media and the *gratifications* produced by those uses can be traced back to a constellation of individual psychological and social needs. Elihu Katz, Jay Blumler, and Michael Gurevitch, three of the founding fathers of the theory, described how its 7-point platform wishes to account for how (1) the social and psychological origins of (2) needs generate (3) expectations of (4) the mass media or other sources, which lead to (5) differential patterns of exposure to the media, resulting in (6) need gratification and (7) other consequences.

The media-oriented needs were typically described as the needs for information, relaxation, companionship, diversion, and escape, and the gratifications were characterized in identical terms—a practice that some uses-and-gratifications practitioners themselves acknowledge to be somewhat circular. Among the basic assumptions of the theory was the idea that both media and content choice are consciously and rationally made and directed toward quite specific goals and satisfactions and that individual utility is more important for media consumption than are values springing from familial or peer group rituals.

Audience Reception Theories

Reception research focuses on the ways in which audience members make sense of mediated meanings. It thus deviates from the mechanistic notion that media messages are merely transmitted to an audience whose understanding of those messages is unproblematic, and it insists that the audience's actualization of mediated meanings must be the object of empirical investigation. Methodologically, reception research has, until recently, adhered rather strongly to the doctrinaire view that only qualitative methods such as depth interviews and ethnographic observation are suitable tools for such exploration.

Reception research is explicitly interdisciplinary and—unlike the previous theories, which are based exclusively in the social sciences—attempts to cross-fertilize scholarship from the social sciences and the humanities. In a catchphrase, it has been claimed that reception research takes its theory from the humanities and its method from the social sciences.

The theoretical platform thus comprises meaning-oriented theories with hermeneutic origins, such as semiotics and discourse theories, whereas the methodological platform is constituted by field-work methods developed within the social sciences. The pioneering practitioners can be characterized as renegades from these two backgrounds who were dissatisfied with the prescribed practices of the parent disciplines: Researchers from the humanities were revolting against analyses in which claims about ideological effects on audiences were made on the basis of inferences drawn from textual analysis. Social science scholars were escaping from the straitjacket of quantitative methodologies and the way in which those methodologies had narrowed notions of what aspects of the audience were researchable at all.

More specifically, in its early years, reception theory was trying to demonstrate that audiences were semiotically *active* in their encounter with mediated meanings, as opposed to the widely held view that media consumption, especially television viewing, was a passive, almost soporific condition. Reception theory's fundamental reconceptualization of audiences was strongly indebted to the British cultural studies scholar Stuart Hall's seminal theory of the meaning-making complementarity of the *encoding* and *decoding* moments of media production and the notion that there was no natural fit between these two moments. In other words, audience members had a relative freedom to interpret the encoded meanings offered to them in the media text, which was consequently regarded as polysemous (i.e., carrying many potential meanings).

Among the handful of inspiring, lasting concepts proposed by Hall were also the notion of the text's *preferred meaning*, or reading, and the three basic ways in which audiences could actualize this preferred meaning. Hall suggested that in the midst of textual polysemy, one meaning would nevertheless hold a privileged position. Since the mass media were firmly lodged within the capitalist social order and therefore logically served the hegemonic interest of the ruling classes, the preferred meaning would be one that conformed to this ideological interest.

Continuing this logic of Marxist cultural theory, the class-divided audiences could actualize the encoded preferred meaning from one of three decoding positions: They could follow a *dominant reading*, in which they conformed to and took over, so to speak, the preferred meaning (for example, agreeing with a news report in which the government urged workers to show wage restraint for the sake of the country); alternatively, they could follow an *oppositional reading*, in which they would contest the ideological implications of the preferred meaning (for example, refusing to comply with the news report about the need for wage restraint); or they could follow the third option of applying a *negotiated reading*, which would lie somewhere between the two extremes (e.g., agreeing in overall terms with the news report's recommended wage restraint but seeing many good reasons to divert from wage restraint in the case of specific social groups).

The particular reading chosen by different audiences would depend on their life circumstances, often corresponding to social class position, and on the specific socioculturally anchored *interpretive repertoires* at their disposal for decoding the media. The specific interpretive repertoires mobilized would also depend on the situational context in which decoding took place. For example, the specific decoding of a Hollywood movie by a teenage youngster would depend heavily on whether the movie was watched in the cinema with a group of peers or in front of the family screen with Mom and Dad. The need to explore such *social uses of the media* empirically was especially pioneered by the American audience ethnographer James Lull in a series of studies of family television.

Finally, empirical fieldwork on audience meaning-making would also lean on the notion of *interpretive communities*, a concept originating in

German and American reception aesthetics based in literary studies. The concept serves to express two different phenomena: first, the idea that the readings of media messages are likely to some extent to follow sociodemographic boundaries of age, gender, ethnicity, and so forth, which may thus be seen as a community in a loose sense of the term (e.g., a music video being read differently by White and African American youth); second, the phenomenon of fan cultures, in which members have a strong sense of cultural belonging to a cultural public, with something approaching membership.

The concepts described here have been heavily discussed and contested in the reception theory literature since the 1980s. Therefore today they have become to some extent divested of some of their original, often Marxist, shades of meaning and have assumed the role of more general stock of the trade. This reinterpretation of theoretical concepts has been inspired by a move toward a more holistic conceptualization of audiences within the larger context of the communication process as a whole and away from the compartmentalized research endeavors of the 20th century. The drive toward *holism in audience research* (as defined by British sociologist David Deacon and his colleagues) is theoretically anchored in the social-constructionist turn in the human sciences, according to which the interdiscursive dimensions of media production and consumption have become a key condition of the mediatized culture. This theoretical development precedes the emergence of the culture of convergence, which in turn has served to corroborate the view that the distinction between media production and consumption is being elided.

Theories of Collective Creativity

The new digital media enable participation on an unprecedented scale. Individuals may participate in the digital, interactive media proper (the Internet, the World Wide Web, Web 2.0), but because all the old media, such as television and newspapers, have been transformed by digitalization into the complex of convergence culture, media users now have opportunities for participating in almost any encounter with any media. This participation includes all three modes of engagement with the media listed at the beginning of this entry: transmission, consultation, and conversation.

As yet there is no full-fledged theory of the participating audience; we have only a rich array of promising theoretical fragments that together make up an incomplete mosaic of this audience. It has been proposed that we may be moving into the age of "disappearing audience," but as U.S. scholar Henry Jenkins, one of the key analysts of convergence culture, warns, it is important that convergence raptures do not mislead us into believing that soon there will be no audiences, only participants.

What we have to take into account in our thinking about audiences of the future is that convergence has to do with the following transformations:

1. The flow of content across multiple media platforms, the cooperation between multiple media industries, and the migratory behavior of media audiences

2. The emergence of a participatory culture, in which media producers and consumers no longer occupy separate roles but become participants who interact with each other according to a new set of logics

3. The development of collective intelligence, when consumer-participants pool their resources and combine their skills in realms where no traditional expertise exists

Since, as Jenkins has admonished us, convergence refers to a process, not an end point, scholars interested in audiences must continue to devote their energies and resources to the building of new theoretical frameworks that enable us to grasp the thoroughly transformed conditions of audiences.

The Scholar's Life in the Habitat of Audience Theories

When the history of audience theories is seen in an evolutionary perspective, as has been done here, it is important to realize that the Darwinian metaphor has its limits: It is not the case that the theories that first appeared in the habitat of audience theories have now become obsolete or even extinct. They continue to live their life, but not "as usual." Time and again, as new animals have appeared, the older inhabitants have had to adapt to the influence of the newcomers, and they may have moved down in the struggle for dominance. Therefore, in audience theory today, all the traditions outlined above are still with us, although in mutually modified forms, and they offer themselves for the qualified judgment of new scholars entering the field.

Kim Christian Schrøder

See also Computer-Mediated Communication; Critical Theory; Cultivation Theory; Cultural Studies; Fans, Fandom, and Fan Studies; Frankfurt School; Interpretive Communities Theory; Journalism and Theories of the Press; Marxist Theory; Media Effects Theories; Network Society; Popular Culture Theories; Public Opinion Theories; Public Sphere; Semiotics and Semiology; Sense-Making; Social Action Media Studies; Spectatorship; Two-Step and Multi-Step Flow; Uses, Gratifications, and Dependency; Violence and Nonviolence in Media Studies

Further Readings

Jenkins, H. (2006). *Convergence culture: Where old and new media collide.* New York: New York University Press.

Jensen, K. B., & Rosengren, K. E. (1990). Five traditions in search of the audience. *European Journal of Communication, 5,* 207–238.

Livingstone, S. (Ed.). (2005). *Audiences and publics: When cultural engagement matters for the public sphere.* Bristol, UK: Intellect Books.

McQuail, D. (2005). *McQuail's mass communication theory* (5th ed.). London: Sage.

Rogers, E. M., & Storey, J. D. (1987). Communication campaigns. In C. R. Berger & S. H. Chaffee (Eds.), *Handbook of communication science* (pp. 817–846). Newbury Park, CA: Sage.

Schrøder, K., Drotner, K., Kline, S., & Murray, C. (2003). *Researching audiences.* London: Arnold.

Windahl, S., & Signitzer, B. (1992). *Using communication theory: An introduction to planned communication.* London: Sage.

AUTOETHNOGRAPHY

The intellectual value of the personal in academic research has long been a debate in communication. From whether to use first person narration in scholarship to the impact of researchers on that which they study, the question of the subjective researching self continues to excite members of the field as an issue of great significance and consequence. At stake for communication theory lies the very worth of the scholarship that researchers publish. On one side of the debate, the inclusion of the personal means giving up the principle and value of objective research, reducing produced knowledge to opinion and hearsay. On the other, the exclusion of the personal perpetuates myths of objectivity that continue to erase the impact of researchers on the knowledge they produce, which obscures the way all knowledge is embedded in cultural and social value systems.

Deeply entrenched in this debate is the narrative-based method of *autoethnography,* a methodology of academic investigation that not only acknowledges the speaking, theorizing researcher but also centers him or her in an effort to illuminate how the experiences of that self are representative of (and in some cases constitutive of) larger social systems. Autoethnographers argue that some questions in communication can be answered only by careful, critical analysis of life experiences. To this end, they take their own self as an entry into culture. Such investigations inform communication theory as a method of *theorizing,* using the self as the location for that communicative work.

Autoethnography can be described best by considering the two central terms that make up the ground of the method: *auto* and *ethnography.* Auto speaks most centrally to the subject (as in the site or location) of the scholarship. As an automethod (like autoperformance or autobiography), the data and evidence one uses in order to theorize communication lie in the authorial self. Autoethnography examines the lived experiences of the self in order to question and open up one's experiences to communicative analysis. Stemming from a belief that new knowledge can be gained by communication scholars' investigating their own communicative lives, autoethnography becomes a mode of scholarship that answers unique questions that deal with the mundane qualities of an individual's life. Questions such as how one experiences racism or sexism, how minute moments of communication done by a self build larger systems of power, or how privilege or domination is experienced can be answered through autoethnography. It is important that they are self-asked and -answered because only the critically reflexive self can probe deeply into the textures of its life to see the everyday, ongoing repetitions in communication that produce cultural configurations.

The *ethnography* in autoethnography is, perhaps, the most significant diversion from other automethods. Ethnography is, most fundamentally, the storying of culture. Autoethnography shares this analytical focus. Thus, any life story may, on some level, count as autobiographical; however, autoethnography requires the link, either directly or implicitly, to the production of cultural systems. A story of how a cultural member experiences his or her disability functions as autoethnography only if the singular story builds an understanding of how disability is understood on a larger cultural level.

Autoethnography's paradigmatic roots are most closely related to *critical theory* as often the narratives circulate around culture and power, asking how the speaking self is constrained or enabled by its participation in society. As a critical methodology, autoethnography "stories" the self in order to resist dominant narratives, complicate taken-for-granted ways of thinking, and disrupt normative communication patterns.

Often, autoethnography seeks to see how everyday communication produces cultural norms. That is, autoethnography is a productive way of investigating how a self is implicated in maintaining the very structures that we live within (often systems of race, gender, sexuality, and/or class). Of course, autoethnography also understands that the self is a product of culture, as well; in this way, self and culture are *co-constructed*, each building and sustaining the other. While other methods can also investigate this phenomenon, autoethnography is a method that allows for a single voice to craft a reflexively textured experience of culture.

Autoethnography, as mentioned in the opening paragraph, often encounters resistance from scholars who advocate a more positivistic approach to research. A key point of contention is the role of truth as a goal of research. That is, if the purpose of research is to determine the truth of communicative interaction, autoethnography, because it is so narratively constructed, can be critiqued for fictionalizing aspects of lived experience to fit the story the storyteller wishes to tell. In other words, if an autoethnographer tells a story of his or her life, how are we to determine the truthfulness of the claims and experiences being narrated? An autoethnographer seeks not to capture some truth, but to expose one's experiences in order to investigate how they are produced by (while producing) culture. In this way, the goal of truth as an outcome of research is secondary to tracing, in a reflexive manner, one's cultural experiences in order to understand how they illuminate communication working in a particular setting.

As a method in communication research, autoethnography is a process of theorizing from one's personal experiences. Whether an addition to more traditional ethnography or a project composed solely in self-narrative, autoethnography works from personal experience to spin a story of culture that examines how an individual's communicative experiences are representative (or constitutive) of culture.

John T. Warren

See also Critical Theory; Ethnography of Communication; Narrative and Narratology; Performative Writing; Phenomenology

Further Readings

Bochner, A., & Ellis, C. (2002). *Ethnographically speaking*. Lanham, MD: AltaMira Press.

Corey, F. C., & Nakayama, T. K. (1997). Sextext. *Text and Performance Quarterly, 17*(1), 58–68.

Goodall, H. L. (2000). *Writing the new ethnography*. Walnut Creek, CA: AltaMira Press.

Holman Jones, S. (2005). Autoethnography: Making the personal political. In N. K. Denzin & Y. S. Lincoln (Eds.), *Handbook of qualitative research* (pp. 763–791). Thousand Oaks, CA: Sage.

Pelias, R. J. (2004). *A methodology of the heart: Evoking academic and daily life*. Walnut Creek, CA: AltaMira Press.

AUTOPOIESIS

See Cybernetics

AXIOLOGY

Axiology is the branch of philosophy that considers the nature of value and what kinds of things have value. The term derives from the Greek language: *axios* (worth or value) and *logos* (study of the nature and properties of, or logic or theory of). Axiologists are broadly concerned with all forms of value, including aesthetic values, ethical values, and epistemic values. In a narrow sense, axiologists are concerned with what is intrinsically valuable or worthwhile—what is desirable for its own sake. All axiological issues are necessarily connected to ontological and epistemological assumptions. With respect to human communication theory, every researcher makes decisions in the theoretical process that reflect his or her axiological position. Axiological decisions guide all facets of research, including the selection of one's topic and the approach one takes toward research.

History of Axiology

The philosophical study of values dates back to the 6th and 5th centuries BCE. In the democracy developed in Athens, Greece, people sought to acquire knowledge for the purpose of building a successful life. Philosophers recognized that the laws and morality of human society differ from country to country and across historical periods. This awareness led the Sophists to take a relativistic, skeptical position on values; they held that one's values can change rapidly without consistency across situations and circumstances. In contrast, Socrates sought to save Athens from the social disorder purportedly created by Sophists by establishing absolute, universal virtues. Socrates taught that there is an important connection between virtue and knowledge. He held that virtue is an attitude of seeking knowledge and that knowledge is necessary for virtuous conduct. Socrates' student Plato asserted that there is an unchangeable world of essence behind the changing world of phenomena. Plato identified four virtues— wisdom, courage, temperance, and justice—as characteristics that everyone in the polis should develop. During the Hellenistic–Roman period, the fall of the city–state (polis) rendered useless Greek theories of value that were centered on the state. Philosophers began to emphasize individualistic ways of living under increasingly unstable social conditions. Individuals became preoccupied with seeking personal safety and peace of mind. During this time, cosmopolitanism, transcending

the bounds of nationality, was enhanced. The Stoic, the Epicurean, and the Skeptic schools of thought dominated this era. The philosophy of the Hellenistic–Roman period culminated in Neoplatonism, a pagan philosophy, which greatly shaped the Christian philosophy that prominently emerged in the medieval period.

During medieval times, Thomas Aquinas argued for the division of religious and natural virtues. He identified as religious virtues the three primary virtues of Christianity—faith, hope, and love. For Aquinas, natural virtues were the four primary virtues of Greek philosophy drawn from Plato— wisdom, courage, temperance, and justice. In the modern period, views of value can be seen as extensions or transformations of both Greek philosophy and Christian virtues. Philosophers began to distinguish judgments of fact from judgments of value. The task of natural science was to provide judgments of fact (objective propositions). The task of philosophy was to address judgments of value (propositions in which a subjective appraisal of a fact is made). Following that shift, fact and value became recognized as separate issues. The 20th century saw the rise of pragmatism. The significance of value theory was partially eclipsed with the rise of evolutionary psychology, the dominance of rationalism, advancing skepticism about the place of values in the world, and changes in the modern view of morality. Values came to be regarded as tools for the effective processing of ideas and things. The intellectual division between natural science and philosophy parallels separations that emerged in the study of ontology and epistemology—all of which are interconnected in the development of communication theory.

Axiological Issues in Communication Scholarship

Axiology is often thought to provide ground for the study of ethics and aesthetics; these philosophical fields depend on particular understandings of value. Ethics is the branch of axiology that attempts to understand the nature of morality. Richard Johannesen notes that ethical issues arise whenever one's behavior could significantly impact another person, when one's behavior involves a conscious choice of means and ends, and when one's behavior can be judged by standards of right and wrong. To develop sound theory, ethical practices must inform one's choices in all aspects of conducting communication research. In these ways, axiological considerations inform the generation and testing of human communication theory.

Communication theorists strive to contribute to shared knowledge about the nature and functioning of human communication. Two axiological issues are significant for the development of communication theory: first, whether research can be value free, and second, the desired purpose or end for conducting research. For communication theorists, a fundamental concern is with the philosophical stability of the research approach. Thinking about axiology at a general level emphasizes the diversity and incommensurability of the variety of scholarly approaches that have value for us in articulating communication theory.

Values in Inquiry

The first axiological issue for communication theorists addresses the extent to which value-free research is possible. Scholars choose to view a research problem through the lens that they believe most accurately describes the world. Thus, some researchers choose theoretical frameworks that are consistent with a realist ontology, whereas others select to work from a nominalist ontology. An ongoing value debate exists between scholars who adhere to the traditional scientific position and those who take an interpretivist approach to communication phenomena.

The *traditional* scientific position (consistent with realist ontology, empiricist epistemology) on axiology is that good science must be value free. This position asserts that scholarship is neutral and that research and theories are value free. The scholar attempts to uncover the facts as they are without biasing the research by imposing personal beliefs. Scientists carefully observe their object of study without the interference of values. This stance enables researchers to represent accurately the phenomena they are studying. Scholars who work from this paradigm generally use quantitative social science protocol to describe and infer regular patterns characterizing a communication phenomenon—whether the theorist is, for example, studying interpersonal affinity-seeking behaviors, conducting a content analysis of political

advertisements, or examining small-group cohesiveness. Most contemporary communication researchers accept that some values inform the research process.

The *interpretivist* approach (consistent with nominalist ontology, rationalist epistemology) asserts that science cannot be value free and maintains that values cannot be avoided in conducting research. A researcher's work is always guided by his or her preferences about what to study and how best to conduct the inquiry. Further, research may be influenced by institutional values as well as political and economic ideologies. These influences make value-free inquiry impossible. Some values are so embedded in a researcher's culture that he or she may not be aware of them (e.g., a European American Christian patriarchal capitalist perspective). Interpretivist researchers assert that since no method of investigation is completely free of distortion, some groups can provide greater insight into different aspects of the social world than others can, due to their position within society. Scholars who work from this paradigm may use qualitative social science methods, rhetorical inquiry, or philosophic ideas as a way to gain insight about communication phenomena, regardless of domain (i.e., interpersonal, small group, organizational, public, or mediated communication) and the specific topic (e.g., conflict management, social control, group socialization, speaker credibility) under consideration.

Purpose of Inquiry

The second axiological issue for communication theorists addresses the purpose or ends for which scholarship is conducted—whether scholarship should be designed to reveal knowledge (basic research) or achieve social change (applied research). The community of scholars who conduct communication research is not homogeneous, and arguments persist over the value of different methods for providing insight about knowledge claims.

The primary consideration in all research is identifying the purpose for which the inquiry is conducted. All decisions related to research flow from a researcher's purpose(s). There are different standards for judging the quality of different types of research. Various types of research have different expectations, audiences, means of reporting, and processes for disseminating conclusions. Because of these differences, the researcher must be clear at the beginning about the purpose of the inquiry.

Basic research seeks to advance knowledge. For basic researchers, the urge to explain the world emerges from their basic human curiosity. Researchers investigate a phenomenon to understand the nature of reality with regard to that phenomenon. The purpose of basic research is to understand and explain, to generate knowledge for the sake of knowledge. Basic researchers work to generate new theories or test existing theories. As we find answers to satisfy our curiosity, our knowledge continues to grow, and further questions emerge. For example, answers about interpersonal conflict management may lead to questions about relationship development and dissolution, which may then lead to questions about symbolic integration in long-term relationships, and so forth. Basic research contributes to the fundamental knowledge and theory in each domain and facet of the communication discipline. Basic researchers see their role as producing knowledge about communication, whether they are examining how power is communicated and responded to via technology in global organizations or whether they are considering the rhetorical features of a speech. Basic researchers do not hold themselves responsible for the ways knowledge is used—their findings can be used for constructive or destructive purposes. Communication knowledge thus becomes a tool for technicians and politicians to use as they will. Academicians in a university community are often basic researchers, free to select their research topics and pursue investigations without being constrained by outside forces.

Applied researchers are driven to solve experiential problems. They conduct research to identify solutions; their findings are directed toward improving the conditions of an organization or the whole of humankind. Applied research contributes to the knowledge of a discipline by helping people make informed choices about how best to respond to a problem. Applied research is value laden in a variety of ways, including subjectivity and researcher bias in solving problems. For example, research problems may be posed by a company or sponsoring agency and require a communication consultant or marketing researcher with the best skills to offer a response to the issue. When a researcher is hired to solve a specific problem, the sponsor usually provides value-laden direction, often identifying the research topic, collaborating to assess the problem, and potentially assisting in conducting the investigation. Research problems may also emerge in response to one's lived experience: A researcher may examine intercultural differences among members in a small group to ensure that productivity is not diminished because of the employees' communication with one another.

The distinctions between basic and applied research are most often reflected in the motives and conditions under which researchers pursue their investigations. For example, the interpretive-critical debate in cultural communication studies centers around whether scholars should simply describe features of a culture they observe or whether they have an obligation to expose oppressive arrangements within the culture. Research should be judged according to the norms of protocol for conducting research as identified by the scholarly community, regardless of the stance the scholar takes toward values in inquiry or the purpose of inquiry. The quality of a research project does not necessarily depend on whether the investigation is commissioned to solve a problem or whether the investigation is conducted by an individual researcher who seeks to advance knowledge. In general, the functions of research—advancing knowledge and solving problems—are not mutually exclusive.

Regardless of whether one holds a value-laden or value-free approach to research or is conducting basic or applied research, researchers have an axiological responsibility to conduct ethical inquiry. Any information to be shared with an audience must reflect professional properties of competent research. Researchers also have a personal responsibility to all stakeholders involved in the research, including subjects. In contributing to the advancement of human knowledge, a researcher must adhere to ethical principles of research.

Axiology is an important consideration in the development of communication theory. Tracing back to antiquity, philosophers have struggled to identify the nature of value and what kinds of things have value. In general, communication theorists face two axiological issues: what scholarship is worth pursuing and how best to conduct research to gain that knowledge. In basic research, scholars conduct inquiry to expand what we know about human communication. In applied research, scholars seek to (re-)solve human problems. Both forms of research co-inform one another and extend our understanding about communication. Operating from varying axiological grounds, ethical scholars enrich our understanding about the value of communication research and theory.

Pat Arneson

See also Critical Theory; Epistemology; Ethics Theories; Inquiry Processes; Metatheory; Ontology; Philosophy of Communication; Realism and the Received View; Social Construction of Reality

Further Readings

Audi, R. (Ed.). (1999). *The Cambridge dictionary of philosophy* (2nd ed.). New York: Cambridge University Press.

Cheney, G. (2008). Encountering the ethics of engaged scholarship. *Journal of Applied Communication Research, 36,* 281–288.

Cherwitz, R. A. (Ed.). (1990). *Rhetoric and philosophy.* Hillsdale, NJ: Lawrence Erlbaum.

Johannesen, R. L., Valde, K. S., & Whedbee, K. E. (2008). *Ethics in human communication* (6th ed.). Long Grove, IL: Waveland Press.

Wood, J. T. (1997). *Communication theories in action: An introduction.* Belmont, CA: Wadsworth.

B

BALANCE THEORY

See Attitude Theory; Co-Orientation Theory; Persuasion and Social Influence Theories

BARGAINING

See Conflict Communication Theories; Negotiation Theory

BEHAVIORISM

See Communication Skills Theories; Humanistic Perspective; Learning and Communication

BIOLOGICAL APPROACHES

See Communibiology

BLACK FEMINIST EPISTEMOLOGY

Black feminist epistemology characterizes U.S. Black women's ways of knowing as distinctive and significant for developing theories of the social world and for attaining social justice for all oppressed groups. This perspective stresses the importance of Black women's social locations for how they create and validate knowledge, claiming that their shared experiences can foster group knowledge that can inform political action. It emphasizes the fact that Black women can face multiple, interlocking oppressions of gender and race as well as classism and heterosexism. Moreover, Black feminist epistemology is a type of critical theory because it aims to empower the oppressed to improve their situation. This theory has implications for communication scholarship because it suggests approaches for theorizing ways that members of nondominant groups construct and disseminate knowledge and provides insights into how communication can effect social change.

Sociologist Patricia Hill Collins grounds Black feminist epistemology in broad goals of Black feminism. Black feminism is a political–social movement that arose from feelings of discontent among Black women and their allies due to frustration with both the civil rights movement and the feminist movement of the 1960s and 1970s. The former neglected gender issues in favor of race, while the latter focused mainly on White, middle-class women's concerns. Consequently, Black women began to develop theory and initiate political action related to their struggles with various oppressions, including sexism, racism, classism, and heterosexism. Based on a commitment to social justice for Black women and other oppressed groups, they, along with other women of color, began to propose alternative feminisms. Black feminist epistemology details one of those alternative perspectives.

Black feminist epistemology contends that although Black women have varying experiences due to differences in age, social class, sexuality, or ethnicity, they are subject to the legacy of struggle against racism and sexism. It argues further that experiencing shared challenges fosters similar angles of vision based on distinctive themes of African American women's experiences, such as work, family, sexual politics, motherhood, and political activism. These common, collective experiences help develop group knowledge and ways of knowing that Black women share with one another.

Collins asserts that Black women have been socialized to create, sustain, and legitimate knowledge in four distinct ways. The first dimension of Black feminist epistemology is *lived experience as a criterion of meaning*. Collins explains that Black women tend to rely on subjective examples as legitimate sources of knowledge. This criterion refers to the use of narratives and practical images to describe experience as a valid form of knowledge or wisdom. For instance, in a famous speech titled *Ain't I a Woman*, to the Ohio Women's Rights Convention in Akron, Ohio, in 1851, emancipated slave Sojourner Truth substantiated her claim to an alternative version of White womanhood with a vivid account of her personal experiences.

The second dimension refers to the *use of dialogue in assessing knowledge claims*. It claims that Black women tend to engage in dialogue with others to develop and legitimate knowledge. A principal assumption of this criterion is that connectedness, not isolation and independent thought, is essential for validating knowledge. Collins traces this dimension to African-based oral traditions, noting that this assumption also undergirds some feminist epistemological theories. For example, Mary Belenky and her coauthors contend that women are socialized to seek connectedness.

The third dimension is the *ethic of caring*, which consists of three components: valuing individual uniqueness, viewing emotionality as appropriate, and developing the capacity for empathy. This criterion counters the mainstream ideology of rationality and objectivity as pivotal to creating and validating knowledge. Collins notes that the ethic of caring also resembles both African-based oral

traditions and feminist perspectives on ways of knowing. For example, the latter refers to women's tendency to value individual personality rather than to seek impersonal sources of knowledge.

The fourth dimension of Black feminist epistemology is the *ethic of personal accountability*. As individuals construct knowledge through experience, dialogue, and an ethic of caring, they also must be accountable for their knowledge claims. Thus, this criterion socializes Black women to validate a knowledge claim based on the perceived credibility of the source of that claim. Collins notes that Black women expect individuals not only to have clear positions on issues that they present but also to assume responsibility for substantiating their validity. She states that Black women are more likely to believe knowledge claims of speakers whom they respect for their moral character and ethical stance.

Collins observes that when Black women politicize these four dimensions and apply them to social projects, they provide a viable framework for Black feminist theorizing and practice. However, she notes that a Black woman's standpoint and its respective epistemology provide but one heuristic approach for analyzing intersections of multiple oppressions. She rejects theories that declare that Black women have a more accurate perspective on oppression because of their race and gender. Rather, she asserts that members of any groups that embody multiply oppressed identities (e.g., other women of color, men of color, poor White women, and lesbians of color) can provide epistemological insights. She concludes that the ultimate value of these types of epistemologies is to challenge enduring processes that persons and groups in power employ to produce and validate knowledge in order to substantiate their right to rule.

Brenda J. Allen

See also Chicana Feminism; Epistemology; Feminist Standpoint Theory; Postcolonial Feminism; Womanism

Further Readings

Allen, B. J. (1996). Feminism and organizational communication: A Black woman's (re)view of organizational socialization. *Communication Studies, 47*, 257–271.

Belenky, M. F., Clinchy, B. M., Goldberger, N. R., & Tarule, J. M. (1986). *Women's ways of knowing*. New York: Basic Books.

Collins, P. H. (2000). *Black feminist thought*. New York: Routledge.

Houston, M., & Davis, O. (2002). *Centering ourselves: African American feminist and womanist studies of discourse*. Cresskill, NJ: Hampton Press.

Bona Fide Group Theory

The bona fide group theory, originally developed by Linda Putnam and Cynthia Stohl, identifies a set of theoretical concepts that enable researchers to move away from studying small groups as if they were isolated, decontextualized, and without history and study groups in context. This perspective was first articulated in a special 1990 issue of the journal *Communication Studies*, in which several well-known communication scholars called for the discipline to pay greater attention to groups within their natural environments. These scholars argued that groups form the foundation of our social lives, our work endeavors, and our cultural and political experiences. Group communication facilitates or hinders a society's ability to thrive. After decades of studying small groups as if they were completely distinct from contexts, it was time for communication researchers to move beyond "container models" of group communication. Collectively, they agreed there was a need to have theories and constructs that enable an understanding of the multilevel, embedded, interpretive, emotional, and rational processes of groups.

Since the early 1990s, several theoretical perspectives have emerged that provide richer, deeper, and more nuanced understandings of groups in context. Going beyond functional approaches, researchers have incorporated structurational, interpretive, feminist, critical, and bona fide theories into small-group studies. Bona fide theory has been used to explore communication processes in contexts such as juries, surgical and health teams, environmental collaborations, management boards, community theater, fund-raising, online support, and adolescent peer groups. Research methodologies have also become more diverse. Discourse analyses, ethnographic studies, quasi-experimental designs, surveys, and laboratory experiments all have been used to study groups from a bona fide perspective.

Bona fide group theory posits that all groups manifest *permeable boundaries* and *interdependence with context*. The theory provides a set of concepts and relationships to explore these essential characteristics regardless of whether groups are experimentally created and manipulated, occur naturally in face-to-face environments, or are computer mediated. The bona fide group theory is a nascent theory insofar as a standard set of postulates and theorems have yet to be developed. However, over the past 18 years, numerous theoretical papers and empirical studies have illustrated the ways in which it is a useful and vibrant framework for the study of group processes as they emerge and are embedded in larger contexts.

In bona fide group theory, group processes (e.g., decision making, conflict management, socialization of members, information processing) are viewed as shaping and being shaped by these two essential characteristics: permeable boundaries and interdependence with immediate context. A third characteristic, *unstable and ambiguous borders*, emerges from the dynamic interplay between the first two distinguishing features. This characteristic focuses on group identities, especially how they emerge and evolve through the ways that members alter their group's boundaries and contexts.

By taking these characteristics into account, bona fide group theory enables scholars to understand the nature of *groupness* as constituted across time and space. The theory posits that the generative mechanism of group dynamics is the continuous communicative interplay between internal and external environments. These dynamics come together through the negotiation of group boundaries, the creation of group identities, and the shaping of the essential nature of the group. By focusing on the two essential characteristics, group scholarship is able to detect associations among contexts, group deliberations, and message systems that remained obscured in traditional laboratory and field research.

The first characteristic, permeable boundaries, challenges the assumption that a group has a fixed location, an existence apart from its environment, and a boundary formed by static, unchanging borders. In traditional studies of groups, boundaries are regarded as given or preexisting structures, and hence the social context is seen as separate from the group. Bona fide group theory is premised on the notion that boundaries are neither previously determined or permanent, nor are they defined by goals, tasks, physical location, or presence of group members. Rather, boundaries are conceived of as socially constructed through interactions that shape group identity; create, reproduce, or sever connections with internal and external environments; live out members' histories; and reflexively define group process.

Theoretically, the ways in which group members change, define, experience, and negotiate boundaries are found in the interactive nexus among (a) multiple group memberships and conflicting role identities, (b) representative roles, (c) fluctuations in membership, and (d) group identity formation. Empirical research suggests a strong association between the ways in which groups manage multiple memberships and overlapping identities and the effectiveness of the group. If boundaries are too volatile and indistinct, the group risks becoming overwhelmed and losing its identity and focus; if boundaries are too stable and exclusionary, the group often becomes isolated, information deprived, and ineffective.

The second major characteristic of bona fide groups is interdependence with immediate context. *Group context* refers to the dynamic ways in which groups depend on and contribute to their physical, social, and task environments. In most group studies of the past (whether in the field or in the laboratory), context was assigned to the group, controlled by the experimenter through laboratory manipulations, or treated as and/or assumed to be a constant. But in bona fide group theory, interdependence is a dynamic variable that is reciprocally negotiated as contexts are socially constructed through (a) intergroup and intragroup communication, (b) coordinated actions among groups, (c) negotiations of jurisdiction or autonomy, and (d) ongoing interpretations in which individuals make sense of current and past intergroup relationships.

Interdependence with immediate context considers the degree to which a particular group depends on other individuals and groups to accomplish its tasks and the degree to which other individuals and groups depend on the focal group. Rather than seeing task dimensions such as complexity, urgency, and accountability as static structural variables that

influence the internal dynamics of a group, bona fide group theory treats these task dimensions as socially constructed activities. Groups may deviate from assigned tasks and actively define what they do and how they do it with little reliance on outside influences whereas other groups may have strong external dependencies. The context shapes and is shaped by a group's ability to control the decisions the group makes, define its priorities, or develop criteria and alternatives to address the issues it faces. Strong as well as weak external linkages may create communicative dilemmas for the group as it struggles to represent adequately what are interpreted as relevant stakeholder positions.

Overall, bona fide group theory privileges neither external nor internal relations. Bona fide group theory posits that all groups, whether found in the laboratory or the field, manifest permeable boundaries and interdependence with context. The theory addresses the complex network of communicative processes that influence group action. From the very conceptualization of what a group is to the methods used to study the groups, the theory requires researchers to explore the production and reproduction of social contexts, social boundaries, and personal and collective identities.

Cynthia Stohl

See also Functional Group Communication Theory; Group and Organizational Structuration Theory; Group Communication Theories; Organizational Communication Theories; Organizational Culture; Organizational Identity Theory; Social Exchange Theory; Symbolic Convergence Theory; System Theory; Uncertainty Reduction Theory

Further Readings

Frey, L. R. (Ed.). (2003). *Group communication in context: Studies of bona fide groups* (2nd ed.). Mahwah, NJ: Lawrence Erlbaum.

Putnam, L. L., & Stohl, C. (1990). Bona fide groups: A reconceptualization of groups in context. *Communication Studies, 41*, 248–265.

Putnam, L. L., & Stohl, C. (1996). Bona fide groups: An alternative perspective for communication and small group decision making. In R. Y. Hirokawa & M. S. Poole (Eds.), *Communication and group decision making* (2nd ed., pp. 147–178). Thousand Oaks, CA: Sage.

Stohl, C., & Holmes, M. (1992). A functional perspective for bona fide groups. In S. A. Deetz (Ed.), *Communication Yearbook 16* (pp. 601–614). Newbury Park, CA: Sage.

BROADCASTING THEORIES

Broadcasting was undoubtedly the most important media development of the 20th century. First radio and then television developed into mass media that could command the attention of virtually the entire nation at times. Interestingly, however, communication theorists have—with some notable exceptions—developed relatively few theories that are specifically about broadcasting. Rather, most theories deal with *media effects*. Many of these theories are quite relevant to broadcasting but also deal with effects of other media, such as newspapers. Thus, to review broadcasting theories, one must first understand theories of media effects in relation to broadcasting as a medium; then one can examine some of the more specialized theories that are specific to broadcasting.

Theories of Media Effects and Broadcasting

Theories of media effects are predominantly a product of the 20th century. While some isolated studies on the effects of newspapers emerged around the turn of the 20th century, most theories were developed and tested as broadcasting emerged and spread as the dominant form of mass media. Traditionally, scholars consider that the first theories of media effects were working with the *powerful effects* hypothesis. Briefly, the hypothesis held that mass media had relatively powerful effects in terms of forming and changing beliefs and that the audience was relatively passive in terms of processing messages and accepting them. These concepts became prominent after World War I, when the *propaganda* used by all sides was eventually seen as a negative phenomenon; Americans began to question whether mass media such as newspapers could be too powerful, convincing people to engage in risky foreign ventures that they might not have undertaken. Harold Lasswell was an influential early figure who also developed the well-known model of communication: "Who says what to whom in what channel with what effect?" He was the first to study propaganda techniques and thus greatly influenced the study of media in general. Other influential figures on the early powerful effects theories were Edward Bernays (considered the "father" of *public relations*), Gustave Le Bon (a French theorist of *crowd psychology*), and John Watson (an important figure in *behaviorism*).

While we may now overestimate the extent to which early scholars viewed the media as having powerful effects, developments in broadcasting began to raise questions along the lines that the media might be too powerful. The rise of Fascism and Communism both relied heavily on propaganda. Hitler used radio and film as key elements of his propaganda policy. For U.S. Americans, the apparently all-too-easy submission of masses of people to totalitarian ideologies brought up queasy feelings about the "dark side" of mass media, especially broadcasting. The famous case of Orson Welles's radio adaptation of H. G. Wells's *War of the Worlds*, in which many Americans thought that a fictional account of an invasion from Mars was real, further heightened concerns. However, Hadley Cantril, in his study of the event—another milestone in mass communication research and one of the first to deal with broadcasting—showed that only a relatively small portion of people panicked; moreover, he was able to show that certain personality characteristics and other conditions predicted a panic reaction, which ran counter to the notion of powerful effects. However, it cannot be denied that developments in radio throughout the 1930s contributed to fears that broadcast mass media might have become too powerful. On the positive side, Franklin Roosevelt's use of radio in his fireside chats was an example of the use of broadcasting to unite people around important issues and causes.

The powerful effects model was effectively struck down in the 1940s. Studies conducted by Paul Lazarsfeld and colleagues showed that people's decisions about political candidates were not much affected by media; rather, people seemed to rely on those closest to them in forming their judgments. This model came to be known as *personal influence*, and it has also been described as a *limited effects* paradigm. By this time, radio was in ascendance as a broadcast mass medium, used widely for both entertainment and information. Thus,

Lazarsfeld's studies were seen by some as confirming that media—even broadcasting—were not so powerful that people could not make their own decisions or that democratic pluralism could not survive in an era of mass broadcasting. However, Lazarsfeld also introduced the notion of the *two-step flow,* in which *opinion leaders* would be more attentive to messages from the media and would use such information within their own primary social networks. Also, studies of the use of films to motivate soldiers during World War II seemed to show little effect. By the end of the 1950s, some scholars were pronouncing the end of communication research. In sum, while radio had been a dominant medium from the 1930s through the 1950s, few scholars had produced research that resulted in radio-specific theories; there was no unified theory of broadcasting. From today's vantage point, however, we can see that broadcast radio was one of the most important developments of the 20th century, playing a role in all the important political, social, and cultural movements of its time.

Critical Theories and Broadcasting

Before examining theories of broadcasting and media effects as they evolved in the United States after the 1950s, it is instructive to look at critical theories of media, most of which came out of Europe from the 1930s onward. Much European research on media is grounded in or is a response to Marxism. Orthodox *Marxist theory* held that all cultural phenomena were formed by economic conditions (the so-called *base–superstructure argument*). However, European scholars, most prominently those from the *Frankfurt School,* found these formulations too simplistic. Theodor Adorno, a prominent member of the school, did research on radio. He thought that it could induce states near brainwashing. Adorno and others in the Frankfurt School, influenced by their experiences with radio, conceived of mass media—especially broadcasting—as a *culture industry,* in which art had been transformed from expression into a mass-produced product with exchange value. Adorno was most insistent in his belief that mass-produced broadcast radio culture devalued the experience of listening to music.

Other critical theorists continued this line of thinking that broadcasting transforms the production of stories, art, and culture into a mass-produced commodity. Herbert Marcuse found that media inculcated patterns of one-dimensional thought. However, other Marxist media scholars saw the media as a potential site for ideological struggle. Gramsci's notion of *hegemony* permitted such a conception. Later scholars such as Stuart Hall and the Birmingham School continued this line of reasoning as the possibility of differing readings of media were accepted. All in all, these critical approaches were in large part responses to both the technological and the economic structures of broadcasting as institutionalized in the capitalist West. As such, they are theories of broadcasting in the broader sense. Todd Gitlin, an American sociologist, underlined the differences between the American limited effects school and the critical research by pointing out that much American research was done under an *administrative model,* serving the needs of the broadcast media, which in turn served the needs of corporate and political elites. However, American research moved beyond the simple polarity between powerful and limited effects, and broadcasting played an important role.

Later Theories of Media Effects and Broadcasting

After the pronouncement of the death of communication research (by Bernard Berelson), media scholars began to offer new theories that addressed concepts of media power that lay somewhere between limited and powerful effects. The theory most directly connected to television (and thus broadcasting) was *cultivation,* developed by George Gerbner and colleagues at the University of Pennsylvania beginning in the late 1960s. Gerbner felt that the many studies of television *violence* were too focused on trying to show that viewers would imitate violence that they had seen on television. While the hundreds of violence studies that have been conducted are also highly relevant to broadcasting, Gerbner conceived of television primarily as a storytelling medium. Thus, his theory was that viewers of television would be more likely to hold conceptions of the world that were congruent with what they had seen on television. Most famously, because heavy viewers of television would see many instances of violence, Gerbner hypothesized that they would also see the world as a more violent place. He called this phenomenon the *mean world syndrome*. Cultivation examined many other concepts in relation to television. For Gerbner, the importance of television was that it was a broadcast medium, dominating the storytelling industry from the 1950s onward. While other media could potentially have had cultivating effects, television was the most important because of its massive reach, a direct result of its broadcast nature.

Another theory that offered a perspective on the effects of media was *agenda setting*. This theory, also developed in the late 1960s, argued that media might tell people, not what to think, but what to think about. Maxwell McCombs and colleagues showed that the agendas of news organizations (including broadcast news) influenced the agenda of the public. Later developments in agenda setting found that exposure to news could *prime* audiences to receive information in certain ways, and that news *frames* are also important in influencing how audiences receive and interpret news. While agenda setting can apply to any journalistic medium, many of the studies within this theory have included television news. The power of television to set political agendas has been recognized since at least the 1960s, and research on agenda setting has confirmed this power time and again.

A third prominent theory of media effects developed after the emergence of television was the *spiral of silence*. Elisabeth Noelle-Neumann argued that public opinion was not just the sum of people's individual beliefs. Rather, public opinion was also characterized by people's beliefs about what others thought. Thus, she argued, people would be less likely to express opinions if they felt that others did not share that opinion. More important, she argued that people would derive their feelings of whether others shared their beliefs from the media; she called this the *media tenor*. Since spiral of silence theory was developed from the 1970s onward, naturally the power of television played a role in terms of its ability to portray opinions as normative to large, heterogeneous audiences.

Indeed, most current theories of media effects have been shaped by television's power to distribute messages to large, heterogeneous audiences. From the 1950s to the 1990s, television's dominance of the mass consciousness was virtually uncontested. Thus, for theories of media effects that were in one way or another informed by conceptions of mass society—a society of disconnected, anonymous individuals—television as a medium represented the apex of mass mediation. In this sense, almost any theory of media effects developed after the 1950s can be seen as a response to television and thus a theory of broadcasting. Not surprisingly, television was seen as a factor in relation to a number of social questions and issues.

Television Research

Most media attract the attention of social critics as the media develop and become important aspects of the culture. This was true of radio, film, popular music, comic books, and most other mass media at various times. However, television seemed to many to be so powerful that it attracted more than its share of criticism and thus the attention of researchers.

Without question, the dominant issue of concern has been television violence. In the 1960s, competition among the three broadcast networks resulted in television lineups that were increasingly filled with action–adventures, Westerns, and crime dramas. While such fare would probably seem tame by today's standards, in comparison with the so-called Golden Age of television (which was characterized by live dramas, quiz shows, variety shows, and similar fare), the new action-oriented lineup was disconcerting to many. The Surgeon General of the United States issued a report in 1972 on television violence, concluding that exposure to television violence does result in a number of deleterious outcomes. The government expanded and updated these findings in 1982. Since then, the dominant view has been that television violence does result in negative outcomes such as desensitization to violence, imitation of violence seen, and acceptance of violence as a way to solve problems. While violence has always been a part of the storytelling landscape, the advent of television as a broadcast medium meant that violent images could now be seen by everyone at virtually any time, in increased vividness and realism. While the government considered regulating violence, not much has been done besides the establishment of a voluntary rating system by television broadcasters and the introduction in 1996 of the V-chip, which allows parents to block programs that they might deem too violent for their children.

Another concern can be found in television's portrayal of minorities and other marginalized groups. Of most concern was the fact that television, especially in its early years, stereotyped groups such as African Americans and women. Research showed that African Americans were much less likely to appear on television programs when compared with their population percentages, and when shown, they were most often portrayed in stereotypical roles, often as either servants or criminals. Women were also shown less frequently, and mostly in "traditional roles," such as mother, secretary, nurse, and so on. When not shown in those roles, they were shown as objects of desire. Much research from a variety of theoretical perspectives has shown that these portrayals did matter in terms of how people viewed the marginalized groups. However, television has proven able to adapt, at least partially, to social change. Blacks and women are now shown more frequently, and the range of roles they can inhabit has also broadened. A similar phenomenon can be seen in the portrayal of gay men and lesbians. Nevertheless, even with some improvements, there are other groups—such as Latinos and Asians—that remain underrepresented on television, and even the groups that have seen their portrayals increase can still make an argument that the dominant—even hegemonic—White male culture of television still has effects at the societal level.

Despite the demise of the powerful effects view of media, television has been blamed at one point or another for almost every social problem: drug abuse, unhealthy behaviors such as smoking or unhealthy eating habits, poor educational performance of children, lack of interest or knowledge in political matters, failure to practice safe sex, and so on. In all, thousands of studies have been conducted linking television viewing to a variety of negative effects. Most studies do show effects for the given variables studied, although effects directly attributable to television are almost always small to moderate when demographic and other factors are controlled for. Still, the simple frequency with which investigators have looked at television as a cause or symptom of social ills is evidence of the enormous power ascribed to television in everyday discourse. While researchers may have bypassed the notion of a *hypodermic needle* or *magic bullet* that could inject passive

viewers with any desired message, there is little doubt that television has been viewed within society as the most powerful mass medium ever devised, at least since the 1960s.

Technological Theories of Broadcasting

It is interesting to note that television's dominance as a mass medium has been challenged—beginning in the 1980s with the rise of cable television and VCRs and more recently with the rise of the Internet. Traditional broadcasting (epitomized by over-the-air broadcasts of television) has lost much of its share to *new media*. At the same time, watching television—in a variety of forms—is still the most common media activity in which people engage. But the rise of new media points to the fact that the form of a technology, in this case broadcasting, can also have important effects.

Modernization theory, popular in the 1960s and 1970s, argued that developing societies could pass more quickly from traditionalism into a modern state with the infusion of mass-mediated communication. Access to information from mass media would help the Third World bypass stages of development by replacing traditional outlooks with those characteristic of "advanced" capitalist democracies. The theory of *diffusion of innovations* also focused on technologies and their adoption as markers of modernity, although this theory also included interpersonal and community-level communication as important determinants of a society's move toward modernization. Broadcasting's technological features—especially its ability to reach illiterate audiences across wide distances—made it a logical candidate for experiments in technological innovation for modernization. The advent of satellite broadcasting made the power of broadcasting as a technology seem even more alluring. Experiments were conducted with the use of television in remote underdeveloped countries, and a variety of nations undertook broadcasting projects—either in radio or television—to advance economic, social, and cultural development. While there were some successes, critics argued that broadcasting would merely serve to transmit the values of dominant, Western capitalist powers. Fears of neo-imperialism or neocolonialism muted much of the hope for broadcasting's power as a tool for positive social change. In any case, by the 1980s and 1990s, broadcasting was reaching more people, and local production was stepping up its output. For many countries where state-sponsored television had been the norm, new commercial outlets were springing up, often through cable and satellite. The fact that local media industries in countries such as India became very large and commercial seemed to confirm some aspects of both advocates of the modernization approach and its opponents. The technology was indeed powerful as countries' economies changed, but broadcasting's quality as the preeminent medium for carrying advertising also meant that the economic model of free-market capitalism was often part and parcel of the technological package. These trends have led to what we now call *globalization.*

Perhaps the most important, though controversial, theory of broadcasting as a technology was that of Marshall McLuhan. He saw media as extensions of human sense faculties, and he was far less concerned with the content of the medium than with its form. He famously said that the medium was the message, by which he meant that use of certain media tended to reorganize the way humans think. Most important for McLuhan was the transition from a literary or written culture (a culture of the "eye") to a mediated, aural culture (a culture of the "ear"). While McLuhan was not the first to point out the importance of the development of writing as the advent of the very essence of modern, rational, scientific, Western thought, he popularized these notions to a very wide audience. Indeed, he became something of a media phenomenon in the 1960s. While McLuhan's ideas were widely circulated, they did not gain much traction among communication theorists. Most commonly, his thoughts have been attacked with the critique of *technological determinism*—the idea that all the effects of a technology can be deduced from its form. Raymond Williams (*Television: Technology and Cultural Form*) is a prominent opponent of technological determinism, arguing that cultural, social, and political decisions affect how a technology will be used. In any case, as we have seen, most theories of broadcasting have been linked with theories of media effect, and thus content and form are inextricably linked.

James Shanahan

See also Agenda-Setting Theory; Computer-Mediated Communication; Diffusion of Innovations; Frankfurt School; Marxist Theory; Media Effects Theories; Medium Theory; New Media Theory; Spiral of Silence; Theory; Two-Step and Multi-Step Flow; Violence and Nonviolence in Media Studies

Further Readings

Adorno, T. (1945). A social critique of radio music. *Kenyon Review, 7,* 208–217.

Cantril, H. (with Hazel Gaudet & Herta Herzog). (1940). *The invasion from Mars: A study in the psychology of panic.* Princeton, NJ: Princeton University Press.

Lasswell, H. (1971). *Propaganda technique in World War I.* Cambridge: MIT Press.

Lazarsfeld, P., Berelson, B., & Gaudet, H. (1948). *The people's choice.* New York: Columbia University Press.

Lerner, D. (1958). *The passing of traditional society.* Glencoe, IL: Macmillan.

McCombs, M., & Shaw, D. (1972). The agenda-setting function of mass media. *Public Opinion Quarterly, 36,* 176–187.

McLuhan, M. (1964). *Understanding media: The extensions of man.* New York: Signet.

Noelle-Neumann, E. (1984). *The spiral of silence: Public opinion—Our social skin.* Chicago: University of Chicago Press.

Shanahan, J., & Morgan, M. (1999). *Television and its viewers: Cultivation theory and research.* London: Cambridge University Press.

U.S. Surgeon General's Scientific Advisory Committee on Television and Social Behavior. (1972). *Television and growing up: The impact of televised violence: Report to the Surgeon General.* U.S. Public Health Service. Rockville, MD: National Institute of Mental Health.

Williams, R. (2003). *Television: Technology and cultural form* (3rd ed.). New York: Routledge.

BUDDHIST COMMUNICATION THEORY

Implicit in all great religions of the world are distinct models of communication. In this regard, Buddhism is no exception. Buddhism refers to a body of doctrines and religious practices expounded by the Buddha—literally, the Enlightened One. The Buddha was born in India in 563 BCE and died 85 years later. There are two main schools of

Buddhism—the *Theravada* and *Mahayana*. The Theravada form of Buddhism, which is the earlier school, is practiced in countries such as Thailand, Sri Lanka, Myanmar, Cambodia, and Laos, while the Mahayana form is practiced in countries such as Japan, South Korea, and Tibet. There are a number of differences between the two, although both have much in common, and both offer important implications for communication theory.

The Buddha himself was a supremely persuasive communicator. He preached to the people in an idiom and vocabulary that were readily understandable. He paid close attention to the psychological makeup of his interlocutors and listeners. He designed his messages in a way that would appeal to ordinary people. In terms of models of communication, he placed the receiver at the center of his communication model—unlike most Western models, which, until recently, focused on the sender. Furthermore, the Buddha always conceptualized communication in terms of a specific context; the act of communication constituted an event, and the context was an integral part of the meaning. Finally, he placed great emphasis on the rhetorical strategies deployed by the communicator. The distinct ways in which he pressed into service allegories, parables, tropes, and stories bear testimony to this fact. Communication, then, is central to Buddhist thought.

Buddhist Phenomenology

Buddhists posit three basic characteristics as defining worldly existence. They are impermanence, suffering, and nonself. The notions of flux and suffering are central to Buddhist phenomenology. The way out of a world of suffering, according to the Buddha, is by pursuing the *Noble Eightfold Path,* consisting of (1) right view, (2) right conception, (3) right speech, (4) right action, (5) right livelihood, (6) right effort, (7) right mindfulness, and (8) right concentration. In addition, there is no permanent personal entity that can be called the self or ego. These three characteristics color the Buddhist approach to communication. In general terms, what is distinctive about the Buddhist understanding of language and verbal communication is that it signifies the middle path—it avoids extremes.

A social aspect is also important to Buddhist thought. There are five main presuppositions associated with the ideal social order, and these have implications for communication theory: (1) The human being is supreme, (2) reason and compassionate understanding rather than blind dogma should guide human action, (3) human beings need to be pragmatic in their behavior, (4) all forms of violence should be eliminated, and (5) peace and harmony are the ideals that underwrite society.

Dimensions of Buddhist Communication Theory

At the foundation of Buddhist views of communication is the Buddhist view of language. Language is seen as always evolving in relation to social contexts and conditions. In the famous discourse on the origins (*agganna sutta*), the Buddha informs the two Brahmins, Vasettha and Bhadrvaja, that human society is a product of evolution. Social institutions, including language, were not fashioned by some divine creator but evolve through processes of social growth. Language, then, is a social practice shaped by convention and agreed on by the people who employ it. In the Buddhist writings, there are copious references to agreement among users (*sammuti*) and the practices of users (*vohara*), evidence of the idea of language as a product of social evolution.

The Buddhist emphasis on language as a social practice also calls attention to the world shared by senders and receivers and how it constitutes a very important facet of the communicated meaning. A communicative event is more than the sending of a message by a solitary sender to a solitary receiver; it takes place within a linguistic context in which both are embedded. The idea of linguistic *embeddedness* constitutes an integral part of the meaning of the communication act and gives it added focus and depth. Embeddedness is present in another way, as well. According to the Buddhist way of thinking, individual consciousness is nurtured on signs and reflects their logic and imperatives. Indeed, consciousness is dependent on the semiotic interactions associated with a given communicative event. Consciousness, then, is forged in the linguistic signs produced and exchanged by the participants; it is not just the subjective experience of the individual but takes into account the social dimensions of context as well.

In fact, theories of interpersonal communication and intrapersonal communication intersect in interesting ways in Buddhist thought. According to Buddhism, language and communication ultimately should pave the way to liberation. Hence, *self-reflexivity* and *critical introspection*—the essence of intrapersonal communication—assume a great importance. For Buddhists, this self-reflexivity is built into the very process of verbal communication. In communicating, one is not merely stringing together a cluster of words but also reflecting on them and evaluating them; to communicate, to use language to interact with others, is to adopt a moral stance. From this flows the notion that linguistic communication involves the imparting of not only information but also feelings and moral assessments. Therefore, to communicate through language is to reflect on how one is constituted as a human being. This is an important area that has been relatively neglected by communication scholars.

Buddhism also contains a well-developed model of interpersonal communication itself, hardly surprising in view of the fact that the aim of Buddhism is to lead people away from worldly suffering; how to live productively and harmoniously with others in society is addressed by Buddhism as a way of alleviating suffering. Furthermore, the concepts of suffering, happiness, rights, duties, goodness, evil, virtues, vices, well-being, truthfulness, and authenticity are discussed in ways that illuminate issues of interpersonal communication. The Buddhist model of interpersonal communication that lies behind moral injunctions, for example, focuses attention on the following components: the sensitive use of language, truthfulness and verifiability of communication, the achievement of consensus and harmony through interaction, the frames of intelligibility we bring to the communicative event, symmetrical relationships in communication, the importance of contexts of interface, and clarification and justification of moral principles underlying social intercourse.

Buddhist communication theory is complex and many sided. The Buddhist approach to language and implications of Buddhism for intrapersonal and interpersonal communication have been presented here as examples of the many implications of Buddhism for communication. Buddhist understandings of communication as a social and moral act have much to offer contemporary communication theorists.

Wimal Dissanayake

See also Asian Communication Theory; Constitutive View of Communication; Epistemology; Ethics Theories; Hindu Communication Theory; Language and Communication

Further Readings

Chuang, R., & Chen, G.-M. (2003). Buddhist perspectives and human communication. *Intercultural Communication Studies, 12*(4), 65–80.

Dissanayake, W. (1983). The communication significance of the Buddhist concept of dependent co-origination. *Communication, 8*(1), 29–45.

Dissanayake, W. (1988). *Communication theory: The Asian perspective.* Singapore: Asian Mass Communication Research and Information Center.

Dissanayake, W. (2007). Nagarjuna and modern communication theory. *China Media Research, 3*(4), 34–41.

Dissanayake, W. (2008). The idea of verbal communication in early Buddhism. *China Media Research, 4*(2), 69–76.

Nordstrom, L. (1979). Zen and the non-duality of communication: The sound of one hand clapping. *Communication, 4*(1), 15–27.

Rahula, W. (1974). *What the Buddha taught.* New York: Grove Press.

C

CAMPAIGN COMMUNICATION THEORIES

Communication campaigns are intended to generate specific outcomes in a relatively large number of individuals, within a specified time, and through an organized set of communication activities. In other words, campaigns employ communication strategies and theories to influence large audiences in some measurable way. Perhaps the objective is to persuade consumers to purchase a particular product, as is the case with commercial marketing campaigns, or to influence an attitude, increase knowledge, promote awareness, or even change a behavior, as is more common in prosocial campaigns. Campaigns can be school- or community-based or regional, national, or international in their reach. Mass media campaigns, frequently used for their large reach, are most successful in increasing awareness and knowledge, while smaller school- or community-based campaigns are more likely to generate higher level changes in attitudes and behavior. Integration of mass media and interpersonal strategies creates the greatest likelihood for behavior change.

Campaigns are complex in that they are an art as well as a science. In other words, high-quality graphics and creative ideas are necessary to attract and maintain attention, but so is a fundamental understanding of communication theory to maximize understanding of audiences, message content, and evaluation strategies. A clear understanding of how theory can inform the campaign process will improve the likelihood of obtaining successful campaign outcomes.

The three major phases of a campaign are planning, implementation, and evaluation. While there are many potential theories that can be used to inform campaigns across the three phases, those theories that are highlighted in this entry are wide in scope and applicable to a broad range of campaign topics. This entry will discuss how theory can be integrated into formative research, message design, and evaluation procedures throughout a campaign's planning, implementation, and evaluation stages.

Theory in Formative Research

The planning stage of formative research is commonly divided into preproduction and production phases. During the *preproduction phase*, research on target audiences is conducted to understand their beliefs, values, knowledge, attitudes, and perceptions about the campaign topic. Preproduction research informs how audiences may be segmented so that campaign messages can be tailored appropriately to an audience's demographics, geographics, and psychographics. During the *production phase*, message concepts are designed on the basis of preproduction findings and then are evaluated by target audience members to determine how they may be revised for the larger campaign. Primary research strategies used in formative research include focus groups, theater testing, surveys, and intercept interviews.

To begin the formative research process, campaigners will first identify relevant literature related to the campaign topic. The relevant literature assists in the identification of a theoretical framework so that campaign researchers can identify factors that might contribute to individuals' willingness to attend to, identify with, process, and ultimately comply with campaign recommendations. Specifically, during the preproduction stage, theory helps inform the questions asked in a moderator guide, survey tool, or interview protocol, and during the production stage, theory provides ideas for message design. Two theories often employed during the formative research phase are the transtheoretical model (TTM) and the theory of planned behavior (TPB).

Stages of Change/Transtheoretical Model

According to James Prochaska and Carlo DiClemente, the TTM is based on the idea that individuals are at different stages of readiness to engage in a recommended behavior, which provides useful information for prioritizing audience segments and identifying who is most likely to be influenced. According to the TTM, people can be in either precontemplation, contemplation, preparation, action, or maintenance stages in terms of their readiness to change a behavior. People who do not believe a problem exists in their current behavior or situation would be in the *precontemplation* stage. Individuals in the *contemplation* stage are aware that a problem exists but have made no serious commitment to change. Individuals in the *preparation* stage intend to take action to change and may seek information about how to facilitate a change. In the *action* stage, people have begun to address the problem behavior by adopting a recommended behavior. When they continue to engage in the recommended behavior over time, individuals have entered the *maintenance* stage. As part of the formative research process, it can be helpful to identify individuals' readiness to change as a strategy to segment audiences. The types of messages that influence people are likely to differ depending on individuals' stage of readiness to make a change.

Associated with each of the TTM stages are activities that help move people through the behavior change process, including consciousness raising, dramatic relief, self-reevaluation, environmental reevaluation, self-liberation, social liberation, counterconditioning, stimulus control,

contingency management, and helping relationships. These processes of change provide campaigners with a toolbox of strategies to incorporate as part of their campaign messages. For example, if a target audience was comprised of individuals in the precontemplation stage (e.g., I did not know anything about blood donation), campaign messages might focus on consciousness raising to increase awareness of the campaign topic (e.g. blood donations are at an extreme low), or if a target audience included individuals in the maintenance phase, campaign messages might focus on helping relationships (e.g., continue to donate blood with a partner) to ensure continued maintenance of the behavior. According to the TTM, people continually go through a *decisional balance*, examining the pros and cons associated with a particular behavior, which should be assessed at the formative research phase (e.g., what are the perceived benefits and barriers to blood donation). Additionally, the TTM notes that *self-efficacy*, one's confidence that he or she can perform a behavior, influences behavior change, which indicates a need to assess factors that may impact self-efficacy (e.g., how confident are you that you are able to donate blood). In sum, the TTM provides information that allows campaigners to segment audiences on the basis of their readiness to change and design messages to test during the formative research phase of campaign development.

Theory of Planned Behavior

Icek Ajzen's TPB provides a useful framework for conducting formative research in campaigns. According to the TPB, three conceptually independent variables contribute to the formation of behavioral intentions that predict actual behavior: individual attitudes, subjective norms, and perceptions of behavioral control. *Attitude* is comprised of behavioral beliefs that have outcome evaluations associated with them (e.g., wearing a seatbelt is a good thing to do); *subjective norm* is defined as a person's beliefs that certain individuals or groups believe he or she should or should not perform a given behavior (e.g., my parents would approve of my wearing a seatbelt); *perceived behavioral control* is the perception that performance of a specific behavior is within a person's control (e.g., it is easy for me to use my seatbelt), and there is a direct link between perceived behavioral control and behavior. The TPB is useful in the formative research phase because it indicates that campaigners need to investigate potential audience members' attitudes about the campaign topic, normative influences that might affect their adoption of campaign recommendations, and perceptions of control, which can identify perceived barriers to adopting campaign recommendations. For example, formative research for a campaign to promote seatbelt use among pregnant women might find that women have a positive attitude toward seatbelt use, as do their significant others, but it might also find that women report discomfort during the later stages of pregnancy. In the production phase of formative research, message concepts can be designed that support positive audience beliefs and address barriers. For example, in the seatbelt scenario, pregnant women might be reminded about keeping their unborn baby safe and be encouraged to purchase a seatbelt extension to improve their comfort level. Thus, while the TTM provides guidance for understanding audience readiness to engage in behavior, the TPB provides insight regarding known predictors of behavior so that campaigners can engage in appropriate research that addresses those predictors in final campaign messages.

Theory in Message Design

The previous section discussed how theory can be used to understand audiences and create message concepts for testing in formative research. This section will elaborate further on the use of theory in message design as a strategy to improve the potential impact of campaign messages. Campaign messages need to be memorable, of high quality, and communicated via a channel appropriate to the audience. While creative messages are essential for society's savvy information consumers, so is the theoretical contribution to message development, because theory provides campaigners with information regarding message structure, argument type, selection of appeals, and repetition, as well as source and channel choices. Many theories can inform message design, but to extend the discussion to other frequently used theories, social cognitive theory (SCT) and the extended parallel process model (EPPM) are discussed as they relate to campaign message design.

Social Cognitive Theory

SCT, a theory by Albert Bandura, is based on the same body of research as social learning theory but focuses more on human thought processes. The central idea of SCT is that people learn from observation and that the reinforcement or punishment of behavior impacts their behavior and subsequent outcome expectancies in similar situations. Also, learning is more likely to occur if a person identifies greatly with the role model and has high self-efficacy. SCT is fundamental to campaign message design because it explicates the idea that people learn and are influenced when they make observations, which includes observation of campaign messages. SCT notes that people are more likely to be influenced by models or message sources with whom they identify; thus, formative research can identify these models for subsequent use in campaign messages. SCT also discusses the importance of rewards and punishments: Campaign messages can promote the positive outcomes associated with adherence to campaign recommendations or highlight the punishments associated with low adherence to a recommended action or belief. For example, a campaign message that encourages individuals to vote on election day may point out that they will feel patriotic and proud to be an American if they exercise their right to do so. And a campaign that encourages individuals to drive the speed limit may also indicate a punishment, such as "If you don't, law enforcement will ticket you."

The theory supports message-design strategies that promote message sources with whom audience members identify, new information for audience members to learn, demonstrations of recommended actions through appropriate channels, and reinforcement or punishment as motivators to comply with message recommendations. SCT is particularly useful when a campaign aims to demonstrate how to engage in a new behavior. For example, health brochures that demonstrate how to appropriately conduct a breast self-exam, a public service announcement that shows how to "click" your seatbelt to avoid a ticket, or a radio message providing directions on how to apply sunscreen appropriately all provide observable examples of SCT. In sum, SCT provides guidelines about observational learning that can translate directly into message design strategies for campaigns.

The Extended Parallel Process Model

The EPPM, a theory developed by Kim Witte, describes conditions when fear appeals will or will not be effective as a campaign message. *Fear appeals* are persuasive messages designed to scare people by describing the terrible things that will happen to them if they do not do what the message recommends. Fear appeals typically use vivid language, personal language, and gory details or pictures, and they are a popular strategy in both health and political campaigns. Everyone can recall health messages that warn of terrible things that will happen if people do not exercise regularly, eat right, get regular checkups, wear safety gear, or take preventive action of some sort. For example, public service announcements about drunk driving that show a crushed car and warn of imminent death if you drink and drive would be considered a fear appeal. And during political campaign seasons, it is easy to recall messages sponsored by a political party that threaten negative consequences and policies should the opposing candidate be elected.

The EPPM describes three components of a fear appeal that predict whether message exposure leads to acceptance, avoidance, or reactance: fear, threat, and perceived efficacy. *Fear* is the emotional part of the message, while *threat* refers to the *perceived severity* (e.g., drinking and driving results in death) and *perceived susceptibility* (e.g., I or my friends could be hit by a drunk driver) of the message. *Perceived efficacy* is comprised of *response efficacy* (e.g., designated drivers reduce drunk driving), as well as the previously discussed construct of *self-efficacy* (e.g., I am confident that I could easily be or use a designated driver). The EPPM states that when threat is high and perceived efficacy is high, target audience members will accept the message because they see there is a problem and feel as though they can do something about it. However, if they perceive a threat to be high and their efficacy to be low, they will not accept the message and engage in avoidance or perhaps reactance, in which they respectively choose to not address the message or do the opposite of what the message recommends. If a fear appeal is the message appeal of choice, this theory identifies message components that need to be present in a campaign message for the fear appeal to be successful. Specifically, a fear appeal needs to promote a threat that is not too intense or scary, but still threatening, and it also needs to recommend an action that people believe will work and is easily done to address the threat. Essentially, the theory provides instructions for campaign messages that aim to scare people into action; however, the theory cautions that those messages should contain both a threat as well as an efficacy component to be successful. For example, campaigners may decide they want to use fear appeals as an antismoking prevention strategy. Messages may include narrative evidence that shows a woman on her deathbed with an oxygen tank and a vivid picture of her tarred, black lung. To be effective, the message would also have to have a strong efficacy component that encourages audience members to remain smoke free by recommending certain actions. While there is much controversy over the use of fear appeals in the campaign literature, they are commonly used in campaigns to illustrate undesirable outcomes for individuals. Campaigners have an ethical imperative to include an efficacy component, and if they do not include an efficacy component, they decrease their likelihood of successfully influencing audience members.

Theory in Evaluating Campaign Effects

In addition to formative research and message design, theory informs the process and summative evaluations of campaigns. *Process evaluation* occurs during the implementation phase of a campaign to ensure that all facets of the campaign are moving along as planned, while *summative evaluation* occurs at the completion of a campaign to determine its effectiveness. During process evaluation, theory provides a map for what variables are critical to monitor during the implementation process. For example, the EPPM would indicate a designated driver message that incorporates a fear appeal should result in acceptance of a message. However, if the message is seen as humorous rather than threatening or if the message does not have as strong an efficacy impact as expected, it would be critical during the implementation phase to assess the message and adjust it accordingly to avoid campaign failure. Process evaluation is often not done despite its importance for accurate evaluation of summative effects.

Social Norms Approach

Summative evaluation to assess the success of a campaign is based minimally on stated campaign objectives, which are informed by theory. At the outset of a campaign, campaigners look to theory to identify what variables (e.g., attitude, personal norms, knowledge) can be impacted by campaign messages and then develop measures that evaluate whether any changes occurred across those variables. Campaign evaluation is difficult as it is not a controlled experiment, but quasi-experimental designs often are used to compare different schools, communities, or regions exposed to a campaign to other equivalent, unexposed groups. Theory plays an integral role in determining campaign objectives, which direct what type of measurement needs to occur to assess effectiveness. *Social norms* campaigns, for example, aim to correct audience misperceptions about a social norm by providing evidence that a perceived norm is different from the actual norm. Social norms campaigns, an approach developed by Alan Berkowitz, are often used on college campuses to address binge drinking, typically providing evidence that most students do not binge drink and only drink a few alcoholic beverages when they do—which is contrary to the common perception that the majority of college students binge drink. Prior to the start of the campaign, campaigners collect baseline data based on the constructs of the theory (e.g., how much each student actually drinks, how much each student thinks other college students at the campus drink). They will then set measurable objectives for the campaign based on the theory (e.g., the campaign will increase student knowledge of campus drinking behavior, increase communication about drinking moderately, decrease drinking by one alcoholic beverage per social activity). During and after implementation, campaigners measure those same constructs to determine whether any changes have occurred within the target group, and they perhaps compare the findings with those from a control campus. In sum, theory identifies important constructs, provides measurement guidance, and contributes to the evaluation of campaign effects.

Kami J. Silk

See also Advertising Theories; Cognitive Theories; Entertainment–Education; Media Effects Theories; Reasoned Action Theory

Further Readings

Ajzen, I. (1985). From intentions to actions: A theory of planned behavior. In J. Kuhl & J. Beckman (Eds.), *Action-control: From cognition to behavior* (pp. 11–39). Heidelberg, Germany: Springer.

Bandura, A. (1986). *Social foundations of thought and action: A social cognitive theory.* Englewood Cliffs, NJ: Prentice Hall.

Berkowitz, A. D. (2003). An overview of the social norms approach. In L. C. Lederman & L. P. Stewart (Eds.), *Changing the culture of college drinking: A socially situated health communication campaign* (pp. 193–214). Cresskill, NJ: Hampton Press.

Hornik, R. C. (Ed.). (2002). *Public health communication: Evidence for behavior change.* Mahwah, NJ: Lawrence Erlbaum.

Pfau, M., & Parrott, R. (1993). *Persuasive communication campaigns.* Boston: Allyn & Bacon.

Prochaska, J. O., & Velicer, W. F. (1997). The transtheoretical model of health behavior change. *American Journal of Health Promotion, 12,* 38–48.

Rice, R. E., & Atkin, C. K. (Eds.). (2001). *Public communication campaigns* (3rd ed.). Thousand Oaks, CA: Sage.

Valente, T. W. (2002). *Evaluating health promotion programs.* New York: Oxford.

Witte, K. (1992). Putting the fear back in fear appeals: The extended parallel process model. *Communication Monographs, 59,* 329–349.

CHICANA FEMINISM

Chicana feminism is a movement that developed in response to the inability of the *Chicano movement* of the 1960s and 1970s and the Anglo *feminist movement* to incorporate the specific experience and social justice issues confronting women of Mexican ancestry in the United States. The experience of Chicanas is rooted historically in the colonization of Mexico and subsequently in the attainment and annexation of most of what was northern Mexico in the 1800s by the United States. Additionally, the Chicana experience is deeply informed by continued *neocolonialist* economic migration and immigration of Mexicans, both temporarily and permanently, to live and work in the United States.

This colonialist past and neocolonialist present combine to create a complex matrix of religion, ethnicity, culture, race, class, sexuality, and gender that characterizes the hybrid and complicated nature of Chicana feminism. Although there has been a history of Mexican women feminists in various forms since colonial times, what sets apart the Chicana feminist who evolved in the 20th century is a focus on political praxis combined with the creation of what Chicana writer Cherríe Moraga calls a *theory in the flesh*—theory that is inherently political in drawing on the contradictions and real-life experiences of Chicana women.

Influence of the Chicano and Feminist Movements

The Chicano movement grew out of a history and experience of labor inequalities and oppression and the efforts of activists and community leaders to correct them. While these efforts had begun as early as the first decades of the 20th century and throughout the southwest United States (chiefly Texas, New Mexico, Colorado, Arizona, and California), the Chicano movement was most strongly influenced by the efforts of the United Farm Workers (UFW), led by César Chávez. This activism was the Chicano counterpart to the civil rights movement in the United States. Chicano university students in the 1960s became involved in supporting the UFW, as well as in questioning the general absence of Chicano experience from university curricula. In response, a Chicano Plan for Higher Education was published—*El Plan de Santa Bárbara*—calling for what would eventually result in the field of Chicano studies and the birth of Chicano studies scholarship. The U.S. feminist movement similarly responded to the fervor around civil rights. Inspired by the history of the women's suffrage movement in the 1920s, this movement worked to secure equality between the sexes in social, economic, and political contexts.

Chicana feminists responded to the ways in which they found themselves essentially absent from these two movements, despite the fact that they were in solidarity with the fundamental goals and purposes of both. The *women's movement,* as the feminist movement was often called, was largely a movement centered around White, Anglo (English-speaking) women, often of higher socioeconomic status than most Chicanas and influenced by very different root experiences and ways of life. Although women shared in the experience of *sexism,* the experience of race and class generally was not reflected in the feminism of the women's movement.

Similarly, although the Chicano movement was making great strides for the Chicano community, even its very name—the masculine form *Chicano*—reflected the taken-for-granted invisibility of Chicana women and of their rights to equal participation with men in the privileges being gained. The emphasis on the family, or *familia,* as the unifying concept or metaphor for Chicanos, like Mexicans, assumed the role of the woman as unquestioning child bearer and mother, sexual partner to the dominant man, and self-sacrificing—as Mary was in the "holy family." The roles of women in Mexican history and in the Chicano movement were largely invisible and unacknowledged; Chicana feminists found themselves bringing the awareness of the history of Mexican feminism to the attention of Chicanos as part of their claim of relevance.

Also absent in the formal rhetoric of the Chicano movement were the tensions between men and women and the influence of *machismo,* or the emphasis on defending and exemplifying male strength, in the domination and subordination of women. While Chicano men were enjoying the prospect of broader horizons and opportunity, Chicanas did not feel included.

Chicana Organizing

In response to these voids, Chicanas began to organize around their specific concerns. In 1971, in Texas, where the Chicano movement had led to the creation of the *Raza Unida* party, women organized a caucus within the party called *Mujeres por la Raza* [literally, Women for the Race]. *La Raza* is a Spanish colloquial term used by Chicanos to refer to themselves as a community united by race. This caucus succeeded in incorporating women's issues into the party's platform, and throughout the early 1970s, Chicanas held repeated conferences, focusing on developing organizational skills and coalition building for women. They also worked against the race and class biases present in Anglo women's politics and officially withdrew from the Texas Women's Political Caucus, endorsing a series of Chicana candidates for various state and local political offices. Although Mujeres ceased to exist when the Raza Unida party ended, the types of issues and activism that had begun did not. Similar efforts existed in other states, including the formation of a national organization for Chicanas—the *Comisión Femenil Mexicana Nacional* (National Mexican Women's Commission).

Chicana efforts to organize themselves were met with much criticism from within the Chicano community. Often they were accused of hurting the overall Chicano cause by emphasizing their own issues. However, the Chicana response was a strategy that recognized the significance of women's roles within the community. It sought to address *all* issues of inequity and to change the overall power dynamics operating: If domination of women within the Chicano community existed, it was not just women but the entire community that was affected by these imbalances of power.

Chicana Theorizing

The dynamics of these efforts would come to influence the nature of the social theories and literature developed by Chicana scholars and activists. Particularly influential was the late Gloria Anzaldúa, a Chicana scholar activist who addressed the tensions experienced by Chicanas by creating a theory of *borderlands* about Chicana experience. Anzaldúa, along with other Chicana feminists, suggested that what a dominant academic audience would consider important might not be similarly significant to Chicana women and their communities. This is a central issue for Chicana feminists: to create theory that can impact academic scholarship while remaining relevant to Chicana women's lives.

Whether traditional academic theory can capture and address the core issues of importance to Chicanas has implications, not just for the content of the theory, but also for the ways in which the theory is written. As such, the style and form of Chicana feminist writing in its purist forms are best described as *multigenre;* Chicana feminist writing includes a combination of different forms, such as poetry, performative writing, autobiography, narrative, and code switching (alternating in a text from one language or linguistic code to another). As a result, the theories and writings produced by Chicana scholars and activists do not often fit neatly into existing academic categories or disciplinary boundaries. This is seen as evidence of its validity rather than as a shortcoming.

Political Nature of Chicana Feminist Theory

Most significant to Chicana theories, and reflecting the political origins of Chicana feminism, is the embedded and explicitly political nature of the work. Chicana feminism seeks to avoid relying on Western theories and forms of thought in order to avoid the risk of reflecting colonialist assumptions present in traditional academic theories. Since Chicanas themselves are the product of colonialist processes of history, one of the more innovative aspects of Chicana feminist theory is that of imagining realities that might counter or resist the colonial.

This is apparent in the use of language, references to history, and narratives in nontraditional and surprising ways in order to move away from dominant modes of representation. The work of lesbian Chicana writers has been exceptionally powerful in challenging many of the colonialist issues embedded in the society they are resisting, calling into question the roles gender and patriarchy play in maintaining existing power relations. Similarly, works that question traditional representations of religious experience and Catholicism, as well as those that utilize indigenous traditions and symbolism to express theoretical concepts, force colonialist assumptions to be laid aside.

Reliance on Lived Experience as Basis for Authority

By drawing on lived experience as the basis for concepts and ideas that are developed in their work, Chicana feminists reflect the early intention of Chicanas not to be made invisible in the light of dominant movements or ideas. Chicana feminists employ a test of real-life validity to their work, where the evaluation must come not only from a scholarly community but from within the cultural *standpoint* the theory is representing. Much Chicana feminist work is *self-reflexive,* applying within itself tests of its own validity by applying cultural knowledge to the ideas as they are expressed.

Attention to Complexity in Chicana Feminism

Chicana feminist scholarship includes the awareness that a good theory will unsettle the dominant order in one or more of the dimensions that Chicanas address in their work. Chicana feminist theories acknowledge that race/ethnicity, religion, sexuality/gender, and social class do not exist separately but in complicated interaction with each other. A good Chicana feminist theory, therefore, is rarely unidimensional, instead focusing on the multiple dimensions that are contested and resisted in Chicanas' work. Their writing attempts to situate the various dimensions together, rather than separately, and the use of a combination of genres is one way of demonstrating the complexity of their arguments.

An example of this is the fact that a commitment to the inclusion of race/ethnicity as an inherent women's issue for Chicanas ultimately implicates the inclusion of Chicano men and Chicano and Chicana youth, along with adult women. The issues affecting the women are part of the social fiber of the communities that birth and nurture the growth of Chicanas. This motivates the historical separation from Anglo women's movements, as well as the view of male–female and other gender-related issues as part of the communication phenomena that must be explored for sound Chicana feminist communication theory.

Gender and complexity of self-representation are thus issues visible within the work of Chicana feminist communication scholars. Rhetorical and performance scholars have been particularly well suited to explore these issues of self-representation in work in keeping with the spirit of Chicana feminism. The work of Jacqueline Martinez utilizes a phenomenological approach to study themes of gender and sexual preference as a Chicana of mixed-race family history within the *habitus* or situated experience of her own life history. Michelle Holling explores the representation of women in Chicana literature, as well as the rhetorical strategies in 20th-century activist efforts that were, and continue to be, issues complicated by race, gender, and politics.

In addition to issues of extended family and historical background, the roles of religion and ritual are included as necessary aspects of Chicana feminist theory. Interdependence and solidarity within multiple Hispanic groups is implicit in theorizing about religion, with communication scholars particularly well suited to approach these interactional dynamics. An example is Sarah Amira De la Garza's book *Maria Speaks,* exploring the topic of self-expression and spiritual–cultural identity as a woman attempting to reconcile issues of matriarchy within a patriarchal, religiously Roman Catholic Chicana upbringing. Her book uses poetry, autobiography, and performative and creative writing as the forms for her ethnographic report, typical of Chicana writing.

In the work of Bernadette Calafell, interdependence and complexity are shown to be an inherent feature of the *gaze,* or perspective, that Chicana communication scholars utilize as part of their standpoint. Calafell explores Chicana and Chicano performance as part of the larger field of Latina and Latino performance but as also distinctly affected by race, gender, and politics.

These dimensions furthermore do not exist in the same patterns or with the same relevance for all Chicanas. Stories of migration, varieties of experience in the labor market, religiosity, and sexual mores and preferences all combine in unpredictable fashion to create what is united by the experience of oppression and domination. Linguistic variation and preferences further complicate the subject of Chicana feminist theory. The struggle to remain united despite the wide range of experiences that create the identities of Chicanas will continue to be a hallmark of Chicana feminist theorizing.

Sarah Amira De la Garza

See also Autoethnography; Critical Race Theory; Feminist Communication Theories; Feminist Rhetorical Criticism; Feminist Standpoint Theory; Latino Perspectives; Muted Group Theory; Narrative and Narratology; Performance Theories; Performative Writing; Power and Power Relations; Social Justice

Further Readings

Anzaldúa, G. (1990). *Haciendo caras/making face, making soul: Creative and critical perspectives by women of color.* San Francisco: Aunt Lute Press.

Arredondo, F., Hurtado, A., Klahn, N., Najera-Ramirez, O., & Zavella, P. (Eds.). (2003). *Chicana feminisms.* Durham, NC: Duke University Press.

Callafel, B. M. (2007). *Latina/o communication studies: Theorizing performance.* New York: Peter Lang.

De la Garza, S. A. (2004). *Maria speaks: Journeys into the mysteries of the mother in my life as a Chicana.* New York: Peter Lang.

DiCochea, P. R. (2004). Chicana critical rhetoric: Recrafting La Causa in Chicana movement discourse, 1970–1979. *Frontiers, 25,* 77–92.

Flores, L. A. (2000). Reclaiming the "other": Toward a Chicana feminist critical perspective. *International Journal of Intercultural Relations, 24,* 687–705.

Garcia, A. M. (1989). The development of Chicana feminist discourse, 1970–1980. *Gender & Society, 3,* 217–238.

Holling, M. A. (2002). Transformation and liberation amidst racist-assimilationist forces. *Review of Communication, 2*(4), 387–391.

Lugones, M. C., & Spelman, E. V. (1983). Have we got a theory for you! Feminist theory, cultural imperialism, and the demand for "the woman's voice." *Women's Studies International Forum, 6,* 573–581.

Martinez, J. M. (2000). *Phenomenology of Chicana experience and identity.* Lanham, MD: Rowman & Littlefield.

CHINESE HARMONY THEORY

Harmony is the cardinal value of Chinese culture. Chinese believe that the universe is in a process of constant change and transformation caused by the dialectical and dialogical interaction between yin and yang, the two opposite but complementary forces; harmony is the key to bringing continuity into this cycle of transformation. Thus, Chinese consider harmony as the end of human communication, in which interactants try to adapt to each other in order to reach a state of interdependence and cooperation.

Based on this Chinese belief, Guo-Ming Chen developed a harmony theory of Chinese communication in 2001, from which a total of four propositions, 23 axioms, and 23 theorems were generated. The theory has been applied to different aspects of Chinese communication behaviors, especially the process of Chinese conflict management.

The theory indicates that the ability to reach a harmonious state of human relationship is the main criterion Chinese use to evaluate communication competence. In other words, from a Chinese perspective, an increase in one's ability to achieve harmony will increase the degree of communication competence. Three principles should be followed to achieve harmony: (1) intrinsically internalize *jen*

(humanism), *yi* (righteousness), and *li* (rite); (2) extrinsically accommodate *shi* (temporal contingencies), *wei* (spatial contingencies), and *ji* (the first imperceptible beginning of movement); and (3) strategically exercise *guanxi* (interrelation), *mientz* (face), and power in the behavioral level.

Jen, Yi, and Li

Jen, embedded in the principle of reciprocity and empathy, is a collective virtue of showing love in interactions. Through a mutually and empathically dependent process, the essence of jen is emitted to sustain the harmonious interaction. Yi, as the internal criterion of appropriate communication behaviors, provides individuals with the capacity to exhibit flexibility and adaptability in a specific context dictated by social norms to reach harmony. Li symbolizes the formality of human interaction and connects an individual's character and social duties by following the rules of conduct and speech in communication. Only through following li can an individual actively adjust to the harmonious and hierarchical order of society, avoid embarrassing confrontations, and handle socially ambiguous situations to uphold the group control over egocentric tendencies. These three intrinsic concepts form the foundation of the inner structure of interactants in creating harmonious Chinese communication.

Shi, Wei, and Ji

Shi requires the ability of knowing the temporal relations to appropriately perform what one ought to in different stages of human interaction. Unable to recognize the change of temporal contingencies in interactions is detrimental to the achievement of harmony and therefore leads to a failure of communication. The spatial contingencies of wei consist of social context and communication environment. Knowing wei refers to the realization and distinctions of who, what, and where in the process of interaction, which is typically reflected in the hierarchical structure of human relationships. Thus, an increase in knowing wei will increase the development of harmony in Chinese communication. Ji is the hidden sign of the beginning of a movement that shows the trace of possible consequences of an ongoing interaction. Being competent to the Chinese means developing a harmonious state by knowing what is hidden and what is evident during the interaction. The way to foster the capacity of knowing ji is based on sensitivity and sincerity.

The intrinsic elements of jen, yi, and li form the latitude of Chinese communication, and the extrinsic elements of shi, wei, and ji form the longitude of Chinese communication; together they weave the contextual network of Chinese communication. This contextual network provides a field in which Chinese exercise various strategic skills to deal with their daily interactions. Chen's Chinese harmony theory stipulates guanxi, mientz, and power as the most fundamental communication strategies employed by the Chinese, which will ultimately decide whether harmony is achieved.

Guanxi, Mientz, and Power

Guanxi dictates the particularistic ties of interactants in the hierarchical structure of Chinese social network. It is treated as a social resource Chinese use to persuade, influence, and control the interaction in order to reach harmony or competence. The ability to distinguish the levels of hierarchical relationships in a social interaction then functions to develop a supportive and harmonious communication climate.

Mientz is the self-esteem or social prestige gained from the respect of one's counterpart in the interaction. A competent Chinese always knows how to make or give face to avoid causing emotional uneasiness of others, which may lead to damage to one's own image as well. In other words, to maintain the face of one's counterpart means to maintain harmonious friendship in the network of guanxi.

Power in Chinese society is embedded in the hierarchical structure of the social network, which ascribes power to the seniority one holds and authority one possesses. The elder and higher-social-status individuals are the locus of power, not only in personal and social interactions, but also in the workplace. These three elements reflect the strategic skills Chinese exercise in the web woven by jen, yi, li, shi, wei, and ji to achieve harmonious and competent communication.

Taken together, harmony is the axis of Chinese communication that is sustained by nine spokes: jen, yi, li, shi, wei, ji, guanxi, mientz, and power. The functions and interrelationships of these concepts form a holistic system of the ideal Chinese communication. The interaction and integration of these nine elements bring continuity into the endless transforming process of Chinese communication. Based on this theory, we understand that, to the Chinese, harmony is a state of equilibrium representing the fulfillment of competent communication by which four ultimate goals of human communication can be reached: a feeling of security, a feeling of togetherness, a joyful feeling of interacting, and a feeling of benefiting from the interaction.

Guo-Ming Chen

See also Confucian Communication Theory; Taoist Communication Theory

Further Readings

Chen, G. M. (2001). Toward transcultural understanding: A harmony theory of Chinese communication. In V. H. Milhouse, M. K. Asante, & P. O. Nwosu (Eds.), *Transcultural realities: Interdisciplinary perspectives on cross-cultural relations* (pp. 55–70). Thousand Oaks, CA: Sage.

Chen, G. M. (2002). The impact of harmony on Chinese conflict management. In G. M. Chen & R. Ma (Eds.), *Chinese conflict management and resolution* (pp. 3–19). Westport, CT: Ablex.

Cheng, C.-Y. (2006). Toward constructing a dialectics of harmonization: Harmony and conflict in Chinese philosophy. *Journal of Chinese Philosophy, 33,* 25–59.

Leung, K., Koch, P. T., & Lu, L. (2002). A dualistic model of harmony and its implications for conflict management in Asia. *Asia Pacific Journal of Management, 19*(2–3), 201–220.

CHRONEMICS

Chronemics is the study of the concepts and processes of human temporality, or connections with time, as they are bound to human communication interactions. Chronemics concerns the study and uses of various kinds of objective time involved in our daily timing and habits associated with our formal and informal obligations. However, chronemics also concerns subjective or personal temporalities. Combinations of subjective and objective time concern our own everyday *personal time*. It is this personal time, a combination of technical timekeeping and personal times and tempos, that is centrally and highly related to human communication. This entry is intended to explain how human temporalities comprise a nonverbal chronemics of human behaviors.

Chronemics is the newest area of nonverbal communication studies, and this new focus seems to link and bind together, for the first time, all other systems of nonverbal communication. All forms of nonverbal communication messages have their own temporalities, beginnings and endings, startings and stoppings, zeros and ones, befores and afters, faster and slower, and so forth. Verbal messages, too, have major temporal features. We could not possibly communicate without human temporality.

Chronemics should provide for a more dynamic study of emotional interactions between people. We are *Homo temporalis;* we all have a complex temporal identity, a composite of personal levels of time experiencing, to be discussed later in this entry. Chronemic studies developed from interdisciplinary time literature and research reports in biology, anthropology, sociology, and psychology.

Objective Time

Objective time concerns behaviors linked to our clocks, timekeeping devices, and calendars. These all deal with our comings and goings, the organization of communication events, and timing our everyday pursuits. Objective time concerns how most people reference time, times, and rates of change. Human attempts to develop timekeeping have been occurring for thousands of years. Marshall McLuhan noted that timekeeping devices are media that transform tasks and create new work and wealth by accelerating the pace of human associations or communication events. Most people do not understand that these devices have not dropped out of the sky; they developed from assumptions made long ago. The single most persistent and ongoing diffusion of innovation continuing its spread on a global scale is objective time.

Clock time was developed for use to standardize needed or valued shared experience, to regularize our meetings, our hellos and goodbyes, our work schedules, our everyday comings and goings. The first characteristic of a developed society is its temporal regularity. Without temporal signposts or objective time markers, our communication meetings would be far less in number. Without calendrical markers, days, dates, weeks, months, and years, made up of seconds, minutes, hours, and other objective markers or intervals, our lives would be very different. We often become somewhat objective in our own repetitive actions, routines, habits, and various forms of redundancies. Most of us are creatures of routine and regularity in our habitual daily schedules. We often seem to create objective *time pacers* to manage our daily behaviors.

Timing devices were created to produce lineally assumed equal intervals in a cyclic sequentiality. This helps people regularize and coordinate divergent personal and sociocultural time, timings, tempos, and rhythms, discussed later. Communication studies have been anchored in an objective time behaviorism that often neglects relativity theory and variable kinds of time. Many people reluctantly perform daily what Lawrence Wright has called a *chronarchy*, or the thoughtless regimentation of people by timekeeping. It should be understood that those who control local clocks control space or proxemics, as well as movements or kinesics though spaces. We develop many kinds of *timetables* and *schedules* in our social and work groups. Most of them have to do with expectancies, due dates, repeat activities, and how we order and structure our communication contacts.

Scientific and Technological Time

Scientific time and technological time are precise kinds of objective time. Unlike subjective or personal time, scientific and technological time, timing, and tempo concern consistent measures reflected in some kind of clock time. Unitizations of processes are critical for any kind of scientific or technological time. Science could not exist without an objective time, clocks, calendars, and other structural features that equally mark off assumed temporal intervals. Seriality and unitized sequentiality are important tools for scientific investigations. More convenient and faster contact speeds seem to parallel more and faster communication contacts. Communication between people is becoming more and more immediate and simultaneous; personally carried media are bringing people into immediate 24/7 contacts not possible before.

Technological time concerns our many kinds of media and their central forms. We often refer to media as channels of communication, not understanding that the brain is the channel of all other media channels. Today's communication media increase exposure to others. Objective time usage is balanced with subjective or personal time use.

Subjective or Personal Time

Genetic and Biological Time

Human genetics concerns a time and tempo, or what has been described as *chronogenetics*. Chronogenetic studies have shown that every gene has a timing structure, with control clocks that supply stabilities and transient clocks that indicate changes. Genetic temporalities interact with any infant's basal endocrinic and metabolic capacities and potentialities. Each of us has a unique biological time because we have inherited biological time from our ancestors. Genetic time concerns the study of the interactions of states and processes of human genes. States are stabilities in the chronogenetic codes, while processes concern transiences or changes in the genetic codes. The stabilities of a gene are called *ergons,* and the transiences or changes of a gene are called *chronons.* The study of *biostationarity* (stabilities) and *bioperiodicity* (rhythmicities) is called *chronobiology.* It is important to understand that genetic timing is what sets our biological clocks and explains why people seem to have widely ranging variations or differences in their biological tempos. Biological variations are always present, but often unconsciously so, and affect our communication processing as senders and receivers of communication throughout our lives.

Biological time involves biological rate variations or biological rhythms, biological drives, and the management of our biologic need tensions. The study of biological time began in 1937, when Pierre Lecomte du Nouy published his book *Biological Time.* While some communication scholars have recently introduced the idea of a communibiology, it should be understood that sociobiology studies are often communication based and have been developing for many decades.

If two people's biological processes are very different, their interactive attention and perceptions become affected. We can then become dysrhythmic in our interactions. When our hormonal, metabolic, and biological rhythms are out of sync during interactions, we personally have problems communicating with others. Whenever biological rhythms, especially daily or circadian rhythms, are involved in mutual contacts, the chances are that we are experiencing communicative entrainment. *Entrainment,* or attempting to become synchronized in interactions between people, is extremely important because it can often result in many communication difficulties or failures.

Our developmental processes and aging are connected to our genetic and biological clocks. The Law of Janet was described by Josef Holubar in his work *The Sense of Time: An Electrophysiological Study of Its Mechanisms in Man.* This law states that the length of a subjective duration of a sensation is inversely proportional to the length of life already lived. H. Hoagland, in his essay "Some Biochemical Considerations of Time," concurs in explaining that the slowing of oxygen consumption in the brain makes time appear to pass faster and faster as one ages, and in children rich in brain oxygen, time passes more slowly.

In short, time seems to crawl when we are young children and appears to rapidly fly when we get older. Time estimations are affected. The amount of oxygen to the cerebral cortex is very high in early developmental stages but decreases as we age and brain temperature drops. Our biological clocks slow down, and clock time seems to speed up as we increasingly age. Also, the acuity of all our sensory systems deteriorates.

Many pharmacological and psychotropic drugs and substances that are ingested in every sociocultural collective affect biological tempos and time estimates. Both illegal and medicinal drugs are often psychotropic stimulants or tranquilizers, and they affect our biological tempos. We also can be hyperaroused or hypoaroused naturally, being alert or not, being active or passive, being extroverted or introverted, and so forth, depending on our inherited biological time. Biological time periodicities help us to regularize and set the characteristics of our perceptual time, timing, and tempos.

Perceptual Time

Perceptual time concerns our processing of nonverbal cues or signals. *Signalic,* or perceptual, communication concerns how we induct the communication of others into our brains. This kind of communication is often called *semiotics,* or how we induct the nonverbal communication signals generated in our various natural, physical, technic, and social environments into our brains. This inducting-of-information process was proposed by Paul Fraisse long ago and concerns rhythmic induction. This requires us to see the world not as objects or spaces, as in objectivity, but as full of rhythmic waves and energy fields of tremendous complexity. We process light waves (seeing), sound waves (hearing), pressure waves (touching), molecular waves (smelling), biochemical waves (tasting), and other rhythmic inputs of stimuli. These waves are converted and channeled in sensory-specific ways into signalic impulses to our brains. The information is converted again when the signals are slowed and the information is spread in thermodynamic lakes of formation within, or information. These lakes of expanding and contracting energy fields are called *holoscapes* or *holograms* in *holonomic brain theory.*

Information that we have already stored in the main cortex of our brains, or old information, is called *déjà vu* (already seen) information. Our brains usually do not process much of this kind of information as it already represents our current, automatic, and familiar realities. When there is new information, it is called *jamais vu* information (never seen, new, novelty). The hippocampus of the human brain acts as a mapping function to screen out déjà vu formations and/or select jamais vu, incoming semiotics for processing. In a top-down fashion, we project our cortical holoscapes, or internal formations, on incoming stimuli, called bottom-up processes. Information processing is recursive and cyclic rather than a simple, in-or-out, linear process, as in older stimulus–response models of human communication. Information processing is an in-and-out-simultaneous process. We project these internal formations on what is received through the senses more and more as we age. This is due to the accumulation of more and more brain memories and the increasing development of the top-down brain axis, discussed later.

This projection on receptions is called *semiosis,* or perceptual time.

When we infer or intend meanings, we are dealing with a psychology of time, not a perceptual time. Meanings are not directly transmitted; only signals or nonverbal messages, perceptual times, timings, and tempos are transmitted. When the nonverbal or signalic world of messages is interpreted and made re-presentable, we are then concerned with meanings and psychological time.

Psychological Time

Psychological time concerns both objective and subjective temporalities, depending on what kinds or modes of consciousness are operative. The human brain not only concerns biological and chemical codes, semiotic or nonverbal communication; it also and basically concerns memories (what we call the past), attention and perception (the present), and anticipation/expectation (futurity), a time system. The human brain is a temporal organ that extends throughout our bodies and is projected by our senses onto our various environments. Our nowness expands and contacts; time must be variable in order for human brains to function as they do.

Karl Pribram, one of the world's leading brain experts and founder of holonomic brain theory, has posited three credible kinds of human consciousness. These three kinds of consciousness are related to how psychological time varies: objective consciousness, narrative consciousness, and transcendental consciousness.

Objective consciousness concerns linearities, serialities, sequences, unitizations, logistics, and ordinary or ordinal thinking. It is left-brained timing and sequentiality, connecting parietal lobe objective, reference memories with frontal lobe anticipations and expectations. This brain connection is called the *back–front brain axis.* Language is objectively ordered linearities and sequentialities. Consequentiality concerns objectively structured goal orientations as to where our objective sequences might lead us.

Narrative consciousness encompasses right-brained, quasi-linear processes: music, aesthetics, stories, poetics, metaphors, plotting, daydreaming, fantasies, and so forth. It concerns human emotions and feelings, as well as the practice of intuitive kinds of empathy, or "feeling into another," or interactions between the objective brain (left hemisphere) and the subjective brain (right hemisphere). This brain connection is called the *left–right axis*. Edward Hall's distinction between monochronic and polychronic time differences seems to be related to this objective–narrative difference. Hall's conclusion was that monochronic time concerns what is here called objective consciousness, and polychronic time concerns the functions of narrative consciousness. Hall was advocating a comparative chronemics to study sociocultural time differences and not merely talking about doing one "thing" at a time as opposed to multitasking.

Transcendental consciousness concerns nonlinear brain processes, including contemplation and meditational states, in which our everyday realities, our objective consciousness, is blocked. Any kind of linear or straight-lined sequential information disappears. We often have no recollection or remembrance of our transcendental journeys. However, many times, upon reentering our objective or everyday consciousness, we are puzzled as to where we have been. Sometimes we can experience insights, new ideas, and uplifting spirituality. Certain individuals and their social groups operate with different systems of psychological time, making for problems during sociocultural interactions.

Sociocultural Time

The manner in which a social group develops a temporal identity concerns how individuals are expected to act and behave in interactions with others. Some sociocultural groupings are focused on a past orientation, some are more present oriented, and some are future oriented. Supposedly, more developed groups are more involved in linear progression and future oriented. Most organizational and work groups of people are purposively bound to objective time, as progress and production are their main concerns. There are groups that are much more into narrative time than Western societies are. Much of the global population is anchored in a narrative time and not an objective temporality. Objective time, when introduced into many narrative-time groupings within nations, tends to significantly alter their cultural temporalities, changing the culture. It is important

for diffusion-of-innovation and intercultural-communication scholars to recognize their own objective-time biases. Some sociocultural groupings, too, are primarily concerned with the spiritual and nonlinear aspects of transcendental consciousness. The rhythms of particular natural environments and particular people-built environments and the communication rhythms in various social environments are all involved in sociocultural time.

The Advent of Chronemics

A number of scholars are responsible for the early development of time and communication studies before the word *chronemics* was coined. George H. Mead was a leading developer of the study of human acts and presentness. Harold Innis, a Canadian communicologist, produced a work entitled *Changing Concepts of Time* in 1952. Also in 1952, Edward T. Hall, under the auspices of the U.S. State Department's Foreign Service Institute, wrote an early work entitled *The Process of Change*. Hall was to write periodically about time and sociocultural relations over the next four decades. Marshall McLuhan, in several works, discussed time and human communication. Kenneth Burke, a rhetorical scholar, produced two early books, *A Grammar of Motives* in 1945 and *Permanence and Change* in 1965. Many other scholars in biology, anthropology, psychology, and sociology wrote about time and human relations.

The actual term *chronemics* was coined in 1972 by Fernando Poyatos, a Canadian linguist and semiotician. Poyatos, in dealing with the communication system of the speaker–actor, briefly discussed a chronemics that concerned conceptions and the handling of time as a biopsychological and cultural element of social interactions. Tom Bruneau developed the first article on time and nonverbal communication in 1974 and attempted to define a chronemics and outline its characteristics in 1977. Since these early works, a number of texts on nonverbal communication have increased commentary about chronemics.

Judee Burgoon, a researcher and theorist in nonverbal communication, outlined a new theory of communication concerning futurity, *Expectancy Violations Theory*, in 1978. In 1983, Edward T. Hall attempted to describe time as *The Dance of Life: The Other Dimension of Time*. Allen Merriam, in 1983, launched one of the first *comparative chronemics* studies, comparing Iranian–American differences in international communication. His work stands as a model that can be used to compare cultural time perspectives. The psychological theory of *planned behavior* has been introduced in communication studies in the area of organizing persuasion tactics.

The works of Joseph McGrath and Janice Kelly were important to the social psychology of time and to a communicatively based temporality. The writings of Eviatar Zerubavel on hidden rhythms and patterns of time in organizational communication are important. The research of John Honeycutt did much to develop the idea of *imagined interactions* in intrapersonal communication, with some futurity perspectives. Another perspective on futurity is the idea of the *consequentiality of communication*. Of course, all communication has some kind of an anticipated, expected, or eventual result, however fleeting. In recent years there has been a dramatic increase in communication publications dealing with *strategic planning*. A model of *organizational time* has been developed in an article by Dawna Ballard, "The Experience of Time at Work."

Chronemic studies need to include more interdisciplinary perspectives in their future developments.

Tom Bruneau

See also Cognitive Theories; Communibiology; Expectancy Violations Theory; Nonverbal Communication Theories

Further Readings

Ballard, D. I. (2008). The experience of time at work. In L. K. Guerrero & M. L. Hecht (Eds.), *The nonverbal communication reader* (pp. 258–269). Prospect Heights, IL: Waveland.

Bruneau, T. J. (1977). Chronemics: The study of time in human interaction. *Journal of the Communication Association of the Pacific, 7*(1), 1–30.

Bruneau, T. J. (1979). The time dimension in intercultural communication. In D. Nimmo (Ed.), *Communication yearbook 3* (pp. 423–434). New Brunswick, NJ: Transaction Books.

Bruneau, T. J. (1996). Subjective time, social interaction, and personal identity. In H. B. Mokros (Ed.), *Interaction and identity* (pp. 97–118). New Brunswick, NJ: Transaction Books.

Bruneau, T. J. (2007). Time, change and intercultural communication: A chronemic perspective. *Sign Systems Studies, 35*(1–2), 89–117.

Cohen, J. (1967). *Psychological time in health and disease.* Springfield, IL: Charles C. Thomas.

Davis, M. (Ed.). (1982). *Interaction rhythms: Periodicity in communication behavior.* New York: Human Sciences Press.

Gedda, L., & Brenci, G. (1978). *Chronogenetics: The inheritance of biological time.* Springfield, IL: Thomas.

Halberg, F. (1977). *Glossary of chronobiology.* Little Rock, AR: International Society of Chronobiology.

Hall, E. T. (1983). *The dance of life: The other dimension of time.* Garden City, NJ: Anchor Press/Doubleday.

Holubar, J. (1969). *The sense of time: An electrophysiological study of its mechanisms in man.* Cambridge: MIT Press.

McGrath, J. E., & Kelly, J. R. (1986). *Time and human interaction: Toward a social psychology of time.* New York: Guilford Press.

Zerubavel, E. (1981). *Hidden rhythms: Schedules and calendars in social life.* Chicago: University of Chicago Press.

Citizenship

Citizenship theory explains the cultural, social, political, economic, and legal processes that regulate national membership and belonging. Citizenship's influence in communication theory has been growing for the past two decades because citizenship theory makes manifest the specific ways in which legal and material systems of society shape cultural processes of basic social participation and enfranchisement. Although the term has been used to address quite a diverse set of questions, the most significant strands of citizenship theory in communication studies treat citizenship as civic practices, as an identity, and as a space for the exercise of political rights.

Civic Practice

Contemporary notions of citizenship began in the 1950s with the work of T. H. Marshall, who understood citizenship as full membership in a community. Marshall proposed three types of citizenship, including *civil citizenship*, which regulates basic liberal rights (e.g., property, liberty of movement, legal representation); *political citizenship*, which influences the individual's participation in the political system (e.g., voting, holding office); and *social citizenship*, which he understood as a person's right to economic and social security (e.g., unemployment insurance, public education). Since Marshall, these three types of citizenship have been used to scrutinize national political realities, including the unequal ways in which civic, political, and social rights are distributed among populations.

Although Marshall clarified the types of rights, responsibilities, and expectations attached to citizenship in modern nations, his emphasis on politics legitimized a most common use of citizenship as political work—as *civics*—here understood as the exercise of the political duties and obligations of individuals. This traditional use of citizenship implies that civics and activism can do the job of assuring substantive justice within and among communities, thus improving democratic structures.

The notion that democracy relies for its functioning on the ongoing civic work of citizens is rooted in particular versions of the political philosophy of *liberalism*. In these versions, liberalism is the path toward having a society that balances personal independence and justice. Often in such theorizing about liberalism, citizenship is understood as an ideal identity that individuals must embrace for the health of the nation and to which the political system should be responsive. Here, the citizen is a civic worker who produces the best conditions for democracy and liberalism.

In communication studies, this understanding of liberalism and citizenship informs work on performance and media activism, broadcasting policy, political communication, liberal feminism, and some versions of critical race theory. Though widely done, understanding citizenship only as civics has theoretical limitations. While perfectly suited for envisioning a more energized civil society and public sphere, this notion of citizenship is less suited for radical critiques of liberalism and democracy, thus limiting its critical uses.

Identity

Some radical critiques were already suggested in Marshall's work. Marshall defined citizenship as

membership, thus underscoring the need to challenge the way citizenship defines who can and who cannot be a member of the nation. At this level, citizenship is an identity that has legal roots. Simply, our original definitions of national citizenship allowed some and precluded others from having access to this legal identity and thus to the portfolio of civic, political, and social rights that Marshall references. Women, children, prisoners, and racial, ethnic, and national minorities, people without property, could not have access to full citizenship. Since, activisms and wars have expanded legal definitions of citizenship, but even today full citizenship is not legally accessible to some. Felons, children, homosexuals, women, disabled people, and immigrants have legally downgraded forms of citizenship.

Although legal definitions of citizenship are at the roots of citizenship understood as an identity, cultural notions of citizenship have some life of their own. This has been the lesson of radical feminism, postcolonial theory, poststructuralism, and critical race theory. Culture does the job of furthering the legal logic by which some people are better suited to embody citizenship than others, and thus culture sets the conditions for belonging. Wealthy, White, heterosexual, able adult males have been traditional icons of citizenship, and although this tradition is changing, these characteristics still play an undue role in limiting the social and political participation of anyone not embodying them.

For instance, cultural forms shaping the public sphere, such as print journalism, political blogging, television news, and political talk shows, are still dominated by the voices of White, heterosexual, able adult males whose perspectives tend to reconstitute political discourses that, within the liberal tradition, naturalize their own existence as the voices of politics. Meanwhile, women, racial minorities, homosexuals, disabled people, and immigrants are relegated to marginal areas of the public sphere (e.g., ethnic and soft news) or relatively trivial cultural forms such as entertainment news, "chick flicks," and "gangsta rap." Not surprisingly, these communities' sense of national belonging can be conflicted.

Political Rights

Narrow cultural and legal definitions of citizenship have had an effect on formal political and economic structures and have given way to the formal marginalization of minority cultural forms. Theorists argue that this marginalization significantly limits the cultural freedom of nonpowerful communities and call for understanding culture as a substantive category of citizenship rights. Often referred to as *cultural citizenship,* this perspective on rights argues that racial, ethnic, sexual, and other minorities are incapable of experiencing basic liberal freedoms if they do not have cultural spaces for expression. Thus, cultural citizenship calls for the creation and maintenance of a broad range of everyday activities such as festivals, ethnic media, theatre, and language preservation that together can function to energize minority expression. In addition, cultural citizenship scholars argue that these cultural spaces eventually can be used to claim civic, political, and social rights and thus improve the workings of democracy.

Hector Amaya

See also Critical Race Theory; Critical Theory; Deliberative Democratic Theories; Feminist Communication Theories; Gay, Lesbian, Bisexual, and Transgender Theories; Identity Theories; Ordinary Democracy; Political Communication Theories; Postcolonial Theory; Poststructuralism; Whiteness Theory

Further Readings

Berlant, L. (1997). *The queen of America goes to Washington city: Essays on sex and citizenship.* Durham, NC: Duke University Press.

Flores, W., & Benmayor, R. (Eds.). (1997). *Latino cultural citizenship: Claiming identity, space and rights.* Boston: Beacon Press.

Honig, B. (2001). *Democracy and the foreigner.* Princeton, NJ: Princeton University Press.

Marshall, T. H. (1973). *Class, citizenship and social developments.* Westport, CT: Greenwood Press.

Miller, T. (1993). *The well-tempered self: Citizenship, culture, and the postmodern subject.* Baltimore: Johns Hopkins University Press.

Mouffe, C. (1993). *The return of the political.* New York: Verso.

Patten, A., & Kymlicka, W. (Eds.). (2003). *Language rights and political theory.* New York: Oxford University Press.

Stevenson, N. (2001). *Culture and citizenship.* Thousand Oaks, CA: Sage.

CLASSICAL RHETORICAL THEORY

Aristotle defined rhetoric as finding all the available means of persuasion. Rhetoric was divided into five parts: *invention, arrangement, style, memory,* and *delivery.* Classical rhetoric can be defined as the period of rhetorical developments from Corax (470–? BCE), author of the first work on rhetoric, *The Art of Rhetoric,* or Socrates (469–399 BCE) to Augustine (354–430). Thomas Benson and Michael Prosser define the period of classical rhetoric generally from Socrates to Augustine; Joseph Miller, Michael Prosser, and Thomas Benson argue that the medieval period began approximately with Augustine and extended to about 1400 and the rediscoveries of classical works.

Plato submitted rhetoric to its first philosophical dissection in his Socratic dialogues. The major Greek classical rhetorical treatise was Aristotle's *The Rhetoric,* followed in Rome by Cicero, Quintilian, and Augustine. Five major classical rhetoricians include Plato (429– or 428–347 BCE or 420–348 BCE), Aristotle (384–322 BCE), Cicero (106–43 BCE), Quintilian (35–95 CE or 40–118 CE), and Augustine.

Plato

Plato, the most significant Western philosopher, articulated Western moral leadership of the universe and developed metaphysical and scientific thinking. In *The Republic,* he proposed the true lover of knowledge as naturally striving for truth and not content with common opinion but understanding the essential nature of things. His protagonist Socrates dialogically searched for truth, justice, high ethics, and goodness. Plato considered the *absolute idea of the good* as the highest form of perfect and invisible *ideas* or *forms* that are developed by inner meditation, in contrast with concrete objects, which he rejected as constituting real knowledge.

For Plato, the ideal republic included a philosopher–king to support virtue, justice, and wisdom; soldiers to protect and control the citizens in acquiring the society's honor; and the civilian members of the society to provide the material needs of the society. He believed that people would act in accordance with virtue if they knew what formed the basis of virtue. Plato excluded poets in his ideal republic since they dealt with illusion rather than reality.

Gorgias

One of Plato's early dialogues, the *Gorgias,* deals with truth, goodness, justice, and ethics but also contrasts monological rhetoric, which he considered like cooking or flattery, and interactive *dialectic,* or discussion, which leads intelligent individuals to reach the truth, perhaps by a kind of authoritarian consensus. Socrates implies that he knows what he doesn't know, while those who think that they are wise often know nothing. The old illustrious teacher of rhetoric, Gorgias, and his followers discuss with Socrates the meaning of a rhetorician and rhetoric. It appears that Socrates leads Gorgias into dialectical traps as Socrates believes that the unknowing rhetorician or orator can persuade crowds or mobs better than the experts in health, medicine, and legislation.

Socrates asks Gorgias what he considers his art to be. Gorgias answers that it is rhetoric. Essentially, Socrates and Gorgias discuss reality as found in philosophical dialectic versus the semblance or pretense of reality as found in rhetorical culture and thus generally untruthful discourse. In ending the dialogue, Socrates makes a geometrical equation that as self-adornment is to gymnastic, so is sophistry to legislation, and as cookery is to medicine, so is rhetoric to justice.

Phaedrus

Plato's later dialogue about rhetoric and love has Socrates and Phaedrus discussing a speech by the famous Greek orator Lysias about love. Socrates praises the speech for its eloquence but critiques its lack of adequate definitions. He offers and then disclaims his own speech but finally gives still another, better speech praising the madness of love. Socrates proposes that if a speech is good, the speaker knows the truth about the matters he speaks about. Socrates indicates that speeches must contrast justice and injustice, good and evil, and reality and the semblance of reality.

In the *Phaedrus,* Plato introduces a noble rhetoric, based on truth, justice, virtue, and goodness.

Socrates discusses both oral and written rhetoric, saying that as speech must lead souls by persuasion, a rhetorician must know the various forms of soul. The speaker or writer must also know the different classes of speech and also proper and improper words. Additionally, like Aristotle later, Socrates proposes that one should speak or write about things that are probable, based on first principles of goodness, justice, truth, virtue, and wisdom.

Plato calls on poets, persuasive orators or writers, and legislators to consider the importance of real knowledge, which leads to truth, supporting it by dialectic. Then, by that serious pursuit he might well be called a philosopher, or a lover of wisdom. Plato ends the dialogue by wishing that his own soul might be beautiful and that all his external possessions would be in harmony with his inner soul.

Aristotle

Aristotle was the Western world's first great encyclopedist, writing many treatises including ones on metaphysics, politics, analytics, logic, physics or natural philosophy, rhetoric, poetry or dramatic arts, music, mathematics, geometry, biology or zoology, and psychology. He called himself a *midwife of ideas.*

Unlike Plato, who saw the soul as a separate nonphysical entity imprisoned in the body, Aristotle viewed the soul as relative and integral to the body. He described psychology as the study of the soul. Through the soul, Aristotle believed that humans develop the moral and intellectual aspects of humanity; thus the orator has the responsibility to lead audiences not only to truth, justice, and goodness but also toward happiness and human perfection.

Aristotle separated the study of logic into *dialectic,* as reasoned and intelligent discussion, and *analytic discourse,* which tests opinions for logical consistency, proceeding through deduction to individual cases. This logic established a major premise, a minor premise, and a conclusion. Logic also includes the process of induction, or individual cases to general principles. Aristotle did not see politics as an abstract idea, as Plato did, but as principles moving toward actual cases with the goal of leading humans toward truth, justice, goodness, and happiness.

Nichomacean Ethics

This treatise by Aristotle dealt with ethics, truth, justice, goodness, and happiness, emphasizing the link between happiness and honor. He identified the causes of human happiness as having a good family, spouse, children, friends, community, education, health, and sufficient wealth for one's station in life, patriotism, and possibly dying gloriously on the battlefield for one's country. In this context, Aristotle argued that life has to be seen in completeness. His concept of happiness was essential in his development of metaphysics, psychology, politics, rhetoric, and poetry, in which he expanded Plato's views on ethics and happiness as being the proper topics of those lines of inquiry and thought.

The Rhetoric

In this treatise with three books, Aristotle defined rhetoric as finding all the available means of persuasion and as the counterpart of dialectics and politics. The first two books emphasized the classes of speeches, role of invention, classes of evidence, and the best ways to persuade the souls of one's audience. The short third book, probably added at a later time, emphasized the three remaining aspects of persuasion: style, memory, and delivery. *The Rhetoric* opened up the compositional, theoretical, analytic, and critical aspects of persuasion throughout Western history, but it was so influential that it has also led many later authors into viewing rhetoric as a mechanical system. Aristotle himself avoided the dilemma that later developed by creating an open and systematic approach to persuasion.

Beginning his treatise, he contrasted rhetoric as the counterpart of dialectic, both of which he claimed belonged to no definite science as all individuals engage in examining and submitting ideas to inquiry. Rhetoric is useful, Aristotle claimed, because truth and justice are naturally stronger than their opposites, and truth and justice will emerge in the process of offering proofs and telling one's story in political terms.

Aristotle defined three classes of speeches: future-oriented *deliberative* speeches, which argue what individuals should or should not do; present-oriented *epideictic* or ceremonial speeches, praising or condemning individuals and their actions; and past-oriented *judicial* or forensic rhetoric,

which persuades judges to decide whether an individual has or has not committed a crime and, if so, what the punishment should be. Aristotle believed that orators should be able to reason on both sides of a question in order to know the whole state of the case, not to promote evil, but to know the difference between good and evil. Unlike Plato, however, who believed that rhetoric itself must lead to moral conclusions, Aristotle argued that rhetoric is neither moral nor immoral, but amoral, as it is the orator who is responsible for leading audiences toward truth, justice, goodness, and happiness.

For Aristotle, persuasive speech must deal with probabilities as orators try to persuade their audiences by what is probable rather than what is absolute, or at least they must argue the difference between the possible and impossible. He said that artistic rhetoric must be concerned with proofs, which are a kind of demonstration, either through *enthymemes*—the most authoritative of proofs—in which the truth of one premise is well known and therefore is omitted, or by *syllogisms,* with the major and minor premises stated, followed by a conclusion. Aristotle's major rhetorical contribution was the notion that there are three kinds of artistic proofs: *ethos,* or ethical proof, which depends on the credibility of the speaker, knowledge of the subject, and good will for the audience; *logos,* or logical proof, which depends on enthymemes and syllogisms; and *pathos,* or emotional proof, depending on appeals to the audience's emotions, such as friendship, joy, anger, or sorrow.

In the second book, about the invention and arrangement of the speech, Aristotle wrote about how these proofs can be organized to persuade one's audience. Specifically addressing the Greek men of his day, he proposed that young men are most likely to accept and be persuaded by emotional proofs, middle-aged men are likely persuaded by a mix of logical and emotional proofs, and old men are persuaded by reasoned logic. Aristotle proposed that all speeches have at least two parts, the thesis and the proof. He also used the analogy of a human body to make this point: the head, the body, and the feet, or an introduction, proof, and conclusion, comprise the parts of a speech.

In the third book of *The Rhetoric,* Aristotle briefly emphasized rhetoric's central role in language, especially in terms of the metaphor, which he had earlier discussed in *The Poetics,* plus simplicity and clarity. He described all words as having denotative and connotative meanings as they may give the audience new knowledge. Aristotle called the metaphor and the simile figures of speech that enrich the orator's artistic proofs by bridging the unknown and the known, but he urged that they should always be used in moderation. Finally, he briefly commented on the quality of the orator's memory in recalling universal and specific commonplaces or topics to use in one's oratory, as well as the need for a proper delivery. These two concepts were much more fully developed in the Roman *Rhetorica CE Herrenium,* written about 85 BCE.

Marcus Tullius Cicero

Cicero was one of Rome's greatest statesmen, elected Consul in 64 BCE, as well as one of the greatest Roman jurists, orators, and rhetoricians. Among his best-known speeches are his Catiline orations, delivered in the Senate in 63 BCE against Lucius Catiline. Cicero claimed Catiline had conspired to overthrow the Roman republic. After Caesar's assassination in 44 BCE, Cicero delivered his 14 Philippic orations against Mark Antony, who then had Cicero assassinated in 43 BCE. Both Cicero's orations against Catiline and his Philippian orations are considered models of nearly perfect classical rhetoric.

Cicero had studied in Greece and was heavily influenced by Isocrates (436–338 BCE), the author of *Antidosis* and *Against the Sophists,* one of the most important Attic orators, and the founder of a rhetorical school in Athens who recommended the importance of rhetoric for the development of citizenship. Aristotle, whose discussion of logical and emotional proofs served as the foundation for invention and arrangement of speeches, was also an important rhetorical influence on Cicero. His own rhetorical influence extended to Quintilian (35–95 or 40–118 CE); Jerome, the translator of the Bible into Latin (347–419 or 420); Augustine (354–430); and Petrarch (1304–1374), who rediscovered many of Cicero's lost works, thus establishing the significance of Cicero's contributions for the Renaissance.

Cicero's rhetorical writings included his history of Roman oratory, *Brutus* (45 BCE); *Orator* (45 BCE), in which he identified the Greek Demosthenes (384 or 383–322 BCE) as the ideal orator, and by implication himself, arguing that the moral orator provided the best source for the advancement of civilization and government; and *On Oratory* (55 BCE), written after finishing his political and military career.

On Oratory

This treatise, replacing his youthful treatise *On Invention,* was written in three books, in what is called a Ciceronian or Aristotelian dialogue style, in contrast to Plato's more interactive Socratic dialogues. In *On Oratory,* Cicero uses an imaginary conversation among friends in 91 BCE to discuss the value of rhetoric; Lucius Licinius Crassus (115–53? BCE), one of the main participants in the dialogue, represented Cicero's own views.

Crassus argued that the power of oratory on assemblies could direct their inclinations wherever the speaker wishes or divert them from whatever the speaker wishes. Furthermore, he suggested that in every free nation, and most of all in communities that have attained the enjoyment of peace and tranquility, rhetoric is always the most superior art as the best source of civilization. After being challenged about this positive argument, Crassus responded that while he was aware of the foolish arguments by Gorgias for the value of the orator's style over knowledge, still the orator must be fully aware of the substance of the matter under discussion, as Socrates had proposed. Essentially, *On Oratory* discussed ethical and emotional proof more in the philosophical views of true rhetoric introduced by Plato's *Phaedrus* and in Aristotle's *Rhetoric* than in Plato's *Gorgias.*

Orator

Cicero's last rhetorical work, in the form of a letter to Marcus Junius Brutus, delineated his view of the ideal orator and argued that true eloquence requires excellence in both thinking and expression, dividing style into appropriate language and delivery. The great orator must master three rhetorical styles—the plain for simple topics, the middle for more profound topics, and the grand style for very important occasions, as was seen in the orations of Greece's perceived best orator,

Demosthenes. For Cicero, the ideal orator can speak in the courts or deliberative assemblies so as to prove, please, or persuade. Cicero called the orator of the grand style magnificent and undoubtedly possessing the greatest power in civilization.

Quintilian

A Spanish Roman, Quintilian was the first teacher of rhetoric in Rome to receive a state salary. His description of the true orator was the good man speaking well.

Quintilian wrote the 12 books of his *Institutes of Oratory* in about 95 CE when his patron, the emperor Domitian, was daily condemning many Roman citizens to death for the slightest expression of disrespect toward himself; he banished all philosophers from Rome for fear that they would turn people against him. Domitian entrusted the rhetorical training of his two young nephews to Quintilian, and Quintilian wrote the *Institutes* for them as a treatise recommending the moral education of young boys as future citizens and leaders. Quintilian emphasized that the orator must above all study morality. Both Jerome and Augustine utilized the values promoted in *The Institutes*.

After being lost, *The Institutes* were rediscovered in 1470 and had a major influence in the Renaissance. Quintilian proclaimed rhetoric as entirely practical and useful, and while admitting that it could be misused, argued that it should be considered a good rather than evil contribution, both to the individual communicator in developing ethical standards and to civilization itself.

Augustine

Augustine is typically considered the figure who bridges the classical and medieval periods. A teacher of rhetoric before converting to Christianity, Augustine in a sense essentially begins rhetoric anew. The contrast between *Verbum* as the word of God and *verbum* as the word of man was debated from the beginning of the Christian church. Jerome, a classical scholar and Christian best known for his translation of the Bible into Latin, frequently argued with Augustine about whether Christians could honorably utilize the ancient pagan rhetorical works. Jerome claimed his Ciceronian training was his great weakness in his moral development, and he gave up his study of classical rhetoric for Christianity. Augustine, however, in the fourth chapter of his treatise, *On Christian Doctrine,* argued that if pagan rhetoric could be used to honor God, then one could still utilize it. *On Christian Doctrine* not only ignores style over substance, it returned to Plato's idea of moving individuals to truth by preaching the word of God. Augustine agreed with Aristotle that rhetoric itself is neither moral nor immoral but that the speaker is responsible for developing wisdom and truth. Nonetheless, wisdom without eloquence is of small benefit to states, but eloquence without wisdom is often extremely injurious and profits no one.

Summary

Classical rhetoric is important as the foundation for the modern field of communication, and the elements of rhetorical training offered by classical rhetoricians continue to be the basis of rhetorical training today. At the same time, there continues to be considerable debate about the nature of rhetoric, its properties, functions, and ends, just as was the case in classical times.

Michael H. Prosser

See also Argumentation Theories; Community; Epistemology; Ethics Theories; Legal Communication Theories; Metaphor; Narrative and Narratology; Ontology; Persuasion and Social Influence Theories; Philosophy of Communication; Rhetorical Theory; Traditions of Communication Theory

Further Readings

Benson, T. W., & Prosser, M. H. (Eds.). (1969). *Readings in classical rhetoric.* Boston: Allyn & Bacon.

Clark, D. L. (1957). *Rhetoric in Greco-Roman education.* New York: Columbia University Press.

Kennedy, G. (1963). *The art of persuasion in Greece.* Princeton, NJ: Princeton University Press.

Kennedy, G. (1972). *The art of rhetoric in the Roman world: 300 BCE–CE 300.* Princeton, NJ: Princeton University Press.

Kennedy, G. (1980). *Classical rhetoric and its Christian and secular tradition from ancient to modern times.* Chapel Hill: University of North Carolina Press.

Kennedy, G. (1994). *A new history of classical rhetoric.* Princeton, NJ: Princeton University Press.

Miller, J., Prosser, M. H., & Benson, T. W. (Eds.). (1973). *Readings in medieval rhetoric*. Bloomington: Indiana University Press.

Murphy, J. J., & Katula R. A (Eds.). (1995). *A synoptic history of classical rhetoric*. Davis, CA: Hermagoras Press.

CO-CULTURAL THEORY

Co-cultural theory is a framework designed to provide insight into the communication behaviors of individuals with little societal power. Generated primarily from the research of Mark Orbe, co-cultural theory focuses on how culture and power affect communication. The theory focuses on various segments of society that have traditionally been described as being a part of subcultural or minority groups. This theory prefers the term *co-cultural group*. Initially, the theory focused on people of color; women; persons with disabilities; gay, lesbian, or bisexual persons; and those from a lower socioeconomic status. More recently, researchers have used the theory to study other groups, including the homeless, first-generation college students, immigrants, and international students.

The core concepts of co-cultural theory emerged from a series of qualitative studies designed to study communication processes from the perspective of those historically marginalized in social structures. These foundational studies drew on the ideas of muted group and standpoint theories and used a phenomenological methodology to gather descriptions of everyday communication inductively. In particular, the theory is based on a specific set of assumptions and related factors that help individuals understand how co-cultural group members use different practices (strategies) that are part of a larger communication orientation.

Co-cultural theory is based on five assumptions, each of which reflects a foundational idea found in *muted group* or *standpoint theory*. The first assumption states that a hierarchy of power exists in each society whereby certain groups of people have greater access to power than others do. In the United States, dominant group members include men, European Americans, able-bodied persons, heterosexuals, and those in the middle or upper class. The second assumption is based on the idea that dominant group members occupy most positions of power throughout society; these positions of influence are used to create and maintain societal structures that inherently benefit their interests. The third assumption of co-cultural theory explores how the reality of dominant group power impacts members of nondominant groups. In particular, it states that dominant group members' societal structures work overtly and covertly against individuals whose cultural realities are different from the cultural realities of those in power. The fourth assumption acknowledges the differences that exist within and between different co-cultural groups; however, it simultaneously recognizes the similarities that also exist within and across groups that occupy similar social positions. The fifth, and final, assumption states that co-cultural group members will be more aware of the importance of strategically adopting communication behaviors that help them negotiate dominant societal structures. Such behaviors will vary within, and across, different co-cultural groups.

According to the theory, co-cultural group members will communicate strategically in a way that reflects a particular *communication orientation*, and not all members of one co-cultural group will have the same communication orientation. How one communicates as a member of a co-cultural group is influenced by six factors: *field of experience, situational context, abilities* to enact different practices, *perceived costs and rewards, preferred outcome* (assimilation, accommodation, or separation), and *communication approach* (nonassertive, assertive, or aggressive). Different co-cultural group members will communicate in strategic ways based on how they negotiate these six factors. For instance, members of a small group of African American women may communicate in different or similar ways, depending on their upbringing, life goals, personalities, or other aspects of their identities. These similarities and differences, according to the theory, may also change depending on situational context. This idea is counter to existing research, which attempts to generalize the communication behaviors of nondominant groups.

Early research by Orbe and colleagues identified 26 different co-cultural practices and determined that different practices were associated with various communication orientations. Co-cultural group members, for example, will use an *assertive assimilation orientation* if they seek to fit in with dominant group members through behaviors that assert their own rights without violating the rights of others. This orientation would involve the co-cultural practices of *extensive preparation* (engaging in extensive amounts of groundwork before interactions with others), *overcompensating* (working extra hard in order to be accepted), *manipulating stereotypes* (exploiting existing stereotypical views for personal and professional gain), and *bargaining* (creating overt or covert agreements to ignore co-cultural differences).

In comparison, an *assertive separation orientation* would be enacted for co-cultural group members seeking to work independent of dominant group members. This orientation involves *communicating self* (interacting with others openly, authentically, and genuinely), *intragroup networking* (working with other co-cultural group members), *exemplifying strength* (promoting the positive attributes of one's co-cultural group), and *embracing stereotypes* (redefining traditional negative stereotypes and incorporating them into a positive self-concept).

In addition to these two orientations, the theory conceptualizes seven others—*nonassertive assimilation, aggressive assimilation, nonassertive accommodation, assertive accommodation, aggressive accommodation, nonassertive separation,* and *aggressive separation*—each of which has several co-cultural practices associated with it. While early research defined this framework, subsequent research has continued to fine-tune these co-cultural orientations by adding, revising, and debating how different practices are used for different purposes in different situational contexts.

Co-cultural theory has been heralded for its effectiveness in creating a theoretical lens to understand the communication behaviors of underrepresented group members from their own respective perspectives. In addition, it is valued for the ways in which it resists cultural generalizations by highlighting the diverse forms of co-cultural communication. Simultaneously, the theory reveals the commonalties inherent in how individuals attempt to negotiate discriminatory societal structures, regardless of the source of their oppression. Critics

of co-cultural theory have questioned the logic of this approach and pointed to the dangers of equating sexism, racism, classism, heterosexism, and other forms of social oppressions. Others have argued that the process of co-cultural communication is not specific to particular groups; instead it is something that all individuals experience as they occupy less powerful positions throughout their lives. Despite some of the limitations associated with this theory, co-cultural theory holds great promise for promoting an increased understanding of the inextricable relationship of culture, power, and communication.

Mark P. Orbe

See also Culture and Communication; Feminist Communication Theories; Feminist Standpoint Theory; Intercultural Communication Theories; Muted Group Theory; Phenomenology

Further Readings

Kirby, E. (2007). Organizing to "meet like real Americans": The case of a Hmong nonprofit organization. In B. J. Allen, L. A. Flores, & M. Orbe (Eds.), *Communication within/across organizations* (pp. 201–228). Washington, DC: National Communication Association.

Lapinski, M. K., & Orbe, M. (2007). Evidence for the construct validity and reliability of the co-cultural theory scales. *Communication Methods and Measures, 1*(2), 137–164.

Orbe, M. (1998). *Constructing co-cultural theory: An explication of culture, power, and communication.* Thousand Oaks, CA: Sage.

Orbe, M., & Spellers, R. E. (2005). From the margins to the center: Utilizing co-cultural theory in diverse contexts. In W. B. Gudykunst (Ed.), *Theorizing about intercultural communication* (pp. 174–191). Thousand Oaks, CA: Sage.

Cognitive Dissonance Theory

Cognitive dissonance theory is concerned with how perception and cognition influence and are influenced by motivation and emotion. Hundreds of experiments have tested dissonance processes. For the most part, these experiments have explored the ways that the experience of cognitive dissonance causes attitude and behavior changes.

Leon Festinger formulated the original theory of cognitive dissonance in the mid-1950s. Festinger theorized that when an individual holds two or more elements of knowledge that are relevant to each other but inconsistent with one another, a state of discomfort is created. He called this unpleasant state *dissonance*. Festinger theorized that the degree of dissonance in relation to a cognition = D/(D + C), where D is the sum of cognitions dissonant with a particular cognition and C is the sum of cognitions consonant with that same particular cognition, with each cognition weighted for importance.

Festinger theorized that persons are motivated by the unpleasant state of dissonance to engage in cognitive work so as to reduce the inconsistency. To reduce the dissonance, individuals could add consonant cognitions, subtract dissonant cognitions, increase the importance of consonant cognitions, or decrease the importance of dissonant cognitions. One of the ways of reducing dissonance assessed most often is change in attitudes. Attitude change in response to a state of dissonance is expected to be in the direction of the cognition that is most resistant to change. Tests of the theory often assume that one's most recent behavior is usually most resistant to change, because it is often very difficult to undo that behavior.

After a decision, all the cognitions that favor the chosen alternative are consonant with the decision, while all the cognitions that favor the rejected alternative are dissonant. The greater the number and importance of dissonant cognitions and the lesser the number and importance of consonant cognitions, the greater the degree of dissonance experienced by the individual. In a decision situation, dissonance is typically greater the closer the alternatives are in attractiveness (as long as each alternative has several distinguishing characteristics).Dissonance caused by a decision can be reduced by viewing the chosen alternative as more attractive and/or viewing the rejected alternative as less attractive.

Dissonance is typically aroused when a person acts in a way that is contrary to his or her attitudes, especially when no one provides encouragement or incentive for doing so. Individuals may reduce this dissonance by changing their attitudes to be more consistent with their actions. Dissonance can also be aroused by exposure to information that is inconsistent with beliefs or attitudes.

Some theorists hypothesized that the effects were due to nonmotivational, cognitive processes or impression-management concerns. However, subsequent research confirmed that dissonance is a motivated process. Beginning in the late 1960s, researchers began to propose motivational explanations for dissonance effects that differed from Festinger's theory. Four revisions have been proposed.

Elliot Aronson proposed that dissonance is not due merely to an inconsistency between cognitions. Instead, he posited that dissonance occurs when a person acts in a way that violates his or her self-concept, that is, when a person performs a behavior inconsistent with his or her sense of self. Since most persons have a positive self-concept, dissonance is most often experienced when a person behaves negatively, behaving in an incompetent, irrational, or immoral manner. One of the primary predictions derived from this revision is that individuals with low self-esteem and individuals with high self-esteem should respond with less and more dissonance reduction (e.g., attitude change), respectively, because in dissonance experiments, individuals with high self-esteem are induced to act in ways that are more discrepant from their positive self-views. Experiments testing this prediction have produced mixed results.

Claude Steele's self-affirmation theory proposed that persons possess a motive to maintain an overall self-image of moral and adaptive adequacy. Accordingly, dissonance-induced attitude change occurs because dissonance threatens this positive self-image. While Festinger's dissonance theory posited that individuals are motivated to reconcile inconsistent cognitions, Steele proposed that individuals are merely motivated to affirm the integrity of the self. In support of this idea, Steele presented experiments in which, following a dissonance induction, participants either were or were not presented with an opportunity to affirm an important value. When participants were allowed to affirm an important value, dissonance-related attitude change did not occur. Other experiments have suggested that making important but non–self-affirming values salient reduces dissonance by reducing the individual's perception of the importance of the dissonant act, consistent with Festinger's theory.

Joel Cooper and Russell Fazio proposed the idea that the discomfort experienced in dissonance experiments was due, not to an inconsistency between the individual's cognitions, but rather to feeling personally responsible for producing an aversive consequence. In support of this idea, experiments revealed that dissonance-related attitude change occurred only in conditions in which an aversive consequence was produced. More recently, experiments have found dissonance-related arousal and attitude change in induced compliance conditions where individuals do not produce aversive consequences.

Several experiments since 1995 have supported the original conception of dissonance theory. But why does dissonance evoke this state? Eddie Harmon-Jones proposed an action-based model of cognitive dissonance in an attempt to answer this question. The action-based model proposes that the perceptions and cognitions likely to arouse dissonance are those that are associated with action tendencies. The action-based model further proposes that dissonance between cognitions evokes an aversive state because it has the potential to interfere with effective and unconflicted action. Dissonance reduction, by bringing cognitions into consonance, serves the function of facilitating the execution of effective and unconflicted action. Experiments have revealed that experimentally increasing the degree of action orientation experienced following difficult decisions increases the degree of dissonance reduction.

Eddie Harmon-Jones

See also Attitude Theory; Persuasion and Social Influence Theories; Power, Interpersonal

Further Readings

Festinger, L. (1957). *A theory of cognitive dissonance.* Stanford, CA: Stanford University Press.

Harmon-Jones, E., & Mills, J. (1999). *Cognitive dissonance: Progress on a pivotal theory in social psychology.* Washington, DC: American Psychological Association.

COGNITIVE RULES MODEL

See Cognitive Theories

COGNITIVE THEORIES

The term *cognition* simply refers to mental activities. Thus, in everyday conversation, when people make reference to *paying attention, planning, forgetting, guessing, daydreaming,* and so on, they are invoking cognitive concepts. The domain of mental activities is obviously very broad, encompassing everything that transpires from the initial perception of a stimulus (e.g., the sight and scent of roses and letter shapes on a card) to evocation of thoughts and emotions, and even production of overt responses (e.g., verbal and nonverbal expressions of joy and appreciation). Cognitive theories provide an important window on communication processes because both message production and message comprehension ultimately transpire in the mind.

The objective of cognitive theories is to describe the mental system(s) that give rise to the various phenomena of interest. In other words, explanation (and prediction and control) comes from specifying the nature of the mental structures and processes responsible for producing a particular phenomenon (in much the same way that one might explain the movement of an automobile by describing the action of the pistons, drive shaft, and so on). At the most fundamental level, cognitive theories focus on explicating foundational mental processes such as the nature of attention, perception, comprehension, memory, and response production. As an approach to illuminating the sorts of issues of interest to communication scholars, cognitive theories have been developed to address phenomena as diverse as communication skill acquisition, social anxiety, memory for messages in the mass media, romantic relationship development, and group decision making.

Historical Background

Cognitive science is a broad, interdisciplinary enterprise that draws from numerous intellectual traditions, among them philosophy, sociology, psychology, linguistics, artificial intelligence, and communication. The systematic, empirical investigation of mental processes dates to the late 19th century, with the work of Wilhelm Wundt and others, but some authors have suggested that the actual inception of *cognitivism* as we know it today did not occur until the mid-1950s. Prior to that time, *experimental psychology* had been dominated by various versions of *behaviorism* that gave little heed to unobservable mental processes. Nevertheless, other fields of study, including *social psychology* and *developmental psychology*, had made ready use of mentalistic concepts at least since the 1920s and 1930s. In that same period, early researchers in speech departments began to focus on topics such as attitude change and the processing of persuasive messages.

By 1970, incorporation of the assumptions, models, and methods of cognitivism into social psychology had led to the development of *social cognition*—an area of study focused on how people acquire, store, and use socially relevant information, especially information about themselves and others. These topics, quite naturally, were of interest to communication scholars, and during the decade of the 1970s, cognitive models of various symbolic and social processes began to appear in the field of communication. By the time Michael Roloff and Charles Berger's edited book, *Social Cognition and Communication,* was published in 1982, the cognitive perspective was firmly ensconced as a way of theorizing about communication processes. The impact of cognitivism in advancing understanding of communication phenomena extends to the present, as evidenced by the work reported in David Roskos-Ewoldsen and Jennifer Monahan's recent volume, *Communication and Social Cognition.*

Types of Cognitive Theories

Cognitivism is a general perspective that encompasses a number of only partially overlapping modes of theorizing. Although it is not exhaustive, one approach to distinguishing types of cognitive models identifies three basic theoretical stances. The first of these seeks to explain behavior by recourse to *brain structures and processes.* A particularly important development driving advances in theories of this sort is the growing use of neuroimaging techniques, such as functional magnetic resonance imaging, which allows researchers to identify areas of the brain involved in communication activities such as processing spoken language or viewing mass media content. In contrast, at the other end of the continuum of cognitive approaches are theories that invoke the terms of *folk psychology* as explanatory constructs. By *folk psychology* is meant the mentalistic terms employed in everyday parlance. Examples of such terms abound, but they include conceptions of *goals, plans, attitudes, self-concept,* and so on. The standard model of theorizing in the tradition of folk psychology is to explain behavior by recourse to one's goals and the information (or beliefs) at one's disposal.

Occupying something of a middle ground between theories cast in neuroanatomical terms and those cast at the level of lay psychology are theories expressed in functional terms. Theories of this sort seek to explain the phenomena of interest by specifying the *functional architecture* (as opposed to the physical architecture) responsible for observed regularities. Thus, functional theories are cast at the level of *mind* rather than *brain.* Theorists working at this level assume that the activities of the mind are instantiated in some way in the brain, but they are not terribly concerned with the precise nature of that link. It is this approach to theorizing that, to date, has been most common among communication scholars pursuing development of cognitive theories. Examples of functional-level theoretical constructs include conceptions of *schemas, scripts, associative networks, procedural records,* and *processing capacity.*

Distinguishing theories whose terms are essentially physical, functional, or of folk psychology is useful for identifying what sort of theoretical "animal" one is dealing with (and what sorts of data are relevant to informing and testing those theories). At the same time, such a simple three-category scheme is limited by the fact that, in practice, theories may blur the line between approaches. It is very common, for example, for hybrid theories to attempt to explicate commonsense terms in functional ways (thus, theories have been developed to specify the nature of the memory structures that represent self-concept, attitudes, etc.). On the other side of the continuum's midpoint, theories developed within the discipline of *cognitive neuroscience* attempt to illuminate the link between brain and mind (i.e., the ways that the physical systems of the brain produce the functional systems of the mind).

Information Processing Systems

One of the key conceptual underpinnings of cognitive science is the notion that the mind is comprised of a series of subsystems, each responsible for carrying out certain operations along the path from stimulus to response. A rudimentary scheme for organizing discussion of these subsystems distinguishes three major processing stages: input processing, memory, and response generation. Although useful as an expository device, such a general scheme comes with the caveat that these processing subsystems overlap, and in fact, each contributes to the functioning of the others.

The input-processing system entails the mechanisms responsible for attention, perception, and comprehension. It is this system that allows us to recognize letters and words on a printed page, to identify facial expressions of emotion, to hear auditory stimuli as music, to follow the plot of a movie, and so on. The response-generation system is responsible for the production of both covert (i.e., mental) and overt (behavioral) outputs. The activities of this system, then, include processes such as goal setting, response planning, behavioral monitoring, and motor control.

The memory system is the repository of information acquired via the activities of the input-processing and response-generation systems. As such, the memory system holds both declarative information (i.e., factual knowledge) and procedural information (i.e., the knowledge that underlies the ability to perform skilled activities such as driving a car or pronouncing the phonemes of one's native language). Cognitive theories typically distinguish between long-term and short-term (or working) memory systems. Long-term memory is an essentially unlimited-capacity system that, as the label suggests, retains information for extended periods of time (i.e., years, or even decades). In contrast, the working-memory system holds a small amount of information, often assumed to be that of which a person is consciously aware, and this only for brief periods of time (i.e., on the order of seconds).

Cognitive Theories Bearing on Communication Processes

Specific examples can help illustrate the nature and range of application of cognitive theories that bear directly on communication processes. Certain cognitive theories (e.g., action assembly theory, heuristic-systematic model) are addressed elsewhere in this encyclopedia and need not be covered here, but other examples are useful for illustrating the diversity of cognitive theories addressing communication phenomena.

Limited-Capacity Model

The idea that humans possess a finite pool of processing resources that can be flexibly allocated to carry out various information-processing tasks, and the corollary notion that some activities make greater demands on processing resources than others, dates to the pioneering work of Daniel Kahneman. Building on these ideas, the limited-capacity model, developed by Annie Lang and her associates, is concerned with processing of messages in the mass media. A general integrative framework, the model incorporates conceptions of limited processing resources, controlled and automatic processing, and appetitive and aversive motivational systems to address how people attend to, store, and retrieve media content. Noteworthy, too, in this approach is the use of physiological operationalizations to tap underlying processing mechanisms.

Construction-Integration Model

A fundamental principle to emerge from the study of perception is that it involves the interplay of bottom-up (or sensory-driven) and top-down (or conceptually driven) processes. This idea is at the heart of Teun van Dijk and Walter Kintsch's model of discourse comprehension. This model addresses the ways that people are able to assign meaning to individual words and clauses (or propositions), to link successive clauses, and to arrive at an understanding of the overall gist of a message. Van Dijk and Kintsch hold that comprehension involves the interaction of perceptual systems, long-term memory of personal experiences and general knowledge (e.g., word meanings), and a dynamic cognitive representation of the message that is being processed. With regard to this final component, a key aspect of the model is the distinction between the representation of the message itself, the *textbase,* and the *situation model*—a representation of what the text is about (e.g., the actors, actions, events). The authors note that memory for the textbase is typically much more limited than memory of the situation model.

Dynamic Memory Theory

In their early work on people's ability to understand and remember narratives, Roger Schank and Robert Abelson gave emphasis to the role of *scripts*—long-term memory structures representing familiar sequences of events (e.g., visiting a restaurant). In light of subsequent empirical research, Schank revised some of his earlier notions in developing *dynamic memory theory,* a description of the memory structures involved in processing current events by relating them to previous similar experiences. In this later formulation, less emphasis is given to the role of structures representing fixed sequences of specific types of events, and more attention is devoted to *memory organization packets* (MOPs)—more general memory structures that apply to whole classes of situated activities (e.g., conducting purchasing transactions). MOPs, then, organize sequences of more specific scenes (e.g., selecting grocery items from store shelves, going through the checkout line). Beyond its obvious implications for understanding the comprehension of narratives, the MOP concept has found application in the study of a variety of other communication phenomena, as is illustrated in the work of Kathy Kellermann and others.

Relational Framing Theory

Studies of interpersonal relationships consistently converge on the finding that they are arrayed along three dimensions: affection–hostility, dominance–submission, and involvement–noninvolvement. In relational framing theory, James Dillard, Denise Solomon, and their associates address the processes by which people make use of cues to draw conclusions about the nature of their relationships along these fundamental dimensions. According to the theory, virtually any statement or other social cue can be interpreted either with respect to its implications regarding the affection–hostility (liking) dimension or the dominance–submission (power) dimension. The theorists propose that cognitive structures, termed *relational frames,* allow people to make sense of, or understand, the relational significance of what would otherwise be ambiguous behaviors. The liking and power relational frames exert mutual inhibitory influence such that activation of one frame tends to suppress the other. The effect of cues relevant to the third relational dimension, involvement, is to intensify interpretations associated with the activated relational frame, whether it be liking or power.

Cognitive Rules Model

One of the pervasive understandings in the study of social behavior is that people act in the pursuit of various goals. Common examples of classes of goals include objectives such as securing material resources, establishing or maintaining interpersonal relationships with certain characteristics, and creating a desired image of oneself in the minds of others. Steven Wilson's cognitive rules model addresses the processes by which a person formulates his or her interaction goals. The model invokes an associative network architecture—an approach to addressing memory phenomena that has found very widespread application in cognitive science. An associative network consists of nodes that represent concepts and links that represent relationships between nodes. In the cognitive rules model, features of social situations, characteristics of one's conversational partner(s), and so on are linked with particular objectives. When a person encounters a specific configuration of situational features, the interaction goals associated with those features tend to be activated, and if this activation exceeds a threshold value, a goal is formed. Other aspects of the theory extend this basic formulation to address the effects of individual differences, situational ambiguity, and familiarity on social-goal formation.

Attitude Accessibility Theory

The attitude construct is a staple of social science, but research suggests that the relationship between attitudes and behavior is more complex than might initially be supposed. In an effort to better understand the link between attitudes and behavior, theorists like Russell Fazio (in psychology) and David Roskos-Ewoldsen (in communication) have pioneered the notion that attitudes may be more or less accessible in memory, and that accessibility, in turn, determines whether and how attitudes play a role in message processing, behavior, and attitude change. Like the cognitive rules model, attitude accessibility theory assumes an associative network architecture in which concepts, corresponding to attitude objects, are linked to evaluations. And, as in standard network models, the links between nodes vary in their strength such that when a given concept is activated, any evaluations with which it is strongly linked will be rapidly and automatically retrieved. In contrast, when associative links are weak, people may have to deliberate to determine their evaluation of a person, thing, or event. Among the predictions suggested by the theory are that readily accessible attitudes are more likely to predict behavior and to persist over time than are attitudes that are less accessible.

Planning Theory

Models of plans and planning were among the earliest developments in cognitive science, dating almost to its inception. Plans are typically held to be mental representations of a sequence of steps leading from some current state of affairs to a desired goal. Charles Berger's planning theory is a noteworthy example of the application of the plan construct to explication of communication phenomena, particularly message-production processes (although the theory also applies to understanding the actions and messages of others). According to Berger, plans are hierarchical, with abstract action specifications at the top (e.g., persuade someone to purchase this used car) and successively more concrete steps below (e.g., offer a 30-day warranty). The theory further asserts that plans vary in their complexity, both with regard to their specificity and in their incorporation of contingencies and alternative paths of action. An important element of the theory is the *hierarchy principle*, which suggests that when a plan is thwarted, people will revise lower level (i.e., more concrete) action specifications rather than the more abstract elements of their plans.

John O. Greene

See also Action Assembly Theory; Attitude Theory; Attribution Theory; Communication and Language Acquisition and Development; Communication Goal Theories; Communication Skills Theories; Elaboration Likelihood Theory; Heuristic-Systematic Model; Intrapersonal Communication Theories; Learning and Communication; Uncertainty Reduction Theory

Further Readings

Berger, C. R. (1997). *Planning strategic interaction: Attaining goals through communicative action.* Mahwah, NJ: Lawrence Erlbaum.

Churchland, P. M. (1988). *Matter and consciousness* (rev. ed.). Cambridge, MA: Bradford.

Dillard, J. P., & Solomon, D. H. (2005). Measuring the relevance of relational frames: A relational framing theory perspective. In V. Manusov (Ed.), *The sourcebook of nonverbal measures: Going beyond words* (pp. 325–334). Mahwah, NJ: Lawrence Erlbaum.

Fazio, R. H., & Roskos-Ewoldsen, D. R. (2005). Acting as we feel: When and how attitudes guide behavior. In T. C. Brock & M. C. Green (Eds.), *Persuasion: Psychological insights and perspectives* (2nd ed., pp. 41–62). Thousand Oaks, CA: Sage.

Gardner, H. (1987). *The mind's new science: A history of the cognitive revolution.* New York: Basic Books.

Greene, J. O. (2008). Information processing. In W. Donsbach (Ed.), *The international encyclopedia of communication* (Vol. 5, pp. 2238–2249). Malden, MA: Blackwell.

Greene, J. O., & Morgan, M. (in press). Cognition and information processing. In W. F. Eadie (Ed.), *21st century communication: A reference handbook.* Thousand Oaks, CA: Sage.

Hewes, D. E. (Ed.). (1995). *The cognitive bases of interpersonal communication.* Hillsdale, NJ: Lawrence Erlbaum.

Jones, E. E. (1998). Major developments in five decades of social psychology. In D.T. Gilbert, S. T. Fiske, & G. Lindzey (Eds.), *The handbook of social psychology* (Vol. 1, pp. 3–57). Boston: McGraw-Hill.

Kellermann, K., & Lim, T. (2008). Scripts. In W. Donsbach (Ed.), *The international encyclopedia of communication* (Vol. 10, pp. 4517–4521). Malden, MA: Blackwell.

Kintsch, W. (2005). An overview of top-down and bottom-up effects in comprehension: The CI perspective. *Discourse Processes, 39,* 125–128.

Lang, A. (2000). The information processing of mediated messages: A framework for communication research. *Journal of Communication, 50,* 46–70.

Roskos-Ewoldsen, D. R., & Monahan, J. L. (Eds.). (2007). *Communication and social cognition: Theories and methods.* Mahwah, NJ: Lawrence Erlbaum.

Schank, R. C. (1982). *Dynamic memory: A theory of reminding in computers and people.* Cambridge, UK: Cambridge University Press.

Wilson, S. R. (1995). Elaborating the cognitive rules model of interaction goals: The problem of accounting for individual differences in goal formation. In B. R. Burleson (Ed.), *Communication yearbook 18* (pp. 3–25). Thousand Oaks, CA: Sage.

COLLECTIVE INFORMATION SAMPLING

Early conceptualizations of collective information sampling (CIS) arose in the mid-1980s in an attempt to give insight into the nature of communication processes and information management within decision-making groups. Garold Stasser and William Titus found that members of decision-making groups tend to communicate and discuss information that all members already know in common (*shared information*) at the expense of discussing information that individual members may uniquely know (*unshared information*). This tendency to favor shared information has a significant impact on the efficacy of group decisions and flies in the face of most intuitive communication thinking. The further development of the theory helps to extend and explain the nature of information sharing within groups, especially those groups that have been given the task of making an important decision within a specific communication context. The major tenets of this theory include not only the explication of the CIS bias toward discussing shared information but also the unpacking of the *mutual enhancement* effect that underpins CIS, as well as a discussion of additional factors that moderate this otherwise robust bias.

Collective Information Sampling Bias

The CIS bias toward discussing shared information is relatively counterintuitive. After all, the assumption is that decision-making groups are formed in order to disseminate information to group members that they may otherwise never discover on their own; groups are then expected to use the collective knowledge of members to make a decision that is better informed than that of any one individual. However, in 1985 Stasser and Titus uncovered the tendency for group discussions to favor *shared information* over *unshared information* to a much greater degree than is predicted by simple probabilities. In a group setting, the probability that a certain piece of information will be discussed, $p(D)$, is based on the following model: $p(D) = 1 - [1 - p(R)]^n$. This model relates the probability that a member will recall and contribute an item of information ($p(R)$) to the number of members who can potentially recall the item (n). This model shows, through basic algebraic computations, that information that is held by more than one member has a significantly higher probability of being mentioned in a group conversation or task. However, actual groups perform much differently than predicted by the model, such that shared information is favored in discussions to a much greater degree than simple probabilities suggest. Unexpectedly, decision-making groups prefer to talk about information that everyone in the group already knows, and they do so significantly more than group organizers likely hope. Essentially, members do not disseminate much new information but instead prefer to discuss information that is likely already known by other group members.

As a result of this lack of new information obtained during discussion, decisional outcomes are often biased toward the prediscussion preferences of individual group members; this bias toward prediscussion preferences is typically found even when the pooled information strongly favors a different decision alternative. Put simply, people often go into groups with a slight bias toward a decision, and other group members do not reveal enough new information to sway that decision; as such, groups are not able to make decisions any better than any one individual within the group.

Mutual Enhancement

In addition to Stasser and Titus's finding that group members are more likely to communicate shared information than unshared information in a decision-making group, later research has found that those group members are also likely to evaluate their group experience more positively when members discuss mostly shared information (similar to those processes present in *groupthink*). That is, members will rate the group interaction more favorably and will report greater satisfaction with the final decision when the group discussion emphasizes shared information that all or most members previously knew. In the late 1990s, this self-congratulatory group effect became known as the *mutual enhancement* effect. *Mutual enhancement* is likely caused by group members' needs to feel validated and affirmed by other group members. Studies show that members tend to repeat shared information in order to affirm themselves, appear credible to the group (*impression management*), receive favorable ratings from members of the group (*face negotiation*), and/or create a rapport with other members of the group. That is, one group member may be likely to mention something that other group members already know to be true, so that he or she can feel validated as other members display their verbal or nonverbal agreement with that statement.

Moderators of Collective Information Sampling

One way that researchers better understand the myriad potential moderators of CIS involves the experimental use of a *hidden profile* information sheet, much in the same manner as the original Stasser and Titus CIS research, which reveals shared and unshared information. By varying the proportion of shared and unshared information that is given about two options in a decision-making task, one can measure the extent to which groups discuss that hidden unshared information based on the proportion of groups that choose the more correct option as the favored alternative.

Using this hidden profile method, many potential variables have been found that decrease this bias toward the discussion of shared information during group decision making. Research has found that group knowledge of individual expertise (through formal or informal channels) allows members the freedom to discuss unshared information to a greater degree. Additionally, group norms that encourage critical interaction often overcome the mutual enhancement needs of members. Structural considerations also have been shown to significantly decrease the otherwise robust nature

of CIS, including the introduction of leadership styles, the delineation of expert roles, the addition of time pressure, and the demarcation of member status.

Jonathan M. Bowman

See also Face Negotiation Theory; Group Communication Theories; Groupthink; Impression Management

Further Readings

Propp, K. M. (1999). Collective information processing in groups. In L. R. Frey, D. S. Gouran, & M. S. Poole (Eds.), *The handbook of group communication theory and research* (pp. 225–250). Thousand Oaks, CA: Sage.

Stasser, G., & Titus, W. (1985). Pooling of unshared information in group decision making: Biased information sampling during discussion. *Journal of Personality and Social Psychology, 48,* 1467–1478.

Wittenbaum, G. M., & Bowman, J. M. (2005). Member status and information exchange in decision-making groups. In B. Mannix, M. Neale, & M. Thomas-Hunt (Eds.), *Research on managing groups and teams: Status and groups* (pp. 143–168). London: Elsevier Press.

COMMUNIBIOLOGY

The communibiological paradigm refers to a perspective on the study of human communication that focuses on the role of neurobiological systems in the production of behavior. Individual differences in communication behavior are conceptualized as reflecting individual differences in neurobiological systems. The initial rationale for the communibiological paradigm was based on the fact that after 30 years of research effort, the learning paradigm had failed to account for acceptable percentages of variance in either traits or behaviors. Similarly, models that suggested that humans can respond spontaneously to the demands of social situations also failed to produce accurate prediction of what people do during social encounters. The communibiological paradigm was proposed to lead to more accurate predictions of communicative behavior.

Within the communibiological literature, it is common for the paradigm to be expressed as a set of propositions parallel to those first proposed in the temperament literature. The propositions evolved as new research findings were published and as social and behavioral scientists changed the way they thought about the nature of social interaction. Before these propositions are examined in detail, it is important to place them in perspective. First, the propositions were not offered as knowledge claims. Instead, they should be viewed as assumptions or axioms on which theories can be constructed. All theories are based on assumptions. One of the most conspicuous characteristics is the explicitness with which theoretical assumptions are stated. Second, each proposition is heavily supported by empirical research. Although the propositions are not knowledge claims, a considerable body of research in support of each proposition is presented to demonstrate that the propositions are reasonable. The propositions presented below represent the most current version of the communibiological paradigm.

The first proposition is that *all mental processes involved in social interaction are reducible to brain activity*. It might seem obvious that all mental processes can be reduced to brain activity, but the implications of that proposition are incompatible with some lines of thought about interpersonal communication. The proposition indicates that communibiology takes a reductionistic perspective on the relationship between the mind and the brain. This means that all mental activity first begins as brain activity. As cognitive psychologist Steven Pinker has argued, to say that we can control our thoughts makes no sense unless by the term *we,* the activity of a cluster of brain cells is implied. Communibiology rejects the notion that some metaphysical force or entity guides thinking. Drawing heavily from the work of neuropsychology, the communibiological paradigm depicts the subjective experience of self-control as an illusion created by the left hemisphere in the cortex.

The second proposition in the communibiological paradigm is that *communicator traits and temperament characteristics represent individual differences in neurobiological functioning*. In the communibiological literature, communicator traits have been conceptualized as expressions of temperament. Traits play a central role in the communibiological paradigm. It should be clear to casual observers that people differ from one another in the way they react to stimuli. When people can be differentiated on the basis of their reactions, trait labels are used to refer to individuals. For example, if someone routinely reacts with anxiety when forced to interact with others in a social situation, that person might be referred to as socially anxious. In this case, social anxiety would represent a trait. According to the communibiological perspective, any theory of communication that ignores communicator traits is necessarily and substantially incomplete. The proponents of communibiology argue that this incompleteness will manifest itself most conspicuously in weak predictive power such as that observed in the learning theories. Studies conducted along the lines suggested in the communibiological literature have resulted in substantially more accurate predictions of behavior than have been observed in the situational paradigm research.

In the development of the second proposition, research was cited that demonstrated that individuals could be sorted correctly into high or low levels of various traits such as extraversion or aggressiveness on the basis of biochemical by-products detectable in body fluids after exposure to a stimulus. For example, the hormones present in the saliva of a person who is inclined toward aggressive behavior are noticeably different from those of a typically passive person after conflict with a stranger. It was primarily this type of research that communibiologists marshaled in support of their proposition. Although more research focused on the trait–behavior relationship is warranted, the linkage between traits and individual differences in neurobiological functioning distinguishes the communibiological perspective from other trait models of behavior.

The third proposition is that *individual differences in the neurobiological systems underlying communicator traits are principally (but not completely) inherited*. Care should be taken not to interpret this proposition as meaning that communication behavior itself is inherited. According to the communibiologist, behavior represents an outcome of traits that are manifestations of neurobiological systems that are mostly heritable. Behavior usually results from more than one trait, and the impacts of situations are not direct but mediated through personality and neurobiological filters. All this makes for a complex relationship among factors that determine behavior. Individual differences in neurobiological systems are not entirely inherited, as prenatal hormone cascades can also shape dimensions of personality. Prenatal hormone effects are neither genetic nor environmental in the social learning sense, but they are biological.

At present, there are no studies that show a direct link between specific genes and the neurobiological systems proposed as determinants of communication traits and behaviors. Rather, the evidence cited in the communibiological literature has shown an indirect connection. This is because linking specific genes to the behaviors that interest communication scholars has not been a priority for geneticists. Nevertheless, the communibiologists maintain that there is more evidence for assuming that neurobiological structures are inborn than for assuming that structures are produced by experience or were assembled randomly. Three lines of research are cited in support of this proposition.

First, a huge body of studies referenced in the communibiological literature indicates that individual differences in temperament, which reflect individual differences in neurobiology, are observable in newborn infants before experience could possibly shape the traits observed. Second, studies link the presence of specific hormone combinations during pregnancy to the development of the infant's personality. Finally, findings from the huge number of studies that have compared similarities of identical twins with those of fraternal twins are persuasive in support of the proposition that neurobiological structures are mostly inherited. Biogeneticists point out that identical twins are genetically identical whereas fraternal twins are no more genetically alike than any other sibling pair. Therefore, high degrees of similarity between identical twins and low degrees of similarity for fraternal twins indicate the presence of hereditary influences. The percentage of influence due to heredity can be estimated from the correlations for the two types of twins. Meta-analyses, which are quantitative summaries of research, show that on average, about 70% of the variance among individuals in a cluster of variables related to interpersonal affiliation (e.g., friendliness, sociability, social competence) is heritable. Furthermore, social anxiety was 65% heritable, and aggressiveness was 58% heritable. Although the results of twin studies are not definitive with respect to the role of heredity, the communibiologists maintain that twin studies, in combination with the newborn temperament observations and the prenatal hormone exposure studies, provide ample evidence to consider the proposition as a reasonable one.

Finally, the fourth proposition advanced in the communibiological paradigm is that *dimensions of situations have only negligible effects on behavior.* Individuals react to situations based on their traits rather than situations. Indeed, research shows that people respond differently to the same situation. Furthermore, research indicates that the nature of the response to a situation is heavily determined by the person's traits. According to communibiologists, individual traits contribute to behaviors in three important ways. First, individuals place themselves in circumstances that are compatible with their traits. Second, individuals' temperaments contribute to the situation itself. Third, interpretations of the situation are strongly influenced by the individual's personality. All these factors are seen as interacting in the production of behavior.

The alternative position is that situations have direct and strong effects on behavior. However, this position stands in contrast to the results of over 20 years of research that does not show strong situational effects. The communibiologists argue that the relatively small direct effects reported in the research are due to the assumption that all people react the same way to a given situation. According to communibiology, individuals show preference for situations and react variously to them.

In the communibiological literature, the four propositions are organized sequentially into a causal chain. Specifically, genetic inheritance and prenatal hormone exposure are seen as leading to the development of neurobiological system parameters, which in turn dispose individuals to different types of temperaments, which in turn dispose the individual to particular behavioral responses. This depiction of a causal chain is proposed in the communibiological literature as the framework for building theories about specific communication constructs.

Michael J. Beatty

See also Interpersonal Communication Theories;
Learning and Communication; Social and
Communicative Anxiety; Social Interaction Theories;
Trait Theory

Further Readings

Beatty, M. J., McCroskey, J. C., & Pence, M. E. (2008).
Communibiological paradigm. In M. J. Beatty, J. C.
McCroskey, & K. Floyd (Eds.), *Biological dimensions
of communication: Theory, methods, and research*
(pp. 1–14). Cresskill, NJ: Hampton Press.
Pinker, S. (1997). *How the mind works.* New York:
W. W. Norton.
Wilson, E. O. (1998). *Consilience: The unity of
knowledge.* New York: Vintage.
Zuckerman, M. (1995). Good and bad humors:
Biochemical bases of personality and its disorders.
Psychological Science, 6, 325–332.

COMMUNICATION
ACCOMMODATION THEORY

See Accommodation Theory

COMMUNICATION ACROSS
THE LIFE SPAN

Humans have considered and written about their
time-bound nature since they had the leisure to
do so. And while the life course probably has not
changed all that much, the way we understand it
has. Life span communication theory should
describe, explain, and predict the modifications
that occur to human communication and thus to
its outcomes over the course of a life span. This is
a tall order, but it goes to the heart of what makes
communication so interesting: It is what makes
us human, what makes us capable of self-change,
and what creates our social worlds. What follows
is a brief history of life span scholarship and how
it informs the specialty of life span communication, a summary of the challenges to studying life
span changes, examples of communication phenomena that have been tested for age differences,

and the current status of life span communication
as a theory.

Background

Scholars of sociology and cognitive psychology
were the first to formally study the life progression of human behavior. Sociologists prefer the
term *life course* to life span and examine the
effects on social policy of changing demographics.
Psychologists are more interested in individual
cognitive changes across the life span. Some, such
as Laura Berk, who did much of the research on
the developmental function of private speech, may
refer to their specialty as *human development.*
Particularly in psychology, life span work arose
from the study of early childhood development. In
the 1920s, Jean Piaget systematically studied the
cognitive development of very young children and
assumed that development ended with the teen
years. But life continues.

The premise of any life span approach to human
behavior is that the potential for human development extends across the life span. In the communication discipline, the key factor in human
development is *spoken symbolic communication,*
which makes possible self-directed change.

In 1989 Jon F. Nussbaum, inspired by the
founding work of other social scientists, was the
first communication scholar to formally articulate a life span perspective. His view is that a life
span perspective can subsume all other communication theories under its umbrella. However,
as both Nussbaum and Nikolas Coupland, a
sociolinguist, pointed out a few years later, the
early work in communication development did
not conceptualize language and interaction as
constitutive of life span experiences, meaning
that people come to understand such experiences
in terms of how they actually communicate
about these experiences. And this is an important distinction for communication theorists to
make. Although sociolinguists and psycholinguists do acknowledge the constitutive nature of
language, communication theorists are best positioned to explain the link from spoken symbolic
interaction to individual identity and distinctively human experience. However, the empirical
research necessary to support this link rarely
appears in the communication literature. One

reason for this gap is that life span methodologies are complicated and take time to execute well. Perhaps a more important reason is the relative newness of life span study and the resulting dearth of graduate-level coursework in life span theory and methods.

Methodological Concerns

Sophisticated methods for studying life span changes arose from the limitations found in existing research designs. In 1988, Paul Baltes, Hayne Reese, and John Nesselroade wrote the book, literally, on research methods for life span developmental psychology. Communication studies of life span change using the simplest appropriate sampling designs—cross-sectional and longitudinal—have appeared in the past decade or two.

Cross-sectional has been the most frequently employed design because the researcher collects data from different age groups at one point in time, thereby avoiding the problems involved in following subjects over many years. The remaining difficulty with gathering data from subjects of different ages is that the samples may not be comparable—in fact, probably are not. Confounding cohort influences may make for a difference between groups; 5-year-olds in 1973 may have had different experiences than 10-year-olds did in the same year. If you ask a set of siblings about that year, you will receive very different answers that are not attributable just to age but to other influences: parenting, teaching practices, access to world events, and so forth. Another source of variation in cross-sectional design is the measurement itself. With very young children, some measures, such as written surveys, are not feasible. And with interviews or observations, the effect of the researcher's attention alone may have unwanted effects. Julie Yingling has interviewed children in treatment for cancer who ranged from age 3 to age 17. Even though the same set of questions was asked of each child, the answers received were not comparable across age groups. The very young children just enjoyed the talking and playing; the teens were serious and thoughtful in their responses. So, results were descriptive but not generalizable, or true for all children in treatment. Cross-sectional designs are quick but not always productive of useful developmental data.

Longitudinal designs, which follow the same person or relationship over time and repeated observations, may seem ideal for examining developmental processes, but they bring different problems. Some measurements (e.g., surveys) are prone to practice effects. If we study the same participants over several months or even years, and use the same survey measure, the participants will become accustomed to it and may remember past responses rather than respond anew. One solution is to use observational measures instead of subject-controlled measures, in which the answers are controlled by the subjects who provide them. Yet another source of variance may be time of testing or observation. If the researcher's plan is to measure at the same time of day over several weeks, months, or years, the time of day itself could be producing an effect (8:00 a.m. can be very different experientially from 8:00 at night). The more severe problems include attrition (no researcher wants to end a longitudinal study with only half of the original subjects), the demands of time (often counted in years) that ignore the tenure clock, and the lack of flexibility to refine study procedures and theory as the field develops past the study. Nonetheless, longitudinal designs are appealing in their capacity to show people as they change. One example of their allure was the very popular British ITV television series that began in 1964 as "Seven Up" and documented a group of 7-year-olds every 7 years, ending with "Forty-Nine Up." Charming and interesting as it was, it could not claim to be solid scholarship about development, although it raised intriguing questions about culture and aging.

Even before life span research began, those who studied child development proposed more-sophisticated designs created to eliminate the disadvantages of both cross-sectional and longitudinal studies. In 1953, Richard Q. Bell suggested alternate sampling to assess differences across sets of cohorts matched on chronological age. A decade later, K. Warner Schaie went further by proposing a *general developmental model* that involves three sequential designs, each of which varies two factors of the three he views as critical to behavioral performance: chronological age, birth cohort, and time of measurement. These three designs (cross-sequential, cohort sequential, and time sequential) require successions of studies, like so: Time 1 observation: ages

10, 15, 20; Time 2 observation (5 years past Time 1): ages 10 (new group), 15 (the original 10s from Time 1), 20 (the original 15s), and so on. The general developmental model controls for many sources of error and can generate solid descriptive data.

Beyond method and design, complex statistical analyses that lend themselves to the study of change have appeared more recently. Two applicable to life span communication data are *linear sequential modeling* and *complexity theory* (also called *chaos theory* or *the new science*). Rather than test mean differences, sequential modeling can solve more complex problems involving analysis of variance and covariance matrices, thus moving beyond simple description to the possibility of prediction.

Complexity theory originally was developed by physicists and biologists to explain nonlinear dynamics in living organisms, and then it excited interest in the social sciences. The biologists were inspired by Ludwig von Bertalanffy's 1968 *general systems theory*. As with systems theory, complexity models are meant to describe the nonlinear and dynamic nature of change and the nature of mutual influence among interacting levels of systems. Complexity theory has been used to examine weather patterns, traffic flow, tipping points, and abuse dynamics in families. However, the nonlinear mathematics involved in modeling these processes are not easily accessible or available to communication scholars, and not likely to be in the near future. At this time, a communication scholar interested in developmental issues must find colleagues in other social sciences to assist in shoring up communication studies' developmental foundations. Those foundations now consist of a few theoretical perspectives and a growing body of descriptive studies.

Developmental Research in Communication

Concepts that recur in life span communication include those that define variables borrowed from psychology: attachment, accommodation, personality, identity, private speech, and social support, and those that are primarily communication variables: persuasiveness, cognitive complexity, conflict management, comforting, dialectical tensions, and turning points.

Regardless of the phenomenon studied, current life span communication practitioners have, for the most part, studied either children's communication or late-life communication rather than developmental changes in communication across the full range of the life span. Only very recently have communication researchers begun to examine systematically points in the human life span other than the first or last.

Scholars examining early development have favored *systems* approaches. In 1993, Laura Stafford and Cherie Bayer plotted the existing research on parent–child interaction by the direction of influence used to explain change: unidirectional, bidirectional, and systems process (or multidirectional), demonstrating the superiority of systems models for examining patterns of interaction and mutual influence. Four years later, Beth Haslett and Wendy Samter acknowledged systems theory as useful to studying *communication and language acquisition,* while emphasizing four structural layers critical to a developmental perspective of children's communication: sound, meaning, grammar, and discourse. Psycholinguists would use the terms *phonetics, semantics, syntax,* and *pragmatics* for those concepts. Regardless of terminology, any scholar of development would have to give some consideration to how these structures are acquired and how they interact in infancy and early childhood. Thus systems theory has been the prevailing choice of those studying early development for its ability to demonstrate mutual influence of communication structures, as well as interactional partners.

On the other end of the spectrum, those examining aging have chosen to test very specific communication theories across age groups to challenge the implicit assumption that studying communication practices in college-age subjects produces reliable explanations. Most communication theories are tested first in college populations, and many go no further. But at least two theories in common usage have been tested across age groups: attachment theory, borrowed from developmental psychology, and accommodation theory, which originated in sociopsychology.

Attachment theory emerged from the 1991 observation by John Bowlby and Mary D. Slater Ainsworth that parent–child interaction affects personality development. Explanations drawn from ethological research support the view that attachment serves a protective function for humans as much as it does for young birds and monkeys. For Ainsworth and Bowlby, the crux of the matter was that early caregiver interaction leads to either security or insecurity; that in turn lays the foundation for the child's personality development and later attachments. With the repetition of a given response to caregivers over time, the child forms one of four working models of self and others, creating a more or less enduring attachment style by adulthood: secure (positive models of self and others), dismissive (positive self model, negative other model), preoccupied (negative self model, positive other model), and fearful (negative models of self and others).

Although it is not featured in early versions of the theory, Laura Guerrero recently noted that communication is a cause of attachment style; the caregiver clearly sets the stage for the infant to learn interaction skills. The nature of the dynamic between them will affect the child's attachments, perhaps for a lifetime. Attachment styles have been considered fairly stable, given a strong early infant–caregiver bond and subsequent reinforcement of that attachment—which is highly likely given that the developing child will be most comfortable participating in the same dynamic over and over. However, critical life events such as death or divorce can precipitate change in attachment style. Not only is communication a cause of attachment style, it can also be a consequence or mediator of style and can certainly reinforce or modify style. Several studies have shown that, in relationships, partners' attachment styles interact to predict communication patterns. Guerrero suggests that the reverse could be true: By developing more socially skilled styles of communication, people could improve their models of self and others, thus modifying their attachment style toward the secure. Attachment theorists have predicted relational satisfaction from style for some time, but this approach can be used much more widely to examine all sorts of influences between communication and working models for self and other as they function and change throughout the life span.

Accommodation theory was developed in 1975 by Howard Giles and Peter Powesland to explain how communication behaviors change depending on whom our interaction partner happens to be. It has since been modified to a communication accommodation theory that explains the process by which we can both reduce and magnify communicative differences between people. *Convergence* toward another by approximating the other's communicative behavior enhances similarities and reduces uncertainty. For example, adopting a conversational partner's accent or vocabulary can lead the partner to perceive the accommodating speaker as more similar to the partner and perhaps as more likable. *Divergence*, on the other hand, can be triggered by dislike of another, by wanting to appear as different as possible from the other. However, accommodation theory is more complex than simply that. Researchers have found that context and perception affect results, thus allowing for the complexity of development. Accommodation theory has proven useful for the study of relational development and intergenerational communication. Mary Lee Hummert's work from the 1990s on suggests that as we age, we develop more sophisticated stereotypes of aging. That is, older adults have more positive views of aging than do younger adults. The use of communication accommodation theory contributes to what we know about life span changes in communication and promises to continue to do so.

Life Span Communication as a Theory

Although there have been studies that examine (a) intergenerational differences, (b) links between self- and other-perceptions and communication behavior, and (c) changes with increasing age, there have been precious few to tackle the developmental questions of life span change in communication from an overall theoretical perspective. Systems theory seems appropriate but is so general as to explain very little about change until all the subsystems and linkages have been first described. One useful attempt to flesh out systems theory is Urie Bronfenbrenner's *ecological systems theory,* first proposed in 1977, which has been used to study the influences of school and home subsystems on early childhood communication but has yet to be used extensively for life span studies.

Jon F. Nussbaum and his colleagues Loretta Pecchioni and Kevin Wright treat the study of the communication life span as an umbrella theory under which all communication theories can fit. Their perspective, set forth in 2005, uses broad assumptions: (a) It is the nature of human communication to foster development, (b) life span communication involves multiple levels of knowledge, (c) change can be both quantitative and qualitative, and (d) unique methods are required to capture communication change. These assumptions are nearly axiomatic; few who study development or communication would argue against them. The theory has served well to pull together disparate communication research programs for a broader view of how communication changes across the life span.

In 2004, Julie Yingling also set out a series of assumptions to support a *relational–dialogical perspective* of communication development. In her view, human communication development is a *dialectical* process that first relies on physiological endowments, then builds symbolically and interactively across the life span. Stated briefly, her assumptions include the following: (a) The human mind is constructed with boundary experiences, or symbolic interactions with others; (b) these are internalized to create an identity that may fluctuate as communication experience fluctuates; and (c) internalizations of experience occur in cycles, the peaks and valleys of which may be viewed as *turning points*. This perspective relies heavily on the theory of *relational dialectics,* in which Leslie Baxter and her colleagues describe the process of *making meaning* between partners from the interplay of competing discourses. The fact that making meaning, a distinctively human symbolic activity, is both diachronic (occurs over time) and synchronic (in one moment in time) gives a clue to the developmental effects of meaning making. As we make meanings, we create and modify identity and social reality. In the process, we learn how to view self, how to view others, and how to view self *with* others. Such a dialectical process is inherently developmental and therefore fitting for the study of life span communication.

Both of the articulated perspectives of life span communication provide a starting point for filling in the blanks in our understanding of how, when, and why shifts in communication, identity, and social meaning occur in the human life span. Both theorists frame the existing communication literature to describe an overview of life span changes in communication.

Julie Yingling

See also Accommodation Theory; Attachment Theory; Communication and Language Acquisition and Development; Communication in Later Life; Communication Theory of Identity; Relational Dialectics; System Theory

Further Readings

Baltes, P. B., Reese, H. W., & Nesselroade, J. R. (1988). *Life-span developmental psychology: Introduction to research methods.* Hillsdale, NJ: Lawrence Erlbaum.

Berk, L. E. (1998). *Development through the lifespan.* Needham Heights, MA: Allyn & Bacon.

Coupland, N., & Nussbaum, J. F. (Eds.). (1993). *Discourse and lifespan identity.* Newbury Park, CA: Sage.

Giles, H., Fox, S., Harwood, J., & Williams, A. (1994). Talking age and aging talk. In M. L. Hummert, J. M. Wiemann, & J. F. Nussbaum (Eds.), *Interpersonal communication in older adulthood* (pp. 130–161). Thousand Oaks, CA: Sage.

Nussbaum, J. F. (1989). *Life-span communication: Normative processes.* Hillsdale, NJ: Lawrence Erlbaum.

Nussbaum, J. F., & Coupland, J. (Eds.). (1995). *Handbook of communication and aging research.* Mahwah, NJ: Lawrence Erlbaum.

Pecchioni, L. L., Wright, K. B., & Nussbaum, J. F. (2005). *Life-span communication.* Mahwah, NJ: Lawrence Erlbaum.

Yingling, J. (2004). *A lifetime of communication: Transformations through relational dialogues.* Mahwah, NJ: Lawrence Erlbaum.

Communication and Language Acquisition and Development

Relationships among communication, language acquisition, and development are deeply involved in what makes us human. While speech scientists and psycholinguists have examined language acquisition, and cognitive psychologists have tied language to developmental issues, most communication scholars have shied away from the question, What exactly does communication have to do with language acquisition and development?

Definitions of Terms and Links Among Them

One of the first scholars of communication to consider the links among communication, language, and development was Frank Dance. This entry will start with the definitions he began to use early in the 1970s. *Communication,* in its simplest sense, is acting on information. *Human communication* is the way humans act on information to communicate by means of spoken language and its derivatives (e.g., writing, symbolic gestures). *Human language* is the systematization of symbols, which is syntactic and culturally determined. According to Frank Dance, yet one other definition is critical in providing the developmental piece. *Speech* is the human, genetically determined, species-specific activity consisting of the voluntary production of phonated, articulated sound through the interaction and coordination of physiological and neural systems.

For Dance, the human capacity for speech is what leads to the inception of the symbol and, further, to the development of human conceptualization. In his view, it is our human speech-making capacity that provides the connections among communication, language, and development. Indeed, cognitive psychologists from Lev Vygotsky through Alexander Luria and Philip Lieberman have agreed with the broad outlines of such a connection. Frank Dance posited more specifically, for the communication field, that when human language is acquired normally, it is spoken, and that the development of spoken language leads to the constitution and effects of specifically human communication.

These kinds of theoretical statements stood out as novelties when they first appeared in the 1970s and early 1980s. Today they are not as controversial, yet neither have they become mainstream. Despite deeper examinations of communication development, we have been unable to either definitively prove or disprove the causality from speech to symbol to human communication effects, but the support is compelling. We look now to the work on these matters that has come to us from other disciplines, then to the current state of thought.

Contributions Across Disciplines

Among the first to systematically link verbal communication with development was the Russian psychologist Lev Vygotsky in the 1920s. He had read Jean Piaget's work of the same era about egocentric thought and speech and found something missing. Piaget claimed that the young child (younger than 7 years) thought and spoke egocentrically, and only later were thought and speech socialized. *Egocentric speech* is language that is not adapted for the listener's needs whereas *socialized speech* is. For example, a 3-year-old is likely to say exactly what is on his or her mind: "I want a cookie." An 8-year-old, however, is more likely to take into account the demands of the situation (e.g., it's near dinner time, Mom is cooking vegetables) and say, for example, "If you let me have a cookie, I'll eat my broccoli." Piaget reasoned that we say what our thought tells us to say; a young child thinks egocentrically and therefore speaks egocentrically. As the brain develops, the child is more capable of more complex, socialized thought.

Vygotsky undertook his own studies of egocentric speech. He made the children's tasks more difficult, and as he did, the amount of egocentric speech increased. He reasoned that the children were using speech *to* figure out problems—that speech indeed helped the child construct trains of thought, not the other way around. Consider this example: A boy, in creating a picture of his home, said, "Where's the blue crayon? I need the blue crayon. Well, never mind, I'll use green and wet it to make it darker." Here, the child, who could not find his blue crayon, is instructing himself how to adapt to its loss and solve his problem. For Vygotsky, speech was the tool children use to create sophisticated cognitive processes. Note that Vygotsky does not attribute this power to language, which is a cultural acquisition, but to speech, which is a genetic endowment subsequently enriched by language. The ability to articulate sound so that the sound can stand for something—to create symbols—is what allows humans to reason in the way they do.

Vygotsky's explanation made sense to many, including Piaget himself, as he admitted in a foreword to one of Vygotsky's translated books. Others who noted and built on Vygotsky's theory include Alexander Luria, another Russian psychologist, and Jerome Bruner, an influential American psychologist. The former is known for his sophisticated work on the making of the mind and the latter for providing the foundations of the *interactionist* school in developmental psychology.

Meanwhile, the discipline of linguistics was changing from the formal study of written language structure to considerations of the language–cognition connection and natural spoken language acquisition. The new cognitive linguists or psycholinguists were interested in questions regarding the role of language in thought and vice versa. Beginning in the late 1950s, Noam Chomsky, a brilliant scholar and lifelong activist, called for a new kind of grammar—transformational—to explain what really happens when we produce language. Chomsky attributed the child's ability to produce grammatical sentences to a brain structure he named the *language acquisition device* (LAD). Again, as with Piaget, the focus is on the role of the mind (i.e., the LAD) in building social behavior rather than the role of social behavior in the development of mind.

When Jerome Bruner discovered the Soviet psychologists in the 1960s, he based his own observations of early child language on their principles. He may be the best known of the developmental school of *social interactionists*. He explained that human development could not be merely a matter of biological propensity or behavioral conditioning. He argued that Chomsky's LAD would not be triggered without a corresponding *language acquisition support system*. More sophisticated and encultured language users provide the scaffolding for a child's construction of symbolic language.

Also concerned with the communicative part of the picture, Philip Lieberman, cognitive scientist and linguist, devised in the early 1970s a theory about the evolution of human language. By the early 1990s, he argued that Chomsky's LAD, or an innate universal grammar structure, was biologically implausible if one examined principles of evolution. Instead, he proposed that children learn language similarly to the ways they learn everything else. The only difference is that they are uniquely equipped to produce and understand speech. Human speech allows us to communicate much faster than in any other mode and to articulate distinctive sounds, thus allowing us to combine sounds in a structured (grammatical) way. This ability to "chunk" bits of sound and attach meaning to them in combination permits us to overcome the ordinary limits of memory. By using

sounds as symbols, we retain their meaning over time. The crux of the matter is the use of sounds for meaning: the symbol.

A *symbol* is one sort of stimulus that allows us to refer to something. In that sense, it shares the communication stage with signs. A *sign* is a stimulus that announces that thing to which it is intrinsically linked. The relationship between a sign and its referent is fixed and concrete; it will always mean the same thing. For example, smoke is a sign of fire and announces to perceiving animals that fire is near. Similarly, a baby's hunger cry announces a hungry baby. And the species' set response in the baby's mother is the letdown of her milk. On the other hand, the relationship between a symbol and its referent is entirely arbitrary. In the example above, mother can choose to perceive her child's cry symbolically in any number of ways. For example, even as her body responds to the child's cry as a sign, her mind can be assigning meanings like "my child loves me" or "my baby is trying to make me crazy from lack of sleep." We create the meanings for symbols, the capacity for which endows us with creative gifts like time shifting—the ability to imagine what will be in the future and to voluntarily consider what has happened in the past. Symbols give us the raw materials for a self-concept in particular and for concepts—complexes of meaning—in general. For example, if Sue is told when she is 3 that she is a girl and the apple of her daddy's eye, that information constructs her idea of self. In preschool she adds pals to her life and so knows herself as a friend. Later, she excels at music, and she is a pianist. By adulthood, we cannot trace back all the sources of self-concept, but it is a pretty firm structure nonetheless.

Given that symbols are critical for developing other human characteristics and abilities, how do they arise? Apparently, the answer is that children grasp how to use speech sounds in a meaningful way with other humans *in interaction*. And it is here that the communication part of the equation links speech with interaction in development to result in language and logical thought. Contrary to Piaget's view that cognition moved from egocentric to socialized thought, it is more likely that human thought develops from a spoken symbolic process worked out in the presence and with the assistance of others to a silent symbolic process worked out internally. Say that Ben has lost his mittens, yet again. As his mother is trying to run him out the door to kindergarten, he says, "But I can't find my mittens, Mom!" She prompts, "Well, where did you last have them? Did you wear them yesterday after school?" He remembers; "Yes." She continues, "Where were you playing? Who were you with?" He now recalls, "Jack was here. We made a snowman in the yard, and I needed a nose and took off my mittens." And off Ben goes to the yard to find his mittens next to the snowman. Alexander Luria and others observed that this kind of learning to use symbols for thought is done with the assistance of more sophisticated thinkers, such as parents, teachers, and tutors. Human communication does not spring into being fully formed; it develops and changes over time. Those who understand this process of development and its dependence on interaction will be those who understand communication changes in the individual.

Communication Scholarship

The first direct treatment of developmental issues in the communication field was in the Frank Dance and Carl Larson text on speech communication in 1972. Ostensibly, it was a basic theory text but included a consideration of the uniqueness of speech communication behavior. Here were ideas from biology, semiotics, philosophy, and more. Further, they stated that the newborn infant is human only in form and potential; what confirms the infant's humanity is the process of interaction with the human environment via symbolic communication. Dance and Larson go on to claim that symbolic communication leads to the development of human cognition. Here is where we see the influence of Lev Vygotsky on Frank Dance's *speech theory of human communication,* formalized a decade later: The gradual internalization of speech communication mirrors the development of complex thought processes.

While Dance and Larson were basing their theory on the Russian theorists who viewed speech as primary, Jesse Delia and Daniel O'Keefe were founding their theory, *constructivism,* on the work of psychologist George Kelly, who actually had little to say about communication development but quite a lot to say about personality and personal constructs. A *construct* is a reference axis—or comparison point between two alternatives—created by a human for setting up a personal orientation to experienced events (including self and others). For example, an early construct might be a comparison point for people as either "nice" or "not nice." One may create a meaning for "nice" only in the context of a meaning for "not nice"—some comparison point. Kelly posited that we devise frames for making sense of our experience in this way.

The *constructivists,* starting in the mid-1970s with Jesse Delia, Ruth Ann Clark, and Daniel O'Keefe, built a communication theory that uses *cognitive complexity* as a explanatory variable for communication behavior. To measure cognitive complexity, they counted the number of *constructs*—descriptive words—that an individual uses to describe others. Their research demonstrated that both complexity and persuasive skill progress with age. They concluded that the more constructs the child has available for distinguishing different kinds of people, the more capable the child is of adapting persuasive speech to influence various others. This sounds as if the child is constructing socialized speech. Notice that a Piagetian would say that cognition is now serving communication. However, a Vygotskian would instead reason that the child's symbol system—developed in interaction with others—has become internalized and has begun to serve cognition. The constructivists have stayed out of this argument, for the most part, but have continued to use cognitive complexity as a primary variable that affects communication.

Others who studied constructivism, such as Brant Burleson, have moved on to study communication behaviors such as comforting while retaining the notion of cognitive complexity as a related necessity for the development of sophisticated comforting behaviors. Indeed, his recent work demonstrates that parents and peers who were skilled in comforting influenced the development of children's comforting skills. Even more interesting is the finding that peers' comforting skills were related to a child's perspective-taking ability. Seemingly, interaction partners contribute a great deal to the child's developing abilities for socialized thought and sophisticated communication skills.

So, interaction, human cognition, and language (spoken symbols) are interrelated. The order in development seems to be (a) interaction, (b) spoken language, and (c) human cognition. Certainly infants think, but their thinking is largely limited to present time and place until symbols serve to stretch their capacities. When spoken language and cognition merge (at about 18 months), a new form of thought begins—conceptual thought—on the basis of internalizing symbols. But it is the interaction with symbolizing others that provides the impetus for such development. Children do not learn to think humanly or to speak meaningfully in the absence of social interaction.

Despite their differences, most scholars of development are thorough *social interactionists*; they believe that interaction is necessary to the development of both communication and language and that we must study interaction to tease out its effects. Thus, much of learning to be a competent communicator is a matter of the interaction we encounter and the sense we make of it.

Current Thought

Although studies about early childhood communication have burgeoned in recent years, complete theoretical treatments about communication/language/development relationships are still relatively rare in the communication field.

One worthy text, by Beth Haslett and Wendy Samter, appeared in 1997. Although they did not offer a communication theory per se in *Children Communicating*, they did frame nicely what we know about early childhood development of language and communication. They offer overviews of Piaget's and Vygostky's theories and then offer an alternative *ecological* approach articulated by developmental psychologist Michael Forrester. For Forrester, the most important social cognitive skill is the ability to understand and participate in conversation. He suggests that young children learn by "overhearing" interaction. Haslett and Samter are content to say that communication, language, and thought all interact and mutually influence each other.

In 2004, Julie Yingling offered a *relational-dialogical* perspective of development, extending it beyond infancy and childhood to the human life span. This approach, owing much to the developmental *interactionists* and to *dialectical* theories of communication, rests on the notion that human thought and self-awareness emerge from the ability to use spoken symbols interactively. Mikhail Bakhtin, another Soviet scholar, suggested that

consciousness lies on the border between the organism and the material world. Further, he claimed that the workings of each human are at such variance as to require the translation found in symbols. Here, at the boundary between self and other, dialogue is what creates meaning. Yingling uses dialogic processes to explain how human communicative development occurs—in a series of progressive internalizations of symbolic interactions or *boundary experiences*.

To explain fully the relationships among communication, language acquisition, and development calls for knowledge of each of these processes, including their physiological and neurological bases, as well as the influence of various interaction sources on the developing human. Much of that knowledge is available and has produced current theories that rely on symbolic interaction as an explanatory variable for many human effects. Refinement and adjustment of these theories is inevitable as relevant communication research continues to proliferate.

Julie Yingling

See also Communication Across the Life Span; Constructivism; Dialogue Theories; Language and Communication; Relational Dialectics; Social Construction of Reality; Social Support; Symbolic Interactionism

Further Readings

Bruner, J. (1975). From communication to language: A psychological perspective. *Cognition, 3,* 255–287.

Burleson, B. R., & Kunkel, A. (2002). Parental and peer contributions to the emotional support skills of the child: From whom do children learn to express support? *Journal of Family Communication, 2,* 79–97.

Chomsky, N. (1957). *Syntactic structures.* The Hague, The Netherlands: Mouton.

Dance, F. E. X. (1982). A speech theory of human communication. In F. E. X. Dance (Ed.), *Human communication theory: Comparative essays* (pp. 120–146). New York: Harper & Row.

Dance, F. E. X., & Larson, C. E. (1972). *Speech communication: Concepts and behavior.* New York: Holt, Rinehart, & Winston.

Haslett, B. B., & Samter, W. (1997). *Children communicating: The first 5 years.* Mahwah, NJ: Lawrence Erlbaum.

Lieberman, P. (1991). *Uniquely human: The evolution of speech, thought, and selfless behavior.* Cambridge, MA: Harvard University Press.

Luria, A. R., Cole, M., & Cole, S. (Eds.). (1979). *The making of mind.* Cambridge, MA: Harvard University Press.

Vygotsky, L. S. (1966). *Thought and language* (A. Hanfmann & G. Vakar, Trans.). Cambridge: MIT Press. (Original work published 1934)

Vygotsky, L. S. (1978). *Mind in society: The development of higher psychological processes.* Cambridge, MA: Harvard University Press.

Yingling, J. (2004). *A lifetime of communication: Transformations through relational dialogues.* Mahwah, NJ: Lawrence Erlbaum.

COMMUNICATION APPREHENSION

See Social and Communicative Anxiety

COMMUNICATION GOAL THEORIES

A goal is some desired end or state of affairs that an individual desires to attain or maintain. Desires become *interaction goals* when communication and coordination with another are required for goal achievement. The majority of our communication with others is goal directed. We pursue goals as we seek to form relationships, convince others of our position, or work to accomplish a task. Goals are a cognitive phenomenon; merely thinking about a goal is not enough to achieve a desired end. The achievement of a goal requires some sort of action designed for attainment. *Planning* consists of producing one or more mental models detailing how a goal might be achieved through interaction. The products of goals and plans are the overt behaviors produced in service of a goal. Goals affect all levels of behavior ranging from the content and structure of verbal messages to nonverbal behaviors. This entry explores theoretical explanations of goals and plans and the ways these cognitive processes inform communication.

Forming Goals

Theories of goal-driven behavior locate goals within a *goals–plans–action* (GPA) sequence initiated by the activation of goal-related concepts from memory. Greene's *action assembly theory* and Wilson's *cognitive rules model* assume that goal-relevant information, including knowledge about goals and situational features relevant to each goal, is stored as nodes within an associative network in long-term memory. The network of goal-relevant information includes concepts such as people, traits, relational qualities, and desired outcomes.

In a given communication situation, relevant concepts are activated in memory. For example, when one is with a romantic partner, concepts related to relationships, romance, and anything relevant to the specific partner may be activated. If one wanted to convince a partner to go to dinner at a certain restaurant, concepts related to persuading the other would be activated as well. Activation is a necessary but not sufficient condition for goal formation. Concepts have an activation threshold, whereby a goal is not formed unless a certain level of activation is received. The probability of particular goal-relevant information being activated is based on three criteria: fit, strength, and recency. For *fit,* there need to be a large number of goal-related concepts that are relevant to the current situation. The *strength* of the activation is determined by how frequently the concepts have been activated in the past; information that has been triggered frequently in the past possesses a stronger activation level than does content that has not been activated as much. Finally, *recency* is defined by when the concepts were last activated, with more recently activated concepts being more accessible in memory than those that have not been activated as recently. Goals are a cognitive product of this activated information, such that what constitutes a goal is assumed to be reflective of the most situationally relevant and appropriate information.

Types and Properties of Goals

There are three general types of goals that people seek to achieve through interpersonal communication. *Self-presentation* or *identity* goals reflect concerns about the image of who we are and how we want to be perceived by others. *Relational* goals include desires to develop, maintain, or neglect particular relationships. *Instrumental* concerns involve obtaining some sort of tangible resource, getting others to do us a favor, or accomplishing some sort of task. These goals often co-occur or shift between one another. Communication is often framed by an instrumental goal such as problem solving or gaining compliance from another, yet identity or relational concerns often become more salient throughout a discussion. For example, a common problem among roommates concerns keeping their apartment clean. One roommate may confront another with the instrumental goal of figuring out a way to solve the problem of cleaning the apartment. However, consider if the other roommate replies, "You are such a slob; it's like we live in a barn!" In response, the roommate may consider it more important to pursue a self-identity–related goal to reestablish that he or she is a neat and good person instead of the initial instrumental concern. This shift in goals during a conversation reflects a shift in goals from *proactive* (i.e., goals that guide a discussion) to *reactive* (i.e., goals in response to another).

Interaction goals are assumed to exist at many levels of *specificity* within a hierarchical goal structure; higher-level goals subsume lower-level goals. Higher-level goals are abstract. For example, a goal "to do well in school" has many meanings and may be achieved in a variety of ways. Higher-level goals are pursued via a variety of lower-level *basic* goals that are more proximal and concrete and facilitate specific behaviors that are pursued in the service of attaining more abstract, higher-level goals. For example, as part of doing well in school, a person could pursue the concrete goal of studying for 3 hours each night. The pursuit and achievement of a goal are more likely if the lower-level goal does not conflict with higher-order goals. Further, clear, attainable goals produce higher levels of performance than general intentions do.

Goals may also be defined and organized in terms of their *importance,* which reflects the particular value or salience of a goal relative to other goals. Important goals are motivating and energizing. Deciding that a goal is important motivates us to pursue the goal as well as to stay committed to its pursuit. Thus, the occurrence of an important goal directs cognitive processing resources toward the pursuit of that goal and encourages the production

of behaviors structured toward the realization of that goal, in place of other behaviors that are not directly related to the most important goal.

While sometimes the most important goal is the one that guides what we say and do, research with Dillard's GPA model suggested that goals may function differently during interactions. The GPA model distinguished between primary and secondary goal functions. *Primary goals* define the focus of an interaction and answer the question, What is going on here? For example, in order to get a good grade on a group project, you may possess a goal to persuade your teammates to start the project early. This goal, in turn, should drive you to confront and persuade your teammates about the project. *Secondary goals* are concerns that shape and constrain what people say as they go about pursuing a primary goal. Dillard specified five categories of secondary goals: (1) identity goals, which reflect desires to act consistent with one's beliefs; (2) interaction goals, or desires to maintain a positive image, saying things that are relevant and appropriate and protective of the image of the other person in the interaction; (3) relational resource goals, which reflect desires to maintain relationships; (4) personal resource goals, which reflect concerns about maintaining one's time, money, or safety; and (5) arousal management goals, as reflected in concerns to reduce anxiety or nervousness. While primary goals define what an interaction is about, secondary goals "pull" the conversation by constraining what people say. For example, a primary goal to persuade teammates to start the project early may be constrained by secondary concerns to get along with the other teammates and to make sure that they like you.

Another defining property of goals is their *difficulty.* Goal difficulty may be defined according to perceived performance in goal pursuit. When self-satisfaction is contingent on the attainment of challenging goals, more effort is expended than if easy goals are adopted as sufficient. In other words, the harder the goal, the more people work to attain it and the greater their performance. Difficulty may also be defined in terms of the number of important goals that an individual attempts to pursue. Managing multiple concerns involves managing more information; thus the more goals a person seeks to pursue at any one time, the more difficult goal achievement will be.

Goals and Planning

GPA theories commonly assume that goals stimulate planning processes designed for goal achievement. *Plans* are cognitive; they constitute knowledge about the preconditions, contingencies, and actions that may facilitate goal pursuit and achievement. Our knowledge of plans may come from a variety of sources, including our own prior experiences, observations of how others have pursued goals, imagined hypothetical interactions, or recommendations from others. *Planning* refers to the psychological and communication processes involved in recalling, generating, selecting, implementing, modifying, and negotiating plans. Planning how to implement a goal occurs to some extent before an interaction; however, quite a bit of planning occurs during an interaction as participants define and negotiate their plans together.

Just as there are a variety of goals, so too are there many types of plans that we may pursue, and some plans are more specific than others. Further, certain plans may be more complex or difficult to implement than others. Complex plans include more actions, more diversity of behavior, and more contingencies than simple plans do. Further, some plans may not be appropriate for every circumstance. Plans are developed and selected with the following considerations in mind: (a) What goals does a situation easily afford? (b) What are the rules and roles associated with the situation? and (c) Is the pursuit of the goal and its associated behaviors socially acceptable?

Monitoring and Revising Goals and Plans

Of course, we are not always conscious of our goals and plans. In some instances, people may behave without any clear goal in mind. This is often the case in routine interactions. But even routine behaviors are reflective of prior conscious and strategic attempts to achieve a goal. Research suggests that although we may not think about our goals and plans all the time, we have a frequent, although fleeting, awareness of our goals and plans during conversations.

While individuals may be able to engage in goal pursuit and achievement with relative ease, some goal pursuit is frequently challenged or thwarted. Sometimes, goals are thwarted when individuals realize that goal pursuit is not proceeding satisfactorily. However, goal pursuit may also be challenged during an interaction with another. For example, suppose someone asks you for directions to the campus library. As you describe the path to the library, your questioner says to you, "I don't understand. Can you tell me a different way?" Thus, the questioner's lack of understanding has blocked your efforts at pursuing the goal of helping the questioner. When a goal or plan is challenged, there are several potential outcomes. An individual may continue a current plan of action toward goal pursuit. Or, an individual may increase his or her efforts in pursuing that goal. Alternatively, an individual may temporarily disengage from goal pursuit or abandon that goal altogether. In giving the directions to the library, you may have to change your plan (the directions) to meet the goal of helping the questioner. Or, you may have to abandon the goal of helping altogether if your repeated efforts fail. Berger's model of planning suggested that revisions are first considered at the lowest or most concrete level of goals and plans and work up the hierarchy to higher-level goal conceptions as goal blockage increases.

A consideration of goals provides a theoretically rich understanding of where communication "comes from" and provides an explanation as to why different people communicate so variably, even in the same situation. As well, the goals-based perspective can provide insight into how intention shapes interaction before, during, and after communication occurs.

Jennifer A. Samp

See also Action Assembly Theory; Cognitive Theories; Interpersonal Communication Theories; Intrapersonal Communication Theories

Further Readings

Berger, C. R. (1997). *Planning strategic interaction: Attaining goals through communicative action.* Mahwah, NJ: Lawrence Erlbaum.
Dillard, J. P. (2004). The goals-plan-action model of interpersonal influence. In J. S. Seiter & R. H. Gass (Eds.), *Perspectives on persuasion, social influence, and compliance gaining* (pp. 185–206). Boston: Allyn & Bacon.

Greene, J. O. (1997). A second generation action assembly theory. In J. O. Greene (Ed.), *Message production: Advances in communication theory* (pp. 151–170). Mahwah, NJ: Lawrence Erlbaum.

Keck, K. L., & Samp, J. A. (2007). The dynamic nature of goals and message production as revealed in a sequential analysis of conflict interactions. *Human Communication Research, 33,* 27–37.

Samp, J. A., & Solomon, D. H. (2005). Toward a theoretical account of goals in microlevel message features. *Communication Monographs, 72,* 23–46.

Waldron, V. R. (1997). Toward a theory of interactive conversational planning. In J. O. Greene (Ed.) *Message production: Advances in communication theory* (pp. 195–220). Mahwah, NJ: Lawrence Erlbaum.

Wilson, S. R. (2002). *Seeking and resisting compliance: Why people say what they do when trying to influence others.* Thousand Oaks: CA: Sage.

COMMUNICATION IN LATER LIFE

Rather sudden and quite dramatic global increases in the proportions of living older adults, together with the ever-expanding horizons of longevity, make the study of aging very timely. Being interdisciplinary, this study is explored from radically different vantage points, from the biological to the sociological. Kofi Anan, then secretary general of the United Nations, pronounced 1999 the International Year of the Elderly and established a task force to explore the pressing implications of what he called this "silent revolution." Although many social and physical disciplines were implicated in this enterprise, communication was not. Nonetheless, in the past few decades, our discipline has made great strides, empirically and theoretically, in enlightening us as to the ways in which communication phenomena and processes are crucial constituents of the social construction of aging.

In what follows, theories outside our discipline that provide an important backdrop to social gerontological theory will be briefly described. While focusing on older adults, these theories, rightly, often take on a so-called life span perspective. In other words, they do not vacuously look at older individuals within a narrow temporal frame (e.g., 65 and older) but, rather, identify how and why the continual management of events across the life span affects people's later wellness. Not surprisingly, perhaps, many of these theoretical positions are also directed toward understanding and predicting *successful aging,* and culturally determined dimensions of self-reported life satisfaction (such as a zest for life and independence) are a critical component of this. Thereafter, communication and aging theories will be introduced.

Theories From Other Disciplines

Much research on communicating to, about, and from older adults has shown distinct signs of ageism, and this is so cross-nationally. In line with this, albeit originally devised to show the social dimensions of aging, one of the first well-cited frameworks was *disengagement theory.* Somewhat discredited these days, this position suggests that older people disengage—as the term suggests—in a seemingly natural way from involving themselves and contributing to society and, moreover, are passively encouraged to do so by younger segments of society. It was felt that disengagement eased the process of ultimate or impending demise for older adults in later life. Erikson's developmental theory similarly proposes that coming to terms with one's own death is, and is also seen to be, an important factor in aging successfully. Indeed, a *terror management theory* perspective on ageism claims that older people are often stereotyped very negatively and hence avoided because their presence can provide anxiety-provoking reminders for younger bystanders of their own inevitable mortality.

In contrast, *activity theory* suggests that socially engaged older adults (e.g., those with hobbies and responsibilities) are happier and survive longer, with the influential, but empirically challenged, position of Robert Kahn and John Rowe claiming that successful aging is, in part, commensurate with a lack of physical disabilities and ill health. Other theories have invested in notions of being internally in control of one's environment and of circumstances that become developmentally more and more important in the second portion of the life span. Indeed, an important adjunct to this idea is being ready and able to effectively compensate for any growing or emergent deficiencies in such areas as memory or agility. Meshing the latter so-called *selective optimization* with *compensation theory* and models of "possible selves" would allow older persons energetically to keep in sight, or strive to be congruent with, their ideal self. This approach would sidestep any discrepant conceptions of a feared (or even dreaded) self. Indeed, *continuity theory* affords particular theoretical weight to people who pay attention to valued aspects of stability and their enduring unique characteristics across the life span. That said, *identity balance theory* suggests that successful aging involves sustaining a demanding equilibrium involving subtly adjusting to or assimilating the former self-concepts and redefining aspects of the self to accommodate necessary changes.

Finally here, Laura Carstensen's *socioemotional selectivity theory* proposes different developmental trajectories across the life span to the extent that in later life, individuals become less and less interested in garnering knowledge about the world around them and in meeting different people but, instead, become increasingly more focused on investing in their very close personal relationships and social networks. This is in line with the *convoy* and *intergenerational conflict models,* which suggest that people opt to associate with those who can provide them solidarity and protect them from disturbing comparisons that can lower self-esteem, such as comparisons to people who are perhaps more socially and cognitively active. Indeed, the resource of being able to reminisce and exchange life narratives (or life reviews) with empathic age peers can be an important buffer to dwelling on self-demise. Yet an important empirically supported aspect of Carstensen's theory is that it is not old age per se that brings on this socioemotional focus but, rather, feelings of or knowledge about being near to death and finitude—an experience also felt by some young people dealing, rather prematurely, with death (e.g., those with HIV or certain cancers).

Communication Theories

Although the foregoing models were not developed within the discipline of communication, they can, nonetheless, be implicitly considered to have communicative dimensions. This is certainly the case when social networks and life narratives come under scrutiny, as well as when people seek for predictability and meaning across the life span in what might be regarded as an extension of uncertainty reduction and management theories. When we turn now to explicitly communication-oriented theories, then models of intergroup relations and communication become pertinent—as they have done with respect to the study of media and aging. One such theory is Jake Harwood's *social identity theory of gratifications and uses,* which shows ways in which older people reinforce their social identities by the media content they select. Communication theories often focus on how certain contexts can make age salient for people and, consequently, induce people not to think of themselves and others with them as idiosyncratic characters but, rather, representative members of age categories. Consequently, the mediating roles of age stereotyping figure prominently in these theories.

The first of these theoretical positions emerged in the mid-1980s, and one that has guided a significant proportion of empirical research is the *communication predicament of aging model.* This framework, which was inspired by communication accommodation theory, proposes vital relationships between intergenerational communication and subjective well-being. It attends to how young people's negative stereotypes of older people (e.g., as frail and despondent) may induce them to adopt overaccommodative communications that are ideationally simple, slowed in speech rate, and exaggerated in intonation. Continued encounters of this nature could lead some older people to wonder if they are truly as incompetent as messages to them from younger people would attest. As a result, and in self-stereotypical fashion, older people may assume the very ageist communication characteristics (such as a slowed gait and voice perturbations) implied by a younger person's stance toward them, despite the fact that they may well be quite competent and independent spirits. Such poor self-perceptions may cumulatively lead to social withdrawal, a lessened sense of self-worth, and even somatic changes accelerating physical demise.

An elaboration of this model, as well as the *communication enhancement of aging model,* attends also to messages that would circumvent the older person experiencing major predicaments and negative outcomes. In the former case, this could be manifest by elders' use of assertive responses to, say, patronizingly stereotyped speech from younger people and, in the latter, by encouraging younger people not to categorize older people by age but to seek the individuality inherent in older adults, encouraging personally accommodative messages toward them and ultimately creating a communicative climate that is empowering to both parties. Indeed, given that older people reciprocally and negatively stereotype younger people too, applied intervention strategies aimed at promoting cross-age healthy relations need to be bilaterally designed. This would inform both (or all) generational parties implicated, as well as encourage media literacy regarding age discrimination and prejudice levied against *both* younger and older age groups.

Mary Lee Hummert and her associates, in their *age stereotypes in interactions model*, also looked at ways in which the negative feedback cycle inherent in the predicament could be interrupted and, instead, yield more favorable outcomes. A number of factors were proposed, including past quality intergenerational contact, high cognitive complexity of the younger person, and attributes of the older person that could trigger positive age substereotyping (e.g., wisdom). In this case, stereotypical speech toward the older person that could be viewed as condescending and debilitating would be avoided—and what is referred to as *normal adult speech* substituted.

Valerie Barker and Howard Giles's so-called *integrative model* not only identified sociostructural factors and filial piety as determinants of successful intergenerational encounters but also drew attention to the fact that *intra*generational communication climates require modeling too. This was a theoretical advance because cross-cultural studies had shown that what predicted poor indices of psychological well-being for certain (particularly Asian) older populations was not poor younger-to-older communication at all but actually nonaccommodative stances from same-aged peers. Finally, life span models that promote successful aging should not be applied simply so as to educate people to appreciate the psychological parameters of aging (e.g., "you're as young as you feel" and "aging is merely a state of mind") but should also encourage people—even in later young adulthood—to resist harmful self-attributions of aging in their face-to-face and electronic communications (e.g., "I must

be getting on!"). In addition, such a position would encourage people to talk about later aging in significantly positive emotional linguistic terms (i.e., as an absorbing adventure).

Much theorizing about human communication implicitly (if often not explicitly) revolves around young people—the empirical mainstay diet of our theorizing. But life circumstances change such that communication management necessarily involves different needs, values, and expressive practices at different age junctures and in different contexts, such as the family and workplace. There is a need for the blending of communication and noncommunication theories of aging on one hand and for forging models more truly centered on life span communication on the other. Such models also need to attend to different subpopulations as they age differently, as well as to perceived age boundaries and transitions, including retirement. As each of us ages, and more of us do so for longer, the role of theory in middle—as well as older—adulthood becomes an imperative challenge. As communication theory illuminates further the work of aging well, the discipline might soon be recognized as a crucial component of any future task forces on matters of aging.

Howard Giles

See also Accommodation Theory; Communication Across the Life Span; Family Communication Theories; Narrative and Narratology; Social Construction of Reality; Social Identity Theory; Social Support; Uncertainty Management Theories; Uncertainty Reduction Theory; Uses, Gratifications, and Dependency

Further Readings

Antonucci, T. C., Jackson, J. S., & Biggs, S. (Eds.). (2007). Intergenerational relations: Theory, research and policy. *Journal of Social Issues, 63*, 679–925.

Baltes, P. B., & Baltes, M. M. (1990). Psychological perspectives on successful aging: The model of selective optimization with compensation. In P. B. Baltes & M. M. Baltes (Eds.), *Successful aging: Perspectives from the behavioral sciences* (pp. 1–34). New York: Cambridge University Press.

Barker, V., & Giles, H. (2003). Integrating the communicative predicament and enhancement of aging models: The case of older Native Americans. *Health Communication, 15*, 255–275.

Carstensen, L. L., Fung, H. H., & Charles, S. T. (2003). Socioemotional selectivity theory and the regulation of emotion in the second half of life. *Motivation and Emotion, 27,* 103–123.

Giles, H. (Ed.). (2004). Communication climates and practices. *Journal of Cross-Cultural Gerontology, 19,* 261–405.

Harwood, J. (2007). *Understanding communication and aging.* Thousand Oaks, CA: Sage.

Nelson, T. D. (Ed.). (2005). Ageism. *Journal of Social Issues, 61,* 207–404.

Nussbaum, J. F., & Coupland, J. (Eds.). (2004). *Handbook of communication and aging research* (2nd ed.). Mahwah, NJ: Lawrence Erlbaum.

Pecchioni, L. L., Wright, K. B., & Nussbaum, J. F. (2005). *Life-span communication.* Mahwah, NJ: Lawrence Erlbaum.

COMMUNICATION SKILLS THEORIES

At the very core, communication skill simply concerns the proficiency or quality of one's communicative performance. Just as people's dancing, driving, or chess playing reflects a certain level of proficiency, so too do their various communication activities, such as listening, public speaking, and making small talk. Communication skill is one of the most extensively and intensively studied of all aspects of human behavior, in part because it is fascinating in its own right, but also because communication skill is vitally important to one's well-being: Skillful communicators are happier and healthier, enjoy more satisfying interpersonal relationships, and perform better in school and in their jobs.

Historical Overview

Questions about communication skill have occupied thinkers for millennia: At least as far back as the Greek Classical Age (5th to 4th centuries BCE), philosophers grappled with identifying effective persuasion techniques. This concern with persuasion has continued as an important area of study to the present day, but in the past century, examinations of communication skill have extended far beyond issues of persuasion and social influence to include practically every aspect of verbal and nonverbal behavior. And the study of social skill has become a broad, interdisciplinary enterprise: Examinations of communication proficiency are found in virtually every branch of scholarly inquiry regarding human social behavior—from political science to neuroscience.

Disciplinary Developments

Amid the breadth and diversity of investigations of communication skill, certain key events and people stand out. Some of these concern the development of broad intellectual traditions and fields of study. For example, because skills are learned rather than innate, the scientific study of *learning processes* that began in the late 19th century bears directly on issues of skilled performance. The study of learning has, itself, undergone various transformations in perspective, progressing through the now familiar epochs of *behaviorism* (based on classical conditioning) in the early part of the 20th century, *radical behaviorism* (based on operant conditioning, most commonly associated with B. F. Skinner) in the middle of that century, and *cognitivism* during the past 50 years. Other pertinent threads are found in examinations of changes in children's cognitive abilities as reflected in the rise of *developmental psychology* in the 1920s and 1930s (with Jean Piaget, Lev Vygotsky, and others) and the study of *child language acquisition*, which began to flower in the late 1950s. In a similar way, *personality psychology*, as represented in pioneering work of people like Gordon Allport in the 1930s, laid the groundwork for a tradition of examining the role of individual differences in behavioral proficiency that continues to the present.

Among these broad disciplinary developments, three others are particularly relevant. Studies of social influence, group and normative forces, empathy, and so on had occupied researchers since the early 1900s, but in the years immediately following World War II, led by scholars like Kurt Lewin, *social psychology* entered something of a golden age that saw the development of many of the classic concepts and theories that continue to infuse that field. Most pertinent to concerns with communication skills is that in the early 1970s, a particular branch of social psychology emerged. *Social cognition* placed emphasis on perception of others, attributions concerning their behavior, and memory for what they said and did—with the attendant assumption that these processes could be systematically biased or flawed.

The second disciplinary thread of particular importance grew from studies of *perceptual and motor performance* that, like allied studies of learning, date to the end of the 19th century, when early researchers investigated topics such as people's ability to send and receive Morse code. With the aforementioned rise of cognitivism, early theorists, such as Frederic Bartlett in the 1950s and two decades later Alan Newell, Herbert Simon, John Anderson, and others, advanced the notion that high-level *cognitive skills* could be studied and understood in ways analogous to those pertaining to perceptual and motor skills.

A third disciplinary movement of special importance was the emergence of *speech communication* as an academic field. American colleges had taught courses in speech since their founding, but most often these courses were taught in English departments. Around 1900, speech departments began to break off from English, and in 1914 the National Association of Academic Teachers of Public Speaking (today the National Communication Association) was founded. Speech communication's central focus on skills training has expanded over the intervening years such that departments now routinely offer classes devoted to enhancing skills for public speaking, group discussion, interviewing, conflict management, and so on.

A Sampling of Milestone Contributions

The emergence of various fields of study bearing on communication skill provided an intellectual milieu in which numerous specific conceptual advances were made. These are too numerous to list, but certain examples merit mention. During the 1960s, Albert Bandura developed *social learning theory*—a rejection of behaviorist, stimulus–response–reinforcement formulations—which instead gave emphasis to the cognitive, symbolic representation of actions and their consequences. Bandura made a compelling case that people can learn from observation and that rather than relying on direct experience of responses and reinforcement, we very often model the behavior of others. People, then, may act in a socially skilled way because they have observed others and are able to anticipate the consequences of their

actions and monitor and regulate their own behavior.

In a series of books appearing in the 1970s, Michael Argyle and his colleagues advanced a general model of skilled interaction behavior that suggested that people pursue social goals via a sequence of steps: (a) perception of the environment—a process that involves attention, interpretation, and so on; (b) translation of perception into performance—a step that includes problem solving and decision making; and (c) motor responses—the generation of overt behaviors. Working from this model, Argyle was able to specify various sources of skill deficits (e.g., in goal setting, planning, behavioral enactment). Moreover, Argyle identified qualities such as expressivity, rewardingness, assertiveness, and so on that distinguish proficient from inadequate interaction behaviors. Yet another contribution of this work was the idea that people could be trained to employ more appropriate perceptual, cognitive, and behavioral responses.

A third example of important contributions to the study of communication skill, also from the decade of the 1970s, is found in John Wiemann's examination of the nature of *communication competence* (and subsequent exploration of that construct by Brian Spitzberg, William Cupach, and others). Wiemann emphasized that competence is a dyadic construct in the sense that the competent communicator not only is able to achieve his or her own goals, but moreover to do so in a way that is satisfying for the other party in the conversation. In Wiemann's formulation, five dimensions of competence are identified: (1) empathy, (2) affiliation and support, (3) social relaxation, (4) behavioral flexibility, and (5) interaction management skills (i.e., handling interruptions, taking turns, etc.).

Theories of Skill Acquisition

Because skills are acquired over time, a great deal of research has focused on understanding the processes that underlie skill development. This research shows that skill acquisition is typically a gradual process; in fact, studies in a variety of domains (not just communication skills) have shown that expert performance requires approximately 10 years of concerted practice. Much of the work on skill development has involved constructing learning curves that graph performance quality on the y-axis and amount of practice on the x-axis. (In many cases the number of practice trials examined in this research is in the hundreds or even thousands.) These learning curves virtually always have a characteristic shape: They show large performance gains early on, but over time, improvements with practice become smaller and smaller.

Significant to note is that although skill-acquisition curves almost always take the same general form, there are individual differences in the course of skill acquisition: Some people start off better, learn faster, and achieve higher levels of performance than others do. Theories of skill acquisition suggest that a variety of personal factors, including intelligence, achievement motivation, and age, will affect the course of performance improvement. Regarding this last point, while it is the case that older adults typically do not acquire new skills as rapidly as their younger counterparts, skills acquired early in life tend to be retained in later years.

The process of skill acquisition is marked by a number of behavioral and cognitive changes, including but not limited to (a) becoming faster or more fluent, (b) making fewer errors, (c) experiencing reduced cognitive load, and (d) being more flexible and adaptive. Various theories have been developed to explain these changes, but the prevailing view focuses on the distinction between *declarative* and *procedural memory*. Each of these refers to information held in long-term memory, but declarative information is essentially memory for facts, while procedural information is memory for how to do things. In the standard model, then, early in the process of skill acquisition, a person learns a set of facts or instructions about what to do. It is possible to act on the basis of this declarative information, but performance tends to be slow, error prone, and cognitively demanding. With continued practice, a person enters a second stage of skill acquisition, in which the information used to carry out the activity is transformed from declarative to procedural form. At this point it is no longer necessary to keep the instructions for the activity in mind, and as a result, he or she gets faster and experiences less cognitive load. Finally, in the third stage of skill acquisition, the procedural memory structures for the activity are strengthened with continued practice (a process which can extend over many years).

Theories of Skilled Performance

The Nature of Communication Skill

Despite the fact that it has been so extensively studied and discussed, there are a number of different theoretical perspectives on what *communication skill* actually entails. In part this diversity in perspectives arises from the fact that the properties or characteristics of a given sample of behavior can be coded at various levels of abstraction. For example, at a molar level, raters might judge whether a person was "friendly" or not. At a more fine-grained level of analysis, however, instances of smiling might be counted and timed. In a similar fashion, the functions served by a given action can be understood at various hierarchical levels (e.g., a person may be "answering a question" or "impressing a job interviewer"). Despite these, and similar, difficulties, it is possible to posit a rough hierarchy of levels of analysis commonly reflected in models of what constitutes communication skill. With no claim of exhaustiveness (i.e., that the framework captures every relevant approach), or of mutual exclusivity (i.e., that any particular model will reflect just one tier), a simple, five-tiered scheme is useful for imposing some order on a complex domain.

At the most molar level of the hierarchy are properties of skilled behavior identified in the aforementioned *communication competence* perspective. Certainly there are differences in the specifics of various formulations, but models in this vein generally emphasize that competent communication is characterized by (a) *effectiveness* and (b) *appropriateness*. That is, the competent communicator is able to accomplish his or her goals while also acting in a socially appropriate way. A person who is effective in achieving his or her objectives, but does so by threatening, bullying, lying, and so on, would not be considered competent, nor would one who is polite, ethical, and pleasant, but unable to "close the deal."

A second hierarchical level for thinking about what constitutes communication skill derives from theoretical perspectives that emphasize that all social interactions involve the mutual *presentation and negotiation of "social reality"*—including the identities of the interactants, the nature of their relationship, and the definition of the social setting (e.g., the purpose of the interaction, standards of appropriate behavior). It is not unusual that one person's view of self, other, relationship, and situation may differ considerably from that of his or her interlocutor. The skilled communicator, then, is sensitive to the implications of his or her own presentation of social reality, the ways in which the perspective of the other may be different, and ways of accommodating those differences or negotiating a mutually acceptable perspective.

Moving yet another step in the direction of more molecular conceptions of communication skill are views that emphasize *general properties of behavior* that are more or less skilled. It is this level of abstraction in the coding of behavior that tends to be reflected in people's everyday characterization of their own and others' actions (so, for example, we commonly think and talk about people as being friendly, rude, and so on). There are obviously a great many of these general dimensions relevant to communication skill, and what counts as skillful varies to some extent with culture and context, but among theories focusing on this level of analysis, emphasis is often given to qualities such as being (a) *other-oriented* (i.e., attentive and responsive to the other), (b) *affirming* (i.e., positive and supportive rather than caustic and punishing), (c) *flexible* (i.e., creative and adaptive), (d) *fluent,* and (e) *relaxed and poised.*

A fourth level reflected in characterizations of communication skill focuses on *information processing capabilities* required to act in an effective and appropriate manner. These mental activities include those related to taking in and making sense of the stimulus environment and those involved in behavioral production. Thus, on the input-processing side of the system, key components of skill include allocation of attention to relevant stimuli, listening, comprehension, social categorization, and appropriate inference making. With respect to behavioral production, the skilled communicator is able to plan and choose among behavioral alternatives, monitor and edit his or her behavior, and translate abstract conceptions of what to do and say into actual, intelligible verbal and nonverbal behaviors.

A final level of analysis seen in conceptions of communication skill is perhaps the most obvious and harkens back to Argyle's pioneering work mentioned earlier. Here the focus is on *overt behavioral features* (e.g., speech rate, occurrence of disfluencies, direction and duration of eye gaze,

discrepancies between message channels). Research dedicated to examining such molecular behavioral features indicates that, among others, behaviors perceived as more socially skilled include more eye contact, more smiling, more gestures, and fewer adaptors (i.e., fidgeting). In the verbal channel, behaviors such as asking more questions and paying compliments are perceived as skillful actions.

Sources of Variation in Communication Skill

One of the primary factors motivating the study of communication skill is the problem of variation in proficiency—a problem that manifests in numerous guises: Why are some people more skilled than other people? Why do people act in a more skillful way at certain times and in certain situations than in others? And why are individuals more skilled in some communication activities (e.g., making casual conversation) than in others (e.g., public speaking)?

These are compelling questions, and a great many theories have been developed to address them, but among these theories, certain themes and approaches are especially noteworthy. Some shortcomings in communication proficiency have their roots in cognitive and information processing deficits, as, for example, in cases of autism and age-related dementia. Among the population not characterized by problems such as these, the study of variation in communication skill very often involves examination of (a) motivation and ability, (b) stable individual-difference factors, or (c) state variables.

Examinations of the role of motivation and ability in communication proficiency are predicated on the notion that skilled performance requires both the ability to act in an effective and appropriate way and the motivation to do so. The person who does not know what to do (or how to do it) is unlikely to act in a socially skilled way. By extension, the individual who does know what to do but is not motivated to put that knowledge into practice is likely to behave in a suboptimal fashion.

Almost certainly, the most common approach to examining variability in communication skill is to locate the source of cross-individual differences in proficiency in relatively enduring trait-like individual-difference factors. Examples of such individual-difference variables are numerous indeed, but among the most prominent are *extroversion, self-monitoring,* and *cognitive complexity.* While the literature on the role of such variables in communication skill is extensive and very often produces statistically significant effects, it is important to note that these relationships tend not to be large, rarely accounting for more than 10% of the variance in actual behavior (as opposed to self-reports of behavior, responses to hypothetical scenarios, etc.).

In contrast to relatively enduring person factors, *state variables* refer to characteristics of persons that change over comparatively short time spans (i.e., days, hours, or even minutes). Among such state variables is the individual's level of *physiological arousal*—a factor that is particularly interesting because some evidence suggests that the relationship between arousal and proficiency is curvilinear: Performance improves with increasing arousal up to some point, but beyond that, still higher levels of arousal result in performance decrements. Other examples of state variables include various moods and emotions, most prominently *social anxiety*—the nervousness and "butterflies" accompanying social interaction that have been shown to be associated with a variety of behavioral manifestations generally taken to be less competent or skillful. In contrast, positive moods tend to be associated with greater creativity and increased social engagement. Still other state variables related to social proficiency include stress, drug ingestion (e.g., "alcohol myopia"), and lack of sufficient sleep.

John O. Greene

See also Cognitive Theories; Communication and Language Acquisition and Development; Competence Theories; Facework Theories; Impression Management; Intercultural Communication Competence; Learning and Communication; Social and Communicative Anxiety

Further Readings

Chen, G.-M., & Starosta, W. J. (1996). Intercultural communication competence: A synthesis. In B. R. Burleson (Ed.), *Communication yearbook 19* (pp. 353–383). Thousand Oaks, CA: Sage.

Delia, J. G. (1987). Communication research: A history. In C. R. Berger & S. H. Chaffee (Eds.), *Handbook of communication science* (pp. 20–98). Newbury Park, CA: Sage.

Greene, J. O. (2009). Communication skills. In H. T. Reis & S. K. Sprecher (Eds.), *Encyclopedia of human relationships.* Thousand Oaks, CA: Sage.

Greene, J. O., & Burleson, B. R. (Eds.). (2003). *Handbook of communication and social interaction skills.* Mahwah, NJ: Lawrence Erlbaum.

Hargie, O. D. W. (Ed.). (2006). *The handbook of communication skills* (3rd ed.). London: Routledge.

Jones, E. E. (1998). Major developments in five decades of social psychology. In D. T. Gilbert, S. T. Fiske, & G. Lindzey (Eds.), *The handbook of social psychology* (4th ed., Vol. 1, pp. 3–57). Boston: McGraw-Hill.

Proctor, R. W., & Dutta, A. (1995). *Skill acquisition and human performance.* Thousand Oaks, CA: Sage.

Spitzberg, B. H., & Cupach, W. R. (1989). *Handbook of interpersonal competence research.* New York: Springer-Verlag.

Spitzberg, B. H., & Dillard, J. P. (2002). Social skills and communication. In M. Allen, R. W. Preiss, B. G. Gayle, & N. A. Burrell (Eds.), *Interpersonal communication research: Advances through meta-analysis* (pp. 89–107). Mahwah, NJ: Lawrence Erlbaum.

COMMUNICATION THEORY OF IDENTITY

The *communication theory of identity* (CTI) was developed by Michael Hecht and colleagues; the theory emerged in the 1980s as part of a shift from considering identity a central element of human existence to identity as a social phenomenon. While earlier views emphasized the Western notion of "self" as a single, unified identity, this broader conceptualization argues that humans are inherently social beings whose lives revolve around communication, relationships, and communities and who operate from *multiple and shifting identities.* As a result, identities and *identification* are key processes through which people and groups orient themselves to each other and the world around them.

From this beginning, a *framed* or *layered perspective* emerged in the early 1990s that described identity as multifaceted, including personal, enacted, relational, and communal frames. Hecht and colleagues were studying interethnic communication with the expectation that identity would influence these processes and they, in turn, would lead to outcomes such as satisfying communication. However, the data did not fit this model. Instead, identity and communication influenced outcomes jointly. The need to explain these findings and emerging research on media representations of identity led to an examination of research conceptualizing identity as a social process and the CTI view of identity as consisting of four frames.

The *personal frame* encompasses what has traditionally been thought of as self and self-concept—the ways an individual conceives of self. The *enacted frame* is the performance or expression of identity. CTI argues that the enactments themselves are a frame of identity—that communication *is* identity and not just caused or influenced by it. As a result, managing or negotiating identity is a central process. Next, the *relational frame* of identity refers to identities that are invested in relationships, exist in relationship to each other, and are *ascribed* in and through relationships. For example, being a parent requires a child, and who we are is established and defined through identities that are ascribed to us by others. Identities also exist as characteristics of communities (*communal frame*). Media tell us, for example, what it means to be successful. Communal identities are held in common by groups rather than individuals. Finally, these identity frames are said to *interpenetrate* or intertwine with each other. For example, one's view of self as a man or women (personal identity) is juxtaposed to how others see us as men or women (relational identity), as well as how one's communities (communal identity) define these social positions.

While the CTI has many other aspects, the conceptualization of identity as social, the interpenetration of the four frames, and the management of these identities form the core of the theory. One implication is that at any time we are likely to be experiencing multiple, intersecting identities, some of which are group based, or communal. People rarely operate out of a single identity; rather multiple identities guide their thoughts and behaviors. This precept had not been well represented in research, and as a result, ethnic communities were

often seen as homogeneous. CTI-related research, in contrast, examined diverse ways of experiencing these identities. For example, studies by Hecht and Sidney Ribeau examined different labels used by members of the African American community and how these labels manifested themselves in relationships, behaviors, and thoughts.

This research also suggested some of the ways in which *identity management* can be problematic. Not only is there a tendency to see members of a group as homogeneous, but the potential conflicts that emerge from competing enactments of identities must be skillfully *negotiated*. For example, the work of Michael Hecht and Sandra Faulkner on Jewish American identity described not only the ascriptions others make to group members but also multiple and fluid communal identities, members' own insider/outsider status, the "closetable" nature of this potentially stigmatized identity, and how all these factors get negotiated inside and outside the group. Specific strategies for revealing identity align along an explicit–implicit dimension that is influenced by the relationship type (especially the presence of romance) and in the greater societal context of isolation and "otherness." In closer relationships and more supportive contexts, identities may be overtly discussed and negotiated (e.g., how all members will get to celebrate their own holidays and even aid in these enactments), as opposed to the more covert practices that go on when discrimination and prejudice are rife. These findings demonstrate the power of the theory to focus on the dynamics of identity—how it changes and evolves.

Another line of work focusing on these dynamics was initiated by Eura Jung in his 2004 dissertation on *identity gaps,* which are defined as disconnects between and among the various frames that challenge identity management. Since communication and human relations are inexact, there are often discrepancies among how we see ourselves (personal identity), how others see us (relational identity), and how we express ourselves (enacted identity). These identities also may differ from communal representations, especially when communal representations are stereotypic. These gaps have proven problematic for effective communication, as well as mental health, across different groups and situations. For example, Jung and Hecht found that Korean immigrants who come from a homogeneous society into a racially segmented and hierarchical U.S. society often experience gaps in identity, especially when they occupy "middle person status" between higher status Whites and lower status Blacks and Latinos in inner cities. These gaps have been shown to produce depression. These gaps also have proven problematic in grandparent–grandchild relationships, as shown in work by Jennifer Kam.

CTI also has directed work on youth identity and health. As a guiding force in Michael Hecht and Michelle Miller-Day's *Drug Resistance Strategies Project*, begun in the late 1980s, CTI has been used to study Latino identity and substance use as well as to develop an evidence-based, multicultural, middle school substance abuse prevention curriculum called "*keepin' it REAL*." The prevention curriculum was infused with the identities of the audience through its basis in *narrative* and narrative performance. The *principle of cultural grounding,* an approach to health-message design developed by Michael Hecht and Janice Krieger, emerged from this work and guides prevention message construction. These messages may address different frames, but it is argued that focusing on indigenous narratives about identity and the identities most salient to these narratives is essential to effective health messages.

Since 2000, CTI has been guiding a number of new lines of research that demonstrate its encompassing and expansive view of identity. Culture has often been defined in terms of nationality, race, and ethnicity; CTI encourages a broader definition consisting of multiple frames of identity. For example, on a communal level, rurality is defined by population density and/or proximity to dense population areas. These definitions have not been useful in public health campaigns except in noting that rural communities tend to be underserved. As a result, Janice Krieger is exploring the construct *rural identity* as it reflects the other frames. *Online communities* also are sources of identity and locations for identity expression. CTI research by Jennifer Warren has demonstrated how different aspects of identity influence online health information seeking by lower income African American women and is being used to develop smoking interventions targeted at members of this ethnic group. From the social-networking sites to health information seeking on the Web, identities are implicated in the online world. Finally, identities have proven useful when *targeting* health messages to groups or *tailoring* them to individuals. Messages designed to include identity representations and to appeal to salient identities are proving effective in health campaigns. The multifaceted nature of CTI makes it ideal for understanding the new global village, with its electronic and face-to-face connectivities and emerging sense of multiple identities.

Michael L. Hecht

See also Co-Cultural Theory; Cultural Contracts Theory; Cultural Identity Theory; Health Communication Theories; Identity Theories; Social Construction of Reality; Social Interaction Theories; Symbolic Interactionism

Further Readings

Hecht, M. L. (1993). 2002—A research odyssey: Toward the development of a communication theory of identity. *Communication Monographs, 60,* 76–82.

Hecht, M. L., Jackson, R. L., & Pitts, M. (2005). Culture: Intersections of intergroup and identity theories. In J. Harwood & H. Giles (Eds.), *Intergroup communication: Multiple perspectives* (pp. 21–42). New York: Peter Lang.

Hecht, M. L., Jackson, R. L., & Ribeau, S. (2003). *African American communication: Exploring identity and culture* (2nd ed.). Mahwah, NJ: Lawrence Erlbaum.

Hecht, M. L., & Miller-Day, M. (in press). The drug resistance strategies project: A communication approach to preventing adolescent drug use. In L. Frey & K. Cissna (Eds.), *Handbook of applied communication.* London: Taylor & Francis.

Hecht, M. L., Warren, J., Jung, E., & Krieger, J. (2004). Communication theory of identity. In W. B. Gudykunst (Ed.), *Theorizing about intercultural communication* (pp. 257–278). Thousand Oaks, CA: Sage.

COMMUNICATIVE ACTION THEORY

Jürgen Habermas, the contemporary German philosopher and social theorist, formulates what are arguably his most important ideas in his theory of communicative action. This account of social action features communication as an integral component and attempts to provide a normative grounding for social and critical theory. Habermas can be considered a second-generation member of the Frankfurt School of social thought, but he differs from such thinkers as Max Horkheimer and Theodor Adorno with his reflective defense of enlightenment themes. While his two-volume work *The Theory of Communicative Action* covers many topics, this entry will focus on those components most relevant to accounts of communicative activity and their normative assessment.

Habermas's theory of communicative action aims to provide a normative basis for social theory and the critique of particular forms of social organization. Instead of selecting norms based on social theories such as Marxism or abandoning any sort of covering norms, as many in postmodern strains of thought do, Habermas wants to continue the project of enlightenment and identify universal notions of truth and freedom. Instead of grounding these in nature or human nature, Habermas places these firmly in the intersubjective action that takes place in certain communicative encounters.

In general, Habermas's account of human action is twofold. Humans can employ what is called *strategic action,* or action that is based on the realization of specific ends by known means. For instance, building a bridge will involve a variety of interactions between humans and material objects, and skilled engineers will be able to predict what actions are necessary to construct a bridge that has certain structural virtues. The second sort of action is *communicative action,* or action oriented toward achieving a rationally held consensus. Whereas many social theories and critiques portray human interaction as merely being the interplay of various forces (as is the case in strategic action), Habermas attempts to build a theory that does justice to another force that is evident in human interaction—the force of reason.

Habermas discusses this distinction between strategic and communicative action by extending the work of speech act theorists such as J. L. Austin. Strategic action in language tends to utilize what Habermas calls *perlocutionary speech acts.* These are uses of language that attempt to achieve some end in the world; the actual utterance is simply the means. These are strategic insofar as they operate on the level of cause–effect and nonrational force.

An example of such utterances would be a shout to "Stop!" that literally stops people in their path, or to lie to individuals who do not know that they are being misled. Both of these cases operate, not on the level of informed and free consensus, but in a causally specifiable fashion. The first utterance is effective because it is loud and arresting; the second utterance is effective because it involves a difference in knowledge between the liar and the lied-to individual.

In contrast to strategic action, communicative action is action that is oriented toward the reaching of understanding and, as such, typically involves *illocutionary speech acts.* These are utterances that attempt to advance some claim about the world to an auditor. Habermas calls these *validity claims,* and they can be divided into three general types. *Constative* claims are representations of some state of affairs in the objective world ("You drove my car yesterday"); these are the sorts of claim that are liable to judgments of truth. Another type of validity claim is a *regulative* claim, or a statement asserting that some state of affairs (actual or possible) in the social world is right or desirable. An example of such a claim would be "It was wrong for you to borrow my car without permission yesterday." The third type of claim is the *expressive* claim. These are claims that assert a certain subjective state of the speaker is the case, and are thus liable to judgments of truthfulness. An example of such a claim is "I am upset that you borrowed my car without permission yesterday." Another important implication of the theory of communicative action is that any utterance having illocutionary force can be criticized on grounds relating to any of these sources of validity. One can criticize any claim insofar as claims all assume some state of affairs in the external world, they involve relations between people (and the assumption that one is justified in making that claim to that hearer in the first place), and they are assumed to represent the actual thoughts of the speaker (and hence be truthful).

Communicative action occurs when individuals are oriented toward exchanging utterances (of the above three types of validity claims) in an attempt to reach an understanding about the claims advanced. In other words, a speaker advances some claim about the objective, social, or subjective world, and a hearer either accepts it or asks for reasons that claim ought to be accepted. The speaker is then under an obligation to provide such reasons. Ideally, rational and free discourse proceeds in communicative action until such an informed consensus is reached on the validity claims in question, although Habermas admits that such progress toward consensus is often rarely achieved in actual practice. Instead, this ideal of communicative action can be used to describe some practices in human society (i.e., deliberative discourse in policy-making) and can be used to critique other communicative practices (such as the use of fear appeals in political advertisements).

These themes are incorporated in Habermas's notion of the *public sphere*, or places where people can openly explore meanings and ideas, as well as in the *ideal speech situation*, which is assumed by all engaging in communicative action. He argues that the mere act of trying to get someone else to agree with the claim you are advancing and the reasons you offer for that claim means you—and the other person—are committed to certain presuppositions: (a) that all individuals are using the same linguistic expressions in a consistent way; (b) that no relevant voices have been excluded or forced out of the interaction; (c) that no force is employed except the force of the better reason (no threats of personal harm, promises of rewards, etc.); (d) that all participants are motivated by the search for consensus and agreement through dialogue; and (e) that no validity claim is immune from challenge by participants. Practices, groups, and organizations can be criticized insofar as they fail to approximate such an ideal speech situation, and they can be reformed to encourage more communicative action.

Scott R. Stroud

See also Critical Rhetoric; Critical Theory; Frankfurt School; Public Sphere; Speech Act Theory

Further Readings

Cooke, M. (1994). *Language and reason: A study of Habermas's pragmatics.* Cambridge: MIT Press.

Habermas, J. (1984). *The theory of communicative action: Vol. 1. Reason and the rationalization of society.* Boston: Beacon Press.

Habermas, J. (1987). *The theory of communicative action: Vol. 2. Lifeworld and system: A critique of functionalist reason.* Boston: Beacon Press.

McCarthy, T. (1994). *The critical theory of Jürgen Habermas.* Cambridge: MIT Press.

Outhwaite, W. (1994). *Habermas: A critical introduction.* Stanford, CA: Stanford University Press.

White, S. K. (1995). *The Cambridge companion to Habermas.* Cambridge, UK: Cambridge University Press.

COMMUNITY

Community is a much-used term in communication research and theorizing, occurring in a variety of everyday senses and as a central concept in several intellectual traditions. As an ordinary term in speech and writing, *community* has (at least) five different meanings. A first and one of the most common ones, $community_1$, is to equate the term with the set of people who inhabit a certain geographic place. In this meaning, community is a geographic unit bigger than family and neighborhood but smaller than the state, region, or nation. $Community_1$ is the name for the people who live in local units such as cities, towns, and school districts (e.g., the Denver community).

A second meaning, $community_2$, is as a term of reference for a discrete set of people who share a culturally marked identity. In the United States, media frequently make claims about the gay or older community, the Hmong or Latino community, the Muslim or Jewish community, and so on. In this second use, community is a synonym for identity groups. $Community_2$ is regularly used to refer to the groups that the larger society has marginalized or stigmatized in some way. Related to this second meaning is a third one, $community_3$, which treats community as a set of people who share an interest or activity (e.g., the snowboarding community, the Facebook community, the vegan community).

Community's fourth meaning, $community_4$, is as a positive sentiment that may be enacted, accomplished, pursued, or endangered. An aim of most groups and organizations, whether they exist face-to-face or virtually, online, is to establish a "sense of community" among participants. Groups that succeed in building community are ones that through their communication have created a sense of caring and connection among the participants.

The last everyday meaning for community, community$_5$, is as a pole in two pairs of political values that both depend on and are in tension with each other. Within this meaning, commitment to the well-being of a group (community) is contrasted with a valuing of individual rights. Here, the needs and demands of people living together with bonds of connection and mutual responsibility, community$_5$, are contrasted with the impersonal, more minimalist rights of society.

These ordinary meanings of community complement as well as contradict each other. Community as a place, an identity, and an interest often come together, and when they intersect, the focal community frequently pursues community as a desired sentiment. At the same time, the demands of community$_1$ and community$_5$ (the social needs of a geographic-based group) may conflict with the needs or wants of identity or interest groups (community$_2$ and community$_3$). These ordinary meanings of community are to be found in many corners of communication scholarship. *Communication Yearbook 28*, a handbook of review articles, made community an organizing concept for 2004. The titles of the articles in this yearbook reflected the multiple meanings of community. Consider but three: "Communication in the Community of Sport," "Meetings: Discursive Sites for Building and Fragmenting Community," and "Ideal Collaboration: A Conceptual Framework of Community Collaboration."

In communication theorizing there are two traditions, or more accurately, two families of traditions, in which community is a key concept. The first family of traditions is descriptive studies of speech, discourse, or practice communities, predominately community$_1$ to community$_3$ meanings; the second family of traditions involves normative theorizing about how communication links to community and the usually positive but sometimes negative effects of community, community$_4$ and community$_5$. Each of these theoretical traditions builds on the ordinary meanings of community, albeit pulling the concept into a theoretical frame that raises very particular issues about communication.

Community as a Descriptive Term

A long-standing tradition in which community is an important concept is *ethnography of communication* studies begun by the anthropologist Dell Hymes and brought to communication in the mid-1970s by Gerry Philipsen. In ethnography of communication, the key unit of analysis is the speech community. Philipsen, for instance, studied a neighborhood of White, ethnic, urban, working-class males in an American city in the 1960s. He named his speech community Teamsterville, and his research made visible how members of this community held distinctive beliefs about categories of people such as women and children and spoke in culturally identifiable ways that differed from middle-class American practices.

While many of the speech communities that have been investigated involved sets of people who lived in a relatively small geographic locale and engaged in face-to-face exchanges, a speech community need not be geographically constrained. Tamar Katriel, for instance, studied the cultural speaking practices of Ashkenazi Jews in Israel, Kristine Fitch studied middle-class Colombians in Bogotá, and Donal Carbaugh investigated middle-class Americans' communicative beliefs and practices.

Research seeking to understand speech communities has a centrally descriptive thrust. Its goal is to make understandable the interpretive and speaking practices, sometimes called *speech codes,* of an identifiable set of people. To facilitate this descriptive enterprise, researchers use the SPEAKING mnemonic, initially developed by Hymes, to direct attention to important facets of a community's symbolic practices. SPEAKING includes the setting (S); the participants (P); the end purpose of an event (E); the sequence of acts that comprise particular events (A); the emotional key (K); the instrumentalities, that is, whether an occasion is face-to-face or mediated (I); the norms of interaction and interpretation (N); and the genre (G) of an activity. Although the kinds of people that could be a speech community has expanded across the years, its center has been a group of people bound by nationality and geography, and often also ethnicity and social class.

A related concept is that of *discourse community.* A discourse community, in John Swales's words, is a "socio-rhetorical network." In contrast to the national, geographic foci of speech communities, discourse communities are created through people's sharing of interests, aims, and activities. Occupational groups such as accountants or social workers are discourse communities, as are people who share a recreational interest in a television series, stamp collecting, or hip-hop. Members of discourse communities come together occasionally for joint activities such as competitions or conferences, and what makes them a *discourse* community is their distinctive ways of communicating. Discourse communities use socially marked vocabularies and engage in specific genres of communication; they also share ways of segmenting and understanding the social world with regard to their foci.

Community of practice is a final way of identifying community in terms of a descriptive unit. Community of practice, a term coined by Jean Lave and Etienne Wenger, refers to a set of people who share a purpose and pursue that purpose jointly in shared practices. Community of practice has much in common with discourse community, but it has been significantly more influential as an idea in communication and related disciplines. Communities of practice look at teams in a workplace, classroom groups, or any set of people spending significant amounts of time together. In education, for instance, the notion of community of practice has changed the way learning is conceptualized, moving it away from an individual, cognitive action and toward seeing learning as distributed among a set of people and accomplished by immersion in shared social practices.

People are generally members of multiple communities of practice. Whenever people come together in groups to do things—in school, at church, in work groups, and in political or recreational groups—they are involved in a community of practice. Most people are central members of some communities of practice and peripheral members in others. It is because community of practice turns attention to the communication processes that create and sustain people's definition of what they are about and fosters connections to others involved in the practice that the idea has been so influential in communication. Ana Ostermann, for example, compared the communicative practices of an all-woman police unit and a feminist crisis center dealing with women who were victims of domestic violence. She found these two occupational groups had very different ways of talking

with the female victims and tied these differences to identifiable values in each community.

Community as a Normative Ideal

A different sense of community can be traced to Aristotle's *Politics*. For Aristotle, every state was a community. Communities were created by a state's men speaking with each other about which proposed courses of action were fair and just. In Aristotle's time a community included only the nonslave adult males in a relatively small geographic area. It was these people who would come together to deliberate and make decisions about the community, and it was the communication about political matters that created a sense of connected caring.

David Depew and John Peters provide a historical overview of how community was taken up by different thinkers in the United States, with each giving the idea a different inflection. At the beginning of the 20th century, George Herbert Mead and Robert Park were interested in exploring how communities in Chicago came into being through communication. Community formation was a major concern. In contrast to the descriptive notion of community, in which people may pursue many types of aims, the normative notion of community foregrounds political aims. A "great community," American Progressives believed, was made possible by the widespread availability of newspapers because newspapers provided different segments of American society the information that would enable the segments to be knit together. Although self and community for people like Rousseau were pitted against each other, for scholars such as Mead and John Dewey, the two terms were interdependent and created through interaction. Selves and communities came into being together.

A problem in contemporary U.S. life is that people much less frequently come together in civic, neighborhood, and church groups to plan and carry out activities together. The relative absence of social ties—what Robert Putnam called *social capital* in his influential book *Bowling Alone*—creates a society in which there is no sense of community, no commitment to a social good that is larger than the needs of individuals.

Although community is usually treated as a solution to the troubles of American life, there is a recognition that communities may also be repressive. In *Democracy and Education,* Dewey advanced two criteria for a good community: First, in a good community, the interests that were shared among members were numerous and varied. Second, the interplay between a community and other forms of association were free and full. In essence, then, a good community is not a walled off cult but a group that is diverse and connected to other associations of people.

Another version of the normative notion of community can be seen in the political movement that has been dubbed *communitarianism.* In the early 1970s, the philosopher John Rawls wrote a widely influential book, *A Theory of Justice.* Rawls argued that the main goal of government is to gain and then distribute fairly to individuals the economic resources and liberties that exist within a society. Many scholars were critical of his position, seeing it as advancing a set of universal criteria for making decisions that unfairly advantaged those who already had power and influence. People, these critics argued, are situated in particular times, places, and cultural groups. Rather than conceiving of citizens as a bundle of individual "rights," communitarians argued that we needed to see people as being part of social and political groups in which groups of people had responsibilities to each other; these groups, not just individuals, were entitled to shape what a society would construe as the societal good.

Concluding Thoughts

In a recent review essay, Erin Underwood and Lawrence Frey examined how the term *community* has been used in communication research. As just about everyone writing about community does, they note that the term is overused, a "purr word" that people use because it generates positive feelings. Underwood and Frey argue for a dialectical conceptualization of community that recognizes how overlapping senses of community frequently co-occur, connecting the traditions of community described above. Drawing on an ethnographic study of a set of people living together in a home for people with AIDS, Maura Adelman and Frey show how the people who lived together created a community of practice that involved physical and communicative ways to help each other, to recognize people's lived

experiences, and to commemorate those who died. In participating in this community of practice, members used communicative rituals to create a sense of community. That is, communicative practices within the community were used to create a sense of community for all who lived there.

Community is a concept rich in association and emotional power; it is a strategically ambiguous idea, but one that treats communication as central to who people are and how connections are built with others. For these reasons, we can expect community will remain a favored concept in communication theorizing and research.

Karen Tracy

See also Bona Fide Group Theory; Community of Practice; Discourse Theory and Analysis; Ethnography of Communication; Interpretive Communities Theory; Network Society; Symbolic-Interpretive Perspective on Groups

Further Readings

Bell, D. (2003). *Communitarianism and its critics.* New York: Oxford University Press.

Bellah, R. N., Madsen, W. M., Swidler, A., & Tipton, S. M. (1985). *Habits of the heart.* New York: Harper & Row.

Depew, D., & Peters, J. D. (2001). Community and communication: The conceptual background. In G. J. Shepherd & E. W. Rothenbuhler (Eds.), *Communication and community* (pp. 3–21). Mahwah, NJ: Lawrence Erlbaum.

Kalbfleisch, P. (Ed.). (2004). *Communication yearbook 28.* Mahwah, NJ: Lawrence Erlbaum.

Lave, J., & Wenger, E. (1991). *Situated learning: Legitimate peripheral participation.* New York: Cambridge University Press.

Milburn, T. (2004). Speech community: Reflections upon communication. In P. Kalbfleisch (Ed.), *Communication yearbook 28* (pp. 411–444). Mahwah, NJ: Lawrence Erlbaum.

Ostermann, A. C. (2003). Communities of practice at work: Gender, facework, and the power of habitus at an all-female police station and a feminist crisis intervention center in Brazil. *Discourse & Society, 14,* 473–505.

Philipsen, G. (1975). Speaking "like a man" in Teamsterville: Cultural patterns of role enactment in an urban neighborhood. *Quarterly Journal of Speech, 61,* 13–22.

Shepherd, G. J., & Rothenbuhler, E. W. (Eds.). (2001). *Communication and community*. Mahwah, NJ: Lawrence Erlbaum.

Swales, J. M. (1990). *Genre analysis: English in academic and research settings*. Cambridge, UK: Cambridge University Press.

Tracy, K., & Dimock, A. (2004). Meetings: Discursive sites for building and fragmenting community. In P. Kalbfleisch (Ed.), *Communication yearbook 28* (pp. 127–164). Mahwah, NJ: Lawrence Erlbaum.

Underwood, E. D., & Frey, L. R. (2008). Communication and community: Clarifying the connection across the communication community. In C. Beck (Ed.), *Communication yearbook 31* (pp. 369–418). Mahwah, NJ: Lawrence Erlbaum.

COMMUNITY OF PRACTICE

Community of practice is a concept emphasizing that learning, knowledge, and identity are ultimately social processes arising from the collective engagement among members of a community. The theory is grounded in the doings, actions, or practices of individuals that take on meaning as the individuals engage with others in shared activities and interests. For communication study, the theory weaves together concerns of joint activity, meaning making, and identity within situated localities.

A community of practice is marked by three characteristics. First, individuals engage in *joint enterprises* reflecting a shared domain of interest. Individuals undertake tasks and activities that are linked to a commonly understood interest or aspect of the community. For example, insurance claim processors in an office individually undertake the collective work of responding to claims submitted by clients for compensation of medical expenses. Second, by undertaking joint activities and discussions, participants build relationships of *mutual engagement;* they assist one another, help each other learn how and what to do, and clarify what is meaningful and what is not, without necessarily being explicit about such concerns. Chatting with colleagues about the day's work provides such opportunities. Third, members of communities develop a *shared repertoire* of resources over time. A shared practice of experiences, tools, stories, strategies for problems, objects, and materials results from members' involvement as practitioners of the community's domain. As claim processors undertake the routine tasks of their day, they acquire and create a host of things to do and say to enable their successful engagements in their work.

While the term was briefly noted in Etienne Wenger's dissertation of 1990, the concept was first introduced to a wider audience the following year by Jean Lave and Etienne Wenger in their book *Situated Learning: Legitimate Peripheral Participation.* Over succeeding years the concept has been articulated further, receiving book-length description by Wenger in his 1998 *Communities of Practice: Learning, Meaning, and Identity.* Since then the concept has been explored by its application to numerous fields and settings in organizations, education, and governmental agencies, among others.

Communities of practice developed from the goal of creating a *social learning theory* to explain the development of knowledge and membership via social practice. Emphasizing the social nature of the process and seeking an alternative to activity theories, the theory is based on four premises: (1) Humans are social beings, (2) knowledge is situated competence in valued undertakings, (3) knowing involves active engagement in such undertakings, and (4) learning ultimately produces meaning. Building from the emphasis of *legitimate peripheral participation,* in which learning is characterized as a feature of community practice as learners move from peripheral to full member status, development of the *community of practice* theory involves integrating concerns of meaning, practice, community, and identity. Broadly, the concept is situated among theories of social practice, which collectively engage the production and reproduction of social resources, coordinated activity, and interpretations, and among theories of identity, which collectively address the social formation of the person and membership among collectives.

Four fundamental dualities make up the concept, each providing a theoretical element extendable in practical application of the theory. The first duality is *participation–reification,* the process of our negotiating meaning by our experience and engagement with the world. As we live, we develop memberships in social communities, participating and taking part in their recognized doings. In addition, we give form to our experiences, which is what *reify* means, by creating tools, symbols, stories, concepts, and material objects that reflect the practices in which we engage as participants. Meaning is manifested by the interplay of our participation and the things we create to reify or represent the practices of our communities. In our claims office, we create forms to aid our classifying of claims and talk to one another about the cases we encounter.

The second duality, *local–global,* emphasizes that practices and identities are locally created and reified. The local ways of undertaking activities, discourses, and materials are particular to this collection of members at this locality. It is emergent as individuals work together in response to what binds them together as a collective. As well, our identities as members are tied to the locale and its practice. For example, an entomology lab may have particular ways of organizing experiments that have developed over time in response to the participants' needs. More broadly, individual communities of practice, sharing a focus or domain of interest, may have connections to broader organizations or *constellations of practices.* All entomology labs share procedures associated with life sciences laboratories in general, presenting *global* concerns in their local practices. Our identities as well represent our multiple memberships in different communities.

Identity is further emphasized in the third duality, *identification–negotiability.* Identification refers to the process of individuals' investing themselves in the meanings of their communities by participating and reifying practice. It is also socially organized, linked to our perceived membership within the community. But with identification is also recognition that we may have different abilities or powers to shape or *negotiate* what is meaningful for us within communities. Not everyone in the claims office may adopt various activities as equally meaningful for their understanding and identification within the office.

The fourth duality emphasizes the continuities and discontinuities of learning by noting that practice involves *design* and *emergence.* Practice is not simply a context for learning about something else. We learn the practice of a community by our engagement in it, developing our memberships as we do. In this perspective, learning is ongoing across one's life in communities. Some aspects of practice may appear designed; new employees are trained to do procedures in ways the supervisor prefers. But collectively, individuals develop ways of undertaking and understanding their activities to be productive members. Practice, then, is an emergent structure created by what and how people learn to jointly undertake the meaningful activities associated with their community. Practice is both stable, resistant to change, and adaptable, capable of responding to new concerns of the community.

Robert C. Swieringa

See also Activity Theory; Community; Identity Theories; Learning and Communication; Organizational Socialization and Assimilation

Further Readings

Lave, J., & Wenger, E. (1991). *Situated learning: Legitimate peripheral participation.* New York: Cambridge University Press.

Wenger, E. (1998). *Communities of practice: Learning, meaning, and identity.* New York: Cambridge University Press.

Wenger, E., McDermott, R., & Snyder, W. M. (2002). *Cultivating communities of practice: A guide to managing knowledge.* Boston: Harvard Business School Press.

COMPETENCE THEORIES

Although competence has been examined from different disciplines and perspectives, it can be simply conceptualized as an individual's ability to interact appropriately and effectively with another person in a specific context. As a basic need of human beings, competence can be understood as the extent to which a person produces the intended effect in the process of interaction. The concept is usually discussed by social scientists and communication scholars under several generic categories, including fundamental competence, linguistic competence, social competence, interpersonal competence, and relational competence.

Fundamental competence concerns the cognitive ability that helps individuals communicate effectively in different situations; *social competence* emphasizes a person's specific skills that lead to an effective interaction; *linguistic competence* focuses more on the knowledge of and the ability to execute language and messages in the process of interaction; *interpersonal competence* is more goal oriented and concerned with the individual's ability to accomplish tasks by demonstrating certain successful communication skills; and *relational competence* highlights the importance of the reciprocal process of interaction, in which the interactants are able to establish relationships with each other to achieve goals. However, all these generic categories can be put under the concept of *communication competence*.

Debates About Communication Competence

Although the definition of competence is commonly accepted, debates continue to exist among scholars regarding whether competence is a trait, state, or perception. The trait approach argues that competence is an inherent predisposition or ability; thus some people are born to be more competent than others. The state approach argues that competence is based on performance or behavioral skills, which are influenced by the particular context, time, or place of interaction. The perception approach argues that competence is neither an intrinsic trait nor extrinsic skills but is the perception or impression resulting from the characteristics and behaviors of the interactants within the relational or interactional context of a communication interaction.

In addition to these debates about the essential nature of competence, another conceptual ambiguity related to defining competence is the use of *competence* and *effectiveness* in similar and overlapping ways. Because effectiveness mainly refers to behavioral performance, and competence requires appropriateness, which is based more on individual knowledge about or motivation toward the situation to complete its meaning, *competence* and *effectiveness* should not be used interchangeably. Instead, effectiveness should be considered one of the criteria in conceptualizing competence.

Theoretical Approaches

An array of theories have been developed to conceptualize the diversity of approaches to competence, including psychological, social, and critical. Theories of communication competence from the psychological perspective basically focus on message processing and production. The psychological perspective of communication competence emphasizes the individual's mental process underlying behaviors. In 2003, Steven Wilson and Christina Sabee specified *expectancy theories* and *attribution theories* as the two categories of communication competence theories for message processing; these theories concern how people attend to, interpret, and evaluate communicative behaviors in interaction. Wilson and Sabee described *goals–plans–action theories* and *hierarchical theories* as the two categories of theories for message production; they concern goal attainment through the process of generating and enacting communicative behaviors.

Theories of communication competence from the social perspective emphasize the relational, functional, and contextual nature of competence. Represented by dialectic theories of human relationship, the social perspective of communication competence takes a dialectical and dialogical stance to examine the change and multiplicity of communicative behaviors in interaction.

The critical perspective for studying communication competence is a less advanced area, drawing on the critical metatheoretical approach developed by Jürgen Habermas. Based on the belief that truth is embedded in the universal pragmatic relations between speech acts, between speakers, and between speech situations, this perspective claims that the emancipated form of life must be anticipated in every act of communication. Thus, competence can be reached only in an open and unconstrained communication context. In other words, communication competence refers to the authentic, accurate, and appropriate exchange of messages in the absence of a dominance–subordination hierarchical structure of social relationship. This approach shows its potential strength when identifying competence in the context of intercultural communication.

Common Themes

The theories contained within each of these perspectives are often incompatible in terms of approaches to communication competence; nonetheless, examining the common themes that cut across these differences is important to a comprehensive understanding of competence. These common themes, based on the criteria of effectiveness and appropriateness as valid indicators of competence, dictate that communication competence should comprise three dimensions: cognitive, affective, and behavioral abilities.

Cognitive Ability

Cognitive abilities are reflected in the individual awareness of relevant communication situations and their requirements. This situational understanding may include knowing the verbal context, in which one should know how to make sense in terms of expression; knowing the relationship context, in which one should know how to match the messages to the particular relationship at hand; and knowing the environmental context, in which one should know the constraints imposed by the symbolic and physical environments on message making. This cognitive knowledge is equivalent to *self-awareness* or *self-monitoring* in the process of communication. Self-awareness or self-monitoring helps one detect the social appropriateness of self-presentation and to further control and modify one's own expressive behaviors to meet the requirements of particular situations.

Affective Elements

The affective perspective of competence mainly concerns personal emotions or changes in feelings caused by different communication contexts or people involved in the interaction. In other words, to be competent in communication, the individual must be able to project and receive positive emotional responses in the process of interaction and demonstrate respect for differences between interactants. Scholars have identified five common personal attributes that reflect affective ability: self-concept, empathy, open-mindedness, social relaxation, and nonjudgment.

Self-concept is the way we see ourselves, which directly impacts how a person communicates and relates to the surrounding world. A person with positive self-concept, especially self-esteem, is more likely not only to think well of himself or herself and be accepted by others, but also to feel more comfortable and perform better in an ambiguous situation. Other aspects of self-concept, including optimism, extroverted personality, and self-reliance, also contribute to the enhancement of communication competence.

Empathy, or *perspective taking,* is the ability to see the event from one's counterpart's perspective during the interaction. Empathic persons are able to project themselves into another person's point of view and feel the same feelings and think the same thoughts as that person. Being able to step into another person's shoes in order to sense what is inside another person's mind helps the individual adopt different roles as required by different communication contexts, which in turn leads to reciprocity, active listening, and the establishment of rapport between the interactants.

Open-mindedness is the willingness to share with others what is on one's mind. It also is the willingness to recognize, appreciate, and accept different views and ideas from others. This process of mutual validation and confirmation of each other's identity is key to fostering a favorable impression in an interaction.

Social relaxation is the ability to regulate anxiety in interactions. A feeling of uneasiness is caused by the uncertainty or unpredictability that is created by an ambiguous situation during an initial encounter. A less competent person tends to feel insecure psychologically when entering a new situation, in which the social anxiety may lead to rigid posture, hesitation, speech disturbances, and limited communication.

Finally, being *nonjudgmental* is an effective way to avoid stereotypes and prejudices that prevent a person from listening sincerely and actively to others during the interaction. In this regard, a lack of communication competence is reflected in a person's tendency to hastily jump to conclusions in conversation without sufficient information. Such evaluative messages often lead to defensive reaction from one's counterparts, putting the interaction and the relationship in jeopardy. In contrast, being nonjudgmental fosters a feeling of enjoyment of personal differences and allows for the development of a satisfactory and supportive communication climate.

Behavioral Aspect

The behavioral aspect of competence is a dimension that concerns the ability to attain communication goals through effective application of behavioral skills. Such skills are demonstrated by adroit verbal and nonverbal behaviors that enable an individual to get the job done effectively and appropriately in communication. Five key factors of competent behavioral skills have been identified by scholars: message skills, interaction management, behavioral flexibility, identity management, and relationship cultivation.

Message skills form the foundation of linguistic competence in communication. They demand the knowledge of linguistic rules and the ability to skillfully use verbal and nonverbal language during the interaction. For example, the effective use of communication codes, the ability to identify and distinguish main ideas and message types, and the capacity for organizing, expressing, and evaluating ideas clearly and precisely are important behavioral skills that lead to a competent communication.

Interaction management is the ability to implement the interactional rules of verbal and nonverbal messages, which mainly refers to conversational turn taking. A competent person is able to make an accurate assessment of the needs of others in order to appropriately initiate, terminate, and take turns in interaction. In other words, in the process of initiating and terminating a conversation, a competent person indicates interest, tolerance, and the ability to orient toward the others in the interaction. A successful interaction management also involves affiliation and support through speech alternation, eye contact, head nods, smiling, and physical proximity, which will naturally manifest the personal abilities of attentiveness, perceptiveness, and responsiveness in terms of communication.

Behavioral flexibility shows a person's ability to adapt to different communication situations by selecting appropriate and effective strategies to achieve personal goals in interaction. Behavioral flexibility is accompanied by a comfortable feeling when interacting with different people in different contexts. In addition to feeling easy and relaxed about getting along with new people and fitting in with different groups of people, a person with behavioral flexibility is also good at making choices in terms of messages to mark the status and relationship of the people involved in the interaction.

Identity management is based on the ability of knowing oneself as an entity, and at the same time being able to inform the counterparts about who they are. Identity cannot be developed alone by oneself; instead, it is formed through the process of negotiation and reinforcement between the interactants in communication, which reflects a dynamic and multifaceted process. Thus, how to display the salience and intensity of each other's identity in different temporal and spatial situations is the sine qua non of being competent in communication.

The last factor of the behavioral aspect of communication competence is the ability to develop a positive relationship with others. *Relationship cultivation* is dictated by the independent and reciprocal interactions between the two parties; only through this dimension can one's needs be satisfied and a positive outcome of interaction be attained. Usually, being friendly, showing concern and commitment, and displaying courtesy and cooperativeness during the interaction will ensure the development of a beneficent relationship.

Assessment of Communication Competence

A final issue for the study of communication competence that needs to be addressed is how to assess communication competence. Scholars have taken three approaches to resolving this problem: (1) soliciting data from individuals through self-assessment of their own abilities, (2) training raters to provide objective and reliable observations of interactants' behaviors, and (3) soliciting interactants' views of their counterparts' communication abilities in communication. The issues and methods of the assessment of communication competence were organized and discussed in depth by Brian Spitzberg in 2003, providing clear direction for future researchers interested in pursuing this specific area of study.

Guo-Ming Chen

See also Cognitive Theories; Communication Goal Theories; Emotion and Communication; Intercultural Communication Competence; Interpersonal Communication Theories; Learning and Communication

Further Readings

Bostrom, R. N. (Ed.). (1984). *Competence in communication: A multidisciplinary approach*. Beverly Hills, CA: Sage.

Chen, G.-M., & Starosta, W. J. (2008). Intercultural communication competence: A synthesis. In M. K. Asante, Y. Miike, & J. Yin (Eds.), *The global intercultural communication reader* (pp. 215–237). New York: Routledge.

Habermas, J. (1970). Toward a theory of communicative competence. In H. P. Dreitzel (Ed.), *Recent sociology No. 2: Pattern of communication behavior* (pp. 114–148). New York: Macmillan.

Rubin, R. B. (1985). Communication competence. In G. M. Phillips & J. T. Wood (Eds.), *Speech communication: Essays to commemorate the 75th anniversary of the Speech Communication Association* (pp. 94–129). Carbondale: Southern Illinois University Press.

Spitzberg, B. H. (2003). Methods of interpersonal skill assessment. In J. O. Greene & B. R. Burleson (Eds.), *Handbook of communication and social interaction skills* (pp. 93–134). Mahwah, NJ: Lawrence Erlbaum.

Spitzberg, B. H., & Cupach, W. R. (1984). *Interpersonal communication competence.* Beverly Hills, CA: Sage.

Wiemann, J. M., & Backlund, P. (1980). Current theory and research in communicative competence. *Review of Educational Research, 50,* 185–199.

Wilson, S. R., & Sabee, C. M. (2003). Explicating communicative competence as a theoretical term. In J. O. Greene & B. R. Burleson (Eds.), *Handbook of communication and social interaction skills* (pp. 3–50). Mahwah, NJ: Lawrence Erlbaum.

COMPLEXITY AND COMMUNICATION

Sir Isaac Newton argued that the relationships between all physical elements can be measured, predicted, and controlled. *Complexity theory,* as developed in the 20th century by scientists such as the Nobel laureate chemist Ilya Prigogine, says otherwise, holding that the relationships of many physical elements and organisms are nonlinear. Some theorists in the social sciences have begun to recognize the adaptability of complexity theory to human systems. For example, one of its classic ideas—that "initial conditions make a difference"—which was originally discovered in meteorology simulations, is transferable to human relationships. Meeting an attractive person, say, or beginning an important project is affected by the precise context of when such an event happens in a sequence of other possibilities.

Inevitably, complexity theory became an umbrella concept that covers a wide span of influences in the hard and soft sciences—from chemistry and physics to communication and social psychology. It has this breadth because the more a focus on any given system, be it social or physical, is widened to include its supersystem (the layer of influences outside it, such as the weather, external politics, or technological change) and its subsystem (the layer below, such as subordinates, commodities, or outsourced functions), the more complex that system becomes. For example, SEMATECH, the computer research consortium developed in the mid-1980s to regain U.S. market share from Japan, has as its supersystem the computer industry; as its subsystem, it has its various suppliers of products and services. Complexity theory would say that it is impossible to understand SEMATECH as an organization without understanding the industry and its suppliers. And, in fact, a team of researchers documenting the SEMATECH story in the 1990s showed that the consortium's leader, Robert Noyce, found it necessary for SEMATECH to invest in the supplier subsystem in order to improve chip-manufacturing performance.

This entry describes two kinds of complexity and then discusses the kinds of communication to be used in response to them. First is *structural* complexity, a set of conditions characterized by numerosity (e.g., the greater the number, the greater the complexity), diversity, and interdependence of system parts. When combined, these three conditions increase the amount of uncertainty that one finds or must deal with in a given system. Structural complexity, then, describes the *conditions* inherent in that system. *Dynamical* complexity, on the other hand, is the actual process of things changing nonlinearly in a structurally complex system. Say, for example, 100 leaders (numerosity) from 100 sovereign nations (diversity), whose fates are connected, must reach a decision concerning the allocation of scarce resources (interdependence of system parts). The process of their decision making is inevitably complex, and the result equally uncertain, which is to say, unpredictable. While traditional Newtonian science may identify main effects and principal features of a system, complexity theorists would argue that total control of elements within that system is impossible because combined effects that are in simultaneous interplay act—and interact—in unpredictable ways, making systems dynamical. When structural and dynamical complexity are applied to human systems, we are reminded anew that people are only occasionally logical and rational. Because they possess imperfect information, they tend to act on the basis of ideology, chance, and perceived individual payoff.

Under conditions of dynamical complexity, the environment shifts around and behind a person such that it is difficult to know what will happen next. For example, in 1980 no one imagined the existence of the Internet and its wide use that followed just 25 years later. At the same time, a picture telephone had existed since the 1960s, but its cost was so high and the quality of the technology so low that no one used it. Who would have predicted 15 years ago that people would be interested in watching a movie on a 5-cm × 5-cm (2-in. × 2-in.) screen held in their hand, as in a smartphone? So, looking at technology alone and how consumers' tastes change in relation to their ability to pay for it exemplifies this kind of complexity.

Nonlinearity includes the idea that the mere behavior of some people taking action has a way of changing the rules for everyone. Since there is no necessarily "right" direction or answer, people, needing a way to gain some modicum of control under conditions of complexity, tend to play off each other and act outward—that is, they use each other's actions as a guide for what to do next. To return to our example of the smartphone, technologists must now be asking themselves, "What does a 5-cm × 5-cm screen mean for the future of our technology? How might such a small screen affect word processing in the future? How might we solve the problem of minute fonts and keyboards?" By the time this little entry is read, even these questions will in all likelihood seem comically dated. This ongoing evolution, in which the system state or condition at any time depends on the preceding condition, defines the system as dynamic and therefore transformative over time.

What happens in the dynamic enactment of structural complexity? Progress is uneven; the varying rate of diffusion of innovations is evidence that players with unequal knowledge innovate at different rates of speed. But there is also a greater chance

for synergy, both positive and negative. There are all kinds of synergies—religious, pharmacological, ideological, practical, and mathematical.

The synergy relating to communication in organizations is of special interest to us here. One such kind of synergy is group synergy. It includes the effect of combining unique individual talents into a team that produces a special outcome, such as a Rodgers and Hammerstein musical, a Lewis and Clark expedition, or a Woodward and Bernstein political investigation. But synergy can also be the way in which complexity increases risks negatively. Just as it is possible to create new technologies that, because of their simplicity, bypass more complicated ones and create transformational results—such as the microchip's replacing the transistor—the opposite can also be true: Negative synergy can generate disastrous results. The combination, in 2001, of the technologies of passenger jets, skyscrapers, and a rudimentary knowledge of piloting an airplane is a poignant example.

Another effect of dynamical complexity is a balancing act between order and disorder within a system. This condition is called *far from equilibrium* (FFE). It has both negative and positive feedback loops and thus is simultaneously capable of stability and instability. Behavior under conditions of FFE is paradoxical because the system moves autonomously back and forth between stability and instability. Take, for example, jazz music. It has stability that is created by the bass and percussion instruments, which establish the basic rhythm of the music. But once this rhythm is in place, variation and improvisation are possible from other instruments because they play off the continuous rhythm. The combination of rhythm and improvisation makes jazz what it is—a complex system that is deliciously FFE.

What does a structural and dynamical interpretation of complexity have to do with communication? This is where the work on integrative complexity in communication and social psychology is applicable. *Integrative complexity* refers to a style of thinking—more particularly, a style of problem solving—that involves recognizing and integrating multiple perspectives and possibilities and their interrelated contingencies. The concept has two features: *differentiation,* which is the number of features of a problem situation recognized and taken into account in decision making, and *integration,* which is the number of complex connections that are drawn from among the characteristics that have been differentiated. Integrative complexity focuses on the extent to which individuals make differentiations in their thinking and integrate those differentiations into workable solutions.

For example, let's say we're a start-up high-tech company aspiring to create technologies that build on the smartphone. All the different pieces of relevant information about that phone—as its price decreases by x percent, its adoption increases by y percent—exemplify differentiation. Meanwhile, the number of connections we manage to make among these pieces of information—for example, the total market for smartphones will be saturated in z years—exemplifies integration.

Let's say, further, that our company aspires to create a superior work environment that will help promote our creation of these technologies. Here, our goal is an environment that is markedly practical, is hospitable to lots of different meanings, and generously takes into account others' points of view. What we do not want is a simplistic environment that prefers black-and-white interpretations of information and that assumes that authoritative figures are more apt to be correct than subordinates who actually operate close to what is going on. Here, then, is the difference between integrative complexity and its opposite, low-integrative complexity.

Integratively complex thinking is affected by the speed and rate of interpretation. Low-complexity thinkers are more likely to (a) be satisfied operating with little information, (b) make snap decisions, and (c) dismiss others into an out-group if the information they provide is disagreeable. Under conditions of complexity, and when creativity is the goal, outsider information increases the quality of decision making because divergent thinkers push against common assumptions.

Integratively complex communication is FFE because it is directed toward the dual goals of processing complex information and making links among the data that provide a workable solution. Integrative complexity involves establishing rules for operating that allow the system to perform without focusing on rules for rules' sake; in addition, those operating under integrative complexity are willing to change rules when they no longer serve the system.

Within integrative complexity, simple social realities are not given as fact but rather constructed and interpreted in complex ways. Any observed phenomenon is the resolution of a large number of mutual, simultaneous, entangled interactions, each of which is constantly shaping and being shaped by all others; there is no simple linear relationship between cause and effect, or even between success and failure. Analytical approaches have generally failed to acknowledge this dynamic nature of organization, analogous to a living process, in which some interdependent parts may experience more comparative degrees of success or failure than others at any given moment. Things tend not to come out even.

Integratively complex systems have checks and balances, multilevel assessments of performance, testing of assumptions with measurement, and public meetings at scheduled intervals to advance arguments so that understanding can mature over time. These practices help show that "the right way to go" is constantly up in the air and dependent on the conversations of participants who are knowledgeable about the problem at hand. Action is valuable under conditions of complexity. It's important to understand the irony of bureaucratic control—that the very attempt to make systems that are perfectly rule-following often results in consequences opposite of what was originally intended.

Integratively complex systems focus on information processing and decision making—especially on how fixed or flexible the interpretation of information is and how, once interpreted, information leads to decision-making structures. An integratively complex system is both stable enough to remain safe from destruction and free enough to experiment and to invent systems that create opportunity.

Larry Browning

See also Cybernetics; Group Communication Theories; Organizational Communication Theories; System Theory

Further Readings

Anderson, P. (1999). Complexity theory and organization science. *Organization Science, 10,* 216–223.

Contractor, N. S., & Seibold, D. R. (1993). Theoretical frameworks for the study of structuring processes in group decision support systems: Adaptive structuration theory and self-organizing systems theory. *Human Communication Research, 19,* 528–563.

Gleick, J. (1987). *Chaos: Making a new science.* New York: Viking Penguin.

Gruenfeld, D. H. (2006). Status, ideology, and integrative complexity on the U.S. Supreme Court: Rethinking the politics of decision making. In J. M. Levine & R. L. Moreland (Eds.), *Small groups: Key readings* (pp. 133–156). New York: Psychology Press.

Harvey, O. J. (1966). *Experience, structure & adaptability.* New York: Springer.

Holland, J. (1998). *Emergence: From chaos to order.* Reading, MA: Perseus.

Huber, G. P. (1991). Organizational learning: The contributing processes and the literatures. *Organization Science, 2,* 88–115.

Maruyama, M. (1963). The second cybernetics: Deviation-amplifying mutual causal processes. *American Scientist, 5,* 164–179.

Perrow, C. (1984). *Normal accidents: Living with high-risk technologies.* New York: Basic Books.

Snowden, D. J., & Boone, M. E. (2007, November). A leader's framework for decision making. *Harvard Business Review,* 68–76, 149.

Suedfeld, P., & Tetlock, P. (1977). Integrative complexity of communications in international crises. *Journal of Conflict Resolution, 21,* 169–184.

Weick, K. E., & Quinn, R. E. (1999). Organizational change and development. *Annual Review of Psychology, 1999, 50,* 361–398.

COMPLIANCE GAINING STRATEGIES

Efforts to gain the compliance of others are ubiquitous. Compliance-gaining communication is a form of persuasion that, in turn, is a form of influence. *Influence* may therefore be understood as an umbrella term that encompasses both intentional and unintentional communication to alter another's beliefs, attitudes, intentions, or behavior. Compliance gaining and compliance resisting are typically viewed as a subset of persuasion that involves intentional efforts to change another's behavior.

Conceptualizing Compliance Gaining

As its name suggests, compliance gaining emphasizes a specific outcome: compliance. Its emphasis is not on attitude change, but rather on *behavioral conformity*. Research on compliance gaining examines various verbal and nonverbal strategies to increase the likelihood of securing another's adherence. Promise of reward and threat of punishment are two of many such strategies. The trajectory of research in this area has emphasized the interpersonal arena, or one-on-one compliance gaining, although other contexts have been studied as well.

Taxonomies and Typologies

Compliance-gaining research dates back to at least 1960, when John French and Bertram Raven identified five bases of power used in social interaction. *Reward power* involves the ability to confer benefits on others. *Coercive power* focuses on the ability to inflict punishments or impose penalties on others. *Expert power* centers on expertise or competence. We tend to comply with people who "know their stuff." *Legitimate power* is based on one's official rank or formal standing. Finally, *referent power* has to do with being admired or respected. A person is more likely to comply with a request from someone she or he reveres.

In the mid-1960s, Gerald Marwell and David Schmidt were among the first to demarcate compliance gaining as a field of study. They identified 16 strategies that they labeled as a *deductive taxonomy,* meaning that all compliance-gaining efforts could be grouped into one of the 16 categories. In the early 1980s, Richard Wiseman and William Schenck-Hamlin questioned such an a priori scheme, noting that some strategies, such as deceit or hinting, were ignored. Wiseman and Schenck-Hamlin formulated their own *inductive taxonomy,* which yielded a total of 14 strategies. Frank Boster, James Stiff, and Rodney Reynolds reconciled the disparity in these two schemes by noting that they were complementary and that combining them produced 24 distinct strategies.

Soon after, a proliferation of taxonomies ensued. In the mid-1990s this taxonomic confusion was remedied somewhat by Kathy Kellermann and Tim Cole. They compared 74 different taxonomies and noted that many strategies were overlapping and/or not conceptually distinct. Similar strategies often carried dissimilar labels (e.g., *threat* and *warning*), and dissimilar strategies often shared confusingly similar labels (e.g., *favor* and *altruism*). After integrating all the strategies, they concluded that 64 separate, distinct strategies had been identified in the literature.

In addition to the patchwork quilt of strategies, compliance-gaining research was problematic on other grounds. First, much of the research was atheoretical in nature. Researchers identified what strategies participants claimed they would use, but not why participants chose those particular strategies. Second, many studies were based on hypothetical checklists. Respondents were presented with hypothetical scenarios, offered a list of potential strategies, and instructed to rate the strategies according to their likelihood of using them. Such an approach risks *social desirability bias*. On paper, respondents might prefer more positive strategies. In practice, however, they might employ more negative strategies. A third limitation is that many studies measured only *strategy preferences*, not behavioral compliance. More recent investigations, thankfully, have focused on actual compliance in real-world settings.

Cialdini's Principles

Robert Cialdini, a leading figure in compliance-gaining research, integrated studies from a variety of disciplines into five basic principles of compliance gaining. The first principle, *reciprocity*, is based on doing another person a favor (called *pre-giving*) and then asking for a different, larger favor in return. Another principle, *commitment and consistency*, centers on a person's desire to maintain psychological consistency among her or his beliefs, attitudes, and behaviors. The third principle, *social proof*, involves comparing oneself to others and modeling others' behavior. The fourth principle, *authority*, relies on source factors such as credibility. The fifth principle, *liking*, is based on warm, ingratiatory behaviors and attractiveness. The sixth and final principle, *scarcity*, has to do with increasing the perceived value of something by making it appear to be in short supply.

Politeness Theory and Influence Attempts

Influence attempts require facework and identity management. Penelope Brown and Stephen Levinson's *politeness theory* highlights the interdependent nature of requesters' and requestees' face needs. A requester usually adapts his or her message to satisfy the requestee's face needs. Some strategies may threaten another's *positive face*—by conveying disapproval, for instance—or another's *negative face*, by constraining the other's freedom or autonomy. When framing requests, then, requesters tend to avoid face-threatening acts and shape their language choices accordingly. The same applies to compliance resisting. When declining a request, the requestee typically chooses language strategies that spare her or him guilt and the other person embarrassment. One of the challenges in making or declining requests is the need to strike a balance between being clear or straightforward and honoring face needs.

Dillard's Goals–Plans–Action Model of Interpersonal Influence

In an effort to understand the bases for strategy development and selection, James Dillard developed the *goals–plans–action* (GPA) *model of interpersonal influence*. The model focuses on the cognitive processes involved in an influence attempt, starting with the source's goals. Goals are future states of affairs that a person wishes to bring about. Compliance gaining often entails multiple goals, which Dillard delineates as *primary* and *secondary goals*. Primary goals are the catalysts for compliance gaining, while secondary goals shape the approach used. When one person asks another out on a date, the requester's primary goal is for the other person to accept the invitation. A secondary goal might be to save face if the invitation is declined. Thus, the requester might test the waters by asking, "Are you doing anything this Saturday night?" Primary and secondary goals may be complementary or contradictory.

Seven types of primary goals have been identified by Dillard. These include *gain assistance* ("Would you help me move?"); *give advice* ("I'd have that looked at if I were you."); *share activity* ("Let's do lunch."); *change orientation*, for example, alter another's perspective ("You should become a vegan: You'll look and feel better."); *change relationship* ("I think we should take a break and just be . . . friends."); *obtain permission* ("Is it OK if I leave early tomorrow?"); and *enforce rights and obligations* ("You promised we would have a destination wedding!"). Primary goals are the impetus for constructing compliance-gaining messages. Dillard does not claim these are the only primary goals. He also acknowledges that goals exist at varying levels of abstraction.

In addition to primary goals, five types of secondary goals have been identified. *Identity goals* involve personal, ethical standards of behavior. *Conversation management goals* focus on identity management and face-saving behavior. *Relational-resource goals* focus on relationship maintenance strategies. *Personal-resource goals* are aimed at improving one's assets. Finally, *affect management goals* emphasize the importance of managing moods and emotions during influence attempts.

Primary and secondary goals vary in their degree of compatibility. According to Dillard, the interplay between them reflects their *goal-structure complexity*. Based on the relationships among all the goals involved, a person develops *plans,* which are possible means of achieving goals. Plans vary in their level of abstraction, complexity, and completeness. Thus, a plan may be half baked or carefully conceived. Plans are developed based on such considerations as ease of execution, likelihood of success, and anticipated resistance.

To implement plans, a compliance gainer must develop *strategies* and *tactics*. Strategies are more abstract, while tactics are more specific or concrete. Thus a parent who used a *strategy* of positive reward to motivate his or her son to try harder in school might employ the tactic "If you get all A's this semester, I'll take you to Disneyland." While independent studies have found support for the GPA model, more empirical testing of the model is needed. At present, the GPA model serves as a useful explanatory framework of how individuals go about designing compliance-gaining messages.

Verbal Strategies

Sequential Requests

Compliance gainers often rely on a series of requests, with an earlier request laying the groundwork for a later request. A variety of sequential strategies have been identified in the literature, including the *low-ball* technique, the *that's-not-all* technique, and the *bait-and-switch* tactic. For brevity's sake, this section examines the two that

have garnered the most research attention: *foot-in-the-door* (FITD) and *door-in-the-face* (DITF).

When using the FITD technique, a source makes a small initial request to soften up the recipient, or target, of the request. Next, a larger, follow-up request is made. Compliance with the initial request significantly increases the likelihood of compliance with the second request, compared with no initial request at all. One explanation for the effectiveness of the FITD is based on Daryl Bem's s*elf-perception theory*. Doing a small good deed activates a person's self-awareness that she or he is a helpful person. Complying with the second, larger request reinforces that self-perception. The FITD strategy has proven to be quite robust, especially when the request is prosocial in nature.

A companion strategy is the DITF technique. This strategy involves making an initial large request, on the assumption that it will be rejected, then following up with a second, more reasonable request. A variety of explanations have been offered for the effectiveness of the DITF. Two of the most common are *reciprocal concessions* and *social responsibility*. For strangers, it appears that targets perceive they are engaged in a negotiation, and compliance with the second request is viewed as a compromise. For friends, a sense of social responsibility or helping behavior seems to be at work. Other explanations, such as the *perceptual-contrast phenomenon,* also have been offered: Compared with the first request, the second request seems much more reasonable. Yet another explanation is *guilt based;* having said no once, the target feels guilty about saying no again. Whatever the underlying mechanism, the DITF has proven to be an effective compliance gaining strategy.

Other Verbal Strategies

Other verbal strategies include the *disrupt-then-reframe* (DTR) strategy, the *even-a-penny-helps* strategy, and the *even-a-few-minutes-helps* strategy. The objective of the DTR strategy is to reduce resistance by using a non sequitur. For example, a requester might ask, "Would you like to buy some raffle tickets? They are $3. That's 300 pennies. What a bargain." The verbal anomaly "300 pennies" tends to interrupt the target's thought process, thereby reducing resistance. Reframing, for example, "What a bargain," redirects attention to the positive features of the request. For the DTR to be effective, both elements—disruption and reframing—are essential.

Making a request and adding "even a penny helps" also has been shown to increase compliance. Yet inserting the phrase "even a few minutes would help" is ineffective. Another study revealed that adding the word "please" to a request for a charitable donation actually backfired, reducing the rate of compliance. Thus, not every verbal appeal is effective.

A variety of other verbal strategies rely on impression management to induce compliance. Two such strategies are *ingratiation* and *self-promotion.* Ingratiatory behaviors include compliments ("I love that tie!") and opinion conformity ("You are so right!"). Self-promotion seeks to enhance another's impression of the source ("I can meet you as soon as I'm done helping at the homeless shelter."). Both positive ("You are so helpful!") and negative *social labeling* ("You should be ashamed!") also have been shown to increase compliance.

Nonverbal Strategies

Immediacy

A number of nonverbal strategies for gaining compliance have been documented in the literature. Many of these are based on *immediacy behaviors,* such as eye contact, smiling, and touch. Peter Andersen's *direct effects model of immediacy* posits that warm, involving behaviors, in and of themselves, generate more favorable impressions of the requester. Greater liking for the requester, in turn, leads to greater compliance.

Touch and Compliance

A number of investigations have demonstrated that a brief, light touch on the shoulder increases compliance. Touch tends to elicit a more favorable impression of the requester, which translates into greater compliance. Touch has been shown to increase tips left by diners, facilitate helping behavior by passersby, improve participation rates in a survey, and increase petition signing. In one study, strangers were asked to watch a large, unruly dog while its owner ran an errand. Strangers who were touched were more likely to comply, compared with strangers who were not touched. These results appear to be generalizable to other settings. A

meta-analysis by Chris Segrin revealed that touch was always as effective and often more effective than no touch. Interestingly, touch appears to be effective even if the target is unaware of it.

Eye Contact

Gaze is another immediacy behavior that has been shown to facilitate compliance. For example, one study found that direct eye contact increased targets' willingness to participate in a survey. Moreover, a verbal request is not necessarily required for eye contact to work. One study found that a person with an arm injury was more likely to receive assistance if she made eye contact with a bystander, as opposed to avoiding eye contact.

One exception to the general finding that eye contact facilitates compliance involves illegitimate requests. Chris Kleinke found that eye contact increased compliance with a legitimate request but decreased compliance with an illegitimate request. Avoiding eye contact while making an illegitimate request may be perceived as a sign of deference or humility. With few exceptions, however, gaze seems to be an effective compliance-gaining strategy.

Smiling

People who smile are perceived as kinder, happier, warmer, more sociable, and more honest than unsmiling people. Not only does smiling tend to engender more favorable impressions of a person, it also increases the likelihood that others will lend assistance. One study found that students who were caught cheating received more lenient punishment when they smiled.

Putting a smile on another's face also appears to facilitate compliance gaining. In one study, a food server who provided a joke for diners received more tips than food servers who did not offer a joke. Smiling, however, is not a foolproof strategy. Smiles can be highly ambiguous. What one person perceives as a genuine smile, another may perceive as disingenuous. The meaning of a smile is thus interpreted against a backdrop of contextual clues, including gender, culture, and the nature of the relationship.

Mirroring and Mimicry

Mirroring or *mimicry* of another's nonverbal behavior also has been shown to facilitate compliance. Mirroring another's nonverbal cues may be construed as a sign of liking or rapport. Mimicry also can facilitate helping behavior. As with many nonverbal cues, mirroring appears to operate at a low level of awareness. The person whose nonverbal behavior is being imitated is typically unaware of the strategy.

Appearance and Apparel

Appearance and apparel are not so much immediacy cues as credibility and status factors. An abundance of research suggests that appearance cues, such as attractiveness and attire, play a role in compliance gaining. Physically attractive people benefit from a variety of positive attributions others make about them. These attributions carry over into behavioral compliance. For example, attractive persons who solicited charity donations received a larger number of donations than did unattractive persons. And strangers were more likely to assist an attractive than an unattractive young woman, and more likely still to help a "traditionally" attractive woman as opposed to an attractive "feminist."

The fairly consistent finding is that well-dressed people are more likely to gain others' compliance than poorly dressed people are. In one study, for example, a well-dressed or casually dressed "shoplifter" pocketed a CD in a retail store in plain view of another customer. Customers were less likely to report the well-dressed thief than the casually dressed thief.

People wearing uniforms are more likely to secure compliance than nonuniformed persons are. In one investigation, a passerby was more likely to help a stranger who needed change for a parking meter when the stranger was dressed as a firefighter rather than as a businessperson or a homeless person.

Contexts for Compliance Gaining

Although early studies on compliance gaining relied heavily on self-reports involving hypothetical situations, recent research centers on compliance in real-world settings. A wide variety of communication contexts have been examined thus far, including bystanders and helping behavior, classroom compliance, computer-mediated influence, food servers and tipping behavior, intimate influence, physician–patient encounters, police interrogation and custodial interviews, retail sales, sexual compliance and resistance, and upward–downward influence in organizational settings. Examining specific strategies in specific contexts has proved much more valuable than the earlier efforts to develop universal, "one size fits all" typologies.

Ethics of Compliance Gaining

As is the case with all persuasion, compliance gaining is fraught with *ethical concerns*. While some view the study of compliance gaining as ethically suspect, equating it with manipulation, others maintain that compliance gaining is a necessary, indispensable feature of human interaction. Robert Gass and John Seiter maintain that particular strategies, such as fear appeals, deception, and ingratiation, are neither good nor bad in and of themselves. Rather, they suggest, the "motives color the means," meaning that the moral quality of an influence attempt depends more on the end(s) sought than the means used. By way of illustration, if one used deception to swindle a person out of his or her life savings, the outcome would be unethical. If one used deception to conceal a surprise party for a friend, however, deception would be justifiable as a means to an end.

Conclusion

Compliance gaining piqued the interest of scholars in the 1960s and has continued ever since. Much of the current research is being conducted in specific communication contexts. While some compliance-gaining contexts may seem mundane, such as studying ways to increase tips, other compliance-gaining research, such as resisting unwanted sexual advances or encouraging patients to follow their doctor's advice, holds important social consequences. Further research in this area offers the prospect not only of how to facilitate compliance, but of how to resist influence attempts as well.

Robert H. Gass

See also Immediacy; Nonverbal Communication
    Theories; Persuasion and Social Influence Theories;
    Politeness Theory

Further Readings

Cialdini, R. (2004). *Influence: Science and practice* (4th ed.). Boston: Allyn & Bacon/Pearson.

Dillard, J. P. (2004). The goals-plans-action model of interpersonal influence. In J. S. Seiter & R. H. Gass (Eds.), *Perspectives on persuasion, social influence, and compliance gaining* (pp. 185–206). Boston: Allyn & Bacon/Pearson.

Gass, R. H., & Seiter, J. T. (2007). *Persuasion, social influence, and compliance gaining* (3rd ed.). Boston: Allyn & Bacon/Pearson.

Goldstein, N. J., Martin, S. J., & Cialdini, R. B. (2008). *Yes! 50 scientifically proven ways to be persuasive.* New York: Free Press.

Guéguen, N., & Fischer-Lokou, J. (2002). An evaluation of touch on a large request: A field setting. *Psychological Reports, 90*, 267–269.

Kellermann, K., & Cole, T. (1994). Classifying compliance gaining messages: Taxonomic disorder and strategic confusion. *Communication Theory, 4*(1), 3–60.

Kleinke, C. (1980). Interaction between gaze and legitimacy of request on compliance in a field setting. *Journal of Nonverbal Behavior, 5*, 3–12.

Segrin, C. (1993). The effects of nonverbal behavior on outcomes of compliance-gaining attempts. *Communication Studies, 44*, 169–187.

van Baaren, R. B., Holland, R. W., Kawakami, K., & van Knippenberg, A. (2004). Mimicry and prosocial behavior. *Psychological Science, 15*, 71–74.

Vrugt, A. (2007). Effects of a smile: Reciprocation and compliance with a request. *Psychological Reports, 101*, 1196–1202.

COMPLICITY THEORY

Complicity theory draws on critical race theory and cultural studies to explore how discourse in opposition to certain groups contributes to the negative social construction of difference as well as identity. Grounded in the *theory of the opposite party* attributed to the ancient Greek Sophist Thrasymachus of Chalcedon, complicity theory begins with the idea that individuals or groups that are at odds fail to see how their positions are implicated in each other's and applies this observation to contemporary conflicts that center on issues of race, gender, class, and classification.

Complicity theory takes the notion that language creates reality to its logical extreme by suggesting that a language of argument and persuasion that rests on rigid definitions of self and other actually cultivates an understanding of difference as fundamentally negative. This account questions the underlying assumption of much Western communication theory that argument and persuasion are "natural" forms of human symbolic interaction.

Theories of complicity are not unique to communication studies. In literary theory, for example, complicity critiques account for the ways that those subjected to oppressive symbolic practices reinforce the institutional and ideological systems that oppress them. Within literary, cultural, and rhetorical studies, theories of complicity have offered powerful and provocative perspectives to view the problems and possibilities of oppositional resistance and emancipatory action.

Within literary and cultural studies, complicity critiques have focused on the ways in which social actors participate socially and symbolically in the creation and maintenance of oppressive symbolic and material practices of late capitalism. Within communication studies, complicity theory has focused on the recognition of the subtle and sometimes insidious ways that individuals are implicated in systems of domination by certain oppositional discursive strategies employed to critique those systems. This conception of complicity as a *theory of negative difference* is grounded in research on rhetoric and race that explores the symbolic and epistemological aspects of oppositional discourse and criticism.

The most sustained considerations of complicity theory have emerged in studies of African American culture, consciousness, and identity. The earliest discussions of complicity as a theory of negative difference emerged in research on the rhetoric of racism that challenged accepted notions of domination and subordination and examined the underlying assumptions of traditional Western communication theories and practices, including notions of Black authenticity and unity. The theory has been adopted by African American communication scholars to examine the complexities of Black nationalism and Black masculinity, as well as notions of racial difference and identity. Complicity theory has also been utilized by scholars writing on reconciliation and reparations to explore the ways in which public and intellectual discourse has actually been reinforced and sustained by oppositional communication.

Complicity theory has also influenced scholarship in studies of Whiteness, gay and lesbian identity, race and gender in higher education, and the power of media to cultivate interracial understanding. In each of these areas, complicity theory offers a useful lens through which the complex character of discursive resistance and reification can be analyzed and explicated. Whiteness studies have drawn on complicity theory to consider how conceptions of racial identity taken to be essentially true contribute to symbolic and social antagonisms and also reinforce White privilege and ideological innocence. Gay and lesbian studies have explored the complex contradictions that emerge at the intersection of Christianity and sexuality and how rigid notions of difference and identity are challenged in this context. Complicity theory has been applied to studies of how educational institutions function with fixed notions of race and gender identity, even as these institutions ostensibly call such notions into question, and has also been used to investigate the potential of film to reshape and transform racial attitudes.

These studies also explore a central concept of complicity theory: the notion of coherence. Coherence focuses on the ways in which seemingly antithetical positions are implicated in each other. While complicity and coherence can be viewed as *contrasting* notions, they can also be understood to exist in a dialogic, or *complementary*, relationship. This understanding of complicity theory assumes that it is not possible to move *beyond* complicity, but only to recognize that we are always complicit in systems of domination. To believe that we can escape our complicity, then, only reinforces the very systems we hope to transform or overcome.

The disease of alcoholism offers a useful analogy: It is only by recognizing and accepting that one is an alcoholic that one can address the disease. When applied to social phenomena such as racism and sexism, complicity theory posits that we can begin to address these conditions only by acknowledging that they always influence our language and behavior, even when we believe that they do not. The notion that one can be "color blind" or "gender blind" is thus a form of self-deception. We are, by virtue of the fact that we live in societies shaped by racism and sexism, complicit in those systems: Only when we can accept our complicity can we begin to understand and address its implications for language, life, and social interaction.

Mark Lawrence McPhail

See also Afrocentricity; Critical Race Theory; Intercultural Communication Theories; Interracial Communication; Social Construction of Reality

Further Readings

Chavez, K. (2004). Beyond complicity: Coherence, queer theory, and the rhetoric of the "gay" Christian movement. *Text and Performance Quarterly, 24,* 255–275.

Hatch, J. (2003). Reconciliation: Building a bridge from complicity to coherence in the rhetoric of race relations. *Rhetoric & Public Affairs, 6,* 737–764.

McPhail, M. (1991). Complicity: The theory of negative difference. *Howard Journal of Communications, 3,* 1–13.

McPhail, M. (1998). From complicity to coherence: Rereading the rhetoric of Afrocentricity. *Western Journal of Communication, 62,* 114–140.

Orbe, M., & Kinefuchi, E. (2008). Crash under investigation: Engaging complications of complicity, coherence, and implicature through critical analysis. *Critical Studies in Media Communication, 25,* 135–156.

Patton, T. (2004). In the guise of civility: The complicitous maintenance of inferential forms of sexism and racism in higher education. *Women's Studies in Communication, 27,* 60–87.

Pfister, J. (2000). Complicity critiques. *American Literary History, 12,* 610–623.

COMPREHENSIVE MODEL OF INFORMATION SEEKING

See Uncertainty Management Theories

COMPUTER-MEDIATED COMMUNICATION

In the broadest sense, computer-mediated communication (CMC) can be any form of communication that is mediated by *digital* technology. Thus, a telephone conversation can be said to be computer mediated if each speech act is converted into digital code, transmitted, and then decoded for the listener.

In relation to the speech acts themselves, such a conversation is no different from that mediated by an analogue or human-operated telephone exchange. However, when the conversation is converted into a form that is managed by computing systems, the spatial, temporal, and social contexts of telephony can be radically transformed. Speech acts can be digitally recorded and digitally recognized in ways that are storable and exchangeable with other digital information. Calls can be screened, forwarded, and blocked, and conversations can be timed in ways that are linked to billing; all these properties impact how people use the telephone, whether they use it at all, and how long they use it.

While CMC can take in the study of telephony and *interactivity* in any computer-mediated form, the most common meaning of it is related to the direct use of personal computers for communication, to the point that today, CMC is often used interchangeably with online Internet communication. Thus e-mail, chat rooms, bulletin boards, and simulated worlds are all forms of CMC. But the distinguishing feature here is that what is being mediated is *communication*—not information or entertainment. Browsing the World Wide Web and downloading information—the primary activity of Web 1.0 (the original use of the Internet)—are not examples of CMC. Rather, communication between individuals, whether one-to-one or many-to-many, sharing text, sounds, and images in Web 2.0, and interacting in next-generation environments are examples. However, the most common forms of CMC are e-mail, with its very low bandwidth, or the broader-banded online social networking outlets, in which users can post images or music. But in each case, text predominates.

A further division here is between synchronous and asynchronous CMC. Many chat sites, such as the early Internet Relay Chat and "I seek you," Multi-User Dungeons (MUDs) and MUDs object oriented (MOOs), and today's Second Life are in real time. The bulk of CMC, however, is asynchronous, with e-mail and online social networking offering the convenience of communication that can be stored in a threaded conversation.

The fact that there are several varieties of CMC, according to temporal and bandwidth qualities, has led some researchers to problematize the status and nature of interactivity in CMC.

Interactivity

Founder of the *Journal of Computer-Mediated Communication*, Sheizaf Rafaeli is a key theorist who can assist in understanding interaction within CMC. In an important 1988 article, Rafaeli distinguishes between connectivity, reactivity, and interactivity. Networks must have a human interface, but they must also have an architecture that makes interactivity possible. Such interactive networks, once established, take on a history of their own, and through such a history, relationships are formed. Two-way communication does not, in itself, guarantee interactivity. Rather, an exchange or action–reaction must develop into a relationship in which one utterance becomes a context for another. Without this form of connectivity, relationships become either circular or solipsistic.

Rafaeli also wants to abandon the dyadic model that is applied to most CMC. Online interactivity is distributed across a network and cannot be reduced to the sum of a point-to-point exchange. Every message takes into account preceding messages, as well as the ways in which previous messages react to one another. This view of interactivity suggests that the actual use of CMC is seldom interactive, particularly in cases of anonymity in CMC discussion groups. For this reason, a fundamental distinction needs to be made between CMC users and groups that have other outside relationships and those that do not.

Computer-Mediated Communication Research Directions

This distinction corresponds to two dominant directions in CMC research—the *cues-filtered-out* approach, which focuses research on users, and *avatar* research. When CMC is experienced as an extension of interpersonal or institutional relationships online, interlocutors are generally referred to as *users*. When interlocutors have no off-line relationship and identities exist only online, they are referred to as *avatars*.

Cues-Filtered-Out Approach

Research into users is distinctively concerned with the way computer-extended communication mediates face-to-face forms of communication. The face-to-face becomes an analogue and benchmark for measuring the "success" of CMC, which is viewed as substituting for the face-to-face. It is known as a cues-filtered-out approach because it examines which cues of nonverbal communication are missing in the communication event and how they are put "back in." Particularly important to this perspective, then, is the study of *emoticons,* the symbols used in e-mail to denote facial expressions, and *netiquette,* the ways that cyberspace demands the forms of polite protocol expected in embodied life.

Nancy Baym argues that in computer-mediated interaction, people are not able to see, hear, or feel one another, which eliminates their ability to use context cues. This leaves them in a kind of social vacuum that is different from face-to-face talk. Because of this, CMC participants typically find ways of "putting back in" the cues that are lost from external contexts. Therefore, much effort goes into bringing these external contexts into the content of interaction.

Baym also identifies five different sources of impact on CMC: (1) external contexts, in which the use of CMC is set (language, city); (2) the temporal structure of the group (synchronistic or asynchronistic); (3) the infrastructure of the computer system (speed, number of computers, capacity for anonymity, user-friendliness); (4) the purposes for which the CMC is used (interest oriented, uses and gratifications); and (5) the characteristics of the group and its members (group size, educational level of participants).

Avatar Research

The second direction of CMC research—avatar research—which was very popular in the late 1990s, champions the exclusion of external contexts of CMC. This research argues that online identities, or avatars, enjoy a neutral space of interaction. Because there are no cues that can spontaneously signify an interlocutor's appearance, gender, class, and ethnicity, avatars are seen to communicate on an equal footing, without any of the social discrimination that accompanies the above categories. An avatar can exist in a number of CMC environments. The avatar's identity may be limited to textual representation, or in the case of many synchronous forms of simulated CMC—such as MUDs, MOOs, and Second Life—an avatar can take on a visual form and adopt voices and behavior that are constructed online. The avatar does not have an identity or a history other than what is formed online.

In the 1990s, the question of online identity represented by the avatar was a major source of fascination for CMC scholars. Social–psychological and psychoanalytic frameworks have been used to understand virtual identity as a unique form of self-identity without the social inhibitions that exist in real life. The notion of cyberpsychology emerged, and new journals, such as *Cyber-Psychology & Behavior,* were established. Much of the work in this approach sought to analyze the way CMC relationships might deviate from real-life relationships with respect to honesty, morality, and empathy. Other writers, such as Sherry Turkle, saw CMC as emancipatory because it allowed people to explore their identity in a socially and physically safe simulated reality.

The euphoria that characterized the social psychology of CMC that was popular in the 1990s came under attack from a number of writers who argued that it ignored empirical research showing that CMC is one medium among many by which the same people interact. The concept of the avatar makes sense only if too sharp a distinction is drawn between the *virtual life* and real life. However, a series of everyday-life types of empirical studies in the late 1990s showed this approach to be unhelpful in explaining why some people spent a great deal of time online while for others, CMC represented a minor part of their communication practices. Moreover, at its height, avatar research could hardly lay claim to providing a representation of some kind of neutral, asocial human nature when it is considered that CMC in the mid-1990s was very much dominated by North American upper-middle-class professionals who shared similar interests.

In recent years, the interest in the avatar has waned and is of little interest to the *net generation* of young people who are born as "digital natives" and have not faced the novelty of having to migrate to digital culture. As Susan Herring has noted, the net generation does not relate well to the utopian speculations or the debates about online democracy, identity, and virtuality of earlier decades.

David Holmes

See also Digital Cultures; Media Equation Theory; Network Society; New Media Theory; Presence Theory

Further Readings

Baym, N. (1998). The emergence of on-line community. In S. Jones (Ed.), *Cybersociety: Computer-mediated communication and community* (pp. 138–163). Thousand Oaks, CA: Sage.

Haythornthwaite, C., & Wellman, B. (2002). The Internet and everyday life: An introduction. In B. Wellman & C. Haythornthwaite (Eds.), *The Internet and everyday life* (pp. 3–41). Malden, MA: Blackwell.

Herring, S. (2004). Slouching towards the ordinary: Current trends in computer-mediated communication. *New Media and Society, 6,* 26–36.

Nancy, J.-L. (1991). *The Inoperative Community* (ed. P. Connor; trans. Peter Connor, Lisa Garbus, Michael Hilland, and Simona Sawhney). Minneapolis: University of Minnesota Press.

Rafaeli, S. (1988). Interactivity: From new media to communication. In R. P. Hawkins, J. M. Wiemann, & S. Pingree (Eds.), *Sage annual review of communication research: Advancing communication science, Vol. 16* (pp. 10–134). Beverly Hills, CA: Sage.

Rafaeli, S., & Sudweeks, F. (1997). Networked interactivity. *Journal of Computer-Mediated Communication, 2*(4). Retrieved February 11, 2009, from http://jcmc.indiana .edu/vol2/issue4/rafaeli.sudweeks.html

Riva, G., & Galimberti, C. (1998). Computer-mediated communication: Identity and social interaction in an electronic environment. *Genetic, Social and General Psychology Monographs, 124,* 434–464.

Turkle, S. (1995). *Life on the screen: Identity in the age of the Internet.* New York: Simon & Schuster.

Wellman, B., & Gulia, M. (1999). Virtual communities as communities: Net surfers don't ride alone. In M. Smith & P. Kollock (Eds.), *Communities in cyberspace* (pp. 167–194). London: Routledge.

Whitty, M. (2002). Liar, liar! An examination of how open, supportive and honest people are in chat rooms. *Computers in Human Behaviour, 18,* 343–352.

Whitty, M., & Gavin, J. (2001). Age/sex/location: Uncovering the social cues in the development of online relationships. *CyberPsychology and Behaviour, 4,* 623–630.

Conflict Communication Theories

In the early 1970s, communication scholars entered the field of conflict theory, dissatisfied by ways previous scholars had treated interactants as solely rational and strategic, communication as binary (communicate or not communicate), and conflict as necessarily destructive. Two implicit assumptions made it impossible to reveal the process or function of communication in conflict: that conflict results from insufficient or ineffective communication and that cooperation is inherently superior. Communication theorists, rather, espoused a view of conflict as an inevitable and necessary social process that when managed well contributes to creativity, cohesiveness, relational growth, and productivity. Most communication theorists prefer the term *conflict management* to *conflict resolution* because the former suggests an ongoing communication process focusing attention on interaction, whereas the latter suggests episodes that must be dealt with as they occur, focusing attention on the discrete content of each episode. The title of a widely cited book, *Working Through Conflict,* captures the essence of communication theorists' presumptions about conflict communication. Not only do individuals communicate to "work through" conflicts; they also accomplish work "through conflict." This entry reviews conceptual issues in the development of communication conflict theory, overviews early models that form the foundation of contemporary communication conflict theory, and summarizes four continuing traditions of communication conflict theory. A great deal of the information herein is drawn from the 2006 *Handbook of Conflict Communication.*

Uniting Conflict and Communication

Communication and conflict are interdependent, simultaneously defining each other. In 1973, Leonard Hawes and David Smith discussed the conceptualization of conflict along three dimensions: *goal, strategy,* and *time.* They delineated prospective and retrospective approaches to goals. The common approach at the time was *prospective,* assuming individuals have clear, direct goals; conflict is defined by contradictory goals. The *retrospective* approach assumes that goals are meaningful only after behaviors are enacted; communication defines the nature of a conflict rather than goals. The second dimension, strategy, refers to resolution versus management of conflict, mentioned previously. The difference lies in the assumption of conflict as destructive or constructive. The third dimension, time, refers to the assumption of whether conflict is episodic or continuous—a temporary disruption to be eliminated or a normal, vital, and integrating aspect of interaction to be managed. Different combinations of assumptions on these three dimensions lead to different conceptualizations of conflict. Prior to the entry of communication scholars, theoretical treatments presumed prospective goals, resolution strategies, and an episodic time frame. This approach was very limited. Communication scholars were called on to take the opposite view (retrospective goals, constructive outcome, and continuous time frame).

In 1978, another communication scholar, Brent Ruben, developed a system-theoretic view that embodies this opposite approach. He argued for a pragmatic or transactional view of communication, presumed by a retrospective view. A prospective view of goals implicitly assumes a mechanistic sender → message → receiver = effect view of communication. Ruben's perspective rejects both this linear view and the prospective view of goals. Ruben also distinguished *paraconflict* (symbolic) from conflict (observable action). As symbolic, conflict is defined as constructive or destructive by how it feels to the individuals. As action, conflict is defined as constructive or destructive by how it functions for the system. Ruben did not allow for an episodic conceptualization because he viewed communication as continual and inevitable. Conflict is defined as the discrepancies between the demands and/or capabilities of the system and the demands and/or capacities of the environment. Conflict is the way a system survives, because adaptation (communication) is constant; conflict and adaptation are inseparable.

Conceptualizing Conflict and Communication

By the 1980s, communication scholars had consensus on a definition for conflict that allows for a prospective, constructive, and continuous view of conflict: the interaction of interdependent people who perceive the opposition of goals, aims, and/or values and who see the other party as potentially interfering with the realization of these goals. Three important features make this definition important to communication theorists: interaction, incompatibility, and interdependence.

Early Conflict Models

Although they rejected basic presumptions underlying much of previous theory, communication conflict theorists found much to build on. The most influential of these early models were game theory and social exchange, integrative and strategic bargaining, the dual-concern model, and mediation competency models.

Game Theory and Social Exchange

Rooted in economic modeling, game theory provides a mathematical system for modeling conflict and predicting conflict behavior. Game theory analyzes rationally conducted conflict between *players*, each of whom pursues well-defined interests and chooses from among alternative actions. Players construct strategies to maximize gain and minimize loss. The underlying premise is that players are consistently rational; a player will necessarily attempt to maximize his or her gains. Game theory failed to capture the social and interactive nature of human intentionality and conflict. The assumption that humans are consistently rational and the inability to account for relational interdependencies are major factors in communication theorists' dissatisfaction. Game theory treated communication as simple information exchange, usually binary (communicate or not). Game theory was unable to account for ambiguities in intentionality, changes in the process, or variations in psychological and relational processes.

Although game theory research in communication declined by the 1980s, its economic presumptions resurfaced in social-exchange models of conflict and negotiation. Social-exchange models presume that disputants hold rational motives to maximize self-interest, which is rooted in symbolic and multiple social resources. Furthermore, the interaction itself can be a social resource. Also unlike game theory, exchange theory allows theorists to account for reciprocity.

Integrative Versus Distributive Bargaining

Integrative negotiation models, introduced in the 1960s, were a key advance in the study of bargaining. Previously, negotiation theory focused on distributive processes, in which participants view their goals as *zero sum* (one party's gain is another's loss). Integrative bargaining is often summarized by the phrase *win–win*; it advocates joint problem solving rather than competition. Communication theorists used models of integrative and distributive negotiation to develop theories of collective bargaining, mediation, and interpersonal conflict. They conceptually differentiated between strategies and tactics. *Strategies* are broad plans of action (e.g., problem solving); *tactics* are specific messages that enact strategies (e.g., information sharing). According to Linda Putnam, in the late 1980s, communication theorists examined the functions of strategies and tactics and how conflict negotiation evolves over time, studying communication patterns and the multiple and various functions served by messages. Communication scholars brought a dynamic view of conflict in their application of integrative and distributive bargaining models.

Dual Concern

The dual-concern model focuses on conflict management styles, predispositions, and behavioral tendencies. The two dimensions are concern for self and concern for others. When these dimensions are arranged to form quadrants, five basic conflict styles can be identified—one in each corner and one in the center. Robert Blake and Jane Mouton developed the original model of management style, the *managerial grid*, in 1964. Their five conflict styles are *forcing* (high concern for results, low concern for people), *confronting* (high concern for results, high concern for people), *smoothing* (low concern for results, high concern for people), *withdrawal* (low concern for results, low concern for people), and *compromising* (moderate on both). In the 1970s, Ralph Kilmann and Kenneth Thomas created an instrument to measure the five conflict styles.

Numerous communication theorists developed dual-concern models and instruments. These models differ in conceptualization of the dimensions and styles, and several collapse the styles into three categories that mirror integrative, distributive, and avoidance behaviors. Early dual-concern models were meant to exemplify typical conflict behaviors that can be predicted for individuals across time and conflict episodes. As this body of theory developed, many scholars enriched it, examining communication competence, emotional valence, hidden tactics, changes in strategy over time, contextual influences, and personality. The dual-concern model is criticized for its cultural bias, reliance on self-report, inability to account for ongoing interaction, and linear approach to the relationship between conflict and communication, yet it continues to be a dominant approach to understanding conflict and communication.

Mediation Competency

Unlike negotiation, in mediation a third party intervenes to help manage the conflict. Relying on negotiation research, early communication mediation theory examined competent mediators' strategies, tactics, phases, and communication patterns. According to Linda Putnam, the earliest of this work focused on persuasion, examining bluffing, coercion, and influence. Tricia Jones pioneered the study of communication and mediation in the 1980s; her taxonomy of mediation communication strategies and tactics allowed her to discover that mediator communication fulfills three basic functions: facilitation, substantive direction, and procedural control. Previously, communication theorists had relied on labor–management mediation theories that did not account for the richness of interaction and relational communication.

Also at this time, William Donohue developed competence models based on appropriate timing of interventions used by mediators. His most important conclusions were that immediate intervention following an attack avoids conflict escalation and that mediators who adjust to disputants' emotional intensity are most successful. Communication theorists' interest in mediator interventions continues to grow, examining such things as peer and community mediation, perceptual and structural factors, transformational processes, empowerment, and meaning creation.

Continuing Traditions

Continuing traditions of communication conflict theory can be organized into four basic contexts:

interpersonal, organizational, community, and intercultural/international. Theory and research are conducted on three basic levels of analysis: cognitive, interactional, or institutional.

The Interpersonal Context

The term *interpersonal conflict* refers to the context of personal relationships, with a large literature focusing on dating and marital relationships. Ted Huston's *social-ecological model* views the environment, individuals, and relational processes as interconnected levels of analysis, each of which varies on a time frame from molar (broad historical/social processes) to micro (individual events). John Caughlin and Anita Vangelisti integrate relational conflict communication theory and research into this model by organizing the literature into categories: conflict behaviors and relational outcomes, individual influences on relational conflict, and contextual/environmental influences.

William Donohue's *relational order theory* specifically applies to mediation of marital conflict. Disputants' relational messages about their feelings for one another and perceptions of power and status create relational frames constraining negotiation. Relational order theory predicts that development of consistent relational frames allows the ability to find common ground on substantive issues. Four basic relational frames arise from combinations of high and low levels of interdependence and affiliation. The mediator must resolve relational paradoxes and find ways to move the partners toward a frame of high interdependence and affiliation.

Ascan Koerner and Mary Anne Fitzpatrick's model of *family conflict socialization* integrates family relationship schemas, family communication patterns, and family conflict behavior in a process of mutual interdependence and reinforcement. Individuals develop mental representations of family members and relationships. These schemas create shared social reality. Shared social realities create family communication patterns with specific conflict behaviors. These behaviors impact the development of the schemas that are at the root of the process.

Psychologist John Gottman's *cascade model* predicts divorce from a cascading of interrelated processes: complaining and criticizing, contempt,

defensiveness, and withdrawal. These negative expressions are associated with *emotional flooding*: When overwhelmed by their partner's negative behavior, people find it difficult to listen and process information, and they alleviate negative emotions by attacking, defending, or withdrawing. Expressions of contempt and disgust are particularly damaging. Expressions of positive emotion can protect against flooding. Communication scholars Laura Guerrero and Angela LaValley advocate for communication theories (*expectancy violations* and *communication competence*) to expand the cascade model by examining the relations among conflict, emotion, and communication.

Michael Roloff and Courtney Waite Miller constructed a rich framework integrating current knowledge of conflict and *social cognition*. Social cognition/knowledge includes frames, beliefs, scripts, rules, and problem appraisal. Roloff and Waite Miller posit that negative events set off cognitive processes (mindful activity), which mediate between social knowledge and cognitive and social effects. The cognitive processes considered include expectation violation, attributions, accommodation, influence goals, and sentiment override (how messages are interpreted based on the emotional state of the relationship). The effects in their model consist of thinking about conflict, information processing, and storytelling (narrative construction).

Daniel Canary developed a model of strategic conflict driven by the idea that competent conflict behavior is *mindful*. The relationship between *conflict instigation* and *message production* is mediated by three factors: *individual differences* (especially locus of control); *interpretations of the conflict* (understood through attribution theory); and instrumental, self-presentation, and relational *goal assessment*. *Goal control* is the extent to which individuals understand what they want and are sensitive to their partner's goals. Canary describes *message production* along two dimensions: levels of directness and cooperativeness. A comprehensive list of specific conflict strategies and tactics is integrated into these four categories: direct cooperative, direct competitive, indirect cooperative, and indirect competitive. Message production is followed by the *other person's response*. This part of the model allows researchers to examine patterns of communication that lead to various outcomes. Patterns and outcomes can cycle back to any previous events in the model.

The Organizational Context

Organizational conflict usually refers to that which takes place in the context of the workplace or institutional setting, and there is an enormous body of theory and research in this area. The management of organizational conflict has been examined on three fundamental levels: dyadic, group, and institutional. At the dyadic level, theory and research that examine processes of interpersonal conflict in the workplace largely follow a *conflict styles* approach based on the dual-concern model. At the workgroup level, three traditions have been identified, according to M. Scott Poole and Johny Garner. These three traditions are the *instrumental,* which focuses on the impact of conflict on group performance and related outcomes; the *developmental,* which treats conflict as a natural part of group development; and the *political,* which views conflict as a struggle for power.

At the institutional level, a sizable body of work examines the transition of organizational conflict management programs from those that focus on dispute resolution to broader and more proactive conflict management systems. Based on a comprehensive review of literature, David Lipsky and Ronald Seeber have developed a comprehensive organizing framework from which to understand this shift. Organizational conflicts manifest themselves in three forms: disagreements, disputes, and litigation. Managing these three forms of conflict differs according to several factors: the responsible party, the type of conflict, the techniques used, the nature of the outcome, and the extent of third-party involvement. *Alternative dispute resolution* programs have been steadily on the rise as large organizations increasingly face the rising human and economic cost of disputes and litigation. Such programs, however, do little to prevent conflicts from escalating to dispute or litigation because they typically do not intervene prior to this escalation. Lipsky and Seeber's organizing model of the research in this area elucidates both the shifts happening in the practice of organizational conflict management and the deeper social processes at play.

The Community Context

Community conflict refers to conflict in the public arena, focusing on communities defined by physical collocation. Community conflict is more polarizing than interpersonal and organizational conflict because the parties lack intimacy and coordinated activity. Barnett Pearce and Stephen Littlejohn developed a theory of moral conflict: When individuals with incommensurate moral orders interact, intractable conflict can result from mutual frustration and entrenchment. Conflict rooted in the worldviews of the opponents is difficult to manage; the logics of the paradigms do not permit cross-translation. Parties become locked into a dispute, perceiving no other choice. Their language differs; even similar terms have disparate meanings. Neither side understands the other, and both fail to see why the other rejects their case. These dynamics lead each to describe the other as misguided, ignorant, evil, or sick. The theory has been developed through a series of descriptive case studies, including the U.S. *Religious Right* movement and the abortion debate. Moral conflicts cannot be solved through traditional dispute resolution; they must be transcended through a process of dialogue. Transcendent communication creates new frames, transforms relationships, and creates opportunities to explore the power and limits of multiple worldviews.

Dialogue theories have their own rich tradition. Kevin Barge has described the relationships among dialogue, conflict, and democratic practice, highlighting three important theoretic movements that bring these things together: community mediation, public participation and dialogue, and appreciative inquiry (a social constructionist perspective on community development, emphasizing the positive core of community life). Dialogic democratic practice faces the dilemmas of several tensions: inclusion–exclusion, deliberative–relational, and macro–micro. Dialogue theories explore how dialogic communication manages conflict and builds community. Dialogue theories include those that are encompassed in the intercultural/international context, as well.

Other areas of theory in community conflict include environmental conflict, racial/ethnic conflict, crisis negotiation, and critical approaches. Theories of environmental conflict explore public participation in environmental decision making. Racial or ethnic community conflict theories examine the potential for positive community-building outcomes from the conflict management process surrounding ethnic identity, minority groups, racial hate incidents, and intercommunal ethnic conflicts. Crisis negotiation, including hostage negotiation, is a unique context for community conflict theory, focusing on the communicative dynamics of conflict as they are complicated by the potential for injury or death of the involved parties. Finally, critical approaches to community conflict take a cultural studies perspective: Conflict is a defining feature of all social systems and threatens identity. Culture, as a site of conflict, becomes an arena in which changing meanings are negotiated.

The Intercultural/International Context

Intercultural/international conflict refers to conflicts between two or more different cultural or identity groups. Many communication theories are directly concerned with or have direct applications to intercultural conflict management. Those with separate entries in this volume include anxiety/uncertainty management theory, expectancy violations theory, cultural types theories, face negotiation theory, accommodation theory, and co-cultural theory. International communication and peace theories also address conflict. Many of these include treatments of racial or ethnic conflict; the field of social psychology also has a rich tradition of ethnic and intergroup conflict theory. Other important theories in the intercultural/international context include *integrated threat theory* (ITT) and the *cultural values dimensional* (CVD) grid.

ITT, developed by Walter Stephan and Cookie White Stephan, assumes that feelings of fear or threat cause prejudice and identifies four antecedent conditions (intergroup conflict history, intergroup knowledge gap, type and frequency of intergroup contact, and societal/group membership power status) that escalate or de-escalate the levels of four types of threat (intergroup anxiety/anticipated consequences, rigid stereotypes, tangible/realistic threats, and values/symbolic threats). Threat escalation creates biased intergroup attitudes (e.g., prejudice) and intergroup conflict cycles, outcomes that then feed off one another.

The CVD grid, developed by Stella Ting-Toomey and John Oetzel, draws from key ideas in anxiety/uncertainty management theory, ITT theory, expectancy violations theory, cultural types theory, and power distance. *Power distance* refers to cultural values for status differences and social hierarchies. Small power distance (SPD) cultures value equal power distributions, symmetrical relations, and reward systems based on merit. Large power distance (LPD) cultures accept unequal power distributions; asymmetrical relations; and reward systems based on rank, role, and status. The CVD grid posits that the individualism–collectivism dimension of cultural types theory interacts with power distance values to create four cultural approaches to conflict: impartial (individualistic, SPD), status–achievement (individualistic, LPD), communal (collectivistic, SPD), and benevolent (collectivistic, LPD).

Conclusion

The study of conflict and communication is broad and diverse at the same time that it espouses a core set of presumptions. These presumptions include the inevitability and constructive nature of conflict, the dynamic nature of goals, and the mutually constitutive relationship between communication and conflict. Regardless of the context in which conflict theories are generated, communication scholars have consensus on these basic issues.

Anne Maydan Nicotera

See also Anxiety/Uncertainty Management Theory; Attribution Theory; Co-Cultural Theory; Constitutive View of Communication; Critical Theory; Cultural Studies; Cultural Types Theories; Expectancy Violations Theory; Face Negotiation Theory; Hawaiian Ho'oponopono Theory; Intercultural Communication Competence; Intercultural Communication Theories; International Communication Theories; Interracial Communication; Peace Theories; Pragmatics; Racial Formation Theory; Social Exchange Theory; System Theory

Further Readings

Blake, R. R., & Mouton, J. S. (1964). *The managerial grid*. Houston, TX: Gulf.

Folger, J. P., Poole, M. S., & Stutman, R. K. (2005). *Working through conflict: Strategies for relationships, groups, and organizations* (5th ed.). New York: Allyn & Bacon.

Hawes, L. C., & Smith, D. H. (1973). A critique of assumptions underlying the study of communication in conflict. *Quarterly Journal of Speech, 59*, 423–435.

Miller, G. R., & Simmons, H. W. (Eds.). (1974). *Perspectives on communication in social conflict.* Englewood Cliffs, NJ: Prentice Hall.

Oetzel, J. G., & Ting-Toomey, S. (2006). *The Sage handbook of conflict communication.* Thousand Oaks, CA: Sage.

Putnam, L. L. (Ed.). (1988). Communication and conflict styles in organizations [Special issue]. *Management Communication Quarterly, 1*(3), 291–445.

Putnam, L. L., & Poole, M. S. (1987). Conflict and negotiation. In F. M. Jablin, L. L. Putnam, K. H. Roberts, & L. W. Porter (Eds.), *Handbook of organizational communication* (pp. 549–599). Newbury Park, CA: Sage.

Ruben, B. D. (1978). Communication and conflict: A system-theoretic perspective. *Quarterly Journal of Speech, 64,* 202–210.

Confucian Communication Theory

Confucianism is a worldview, a political ideology, a social ethic, a scholarly tradition, and a way of life. As one of the most prominent traditions of thought, Confucianism has lasting and profound bearings on social, political, and value systems in East Asia. This entry (a) outlines the cardinal principles of Confucianism, (b) discusses the Confucian view of language, and (c) illustrates the impact of Confucianism on interpersonal relationships and communication patterns in East Asian cultures.

Confucius (551–479 BCE) viewed the universe as an organic whole and all modalities of beings in it as interconnected and governed by a unifying force, *Dao* (the Way). Dao and *tao* are the same thing, the Daoist/Taoist notion of the Way. This term is romanized as tao in the older Wade-Giles system and as dao in the modern pinyin system. This entry uses the latter because it is phonetically closer to the actual pronunciation of the word in Mandarin, and these days more and more Sinologists and communication scholars on Chinese communication have started to make the switch. Dao constitutes the harmonious organization of life that upholds and perpetuates a moral order. Through following Dao, human beings can gain a sense of self-knowledge; gain insights into the human condition as a whole, as well as one's own

particular location in it; and acquire *de* (virtues), the ability to achieve harmony both within oneself and with others.

Cardinal Principles

Confucian teaching lays out three principal virtues to define proper human relationships: *ren* (humanness), *yi* (righteousness), and *li* (propriety, rite, and ritual). The fundamental concern of Confucianism is ren, to learn to be humane. A person of *ren* is one who (a) loves all human beings; (b) desiring to develop and nourish oneself, develops and nourishes others; and (c) does not do to others what one does not wish done to oneself. Ren can be attained through a process of ceaseless self-cultivation that transforms the private ego to the all-encompassing self, a holistic human existence in harmony with all other beings in the universe.

The second cardinal principle, yi (righteousness), states the duties or moral obligations associated with people as they are located within networks of social relations. In Confucian teaching, the realization of the self, or the worth of the person, is essentially tied to his or her ability to fulfill his or her social responsibilities. Although Confucius conceived social relationships as often hierarchical, obligations are mutual or reciprocal and required for all parties concerned. The mutuality and reciprocity tenets render fulfillment of obligations a moral imperative for everyone. Those who have more power and privilege are given more responsibilities than those who have less.

The third fundamental concept of the Confucian doctrine, li (propriety, rite, and ritual), is the social norms that regulate human actions. Li prescribes the appropriate human conduct with a keen awareness of the principle of ren and genuine concern for others. Only through following li can people discipline their mind and action until the proper principles can be enacted in a genuine nature.

Confucianism views the human community as an intrinsic part of people's quest for self-realization. Self-cultivation is understood as a social or communal act that does not happen in seclusion. Self-cultivation is essentially to transcend all forms of human insensitivity, such as egocentrism, selfishness, nepotism, parochialism, and ethnocentrism, and to learn to be sensitive to an ever-expanding network of relationships. Through self-cultivation, one makes oneself available to the human community and contributes to a social order that enables and encourages self-cultivation.

Confucian View of Language

Based on her close reading of the classical text the *Analects* of Confucius, Hui-Ching Chang explicated Confucius's view of language in human interactions and social affairs. Confucius envisaged the purpose of communication as ethical, that is, to adhere to and sustain the moral order of the human community. Communication is necessary for people to learn and experience their connection and commonality with others and thus to develop sensitivity to them. In this sense, communication is not a functional instrument to accomplish certain tasks. Rather, it is the means of facilitating and reflecting a person's self-cultivation or moral development. Proper speaking ought to follow the principle of li (propriety) and should be appropriate according to the particulars of the context. The moral imperative in Confucianism distrusts and discourages overly ornamented words that do not have substance and do not correspond to the person's morality. Confucius weighted actions more than words in his assessment of a person's integrity.

Confucian Influence on Interpersonal Relationships

Because Confucianism has had a lasting impact on the society, government, education, and family in East Asia (e.g., Japan, mainland China, Hong Kong, Taiwan, Singapore, South Korea, North Korea, and Vietnam), interpersonal relationships in these countries are conceived and developed in ways that differ from those of the cultures informed by individualism. June Ock Yum has discussed Confucian influences on interpersonal relationships and communication patterns in East Asia. According to Yum, East Asians are more attentive to relational contexts in social interaction. Instead of employing universal rules in interaction with all people, East Asian people are more conscious of the position of a person in the complex web of human relations. Socialized in the Confucian tradition that places ultimate emphasis on sensitivity to human relations, as expressed in all three cardinal principles, East Asian people are apt to relate to

others differently in accordance with their relationships with them and different communicative contexts.

In East Asian cultures, reciprocity is envisioned as long-term and asymmetrical. People in individualistic cultures, such as Canada and the United States, largely define their commitments and obligations to others and to organizations as short-term, symmetrical, or contractual. In the Confucian view, every person is connected with all other beings across time and space as defined by the principle of ren. The very existence of a person is indebted to other beings. Thus, East Asians do not try to "keep score" or "make it even" as soon as possible in their interactions with others. Instead, reciprocity as the organizing principle of relationships entails a never-ending project of self-cultivation. It is precisely because in East Asia relationships are recognized as long-term and all encompassing in social affairs that the distinction between public and private domains disappears. People in East Asian cultures tend to develop relationships across the public and private spheres to ensure mutual trust and reciprocity. On the other hand, the long-term relationships in almost every aspect of life may result in a sharp distinction between in-group members and out-group members.

Another distinctive characteristic of East Asian relationships is the employment of informal intermediaries. In East Asian cultures, with their emphasis on the principles of yi and li, it is not what is said but who says it that is more important. East Asians prefer mutual acquaintances who have proper relationships with both parties concerned instead of contract professionals (e.g., lawyers, negotiators, marriage counselors) when mediating, negotiating, or resolving conflicts.

Confucianism and Communication Patterns

The influence of Confucianism can also be observed in communication patterns in East Asian cultures. The Confucian concern with morality and ever-expanding relationships is reflected in the process-oriented view of communication in East Asia. Communication is viewed as an infinite process of interpretation and interaction. Grounded in the Confucian awareness of particularity in relationships, East Asian people prefer a differentiated linguistic code that is responsive to different relational contexts in communication. For instance, East Asian languages have more elaborate honorific linguistic systems than English does. Communication competence in East Asian cultures thus includes the ability to correctly assess where one stands in relation to the other and to make the appropriate linguistic choice accordingly. The care for harmonious relationships in Confucian teaching steers East Asians away from overreliance on direct communication. Indirect modes of communication are valued precisely because of the concern for the other person's face. Finally, communication in East Asian cultures is more receiver centered than sender centered, which is the dominant model in Western cultures. The use of indirect communication leaves more room for interpretation. Receiver-centered communication requires the listener to attend to different situations and relationships as well as to the speaker's emotional and material needs in order to discern the implicit meanings the message contains. This mode of communication is a practice of the Confucian cardinal principle of ren, ultimate sensitivity toward others.

Jing Yin

See also Asian Communication Theory; Chinese Harmony Theory; Taoist Communication Theory

Further Readings

Chang, H.-C. (2008). Language and words: Communication in the *Analects* of Confucius. In M. K. Asante, Y. Miike, & J. Yin (Eds.), *The global intercultural communication reader* (pp. 95–112). New York: Routledge.

Chen, G.-M., & Chung, J. (1994). The impact of Confucianism on organizational communication. *Communication Quarterly, 42*(2), 93–105.

Tu, W. (1985). *Confucian thought: Selfhood as creative transformation.* Albany: State University of New York Press.

Tu, W. (1995). Confucianism. In A. Sharma (Ed.), *Our religions* (pp. 140–227). San Francisco: HarperCollins.

Yum, J. O. (1988). The impact of Confucianism on interpersonal relationships and communication patterns in East Asia. *Communication Monographs, 55*(4), 374–388.

CONSEQUENTIALITY OF COMMUNICATION

Consequentiality is a framework for understanding the features and dynamics of the communication process that enable it to have an impact on social and cultural life. It focuses attention on the continuous production of behavior by communicators, the coordination required as each communicator adjusts to the unfolding scene or situation, and the meanings that arise in and through this process. Consequentiality serves as a contrast to alternative frameworks that study the effects of particular behavioral acts ("independent variables") on other behavior ("dependent variables") or the effects of mental or emotional states on behavior.

The consequentiality framework acknowledges the contingent and unpredictable quality of communication. The behavior communicators produce at any one time is dependent on what else is happening in the immediate circumstances: what all the participants have contributed to the scene up to that point; what is occurring simultaneously; and participants' calculation of what might happen next in the sequence to confirm, clarify, or even reshape the meaning and direction of the event. However, unpredictability does not mean that the communication process occurs randomly. Rather, it is recognition of communicators' ability to deploy selectively various resources for behavior (e.g., language, cultural expectations, social obligations) and, in doing so, to bring order and meaning to each unique communication event. Thus, the framework posits that the communication process makes use of cultural, psychological, and social resources but is a phenomenon sui generis, requiring its own explanations.

Consequentiality is not a single theory or research approach. Rather, the consequentiality framework permits study of the communication process by means of a wide variety of theories and methods, including conversation analysis, coordinated management of meaning, the ethnography of speaking, and social communication.

The framework was initially proposed as a direction for communication theory in an anthology titled *The Consequentiality of Communication*, edited by Stuart J. Sigman in 1995, with contributions from scholars representing a variety of perspectives. It developed from the concern that communication scholars began to address in the late 1970s and early 1980s that the communication discipline borrowed extensively from psychology; focused on the cognitive, emotional, and personality traits that appeared to influence the production of behavior; and did not consider how the ongoing process unfolded and was managed by communicators. Rather than provide a single communication theory, the initial articulation of consequentiality was intended to serve as a unifying framework for theory development and as a pointer to a set of observations about communication that theorists should attempt to explain.

The aforementioned studies from the 1970s onward acknowledged that the communication process itself, rather than cultural, psychological, or social antecedents to communication, is the proper study for the discipline. These early studies on the "doing" of communication primarily focused on the cultural and social resources that membership in a community makes available to communicators—the "codes," "rules," or "scripts" for behavior. The consequentiality framework acknowledges the important direction in the discipline's history represented by a rules approach. Consequentiality pushes the analysis further by focusing on the use and appearance of code resources in actual situations and on the constitutive role played by communication in bringing into existence social categories, cultural patterns, and psychological conditions.

Research within the consequentiality framework asks what is done *with* the codes and *how* behavior produces social reality. As such, the framework acknowledges the following observations about communication and encourages investigation of their structure and import:

Diversity: The consequentiality framework notes that in any given situation, there may be multiple codes that are appropriate and may be invoked. As such, communicators may face uncertainty as to which goals, purposes, and roles are operative at any one time and may need to negotiate the definition of the situation and adjust their unfolding behavioral contributions accordingly.

Optionality: Even in those situations in which the range of applicable codes is minimal (or a single script from multiple possibilities has apparently been invoked and made operative), the rules may be

structured with *choice nodes*—moments when a collection of behaviors might be selected from and when each particular selection may move the scene in one direction or another. As Ferdinand de Saussure taught, scripts and rules have multiple levels and paradigmatic options for behavioral production, and it is only in the actual behavioral moment that the codes exact normative force.

Fluid contextuality: The definition of a situation and the associated codes for behavior may change during the unfolding event. Communication acts may not only establish a normative trajectory for the encounter but may also retrospectively formulate the meaning and import of earlier behavior. This may require communicators to confirm their understanding of their communication engagement and produce new entailments for subsequent action. Thus, according to Saussure, behavioral units can be seen in syntagmatic relationship, that is, as part of patterned sequences that unfold across time.

Metacommunication: Human beings exhibit the capacity to engage in communication with their fellows and to engage in communication about their communication. They may be called on to account for their behavior and to engage in repair work when misunderstanding, offenses, and misalignments have been produced. New rule systems, role relationships, and institutional structures may emerge from the alignments that communicators make as part of this metacommunication.

Consequentiality cannot be studied apart from particular communication situations and the license that persons may exercise in shaping the significance and direction of those situations. Communication theorist Robert E. Sanders offers a useful heuristic for considering the extent to which the consequentiality framework can be applied to any particular situation. Sanders, who refers to his approach as *neo-rhetorical,* suggests a distinction between weak and strong senses of consequentiality. Focusing on communicators' identities, Sanders suggests that in the *weak sense of consequentiality,* communication is used to provide information about the communicators' social identities and relationships and their behavioral obligations in the situation. Events in which the communication process is weakly consequential are those with normatively rigid cultural and social codes; the codes must be taken for granted and require communicators to confirm and inform each other about their unquestionable roles. In contrast, the *strong sense of consequentiality* is relevant to those situations for which identities are unknown, ambiguous, and/or contested, and considers the process by which identities, relationships, and roles are actively constructed and negotiated—and not merely conveyed—by the participants.

Broadening the view from communication about identity, weak consequentiality refers to those events for which there is a rigid behavioral script, with minimal choice nodes and severe penalty for deviations and modifications. A church service might serve as an example of an event for which the communication of the participants is weakly consequential. Communicators must be able to know what scene is being enacted and what the obligations for their specific behavioral contributions to that scene are, but adherence to the script is paramount.

Strong consequentiality encompasses situations for which the behavioral script is multifaceted, with opportunities for multiple actors, intentions, and behavioral options to develop and be acted on during the course of the event. The trajectory or outcome of an event with strong consequentiality is not determined at the outset and instead unfolds through moment-by-moment behavioral production. Initial encounters such as dating, job interviews, and unplanned conversations are examples of this type of situation.

The weak-versus-strong distinction is not intended to lead to the characterization of situations as absolutely one or the other. The heuristic assumes that communication across acts and situations is consequential. In the case of the church service, for example, the demonstrated skill of the priest during a religious service, the attentiveness of the parishioners, and other acts that transpire may result in differing spiritual feelings being generated. Thus, the existence of a prescribed liturgy does not detract from the fact that the liturgy must be enacted and that enactment may evidence communication consequentiality. Conversely, while first social encounters such as a romantic date or professional interview may not have a clear end state or narrative arc, they are bound by protocols and expectations. Thus, even strong consequentiality is constrained by codes for behavior.

The notion of consequentiality harkens back to earlier distinctions within the field of structural and sociolinguistics, that between *langue* (language) and *parole* (word; Ferdinand de Saussure) and *competence* and *performance* (Noam Chomsky, Dell Hymes). These pairs of distinctions posit, respectively, a grammar consisting of an idealized set of rules for behavior—both verbal and nonverbal—and the actual, moment-by-moment behavioral production that inexactly manifests the grammar. However, for the consequentiality framework, performance (the communication process) is not a lesser manifestation of codes but rather the selective and strategic employment of codes. Humans make selections from a repertoire of symbols, values, and strategies, and these selections shape subsequent behavior, institutional commitments, and social identities. Equally, meanings and patterns may emerge from communication situations, and these may yield new institutional and relational arrangements and thus new codes for subsequent behavior.

Though primarily concerned with interpersonal (face-to-face) communication, the consequentiality framework has been employed in journalism, mass communication, and organizational communication scholarship. Research has examined the writing process, in which each draft produces a rhetorical strategy and logic that may influence and be refined by subsequent drafts. Others have studied how organizations invoke their cultural narratives and subtly shape their future course through ritualized reenactment and modification of these narratives and the creation of new ones. Another direction that has been taken is the application of consequentiality to the development of a theory of *ludicity*, the human capacity for play and recreation. Complementing earlier scholarship on the universal and biological origins of play, this work suggests that individual acts of playmaking, while subject to rules of engagement, exhibit ludic consequentiality, or the capacity for play to establish (and not merely reflect) identities and relational meanings for the participants.

In brief, while theorists may refer to the *consequences* of any single act of behavior or cognition, one does not generally refer to an act's *consequentiality;* the latter term is applicable to the more inclusive communication process.

Stuart J. Sigman

Further Readings

Bamberg, M. (2004). Narrative discourse and identities.
In J. C. Meister, T. Kindt, W. Schernus, & M. Stein
(Eds.), *Narratology beyond literary criticism*
(pp. 213–237). Berlin, Germany: Walter de Gruyter.

Penman, R. (2000). *Reconstructing communicating:
Looking to a future.* Mahwah, NJ: Lawrence
Erlbaum.

Sigman, S. J. (Ed.). (1995). *The consequentiality of
communication.* Hillsdale, NJ: Lawrence Erlbaum.

Sigman, S. J. (1995). Question: Evidence of what?
Answer: Communication. *Western Journal of
Communication, 59,* 79–84.

Consistency Theories

See Attitude Theory; Cognitive Dissonance
Theory; Co-Orientation Theory;
Persuasion and Social Influence Theories

Constitutive View
of Communication

To take a constitutive view of communication
means to presume that communication, or interaction, is a process of meaning creation or social
construction. The fundamental idea of *constitution* has had enormous influence on the field of
communication, especially in the areas of interpersonal communication and organizational communication. An important implication of a constitutive
view is that communication is assumed to be the
basic building block for social entities, such as
personal relationships and organizations. This
entry provides a brief history of the origins of the
constitutive view, explains its basic assumptions,
and examines examples of applications in interpersonal and organizational communication.

Background: Communication Models

Early communication theory took the form of
models. In a classic communication theory textbook published in 1972, C. David Mortenson
defined a model as a systematic representation
of an object or event in idealized and abstract
form. A model of communication is a still picture of a moving process. Models of communication are useful in identifying the basic
components of the communication process and
how they are related. A model aids in concic-
alizing processes of interest and in generating
questions for richer forms of theory. Models are
helpful as metaphors that guide our ability to
visualize concepts of interest in terms of one
another as they help us to clarify complex processes. However, communication models are
oversimplified and mask complex processes that
cannot be modeled, often leading to premature
conclusions. Models are very limited and thus
are best thought of as only a most rudimentary
form of theory. The earliest known models of
communication were developed by Aristotle in
his theories of rhetoric and proof. Aristotle's
purpose was *prescriptive*—to instruct others to
be effective persuasive speakers.

Contemporary communication theory is
descriptive—its purpose is to describe, explain,
predict, and/or control communication phenomena. Early-20th-century views of communication
were highly mechanistic, treating communication
as a machine-like process wherein information or
messages are depicted as traveling through channels. These mechanistic models are also known as
linear models because the communication process
is depicted as a line. The most influential linear
model is Shannon and Weaver's mathematical
model, developed to help telephone engineers
design efficient ways to transmit electrical signals
from place to place. The Shannon–Weaver mathematical model was essentially a line from left to
right that traveled through boxes, depicting an
information source sending a *message* through a
transmitter (encoder), which transforms the message to a *signal*, sending it through a *channel* that
is affected by *noise*. The *signal* then passes through
a *receiver* (decoder), which transforms the signal
back to a *message* that finally reaches its *destination*. The Shannon–Weaver model was not meant

to describe face-to-face human communication, but it provided a baseline from which to do so.

Numerous models of face-to-face human communication were based on the Shannon–Weaver linear model. Scholars of human communication took a message-centered approach in modeling communication. The most basic form of linear communication models is often called a model of *communication-as-action*, depicting a *sender* (or a source or a speaker) transmitting a message through some *channel* to a *receiver*—still a line drawn from left to right. In 1960, communication scholar David Berlo coined the term *SMCR* to describe this type of linear model, denoting the model components of sender (or speaker or source), message, channel, and receiver. Models that depicted communication-as-action were unsatisfactory because they were too heavily focused on the sender or source of the originating message.

In 1954, Wilbur Schramm created one of the first models of face-to-face human communication. Rather than a sender and a receiver, Schramm's model depicted *interpreters* who were simultaneously *encoders* and *decoders*. Though messages were still depicted as traveling along a line, the line was circular, beginning with the first interpreter as an encoder, traveling to the second interpreter as a decoder, and then returning from the second interpreter as an encoder back to the original interpreter as a decoder. Schramm was the first scholar to model communication as an interactive process. This form of model is known as a *circular model*, also called a model of *communication-as-interaction*. Schramm's inclusion of the notion of *interpretation* is the conceptual basis for the meaning-centered approach at the heart of the constitutive view.

These basic models of communication (linear/action and circular/interaction) are often referred to as a *transmissive view of communication* because they depict communication as a process by which something (a message, information, etc.) is *transmitted* from person to person. But even models of communication-as-interaction quickly became unsatisfactory as our thinking became more sophisticated and our focus shifted from messages to meaning. Communication scholars began to focus on the communication process not as the *exchange* of messages or mere *transmission* of meaning but as the *creation* of meaning.

The third generation of communication models was *nonlinear* models, also called models of *communication as transaction*. Transactional models focus on the functions of communication and represent the origins of the *constitutive view of communication*. The most famous of these models was developed by Dean Barnlund in 1970. Barnlund used a complex graphic representation of spirals and curved arrows to represent the continuous, unrepeatable, irreversible nature of communication. Meaning was seen as assigned or attributed rather than received. Along with *interactants*, *decoding*, *encoding*, and *messages*, Barnlund's model included a set of valenced cues: *public cues* (in the environment), *private cues* (in or on the persons), and *deliberate behavioral cues* (nonverbal and verbal). All these components were depicted as interrelated and constantly evolving.

The idea of communication as a transaction through which communicators created meaning had a profound effect on the field. Scholars quickly moved beyond creating additional graphic representations of communication processes in the form of pictorial models. The rudimentary nature of pictorial representation can only roughly approximate the process of meaning creation. This shift from linear to nonlinear modeling represents a shift in thinking from a transmissive to a constitutive view of communication.

First-Order Model or Metamodel

In 1999, Robert Craig described the constitutive view by distinguishing first-order from second-order phenomena. A *first-order phenomenon* explains *second-order phenomena*. According to Craig, the constitutive view of communication posits that communication is not a secondary phenomenon that can be explained by antecedent factors (such as psychological, sociological, cultural, or economic factors). Instead, communication is the primary, constitutive social process that explains all these other factors. Basically, communication is the root of other social processes rather than the result.

Craig also distinguished between *first-order models* and *metamodels*. A first-order model is a symbolic representation of communication processes themselves. A first-order model describes the characteristics of phenomena in the world. A metamodel is a model of communication models. A metamodel describes the characteristics of theoretic representations of phenomena. Craig argued that the constitutive view should be seen both as a first-order model of communication processes themselves and as a metamodel that explains the process of theorizing.

As a first-order model, the constitutive view depicts communication as a process of meaning making, as described above. As a metamodel, the constitutive view allows us to think of different communication models as different ways of constituting the communication process symbolically for particular purposes. The advantage of this way of thinking is that first-order constitutive models do not necessarily mean the rejection of transmissive models, as had been traditionally thought. As a metamodel, the constitutive view does not address the nature of communication itself but rather the ways in which we think about it as theorists. Hence, we can comfortably constitute communication as constitutive (as in a transactional model) for one purpose and constitute communication as transmissive (as in SMCR models) for another. For example, when we seek to understand the creation of complex organizational systems, a constitutive view suits our purposes. However, when we seek to understand how information originates, is disseminated among people and groups, and achieves goals within these complex organizational systems, a transmissive view may be more fruitful. Craig's views were somewhat controversial and sparked a great deal of debate. However, his careful conceptual distinctions were important for the field.

Communication Theories

We will now turn our attention to two theoretical perspectives grounded in a constitutive view of communication: the relational perspective and communicative constitution of organization (CCO). Both of these traditions take the constitutive view further than simple meaning creation. Communication is seen not only as creating meaning but as creating, or constituting, social entities (personal relationships and organizations, respectively). In other words, personal relationships and organizations are seen as made of or made from communication. This is a fundamentally constitutive view because communication is theorized not as merely one factor that influences the formation of the social entities but rather as the very essence of their nature.

The Relational Perspective

The relational perspective is also known as *the interactive view* and as *pragmatics;* it rests on systems theory. Because this volume has entries devoted to pragmatics and systems theory, our treatment here will be quite brief, focusing only on the way in which this perspective is grounded in the constitutive view. Because it stems from a constitutive view, the relational perspective was able to accomplish three basic analytic shifts from earlier theories of relationships. First, the focus of analysis changed from the individual to interaction. Second, observation shifted from psychological processes to systemic processes. Finally, whereas previous perspectives on relationships studied individuals in the context of relationships, the relational perspective studied relationships themselves. In short, a constitutive view allows the assumption that a relationship is *between* people, not within them. Pragmatics scholars define *relationship* as an emergent social structuring created by and defined by communication patterns. As such, relational process and relational form are seen as mutually constitutive—each creating and defining the other. As things or entities, then, relationships are communicatively constituted (made of or made by communication).

Communicative Constitution of Organization

CCO theory is a relatively recent and rapidly growing body of organizational communication theory grounded in a constitutive view. The notion of CCO has a variety of theoretic roots, among them (in alphabetical order) critical discourse analysis, critical theory, ethnomethodology, Marxist theory, narrative theory, philosophy, pragmatics, rules theory, semiology, speech act theory, structuration theory, and systems theory. In 2000, a special issue of the *Electronic Journal of Communication* focused on communication as a constitutive process in organizations and organizing. This issue focused attention on CCO as a particular theoretic tradition. One of the most prolific scholars in the CCO tradition is James R. Taylor, emeritus professor from the University of Montréal. Taylor's work has been so influential that it has initiated a focused theoretical perspective in CCO, which has come to be known as the Montréal School. Scholars affiliated with the Montréal School include François Cooren, Daniel Robichaud, Hélène Giroux, Boris Brummans, and Mathieu Chaput, among others. One of the key constructs focused on by Montréal School scholars is *agency*—the ability to act on the world. One of their more controversial claims is that nonhumans (such as documents and road signs) have agency. Other organizational communication scholars pursuing CCO theory include Linda L. Putnam, Robert D. McPhee, Gail Fairhurst, Lawrence D. Browning, Timothy Kuhn, Karen Ashcraft, Anne M. Nicotera, and several others. There is a great deal of variation and debate among CCO scholars, but all are united in the constitutive view of communication. It must also be noted that CCO theory is not unique to the discipline of communication; *organizational studies* is a multidisciplinary and international body of work that spans many social disciplines, each of which makes contributions to CCO theory. Some of the most influential CCO research has originated in other disciplines.

Two Specific CCO Theories

Although many communication scholars theorize about CCO processes, two theories stand out as most influential: Taylor's conversation and text theory and McPhee's four flows. Each of these is described briefly, highlighting their grounding in the constitutive view. Taylor's *conversation and text theory* rests on a simple distinction between two key concepts: conversation and text. *Text* can be defined as both the content and the outcome of interaction. A text can be in written form (such as policy manuals) or unwritten form (such as decisions made in a meeting that are repeated to others). *Conversation* is the communicative interaction itself. Text is meaning and outcome; conversation is activity. Conversation is about text and produces/reproduces text. Taylor and his many coauthors, most notably Elizabeth VanEvery, discuss the translation process from conversation to text. Conversations must be interpreted through processes of punctuation and sensemaking. Sensemaking will depend on the interactants' interpretive frames. This sensemaking could occur psychologically (in the minds of the interactants) or might be formalized (such as providing a glossary of terms to an audience).

Organizational communication is *created by interaction* in this way. In mutually constitutive fashion, organizational communication then defines the context through which we transform text into conversation. Organizational communication becomes formalized through processes of *distanciation*—the distance between the intended meaning of the speaker(s) and what is created and retained in interaction. Taylor and his colleagues posit "six degrees of separation" by which text and conversation become translated to complex organizational forms. The capsule summaries here appeared in Katherine Miller's communication theory textbook published in 2005.

First degree: Intent of the speaker is translated into action and embedded in conversation.

Second degree: Events of the conversation are translated into a narrative representation, making it possible to understand the meaning of the exchange.

Third degree: The text is transcribed (objectified) on some permanent or semipermanent medium (e.g., the minutes of a meeting).

Fourth degree: A specialized language is developed to encourage and channel subsequent texts and conversations.

Fifth degree: The text and conversations are transformed into material and physical frames (e.g., laboratories, conference rooms, organizational charts, procedural manuals).

Sixth degree: A standardized form is disseminated and defused to a broader public (e.g., media reports and representations of organizational forms and practices).

In this way, organization—both as a process and as a social entity—can be seen to be communicatively constituted.

Robert D. McPhee takes a very different approach, suggesting that communication processes are comprised of four *flows* that constitute organization. The four flows are membership negotiation, organizational self-structuring, activity coordination, and institutional positioning (in the social order of institutions). The flows are separate only for the purposes of analysis. Any message or episode of interaction can contribute to multiple flows, and processes identified with a specific flow can overlap with those identified with one or more other flows.

The four are distinct because any one is constitutive of the organization. Flows are multidirectional and topically variable. Communication in the *membership negotiation* flow focuses on the relationship of members to the organization. The *organizational self-structuring* flow includes communication related to the organization's form, boundaries, goals, policies, procedures, and any other process related to its identity. The third flow, *activity coordination*, includes all interaction related to connecting and shaping work processes and joint actions. This includes both cooperative and conflicted interaction. Fourth, the *institutional positioning* flow is comprised of communication related to the organization's relationship to other organizations in its societal environment. In each flow a social structure is generated through interaction. The flows can control or condition one another. Together, these communication flows constitute organization—both as a process and as a social entity.

Conclusion

The relational perspective and CCO theory are only two examples of theoretic traditions in communication that are grounded in a constitutive view. The field of communication has numerous theories grounded in this view. Any scholar who defines communication as a meaning-making process is following a *constitutive view*, quite distinct from a *transmissive view*, which defines communication as a process by which something is transmitted or exchanged.

Anne Maydan Nicotera

See also Cultural Studies; Language and Communication; Meaning Theories; Narrative and Narratology; Organizational Culture; Pragmatics; Process of Communication; Relational Communication Theory; Rules Theories; Semiotics and Semiology; Sense-Making; Social Construction of Reality; Social Interaction Theories; Speech Act Theory; Structuration Theory; Symbolic Interactionism

Further Readings

Barnlund, D. C. (1970). A transactional model of communication. In K. K. Sereno & C. D. Mortensen (Eds.), *Foundations of communication theory* (pp. 83–102). New York: Harper & Row.

Craig, R. T. (1999). Communication theory as a field. *Communication Theory, 9,* 119–161.

Craig, R. T. (2001). Minding my metamodel, mending Myers. *Communication Theory, 11,* 133–142.

Craig, R. T. (2007). Pragmatism in the field of communication theory. *Communication Theory, 17,* 125–145.

Myers, D. (2001). A pox on all compromises: Reply to Craig (1999). *Communication Theory, 11,* 231–240.

Putnam, L. L., & Nicotera, A. M. (Eds.). (2008). *Building theories of organization: The constitutive role of communication.* New York: Routledge.

Rogers, L. E., & Escudero, V. (Eds.). (2003). *Relational communication: An interactional perspective to the study of process and form.* Mahwah, NJ: Lawrence Erlbaum.

Taylor, J. R., & Van Every, E. J. (2000). *The emergent organization: Communication as its site and surface.* Mahwah, NJ: Lawrence Erlbaum.

CONSTRUCTION-INTEGRATION MODEL

See Cognitive Theories

CONSTRUCTIVISM

In its original form, constructivism refers to the study of how individual human mental structures are constructed over time and how neuronal networks previously trained to perform given symbolic actions become conditions to subsequent ones. As mental structures develop, they define a person's ability to engage in other actions in the future. This means that certain symbolic actions cannot be performed if certain previous ones have not matured. For example, abstract hypotheses such as those found in mathematics or physics can be formulated only if the individual has previously learned to formulate hypotheses based on empirical data emerging from concrete experiences. Therefore, the mental exercise leading the person to perform a symbolic action takes place only if necessary (organic) and sufficient (experiential) conditions for further construction have previously been met.

As with many other schools of thought that produced fertile terms that became fashionable and lost their original meanings, many variations on the use of the term *constructivism* unrelated to its original formulation have arisen over the years. There are, thus, many constructivisms, each proposed by different authors and anchored in different epistemologies. This entry provides an overview of various uses of this term in different disciplines, such as biology and psychology, that contributed to communication theories.

Historic Context

Constructivism, originally known as genetic epistemology, was first introduced and coined by the Swiss thinker Jean Piaget, who studied the biological roots of knowledge. He was interested in unveiling how human beings know the world and empirically investigated how knowledge emerges and progresses through individual mental transformations in social environments. The human process of knowing, according to Piaget, can be understood only through a carefully designed research program aiming to unveil how knowledge develops over time through biological processes of assimilation and accommodation, leading to adaptation. Although these terms are common in general biology, Piaget proposed a biology of knowing, in which assimilation, accommodation, and adaptation are considered stages of the symbolic processes, necessary for knowledge learning that will enable people to make sense of the world.

In cognitive terms, *assimilation* accounts for absorbing the meaning related to a given content without changing structured knowledge previously embedded in the neural networks, while accommodation leads to reorganization of neural systems and conceptual change. Both assimilation and accommodation processes are necessary for symbolic adaptation to or sense making about the environment. Piaget chose to study children of all ages and use the methodological tools of psychology in order to verify the hypothesis that knowledge is constructed over time through complex interactions in which the individual makes sense of self and of the world. Construction, then, occurs when the neural pathways of the mind are progressively shaped through interactions with the world. Once knowledge is achieved (learned), the individual cannot unlearn it unless there is brain injury or a degenerative mental illness. This developmental process starts with the body. Movements translate a logic of brain functioning (logic of actions) that lies below the surface, followed by language acquisition and the development of logical reasoning founded on empirical experiences (concrete logic), followed by the development of reflective abstraction—or metacognition—that enables the individual to solve complex symbolic problems in the absence of empirical verification (operatory logic).

Piaget's ideas turned out to be very influential in many fields. Unfortunately, his contributions to communication were overshadowed by the revolution triggered by his theory in psychology and education. Piaget also provided epistemological contributions to sociology, biology, mathematics, physics, and, to a lesser extent, logic. His work resonated with certain "ecological" approaches in cybernetics that would later lead to systems theory, and it also had a direct impact on cognitive science.

These two main developments (ecological-systemic and cognitive approaches) helped to shape the ideas of certain scholars in the emerging field of communication studies who called themselves constructivists and their theories constructivism. Ecological-systemic theorists borrowed the term *constructivist* that gave academic celebrity to Piaget's scientific discoveries while taking away its original meaning. In contrast, the cognitive scientists translated concepts issued from constructivist epistemology and its qualitative and logical approaches into empiricist epistemology, thanks to the introduction of neobehaviorist experimental methodologies.

Common to all these approaches was the importance given to biology—the idea of organic development and organic systems—and the interest in discourse, in terms of both structure (logics, argumentation) and content (meanings).

The Constructivist Communication Schools

The School of Neuchâtel

Jean-Blaise Grize, a Swiss logician of the University of Neuchâtel in Switzerland who collaborated on

Piaget's research, assumed the challenge of developing the field of communication from a genetic standpoint. Trained as a logician and mathematician, Grize became particularly interested in unveiling the logic behind everyday communication that enables human beings to reason and make sense of the world. His communication theory, *schematizzation,* derives from the Piagetian notion of *scheme,* later incorporated by cognitive science. In Grize's theory, all communication actions are schematizations because interlocutors base their communication efforts on constructed symbolic schemes.

These constructed schemes have a natural logical structure that carries meaning resulting from complex psychosocial processes. Each word uttered in a sentence carries with it individual motivations that are translated into action as goals. Individual and social representations formed in the mind of the communicator are made available to others to be reinterpreted and rebuilt. In addition, sociocultural constructs enable those representations to be translated as words and sentences. Language is understood as a permanent sociohistorical building process that individuals rebuild constantly while communicating.

In addition to schematization, Grize and his collaborators, Denis Miéville and Marie-Jeanne Borel, developed a new branch of logic, *natural logic,* to focus on how the mind reasons through language. Natural logic studies the thinking operations that enable the construction of meanings in argumentation processes, distancing itself from both formal logic and empiricist informal logic approaches such as those of Stephen Toulmin, John R. Searle, and John L. Austin. In addition to being a specific branch of logic, natural logic can also be seen as a *method* to study schematizations in the communication process. In addition to previous developments in Europe, the study of natural logic, under the coordination of Grize and Miéville, has recently been expanded by the research of Emilio Gattico in Italy and Milton N. Campos in Canada.

The North American Constructivist School

North American communication constructivists base their use of the term *constructivism* on George Kelly's influential psychological work,

namely, *The Psychology of Personal Constructs,* published in 1955. Kelly postulates that people understand experience in terms of categories that distinguish one thing from another in sets of opposites. These contrasts (black–white, tall–short, fast–slow) are constructs that comprise a system of ideas with which individuals come to understand their experience and anticipate future events, an idea quite distant from Piaget's original constructivist epistemology.

Certain scholars in the interpersonal or "speech" branch of communication studies were strongly influenced by Kelly and developed an openly constructivist perspective in their research. The most influential is Jesse G. Delia, who inaugurated what is known as the *communication constructivist school.* Delia and his colleagues (James L. Applegate, Brant R. Burleson, Ruth Anne Clark, and Daniel J. O'Keefe, among others) promoted the core functionalist idea that people develop personal constructs out of experience and apply these when they face new experiences. The repetitive character of *constructs* borrowed by Delia from Kelly is very similar to the notion of scheme in Piagetian theory. In fact, constructivist scholars in the Delia tradition refer to sets of constructs as *interpretive schemes.* What is different and very original is that this research program, borrowing procedures from neobehaviorist experimental science, focuses on how constructs lead the individual to anticipate and respond to situations in terms of the communicative messages that will be used.

A person's communication is influenced by his or her *cognitive complexity,* related to the number of constructs in a person's cognitive system, or the degree of differentiation a person is able to make. Cognitive complexity is developmental. As individuals mature, the cognitive system moves from relative simplicity to relative complexity, but some persons are more complex than others, so cognitive complexity is dependent as well on the individual. In addition, a given individual will have greater complexity in some subjects than in others. The primary claim of this version of constructivism is that the increased differentiation that comes with cognitive complexity enables individuals to craft messages that adapt more effectively to listeners, so-called *person-centered* messages.

The Ecology-of-Mind Constructivist Scholars

Information processing theory and other theoretical approaches influenced by cybernetics have presented themselves as challenges to traditional behaviorism in that they all converge to the idea that it is possible to study mental processes, considered doubtful by behaviorist thinkers such as John B. Watson and B. F. Skinner. This was the approach of the North American scholars who developed different versions of *mind ecology,* also known to be constructivists.

Although in many ways the different constructivists discussed previously were connected with the cybernetic movement and considered biology fundamental for understanding communication, the constructivism that is presently mainstream is the one derived from the works of Gregory Bateson, a British anthropologist who immigrated to the United States, and is to a certain extent epistemologically consistent with the *constructionism* of Bruno Latour, a French sociologist of science. Later, others such as Ernst von Glasersfeld from Germany and Humberto Maturana and Francisco Varela from Chile also developed mind-ecology approaches that were rapidly adapted to communication studies. The phrase *ecology of the mind,* however, was coined by Gregory Bateson.

Bateson is the most influential of the ecology group and helped shape the destiny of communication studies from an empiricist system perspective. He argued that both logical and quantitative accounts were inappropriate to study how communication systems evolve. His work influenced communication schools such as the Palo Alto group, whose main theoretician is Paul Watzlawick.

In contrast to Bateson, Ernst von Glasersfeld, a German psychologist, cyberneticist, and journalist, proposed the term *radical constructivism* as a way to counter the growing influence of ecology-of-mind constructivists who reduced communication to meanings. For von Glasersfeld, the construction of communication is revealed by its formal structure and dynamics, that is, signals on which meanings are molded. People attribute meanings to words by interpreting the signals of language, translating them in the context of their experiences, and constructing communication structures that are both syntactical and semantic. From this viewpoint, von Glasersfeld was indebted to Piaget, who

highlighted that interaction occurs between the structuring activity of the subject (neural networks) and his or her subjectivity (the content of experience). However, and differently from genetic epistemology, von Glasersfeld tended to agree with the lack of differentiation between subject and object advanced by phenomenological epistemology.

Humberto Maturana, and later Francisco Varela, both phenomenologists, not only contributed to von Glasersfeld's radical constructivism but also had a huge influence in what became known as *second-order cybernetics,* a movement with direct consequences for communication studies. Maturana, who considered cognition as the other side of perception, was decidedly phenomenological. His biological phenomenology, which was later theorized by Varela as *naturalizing phenomenology,* kept subject and object indistinct from one another. Applied to communication theory, naturalizing phenomenology sees interaction as totalities of forever-emerging subjects. These phenomena form *autopoietic systems,* or the autoproduction of communication systems in which subject and object are dissolved into one another, and boundaries traditionally attributed to the subject–object pair by all other epistemologies are destroyed. *Autopoiesis* is consistent with philosophical phenomenology, according to which reality is a totality in which no part can be studied separately to understand the whole.

This view has very little to do with any idea of construction, genetic or otherwise, because it is based on the premise that communication is an emerging process of living, denying any possibility of studying parts such as what is communicated (message), the timing of the communication (dynamics of interaction), and the parties transmitting or receiving the communication (subjects). All the preceding perspectives demand that the researcher assume a separation between cognitive representations, or mental entities, and the subject or object being represented. In contrast with this view, phenomenologists, and more recently empiricists in the pragmatic tradition, completely deny representation as being possible. In the "place" of representation (or better put, the "absence of a possibility of place"), Maturana and Varela propose *enaction* as the process of the emergence of living that enables the possibility of communication.

What is curious in Maturana and Varela's constructivism is that although it inspired many thinkers to reconceptualize communication in autopoietic terms, these same thinkers would probably answer a resounding no to the question, Are you a phenomenologist? The second-order cybernetics is, thus, an "unframed" school of thought that invented *phenomenological constructivism*.

Recognized authors working from this perspective in communication studies include Klaus Krippendorff, who proposed the *recursive communication theory*. According to Krippendorff, communication is a reflexive process, meaning that each aspect of communication can be understood only in terms of other aspects of communication. Therefore, communication needs to be studied from within itself. In other words, communication can be studied only from the perspective of the discourse it produces. According to the theory, individual practices are fed by constructions of reality that, in turn, feed practices, both issued from human understanding. The main elements of the theory are the following:

1. Understanding is the core of communication processes; "construction" is to be found in the way individual practices lead to how reality is understood.

2. Communication processes are social phenomena that are reflexively built.

3. Language is constitutive of communication construction.

4. The recursive theory has no fixed model of communication, and participants in the communication process do not need to be in agreement with any given theory.

5. Communication makes possible virtual construction of "others" in the mind.

Krippendorff's theory, consistent with the core idea of Bruno Latour's sociology of science (in that theories are social constructions), inspired followers such as James Taylor, who helped establish the field of organizational communication; Niklas Luhmann, who influenced the social sciences in general and communication in particular, from a system perspective; and Pierre Levy, who developed the notion of collective intelligence in the field of cybercommunication.

Milton N. Campos

See also Argumentation Theories; Cognitive Theories; Communibiology; Critical Constructivism; Cybernetics; Interpersonal Communication Theories; Language and Communication; Learning and Communication; Palo Alto Group; Phenomenology; Speech Act Theory

Further Readings

Bateson, G. (1979). *Mind and nature: A necessary unity.* New York: E. P. Dutton.

Borel, M. J., Grize, J.-B., & Miéville, D. (1992). *Essai de logique naturelle* [Essay on natural logic]. Bern, Switzerland: Peter Lang.

Campos, M. N. (2007). Ecology of meanings: A critical constructivist communication model. *Communication Theory, 17,* 386–410.

Delia, J. G., O'Keefe, B. J., & O'Keefe, D. J. (1982). The constructivist approach to communication. In F. E. X. Dance (Ed.), *Human communication theory* (pp. 147–191). New York: Harper & Row.

Fosnot, C. T. (2005). *Constructivism: Theory, perspectives and practice* (2nd ed.). Williston, VT: Teachers College Press.

Grize, J.-B. (1996). *Logique naturelle & communications* [Natural logic & communications]. Paris: Presses Universitaires de France.

Kelly, G. A. (1955). *The psychology of personal constructs: Vol. 1.* New York: W. W. Norton.

Krippendorff, K. (1994). A recursive theory of communication. In D. Crowley & D. Mitchell (Eds.), *Communication theory today* (pp. 78–104). Stanford, CA: Stanford University Press.

Piaget, J. (1995). *Sociological studies* (T. Brown, R. Campbell, N. Emler, M. Ferrari, M. Gribetz, R. Kitchener, et al., Trans.). London: Routledge.

Steffe, L. (2000). *Radical constructivism in action: Building on the pioneering work of Ernst von Glasersfeld.* New York: RoutledgeFalmer.

Varela, F. J., Thompson, E., & Rosch, E. (1993). *L'inscription corporelle de l'esprit. Sciences cognitives et expérience humaine* [The embodied mind: Cognitive science and human experience] (Pierre Lavoie, Trans.; 9th ed.). Paris: Éditions du Seuil.

von Glasersfeld, E. (1996). *Radical constructivism: A way of knowing and learning.* London: Routledge.

Contextual Theory of Interethnic Communication

Ethnic diversity has become an increasingly salient and significant social issue in many societies around the world. Even as individuals of differing ethnic backgrounds live and work more closely than ever before, issues of ethnicity continue to invoke intense and often volatile responses. Young Yun Kim's contextual theory of interethnic communication addresses a full spectrum of behaviors displayed by individuals at their grassroots-level encounters with people who are ethnically different from them.

Applying a psychological perspective, Kim defines *interethnic communication* as an event, or a series of events, that occurs whenever at least one of the participants sees himself or herself and an interaction partner according to ethnic group categories. In this approach, not all communication encounters between individuals of dissimilar ethnicities are to be considered *interethnic* in character. The term *ethnicity* is broadly employed as a social category associated with some combinations of common national origin, race, religion, culture, and language. Ethnicity thus differentiates one group from another based on *extrinsic ethnic markers* such as physical features and speech patterns, and *intrinsic ethnic markers,* including cultural norms, beliefs, values, and thought patterns.

This theory grew out of Kim's research on the cross-cultural adaptation phenomenon of cultural strangers striving for a successful functional and psychological relationship with the host environment. During the 1980s and 1990s, Kim broadened her cross-cultural adaptation research to include the general phenomenon of interethnic communication involving all individuals living in an ethnically diverse society, regardless of their native-born or foreign-born backgrounds. Several initial theoretical papers on interethnic communication were published in the 1990s, followed by a formal presentation of the theory in 2005.

Interethnic Communication as a Dynamic System

Kim's theory is built on a keen recognition that specific interethnic communication events cannot be meaningfully understood without taking into account a set of historical, situational, and psychological forces that make up the context for particular interethnic behaviors. Kim conceives the behavior and the context as together co-constituting the basic interethnic communication system, operating simultaneously in a dynamic interplay, each affecting the other. Interethnic communication is thus treated not as a specific analytic unit (or variable) but as an entire system in which the behavior and the context are taken together into a fusion. Kim further conceives the interplay between the behavior and the context not as a one-directional cause and effect but as what Gregory Bateson described as a back and forth or circular stimulus and response.

Accordingly, the theory offers an integrative model of a basic interethnic communication system, a hierarchical arrangement that includes the behavior and a progression of three levels of context: the communicator at the center, the immediate social situation at the next level, and the larger environment at the macrolevel. The model serves as a matrix of transactions among these levels that can be thought of visually as a set of concentric circles that surround the behavior.

Levels of Context

With the integrative model, the theory places the behavior within three contextual layers: the communicator, the situation, and the environment, thereby offering a comprehensive account for the nature of the relationship between interethnic behavior and key factors of the surrounding context. In varying degrees of salience and significance, all contextual forces are regarded in Kim's theory to operate in any given interethnic communication event, potentially influencing, and being influenced by, the nature of individual behaviors.

Although these three levels are used to capture the major parts of the process, the outermost environmental context actually can include many sublevels, such as international settings, nations, regions, cities, neighborhoods, institutions, organizations, and other social entities. Within this organizing framework, the theory examines interethnic communication in its simplest and most general form, a single person communicating. The behavior (or activity) constitutes the stuff of an interethnic communication event, or the "what and how" of the messages sent and received.

At the same time, the conditions that surround the communication behavior comprise the contextual layers, or covert factors, that shape, as well as are shaped by, the behavior. Silently present in the context of this single-person interethnic communication system is one or more persons with whom the focal communicator interacts. Temporality also is built into this communication system, even though it is treated as frozen in time for the sake of analysis—rather like a motion picture is stopped so that it can be studied one frame or a set of frames at a time.

The Behavior: Association–Dissociation Continuum

The behavior, the focal point of this contextual theory, consists of a full spectrum of interethnic communication behaviors and actions. Included in this behavior spectrum are not only overtly observable verbal and nonverbal encoding activities but also intrapersonal decoding activities taking place within the person and hidden from other communicators. Encoding and decoding behaviors lie along a bipolar continuum between association and dissociation and vary in the extent to which they facilitate mutual understanding, cooperation, and convergence (the coming together of the involved persons, or *association*) or cause misunderstanding, competition, and divergence (the coming apart of the relationship between interactants, or *dissociation*). Behaviors seldom do one or the other exclusively but display some degree that may be more or less associative/dissociative.

Based on an extensive array of research findings, Kim explains that communicators in interethnic encounters behave associatively when they perceive and respond to others as unique individuals rather than as representatives of an out-group category; when they focus on others as unique individuals; and when they are attentive and display friendly facial expressions, complementary or mirroring bodily movements, and personalized (rather than impersonal) speech patterns. In contrast, a communication behavior is characterized as dissociative when it is based on a categorical, stereotypical, and depersonalized perception that accentuates differences. Dissociative behaviors

also include many forms of divergent verbal and nonverbal behaviors that indicate psychological distance and emotional intensity, from subtle expressions to blatantly dehumanizing name-calling, ethnic jokes, and hate speeches. Nonverbally, a communicator acts dissociatively through a range of behaviors, from subtle facial, vocal, and bodily expressions of lack of interest, disrespect, arrogance, and anger to more intense expressions of hatred and aggression, such as rioting and acts of violence.

The Communicator

Associative/dissociative interethnic communication behaviors are directly linked to the internal characteristics of the communicator. Incorporating various pertinent theoretical ideas and related research findings in the literature, the theory presents two communicator factors: (1) *identity inclusivity/exclusivity* and (2) *identity security/ insecurity*. The theory argues that, as functionally interrelated but conceptually distinct concepts, these identity orientations are significantly and reciprocally linked to an individual's associative/ dissociative interethnic behavior.

Identity inclusivity/exclusivity refers to the tendency of individuals to categorize themselves and others as in-group or out-group members. Inclusive identity orientation serves as a cognitive and motivational basis of associative behavior, whereas exclusive identity orientation is closely linked to a more rigid differentiation of oneself from ethnically dissimilar others. A substantial body of studies supports this theoretical claim. In interviews with Native Americans throughout Oklahoma, for instance, Kim and her coauthors found that those interviewees whose identity orientations were more inclusive (or less exclusive) were more actively engaged in interpersonal relationships with non-Indian acquaintances and friends. These interviewees also reported greater psychological health and functional fitness with respect to American society at large.

Identity security/insecurity is reflected in the degree of self-confidence and the sense of self-efficacy. The level of *identity security* indicates an individual's overall sense of self-confidence, or internal strength, with which to react to stressful situations with composure and clear and rational thinking. Identity security, as such, is a kind of personal resource that accords the capacity to empathize with others and to be creative in responding to impending problems. Identity security is also expressed in a sense of self-assuredness and positive attitudes toward others. In comparison, identity insecurity often manifests itself in feelings of inferiority or defensiveness when interacting with ethnically dissimilar others.

The Situation

Next to the communicator layer is the situational layer in which an interethnic encounter takes place. The theory identifies three key situational factors as being significant to understanding the nature of the communicator's interethnic behavior: (1) *ethnic proximity/distance;* (2) *shared/separate goal structure;* and (3) *personal network integration/segregation.*

Ethnic proximity/distance refers to the level of homogeneity or heterogeneity between the interactants. This situational factor arises from the degree of *extrinsic ethnic markers,* such as physical features and speech accents, and from the degree of compatibility or incompatibility stemming from *intrinsic ethnic markers* such as internalized beliefs and values associated with a specific ethnic group. The theory argues that ethnic proximity encourages associative behaviors, whereas ethnic distance increases psychological distance between the interactants and keeps them from noticing their underlying similarities.

Shared/separate goal structure is defined as the extent to which the communicators come together with mutuality of interests. Shared goals foster and are fostered by associative behaviors and cooperative relationships between the involved parties. In contrast, communicators who see in the other interactant(s) few shared goals are less likely to be motivated to engage in associative behaviors. In ethnically diverse athletic teams, for instance, team members with a strong commitment to the collective goal of achieving a winning season tend to subsume their ethnic group interests more willingly to those of the team.

Personal network integration is identified in the theory as having a significant relevance to interethnic behavior. *Personal network,* also referred to by network analysts as *interpersonal network, egocentric network,* and *personal community,* is largely a product of voluntary association. Accordingly, the ethnic composition of a given communicator's personal network is indicative of the extent to which he or she has, or has not, already participated in associative activities with ethnically dissimilar others. Hence, the theory argues that communicators whose personal networks are already more integrated are likely to act more associatively in dealing with other ethnically dissimilar others.

The Environment

Surrounding the situational contextual layer is the environment, the outer social milieu, which is comprised of multiple sublevels as described earlier in this entry. Directly or indirectly, strongly or weakly, certain conditions of each environmental layer potentially influence, and are influenced by, the associative–dissociative interethnic behavior of the individual communicator. The theory identifies three factors of the environment: (1) *institutional equity/inequity,* (2) *in-group strength,* and (3) *environmental stress.*

Institutional equity/inequity addresses issues of fairness and justice. Through the activities of social comparison, individual communicators are less likely to act associatively if they perceive, correctly or not, some form of unfair rules or practices directed against their own ethnic group. Many of the contemporary incidents of institutional inequity can be traced to the history of subjugation of one ethnic group by another in various forms, including slavery and colonization. Societies such as the United States have undergone a significant transformation toward greater institutional equity, thereby rendering a substantial increase over time in interethnic associations across ethnic boundaries.

Interethnic behaviors are further linked to *ethnic group strength.* The overall strength of an ethnic group is closely tied to objective properties such as its relative size, economic resources, and institutional and organizational strengths. Individuals in a large, active, and well-organized ethnic community (such as the Cuban American community in Florida) are more likely to maintain ethnic relational ties than to reach out actively to individuals outside their ethnic community. Conversely, an individual whose ethnic community is small and less institutionalized tends to be more motivated to associate himself or herself with out-group members.

The third environmental factor, *environmental stress*, pertains to the tension in an organization, community, or society at large. Interethnic tension is also likely to increase when the environment is under duress because of events that are linked to a particular out-group. Such was the case when violent or otherwise dissociative acts increased against individuals of Middle Eastern origins following the acts of terrorism on September 11, 2001. Dissociative behaviors also tend to increase when a society undergoes certain challenging circumstances caused by economic hardship, shortage of resources, or involvement in an international crisis.

Theorems

As outlined above, Kim's theory identifies eight contextual factors of the communicator, the situation, and the environment as being significant to understanding interethnic behavior. Conversely, the theory argues that specific associative or dissociative interethnic behaviors can influence the nature of the eight contextual factors. Linking each of the contextual factors to associative/dissociative behavior in a reciprocal functional relationship, the theory proposes eight testable theorems.

Theorems 1 and 2 propose a profile of a communicator who is likely to act more associatively as someone with a more inclusive and secure identity orientation. These two theorems further predict that a communicator who acts associatively is likely to find his or her identity orientation becoming more inclusive and secure.

Addressing three situational factors, Theorems 3 through 5 predict that interethnic behavior is likely to be more associative when the communication situation created by the communicator and the other interactant(s) presents greater ethnic proximity (similarity and compatibility) and shared goals (common interests) and when the communicator's existing personal network is ethnically more integrated. Conversely, these three theorems suggest that the same situational factors of cultural proximity, shared goal structure, and integrated personal network can be fostered through associative behaviors.

Theorems 6 through 8 posit that the communicator is likely to behave more associatively when the larger environment offers him or her a system of law, rules, policies, and practices that are, or are perceived to be, more equitable; when the communicator's own ethnic group is smaller in size and weaker in collective strength; and when the relevant environment is calmer and more prosperous. At the same time, the theorems also predict that, directly or indirectly, associative behaviors of individual communicators can help foster greater fairness for all parties involved; counter potentially adversarial conditions stemming from unequal strengths of the ethnic groups involved; and mitigate the potential dissociative impact of serious economic, political, or social challenges confronting the surrounding environment on the interethnic relations between individuals.

The Theory and the Reality

In addition to the generalizable patterns of behavior–context relationships identified in the eight theorems, the theory provides a broadly based conceptual roadmap that can guide case studies of specific interethnic communication events. The theory offers an integrative analytic framework with which to survey the entire field of behavior–context interface in a given case, directing an analyst's attention to the particularities of behavioral and contextual forces operating in a given interethnic event or a series of related events.

The theory allows that each event presents a unique circumstance in which some factors may be of greater relevance and play a more prominent role than others. Once all the constituent dimensions and factors are identified, the analyst may zero in on those factors that are most salient and significant to understanding and explaining that event. Even a single factor may be so powerful as to overshadow every other force operating in a given encounter. Such would be the case when two individuals respond to an identical set of situational and environmental conditions in vastly different manners or when commitment to a shared goal (a situational factor) is so strong that interactants are able to overcome many of the adversarial environmental factors and manage to engage in associative behaviors and activities.

For everyday practitioners of interethnic communication, the systemic conception of interethnic communication depicted in this theory suggests that change in the status quo in interethnic relations can be initiated at any level. Those who desire change may begin by looking inwardly and reflecting on the extent of inclusiveness and security in their own sense of who they are and how they orient themselves to ethnically dissimilar others. By practicing associative behaviors at the individual level, they may work to improve the quality of interethnic relations in organizations and communities around us. They may further anticipate that, by creating a situation around them in which all involved parties see the mutuality of their respective interests and aspirations, they can engender a strong sense of community and active interpersonal associations that transcend ethnic categories.

Ultimately, the contextual theory of interethnic communication speaks to the real possibility that a single communicator can make a difference for all others involved in an interethnic encounter. When sufficiently multiplied by many others, a communicator's behavior can resonate broadly to help shape the quality of interethnic communication in a given neighborhood, organization, community, society, and beyond. It is this grassroots-level reality of individual communicators that the theory illuminates in its full complexity.

Young Yun Kim

See also Accommodation Theory; Actor–Network Theory; Communication Theory of Identity; Cross-Cultural Adaptation Theory; Culture and Communication; Intercultural Communication Theories; Interracial Communication; Self-Categorization Theory; Social Identity Theory; System Theory

Further Readings

Bateson, G. (1972). *Steps to an ecology of mind.* New York: Ballantine Books.

Kim, Y. Y. (1978). Inter-ethnic and intra-ethnic communication. *International and Intercultural Communication Annual, 4*(1), 53–68.

Kim, Y. Y. (1986). Understanding the social context of intergroup communication: A personal network theory. In W. Gudykunst (Ed.), *Intergroup communication* (pp. 86–95). London: Edward Arnold.

Kim, Y. Y. (1989). Explaining interethnic conflict: An interdisciplinary overview. In J. Gittler (Ed.), *Annual review of conflict knowledge and conflict resolution: Vol. 1* (pp. 101–125). New York: Garland.

Kim, Y. Y. (1997). The context-behavior interface in interethnic communication. In J. Owen (Ed.), *Context and communication behavior* (pp. 261–291). Reno, NV: Context Press.

Kim, Y. Y. (1999). *Unum* and *Pluribus:* Ideological underpinnings of interethnic communication in the United States. *International Journal of Intercultural Relations, 23*(4), 591–611.

Kim, Y. Y. (2003). Unum vs. Pluribus: Ideology and differing academic conceptions of ethnic identity. In W. Gudykunst (Ed.), *Communication yearbook 26* (pp. 298–325). Mahwah, NJ: Lawrence Erlbaum.

Kim, Y. Y. (2005). Association and dissociation: A contextual theory of interethnic communication. In W. Gudykunst (Ed.), *Theorizing about intercultural communication* (pp. 323–349). Thousand Oaks, CA: Sage.

Kim, Y. Y., Lujan, P., & Dixon, L. (1998). "I can walk both ways": Identity integration of American Indians in Oklahoma. *Human Communication Research, 25,* 252–274.

CONVERGENCE THEORY

The convergence theory of communication was developed in 1979 by D. Lawrence Kincaid to provide a general model of communication that would overcome the criticisms and shortcomings of prevailing models, especially information transmission models such as the one used in Shannon and Weaver's mathematical theory of communication. The model represented communication as (a) a process rather than a single action; (b) sharing or exchange of information rather than one-way transmission; (c) two or more participants in dialogue; (d) a means to clarify the confusion between information, knowledge, messages, symbols, and meaning; and (e) a self-correcting feedback process, defined dynamically as a diminishing series of corrections that enable communicators to *converge* on a goal. The theoretical implications of the convergence model became readily apparent, leading to theoretical propositions that could be tested empirically. It also became apparent that *convergence*, the general principle underlying the model, is central to many specific theories found in the field of communication.

Convergence is often mistakenly equated with consensus. Convergence is *movement* toward one point, toward another communicator, toward a common interest, and toward greater uniformity, never quite reaching that point. It is assumed, for example, that no two people can ever reach the same meaning for information, only a greater degree of similarity. In communication, the goal of this feedback process is mutual understanding, a reduction in the set of all possible individual understandings to a more limited one that is shared.

The Convergence Model

The latest version of the convergence model depicts a cyclical, iterative process involving at least two participants. Participants are connected by sharing the same information with one another. Information, lying at the central core of the model, is physical—something endowed with form. Sound waves created by the vocal chords, text messages on paper or sand, patterns on a television monitor, tone of voice, body language and position, and so forth are physical phenomena and hence potentially sources of information for communication. Limiting the concept of information to its physical manifestation makes it possible to treat it as the *means* by which thoughts and meaning are expressed and shared with others. Thoughts and meaning are defined purely as cognitive phenomena, which are *psychological*. The psychological realities toward which communicators converge consist of perceptions, interpretations, understandings, and beliefs. Emotional responses to information can affect each one of these cognitive processes. The relationship formed between participants by sharing information is *social*. Information is created and/or shared by the actions of two or more participants, groups, organizations, or cultures engaged in intergroup, interorganizational, and intercultural communication. The collective action of individuals, including the coordinated actions required for communication itself, is also a source of information.

Power—the capacity to exercise control over others—is not an inherent part of communication per se but rather an attribute of the relationship between participants. To have an effect on communication, power must first be made apparent by means of information. Physical size, posture, tone of voice, clothing, titles, signs of wealth, and so forth provide information about the respective power of each participant. Power can also be communicated by overt threats of positive and negative sanctions, and ultimately by physical action (force) itself. Information that reflects power can also induce an emotional response, such as respect or fear, which in turn is expected to influence the communication process, increasing the likelihood that the position of the one with more power will be accepted.

In 2002, Kincaid introduced an extended model that allowed for divergence and conflict as well as convergence and cooperation. Communication as convergence or divergence consists of six phases: (1) a *scene-setting* phase that creates an informationally closed system for dialogue; (2) a *buildup* phase leading to final positions taken within a common frame of reference (mutual understanding); and (3) a *resolution* phase, in which participants mutually agree on a common position they trust each other to implement. Mutual understanding helps to ensure each participant's trustworthiness, but if flaws are revealed in the resolution stage, mistrust can arise and throw participants back into a new buildup phase with an increased possibility of (4) a *climax* phase, when emotion and reason do not lead to changes in position and mutual understanding, leading to (5) a *conflict* phase, in which neither participant will change and hence must resort to their threatened fallback positions. In the final (6) *resolution* phase, either cooperation or conflict is implemented. If participants agree on a *common position* that they can trust each other to implement, then the outcome will be cooperation.

Following this new model, *communication* is defined as a process in which two or more participants share information and converge toward a state of greater mutual understanding and agreement leading to cooperation or, as explained later in this entry, diverge toward a state of incompatible viewpoints and disagreement, leading to conflict. Cooperation requires some minimal level of mutual understanding and agreement. Even when conflict occurs, communication has still created a state of greater mutual understanding of each participant's point of view.

Convergence Theory at the Aggregate Level of Analysis

The most important principle of semantics is that there is no one-to-one correspondence between symbolic information and its meaning. If that were the case, a new symbol would be required for every different circumstance in which communication occurs. There are no perfectly equivalent circumstances, only variety. Meaning is possible because of variation, and that variation includes silence and the nonoccurrence of other symbols (e.g., "no" instead of "yes" or "maybe"). This semantic principle implies that information is a physical difference (pattern) that affects uncertainty in a situation in which a choice exists among a set of alternatives. When uncertainty is too high to permit one to decide (interpret or understand), then additional information is sought. This feedback process reduces the initial levels of uncertainty regarding each participant's interpretation and understanding, leading to an increased level of mutual understanding.

When the convergence model is applied at the *aggregate level of analysis* to groups, organizations, and cultures, then theoretical propositions can be proposed that use formulas for statistical averages and variances. Here the theory predicts that when messages constructed with multiple concepts are shared, the average position of each concept will converge on the statistical center. Thus, the association of concepts in a message leads to the mutual convergence of all concepts toward one another. The average position of a set of measured concepts of two or more local subcultures that share information is expected to converge over time toward a global mean. This hypothesis was tested by measuring the average difference in the multidimensional space of Eastern and Western cultural values (e.g., individual freedom, saving face, happiness, success) of Korean immigrants who had lived in Hawaii from 1 to 15 years. During this period, a statistical measure of meaning of successive Korean immigrant cohorts converged toward that of the host culture in the form of damped harmonic motion, which is a statistical concept related to changes in variation. The results were also expressed mathematically as a convergence toward a state of greater uniformity (less diversity) of values, as measured by the reduction in the statistical variance.

This work led to the following two complementary convergence theorems for the aggregate level of analysis of communication in social networks, groups, organizations, and subcultures in a population:

Theorem 1: In a relatively closed social system in which communication among members is *unrestricted,* the system as a whole will tend to converge over time toward a state of greater cultural *uniformity.*

Theorem 2: In a relatively closed social system in which communication among members is *restricted,* the system as a whole will tend to diverge over time toward a state of greater cultural *diversity.*

Homogeneity of information leads to uniformity of belief and behavior; heterogeneity leads to diversity. For initially diverse subgroups who share information within a relatively bounded social system, the statistical variance around the mean of a continuous measure is expected to decrease over time, as the Korean immigrant case confirmed. If a boundary is imposed between two groups (restricting information sharing), then the variance of the system as a whole is expected to increase over time (toward greater diversity) and *simultaneously* decrease within each subculture around its local mean. Boundaries can be created by the lack of interpersonal contact (social network clustering), by lack of a common language, by the use of different channels of mass media, and by geographical barriers. Conversely, with less restricted information sharing, *diversity decreases over time* (hence, uniformity increases).

In 1983, before the theorems were formally proposed, Everett Rogers and Kincaid measured the diversity of contraceptive behavior among women in 24 Korean villages. Because contraceptive practice is a discrete behavior, it was possible to calculate the percentage of adoption of each contraceptive method within the relatively bounded *social networks* of each village and then compute the average degree of diversity–uniformity. Surprisingly, the most popular method of birth control varied across the 24 villages: Some were predominantly oral-pill villages, others IUD villages, others condom villages, and so forth. In other words, the distribution of behavior within each village's social network appeared as if it had been a collective decision rather than the sum of many individual choices. The average uniformity–diversity was positively correlated with the degree of interconnectedness of the social networks within the village, a measure of the degree of restriction of information flow and absence of bounded clusters. Villages with less connected communication networks had a flatter, more diverse distribution of behavior; those with more densely connected networks had a narrower, more uniform distribution, which is characteristic of a prevailing social norm.

Bounded Normative Influence

The two convergence theorems are valid because of the nature of information processing and the role played by boundaries. When the boundary of a group expands to include new members with different points of view, diversity increases. When people who disagree leave, uniformity among those who remain automatically increases. At the same time, the group becomes more diverse with respect to outsiders. This convergence process is enhanced by *bounded normative influence*—the tendency of social norms to influence behavior within relatively bounded local subgroups of a social system rather than in the system as a whole. This cultural and social network principle resolves the paradox of how *innovation* (a new minority position) can survive the social pressure of the majority and eventually grow to become the new majority: subgroups insulate themselves by forming boundaries within which they are the majority, and they then expand by recruiting new members from the outside.

Bounded normative influence is evident in Gerry Mackie's explanation of how the deeply embedded social norm of women's foot binding in China was totally overcome in one generation at the beginning of the 19th century by the organization of cohesive, local societies in which families pledged to raise girls with natural feet and have their sons marry only girls with natural feet. In a recent network analysis of the 30-year decline of smoking in the United States, Nickolas Christakis and James Fowler discovered that while smoking declined overall, the size of clusters of those who continued to smoke remained the same across time (appearing progressively in the periphery of social networks), suggesting that clusters of connected people were quitting together. In their recent book

The Big Sort, Bill Bishop and Robert Cushing described the profound ideological clustering and polarization that has been taking place in the United States over the past 30 years as a result of geographical mobility to places of like-minded people, a voluntary narrowing of exposure to cable television channels and Internet sites, and a growing unwillingness of people to be exposed to contrary points of view. All three societal changes can be explained by—and could have been predicted by—the two basic theorems of the convergence theory of communication.

D. Lawrence Kincaid

See also Cybernetics; Information Theory; Semiotics and Semiology; Symbolic Convergence Theory; System Theory

Further Readings

Barnett, G. A., & Kincaid, D. L. (1983). Cultural convergence: A mathematical theory. In W. B. Gudykunst (Ed.), *Intercultural communication theory: Current perspectives: Vol. VII. International and intercultural communication annual* (pp. 171–194). Beverly Hills, CA: Sage.

Kincaid, D. L. (1988). The convergence theory of communication: Its implications for intercultural communication. In Y. Y. Kim (Ed.), *Theoretical perspectives on international communication: Vol. XII. International and intercultural annual* (pp. 280–298). Beverly Hills, CA: Sage.

Kincaid, D. L. (2002). Drama, emotion, and cultural convergence. *Communication Theory, 12,* 136–152.

Kincaid, D. L. (2004). From innovation to social norm: Bounded normative influence. *Journal of Health Communication, 9,* 37–57.

Rogers, E. M., & Kincaid, D. L. (1981). *Communication networks: Toward a new paradigm for research.* New York: Free Press.

Woelfel, J., & Fink, E. L. (1980). *The measurement of communication processes: Galileo theory and method.* New York: Academic Press.

CONVERSATIONAL CONSTRAINTS THEORY

Culture-based conversational constraints theory, developed by Min-Sun Kim and her colleagues, explains why people from different cultures say what they say. In contrast with mostly descriptive research on cross-cultural strategy choices, the major goal of this research program has been to understand, from a goals perspective, why a particular conversational strategy is chosen cross-culturally. This theory derives, in part, from research on metagoals in interpersonal communication contexts. However, the focus of the culture-based conversational constraints theory has been to understand the cognitive underpinnings of message production across cultures.

Most cross-cultural studies explain away the stereotypical communication differences as some "cultural" difference, such as being Asian or being American. The influence of norms, customs, and rules can be applied only according to a given situation and thus has limited explanatory power. The central focus of conversational constraints relates not to what is said but rather to how what is said is to be said. Kim proposes the existence of five interactional concerns (i.e., conversational constraints) that are assumed to guide message production: (1) concern for clarity, (2) concern for minimizing imposition, (3) concern for avoiding damage to the hearer's feelings, (4) concern for avoiding negative evaluation, and (5) concern for effectiveness. Although this line of research does not directly assess message production, a likelihood-of-use measure is usually included that is intended to capture a portion of individuals' implicit theories of interaction goals.

Genesis of Culture-Based Conversational Constraints

As people pursue interaction goals such as gaining compliance, seeking information, or altering relationships, they generate messages within a variety of constraints. In conversation, actors face constraints on how they speak. This is the backdrop against which people pursue their conversational goals. These higher-level constraints have been named *supergoals, cross-situational goals, super-maxims, metastrategies, metagoals, metaplans, ritual-constraints,* and *sociopragmatic interactional principles.* The main implication is that, regardless of one's interaction goal(s), there exist higher-level concerns regarding how one will achieve the goal(s).

Researchers from communication, artificial intelligence, psychology, linguistics, and other related fields have suggested two major dimensions that may serve as global constraints in conversational and planning situations—appropriateness and effectiveness. In the past, several authors have suggested similar dualities that are motivating forces in communication: being clear and being polite, concern for clarity and concern with support, directness and politeness, and efficiency and social appropriateness. Grice put forward the *maxim of manner* in the use of language (e.g., be clear, be brief, try to avoid obscurity), which can be seen as offering guidelines for direct communication. Brown and Levinson also posit such wants as (a) the want to be efficient or indicate urgency and (b) the want to maintain the hearer's face to some degree.

Based on the above literature, most theorists in interpersonal communication seem to have accepted, either implicitly or explicitly, the importance of appropriateness and effectiveness (or efficiency) in defining communication competence. The notion of social appropriateness as a communication constraint, however, presupposes some accepted standards of what constitutes appropriate communication performance. It inherently requires a culturally homogeneous community. Thus, appropriateness runs the risk of being meaningless in cross-cultural comparisons. When people do not share social conventions, their notions of appropriateness are different. For instance, a use of a request strategy by a person from one culture, where the choice would be appropriate, may be considered inappropriate when used with a person from another culture.

Contents of Culture-Based Conversational Constraints

Kim proposed a set of culture-based conversational constraints to account for the use of different conversational strategies in different cultures. The previous set of two interactive constraints (i.e., social appropriateness and efficiency) is broken down into three more specific social-relational categories (imposition, other's feelings, and negative evaluation). Two other task-related constraints are added (clarity and effectiveness). This section defines each dimension (see Figure 1) in the context of requesting behavior.

Clarity

Clarity is defined as the likelihood of an utterance's making one's intention clear and explicit. Clarity is discussed frequently in the literature on conversation. For instance, Grice's maxim of manner (e.g., be clear, be brief, avoid obscurity) can be seen as a guideline for clear communication. The current typology of request strategies varies on a clarity dimension. If one's primary goal is to request an action, direct imperatives (e.g., "Repay the loan" or "Lend me your book") make the speaker's illocutionary point—his or her intent—explicit. The hint strategy—the other end of the continuum—should be least clear, since clarity of intent is not necessarily derivable from the literal meaning of the utterances.

Minimizing Imposition

This dimension pertains to the degree to which an utterance avoids imposing on the hearer's autonomy or interfering with the hearer's freedom of action. This type of concern has been referred to in more abstract terms as *negative politeness* or *deference politeness*. What is desired is to avoid imposing on others. Concern for minimizing imposition has primarily been conceived as a means of protecting the hearer's face. Several authors argue that in the Western world, the notion of politeness usually is associated with showing deference by not expecting the hearer's cooperation and by leaving the hearer the option of noncompliance. While the salience of this constraint might differ across cultures, prior research confirms the importance of minimizing imposition in many cultures.

Consideration for the Other's Feelings

When making a request, people also may consider how their projected action will affect the hearer's feelings. "Concern for the other's feelings" relates to the speaker's perceived obligation to help the hearer claim and sustain a positive self-image. The degree to which a strategy shows a consideration for the hearer's

Concern for clarity

1. In this situation, I feel it is very important to make my point as clearly and directly as possible.
2. In this situation, I want to directly come to the point while conveying my message.

Concern for not hurting the other's feelings

1. In this situation, I feel it is very important to avoid hurting the other's feelings.
2. In this situation, being considerate toward the other's feelings is a major concern to me.

Concern for nonimposition

1. In this situation, it is very important *not* to intrude on the other person.
2. In this situation, it is very important to avoid inconveniencing the other.

Concern for avoiding negative evaluation by the hearer

1. In this situation, it is very important that the other person does *not* see me in a negative light.
2. In this situation, it is very important that my message does *not* cause the other person to dislike me.

Concern for effectiveness

1. In this situation, it is very important to get the other person to do what I want.
2. In this situation, making the other person comply with my request is very important.

Figure 1 List of Culture-Based Conversational Constraints: Scale Items

Source: Kim, M. S. (1992). *Cross-cultural variations in implicit theories of requesting behavior.* Unpublished doctoral dissertation, Michigan State University.

feelings has been proposed under various labels, including *positive face, identity goals,* and *concern with support.* Direct statements with a lack of request mitigation (e.g., "Do X!") may risk a higher chance of hurting the other's feelings than hints that communicate the implicit message that the speaker is not concerned about the relationship but only with accomplishing the instrumental outcome.

Risking Disapproval for Self

This dimension represents the desire to avoid negative evaluation by the conversational partner. This constraint is consistent with Brown and Levinson's notion of a speaker's desire to save his or her own positive face. In recent years, several authors have suggested similar interactive constraints in communication, including *impression-management goals* and *approval-seeking strategies.* The direct-statement strategy potentially could risk devaluation for self since it is more demanding than the hint strategy.

Effectiveness

Effectiveness is another major dimension that influences choice of conversational tactics and strategies. If speakers undertake communicative acts to accomplish a primary goal, then it seems likely that they are concerned with whether that goal will be accomplished. While effectiveness alone is not a sufficient condition of competence, it nonetheless indicates the importance of this constraint in social interaction.

Cultural Variability in Perceived Importance of Constraints

Kim's conversational-constraints studies seek to generate knowledge about the cultural precursors of conversational concerns, in contrast to situational and individual difference predictors that have been the focus of most previous studies. Hence her research program is distinguished by its use of multiple-culture samples. Some of the research treats cultural membership as the independent variable and the importance of the constraints as the dependent variables.

A major issue that Kim and her colleagues have pursued involves linking the differences between *individualist* and *collectivist* communication styles to the importance of the conversational constraints. Individualism–collectivism has been considered the single most important dimension of cultural difference in social behavior. Kim has investigated how cultural groups may differ in the structure and content of their perceptions about preferred communication behavior, focusing on the importance attached to interactive concerns in conversation. The results indicate that the dimension of individualism–collectivism (as operationalized by nationality) is systematically related to the perceived importance of clarity, avoiding hurting the hearer's feelings, and minimizing imposition. For example, U.S. Americans perceive clearer tactics as more effective, whereas Koreans believe just the opposite. Elsewhere, Kim and her colleagues have attempted to trace the effects of cultural membership from self-concept variables through judgments of constraint importance.

Claims of cultural distinctions between East Asians and U.S. Americans on relationship orientation versus task orientation abound in the literature. This line of research shows that the popular claims regarding relationship orientation (East Asian) versus task orientation (U.S. American) in verbal styles may in fact be grounded in shared cognitive knowledge about communication behavior. Later, *self-construal,* how we depict ourselves, has been introduced into the research to account for both the between- and within-culture variation in the expression of communication behavior. By the use of this individual-level approach to cross-cultural differences in conjunction with the prior culture-level approach, hypotheses can be examined both intraculturally and cross-culturally so that explanatory variables may be tested at two levels.

This theory extends our knowledge about what kinds of general conversational constraints shape peoples' beliefs concerning competent behavior. Because goals arise from culture and self-concept, the model highlights the goal formation portion of the message-production process. In addition, because conversational constraints limit message choice prior to enactment, the model speaks to the planning stage as well.

Conversational constraints are essentially cognitive generators of tactical preferences. Without these overarching concerns, people's choice of tactics would appear as isolated entities without connection to the rest of their knowledge. The conversational constraints seem self-evident to native speakers but, in fact, are culturally specific, which helps to explain culture's effect on conversational behavior in different societies. The current theory, despite its obvious need of further testing and theoretical refinement, provides a theoretical framework that can systematically explain how the interactive constraints guide the cultural preference of communication tactics and the perceptions of intercultural communicative competence.

The main practical implication of the theory is that when speakers of different cultural backgrounds interact, the problems that develop in communication can be accounted for by the salience of global goals or constraints in conversation. Given that global constraints contribute to consistent performances across different contexts, the concept of the different restraining forces of various conversational constraints can provide a useful framework for explaining intercultural communication and misunderstandings.

Min-Sun Kim

See also Competence Theories

Further Readings

Gudykunst, W. B., & Lee, C. M. (2003). Cross-cultural communication theories. In W. B. Gudykunst (Ed.), *Cross-cultural and intercultural communication* (pp. 7–34). Thousand Oaks, CA: Sage.

Kim, M.-S. (1992). *Cross-cultural variations in implicit theories of requesting behavior.* Unpublished doctoral dissertation, Michigan State University.

Kim, M.-S. (1993). Culture-based conversational constraints in explaining cross-cultural strategic competence. In R. L. Wiseman & J. Koester (Eds.), *Intercultural communication competence* (pp. 132–150). Newbury Park, CA: Sage.

Kim, M.-S. (1994). Cross-cultural comparisons of the perceived importance of conversational constraints. *Human Communication Research, 21,* 128–151.

Kim, M.-S. (1995). Toward a theory of conversational constraints. In R. L. Wiseman (Ed.), *Intercultural communication theory* (pp. 148–169). Thousand Oaks, CA: Sage.

Kim, M.-S. (2004). Culture-based conversational constraints theory: Individual- and culture-level analyses. In W. B. Gudykunst (Ed.), *Theorizing about intercultural communication* (pp. 93–117). Thousand Oaks, CA: Sage.

Kim, M.-S., Hunter, J. E., Miyahara, A., Horvath, A., Bresnahan, M., & Yoon, H. J. (1996). Individual- vs. culture-level dimensions of individualism and collectivism: Effects on preferred conversational styles. *Communication Monographs, 63,* 29–49.

Conversation Analysis

Conversation analysis (CA), initially developed by Harvey Sacks with Emanuel Schegloff, David Sudnow, and others, seeks to provide a descriptive study of human conduct via empirical data of naturally occurring interaction. CA attempts to provide an approach to investigating the sequential nature of social action from the perspective of the participants' display of methods and procedures utilized in the organization of their interaction. From its inception in the early 1960s, CA has developed a set of concerns centered on the observable features of interaction as they arise in a range of circumstances and situations and for undertaking various actions via talk. While originally presented as a means of extending sociological analysis, CA, as an approach to activity, has grown to be incorporated into numerous fields and explorations regarding human communication.

Early Development

Harvey Sacks initiated the idea of CA while a graduate student with Emanuel Schegloff and David Sudnow in the Sociology Department at the University of California, Berkeley. All three were students of Erving Goffman, who was developing his personal approach to examining the everyday social activities of individuals in an attempt to describe what he called the *interaction order*. Sacks and Schegloff were seeking to develop a new way, independent of then current sociological methods, for conceptualizing and approaching social activity. In so doing, they avoided the reliance on commonly employed sociological concepts (e.g., culture, norms, organizations, or states) to provide means of describing and explaining data. Rather, they sought an approach rooted in the observable displays of what individuals do during interaction to make their understandings of the activity in which they were involved known to participants.

Sacks became a fellow at the Los Angeles Suicide Prevention Center in 1963. As part of the procedure of handling incoming helpline phone calls, the center routinely made audio recordings of these calls. These materials provided a set of naturally occurring data that Sacks could examine. While Sacks was not initially interested in studying conversation, the recorded phone calls provided a means to analytically investigate social action as undertaken via the interaction of caller and counselor. The recent developments of recording technology provided the ability to capture natural instances of human conduct without the direct intervention of the researcher to filter observations, such as through note taking. This noninterference of the analyst became one of the assumptions of CA data collection.

Even though the initial set of recordings was produced in an institutional setting (the Suicide Prevention Center), the focus was on the observable elements of conversation practice generally rather than on any situated features of the interaction. While these recordings provided the initial corpus from which Sacks drew his material as he developed his lectures on CA, the data set quickly grew to include instances of conversation that were not institutionally connected. These data allowed for the development of arguments regarding the general use of conversational devices (such as turn taking and sequential organization) across situations rather than in one particular institutional setting. As a faculty member, Sacks attracted several students, such as Gail Jefferson, Anita Pomerantz, and Jim Schenkein, among others, with whom (in addition to Schegloff) he would develop initial concepts of conversational practice and who would be among those carrying on Sacks's research tradition following his early death in a traffic accident in 1975.

Goffman's work investigating the ritual and social order of face-to-face interaction was one early influence on the development of CA as a sociological approach. Goffman created unique and informative descriptions of routine activity that illustrated the social, rather than individual, organization of our interactions. For Goffman, the organization of activity and interaction was not independent of situation; the social organization provided a framework from which to examine situations and interactions within. Similarly *ethnomethodology,* developed by Harold Garfinkel, influenced the initial conceptions of CA. Ethnomethodology provided a specific approach to the investigation of the lived social world by problematizing the commonsense reasoning employed by individuals as they engage in their routine, day-to-day activities. In essence, ethnomethodology sought to illustrate how social actors' reliance on the procedures of social norms served as the manifestation of their understandings of those norms.

Basic Assumptions

As an investigation into human activity, CA seeks to discover and describe the routine competencies relied on by individuals to manage and display their understandings of the moment during interaction. It tries to develop accounts for how participants produce their own contributions and indicate recognition and understanding of contributions by others. As joint activity, interaction requires the coordination of participants to place their respective turns in a fitting and understandable manner relative to one another. Consequently, each turn of talk stands in relation to its prior turn, so that a subsequent turn may be observed as recognizing and responding to it, based on its display. CA examines the sequential nature of how participants display their ongoing comprehension of the interaction by considering the observable features of interaction to which participants orient themselves during sequences of talk. Features highlighted by participants during their interaction become examinable by the analyst.

Researcher emphasis on those features that participants display themselves highlights an important facet in the design and undertaking of CA work. Unlike approaches that make use of theoretical concepts and orientations to help unpack and understand the activities in which people engage and organize their social worlds, CA eschews theoretical constructs that do not originate in the interactional realm under investigation. That is, CA does not promote or develop generalizable theoretical explanations for observed phenomena beyond (a) those concepts and explanations developed from prior empirical investigation into talk-in-interaction and (b) the commonplace understandings of how interaction works based on our engagement as conversational practitioners. Thus, analyst-selected categories of description are not used to identify or explain the undertakings within interactions; instead, the observable details indicated by participants as relevant to the present engagement in and understanding of the interaction are utilized as necessary and useful for comprehending the current moment. For example, from within the CA approach, the concept of power is not used as an explanatory concept to account for the unfolding of interaction among participants unless those involved display their orientation to that issue for the management of the unfolding interaction.

Topics of Investigation

Four basic topics represent the fundamental concerns of CA: membership categorization, turn design, turn taking, and sequential organization.

Membership Categorization

Membership categorization was an early focus of Sacks in his development of CA. *Membership categories* refers to the social types people may use to classify and describe one another. These include such things as the occupation a person may hold, such as teacher, doctor, secretary; a relationship one may have to another, such as mother, friend, coworker; and general types used to distinguish some aspect of a group, such as nerd, fan, or jock. Categories are consequential for interaction, for people design their contributions in part based on the categories into which they place their participants and themselves.

Participants use categories as a way to provide understandings about the various activities, rights, responsibilities, motives, and competencies that they attach to members of categories. This information is consequential for how one designs turns of talk, the selection of recipients for the talk, and for interpretations of the recipient's talk. For example,

a supervising physician may introduce himself or herself to a patient who has been examined by an intern in a way that shows the intern as an equal. Such a display may be taken to indicate the physician's assumption that interns are concerned about maintaining their authority in front of patients.

Turn Design

A second key topic for CA is the design of turns of talk. Turns are highly fluid creations, having no set size, topic, form, or order among speakers. Turns can be constructed out of many different types of units, from complete sentences to individual words or even sounds. The syntactic structure of a turn does not define the talk as a turn by the current speaker. Speakers select the form of a turn to help undertake the projected action (e.g., telling a joke). Given that turns are unpredictable in length or composition, a question arises as to how listeners know when a speaker is about to complete his or her turn of talk. Complicating matters is that, overall, a rule participants orient themselves to during talk is that one person speaks at a time. While the overlap of turns of talk of speakers is fairly common, these overlaps tend to be brief moments; additional speakers will stop speaking so that only one continues. In addition, analysts note that there are relatively minimal gaps and overlaps at points of speaker change.

Consequently, there must be ways that participants can determine when a current speaker will end his or her turn of talk. These points of possible completion for the current speaker, places the turn could be projected to end—even if it does not end at any one of them—are referred to as *transition relevance places*. Participants in interaction can note these upcoming places in a speaker's turn as a spot at which they could begin speaking if the speaker ends. This matters for the creation of turns; for example, if a speaker wishes to take a long turn of uninterrupted talk, perhaps to tell a story, the speaker will need to forestall listeners from beginning a turn of talk at a transition relevance point by indicating a desire for an extended turn. In such occasions, speakers may first create a *story preface*, such as "Did I tell you what happened yesterday?" to indicate that their upcoming turn will need to be uninterrupted by listeners. Routinely, participants negotiate their turns as next speakers in part via the construction of their own turns of talk.

Turn Taking

The recognition of a basic rule for organizing turns of talk, that one speaker talks at a time, and that speakers can project where a current speaker's turn may end, connects to a third key topic of CA: Who talks when. Since more than one listener may wish to speak next, a system of *turn taking* arises in interaction to help distribute turns of talk among potential speakers. Early research established a set of three ordered rules participants utilize for allocating their turns of talk. The set is ordered in that the first takes precedence over the second and third, the second takes precedence over the third, and if neither of those two occurs, the third may.

The first turn-taking rule is that the current speaker may select the next speaker. Current speakers have numerous ways in which they may distinguish who is to talk next, from individual speakers ("Fred, what is that?") to any one of several fitting respondents ("Does anyone know the time?"). The second rule is that if the current speaker does not select the next speaker, a listener may self-select, often by being the first to respond. The third rule is that if neither of these first two occurs, the current speaker may continue as next speaker. In orienting to this feature of interaction, CA describes a fundamental organizing principle but also identifies a practice that speakers may exploit for immediate purposes, indicating their awareness of the system and its potential use. Speaker change indicates another key topic of CA investigation, the sequential organization of interaction.

Sequential Organization

A primary focus of CA is describing how the placement of a turn of talk is consequential for understandings and their display among participants. Certain turns seem fitting to occur where they do. For example, responding with "Bye" to someone's "Hello" would not seem fitting at the start of a conversation. The projection of an upcoming turn by a current utterance and the relation between utterances form a key organizational feature of explaining interaction.

A foundational structure in CA is the *adjacency pair*: two utterances (referred to as the *first pair-part, FPP,* and the *second pair-part, SPP*), each created by different speakers, that form a pair, with a particular relation of *conditional relevance* between them. Adjacency pairs occur in different types, such as *greeting–greeting, summons–answer,* and *request–response.* For example, many conversations begin with a greeting–greeting adjacency pair, in which one person offers a greeting and another responds with a similarly recognized turn. We understand that such a pairing does not obligate us to stop and have a conversation; we can simply exchange greetings and move on. In contrast, a summons–answer pair does create a situation requiring further talk. If someone issues a summons, such as a parent calling for a child, and an answer is not forthcoming (the child does not respond), the summons may be reissued until it is answered ("What?"). At that time the pair is closed and a reissue of the summons would be understood as not maintaining the structure of the pair. Unlike the greeting–greeting pair, once the summons is answered, the initial speaker is under obligation to continue the interaction or to account for issuing the summons in the first place.

CA explains the hanging together of the pair as *conditional relevance* of the SPP on the FPP. That is, given an FPP (such as a summons), the SPP is expectable (an answer to the summons is expected). Further, what follows the FPP in sequence will be heard as a second to that first. What follows the summons will be heard and interpreted for its relevance in relation to that summons. Finally, if the second does not occur—nothing understandable as an "answer" to the summons occurs—the second will be "officially absent": taken to be consequential for the developing organization by its absence as an SPP. Adjacency pairs highlight the sequential nature of interaction, that what precedes a turn is consequential for the recognition and comprehension of a subsequent turn and that a following turn is designed by speakers to display their understanding of the activity at hand.

The term *adjacency pairs* does not require a literal adjacency among turns of talk. The sequential ordering of pairs may be extended and momentarily suspended. For example, early work identified *insertion sequences*—sequences of adjacency pairs inserted into another adjacency pair (e.g., a question–answer pair inserted into another question–answer so that the initial question and its answer are separated by another pair, Q-Q-A-A). Such organization points to the ability of participants to suspend a current activity to jointly orient to and complete another activity before returning to the original one. *Presequences* (pre's) are adjacency pair structures in which the FPP is used to check on the conditions for performing a subsequent action. For example, we may want our invitation to be accepted, and to help avoid its being turned down, we ask before making the invitation, "What are you doing Saturday night?" If conditions are right (the other person is not busy), we can then go on and provide the invitation itself. Also, from the creation of the pre (the FPP), participants orient to the likely upcoming activity and display that orientation by offering a response to the pre that properly prevents its creation (for example, saying "I am busy" to the sample question).

Presequences and their strategic use displayed by participants bring up another organizational feature identified in CA work: *preference for agreement*. Here, the preference is of the speaker for responses that facilitate the undertaken activity and help to foster social solidarity among participants. Preference impacts sequential organization in that turns of talk may be constructed so as to facilitate a preferred response.

Sequential organization of interaction highlights the observable nature of human conduct for participants. Speakers are held accountable for their actions, the turns of talk created, by others and selves. Sometimes, turns do not readily illustrate the preferred action of the speaker, and *repair* of the utterance is needed, often in the form of *self-repair* (where a speaker "fixes" his or her own turn-construction problem). Such repair may be initiated (the momentary problem highlighted) by either the speaker or one of the hearers. The organization of repair indicates the awareness of participants of apparent expectations of the fit between the form of the utterance, the action being performed, and the location within the unfolding sequence.

Methods Applied

Typical Analytic Approach

While there is no one set way to undertake CA, there are aspects of the method that appear common. Applications of CA revolve around the comparative analysis of features drawn from a collection of samples. A description is developed to explain regular forms of organization from across a range of samples from different speakers in different settings. As samples are collected, deviations from the common structure appear. Developing accounts are broadened to include these forms, to provide an explanation of how the features of the performed interaction work within the sequences in which it appeared.

The approach to data is exemplary in that the researcher seeks to examine a collection of examples for their commonality in structure and difference in application. CA is empirical research, building claims about social organization among participants from materials available in the talk itself. It relies on the shared understanding of interaction to develop explanations: specific knowledge from prior investigations shared among analysts and the routine understandings shared by being members of the broader community.

Theory

CA does not seek to develop abstract, generalizable accounts of human interaction or activity. Such approaches would not adequately describe the consequential but mundane features of interaction relevant for participants' understanding of their lived-in worlds. Rather, what CA seeks to uncover is the highly situated organization of members' lived practices as they display them in day-to-day talk; these are the "theories" interlocutors employ to make sense of and respond to the activities they jointly undertake with others.

With its focus on human interaction and action, CA does relate to pragmatic examinations of communication. With other discourse approaches, it shares the move away from describing and explaining causes of human behavior and toward describing how such conduct is created and recognized. At the same time, CA's unique focus on the sequential nature of interaction, the relations among turns of talk, and the reliance of CA on only those features observable to participant and researcher as sources of explanations, sets it apart from other discourse approaches that take a more social-situated focus for explanation (e.g., ethnography of communication or sociolinguistics) or that impose concepts and explanations from outside the source material (for example, critical theory and some forms of discourse analysis).

Robert C. Swieringa

See also Discourse Theory and Analysis; Ethnomethodology; Interpersonal Communication Theories; Language and Communication; Membership Categorization Analysis

Further Readings

Atkinson, J. M., & Heritage, J. (Eds.). (1984). *Structures of social action: Studies in conversation analysis.* Cambridge, UK: Cambridge University Press.

Drew, P., & Heritage, J. (Eds.). (1992). *Talk at work: Interaction in institutional settings.* Cambridge, UK: Cambridge University Press.

Sacks, H., Schegloff, E. A., & Jefferson, G. (1974). A simplest systematics for the organization of turn taking for conversation. *Language, 50,* 696–735.

Schegloff, E. A. (1979). Identification and recognition in telephone conversation openings. In G. Psathas (Ed.), *Everyday language: Studies in ethnomethodology* (pp. 23–78). New York: Irvington.

COORDINATED MANAGEMENT OF MEANING

The coordinated management of meaning (CMM) theory, developed by W. Barnett Pearce, Vernon Cronen, and their colleagues, explains how communicators organize interaction. Since its inception in the 1970s, this theory has been included consistently in the canon of communication theory and applied to a variety of settings. It is a wide-ranging theory that touches many aspects of the field and presents a way of analyzing all kinds of human activity in terms of the *communication perspective,* or how reality is constructed in social interaction. The major tenets of the theory today can be summarized in the categories of meaning and action, coordination, and story telling.

The theory first appeared in print in the mid-1970s, with its first full-blown explanation following in 1980 in Pearce and Cronen's book *Communication, Action, and Meaning: The Creation of Social Realities.* Having undergone considerable expansion and refinement over the years, the theory continues to develop and has been influenced by thinking in social constructionism, cybernetics, philosophy of language, logic, rules theory, dialogue theory, action research, and other traditions. It originated as a general descriptive theory of communication but today is most often regarded as a practical theory.

Meaning and Action

Communicators do two things in every encounter. They interpret, or ascribe meaning, and they act—two functions closely tied to one another: *Meaning* leads to *action,* and action forms meaning. Communicators must coordinate their meanings and actions as they interact over time. In all social situations, then, communicators must manage their own meanings and actions, while responding to the meanings and actions of others. This is the central claim of the theory.

Contexts of Meaning and Action

Communicators interpret and act on the basis of their experience, and this experience forms a *context* that establishes a basis for meaning and action within the situation. Initially in CMM, contexts were presented in a hierarchy in which one context was always embedded within other contexts. In this classical version, the act is understood in terms of the relationship, the relationship in terms of the episode, the episode in terms of the self, and the self in terms of the archetype. However, contexts can shift so that, for example, the episode could be understood within the context of self, or the self could be understood within the context of the act. Even a single communicator can shift back and forth among contexts from moment to moment and situation to situation.

Thus, contexts are fluid and dynamic. For this reason, CMM now most often uses the more powerful metaphor of *loops,* which emphasizes the mutual entailment, or *reflexive relationship,* among contexts. In the above example, self and episode form a reflexive loop. The loop metaphor is infused throughout CMM to capture the systemic nature of meaning and action.

Rules

Heavily influenced by the philosophy of language, particularly the language-in-use movement and the associated theory of speech acts, CMM explains meaning and action according to rules. A *rule* is a guideline that helps a person assign meaning and take action. There are two types of rules—rules of meaning and rules of action.

Rules of meaning, commonly called *constitutive rules,* tell what something should be taken to mean—what it "counts as." Such rules help answer the question, What is going on here? or, What does this mean? For example, a smile may count as being pleased or amused, or it might be seen as a smirk implying cynicism, disagreement, or displeasure. The word *cool* might designate *not warm,* or it might mean *good, special,* or *nice.* People can assign meanings to virtually anything—language, actions, statements, behaviors, situations, events, episodes, groups, the self, other people, and so forth. Sometimes the rules governing one's interpretations are quite stable, giving rise to tenacious meanings, and other times they are dynamic and shift around.

Rules of action, commonly known as *regulative rules,* tell what actions should be undertaken. For example, one common rule is that when someone smiles, the other person should smile back. If someone responds to a story with the word "cool," the other person may be obligated to say "Thanks."

Logical Force

In CMM, rules of meaning and action constitute a *logical force* that arises within salient contexts. A logical force is a cognitive connection among meanings and actions. Given a particular state of affairs, a certain meaning and/or action feels logically right. For example, if a person perceives that a smile means pleasure, that person feels that it is right to smile back. If, however, the person perceives that the smile means displeasure, a different response may be called for. Four types of logical force are featured in CMM.

The first is *prefigurative force.* Here an antecedent event is believed to cause a consequent action. A communicator feels that his behavior is determined by something that happened before. For example, one might respond to criticism with an angry and defensive statement, feeling that one has no choice.

The second type is *contextual force.* This has the same deterministic tone but is less connected to specific prior acts and more associated with meanings in the context. The communicator feels that in a situation like this, he or she must act a certain way. For example, one might reason that within the context of "competent self," criticism must be ignored.

The third type of logical force is *implicative force,* in which action is designed to transform the context. For example, one might decide to respond to criticism in a friendly, accepting way in order to shift the meaning of the episode from "giving criticism" to "providing mutual help."

The fourth type is *practical force.* Also goal oriented, this force has achievement of practical outcomes as the aim. Here, for example, one might respond to criticism by criticizing the other person in return in order to be left alone in the future.

Logical force employs *deontic logic,* in which one state of affairs creates an expectation or obligation in if–then form. For example, one might think, "If you criticize me, I am obligated to defend myself." Here, the context is "self as competent," and in this context, a complaint is taken as illegitimate. Rules are not immutable but are socially constructed by the communicators over time as various contexts assume importance. CMM likens the individual to a daisy: The person at the center of the flower is surrounded by petals representing the many social worlds in which he or she participates.

Because every person lives in many social worlds, numerous "logics" of meaning and action are available to them. A set of rules in one situation or point in time may fade away completely as new ones take their place. Because individuals do use potentially contradictory rules of meaning and action, they can experience confusion from time to time. A person can be torn between competing interpretations and actions. Other times, one experiences a high level of *coherence,* or consistency and clarity. Sometimes, as well, individuals feel unable to find any context or set of rules to make sense of a state of affairs, a condition called *mystery.*

Meaning and Action Loops

When meanings and actions are consistent and reproduce one another, a *charmed loop* exists. For example, when moral beliefs are rigid, one's actions may be limited to a prescribed set of behaviors, which in turn constructs moral rigidity. Here the contexts of moral belief and moral action reinforce one another in a highly coherent closed system. When meanings and actions are inconsistent and contradict one another, a *strange loop* is experienced. This happens when the contexts or the meanings within a context shift, causing a change in the rules of meaning and action. The alcoholic's paradox is a classic example: "When I drink, I am out of control, and when I am out of control, I must not drink; however, when I do not drink, this shows I am in control, and when I am in control, I should be able to drink." In this repetitive pattern, the drinker shifts meaning from "self as in control" to "self as out of control," and the rule connecting self to action then also shifts from drinking to not drinking.

Coordination

The second key concept in CMM, *coordination,* is the process in which two or more communicators organize their meanings and action into some kind of pattern that makes sense to them. When one person acts, the other person must interpret the action. The second person then will act or respond on the basis of this meaning. The first person must then interpret and act. Each is privately asking the question, What does this action mean, and how should I respond? If successful, the participants will feel that their interaction is coordinated or that it has some kind of logical pattern to it. In highly socialized situations in which standard patterns can be used, coordination is not a problem. Neither is it difficult when the parties themselves have worked out a clear set of expectations over time. However, coordination can be difficult in new situations, with new conversation partners, or in unexpected

circumstances. The basic task of all communication is to maintain some level of coordination.

A lack of coordination occurs when communicators cannot seem to mesh their actions in a meaningful way. Each believes the other's actions make no logical sense. They share no frame of logic that enables them to understand the pattern of interaction. Communicators achieve coordination when interaction feels appropriate and logical. They do not need to share a common set of rules of meaning and action in order for coordination to occur. Sometimes the parties do not understand an interaction the same way. This is not necessarily a problem, as long as partners are able to work together smoothly.

At the same time, however, coordination is not always a good thing. An *unwanted repetitive pattern* is a highly coordinated set of actions that neither person wants. Meanings and actions are tied in a tight loop that the parties cannot break. They seem unable to find new rules of meaning and action or new contexts in which a transformed pattern might emerge. Relational violence is a good example.

Story Telling

Providing a way to frame experience, *stories* are the means for achieving coherence in a situation. We create contexts, establish meanings, and define actions through story telling. Through stories, we codify our logics of meaning and action and explore our own and others' social worlds.

CMM uses a tool called LUUUTT to explore this idea. The LUUUTT model identifies six dimensions: stories *Lived,* stories *Untold,* stories *Unheard,* stories *Unknown,* stories *Told,* and story *Telling. Stories lived* provide the data of life experience, but we can never tell all our experience. Instead, we can tell only part of the stories we live at any given time, and the *stories we tell* construct a world of meanings and actions. *Unheard stories* are missed because communicators do not have mutual resources for engaging one another's stories sufficiently to get these. And stories that are either untold or unheard become *unknown stories* that might otherwise help add coherence and coordination to an otherwise confusing situation.

Story telling, then, provides the resources with which our social worlds are made—the rules of meaning and action and context that give life to these. When stories lived match stories told, a high level of coherence results. When stories told match stories heard, meanings come to be mutually understood. Patterns of communication can be changed and expanded and coordination achieved by telling and hearing different stories.

Stephen W. Littlejohn

See also Philosophy of Communication; Rules Theories; Social Construction of Reality; Speech Act Theory; System Theory

Further Readings

Cronen, V. E. (2001). Practical theory, practical art, and the pragmatic-systemic account of inquiry. *Communication Theory, 11,* 14–25.

Pearce, W. B. (1989). *Communication and the human condition.* Carbondale: Southern Illinois University Press.

Pearce, W. B. (2008). *Making social worlds.* Boston: Blackwell.

Pearce, W. B., & Cronen, V. E. (1980). *Communication, action, and meaning.* New York: Praeger.

Co-Orientation Theory

The original source of co-orientation theory is an article written by Theodore M. Newcomb, published in the *Psychological Review* in 1953, under the title "An Approach to the Study of Communicative Acts." Newcomb outlined his framework of analysis in this way: Communication, in its essence, serves two ends, to establish a common orientation of two (or more) individuals with respect to each other and, *simultaneously,* to link them to a shared object of concern. The originality of his conception resides in this recognition of interpersonal adaptation as mediated by a joint interest in the state of an objective world, one that communicators are mutually connected *to* and *by.* Interaction is now seen through a new lens, that of some aspect of the world to which more than one person orients. This idea of social interaction contrasted with the then popular mathematical theory of communication associated with Claude Shannon, commonly called *information theory,* which concentrated on information quantities in messages and how to encode messages most efficiently in linking a source to a destination. Shannon and his colleagues had denuded messages of reference to interaction. Newcomb's innovation served to correct this abstraction from ordinary reality by reestablishing communicative acts as embedded within both a social and a material reality.

In taking this step, Newcomb was reflecting the influence of his mentor, Kurt Lewin, one of the great innovators in social psychology of the first part of the 20th century. Lewin came out of the tradition of Gestalt theory, and thus his attention was focused less on intrapersonal psychological states and more on how individuals fit themselves into fields of internal and external influences that are both social and material in nature. Newcomb's innovation was to systematize this perception by mapping it onto a simple model that he called an *A-B-X system:* two individuals, A and B, and one object, X. The resulting triadic unit, he noted, could be regarded from two different perspectives, either that of the participants themselves, as seen from within their respective *life spaces* (a *phenomenal* view that sees attitudes as a state of mind), or that of an external observer for whom the whole A-B-X system is in view. Newcomb then identified what he called a *system.* An instance of communication can be depicted as an *A-to-B-re-X* system, in which A communicates with B about X. For example, professor and student communicate with one another about some aspect of the history of Canada. What the system amounts to, beyond an interpersonal relationship or a common group membership, however, remained largely unexplored in his essay. He did not probe the organizational implications of co-orientation, and yet presumably in any moderately complex system, there are many concurrent instances of A to B re X (people speaking to people about topics of mutual interest). How they link to each other to compose a more complex system of communicative acts was left to later theorists to elaborate.

Newcomb did probe, to some extent, the unfolding dynamic of A-B-X relationships. The key factor, as he saw it, is attitude, although his article appeared before the word *attitude* became identified as a strictly cognitive state. In earlier work, it also meant something closer to the positioning of someone in an encounter, or a visible orientation. Attitudes might be positive or negative, A to B, B to A, A and/or B to X. In our example, the professor and student have attitudes toward one another, and they have attitudes toward the historical topic of mutual interest. Co-orientation, which is to say the lining up of attitudinal orientations in a compatible way, is an essential aspect of human life.

Systems of relationship that are in equilibrium (e.g., A and B share compatible orientations to each other and to the object X) tend to be stable. This would be the case, for example, when the professor and student like each other and share a common attitude toward the historical topic. It would also be true, by the way, if they had opposing attitudes toward the topic and really did not like each other very much. In contrast, incompatibility provides an impulse toward resolving the tension—what Newcomb designated a *strain toward symmetry*. When facing an asymmetrical relationship, A and B could simply go their own ways, or perhaps they might find themselves progressively moderating their orientations in the interest of maintaining co-orientation. Imagine, for example, that the professor had a very favorable attitude toward the historical topic but found that a particular student, whom the professor quite liked, hated this topic. This would create a strain toward symmetry that could lead the professor to respect the student less, reevaluate the favorable opinion of the topic, or disengage from the student. The student, on becoming aware of the asymmetry, might go through a similar adjustment process.

Newcomb assembled a good deal of empirical evidence to support his thesis of a strain toward symmetry. Groups, he noted, tend to develop homogeneous attitudes over time through communicating frequently. The pressure on people to conform is also considerable since attitudes that are stubbornly incompatible with those of the majority will isolate their holders and eventually lose them their status as members. A good deal depends, however, on the salience of the object and the relationship: obviously, some things are more important than others. Newcomb termed this factor *valence*: not merely plus or minus, but more or less so. And this in turn implies that it is possible for people to agree to disagree since the bonds that hold people together involve multiple objects, not all of the same

valence. He also opened the possibility that the object might be less an object in the material sense than role prescriptions or norms. For example, the professor and student may be able to sustain a good relationship with mutual respect that allows for the norm of scholarly disagreement about history within their roles as student and teacher.

Newcomb's introduction to co-orientation left little imprint on the thinking of his contemporaries. Attitude research exploded in the 1950s, but it was largely impelled by other influences. Newcomb's article did influence the thinking of one of his students, Bruce Westley, who, in collaboration with Malcolm MacLean, published an article in 1957 that explored the topic of *gatekeeping*. They adapted A-B-X theory by adding a C, the *gatekeeper*, who intervenes to bias the *A to B* channel by inserting an alternative reading. Although this addition to the co-orientation model provided additional detail, the full potential of the model was not seen until many years later, when it was taken up by organizational communication scholars as part of complex systems of communication.

James Taylor

See also Attitude Theory; Organizational Co-Orientation Theory

Further Readings

Newcomb, T. M. (1953). An approach to the study of communicative acts. *Psychological Review, 60,* 393–404.

Westley, B. H., & MacLean, M. S. (1957). A conceptual model for communications research. *Journalism Quarterly, 34,* 31–38.

CORPORATE CAMPAIGN THEORIES

The concept of corporate campaign theories can be discussed from at least two major perspectives: promotional product or service advertising campaigns, most relevant to the field of marketing, or the less visible corporate issues campaigns, most relevant to the field of public relations and issues management. This entry explores the corporate issues campaigns perspective and associated theoretical frameworks.

In the corporate environment, issues campaigns focus on either opportunities or threats. Every corporation wants to function as autonomously as possible in its economic environment. In that environment, an issue that could result in additional regulatory, legislative, or legal restriction is perceived as a threat to the organization's ability to function, and the organization attempts to resolve the issue before these restrictions become necessary. In a parallel scenario, when the regulatory, legislative, or legal outcome is perceived as beneficial to the organization, the organization will attempt to further these actions. Whether beneficial or restrictive, corporate efforts frequently take the form of management-level information campaigns that could involve coalition building, mass media or interpersonal contact, and usually behavior change in the relevant organization.

Because these issues campaigns frequently involve or potentially involve regulatory agencies, legislative bodies, or court decisions, the issues both attract and compete for attention in the public arena, including media coverage. An issue may also attract activist interest groups. Management of these corporate issues campaigns therefore involves negotiation with activist groups, included in the theoretical framework of powerful stakeholders. The concept has been tied directly to at least five theoretical frameworks: systems theory, issue life-cycle theory, legitimacy-gap theory, powerful stakeholder theory, and social exchange theory.

The concept of corporate issues campaigns and their resolution draws on several disciplines, most notably the public policy side of political science and business management, and includes much of public relations' emphasis on management-level communication that prepares and negotiates. But the concept as a unit was strongly positioned theoretically in the field of communication first through Robert Heath and Richard Nelson's 1989 book, *Issues Management: Corporate Public Policy Making in an Information Society.* Heath's 1997 book, *Strategic Issues Management: Organizations and Public Policy Challenges,* brought the concept into the management boardroom through concern for issue anticipation and established corporate issues management campaigns as an academic field in communication. The emphasis moved to corporate campaigns in anticipation and prevention of issue development, including negotiation with

relevant stakeholders, changes in corporate behavior, and communication of these changes. This latter academic approach is of interest here.

Systems Theory

Systems theory is based on a generic concept that has been applied to organizational communication, public relations processes, and corporate issues management and campaigns. Applied to corporate campaigns, the premise of systems theory is simply that no corporation or part of the corporation exists or functions by itself. The corporation is a complex system of connected, interdependent internal parts connected to a broader external suprasystem that encompasses not only other similar units but also interdependent organizations that influence and are influenced by the original corporation. Whether internal or external, these interdependent units are potential *stakeholders* that have the ability to affect the corporation in a positive or negative way. Thus the systems environment is broader than one corporation and has the potential to create a turbulent setting where the corporation attempts to survive and prosper. Turbulence can result from social, political, or economic change. Change in the external environment generally requires change in the internal environment that can distract the corporation from its mission. Therefore, consistent with systems theory, the organization will strive for a level of what is called *homeostasis,* or balance, in order to regain stability or a nondisruptive state. Relevant management personnel should continually practice *environmental scanning,* monitoring the environment in order to avoid surprises.

Systems theory would suggest that any organism that fails to adapt to its environment challenges its own survival, and a corporation that ignores incoming information regarding change becomes a closed system that eventually will be unable to survive. However, a corporation cannot deal with every environmental disruption or issue. Neither can it respond to an issue without careful analysis of the issue's potential effect on the organization, its potential effect on powerful stakeholders, the potential for the issue to develop or be disrupted, and potential media interest.

Organizational systems theorists suggest that organizational response can take one of two forms. If the organization feels the problem or issue is routine or has been dealt with previously, established procedures may already be in place. Assuming the organization was satisfied with the earlier outcome, routine response procedures should be sufficient. If the problem or opportunity has not been addressed, the organization should search for both similar issues and coalitions and evaluate the new information before acting. *Cybernetics* suggests that the organization will respond by either increasing or decreasing information from the organization to relevant stakeholders. However, issues management theorists recommend two-way negotiation to establish mutually beneficial relationships.

Issue Life-Cycle Theory

Issue life-cycle theory in effect extends systems theory by explaining the components that predict whether an issue will grow or will safely move out of the corporate system. The theory suggests that negative corporate issues begin when a recognizable group begins to register discontent with the corporation or when a specialist group recognizes a corporate-related problem. Positive-outcome issues may be supported by the organization. Regardless, at least three stages exist: first, the beginning of an issue, when a problem begins to surface and attract attention; then the stage when the organization is expected to react; and the final stage, when the organization makes changes to resolve the issue or when the issue disappears.

A negative issue that is not resolved in its early stages can escalate to the point that a political solution, such as regulation or litigation, is expected. When mass media become aware of an issue and find it of interest, at least in the short term the issue grows. Media coverage legitimizes an issue, attracts other media, creates an awareness of the issue in a broader public whose activities can attract additional media coverage, and can even create a label or name for the issue. It also can provide a means of activity for groups, or stakeholders, who thought the issue was unresolvable.

These activist groups may pressure an organization for unilateral change. Even after mutual resolution of an issue, the activist groups have developed coalitions that can be quickly mobilized if another related problem arises. Organizations generally wish to avoid a litigated solution, which can be precedent setting, affect other organizations, and

move an ethical issue into the legal system. Social issues generally have a limited life cycle as they share public interest with other issues. Regardless of the issue focus, life-cycle theory says that no issue stays in the forefront forever. Other issues move into the cycle and attract attention of relevant groups and organizations.

Legitimacy-Gap Theory

Theorists have attempted to identify the reasons a corporate issue moves into the issue cycle, generates problematic attention, or fails to generate desired attention. One of these explanations is *legitimacy-gap theory*, discussed at length by Suresh Sethi. If we consider an organization a legitimate member of the business or nonprofit community, any activity or information that creates a discrepancy between society's expectations of the organization and the organization's perceived behavior creates a gap that could threaten the organization's status. Two scenarios can explain this gap. In the first scenario, the organization's behavior is knowingly inappropriate. The organization has either changed from acceptable to unacceptable behavior, or it had hidden inappropriate behavior that has been discovered. In the second scenario, the organization has neither changed its behavior nor tried to hide inappropriate behavior, but society's expectations or norms have changed, and the organization no longer meets these standards.

These scenarios often appear when an organization focuses only on financial success, and the effects can be traced through analysis of corporate history and development of corporate public relations in this country. Financial success enables an organization to survive, but this narrow focus relates to only one stakeholder, the shareholders of the corporation. To close or avoid a legitimacy gap, corporate citizenship suggests that a successful organization needs to maintain awareness and consideration of changing social mores and exhibit behavior that is perceived as not only financially sound but also socially responsive to other stakeholders in the organizational system.

The issue is one of corporate ethics and social responsibility. Even when government attempts to promote a favorable business climate, social and environmental regulation will follow irresponsible behavior, especially behavior that is perceived as causing social risk. Social responsibility is also becoming a criterion for financial investors. Research enables an organization to maintain awareness of social norms.

Powerful Stakeholder Theory

Different stakeholders have different roles in the organizational system, and the amount of attention needed to engage a particular stakeholder group will vary with the issue. When an issue campaign becomes an organizational priority because of the behavior, needs, or influence of one stakeholder group, that stakeholder group assumes the role of or rises to status of a *powerful stakeholder* and generally behaves as and is treated as an activist group. Vincent Price reminds us that the political process, in which regulatory decisions are made, focuses either on recruiting specific groups, or publics, for individual problems or on defining these issues so the identified groups do not form or become active. These powerful stakeholders can include media that focus on an issue.

At minimum, interested stakeholders are perceived as having two roles. The first role is that of smaller activist groups that focus intently and actively on the issue, identified by Walter Lippmann as *actors*. These active groups are problematic if they have power in regard to the relevant issue, beneficial if the organization supports the issue. The second role is that of a support group, or in Lippmann's terms, *spectators*, who provide support or perceived support to the actors. This spectator group could also include James Grunig's *aware publics*, those who are aware of the issue but see barriers to the issue's resolution. Perceived support can encourage the actors to continue their behavior in support of or opposition to the issue in question. While shareholders and regulatory bodies will always hold a powerful stakeholder role in the organization, employees, residents in the organization's community, customers, and even suppliers can become powerful by organizing around an issue. If these groups begin forming coalitions, the issue will escalate.

As issue life-cycle theory proposes, individual issues do not maintain priority status forever. But even if an issue is resolved, the original coalitions can materialize faster if another relevant issue develops. Corporate campaign managers should be aware of these group linkages as well as their interests.

Social Exchange Theory

Successful corporate campaign interaction requires communication that is understood by all participants, and this interaction includes words, symbols, and actual behavior, such as demonstrations by activist groups and corporate change by organizations. Without analysis of the interaction rhetoric, *rhetorical analysis,* differing viewpoints, values, and issue perspectives will not come forward and cannot be resolved, or disagreement between an organization and stakeholders may inaccurately be perceived to exist.

One particular type of interaction, *social exchange,* is specifically appropriate for resolution of issues. Corporate interaction with activist groups and other issue-related stakeholders suggests that during negotiation each group expects something from the other. Thus, one concession can be traded for a reciprocal concession, or an exchange. However, Blau reminds us that these mutual concessions are not necessarily social exchange. In his (and Emerson's) analysis, these concessions or exchanges are discrete, even economic, in that they resemble a purchase in which one value is traded for another.

Social exchange as a concept is more relational; trust is built. In this approach, if an organization exhibits responsible behavior, the return or reward may not be immediate. Rather, the organization builds intangible goodwill that will hopefully result in support and future goodwill with the affected stakeholders. The recipient of the intangible goodwill theoretically incurs an obligation to the responsible organization.

The organization's responsible behavior cannot be short-term and must address the needs of the relevant stakeholder group. Blau noted that this responsible behavior also builds power for the giver, the organization, as long as the benefit has value to the recipient and if the benefit cannot be obtained elsewhere. Thus corporate issues campaigns are long-term efforts to maintain an organization's reputation and build goodwill with relevant stakeholders.

Janet A. Bridges

See also Campaign Communication Theories; Cybernetics; Institutional Theories of Organizational Communication; Organizational Communication

Theories; Organizing, Process of; Public Opinion Theories; Social Exchange Theory; Stakeholder Theory; System Theory

Further Readings

Blau, P. M. (1968). Interaction: Social exchange. In D. L. Sills (Ed.), *International encyclopedia for the social sciences: Vol. 7* (pp. 452–458). New York: Macmillan.

Bridges, J. A. (2004). Corporate issues campaigns: Six theoretical approaches. *Communication Theory, 14,* 51–77.

Bridges, J. A., & Nelson, R. A. (2000). Issues management: A relational approach. In J. A. Ledingham & S. D. Bruning (Eds.), *Public relations as relationship management: A relational approach to the study and practice of public relations* (pp. 95–115). Mahwah, NJ: Lawrence Erlbaum.

Donaldson, T., & Preston, L. E. (1998). The stakeholder theory of the corporation: Concepts, evidence and implications. In M. B. E. Clarkson (Ed.), *The corporation and its stakeholders: Classic and contemporary readings* (pp. 173–203). Toronto, Ontario, Canada: University of Toronto Press.

Emerson, R. M. (1981). Social exchange theory. In M. Rosenberg & R. H. Turner (Eds.), *Social psychology: Sociological perspectives* (pp. 2–65). New York: Basic Books.

Grunig, J. E., & Grunig, L. A. (1992). Models of public relations and communication. In J. E. Grunig (Ed.), *Excellence in public relations and communication management* (pp. 285–325). Hillsdale, NJ: Lawrence Erlbaum.

Heath, R. L. (1997). *Strategic issues management: Organizations and public policy challenges.* Thousand Oaks, CA: Sage.

Heath, R. L., & Nelson, R. A. (1986). *Issues management: Corporate public policymaking in an information society.* Beverly Hills, CA: Sage.

Lippmann, W. (1925). *The phantom public.* New York: Harcourt Brace.

Price, V. (1992). *Public opinion.* Newbury Park, CA: Sage.

Sethi, S. P. (1979). A conceptual framework for environmental analysis of social issues and evaluation of business response patterns. *Academy of Management Review, 4,* 63–74.

Wartick, S. L., & Mahon, J. F. (1994). Toward a substantive definition of the corporate issue construct: A review and synthesis of the literature. *Business & Society, 33,* 293–311.

Weick, K. E. (1969). *The social psychology of organizing.* Reading, MA: Addison-Wesley.

CORPORATE COLONIZATION THEORY

Corporate colonization refers to domination by corporate organizations. *Colonization* has usually referred to one country or society invading or taking over another. In the 1970s and 1980s, Jürgen Habermas used the term to discuss the way different parts of society can dominate the *lifeworld*—the everyday meaning and experience of individuals through various asymmetrical structural and system relations. In his 1992 book, *Democracy in an Age of Corporate Colonization,* Stanley Deetz detailed the ways in which this happens within corporations.

Scholars have been concerned for some time with the *politics of the personal*—the political processes by which meanings, identities, and experience are formed. Much of this was gradually organized and connected to communication processes by critical theorists from the Frankfurt School in the 1930s. The central issue has been with how language and communication processes affect the formation of the *interior,* meaning the very identities and meanings that individuals and groups espouse. This work has contrasted with more common concern in communication studies with expression.

Most scholars interested in this *inner* colonization have worked from a constitutive theory of communication, providing a nonpsychological understanding of meaning and experience, focusing on how the relational positioning of the human subject is put into play and interactively with the world and others produces experience. In the corporate world, the large economic corporations rather than general economic relations were seen as the locus of meaning, experience, and reasoning domination. Deetz's work pays attention to political relationships, using a social constructionist view. Using this "political-attention-relation-constructionist" theory of communication, Deetz critiqued liberal democratic communication theory as inadequate to deal with a colonized world, positioned the everyday world as the central site of democracy, and proposed the development of more participatory conceptions and practices of communication as core to reciprocal open formation of self and society.

Understood in this way, the concept of corporate colonization draws attention to the ways workplace organizations have usurped the functions of lifeworld institutions that tie meaning to such groups as religion, family, and community. In different historical periods, other institutions have dominated meaning, and personal identities may have been more firmly located in them. In an age of corporate colonization, corporations shape decision-making processes and ways of life more powerfully than in the past, and personal identity is often derived from the workplace and work processes.

Conceptually, colonization of this sort might be represented in the following way. Imagine three spheres of life—private, public, and economic. Through history these have resided in a dynamic tension-filled relationship, each having its own logic and demands. Many of the decisions about how to raise children, live a good living, and value events and others arose out of meaning structures developed in the private sphere of homes, communities, and churches. Public sector institutions—governments, legislatures, and so forth—made decisions about public welfare, defense, and intercommunity relationships. Business and work made decisions about what goods and services to produce and how work processes were to be organized. Throughout history some struggle has existed among these three sectors, with one or another becoming more dominant and the others providing a supportive role. Occasionally, for example, governments have become deeply involved in business and decisions of the home and community or the church in business and government.

In domination, one of the spheres begins to encroach on the others, replacing the logic and demands in those spheres with its own. In corporate colonization, a particular form of workplace and economic relations becomes dominant. For example, in cases of corporate colonization of the public sphere, work organizations have increased power in legislative and policy-making processes; economic decision processes might gradually replace political processes. In inner colonization, corporations encroach on the private space, the colonization of the personal. Both through their own internal practices and through their external advertising and media control, personal identities,

values, concepts of civility and worth, child rearing practices, and conceptions of progress are increasingly derived from corporations. The development of consumption life styles becomes both an effect and a continuing cause of corporate identification. In corporate colonization, instrumental reasoning becomes the primary form of reasoning. Ends are stressed over means, resulting in people, things, and processes being assessed in terms of their rational, measurable impacts on the world.

This has been both good and bad. On the positive side, economic institutions have sometimes been more peaceful, accepting of group differences, and efficient than their community and public counterparts. But raw, short-term economic logics without counterbalance have also been disastrous for people and the environment. The traditional state democracies struggle when the leading social decisions are made in nondemocratic sites and institutions. Both possibilities and difficulties of inclusion of social and ecological values in the decision processes in economic sites exist. The concern of communication scholars has been to understand the communication dynamics of colonizing processes and to reconstruct communication theory to be more attentive to these dynamics since much of current theory was developed for the traditional private and public spheres.

Critical communication theories have been very helpful in understanding this new politics of everyday life. These theories have focused on the communicative production and reproduction of structures of discourse that recruit, call, or position subjects in particular ways, the communicative processes by which some formations become more dominant, and processes of closing off certain ways of thinking and acting by suppressing conflict and preventing different discourses that might challenge or change the existing order of things. In workplace studies the attention has been to communicative processes of power control and resistance.

Stanley A. Deetz

See also Constitutive View of Communication; Critical Discourse Analysis; Critical Organizational Communication; Critical Theory; Cultural Studies; Frankfurt School; Organizational Control Theory; Postmodern Theory; Stakeholder Theory

Further Readings

Ashcraft, K., & Mumby, D. (2004). *Reworking gender: Toward a feminist communicology of organizations.* Thousand Oaks, CA: Sage.

Deetz, S. A. (1992). *Democracy in an age of corporate colonization: Developments in the communication and politics of everyday life.* Albany: State University of New York Press.

du Gay, P. (1996). *Consumption and identity at work.* Thousand Oaks, CA: Sage.

Fleming, P., & Spicer, A. (2008). *Contesting the organization: Struggle, power and resistance in organizations.* Cambridge, UK: Cambridge University Press.

McCabe, D. (2007). *Power at work: How employees reproduce the corporate machine.* London: Routledge.

Mumby, D. K. (1997). The problem of hegemony: Rereading Gramsci for organizational communication studies. *Western Journal of Communication, 61,* 343–375.

Nace, T. (2003). *Gangs of America: The rise of corporate power and the disabling of democracy.* San Francisco: Berrett-Koehler.

Thackaberry, J. A. (2004). Discursive opening and closing in organizational self study: Culture as the culprit for safety problems in wildland firefighting. *Management Communication Quarterly, 17,* 319–359.

Wieland, S., Bauer, J., & Deetz, S. (in press). Excess careerism and destructive life stresses: The role of entrepreneurialism in colonizing identities. In P. Lutgen-Sandvik and B. Sypher (Eds.), *Destructive organizational communication: Processes, consequences, and constructive ways of organizing.* New York: Routledge.

CORRESPONDENCE THEORY

See Language and Communication; Meaning Theories; Metatheory

CREATIVITY IN GROUPS

Creativity in groups is an emergent process that results in novel and relevant ideas, responses, processes, or products. This definition of creativity weds process and outcome—which will be addressed later in this entry. Although creativity in groups has a long history of being studied in disciplines such as business and psychology, only recently have communication scholars paid systematic attention to how group communication and creativity are related. This entry explores the concept of creativity in a group context, examining how creativity differs from related concepts such as learning and innovation, the different factors that seem to hinder as well as facilitate creativity, and theoretical developments in the group communication field.

The term *creativity* is sometimes used interchangeably with related concepts such as *learning* and *innovation*. Careful examination, however, reveals that creativity is related to, yet distinct from, these processes. *Learning* may be considered to be the increased capacity of a group to adapt and change on the basis of newly acquired information, skills, or understanding. So while creativity generally indicates learning has taken place, not all learning results in creativity. While a group may increase knowledge, skills, and understanding of information, for example, it is when that knowledge, skill, or understanding is applied in ways that serve to yield novel products, processes, or ideas that are directly relevant to the task at hand that members engage in creativity. Thus learning paves the way for creativity and creative activity.

In addition to the production of novel and relevant ideas, responses, processes, or products, *innovation* adds the criterion of implementation. The main difference between creativity and innovation is that the latter requires a plan for how the group's creative product will be put into effect as well as the actual enactment of that plan. Creativity is part of the innovation process.

Factors Affecting Group Creativity

One might think that part of the answer to having groups produce highly creative and imaginative solutions to problems is to compose them of highly intelligent or creative individuals. While this may make intuitive sense, it is not always the case that groups composed of such individuals will produce more creative solutions than groups not composed of such individuals or than individuals working alone. Part of the reason is that bringing individuals together to work in a group setting sometimes results in the manifestation of factors that hinder creativity. Some of these factors are associated with the individuals who compose the group, some are associated with the larger environment or broader context in which the group is situated, and some are associated with the exchange of communication messages themselves.

Among the factors associated with individual hindrances to creativity are functional fixedness and evaluation apprehension. *Functional fixedness* refers to a person's propensity to think about things in ways in which they have traditionally been used. A claw hammer, for example, is a tool used to pound nails into a material or pull them out. Yet, depending on the situation, the tool may also be used as a lever or a glass smasher. A person who is prone to functional fixedness will have difficulty using the hammer in the latter two ways because he or she is rigid in his or her thinking about how a hammer can or should be used. With *evaluation apprehension,* group members may fear being judged or seen in a negative light by other group members. In an effort to minimize this fear, such members will refrain from expressing ideas.

Factors associated with the larger environment in which the group operates also may serve to hinder group creativity. These factors include organizational resources that are available to group members, such as time and information. *Time pressures* imposed on the group by the organization, for example, will have an adverse effect on creativity as members are not allowed to adequately express and search for information and ideas. Another broader environment factor concerns *organizational culture.* Here, an organization that has had a past history of financial, social, or other failures may have developed procedures, policies, language and/or reward systems that are indicative of being risk-averse. Consequently, original, novel, and divergent problem solving is not valued. A group charged with creative problem solving is affected by the risk-averse culture of the organization in which it is embedded. Group creativity suffers as a result.

Among the factors related to communication messages that may hinder group creativity are production blocking and the communication network structure that is characteristic of the group. *Production blocking* occurs when group members are limited in their generation of ideas because of the sequential flow of communication messages. That is, every time a group member speaks, others are essentially blocked from expressing their ideas. *Network structure* refers to the patterning of communication messages among group members, or who talks to whom and with what frequency. Group members may communicate little with each other and may direct most if not all messages to the group leader. The group leader, then, acts as a gatekeeper for information and ideas.

Communication View

In addition to factors associated with communication messages themselves, communication is related to group creativity in at least two other ways. First, and perhaps most basic, communication is a *symbolic activity,* and creativity is always expressed symbolically. When group members wish to convey information, thoughts, and ideas to one another, they do so through the use of language. Ideas are expressed, assessed, and validated though the use of language, the exemplar of human symbolic activity. Second, symbols, their use, and the meanings attached to them serve to create the very group environments in which creativity takes place. Group environments may be described in different ways, and regardless of how described, communication serves to give life to them. For example, notions of how things should be done, what is to count as acceptable or right or wrong, and the general atmosphere of group relations are all communicatively and symbolically constituted and maintained. The manner in which group members communicate with one another serves to give life to these notions and, in short, to the immediate environment in which creativity occurs.

Given that the communication process is essentially tied to group creativity, a variety of communication techniques, tools, and formats have been designed to enhance creativity. One of the ways in which group creativity may be fostered is by attempting to minimize the effects of those individual, environmental, and communicative factors that hinder it. Such fostering may be accomplished, for example, by structuring the communication that takes place in the group.

A variety of methods, or *formats,* have been developed for structuring communicative activity, with arguably the most famous being the brainstorming technique developed by advertising executive Alex Osborn. One of the central arguments justifying the use of the brainstorming technique concerns the role of the evaluation of ideas. Sometimes group members place an emphasis on evaluating ideas instead of generating them. As well, some group members may become apprehensive about having their ideas being negatively evaluated by other members. Consequently, those ideas are never expressed in discussion. The brainstorming technique is designed to reduce the adverse impact of evaluation on idea generation. Despite its widespread use, the brainstorming technique has met with equivocal empirical results.

Theoretical Approaches

Abran Salazar has put forward a theoretical view of the connection between communication and group creativity. His view is influenced by a complex-systems orientation to the study of groups. There are many different systems, and groups are but one type. A complex system is one that is marked by increased dynamism and variety of group activities. It is a system that operates at the boundary between order and chaos.

Picture a match that has just been put out. Left alone, smoke rises from the match head in a steady column (order). A few inches above the match head, there is a noticeable disturbance in this orderly rise: The smoke displays an increased dynamism (complexity) among the particles that compose it, with the result being a visible change in the column. Just beyond this disturbance, the smoke loses coherence and dissipates (chaos) into the surrounding air. The point at which the smoke seems ready to dissipate may be said to be the "edge of chaos"; it is the point at which the smoke has reached a complex and dynamic state but has not yet lost coherence.

At times, groups also operate in an analogous complex state. Salazar claims that in order for a group to be creative, it should function in this complex state. That is, a group's chances of being creative are small if it continues to function in the ways it always has—by displaying a characteristic order. By the same token, a group will not be creative if it is in a state of chaos. Rather, a group should

function between order and chaos. How group members communicate with one another informs us about whether a group is in a complex state.

One can observe how members target other members through their communication, that is, who tends to talk to whom and with what frequency; this is the group's *structural system*. One can also observe the procedure group members use when working on a task (*technical system*); the roles group members occupy (*relational system*); and the assumptions about what is right or wrong, and good and bad, which is inherent in how group members communicate about information (*information system*). Whenever we see group members changing their interaction patterns, whether by changing the frequency and directional flow of communication, using new procedures to solve problems or make decisions, displaying little or no discussion typical of group member roles, or questioning or supplanting assumptions about what counts as good or bad information, the group is showing evidence of operating in a complex state. This complex state lays the fertile ground for the emergence of the creative process and outcomes. Hence, as far as creativity is concerned, there is no differentiation to be made between process and outcome.

John Gastil has built on Salazar's ideas, focusing on how groups can come to a state of complexity. He discusses a three-stage process. The first of these stages is taking an *inventory* of the group. Here, group members come to know how each of the four systems described in the previous paragraph work. Group members take stock of their group in an effort to come to know how to change it. In the second stage, *perturbation*, group members introduce disturbances that serve to shake up the group in some way pertaining to one or more of the four systems. Such perturbations may include changing group roles, employing different standards for evaluating information, or using a new procedure for solving problems. Finally, in *amplification and extension*, group members employ the changed features, integrate them into everyday group functioning, and recognize the implications of the change(s) for other aspects of group work, such as impact on roles and power differences.

As of today these theoretical ideas have not been empirically tested. While the models identified above have intuitive appeal, future development in the field of communication will benefit from further theoretical honing and empirical scrutiny. After all, there may be an element of chance or serendipity associated with creativity that no model may be able to capture. Clearly the study of communication and group creativity is still in incipient stages. However, if group communication scholars' attention to creativity in some degree parallels that paid to it by psychology scholars after J. P. Guilford's call to engage in creativity study in his 1950 address to the American Psychological Association, it will have been a very promising beginning indeed.

Abran J. Salazar

See also Functional Group Communication Theory; Group Communication Theories; Groupthink; System Theory

Further Readings

Gastil, J. (2009). *The group in society.* Thousand Oaks, CA: Sage.

Jarboe, S. (1999). Group communication and creativity processes. In L. R. Frey, D. S. Gouran, & M. S. Poole (Eds.), *The handbook of group communication theory and research* (pp. 335–368). Thousand Oaks, CA: Sage.

Johnson, C. E., & Hackman, M. Z. (1995). *Creative communication: Principles and applications.* Prospect Heights, IL: Waveland.

Mongeau, P. A., & Morr, M. C. (1999). Brainstorming reconsidered. *Group Facilitation, 1,* 14–21.

Salazar, A. J. (2002). Self-organizing and complexity perspectives of group creativity: Implications for group communication. In L. R. Frey (Ed.), *New directions in group communication* (pp. 179–199). Thousand Oaks, CA: Sage.

Simonton, D. K. (2004). Creativity as a constrained stochastic process. In R. J. Sternberg, E. L. Grigorenko, & J. L. Singer (Eds.), *Creativity: From potential to realization* (pp. 83–101). Washington, DC: American Psychological Association.

Sunwolf. (2002). Getting to "GroupAha!": Provoking creative processes in task groups. In L. R. Frey (Ed.), *New directions in group communication* (pp. 203–217). Thousand Oaks, CA: Sage.

Whetton, D. A., & Cameron, K. S. (2005). *Developing management skills* (6th ed.). Upper Saddle River, NJ: Pearson Education.

CRITICAL COMMUNICATION PEDAGOGY

Named by Deanna L. Fassett and John T. Warren in their book of the same name, critical communication pedagogy is both a paradigm and an area of study. As a paradigm, this worldview contextualizes and provides a lens to view recent initiatives at the intersection of communication and education that deal with power relations as they arise from social systems of race, gender, class, disability, and sexuality. Critical communication pedagogy, at this level, serves as a framework that collects and provides coherence for the diverse work that takes a critical lens to issues of communication in pedagogical contexts.

As an area of study, critical communication pedagogy is also a subdiscipline that is beginning to develop on campuses across the United States. From site-specific studies to expansive views of educational practice, scholars use critical communication pedagogy to investigate power within a variety of contexts. By building on an interdisciplinary base, this communication-centered approach builds new ways of knowing and thinking about how (and to what effect) communication happens within classrooms.

Historical Origins

When the National Communication Association (then called the National Association of Academic Teachers of Public Speaking) began the formal study of communication, the focus of the organization was dedicated to the teaching of public speaking. These early teachers studied and wrote on how best to teach speech. Since then, the study of pedagogy has always been the center of the formal study of communication, even as it traces its roots to the rhetors of ancient Greece. As a subdiscipline of communication studies, communication education continues to investigate how best to teach the principles of communication, including the best instructional practices for the teaching of such topics as nonverbal communication, persuasive speaking, rhetorical theory, interpersonal communication, and communication theory, to name but a few content areas. The teaching of speech, as a research area, centers on pedagogical practices, claiming that the teaching of communication is unique and requires a discipline-specific pedagogy to meet the needs of communication classrooms.

Often credited with beginning in the 1970s, instructional communication shifts the focus from the teaching of speech to the study of communication in classroom settings, regardless of the discipline. With the careful application of communication theory, scholars investigated a variety of communication phenomena in the context of classrooms, including teacher–student immediacy, student–teacher facework management, communication apprehension, and communication competence. Today, researchers seek to provide useful ways of understanding misbehaviors and miscommunication in the classroom in order to counter them, building more effective classrooms where learning can be enhanced.

The field of education, also in the early 1970s, was beginning to witness the influx of critical theory, the most significant of which was Paulo Freire's book *Pedagogy of the Oppressed,* first published in English in 1970. From the workings of Marxist, feminist, and other schools of critical thought, critical pedagogy was taking root as a major force within education. Critical pedagogy examines the institution of education (and the practices that sustain it), arguing that education is deeply rooted in power and serves to reproduce the ideologies of the dominant class. Today, hundreds of books have been written on the topic of critical pedagogy; however, the communication scholar, with his or her attention to the workings of discourse and embodied communication, still struggled to find a place within this conversation. In the early 1990s, Jo Sprague began, in earnest, to introduce critical pedagogy to the field of communication, arguing that communication scholars could offer the research much in terms of focus and analytical precision.

Critical communication pedagogy ultimately stands as the evolutionary outcome of these diverse threads. While not communication education, the import of communication as a unique area of study is recognized. While not instructional communication, the fine attention to the workings of communication remains central. While not critical pedagogy, the focus on examining larger institutional forces guides critical communication pedagogy researchers. Together, these form a paradigm of research characterized by critical theory's dedication to social change as a goal of research as well as communication studies' analytical focus on mundane practices. Critical communication pedagogy provides specialized attention to the functioning of power, asking how communication works to sustain (and possibly counter) systems of domination.

Commitments of Critical Communication Pedagogy

In *Critical Communication Pedagogy,* Fassett and Warren use the framework of 10 *commitments* to name the stakes and issues that together assemble the logic, paradigm, and area of study that are critical communication pedagogy. The first addresses identity, arguing that constitutive approaches allow the researcher to see identity as produced in and through communication, not as something taken for granted from which communication originates. This communicative way of seeing the self foregrounds how identity is constituted in interaction, reflecting basic principles of performance and ethnomethodology (careful attention to the details of actual interactions), which both grant that subjects are the result of undergoing interaction. In sum, identity is conceptualized as produced or made by our communicative experiences.

The second commitment sees power as fluid and complex, rather than as a force that can be possessed. Power, within this framework, is shared, even if the players are not equal. For instance, while teachers certainly have power in the classroom, students also have power to use, manipulate, and resist the structure of education that circulates around them. This leads to the third commitment, which defines how culture is seen within critical communication pedagogy. Culture infuses everything, and a critical communication pedagogy researcher would do well to remember that any examination of the classroom that fails to account for culture is problematic.

Commitments four and five focus on the relationship between communication's dedication to mundane and minute communication practices (fourth commitment) and critical theory's examination of larger social structural systems (fifth commitment). Critical communication pedagogy, as a paradigm, sees mundane practices and larger social systems as co-constructed, meaning that they affect one another. So, while mundane communication practices constitute larger institutional norms, those norms in turn place everyday communication in context. This co-constructive process is used as the basis for critique. For instance, school uniforms surely help discipline students by reproducing idealized notions of how cultural citizens should look; however, any examination of uniforms must be seen within the larger system, and any focus on one piece to the exclusion of another limits one's ability to understand the phenomena.

Philosophy of language is the primary concern of commitment six, again focusing on how language constitutes or generates meaning. Critical communication educators argue that language always does more than reflect or represent some idea or ideal; language creates meaning and produces relationships. Each utterance makes the world; other choices would make different worlds. This is why commitment seven centers on reflexivity, arguing that a radical (as in, *at the root*) reflexivity is needed to see ourselves critically, to be accountable for what we say and how that saying affects others. Reflexivity is not just the ability to look back on one's self and understand how one is involved in power; rather, reflexivity also includes the understanding that all social activity is achieved through communication—it frames all the taken-for-granted aspects of life and recognizes that they are, in the end, produced by human interaction. So, just as language produces the world, it also produces, for instance, speaking subjects, social institutions, and created categories such as race and gender that govern or shape the communicators who use language.

In commitment eight, which borrows from the philosophy of Paulo Freire, critical communication educators embrace praxis, simply defined by Freire as theory-infused action designed to transform the world. Action without continual thought and critique does not necessarily transform the world in liberating ways; for instance, before anyone would intervene in a community (especially a community one is not a member of), he or she would want to balance the desire to act with careful reflection, built from the members themselves. Such action then will be hopeful rather than simply a different version of domination. From praxis, or thoughtful practice, comes our ability to act, to meet the world with a willingness to challenge it. Often, critical communication educators see such agency in the most mundane of sites—their classrooms, their neighborhoods, and so forth. Regardless of the context of action, what counts is how one engages—the effort to see the self and other as complex beings, each striving for meaning and purpose, is to engage them with a kind of care that embraces the ethics of a critically compassionate communication pedagogy. Often, this results in dialogue, the last of the 10 commitments. Dialogue as method, metaphor, and ethic serves as a key principle of critical communication pedagogy. Ultimately, dialogue is constructive and deconstructive at the same time. That is, it is both a basis for changing customary power relations and a basis for building new ways of thinking and seeing relationships.

Together, these 10 commitments build a foundation on which one can construct a productive ground to study and enact a critical communication pedagogy. As both a theory and a guiding praxis of pedagogy, critical communication pedagogy enables one to see the site of education as a institution that is produced through communicative interaction. Such institutions are necessarily reproductive of the very social forces that are ingrained in the culture itself—because power and privilege are pervasive, schools can be seen as sites where these systems are reiterated and normalized.

Critical Communication Pedagogy as a Communication Theory

Communication and education as disciplines often ask different questions, drawing readers and thinkers to different ways of seeing what happens in pedagogical sites. Because of these different lenses, there is often little shared dialogue between the two programs of study. In contrast, critical communication pedagogy does more than simply link these two literatures; rather, it theoretically demonstrates that the subject of critical pedagogy (the institutions of education and systems of domination) are produced through communication (the constitutive, mundane moments of interaction). As such, as a theory, critical communication pedagogy enables scholars to see how the institutions of which we are members are produced and normalized through our everyday talk, gesture, and so forth. By analyzing communication, scholars can talk about institutions not as amorphous structures under which we labor, but rather as crafted spaces that exist in, through, and because of our communicative practices.

Because critical communication pedagogy enables such dynamic and vivid analyses of educational settings, it also enables innovative ways of resisting oppression. Take, for example, deeply embedded sexist talk and practices among students in a classroom setting. One could study, from the standpoint of critical communication pedagogy, how sexism plays out in classrooms in ways that reproduce and normalize it. As a result, such a study offers a lens by which to understand the complexities involved in how gender gets enacted in that classroom and beyond; this information can provide the basis for creating new policies, new ways of teaching, and new ways of thinking about gender in the classroom that might provide different possibilities for enacting gender.

The classroom is often cited as a place ripe for social change—it is a place where progressive change has historically been enacted (think school integration, for example). As such, critical communication pedagogy is hopeful in part because it builds on a long-standing tradition of making education a site where one learns not only content, but ways of being critically reflexive citizens of the world. Here lies a source of its potential as a communication theory.

John T. Warren

See also Autoethnography; Constitutive View of Communication; Critical Race Theory; Critical Theory; Culture and Communication; Ethnomethodology; Feminist Communication Theories; Power and Power Relations; Social Construction of Reality

Further Readings

Fassett, D. L., & Warren, J. T. (2007). *Critical communication pedagogy*. Thousand Oaks, CA: Sage.

Freire, P. (2003). *Pedagogy of the oppressed: Thirtieth anniversary edition*. New York: Continuum. (Original work published 1970)

Nainby, K. E., Warren, J. T., & Bollinger, C. M. (2003). Articulating contact in the classroom: Toward a constitutive focus in critical pedagogy. *Language and Intercultural Communication, 3,* 198–212.

Sprague, J. (1992). Expanding the research agenda for instructional communication: Raising some unasked questions. *Communication Education, 41,* 1–25.

Sprague, J. (1994). Ontology, politics, and instructional communication research: Why we can't just "agree to disagree" about power? *Communication Education, 43,* 273–290.

Willis, P. (1977). *Learning to labor: How working class kids get working class jobs.* New York: Columbia University Press.

CRITICAL CONSTRUCTIVISM

Critical constructivism stands for the merging of *constructivist* or *constructionist* views with *critical* epistemology developed by the Frankfurt School. This involves combining ideas related to how people think while interacting with the social environment (constructivist) or how meanings are socially derived (constructionist) and impacted by power structures in society, as well as the ethical consequences of people's choices (critical). The term *critical constructivism* was first used in the 1960s in the field of education and then, with similar meaning, in psychology. Later, critical constructivism was incorporated into political science and sociology; it found its way into communication studies with the work of Andrew Feenberg, Maria Bakardjieva, and Milton Campos. This entry describes these lines of work and their confluence.

Origins in Education

The *critical constructivist school* in education was built around the tradition known as *critical thinking,* which emerged from the application in education of informal logic approaches, such as those of the British logician Stephen Toulmin, who became disillusioned with the power of formal logic as a tool for understanding commonsense communication. He developed a method for analyzing arguments based on constructs analogous to those found in legal procedures and tribunals, and this method led to the development of the informal logic school in the United States in the early 1960s.

The general idea of the critical constructivists in education was to integrate these contributions regarding informal logic to notions of cognitive development, originally based on traditional Piagetian theory and/or contemporary cognitive theories. According to this view, critical-thinking abilities can scaffold the development of more and more complex cognitive abilities through well-designed pedagogical activities based on argumentation. Certain educational strategies would "wake up" children's awareness of the underlying logical structures of their own reasoning through critical inquiry. It was believed that good teaching designed to enhance critical thinking could speed up cognitive development, that pedagogical activities developed on this basis would enhance learning.

Strategies of this kind were further developed by the introduction of sociocognitive approaches in North America, adapted largely from the learning theory by the Russian psychologist Lev Vygotsky. Some cognitive psychologists and educators, who came to believe in the integration of Vygotsky's psychology with cognitive theories issued from cybernetics (such as the information processing theory), found ways to assess argumentation as a critical process of construction.

Thus, the *critical* component of this educational tradition refers not to power structures in society but to critical-thinking processes within the individual's discourse. Although these educational applications introduced the term *critical constructivism*, the term took an entirely different turn in communication, as reflected in the critiques of technology offered by Feenberg and Bakardjieva.

Feenberg's and Bakardjieva's Critique of Technology

The term *critical constructivism*—which could also be called *critical constructionism*—was first published in communication studies in 1999 in the foundational book *Questioning Technology,* by the American philosopher of technology Andrew Feenberg. Later, and very curiously, Maria Bakardjieva proposed the term independently in her 2002 dissertation for a doctorate in communication (she also has a PhD in sociology), which led to the world-renowned book *The Internet in Everyday Life,* published in 2005. Today, Feenberg

and Bakardjieva are the most important scholars of this tradition.

Both share common ground with the educational critical constructivist approaches developed by the critical thinking school in terms of a view toward change and a focus on the idea of construction to account for the process of understanding. But these scholars depart from this common ground in their approach to critique. From their perspective, critical constructivism refers to the integration of the *social construction of reality theory,* proposed within the tradition of the sociology of science and technology, and critical theory, namely, the contributions of the German philosophers Herbert Marcuse and Jürgen Habermas.

According to Feenberg, the critical constructivist approach criticizes deterministic views, according to which technology shapes society by itself, silently or independently of major political and cultural developments. Feenberg makes three propositions: (1) Technology is defined by a social process in which technology choices are influenced by a variety of contextual criteria; (2) this social process satisfies various cultural needs related to technology; and (3) competitive definitions of technology mirror conflictive views of society. Thus, technology choices are influenced by power arrangements in society.

This approach draws from the critique of traditional Marxism made by Frankfurt intellectuals, namely Herbert Marcuse. According to Feenberg, Marcuse understands social progress as mirroring historical conflicts and artistic representations that are based on experience, that provide meaning to art, and that place technology at the core of social processes. This approach is consistent with the views of Jürgen Habermas about democracy as an intersubjective process of understanding (created through interaction with others), through which communication integrates public and private realms of life. Feenberg synthesizes these ideas but distances himself from Habermas because of the latter's supposed silence about the role of technology, thoroughly discussed by Marcuse. In addition, Feenberg absorbed a number of Michel Foucault's reservations about critical theory and embraced the critique of technological determinism from the *actor network theory* by Bruno Latour, one of the main theorists who shaped the constructionist tradition. Feenberg's critical constructivism is, thus, a philosophical critique of technology integrating the contributions of postmodern structuralism and critical theory.

Maria Bakardjieva has made contributions to advance this line of inquiry with in-depth reflections derived from extensive empirical work done with Internet users that highlights the importance of a normative or prescriptive approach in social communication processes. Her empirical research provided qualitative evidence that Habermas's critique of reason can be regarded as a suitable progressive framework to understand people's experiences with technology. Moreover, in line with Feenberg's critique, Bakardjieva points to the fact that the uses of technology in the practice of communication empower people, provided that the conditions of democratic engagement are met.

The work of Feenberg and Bakardjieva do not constitute the formulation of a new communication theory, but rather a philosophical and sociological inquiry grounded on empirical studies and critical social and political intervention into the role of technology in contemporary society. In other words, their work proposes a critical constructivist view of science and technology that uses the social construction of reality to show the role of active citizens in political engagement. Empowered citizens can build democratic societies by shaping and using communication technology to change society and achieve democracy and justice. Feenberg's and Bakardjieva's approaches to communication do provide insightful contributions about active normative models in which technology could be meaningfully integrated in life and in society. Milton Campos took critical constructivism in a somewhat different direction in his ecology of meanings theory.

Campos's Ecology of Meanings Communication Theory

Milton N. Campos used the term *critical constructivism,* also independently, in 2005, when he proposed a general critical constructivist theory of communication known as *ecology of meanings.* Communication is seen as a biological mechanism that enables a person to make sense of the self and the outside world. The term *ecology* stands for blended natural, or biological, and cultural interaction processes. As for *meaning,* it is understood as the process of permanently making "sense" of the others and of the world, which is different from the semiotic idea of *signification,* in which meaning is simply the denotation of a word or symbol. According to the theory of ecology of meanings, communication should be understood as a *transversal discipline* that crosses all others because it is both psychological and social and because it accounts for necessary universal and particular contingent knowledge. Communication is the foundation of all scientific disciplines and all forms of human expression (e.g., art, common sense, codes) because it is simultaneously a *condition* and a *result* of all possible human knowledge.

Ecologies of meanings can be considered as open, dynamic, and progressive symbolic universes, analogous to the expansion of the physical universe or to the expansion of the human population. Ecologies of meanings have structure and dynamics. The structure lying beneath developmental and evolutionary interactive processes can be explained as three interconnected layers that evolve altogether along time: (1) internal cognitive and affective structures; (2) consciousness and will; and (3) the external natural and social environments. The internal cognitive and affective structures emerge from the functioning of the brain. Underlying psychological states enable communication in the social environment. Consciousness and will shape moral values within the person (*morality*) and action outside the person (*ethics* and *politics*).

The external natural and social environments on one hand provide the conditions of existence such as the accessibility to material and spiritual resources needed for development (food, shelter, and care, as well as ideas) and, on the other hand, trigger actions on the world that lead to transformation and change.

As for the dynamics, the above-mentioned three interconnected structural and functional layers account for the concept of biological construction advanced by Jean Piaget and the notion of cultural molding of meanings and judgment making underlying Jean-Blaise Grize's and Jürgen Habermas's works. Dynamics express how people, while communicating through language (e.g., spoken, written, symbolic, bodily), construct and co-construct images of themselves, of one another, and of the world. These constructions and co-constructions are accounts or glimpses of progressively represented reality that are reflexively and critically assessed. Interpretations resulting from these processes, or *configuration of meanings,* can be just ephemeral through assimilation of outside influences or more permanent through both assimilation *and* accommodation to the social environment, leading the individual to change himself or herself and the world.

Ecology of meanings is, thus, a critical constructive communication theory accounting for interactions of configurations of meanings that express constructed and co-constructed images of the world. The theory traverses both the universal (ever-moving, organic, logical structures) and the situational contents of communication that emerge from culture, including language, history, geography, and other cultural factors.

Campos integrates the theories of Piaget, Grize, and Habermas to describe different layers of ecologies of meanings:

1. Piaget's *model of values exchange* accounts for the biology of interaction in which the exchange of affective and moral values evolves in circumstances of equilibrium or disequilibrium. Equilibrium is a state in which the individual truly cooperates and one in which moral values are consistent with equality and democracy. Disequilibrium results from constraint, as when a ruling authority imposes his or her will on others, and moral values of manipulation and control prevail.

2. Grize's theory of *schematization* accounts for the sense-making process that emerges in communication exchanges. Researchers can use the *natural logic* developed by Grize to study the thinking operations, expressed by language, that lead to the construction and co-construction of the discourse, to extract ethical possibilities from the language used. In terms of moral values, for example, when a president announces to the citizens of a given country, "I decided to go to war," the predicate "to decide to go" reflects a double moral stance (to *make a decision* and to decide in favor of *disequilibrium*). This stance has psychological and social consequences.

3. Habermas's *theory of communicative action* accounts for the political inscription of moral behavior in communicative action that projects values in how language is used. Habermas's "taxonomy" of reason expressed in discourse includes two poles—the *teleological,* or instrumental reason (standing for disequilibrium, constraint), and *communicative* (equilibrium, cooperation). Communicators, thus, *do* have a choice in terms of what moral behavior and subsequent social actions will be taken.

These three theories are taken altogether in the ecology of meanings theory in that they allow a holistic understanding of the communication process. According to the ecology of meanings theory, communication, as all biological mechanisms, is a never-ending, progressive process of disequilibrium, in which interlocutors search for equilibrium, fighting for autonomy instead of multiplicity, and shared understanding instead of conflict. Communication thus crosses science, philosophy, the arts, religion, and the daily-lived world.

This transversal discipline, considered as a knowledge field, needs formal and informal methods to provide the necessary ways to verify and interpret progressive communicative constructions, co-constructions, reconstructions, and so on. The knowledge scale is not only that of science: it goes from the phenomenological experience of living and social-political action in the world to the possibility of symbolically expressing the empirical world through the mysterious forms of logic and mathematics. Whatever symbolic course of action people take, it leads to communicative behavior and ethical choices that have moral consequences. *Communication is, in fact, an Ethics* that triggers the amazing human ability of constructing multiple universes of love, understanding, and cooperation, or hate, war, and destruction.

Milton N. Campos

See also Archeology and Genealogy; Argumentation Theories; Communication and Language Acquisition and Development; Constructivism; Critical Theory; Cybernetics; Frankfurt School; Social Construction of Reality

Further Readings

Bakardjieva, M. (2005). *Internet society: The Internet in everyday life.* London: Sage.

Campos, M. N. (2007). Ecology of meanings: A critical constructivist communication model. *Communication Theory, 17,* 386–410.

Feenberg, A. (1999). *Questioning technology.* London: Routledge.

Feenberg, A. (2003). Modernity theory and technology studies: Reflections on bridging the gap. In T. J. Misa, P. Brey, & A. Feenberg (Eds.), *Modernity and technology* (pp. 73–104). Cambridge: MIT Press.

Grize, J.-B. (1996). *Logique naturelle & communications* [Natural logic & communications]. Paris: Presses Universitaires de France.

Habermas, J. (1984). *The theory of communicative action* (Thomas McCarthy, Trans.). Boston: Beacon Press.

Piaget, J. (1995). *Sociological studies* (T. Brown, R. Campbell, N. Emler, M. Ferrari, M. Gribetz, R. Kitchener, et al., Trans.). London: Routledge.

Toulmin, S. (1969). *The uses of argument.* Cambridge, UK: Cambridge University Press.

CRITICAL CULTURAL STUDIES

See Cultural Studies

CRITICAL DISCOURSE ANALYSIS

Critical discourse analysis represents a variety of theories, methodologies, and definitions. Encompassing the theoretical concepts of discourse theory and critical theory, as well as suggesting a method for uncovering the relationships among these various perspectives, critical discourse analysis (abbreviated as CDA in most contexts) is the study of texts, speech, and visual images to uncover the shared meanings that contribute to, or represent, social structures and ideologies. CDA is distinguished from discourse analysis by its explicit political and social goals; it assumes that discourse structures constitute social inequality and injustice and seeks to expose those structures in both the production and reception of written, spoken, and/or visual messages. CDA is concerned with studying and analyzing how power relations, inequality, and dominance are created and perpetuated through discourse within various political, social, and historical contexts. By unmasking the workings of such discourse practices, CDA

scholars hope to subvert—or at least resist—those practices in the interests of social justice.

CDA does not provide one single or specific theory or research methodology. Rather, various theories and research methods have influenced the development of CDA. Epistemological theories, social theories, sociopsychological theories, discourse theories, and linguistic theories, to name only a handful, can be found in CDA. In essence, CDA brings a variety of theories into play by focusing both on the micro aspects of discourse (e.g., words, sentences, and images) and the macro aspects of social structures (e.g., production and reception of texts within a broader order of discourse). On the micro level, CDA assumes that power manifests in the usage patterns of words and images and that individuals participate in these construction processes in their use of language. On the macro level, CDA assumes that our identities (subjectivities) are constructed in and through the ways we produce and consume discourses and that language constructs our social and cultural worlds. Within both contexts, CDA assumes that social, cultural, identity, and power structures are not fixed—that changes in language usage can and do change that which is constructed. This social change is the goal of CDA.

The key terms of CDA are *discourse* and *critical.* In most usage related to CDA, discourse is distinguished from *texts,* which are specific utterances, images, or writings. Discourse is an overall form of knowledge and an arena that delimits certain expression. According to Michel Foucault, whose work influenced the development of CDA, the use of language and words is regulated through *discursive formations*—conventions and rules that constrain our knowledge and the meanings of things. Discourse, then, is the arena in which social relations, practices, and behaviors are constructed and maintained.

Concerns regarding the manifestation of power and the workings of ideology characterize the critical aspect of CDA. These concerns can be traced to the work of Marxists and the influence of Frankfurt School scholars who argued that certain ideologies are conveyed through textual and cultural forms. Ideology is an important concept in CDA because it is through ideology that power and inequality are maintained. Textual production and reception are social processes. The meanings of texts are often encoded by those in power, although the meanings and effects of language are also products of negotiation between producers, consumers, and the broader social/cultural context. Texts, then, can be open to contestation as various individuals and groups—producers and receivers—struggle over meanings and effects. The role of ideology, however, is to naturalize dominant structures so that the processes of meaning making and social construction are obscured. CDA aims to make these processes visible by asking whether texts serve powerful interests or structures of domination, by evaluating whether one representation or identity is selected or constructed in particular ways, and by asking who produces the representations and what their motivations might be.

Finally, CDA considers the social, political, cultural, and historical contexts of discourses and how discourses have evolved or developed over time. It is important to understand context in order to analyze *intertextuality*, a concept used by Norman Fairclough to analyze the structure and organization of texts in relationship to other texts and their contexts. Intertextuality refers to the ways that texts are implicated in other texts or draw on prior texts. It is through an analysis of intertextuality that the relationship between texts and social structures may be uncovered. This analysis becomes especially meaningful when the various contexts in which discourse practices and texts occur are taken into consideration.

Concerns and Focus of Critical Discourse Analysis

CDA has several intellectual traditions that have produced various forms of analysis over the years. In addition to Marxist theory and the insights of the Frankfurt School, the work of Jürgen Habermas, Antonio Gramsci, Louis Althusser, Michel Foucault, Stuart Hall, and British cultural studies scholars have influenced the direction and concerns of CDA since its beginnings in the 1970s. A group of scholars in the United Kingdom, who were influenced by the work of linguist Michael Halliday (although some used approaches from Noam Chomsky, the work of Roland Barthes, and early French semioticians), developed an approach called critical linguistics in the 1970s. Critical linguistics sought to analyze

texts as instruments of social and political power. Borrowing from the structuralist–functionalist tradition and Russian formalism, critical linguists used words and sentences as their units of analysis. They structured their interpretations in three areas identified by Halliday: the ideational dimension (which is similar to the ideological focus on the relationship between language and social structure); the interpersonal function (which is that aspect of language that defines how relationships are structured in language—whether one-way or two-way, argument, or dialogue, for instance—and how identities are constructed); and the textual function (which considers the structure and form of the text itself and its genre). Despite the three-pronged analysis, critics charged that this approach was too centered on the text itself and did not consider the practices of production or the possible interpretations of texts, which would lead to an analysis of meaning as changeable and as the result of social struggle. Building on these concerns, Australian social semioticians in the 1980s and 1990s incorporated poststructuralist ideas as well as the insights of French structuralism and semiotics into their work and developed a focus on intertextuality and the ways that discourses constitute identities and subjectivities.

Norman Fairclough built on the work of the Australian scholars to produce his theory of discourse and social change. He combined the mostly linguistic study of words and texts with an emphasis on Foucault's notion of discursive formations to study more specifically the ways that texts are implicated in social and cultural forms. In the late 1980s, Fairclough developed an analytical framework for researching language in relation to power and ideology and in relation to social and cultural change. He also suggested that mass media are powerful sites for research both in their use of language and in their manifestation of particular routines—or practices—that influence the character and meaning of a text. In addition, Fairclough argued that discourses needed to be analyzed within the broader arena of discursive formations and their interrelations (what he called *orders of discourse*). Thus, CDA expanded to include not just individual texts (and the internal linguistic structure of texts) but also the ways in which they intersect with other texts and with other discourses to form powerful, constitutive orders of discourse.

Other scholars have contributed to the theoretical and methodological development of CDA. In the late 1980s, Michel Pêcheux, who also was influenced by Althusser and Foucault, developed the notion of interdiscursivity, noting that various discourses can interact and intersect (for instance, the discourses of economics and politics). During this same period, Teun van Dijk developed cognitive models in order to understand how individuals process the meanings of texts and how meanings circulate socially and culturally. Van Dijk is known for his critical analysis of discourses that encode prejudice and racism, for example. This contribution added to the theoretical base of CDA that concerns itself with the reception and consumption of texts as well as the theoretical concerns regarding the ideological power of texts. The Vienna School of CDA in the late 1990s focused on language use in institutional settings and introduced the historical perspective. In addition, scholars in this tradition study the construction of identity at national and transnational levels. Scholars associated with this school are Ruth Wodak and Gilbert Weiss. At the end of the 1990s, CDA scholars began to turn away from the purely linguistic analysis of texts to include visual texts and the meaning of images. This "semiotic turn" expanded the range of CDA studies to include film, television, and music.

Approaches to Critical Discourse Analysis

Practitioners of CDA use different tools or methods for uncovering the mechanisms by which discourse functions. As defined above, texts are the primary unit of analysis—whether spoken, written, or visual. Analysts consider the various representations in texts, the framing techniques, linguistic features such as grammatical structure and modality, what is excluded from the text, how individuals are implicated in the text, and how texts interact with other texts in a discursive field. The form of a text—or its genre—is also considered. Genres are identifiable, repeated forms of communication such as the news broadcast, the television Western, political speeches, textbooks, business letters, and so on. These forms of communication follow certain conventions; as such, they are seen to have ideological effects. The validity of a message, for instance, may be strengthened if it is delivered in the form of a policy or newscast because individuals are used to hearing and responding to messages of these genres in particular ways. In addition, specific ideas or discourses may be found repeatedly in certain genres; for example, television Westerns feature discourses of gender and heroism; political speeches may contain discourses of patriotism and public service. Thus, in addition to the actual messages contained within them, genres communicate ideas and meanings that are shared socially and culturally because of the form in which they are delivered.

Fairclough's approach to CDA considers three levels of analysis: the text itself; the processes of producing (creating, writing, speaking) and receiving (reading, hearing, interpreting) texts (what he calls *discursive practices*); and the larger social context in which texts are created and consumed. Texts perform the ideational and interpersonal aspects identified by Halliday—that is, they convey certain representations of the world and establish relations among participants. In addition, they provide the building blocks for identity construction, both in the ways that people identify themselves and how they are identified by others. Discursive practices refer to the rules and conventions by which texts are produced and consumed. One may consider, for instance, the economic considerations of producers who tailor their products to fit audience demands as well as the viewing or reading habits of particular demographic groups. But it also implicates the more subtle, socially conditioned ways that messages are produced, circulate, and are interpreted—why some messages predominate, are taken as common sense, or are difficult to dismantle (ideas regarding gender, race, and age are examples). Texts and their practices of production and consumption are considered within the broader arena of discursive formations and interdiscursivity (orders of discourse) to uncover their ideological and social construction effects. Finally, a consideration of specific political, historical, and social contexts provides a necessary frame for understanding the power and meaning of texts and discourse.

In spite of myriad, interdisciplinary approaches, CDA is unified around basic principles, identified by Ruth Wodak and Norman Fairclough, which include an orientation toward social problems such as racism, sexism, and social change; eclecticism in theories and methods; investigation "from the inside," which means that analysis begins with the textual artifact first, rather than making the data fit a theory; consideration of intertextual and interdiscursive relationships; an accounting of historical context; specification of the precise method of analysis used in a given study (due to the eclectic approach); and application of the results of analysis—often toward the goal of changing oppressive discursive and social practices.

Janet M. Cramer

See also Constitutive View of Communication; Critical Theory; Discourse Theory and Analysis; Language and Communication; Materiality of Discourse; Meaning Theories; Social Justice

Further Readings

Fairclough, N. (1995). *Critical discourse analysis*. New York: Longman.

Fairclough, N. (1995). *Media discourse*. New York: Edward Arnold.

Hodge, R., & Kress, G. (1979). *Language as ideology*. New York: Routledge.

van Dijk, T. (1991). *Racism and the press*. New York: Routledge.

Wodak, R., & Meyer, M. (Eds.). (2001). *Methods of critical discourse analysis*. Thousand Oaks, CA: Sage.

CRITICAL ETHNOGRAPHY

Critical ethnography is a way to study communities and cultures that seeks to dismantle unfair power hierarchies, promote emancipation, and reduce the oppression of underprivileged people worldwide. Ethnographers who use this form of research claim that it is not enough to report "objective" findings on peoples' cultures but feel instead that it is the responsibility of an ethnographer to engage in various forms of political action on behalf of and together with the group they study.

Critical ethnography is not a theory per se, but rather a research strategy and methodology that rely heavily on the theoretical foundations of *critical theory*. Relatedly, critical ethnography is a tool for the construction of theory and for the translation of critical theory into practice. In essence

critical ethnography is a way to do critical theory, or as many scholars have stated, the practice of critical theory. Critical ethnography, then, is a methodological and practical undertaking through which critical ethnographers question the boundaries between theory and method.

The entire process of critical ethnographic research is based on critical principles: From the various ways to collect data to how data are interpreted and represented to various audiences to the ethical involvement of researchers and collaborators to the application and generation of theory and knowledge, the end goal of critical ethnography is to create transformational change. This entry will examine the theoretical foundations, methodological processes, and ethical commitment of critical ethnographers. As a resource for examples it will look at the critical ethnographic work of Dwight Conquergood, who in his life conducted critical ethnographies among the urban poor of Chicago, within a Southeast Asian refugee camp, and at vigils held at prisons for death row inmates on the eve of their executions.

Theoretical Foundations

Critical ethnography shares several things with interpretive, noncritical approaches. It explores, describes, and interprets norms, rules, everyday rituals, and epistemologies that identify people within a culture or institution. This is done not in order to test hypotheses or even to collect empirical information subject to tests of validity and reliability, but rather to better understand social phenomena. Also critical ethnographers are not keen on statistical generalizability but prefer analytical generalizability, which emphasizes the potential of ethnographic research for theoretical development. When ethnographic research allows scholars to create and expand concepts or understand generic processes or social systems, ethnographic research can be said to have value for theoretical/analytical development.

However, where critical ethnography diverges from interpretive ethnography is in the epistemological and theoretical orientation of the ethnographer and his or her role as an engaged citizen, activist, and scholar. Critical ethnography seeks to move beyond mere description and interpretation and move instead toward a critical approach that seeks to question hegemonic discourses that allow certain groups to exert power over others, to equalize power structures, and to criticize the actions and policies faced by people enmeshed in subordinate relations. In his work, for instance, Dwight Conquergood took it on himself to testify in court as an expert witness on the groups he studied on several occasions.

Historically, ethnographers—even many interpretive ones—have adopted an ethnographic approach based on detachment from the people under study, the desire to maintain and gather value-free knowledge, and the relativist view that cultures are different but equal. In contrast, critical ethnographers' main assumption and interest are in the ways cultures are positioned unequally in power relations. Critical ethnography takes its roots from critical theory, following in particular the idea that institutions create unequal power structures and produce a false consciousness in which the people cannot see this and actually work to maintain the status quo. This translates into full-blown attempts to create communities and relationships based on ideals of equality, as Dwight Conquergood did by forming surrogate families both among the Hmong in Southeast Asia and in Albany Park.

Much of critical ethnography's underpinnings are rooted in other theoretical traditions, such as critical race theory, feminist theory, queer theory, postcolonialist theory, and critical performance pedagogy. It follows that much of critical ethnography is based on theoretical perspectives that valorize the value of class, race and ethnicity, gender, sexual preference, and nationality.

Methodological Process

Methodology is study and reflection on methods of data collection and strategies of data analysis and representation. Whereas methods are practical techniques, methodologies are theoretical endeavors. Thus a particular methodology, ethnographic methodology for example, is the overall theory and paradigm that guide the ethnographer throughout the research process, including the research question, the development of a research design and proposal, the collection of data, data analysis, and presentation of the research. Methodological reflections—just like theoretical reflections—act as guides to help researchers conduct research and move through the process of engaging in scholarship.

More specifically, critical ethnographers' method includes participant observation and various types of interviewing. Ethnographers collect these kinds of data together with, at times, textual data to produce an account of a community or phenomenon under study. Other methods, less frequently used, are surveys, diaries, personal introspection, and other similar forms of nonparticipant observation. It is important to emphasize that these are methods and not methodologies. In the following paragraphs, this broad realm of activity is divided into three areas: collection of data, data analysis, and representation of data.

Collecting Data

A critical approach to ethnography begins with the selection of a research site and the collection of data from the field. Critical ethnographers select research sites where they feel injustices need to be brought to light and wrongs need to be righted—as Conquergood's selection of research topics shows. Thus, rather than the need to accumulate knowledge for knowledge's sake, critical ethnographic research designs begin with the impetus of putting critical theory into practice.

With regard to data collection, like all forms of ethnography, critical ethnography revolves around the method of participant observation conducted within a clearly bounded research setting. Ethnographers go directly into the communities that they are studying or collaborating with and interact with them in order to gather research data and solve practical problems. Ethnographers take notes, talk to people, live within the community or as close as possible to it, and spend a great deal of time learning about (and with) the people or phenomenon they are studying. At times this may also result in ethnographers teaching and sharing knowledge. Conquergood, for example, used performances to teach public health and sanitation principles to Hmong refugees in Thailand.

Critical ethnographers utilize an inductive theoretical approach to collecting and interpreting data. This means that ethnographers go into the field without the need to test a preformulated hypothesis and without preconceived notions, categories, themes, or conclusions in mind. Thus the research is an emergent process in which categories, themes, and analysis take shape as the research is in progress. The only limitation to this induction comes from the researcher's moral stance, which is unchangeably grounded in communitarian ethics and the will to suppress oppression and injustice. Thus, in opposition to other forms of ethnography, critical ethnography is driven first and foremost by a theoretical perspective, philosophy, or ideology. Being so critical and still maintaining an inductive approach is often very complex.

Where interpretive and critical ethnography diverge in relation to collecting data is in their approach to collaborative dialogue. Coparticipation and collaboration are often crucial in critical ethnography. Critical ethnographers believe that it is ethical and morally essential for research to take a collaborative and participatory approach. Collaboration is not only part of the data collection but begins from the research design and moves into the data analysis and representation of research. Critical ethnographers wish to enact a multivocal process in which all perspectives are expressed. This means that the data collection is dialogic and democratic, which means involving research participants at every step of the process.

One key aspect in data collection is the constant reflection, negotiation, and renegotiation of the researcher's position and power differences in relation to informants. Critical ethnographers realize that power difference between researcher and informants cannot be entirely eliminated but believe that the reflection process allows researchers to understand and manage how power differences influence the data gathered. This reflexive process allows the researcher to see how outside forces create the culture under study, beginning from the study itself.

Data Analysis

After data collection, ethnographers engage in data analysis. However, unlike much of conventional ethnography, which is interested in the formation of theoretical categories or even—in the case of some realist ethnography—lawlike statements, critical ethnography attempts to avoid reducing lived experience to excessively abstract categories. Instead, critical ethnography seeks to expose the complexity and nuances of everyday experiences and to unravel and dismantle the categories of knowledge that structure those experiences. This requires critical ethnographers to approach the data analysis process using a reflexive approach that allows researchers to understand their position in the research process. In this sense, gathering and sharing knowledge and doing theory become enlightened and situated practices, rather than constructions by fiat.

Reflexivity enables the researcher to examine oneself and one's position during data analysis. This process reveals one's background, history, and daily experiences and how these factors ultimately influence the ethnographer's epistemological views, theoretical perspectives, and assumptions. Not only does critical ethnography take on an emic approach (viewing things from the perspective of the participants), but it also requires that in order to dismantle ideologies, it is necessary to use an etic approach (researcher's perspective) in order to reflect on biases that shape the process of conducting and writing ethnographies.

Data analysis is done inductively, from specific data to general conclusions. Working from an inductive frame requires the researcher to address research questions and analysis as the research unfolds and takes form. Thus categories and patterns are shaped as the data collection proceeds rather than being predetermined and fixed.

Representation of Data

A third element of the methodological process is reflection on the writing of ethnographic data and how informants are represented through the words and eyes of the researcher. Methodological discussions about how to present the data—the genres and media of ethnographic presentation—are an important part of the writings of critical theorists. Whereas many academics write up research using dispassionate, impersonal, scientific prose that disconnects informants from the audience, critical ethnographers reject this type of representation and instead seek to create ethnographies that engage their readers and informants directly, experimenting with different genres and media. Critical ethnographers in their research and writing openly display a standpoint, political motivation, and the partiality of research practices. They seek to create a plural and inclusive text that infuses a variety of voices rather than just the dominant scientific voice of the ethnographer. Conquergood's several essays and staged performances—for instance his work on the death penalty and what he called lethal theater—utilized this approach to garner attention for the plight of death row inmates.

Collaboration with informants on all aspects of the research process is essential for developing a multivocal, or inclusive, text. In many cases critical ethnographers ask informants to participate in the entire development of the research, including the final writing or other forms of production and performance, in turn creating co-constructed texts. Informant collaboration allows the development of a representational style that includes the voices of the people rather than excludes them under the guise of anonymity. Following the lead of critical theory interventions that blur the boundaries across disciplines, some scholars purposefully seek less traditional academic prose and engage in experimental writing styles seen more in the humanities than in the social sciences. For example, a critical ethnographer may use poetic stanzas in order to represent conversations or interviews with informants. This is usually done to enable rhythms of dialogue and speech to flow naturally, allowing the interview and persons involved to come to life. Other common styles adopted are performative writing styles as well as actual dramas and performances to present the study, as well as—again in the case of Conquergood's work—films and documentaries. In most cases the voices of the informants, ethnographer, institutions, and other informants are all included in the text, creating a plural perspective of voices that disperse the authority of the academic voice.

April Vannini

See also Critical Discourse Analysis; Critical Theory; Cultural Identity Theory; Cultural Studies; Ethnography of Communication; Performance Theories; Performative Writing; Power and Power Relations; Privilege

Further Readings

Conquergood, D. (1991). Rethinking ethnography: Towards a critical cultural politics. *Communication Monographs, 58,* 179–194.

Denzin, N. K. (2003). *Performance ethnography: Critical pedagogy and the politics of culture.* Thousand Oaks, CA: Sage.

Madison, D. S. (2005). *Critical ethnography: Method, ethics, and performance.* Thousand Oaks, CA: Sage.

CRITICAL ORGANIZATIONAL COMMUNICATION

Critical organizational communication is concerned with understanding issues of power in organizational settings. Critical organizational communication studies now cover a wide array of more specific approaches to and theories about the study of organizational communication, drawing significantly from critical modernism, poststructural, and feminist scholarship on the subject. Critical approaches to organizational communication first were developed in the 1980s, with the interpretive turn in organizational communication theory. These approaches became increasingly complex as they were influenced by and became mutually intertwined with the emergence of feminist thought, the popularity of poststructural approaches, and ever-widening empirical contexts for inquiry.

The Interpretive Turn

In the 1980s many scholars began to highlight the centrality of subjectivity, meaning, and context in organizational communication, thereby paying attention to the cultural life of organizations. Formerly, scholarship had been built primarily on a container metaphor for organizations, which entailed looking at how communication, in the form of messages, was transmitted "in" preexisting organizations. However, the interpretive turn led scholars to become especially interested in examining connections between communication and the ontology, or nature, of organizations, that is, how communication actually created the apparently solid things that we called organizations. Thus, scholars started taking apart phenomena that were earlier taken for granted and began to look at how they were communicatively constructed. For instance, instead of measuring how much workers participated in decision making in their organizations, scholars interested in studying participation began to study how workers ascribed definite meanings to participation and then acted on those meanings. And so, the interpretive turn led to the demise of the idea of an organization as a container and led instead to an abiding concern with understanding the connections between organizations and the rest of society.

Critical approaches grew quickly with the advent of the interpretive turn because power was such a valuable concept in enabling us to understand why particular meanings came to be dominant, why organizations were constructed in specific ways, and what that had to do with the larger political economy of capitalism. While scholars had always studied power in organizational settings, with the advent of the interpretive approach, power became an altogether multidimensional concept. Researchers became increasingly eclectic, drawing from such sources as the *community power* debates in sociology in order to explain why individuals and collectives did not agitate against visibly oppressive conditions. As scholars paid attention to such acquiescence to control, they expanded their conception of power to include not just issues of obedience and direct control through such mechanisms as reward and punishment, but also social and cultural norms, discipline, and unobtrusive forms of control. In the process, four terms became particularly important in critical conceptions of organizational life: *concertive control, hegemony, systematically distorted communication,* and *identification.*

A First Generation of Concepts

The four terms—*concertive control, hegemony, systematically distorted communication,* and *identification*—might be taken as the cornerstones of a first generation of critical organizational communication studies, which still have currency today. The term *concertive control* was developed by Phil Tompkins, George Cheney, and their associates, as an extension of the work of Richard Edwards, in order to describe a form of organizational control that did not rely on coercion, bureaucracy, or even technology. They described early systems of workplace control as "simple" in that they were based on arbitrary and ad hoc rules set by owners. The advent of the industrial age

resulted in the development of more elaborate systems of control that were technical and/or bureaucratic. Technical systems of control were exemplified by the Fordist production line, which rigidly controlled the speed and output of work, even as it deskilled workers, forcing them to learn specific tasks at the expense of developing their knowledge base. Bureaucratic systems of control are exemplified by large modern organizations such as universities, which involve formal, codified, rationalized systems of rules and regulations that govern conduct. Concertive control systems, on the other hand, are epitomized by organizations that involve significant amounts of teamwork, control via a system of informal values, and norms and codes that are constructed by workers themselves and that serve to regulate their behavior. While it is evident that simple, technical, and bureaucratic control systems are made possible through communication processes between superiors and subordinates, it is especially easy to see how concertive control systems are constructed through communicative dynamics among employees.

The term *hegemony,* coined by Antonio Gramsci to describe antagonistic and mutually negotiated relationships between social classes, was adopted by organizational communication scholars such as Dennis Mumby to describe the idea that organizational members might consent to the domination of powerful groups over them. This was found to happen where an apparent consensus about the cultural meanings of key workplace practices and vocabularies benefits one group more than others. Hegemony is seen to operate through ideologies, or systems of values and beliefs, and discourses, or broad patterns in talk and text, that, taken together, produce social relationships. Thus, critical scholars interested in hegemonic work practices are prone to deconstruct, or show alternative ways of understanding, the meanings of dominant organizational values such as excellence or hard work in terms of which groups benefit most from those particular constructions. A specific focus in early research on the subject was to examine how organizational and broader vocabularies and patterns of communication served to further the interests of management, an idea called *managerialism,* which in turn was taken to refer to conceptions of organizations as primarily sites of profit rather than cooperation or community.

A third key term in the first generation of critical organizational communication studies was *systematically distorted communication,* a term coined by Jürgen Habermas and developed in the context of organizational studies by scholars like Stan Deetz and Dennis Mumby. In Habermasian terms, systematically distorted communication refers to the instrumental manipulation of language by the systemic interests of money and power that result in the corruption of the *lifeworld,* or our everyday networks of communicative practice. Systematically distorted communication is achieved through a broad plethora of strategies—*universalization,* for example, or the treatment of sectional organizational interests as universal; *disqualification,* or treating the subject or source as petty and trivial; and *neutralization,* or the treatment of topics as not having any kind of political significance. Stan Deetz's early work on the subject focused particularly on what he called the *corporate colonization* of the lifeworld—a phrase that drew attention to the deep structuring of corporate interests into the very fabric of society and that affected where individuals lived, how they chose to educate themselves and their children, the structure of their community relationships, and their expectations of government and public life.

A fourth key term in early critical organizational communication might be said to be *identification,* or the rhetorical process through which organizations persuaded their members to construct their selves in alignment with the organization's key goals and values. The term was made popular by George Cheney, who used rhetorical critic Kenneth Burke's work to launch an entire tradition of rhetorical inquiry in organizational communication. Cheney argued that organizations most often persuaded members through persuasive techniques such as building common ground over subjects and issues (thesis), identifying an enemy against which members were exhorted to act (antithesis), or simply by assuming a sense of "we" or togetherness. Identification, said Cheney, was necessary in contemporary organizations precisely because of the vast differences in incomes and values between organizational members: In this sense, identification could be interpreted as a form of systematically distorted communication.

As scholars grappled with a range of concepts that shed light on the communicative character of systems of domination and oppression, they retained a core concern of classical critical theory with the idea of *praxis,* or transformative social practice. A key concern of critical scholars is to stay engaged in a practical sense with structures of domination and oppression. This concern has taken many forms in critical organizational communication, most visibly in the attention that critical scholars have paid to activism, as well as their extensive theorization of the notion of *empowerment*—the ability of individuals and communities to engage in decision making and take action in the face of larger power inequities.

A Second Generation of Concepts

In the 1990s, critical organizational communication researchers continued to elaborate on and refine the terms outlined above, and as they did so, they made at least two immensely significant moves that characterized an entire new generation of studies. The first was the explicit recognition of the dialectical character of power. Mumby in particular argued that researchers needed to conceptualize broad systems of control and processes of discipline in terms of the conditions for *resistance* that they engendered. Considerable attention began to be paid to exploring how domination and resistance occur simultaneously. Critical organizational communication researchers studied this by mapping out the conditions and possibilities for resistance in systems of disciplinary control, drawing on the work of scholars like Michel Foucault and James Scott as they did so. Among other things, researchers studied how flight attendants resisted patriarchal conventions, how secretaries resisted administrative control, and how service workers reinterpreted and resisted dominant constructions of their jobs.

A second major move that changed critical organizational communication studies in the 1990s was the emergence of a robust corpus of *feminist inquiry* in organizational communication studies. Feminist researchers capitalized on the ascendance of critical modes of inquiry in organizational communication in order to draw attention to the inherently gendered character of organizational formations. As might be evident from the examples in the previous paragraph, feminist researchers paid considerable time and energy to understanding how individuals resisted patriarchal practices in organizational contexts, developing sophisticated and nuanced understandings of self, identity, and voice in the process. Indeed, the term *feminism* encapsulated a variety of approaches to understanding gender that could not be fully subsumed under the term *critical* as it was traditionally articulated. Feminist scholars were therefore responsible for bringing more modernist and poststructural approaches into the study of organizations, ultimately putting in dialogue various philosophical frameworks to question organizational processes and practices.

While both poststructuralist and critical late-modern approaches to organizational communication treat the analysis of power as central to the understanding of communicative phenomena, poststructuralist thought makes at least two moves beyond "traditional" critical approaches to organizational communication studies, thereby transforming the terrain of critical organizational communication. First, poststructural studies are much more likely to treat power in broad and diffuse terms, understanding it not so much as a property of structure evidenced by hierarchy, but as dispersed, decentralized, and disciplinary mechanisms that operate through language. So, poststructural perspectives are much more likely to treat organizational structure as a property of power, arguing that diffuse systems of disciplinary power themselves constitute what are presented to us as organizational structures. Second, poststructural studies are much more prone to understanding selfhood and identity as fragmented, disjointed, and contingent and are thus much more likely to treat individual agency as vulnerable to the point of extinction.

The advent of poststructuralism as a significant influence on critical organizational communication was most evident in the 1990s, in the increasing emphasis of critical scholars on the notion of *discourse* and a focus on *contradiction* and *paradox* in organizational life. The concept of discourse, which was taken largely from Foucault, referred to the broad expression of power in language, from which our notions of logic, truth, and action are derived. The term allowed researchers to identify multiple and competing logics and truths in organizational life. For instance, discourses of technical excellence in organizations are often seen to compete with discourses of managerial efficiency.

Therefore, critical scholars began to take the contradictory and paradoxical character of organizational communication seriously, even understanding key critical terms such as *participation* and *empowerment* from the standpoint of paradox, contradiction, silence, and voice.

Discourses of Suspicion and Vulnerability

Contemporary critical organizational communication researchers are thus irrevocably influenced by both feminist thought and poststructural sensibilities, embracing both a discourse of suspicion and a discourse of vulnerability. Mumby uses the term *discourse of suspicion,* drawn from Paul Ricoeur's notion of the hermeneutic of suspicion, to characterize scholarship in the area because such studies do not take the surface of organizational life for granted. Instead, their central concern still is to uncover the deeper structural, systemic, and discursive power inequities that underlie everyday communication practices. Simultaneously, however, a *discourse of vulnerability* also underlies contemporary critical organizational communication scholarship. The term *vulnerability* turns our attention to several related ideas. First, the term refers to what one might call the *crisis of representation* in that several critical researchers now balk at the claim to unilaterally present their research as the single, unified, authoritative account of a phenomenon. Moreover, the term refers to the idea that organizational and societal discourses make the notion of an agentic, or choice-making, individual extremely problematic. In other words, we very rarely enact unified selves: Our sense of who we are varies and shifts dramatically in different times and situations and is significantly impacted by a range of different discourses; thus, the idea that we make "free" choices is problematic.

Scholars have developed the versatile and hybrid space at the crossroads of discourses of suspicion and discourses of vulnerability to engage in a series of diverse and specific conceptual and empirical moves that are sometimes explicitly linked with critical approaches or sometimes with poststructural approaches. Three are especially worth discussing. First, scholars have studied organizational identity and difference in terms of *intersectionality,* lending credence to the idea that our organizational selves are, in a sense, crystallized from a vast set of discourses, including those of gender, sexuality, ability, race, age, and class; the study of one of these points of difference necessarily entails the examination of myriad others. For instance, trying to understand popular conceptions of the empowered entrepreneur now involves examining how our notions of professional entrepreneurial identity are guided by assumptions about class, gender, and race. Second, scholars have drawn on discourses of suspicion as well as vulnerability to examine the *effects of economic globalization,* and such work has taken a wide variety of forms. For instance, some scholars have analyzed in great detail the potential and problems of corporate social responsibility in the face of looming global environmental crises. Others have examined resistance to corporate globalization in the form of contemporary global justice activism, using it as a platform to critique the focus of earlier studies of resistance and power on individualized resistance. Still others have examined the effects of globalization on the nongovernmental and nonprofit sector, focusing on such issues as information technology and accountability.

Third, critical researchers have written considerably about discursively constructed boundaries between *life* and *work* in the context of gender, race, sexuality, and class. As they have done so, they have drawn from a wide variety of theories in organizational communication, including structuration, relational dialectics, and poststructuralism. Throughout, however, they have paid close attention to a core concern of critical studies, empowerment, asking questions about how individuals and families enact empowerment in the context of discursive constraints at home and at work. As they have done so, they have created a genre of scholarship that blurs the lines between the hitherto distinct domains of inquiry in organizational and family communication, while retaining key critical overtones.

In sum, what might now be called critical organizational communication has grown increasingly eclectic over the years, with wide-ranging and multidisciplinary influences. Indeed, researchers have also gone back to some of the more classic concerns of critical organizational communication, using contemporary sensibilities to re-understand key concerns about concertive control and resistance and renewing interest in the study of organizational rhetoric. Researchers have just begun to concern themselves with an ever-broadening array of topics, including environmental activism, postcolonial politics, sexuality in organizations, and community engagement. It is reasonably safe to suppose that such directions are more likely than not to be multiple and fragmented, as distinct from the relatively homogeneous conceptual growth evident in an earlier generation.

Shiv Ganesh

See also Corporate Colonization Theory; Critical Theory; Discourse Theory and Analysis; Feminist Communication Theories; Globalization Theories; Hybridity; Identification; Interpretive Theory; Intersectionality; Organizational Communication Theories; Organizational Control Theory; Organizational Culture; Organizational Identity Theory; Poststructuralism

Further Readings

Ashcraft, K. L., & Mumby, D. K. (2004). *Reworking gender: A feminist communicology of organization.* Thousand Oaks, CA: Sage.

Clair, R. P. (1998). *Organizing silence: A world of possibilities.* Albany: State University of New York Press.

Deetz, S. (1992). *Democracy in an age of corporate colonization: Developments in communication and the politics of everyday life.* Albany: State University of New York Press.

Ganesh, S., Zoller, H. M., & Cheney, G. (2005). Transforming resistance, broadening our boundaries: Critical organizational communication studies meets globalization from below. *Communication Monographs, 72,* 169–191.

Golden, A., Kirby, E., & Jorgensen, J. (2006). Work-life research from both sides now: An integrative perspective for organizational and family communication. *Communication Yearbook, 30,* 143–195.

Larson, G., & Tompkins, P. (2005). Ambivalence and resistance: A study of management and resistance in a concertive control system. *Communication Monographs, 72,* 1–21.

May, S., Cheney, G., & Roper, J. (Eds.). (2007). *The debate over corporate social responsibility.* Oxford, UK: Oxford University Press.

Meisenbach, R., & McMillan, J. J. (2006). Blurring the boundaries: Historical developments and future directions in organizational rhetoric. *Communication Yearbook, 30,* 99–141.

Mumby, D. K. (1988). *Communication and power in organizations: Discourse, ideology and domination.* Norwood, NJ: Ablex.

Mumby, D. K. (1993). Critical organizational communication studies: The next ten years. *Communication Monographs, 60,* 8–25.

Stohl, C., & Cheney, G. (2001). Participatory processes/paradoxical practices: Communication and the dilemmas of organizational democracy. *Management Communication Quarterly, 14,* 349–407.

Tompkins, P. K., & Cheney, G. (1985). Communication and unobtrusive control in contemporary organizations. In R. D. McPhee & P. K. Tompkins (Eds.), *Organizational communication: Traditional themes and new directions* (pp. 179–210). Beverly Hills, CA: Sage.

CRITICAL RACE THEORY

Critical race theory (CRT) is perhaps best characterized as a loosely knit body of work that centers on the study of race and racism. Committed to a complex notion of race as simultaneously socially constructed and deeply material, at least in its lived experience and its effects, CRT offers a historicized and dynamic study of race and racism that traces the roots of racial thinking and racist practice as it also carefully tracks contemporary discourses and practices of race and racism.

Origins

Though the origins of CRT can be traced to the influential writings of early figures such as W. E. B. DuBois and civil rights leaders, such as Martin Luther King Jr. and César Chávez, its formal emergence dates to the mid-1970s and the writings of legal scholar Derrick Bell. Bell, among others, launched a critique of the legal system, arguing that its methods and practices perpetuated a racially stratified society. Though his considerable body of work offers numerous specific critiques, his larger argument can perhaps best be summarized as follows: Racial thinking is ingrained in U.S. history, culture, politics, law, and society in ways that often mask it, making both the racial thinking and the racist manifestations appear neutral. Moreover, the intersection of that racial thinking with the U.S. tradition of liberalism promotes practices and policies that appear to motivate change but that traditionally have enabled the perpetuation of both racial thinking and racist practice. A central such instance for Bell and other CRT scholars is civil rights legislation. While not denying the clear material changes brought about by civil rights, Bell argued, in instances such as the increasing attacks on affirmative action, that the gains made were being lost. CRT also owes debt for its emergence to the critical legal studies (CLS) movement. CLS scholars, writing mainly in the 1970s and 1980s, argued that while law tends to be thought of as neutral, it is heavily political. Indeed, they coined the argument that law is politics. By this, they sought to draw attention to the power-laden biases that drive legal thought and policy. Influenced by the writings of continental social theorists, CLS maintains that U.S. law has mostly served the interests of the dominant and functioned to justify the injustices that it enables. For CRT scholars, such arguments help illustrate the Whiteness that permeates law and society more generally. In response, Bell and the growing community of CRT scholars advocate new approaches to law and legal thinking that would both revise conceptions of race and racism and advocate for racial justice.

Fundamental Assumptions

The writings of CRT scholars are increasingly interdisciplinary and varied. Still, several assumptions are widely shared. United in its investment in the study of race, CRT argues that racism is not merely the seemingly pathological acts of a few extremists, such as members of the Ku Klux Klan, nor is it only the overt expressions of discrimination, such as expressed in Jim Crow laws. Instead, racism is expressed in everyday discourse and practice by much or even all society. In explanation, they argue that racism is a normal, not an exceptional, part of U.S. society; that is, race and racism are so deeply a part of U.S. thought and culture that racial thinking and racist practice have come to look "normal." Given the invisibility of race and racism, CRT advocates careful historicized and localized studies of race and racism. In a sense, CRT argues for a constant mapping of the racial landscape. CRT argues that racist thought and practice are historically and contextually specific; this dynamism requires that scholars attend to its various manifestations. CRT scholars argue, for instance, that racism looks very different in a post–civil rights world than it did previously. Civil rights legislation required the ending of overt acts of racism—such as school segregation—but did not and does not end covert or institutionalized forms of racism. Thus, for instance, while de jure racial segregation is illegal, de facto racial segregation, in housing and education, continues, though its racial component is easily masked by its class component. These ways of thinking about race and racism are then closely linked to a third assumption, that traditional legal thinking is both racial and racist. Grounded in an ideology of liberalism, traditional legal thinking is invested in universalism and formal equality, both of which advantage dominant cultures and disadvantage marginalized ones. Here, CRT maintains, for instance, that universalism—or the argument that all similar instances be treated identically—protects some populations over others. It argues that all people, regardless of race, class, and gender, should be treated the same, but in doing so, it ignores the reality that race, class, and gender mean that people's experiences are not the same. Universalism, for instance, underlies arguments for formal equal opportunity as manifest in such practices as standardized testing. CRT scholars, however, note that, conceptualized as such, equal opportunity is in fact not equal, for standardized testing benefits racially and class-privileged populations. The critiques of the legal field captured in CRT discussions of liberalism, equality, and universalism all express the larger foundational argument that racial justice is unlikely to occur via traditional legal routes, which typically do not require rethinking of racial reasoning and racism.

Core Themes

Spurred by the fundamental assumptions about race and racism, along with law and legal change, CRT asks several key questions about racial justice and social change. While these questions do not capture the entirety of the CRT agenda, they do point to overarching issues that drive much of this interdisciplinary body of research.

The guiding concern for CRT is, of course, race and racism, and much scholarship is designed to uncover the ways in which racism continues to be the norm. In assessing this question, Bell introduced *interest convergence theory,* or the idea that dominant populations, such as Whites, will support an antiracist policy or practice only when they perceive it to benefit them. Others within CRT, such as legal scholar Stephanie Wildman and communication theorist Dreama Moon, turn to the notion of *privilege,* which has also been carefully addressed outside CRT. Privilege, as the feminist and antiracist scholar Peggy McIntosh explains, is the system in which some populations, for instance Whites, enjoy unearned advantages to which people of color do not have access. One example is the presumed racial neutrality of the opinions and arguments made by Whites; people of color are often perceived as pursuing a racial agenda in their arguments or as being racially biased. Making a related argument, Cheryl Harris has coined the idea of Whiteness as property; it is something of value—a privilege—that only some people own and/or have access to.

A second theme within CRT might be framed as the attention given to absences and invisibilities in racial thinking. For instance, a number of scholars have looked at the limitations of what they refer to as the *Black/White binary.* Tracing the ways in which race is understood as an either/or between Black and White, CRT scholars identify the resulting gaps in how both race and racism are understood and perceived. They note that the histories, experiences, identities, and legacies of Latinos/as, Asian Americans, and American Indians have been largely neglected in both popular and academic literature. In addition, some have argued that racist and racial policies that predominantly affect Latinos/as and Asian Americans, such as English-only laws, are not as readily seen as racist because the policies do not directly affect Blacks.

A second primary emphasis in the assessment of absences and invisibilities is discussion of *intersectionality.* Like research on the Black/White binary, this work challenges either/or thinking and asks for more complex understandings of race that attend to the intersections of race with other aspects of social location, such as gender, class, sexuality, and nation. In her groundbreaking work, Kimberlé Crenshaw explored the invisibility of women of color and delineated the ways in which women of color are systematically disadvantaged by a logic that, for instance, keeps track of "women and minorities." She and others have argued that this language, so firmly rooted in social practice, fails to recognize that women of color are simultaneously women *and* minorities.

Storytelling provides a third way in which CRT seeks to fill in existing gaps in knowledge and ways of thinking. Convinced that traditional theoretical models and academic modes of writing provide only a partial accounting of the range of social experiences, CRT advocates nontraditional modes of writing that emphasize the use of personal and community knowledge, including the relating of narratives, both auto/biographical and fictional. These *counternarratives,* often grounded in the everyday racialized experience of people of color, provide correctives to traditional narratives and historic accounts, as well as offering evidence of the multiple ways of knowing that exist.

A final area of interest for CRT includes the development of new theoretical accounts of race and racism. Two recurring arguments are the discussions of *particularism* and *microaggressions.* Continuing its critique of liberalism and universalism, CRT advocates particularism, or what has come to be known as the *call to context.* As noted earlier, CRT challenges the liberalism of traditional legal theory, with particular attention to the tendency in legal thought, law, and policy to advocate universalism. But CRT maintains that all people and all experiences are not the same; race, as well as gender and class, means that people's lives are vastly different. Thus, CRT continues, we cannot treat all crimes or all people in the same way. Instead, CRT asks that we account for the particulars of one's life or the context in which a particular event occurred and in this way gather greater insight into how race works on an everyday basis.

In assessing racism and tracking its continual evolution, scholars have also drawn attention not just to the overt acts of racism that prevailed prior to the civil rights movement but also to the more covert acts of racism pervasive today. These include everyday acts that traditional scholarship has largely ignored, such as *microaggressions,* or acts that are easily dismissed or negated. One such instance might be the tendency, particularly

though not exclusively among White women, to hold their purse tightly, to lock their car doors, or to cross to the other side of the street when they encounter Black men. CRT scholars have argued that these microaggressions take place frequently, even daily, for people of color and become one of the more emotionally exhausting forms of racism; the larger society generally fails to acknowledge the racial component of these acts as well as the toll they take.

Interdisciplinary and Cross-Disciplinary Developments

Though CRT initially emerged among legal scholars, it has increasingly grown such that CRT scholarship is now a truly interdisciplinary venture, with work being done in such fields as sociology, education, and, of course, communication. Continuing to examine the broad themes discussed above, the interdisciplinary scholarship also directs attention to the particularities of each discipline. For instance, education scholars examine the racial assumptions of educational institutions. Looking at practices such as standardized testing, classroom interactions, and epistemologies, they question whether schooling can be considered to include being schooled into racial thinking. Communication scholars have asked a number of critical questions, many of which examine the discursivity of race. Some look at issues of free speech, while others pursue questions of hate speech. A considerable body of scholarship explores larger social discourses, such as those surrounding immigration, hate crimes, affirmative action, and English-only laws.

In addition to these interdisciplinary ventures, CRT has generated several closely related bodies of literature, including three projects examining the racial dynamics of Latinos/as, Asian Americans, and Native Americans. These are commonly referred to as *Latcrit, Asiacrit,* and *Tribalcrit. Critical race feminism,* another offshoot, regularly considers the intersections of race and gender. Finally, *critical Whiteness studies,* while not necessarily an outgrowth of CRT, are a closely related body of work. All these projects include both legal and interdisciplinary scholars. Across both the interdisciplinary and cross-disciplinary studies, one finds work that both extends the core focus of CRT and adds to that study with the specific interests of the particular fields.

Lisa A. Flores

See also Critical Theory; Feminist Communication Theories; Frankfurt School; Intersectionality; Privilege; Whiteness Theory

Further Readings

Bell, D. (1987). *And we are not saved: The elusive quest for racial justice.* New York: Basic Books.

Crenshaw, K. (1991). Mapping the margins: Intersectionality, identity politics, and violence against women of color. *Stanford Law Review, 43,* 1241–1297.

Crenshaw, K., Gotanda, N., Peller, G., & Thomas, K. (1996). *Critical race theory: The key writings that formed the movement.* New York: New Press.

Delgado, R. (1995): *The Rodrigo chronicles: Conversations about America and race.* New York: New York University Press.

Delgado, R., & Stefanic, J. (1998). *The Latino/a condition: A critical reader.* New York: New York University Press.

Flores, L. A., & Moon, D. G. (2002). Rethinking race, revealing dilemmas: Imagining a new racial subject in Race Traitor. *Western Journal of Communication, 66,* 181–207.

Hasian, M., Jr., & Delgado, F. P. (1998). The trials and tribulations of racialized critical rhetorical theory: Understanding the ambiguities of Proposition 187. *Communication Theory, 8,* 245–270.

Holmes, D. G. (2007). Affirmative reaction: Kennedy, Nixon, King, and the evolution of color-blind rhetoric. *Rhetoric Review, 26,* 25–41.

Ladson-Billings, G. (1995). Toward a critical race theory of education. *Teachers College Record, 97,* 47–68.

CRITICAL RHETORIC

The *critical rhetoric project* began in the early 1980s in the communication discipline principally with the work of Raymie McKerrow and Michael Calvin McGee. The phrase *critical rhetoric* in particular owes its genesis to McGee. Work by Phillip Wander, Michael McGee, Maurice Charland, Robert Hariman, and Celeste Condit, among others, was instrumental in building the arguments that led to the publication of the essay "Critical Rhetoric: Theory and Praxis" by McKerrow in 1989. While the designation of a *critique of domination* and *critique of freedom,* and the principles that encompassed a new formulation of rhetoric's provenance, may have been seen as original or new, they were premised on the ongoing conversation among scholars begun in the late 1970s and early 1980s.

Reason, in all of its forms, has had a dominant role in Western theories of rhetoric. Derived from both Plato and Aristotle, the sense that rhetoric should be *reasoned discourse* lives on in the work of deliberative democracy theorists in the 21st century. While not seeking to eliminate reason or rational discourse from the playing field, a critical rhetoric perspective recognizes that not all communication between people will be, or necessarily should be, "reasoned," especially if the sense of rationality that is meant is that dictated by those "in charge." The power of the entrenched establishment in determining who can say what to whom and in what way is not to be ignored. But it is to be challenged, and that is, from the outset, the orientation of a *critical* perspective on rhetoric's role. As noted above, the critical practice encompasses two distinct (yet not mutually exclusive) perspectives: What is styled a *critique of domination* is oriented toward emancipation and may be best seen in terms of a "freedom from" domination. On the other hand, what is styled a *critique of freedom* is an attempt to place the focus on a not-yet-determined future, captured as a freedom to become other than we are at this moment. A focus on power relations (derived from Michel Foucault's analysis) places repressive power in the camp of domination, while a productive sense of power—what it can create in positive terms—is placed in the camp of freedom. While seeing these as two sides of the same coin is appropriate, they may function in a blended perspective, wherein one both seeks to escape (freedom from) and, at the same time, considers what one might be free to escape to.

In addition, the hope is that the critic is willing to go beyond a simple criticism to interrogate the very assumptions on which either domination or freedom rests. Nothing is privileged in an ultimate or permanent sense in the process of critiquing present reality. Thus, the grounding assumptions underlying democracy, for example, become subject to examination. This implies a commitment to *recursivity,* or constant critique: that which is "decided" as a preferred state of affairs for a people becomes, once instantiated, the subject of renewed examination. Nothing is held constant—unless one wishes it to remain. That is, critique is not committed to change as the only outcome but is committed to a reexamination of social relations (wherein power is seen as relational). What is "critical" in this scene is that, once advocacy stops and change is instantiated, it becomes a subject for continual critique. The constancy of a continual critique does not, in and of itself, blind one to ever taking action. Action may be the outcome of a specific critique at some point in time. The changes that occur in relations between people may be "a better world" (as one might hope in advocating a change), but that better world is not, by virtue of that change, a perfect place for all people.

Critical rhetoric is not a method of analysis. Rather, it is an orientation toward critical practice that does not seek to advance a specific approach or a specific set of terms that one might use in illuminating an object of inquiry. Drawing on Foucault, it seeks instead to understand how a particular discursive formation comes to be, in a particular place and time. Thus, it resists being named, as naming may result in any particular act of critique being reified as "the way this is done." In reversing traditional approaches to public address, however, it does follow what McGee termed an *inventional* approach in critical practice. McGee was not seeking—nor does a critical rhetoric perspective seek—to destroy the agent as a formulator of change. Instead, the approach seeks to place the agent in a larger context of contingent forces that shape discursive acts. Thus, the agent is implicated in a past and future in an ongoing and contingently derived process. Any rhetorical act is premised on those that preceded its enunciation; rhetors seek change in a context that is not of their own making, yet may influence new relationships through their efforts to give voice to that which should be said. Once said, the new future is itself subject to further critique.

McKerrow's 1989 article advanced eight principles that sought, collectively, to reshape and redirect criticism. Borrowing directly from McGee, the first principle announces an inventional theme that orients criticism toward praxis. What is altered in this expression is not that practice is "unmethodical," but rather that one's approach is not constrained by any specific tactics or strategies in ordering one's thought about an event or text. One may be methodical in assessing an event without claiming allegiance to any precise "do this, and then do this" approach. What is privileged is a question: What does this context determine to be necessary in best understanding and analyzing its features?

The second principle recognizes that discourse is itself a material entity. While there are varying analyses that make this a controversial claim (for example, the work of Carole Blair, Dana Cloud, and Ronald Greene), the point being advanced here is simply that words matter—discourse makes a difference.

The third principle asserts that rhetoric is more properly seen as *doxastic* rather than *epistemic.* Given rhetoric's relation to contingency (that which could be otherwise), *doxa,* or grounded opinion, rejects a true-or-false knowledge in favor of a way of knowing that is contingent; words are seen as constituting a social reality, and what brings these words rather than others into the scene at this time is the focus of analysis.

The fourth principle follows on the heels of the previous commitment to a relativized sense of knowledge in noting that naming is central to rhetoric. Implicit in a recognition of the power of naming is Kenneth Burke's perspective: Naming is neither final nor absolute, but rather an interpretive move in assessing what "is" perceived to be true at this moment. Through naming, one fixes that which is named (consider the attempt to remove the stigma of *ex-con* from one's existence after serving time) and thereby asserts one's relation to that which is named. Power is never far removed as a relational force that influences social relations; it asserts who can name, as well as the possibility of resistance to being so named. Should resistance be successful, the change in naming also changes the social relations between those involved. Recognizing the ex-con as a person who is more than what is carried in that name and refusing to continue using that attribution alters the social connection that exists.

The fifth principle suggests that influence is not, in and of itself, proof of a causal force or relationship. Drawing again on the work of Michel Foucault, the question is, Why this discourse rather than another at this time? This implies a causal force may be at work in forcing or determining the direction of discourse, thereby further removing the agent as one who might make his or her own decisions about such matters. What is intended by this principle is a simple recognition that whatever is going on may not be reducible to causal claims. Were this the case, we would be mired in modernity—in a linear evolution of determinative events that forecast the future. The continuity of history would be a pregiven attitude. Such a perspective is limiting in terms of what actually happens.

From an understanding that influence may not be causal, we come to the sixth principle, which focuses attention on the relationship between presence and absence. There is a natural tendency to gravitate toward that which is observable—that which is present in the social scene. What this principle seeks is a reminder: Absence may be more important, more potent, as a source of information than mere presence. The examination of media events, for example, is surely informed by who is seen. Nevertheless, who is not present is equally telling—as years of awards going to Caucasians, as years of movies with Whites playing the role of Native Americans, as years of noting the absence of Black head coaches in the National Football League would tell us, if only we would pay attention.

The seventh principle further complicates the critical act by noting that *polysemy,* or multiple perspectives, is far more common in interpretive work. Critiquing from an ideological perspective does not imply that one, and only one, conclusion is possible from one's understanding of a scene. Rather, multiple perspectives, each perhaps emanating from slightly different questions being asked, will generate equally different takes on the meaning or significance of an event or text. *Defeasibility* rules in the critical, interpretive realm. This does not mean a position is inherently indefensible, but it does mean that its defense is open to question and validation. That different views can be taken on the same event does not mean everyone is entitled to his or her own opinion—extreme relativism is not intended to be the result. Rather, it means that, just because I believe X, I still must show, and not just tell, why I believe in this way. Making the best case for an interpretive claim is tantamount to defending one's critical assessment, while recognizing that changing one's mind is an open option in the face of alternative interpretations.

The critical act culminates in a performance of oneself, hence the final principle. The critic, just as the rhetor, advocates and hence commits self in the world to this position rather than another. In so doing, the critic goes beyond mere description (this is what I think happened) to an evaluation of what that action means. The performance may be more than one of conveying information; it also may well be a political act—privileging one form of discourse over another or noting the ill effects that a continued exposure to or belief in a form of discourse may have for society. To advocate, especially in the context of advancing one's own ideological stance toward the world, is not done from a position of having the only or "right" answer. The principle of recursivity accompanies the critical act, just as it does the potential to engage others in a new or different power matrix.

To close, the critical rhetorician, in the guise of an inventor, takes an orientation toward the symbolic world that commits one to the possibility of error. At the same time, to risk failure does not imply a paralysis of will. The critical rhetorician seeks change via her or his own assessment of discursive formations, knowing full well that the instantiation of a new universe, with different possibilities for discursive interactions, lays itself open to renewed critique.

Raymie E. McKerrow

See also Critical Discourse Analysis; Critical Theory; Ideological Rhetoric; Ideology; Materiality of Discourse; Power and Power Relations; Rhetorical Theory

Further Readings

Blair, C. (2001). Reflections on criticism and bodies: Parables from public places. *Western Journal of Communication, 65,* 271–294.

Charland, M. (1987). Constitutive rhetoric: The case of the *Peuple Quebecois. Quarterly Journal of Speech, 73,* 133–150.

Cloud, D. (1994). The materiality of discourse as oxymoron: A challenge to critical rhetoric. *Western Journal of Communication, 58,* 141–163.

Condit, C. (1987). Democracy and civil rights: The universalizing influence of public argumentation. *Communication Monographs, 54,* 1–18.

Foucault, M. (1972). *The archaeology of knowledge* (A. M. Sheridan Smith, Trans.). New York: Harper & Row.

Greene, R. W. (2004). Rhetoric and capitalism: Rhetorical agency as communicative labor. *Philosophy and Rhetoric, 37,* 188–206.

Hariman, R. (1986). Status, marginality and rhetorical theory. *Quarterly Journal of Speech, 72,* 38–54.

McGee, M. C. (1975). In search of the "People": A rhetorical alternative. *Quarterly Journal of Speech, 61,* 235–249.

McGee, M. C. (1980). The "ideograph": A link between rhetoric and ideology. *Quarterly Journal of Speech, 66,* 1–16.

McGee, M. C. (1984). Another Philippic: Notes on the ideological turn in criticism. *Central States Speech Journal, 35,* 43–50.

McGee, M, C. (1990). Text, context, and the fragmentation of contemporary culture. *Western Journal of Speech Communication, 54,* 274–289.

McKerrow, R. E. (1989). Critical rhetoric: Theory and praxis. *Communication Monographs, 56,* 91–111.

McKerrow, R. E. (1991). Critical rhetoric in a postmodern world. *Quarterly Journal of Speech, 77,* 75–78.

McKerrow, R. E. (1993). Critical rhetoric and the possibility of the subject. In I. Angus & L. Langsdorf, (Eds.), *The critical turn: Rhetoric and philosophy in postmodern discourse* (pp. 51–67). Carbondale: Southern Illinois University.

McKerrow, R. E., & St. John, J. (2005). Critical rhetoric: A context for continual critique. In J. Kuypers (Ed.), *The art of rhetorical criticism* (pp. 345–366). Boston: Allyn & Bacon.

Ono, K. A., & Sloop, J. M. (1992). Commitment to *telos*: A sustained critical rhetoric. *Communication Monographs, 59,* 48–60.

Wander, P. (1983). The ideological turn in modern criticism. *Central States Speech Journal, 34,* 1–18.

CRITICAL THEORY

At first glance, critical theory appears to be quite negative. It sounds like a tool of analysis to denigrate things, people, and ideas. Criticism is something many associate with negativity, disparagement, and disapproval, yet despite the severe name, critical theory is very useful to the study of communication. Specifically, critical theory offers frameworks to analyze the complexities and contradictions of marginalization and resistance in societies. It is important to note at the outset that critical theory is not a theory proper but a set of complementary theoretical frames that examine structures of *domination* in society in order to open possibilities for the *emancipation* of people, meanings, and values. This two-pronged approach means that critical theorists see theory and action as inextricably interwoven. Critical theory is also oriented toward people, meaning that critical theorists use social life and lived experience as the site of inquiry for analysis and interpretation with the hope that they might find ways to make societies more open and equitable for marginalized groups. Finally, critical theorists are interested in the discursive and material practices of oppression and resistance. To understand how critical theorists arrive at this intellectual focus, this entry will discuss the historical emergence of critical theory, the primary concepts of critical theory, the contemporary forms of criticism in critical theory, and the applications of critical theory in communication studies.

Historical Foundations

Most contemporary scholars attribute the emergence of critical theory to Max Horkheimer and the Frankfurt School of Social Research in Frankfurt, Germany, popularly known as the *Frankfurt School.* In 1937, Horkheimer published a now famous essay entitled "Traditional and Critical Theory," in which he outlined a needed change in the scholarly pursuit of knowledge. The traditional approach to research at the time privileged objective scientific methods and implicitly emphasized strict interpretations of Marx and, ultimately, Communist values for social organizing and governance.

Largely responsive to the time period, Horkheimer called his colleagues to shift their energies to a new focus that would use Marxist theory in unorthodox and resistant ways, what is now understood as *neo-Marxism.* This approach uses Marxism as a theory to understand inequalities within a society. Unlike traditional approaches that used Marx as a universalizing theory, critical theorists use Marxist concepts such as exploitation, alienation, ideology, and class consciousness to understand the dynamics of marginalization. In reinterpreting Marx, Horkheimer specifically called his colleagues to use theory as a mode of critique to understand and ultimately change the organization of society. The first dimension of this new criticism was to historically examine the way a social structure forms and marginalizes particular groups. Second, Horkheimer believed that critical theorists should do interdisciplinary social research, analyzing politics, economics, sociology, and history, among other disciplines, to holistically understand relations of domination within a society.

The writings of Marx are certainly a cornerstone of critical theory, but so is Freudian psychoanalysis. The Frankfurt School theorist most interested in the psychoanalytic dimension of social critique was Erich Fromm. In particular, Fromm examined the relationship between personal freedom and social control, believing that the minute individuals achieve freedom, they search for some authority for affirmation of that freedom. While Fromm was questioned by others at the school for this focus, later it would become well accepted that, in addition to understanding how social structures exist external to individuals, scholars should also examine the ways structures embed themselves in the psyches of individuals and classes of people.

In addition to these theorists, the emergence of critical theory must also be attributed to Theodor Adorno, Walter Benjamin, Herbert Marcuse, and Friedrich Pollock. Furthermore, since the 1960s, Jürgen Habermas has contributed greatly to critical theory. Specifically, his theorizing has broadened the utility of critical theory by disconnecting it strictly from Marx. In addition to his work regarding the *public sphere,* Habermas argues that critical knowledge is information that allows individuals to break away from forms of domination. The process of gaining this critical knowledge involves reflexivity, or the process of reflecting on one's participation in structures of domination. While domination was certainly still relevant in the Marxist sense in Habermas's work, Habermas called on critics to recognize other modes of

domination in society in need of critical attention. This point really helped open up critical theory to other modes of analysis. In particular, the founding work of these theorists is influential today in examinations of capitalism, social institutions, culture industries, and popular culture. As will be elaborated in the next section, the foundational work in the Frankfurt School has led to a set of useful concepts that inform critical theorists' interrogations of social structures.

Key Terms

As mentioned above, contemporary critical theory is not a unified theory but should be understood as a loose set of theoretical frameworks that all share the goal of critiquing domination with the end goal of social change. Because of this, there are innumerable concepts that critical theorists use to evaluate society. Most of these concepts—including false consciousness, alienation, the death drive, and melancholia—are situationally useful to critical theorists, depending on the focus of their analyses. There are, however, overarching concepts that inform most critical theory analyses.

Critique of Domination

A central thread in critical theory research is the examination of social conditions for the hidden productive structures of marginalization. This sort of examination looks at the constraints placed on people's subjectivity, agency, and access to resources in particular contexts. Critical theorists understand that structures such as language, social institutions, and government produce meaning systems and knowledge about particular groups. Structures also produce, or reinforce, rules and norms for distributing resources and recognition across groups. In both creating knowledge about people and allocating resources to those people, these structures privilege some while marginalizing others. It is this inequality that is at the heart of critical theory's analysis. The goal in critiquing such structures of domination, however, is to produce possibilities for transforming social relations.

Ideology

Most critical theorists would agree that one of the foundational dimensions of domination is ideology, or systems of beliefs that serve as the foundation of a group's worldview and perception of reality and consciousness. These ideas structure what people believe about others and the world. While some theorists, such as Louis Althusser, attribute the formation of ideologies to superstructures that he names as state apparatuses, other critical theorists reject such a realistic source for ideology. Instead, many understand predominant ideologies to be constituted from dominant discourses and discursive practices within a society or institution. This does not mean that there are not alternative ideologies within a society, but that through deployment in language, some ideologies come to appear more normative and natural. This is the process that produces structures of domination, or what scholars name as *hegemony*.

Hegemony

Studies of hegemony examine the struggle over ideologies and interests between differently classed individuals in a society. Hegemony happens when one group or one set of ideas is privileged over others, often through subversion or co-optation. Hegemony works in subtlety and soft suggestion rather than direct coercion. It happens when one group's interests are shaped and shifted to reinforce the power of and benefit the dominant group's interests. Hegemony is an important area of inquiry for critical theorists because people often are unaware that their actions and beliefs reinforce the dominant group's interests. It is here, then, that critical scholars are called to intervene by analyzing social practices, norms, and conditions to challenge the eminence of particular ideologies. This task is called the social transformation objective of critical theory.

Social Transformation/Emancipation

Transformation is what sets critical theory apart from most other theories. In addition to analyzing, those who use this framework must provide possibilities for or institute social change. In this vein, theorists of this tradition understand description and social reform as co-constituting goals of theory. Importantly, however, social transformation is not limited to physical activism, but change also happens through discursive interventions, or offering

emancipatory readings of domination that might lead individuals to change their participation in oppressive systems and ideas.

Contemporary Approaches

Depending on who is asked, theoretical approaches including Marxist analysis, psychoanalysis, public sphere theory, feminist theory, critical race theory, Foucaultian analyses, poststructuralism, disabilities studies, queer theory, postcolonial theory, and critical legal theory are included in the purview of critical theory. This inclusion is in many ways representative of critical theory, and yet there are major foundational dissonances among these frameworks if they are conceived of as a unified body of theory. These dissonances include disagreements about the nature of reality, the nature of knowledge, and the preferred methods of analysis. And yet, broadly concerned, there are primary resonances among these trajectories of critical theory. The primary modes of criticism that are useful to communication studies are reviewed in the following section.

Marxist Criticism

Critical theory began with Martin Heidegger's reinterpretation of Marxist theory, and so it makes sense that neo-Marxism is still the foundation of critical theory approaches. Marx was centrally concerned with the ways that dominant modes of production determine relations between people in society. Specifically, he believed that the focus on profit in capitalist societies created relations of domination between those that labor and those that benefit from labor. Heidegger's revisioning of Marxism allowed contemporary scholars of Marx to complicate their analysis of oppression in society. Instead of a strict class analysis, neo-Marxists see domination as the result of multiple interlocking systems of oppression, with class as one contributing factor to that marginalization.

Psychoanalytic Criticism

While not completely accepted when critical theory first emerged, psychoanalysis is now a part of a long tradition of examining domination, particularly in regard to questions of human nature and subjectivity. Psychoanalysis provides theoretical tools to understand how domination manifests in individuals. While Sigmund Freud posited that adult behavior can be explained by childhood and familial situations, psychoanalytic criticism today applies important Freudian and Lacanian (from the work of Jacques Lacan, who followed and elaborated on Freud's work) concepts such as *melancholia* and *displacement* to examine the ways that groups of people respond to their positions of marginalization and privilege. This criticism differs from many other forms of critical theory in that it calls theorists to examine the effects of social structures through a focus on human behavior.

Poststructuralist Criticism

While psychoanalysis calls for an examination of human behavior, poststructuralist criticism investigates structures of language for the ways that they create and maintain social domination. Most of our lives we take language for granted and use it without reflection. Poststructuralist criticism offers the tool to investigate the hidden meanings and implications of language choices. Specifically, the tool of deconstruction is used to interrogate ideologies veiled in language and language structures such as the binary. This criticism contributes to critical theory in that it provides a way of examining structures of domination that are produced and reproduced through language.

Foucaultian Criticism

Michel Foucault was never a member of the Frankfurt School, but his research resonates greatly with the basic premises of the critical theory approach. First, Foucault contributed greatly to discussions of power, believing that power was not only destructive, but that there is an affirmative, or productive, dimension to power. This contribution has greatly shaped the work of critical theorists as they now question both the way power marginalizes and how people resist in the face of marginalization.

Like other critical theorists, Foucault's work focuses on social life and subjugation in institutions of society. In particular, Foucault offers important theoretical and methodological tools

for examining social institutions and people's relationship to institutions. For example, Foucault himself investigated the psychological institution (psychologically based institutions and norms), the prison system, and religion. In particular, his work provides critical theorists with tools to understand discourse, the relationship between power and knowledge, *governmentality* (the organized practices through which people are governed), and ethics. Critical theorists using Foucault in their analyses may approach their investigation using his methodological tools of archeology and genealogy, or they may examine structures of dominance via Foucaultian concepts.

Feminist Criticism

The previous modes of criticism offered tools to examine marginalization in class structures, language structures, and social institutions. Feminist criticism is considered by many a dimension of critical theory for its primary focus on gender inequality and patriarchy as a system of gender oppression. Many feminist critics conjoin feminist analysis with other forms of criticism to focus on particular manifestations of gender oppression in society. For example, many feminists take a poststructuralist perspective to understand the function of language in maintaining gender oppression. Others employ a Marxist or Foucaultian emphasis in their examinations of gendered social structures.

Postcolonial Criticism

Most strands of critical theory provide tools to examine structures of domination within societies, but postcolonial criticism interrogates the relations of domination between societies. Informed by the processes of colonization and decolonization around the world, postcolonial criticism examines the way knowledge, discourse, economics, politics, and many other facets of social life exist in unequal relationships between nation-states. In particular, postcolonial critics interrogate the dominance of Western discourse, media, and intellectualism in producing knowledge about colonial subjects and states. Postcolonial criticism also provides tools to examine the effects of colonization and decolonization on subjects within societies. This mode of criticism is not only greatly informed by Marx, but much of the research also takes a psychoanalytic or poststructuralist approach to understanding subjectivity and subjugation.

Influence in Communication Studies

Critical theory has broadly influenced the ways scholars in the social sciences and humanities approach research, and communication studies is certainly no exception. While critical theory began to emerge in Europe around the 1940s and 1950s, U.S. American communication scholars did not begin to fully engage with it until the 1980s and 1990s. The latency of critical theory's application in communication studies is due in large part to the dominance of functionalist assumptions about research, including the privileging of objectivity and generalizability in many strands of communication research. Furthermore, many classic critical theorists were not accessible to U.S. American communication scholars because they were not translated into English, and most U.S. communication scholars were not required to be fluent in texts outside the English-speaking world. Despite the late arrival, critical theory has had enormous influence in communication studies, specifically in the areas of rhetoric, performance studies, organizational communication, and, to some extent, intercultural communication.

Rhetoric

As noted above, many of the areas in communication studies have taken up critical theory as a mode of analysis, but perhaps none as completely as rhetorical studies. Scholars concerned with society have had an important—and sometimes contested—relationship with rhetoric, or the study of public discourse and deliberation. Critical theory's focus on structures of domination, however, melds nicely with rhetoric's examination of discourse in action via speech and public texts. Much like social researchers who examine class, language, or colonial relations of domination, rhetorical scholars are interested in the way domination plays out in people's speech, including who speaks and what/when/where they speak. The relevance of critical theory is evident in rhetoric's focus on key critical theorists such as Heidegger, Habermas, and Marcuse. Critical theory is also evident in the

deployment of particular forms of critical theory to study public discourse. For example, feminist rhetorician Cindy Griffin makes use of the Marxist concept of *alienation* in her analysis of Mary Wollstonecraft's rhetoric. In examining Wollstonecraft's writings on the conditions of women, Griffin calls rhetorical scholars to see that alienation is not only material but that it exists in the discursive realm through language that positions women in passivity and objectivity rather than as active agents. These discursive alienations of women then are materially reproduced and reinforced through the lack of women's access to public recognition and resources.

In addition to forms of criticism, rhetoricians have developed methods of analysis centrally informed by critical theory. Two of the most utilized modes of critical analysis are the ideographic analysis, conceptualized by Michael McGee, and critical rhetoric, formulated by Raymie McKerrow. Critical rhetoric directly ties to the project of critical theory, taking a two-pronged approach to a critique of domination and a critique of freedom. Here McKerrow aligns with Foucault in understanding power as both marginalizing (critique of domination) and productive (critique of freedom). Additionally, the transformative project of critical rhetoric as conceived by McKerrow is discursive intervention.

Performance Studies

Much like rhetoric, performance is an important site for the intervention of critical theory. In the 1980s, performance scholars debated the utility of critical theories in the interpretation of literature. In particular, the work of Marcuse and Adorno was influential early on in performance studies because of these two theorists' emphasis on aesthetics. Additionally, poststructuralist criticism provided ways of reading below the surface of literature to examine the undergirding ideologies in literary texts. Poststructuralism is also influential because it provides tools to understand how discourse constructs what people know and what they do. In particular, performance scholars are interested in Jacques Derrida's notion of *citationality*— that people's everyday verbal and corporeal performances are nonoriginal, constantly referencing past performances.

Finally, performance scholars are very much concerned with the second dimension of critical theory's intent—social transformation. Not only do performance scholars work toward social reform through discursive interventions, but they actively engage in reform through actual performance to change what people know, believe, and do.

Organizational Communication

Scholars of organizational communication have largely welcomed critical forms of analysis to the study of organizations and organizing. In particular, they have been interested in the ways that particular individuals or groups come to hold power in organizations. Additionally, they examine the way power functions in discursive and material practices within organizations. For example, Angela Trethewey uses critical theory as a framework to explore how ideologies of aging shape professional women's experiences at work. She finds that as they age, professional women experience loss, isolation, and diminished access to resources and at the same time deploy resistance strategies against the "decline" story offered by age ideology.

Intercultural Communication

It might seem obvious that scholars of culture and communication would be interested in dynamics of power among cultural groups, but critical studies of intercultural dynamics had a relatively late start in comparison to other foci within communication. Despite this late start, there is a growing contingent of intercultural work that examines the relations of power evident in dynamics between cultural groups. Much of this work explores the meanings attributed to differently classed, raced, gendered, national, sexual, or able-bodied individuals. For example, scholar Lisa Flores examines the mediated representations of Mexican immigrants to the United States in the 1920s and 1930s, finding that immigrants are not only represented as other to White U.S. citizens but are dehumanized in mediated accounts to justify deportation. Other critical modes of intercultural work involve investigating the ways that marginalized groups respond or resist oppression and examining the way power plays out in actual intercultural encounters and relations.

Conclusion

This review of critical theory has explicated the basic tenets of this school of research, identified its historical foundations, reviewed key terms, discussed prominent modes of criticism, and reviewed the influence of critical theory on the communication discipline. While no accounting of a school of inquiry such as critical theory can be complete, this discussion has hopefully provided an opening into the exciting possibilities of critical modes of analysis.

Sara L. McKinnon

See also Archeology and Genealogy; Critical Organizational Communication; Deconstruction; Feminist Communication Theories; Frankfurt School; Ideological Rhetoric; Ideology; Intercultural Communication Theories; Marxist Theory; Performance Theories; Postcolonial Theory; Poststructuralism; Pragmatics; Public Sphere; Rhetorical Theory

Further Readings

Farrell, T. B., & Aune, J. A. (1979). Critical theory and communication: A selective literature review. *Quarterly Journal of Speech, 65,* 93–120.

Flores, L. (2003). Constructing rhetorical borders: Peons, illegal aliens, and competing narratives of immigration. *Critical Studies in Mass Communication, 20,* 362–387.

Griffin, C. L. (2000). Rhetoricizing alienation: Mary Wollstonecraft and the rhetorical construction of women's oppression. In C. R. Burgchardt (Ed.), *Readings in rhetorical criticism* (2nd ed., pp. 507–526). State College, PA: Strata.

Hardt, H. (1992). *Critical communication studies: Communication, history, and theory in America.* New York: Routledge.

McGee, M. C. (1980). The "ideograph": A link between rhetoric and ideology. *Quarterly Journal of Speech, 66,* 1–16.

McKerrow, R. E. (1989). Critical rhetoric: Theory and praxis. *Communication Monographs, 56,* 91–111.

Mumby, D. K. (1997). The problem of hegemony: Rereading Gramsci for organizational communication studies. *Western Journal of Communication, 61,* 343–375.

Pollock, D., & Cox, R. J. (1991). Historicizing "reason": Critical theory, practice and postmodernity. *Communication Monographs, 58,* 170–178.

Trethewey, A. (2001). Reproducing and resisting the master narrative of decline: Midlife professional women's experiences of aging. *Management Communication Quarterly, 15*, 183–226.

Tyson, L. (2006). *Critical theory today: A user-friendly guide.* New York: Routledge.

CROSS-CULTURAL ADAPTATION THEORY

Around the world, millions of people relocate and cross cultural or subcultural boundaries each year. Although unique in individual circumstances, all strangers in an unfamiliar environment embark on the common project of establishing and maintaining, over time, a relatively stable and reciprocal relationship with the host environment. Young Yun Kim explains this phenomenon in her cross-cultural adaptation theory.

The theory is framed by three boundary conditions: (1) The strangers have had a primary socialization in one culture or subculture and have moved into a different and unfamiliar culture (or subculture), (2) they are at least minimally dependent on the host environment for meeting their personal and social needs, and (3) they are regularly engaged in firsthand communication experiences with that environment.

Kim laid the initial groundwork for this theory in 1976 in a study of Korean immigrants in the Chicago area, followed by a series of studies conducted among various other immigrant groups. A full-fledged theory was first presented in 1988, and a further updated and refined version in 2001. This theory has been widely utilized in research studies across social science disciplines including intercultural communication, mass communication, cross-cultural and social psychology, migration studies, education, social work, and business management.

A Communication Phenomenon

The theory is built on the premise that a person is an *open system* that coevolves with the sociocultural environment. Plasticity, or the ability to learn and change through communicative exchanges with the environment, is one of the most profound characteristics of the human mind and the very basis on which individuals adapt to conditions of the environment. Cross-cultural adaptation is, thus, regarded in this theory as the unfolding of the natural human tendency to struggle to regain an internal equilibrium in the face of adversarial environmental conditions.

By placing adaptation at the intersection of the person and the environment, the theory explains cross-cultural adaptation essentially as a process that occurs in and through communication activities. Underscored in this view is that communication is the necessary vehicle without which adaptation cannot take place, and that some degree of cross-cultural adaptation, no matter how minuscule, occurs as long as the individual remains engaged with the host environment. This systemic, communication-based conception elevates the ontological status of cross-cultural adaptation to the level of a panhuman phenomenon that must be treated not merely as a specific analytic research unit (such as an independent or dependent variable), but as the entirety of the evolutionary process an individual undergoes in relation to an unfamiliar environment.

The theory addresses two central questions: (1) How does the cross-cultural adaptation process unfold over time? and (2) What are the key factors that help explain the different speeds with which individuals achieve adaptive changes?

Process

The first question concerning the unfolding of cross-cultural adaptation over time is answered in the form of a *process model,* a theoretical representation of the process of a person's evolution toward increased person–environment fit. The theory explains that this evolutionary process inevitably accompanies *stress* in the individual psyche, a kind of identity conflict rooted in the desire to retain the habitual mind, on one hand, and the necessity to seek congruence with the new milieu on the other. The experience of stress produces a state of disequilibrium, often manifested in emotional lows of uncertainty, confusion, anxiety, cynicism, hostility, avoidance, or withdrawal.

Yet, no open system can stabilize itself forever. If it were so, nothing would come of evolution. The heightened self-awareness in the state of stress serves as the very force that propels strangers to overcome the predicament and partake in the act of *adaptation* through the active development of new habits. This is possible as they engage in forward-looking moves, striving to meet the challenge by acting on and responding to the environment. Stress, in this regard, is intrinsic to self-(re)organization and self-renewal.

What emerges from successful, long-term, and cumulative experiences of managing the stress–adaptation dialectic is a subtle and often imperceptible psychological *growth*. This growth entails an increased complexity in an individual's meaning system. Periods of stress pass as an individual works out new ways of handling problems, owing to the creative forces of self-reflexivity of the human mind.

The theory explains that, together, the three-pronged psychological phenomenon of stress, adaptation, and growth serves as the very force behind an individual's adaptive change over time. The *stress–adaptation–growth dynamic* does not play out in a smooth, steady, and linear progression, but in a dialectic, cyclic, and continual draw-back-to-leap pattern. Each stressful experience is responded to with a "draw-back," which, in turn, activates adaptive energy to help individuals reorganize themselves and leap forward. As growth in some areas always occurs at the expense of others, the adaptation process follows a pattern that juxtaposes psychological integration and disintegration, progression and regression.

The stress–adaptation–growth dynamic continues as new challenges present themselves in the host environment, with the generally forward and upward movement in the direction of less stress and of greater adaptation and growth. In this process, large and sudden changes indicative of the severity of difficulties an individual experiences in the host environment are likely to occur during the initial phase of exposure to a new culture. Over a prolonged period of undergoing internal change, the fluctuations of stress and adaptation become less intense or severe, leading to an overall calming trend.

Structure

The second question driving this theory calls for a set of key factors that account for the different speeds with which individuals move along the cross-cultural adaptation process. The theory answers this question in a *structural model*, in which key dimensions of factors that facilitate or impede the adaptation process are identified and their interrelationships articulated.

The theory locates the explanatory factors within the communicative interface of the stranger and the environment. In this communication framework, strangers' communication activities are grouped in two basic, interdependent categories: (1) (intra)*personal communication*, or the internal mental activities that occur within individuals, disposing and preparing them to act and react in certain ways in actual social situations; and (2) *social communication* that takes place whenever they participate in face-to-face or mediated forms of interactions with other people.

Personal Communication: Host Communication Competence

The successful adaptation of strangers is realized only when their personal communication systems sufficiently overlap with those of the natives. The capacity of strangers to appropriately and effectively receive and process information and to design and execute mental plans in initiating or responding to messages is labeled as *host communication competence*. Host communication competence facilitates the cross-cultural adaptation process directly and significantly. It serves as an instrumental, interpretive, and expressive means of coming to terms with the host environment.

The theory identifies key elements of host communication competence in three categories: (1) cognitive, (2) affective, and (3) operational. *Cognitive competence* includes such internal capabilities as the knowledge of the host culture and language, including the history, institutions, worldviews, beliefs, mores, norms, and rules of interpersonal conduct, among others. Language/culture learning is accompanied by a development of cognitive complexity, the structural refinement in an individual's internal information-processing ability. *Affective competence* facilitates cross-cultural adaptation by providing a motivational capacity to deal with various challenges of living in the host environment, including the willingness to make necessary changes in one's original cultural habits. It also includes the openness to new learning and the capacity to partake in the natives' emotional and aesthetic sensibilities. *Operational competence* allows strangers to enact their cognitive and affective capabilities outwardly, making it possible for them to choose the combinations of verbal and nonverbal behaviors that are appropriate and effective in specific social situations.

Host and Ethnic Social Communication

Directly and reciprocally, the development of host communication competence influences, and is influenced by, an increased participation in host social communication activities of the host environment. A stranger's interpersonal and mass communication experiences of the host environment are constrained by his or her host communication competence, while every host social communication event offers the stranger an opportunity for new cultural learning. *Host interpersonal communication*, in particular, helps strangers to obtain vital information and insight into the mind-sets and behaviors of the local people, thereby serving as the points of reference for a check and validation of their own behaviors. *Host mass communication* facilitates the adaptation of strangers by exposing strangers to the larger environment. Serving this function are various forms of mass communication such as radio and television programs, magazine and newspaper articles, movies, museum exhibits, theater performances, Internet Web sites, audiotapes, videotapes, and posters.

In many communities in contemporary societies, strangers' interpersonal and mass communication activities involve co-ethnics or co-nationals and home cultural experiences. *Ethnic interpersonal communication* activities provide strangers with access to their original cultural experiences, often rendering assistance to those who need material, informational, emotional, and other forms of social support. With the advent of Internet Web sites and direct satellite and cable broadcasts, strangers enjoy an increased access to various sources of *ethnic mass communication* that are produced locally or in their home country.

During the initial phases of relocation, when strangers lack host communication competence, ethnic social communication activities may serve adaptation-facilitating functions. Due to the relatively stress-free communication experience in dealing with their own ethnic individuals and media, ethnic communication experiences can offer temporary refuge and a support system. The theory explains, however, that heavy and prolonged reliance on ethnic social communication activities tends to help maintain strangers' original cultural habits and limit their opportunities to participate in the host environment.

Environment

To the extent that strangers participate in host social communication activities, the host environment exerts potentially adaptive influences on them. The nature of such influence, in turn, is shaped by the various characteristics of the host environment itself. The theory identifies three key environmental conditions affecting the stranger's adaptation process: (1) host receptivity, (2) host conformity pressure, and (3) ethnic group strength.

Host receptivity refers to the degree to which a given environment is structurally and psychologically accessible and open to strangers. A given society or community may extend welcoming attitudes toward particular groups of strangers, but not toward certain other groups. *Host conformity pressure*, the extent to which the environment challenges strangers to act in accordance with its language and cultural norms, varies as well across societies and communities. Culturally and ethnically heterogeneous environments such as large cosmopolitan cities tend to exert less conformity pressure on newcomers to change their original habitual ways. *Ethnic group strength*, on the other hand, tends to discourage the cross-cultural adaptation process of individual members. Large and active ethnic communities offer their members informational, emotional, and material support systems. Although such an ethnic support system can aid newcomers' initial cross-cultural adaptation, it also tends to exert a level of social pressure to maintain the ethnic practices and discourage an active participation in the host social communication activities.

Predisposition

Along with the conditions of the environment, the process of cross-cultural adaptation is affected by the internal conditions of individual strangers themselves. The theory identifies three key predispositional factors: (1) *preparedness,* (2) *ethnic proximity/distance,* and (3) *personality.*

Strangers come to their new environment with differing levels of *preparedness,* that is, the mental, emotional, and motivational readiness to deal with the new cultural environment, including the understanding of the host language and culture. Affecting such preparedness are formal and informal schooling and training in, and media exposure to, the host language and culture, contacts and experiences with members of the host society, as well as prior cross-cultural adaptation experiences in general. Strangers also differ in cultural, racial, and linguistic backgrounds. *Ethnic proximity* (or *ethnic distance*) serves as a relational concept with which a given stranger's ethnicity and the predominant ethnicity of the host environment are compared. A stranger whose ethnicity is similar to and compatible with that of the mainstream ethnicity of the surrounding community is likely to blend in with relative ease. In addition, strangers differ in their more or less enduring *personality traits.* Of particular interest are those personality resources that would help facilitate an individual's ability to endure adaptive stresses. The theory identifies *openness, strength,* and *positivity* as three particularly significant personality characteristics that enhance one's chances for successful cross-cultural adaptation.

Intercultural Transformation

Through a progression of internal change, strangers undergo a set of identifiable changes in their habitual patterns of cognitive, affective, and behavioral responses. The theory identifies three interrelated aspects of adaptive changes: (1) *functional fitness,* (2) *psychological health,* and (3) the emergence of an *intercultural identity.*

Through the repeated activities resulting in new cultural learning and self-organizing and reorganizing, strangers in time achieve an increased *functional fitness* vis-à-vis the demands of the host environment. Successfully adapted strangers have accomplished a sense of ease, efficacy, and a desired level of effective working relationship with the host environment. Closely associated with the increased functional fitness is a higher level of *psychological health* reflected in an increased sense of personal well-being and satisfaction in one's life in the host environment. These functional and psychological facets of intercultural transformation are often accompanied by a subtle change in one's identity. Employing the concept *intercultural identity,* the theory explains that as individuals advance in the cross-cultural adaptation process, their identity orientations undergo a gradual and largely unconscious transformation toward less categorical and more complex ones. That is, individuals become better able to see the common humanity among different cultures and ethnicities and locate the points of consent and complementarity beyond obvious difference and contention.

Theorems

The above-described dimensions of factors constitute the structural model in Kim's cross-cultural adaptation theory. In this model, all the linkages indicate mutual stimulations (and not unidirectional causations). Directly or indirectly, each of these factors facilitates or impedes the adaptation process of an individual. Like a locomotive engine, the workings of each unit operating in this process affect, and are affected by, the workings of all other units. Out of this dynamic interface among the dimensions and factors arise the fluctuating experiences of stress, adaptation, and growth—an emerging development accompanying an increasing level of congruence and ease with respect to the host environment, the original culture, and the ongoing identity transformation itself.

Together, these factors offer a system of explanations as to why every incidence of cross-cultural adaptation takes place at its own pace and why some individuals are more successful than others in their cross-cultural transitions and eventual attainment of fitness vis-à-vis the host environment. The interlocking relationships identified in the structural model are formally specified in a total of 21 theorems, generalizable and predictive statements of a functional relationship, such as: The greater the host communication competence, the greater the participation in host social (interpersonal, mass) communication (Theorem 1).

Looking Ahead

Although intended to explain the adaptive experiences of individuals who relocate to a new and different cultural or subcultural environment, the core concepts and the theoretical arguments are applicable to the broader context of increasing intercultural exposures brought about by the process of globalization. Whether at home or on foreign soil, numerous people the world over are being challenged to undergo at least some experiences of the stress–adaptation–growth dynamic. Through direct contacts as well as via mass media and other technological means of communication, people around the world are increasingly exposed to the images and sounds of once-distant cultures. In many urban centers, local people are routinely coming in contact with foreign-born individuals.

This emerging phenomenon of crossing cultures at home promises a new chapter in the continuing development of the cross-cultural adaptation theory. For now, the theory speaks to a uniquely human plasticity to adapt to the increasingly intercultural environment. Through the concept of *intercultural identity*, the theory suggests a potentially viable vision of being oriented to oneself and to the world in an open and flexible manner. In the project of cross-cultural adaptation, the theory suggests the new possibility for individuals anywhere in the world to embark on a path of personal growth, in which they stretch themselves out of the familiar and reach for a deepened and more inclusive understanding of human conditions, including their own.

Young Yun Kim

See also Communibiology; Communication Theory of Identity; Competence Theories; Complexity and Communication; Contextual Theory of Interethnic Communication; Co-Orientation Theory; Cross-Cultural Communication; Intercultural Communication Competence; Intercultural Communication Theories; System Theory; Transculturation

Further Readings

Bertalanffy, L. (1975). General system theory. In B. D. Ruben & J. Y. Kim (Eds.), *General systems theory and human communication* (pp. 6–32). Rochelle Park, NJ: Hayden Books.

Ford, D. H., & Lerner, R. M. (1992). *Developmental systems theory: An integrative approach*. Newbury Park, CA: Sage.

Jantsch, E. (1980). *The self-organizing universe: Scientific and human implications of the emerging paradigm of evolution*. New York: Pergamon.

Kim, Y. Y. (1988). *Communication and cross-cultural adaptation: An integrative theory*. Clevedon, UK: Multilingual Matters.

Kim, Y. Y. (2001). *Becoming intercultural: An integrative theory of communication and cross-cultural adaptation*. Thousand Oaks, CA: Sage.

Kim, Y. Y. (2008). Toward intercultural personhood: Globalization and a way of being [Special issue]. *International Journal of Intercultural Relations, 32,* 359–368.

Kim, Y. Y., & Kim, Y. S. (2004). The role of the host environment in cross-cultural adaptation: A comparative analysis of Korean expatriates in the United States and their American counterparts in South Korea. *Asian Communication Research, 1,* 5–25.

Kim, Y. Y., Lujan, P., & Dixon, L. (1998). "I can walk both ways": Identity integration of American Indians in Oklahoma. *Human Communication Research, 25,* 252–274.

CROSS-CULTURAL COMMUNICATION

Cross-cultural communication is normally thought of as communication that takes place between members of whole cultures in contact or between their cultural spokespersons or representatives. Cross-cultural communication is distinguished from *intracultural communication,* which occurs between people sharing a common culture, and *intercultural communication,* which refers to exchanges in interpersonal settings between individuals from different cultures. William B. Gudykunst identifies both *intercultural communication* and *cross-cultural communication* as segments of *intergroup communication.*

When researchers want to compare or contrast the communication of people from different cultures and explain how communication varies from one culture to another, then a *cross-cultural communication* study occurs. William B. Gudykunst and Carmen M. Lee identify this type of research as among the several approaches for incorporating culture into communication theories. Such theorizing must link dimensions of cultural variability directly with the cultural norms and rules that influence the communication behavior being explained. It must avoid oversimplifying the process or inappropriately coupling the way that the cultural variables influence cultural norms and rules or the reverse. This kind of work is of interest to several academic fields, including anthropology, communication, international relations, psychology, and sociology, and has been applied to concepts such as attitudes, beliefs, cognition, cross-cultural business and training, journalism, language and linguistics, mass media, nonverbal cues, organizational culture, perceptions, stereotypes, thought-patterning, and values.

Theoretical Dimensions

Several sources of cultural variation have been investigated. These include (a) *power distance,* or the degree to which cultures include status and power hierarchies versus relative equality; (b) *individualism–collectivism,* or the extent to which cultures value individual personal identity versus community identity; (c) *self-construals,* or the ways that people see themselves; and (d) *low and high context,* or the degree to which a culture relies on unstated relational dynamics versus direct verbal communication.

A number of important theories have made use of these cross-cultural distinctions. Examples include Stella Ting-Toomey's 1985 *face negotiation theory,* which illustrates how communicators from different cultures manage varying practices of facework; Young Yun Kim's 1993 *conversational constraints theory,* which looks at how people from different cultures choose various strategies of communication; Judee Burgoon's 1978 *expectancy violations theory,* focusing on how communicators from different cultures respond when their expectations are violated; and William B. Gudykunst's 1995 *anxiety/uncertainty management theory,* which focuses on how communicators reduce uncertainty and anxiety in cross-cultural situations. As another example, *communication accommodation theory,* attributed to Howard Giles and others,

looks at the ways in which communicators accommodate various cultural practices in cross-cultural situations.

In addition, cross-cultural investigations could focus on a variety of other important variables. Michael H. Prosser in his 1978 book, *The Cultural Dialogue,* identified several problems that could guide this work. Among other things, it could investigate the role of conflict and conflict resolution, the ways in which communication is used for control and power, the impact of technology and especially information technology, cultural stability and cultural change, cultural imperialism, and cultural dependency or interdependency.

Steve J. Kulich recommends a nine-level analysis offering themes for cross-cultural research in which culture can be viewed in terms of (1) propagated mythic ideals; (2) mainstream promotion or mass trends; (3) model-citizen norms; (4) expected behavior mechanics; (5) integrated meshworks, which includes a set of real or imagined networks; (6) mediated metaphors; (7) mindless personal responses to familiarity; (8) personal matrix options, such as recognizing that binary theories at each extreme end of a spectrum must realize that instead some cultures are both traditional and modern at the same time; and (9) personalized meaning. In the context of social science research, Kulich proposes that an integrated grid can be developed in the cross-cultural study of communication that incorporates cultural, subcultural, contextual, and individual levels of culture. An integrated grid includes cultural socialization that is passed down vertically or horizontally within a culture; socially constructed perceptions within the context of cultural groups; and personally interpreted meanings, which include conceptual perceptions within social groups and reflective and relative meanings, leading to intercontextual studies. Kulich explains that at the cultural level, one needs to consider such issues as ideal myths, mass trends, and model citizen norms. At the subcultural or contextual level, he proposes that expected behavioral mechanics, integrated meshworks, and mediated metaphors need to be considered, and at the individual level, scholars need to interpret their own mindless responses, personal matrix options, and personalized meanings.

Illustrative Examples

An early longitudinal example of major cross-cultural research efforts includes Charles E. Osgood's *Cross-Cultural Universals of Affective Meaning Project,* designed to find nearly universal factors of meaning across approximately 50 cultures. In this multinational study, 100 teenaged boys in each culture were chosen to assess 100 terms for their understandings of *goodness* or *badness, power* or *lack of power,* and *swiftness* or *slowness.* This study tested and confirmed the hypotheses that regardless of language or culture, human beings use the same qualifying and descriptive framework in allocating affective meanings of concepts involving attitudes, feelings, stereotypes, and values.

Desmond Morris's study of middle-aged male usage of nonverbal gesture cues in 25 European cultures, described in his 1980 book *Gestures,* hypothesized and confirmed that middle-aged men living closer to the Mediterranean Sea, and already strongly fixed in their own national culture behaviors, would utilize far more exaggerated and bolder gestures than would those middle-aged men living in the northern European or Scandinavian countries. Also, the hypothesis that the former group would have more gestures with sexual implications than the northern European or Scandinavian cultures was generally confirmed. Later, in his 1994 book, *Bodytalk: A World Guide to Gestures,* more cross-cultural nonverbal studies were significantly explored in a much wider geographical range.

In the 9-day 1974 bicultural Japanese–American research conference in Nihonmatsu, Japan, the research team hypothesized that Japanese participants would be more task oriented and Americans would be more process oriented. Not surprisingly, it was found that the younger Japanese and American participants were more process oriented, while the older Japanese and Americans were more task oriented, thus disconfirming the hypothesis. Michael H. Prosser's book *The Cultural Dialogue* discusses this research conference, providing the essence of the bicultural dialogue that occurred there.

One of the most important cross-cultural studies of national attitudes and values was Dutch sociologist Geert Hofstede's analysis of 116,000 responses. Based on this study, he initially proposed the development of four national cultural dimensions—*uncertainty avoidance, power distance, individualism versus collectivism,* and *masculinity versus femininity.* Michael Harris Bond added a fifth dimension in 1987 called *Confucian dynamism,* also known as *short-term versus long-term orientation.* Uncertainty avoidance specifies the level to which members of a national culture avoid or accept uncertainty; power distance is the extent to which less powerful members of organizations and institutions accept unequal distributions of power. Masculinity versus femininity, more recently described as *aggressiveness versus nurturing,* emphasizes how a national culture manages its gender issues.

Individualism versus collectivism, initially proposed by cross-cultural psychologist Harry C. Triandis, focuses on whether members of a national culture are more oriented to *individual* versus *collective* or *communitarian values.* The Chinese Culture Connection in 1987 proposed that Hofstede's Western bias needs to be supplemented by a Chinese methodological bias of Confucianism. This cultural variability dimension has three aspects: *status relationships; integration,* or *harmony with others;* and *moral discipline.* In 2008, Hofstede added two new dimensions: *indulgence versus restraint* and *monumentalism versus fleximility* or *flexible humility.* These new dimensions have been articulated in his essay "Dimensionalizing Culture: Hofstede Model Context," in Steve J. Kulich and Michael H. Prosser's forthcoming coedited book *Cross-Cultural Value Studies,* and still need testing.

Western Versus Non-Western Cross-Cultural Problems

Many early cross-cultural studies focused on comparisons between American and Japanese, American and European, or American and Soviet cultural patterns. More recently, considerable research has emphasized contrasting cultural aspects of the Americans and Chinese or Chinese and other Westerners. Michael Harris Bond recommends that while these bicultural studies are useful, including those by cross-cultural psychologists, they use Western research methods to deal with indigenous cultural patterns. He urges cross-cultural researchers to move toward more pancultural studies, as Hofstede's studies have done, and that for serious reliability, at least 10 cultural groups are needed when standard social science statistical measurements are used.

CHANG, Hui-ching proposes that in building cross-cultural theory incorporating both Western and Asian ideologies, the central starting point for several Asian societies must be Confucianism. This requires the recognition that Asian cross-cultural theories about relationships, intimacy, interpersonal communication, and intercultural communication have Confucian roots. However, at the same time, Confucianism must be integrated with modern theories and must compete with both ancient and contemporary Western and other Asian theories. Her research program, leading to the potential construction of cross-cultural theories, first explored folk concepts leading to relationships developed in Chinese society and then showed how these relationships develop between the East and the West through cultural exchanges such as popular books, workshops, and seminars. Finally, she shows how these relationship ideals develop and expand microculturally through the ordinary language that Chinese use in their daily lives. Fundamentally, she believes that cross-cultural theory construction for a society such as China must concentrate on how the Chinese create these relationships through their modern daily use of language. Cross-cultural researchers in such a setting ideally should be bilingual, both in a Western language and in Chinese.

HWANG, Kwang-Kuo also argues that the development of social scientific cross-cultural research in the indigenous Asian setting is problematic because Western social science methods are not always appropriate to study indigenous Asian cultural factors. He believes that Western social science theories, or the *scientific microworld* versus the indigenous *Asian lifeworld* for intellectuals in non-Western countries, have serious limitations as the philosophy of science for constructing a scientific microworld is essentially a product of alien cultures inconsistent with practical Asian cultural traditions. Thus, a cross-cultural communication researcher must construct a tentative theory to solve scientific problems caused by inconsistencies between Western theories and the observed phenomena or results of experiments in more traditional Asian societies, contradictions within a system or theory, and conflicts between the two types of theories. For example, formal justice in Western scientific cross-cultural studies includes such basic elements as authority in an unequal relationship but does not practically consider the notion of Confucian respect for the superior in determining what is just.

Referring to cross-cultural communication studies for Chinese scholars as illustrative, GUAN, Shije notes several problems for China, and by implication for other Asian cultures: (a) More dialectical research is conducted than empirical studies; (b) too much research is conducted in individual disciplines rather than on an interdisciplinary basis; (c) more general introductions are provided than on specific topics with Chinese characteristics; (d) more Sino–U.S. research is done than comparisons of China with other countries; and (e) more international studies than domestic cross-cultural research are done of different Chinese communities in the mainland, Hong Kong, Taiwan, and in the Chinese diaspora. He argues that this singularity of research methodology and focus has been a bottleneck in restraining further in-depth cross-cultural Chinese and Asian communication research.

Summary

It is impossible to completely separate the theoretical study of intercultural and cross-cultural communication. Gudykunst notes that before the late 1970s, when he began his doctoral studies, there were few, if any, reliable and valid theories for the study of either type of communication. As the study of intercultural and cross-cultural theories has matured, many new actual theories have been developed, tested, and confirmed or disconfirmed. Still more cross-cultural theories will develop over time that can be tested in a reliable and valid manner. New social science statistical measurements can help researchers hypothesize and test these theories, adding to the mature development of cross-cultural theoretical constructs.

Michael H. Prosser

See also Accommodation Theory; Asian Communication Theory; Confucian Communication Theory; Conversational Constraints Theory; Cultural Types Theories; Culture and Communication; Expectancy Violations Theory; Face Negotiation Theory; Facework Theories; Intercultural Communication

Theories; International Communication Theories; Uncertainty Management Theories; Values Studies: History and Concepts; Values Theory: Sociocultural Dimensions and Frameworks

Further Readings

Chen, G.-M., & Starosta, W. J. (2005). *Foundations of intercultural communication*. Lanham, MD: UPA.

Gudykunst, W. B. (Ed.). (2003). *Cross-cultural and intercultural communication*. Thousand Oaks, CA: Sage.

Hofstede, G. (2001). *Culture's consequences* (2nd ed.). Thousand Oaks, CA: Sage.

Kulich, S. J., & Prosser, M. H. (Eds.). (2007). *Intercultural perspectives on Chinese communication*. Shanghai: Shanghai Foreign Language Education Press.

Kulich, S. J., & Prosser, M. H. (Eds.). (in press). *Cross-cultural value applications*. Shanghai: Shanghai Foreign Education Language Press.

Kulich, S. J., & Prosser, M. H. (Eds.). (in press). *Cross-cultural value studies*. Shanghai: Shanghai Foreign Education Language Press.

Prosser, M. H. (Ed.). (1973). *Intercommunication among nations and peoples*. New York: Harper & Row.

Prosser, M. H. (1978). *The cultural dialogue: An introduction to intercultural communication*. Boston: Houghton Mifflin.

Prosser, M. H., & Sitaram, K. S. (Eds.). (1999). *Civic discourse: Intercultural, international and global media*. Westport, CT: Ablex.

Samovar, L. A., Porter, R. E., & McDonald, E. R. (2008). *Intercultural communication: A reader* (12th ed.). Belmont, CA: Wadsworth.

Sitaram, K. S., & Prosser, M. H. (Eds.). (1998). *Civic discourse: Multiculturalism, cultural diversity, and global communication*. Westport, CT: Ablex.

CROSS-CULTURAL DECISION MAKING

Organizations of today are becoming increasingly multicultural. Workers, managers, as well as professionals are crossing national boundaries and, as a result, facing a variety of intercultural conflicts. While there are numerous factors involved in such conflicts, differences in the nature and style of decision making seem to be one of the major sources of confusion and frustration among the interacting members of such organizations.

Organizational theorists and psychologists as well as small-group communication scholars have argued for years about how people make decisions. Many articles and books have been written on decision making in relation to leadership, planning, and group process. Statistical decision making is also a popular area for study in the West, where decision making has generally been considered as an individual mental process involving the identification of a problem, consideration of the problem, and selection of the course of action for solving the problem. However, in Japan, for example, people do not seem to make decisions in the Western sense of the word. Decisions might be made somewhere by someone, but it is difficult to clearly identify the locus of the decision.

The realities of decision making in various parts of the world have not been thoroughly examined. In 1951, Fred N. Kerlinger asserted that the manner of reaching decisions is related to the patterns of thinking, because most people use, almost without thinking about or questioning it, the processes that have been handed down to them as part of their cultural heritage. Edward Stewart developed a theory of cross-cultural decision making by asserting that although decision making is rooted in a universal structure of cognition, once these structures are transformed and function as processes or operations, their evaluation and frequency differ from society to society. He further argues that decision making is a process or form bridging the gap between the internal mental process and action, and therefore, the values and assumptions embodied in different cultures affect the manner and rationality of decision making. Hence, more research is needed on cross-cultural decision making, comparing decision-making styles across cultures.

U.S. American and Japanese Decision Making

Decision making in organizations is complex in nature and form and differs greatly, depending on the particular context in which such decisions are made. For the purpose of comparison, however, research indicates that there are at least four components that can be examined cross-culturally: (1) the decision maker, (2) the process and nature of discussion, (3) temporal aspects of decision making, and (4) mode of arriving at a decision.

The first component in decision making is the decision maker. In most U.S. organizations, the individual is the decision maker. The leader of the group is in a position to perceive a problem that requires solution. After consulting with some specialists or collecting relevant information, the leader selects one of the alternative plans for solution. Stewart argues that throughout one's upbringing, the American individual is encouraged to decide for himself, develop her own opinion, solve his own problems, have her own things, and in general learn to view the world through the point of the self. Because of these strong attachments of the self to the decision maker, the individual is likely to believe he or she is the locus of decision making even when forced to accept the effects of others' decisions on his or her life.

In contrast, it is difficult to see who the actual decision maker is in Japanese organizations. The role of the leader is to bring up the proposed idea and facilitate the discussion among small groups. The leader does not have to have special, professional, or technical knowledge about the subject matter. Rather, what is needed as a leader is to grasp the flow of discussion by being sensitive to the emotional feelings of participants.

In the second component of decision making—the process and nature of discussion—the leader of the group in U.S. organizations often holds meetings where the leader proposes an idea, explains the background leading to the proposal, and asks participants to judge whether the proposal is good enough to be approved or not. In other words, discussion continues through the stated agenda, and agreement is often reached after frank exchange of opinions among group members.

Discussion in Japanese meetings, on the other hand, might be perceived as somewhat ceremonial or ritualistic. The proposal, mostly agreed on through prior consultation among the members concerned, will be presented at the meeting. Even if the group is unable to reach agreement in prior discussion, the leader will not put the proposed idea on the agenda at the formal meeting.

In the third component of decision making or its temporal dimension, promptness is the utmost concern of members in U.S. organizations. Before the meeting is held, the agenda will be sent out in advance to group members, either as documents or in e-mails. At the meeting, the time will be spent sequentially moving from proposal to explanation, and then to question and answers, often to be followed by voting. While decisions themselves are made swiftly, chances are that the implementation of decisions will be slow as the members concerned must be persuaded to go along with it.

In Japanese organizations, the meeting is likely to last until agreement is reached. What is valued in the meeting is that everyone spends some time together sitting face-to-face to consider the proposal. The participants may disclose their own opinions with much reservation. In such a case, the meeting will take an extremely long time until a decision is reached. However, once the decision is made, its execution is swift and thorough, as everyone concerned is well aware of how to carry out the proposed decision.

In the fourth component, mode of arriving at a decision, the typical U.S. American mode of decision making is either by announcement on the part of the leader or by majority voting. The leader tries hard to push through the proposal. The leader is expected to explain the decision and to offer the others reasons for considering such a proposal. The deliberation is focused on whether the proposal can be either supported or rejected.

In Japan, all possible effort will be made to achieve consensus before and during the meeting. The leader serves as a moderator, presiding over the meeting and working to reach consensus on the proposal. In the process, participants might say that the meeting went well, and the will of all the members is solidified so that acceptance and implementation of the proposal becomes possible.

Communication Styles

Communication style also differs cross-culturally during the process of decision making. According to Kume, two contrastive prototypes of communication styles in the process of decision making have emerged from the research: *mawashi* and *tooshi. Mawashi* (a Japanese expression that means to circulate or rotate) is defined as a way of reaching consensus by passing around a particular view almost endlessly among members of a group, whereas *tooshi* (which in Japanese means to push through or have one's own way) is defined as a direct communication style of an individual's expressing his or her view clearly so that the idea can be accepted by all the members concerned or at least accepted by all through majority voting.

In *mawashi* style, people communicate by circulating their ideas or hinting at something indirectly, while in *tooshi* style a leader's idea is adopted as long as it is convincing enough to everyone concerned. What is emphasized in *tooshi* style is the persuasiveness on the part of the leader, which is in a sharp contrast to *mawashi* style, in which you are concerned about how your message is interpreted by the other people involved. By circulating your ideas in the form of indirection, polite expressions, or even self-deprecatory expressions, the other members of the groups are engaged, so to speak, in a synchronization of thoughts and feelings.

This simplistic dichotomy of *mawashi* and *tooshi* is merely intended to emphasize that there might be profound differences in the manner by which people of different cultural backgrounds communicate. This also indicates that any two cultural groups might have different perceptions and approaches to decision making in meetings. It also implies that even within the same organization, the above two styles can be interchangeably employed, depending on the nature of the organization, its leadership, the kind of decision to be made, and the attitudes of participants toward the meeting.

The understanding of culture in decision making should not be limited to national culture, but could be extended to subcultures or co-cultures. For example, a detailed case study was conducted by Lea P. Stewart in 1985 to illustrate the conflict resulting from sharply different styles of decision making between engineers and nontechnical managers. Furthermore, because decision making naturally involves an ethical dimension, the question of who should be responsible for the decision can be cross-culturally explored, even though the question of accountability in another culture is not considered as important as in the United States. Continued research on cross-cultural decision making can be expected to continue to provide useful information for those who are working in multicultural organizations.

Teruyuki Kume

See also Cross-Cultural Communication; Culture and Communication; Effective Intercultural Workgroup Communication Theory; Group Communication Theories; Organizational Communication Theories

Further Readings

Adler, N. J. (2002). *International dimensions of organizational behavior*. Cincinnati, OH: South-Western/Thomson.

Kume, T. (2007). Contrastive prototypes of communication styles in decision-making: *Mawashi* style vs. *tooshi* style. In M. Hinner (Ed.), *The influence of culture in the world of business* (pp. 211–227). New York: Peter Lang.

Oetzel, J. G. (2005). Effective intercultural workgroup communication theory. In W. B. Gudykunst (Ed.), *Theorizing about intercultural communication* (pp. 351–371). Thousand Oaks, CA: Sage.

Stewart, E. C. (1985). Culture and decision-making. In W. Gudykunst, L. P. Stewart, & S. Ting-Toomey (Eds.), *Communication, culture and organizational processes* (pp. 177–211). Beverly Hills, CA: Sage.

Stewart, L. P. (1985). Subjective culture and organizational decision-making. In W. B. Gudykunst, L. P. Stewart, & S. Ting-Toomey (Eds.), *Communication, culture and organizational processes* (pp. 212–230). Beverly Hills, CA: Sage.

CULTIVATION THEORY

Cultivation, also known as *cultivation theory* or *cultivation analysis*, is the area of communication research that investigates relationships between exposure to television and beliefs and attitudes about the world. Briefly, cultivation hypothesizes that heavy viewers of television will be more likely to hold beliefs and conceptions about the world that are congruent with what they see on television. For example, television programs are often seen to be highly violent; cultivation hypothesizes that heavy viewers of television will be more likely to see the world as a violent place.

Cultivation was an outgrowth of the *Cultural Indicators* project, a research program begun by George Gerbner at the Annenberg School for Communication in the late 1960s. The Cultural Indicators project began by documenting levels of violence and other socially relevant information (such as portrayals of women and minorities) in prime-time and children's programs. As the project began to assert that, for instance, television was overtly and overly violent, cultivation was developed as a way to ascertain whether viewing contributed in any way to viewers' conceptions and beliefs about the world.

The basic hypothesis of cultivation, though questioned by some, is that watching a great deal of television will be associated with a tendency to hold specific and distinct conceptions of reality, conceptions that are congruent with the most consistent and pervasive images and values of the medium. Yet there has been a great deal of interest in, criticism of, debate about, and support for the basic idea of cultivation, a research tradition that continues to be strong over 30 years after its inception.

The first cultivation results were introduced by George Gerbner and Larry Gross in 1976, in a *Journal of Communication* article titled "Living With Television: The Violence Profile." In addition to presenting results showing relatively high levels of televised violence on the major networks, Gerbner and Gross showed that heavy television viewers were more likely to overestimate the proportion of people involved in law enforcement and were more likely to say that others can't be trusted and to overestimate their own chances of being a victim of violence. Such findings eventually led to the notion of the *mean world syndrome*, in which heavy viewers are more likely to see the world as a scary, mean, violent, and dangerous place. This work led to a profusion of tests of the cultivation hypothesis in many different domains, but first there were criticisms to deal with.

Criticisms

Soon after the appearance of the cultivation hypothesis and its early tests, various criticisms were leveled from social scientists. Some criticisms were offered from a "humanistic" perspective, arguing that viewers interpret violence very differently and that aggregating responses to survey questions would miss these differences. Gerbner and Gross defended cultivation theory against these criticisms, arguing that individuals would certainly be likely to have different interpretations of violence but that aggregate patterns were also meaningful. They suggested that tests of such

patterns were themselves useful for determining whether or not television's messages, seen as an overall system, were in any way related to viewers' conceptions. As has been found consistently since Gerbner and Gross's original study, viewing has shown a small but significant relationship with viewers' conceptions, often over and above controls for other important variables.

Other criticisms claiming to disconfirm cultivation were offered from countries such as Great Britain, where similar results were not found. In this case, however, it seemed clear that differences in the programming systems between the two countries could be a major explanatory factor. Since then, numerous studies of cultivation have been carried out in countries other than the United States, many confirming cultivation.

Another criticism was that cultivation might really be an artifact of the fact that people living in high-crime areas might watch more television; thus, cultivation would be a spurious artifact of this three-way relationship. In response to these criticisms, Gerbner and his colleagues found that fear of crime was actually enhanced by television viewing in the high-crime areas, a phenomenon they termed *resonance*. This term was meant to denote a phenomenon in which the lived experience of the individual would be confirmed in the television world, resulting in higher cultivation relationships for those individuals.

Mainstreaming

Other criticisms used multivariate statistical techniques to show that cultivation relationships would disappear if researchers controlled for other important variables. Indeed, in most cases, simple cultivation relationships are often reduced or eliminated when multiple controls are applied. However, at about the time these criticisms were appearing, Gerbner and his colleagues were reanalyzing data with an eye toward specifying when and where the cultivation relationships might be stronger. The most important idea to emerge from these analyses was that of *mainstreaming*.

Mainstreaming is the phenomenon in which groups that would otherwise differ on opinions and beliefs about issues become more similar to one another when they view television heavily. The idea is that television's message system draws its heavy viewers closer to a mainstream position. Thus, for instance, while liberals and conservatives would be expected to disagree on an issue such as whether abortion should be available (and they do), the difference is much smaller between liberals and conservatives who are heavy viewers. Gerbner and his colleagues eventually saw mainstreaming as working toward a blurring of views and ideology toward a somewhat conservative mainstream that would be favored by the corporate-controlled media system. Mainstreaming and resonance did not completely resolve the debates about cultivation, but the cultivation hypothesis did not go away and has been tested dozens of times in various studies since the 1970s.

Findings

After the violence results emerged, cultivation studies were carried out on a variety of issues. Studies found that television viewing was associated with a tendency toward greater conservatism. Television appeared to cultivate less tolerance of minorities and out-groups. For instance, several studies showed that heavy viewers were more likely to favor keeping women in "traditional" sex roles, which was not surprising given that women were outnumbered by men on television and often shown in traditional roles such as housewife, secretary, or nurse. Television was shown to also cultivate less tolerance for groups that were not shown very much, such as gay men and lesbians. The notion of *symbolic annihilation* suggested that invisibility in the world of television could be as important as actively negative portrayals.

The list of issues that cultivation has addressed is virtually endless. While a majority of studies have concentrated on issues such as violence and crime, ideology, and the roles of different demographic groups, other questions have been investigated. These include perceptions of science, religion, the environment, and belief in the paranormal, among many others. Overall, the published studies have consistently shown that television viewing shows small but significant relationships with perceptions about many phenomena, often after controlling for a variety of other variables. As would be expected, the studies have grown in methodological sophistication. Also, the community of researchers testing cultivation grew; while Gerbner and colleagues conducted many of the original studies, researchers around the world have picked up cultivation ideas. Even now, and despite enormous changes in the media system, cultivation is still generally accepted as one of the most important and testable propositions within media effects research.

Meta-Analysis

In 1997, Michael Morgan and James Shanahan meta-analyzed 52 independent studies of cultivation, representing over 20 years of cultivation work. Meta-analysis is used as an alternative to the traditional narrative literature review. It compiles results from all extant studies, converts their findings to a similar metric, and then weights the effects for sample size to produce an overall estimate of the "true" cultivation effect. While single studies are more open to problems such as sampling error, meta-analyses can give a truer picture by virtue of their compilation of many studies, resulting in a much larger sample. Morgan and Shanahan found that, on average, the cultivation effect was about .09 (expressed in Pearson's r). Thus, they argued, as Gerbner and Gross had done earlier, that television viewing does make a small but significant contribution to viewers' perceptions of reality.

They found, however, that the effect size differed when tested in different ways. Small sample sizes tended to yield larger estimates, for instance. Expanding on this meta-analysis in 1999, Shanahan and Morgan found, for instance, that cultivation effects were higher for self-identified liberals than moderates or conservatives. That is, while self-identified liberals differ from conservatives on many issues, the differences between light- and heavy-viewing self-identified liberals are the most marked, with heavy-viewing liberals scoring much closer to the moderates and conservatives. This finding is very consistent with the notion of mainstreaming discussed above. All in all, then, the meta-analysis showed that cultivation has revealed a fairly consistent pattern of effect, with an effect size not dissimilar to that revealed in meta-analyses of other theories of media effects.

Psychological Mechanisms

Early on, some investigators opined that cultivation contained no psychological or cognitive explanation of how cultivation worked. While Gerbner and his colleagues were less interested in this question—they tended to be more focused on television from the macrosocial perspective—others put forth tentative explanations. Some early studies sought to break down the cultivation process into steps, such as *acquisition* and *construction*. In the first step, viewers would acquire knowledge from their accumulated viewing experience, which would then be cognitively aggregated into a view of the world consistent with television's messages. Such explanations tended to differ between *first-order beliefs* (simple perceptions of facts about the world) and *second-order beliefs* (more complex views of the world, such as attitudes or ideology). However, while these terms remain in use in some studies, Gerbner and associates did not find them useful and abandoned them as a potential cognitive explanation.

Perceived reality was another mechanism offered to explain cultivation. It was argued that viewers who saw television as more real would be more likely to show evidence of cultivation. Though some studies were done with suggestive results, perceived reality never gained acceptance as the cognitive explanation of cultivation.

Another approach focused on memory. Researchers argued that viewers' memories about a topic could provide a better prediction of beliefs than media exposure. However, few convincing tests of this idea were offered. Elaborating on this idea, other researchers proposed that people who confuse news for fiction would be more likely to give television answers (i.e., answer questions with information received from television), and some evidence was shown for this.

However, the most convincing evidence for a cognitive explanation of cultivation came from L. J. Shrum, who wondered whether viewers consider judgments of reality at all when answering questions about the world. He used a heuristic model to explain why heavy viewers would give television answers. Simply put, he argues that most people do not give thoughtful answers to questions; rather, they rely on whatever information seems most readily available to them. They do not systematically scan their memories for relevant information; rather, they take what is most readily available. Shrum has conducted many studies that show that heavy television viewers will give

television answers to questions (such as, for instance, perceptions about material wealth), and they will give answers more quickly than light viewers will. These results suggest that television viewers have simply accumulated more information about various television-related topics from television than light viewers have. The fact that they answer more quickly indicates that they are accessing this information more heuristically than systematically. That is, heavy viewers are not rationally considering their options; they are just drawing from the stories, images, and representations they have seen on television more frequently and more rapidly than light viewers are. As of now, Shrum's ideas stand as the most plausible account of how cultivation works psychologically.

Future of Cultivation

Much is changing in the media world. When Gerbner began investigating cultivation, there were three dominant television networks; now there is a plethora of cable channels available. And other sources of information and entertainment exist that can compete with television: videogames, the Internet, VCRs/DVDs, and the like. For some, this means that the era of cultivation is over, as viewers can choose and manage their own program choices. As some of these changes emerged, however, Gerbner argued that the media world was still a corporate-controlled entity and that media industries would find ways to dominate the world of storytelling and connect it to advertising.

Nevertheless, it remains to be seen whether cultivation effects will hold up over the long term. Other investigators are pushing toward questions such as whether exposure to specific genres of television produces cultivation effects. Others are looking at long-term questions, such as whether cultivation is a theory of social stasis, or how cultivation deals with social changes. With the existence of data sets that now cover more than 40 years, researchers are only beginning to speculate about television's role in the processes of social change.

James Shanahan

See also Broadcasting Theories; Cultural Indicators; Media and Mass Communication Theories; Media Effects Theories

Further Readings

Gerbner, G., & Gross, L. (1976). Living with television: The violence profile. *Journal of Communication, 26,* 173–199.

Morgan, M. (Ed.). (2002). *Against the mainstream: Selected writings of George Gerbner.* New York: Peter Lang.

Morgan, M., & Shanahan, J. (1997). Two decades of cultivation research: An appraisal and meta-analysis. In B. Burleson (Ed.), *Communication yearbook 20* (pp. 1–45). Thousand Oaks, CA: Sage.

Shanahan, J., & Morgan, M. (1999). *Television and its viewers: Cultivation theory and research.* London: Cambridge University Press.

Shrum, L. J. (1995). Assessing the social influence of television: A social cognition perspective. *Communication Research, 22,* 402–429.

Signorielli, N., & Morgan, M. (Eds.). (1990). *Cultivation analysis: New directions in media effects research.* Newbury Park, CA: Sage.

CULTURAL CONTRACTS THEORY

Cultural contracts theory was created by Ronald L. Jackson II in 2002 to respond to the ongoing discussion about identity negotiation throughout research in the humanities and social sciences. While it might seem obvious that this theory emanated from sociologist Charles W. Mills's 1997 *racial contracts* treatise, the author was unaware of Mills's work until nearly 3 years after the cultural contracts theory was established. The theory actually has its roots in Jean-Jacques Rousseau's 1762 explication of the social contract, which was a moral and philosophical essay on the implications of national sovereignty and the maintenance of social order. This early document spawned a lot of debate about freedom, independence, autonomy, and citizen obligation to social order. The cultural contracts theory is aligned with Mills's theory to the extent that it is aware of and responsive to power inequities that destabilize or imbalance interaction and ultimately instigate cultural identity negotiation.

Jackson actually thought about the contracts metaphor when buying a home. He noted the similarities between communicating one's preferences in important life negotiations such as buying a home and negotiating one's identity with a stranger whom we expect to behave or proceed in a certain way. In these kinds of interactions, one's values, norms, beliefs, and patterns of communication—indeed one's culture—are revealed within the encounter. Likewise, people negotiate differences in opinion, style, and orientation in these sorts of transactions. Whether two people are meeting one another for the first time or have been acquainted for years, they must still coordinate their relationship by understanding the other's culture. Just as in a home-purchase contract, everyday communication contains "small print," with hidden features of a relationship. In identity negotiation, the small print can be about hidden motives but is often about hidden insecurities that come as a result of past experiences. All of this complicates the encounter and is exacerbated in intercultural interactions where race, gender, and class all come to bear.

Cultural Contracts in Operation

Drawing from the literature on identities as well as previous studies conducted on how intercultural relationships are formed and sustained, Jackson asked, what about one's identity is actually being negotiated, and how does that happen? When people interact, their identities will overlap to a greater or lesser extent. The co-orientation process that occurs in interaction can be seen as *identity negotiation*, which involves varying degrees of cooperation. The resulting agreement is a "contract" that specifies the rules and conditions for mutual identity management. These contracts function to preserve, protect, and define the self as it meets up with others.

At the core of cultural contracts theory is the metaphor of *negotiation*. Identities are not simply conceded while communicating; rather, there is an attempt to hold onto and negotiate aspects that define who one is. This process permits at least two options: One can elect to assimilate or accommodate, or one can negotiate the relationship anew by signing another contract.

What happens if both interactants see themselves as "leader"? What if there are cultural differences in their definitions of leadership? What if both want to enact their identities in response to another? These are all critical questions. In every communication encounter, people are communicating their worldviews and what they value, and they must continuously engage this process in juxtaposition with others.

Use of the word *cultural* in the theory is deliberate. Even if one is incapable of articulating the specificities of his or her worldview, there are still cultural norms and beliefs that influence how people behave on a daily basis. So, the theory maintains that everyone has a cultural contract. It is impossible to be without at least one; otherwise there would be no means of knowing what is appropriate or effective in a given culture.

Cultural contracts theory is based on three premises or axioms about the processes and outcomes of identity negotiation engagement: (1) identities require affirmation, (2) identities are constantly being exchanged, and (3) identities are contractual. To say that identities require affirmation is to say that there are multiple ways to think of identity. It essentially refers to a self-definition that is communicatively affirmed or validated by others. Postcolonialist and psychiatrist Frantz Fanon goes so far as to say that speaking enables one to be alive for others, which suggests that there is an interdependent function to human interaction; each of us comes to understand the self by knowing what the self is not. We know what it means to be *rich* by contrast to what it means to be *poor*. We know what is *right* by acknowledging what is *wrong*.

In the process of establishing who one is, there is a sharing and exchange of self-definitions and worldviews—and this is the second axiom of cultural contracts theory. Communication is inevitable and happens all the time; even when we think we are not communicating, we are. And while it is simple to suggest that humans communicate constantly, it is much more complicated to argue effectively for how one exchanges identities or portions of identities while interacting. Clearly, differences of identities imply a need for relational coordination.

Metaphorically speaking, then, there is a need for "contracts" that figuratively stipulate the rules of engagement among cultural group members within and outside a given culture. Social rules and laws become guideposts for acceptable and normal interaction; compliant behavior confirms your signature on the contract. The term *cultural contracts* refers to the end product of identity negotiation; hence, every "signed" or agreed-on cultural contract has a direct impact on one's identity.

At some point in their lives, people all have to decide to accept and abide by the cultural values, norms, beliefs, and communication patterns of a given culture as a template for how to behave; hence, our cultural contracts reflect our worldviews. This worldview shifts over time and during critical incidents with relational partners. The effect on identities, whether it is a shifting or solidifying move, depends on the significance of the initiating incident and/or nature of the identity negotiation process. At times, the negotiated shift in identity is so dramatic that a contract breach or violation occurs, with one of three possible outcomes: ending or disrupting the relationship; devising an original or amended contract; or conceding, usually because of the high value given to the relationship or the high costs of leaving the relationship.

Types of Cultural Contracts

Three basic types of cultural contract have been identified: Ready-to-sign, quasi-completed, and cocreated. Each kind of contract reveals how people have personally and socially constructed how they define themselves. *Ready-to-sign cultural contracts* are prenegotiated; the parties do not permit any further negotiation of the contract. These contracts are designed to promote assimilation or maintain one's own worldview. Those who seek to introduce a ready-to-sign contract are often firmly entrenched in their own perspective and are not interested in others' worldviews. Essentially, they take their cultural understandings into every encounter and have no interest in learning about other cultural traditions, values, norms, and beliefs. As the most rigid of the contract types, the ready-to-sign cultural contract is the type that dominant groups often "hold in their pocket," ready to present to marginalized group members. The reason that language forms such as Ebonics have not reached full political legitimacy as a language form can be explained by the ready-to-sign contract prevalent in Canada and the United States that refuses to recognize the standards, structure, and function of Ebonics—or of any language or language variation that contests one form of English as the appropriate and normal standard of American speech.

Quasi-completed cultural contracts consist of some prenegotiated agreements and some agreements to agree to relationally coordinate one's identities with those of another. These are perhaps the most common type of cultural contract, and they are ordinarily short-term episodes of identity shifting. People code switch every day when they go to work or school or participate in formal public events and activities. People also use different contracts for different people. The person who feels compelled to code switch with you may not code switch with someone else, or perhaps not in the same way. Signers of the quasi-completed contract may do so because they want both options available: They want to have the option of maintaining their own worldviews, and they want to have the option of cocreating with others. These individuals, in other words, waver in their interest to relationally coordinate. In addition, some quasi-completed contacts are "signed" as self-protection in order to avoid stress. For example, some African Americans try to "talk proper" on the telephone by changing their tonality and inflection to "sound White" in order to avoid racially biased treatment such as linguistic profiling.

The third kind of contract, the *cocreated cultural contract,* is fully negotiable. Cocreated cultural contracts are the ideal kinds of social agreements we would like to have with cultural others because people from cultures other than our own are interested in fully valuing difference. If a cultural contract is cocreated, differences are fully acknowledged and valued. Cultural differences are not ignored, and they are not the only reason the two partners are in relationship. "Signing" this type of contract indicates an openness and embrace of other ways of seeing the world. Mutual satisfaction, rather than obligation to the requirements of the other's culture, is the centerpiece of such relationships.

Cocreated contracts, in the end, however, are behavioral. That is, mere talk about harmony and cohesiveness does not manifest into a cocreated contract; one must also demonstrate the unconditional appreciation and valuation of the other person. This is perhaps discussed and exhibited most as it relates to romantic interpersonal relationships, especially interracial ones. The cocreated contract stipulations for interracial romantic relationships, for example, typically include acknowledgment and appreciation of the cultural ancestries, values, norms, beliefs, practices, and patterns that govern the partners' behaviors as individuals and as partners.

Limitations

While cultural contracts theory asserts that taking into account others' values is routine in daily interactions, what is not so clear in this theory is how each of us develops, sustains, or shifts our cultural contracts over time. Also, how does one move from one contract to another with different people? When and why do we identity shift or code switch with different people? All of these questions are raised in this paradigm. At the same time, it cannot reasonably answer every question about human interaction; nor should it be expected to. Rather, it points out dynamics familiar to marriages, teams, corporations, churches, schools, and everyday acquaintances, offering a way to understand a phenomenon that occurs instantly when we interact with others in one episode or throughout time. We negotiate identities so quickly that we are not always aware that it is happening.

Unlike uncertainty reduction theory, which is mainly about initial interaction, cultural contracts theory holds that we all have at least one culture we claim and that serves as a guide for how we interact with others. Even in our attempts to be elusive and try not to claim any given culture, the way we behave tattles on us and reminds us about how we live in the world and about what we value. Such values sometimes affirm and sometimes violate our expectancies about others and lead to negotiation, accommodation, and reassessment of contracts.

Ronald L. Jackson II

See also Accommodation Theory; Communication Theory of Identity; Cultural Identity Theory; Cultural Performance Theory; Culture and Communication; Expectancy Violations Theory; Face Negotiation Theory; Identity Theories; Relational Development

Further Readings

Baugh, J. (2000). Racial identification by speech. *American Speech, 75*(4), 362–364.

Fanon, F. (1967). *Black skin, white masks.* New York: Grove.

Hecht, M. L., Jackson, R. L., & Ribeau, S. A. (2003). *African American communication: Exploring identity and culture* (2nd ed.). Mahwah, NJ: Lawrence Erlbaum.

Jackson, R. L. (1999). *The negotiation of cultural identity.* Westport, CT: Praeger.

Jackson, R. L. (2002). Cultural contracts theory: Toward an understanding of identity negotiation. *Communication Quarterly, 50,* 359–367.

Jackson, R. L. (2002). Exploring African American identity negotiation in the academy: Toward a transformative vision of African American communication scholarship. *Howard Journal of Communication, 2,* 43–57.

Jackson, R. L., & Crawley, R. L. (2003). White student confessions about a Black male professor: A cultural contracts theory approach to intimate conversations about race and worldview. *Journal of Men's Studies, 12,* 25–41.

Cultural Identity Theory

Cultural identity theory (CIT) is one of several theories developed to build knowledge about the communicative processes in use by individuals to construct and negotiate their cultural group identities and relationships in particular contexts. Originally developed in the late 1980s, the theory has significantly evolved through continuing collaborative projects in various international sites and diverse regions in the United States. Early versions emphasized an interpretive theoretical perspective, social construction, and individuals' discursive accounts of experiences, while versions after 2000 have been broadened to incorporate a critical perspective and to include attention to contextual structures, ideologies, and status hierarchies. Research guided by the theory today most often includes discursive analysis of public and interview texts focusing on the forms through which cultural-identity positions and intercultural relationships are negotiated, the role of privilege in the outcomes of discourse, and implications for intercultural relations and social justice.

Early Interpretive Versions of Cultural Identity Theory

Early CIT work was characterized by an interpretive theoretical perspective, in which cultural identity processes were described, but not critiqued. Mary Jane Collier and Milt Thomas combined the ethnography of communication and social construction and from there proposed several properties of the enactment, or creation, of cultural identity evident in communication texts. First they argued that individuals' messages during interaction may contain multiple types of cultural identities, such as national, racial, ethnic, class related, sex and gender based, political, and religious. Because individuals enact multiple identities, all voices within each identity group do not speak in the same way or have the same recognition by others.

Diversity, both within and between groups, became a key principle and was examined in several research studies. For instance, in the mid-1990s, Mary Jane Collier, Michael Hecht, and Sidney Ribeau demonstrated the multivocality, or different expressions, of African American identity, as well as some broad patterns of conduct and norms providing evidence of various ethnic identities among African Americans.

Early CIT also proposed that individuals' cultural identities differ in salience and relative importance across situational contexts, time, and interactions. In a study on ethnically identified college students' communication with acquaintances in the mid-1980s, Collier found that ethnic similarity and difference between the individual and his or her acquaintance were factors that affected how much cultural identity stands out.

A third property of this early work was the varying scope or prevalence with which the particular forms of cultural identities are visible. When Collier studied conflict among friends identifying as Latino/a, Asian American, African American, and Anglo American in the United States, she found that there were some similarities in cultural norms for members of each ethnic group, as well as within-group differences with regard to gender and the nature of the relationship.

A fourth property of early CIT work was related to who constructs or produces the cultural identity and the ways in which these identities are communicated. Two processes were found—avowal and ascription. *Avowal* was defined as personal articulation of one's views about group identity, and *ascription* referred to how one refers to others. The most common forms of ascriptions are stereotypes of other groups. CIT scholars argued that identity construction is part reaction to past ascriptions and part ongoing and dynamic avowal of identity claims, and therefore both avowed and ascribed cultural identities are important. In interviews with South Africans in the early 1990s, Collier found that there was often a difference in described qualities of avowed cultural identities by insiders and the qualities ascribed to that group by outsiders. She argued that this mismatch could be a factor in continuing or intensifying conflict, but that the consequences depended on the status positioning of group members.

CIT scholars such as Collier also proposed that cultural identities are negotiated within a social context and are affected not only by historical events and political conditions but also by who is present and the situation or site of interaction or public discourse. For example, Collier, Hecht, and Ribeau defined African American ethnic identity as a "problematic event" that is historically and politically situated; they pointed to insider-avowed and outsider-ascribed descriptions of ethnic identities in order to provide a view of the communication through which African American ethnic identities are negotiated.

The intensity with which particular cultural identities are avowed and ascribed was described in CIT as differing depending on context, situation, topic, and relationship. Intensity of avowal and ascription was also linked with the salience, or prominence, of cultural identity, as born out in research by Collier related to South African racial, ethnic, and gendered identities. Cultural identities also have been shown to change in significant ways. *Othering* (placing one group as *other than one's own*) in the form of racism against Blacks by Whites has endured over the years and appears even in certain color-blind forms, according to research on interracial marriages in the United States conducted by Jennifer Thompson and Mary Jane Collier.

Along with other theorists, CIT scholars noted that cultural identities become evident through social comparison. On other words, speakers compare the status position of their own groups to those of other groups. For instance, when South African Afrikaners described their views about the social and economic future of the country in the early 1990s, they did so by using positive self-references for Whites and negative descriptions for Blacks.

Critical and Interpretive Cultural Identity Negotiation Theory

Critiques of research guided by CIT emerged in the late 1990s. Critical scholars called for researchers to recognize the influence of ascriptions and representations found in public texts and the role of structures such as institutional policies and ideologies on identity politics and negotiation. To respond, Collier broadened her work through integrating critical and interpretive perspectives. Stressing the role of contextual negotiation of multiple identities and relationships, CIT evolved into *cultural identity negotiation theory* (CINT). Collier's more recent work in CINT emphasizes researcher reflexivity, or scholars' reflections on their impact on the work they do as well as the way in which that work influences them. CINT work from early 2000 forward calls for attention to the material and social consequences of cultural identity negotiation and increasingly reflects attention to concerns with social equality and justice.

CINT research incorporates attention to forms of discourse such as ascriptions that subjugate certain groups of people as a type of racism, including the discourse that appears in both overt and less visible ways. These types of subjugating discourse are sometimes found in interviews with U.S. courtroom personnel, who pride themselves on being "objective." It has also been found in comments from wives who identify as White in interracial marriages in the United States. As well, views of "others" have been shown to emerge in contradictory ways. CINT research shows how political histories and government institutional actions are described by representatives of marginalized and privileged groups, such as those identified as Palestinian and Israeli in a peace-building program. Further, research methods such as focus group, interviews, and analysis of public discourse can involve the reproduction of Whiteness and class privilege and thereby reinforce and extend the status and resources of particular groups. Reflexively, then, scholars and practitioners can uncover their own systems of oppression as well as identify what can be changed.

To make a new, less oppressive move in CINT research, interpretation and coding procedures often involve multiple coders in dialogue with one another working with transcriptions from videotapes and audiotapes. CINT works to build relevant bodies of knowledge about lived experiences and provides data to inform research, add relevance to instruction, and potentially transform oppressive structures, institutions, and relationships.

Mary Jane Collier

See also Contextual Theory of Interethnic Communication; Critical Ethnography; Critical Race Theory; Critical Theory; Cultural Contracts Theory; Culture and Communication; Identity Theories; Whiteness Theory

Further Readings

Collier, M. J. (1998). Research on cultural identity: Reconciling post-colonial and interpretive approaches. In D. Tanno (Ed.), *Cultural identity and intercultural communication. International and intercultural communication annual: Vol. 21* (pp. 122–147). Thousand Oaks, CA: Sage.

Collier, M. J. (2005). Enacting and contesting privilege: Cultural identifications in South African focus group discourses. *Western Journal of Communication, 69,* 295–318.

Collier, M. J. (2005). Theorizing cultural identifications: Critical updates and continuing evolution. In W. B. Gudykunst (Ed.), *Theorizing about intercultural communication.* (pp. 235–256). Thousand Oaks, CA: Sage.

Myers, M., & Collier, M. J. (2005). Cultural ascriptions displayed by restraining order court representatives: Implicating patriarchy and cultural dominance. *Women's Studies in Communication, 28,* 258–289.

Thompson, J., & Collier, M. J. (2006). Toward contingent understandings of intersecting identifications among selected U.S. interracial couples: Integrating interpretive and critical views. *Communication Quarterly, 54,* 487–506.

CULTURAL INDICATORS

Cultural indicators (CI), in communication theory, refers to several different concepts and entities. Most commonly, it refers to the research program begun by George Gerbner at the Annenberg School for Communication in the 1960s. The purpose of this research program was to establish a method to document and measure cultural phenomena in a way that would complement existing social and economic indicators. Gerbner believed that culture, in its broadest forms and manifestations, would give important evidence about the direction that a society was taking. Working from this viewpoint, he sought to establish measures of culture that could complement existing economic indicators (such as gross domestic product) or social indicators (such as the crime rate).

Gerbner began his career in communication theory by working on a general model of communication, but his contributions in CI and related areas of inquiry were much more lasting. Gerbner began articulating the need for cultural indicators as early as 1969, though even his earlier research was setting the stage for assessing the importance of cultural products in society. In 1973, Gerbner put forth a formulation for a CI research paradigm, which became so well known that it could eventually be capitalized; we now use *Cultural Indicators* to refer to the long-term research project led by Gerbner, often in collaboration with colleagues Larry Gross, Michael Morgan, and Nancy Signorielli.

Gerbner put forth three prongs for a CI research paradigm: institutional process analysis, message system analysis, and cultivation. Institutional process involved the study of the structures of media industries that controlled the mass production of messages. Such a study would involve detailed examination of various roles in media production, focusing on power roles, types of leverage exerted, and typical functions performed within the media. Such studies would serve to indicate the cultural, social, political, and economic bases and purposes for the production of media messages.

Message system analysis focused on the systematic analysis of media content, specifically with an eye toward determining not only what was being portrayed, but how messages were related to the needs, desires, and interests of those producing the messages. Gerbner was building on his own prior interest in content analysis, but also connecting such study to a more overarching view that messages were not just the random output of a purposeless machine, but a product of a system serving specific social, economic, and political needs and functions.

Cultivation was the attempt to connect messages with their potential impact. Although Gerbner eschewed then-traditional notions of media effects, he felt that it would be possible to see to what extent consumers of media messages had absorbed the lessons and morals embedded within those messages. Thus, cultivation focused mostly on the relationships between consumption of messages and the extent to which consumers held worldviews consistent with those messages. This was something of a departure from the then-common method of examining media effects, which often focused on simplistic stimulus–response models of media effects tested under laboratory conditions. Rather, Gerbner was interested in the extent to which consumers of media messages would absorb, retain, and hold beliefs consistent with those found in media messages. Thus, CI research most often combined content analyses of media messages with survey data on the beliefs of heavier consumers of those media. The extent to which heavier users of those media held beliefs consistent with media messages was seen as the extent to which they had been "cultivated" to hold those beliefs.

While Gerbner's research program could have been applied to any aspect of the message system, it became almost synonomous with the media effects of television. During the time in which Gerbner began the CI project, television was far and away the dominant medium. The three major networks dominated the distribution of entertainment and news messages, eclipsing other media such as radio, newspapers, and films. Gerbner argued that corporate control of television meant that the goals of political and economic elites would find their way into television's messages and that heavy viewers of television would inevitably absorb the conceptions and morals found in those stories. While the institutional analysis portion of the research program was not completely abandoned, CI research became most associated with research on the nature of television's stories and its impacts.

The issue on which CI research came to the forefront was that of televised violence. As early as 1967, Gerbner began collecting content data on television as part of what would become the ongoing CI research program. These data focused on a variety of issues, such as the roles of men and women and occupational roles on television and portrayals of minorities. Also included were data on violence. Trained coders would examine programs for the number of violent acts, describing in detail not just the act itself, but also who committed it and its victim. Eventually, Gerbner and colleagues developed a *Violence Index,* which has become one of the better known products of the project. Data using this method have been collected essentially continuously since 1967.

The index itself was a composite of the percentage of programs (usually either prime-time programs or children's programs) with violence, the rate of violent acts per program, the rate of violent acts per hour, the percentage of characters involved in violence, and the percentage of characters involved in killing. The numbers resulting from this anaysis were found to range from about 115 to 185, usually averaging about 160. Building from this start, Gerbner and his colleagues went on to produce *Violence Profiles,* which would track the ups and downs of violence in any given year.

In 1976, Gerbner and Larry Gross published *Living With Television,* which tracked violence levels from 1967 to 1975. Across the years sampled, violence did not change much, though it was higher in childrens' programming, declining in the then-popular family viewing hour, and increasing during the late evening period. Mostly, since then, CI research has found that violence levels do not vary much. While there may be ups and downs in particular years—due either to change in programming fashion or perhaps during periods when politicians are paying more attention—in general, television has remained fairly violent. This particular measure is one of the continuing and most lasting contributions of CI research.

The measure was and still is controversial. Some argued that the definition of violence used was too liberal. Critics argued that "cartoon" or "slapstick" violence should not really count. Gerbner retorted that "happy violence" could be as pernicious or more so than "sinister" or obvious violence. Later studies of television violence, some commissioned by the industry, have sought to refine or revise the conceptions introduced by Gerbner. Nevertheless, the Violence Profiles were the first to set the critical debate on the levels of violence on television on some firm scientific footing.

While the issue of violence took much of the attention, the CI project has also collected much data on other issues. CI researchers noted the persistent underrepresentation of women and minorities in television's early years. Men often outnumbered women by 2 or 3 to 1. Blacks, gays, and other minorities were also underrepresented. In general, the CI project began by concerning itself with a very wide array of issues and portrayals on television; this has continued to this day, as other researchers have taken up the research tactics first promulgated by Gerbner and his colleagues.

With respect to cultivation, Gerbner and Gross found that heavier viewers of television were more likely to see the world as a violent place and to be less trusting of others. This phenomenon came to be known as the *mean world syndrome.* This was a fairly marked turn from the traditional research focusing on whether viewers imitated television violence. While Gerbner never denied that televised violence could have some role in promoting real social violence, he was more interested in what the viewer would learn about violence. While many murders are committed on television, few people imitate them. But the early cultivation findings showed that people did derive impressions of society from the scenes of violence they saw on television. For Gerbner, ultimately, this was a question dealing with social control. Violence on television was not just "for fun"; it also taught lessons about who could and did commit violence and who would be the victims of it. The idea that such violence might convince people to support stronger legislation on crime was not far removed from Gerbner's original conception that the study of communication should be seen as *basic cultural inquiry.* Thus, violence, while it may have entertained, was also there to help sell products, meeting the commercial needs of the medium. Moreover, it helped to establish perceptions of what was wrong in society, and who could or should control it.

CI research has spawned literally hundreds of studies, both by the original research team and others who have continued, extended, and even criticized the paradigm. Almost always it has focused on television. Even as the television medium has fractured and splintered, researchers are still finding evidence of cultivation on a variety of issues. Researchers are finding, for example, that television interacts with culture in complex ways. Television by no means controls the direction of

society. As minorities and women, for instance, have made strides through civil rights activism, television programs slowly came to recognize these achievments and embody them in their programs. The fact that CI researchers are still collecting data, and have been doing so since the late 1960s, is now allowing scholars to pursue questions about media and social change that have been impossible to address until recently.

In the cultivation arena, research continues to proliferate. Despite heavy criticism early on, studies continue to accumulate that show that there is a fundamental relationship between what people see in the "television world" and what they believe about the "real world." Researchers have even begun to establish a cognitive basis for cultivation, which shows that heavy viewers of television are more likely to draw on memories and cognitions from their television experience when answering questions about their real-world preceptions or experience.

CI can also refer to statistics gathered by countries or international institutions about cultural activities. Data on phenomena such as media penetration rates and production of cultural artifacts such as books, films, and television programs are normally collected for many countries. As such, they often represent economic indicators of cultural activity. Such data were often used to argue that powerful and wealthy Western countries, especially the United States, were dominating poorer countries culturally, dumping cultural products on markets that could not afford to produce their own. This argument for *media imperialism* was a subspecies of the argument for *neocolonialism:* Powerful countries no longer relied on direct military and political control to extract resources from client states. Communication technology permitted powerful states to maintain hegemonic relations through the domination of culture. Such arguments have diminished, especially as many formerly media-dependent countries have developed their own local media systems. However, the production and flow of culture across borders continues to be of interest, especially as globalization has turned the production and reception of messages into an international enterprise with ramifications and effects that are not yet well understood.

Finally, in 1994, William Bennett published *The Index of Leading Cultural Indicators,* which he updated and revised in 1999. He was secretary of education under Ronald Reagan. The book is actually a compendium of a variety of economic, social, and cultural statistics. Bennett treats culture in a macro sense; all phenomena, whether economic, social, or political, tell us something about culture. However, the book has relatively little to offer to communication theorists; most of its data on communication phenomena are available from primary sources. Also, note that the title is somewhat misleading: no single index is offered.

James Shanahan

See also Americanization of Media; Cultivation Theory; Media and Mass Communication Theories; Media Effects Theories; Neocolonialism

Further Readings

Bennett, W. (1999). *The index of leading cultural indicators*. New York: Broadway.

Gerbner, G. (1973). Cultural indicators: The third voice. In G. Gerbner, L. Gross, & W. H. Melody (Eds.), *Communications technology and social policy* (pp. 555–573). New York: Wiley.

Gerbner, G., & Gross, L. (1976). Living with television: The violence profile. *Journal of Communication, 26,* 173–199.

Morgan, M. (Ed.). (2002). *Against the mainstream: Selected writings of George Gerbner*. New York: Peter Lang.

Shanahan, J., & Morgan, M. (1999). *Television and its viewers: Cultivation theory and research*. London: Cambridge University Press.

Signorielli, N., & Morgan, M. (Eds.). (1990). *Cultivation analysis: New directions in media effects research*. Thousand Oaks, CA: Sage.

CULTURAL PERFORMANCE THEORY

Cultural performance theory offers an approach for understanding culture within the activity of everyday life. It serves as a means to conceptualize culture by placing culture at the center of hegemonic, or dominating, messages and revealing the hierarchical structure of society through lived experience. Performance is foundational to the study of human communication. *Performance* has no singular definition, nor is it situated in any singular discipline of study. Performance offers value and insight to theater studies and to social sciences, and it can be viewed through the lens of cultural and critical studies. Performance theory views humans as *Homo narrans*, or creatures who communicate through stories as a way of crafting their social world and making meaning of it.

Performance implies an act of doing, practice, and theatricality, while simultaneously encompassing both the subject of research and the method of doing research. Created from perspectives on human behavior, culture, and ritual, cultural performance theory explores the relationship between the foundations of human experience: community, culture, and performance. It also serves as a challenge to traditional theory by bringing together differing domains of knowledge—the objective, scientific, and observable—with the embodied, practical, and everyday. Cultural performance theory radicalizes, or identifies as the root issue, the binary opposition between theory and practice by providing a model of communicative practice in which culture and performance are inextricably joined and integral to the communal experience of everyday life.

The term *cultural performance* refers to discrete events, or cultural performances that can be observed and understood in any cultural structure. These events include, for example, traditional theater and dance, concerts, recitations, religious festivals, weddings, and funerals, all of which possess certain characteristics: limited time span, a beginning and an end, a set of performers, an audience, a place and occasion, and an organized program of activity. This approach to cultural performances would later influence anthropological and theatrical theory in the 1970s and give rise to the study of folklore from the perspective of culture and performance.

The disciplines involved in cultural performance theory extend broadly. Erving Goffman, a sociologist, explored the social construction of the self in everyday life. Theater scholar Richard Schechner offered the study of social drama and performance as a lens to examine human communication. Anthropologists Victor Turner and Dwight Conquergood employed performance as a means of interpreting cultures and understanding historical, social, and cultural processes—from ritualistic modes of expression to ethnographic performance. Communication scholars extend culture to include knowledge formation and culture as a force for intercultural exchange, understanding, and equality. The major tenets of cultural performance theory are illuminated in four features specific to culture: process, play, poetics, and power.

Culture as Process

Culture as process assumes that human communication in and through performance is active; all that makes us human is ever-changing, ongoing, and not static. Culture is the sum total of all that we are; a way of life; a blueprint for maintaining traditions; how we celebrate occasions, make memories, ritualize events, and understand the ordinariness of everyday life in our families and communities. Culture also provides the possibility for creating and discovering new ways of crafting and negotiating meaning of the world. Culture is embedded in human communication and is an aspect of all humans. Human behavior is performative when the act is telling a story, creating reality, critiquing society, or remembering history through oral communication, the primacy of the spoken word. A theory of cultural performance illuminates how humans participate in political and cultural aspects of everyday life in creative and expressive ways. For example, oral history performance creates opportunities to understand how culture, identity, and discourse are situated within a historical context of the times. For Africans living in America, for example, various forms of ritual served as a way to articulate the ways in which cultural differences are created between cultures, while illuminating meanings that are contested, as well as the tensions, the complexities, and the commonalities of human existence and meaning making within the context of social interaction.

Performance encompasses a wide range of human activity and is embedded in all human communication while providing a framework for rethinking the body, or self, in ways that critically assess subjectivity and identity, negotiate structures of power and resistance to domination, and challenge predominant ideologies of sexuality, class, gender, race, and ethnicity. Performance is a human act that sees culture as a way of knowing and of discovering new ways of experiencing and making

meaning of the world. Cultural performance, then, becomes an active, engaging, symbiotic exchange in which culture is transacted through performance—a process of throwing off and pulling in cultural forms centered in conflict and dynamic to the total sensual experience of a culture.

Culture as Play

The idea of *culture as play* illuminates the ways in which humans craft meaning of the world in and through the performative experience of play. Play is a specific, special, and significant form of human activity. This aspect of cultural performance aims to analyze the cultural functions of play that provide a deepening communal experience of norms and values subscribed by the culture. The relationship between culture and play is viewed as a representation of culturally constructed and articulated forms of playful activity such as tournaments, exhibitions, pageants, and contests, including playful activities of children and animals. Play is a voluntary act freely selected and capable of suspension at any time. Play is socially associated with "free time," nonworking, and leisure; it promotes social group cohesion within culture. Scholars of play theory reject notions that play must serve some purpose. Rather, they construct theory around performance that examines what play is and what it means to the player. Other perspectives interested in culture as play note the reflexivity and creativity of the self in play and embrace a communications-based approach to the performance of play.

Culture as Poetics

Culture as poetics elucidates the social and symbolic constructions of culture. It emphasizes the ordinariness of everyday life. Such constructions include rites of passage, social rituals, and those social performances that instantiate and reconstitute values and norms of the culture. Rites of passage are cultural instances of performance that explain the ways in which people move from one point in time to another on their journey of life. Humans engage in life crises and enact ceremonies, such as rites of passage, in order to offer safe travel from one instance in life to another. Other categories of cultural performance include ceremonies with strangers, pregnancy and childbirth rites, initiation rites, betrothal and marriage rites, and separation or funeral rites.

Research on rites of passage was further advanced by exploring the role of ritual in everyday life. The traditional and largely descriptive approach to the study of humans advanced to the point of viewing culture as performance, which revolutionized and ushered in a new way of studying human poetics, communication, and behavior. In the area of performance studies, concepts such as *liminality* (the threshold of "betweenness"), *communitas* (group intimacy), and *social drama* (cultural conventions) moved beyond description of cultural performance and its constitutive elements to posit the structures and functions of performances as both reflective and reflexive. As *reflective,* cultural performances have sensory codes, which are meaningful messages about a material world picked up at once by all the senses. A vision of the world through the lens of cultural performance reflects the ongoing social processes, claiming what is important, what is valued, and how society functions. The *reflexive* function relates to the ways in which cultural performances can lead to change. Cultural performances provide moments to enact, comment, critique, and evaluate the norms and values of a culture. Performance reflexivity is engaged when a sociocultural group turns, bends, reflects back on itself, on the relations, actions, symbols, meanings, codes, roles, statuses, social structures, ethical and legal rules, and other components that make up the members' public selves.

Conquergood underscores the importance of performance as a means toward intercultural understanding; privileging the stories, lived experiences, and everyday constructed performances of ordinary people. He views cultural performance theory as a model of intellectual inquiry and a way for understanding the interrelationship among cultures. Guillermo Gomez-Pena reminds us that culture embraces the ordinariness of life by linking us together as humans in expressive, creative, and dialogic ways. Thus, through means of dialogue, we learn the ways of others, their ideas manifested in language, history, art, literature, and politics.

Culture as Power

Culture as power is a perspective that shows how performance can reveal the state of displaced persons moving between cultures. From this view, cultural performance theory becomes a dynamic means for critiquing culture and a way to articulate the struggle of the lived experience of colonized and oppressed peoples. The theory provides a framework for analyzing what Turner calls the *sensory codes* of a culture. Such codes can range from food performances to political campaigns to cultural expressions of the body and its identity. Culture as power offers performance the inroad to reflect the dynamics of cultural processes and claims about which stories are important, who gets to tell those stories, how we shape the social canvas of cultural transformation, what is valued in a culture, and how we participate in creating a different vision for the future. Culture as power deconstructs the notions of identity by examining how humans negotiate, navigate, and transform systems of domination and control and explores the process by which self and social identity are crafted. Power is performed within the cultural context of *the other* and illuminates the dynamics of domination. By *other* is meant those in society marginalized due to sexuality, race, gender, socioeconomic status, or ethnicity.

The notion of the other reveals dynamics between the marginalized and the privileged. As a symbolic act of resistance, subversive performances are cultural expressions that disrupt and transgress customary boundaries in a nuanced way. For example, performance artists of color in the United States draw on the communal aspects of indigenous ancestral people to reclaim tradition, political struggle, and self-empowerment. These performances place culture at the center, show how the manifestations of being on the margins of society occur at the edge of survival, and transform existence in a way that can facilitate change. For example, Dwight Conquergood's ethnographic fieldwork with refugees and migrants in Thailand, the Gaza Strip, and inner-city Chicago gangs points to the ways in which cultural performance theory is a lens for seeing how people construct their identities in the face of struggle, liberation, and ultimately change through persuasive means of telling their stories.

Dominant cultural performances have the privilege of living out loud, being explicit, speaking directly without fear of retribution, while subordinate voices perform counterintuitively in ways that are masked, covered, and embedded ways of existence. Mikhail Bakhtin recognizes the value of culture and living on the margins of society, suggesting that the most intense life of a culture occurs at its boundaries. Cultural performance theory, then, reveals the underbelly of culture as the expression of power and dominance. However, a performance paradigm also privileges the dynamic, precarious, and embodied experience grounded in a historical process and reveals how marginal voices resist domination through performance: for example, Myron Beasley's critique on ritual performances of same-gender-loving men as transgressive and transformative; Bryant Keith Alexander's reading on performing Black masculine identity; or Olga Davis's illumination of the performative act of survival of 20th-century race riots through the lens of cultural memory. Each speaks to the transformational quality of culture performances with the objective of challenging systems of power and control.

Olga Idriss Davis

See also Cultural Studies; Culture and Communication; Narrative and Narratology; Performance Ethnography; Performance Theories; Performative Writing; Stories and Storytelling

Further Readings

Alexander, B. (2004). Passing, cultural performance, and individual agency: Performative reflections on Black masculine identity. *Cultural Studies/Critical Methodologies, 4*, 377–404.

Beasley, M. (2008). Popica/popcorn: Resistance and ritual performance. *Performance Research, 12*(4), 167–172.

Beasley, M. (2008). Tribute to the ancestors: Ritual performance and same-gender-loving men of African descent. *Text and Performance Quarterly, 28*, 416–440.

Bell, E. (2008). *Theories of performance*. Thousand Oaks, CA: Sage.

Carlson, M. (1996). *Performance: A critical introduction*. New York: Routledge.

Conquergood, D. (1989). Poetics, play, process, and power: The performative turn in anthropology. *Text and Performance Quarterly, 1*, 82–95.

Davis, O. I. (2008). Locating Tulsa in the souls of Black women folk: Performing memory as survival. *Performance Research, 12*, 124–136.

Fine, E. C., & Speer, J. H. (Eds.). (1992). *Performance, culture, and identity*. Westport, CT: Praeger.

Goffman, E. (1959). *The presentation of self in everyday life*. Garden City, NY: Doubleday.

Gomez-Pena, G. (1994). The multicultural paradigm: An open letter to the national arts community. In D. Taylor & J. Villegas (Eds.), *Negotiating performance: Gender, sexuality, and theatricality in Latin/o America* (pp. 17–29). Durham, NC: Duke University Press.

Huizinga, J. (1938/1950). *Homo ludens: A study of the play-element in culture*. Boston: Beacon.

Madison, D. S., & Hamera, J. (Eds.). (2006). *The Sage handbook of performance studies*. Thousand Oaks, CA: Sage.

Pelias, R. J., & VanOosting, J. (1987). A paradigm for performance studies. *Quarterly Journal of Speech, 73*, 219–231.

Schechner, R. (1993). *The future of ritual: Writing on culture and performance*. New York: Routledge.

Singer, M. (1972). *When a great tradition modernizes: An anthropological approach to Indian civilization*. New York: Praeger.

Striff, E. (2003). *Readers in cultural criticism: Performance studies*. New York: Palgrave Macmillan.

Thiong'o, N. (1998). *Penpoints, gunpoints, and dreams: The performance of literature and power in postcolonial Africa*. New York: Oxford University Press.

Turner, V. (1988). *The anthropology of performance*. New York: PAJ.

Van Gennep, A. (1960). *The rites of passage* (M. B. Vizedom & G. L. Caffee, Trans.). Chicago: University of Chicago Press.

CULTURAL STUDIES

Cultural studies can be loosely defined as an academic field of study that crosses disciplinary boundaries such as political economy, literary studies, cultural anthropology, philosophy, American studies, gender studies, film studies, and communication studies. Early cultural studies, which emerged from the Birmingham Centre for Contemporary Cultural Studies (CCCS) in Great Britain, generally utilized *Marxist* and *structuralist* perspectives to investigate the complex relationships between political economy and culture. Particularly, cultural studies explored the mundane and the "popular" as opposed to what might be called high culture.

Contemporarily, cultural studies has fractured into numerous strands of thought that do not share theoretical or methodological unity, although the emphasis on ordinary and popular culture remains central. Communication, which was one of the first disciplines to offer cultural studies legitimacy in the United States, has most often seen a cultural studies influence in assessments of articulations of power and knowledge within popular media texts. Understanding the importance of cultural studies requires an exploration of its creation as an academic field of study, a look at the central issues for nearly all cultural studies scholars, a brief discussion of its relevance in the field of communication, and a summary of persistent criticisms.

Creation of Cultural Studies

The emergence of British cultural studies, in connection with the CCCS, can be traced to post–World War II Great Britain. A number of cultural and social changes faced Great Britain during this time period, including its decline as a world superpower, the development and proliferation of mass media, and the loss of "imperial" identity and homogeneity with an influx of new populations, many of whom were formerly colonized peoples. Moreover, with the expansion of educational opportunities in Great Britain, students who once would have had no access to higher education were now afforded scholarships so they could attend school. These "scholarship" students eventually became intellectuals who did not espouse the same perspectives or values of the middle and upper class who comprised much of the intellectual class. The traditional intellectual class contained many of those who privileged the high arts and condemned the "popular" ones. Thus, a collection of working class intellectuals, including Richard Hoggart and Raymond Williams, two of those credited with the creation of cultural studies, began emphasizing the importance of popular culture. Additionally, several individuals involved in the teaching profession, including Stuart Hall, another founder of contemporary cultural studies, began noticing a disconnect between themselves and their knowledge and the cultural communities of their students. A desire to narrow this gap also led to early explorations of popular culture.

Hoggart, Williams, and others, such as E. P. Thompson, set many of the modern foundations for cultural studies. Stuart Hall's theories and writings perhaps have left the longest lasting impression, especially on U.S. audiences. Hall took over for Hoggart as director of the CCCS in 1969. Under Hall's leadership, the CCCS shifted its focus from "everyday" cultures to an emphasis on the mass media and the ideological functions and effects of the media. Hall also centered his approach to cultural studies on dynamics of race and empire, an influence that remains strong today. Hall left the directorship of the CCCS in 1979 to become a professor of sociology at the Open University, and it was also during this time that other centers and university departments began to more seriously aid in constructing the field of cultural studies. The Open University, with the help of Hall, became central in offering innovative tools for cultural studies. Additionally, numerous journals and working groups produced a vibrant body of cultural studies literature.

In the mid- to late 1980s, centers and departments in the United States began to produce a plethora of cultural studies research projects. Several collections of scholarly writing emerged from these collaborations, including Cary Nelson and Lawrence Grossberg's edited collection, *Marxism and the Interpretation of Culture*, and Grossberg, Nelson, and Paul Treichler's collection, *Cultural Studies*. Additionally, in 1987, the journal *Cultural Studies* launched its inaugural issue in the United States, featuring an internationally acclaimed editorial board. Today, numerous cultural studies journals, anthologies, and academic conferences as well as departments, programs, and centers have been created around the world.

Key Issues in Cultural Studies

In spite of the growth of the field of cultural studies, its increasing legitimacy within the academy, and the substantial number of scholars who identify with it, cultural studies has maintained its refusal of disciplinary and methodological purity. Nevertheless, a number of key issues serve a central function to many cultural studies scholars. Foremost in this arena is the term *culture*, which has numerous definitions, including Raymond Williams's famous definition of culture as a "way of life." Others, such as Grossberg, contend that the *culture* of cultural studies is always a contextual and ambiguous space. No singular definition will do; thus reading *culture* in relation to the following collection of concepts is an imperative of cultural studies.

Language and Signification

The relationship between language and culture is hotly contested, but for most cultural studies scholars, language and processes of signification provide the only access we have to understanding culture. Because meaning is paramount to any definition of culture, the processes of meaning creation must remain in focus. Meaning is constructed, and the site of its construction is language. Cultural studies scholars most typically follow the tradition of Swiss linguist Ferdinand de Saussure, who argued that meaning is arbitrary and that no necessary relationship exists between an object and the word that represents it. Investigating the meaning of *signs,* the arbitrary relationship between the *signifier* (word) and the *signified* (object), provides a way to understand culturally specific modes of meaning making.

Language is one site to interrogate this relationship; signifying processes, more broadly speaking, are another. Images, film, and various nonlinguistic signs can be analyzed as processes of signification that reinforce particular cultural *myths,* or social meanings that attach themselves to particular signs. For example, an advertisement or photograph may contain several signifiers that attach to multiple signifieds, depending on the cultural context. An image of Barack Obama after winning the U.S. presidency in 2008 offers an example. The signifiers in the image might include Obama's smile, his suit and tie, his maleness, and his brown skin. The signifieds, however, could include a shift in the United States' history of racism, a young and attractive president who suggests a change in policy course, or a continuation of the masculine-dominated political system. Any of these meanings are possible, and by understanding these processes of signification, cultural studies scholars can better understand cultural stagnation and change.

Text and Audience

The exploration of signs usually works by featuring the cultural artifact in question as a *text.* In cultural studies, a text can refer to a written text, but it is more often used to refer to any artifact that requires *reading* or interpretation. *Textual analysis* remains the primary methodological approach in cultural studies. Because of the emphasis on media, cultural studies scholars are interested in both the analysis of media as *polysemic* texts that can be read in multiple ways and in how audiences make use of those texts in culturally and historically specific contexts. Drawing on *poststructuralism* and *postmodern* theories, cultural studies assumes that no text has an intended or singular meaning. Texts interact with audiences in different contexts to create different meanings. For instance, a song written by a U.S. American artist has very different meanings for audiences at a club in New York City, a boutique in Paris, or a shopping mall in Tokyo. Hall's notions of *encoding* and *decoding,* or the interaction between producer and audience to create meaning, have proved especially helpful in understanding these processes.

Ideology and Hegemony

Texts and audiences within any context are not innocent. Because cultural studies research typically produces and adds to *critical theory,* theorizing ideology and hegemony are key enterprises for cultural studies scholars. Generally following Marxist tradition, a key question is, how do mass media uphold and reinforce the ideology of the dominant class? Related to this question is the issue of *discourse,* or the web of cultural meanings that congeal on a particular topic or idea, and how some discourses get naturalized to seem as if they are the only one. Ideology is a difficult concept, and cultural studies scholars early on followed the theorization of Louis Althusser, who offered a deterministic perspective on the discursive and material functioning of ideology. Althusser's theory of ideology promoted a perspective that essentially said ideology produces culture, and people have little agency to challenge it.

Cultural studies scholars mitigate Althusser's deterministic conceptualization of ideology by turning toward Antonio Gramsci's notion of *hegemony.* Rather than depicting ideology as all-encompassing, he argues that dominant ideologies and domination are rarely instituted by force or coercion; rather, people consent to their own domination. Consent is achieved when the dominant group acknowledges oppositional positions and viewpoints enough so those who are disempowered feel that their interests are taken into consideration. Though little actual change may happen, the accommodations the dominant group offers provide enough recompense to keep the marginalized complacent. Thus hegemony affords the possibility for people to enact social change since they take part in their own domination. Cultural studies scholars often investigate the functioning of ideology and hegemony, as well as the ruptures in dominant discourses that leave possibility for agency and revolution.

Identity and Subjectivity

Questions of agency remain crucial for cultural studies scholars. Ideology not only functions to produce particular manifestations of culture, but beliefs about the self are also ideological. An assumption that is present in both Althusser and Gramsci is that ideologies are internalized and help constitute people's sense of who they are in a given cultural space. Because ideologies are found in the language, texts, and signifying practices, what those things mean comes to reside in people. This means that who people understand themselves to be and how others understand them in terms of factors such as race, class, gender, and sexual orientation are not "natural," but "naturalized." A person's relationship to a particular text is thus a product of a range of cultural processes that are heavily infused with specific ideologies about who they are and how they should be.

Methodological Approaches

Investigating the aforementioned concerns proves to be a complicated methodological task. One of the key strengths and most often identified weaknesses of cultural studies is its refusal to adopt a unified methodological approach. On one hand, this refusal leads cultural studies scholars to conduct research that is driven by their research questions. Cultural studies scholars thus utilize an array of methods including, but not limited to, archival research, textual analyses, interviews and ethnographic methods, surveys, content analysis, psychoanalysis, semiotics, and deconstruction. Scholars who have long

critiqued the methodological limitations of those disciplines that demand adherence to a unified or consistent method have championed this plurality. On the other hand, without a coherent methodological approach, critics have maintained that cultural studies will always lack validity.

One of the most well-known examples of a cultural studies approach to the study of cultural artifacts is *Doing Cultural Studies: The Story of the Sony Walkman*. This book, which provides a step-by-step analysis of the culture of the Walkman, identifies the necessity of unpacking the *articulation* of five related cultural processes: representation, consumption, identity, production, and regulation. These processes create a *circuit of culture* that one must investigate in order to offer a comprehensive look at the function, use, and meanings connected to cultural artifacts. Though many cultural studies projects do not take this particular approach, this case study serves as an exemplar for how to critique the numerous *culture industries* and their products.

Cultural Studies and Communication

Importantly, the discipline of communication studies was among the first to embrace cultural studies in the United States. Specifically, those who study media and cultural processes have been most interested in the cultural studies project. Lawrence Grossberg has been one of the leaders in bringing cultural studies to communication, having written extensively about cultural studies. His work on topics such as youth culture, conservatism, and popular music has laid the groundwork for an entire body of scholarship connecting communication and cultural studies. Similarly, a number of feminist and queer scholars have done important work that conjoins the two areas of study, including Raka Shome, Radhika Parameswaran, Katherine Sender, and others. In her work on Princess Diana, for instance, Shome analyzes British media representations of Diana after her death. Shome demonstrates the connections between White femininity and national identity during the crisis. Sender has also created a body of work analyzing the relationships between gender and sexuality in the media within a broader context of *neoliberalism*. Sender's research highlights representation in relation to matters of consumption, production, regulation, and identity, connecting it strongly with the cultural studies tradition practiced at the Open University. Others such as Toby Miller have intervened in cultural studies practice by insisting on an internationalization of research and a connection with other dimensions of cultural reality such as law, policy, and money. For media analyses to have relevance to public audiences, scholars must push for more complex analyses that lead to radical critique and social transformation.

Criticisms

No field of study that has changed the academic landscape like cultural studies could be without its critics. Cultural studies has taken hits from an array of scholars for both its political agenda and its methodological fluidity. By now it should be clear that cultural studies has no use for conventional scholarly expectations of objectivity or neutrality. To the contrary, cultural studies scholars are overt in their political commitments, and they often maintain that their critical reflexivity about politics makes their work more honest than that which denies any political investment at all. Not all critics find this premise persuasive. Moreover, some critics hardly consider cultural studies scholarly. Physicist Alan Sokal wrote a parody, which appeared as a hoax, in the cultural studies journal *Social Text,* of what he described as the "nonsense" of cultural studies scholars writing from a postmodern tradition. In explaining his hoax, Sokal argued that the political turn away from analyses of objective realities toward the social construction of reality undermines possibilities for scholarship to affect genuine social change. Sokal's work created a significant controversy within and outside the field both because he fooled the editors and reviewers of a leading cultural studies journal and because of the scathing nature of his critique.

The Sokal hoax also points to the methodological critiques leveled at cultural studies, from those both within and outside the approach. For example, cultural studies scholars have long squabbled over the relationship between culture and political economy, with some critics arguing that cultural studies has reduced everything to culture, denying the impact of political economy. Additionally, cultural studies scholars have critiqued each other

for using whatever method suits their fancy, relying on a critique of the conditions of knowledge production as a justification for less-than-rigorous methodology. At the same time, because textual analysis remains a primary method, some have suggested that cultural studies research has not advanced beyond the literary criticism generally applied to "high arts."

Outside cultural studies, the methodological critiques have been no less severe. Some practitioners of journalism maintain that the influence of cultural studies corrupts journalistic practice as it emerges from radical theory rather than empirical investigation. Harold Bloom, a Yale literature professor, argues that cultural studies is destructive to literary studies and an enterprise designed to advance people's careers rather than engage in serious analysis of literary texts.

Probably one of the biggest critiques of cultural studies remains its profound Eurocentrism. Though the complex phenomenon of globalization has been studied extensively, and *postcolonial theory* has long impacted the thinking of a number of people in cultural studies, the *ethnocentrism* of much of the work has stayed firmly intact. Scholars from traditions in Asia and Latin America in particular have suggested that cultural studies remains a very limited enterprise as long as its perspective emerges from only a small collection of powerful regions (Europe, Australia, and the United States). Latin American cultural studies scholars, for example, demonstrate a long-standing and rich tradition of critical writing and research in Central and South America that predates many of these same conversations in Eurocentric cultural studies. Still, very little of that Latin American tradition is regarded in the Eurocentric one. Despite its obvious shortcomings, cultural studies remains a vibrant and constantly changing project that will no doubt continue to influence generations of communication scholars.

Karma R. Chávez

See also Critical Discourse Analysis; Critical Theory; Feminist Communication Theories; Language and Communication; Marxist Theory; Materiality of Discourse; Postcolonial Feminism; Postcolonial Theory; Postmodern Theory; Poststructuralism; Semiotics and Semiology

Further Readings

Abbas, A., & Erni, J. N. (Eds.). (2005). *Internationalizing cultural studies: An anthology*. Malden, MA: Blackwell.

Del Sarto, A., Ríos, A., & Trigo, A. (Eds.). (2004). *The Latin American cultural studies reader*. Durham, NC: Duke University Press.

du Gay, P., Hall, S., Janes, L., Mackay, H., & Negus, K. (1997). *Doing cultural studies: The story of the Sony Walkman*. London: Sage.

Erni, J. N., & Chua, S. K. (Eds.). (2005). *Asian media studies: Politics of subjectivities*. Malden, MA: Blackwell.

Grossberg, L. (1993). Cultural studies and/in new worlds. *Critical Studies in Mass Communication, 10*, 1–22.

Grossberg, L., Nelson, C., & Treichler, P. (Eds.). (1992). *Cultural studies*. New York: Routledge.

Hall, S. (1992). *Culture, media, language: Working papers in cultural studies, 1972–79*. London: Hutchinson Centre for Contemporary Cultural Studies, University of Birmingham.

Hasian, M. A., Jr., & Nakayama, T. K. (1997). The empires strike back: The Sokal controversy and the vilification of cultural studies. *Journal of Communication Inquiry, 21*(2), 45–55.

Johnson, R., Chambers, D., Raghuram, P., & Tincknell, E. (2004). *The practice of cultural studies*. Thousand Oaks, CA: Sage.

Lewis, J. (2008). *Cultural studies: The basics* (2nd ed.). Thousand Oaks, CA: Sage.

McRobbie, A. (Ed.). (1997). *Back to reality? Social experience and cultural studies*. Manchester, UK: Manchester University Press.

Miller, T. (Ed.). (2001). *A companion to cultural studies*. Malden, MA: Wiley/Blackwell.

Nelson, C., & Grossberg, L. (Eds.). (1988). *Marxism and the interpretation of culture*. Urbana: University of Illinois Press.

Sokal, A. (1996). Transgressing the boundaries: Toward a transformative hermeneutics of quantum gravity. *Social Text, 14*(1/2), 217–252.

Turner, G. (2002). *British cultural studies: An introduction* (3rd ed.). New York: Routledge.

CULTURAL THEORIES OF HEALTH COMMUNICATION

According to an Institute of Medicine report published in 2003, the concept of culture has increasingly become a core component in the development of health communication theory and application. The field of health communication has recently seen a growing interest in the concept of culture, with the idea that culturally based theories of health communication should guide effective health communication applications. This emphasis on culture in health communication has been brought about by (a) the increasing diversity within the United States against the backdrop of shifting global migration patterns and (b) the increasing postcolonial criticism of traditionally top-down health communication programs. As a result of this emphasis, the hegemonic, or oppressive, assumptions underlying mainstream conceptualizations of health and communication about health have been questioned by health communication scholars.

In order to address the concept of culture in health communication, scholars and practitioners have introduced culturally based constructs into existing health communication theories, developed culturally based theories of health communication, and outlined communication processes and strategies that take culture into account. This work may broadly be categorized into (a) culturally sensitive and (b) culture-centered approaches.

Whereas the *culturally sensitive approach* focuses on developing communication materials that are responsive to the characteristics of the culture as identified by expert scholars and communication practitioners, the *culture-centered approach* relies on developing culture-based processes for listening to cultural members and developing strategies for addressing problems articulated by participants in important health-related discursive spaces, or places and situations in which communication occurs and in which meaning is created. These are situations that traditionally have neglected or erased the voices of various cultural groups. With their diverse roots, the culturally sensitive and culture-centered approaches vary widely in their concepts of culture, in their theorizing of the role of communication in the realm of culture, and in the nature of health communication applications that are developed on the basis of culture.

Culturally Sensitive Health Communication

Culturally sensitive health communication theories aim to develop communication solutions to preconfigured health problems in local communities. In these theories, culture is treated as a variable that modifies the traditional elements of communication and persuasion. The goal of culturally sensitive health communication theories is to utilize the concept of culture to develop more effective and efficient health communication programs among the members of various cultures.

Researchers and providers segment target audiences of health communication programs according to certain cultural variables and subsequently carry out health communication interventions with the idea that culturally relevant communication materials are more effective than materials that are not relevant. This notion of adapting communication materials to the salient characteristics of the culture lies at the heart of culturally sensitive health communication. Communication is thus conceptualized in terms of health messages. For example, Matthew Kreuter and Stephanie McClure offer a comprehensive review of culturally sensitive health communication programs, incorporating elements of culture into the widely used communication–persuasion model developed by William McGuire, which deals with how to induce resistance to messages that may influence people in unwanted ways. In their review, the authors offer a framework for examining the effectiveness of source characteristics, message characteristics, and channel characteristics in the context of cultural variables.

The Concept of Culture

Culture is seen as a repository of values, beliefs, and practices that are typically categorized in the realm of certain geographically defined spaces or clearly defined communities. These values, beliefs, and practices are conceptualized as variables that guide the development of culturally appropriate health messages. The emphasis here is on noting the cultural differences within populations with respect to the beliefs and values and their communicative and health practices. Cultural variables are incorporated into existing health communication theories with the idea that these variables would enhance the applicability of the theories in the target populations. Examples of such cultural variables include individualism–collectivism, power distance, uncertainty avoidance, and masculinity–femininity.

Culture, therefore, is treated as a static entity that could be measured through instruments and then be utilized for the purpose of guiding health communication applications.

The Role of Communication in Culture

Communication is seen in terms of interventions that are directed toward changing certain undesirable characteristics within the culture that are typically associated with poor health outcomes. In the culturally sensitive approach, communication is treated as messages, and the goal is to create the most effective message for the target culture. Based on an individualistic framework, the culturally sensitive approach is directed toward changing the underlying belief structures associated with a proposed health behavior as might be encountered within the realm of individual lifestyles. Therefore, communication in culturally sensitive health communication is behavior-change persuasion that is built on the idea that sending out the appropriate culturally situated message will be effective in bringing about behavior change in the target culture. The health problem in the community is predetermined, and formative research is conducted in order to identify the salient cultural characteristics that would guide the culturally sensitive health communication intervention. In the culturally sensitive approach, communication is linear and top-down, and the cultural information obtained from the target audience is utilized in order to develop a more effective health communication program promoting a specific behavior.

For culturally sensitive scholars, the health communication intervention is likely to be more effective when it takes into account source, message, and channel characteristics that are appropriate for the predefined characteristics of the culture. Therefore, the emphasis in culturally sensitive health communication is on identifying those cultural variables that would be informative in the selection of sources, message content, and the appropriate channels for targeting the cultural members. Culturally relevant health communication strategies might range from the selection of similar sources, to the selection of surface-level message characteristics such as color and sound that are aligned with cultural beliefs and values, to the development of messages that are aligned with the underlying social and cultural dimensions of the target community.

The Nature of Health Communication Applications

Health communication applications in the culturally sensitive health communication approach are typically interventions that are directed toward addressing the culturally based barriers that may interfere with the adoption of a recommended behavior. These applications are therefore top-down in their implementation of communication strategies, with communication continuing to flow from the centers of expertise to the cultural communities at the peripheries. Health communication applications in the cultural sensitivity approach ultimately work with cultural variables to produce effective messages that are directed toward bringing about attitudinal and behavioral changes in the population. Relevant cultural variables are selected in order to guide the strategic selection of channel, source, and message characteristics for the health communication intervention promoting the predetermined behavior in the community.

Culture-Centered Health Communication

In response to the criticisms articulated by Deborah Lupton and Collins Airhihenbuwa, the culture-centered approach developed in the work of Mohan Dutta critiques the dominant framework of health communication for its West-centric assumptions and opens up the discursive space to include alternative meanings of health. It does this through joining in solidarity with cultural communities that are otherwise erased from the discursive spaces of knowledge. Here cultural participants themselves are agents in seeking out, making sense of, and transforming unhealthy social structures.

The Concept of Culture

Culture is dynamic and is embodied in the locally situated contexts within which cultural members negotiate their meanings of health. Therefore, central to the concept of culture in this approach is the intersection between communication and continually shifting local contexts. Culture is constituted through communicative practices and constitutes the broader framework within which communication takes place and meanings are shared. The dynamic nature of culture as conceptualized in the culture-centered approach leaves openings for meanings, values, and rituals to be articulated, co-constructed in participatory spaces, and renegotiated through cultural interpretations. Dynamic culture is constituted through participatory communication, making listening and dialogue two of the central concepts in the culture-centered approach. It is through the communicative act of listening that opportunities are created for the articulation of hitherto unheard problem configurations from the standpoints of cultural members.

The Role of Communication in Culture

Communication in the culture-centered approach lies at the intersection of culture, structure, and agency. *Structure* refers to the forms of organization and resources within the social system that provide and/or limit access to the fundamental necessities of health. Examples of structures include hospitals, health service agencies, shelters, workplaces, forms of transportation, and food resources that are related to experiences and meanings of health. *Agency* refers to the capacity of cultural members to define their own problems, articulate their needs, and participate in communicative processes and practices that seek to address their articulated needs. *Communication* here is seen as a process through which agency is expressed, as meanings are shared locally, nationally, and globally in order to address the structures that facilitate and constrain the possibilities for health. This approach emphasizes the meanings that are co-constructed by cultural members as they participate in a variety of transformative practices that seek to change unhealthy social structures even as they work with these structures. Therefore, communication serves as a process for creating participatory spaces for listening to the voices of local communities and for dialoguing with cultural members in order to address the broader structures that impede the possibilities for health. Furthermore, the culture-centered approach offers a deconstructive lens for continually interrogating the hegemonic assumptions of mainstream health communication programs, as well as an entry point for engaging in dialogue with those communities at the margins that remain hidden from dominant discursive spaces.

Nature of Health Communication Applications

The health communication applications developed in the culture-centered approach are fundamentally transformative in nature as they seek to address the social structures that create and sustain the unhealthy conditions at the margins of society. Therefore, many of the applications in this approach are directed toward addressing the broader social structures surrounding the health experiences of cultural communities. Examples include projects of community activism, political mobilization, and citizen participation that are typically directed at health policies. In addition, culture-centered health communication applications are based on principles of participation as scholars engage with local communities in order to listen to the voices of community members by creating participatory platforms that voice the stories of local community members.

Conclusion

The cultural sensitivity approach and the culture-centered approach offer largely different understandings of culture, the relationship between communication and culture, and the role of social structures in the realm of health experiences of individuals, groups, and communities. Whereas the cultural sensitivity approach takes an individualistic approach to health problems, with the locus of control being in the realm of individual lifestyles, the culture-centered approach seeks to address the social structures underlying health problems. The cultural sensitivity approach responds to culture by taking cultural variables into account in the development of culturally appropriate health interventions, and the culture-centered approach takes culture as an entry point for listening to voices of local communities in participatory processes that are directed toward addressing unhealthy social structures.

Mohan J. Dutta

See also Cultural Types Theories; Culture and Communication; Health Communication Theories

Further Readings

Airhihenbuwa, C. (1995). *Health and culture: Beyond the Western paradigm*. Thousand Oaks, CA: Sage.

Dutta, M. (2007). *Communicating health: A culture-centered approach*. London: Polity Press.

Dutta-Bergman, M. (2004). The unheard voices of Santalis: Communicating about health from the margins of India. *Communication Theory, 14*, 237–263.

Krueter, M., & McClure, S. M. (2004). The role of culture in health communication. *Annual Review of Public Health, 25*, 439–455.

Lupton, D. (1994). Toward the development of a critical health communication praxis. *Health Communication, 6*(1), 55–67.

McGuire, W. (1989). Theoretical foundations of campaigns. In R. E. Rice & C. K. Atkin (Eds.), *Public communication campaigns* (2nd ed., pp. 43–65). Newbury Park, CA: Sage.

CULTURAL TYPES THEORIES

Cultural types have assumed great importance in those areas of the communication field related to culture. The phrase *cultural types* has three primary usages in the social science literature: (1) culture and personality, (2) national character, and (3) high versus low context. This entry discusses these concepts, their origins and relationships, and their relevance to scholarship in communication.

Culture and Personality

The academic concept of cultural types first appeared in the early 19th century, likely based on existing ethnocentric cultural prejudices between peoples of newly emerging nation-states. The cultural types notion suggested a relationship between upbringing in a culture and the character and personality of its people. Traditional religious concepts had been accepted for centuries as explanations of adult behavior, based in part on the idea of karma, the summative moral result of past behavior, or the soul, granted to the child by a higher power before birth. The academic study of culture and personality attempted to understand personality development and its relationship to the social environment in which it developed.

The emerging fields of anthropology and psychology approached the explanation of behavior independently for most of the 19th century until Sigmund Freud's theories of psychoanalysis provided a potential bridge between them. Charles Darwin's theories became a strong influence on each of the social sciences, and the newly conceived differences proposed between human cultures were classified by some anthropologists according to their presumed level of development along an evolutionary scale, from primitive to civilized. Anthropologists searched for common features of personalities in a given culture that might allow the characterization of peoples by their cultures. Generalizations were sought about each culture, such as national character, modal personality types, and particular personality configurations.

Other anthropologists, led by Franz Boas and his students Edward Sapir and Ruth Benedict, developed a position arguing for the equivalence of humans and their social institutions across cultural groups. By the second decade of the 20th century, Sapir was integrating work from his linguistic studies with concepts relating psychology and psychotherapy to cultural anthropology, suggesting that all members of a culture possess related personalities and that these can be subanalyzed into types. This greatly expanded the new culture and personality approach, shifting thinking from the presumed evolution of cultures toward the importance of the individual, arguing that culture assumes the character and form of its members' personality structure.

Much of this thinking was influenced by Boas's and Benedict's work on Native American cultures. Boas defined culture as a collection of individuals with their own institutions and societies, introducing the modern definition of culture, and rejected a hierarchy of cultures. This work patterned culture at an individual level, seeking the source of individual differences in behavior and the meaning attached to the variations, opening a wider discussion between anthropologists and psychologists culminating in the 1920s and 1930s.

During World War II, the Office of Strategic Services employed both Benedict and her student Margaret Mead in a U.S. Army–motivated project to understand the culture of the enemy, particularly the Japanese. Conducted by Benedict and designated as a study of national character, the research was necessarily based on existing written accounts together with interviews of Japanese Americans, and published after the war. The Office of Strategic Services expanded the national character studies directed by Benedict and Mead as a preemptive attempt to understand different countries and the threats they might pose. Mead's main work was for the Committee for National Morale, to apply anthropology and psychology to the issue of building American morale.

Benedict's work compared the national characters of two similar cultures, England and the United States, finding that while Americans taught young women to exercise control over men's sexual urges in dating, young women in England were brought up not to worry about holding this line since young English males were taught to control themselves. These gender norms for male/female interactions were seen as sufficiently different between the countries that the cultures could easily appear different if analyses of variables other than culture and personality were not undertaken. This also implied that gender characteristics were not shaped by biology or genetics but by culture, implying that gender roles might be modified by changing cultural prescriptions and that culture could change personality.

National Character

When the notion of cultural types first appeared, it formed the basis for the concept of national character, particularly in Europe and East Asia. It was employed as the basis for prejudice and discrimination against minorities or against opposing nations and their populations, or, correspondingly, as the basis for the presumed superiority and right to power of a majority culture. In 19th-century Russia, interpretation of events was closely identified with the concept of the *Russian soul,* a clearly defined notion of national character that is still in use in some modern Russian institutions. Chinese Communist leaders from Mao Tse-tung to Deng Xiaoping employed cultural types notions, particularly with reference to interactions with Russia, and many Russians still respond to the *Russian soul* concept.

In the 1950s and 1960s, national character studies were criticized severely as ethnocentric and reductionistic because they evaluated each culture on the basis of a small number of characteristics that used Western values, reducing cultural and social complexity to simple descriptions. The similarity of the national character concept to the Nazi use of Aryan superman notions together with its characterizations of inferior populations led to further discrediting. British social anthropologists led by Alfred Reginald Radcliffe-Brown critically examined the entire field of culture and personality studies, referring to them in general as a vague abstraction. He saw the studies as based on Western philosophical and religious assumptions concerning the nature of humanity and suggested that the proposed personality types were not empirically evaluated through a comparison with alternative theories.

While these criticisms were valid, seeking relationships between psychology and culture can produce valuable insights. The culture and personality approach continued as *cognitive* or *psychological anthropology* with a new emphasis on the individual, recognizing that all humans are basically similar and seeking possible cultural and social effects on personality. Understanding this history is important when considering the work of Edward T. Hall, Geert Hofstede, and others in the study of relationships between cultural contexts and communication.

High-Context and Low-Context Communication

Although several different schemes have been used to distinguish among cultures, the ideal types of *high context* and *low context* have been especially important in the communication field. For this reason, this entry features this particular distinction in somewhat greater detail than others. High and low context are ideal types referring to the amount of information directly stated in a communication message versus any additional amount needed to understand it. These concepts were introduced by Edward T. Hall in his 1976 book *Beyond Culture*. In any culture, people require contextual information beyond the words of a message in order to assign meaning. The context needed is higher in some cultures and messages and lower in others.

In the 1930s, Hall was strongly influenced by the work of Franz Boas and Ruth Benedict and lived with Navajo and Hopi on reservations in Arizona. By the 1950s he was employed by the U.S. State Department to teach intercultural communication to State Department personnel about to be assigned to foreign posts. Hall's students expressed little use for anthropological descriptions of the cultural systems of the Hopi in their attempts to understand the culture they would face in their assigned country. Yet Hall found it difficult to describe the specific culture of entry for each of the students going to a dozen or more different cultures. To address these problems Hall began his initial work on *intercultural communication proper*, generalizations about intercultural communication that hold across cultures. Such generalizations are within Kenneth Pike's *etic* approach, considering multiple cultures from an outside viewpoint to determine their commonalities. The distinction between high- and low-context cultures formed a portion of Hall's work in this regard.

High-Context Communication

In a high-context culture, the significance intended by a message is located largely in the situation; the relationships of the communicators; and their beliefs, values, and cultural norm prescriptions. Thus context is important in interpreting high-context communication since the amount of information carried in the context is high. High-context cultures usually emphasize politeness, nonverbal communication, and indirect phrasings, rather than frankness and directness, in order to avoid hurt feelings. They emphasize the group over the individual and tend to encourage in-groups and group reliance. Messages in many high-context conversations are ambiguous, with multiple possible interpretations that may drift into vagueness, seemingly indefinite in form and imprecise in thought.

Hall's *high context* concept is similar to Ferdinand Tönnies' concept of *Gemeinschaft*. Gemeinschaft refers to community or family-type relationships between people with strong personal ties. *Gesellschaf* is similar to Hall's *low context*, emphasizing secondary relationships such as at a job, where the motivation to be together is principally a self-interest in making money, generally with less individual loyalty to the social group. *Gemeinschaft* and *high context* are also related to Basil Bernstein's notion of *restricted codes* that occur where there are closely shared identifications, expectations, and assumptions in a subculture that raises "we" above "I." Geert Hofstede's 1980 study of IBM employees identified four bipolar dimensions that characterize culture. The *individualism–collectivism* distinction Hofstede describes is related to the above conceptions of Tönnies, Bernstein, and Hall.

The defining feature of high-context communication remains one in which the context of the message is a greater determinant of its intended meaning than are the words. Thus "kill the umpire" is understood to express great displeasure with the decisions of the official behind home plate if spoken by a spectator after a questionable call during a baseball game. It is not intended as a literal call for the death of an individual. This message is highly contextual and would be understood in the same way by almost everyone in the co-culture of baseball fans, despite its lack of concern for the feelings of the umpire being berated, and its directness.

Low-Context Communication

In a low-context culture, the meanings intended by a message are located in the interpretations of its words and their arrangement. These are carefully selected in an attempt to express those meanings clearly and explicitly. Thus, there is low dependence on the surrounding context when interpreting low-context communication. Low-context cultures often place a high value on the individual, encouraging self-reliance. The predominant culture of the United States provides an example in which the presumed need is minimal for context surrounding a message in order to understand it.

If a professor states, "The paper is due on Thursday at noon, no exceptions," the statement means the paper is due on Thursday at noon, no exceptions. Little understanding of the situation or context in which the message exchange occurred, beyond the words of the message itself, is needed in order to assign meaning to the message. Yet even low-context communication requires a degree of consideration of the surrounding context and nonverbals, since the tone of voice of the professor, the situation in which the message occurred, and the past history of the interaction between the

particular participants might create the understanding that this message was intended as a joke or as a facetious response.

The concepts of high- and low-context communication are best seen as end points on a continuum rather than as either/or positions. They should be understood historically, in the context of difficulties with earlier attempts to relate properties of culture to individual behavior.

Thomas M. Steinfatt

See also Culture and Communication; Elaborated and Restricted Codes; Face Negotiation Theory; Intercultural Communication Theories; Linguistic Relativity; Nonverbal Communication Theories; Organizational Culture

Further Readings

Barnouw, V. (1963). *Culture and personality.* Homewood, IL: Dorsey.

Hall, E. T. (1976). *Beyond culture.* Garden City, NY: Anchor Press.

Hofstede, G. H. (2001). *Culture's consequences: Comparing values, behaviors, institutions, and organizations across nations.* Thousand Oaks, CA: Sage.

LeVine, R. A. (1974). *Culture, behavior, and personality.* Chicago: Aldine.

Sapir, E. (1949). *Culture, language, and personality.* Berkeley, CA: Language Behavior Research Laboratory.

Stocking, G. W., Jr. (1988). *Malinowski, Rivers, Benedict and Others: Essays on culture and personality. History of anthropology series, Vol. 4.* Madison: University of Wisconsin Press.

CULTURE AND COMMUNICATION

The goal of this entry is to broadly outline selected conceptualizations and approaches linking culture and communication in order to demonstrate the range of theoretical assumptions that guide research. The information is designed to enable the reader to understand a few of the contextual factors that have enabled particular approaches to emerge and to appreciate areas of similarity and difference. Readers are encouraged to remember that even scholars who align with similar perspectives may have different views of how to approach culture in their work.

Selected Approaches

Frankfurt School and Critical Theory

The Frankfurt School refers to a group of German economists, social theorists, and philosophers at the Institute for Social Research in Frankfurt, originally established in 1923. Influenced by Marxism and World War I, they were interested in elucidating the links between economic systems and structures within society, concerned with how capitalism produces and reproduces forms of domination, and ultimately driven by the purpose of emancipation and changing the social order. Their work was oriented toward examining conflict and predominant tensions between working classes and dominant classes. They recognized the abilities of the working classes to challenge and change the resulting social order, and therefore their work is credited as originating what is now called critical theory. Well-known members of the Frankfurt School include Max Horkheimer, Theodor Adorno, Herbert Marcuse, and Jürgen Habermas.

As the sociopolitical landscape in Germany became dominated by the Nazi movement in the 1930s, several scholars immigrated to the United States and established the Institute for Social Research at Columbia University. They turned their attention from the role of activism and working-class movements to a focus on objective conditions and advocated for the role of reason and intellect in determining and changing the social order. They also began to address mass communication and media as structures of oppression in capitalistic societies.

The work of these critical theorists includes views of individuals as agents of change and attention to both discovering societal structures and then changing them through public deliberation. Trained primarily as philosophers, some scholars from the Frankfurt School emphasized intellectual and rational orientations to building knowledge about culture and society in contrast to focusing on popular or widely accessible aspects of culture.

In general among Frankfurt School critical theorists, culture is the communicative structure that reflects the social order; culture is revealed in texts and discourses that are produced by institutions, organizations, and public spokespersons. With regard to ontology (that which is) and praxis (practical action), critical theorists suggest that individuals have the ability and agency to advocate for change, and this often occurs in public deliberation and debate in public spaces.

Intercultural Communication and Foreign Service Institute

Another significant group of scholars doing work on culture and communication in the United States just after World War II included Edward T. Hall, a cultural anthropologist. The Foreign Services Act had just been passed by the U.S. Congress in 1946 to establish a Foreign Service Institute (FSI) in the Department of State. Hall worked at the FSI with linguists and other academics to prepare U.S. diplomats for their overseas sojourns.

Hall's work is noteworthy because he brought attention to face-to-face interaction between members of different cultural groups and also introduced the importance of nonverbal forms of communication. He focused on contextually specific interactions and brought more attention to the role of nonverbal cues such as proxemics (use of space), kinesics (body language), paralanguage (tone of voice and vocal cues), and temporality in establishing the meanings of messages. This was a significant expansion of more traditional anthropological orientations that focused on one specific cultural group at a time, such as ethnographic descriptions of Hopi Indians, or performed cross-cultural comparisons of communication practices within one cultural group, such as U.S. Americans, with those used by another cultural group, such as Japanese.

Hall argued that culture can be identified when groups use patterned, learned, and analyzable codes of communication. With regard to ontology, his work showcases the idea that culture is communicatively constructed and that realities experienced by humans are culturally patterned. He showed the benefits of microanalysis, studying specific interactions and contextual cues as they affect meanings and behavior. In his training of diplomats for foreign service, he discovered that the diplomats wanted practical and concrete recommendations about what would be effective conduct in the various countries where they were to be posted. They were most concerned with learning what behaviors they should use and what behaviors they should avoid in order to be effective communicators. Thus, Hall brought academic and popular attention to intercultural communication effectiveness starting in the 1950s.

The context of the FSI work is therefore important in understanding the popularity of intercultural communication competence research, training programs, courses, and workshops, as well as popular books that offer "tool kits" and prescriptions for more effective conduct in particular countries. The work of the FSI laid the foundation for laypeople, corporate managers, international trainers, educators, and academics to link communication patterns with national, racial, and ethnic groups who live in particular places.

Cultural Studies Orientations

The label of *cultural studies* originally emerged from an interdisciplinary enterprise at the Centre for Contemporary Cultural Studies in Birmingham, England, in 1964. Scholars in the United States who align with a cultural studies orientation are interested in uncovering ideologies that dominate, along with maintaining a commitment to create emancipation and social change. Steeped in the events of previous decades of social and political unrest, some academics began studying how capitalist political systems and the policies and practices of the governments, multinational corporations, courts, and educational institutions positioned U.S. national culture as primary and acted to privilege some groups and marginalize others.

Scholars aligning with this perspective argue that there is not nor should there be one overarching conceptualization of culture; they focus on relationships between discourse, power, and ideologies. Discourse systems refer to what is talked about or expressed, the structure or rules about what can and cannot be said, who may speak, and what is accomplished for whom. Discourses are produced by institutions such as governments, professional groups such as the medical community, or social groups. According to a key figure among cultural studies scholars, Stuart Hall, culture is a site of struggle because these discourse systems are contested. In other words, some are found more often and are given more value than others, and there is ongoing negotiation about which discourse systems should be more important. For example, there are competing discourse systems related to different diseases and the relative stigma of having HIV/AIDS. Talking about HIV/AIDS as an "African" or "gay" disease or as a virus positions those with the disease into different levels of stigma and status and provides different levels of access to resources for treatment.

Culture, therefore, is defined as a complex and contested communicative system through which ideologies and status are negotiated. Ideologies are fundamental assumptions about reality that are both institutionally and socially patterned and function to position groups with higher and lower status. For example, consider ideologies related to financial aid for college students, such as the following: (a) Financial aid for any group member should be awarded on the basis of individual merit, or (b) financial aid for any group should be awarded on the basis of past histories of discrimination against the group and current levels of underrepresentation in higher status professions. Neither of these ideologies is mutually exclusive and both "compete" for priority in policy discussions among college administrators, faculty, and students.

The negotiation of ideologies, and therefore of culture, takes place in part through discourses that include verbal codes and nonverbal images, and products, as well as policies and procedures or organizations and institutions. Also important for cultural studies scholars is to look at what is accomplished by certain ideologies being reinforced, such as some groups having higher or lower socioeconomic status and social practices that include material conditions of living.

Because these relationships between discourse, ideologies, and power influence public audiences, and because domination and oppression are constructed in patterns of discourse, in normative practice, and in historical context, most cultural studies scholars turn their attention to mediated and public messages as the forms through which power relations become visible. Scholars additionally became interested in intersections of race, ethnicity, class, and sexuality; they began to examine representations and interpretations of particular groups and how these were positioned in relationship to one another.

There was a move among some of these academics to question dominant paradigms, as well as objective, rational, and scientific determinism. Questions about what scaled measurements actually measure, who is conducting social-scientific research about racial and ethnic groups, and consequences of naming some groups as *minority* and generalizing about ethnic group communication styles were raised. Many cultural studies scholars argued for seeking alternative views, advocated for the value of culturally relative knowledge, and viewed closure and objective certainty as dubious. There were calls to recognize more fully the existence of multiple histories and truths and to acknowledge the role of structures and institutions, hence macro contexts, in producing what is believed, as well as what is considered to be real and valued.

With regard to both axiology (values) and praxis (practical action), cultural studies scholars advocate a reformist orientation and methods that both uncover domination as well as point to social practices that can be changed. What is also unique in this approach to culture and communication is the discussion of group identities and representations as multiple, intersecting, and often contradictory, and the emphasis on the ways in which discourse, ideologies, and power are related.

Ethnography of Communication

While cultural studies scholars were calling for attention to social structures, Dell Hymes, a cultural anthropologist, was arguing for the merits of studying culture and communication in context. Similarly to the work of Edward T. Hall, ethnography of communication builds and expands foundations from the study of culture by anthropologists. In the 1970s, Hymes offered a framework for analyzing naturally occurring speech and conduct in situ, which means in the field or community setting in which it emerges. For ethnographers of communication, culture is a code of speaking and acting, a historically transmitted pattern of symbols, meanings, premises, and rules.

The ontological assumptions held by ethnographers of communication are that individuals learn and communicate through shared patterns of conduct, and these codes provide ways of identifying who is a group member. Researchers come to know and understand these patterns through extensive observation and/or participant observation often combined with in-depth, open-ended interviews. The observed social practices reveal ontological processes related to what it means to have a particular group identity, what is appropriate and prescribed conduct, the scenes and spaces in which particular activities take place, and ways in which people assign meaning and make sense of their lives. Context is revealed, for example, by categorizing the location in which contact occurs as well as noting discursive references to places and spaces or descriptions of institutions as people talk together. Ethnographers define culture as socially constructed through human conduct.

Postcolonial Approaches

Postcolonial studies emerged in the 1970s as economies were becoming multinational, computer technology was bringing in an information age, and academics were entering into a postmodern era. What is unique about postcolonial studies is the call for identifying historical links, uncovering erasures of historical events, and carefully examining geopolitical relations and inter/national histories in the study of culture and communication. Along with cultural studies scholars, postcolonial studies scholars also examine forms of intersecting nationalities, race, sex, and class positions. A prominent figure in postcolonial studies is Edward Said, who critiqued the ways in which discourses such as those dealing with "Orientalism" colonize and position groups into marginalized or subordinate positions. This movement seeks to understand the effects of macrocontextual factors such as histories and economies, institutional norms such as government and political policies, and international orientations such as imperialism on national and regional cultures.

Cultural Types Theories

Interested in increasing contact among peoples of the world, Geert Hofstede, a social psychologist, conducted research on IBM multinational sites and identified dimensions of cultural variability based on scaled measurements of business employees in 70 countries. His work on dimensions of cultural variability addressed such dimensions as individualism–collectivism, high–low power distance, masculinity–femininity, and high–low tolerance for uncertainty. These dimensions became widely researched in psychology, sociology, business, and communication and were adopted widely by trainers in corporate and international relations settings.

Hofstede conceptualized culture as a mental program or software of the mind. He operationalized these patterns of mental programs through measuring group members' preferences (social–psychological orientations across four dimensions of cultural variability). These mental programs are learned and shared among group members who share a cultural affiliation such as national citizenship. Because ontologically, group members from a particular nation are socialized with similar mental programs and behavioral norms, they learn to prefer similar behaviors. Scholars approach knowledge generation by assuming not only that these dimensions or types can be measured, but also that they are useful to describe, predict, and explain cultural preferences for conduct. The types have been applied to account for the behavior of over 50 national groups.

William Gudykunst, building on experience in Asia, studied personal relationship development among strangers and acquaintances from different nations. He developed a theory of anxiety and uncertainty management in the 1980s and argued for giving primary attention to intercultural encounters rather than cross-cultural comparisons of cultural communication styles. His own work on culture and communication features theorizing in the form of axioms or verifiable relationships among variables, such as levels of self-esteem and tolerance for anxiety, and use of scaled instruments. These allow for objectivity, quantification and measurement, consistency across different groups since the same instruments are used with diverse samples, statistically verifiable prediction, and generalization to wider populations.

Cultural types theorists, therefore, conceptualize culture as social–psychological patterns that can be measured based on dimensions such as individualism–collectivism. This work has been credited with increasing the rigor and precision of theorizing, extending social–psychological research about intercultural relating, and demonstrating the value of empirically testing and systematically building particular theories.

International Communication

Given the information age and the globalization of economic systems, scholars interested in mass communication became interested in issues related to information flow, social marketing, and influence of products and strategies across national borders. For international communication scholars, culture was thus conceived in terms of information, the various media forms through which broadcast and print media traveled and their impacts on diverse groups, as well as multinational products that were marketed internationally.

Such scholars also study the role of information and communication in developing countries. Scholars interested in development often approached culture as a set of living conditions that were characterized by poverty or lack of technological innovation as well as attitudes, values, and beliefs that impacted particular ways of life. Communication strategies were developed by U.S. and European scholars to introduce cultural change in such regions as India, Africa, and Latin America.

A leading development scholar was Everett Rogers. His model of diffusion of innovations includes stages of social change ranging from knowledge acquisition, persuasion, reaching a decision, implementation of a new innovation, and confirmation of use. As time progressed, other development scholars turned their attention to community-based participative action approaches that centered on enhancement of social justice, communities defining what they needed and how to introduce change, and the collaborative development of sustainable strategies. In the newer approaches to development, culture is viewed as a set of communicative actions and identities that the community constructs, as well as a set of contextual structures such as government policies and economic systems that both enable and constrain the lives and relationships of community members.

Interpretive Theories of Cultural Identities

During the 1980s in the United States, other scholars became interested in building knowledge about cultural identities in a more contextually based and experientially relevant manner. Scholars such as Mary Jane Collier, among others, theorized that in various interactional settings, individuals enact multiple cultural identities that overlap and are sometimes contradictory and that there is a diversity of voices within discourses from those aligning with the same national or ethnic group.

Culture, in this orientation, is seen as an enacted, emergent, contextual alignment with a cultural system or cultural group. In this orientation, culture is defined as an emergent group identity that becomes evident in a set of communicative codes, norms for conduct, patterns of premises and interpretations, and outcomes, such as relationship or status positioning. Epistemologically, scholars ask individuals to share narratives about their cultural group identities or to describe recalled conversations that constructed or impacted cultural identities and/or analyzed public discourses.

Some interpretive scholars place attention on individuals' accounts of their experiences of enacting different cultural identities and/or accounts of being ascribed stereotypical cultural identities. Other interpretive scholars look for culture in group and public discourses, examining such factors as membership categorization practices, avowal and ascription of cultural identities, and negotiation of racial contracts.

This interpretive emphasis emerged, in part, as a move away from social–psychological theories that linked national or ethnic background to communication style or psychological preference and a desire to better account for the role of context in cultural identity negotiation. Furthermore there was a recognition that cultural identities emerge in social relationships in which individuals are negotiating diverse status positions, and later, acknowledgment that power relations and structural factors impact cultural identity negotiation.

Some interpretive research was also consistent with the call from cultural studies and feminist scholars to understand multiple and contradictory cultural identities that could emerge in one relationship or in one setting. For example, approaches were developed that emphasized cultures and cultural identities as plural and as both socially constructed in interaction and institutionally produced by educational, political, and legal policies and economic conditions. Scholars began to advocate for recognizing broader contextual factors as well as the immediate environment of interaction, and knowledge claims included recognition of diverse cultural identity locations such as nationality, race, ethnicity, sexual orientation, class, gender, level of education, and so on.

Emphasizing experiences and accounts of individuals about their group memberships and identity negotiations, which places value on subjectivity, some interpretive scholars also began to call for more self-reflexivity on the part of researchers. In other words they acknowledged that the researchers' respective cultural identities and training influence research orientations and interpretations and should be recognized as a source of cultural bias. More recent work on cultural identities features scholarship based on integrating critically oriented approaches to critiquing contextual factors and structures, building understanding of socially constructed communicative texts and discourses, and summarizing what these communicative moves accomplish in the way of status and levels of privilege.

Summary

These are just a few of the very different orientations to theorizing culture and communication that have emerged as influential in U.S. research. In the programs of research discussed here, there are similarities as well as differences in assumptions about what it means to be members of multiple cultural groups, what representations of cultural groups mean to audiences and consumers, the extent to which context is important and how it is defined, and ideas about how to build knowledge.

Mary Jane Collier

See also Critical Theory; Cultural Contracts Theory; Cultural Identity Theory; Cultural Studies; Cultural Types Theories; Diffusion of Innovations; Ethnography of Communication; Identity Theories; Intercultural Communication Theories; Postcolonial Theory

Further Readings

Collier, M. J. (1998). Research on cultural identity: Reconciling post-colonial and interpretive approaches. In D. Tanno (Ed.), *Cultural identity and intercultural* communication. *International and intercultural communication annual: Vol. 21* (pp. 122–147). Thousand Oaks, CA: Sage.

Gudykunst, W. B. (1985). A model of uncertainty reduction in intercultural encounters. *Journal of Language and Social Psychology, 4,* 79–98.

Habermas, J. (1984). *The theory of communicative action: Vol. 1. Reason and the rationalization of society* (T. McCarthy, Trans.). Boston: Beacon.

Hall, E. T. (1976). *Beyond culture.* New York: Doubleday.

Hall, S. (1986). Cultural studies: Two paradigms. In R. Collins (Ed.), *Media, culture, and society: A critical reader* (pp. 57–72). London: Sage.

Hofstede, G. (1980). *Culture's consequences.* Beverly Hills, CA: Sage.

Hymes, D. (1974). *Foundations in sociolinguistics: An ethnographic approach.* Philadelphia: University of Pennsylvania Press.

Rogers, E. M. (1983). *Diffusion of innovations.* New York: Free Press.

Said, E. W. (1978). *Orientalism.* New York: Random House.

CULTURE INDUSTRIES

See Cultural Studies; Postmodern Theory

CYBERNETICS

Massachusetts Institute of Technology mathematician Norbert Wiener defined *cybernetics* as the science of "control and communication," and to indicate its generality, he added "in the animal and machine." Wiener derived the term *cybernetics* from the Greek *kybernetes,* the steersman, who observes deviations from the intended course of the boat and communicates with the rudder to counteract them. Wiener recognized the revolutionary potential of cybernetics for the development of technology and advances in the biological and social sciences. Cybernetics continues to offer a unique vocabulary for the study of communication.

The object of cybernetics has ancient roots. Heron of Alexandria (10–70 CE) was the first chronicler of a peculiar mechanism capable of holding the flame of oil lamps steady. Later, similar mechanisms were found in water clocks. In the 18th century, they reappeared as James Watt's centrifugal governor of steam engines, which drove the industrial era. Since 1910, engineers called them *servomechanisms.* However, it was Wiener who realized that feedback loops and communication processes formed a unity not heretofore conceptualized.

Cybernetics became established during a series of interdisciplinary meetings held between 1944 and 1953 and known as the Macy Conferences on Cybernetics. They brought together some of the most important postwar intellectuals: Norbert Wiener, Ross Ashby, Gregory Bateson, Heinz von Foerster, Warren McCulloch, Margaret Mead, John von Neumann, Claude Shannon, and Erving Goffman, who presented his early sociological ideas there. Cybernetics quickly expanded to embrace neuronal networks (McCulloch), communication patterns in groups (Alex Bavelas), anthropological concerns (Mead), mind (Ashby, Bateson), management (Stafford Beer), political systems (Karl Deutsch), family systems therapy (Bateson, Jay Haley), and of course computation (von Neumann, Shannon).

Cybernetics was too radical to fit traditional academic distinctions and remains an enormously productive interdiscipline that gave birth to numerous specializations—mathematical communication theory, control theory, automata theory, neuronal networks, computer science, artificial intelligence, game theory, information systems, family systems theory, constructivism—and continues to challenge various ontologies (philosophies of being). In the late 1970s, cybernetics took a reflexive turn, recognizing that the known reality cannot be separated from the process by which it is explored, giving rise to second-order cybernetics, fundamental to all sciences.

The use of the prefix *cyber-* in popular literature about intelligent artifacts, digital media, and globalization of communication—fueling a sense of liberation from authoritarianism, technological determinism, and geographical, even bodily, limitations—attests to how well the fruits of cybernetics are growing in contemporary culture, albeit somewhat shallowly.

Feedback

Autonomy as operational consequence of *circular forms of organization* unites most cybernetic conceptions. In traditional communication theory, feedback, based on circularity, is the response to intentional communication—interpersonally, listeners' responses indicating comprehension of what one said, and institutionally, statistics of audience reactions to media content. This popular conception of feedback amounts to control *of* something. In cybernetics, feedback means circular communication, and control is seen as residing *within* a system embodying circularities. For example, when A affects B, B affects C, and C affects A in return. This circularity has several implications:

1. All components involved affect each other but also themselves via the others. It would therefore be difficult to single out one as in control of all others.

2. Circularities bring a system either to converge on an equilibrium at which it no longer changes or to escalate in some of its variables, perhaps beyond its breaking point.

The former is called *deviation reducing, negative,* or *purposive feedback,* the latter *deviation amplifying, positive,* or *morphogenetic* (change of form) *feedback.* In conversations, negative feedback might lead to consensus, while positive feedback may escalate into a fight. Positive feedback may be carefully monitored, as in the steady growth of a business enterprise, or create unanticipated forms. An arms race, for example, can lead to war and political or economic reorganization. Therapeutic discourse may destabilize a burdensome situation and spiral into a more desirable practice of living.

3. In the presence of disturbances from its environment, negative feedback may lead a system to adjust. For example, home heating systems, including a thermostat, render the variation in external temperature no longer noticeable from inside the home.

Bateson suggested that virtually all naturally evolved systems, from simple organisms to ecologies and from conversations to social institutions, sustain themselves in multiple circularities. The preference for linear causal explanations, including for one-way communication, amounts to cutting these circularities open, effectively preventing understanding of the purpose, intelligence, morphogenesis, autonomy, and life of such systems.

Information

Cybernetic conceptions of information emerged largely in explorations of purpose. Bateson observed that circularities—from simple feedback loops and manifestations of mind to social systems—do not respond to stimuli but to *differences.* They are triggered by differences between what is and what should be; they transmit these differences to other parts of the system, which effectively process differences of differences, and so on; and they ultimately replace the very differences that triggered the circular process. He defined *information* as *the differences that make a difference at a later point.* Bateson's differences are related to George Spencer-Brown's *distinctions,* Shannon's *choices,* and Ashby's *variety.* What they share is a reliance on relations among multiple events, not their nature.

Hence, cybernetic explanations of behavior in terms of information fundamentally differ from the causal explanations that physics has to offer. For example, kicking a stone propels the stone in the direction of the physical force applied, but kicking a dog yields a response that is explainable largely from what the dog knows about the kicker—information made that difference. Francisco Varela appropriately called the flow of these differences *in-formation,* and Ashby once characterized cybernetics as the study of systems that are *closed to information.*

The cybernetic conception of information is at variance with the popular notion of information as contained in or a property of messages, that is, without reference to whom, in which context, and relative to which prior messages they inform. Obviously, data generated for an analysis can inform only those researchers who know how they were generated. The Internet can provide information only to those who believe they read the documents they retrieve as intended by those who wrote them. Thus, information resides *within* a system of coordinated interpretations.

Self-Reference

The paradoxical nature of self-referential statements like "do not read this sentence" or the interpersonal injunction "be spontaneous" has been puzzling logicians for centuries. Alfred North Whitehead and Bertrand Russell identified self-reference as the chief villain in logic, considered the paradoxes to which self-reference leads an abnormality of language, and proposed the *theory of logical types,* which exorcises self-reference from scientific discourse. Yet, everyday life is full of nonthreatening paradoxes. Zen Buddhists employ them as powerful teaching devices, therapists rely on them for identifying and treating communication pathologies, and many cybernetic concepts would be inaccessible without addressing their circularity.

Based on Spencer-Brown's *Laws of Form,* Louis Kauffman and Varela dissolved the viciousness of paradoxes of self-reference by describing the dynamics they set in motion. So, the paradox of Epimenides, the Cretan, who claimed "all Cretans are liars," can be dissolved into this time series: From assuming he is telling the truth follows he is lying follows he is telling the truth follows he is lying, . . . ad infinitum. This dynamics renders self-reference no longer threatening.

Recursive Computation

Arguably the most important contribution of cybernetics is the development of modern computers. The problem of self-reference was solved by adding time to propositional logic, meant to state facts. This move lies at the root of the development of recursive algorithms. *Algorithms* are step-by-step instructions for actions, like recipes and software that make general computers perform specific functions. *Recursive functions* are circular by repeatedly operating on themselves, ideally converging to the solution of a problem. Recursive computation transformed mechanical calculators into modern computers.

Much of computer-aided communication amounts to the reproduction of messages. Expanding on the choices thereby transmitted, Ashby developed another concept of communication, *intelligence amplification.* Technologies of intelligence amplification utilize algorithms that iteratively expand the capacity of humans for selecting among alternatives. Internet browsers, for example, go through millions of documents within seconds and select among them according to users' search criteria. In the social domain, one can observe intelligence amplification in many situations, for example, when CEOs distribute decisions among the members of a corporation, communicating to them only how to coordinate their actions in communication.

The cybernetics of recursive computation and intelligence amplification has ushered in the computer revolution that drastically transformed contemporary society, globalized business and politics, democratized communication structures, and undermined centrally controlled dictatorships. Cyberspace is a computational space, widely accessible due to the development of algorithms for user-friendly computer interfaces.

Stating scientific theories algorithmically rather than in natural language enables computer simulations of their entailments well beyond human imagination. Algorithmic theories of social phenomena, especially of the economy, communication networks, ecologies of messages, artificial life, and systems with very many variables have become indispensable tools, vastly expanding scientific knowledge.

Self-Organization

Self-organizing systems develop indigenous patterns of communication and identities and protect them in the presence of interferences from their environment. They are *organizationally closed* by being immune to instructions from their outside. Interactions within social organizations, families, for example, can hardly be explained from where they reside. Families develop, reproduce, and maintain indigenous forms, a culture, secrets, and unique patterns of communication. Their manner of self-organization cannot be understood from their outside by detached observers.

Ashby's *law of self-organization* identifies three properties: (1) *Circular networks of recurrent communication* stabilize such systems while (2) internal variation ensures their *ability to move from one stability to another,* in the course of which (3) communication becomes *increasingly orderly* and *resistant to outside intervention.* Humberto Maturana and Varela add to these

(4) the ability to *maintain their boundary*, their identity. von Foerster demonstrated that self-organizing systems decrease their entropy (increase order) inside, and/or increase the entropy (decrease order) in their environment. Governments, for example, govern largely by keeping those governed relatively unorganized—a collectivity of citizens—and prevent competing organizational forms from emerging. von Foerster also showed that random disturbances can speed up self-organization and called this phenomenon the *order from noise principle*. Self-organization presents profound methodological challenges to the study of social phenomena.

Autopoiesis

Maturana and Varela identify *autopoiesis*—literally self-production—as the process that distinguishes living from nonliving systems. Autopoietic systems consist of *recursive networks of interactions among components that produce all and only the components necessary for such networks to continue producing them within a boundary.* (Notice the necessary self-reference in the definition of this operationally closed system.) Accordingly, biological organisms are autopoietic as they continually regenerate their physical infrastructure in their location and in the presence of internal decay and external disturbances.

Autopoietic systems "serve" no function. Reproduction, purposiveness, adaptation, cognition, even survival are epiphenomena of the autopoietic organization of living systems. Allopoietic systems, by contrast, produce something other than what constitutes them. Designed *for* a purpose, artifacts like automobiles and factories produce something needed elsewhere.

Niklas Luhmann adopted the word *autopoiesis* in his sociological systems theory. He observed that social systems do not merely organize themselves but metaphorically produce their own sociology. For Luhmann social systems are constituted in the communications that circulate within them. Their environment exists only in communications about it, and human beings, while necessary to understand and rearticulate communications, are excluded from his theory for being a mere medium for communications to create further communications.

Cognitive Autonomy

Cybernetics made numerous contributions by applying the principles of cybernetics to itself. One is Ernst von Glasersfeld's *radical constructivism* and Maturana and Varela's *biology of cognition*. Their epistemologies (ways of knowing) acknowledge that we humans cannot step out of our nervous system and determine the external causes of our perceptions. Early work on neural networks suggested that cognition recursively operates on its own processes.

From this fundamental cognitive autonomy follows that the realities we see are constructed within our nervous system, including our interactions with an environment. Our realities do not represent what exists outside cognition but merely conserve our autopoiesis. Reality constructions are retained when acting on them succeeds to expected experiences. They may be revised or expanded when unexpected experiences are taken as opportunities for learning. But they are extinguished whenever acting on them has fatal consequences to those who hold them. Thus, in ordinary life as well as in science, cognitive constructions of reality are variable and subject to an evolutionary mechanism.

Cognitive autonomy puts the cherished role of scientific observers in question. von Foerster noted that objectivity is the illusion of being able to describe the world without an observer, and encouraged cyberneticians, similar to what Mead had suggested, to include themselves in the domain of their observations. He called the practice of describing and observing one's observations *second-order cybernetics*. Although describing one's observing rather than its presumed causes introduces a circular epistemology, its attendant reliance on descriptions, on a representational conception of language, and on cognition does not quite escape the enlightenment project of describing the world as is, even when acknowledging observers in their descriptions.

Language and Discourse

Language is a *social*, not a cognitive, artifact. Conventionally, language is an abstraction from what happens in naturally occurring conversations. For Maturana, language is *consensual coordination of actions,* which is the root of conversation and related to co-orientation theory.

Cybernetics considers conversations as self-organizing, requiring no outside support. Conversations cannot be analyzed in terms of the logic of propositions, syntax, and semantics, but as language games (Ludwig Wittgenstein) consisting of speech acts (John Austin, John Searle) or conversational moves that coordinate the cognition participants bring to them. Conversations *perform or enact the very social realities that participants conversationally co-construct.* Being self-organizing, the responsibility of directing conversations is shared among their participants.

Systematically constrained conversations are called discourses. A *discourse* (a) *creates its own reality;* (b) its *objects are continuously elaborated* within its discourse community, which (c) *institutionalizes its recurrent practices,* (d) *maintains a boundary* around what does and does not belong, and (e) *justifies the reality it constructs* to other discourse communities on which it depends for material support. Scientific discourse, for example, constructs realities so as to be amenable to investigation by scientific methods and in conformity with what a discourse community considers its subject matter. It is instituted in universities, methodologies, equipment, and publications. It draws a boundary around everything to which relevant truth criteria apply and justifies its theories and models in terms of their usefulness outside science. The coexistence of many discourses puts the idea of a universe in doubt.

Because discourses need to justify themselves, they are not entirely autonomous, however. *Scientific theories,* for example, are discursive products of specialized conversations, may occur in publications outside their discourse, and can affect the truth of what they claim to describe. Especially social theories, when entering the conversations of those theorized therein, may become self-fulfilling, self-defeating, or remain irrelevant. The making or breaking of candidates for political offices by the media exemplifies how social realities are languaged into being.

An example from public opinion research is Elizabeth Noelle-Neumann's spiral of silence, a process in which citizens feel discouraged to speak in public when seemingly facing overwhelming opposition. Noticing the relative absence of their own opinions in the mass media discourages citizens from asserting their opinions, which thus converges on silence as the attractor of this negative feedback.

Unless irrelevant, the communication of theories can modify realities despite their proponents' descriptive intentions. Since all communication theories must also be communicated, communication theorists should recognize the epistemological implications of this fundamental self-reference and account for the dynamics their theories can set in motion whenever their theories enter the conversations among interested parties.

Participatory Epistemology

Ashby initiated another reflexive turn. He demonstrated that understanding systems solely from observational data is limited to trivial machines. Nontrivial systems, such as contemporary computers, humans, and social forms, embody various kinds of autonomy. They may become known in two ways—by building them or by interacting with them. Computers may be understood either way. Humans, however, cannot be designed or manufactured. They evolve with their environment, and understanding them results from interacting with them. Ashby suggested that experimenters and their objects, analysts and their analyzed, and interviewers and their interviewees form a system of which experimenters/analysts/interviewers can know only the consequences of their own actions, their manner of participating, neither the whole system nor their objects of interest.

Similarly, networks of conversation, whether constitutive of one's family, corporation, discourse community, or government, defy not only outside instruction but also comprehension by external observers. One has to join them to experience their progression—not as self-reflecting observers, but as active participants. Traditional conversation analysis, for example, limits itself to analyzing transcripts of verbal interactions, which omit what is essential to conversations: the experience of codirecting their flow.

Noting the many sociopolitical transformations that cybernetic discourse is creating in society, Mead went beyond Ashby and invited cyberneticians to expand cybernetics to include the consequences of their discourse and consider themselves as responsible participants or change agents in/of their own society. This reflexive turn encourages an epistemology of participation in systems under continuous reconstruction in which human constituents hold each other accountable for what they say and do.

Cybernetic epistemology explicitly abandons the unattainable and unethical God's-eye view of the universe, common to objectivist scientists, for the admission that one can understand always only one's contributions to a continuously evolving reality. By locating abstractions and metaperspectives in the language used during conversations, it is a bottom-up epistemology. It invokes a communication ethic that grants the human constituents of a system of interest a measure of equality, agency (accountability), cognitive autonomy (individually owned and potentially unlike conceptions), and the ability to communicate with one another (coordinating participants' understandings). It acknowledges that promoting theories, proposing actions, using artifacts commensurate with one's understanding of one's system, and communicating with other constituents about that understanding change the very system as understood. The difference between unreflective participation in one's world and scientifically guided participation lies not in the latter having privileged access to reality but in accepting accountability to those who may have to live in the realities being advanced. It means constructing realities that preserve the circularity of human communication.

Klaus Krippendorff

See also Constitutive View of Communication; Constructivism; Co-Orientation Theory; Epistemology; Information Theory; Language and Communication; Network Society; Organizational Co-Orientation Theory; Palo Alto Group; Philosophy of Communication; Relational Communication Theory; Social Construction of Reality; Spiral of Silence; System Theory

Further Readings

Ashby, W. R. (1956). *An introduction to cybernetics.* London: Chapman & Hall.

Bateson, G. (1972). *Steps to an ecology of mind.* New York: Ballantine.

Heims, S. J. (1991). *The cybernetics group.* Cambridge: MIT Press.

Maturana, H. R., & Varela, F. J. (1987). *The tree of knowledge: Biological roots of human understanding.* Boston: Shambhala.

Mead, M. (1968). Cybernetics of cybernetics. In H. von Foerster, J. D. White, L. J. Peterson, & J. K. Russell (Eds.), *Purposive systems* (pp. 1–11). New York: Spartan Books.

Varela, F. J. (1979). *Principles of biological autonomy.* New York: North Holland.

von Foerster, H., et al. (Eds.). (1974/1996). *Cybernetics of cybernetics* (2nd ed.). Minneapolis, MN: Future Systems.

von Glasersfeld, E. (1995). *Radical constructivism.* Washington, DC: Falmer Press.

Watzlawick, P., Beavin, J. H., & Jackson, D. D. (1967). *Pragmatics of human communication: A study of interactional patterns, pathologies, and paradoxes.* New York: Norton.

Wiener, N. (1948). *Cybernetics, or control and communication in the animal and machine.* New York: Wiley.

Wiener, N. (1950). *The human use of human beings: Cybernetics and society.* Boston: Houghton Mifflin.

D

Daoism

See Taoist Communication Theory

Deception Detection

Deception refers to the successful or unsuccessful deliberate attempt, without forewarning, to create in another a belief that the communicator considers to be false. This definition emphasizes that deception is an intentional, strategic act and does not necessarily require the use of words. Although many consider lying to include only outright fabrications, deception can take many forms, including concealment, omissions, exaggerations, half-truths, misdirection, and even playings such as tricking or bluffing. Telling literal truths that are designed to mislead should be considered deception, as well. This entry explores how humans detect deception and the theories that have been posited to explain deception detection. The considerable research on deception and deception detection, along with practical concerns about deception in everyday life, demonstrates the significance of this topic to communication theory.

Studies About Deception Detection

The study of deception detection has a long history. Questions about the morality of deception and how to detect it have been explored by Aristotle, St. Augustine, Aquinas, Kant, Machiavelli, Darwin, and Freud, to name just a few. Despite recent developments in technology used to detect deception, such as polygraphs, MRIs, and voice stress analyzers, most deception detection is done by humans. In the U.S. legal system, as well as in others worldwide, jurors are the sole determinant of honesty and believability of witnesses and the accused. They rely on the person's demeanor and manner of testifying to distinguish between truth and falsehood. Unfortunately, humans lack a high degree of accuracy in their deception detection abilities, rarely perform better than chance when attempting to distinguish lies from truth in research studies, and do even worse when the lie is against the self-interest of the deceiver (such as false confessions). Even deception experts such as law enforcement personnel, judges, psychiatrists, job interviewers, and auditors do not appear to detect deception with greater accuracy than nonexperts.

In order to improve accuracy, many studies have attempted to identify specific cues that differentiate liars from truth-tellers. Specific nonverbal cues, such as a lack of eye contact or foot tapping, are often thought to be associated with deception; however, few cues are reliable indicators of deception, and many behaviors show no discernible links, or only weak links, to deceit. In reality, people often do not discover lies for days, weeks, or even months afterward, and deception is typically revealed by a third party, making nonverbal cues leaked during the deception quite irrelevant. Verbal cues are only slightly more reliable, and research has suggested that deceivers are less forthcoming than those who tell the truth; furthermore, their lies are less plausible, less likely to be structured in a logical, sensible way, and more likely to be internally discrepant or to convey ambivalence than truthful statements. However, given the inconsistency of these findings in the research literature, the best method of deception detection is most likely to be verification of the information presented in a message.

Theories About Deception Detection

Through a series of lectures delivered at Harvard in 1967, Paul Grice presented a theory of language use that has come to be known as his theory of *conversational implicature*. Among others, one of his principles is the *quality maxim*—that speakers should try to make their contributions true, refraining from saying anything they know to be false or for which they have inadequate grounds for belief. This maxim, like Grice's other maxims, is an assumption that communicators must make in order to perceive others as cooperative in a conversation. Even deliberate and obvious violations of this maxim, such as irony, require communicators to use mechanisms called *implicatures* to indicate that the speaker is being truthful and therefore cooperative.

Steven McCornack created *information manipulation theory* in an attempt to understand the covert violation of Grice's maxims through the use of deceptive messages. He argues that speakers can produce messages that violate the norms of cooperative conversational exchanges either by violating Grice's rules or by adhering to Grice's rules but presenting the messages in such a way that the listener is misled (e.g., through sarcasm). Recently Kelly Aune and his colleagues presented the *theory of communicative responsibility,* in which they attempt to take Grice's principles a step further by examining the process by which communicators determine what their communicative responsibilities (including truthfulness) are and how they should satisfy those responsibilities.

David Buller and Judee Burgoon have also recently posed a theory of *interpersonal deception*, which attempts to explain how senders produce credible messages, how receivers process and judge such messages, and how the coordination between sender and receiver influences the process of deception detection. Consistent with Burgoon's previous *expectancy violations theory*, the theory of interpersonal deception suggests that understanding both the structural and the functional features of communication is crucial to understanding the interactive nature of deception.

Norah E. Dunbar

See also Conversation Analysis; Expectancy Violations Theory; Interpersonal Communication Theories; Interpersonal Deception Theory

Further Readings

Aune, R. K., Levine, T. R., Park, H. S., Asada, K. J. K., & Banas, J. A. (2005). Tests of a theory of communicative responsibility. *Journal of Language and Social Psychology, 24,* 358–381.

Bond, C. F., Jr., & DePaulo, B. M. (2006). Accuracy of deception judgments. *Personality and Social Psychology Review, 10,* 214–234.

Buller, D. B., & Burgoon, J. K. (1996). Interpersonal deception theory. *Communication Theory, 6,* 203–242.

Ekman, P. (1985). *Telling lies.* New York: W. W. Norton.

Grice, H. P. (1975). Logic and conversation. In P. Cole & J. Morgan (Eds.), *Syntax and semantics: Vol. 3* (pp. 41–58). New York: Academic.

McCornack, S. A. (1992). Information manipulation theory. *Communication Monographs, 59,* 203–242.

Park, H., Levine, T. R., McCornack, S. A., Morrison, K., & Ferrara, M. (2002). How people really detect lies. *Communication Monographs, 69,* 144–157.

Vrij, A. (2000). *Detecting lies and deceit: The psychology of lying and the implications for professional practice.* Chichester, UK: Wiley.

DECONSTRUCTION

Deconstruction is famously associated with the Algerian-born French philosopher Jacques Derrida (1930–2004). One of the most influential thinkers of the 20th century, Derrida is also known as one of the leading voices of what is loosely called *poststructuralism*. Over a distinguished career that began in the 1960s, he produced a large body of work that has irrevocably unmoored many of the most securely anchored ideas in Western philosophical thinking. Through careful and ingenious readings of key texts in philosophy and literature, both ancient and modern, Derrida managed to uncover in them a set of hidden contradictions that work against the best intentions of their authors. According to Derrida's critical readings, philosophical arguments are no different from those in literature and, like them, are subject to all sorts of alternative interpretations, equivocations, paradoxes, even unacknowledged mistakes, in other words, various "accidents" caused by what he called the loose play of language traditionally considered to be the standard, even desirable, form of literary writing.

After the publication of *Writing and Difference, Of Grammatology,* and *Speech and Phenomenon* in 1967, Derrida was quickly recognized as a uniquely iconoclastic critic of Western philosophy, and his ideas, now called *deconstructionism,* began to circulate widely, crossing disciplinary boundaries and wielding ever-increasing influence in the humanities, social sciences, and beyond.

The result was a sizable quake under philosophers' feet, a violent shaking that weakened philosophy's boasting claim to being the first science of all sciences. Derrida showed that philosophy is not immune from the figurative exuberance of language and is essentially *textual*—a kind of writing no more and no less serious than nonphilosophical ones—and, as a result, the long-accepted tenet that philosophy is the most logical and judicious path to truth, goodness, and beauty is shown to be one of disillusionment and misconception.

It is important to note that Derrida hardly used the word *deconstruction* in his early writings and expressed his disfavor toward the term because of its negative semantic associations. However, after this term gained wide circulation and began to take root in contemporary critical vocabulary, he came to accept its currency and often commented on the word's negative associations in an effort to clarify what deconstruction means and how it ought to be understood. One of the points he made repeatedly is that deconstruction does not affirm or assert a thesis of its own per se. Instead, Derrida prefers to define the term by saying what it is not, instead of stating straightforwardly what it is. Here he intends to impart two things.

First, in principle and in practice deconstruction does not and cannot affirm any position in relation to its object of analysis. Instead of attempting to ground philosophy on a single unifying principle, as philosophers always do, deconstruction, by design, proposes no unifying principle on which to build anything new. Having no position to call its own, deconstruction is a kind of reading, which consists of reading with a fidelity that finally betrays the contradictions hidden within the text—fundamental contradictions that cause what is built on them to falter and collapse. This studied way of reading can properly be called deconstructive rather than destructive; in fact, this way of reading is as far from being destructive as the text is from achieving its claims in that it *follows* the text in good faith, teasing out through this faithful following the warring forces that are within the text. Deconstructive reading, therefore, is parasitic; it is always dependent on the text to which it is applied for meaning.

Second, following from the idea that it affirms no position of its own, deconstruction must also be understood to be a practice that eliminates itself. Deconstructive reading is possible only by virtue of the text it follows and cannot exist apart from the text to which it is applied. By allowing the text to speak for itself, deconstruction necessarily falls prey to its own operation. Being parasitic, deconstruction proceeds only to deconstruct itself. It cannot make truth claims because it would have to cause its own truth claims to disappear.

Although deconstruction is without a thesis of its own, it is not voiceless or without basis. As a parasitic practice, it cannot survive without a medium through which to operate. It would not be able to unfold unless there is a *co-text,* or discourse with which it is compared or understood, or *con-text,* a larger set of discourses that provide a basis for deconstruction. These co- or con-texts provide a frame in and against which deconstruction enacts the unweaving of the host text. This medium is language and what language makes possible; it is writing, including what writing means to say. Deconstruction takes place in writing: It reads the host text, rereads what is written, and rewrites what the host text claims to construct. Writing matters for deconstruction because it is where the problem of philosophy begins and ends, and it is also where deconstruction begins and continues to begin without end. This attention to writing, to how language works, explains Derrida's obsession with texts; it also explains the notoriety of the phrase, for which deconstruction is popularly, albeit regrettably to its proponents, known: "*il n'y a pas d'hors texte*" (there is nothing outside the text).

This careful attention to text helps us understand how deconstruction operates, how it positions itself to begin to cut into a text in the way it does, and how this cut disrupts what the philosopher intends to say. To illustrate this, let's imagine the following situation: After a hard day in the office, John and Etsuko decide to go for a quick meal before heading home. Driving along a strip in town where fast food chains are located, they agree to stop for a burger. Thinking about the options, John turns to Etsuko and asks, "McDonald's or Burger King?" Perhaps out of politeness, Etsuko responds by saying, "Which one do you like?" Out of politeness, too, John quickly replies, "Why don't you pick? They are the same to me." Instead of making an apparently simple choice, however, Etsuko murmurs to herself, "Oh, no! They are not the same," and starts to explain to John the different ingredients used by McDonald's and Burger King and the different ways they prepare their meals. Little amused by Etsuko's long-winded report and desperate to find a parking place, John bursts out, "Just pick one! What difference does it make?" On hearing this, Etsuko proceeds to discuss in great detail the differences in tastes and nutrition values between a Whopper and a burger sold under the Golden Arches.

It is not difficult for us to imagine the frustration John experiences as he listens to Etsuko's lecture on hamburgers while searching for parking, and it is not difficult for us to appreciate the comic effect brought about by Etsuko's sublime response to John's apparently straightforward question. Etsuko is faultless in her literal interpretation: She understands the question, "What difference does it make?" and answers it accordingly. Pragmatically, however, she fails to decode John's message according to its context, thus misunderstanding what John means. It is this misunderstanding on Etsuko's part that makes us smile, and, more fundamentally, it is language—language as it is used by us to do things—that makes both Etsuko's misunderstanding and our smile possible.

This example suggests that language and meaning are thorny affairs that often unfold beyond speakers' control, catching them by surprise and generating effects they hardly expect. Contextual variations notwithstanding, John's utterance is not ambiguous or equivocal: It means what it says, and John intends it to mean what it is supposed to mean. From Etsuko's perspective, the meaning of John's utterance is equally clear: Phrased as a question, John's speech is seen by Etsuko as a request to spell out the differences between the hamburgers sold at two different restaurants. However, we, as outside observers, may analyze the complication of meaning exhibited by this example. The fact remains that a seemingly simple sentence, "What difference does it make?" is capable of yielding meanings that are contradictory, meanings that end up neutralizing or negating one another. On one hand, it means, as John intends it, expressly that between two choices, McDonald's or Burger King, there is no difference; on the other hand, since it comes forward as a question, the sentence can be properly interpreted as a direct request for the interlocutor, Etsuko, to specify the differences between two choices. To the extent the sentence requests a specification of the differences between two choices, it implies that there are indeed differences between them. The two readings are equally valid, and they can be given, or rather give themselves, only to negate each other. It is contradiction like this—a contradiction inherent in language when and especially when things seem to go on as usual—that causes a text to undo itself, to unsay what is said, and hence to make the meaning of the said finally *undecidable*.

Philosophical and literary texts are undoubtedly more complex and complicated than is an offhanded remark addressed to a fellow hamburger lover. So if a verbal riposte such as John's and Etsuko's can have contradictory meanings, then a text—philosophical, literary, or otherwise—will also speak inevitably and unknowingly against itself and fall victim to what cannot be controlled. To write, as Plato recognized, is to fight against the possible tailspins of what one intends to say, yet in writing, in making language say what one wants it to say, the writing itself also brings down what one thinks one is saying. Deconstruction takes place as long as writing takes place, as long as one writes.

Critics of deconstructive writings, particularly those by Derrida, often complain that such writings are difficult to understand and even incomprehensible. Where does this sense of frustration come from? Is it not the case that reading and writing have never been and never will be easy? It is out of the difficulty of reading and writing—a difficulty *of* that which we call language—that deconstruction comes to pass. It is this difficulty of language that deconstruction boldly confronts. It is also to this difficulty that deconstruction, nonthetic notwithstanding, ceaselessly turns and returns.

Briankle G. Chang

See also Critical Theory; Postmodern Theory; Poststructuralism

Further Readings

Bennington, G. (1993). *Jacques Derrida*. Chicago: University of Chicago Press.

Derrida, J. (1973). *Speech and phenomena*. Evanston, IL: Northwestern University Press.

Derrida, J. (1988). *Limited Inc.* (G. Graff, Ed.). Evanston, IL: Northwestern University Press.

Derrida, J. (1997). *Of grammatology* (G. Spivak, Trans.). Baltimore: Johns Hopkins University Press.

Stocker, B. (2007). *Jacques Derrida: Basic writings*. New York: Routledge.

DEFINITIONS OF COMMUNICATION

The central thrust of human communication concerns mutually understood symbolic exchange. This entry considers the purpose and form of definitions, and the function of message, source, receiver, and channel considerations in defining the term *communication*. It discusses the consequences of different definitions of communication for the meaningful use of the term.

Characteristics of Definitions

Broad Versus Narrow

The term *communication* is commonly used in both broad and narrow senses, from simple human contact to technical uses as in information theory. Defining *communication* broadly, perhaps as the transfer of information, provides the advantage of including most or all the possible instances that the term *communication* might ever be used to reference.

This large number of possibilities will also include many actual instances that the user likely neither intended nor had in mind. Overly broad definitions are not "wrong," but in many cases their breadth precludes their utility in delineating the area under study. Related problems are encountered when definitions become too narrow, thereby excluding portions of what is actually under study. To be useful, definitions in any scholarly area need to describe what is actually studied and to represent accurately the manner in which the term is used in practice in the discipline.

Inherent Meaning Versus Human Creations

One form of definition states "Communication is…" and lists its defining characteristics. This form assumes that words have fixed or relatively fixed meanings and that the function of definitions is one of discovery of the *correct meaning* of a term. The concept of fixed definitions implies that there are correct definitions and meanings that are inherent in objects—that all tables possess a form of "tableness," for example—where tableness is conceived to be a known, preexisting, and relatively permanent property of nature. It also presumes that the definitional process involves seeking out this inherent preexisting meaning and then phrasing this meaning accurately in *the* definition. Alternately, definitions can be regarded as human creations that are changeable over time, context, sociocultural language group, and purpose. The definitional process in the second approach is seen as a search for utility of usage wherein definitions can be discarded or changed according to that utility. This second approach suggests "Let us use the term *communication* to mean…" rather than "Communication is…." The human creation approach involves evaluating definitions according to their ability to further the purposes of the persons involved in the communication transactions in question and is often more useful in studying communication.

Clear Boundary Versus Central Thrust

Definitions can also be used in an attempt to place all events qualifying as communication in one box and all events not so qualifying in another. The goal of such *clear boundary* definitions is to create certainty as to what is and what is not included in the defined term. An alternative goal of definitions is represented by the *central thrust* approach, wherein the major properties of the defined concept are stated and concern for boundary conditions is left for those instances that require such clear delineation when employing the definition in practice.

Characteristics Affecting Definitions

The Message: Signs and Symbols

Charles Peirce uses the term *sign* as an overarching category in his system of semiotics, with *indexical, iconic,* and *symbolic* signs as principal subdivisions. Each of these subdivisions is intended to overlap with other subdivisions in Peirce's system and is purposely ambiguously defined. For example, a defining characteristic of *symbols* in Peirce's system is the need for symbols to be learned. Yet both his *indexical* and *iconic* signs also require learning, as none are innate. For the purpose of defining communication, a more useful system may be provided by regarding *signals* as the overarching category, where signals are all stimuli normally detectable by humans through any of their five senses. Two nonoverlapping and clearly defined subdivisions of signals then become *signs* and *symbols*. *Signs* in this method are detectable stimuli characterized by a direct, fixed, physical connection to their referent, while s*ymbols* have only an arbitrarily defined connection to their referent. Thus symbols require some form of prior agreement between the communicating parties specifying the relationship between symbol and referent. Signs require learning, but not prior agreement, since they have a physical connection to their referent. *Icons* in this system are simply symbols that attempt to employ some form of resemblance to some property of their referent in the construction of the representation used to denote them. Any such resemblance must be specified through prior agreement in creating the intended symbolic usage, and that usage can be changed and manipulated in the same way as with all other symbols. Thus icons do not require a special category. They are symbols. And signs and symbols are each unique categories that taken together cover the domain of perceived signals.

Language is one way of providing prior agreement. A language provides one or more definitions of detectable sound, light, odor, taste, and/or touch patterns that will be used as symbols to represent ordered symbolic events within a message. While signs, as defined, can represent only physical events, often only in the here and now, symbols can be used to represent any form of event: physical, phenomenological, the dreamed of and hoped for, unreal ideas and conceptions, the here and now, or the not-here and the not-now. Symbols also allow for great latitude in lying, where the ability to lie may itself be treated as a defining characteristic of human communication. Some animals and plants use signs as determined by their DNA in order to disguise, deceive, and mislead. But a direct conscious deliberate lie so intended by an individual requires some involvement with symbols.

Source and Receiver Considerations

Plants, Animals, and Machines

Broad divisions of source and receiver include humans, animals, plants, and machines. Machines communicate through simple information transfer, as in radio transmission and computer functions. Machine communication differs from the simple physical contact of objects. Information about course and position relative to an approaching vessel obtained by a ship's radar and sent to an autopilot is clearly of a different order from contact between the hulls of the two vessels. Physical contact may produce knowledge if it is detected by a communicative system, but the phenomenological information thereby produced is of a different nature from the physical contact that produced it. This distinction recognizes the difference between the physical and phenomenological planes on which humans exist. Communication ultimately concerns the phenomenological plane, involving knowledge, beliefs, and feelings and the relationship of information in this plane to the physical.

Human communication differs from the signaling behavior of plants and animals by transferring information in a way that fundamentally defines human communication: *Human communication occurs through the use of at least some mutually understood symbols* and may include other forms of information transfer as well. While human symbols are completely arbitrary, requiring prior agreement among the parties for communication to occur, no such agreement is required by animals and plants. Animal and plant message systems are signlike, essentially determined by DNA. Plants and animals employing these message forms cannot alter them or their meanings at will. Humans can and do alter forms and meanings and can carry their arbitrarily defined symbols with them rather than lugging along the objects or bringing forth the concepts they represent. This apparently minor distinction—the ability to change the meaning of symbols by agreement—is the basis for all human knowledge, stored symbolically within the human brain, libraries, and hard drives. It is also the basis of human communication.

Intent of the Source

Human communication can be defined either with or without the involvement of intent on the part of the source. In the study of persuasion, knowledge of the intent of a source regarding the desired effect of a message on a receiver is needed in order to determine the relative success of a persuasive message. Aside from the evaluation of the efficacy of persuasive messages, intent is not required as a definitional requirement for human communication unless unintentional messages, such as in much of nonverbal behavior, are specifically intended to be ruled out of consideration.

One Cannot Not Communicate

Related to the definitional consideration of intent is Paul Watzlawick, Janet Beavin, and Donald Jackson's suggestion that one *cannot not communicate*. To accept this suggestion requires an exceptionally broad and unusual definition of communication. This broad usage implies that communication occurs whenever any human is simply present, regardless of whether the person is alone or whether any communicative actions are taken or avoided by the human. In the narrower original sense, the phrase refers to the inability of any potential source or situational actor to stop a potential receiver from making inferences about the potential source's actions or lack thereof. Nonverbal cues can always be interpreted by a receiver regardless of whether the source actually did or did not emit the cues, did or did not intend to emit the cues, or was asleep or deceased. A more direct phrasing of *one cannot not communicate* might suggest that people will invariably make inferences about the behavior of another person, though they may be incorrect in those inferences and though the behaviors that may have led to the inferences may have been imagined by the receiver rather than emitted by the source. Nothing in the phrase *one cannot not communicate* implies the need for symbolic or signlike behavior by a source, the existence of a message, the existence of a communicative interaction, or the existence of any degree of source–receiver shared meaning. Rather, communication is judged to exist whenever an observer creates meaning. The phrase operates heuristically concerning how the term *communication* might most usefully be defined. If communication is defined only as *meaning creation by one person through observation of anything about another person*, then we could conclude that one cannot not communicate. With other definitions of communication, it is quite possible to not communicate.

Considerations Related to Channel

A third consideration in defining communication, beyond those of the message and source–receiver considerations, involves the channel. The term *communications* is often used in reference to the media or channels of communication. Three principal issues relevant to defining human communication concern nonverbal communication, intrapersonal communication, and the extent of completion of the transmission–interaction process.

Nonverbal Behavior and Nonverbal Communication

In 1904 a retired German schoolteacher owned a horse named Hans. The teacher spoke to the horse and taught the horse to send messages back to him using hoof tapping as the coding system. Hans could do simple numerical calculations when given the arithmetic problems orally and could encode words by converting letters into a number of taps. This implied that the horse had communicative ability since he could receive and apparently understand symbolic messages and could respond to them in a reasonable manner. This was truly remarkable for a horse, who was thus renamed Clever Hans. In fact, Hans could behave, but he could not communicate. Hans's "communication" occurred solely in the minds of his human listeners. Hans could tell when his listeners wanted him to stop tapping through an awareness of their nonverbal behaviors. He wanted the rewards he received from them when he stopped but received the rewards only if he stopped when people wanted him to stop. This occurred when he reached a number of taps that had a specific mental significance for the people, significance not shared by the horse. Hoof tapping is nonverbal behavior, not nonverbal communication. The fact of meaning assignment occurring inside the heads of listeners with respect to the horse's behavior does not provide a particularly useful definition of communication. No common meanings for the communicative behaviors of the horse were shared between the people and the horse. It may be useful to suggest that some degree of shared common meaning between a source and a receiver must occur before any behavior, verbal or nonverbal, is considered communicative.

Intrapersonal Communication

Intrapersonal communication, communication within a person or between a person and himself or herself, is a form or class of thinking, just as nonverbal communication is a form or class of nonverbal behavior. Intrapersonal communication cannot be identical to thinking or it would be nothing more than thinking. There would be no reason for its existence as a concept. It differs from thinking as a generic concept in its emphasis on the existence of a dialogue occurring within one person and its focus on the message-creation and meaning-creation processes. Intrapersonal communication is often conceived as involving a conversation or sharing of meaning between two positions or modes of thought within a person. It involves shared meanings between the dialogic entities. Unlike generic nonverbal behavior, thinking itself involves the use of symbolic forms. Thus its subsets such as intrapersonal communication inherently involve the symbolic transfer of meaning, possibly between two dialogic positions within a person.

The Transmission Process

Communication involves a sequence of communicative events that, individually, constitute insufficient conditions for its existence. The boundary conditions for the departure and end points of each event in the sequence are clearly elastic, with the ordering sequence of the events relatively but not absolutely fixed and the departure point for analysis within the sequence arbitrary.

The following communicative events both specify a sequence and provide a template for considering the difference between *attempts to communicate* and *communication*. They assume a written message but are adaptable to all channels and are but one way of punctuating a communication situation. The question becomes, would a specific punctuated instance or sequence of events be *communication* or simply *an attempt to communicate* if the sequence progressed only to the first element of the sequence, to the second element, and so forth:

1. The possibility of composing a message is considered.

2. A message is considered and intended, but not composed.

3. A message is intended to be sent and is composed, but is not sent.

4. The message is composed, intended, and sent but not received.

5. The message is composed, intended, sent, and received but not detectible as received by the receiver.

6. The message is detectible, received with the source's knowledge, but not opened.

7. The message is received, recognized as such by the receiver, opened but not processed.

8. The message is received, opened, and partially processed.

9. The message is opened and processed, but not understood.

10. The message is processed and understood to an extent but with no measurable cognitive or emotional change in the receiver.

11. The message is understood to an extent with consequent phenomenological change, but without any externally observable response.

12. The message is intended, composed, sent, received, detected, recognized as a message, opened, processed, understood, and interpreted, with an externally observable response, but without a reply.

13. The message is composed and so forth, with an externally observable response, and sending a reply is considered.

And so forth.

This sequence is one way of segmenting a communication process. The lines between the given event segments could be drawn at other points, and different elements of the process could be selected for discussion. In this sequence of events, Event 13 is similar for the receiver to Event 1 for the source. The unstated continuation of the sequence through Events 14 to 25 if phrased similarly to Events 1 to 13 would complete the feedback loop, with Event 26 for the original source in the event sequence similar to Event 1 for that source, the possibility of composing a reply to the reply. Defining communication as any set of events that does not include at least Segments 1 to 11 would suggest that speaking to someone in language X who does not understand X is *communication*, rather than simply *a communicative attempt*.

Similarly, when an academic area concerns itself almost exclusively with message construction, as in Events 1 to 5 and little beyond, it may be more accurately named as an area concerned with one or more such forms of message construction rather than one of communication itself. Persons studying communication implicitly assume the existence of some or all these elements within the context of their work. Making the elements included in their work explicit may be useful in furthering the study of communication. As with all fields, that of communication is usefully informed by work in many areas of study that do not in and of themselves constitute the central thrust of communication, but are of fundamental importance to its understanding.

Thomas M. Steinfatt

See also Constitutive View of Communication; General Semantics; Nonverbal Communication Theories; Process of Communication; Semiotics and Semiology

Further Readings

Berlo, D. K. (1960). *The process of communication.* New York: Holt, Rinehart, & Winston.

Berlo, D. K. (1977). Human communication: The basic proposition. In T. M. Steinfatt (Ed.), *Readings in interpersonal communication* (pp. 15–25). Indianapolis, IN: Bobbs-Merrill.

Littlejohn, S. W., & Foss, K. A. (2008). *Theories of human communication* (9th ed.). Belmont, CA: Thomson Wadsworth.

Newman, J. (1960). A rationale for a definition of communication. *Journal of Communication, 10,* 115–124.

Sebeok, T. A., & Rosenlthal, R. (Eds.). (1981). *The Clever Hans phenomenon: Communication with horses, whales, apes, and people.* New York: Academy of Sciences.

Steinfatt, T. M. (1976). *Human communication.* Indianapolis, IN: Bobbs-Merrill.

Watzlawick, P., Beavin, J., & Jackson, D. (1967). *Pragmatics of human communication.* New York: Norton.

Winer, M., Devoe, S., Rubinow, S., & Geller, J. (1972). Nonverbal behavior and nonverbal communication. *Psychological Review, 79,* 185–214.

DELIBERATIVE DEMOCRATIC THEORIES

Deliberative democratic theories comprise a diverse array of approaches and insights on *deliberative democracy,* the idea that citizens directly contribute to ongoing substantive and inclusive public discussion and debate and seek to arrive at *reasoned consensus* through appeals to the public good. Deliberative democratic theories also emphasize the necessity of deliberation within government itself and especially in those *governance* practices in which public officials and citizens work together. This body of work consists of insights from many sources—from advances in moral or political philosophy to the testing of novel empirical hypotheses. With origins in critiques of existing political practices, deliberative democratic theory has grown into a complex interdisciplinary body of intellectual, methodological, and practical scholarship.

Conceptualizing Deliberation and Democracy

Contemporary work on deliberation often traces back to the writings of German social theorist Jürgen Habermas, who argued that modern political systems needed to sustain a vibrant *public sphere*, a space in which diverse members of a society freely interact and address common concerns outside formal public institutions. In an *ideal speech situation*, people could debate issues based solely on the merits of their arguments, uninfluenced by inequalities in participants' social, economic, or legal standing.

Though suggested as a philosophical abstraction (and background assumption underlying democratic political and legal discourse), early deliberative theory written or inspired by Habermas drew criticism for its lack of realism. In particular, the *difference critique* holds that unfettered deliberation cannot occur, owing to pervasive inequalities among citizens in any society. In this view, promoting deliberative ideals glosses over such differences and confers unwarranted political legitimacy on public institutions. Public discourse norms should never promote deliberation to the exclusion of alternative forms of speech, such as personal testimony and advocacy, particularly within and between different subpublics unlikely to share common interests. Even amid this critique, however, some theorists developed full-scale conceptions of democracy inspired by the deliberative ideal.

Empirical Deliberative Theory and Practice

Since the late 1990s, much deliberative democratic theory and research have focused on the actual practice of political conversation, discussion, debate, dialogue, and other communicative practices that can, at times, represent aspects of the deliberative ideal. Empirical theories vary in their definitions of deliberation but generally understand it to be a discursive process of carefully weighing diverse arguments about the most appropriate form of action to take in addressing a public problem. Deliberation involves gaining background knowledge and exploring alternative solutions, all respecting the equality of speaking opportunities and the full diversity of participant viewpoints and experiences.

This conception of deliberation grounds in the actual *practice* of deliberation. Beginning with citizens' juries and planning cells in the 1970s, a range of deliberative designs have been developed that involve lay citizens in governance, public debate, and civic education. In some ways, this represents a resurgence of the *forum movement* of the early-20th-century United States, but modern deliberative models often give citizens a more direct role in policymaking and draw from international experiments with consensus conferences, deliberative polls, national issues forums, participatory budgeting, study circles, 21st-century town meetings, and other processes.

The bulk of empirical work on deliberation has scrutinized the effects of these deliberative practices (or lower-grade simulations of them). In particular, theorists have devoted considerable attention to how participants in deliberative events change the quality and direction of their policy-relevant attitudes. The general hypothesis animating much deliberative research maintains that participants refine their unreflective opinions into considered judgments through the experience of hearing and advancing arguments that are interwoven with both personal experiences and general information. In some cases, theorists maintain that participants are likely to change their basic position on an issue, shifting from one point of view to another. In the aggregate, this could produce something approaching the elusive ideal of a broad public consensus.

The findings of numerous studies, however, show that deliberative events only crystallize public opinion around a shared judgment under special circumstances. Studies of political conversations, loosely structured discussions, and mediated deliberative experiences, such as watching a news program on an issue, are more likely to sharpen the clarity and consistency of participants' original views, particularly when the activity involves sophisticated participants who can recognize the others present who share their own views. By contrast, a broad consensus often emerges in carefully designed events that ensure sustained deliberation among a diverse cross-section of the public. For example, the British Columbia Citizens Assembly brought together a large random sample of that province's citizens to discuss electoral reform over the course of several months. By the end, the participants reached a near consensus on advocating a new voting system that, prior to deliberation, almost none had even known existed.

Other deliberative theories under development explore how deliberation in juries, forums, and other venues shapes participants' subsequent civic attitudes and behavior. Additional work seeks to clarify the circumstances under which public deliberation influences public policy or the local community's future civic capacity and appetite for a more deliberative approach to politics in general.

Both qualitative and quantitative research also investigates what kind of communication actually takes place during ostensibly deliberative events face-to-face and online. Early findings suggest that deliberation involves a considerable amount of storytelling and quasi-narrative speech. Formal argument and counterargument appear less common, unless built into the structure of the event itself. These early findings complicate empirical deliberative theory by pointing to the importance of clarifying precisely what kinds of communication behavior (and cognition) operate in deliberation and the long-term attitudinal and behavioral impacts of these differences on participants, policymaking, and community politics.

John Gastil

See also Critical Theory; Dialogue Theories; Ordinary Democracy; Political Communication Theories; Public Sphere

Further Readings

Chambers, S. (2003). Deliberative democratic theory. *Annual Review of Political Science, 6,* 307–326.

Dahlberg, L. (2005). The Habermasian public sphere: Taking difference seriously. *Theory and Society, 34,* 111–136.

Delli Carpini, M. X., Cook, F. L., & Jacobs, L. R. (2004). Public deliberation, discursive participation, and citizen engagement: A review of the empirical literature. *Annual Review of Political Science, 7,* 315–344.

Gastil, J. (2008). *Political communication and deliberation.* Thousand Oaks, CA: Sage.

DEPENDENCY THEORIES

See Asian Communication Theory; Digital Divide; Flow and Contra-Flow; Free Flow Doctrine; Informatization; International Communication Theories; International Development Theories; New World Information and Communication Order (NWICO); Uses, Gratifications, and Dependency

DIALOGUE THEORIES

From a communication perspective, dialogue represents a form of discourse that emphasizes listening and inquiry, with the aims of fostering mutual respect and understanding. Dialogue allows communicators to become aware of the different ways that individuals interpret and give meaning to similar experiences. It is viewed as a dynamic, transactional process, with a special focus on the quality of the relationship between participants.

The term *dialogue* derives from the Greek *dialogos,* in which *logos* refers to meaning and *dia* is a prefix that translates as *through* or *across.* Implied in its Greek roots is the notion that meaning emerges from interaction; it is not something that already exists, waiting to be discovered. Meaning is co-constituted through communication, reflecting both the form of message exchange and the relationship between individuals. Dialogue is made possible by the attitudes with which participants approach each other, the ways they talk and act, and the context within which they meet.

Dialogue is often contrasted with monologue, a transmission-focused process that is primarily concerned with control of the other and of the situation, and with discussion and debate, both of which involve dissecting or breaking things apart, with an emphasis on the presentation and defense of positions. Dialogue points beyond the everyday exchange of messages, implying a particular quality of communication that makes possible learning and change, in both self and others. Dialogue does not preclude disagreement; indeed it allows participants to explore complexities of their own perspectives as well as those of others. Scholars advocate dialogue as a constructive way for individuals to navigate their differences in interpersonal, organizational, community, and public realms. This entry provides a brief overview of the primary "thought leaders" in dialogue theory and traces the way in which dialogue theory was incorporated into and developed within the communication discipline.

Thought Leaders in Dialogue Theory

There are many important contributors to dialogue theory, but the following are considered to be those who most directly addressed dialogue in their writings: Martin Buber, Carl Rogers, Hans-Georg Gadamer, Mikhail Bakhtin, David Bohm, and Paulo Freire.

The existentialist philosopher Martin Buber placed the concept of dialogue at the center of his approach to human communication and human existence. His distinction between two types of human relationships, *I-It* and *I-Thou,* became a key focus of dialogue theory. In an I-It relationship, the communicator views the other as an object and manipulates the other for the communicator's own selfish ends. The communication in an I-It relationship is characterized by self-centeredness, deception, pretense, appearance, domination, and even exploitation. Persuasion, prestige, and power characterize the exchange. In an I-Thou relationship, on the other hand, the attitudes and behavior of each communicator revolve around honesty, directness, spontaneity, and mutual responsibility. Individuals in a dialogic relationship do not attempt to impose their own views on each other, and each person accepts the other unconditionally, without attempts to change the other. Dialogic partners show an awareness that others are unique and whole persons, exhibit a *genuineness* or *authenticity* toward each other, and demonstrate a *respect* for each other that encourages mutual growth and development.

Buber also introduced the concept of the *between* as a guiding communication metaphor. He understood dialogue as rooted in the space that exists between persons in a relationship. It is this common center of discourse that brings people together in conversation, not the individual psyche of the interactants. His emphasis on the sphere of the

between and the way in which meaning is co-constituted during dialogue takes the focus away from both individualism and collectivism and places it on the relational. This gives recognition to the *interdependence* of self and other, the *intersubjectivity* of meaning, and the *emergent* nature of reality.

Carl Rogers, considered by many to be the most influential American psychologist and psychotherapist, was a central figure in advancing a dialogic view of communication. One of the founders of the humanistic approach to psychology, he developed a *client-centered* approach to therapy, which he later termed *person-centered* as the application of his work broadened to include relationships in other contexts. He believed that *listening* was central to therapy and to all relationships, and he popularized the term *empathy* as key to meaningful communication. Perhaps more than any other leader of the humanistic psychological movement, Rogers shifted the focus of communication to the *self.* He believed that communication and relationships must center on concern for human feelings, human relationships, and human potential. He placed a great deal of trust in the innate wisdom of human beings, believing that if one could get in touch with the deepest sense of self, direction will emerge and constructive changes would occur without the need to be instructed, shown, or directed by others. He encouraged stripping away facades and moving away from "oughts," expectations of others, and attempts to please others. Rogers believed that a space could be opened for dialogue when relationships are characterized by a willingness to listen and to enter into a meaningful relationship with the other, genuineness in sharing feelings and ideas with the other, respect and regard for the other, and empathic understanding, which he viewed as entering the private perceptual world of the other and becoming "at home" in it.

Hans-Georg Gadamer was a philosopher who studied and worked closely with Martin Heidegger; Gadamer became interested in hermeneutics, or interpreting the meaning of written texts and symbolic artifacts, from his association with Heidegger. Gadamer's goal was to uncover the nature of human understanding. In his treatise *Truth and Method,* he argued that humans above all seek understanding, and it is through language that this understanding is built. Both language and understanding are living, dynamic processes, open to continual development and change. Meanings that evolve between oneself and the other are open, fluid, and dependent on both the context of the encounter and the prior understandings and prejudices of interpreters. He wrote about the positive impact of prejudice, which he argued needs to be recognized as inherent in all communicators and forms the basis for human understanding. Gadamer used the phrase *fusion of horizons* to characterize the understanding that develops between persons. He believed that the process of understanding is not based on empathy for another but involves the attainment of a "higher universality" that overcomes the limited horizons of each participant. It is a move from the separate positions of individuals to a synthesizing position that includes relevant aspects of each person's views.

Mikhail Bakhtin was a Russian scholar of literature, culture, language, and philosophy who produced the bulk of his writings in the 1920s through the 1940s but who was not discovered by Western scholars until the 1970s and 1980s. Though he addressed a wide range of topics, the concept of dialogue was central to his thinking. He believed that dialogue reflects both unity and difference, and at the heart of dialogue is the simultaneous fusion and differentiation of perspectives. For dialogue to occur, participants must build a common base of understanding and at the same time maintain the uniqueness of their individual perspectives. Bakhtin views dialogue as embodying a dialectical *tensionality* that inherently gives it a fluid and dynamic nature. As participants engage in dialogic interaction, there is a dynamic interplay of expression and nonexpression, certainty and uncertainty, conventionality and uniqueness, integration and separation. Dialogue, to Bakhtin, is an emergent process in which the *interplay of contradictory forces* creates a constant state of unrest and instability, while also bringing moments of *unity and synthesis*.

David Bohm, an American physicist and colleague of Albert Einstein, spent most of his career in London. His early works dealt with topics such as quantum theory and the theory of relativity; later in his career he brought his understanding of theoretical physics into the realm of dialogue. He warned against the dangers of *fragmentation,* of breaking the interaction process into separate elements that are treated as if they are independent of each other. Instead, he argued, dialogue must be

understood as a *holistic* process rather than as a collection of separate exchanges. This undivided whole is in a constant state of flow and change, part of an unbroken movement. Bohm believed that for dialogue to occur and be sustained, communicators must suspend judgment about both their own and others' beliefs and opinions. This *suspension* implies allowing a variety of perspectives to exist in tension, without premature attempts to resolve them.

The Brazilian educator Paulo Freire is best known for his influential book *Pedagogy of the Oppressed*. In Freire's view, dialogue allows us to move away from individualism and the focus on self to jointly build a learning community. He advocated a dialogic style of education in which the student's own historical situation provides the starting point for learning. In his work with nontraditional students, he sought, through dialogue, to protect the dignity of learners, allowing them to explore new ideas without fear of humiliation. According to Freire, it is important to affirm the other, thereby helping to instill a sense of hope in the minds of an otherwise oppressed community. For Freire, dialogue can transform the world by enabling us to explore the type of world we desire and shape it together. Dialogue is built on *humility* to learn from the other, guided by *trust* between communicators, and pushed forward by *hope* for liberation from oppression. He insists on the unity of word and action: Unless dialogue leads to changes, it is just "idle chatter." Although he also believed that action without dialogue was also inappropriate, he saw dialogue as the way to challenge the existing domination that was responsible for oppression.

Dialogue Theories in Communication

Communication scholars have been concerned with the concept of dialogue from the field's earliest days, starting with study of the Socratic dialogues written by Plato. Until around 1970, however, the focus of dialogue studies in communication was primarily on rhetorical inquiry. This began to change when Floyd Matson and Ashley Montagu published their influential volume *The Human Dialogue,* which appeared in 1967. The authors drew heavily from the work of Martin Buber, adopting his contrast of dialogue with monologue. They described how dialogue promotes both development of self and knowing the other in the context of strengthening the relationship between individuals. They characterized dialogue as the "unfinished third revolution" in communication theory, sketching out a vision of communication that would move from detachment to connection, from objectivity and subjectivity to intersubjectivity, and from estranged aloofness to "something resembling an act of love." Although Matson and Montagu's works were not from the communication discipline, their book helped turn attention toward new ways of conceptualizing the speaker–listener relationship.

Communication scholar Richard Johannesen's 1971 article "The Emerging Concept of Communication as Dialogue" provided an important impetus for the development of dialogic studies in the communication discipline. Drawing heavily from Martin Buber and Carl Rogers, he described what he called the major components essential for dialogic communication: (a) genuineness—avoiding a façade, stratagem, or projection of an image; (b) accurate empathic understanding—reflecting feelings as seen from the other's viewpoint; (c) unconditional positive regard—confirmation and nonpossessive warmth for the other, without necessarily approving the behavior of the other; (d) presentness—avoiding distractions and being communicatively accessible; (e) spirit of mutual equality—viewing each other as persons, not objects, avoiding superiority and power; and (f) supportive psychological climate—listening without anticipating, interfering, competing, refuting, or warping meanings. Johannesen raised a number of questions that were given attention by subsequent scholars: Should monologue and dialogue be viewed as mutually exclusive opposites? How does one study dialogue? Can it be subjected to empirical research? Can people be taught to engage in dialogue? What ethical issues are inherent in the concept of dialogue? What is the role of nonverbal communication in dialogue? In what communication contexts can dialogue function most effectively?

As the study of interpersonal communication advanced in the 1970s, a number of dialogically oriented textbooks were published. John Keltner's *Interpersonal Speech Communication*, Kim Giffin and Bobby Patton's *Fundamentals of Interpersonal Communication*, Charles Brown and Paul Keller's *Monologue to Dialogue: An Exploration of Interpersonal Communication*, and John Stewart's classic reader *Bridges Not Walls* all reflected a shift away from the older rhetorical traditions in communication to increased emphasis on the humanistic orientation of the 1960s. This new focus on dialogue was not without its critics, and some even characterized the new dialogic focus as an "academic fad."

In "Foundations of Dialogic Communication," written in 1978, John Stewart helped clarify communication scholars' basic understanding of the dialogic phenomenon by articulating the philosophical positions in which the study of dialogue is grounded. He showed how (a) phenomenology's emphasis on the metaphysical and epistemological primacy of *relationship* contributed a *relational perspective* to dialogic studies and an emphasis on the nature of the *transaction* between human beings engaged in dialogue; (b) the phenomenological notion of *intuition* grounds dialogic communication's *experiential focus*; (c) existentialism leads to a focus on self and self-awareness, leading to the importance placed on developing awareness of one's own idiosyncratic communication values and behavior through dialogue; and (d) philosophical anthropology channels dialogic studies toward *holism*, in which emphasis is given to integrating cognitive, affective, and behavioral elements of communication.

Stewart's grounding of dialogue studies in philosophical inquiry helped move the study of dialogue beyond its early emphasis on humanistic psychology and encouraged the further development of dialogue theory within the communication discipline. Additional textbooks with a dialogic focus appeared, but there were also scholarly books and journal articles. A review in 1998 by Kenneth Cissna and Rob Anderson listed more than 100 citations on the topic of dialogue, most of them published during the 1990s. The number has continued to grow in the 21st century, and dialogue has become a concept that carries across all communication studies. New books went beyond interpersonal communication, as dialogue theory was embraced also by rhetorical studies, organizational communication, media studies, and intercultural communication. At the same time, dialogue studies in communication expanded to include a broader range of thinkers, including feminist theorists such as Carol Gilligan. Her 1982 book, *In a Different Voice,* described moral development from a female perspective, showing how women give more emphasis to connection, relationship, inclusion, and caring, all of which are part of a dialogic perspective.

As works on dialogue grew rapidly, however, there was a tendency to define it so broadly that it became a synonym for all human contact. In their 2000 article "Dialogue as Tensional, Ethical Practice," John Stewart and Karen Zediker advocated a more focused understanding of dialogue. They differentiated between what they termed "descriptive" and "prescriptive" approaches to dialogue. The former refers to an approach that views all human life as inherently dialogic, while the latter approach reserves the term *dialogue* for a particular quality or type of relating. Those who draw heavily from Bakhtin's work, such as Leslie Baxter and Barbara Montgomery in their 1996 book *Relating: Dialogue and Dialectics,* fall within the descriptive approach. They argue that dimensions of personal relationships such as the self, competence, and relational development should be reconceptualized dialogically. For descriptive theorists, the essential human condition is relational, and dialogue is an omnipresent and significant feature of daily interaction.

Prescriptive approaches to dialogue, which also emphasize the relational nature of the human condition, are equally concerned with urging their listeners to change their communication patterns toward more dialogic modes of interaction. Dialogue, in this case, is a goal toward which participants can work. Interactants can make communicative choices that will help create conditions for dialogue to occur. Those who base their work on Buber's approach, such as Barnett Pearce and Stephen Littlejohn in *Moral Conflict: When Social Worlds Collide,* are more prescriptive in their orientation. These authors suggest specific communication practices that are designed to promote higher quality public discourse on divisive issues.

Many communication scholars believe that prescriptive approaches to dialogue are particularly needed in today's multicultural and conflicted world in which value differences and struggles over scarce resources often lead to alienation, marginalization, community breakdowns, violent confrontations, and other dysfunctional and destructive consequences. Although the characteristics of communication and relationships advocated by prescriptive theorists and practitioners may be difficult or in some cases impossible to realize, they can serve as an ideal toward which communication can be directed. Dialogic practices apply to a wide variety of contexts, including personal relationships, organizational environments, educational settings, health care systems, and public discourse, as Ronald Arnett and Pat Arneson demonstrate in their book, *Dialogic Civility in a Cynical Age.* Although the situated and emergent nature of dialogue makes it inappropriate to offer a set of specific steps that will guarantee a dialogic experience from a particular encounter, the acts of turning toward the other, focusing on the between, listening with respect to differences, and other dialogic moves all increase the likelihood that communication will be enhanced and relationships will become more creative, fruitful, and rewarding.

Benjamin J. Broome

See also Critical Communication Pedagogy; Empathy; Hermeneutics; I and Thou; Interpersonal Communication Theories; Phenomenology; Rogerian Dialogue Theory; Social Interaction Theories

Further Readings

Anderson, R., Baxter, L. A., & Cissna, K. N. (Eds.). (2004). *Dialogue: Theorizing difference in communication studies.* Thousand Oaks, CA: Sage.

Anderson, R., Cissna, K. N., & Arnett, R. C. (Eds.). (1994). *The reach of dialogue: Confirmation, voice, and community.* Cresskill, NJ: Hampton Press.

Arnett, R., & Arneson, P. (Eds.). (1999). *Dialogic civility in a cynical age: Community, hope, and interpersonal relationships* (pp. 83–102). Albany: State University of New York Press.

Bakhtin, M. M. (1981). *The dialogic imagination: Four essays by M. M. Bakhtin* (M. Holquist, Ed.; C. Emerson & N. Holquist, Trans.). Austin: University of Texas Press.

Baxter, L. A., & Montgomery, B. M. (1996). *Relating: Dialogues and dialectics.* New York: Guilford Press.

Bohm, D. (1996). *On dialogue* (L. Nichol, Ed.). London: Routledge.

Buber, M. (1958). *I and Thou* (2nd ed.; R. G. Smith, Trans.). New York: Scribner. (Original work published 1923)

Cissna, K. N., & Anderson, R. (1998). Theorizing about dialogic moments: The Buber-Rogers position and postmodern themes. *Communication Theory, 8,* 63–104.

Gilligan, C. (1982). *In a different voice: Psychological theory and women's development.* Cambridge, MA: Harvard University Press.

Matson, F. W., & Montagu, A. (Eds.). (1967). *The human dialogue: Perspectives on communication.* New York: Free Press.

Pearce, W. B., & Littlejohn, S. W. (1997). *Moral conflict: When social worlds collide.* Thousand Oaks, CA: Sage.

Stewart, J. (1978). Foundations of dialogic communication. *Quarterly Journal of Speech, 64,* 183–201.

Stewart, J., & Zediker, K. (2000). Dialogue as tensional, ethical practice. *Southern Communication Journal, 65,* 224–242.

DIASPORA

Diaspora means dispersal, the scattering of a people. Originally referring to the Jewish peoples, diaspora dates from ancient times. Commenting on the revival of the concept in the late 1980s, Khachig Tölölyan observed that *diaspora* was now used as a synonym for distinct terms such as *expatriate, exile, ethnic, minority, refugee, migrant, sojourner,* and *overseas community.* The term now operates as a significant sociological and critical category imported into communication studies that puts into play the human and social dimensions of globalization through the increasing movement of peoples demographically across and around the globe.

This angle on globalization—globalization-from-below—has been often neglected in the focus on the latest exploits of the American, British, European, or Japanese world-spanning multinationals. Arjun Appadurai, in an influential analysis, lists the new flow patterns of media and people (which he calls *mediascapes* and *ethnoscapes,* respectively) alongside the flows of technologies, capital, and ideas as constituting the current globalizing era. Importantly, he sees all these flows as *disjunctive*—they are occurring together in related, but unsystematic, ways.

Communication, media, and cultural studies about contemporary diasporas have been a corrective to critical analyses that focus on the inadequacies of media representations of minority cultures in Western societies. Indeed, a number of basic theoretical shifts well underway in these fields reflect the significance of global flows, or movements, of audiovisual media for actually existing diasporas. These theoretical changes are important because they show how peoples displaced from homelands by migration, refugee status, or business and economic imperatives use video, television, cinema, music, and the Internet to rebuild cultural identities. Such shifts could move from a social problem or welfare conception of the migrant to an appreciation of cultural difference; from a view of the media as an imposed force to a recognition of audience activity and selectiveness; and from an essentialist or "heritage" model to a more dynamic, adaptive model of culture.

There is considerable research on the problems associated with diasporic cultures. As one example, Hamid Naficy's study of what he calls the *exilic television* produced by Iranians in Los Angeles in the 1980s is a model for how communication media can be used to negotiate the cultural politics of both *home* and *host.* Naficy's is the most theorized account of diasporic, hybrid cultural identity yet produced in its relation to audiovisual media. Naficy incorporates both the industrial and the narrative features of the television services and program genres developed by the Iranian exile community to show the relationship, as depicted on television, between the transnational experiences of displacement and migration, which in this case was enforced, and strategies of cultural maintenance and negotiation within the borderline "slipzone" between home and host.

The same attention that Hamid Naficy pays to the threshold experiences of exile from a broken national community is seen in Dana Kolar-Panov's research. Kolar-Panov's work goes below the level of consumption of mainstream media in capturing the role played by *video letters* used by overseas citizens of the former Yugoslavia to convey news as their country broke up during the early 1990s. This work illustrates the politics of discord between communities in the homelands as they are played out in the diasporas and the dramatic alternative textual representations of "atrocity videos," which show the real-time destruction of the homelands. These videos perform the role of virtual palimpsests—old "writings" that show through new ones—demonstrating the powerful role of the media in contemporary diasporas.

Marie Gillespie's 1995 study set a benchmark in its detailed audience ethnography and its demonstration of the need for different methodologies to capture consumption of various media formats (mainstream soaps; news; advertising; and community-specific, or *narrowcast,* media, such as Hindi television and film) among diasporic communities. This study examined the microprocesses, or daily practices, involved in the creation of a British Asian identity among young people in Southall, in West London. This new identity emerged against a backdrop of *new ethnicities* that surfaced within the framework of postcolonial migration and the globalization of communications.

The study of the diasporic ethnoscape and the world-spanning media flows—to a significant extent a condition of the ethnoscape's existence—are dynamic internationally as well as locally. Such work enables cross-disciplinary intersections of cultural and media studies with anthropology, political science, demography, and geography. Cultural and media studies' nuanced attention to structures of feeling, identity, and community dynamics lend qualitative depth and texture to the more data-driven approaches to all aspects of minority cultures seen in the social science disciplines.

Studies of diasporic cultures, then, are as much about innovative uses of the Internet and other newer technologies as they are about heritage, preservation of identity, and nostalgia. As showcased in *Floating Lives: The Media and Asian Diasporas,* the prevalence of computers in the home, use of the Internet, and participation in globally oriented Web forums were higher among economic migrants from east Asia to Australia than among the general population. An outward-looking, cosmopolitan *ethos* was a major part of the cultural capital of such households.

Stuart Cunningham

See also Cultural Studies; Globalization Theories; Hybridity; Neocolonialism; Postcolonial Theory; Transculturation

Further Readings

Appadurai, A. (1990). Disjunction and difference in the global cultural economy. *Public Culture, 2,* 1–24.

Cunningham, S., & Sinclair, J. (Eds.). (2001). *Floating lives: The media and Asian diasporas.* Lanham, MD: Rowman & Littlefield.

Gillespie, M. (1995). *Television, ethnicity and social change.* London: Routledge.

Kolar-Panov, D. (1997). *Video, war and the diasporic imagination.* London: Routledge.

Naficy, H. (1993). *The making of exile cultures: Iranian television in Los Angeles.* Minneapolis: University of Minnesota Press.

Rogers, E. (1969). *Modernization among peasants: The impact of communication.* New York: Holt, Rinehart, & Winston.

Tölölyan, K. (1996). Rethinking diaspora(s): Stateless power in the transnational moment. *Diaspora, 5,* 3–86.

DIFFUSION OF INNOVATIONS

Diffusion is the process by which an innovation makes its way over time to members of a social system. An *innovation* is the introduction of something new—a project, practice, or idea. The *innovation–decision process* is the process of progression an individual goes through from first encountering an innovation to its adoption. *Innovativeness* is a measure of early adoption; individuals are considered innovative and potential *change agents* if they are more willing to adopt new ideas than other members of a system and likely to do so earlier than others. Finally, the *rate of adoption* of an innovation is the relative speed with which an innovation is adopted.

Background

The French sociologist and legal scholar Gabriel Tarde can be said to be the originator of the basic idea of the diffusion of innovations; he coined and developed concepts that would become basic to diffusion research, such as *opinion leadership* and the *S curve of adoption* (although he used different terms). Tarde's work was followed by anthropologists such as Clark Wissler, who analyzed the diffusion of the horse among the Plains Indians—an innovative practice that allowed them to engage in almost constant warfare with neighboring tribes.

All the components of what is associated with the contemporary research paradigm of diffusion of innovations came together in a study in 1942 by Bruce Ryan and Neil Gross about how the adoption of hybrid seed corn diffused among Iowa farmers. Agricultural officials wondered why this technology—which resulted in as much as a 20% increase in production per acre—was not adopted more quickly (it took about 12 years from initial introduction to widespread adoption of hybrid corn). Ryan and Gross discovered that the farmers had to change virtually all their practices in relation to growing corn, including purchasing corn from a company rather than using corn from the previous year as seed (especially difficult during the Depression). This study also suggested that the rate of adoption of most innovations will form a bell-shaped or S curve, with a few people adopting in the beginning, followed by mass adoption, and then a dropping off because of the success of the diffusion and adoption processes. This study became the model for many diffusion studies during the 1950s, conducted by rural sociologists studying a host of other agricultural innovations.

Meanwhile, the diffusion approach moved beyond rural sociology to influence other social sciences, including marketing, political science, education, geography, public health, and economics. A major impetus to diffusion research in the social sciences was the work of Everett Rogers. Rogers earned his PhD in sociology at Iowa State University, where the studies of the diffusion of hybrid corn were done; his dissertation summarized what had been done on the subject. This dissertation became the basis for his now classic book, *Diffusion of Innovations*, published in 1962, in which Rogers provided a general model of diffusion, appropriate across disciplines and research paradigms.

While diffusion has been studied by scholars across disciplines, it has been of particular interest to communication scholars because at its core, the diffusion of innovations is a communication process. First, the innovation is made known through communication channels; if individuals are unable to find out about an innovation, diffusion simply cannot occur. Mass media and mass communication are involved in the process in that they contribute to awareness about the new idea or product. Interpersonal communication is also critical to the diffusion process: The decision to adopt an innovation depends largely on discussions with peers who have already evaluated and made a decision about whether to adopt the innovation. Today, of course, with cell phones, smartphones, and the Internet, the interpersonal–mass communication link is blurred, and potential innovators are just as likely to find out about an innovation via a computer-mediated format and to evaluate it the same way—through Internet chat rooms and online product reviews.

Other communication processes are involved as the potential innovator considers the information received. Because of the novelty of the innovation, the individual experiences a high degree of uncertainty about it. Thus, studies of attitude change, uncertainty reduction, and decision making come into play in the diffusion process, especially as they impact behavior change since diffusion ultimately is about adopting a new behavior.

Over the years, diffusion of innovation has explained the process of adoption of many new innovations, from family planning among women in Korea to doctors prescribing tetracycline to safe-sex practices among gay men in San Francisco to the adoption of the Internet. How quickly news is diffused about events, such as September 11 and the explosion of the space shuttle Columbia, is another avenue of diffusion research. And the diffusion-of-innovation paradigm has also been used to study resistance to innovations—why a keyboard arranged so that the strongest fingers strike the most frequently used letters of the alphabet has never caught on.

Arvind Singhal

See also Media and Mass Communication Theories; Two-Step and Multi-Step Flow

Further Readings

Coleman, J. S., Katz, E., & Menzel, H. (1966). *Medical innovation: A diffusion study*. Indianapolis, IN: Bobbs-Merrill.

Dearing, J. W., & Meyer, G. (2006). Revisiting diffusion theory. In A. Singhal & J. W. Dearing (Eds.), *Communication of innovations: A journey with Ev Rogers* (pp. 29–60). Thousand Oaks, CA: Sage.

Rogers, E. M. (2003). *Diffusion of innovations* (5th ed.). New York: Free Press.

Rogers, E. M., Singhal, A., & Quinlan, M. M. (2008). Diffusion of innovations. In M. Salwen & D. Stacks (Eds.), *An integrated approach to communication theory and research* (2nd ed.). Mahwah, NJ: Lawrence Erlbaum.

Ryan, B., & Gross, N. C. (1943). The diffusion of hybrid seed corn in two Iowa communities. *Rural Sociology, 8*, 15–24.

Singhal, A., & Dearing, J. W. (Eds.). (2006). *Communication of innovations: A journey with Ev Rogers*. Thousand Oaks, CA: Sage.

Tarde, G. (1903). *The laws of imitation* (E. C. Parsons, Trans.). New York: Holt, Rinehart, & Winston.

Valente, T. W. (2006). Communication network analysis and the diffusion of innovations. In A. Singhal & J. W. Dearing (Eds.), *Communication of innovations: A journey with Ev Rogers* (pp. 61–82). Thousand Oaks, CA: Sage.

Wissler, C. (1927). *North American Indians of the Plains*. New York: American Museum Press.

DIGITAL CULTURES

Digital cultures are social formations produced exclusively through engagement with information and communication technologies (ICTs). Also referred to as *cybercultures, virtual communities, online communities,* or *Internet communities,* they encompass a wide array of cultural interests and practices in different types of forums that are accessible only by a computer or other device with Internet connectivity. At the heart of any digital culture are social interaction and a network of relationships; communication scholars have an abiding interest in studying issues of identity, community, and access in relation to them.

These terms can be traced back to and continue to be informed by the concept of *cyberspace.* In the early 1980s, William Gibson coined the term in his cyberpunk novel, *Neuromancer.* Bodies are described as mere "meat" that is discarded when the characters "jack in" to their computers to immerse themselves in a virtual reality. In the early 1990s, scholarly and popular accounts of ICTs borrowed Gibson's term to imagine a spatial context for *computer-mediated communication.* The

majority of these accounts were celebratory, emphasizing the advantages of leaving behind the body and its problematic identities (e.g., race and gender). Cyberspace was seen as having the potential to revitalize the public sphere politically and socially and forge new connections and commonalities among disparate groups.

Howard Rheingold can be credited with expanding the focus of discussion to the digital cultures that comprise cyberspace. He argued that the search for community was central to the social use of ICTs and described his experiences in the virtual pubs and salons of the Whole Earth 'lectronic Link, a San Francisco–based bulletin board service in the pre–World Wide Web era. The other technologies that enabled the creation of text-based virtual communities at that time included Internet relay chat (chat rooms), Listserv (electronic mailing lists), Multi-User Domain (MUD; multiplayer computer games), and Usenet (newsgroups).

A number of scholars have theorized about cyberspace and digital culture based on behaviors observed on MUDs and Usenet groups. MUDs involve fantasy and action role-play, loosely based on the game Dungeons and Dragons, but also social interaction. One of the most popular social MUDs was LambdaMOO, founded in 1990. Participants interact in various rooms of a large house. According to Sherry Turkle, the value of virtual role-play is being able to experience the fluidity of identity as characterized by postmodern theory. The reverse is also true: There can be real-life negative consequences of cyberspace interactions. The virtual rape that took place in LambdaMOO is perhaps the most infamous example. The "cyberrape" was performed by an avatar named Mr. Bungle, who ran a "voodoo doll" subprogram that allowed him to engage in sexual acts that could be attributed to other characters in the virtual community. The duration and intensity of these acts resulted in feelings of violation for participants in real life, raising questions about the boundaries between real-life and virtual communities.

As for the Usenet, it is seen by some as the original Internet community. Started by two Duke University computer science students in 1979, it began with five overarching categories to organize its newsgroups: alt.* (alternative), bus.* (business), comp.* (computing), rec.* (recreation and leisure), and soc.* (social issues). When America

Online (AOL) gave its subscribers open access to the Internet in 1993, many long-time Usenet participants complained bitterly that the presence of the AOL subscribers increased the number of groups and quantity of posts dramatically while degrading the quality of discussion.

With rapid advancements in ICTs, cyberspace and digital culture have expanded exponentially and changed form. By 1995, dial-up bulletin board systems were largely replaced by pay-based online services such as CompuServe, Genie, and AOL, with their own discussion forums. By 2000, those forums, as well as the Usenet, had been eclipsed by Web-based forums (e.g., Yahoo groups and Delphi forums). Similarly, MUDs were complemented by *graphical multiuser konversations* and then eventually overshadowed by *massively multiplayer online role-playing games* such as World of Warcraft and three-dimensional virtual worlds such as the Sims and Second Life. The most recent cluster of digital cultures, considered by some to herald the *Web 2.0* era, includes social networking sites such as Facebook, blogging communities, and YouTube.

Media fans continue to comprise one of the largest segments of digital culture. One of the first mailing lists used for nonmilitary and nongovernment purposes was on the topic of science fiction. Research indicates that the Usenet newsgroups with the highest volume of daily postings were those related to the discussion of television, movies, and sports. Today, networks and fans alike maintain discussion forums for every current television program. There are also virtual communities dedicated to fan-produced fiction, art, music, and videos.

The scholarship on digital cultures has taken a critical turn since the early 1990s. Gender, race, class, and sexuality—informed by poststructuralist, postcolonial, and feminist theories—are understood as shaping and affecting social relations in cyberspace even if not exactly in the same ways as "in real life." Until 2000, when gender parity was reached, most forums were dominated by men, with women reporting exclusion, harassment, and marginalization. Even today, the majority remains dominated by White, English-speaking, and middle-class participants. That said, members of real-life marginalized groups such as gays, lesbians, bisexuals, as well as other self-identified queer and transgendered people, are claiming a piece of cyberspace as their own. Queer youth in isolated, rural communities, for example, have benefited from queer-centered Web sites and discussion forums.

The cultural norms of the West still dominate cyberspace, despite the increasing number of Internet users in wealthier Asian countries, notably Japan and South Korea, as well as in India. The World Wide Web has always been a misnomer, and access, with the exception of a few pockets, remains very limited in the Global South (Africa, South America, Southeast Asia). The digital divide also manifests itself in the West. In the United States, for example, some poor African American and Hispanic neighborhoods still remain without an advanced telecommunications infrastructure. Hence, the digital divide affects which cybercultures are formed and under what conditions.

Rhiannon Bury

See also Community; Computer-Mediated Communication; Digital Divide; Fans, Fandom, and Fan Studies; Network Society

Further Readings

Bell, D. (2001). *An introduction to cybercultures.* London: Routledge.

Bury, R. (2005). *Cyberspaces of their own: Female fandoms online.* New York: Peter Lang.

Dibbell, J. (2001). A rape in cyberspace; or how an evil clown, a Haitian trickster spirit, two wizards, and a cast of dozens turned a database into a society. In D. Trend (Ed.), *Reading digital culture* (pp. 199–213). Malden, MA: Blackwell.

O'Riordan, K., & Phillips, D. J. (2007). *Queer online: Media technology & sexuality.* New York: Peter Lang.

Smith, M., & Kollock, P. (Eds.). (1999). *Communities in cyberspace.* New York: Routledge.

Turkle, S. (1995). *Life on the screen: Identity in the age of the Internet.* New York: Simon & Schuster.

DIGITAL DIVIDE

Digital divide is a term representing the gap between populations that have easy access to communication and information technologies and those who remain underserved by these technologies. Issues related to the digital divide are salient worldwide because of the widely held belief that inclusion and involvement in the global information and knowledge economy is an important measure of the "quality of life" in the 21st century. Consequently, being excluded by this emerging economy is deemed a significant deprivation. The digital divide is an important concern for communication and social change theorists and practitioners. This essay highlights and describes key facets of the digital divide.

While liberals, libertarians, and conservatives are united in their determination to tackle this divide, their solutions vary in scope and substance. Empowerment, digital competency for economic development, and open access for all are just some of the objectives of digital-inclusion projects. Making provisions for digital dividends has become a priority concern for organizations such as the World Resources Institute and the World Bank. The World Bank, for instance, supported the Virtual Souk project in North Africa that has enabled rural artisans to connect to a larger, international market for their crafts.

While access to and the affordable uses of information and knowledge have increasingly become a yardstick for development as defined by the International Telecommunications Union, the United Nations Development Program, and a range of multilateral and international aid agencies, the preponderance of technologically determinist thinking and the tendency to advocate one-size-fits-all solutions have seriously affected the efficacy of the global response to the digital divide. While there is certainly a case to be made for *leapfrogging technologies,* such as the use of mobile telephony in contexts previously discounted by or beyond the shapings of telecommunications, it would be shortsighted to infer from such examples that a single application such as mobile telephony is the answer to the world's digital divide.

What, then, are some of the key issues related to the digital divide? First, there is, unlike in the past, a willingness to interpret the digital divide as an aspect of other divides in society. In other words, the digital divide cannot be seen in isolation from other social differences resulting from poverty, status, caste, class, and inequity; solutions must factor in this larger context of social deprivation. A second issue relates to the belief that because information and communication technologies (ICTs) can effect change in society, the deployment of ICTs must be accompanied by parallel changes in local social structures given that these structures can either support access or indeed block access to those who stand to gain from digital inclusion projects. A case in point is whether issues related to caste are factored into ICT projects in Indian villages.

There is also greater appreciation for the fact that solutions to the digital divide—whether they be e-governance projects, ICT kiosks, online marketing, or the computerization of village-level information—require more than just a technological solution. Sustainable projects require political will, capacity building at local levels, the availability of language-specific software, intentional networking strategies with a range of institutions, training in software and hardware skills, and last but not least, regular access to uninterrupted power supplies. Telecenters in South Africa, for instance, provide a range of services, from faxing to voice telephony. The more sophisticated versions of telecenters offer e-governance, e-health, e-education, and other services. Issues related to scalability remain widespread, with the result that a number of digital-divide projects continue to be pilot projects with little or no possibility for upgrading or extension.

While there is enough evidence to suggest that digitalization can have a positive impact on the lives of people, more often than not digital solutions are imposed by well-meaning outsiders. Such imposed solutions, based on minimal consultation with local people, can result in people's rejecting the technology for the simple reason that they have not been convinced of its worth. It is necessary for local people to be involved in defining their information and communication deficits and for them to prioritize the deficits that they see to be most important. Today, for the most part, the impetus for change solutions comes from governments, nongovernmental organizations, and international nongovernmental organizations, and also from hardware and software companies that stand to gain from increased connectivity.

There is also greater acknowledgment, particularly in communication and social change theory, of the fact that the issue with respect to the digital divide is not just access but affordable, sustainable access. This is a critical concern not only in the developing world but also in the developed world, where significant pockets of people, including the rural and urban poor in the United States, the socioeconomically disadvantaged living on housing estates in all large cities in the United Kingdom, and small farmers in rural Australia, are yet to benefit from digital dividends. The reduction of mobile telephony charges in many parts of South Asia, coupled with the steady decline in the price of handsets, has led to a massive increase in rural mobile telephony and a consequent decline in the need for land lines.

Today, there is more openness to the need for appropriate technological solutions. Mounting concerns related to electronic waste (e-waste) have demonstrated the need for a better use of existing technologies and the need for adaptability, appropriateness, and maximization of the potential of hardware and software. The digital divide is of key concern in communication and social change theory, communication and social movement theory, and theories related to global media governance.

The financing of digital divide solutions remains a thorny issue. While there are numerous initiatives—both governmental and intergovernmental—that are aimed at bridging the digital divide, funding tends to be project driven, dependency remains a critical concern, and issues related to sustainability remain a recurrent concern. The *Global Digital Divide Fund*, proposed by the president of Senegal at the United Nations–sponsored World Summit on the Information Society held in 2003, received very little support from Group-of-Eight countries or from industry. While there literally are thousands of digital-inclusion projects spread throughout the world and supported by civil society and state, intergovernmental, and commercial sectors, there is as yet very little evidence to suggest that these projects are providing answers to the need for long-term solutions to contemporary information and knowledge deficits.

As globalization continues to integrate the world into a global market on one hand, it is also responsible for marginalizing regions and people who have nothing to offer the market economy. These people in parts of sub-Saharan Africa, Latin America, and South Asia who live lives that are, in effect, beyond the market, need solutions to issues related to basic needs—access to food, water, shelter, education, and employment. How to integrate these people into the knowledge era remains a knotty issue for all those concerned with the digital divide.

Pradip Thomas

See also International Communication Theories; International Development Theories; Media Democracy; Media Sovereignty; Network Society; New Media Theory

Further Readings

Communication Initiative, Food and Agriculture Organization of the United Nations, & World Bank. (2007). *World congress on communication for development: Lessons, challenges, and the way forward.* Washington, DC: World Bank Publications.

Mansell, R., & Wehn, U. (1998). *Knowledge societies: Information technology for sustainable development.* Oxford, UK: Oxford University Press.

Yoon, C. S. (Ed.). (2003). *Digital Review of Asia-Pacific, 2003–2004.* Penang: Southbound.

DIPLOMACY

See Media Diplomacy

DISCOURSE THEORY AND ANALYSIS

Discourse analysis is a term that comprises many different approaches to language, both in theory and in method. Some approaches find their provenance in linguistics and literary studies, yet others in sociology, psychology, or anthropology. They all share an interest in the analysis of text and talk, and their focus is language in use. In the theoretical and methodological underpinning of this starting point, however, discourse analysis arises as a contested terrain. After a historical introduction, this entry will focus on the forms of discourse theory and analysis that are applied in, or originate from, the social sciences. Most of them have also adopted the term *discourse analysis* as a way to present their approach.

Historical Developments

One of the greatest achievements of the earliest forms of discourse analysis was a departure from the traditional linguistic approach that started from invented or written data. Zelig Harris, a prominent linguist in the 1950s and founder of the first linguistics department in the United States, is probably also the first person to have used the term *discourse analysis*. He launched a research program aimed at unraveling general principles in language production by looking at regularities in actual usage. In practice, however, the focus on empirical data was still limited, in part because of the program's taxonomic ambitions.

Some 25 years later, John Sinclair and Malcolm Coulthard developed a model of teacher–student interaction that started from a prototypical three-part sequence of teacher initiation, student response, and teacher feedback (evaluation). They found that departures from this sequence were "noticeably absent" for students. A missing feedback was, for example, treated as a clue for having given the wrong answer. The comparative work of Coulthard and Sinclair was designed to provide insight into structures of interaction across different institutional settings. Although they drew on simplified transcripts, their approach put forward a substantial argument for the importance of studying *real-life interaction*. At the same time, this and related approaches were criticized for their urge to characterize everyday verbal interaction in terms of quasi-syntactical rules. Introductions on discourse analysis from that period, for example from Gillian Brown and George Yule, display the same emphasis on formal rule seeking.

Discourse Analysis in the Social Sciences

Apart from the shift toward studying real-life materials, or the ambition to do so, discourse analysts proposed a move in thinking about the nature of language, especially within those forms of discourse analysis associated with *poststructuralism* and *postmodernism*. Language was no longer seen as a passive medium that smoothly conveys information about the world out there and what people think about this world. Instead, it was conceptualized as an active and constructed tool that co-constitutes the world around us. Accounts of reality are necessarily selective and should therefore be understood as constructions rather than reflections of what is "really the case."

This conception of language was not entirely new but inspired researchers to actively criticize the tacit assumption of *language as a neutral vehicle* that was still prevalent in most social science research. Different forms of discourse analysis have evolved, depending on how the notion of context was understood and the influence that was attributed to *people versus structures*. Some discourse analysts emphasize the role of people as active sense-makers who use the context flexibly to perform particular actions such as blaming, mitigating, and building expertise. Context is taken to refer to the local surroundings of talk and to broader cultural reservoirs made relevant in the interaction. Others were encouraged by the work of the French historian and philosopher Michel Foucault and lay more emphasis on discourse as a constitutive power in itself.

The Influence of Foucault

In the 1970s Foucault firmly introduced the element of power into discourse analysis. While not at all concerned with the analysis of verbal interaction, his influence on discourse theory and analysis has been huge. The French *discours* denotes something radically different from the conception of discourse in the Anglo-Saxon tradition. Instead of referring to everyday interaction, it refers to institutionalized rules that govern the way a certain topic—sexuality, hysteria, romantic love, punishment, and imprisonment—can be meaningfully talked about. Discourse itself is power but not so much in the hands of people. Foucault focuses on discourses as constitutive of knowledge and meaning. Everything outside such a *discours* is without sense and significance.

Foucault's so-called genealogical studies were historical and did not draw on records of interaction. The studies show how particular "sets of statements" acquire authority and act as rules, prescribing if and how certain topics should be thematized. Finally they come to manifest themselves as institutions. In the context of mental illnesses, for example, medical records of the insane are not decontextualized, neutral statements but powerful tools that help to fill in the very definition of what madness is and what or who represents sanity.

Foucault's illuminating analyses show historically embedded discourses that perform their work on the level of structures rather than through active agents. His approach, however, has not resulted in a distinct methodological perspective that acquired followers in the strict sense of the word.

Discourse Analysis and Sociology of Science

Unlike Foucault's work, the form of discourse analysis that was developed within sociology of science in the 1980s positioned participants' performative work at the heart of its approach. In a study among biochemists, Nigel Gilbert and Michael Mulkay revealed the use of two contradictory *interpretative repertoires* (broadly discernible clusters of terms and figures of speech often assembled around metaphors or vivid images) with which the scientists accounted for the truthfulness of their and other people's scientific work. The *empiricist repertoire* was dominant in scientific articles and was drawn on to explain results in terms of impersonal rules, with experimental data getting chronological and logical priority over interpretation. The *contingent repertoire,* on the other hand, was popular in more informal settings and referred to speculation, personal commitment, and social networks as important explanatory sources. Gilbert and Mulkay were particularly interested in the fact that the scientists needed, not one, but two different sets of accounts to explain their results in a satisfactory manner.

By the end of the 1980s Jonathan Potter and Margaret Wetherell used the repertoire concept in developing an approach that first emerged as a discourse-based alternative for social psychology. The book *Discourse and Social Psychology* marked the beginning of a discourse tradition that had its roots in diverse disciplines such as the philosophy of Ludwig Wittgenstein, ethnomethodology, and poststructuralism. The notion of an interpretative repertoire was coined to capture the ostensible inconsistencies in people's accounts of mind and reality that were not explained by the social–psychological attitude concept. Potter and Wetherell's most important criticism concerned the interpretation of an attitude as an abstract, cognitive state of mind. When people give their opinion they do not so much express a mental state but rather perform a social action such as blaming

someone, reducing one's own responsibility, or giving a compliment. Views are designed and redesigned to fit a certain functional context, and it is for this reason that they show considerable variation across different interactional situations. The repertoire notion was applied in a wide range of disciplines, including sociology, health studies, and communication, and to a diverse set of topics, such as science discourse, racism, gender, and politics. At the same time, it has been criticized for its broadness and its tendency to overlook crucial details in talk.

Discourse and Ideological Dilemmas

With a similar eye for the importance of inconsistency rather than steadiness and uniformity, the social psychologist Michael Billig and colleagues made a case for paying more attention to the role of *ideological dilemmas* in discourse. Their interest in ideologies and in dilemmas was in how ideologies and dilemmas appeared in everyday life and, more specifically, in everyday talk. Ideologies were identified as always containing or invoking counterideologies, for example when the demands of intellectual theory clash with the routines of everyday life. Participants shift alignment flexibly from one theme to another and back ("that's all very well in theory, but in practice…"), thereby tailoring their ideological repertoire to the interactional business at stake. The notion of individual freedom may be drawn on to make up for the flaws of social responsibility and collective ideals and vice versa. In this sense, contrary themes within or between ideologies function as suitable "error accounts." Rather than belonging to some ideological periphery, they are mutually implicative and therefore part of how ideologies work.

Critical Discourse Analysis and Foucauldian Discourse Analysis

In the 1990s, critical discourse analysis combined more fine-grained, linguistically inspired analyses with an interest in power and social inequality. Despite their different accents, critical discourse analysts are united in their attempts to reveal the workings of language within social relations of power and the *normalizing effects of discourse* in this respect. They show a strong preference for data related to social issues such as gender inequalities and racism—for example, research on how men and women are represented in the media or how different ethnic categories appear in policy documents. Critical discourse analysts have been inspired by predecessors as diverse as the Frankfurt School and Jürgen Habermas, the Italian activist and theorist Antonio Gramsci, Michel Foucault, and the Russian philosopher and linguist Mikhail Bakhtin. Michael Halliday's functional grammar has been another important influence. Critical sociolinguists such as Robert Hodge and Günther Kress have stressed the role of power in producing linguistic form and difference.

Despite the similarities in perspective, there are notable differences when it comes to the actual analyses. Some critical analysts focus on the *cognitive basis of representations,* for example, the sociocognitive processes underlying racist discourse (Teun van Dijk). Others (such as Norman Fairclough) are particularly interested in the relationship between different levels of social practices constituting a social order (such as of education in a particular country) and its related order of discourse (marginal and dominant ways of "making meaning," for example, about what counts as proper education).

Critical discourse analysts have an interest in the subtle properties and workings of power. The concept of *hegemony* is often used to capture those aspects of power that sustain practices of dominance (over women, over the poor) with seeming consent of those oppressed. These forms of dominance are considered "jointly constructed" rather than simply imposed. Dominant discourses play a crucial role in sustaining such practices. Critical discourse analysts are not only interested in revealing the mediating role of discourse but also make a plea for political engagement—finding points of entry to support marginalized groups in society.

A more recently evolved branch of discourse analysis is Foucauldian discourse analysis. It shares the critically engaged focus of critical discourse analysis but presents itself as more directly informed by the work of Michel Foucault. In line with Foucault's notion of discourse, it highlights the productive side of language in that it establishes groups, categories, and subjects rather than laying stress on how language conveys meaning. Perhaps confusingly, Foucauldian discourse analysis often departs from the kind of genealogical studies as Foucault propagated them. While some studies make use of historical texts, most seem to draw on interview materials. The concept of interpretative repertoire is often deployed as a starting point for analysis. It is doubtful whether Foucault would have pursued such analyses himself, since it seems to put active meaning construction by subjects at the center of analysis. Foucauldian discourse analysts stress that it is not methodological rigor per se that makes up for the quality of the analysis. Corresponding with Foucault's focus on power–knowledge networks, the notion of an objective truth is eschewed in favor of sustained *reflexivity* about one's own production of "truth" or theory.

Discursive Psychology

Derek Edwards and Jonathan Potter are the founders of what is now called discursive psychology. Discursive psychology developed out of the strand of discourse analytic repertoire research as it was developed by Gilbert and Mulkay and applied to social psychology by Potter and Wetherell. In its current form, it is very much akin to conversation analytic research. Like conversation analysts, discursive psychologists are interested in close empirical investigation of naturally occurring data. They work from detailed transcripts of audio or video recordings derived from a variety of "natural" settings, such as talk between peers, counseling sessions, or mealtime conversations. Discursive psychology examines how psychological issues are made relevant in everyday interactions. The question of what psychology comprises is, however, approached from participants' so-called *emic point of view.* How are attitudes, emotions, scripts, and the like made available, and how are they ascribed and resisted by people *themselves,* as part of the social actions performed in and through talk? Limited memories may, for instance, account for a forgotten action, while gustatory "mmms" may enhance the genuineness of food pleasure. The action-oriented approach to language marks a shift away from cognitivist traditions in psychology that treat mental states as the source or cause of what is being said.

For discursive psychologists, as for conversation analysts, it is *action in sequence* rather than the isolated sentence or utterance that is the basic unit of analysis. Many actions are accomplished in pairs, such as question–answer and invitation–acceptance pairs. The *normative* character of these paired actions enables people to make sense of deviations. Precisely because they have a common expectation that questions are followed by answers, they can make inferences about the nature of the deviation and the action that it accomplishes. These publicly displayed and continuously updated understandings are available, not only for conversationalists, but also for analysts, who use them as an important *proof procedure* by which they can check their own interpretations.

Recently, Edwards and Potter have distinguished three major strands in discursive psychology. The first strand focuses on reformulations of traditional psychological topics such as attitude, motives, memory, and scripts, into discourse practices. Someone who expresses a complaint is at risk of being treated as a dispositional moaner. Humor can be used to negotiate the *motive* of the complainer by showing that he or she is not disposed to make too much of it. The second strand involves studies of how psychological terms are deployed in everyday talk (*intent, remember, see, know,* for example). When people display uncertainty about something they are saying ("What is it I was reading somewhere?"), the statement may not simply claim that one has not quite remembered but may also display disinterestedness precisely at a point where it could be an issue ("She would say that, wouldn't she?"). A third line of research focuses on psychology-in-interaction as it appears in less overt ways. Attributions of agency and intent and the corresponding accusations of stake and interest are, for example, typically performed not by explicit blame but through apparently straightforward, factual descriptions.

Bones of Contention in Contemporary Discourse Analysis

There have been vibrant debates about virtually all basic assumptions in discourse theory and analysis. An ongoing discussion is the relationship between discursive practices and the "world-out-there." Are they intricately bound up with each other, or does the material world deserve a more detached or even autonomous position? Another notable discussion concerns the notion of context: Must a discourse analysis include an analysis of cultural and historical resources, or should a proper study be grounded in how these resources are actually used in the interaction (see for example the debates between Emanuel Schegloff, Margaret Wetherell, and Michael Billig). Often interwoven is the issue of how far analysts should take into account the detail of talk-in-interaction (for example, transcribed hesitations, timed pauses, and intonation). Can we find everything in the talk as long as we look closely enough, or do we need to take a broader perspective and necessarily leave out some of the particulars?

Hedwig te Molder and Jonathan Potter explored the role of mental concepts in the analysis of interaction. The status of cognition is a gray zone of disagreement between conversation analysts and discursive psychologists and is a clear bone of contention in the debate between the latter and cognitive (social) psychologists. Is cognition first and foremost a topic and interactional resource for participants themselves, or does it count as an empirically grounded explanation for why people say the things they do? Another area of dispute focuses on the critical potential of the various discourse approaches: Does political engagement need to be an explicit part of one's research program in order to be effective, or does such an "imposed" critical stance obscure the relevance of participants' own orientations and thus become counterproductive? Related to the issue of political involvement is the status of the analyst's observations. While the majority of discourse analysts in the social sciences have adopted the conceptualization of discourse as oriented to action rather than merely conveying truth, still open to discussion is to what extent and how this should apply to the analyst himself or herself. How detached or self-reflexive can or need one be?

Despite the differences in opinion and approach, the lively debates in journals such as *Discourse Studies, Discourse & Society,* and more recently *Discourse & Communication* and the growing applications of discourse analysis in a variety of disciplines prove discourse theory and analysis to be a dynamic and innovative field of research.

Hedwig te Molder

See also Accounts and Account Giving; Action-Implicative Discourse Analysis; Conversation Analysis; Critical Discourse Analysis; Ethnomethodology; Language and Communication; Poststructuralism; Semiotics and Semiology

Further Readings

Billig, M., Condor, S., Edwards, D., Gane, M., Middleton, D. J., & Radley, A. R. (1988). *Ideological dilemmas: A social psychology of everyday thinking.* London: Sage.

Edwards, D., & Potter, J. (1992). *Discursive psychology.* London: Sage.

Phillips, L. J., & Jørgensen, M. W. (2002). *Discourse analysis as theory and method.* London: Sage.

Potter, J., & Wetherell, M. (1987). *Discourse and social psychology: Beyond attitudes and behaviour.* London: Sage.

te Molder, H., & Potter, J. (Eds.). (2005). *Conversation and cognition.* Cambridge, UK: Cambridge University Press.

Wetherell, M. (1998). Positioning and interpretative repertoires: Conversation analysis and post-structuralism in dialogue, *Discourse and Society, 9,* 387–412.

Wetherell, M., Taylor, S., & Yates, S. (Eds.). (2001). *Discourse as data: A guide for analysis.* London: Sage.

Wetherell, M., Taylor, S., & Yates, S. (Eds.). (2001). *Discourse theory and practice: A reader.* London: Sage.

Wooffitt, R. (2005). *Conversation analysis and discourse analysis: A comparative and critical introduction.* London: Sage.

DOCUMENTARY FILM THEORIES

Documentary film theories attempt to accomplish several goals, which include defining the genre of documentary film, articulating its components, and describing its effects and use in society. This entry explores the various definitions of documentary film, the evolving set of documentary filmic components and practices, and how the definitions and construction of documentary films inform documentary film theories. These issues are particularly relevant for the field of communication and rhetoric because most documentary films engage in various forms of persuasion.

Definitions of Documentary

The term *documentary* was coined in 1926 by British filmmaker John Grierson in his review of Robert Flaherty's film *Moana.* Grierson described the film as visually capturing the daily life of young Polynesians. In the 1930s, Grierson became a documentary filmmaker and producer, and he expanded his definition of documentary film to the "creative treatment of actuality," which was largely uncontested until the early 1960s. Erik Barnouw, who wrote one of the most popular books on documentary film history, *Documentary: A History of the Non-Fiction Film,* defines this genre by the films' place in history and societal use. Barnouw distinguishes documentaries from earlier nonfiction films (which were known as travelogues) by their incorporation of a narrative structure and use of multiple close-ups. The use of narrative and close-ups came directly from the influence of fiction film, and one result of their use was a clearer manifestation of the filmmaker's point of view.

One of the tensions that concerns definitions and theories of documentary film is grounded in claims of neutral representation. The film *Nanook of the North,* directed by Robert Flaherty, is generally regarded as one of the first documentaries even though the film is critiqued for its romanticized portrayal of Inuit life and its use of historic recreations. Flaherty's first attempt to depict Inuit life resembled a travelogue (with which he was not happy), and it was destroyed in a fire. He returned to northern Canada determined to create an empathetic depiction of the rapidly disappearing Inuit culture. He decided to focus the film on the life of Nanook and his family in order to more fully engage audiences with their plight and daily struggle for existence. Despite the film's questionable depictions of authentic Inuit life (many scenes were staged), *Nanook of the North* retains its position in documentary film history.

Documentary Practices

Many early documentary film practitioners were primarily interested in making their films persuasive, and they incorporated additional narrative components into their films. Robert Flaherty (father of British documentary), John Grierson (father of American documentary), Dziga Vertov (father of Soviet experimental documentary): all were attracted to what we have come to recognize as a documentary form; however, there was not the concomitant understanding that their films were to be "objective." A prominent critic of voice-over narration was Leni Riefenstahl, the director of *Triumph of Will*, who believed that her images were more persuasive without an omniscient narrator telling the audience how to interpret her films' images. Although early documentaries clearly embraced nonneutral representation, there was criticism of this approach. Luis Buñuel's 1932 film, *Land Without Bread*, illustrated the inherent biases in the documentary film form by clearly staging scenes and having the film's narrator criticize the film's characters.

The tension between persuasion and authentic neutral representation did not stop several documentary practitioners from using the form for social action. During the 1930s, John Grierson used documentaries to instigate British government economic reforms for the poor. In the 1930s and 1940s, governments around the world used documentary films to inspire their citizenry to support their country's wartime goals. In 1948, Standard Oil of New Jersey hired Robert Flaherty to make the documentary *Louisiana Story*, which would ease fears of oil exploration in the Louisiana bayous. In 1988, Errol Morris's film *Thin Blue Line* played a key role in overturning the murder conviction of an innocent man. In the early 2000s, community activists used the making of a documentary film as a community-organizing tool and as part of a civil disobedience action. The use of documentary film by individuals, governments, and businesses to influence public opinion has been a part of the documentary tradition.

Documentary Components

The filmic component that has been part of the documentary form from the beginning, but still raises issues regarding its role in documentary film, is *historic recreation*. One of the most famous incidents of historic recreation in a documentary film occurred during the making of *Nanook of the North*. Director Robert Flaherty instructed Nanook and his fellow Inuit to use harpoons to capture a walrus although these men were using rifles by that time. The creation of this scene reportedly endangered the lives of the men, but Flaherty insisted on recreating the scene in order to depict a former way of Inuit life. Some documentarists and critics shun this particular filmic component, claiming its inappropriateness for documentary,

while others view the historic recreation as just another filmic device available to tell a story, one that is necessary if no actual film footage of the event exists.

Additional elements from fiction film that appear in documentaries include voice-over narration, graphics, animation, scripts, actors, music, and B roll (images that illustrate a speaker's point). From the 1930s through the 1950s, governments and corporations around the world rapidly adopted these components into documentary filmmaking, which allowed their critics to label some of this output as propagandistic. One reaction to this evolution of the documentary film form came in the early 1960s with the practitioners of *cinema verité*. These filmmakers and theorists sought to make the documentary form free of the filmmakers' point of view by eschewing fiction film elements and using only location sound and unstructured filming (e.g., only location sound, no interviews, no voice-over narration, and no scripting of any form). This move to include objectivity in the definition of documentary film forced documentary film theorists to more carefully examine the relationship between documentary film and its representation of reality.

Evolving Theories

Due to the historic belief in a camera's ability to authentically record reality, most early documentary theories included an assumption that documentary film could record reality with no imprint of human interpretation. This belief in the camera as able to record the truth was challenged in the late 1960s and early 1970s with *poststructuralist* theories that observed how the camera and filmmaking were part of a system of cultural values and beliefs. During this time, many film theorists employed the literary theory of *semiotics* in their film analyses. Semiotics is a meaning-centered theory of language in which the critic examines language as *symbols*. In semiotic theory, language is analyzed as a set of symbols in which the symbols themselves contain their own meanings. According to semiotic theory, meaning is the point between the actual object in the world and the language or symbol that describes the object. The study of language as a system of symbols enables the critic to discover the sets of meanings each culture develops in its understandings of the world and the world's social relationships. Semioticians used the work of linguist Ferdinand de Saussure, who described this process as analyzing *signs,* and he assigned the term *signifier* to the language (or symbol) used to describe the *signified,* which is the actual image we see in our minds of the described object. Previous approaches to documentary film theory assumed a denotative relationship between the subject and the filmed image. This relationship came under scrutiny with a new generation of documentary film theorists influenced by semiotics.

The recognition that the camera and all filmic choices are part of a cultural sign system challenged the view of documentary films as objective or representing authentic reality. Roland Barthes wrote in *Image, Music, and Text* of the multitude of interpretations in the cultural signs themselves. Scholars of *postmodernism,* who examine the relationships between representation and reality, observed that reality does not exist outside the individual. With these particular philosophical issues in mind, documentary film's use of cinematic realism came under pressure. Critical issues arose concerning whose reality was in fact being depicted. By the late 1980s and early 1990s, the study of documentary film became highly interdisciplinary as theorists used Marxism, feminism, and rhetoric to analyze the implications of documentary's use of cinematic realism. Marxist theorists questioned which events were covered in documentary films and whether their representations empowered the working classes with revolutionary insights into their oppressive conditions. Feminist documentary theorists critiqued the documentary form as primarily representing a male-centered view that perpetuated not only patriarchy but also a mainstream bourgeois reality.

Contemporary documentary theorist Bill Nichols incorporates rhetorical theories in his approach to analyzing the documentary. In particular, he uses a neo-Aristotelian model to analyze a documentary's persuasive arguments. In addition to using the canons of invention, arrangement, style, memory, and delivery as a theoretical approach to understanding a documentary's persuasive qualities, Nichols developed six categories of documentary film that do not question the films' ability to record authentic representations but instead focus on *how* different styles of documentary films tell their stories. Nichols's categories include poetic (abstract films using pieces of filmed actuality), expository (the most common form, similar to an expository essay), observational (similar to cinema verité), participatory (the filmmaker on camera interviewing or as part of the story), reflexive (challenges documentary format and is more abstract), and performative (emphasis on subjective observations).

Audience and Ethics

In addition to the analysis of the films as texts, documentary film theorists began to incorporate the role of the audience, the filmmakers' ethics, and the filmmakers' identity in their theorization. Documentary film theorist Brian Winston considers audience reception as key to defining the documentary as well as essential for evaluating any documentary film's truth claims. He observes that the various forms of documentary have no inherent claim to representing authenticity or the truth but that it is up to the audience to evaluate the documentary filmmakers' relationship to the subject and the filmmakers' methodological choices in that representation. Most documentary film theorists also include the role of the filmmaker's ethics in defining and analyzing documentary film. Erik Barnouw notes the problems in the 1920s, when anthropological documentary filmmakers of foreign cultures staged unflattering depictions of their subjects. Several years after the philosophical impact of cinema verité, one of its foremost U.S. practitioners, Frederick Wiseman, acknowledged the large role that his point of view played in his topic and editing choices. Considering the popularity of Michael Moore and other documentarists who insert themselves into their films, documentary theorist Garnet C. Butchart emphasizes how the entire truth claim of documentaries rests on the filmmakers' ethics in making their films. Documentary theorist Michael Renov views the autobiographical documentary film as the evolution of the documentary form and argues that it has powerful possibilities of oppositional representation. For Renov, theorizing the filmmaker's positionality, or place, in terms of race, class, gender, and sexual orientation is the subject of many contemporary documentaries.

The combination of audience expectations, filmic components, the filmmaker's ethics, and the use of documentary films to promote social goals have all come to both define the genre and inform documentary film theories. For some documentary theorists, the definition of a documentary film is tied to neutral representation and the claim that a documentary film can make objective truth claims. For other documentary theorists, the influence of the filmmaker, the audience, and the film's form demand interrogation and are part of analyzing any documentary film. For these theorists, visual representation is deeply symbolic and embedded with myriad value-laden images and audio, and their role as theorists is to articulate these values and evaluate their persuasiveness.

Teresa Bergman

See also Feminist Communication Theories; Film Theories; Marxist Theory; Media and Mass Communication Theories; Postmodern Theory; Poststructuralism; Semiotics and Semiology

Further Readings

Barnouw, E. (1993). *Documentary: A history of the non-fiction film*. New York: Oxford University Press.

Barthes, R. (1997). *Image, music, text*. New York: Hill and Wang.

Benson, T. W., & Snee, B. J. (2008). *The rhetoric of the new political documentary*. Carbondale: Southern Illinois University Press.

Butchart, G. C. (2006). On ethics and documentary. *Communication Theory, 16*, 427–452.

Gaines, J., & Renov M. (Eds.). (1999). *Collecting visible evidence*. Minneapolis: University of Minnesota Press.

Nichols, B. (2001). *Introduction to documentary*. Bloomington: Indiana University Press.

Renov, M. (2004). *The subject of documentary*. Minneapolis: University of Minnesota Press.

Winston, B. (1995). *Claiming the real*. British Film Institute: BFI Publishing.

DRAMATISM AND DRAMATISTIC PENTAD

Dramatism, or *dramaturgy*, is an approach taken to understand the uses of symbols in the social world. This approach is important to communication theory because a primary use of symbols occurs through language. Such a focus on the symbolic uses of language to influence is inherently rhetorical. In addition, dramatism seeks to understand the human world as a symbolic world of drama in which language is a strategic, motivated response to specific situations. As such, language is viewed as a mode of symbolic action rather than a repository of knowledge, and the use of language or other symbols to induce cooperation among human beings is the focus of investigation. To develop the concept of dramatism further, this entry will look at the contributors to and key assumptions of dramatism and its associated method, the dramatistic pentad.

Introduced by literary theorist Kenneth Burke in the early 1950s, dramatism has penetrated many disciplines, including political science, sociology, literary criticism, rhetoric, organizational communication, and interpersonal communication. Burke's students have applied the concept of dramatism in philosophy (Susan Sontag), sociology (Hugh Dalziel Duncan), political science (Doris Graber), and interpersonal communication (Erving Goffman). Still others in many additional disciplines have been influenced by dramatism, including Harold Bloom, Stanley Cavell, Clifford Geertz, Rene Girard, Frederic Jameson, Geoffrey Hartman, and Edward Said. Dramatism continues to develop as an aid to understanding the complexity of human symbol use.

Several assumptions undergird dramatism, the most important of which is the understanding of human beings as symbol-using animals. Humans create symbols (language is the most obvious example of a human symbol system), respond to symbols, and understand their circumstances through symbols. It is by way of symbols that humans have the unique ability to conceive of the *negative* or the absence of something. Symbols function to create and sustain hierarchies of power and identification among dissimilar groups. Symbols also allow for incongruities, such as creating the conditions for conflict while simultaneously unifying individuals to resist conflict.

Another assumption is that human interaction can be approached as a drama, hence the name *dramatism*. For Burke, the relationship between life and theater is literal rather than metaphorical. Humans enact real roles on live stages as they attempt to impact others. These dramas guide the ways that individuals, groups, and organizations conduct their behaviors. Dramatism also acknowledges that human beings act rather than move. The distinction between action and motion is that human beings make choices to act, often through symbols, while animals, plants, and other physical objects simply engage in motion. This human choice to act is the basis of all human motivation. Thus, symbols become sites for discovering motivation.

Finally, dramatism suggests that symbols form a grid or screen through which the world is viewed. Such *terministic screens* select or favor some realities and deflect others; doctors arriving at the scene of a car accident will look first for injuries because of the medical terministic screen operating for them; lawyers, while equally concerned with injury, will also note possible factors of blame because of the terministic screen implicit in their training. The terministic screens through which we apprehend our worlds have larger implications as well; they bristle with embedded values that, in turn, form belief systems or ideologies. These ideologies filter our understanding of others, our communication to them, as well as our choices of action.

The *dramatistic pentad* is the key model used by critics to analyze human use of symbols in communication. The pentad is made up of five elements or terms (hence the name *pentad*): *act,* or what was or will be done; *scene,* or the context of the act that answers the questions of where and when the act occurred; *agent,* or who performed the act; *agency,* or the way the act was performed; and *purpose,* or the goal of the act. These five terms answer the what, where, who, how, and why of human communication. The act serves a pivotal place in the pentad because human society is fundamentally dramatic or driven by action. Later, Burke suggested that *incipient act,* or the first steps toward the act, can substitute for the act in pentadic analysis. The incipient act recognizes the vital connection between thought and behavior. He also later added a sixth term, *attitude,* to further clarify the manner in which the agent approached the doing of the act.

While all human use of symbols in communication shares the same elements or terms, the proportion of those terms varies. Often, pairs of terms, or *ratios,* surface to dominate communication. For example, when communication focuses on what occurred and who performed the action, a ratio of agent–act dominates, or surfaces. For example, in a courtroom, a prosecuting attorney might argue that the accused did indeed unlawfully enter a house—an agent–act ratio. The defense attorney might prefer to make use of a scene–agent ratio instead, arguing that the accused came on a house with the door broken in and entered to see if there was a problem; in this case, scene dominates the act.

Application of the dramatistic pentad also helps to identify the ideology or worldview from which the communicator constructs the message. Generally, one term of the pentad dominates the communication, providing an ideology that accompanies it. If the act is the central term of the communication, then the form of the communication is realism. In such communication, active language such as verbs would dominate. On the other hand, if the central term is the scene or the setting for the action, we are urged to view the drama as dominated by the material situation, or materialism. If the agent, or the actor in the drama, is featured, then idealism is the corresponding orientation. Agency and purpose both locate the importance of the drama in how action is accomplished. Agency, or the way the act is performed, suggests pragmatism, while purpose, or goal, makes mysticism its compulsive force because the individual is less important than the final objective. For each of these central terms, a corresponding philosophical orientation arises, and when the term dominates the communication, its philosophical orientation forms the point of embarkation.

Burke used the illustration of the human hand to explain the working of the pentad. Each finger becomes a separate term of the pentad, distinct in its form. However, the palm of the hand unifies the fingers so that even though the fingers are separate, they are also united. Through the pentad, human actions are viewed from five interrelated points of motivation that are overlapping. By identifying the separate terms of the pentad, the critic can ultimately understand their common connection.

Kathleen M. German

See also Ideological Rhetoric; Ideology; Meaning Theories; Rhetorical Theory; Symbolic Interactionism

Further Readings

Burke, K. D. (1945). *A grammar of motives*. Berkeley: University of California Press.

Burke, K. D. (1976). Dramatism. In J. E. Combs & M. W. Mansfield (Eds.), *Drama in life: The uses of communication in society* (pp. 7–17). New York: Hastings House.

Duncan, H. D. (1962). *Communication and social order*. London: Oxford University Press.

Goffman, E. (1956). *The presentation of self in everyday life*. Edinburgh, Scotland: University of Edinburgh Social Sciences Research Center.

Graber, D. (1976). *Verbal behavior and politics*. Urbana: University of Illinois Press.

Ling, D. A. (1970). A pentadic analysis of Senator Edward Kennedy's address to the people of Massachusetts, July 25, 1969. *Central States Speech Journal, 21*, 80–86.

Dual-Level Connectionist Models of Group Cognition and Social Influence

Dual-level connectionist models (DLCMs) of group communication arose from two very different strains of work in individual psychology—the activation of links in semantic memory and parallel processing models of pattern recognition and learning. Unlike their psychological roots, however, DLCMs integrate individual psychological concepts with group communication. They explain how cognitive states (beliefs, feelings, etc.) are changed by communication among group members. These changes result in changes in the content of communication events, which then influence patterns of group communication. In turn the cognitive states of group members may be changed, and so on. DLCMs go beyond important dual-level theories of influence such as Richard Petty and John Cacioppo's elaboration likelihood theory and Shelly Chaiken's heuristic processing model, which focus primarily on mental processes rather than on the integration of mental processing and temporally embedded social processes. DLCMs have been applied broadly by Dean Hewes to group emotional dynamics, group phase development, and argumentation and influence in groups. But to understand how DLCMs accomplish this, we need to examine them in detail, sketching their elements and processes and discussing their promise.

Elements and Processes

Regardless of the specific applications, DLCMs contain a common set of components: *nodes, links, dynamic processes,* and *modules*. Nodes are perceived communication events (inputs), mental states associated with them (processing nodes such as beliefs, policies, and emotions), and communication outputs connected to mental states (arguments, emotional statements, etc.). For example, in a DLCM theory of argumentation and influence in groups, input nodes might be policy-relevant arguments from other group members as perceived by a particular member, the set of policy options relevant to those (processing nodes), and a set of arguments produced by that group member and transmitted to the other group members, and so on for all group members. These nodes are connected to each other, although not fully, and are the potential sites of change, both communicative and mental. Thus, DLCMs are *connectionist* because of the connections between the nodes and *dual-level* since change can occur in both the communicative and cognitive levels.

Connections between nodes, or links, have *constraints, valences,* and *activation weights*. Constraints determine the connections between types of nodes. For instance, in the example above, links run (a) from perceived messages (inputs) to policy options, (b) among policy options (processing nodes), (c) from policy options to generated arguments, and (d) from members' arguments to other members' received messages. In a DLCM group argument theory, (a), (c), and (d) are unidirectional flowing forward as described above. Unidirectional links, for example, can run from perceived messages to mental states but not the reverse. Thus, a theoretical constraint is placed on types of links.

Valences specify the negative or positive implications of the links between nodes. For example, a negatively valenced link between a mental state, say an emotion, and an emotional message indicates that the more an emotion is experienced, the less likely it is to be expressed—feeling anger leads to the repression of expressed anger. A positively valenced link indicates the reverse. Moreover, each link has an activation weight that indexes the strength of a link. Stronger arguments for a policy option have larger activation weights for links to policy options than do weaker arguments.

DLCMs possess dynamic processes that explain how the activation weights can be changed. The continued reception of perceived messages with a positive valance can strengthen those links to thinking processes (processing nodes). In other words, if the links are positive, the more frequently a group member receives a perceived message, the stronger the link between that message and processing node, and the more readily the group member calls the relevant processing node to mind. This, in turn, influences the production of messages because frequently activated processing nodes strengthen the link between them and the produced message, again assuming these links are positive. For example, in a DLCM theory of group development, there might exist a positive link between some functional statement made by other members of a group (say, "defining the problem") and the receiver thinking about that function. A subsequent functional statement of the same type will move the increment of the activation weight for that link upward. This makes the person more inclined to think about that function over time as functional messages of that type recur. Mixed functional messages (positively valenced links) from other group members, on the other hand, lead to the leveling of weights across nodes for individual members, which, in turn, would lead to more confused thinking about functions and mixed expression of those functions to others. Of course, if the weights are negatively valenced, the weights build up negatively through repeated activation and tend to inhibit the activation of those nodes subsequently.

These dynamic processes are the heart of the DLCMs. They make it possible to track both communication and psychological processes over time. For example, in the study of policy decision making, they can produce increasing differentiation, integration, vacillation, or ambivalence among policy options both within and between individuals, depending on the input messages and structure of links between and among the nodes. They can

also predict both steady movement toward a decision and abrupt shifts in group preferences, as well as tendencies toward *self-organization* or *chaos*.

Modules, the fourth set of elements, are also dynamic mechanisms that, while essential to the complete development of DLCMs, are conceptualized as processes that are distinct from the elements discussed so far. Four modules are posited—the *interpretive, strategy production,* and *accessibility modules,* as well as the *turn-taking management device.* The turn-taking management device regulates turn exchanges among the group members. The accessibility module describes when interactions among people do not occur, allowing for predictions of group behavior across multiple meetings, and effects of subgroup meetings and consultation that occur between meetings. Interpretive modules bridge the gap between the meaning of a message for the sender and the meaning given it by its recipient. The strategy production modules serve to edit messages considered by senders before transmission based on their perceived appropriateness, effectiveness, and timeliness.

Conclusions

DLCMs are complex theories of group interaction necessary to explain the integration of individual cognition of all group members and ongoing communication, something beyond the scope of any current theory of group communication. DLCMs have heuristic value because they apply to a range of group phenomena. A DLCM theory of group development explains current data on group phases, presents an account of intrusions in phase development that differs from explanations by Marshall Scott Poole and Joel Doelger and Poole and Carolyn Baldwin, and does so by integrating individual cognitive processes and sequential patterns of communication where these theories do not. A DLCM theory of emotional dynamics fills a gap in available theorizing since virtually all treatments of emotion in groups address individual states rather than the emotional dynamics of those states among group members. A DLCM theory of group argument and social influence integrates separate explanations based on cognitive processes with those primarily anchored in communication processes such as that of Marshall Scott Poole,

David Seibold, and Robert McPhee, to the benefit of both. Thus, the DLCM framework of group communication has considerable promise, though more theoretical and empirical work is needed.

Recently, a number of critics have evaluated this framework, highlighting both its potential and its gaps in coverage. The reviews have been positive but do leave some questions for further development. For example, the dynamic processes in such models need further clarification. Concerns have been raised about the testability of these models. An important question deals with the long-term effects of messages received during the initial stages of group discussion compared to those received later. Some of these objections have been addressed while others need further clarification. All these critiques have proven useful for the subsequent advancement of the DLCM framework or its various instantiations.

DLCMs provide a handle on the most serious gap in the study of group communication. We have been driven to date by purely psychological theories on one hand and those purely sociological on the other. As a field standing between these two monoliths, our task is to find the connection between them through the communication processes connecting them. Even if the DLCMs prove to be incapable of serving this function, they identify the problems and point the way to those frameworks that will.

Dean E. Hewes

See also Cognitive Theories; Elaboration Likelihood Theory; Group Communication Theories; Heuristic-Systematic Model

Further Readings

Anderson, J. (1973). A spreading activation theory of memory. *Journal of Verbal Learning and Verbal Behavior, 22,* 261–295.

Arrow, H., McGrath, J., & Berdahl, J. (2000). *Small groups as complex systems.* Thousand Oaks, CA: Sage.

Bonito, J., & Sanders, R. (in press). A different approach to answering a good question: A response to Hewes's models of communication effects on small group outcomes. *Human Communication Research.*

Chaiken, S. (1980). The heuristic model of persuasion. In M. P. Zanna, J. M. Olsen, & C. P. Herman (Eds.),

Social influence: The Ontario symposium: Vol. 5 (pp. 3–39). Hillsdale, NJ: Lawrence Erlbaum.

Gouran, D. (in press). A response to Hewes's "The influence of communication processes on group outcomes: Antithesis and thesis." *Human Communication Research.*

Hewes, D. (1986). A socio-egocentric model of group decision making. In R. Hirokawa & M. S. Poole (Eds.), *Communication and group decision making* (1st ed., pp. 265–291). Beverly Hills, CA: Sage.

Hewes, D. (1996). Small group communication may not influence group decision making: An amplification of the socio-egocentric model. In R. Hirokawa & M. S. Poole (Eds.), *Communication and group decision making* (2nd ed., pp. 179–214). Thousand Oaks, CA: Sage.

Hewes, D. (in press). Elaborations on the socio-egocentric and dual-level connectionist models of group interaction processes. *Human Communication Research.*

Hewes, D. (in press). The influence of communication processes on group outcomes: Antithesis and thesis. *Human Communication Research.*

McClelland, J., Rumelhart, D., & Hilton, G. (1988). The appeal of parallel distributed processing. In McClelland, J., Rumelhart, D., & the PDP Research Group (Eds.), *Parallel distributed processing: Vol. 1* (pp. 3–44). Cambridge: MIT Press.

Meyers, R., & Seibold, D. (in press). Making foundational assumptions transparent: Framing the discussion about group communication and influence. *Human Communication Research.*

Pavitt, C. (in press). A sympathetic reaction to the SM and DLCM as group communication theories. *Human Communication Research.*

Petty, R. E., & Cacioppo, J. R. (1986). *Communication and persuasion: Central and peripheral routes to persuasion.* New York: Springer-Verlag.

Poole, M. S., & Baldwin, C. (1996). Developmental processes in group decision making. In R. Hirokawa & M. S. Poole (Eds.), *Communication and group decision making* (2nd ed., pp. 215–241). Thousand Oaks, CA: Sage.

Poole, M. S., & Doelger, J. (1986). Developmental processes in group decision making. In R. Hirokawa & M. S. Poole (Eds.), *Communication and group decision making* (1st ed., pp. 35–61). Beverly Hills, CA: Sage.

Poole, M. S., Seibold, D., & McPhee, R. (1982). A comparison of normative and interactional explanations of group decision making: Social decision schemes versus valence distributions. *Communication Monographs, 49,* 1–19.

DYADIC POWER THEORY

First proposed by Boyd Rollins and Stephen Bahr in 1976 and later revised by Norah Dunbar, dyadic power theory (DPT) emphasizes the relative perceived power of partners in a relationship. From a social–psychological perspective, *power* is generally defined as the capacity to produce intended effects and, in particular, the ability to influence the behavior of another person even in the face of resistance. Dunbar asserts that power is an integral part of any relationship but is especially important in close romantic relationships because it determines how the partners relate to each other and how decisions are made. The theory assumes that perceptions of legitimate authority to make decisions and to exert control over a variety of resources increase individuals' perceptions of their own power compared with that of their partner. Perceptions of power, in turn, increase the likelihood of using dominance as a way to control the interaction through a mechanism Rollins and Bahr call *control attempts* but what Dunbar often refers to as *dominance*.

Rollins and Bahr originally argued for a linear relationship between dominance and power, stating that an increase in a spouse's perception of power in a marriage role relative to that of the partner will produce an increase in attempts to control her or his spouse in the role. Furthermore, they argued that the effectiveness of the control attempts is influenced by the relative power perceived by the recipient such that the greater the relative power of the initiator, the more likely the control attempts will result in compliance. From this perspective, the more powerful someone is, the more dominance he or she will exert through control attempts, and the more his or her partner will comply with his or her requests.

However, recent tests of DPT by Dunbar have not supported Rollins and Bahr's linear proposition but have indicated that the relationship between perceived relative power and manifest dominance is curvilinear, such that partners who perceive their relative power difference as extremely high will use fewer control attempts than partners who perceive their relative power difference as low. This is because high-power individuals do not need to make a large number of control attempts over low-power individuals; by virtue of their latent power, they can maintain control without dominant behaviors. On the other hand, in line with Michael Roloff and Denise Cloven's research that suggests a lack of power creates a *chilling effect* in conflict situations, low-power individuals are unlikely to express grievances to high-power individuals if they fear that retaliation, violence, or termination of the relationship will result from their control attempt. For example, a battered wife may not openly disagree with her husband, or a subordinate may lie to his or her superior at work for fear of reprisal.

The process of displaying verbal and nonverbal dominance during interaction is central to DPT, but the outcomes of such displays must be examined as well. The model proposed by Rollins and Bahr ends with one partner's compliance, or the outcome of the conflict interaction, but Dunbar extended it to examine the outcomes of the interaction for the health of the relationship and satisfaction with the interaction itself. In ongoing relationships, satisfaction is an especially important outcome to examine because dissatisfaction can "erode" the relationship and lead to distress if left unchecked. For example, in the context of marriages, many researchers have found power equality to be a large determinant of marital satisfaction.

While power equality can enhance satisfaction, the perception of a loss of power can be particularly destructive to relational or interactional satisfaction. Perceived imbalance in the resources of exchange, inequity, and unequal distribution of power are often cited as sources of conflict and reasons for relational dissatisfaction. Powerlessness also should have an influence on an individual's satisfaction within a particular interaction, even one with a total stranger.

Although Rollins and Bahr's theory was originally conceived as a model of marital power, DPT's scope should not be limited to marriage. It has the potential to be applied to friendships, familial relationships, dating relationships, work relationships, and any other setting in which interactants have an established history and expect to have continued interaction in the future.

Norah E. Dunbar

See also Interpersonal Communication Theories; Power, Interpersonal; Relational Communication Theory

Further Readings

Berger, C. R. (1994). Power, dominance, and social interaction. In M. L. Knapp & G. R. Miller (Eds.), *Handbook of interpersonal communication* (pp. 450–507). Thousand Oaks, CA: Sage.

Dunbar, N. E. (2004). Dyadic power theory: Constructing a communication-based theory of relational power. *Journal of Family Communication, 4*(3 & 4), 235–248.

Dunbar, N. E., & Burgoon, J. K. (2005). Perceptions of power and interactional dominance in interpersonal relationships. *Journal of Social and Personal Relationships, 22,* 207–233.

French, J. R. P., Jr., & Raven, B. (1959). The bases of social power. In D. Cartwright (Ed.), *Studies in social power* (pp. 150–167). Ann Arbor, MI: Institute for Social Research.

Huston, T. (1983). Power. In H. H. Kelley, E. Berscheid, A. Christensen, J. Harvey, T. Huston, G. Levinger, et al. (Eds.), *Close relationships* (pp. 169–219). New York: W. H. Freeman.

Rollins, B. C., & Bahr, S. J. (1976). A theory of power relationships in marriage. *Journal of Marriage and Family, 38,* 619–627.

Roloff, M. E., & Cloven, D. H. (1990). The chilling effect in interpersonal relationships: The reluctance to speak one's mind. In D. D. Cahn (Ed.), *Intimates in conflict: A communication perspective* (pp. 49–76). Hillsdale, NJ: Lawrence Erlbaum.

DYNAMIC MEMORY MODEL

See Cognitive Theories

E

EFFECTIVE INTERCULTURAL WORKGROUP COMMUNICATION THEORY

The effective intercultural workgroup communication theory (IWCT), developed by John Oetzel in 1995, explains how cultural variability and diversity influence communication processes and the subsequent outcomes that occur in workgroups. This theory addresses limitations in explaining workgroup communication in culturally diverse groups and has been refined over the past 10 years as more complex understandings of how culture influences communication have been identified.

The theory was developed from the literature attempting to identify models of effective workgroups. The predominant models of workgroup effectiveness ignore culture and emphasize work or task communication only. These models privilege one particular view of how groups should work by emphasizing work outcomes over relational outcomes. The IWCT recognizes that group processes and outcomes include both task and relational aspects. The literature on cultural variability provides a strong theoretical explanation as to why both task and relational aspects are important in effective workgroups. Hence, IWCI merges these two different literatures in providing a practical theory of workgroup communication. This entry examines the three key components of the theory—inputs, processes, and outcomes—and the relationships among these concepts.

Key Concepts

The theory includes three broad inputs in culturally diverse workgroups: contextual factors, group composition, and cultural–individual factors. *Contextual factors* include the following: (a) a history of unresolved conflict among cultural or ethnic groups (e.g., the conflict between Israelis and Palestinians); (b) in-group–out-group balance (i.e., the number of group members from each cultural group); (c) cooperative versus competitive tasks (i.e., does the task require collaboration among members or encourage members to work for their own interests?); and (d) status differences among members (e.g., boss and employee). Essentially, each of these four factors is a condition that helps or hinders the creation of a common identity in a culturally diverse workgroup. *Group composition* is the degree of cultural diversity (or similarity) in the group and ranges from homogeneous to heterogeneous. *Cultural–individual factors* are the values and identities that individual group members have. The primary cultural value difference considered is variability of individualism and collectivism. Individualism is a social pattern that consists of loosely linked individuals who view themselves as independent of collectives and who give priority to their personal goals over the goals of others, while collectivism is a social pattern consisting of closely linked individuals who see themselves as part of one or more collectives (family, coworkers, tribe, nation) and are willing to give priority to the goals of these collectives over their own personal goals.

Processes refer to the communication among members of a workgroup. The theory distinguishes between effective and ineffective communication. *Effective communication* consists of four workgroup behaviors: equal participation, consensus decision making, cooperative conflict, and respectful communication. These four behaviors are culturally appropriate in that they relate to both task and relational aspects. Outcomes are the work output of the group and/or the relationships of the members and include such factors as decisions, solutions, creative ideas, satisfaction of members, and cohesion among members. Outcomes are categorized as either task (e.g., decision, solutions, and plans) or relational (e.g., satisfaction and cohesion).

Relationships Among Concepts

The theory has a strong foundation in system theory. From this foundation, IWCT provides a series of general assumptions and specific propositions. The general assumptions of the theory are threefold. First, the context of the group frames the relationships among inputs, processes, and outputs. Second, within a particular context, the inputs influence the communication processes of a group; subsequently the communication processes impact the outcomes of the group. Third, the processes and outcomes serve as feedback for context and input.

IWCT has nine propositions that explain these general assumptions within intercultural workgroups. For the input–process relationship, the propositions specify the inputs that lead to effective or ineffective communication in culturally diverse workgroups. Specifically, the theory proposes the following: (1) the more negative contextual factors that a culturally diverse group faces, the less likely the group will experience effective communication; (2) the more culturally heterogeneous a group, the less likely it will experience effective communication; (3) the more individualistic (or independent) a culturally diverse group, the more likely the group will utilize dominating conflict strategies; (4) the more collectivistic (or interdependent) a culturally diverse group, the more likely the group will utilize collaborating conflict strategies; (5) the more individualistic (or independent) individuals in a culturally diverse group, the more likely they will take turns; (6) the more collectivist (or interdependent) a culturally diverse group, the more likely the group will have equal participation; and (7) the more members of a culturally diverse group have other- or mutual-face concerns, the more likely the group will have effective communication.

For the process–outcome relationship, the propositions explain how communication processes relate to task and relational outcomes. Specifically, IWCT proposes the following: (8) the more a culturally diverse group utilizes effective communication processes, the more likely the group will achieve task effectiveness; and (9) the more a culturally diverse group utilizes effective communication processes, the more likely the group will achieve relational effectiveness.

In terms of feedback, the theory argues that the outcomes of a group reinforce individual decisions and satisfaction and may influence future work effort in the group. Further, if a culturally diverse workgroup has effective communication, it may improve the quality of intercultural relations that members have with people outside the workgroup (e.g., by encouraging them to see members of other cultural groups in a positive light).

John G. Oetzel

See also Cultural Types Theories; Functional Group Communication Theory; Group Communication Theories; Intercultural Communication Theories; System Theory

Further Readings

Oetzel, J. G. (1995). Intercultural small groups: An effective decision-making theory. In R. L. Wiseman (Ed.), *Intercultural communication theories* (pp. 247–270). Thousand Oaks, CA: Sage.

Oetzel, J. G. (1998). Explaining individual communication processes in homogeneous and heterogeneous groups through individualism-collectivism and self-construal. *Human Communication Research, 25*, 202–224.

Oetzel, J. G. (2005). Intercultural work group communication theory. In W. B. Gudykunst (Ed.), *Theorizing about intercultural communication* (pp. 351–371). Thousand Oaks, CA: Sage.

ELABORATED AND RESTRICTED CODES

Codes used in communication may be characterized according to the extent of their elaboration within a specific message or in a communicative style. A message in an elaborated code carries all information needed to understand it within the message itself. Thus, elaborated codes are relatively context free. Restricted codes are context bound and cannot be easily understood without additional information beyond that in the message. This entry describes elaborated and restricted codes, discussing the implications of the elaborated–restricted code distinction for the study of communication.

Description of Elaborated and Restricted Codes

The elaborated–restricted code distinction was proposed by Basil Bernstein in response to questions concerning learning differences among children. Bernstein held that restricted codes occur where social relations are based on closely shared identifications, expectations, and assumptions, where the subculture raises "we" above "I." Their use creates social solidarity by restricting verbal elaboration of individual experience. In a restricted code, the intentions of a speaker are verbally unelaborated. Speech is normally conducted rapidly and fluently, often with few articulatory clues to the context of the message. From the viewpoint of a third-party listener who is unaware of the topic or context, the meaning gathered from a restricted-code conversation is discontinuous, condensed, and local. Meaning in a restricted code is implicit rather than verbally explicit and is carried in the *how* of saying more than in the *what*. Notions of causality, if present, are limited.

Example of an overheard conversation in a restricted code between A and B:

A: So?

B: No.

A: No?

B: Jim.

A: Jim.

B: Jim.

A: Umm.

B: Mmn.

In contrast, an elaborated code encourages the speaker to focus on the experience of others as different from one's own. Elaboration is required due to a gap between speaker and listener. The other is presumed to be a different person with no direct knowledge of the speaker's phenomenology. With a restricted code, the gap is presumed to occur, not between speaker and listener, but between those who share the code and those who do not. A restricted code presumes a generalized undifferentiated other, while an elaborated code presumes a single differentiated other.

Example of a somewhat more elaborated code, for the same overheard conversation:

A: What happened?

B: The answer was no.

A: No? Why not?

B: Unexpectedly, Jim was there.

A: Oh no, Jim. You're kidding.

B: Jim was there and, you know, they just can't talk in front of him.

A: So, none of this is going to happen just because Jim showed up unexpectedly.

B: Right, it's not going to happen.

Implications for Communication

The degree of code elaboration has been proposed as an explanatory mechanism for learning differences among children. Code elaboration requires a form of perspective taking not needed when the code is restricted. A restricted-code speaker is presumed to communicate primarily or exclusively with sharers of the restricted code. Speaking is easy when composing a restricted-code message since the receiver is presumed to possess prior awareness of the topic, situation, and context. These need not be specified. Speaking is a more difficult and complex process when composing an elaborated code. An elaborated-code speaker must consider the phenomenology of the other and compare what is likely to be known with what is expressed in the message. The required but missing portion of the message, if any, may then be determined by a form of subtraction. The missing information may be composed into an acceptable message format, and the formatted message information may be integrated with that contained in the restricted message. The finalized elaborated message can then be delivered to the listener.

Listening is also more difficult within an elaborated code. While background, situation, context, and topic are clearly specified in an ideal elaborated message, the listener must decode this information from the message, integrate it into the listener's belief system, check it for internal and multiple external consistencies, and evaluate it for credibility, intended humor, and important implications. In a restricted code, that information is already present in the receiver.

Intercultural Implications

In the 1950s, as educational test scores of children became widely used indicators of learning, large differences between mean test scores for Black and White children in some American schools became apparent. In searching for reasons for this disparity beyond genetics, scholars in education examined multiple possible correlated factors, including language. Black English was held by some to be a restricted code. Children learn through language, and restricted codes might lead to restricted abilities and thus restricted learning. Elaborated codes give the child more of the grounds for action and lead to thought in terms of cause, effect, and consequences. Other scholars suggested multiple flaws in this possible explanatory mechanism. Among these are the possible ethnocentrism involved in presuming that structures deemed to be logical in standard English were more than simple habitual conventions of upper-class message construction. Another is the self-fulfilling prophecy effect of teachers' expectations on children's performance, as teachers are taught to be particularly aware of proper use of elaborated codes.

Linguistic Relativity

The possible relation of language structure to thought in the elaborated–restricted code distinction has potential implications for the concept of linguistic relativity. For example, some educators believe language is the common denominator in and the core of the difficulty for disadvantaged children. Children learn their culture's social structure, according to elaborated–restricted codes theory, through the social structure embedded in speech. The form of a child's speech reinforces the social structure, with the social identity becoming the child's psychological reality. Children who learn different roles due to their families' class positions may adopt different social and intellectual orientations and procedures despite equal intelligence.

Thomas M. Steinfatt

See also Communication and Language Acquisition and Development; Culture and Communication; Ethnography of Communication; Language and Communication; Linguistic Relativity; Speech Codes Theory

Further Readings

Bernstein, B. (1964). Elaborated and restricted codes: Their social origins and some consequences. *American Anthropologist, 66*(6), Pt. 2, 55–69.

Herrnstein , R. J., & Murray, C. (1994). *The bell curve: Intelligence and class structure in American life.* New York: Free Press.

Labov, W. (1972). *Sociolinguistic patterns.* Philadelphia: Pennsylvania University Press.

Williams, F. (1970). *Language and poverty: Perspectives on a theme.* Chicago: Markham.

ELABORATION LIKELIHOOD THEORY

John Cacioppo and Richard E. Petty's elaboration likelihood theory (ELT) deals with the ways in which communicators process persuasive messages. The theory describes two cognitive levels through which communicators process issue-related arguments and explains how these two routes differ. Human beings want to hold correct attitudes and opinions but are not always willing or able to evaluate the merits of the issue-related arguments presented in support of an appeal. The persuasive message recipient evaluates some messages in an elaborate way and deals with others with much less critical thinking, if at all. Relevant to communication theory, ELT acknowledges and tries to explain the two different means by which the recipient evaluates issue-related content. ELT tries to predict when and how the recipient will and will not be persuaded.

Cacioppo and Petty's use of the term *elaboration* refers to the extent of critical thinking that an audience member gives to the persuasive message. *Elaboration likelihood* is the two social scientists' metaphor for variable; it can change from little to great, depending on the way the message is evaluated. Cacioppo and Petty posit that a receiver of a persuasive message processes the information through one of two routes—central or peripheral—or sometimes both, toward attitude change.

The Central Route

The *central route* to persuasion is taken when the recipient is guided by an elaborate amount of critical thinking about what is said in the persuasive message. In the central scenario arguments are considered carefully. The compatibility between the message and the receiver's attitude plays a role in persuasion.

The potency of the message also plays a part. Centrally, the message recipient is identifying weak arguments and is being influenced by strong arguments. When the recipient realizes that the message is significant to his or her life, the likelihood of cognitively elaborating on the message increases. After this increase occurs, attitude changes will likely have a long-lasting behavioral effect.

The amount of critical thinking expended is dependent on two general factors: the receiver's motivation and the receiver's ability, *ability* meaning being knowledgeable about the issue involved in the persuasive message and not being distracted from the message. At least three components comprise the motivation factor. The first is the relevance of the topic to the receiver; the more relevant the topic, the more likely the receiver will think critically about the issues involved. The second

component in the receiver's motivation is the variety of credible sources. When listening to several experts speak about the issue, the receiver will typically tend to centrally process the content. In disagreement with this point, however, Ann Bainbridge Frymier and Marjorie Keeshan Nadler, two persuasion scholars, contend that accountability is a determinant of motivation, not the variety of credible sources.

The third component in the receiver's motivation is the penchant for mulling over arguments. Frymier and Nadler point out that this factor affects motivation, but so does the degree of personal responsibility and incongruent information.

The issue-related message recipient, no matter how motivated, cannot use the central route if the recipient is ignorant of the issue. For example, most college students would probably engage in a high elaboration about an informative speech on downloading music rather than a speech on Beverly Sills.

Peripheral Route

Cacioppo and Petty use the term *peripheral* because the receiver looks to less central considerations in processing the message. The decision is not based on the message itself. *Peripheral cues* include an appropriate guiding principle that comes to mind during the message, source credibility, the style and format of the message, and the mood of the receiver. Instead of the receiver's taking into consideration the argument's strength, he or she depends on *heuristics*, the receiver's use of simple decision rules, which are activated by peripheral cues during the persuasive message. Three major heuristics are credibility, likableness, and consensus. The *credibility heuristic* is the propensity to believe sources who have credibility. The *likableness heuristic* is the receiver's propensity to agree with individuals he or she likes. When source credibility is high, the message may be believed regardless of the arguments presented. Moreover, it is natural for a receiver to believe individuals he or she likes, or to be persuaded if there is a variety of credible sources.

An example of persuasion through the peripheral route might involve someone who wants to purchase a cell phone but does not want to take the time to read about and shop for the various models. Such a person might take a friend's suggestions for which one to buy or base a decision on a 30-second commercial on a radio station's morning show. In this case the liking heuristic and the credibility heuristic are being used. Someone might be persuaded to set out tomato plants simply because neighbors are setting out tomato plants (the consensus heuristic); yet, that person is not persuaded to follow the tips about growing tomatoes given on a horticulturist's television program.

Because elaboration likelihood is a variable, the receiver of a persuasive message will probably use both routes. Persuasion can take place with either route. The two routes to persuasion are not mutually exclusive.

Since the mid-1980s, the elaboration likelihood theory has generated ample research and continues to do so. Daniel O'Keefe has assessed Cacioppo and Petty's theory as the most promising theoretical development, surpassing the theory of cognitive dissonance. ELT, the dominant persuasive theory, is seen in communication, psychology, marketing, health fields, and the like. It is certainly a central topic of communication theory.

Don Rodney Vaughan

See also Attitude Theory; Cognitive Theories; Dual-Level Connectionist Models of Group Cognition and Social Influence; Intrapersonal Communication Theories; Persuasion and Social Influence Theories; Social Judgment Theory

Further Readings

Frymier, A. B., & Nadler, M. K. (2006). *Persuasion: Integrating theory, research, and practice.* Dubuque, IA: Kendall/Hunt.

Infante, D. A., Rancer, A. S., & Womack, D. F. (1997). *Building communication theory* (3rd ed.). Prospect Heights, IL: Waveland.

Littlejohn, S. W., & Foss, K. A. (2005). *Theories of human communication* (8th ed.). Belmont, CA: Thomson Wadsworth.

O'Keefe, D. J. (1990). *Persuasion: Theory and research.* Newbury Park, CA: Sage.

Petty, R. E., & Cacioppo, J. T. (1986). *Communication and persuasion: Central and peripheral routes to attitude change.* New York: Springer-Verlag.

Emotion and Communication

The human experience of emotion is ubiquitous. Recently, however, communication theorists and researchers have discovered that the *communication* of emotion is similarly omnipresent. Emotions are not just private, subjective experiences; universal communication systems are designed to verbally and nonverbally communicate emotions to others.

Social evolutionary theorists recognize that emotional communication evolved because it conferred a selective advantage on expressive individuals. Fear displays, for example, evolved because they provide rapid danger signals to other members of the group, enhancing their collective survival. Across the gamut of human emotions, social evolutionary theorists have shown that every human emotion developed as more than an internal control system; emotions are consistently communicated because they provide powerful survival advantages.

Throughout primate evolution and human history, emotions have been communicated primarily through nonverbal communication. Emotional expression evolved long before the dawn of human language. Indeed, intercultural communication theorists have shown that human nonverbal emotional displays are primarily universal, though small regional "accents" or cultural variations exist. Cross-cultural similarity of emotional expressions indicates human evolutionary adaptations have occurred across the millennia.

Developmental communication theory also supports the primacy of emotional communication. Nonverbal emotional expression precedes verbal communication in each human's life. Every human infant is well-equipped at birth to express a variety of emotions. Successful communication depends on infants' being well-equipped emotional senders and the skill of adults who vary widely in their ability to read infant displays. Infants show little control over emotional expression; they are biologically adapted to automatically communicate emotions. While socialization inculcates display rules for appropriate emotional communication, even adults frequently produce automatic, spontaneous nonverbal expressions communicated through one's voice, body, arms, and predominantly facial expression.

Every emotion produces recognizable nonverbal displays. Similarly, emotions produce patterns of verbal communication designed to elicit appropriate responses in receivers. Paul Ekman's landmark research revealed that at least six basic emotions are primarily pancultural and communicated similarly in cultures worldwide. Cultural display rules teach each developing individual to mask, amplify, minimize, magnify, substitute, or conceal emotional communication. Recent research and theory suggest that emotions display regional variations or accents in how they are communicated. Nonetheless, the six emotions discussed next—fear, anger, sadness, disgust, happiness, and surprise—are culturally universal and communicated similarly across culture.

Fear

One of Ekman's six basic emotional expressions, fear, is among the most disturbing, but most important. Fear is contagious, and its expression warns others of impending danger, producing both functional danger avoidance behaviors and dysfunctional phobic responses. Like birds on a wire, fear evokes collective avoidance and panic reactions in people. Fear is usually a transient emotion, though long-term fear can produce severe anxiety, paranoia, and phobic responses at both the interpersonal and collective levels. Throughout history, leaders of nations have often kept their citizens in a state of excessive fear, particularly fear of external threats, to control their behavior and enact draconian polices. Machiavelli was the first to write that fear was the most powerful means of social control that a leader could employ.

Fearful expressions accompany fear's experience, providing instant, typically nonverbal warnings to others about impending danger. Fear produces a distinctive facial expression, vocal exclamations, and flight-or-fight response. The classic fear expression is displayed by raised eyebrows and narrowed, triangular-shaped eyes produced by raising the upper eyelid and tightening the lower eyelid, with lips stretched across bared lower teeth. Fear produces functional, spontaneous ducking, fleeing, and cowering and nonverbal paralinguistics that include shouts, screams, and cries. Fear appeals have great pragmatic utility when used by parents, teachers, politicians, and health agencies to influence attitudes and change behavior.

Anger

The second basic universal emotional expression is anger, an intense feeling of displeasure resulting from injury, harm, or mistreatment by others. Anger results from troubling social events, insults, verbal attacks, injuries, thoughtlessness, rudeness, frustration of a person's goals by another person, threats to a person's identity or reputation, or relational threats such as infidelity or disloyalty.

Anger is communicated rapidly and spontaneously through nonverbal and verbal expressions. Anger feels unpleasant, and though its display is frightening and detestable, it is a crucial form of communication that warns interactants of an angry person's dangerous state and the possibility of impending attack. Without such a warning, anger could result in death or injury to the interactants.

Despite societal norms prohibiting the expression of anger, angry outbursts are relatively common. Angry communication is usually directed at the alleged perpetrator of hurt or harm but may also be shared with friends, family, and health providers for catharsis or to elicit sympathy or social support.

Angry facial expressions include the clenched jaw, knit and lowered eyebrows, and menacing stares that are innate and culturally universal. Vocal behavior communicates anger via loud, harsh, low-pitched vocalizations. Angry verbal behaviors include profanity, berating the perpetrator, threats, or guilt inductions. Anger may result in "getting in one's face," shaking fists, or walking out on the presumed perpetrator. Angry expressions include foot stomping, slamming doors, breaking things, throwing tantrums, threatening gestures, becoming withdrawn, and terminating relationships.

Sadness

Sadness, depression, and grief result from and are expressed through communication. The primary source of sadness is interpersonal loss or troubled social interaction. Infants display sadness and distress in response to parents' sadness displays. Depression, a chronic melancholic state, both results from and causes troubled relationships.

Sadness displays are produced by every healthy infant to communicate distress to caregivers. These innate, spontaneous displays can also be intentionally reproduced to communicate sadness through crying, a downturned mouth, and fussing. People also communicate sadness verbally to potential comforters to elicit relief from this unpleasant state. Sad individuals may speak softly, slowly, and unenthusiastically, without variation, and pause longer. Sad people avoid social interaction, become immobilized, and engage in a number of nonverbal behaviors, including sad facial expressions, slouching, reduced smiling and eye contact, and less open body positions.

Disgust

A fourth basic emotion originated when humans encountered the taste or smell of rotten food, decaying animals, or bodily excrement. The disgust expression is recognized even by preschool children: a downturned mouth, sometimes accompanied by a protruding tongue, a wrinkled nose, with the eyes nearly shut. Theorists reason that the original function of the disgust expression was to close sensory inputs and to eject noxious substances. Disgust is communicated vocally with utterances such as "yuck" or "ick" and by verbal statements such as "gross" or "disgusting."

Across the millennia humans have applied the disgust expression to distasteful people, relationships, and interactions. Whether gustatory or social, the disgust expression is an innate, cross-cultural response to noxious stimuli. Disgust was one of Darwin's fundamental emotions and among Ekman's basic facial expressions.

Happiness

The fourth basic emotion, happiness, is expressed and recognized worldwide as a universal sign of positive affect. An authentic, felt smile includes more than an upturned mouth; it includes raised cheeks, squinting, and smile lines around the eyes. The happiness display typically occurs during social interaction and is seldom displayed in private, suggesting the innately social roots of the experience and expression.

Smiling is an appeasement gesture signaling friendliness and low threat. Smiling occurs among all primates and evolved as a sign of nonviolence designed to calm other individuals and establish positive relationships. Happiness motivates closer interpersonal distances and friendly tactile communication such as hugs and reduces violent, hostile touch. Happiness produces warm vocal tones and higher pitch during speech.

Surprise

Unlike the other five basic emotions, surprise lacks positive or negative evaluative content. Surprise is an orienting emotion in response to rapidly changing interpersonal or environmental circumstances. The surprise facial expression consists of an open mouth, raised eyebrows, open eyes, widened nostrils, head orientation toward the stimulus, and startled verbal or paralinguistic vocalizations. The universal, cross-cultural recognizability of surprise suggests its evolutionary interpersonal origins. Surprise is the most fleeting emotion, lasting a fraction of a second and quickly blending into expressions such as happiness, fear, or anger.

The Social Emotions

Beyond the six basic emotions are the social emotions, so named because they both result from and are displayed during interpersonal communication. Social emotions evolved to socialize, reward, sanction, and discourage specific behaviors. Appropriate emotional displays and their accurate recognition are taught in every culture to facilitate smooth, harmonious social interaction.

Embarrassment evolved as an inherently social emotion during interaction from failed self-presentation, loss of face, or threats to self-esteem. Remediation of embarrassment occurs through verbal accounts and excuses along with nonverbal apologies including shrugs, sheepish looks, blushing, gaze aversion, feeble smiles, and interpersonal avoidance.

Similarly, *guilt* is a cross-cultural, social emotion functioning as a sanction for hurtful behavior or interpersonal transgressions. Guilt is communicated nonverbally via hiding, isolation, and contrite, apologetic behaviors. Though a specific "guilt" facial expression has not been identified, sad, worried, or sorry facial expressions, particularly during apologies, typify communication of guilt. Similarly, avoidance, bodily shrinking, and silence typify guilt in most cultures. People failing to display guilt and remorse following improper actions may be ostracized, banished, or even killed. Guilty communication demonstrates a remorseful attitude that reassures other group members. *Guilt trips* are strategic actions that attempt to change another person's behavior.

Closely related to embarrassment and guilt is *shame*, a social emotion in both cause and manifestation. It results from perceived transgressions against others and their negative reactions. Shame is an intense, negative feeling of inferiority and loss of respect from failing to live up to others and one's own expectations. Emotions theorists disagree about whether shame is a primary emotion or an emotional blend including sadness, dejection, anger, and helplessness. Ashamed individuals attempt to disappear, sulk, hide, slouch, cover the face, and avoid social interaction. Verbally, shamed individuals may declare their worthlessness or helplessness, ask for forgiveness, and promise to improve.

Pride is often viewed as a positive emotion though it is also one of the "seven deadly sins" that is said to come before a fall. Excessive pride communicates arrogance and conceit. Nonetheless, a modicum of pride is the basis of self-esteem and a natural reaction to compliments and accomplishments. Pride is inherently social; it depends on a real or imagined audience. Nonverbally, proud individuals stand and sit taller, exhibit signs of strength, expand and display their bodies, smile broadly, and produce celebratory behaviors such as hugs or "high fives." Verbally, pride is displayed through both appropriate disclosure and inappropriate boasting.

Love is a powerful primary emotion that is universally experienced throughout the world. It occurs among people who seek or share a long, rich relationship. Love evolved to create lasting bonds between people that helped ensure the survival of pairs or groups in a dangerous world. It is overtly expressed by saying "I love you" and through nonverbal expressions such as prolonged eye contact; intimate touch including hugging, kissing, or sexual activity; increased smiling; more time spent together; and protective or nurturant actions.

Jealousy, which sometimes accompanies love, occurs when a person perceives that a third-party rival threatens a primary relationship. Jealousy evolved as friend- and mate-protection from defection into other relationships. Although jealousy is a unique emotion, it is accompanied by other emotions, including sadness, anger, fear, hate, and hurt. Jealousy occurs in close relationships and results in numerous communication behaviors, including negative affect displays toward one's partner and rival through both verbal and nonverbal communication. Jealousy may lead to constructive communication, avoidance behaviors, denial, threats, violence, increased affection, flirtation with potential partners, improvement of appearance or image, and stalking and other surveillance behaviors.

The Unique Role of Emotions

Theorists maintain that in the short term, emotions short-circuit cognitions. Feelings of emotion and their display occur rapidly, often faster than cognitive processing. Emotions evolved to provide rapid, quick, short-term reactions to changing environmental and interpersonal circumstances and long-term information to plan and execute strategic communication. Emotional communication is the result of both biology and learning. Emotional communication evolved to help the individual, the group, and the human species survive. However, culture and individual decisions always play a role in emotional expression. The communication of emotion is a complex mix of inherited, spontaneous emotional expressions along with enculturated displays under the strategic control of individuals.

Peter A. Andersen

See also Communibiology; Kinesics; Nonverbal Communication Theories

Further Readings

Andersen, P. A. (2008). *Nonverbal communication: Forms and functions.* Long Grove IL: Waveland.

Andersen, P. A., & Guerrero, L. K. (1998). *Handbook of communication and emotion: Research, theory, applications and contexts.* San Diego, CA: Academic Press.

Darwin, C. (1998). *The expression of emotion in man and animals* (3rd ed.). London: Harper Collins.

Ekman, P. (1973). *Darwin and facial expression: A century of research in review.* New York: Academic Press.

Ekman, P. (1993). Facial expression and emotion. *American Psychologist, 38,* 384–392.

EMPATHY

Empathy means to feel into another person's biological processes, perceptions, emotional states, and their kinds and forms of consciousness in order to assess their feelings. Further, empathy means not only assessing another's affective communication, but using one's assessments in order to be eventually helpful to another person's communication development. Empathy also means having a purpose to help others with their struggles, their problems, their goals, and so forth. The purpose of practicing empathy is to improve communication between people. Empathy is natural and basic to decent and respectful human communication altogether. Empathy is central to improving human communication in that it helps to develop trust, predictability, and friendlier and more open communication between people. The nature of empathic sharing, a brief history of the study of empathy, and empathic processes will be the focus of this entry.

The Nature of Empathic Sharing

The meanings of the idea of empathy are complex, indicating that various systems of the brain and body are involved in being empathic toward others. Practicing empathy concerns a complex of nonverbal systems. The empathic system is mainly nonverbal in that empathy is mainly an emotional rather than a rational or logical kind of human processing. Sometimes one sensory or nonverbal system is dominant, and at another time several of the senses are involved, depending on levels of friendship and intimacy.

The initiation or avoidance of touching is very important to empathy. How someone touches, the placement of the touch, the length of the touch, the intensity of the touch, can influence empathy acquired and/or intended. The manner of looking, too, can be very important as there are warm stares and glances, warm and avoiding eye contacts, cold looks, and many other characteristics of visual contacts. One's hearing and auditory acuity are extremely important in the practice of empathy because how someone speaks carries much of the emotional meanings involved. The rate of speech, the loudness, the length of vowels, intonation patterns, pitch, and many other factors involved in vocal variety concern empathic processing of the other. The lengthening and shortening of vowels are especially important, as they carry attitudinal and emotional information from the right hemisphere of the brain into words spoken. The *paralinguistics*, or qualities of voice, are main factors in detecting and deciphering emotions in another person. Also, the kinesics, or movements, of a person are very important. There are *microkinesics*, blinks, facial expressions, twitches, finger movements, and many other small movements that indicate emotional presence. There are *macrokinesics*, or large movements that can also reveal a person's emotional states. It is in recognizing and processing nonverbal communication characteristics, then, that much of empathic information can be collected.

Most people think of empathy as putting yourself into someone else's shoes or walking a mile in those shoes. This is a simple but important definition. What it means is that one should try to see the world from others' perspectives, from their point of view, from their emotions and problem situations, and circumstances in their lives, and not one's own. Stereotyping, mistrustful relationships, and misunderstandings arise when caring and empathic regard are not practiced. Some people are very adept at empathy and are very telepathic. *Telepathy* means *feeling across*, a direct contact by one person and the very accurate description of what another is thinking about or feeling. Most people have some telepathic abilities at certain times.

There are many factors involved in why some people cannot or will not practice empathy with others. Related to the idea of empathy is the notion of apathy, or no feeling, not caring. Many people guard their feelings and emotions, hiding them, and are careful not to reveal how they feel. They do not trust others and keep to themselves. They imagine themselves to be perfectly logical and rational and see feelings and sharing them as a sort of weakness. Some people, although they reveal much to one another, are not willing to change themselves or their dysfunctional kinds of communication. It is not easy to help others who are angry, hurt, or horribly repressed, and a helper must be cautious. While there are trained therapists, counselors, social workers, and the like, even trained helpers are sometimes not successful with clients who are dysfunctional.

Brief History

The derivation of the concept and meaning of the word *empathy* is informative. In 1897 the word was translated from the Greek language into the German language as *einfuhlung*, meaning to "feel oneself into" something during aesthetic perception and appreciation, "feel into" an art object or painting, into a crystal, or into any object to understand its interior structures. The term was adapted from the Greek word *empatheia*, which means feeling into, finding or searching one's way into, or experiencing another. According to *Webster's Third New International Dictionary*, the suffixes *em-* or *en-* mean to *put into* or *go into*, while *path* or *patho*, from the Greek, implies emotion, passion, or suffering. *Pathos* concerns an emotion or sympathetic pity. The *Oxford English Dictionary* defines *empathy* as the power of projecting one's personality into an object or person of contemplation.

The scholarship of the French child psychologist Jean Paul Piaget did much to develop the study of how children develop empathy in terms of role taking, or taking into oneself the imagined roles of others. Piaget's students carried on his investigations, showing that empathic role taking develops rapidly just before and during puberty, while other perceptual forms are developed even earlier.

The Chicago school of sociology did much to carry on the early work in describing empathic processes. George H. Mead and his students began the study of mind, self, and society, studying the smallest of human acts and what was taking place in the moment of interactions, in the here and now. More and more study and writing were developed by professionals in therapeutic circles— psychotherapists, psychologists, counselors, social workers, clergy, and helpers of others of many kinds. The work of Carl Rogers and others developed new ideas about helping and training people who were to practice empathy with clients.

Empathic Processes

Object Identification

One often tries to figure out another person by categorizing him or her. This is a common but limited form of empathy. One tries to localize the other, to find some means of coping with a new person or problems in their lives. Objective kinds of empathy can be very important to classify others, to define them vis-à-vis oneself. This kind of empathy is basic to later forms of empathy based in conceptual and psychological processes. One must be able to identify another for ongoing relationships to develop. What happens is that many people, in order to keep others at a distance, invent names, convenient slots, for those they meet, and put them into categories as a quick way to describe them without getting to know them at all.

Imitation and Simulation

One of the most important aspects of the empathic process concerns early developmental forms of biological, sensory, and perceptual behaviors. This kind of empathic ability seems to develop before cognitive or psychological kinds of empathy process. We often imitate and replicate the behaviors of others close to us. We attempt to act, speak, move, and enact the behaviors of significant others in our lives. Much of early play is the attempt to pretend and create enactments of other people's behaviors.

The essence of imitation and simulation concerns the sharing of biological and sensory rhythms that people do not realize they are projecting. Indeed, most cues or signs or signals are wave-based neural processes and are processed without conscious recognition. It is an invisible kind of nonverbal communication. The newest field of nonverbal communication is called *chronemics*. Chronemics is very much involved as a silent and hidden language that is an important basis of empathy development. This level of communication continues into adulthood and is not something that is forgotten or overcome.

We attempt to imitate the motorality of another in our own musculature. We respond to others by reproducing the acts of the other(s). Kenneth Burke's theory of identification noted that we overcome differences when we transcend them by adopting similar dress, behavior, language, and attitudes. William S. Howell elegantly described this kind of empathy when he discussed empathy as the ability to replicate what one perceives. One can improve one's empathic abilities by learning to process a host of biological and perceptual cues available to anyone. A person need not be a physician or medical expert to begin to pick up these vital kinds of information from another's presence and nonverbal communication.

To be mutually entrained to another means that one is beginning to feel a *synchronicity*, a developing synching or bonding with another person. These synching behaviors are what have been called bonding experiences between people, shared and reflected smiles, shared tears, similar laughings, and many other forms of interaction that become synchronous. *Mirrored reciprocities*, reciprocal interactions, develop that help people to bond with one another. Friendships and intimacies develop from the careful uses of imitations and simulations.

Recently, in brain studies, there has been an attempt to discover the neurology of imitation and simulation. This concerns what have been described as the actions of *mirror neurons*. Mirror neurons are clusters of neurons that seem to be activated in a monkey when it sees another monkey eating or doing something necessary. Both monkeys activate similar neuronal areas in the brain simultaneously. At first, this activity was touted as being basic to all kinds of empathy, but later it was shown to be involved only at the imitation or simulation levels of empathic processing—the biological and signalic levels. However, it seems improbable that some minor clusters of neurons alone could be responsible for many psychological and social aspects of empathy.

Empathic Psychological Processes

Most of the writings about empathy have come from various fields of psychology. Each particular field seems to have some differences of focus in its discussions of empathy. Most views of this topic are what David Berlo defined as a kind of mental empathy related to making inferences about others, the *inference theory of empathy*. Basically, the inference-making process is involved somewhat in all psychological or cognitive-making thinking about others. Losing consciousness of one's self in the other and the experience of foreign consciousness in general are also common descriptions of empathy as a psychological mode. Some other descriptions of the psychological process are *I-and-the-other*; the *nowness of youness*; trial identification; identification; a creative act; personal introspection about another in the here and now; vicarious introspection; sudden intuition; a mode of cognition; an information-gathering activity; predicting what others will feel, say, or do about you, themselves, and others; projecting one's consciousness into another; resonating the other as a special unconscious ability; and creating an interpersonal space in the analytic and therapeutic situation.

Empathy as Steps in the Interactive Process

Some scholars have tried to describe a step-by-step prescription for counselors, therapists, and helpers to use in their practices. Some of them pertain to professional uses, and some are merely to change the sequence of the therapeutic processes of empathizing. The earliest description was outlined by Theodor Lipps in 1907: (a) one is stimulated by another person and imitates the person; (b) the observer feels himself or herself into the other person; (c) the observer loses consciousness of himself or herself; and then (d) the observer experiences the other, as if he or she had become the other. Another example of a step-by-step empathic process is (a) identifying with the other person by becoming absorbed in the other; (b) capturing and incorporating the experience of the other into ourselves; (c) having the other's experience echo and reverberate within ourselves; and (d) then distancing ourselves from the other by detached, objective analysis.

Others discussed empathic methods more colorfully in the actual, here and now, in the momentary interactive context: There is a meeting of us two, eye to eye, face to face. When you are near I will take your eyes out and place them in my sockets instead of yours, and you will take my eyes out and place them into your sockets. Then, I will look at you with your eyes and you will look at me with mine. This is one of the very first descriptions of what can be called *mutual empathy*, a sharing of empathy in the interactive moment.

Another way in which empathy can have different steps, or kinds of activities in sequences, is the idea of the interplay of three kinds of empathy: *interactive empathy*, *reflective empathy*, and *projective empathy*. Interactive empathy concerns our focus and levels of attention as well as how perception is involved in the here and now. It is in the actualities, the dynamics of the using one's very high levels of attentional focus and vigilance. High levels of attention are necessary for memories to be remembered by the helper, later. The focus must be highly variable and carefully selective. It requires much practice, with trials and errors as a methodology. One must separate verbal and nonverbal communication, jumping from one to the other, over and over during the actual interactions between a helper and another. One listens carefully so as to attempt to separate what a person is saying from what that person is feeling when speaking. This takes practice. One must create a model of the other's nonverbal behaviors to be remembered later, by focusing on different kinds of nonverbal communication and being highly alert to processing semiotic, emotional, or nonverbal information. One can and should increase one's levels of attention and awareness to a very high degree.

Reflective empathy concerns being away from interactive exchanges, being alone, later. One reflects on the other, seeing him or her again as imagery. It is a re-search, or searching again. One re-sees and re-hears the person. One re-spects the other, or sees them again; one focuses on visual and auditory memories, as well as memories of all the nonverbal systems observed. One reflects on the other's emotions and attitudes expressed in the other's voice and movements. Re-membering means putting the members of a past communication interaction back together again. This also helps to preserve the memory of the interaction and its recall. This stage is a movement toward the final step, the use of projective or predictive empathy.

Projective empathy is doing imagined interactions, seeing ahead into the future and imaging the next interaction to take place with the other. Projective empathy is sometimes called predictive empathy, if it actually becomes successful. In projective empathy, one thinks ahead with interactive and reflective forms of empathy already in mind. One uses this forecasting information to plan what to say, when and how to say it, and why one should say something or act in some manner when seeing the other person again.

These three kinds of empathy are congruent with all major psychological processes, present, past, and future. Interactive empathy concerns attention and perceptions, sensing in the present moment, in the nowness of the interactions. Reflective empathy concerns the past, preserving memories of the interactive event. Reflections on the interactive event help to recollect and solidify memories of the event, putting them together again, remembering. It concerns human memory and mnemonics, the past. Projective empathy concerns planning; thinking ahead; using futurity, imagined interactions, anticipation and expectancy, the future. These activities are main functions of the human brain and, if used carefully, have much promise for the development of better empathic skills.

Social Role Taking as an Empathic Process

Role taking develops very early in a person's development, as role taking is built on imitating and simulating others in one's communication environments. With maturity and increasing socialization comes the increasing potential to walk a mile in someone else's shoes, and one begins to think about another person's viewpoint. One begins to empathize with the other's life roles and occupational roles.

Life roles are those concerned with family relatives and intimates, important, significant others. One attempts to take the role of others in one's imagination. The nature of the role obligations of that person is of major concern. Take your own mother's role, seeing how she sees her motherhood, and you. Think of acting like your mother. See her many viewpoints. Role enactments are excellent family therapy tools.

One can mentally take on the role obligations, attitudes, beliefs, behaviors, and values of others. Actors and actresses do role-playing continually. Taking or playing life roles is very important as learning devices, in that these social roles concern our primary connections with significant others. How we perceive another's occupational role, too, can give us important clues, important information, in how we can or should communicate with others in organizations and elsewhere.

Tom Bruneau

See also Chronemics; Emotion and Communication; I and Thou; Identification; Nonverbal Communication Theories; Rhetorical Sensitivity; Rogerian Dialogue Theory; Symbolic Interactionism

Further Readings

Berlo, D. K. (1960). *The process of communication.* New York: Holt, Rinehart, & Winston.

Bruneau, T. J. (1989). Empathy and listening: A conceptual review and theoretical directions. *Journal of the International Listening Association, 3,* 1–20.

Bruneau, T. J. (1993). Empathy and listening. In A. D. Wolvin & C. G. Coakley (Eds.), *Perspectives on listening* (pp. 185–200). Norwood, NJ: Ablex.

Bruneau, T. J. (2000). Peace communication: The ethics of caring across cultures. In L. A. Samovar & R. E. Porter (Eds.), *Intercultural communication: A reader* (pp. 455–463). Belmont, CA: Wadsworth.

Clark, A. J. (2006). *Empathy in counseling and psychotherapy: Perspectives and practices.* Mahwah, NJ: Lawrence Erlbaum.

Davis, M. H. (1996). *Empathy: A social psychological approach.* Boulder, CO: Westview Press.

Howell, W. S. (1982). *The empathic communicator.* Belmont, CA: Wadsworth.

Katz, R. L. (1963). *Empathy: Its nature and uses.* New York: Free Press of Glencoe.

Lichtenberg, J., Bornstein, M., & Silver, D. (1984). *Empathy: Vols. 1 & 2.* Hillsdale, NJ: Analytic Press.

Malle, B. F., & Hodges, S. D. (2005). *Other minds: How humans bridge the divide between self and others.* New York: Guilford Press.

Scheler, R. (1959). *The nature of empathy* (P. Heath, Trans.). New Haven, CT: Yale University Press.

Stein, E. (1989). *On the problem of empathy* (3rd ed.; W. Stein, Trans.). Washington, DC: ICS Publications.

EMPIRICISM

Empiricism is not a theory as such; it is a foundational system that governs the elements and relationships from which theories are formed. One may think of it as a set of specifications that determine what theories can be and what they might be able to do. Empiricists believe that knowledge comes to us via observation through our senses or that its claims should be based on observations. Statements not validated by an observation of a physical event do not qualify as knowledge. This rules out theories about the Flying Spaghetti Monster or the Great Pumpkin, because no valid observations are available about either entity. At the same time, empiricists find certain unobservable concepts acceptable because they are based on other, more fundamental observations. Examples are the orbit of Mars, behavioral intentions, comforting communication, or couple types.

Empiricism relies on a further assumption that events can be observed, recorded, and compared in sensible ways and that these records are the equivalent of direct observations. This assumption depends on the usefulness of various procedures, such as controlled experiments and validated instruments that remove the subjectivity inherent in human information processing. Empiricists also believe that there is a real world separate from our evaluation of it. For example, many persons believe in "metaphysical" entities such as the soul, but empiricists deny that such nonphysical elements are real because they cannot be observed through the senses.

Historical Roots

Ancient skeptics were atheists, the most prominent of which was Sextus Empiricus (about 150 CE). Skeptics denied Plato's assertion that there existed a *noumenal*, or real, world (in contrast to a phenomenal world, which is inside the person) in which entities such as justice and honor had their true existence. This naive skepticism is not very useful, because we all believe in things we have not seen. Few persons have ever seen their liver, but most of us believe that we have one. Emily Dickinson never saw the sea (even though Amherst is only about 100 miles from the ocean) but felt that she was justified in believing in its existence. So most empiricists not only believe in the evidence of one's senses but also extend that belief to descriptions of entities furnished by other persons and, in addition, entities that could *possibly* be observed given sufficient effort and expenditure to do so.

Most historians of philosophy agree with Bertrand Russell that Western thought has long been divided into two basic groups: those inspired by the nature of mathematics, and those who rely instead on empirical principles. Russell placed

Plato, Thomas Aquinas, Spinoza, and Immanuel Kant in the former group because they relied on a priori principles derivable from language as the source of fundamental knowledge. In the other group Russell placed Democritus, Aristotle, and empiricists from John Locke onward.

Values of Empirical Research

Because empiricism seems so obvious, many people wonder why theorists need to argue for it as a foundation of theory building. The answer is that human history is riddled with nonempirical beliefs that have had significant harmful effects. For example, Aristotle believed that women had fewer teeth than men and that this was a manifestation of woman's "essence," which was inferior to that of men. This view was accepted for centuries without question because Aristotle said it. An empiricist would insist on counting teeth rather than believing Aristotle. When one does so, the dentition of men and women proves to be the same. Today a few people still believe that race and intelligence are associated in a causal fashion, in spite of the mountains of empirical evidence to the contrary.

Many researchers believe that communication (as well as sociology and psychology) can be studied using a variety of methods. Probably the most fundamental paradigmatic division in communication theory is a separation between interpretive/critical and empirical (or objective) thought. This distinction provides support for such formulations as rules theory, social construction theory, cultural climates, narrative theory, and other interpretive schemes. A currently popular manifestation of interpretive thought finds its justification in qualitative, as opposed to quantitative, research.

Most proponents of empirical method feel it is necessary to separate observation from evaluation, worrying that empirical issues should not be mixed with moral ones. They argue that confusing observed fact with evaluation has historically created terrible problems. The holocaust resulted from Hitler's position that Blacks, Gypsies, homosexuals, and Jews were *Untermenschen*, or less than human. The attribution of subhuman characteristics to other persons is a value claim masquerading as a factual one. Today the AIDS epidemic is one of the most serious public health problems facing the world, yet the efforts of the U.S. government to deal with it have been hampered by the intrusion of moral evaluations, such as the characterization of AIDS as a "gay disease" and condemnation of alternate lifestyles. This is not to say that moral issues and values are unimportant but to argue against confusing them with factual observations. This is a value of empiricism.

Problems With Empiricism

Strict empiricism, however, can lead to problems of its own. Reliance only on sensory experience ignores a good deal of information that may be quite useful, making logical inference essential. Health care, for example, must rely on causal assumptions that are not actually observed. If an individual's blood reacts in a particular way in a laboratory, a physician examining the results of this test may conclude that the individual's circulatory system has a good deal of a substance called cholesterol and that this condition might result in heart disease. If the patient agrees, the physician may ask the patient to take medicine to reduce the condition. A later, more favorable test leads the physician to conclude that the patient's cholesterol is reduced and that the risk is alleviated. Notice that at no point does either the doctor or the patient actually see any of this substance in the circulatory system. Both of them are satisfied that the blood test in and of itself is a satisfactory index of the cholesterol level. The doctor might explain that persons with a certain kind of blood have been observed to have more heart disease and shorter life spans. These direct observations are taken for granted. However, there is a good deal of medical research for which no direct cause and effects can be cited, and here empirical principles fail, and logic and judgment have to be relied on.

Most communication researchers in the empirical tradition also rely on logic and judgment to complete the picture started with empirical observations. Every published experimental study, for example, has a discussion section in which the authors speculate about possible logical connections and conclusions based on the data. These interpretations are important because they open areas for further exploration and observation and the development of theory.

Many theorists see inherent difficulty in empirical research stemming from a tendency of a researcher to see what he or she wants to see. This is a problem everywhere. One classic example occurred in the debate about evolution. Almost every textbook in biology cites the example of the spotted moth evolving as the atmosphere changed in Britain. As the air became more sooty, the moths supposedly evolved their wing colors, making them more difficult for predators to find. Actually, the data cited in this effect were highly suspect.

If theories begin with observations, then induction is required to analyze them and point out similarities and formulate general principles. But induction from observables is sharply limited. A valuable extension is to formulate principles through inductive observation and then derive new principles from these through deduction. Indeed, theories are always more than single generalizations based on a set of observations. They must connect these general ideas with other ideas in a logical system. Albert Einstein once observed that the more general and far-reaching the theory becomes, the less value basic observation could be for building theory.

Robert Bostrom

See also Epistemology; Humanistic Perspective; Inquiry Processes; Interpretive Theory; Phenomenology; Realism and the Received View

Further Readings

Berkeley, G. (1957). *A treatise concerning the principles of human knowledge.* Indianapolis, IN: Bobbs-Merrill. (Original work published 1710)

Bostrom, R. N. (2003). Theories, data, and communication research. *Communication Monographs, 70,* 275–294.

Harrington, N., & Bostrom, R. (1996). Objectivism as the basic context for theory and research in communication. In J. L. Owen (Ed.), *Context and communication behavior* (pp. 118–143). Reno, NV: Context Press.

Hooper, J. (2002). *Of moths and men.* New York: Norton.

Isaacson, W. (2007). *Einstein: His life and his universe.* New York: Simon & Schuster.

Russell, B. (1945). *A history of Western philosophy.* New York: Simon & Schuster.

ENTERTAINMENT–EDUCATION

Entertainment–education (E-E) is a theory-based communication strategy for purposefully embedding educational and social issues in the creation, production, processing, and dissemination process of an entertainment program in order to achieve desired individual, community, institutional, and societal changes among the intended media user populations.

Theorizing is an integral part of every aspect of the E-E strategy, from designing a program to its evaluation. For example, Miguel Sabido, a television writer–producer–director in Mexico, developed a methodology for E-E soap operas, centering on Stanford psychologist Albert Bandura's social learning theory, which explains how human beings learn new behaviors by observing mass-mediated role models. In operationalizing Bandura's concept of role modeling, Sabido hypothesized that the relationship between an audience member and a media role model goes beyond the cognitive information-processing domain. For instance, audience members participate in *parasocial relationships,* analogous to real relationships, with media personalities and readily invite these people into their homes via television or radio. They may even talk to these characters by addressing the television or radio set.

Thoughtful, deliberate, and purposeful embedding of educational messages in entertainment genres, in all their nuance and complexity, is central to the E-E strategy. That is, E-E is not just inserting an educational message in an entertainment program but involves the development of creative ideas for programming, the actual production and dissemination, audience-centered information processing and interpersonal dialogue, and individual and collective decisions and actions. E-E programs often contribute to social change at the middle- and macrolevel by influencing social dynamics between and among individuals, cultural groups, communities, organizations, and social systems at large. An E-E strategy is directed at an intended media user population, comprising audiences of mass media products (newspapers, films, television, and radio) and/or consumers of games and virtual environments. Consider the following examples of mass media–sparked social changes in three locations on three continents.

In 1996, All India Radio in New Delhi, India, then broadcasting a radio soap opera *Tinka Tinka Sukh* (Happiness Lies in Small Things), received a colorful poster–letter signed by 184 community members from a village named Lutsaan in India's Uttar Pradesh state. It stated that listening to *Tinka Tinka Sukh* had benefited the village, particularly the women, and that listeners came to oppose dowries and would not participate in this practice. Listeners in Lutsaan said they were stirred by Poonam's character—a young bride, who is beaten and verbally abused by her husband and in-laws for not providing an adequate dowry, the payment by a bride's parents to the groom's parents.

In 2000, when Camilla, the protagonist on *Lazos de Sangre* (Blood Ties), a popular Brazilian *telenovela*, was diagnosed with leukemia, the Brazilian National Registry of Bone Marrow Donors reported that new donor registrations increased by 45 times: from about 20 a month to 900 a month.

On August 3, 2001, when Tony was diagnosed with HIV on an episode of the popular soap opera *The Bold and the Beautiful*, the number of calls within the hour to the Centers for Disease Control and Prevention's AIDS hotline increased 16 times over the previous hour. This storyline, which ran during 7 months, was seen in over 100 countries, for an estimated audience of about 400 million people.

Theoretical Bases of E-E

Albert Bandura's social learning/cognitive theory has dominated the theory-based production and investigation of E-E programs—not surprising, since E-E programs seek to influence the behaviors of audience members through positive and negative role models. Bandura's theory states that individuals learn through modeling by observing and imitating others. Social learning theory is both behaviorist, in that it explains behavior, and cognitive, in that it explains behavior in terms of individuals' cognitive processes of attention, memory, and motivation.

Most E-E investigations have focused on providing cognitive and rational explanations of audience effects, utilizing theoretical frameworks such as the elaboration likelihood model, which shows when people are more likely to evaluate arguments critically and when they are more likely to be influenced by peripheral concerns, and the health belief

model. This work also relies in part on theories related to the hierarchy of communication effects, stages of change, and others. However, scholarly interest in focusing on the rhetorical, play, and affective aspects of E-E, emphasizing the entertainment rather than the education aspect of E-E, is on the rise.

Scholars realize that E-E interventions that are soap opera centered represent highly complex narratives with multiple plotlines, protagonists and antagonists, and twists and turns. E-E investigations now theoretically seek to explain why certain narratives may be perceived by audience members as more involving, engaging, coherent, and believable than certain others. Questions are being broached about how a narrative's rhetorical punch may be influenced by the E-E intervention's medium, broadcast frequency, length, time of broadcast, and other attributes. Scholars now conduct research on how a complex E-E narrative may "transport" audience members from their present situation into a hypothetical situation, influencing their repertoire of possible actions. Scholars also investigate how an audience member's repeated and prolonged distress from seeing a favorite character in deep trouble enhances the involvement and enjoyment of the drama and its resolution.

Theoretical investigations of E-E now have begun to take the role of audience emotions more seriously. While emotions have primarily been investigated in interpersonal contexts, and on a limited basis in organizational contexts, they were not systematically broached in mass-mediated contexts. E-E investigations now increasingly focus on the communication of affect from media characters to audience members. For instance, how are audience members "infected" by the emotional state of characters? Might witnessing the death of a favorite character from AIDS, and the grief experienced by his parents, widow, and three young children, serve as a more powerful trigger to adopting a health prevention behavior than a rational media message that promotes condom use? The field of E-E is charting new directions in terms of theory, characterized by increasing breadth and depth.

Today and Tomorrow

E-E today is a worldwide phenomenon, with almost every nation and every well-known social change agency having, or having had, an E-E project. Diverse opinions now characterize the E-E field, including the voices of enthusiasts, dissenters, and skeptics. More organizations are engaged in the practice of E-E, and now teaching and scholarship on E-E are finding their way into university-based schools of communication, public health, and international development. Evaluations of E-E interventions, over the years, have become increasingly sophisticated, employing multiple theoretical perspectives and research methods. In the past decade or so, the E-E strategy emerged as an important issue in the fields of communication, health, and development practice and research.

The field of E-E will move into various expressive forms such as arts, crafts, textiles, murals, and other forms well beyond mass-mediated communication. In South Africa, for example, *positive pottery* includes colorful AIDS ribbons, made by individuals with HIV, etched with various African images. E-E is expected in the future to integrate "modern" and "traditional" entertainment outlets, along with "big" and "little" media technologies, an eventuality made possible by advances in the Internet. Web-based delivery makes it possible to tailor a communication message to audience members. Further, such interventions will probably become more closely in touch with participatory methods, as the work of Brazilian theater director Augusto Boal illustrates. Boal, who founded the Theatre of the Oppressed (TO) movement, based his work on Paulo Freire's principles of dialogue and interaction. Here active spectators ("spect-actors") address and reflect on problems and take control of situations so that they are not put in the role of passive receiver or victim.

E-E is already starting to go beyond traditional communication forms in areas such as family planning and HIV prevention to address other pressing social issues, including, for example, peace, conflict mediation, terrorism, and race relations. The role of E-E will be recognized as a factor in understanding how people work toward liberation and empowerment through using traditional songs and performances to protest, resist, invite dialogue, engage in debate, and cope with the circumstances in which they live.

Arvind Singhal

See also Elaboration Likelihood Theory; Media and Mass Communication Theories

Further Readings

Papa, M. J., Singhal, A., Law, S., Sood, S., Rogers, E. M., & Shefner, C. L. (2000). Entertainment-education and social change: An analysis of parasocial interaction, social learning, collective efficacy, and paradoxical communication. *Journal of Communication, 50,* 31–55.

Singhal, A., Cody, M. J., Rogers, E. M., & Sabido, M. (2004). *Entertainment-education and social change: History, research, practice.* Mahwah, NJ: Lawrence Erlbaum.

Singhal, A., & Rogers, E. M. (1999). *Entertainment-education: A communication strategy for social change.* Mahwah, NJ: Lawrence Erlbaum.

Singhal, A., & Rogers, E. M. (2002). A theoretical agenda for entertainment-education. *Communication Theory, 12,* 117–135.

ENVIRONMENTAL COMMUNICATION THEORIES

Environmental communication is a field within the communication discipline, as well as a meta-field that cuts across disciplines. Research and theory within the field are united by the topical focus on communication and human relations with the environment. Scholars who study environmental communication are particularly concerned with the ways people communicate about the natural world because they believe that such communication has far-reaching effects at a time of largely human-caused environmental crises. This entry outlines some ways researchers who study environmental communication use existing theory to investigate their particular questions about *human–nature relations*. The entry also illustrates ways scholars have developed and are currently developing theory that is specific to environmental communication. The final section of this entry explores the ways some environmental communication scholars see their goals of applying and creating theory not only as trying to understand and explain but also as striving to improve human relations with nature.

Central to environmental communication theory are these assumptions: The ways we communicate powerfully affect our perceptions of the living world; in turn, these perceptions help shape how we define our relations with and within nature and how we act toward nature. Thus, environmental communication scholars often speak of communication as not only reflecting but also constructing, producing, and naturalizing particular human relations with the environment.

Many environmental communication theories include the assumption that human representations of nature, be they verbal or nonverbal, public or interpersonal, face-to-face or mediated communication, are *interested*. This, in part, means that communication about nature is informed by social, economic, and political contexts and interests. These contexts and interests help to shape our communication, often in ways we are unaware of, and direct us to see nature through particular lenses while also obscuring other views of nature.

The theories that scholars use to investigate these assumptions range widely in their epistemological and methodological orientations. Because human relations with nature are negotiated within cultural communication, mass media, public communication, interpersonal communication, popular culture, and so forth, environmental communication theory draws from cultural theory, media theory, rhetorical theory, social movement theory, pop-culture theory, and many other areas. In this way, environmental communication researchers have accessed existing theories to serve as conceptual frameworks for their questions and studies.

For example, in media studies of environmental communication, researchers have at times used framing theory to analyze media coverage of the environment, finding, for example, that the mainstream media increasingly frame environmental activist *ecotage* (eco-sabotage) as ecoterrorism. In examining cultural manifestations of human–nature relations in face-to-face communication, some researchers have used ethnographic approaches, finding, for example, that members of a particular non-Western culture speak of "listening" to nature, a cultural form of communication that supports a highly reflective and revelatory mode of communication that opens one to the relationships between natural and human forms.

Environmental communication scholars also borrow from and add to transdisciplinary theory that is both environment specific, such as ecofeminist theory and political ecology, and non-environment-specific, such as social constructionist theory, systems theory, and performance theory. In addition, scholars have created theories that emanate specifically from environmental communication issues. These borrowed and generated theories are applied to a variety of sites of human–nature relations. For instance, some theories focus on explaining public dialogue about the environment, including political, media, and advocate discourses, while some focus on explaining cultural views or everyday communication about the environment. Other, more general theories span these and other sites of communication because they deal with fundamental ways humans communicate about nature.

Origins of Environmental Communication

Environmental communication is thought to have emerged as a distinct field in the United States in the early 1980s from the tradition of rhetorical theory. In historical accounts of the young discipline, scholars often cite the 1984 publication of a generative rhetorical study as definitively announcing the field to the rest of the communication discipline. In this study, Christine Oravec analyzed the discourse of early-1900s preservationists and conservationists, two sides of a controversy over whether to build a dam in a highly regarded natural site. Oravec illustrated how conservationists won—and the dam was built—by appealing to a "progressive" view of the "public" and its relationship to nature. The debate signaled the defeat of one view of society—the preservationist view that the intact beauty of nature served the nation as an organic whole—and the rise of the conservationist view of progressivism, in which the material needs of individuals determine the uses of nature, a view which is still a dominant discursive force in the ways environmental decisions are made today.

While early environmental communication work was not limited to rhetorical theory, a range of important environmental communication theory has emerged from the application of rhetorical theory, including historical explorations of the *sublime response* to nature and explanations of the rhetorical uses of the *locus of the irreparable* in environmental issues. More recent rhetorical research has theorized about the ways environmental activists use widely televised *image events*, such as the positioning of activist boats between whaling harpoon and whale or the occupying of old-growth trees marked for logging, in efforts to confront profit-motive-driven industrialism with community and ecological needs. Other scholars have used rhetorical theory to grapple with ways the inventional resources of melodrama might transform environmental controversies and oppose dominant discourses that rationalize or obscure environmental threats and to explore how certain Native communities' arguments are excluded from decisions about where to store nuclear waste. Many of these studies critically expand on notions and theories of rhetoric by focusing on the reproductive and transformative potentials of such forms of environmental communication.

Recent work using critical rhetorical theory also points to crossovers with critical discourse analysis, a largely European theoretical and methodological tradition. Critical discourse analysis is often used to explore human–nature issues in the discipline of ecolinguistics, the parallel or sister discipline of environmental communication, which has a strong presence in Europe. As in critical discourse analysis and ecolinguistics, critical efforts to ground rhetorical theory in issues of power and the material world have been central to environmental communication research. Some environmental communication rhetorical theorists have turned to theories outside rhetoric and communication to purposefully ground their work in the environmental and social spheres. For instance, some environmental communication rhetoric scholars have incorporated social systems theory to explore more holistic analyses of human–nature relations. Others have turned to political economy and political ecology to explain how rhetorical representations of the environment reflect and reproduce a particular political economy of interests.

Material–Symbolic Discourse

Because environmental communication research looks at human society as well as the natural world beyond the human, many environmental communication scholars have been interested in discourse theory informed by poststructuralism, as well as contemporary disciplines such as science studies and cultural studies. Informed by these traditions, many environmental communication scholars view our systems of representation as both symbolic and material. This means that scholars view the material world as helping to shape communication and communication as helping to shape the material world.

An example is the word *environment*. *Environment* is a symbol we dominantly use in Western culture to describe the natural world in a way that connotes a material nature that surrounds us and is separate from us. The symbol, or metaphor, of *environment* is not only shaped by material and symbolic Western historical and contemporary relations with nature, but also helps to shape our contemporary ideas of and actions toward nature, allowing us to perceive and treat the living world as separate from and often as secondary to the human species. Environmental communication scholars explain that the word *environment* reflects anthropocentric, or human-centered, cultural views of and relations with the living Earth. At the same time, the dominant use of the term *environment* to describe nature helps to reproduce such anthropocentric views, reconstructing perceptions that allow for exploitive and destructive actions that continuously materially shape the biosphere.

The ontological orientation of viewing discourse as both material and symbolic necessarily brings issues of power to the forefront of theories of environmental communication. Communication about the "environment" is embedded within social systems and within the power that is negotiated within these systems. As such, social, cultural, economic, and ideological forces inform representations of nature, constraining or allowing for particular ways of communicating about the "environment." Societal responses to ecological degradation are filtered through dominant systems of environmental representation. Environmental communication scholars critique and raise awareness about existing dominant discourses that are harmful to the environment. In doing so, they look, not only at communication that is directly about the environment, but also at communication that is not necessarily about the environment but that has an impact on the environment—such as neoliberal discourses of free trade that indirectly cause enormous environmental damage.

In addition, environmental communication scholars explore and theorize about alternative ways of speaking about human relations with nature that may be beneficial to the biosphere. Some environmental communication scholars theorize that such alternative ways of communicating about nature may help human society overcome or subvert destructive culturally dominant ways of relating with nature. In this way, while environmental communication scholars are interested in exploring the ways symbols, such as "environment," might be shaped by worldviews that situate humans as separate from and often superior to nature, scholars are also often interested in illustrating other representations of human–nature relations that might allow for different views and inform different actions.

Mediating Human–Nature Relations

Environmental communication scholars have explored the notion that communication *mediates* human–nature relations in a variety of ways and from a variety of orientations. On one hand, much like a material–symbolic discursive approach to environmental communication, this theory of communication mediating nature understands human communication as mediating human views and actions toward nature. Studies that explore this notion include rhetorical critiques of core cultural environmental narratives that find human–nature or culture–nature binaries as ideological organizing factors; critical reads of popular media representations of nature that find the reproduction or the undoing of dominant environmental narratives; and interpretations of ways that attitudes of ethnocentrism, anthropocentrism, or ecocentrism might inform the communication of everyone, from the average citizen to environmental advocates. Still others have investigated how multiple and varied discourses mediate notions and relations with nature in single everyday utterances.

On the other hand, some environmental communication scholars are also interested in how nature might mediate communication. In this sense, these scholars are interested not only in how human representations of nature mediate views of and actions toward nature, but also in how nature "speaks." This theoretical move is symptomatic of an environmental communication scholarly orientation that sees importance in how nature is represented in research. Just as many environmental communication scholars view dominant Western environmental discourse as separating nature from the human, many also see much academic research as doing the same kind of work in creating culture–nature binaries. In countless examples of communication research and other humanities, social-science, and physical-science research, nature is represented as a mute object, separated from humans, which exists as a static background, as an economic resource, or as an object to which things are done.

In situating nature as an integrated and dynamic communicatory participant that has a role in mediating human–nature relations, environmental communication scholars explore ways of understanding and articulating environmental copresence. This more recent theoretical move in environmental communication scholarship is an attempt not only to explain but also to subvert anthropocentric and hierarchical articulations of human–nature relations. To aid in this endeavor, some environmental communication scholars have turned to existing theory, such as phenomenology, which stitches the human back into the fabric of the Earth. Others have worked to articulate a materialist theory of communication in order to overcome the objectification of nature in constitutive theories. Others have empirically illustrated ways people of Western cultures discuss nature "speaking." Still others argue that nature, or the "extrahuman," must be included not only in communication but also in democratic practices.

All these approaches represent a notable departure from a traditional communication scholarship theoretical assumption that communication is what makes humans different from other animals or delineates us from nature as human. Here, instead, the scholarly effort is to undo such binary assumptions and to include nature in an effort to hear the interaction of myriad voices of the ecosystems of which humanity is a part.

Applied and Activist Theory

Much environmental communication scholarship is critically engaged not only with understanding human–nature relations but also in aiding somehow in social-environmental change. This aid ranges from scholars articulating via theory and research how communication helps to shape and shift nature all the way to explicitly activist research in which theory directly emerges and/or is directly applied to particular socioenvironmental situations in an effort to help enact transformation.

Recent conversations within environmental communication have been particularly interested in the ethical role of scholars. Some researchers have gone so far as to claim that environmental communication is a *crisis discipline* because it deals either directly or indirectly with pressing issues such as climate crisis, endangered species, and toxic pollution. Much as the trans-discipline of conservation biology strives to illustrate and explain the biological elements of ecological collapse in an attempt to both halt and reverse this collapse, some claim environmental communication scholars have an ethical duty to not only try to explain but also help change the society that has caused ecological collapse and at the same time not responded adequately to this crisis.

Environmental communication scholars who are driven by this urgency to address the environmental failures and healing possibilities of communication not only explore and critique discourses but also often engage directly in these discourses by facilitating public processes, sharing critiques with discourse producers, and even providing alternative discourses that are more sustainable. Some environmental communication scholars choose research sites that involve environmental activism and in turn raise awareness about existing alternative or resistant discourses by writing about such practices (e.g., toxic tours led by marginalized communities). Some scholars study emerging sites of environmental action in an effort to articulate effective activist practices (e.g., studies of climate crisis activism such as the recent nationally networked Step It Up actions designed to address global warming). Still others choose sites and approaches to their research that ensure they are not only observers but also participants in the environmental work going on in their research sites (e.g., as volunteers for environmental protection groups or as active participants in environmental movements).

Many of these scholars develop theories that they apply directly to the sites they study in an effort to try to change unjust or unproductive environmental practices in these settings. For instance, the theory of the *trinity of public participation* attempts to illustrate the role of practical theory in both planning and evaluating the effectiveness of participatory processes regarding contentious environmental issues. Another example includes the theory of *self-in-place*, which has been applied to everything from public participation in informing adaptive environmental management to exploring ways to understand and combat urban sprawl. Thus, in a variety of ways, some environmental communication scholars both apply existing theory and generate new theory in efforts to contribute to the empowerment of citizens to act on environmental issues.

Tema Milstein

See also Constructivism; Critical Discourse Analysis; Critical Rhetoric; Critical Theory; Cultural Studies; Culture and Communication; Ideology; Materiality of Discourse; Performance Theories; Phenomenology; Popular Culture Theories; Poststructuralism; Power and Power Relations; Rhetorical Theory

Further Readings

Cantrill, J. G., & Oravec, C. L. (Eds.). (1996). *The symbolic earth: Discourse and our creation of the environment.* Lexington: University Press of Kentucky.

Carbaugh, D. (1999). "Just listen": "Listening" and landscape among the Blackfeet. *Western Journal of Communication, 63*(3), 250–270.

Cox, R. (2007). Nature's "crisis disciplines": Does environmental communication have an ethical duty? *Environmental Communication: A Journal of Culture and Nature, 1,* 5–20.

DeLuca, K. M. (1999). *Image politics: The new rhetoric of environmental activism.* New York: Guilford.

Herndl, C. G., & Brown, S. C. (Eds.). (1996). *Green culture: Environmental rhetoric in contemporary America.* Madison: University of Wisconsin Press.

Marafiote, T., & Plec, E. (2006). From dualisms to dialogism: Hybridity in discourse about the natural world. *The Environmental Communication Yearbook, 3,* 49–75.

Milstein, T. (2008). When whales "speak for themselves": Communication as a mediating force in wildlife tourism. *Environmental Communication: A Journal of Nature and Culture, 2,* 173–192.

Muir, S. A., & Veenendall, T. L. (Eds.). (1996). *Earthtalk: Communication empowerment for environmental action.* Westport, CT: Praeger Press.

Oravec, C. L. (1984). Conservationism vs. preservationism: The public interest in the Hetch-Hetchy controversy. *Quarterly Journal of Speech*, 70, 444–458.

Peterson, M. N., Peterson, M. J., & Peterson, T. R. (2007). Environmental communication: Why this crisis discipline should facilitate environmental democracy. *Environmental Communication: A Journal of Nature and Culture*, 1, 74–86.

Pezzullo, P. C. (2007). *Toxic tourism: Rhetorics of pollution, travel, and environmental justice.* Tuscaloosa: University of Alabama Press.

Rogers, R. A. (1998). Overcoming the objectification of nature in constitutive theories: Toward a transhuman, materialist theory of communication. *Western Journal of Communication*, 62, 244–272.

Schwarze, S. (2006). Environmental melodrama. *Quarterly Journal of Speech*, 92, 239–261.

Senecah, S. (2004). The trinity of voice: The role of practical theory in planning and evaluating the effectiveness of environmental participatory processes. In S. P. Depoe, J. W. Delicath, & M.-F. A. Elsenbeer (Eds.), *Communication and public participation in environmental decision making* (pp. 13–33). Albany: State University of New York Press.

EPISTEMOLOGY

Epistemology is the branch of philosophy that considers the nature, scope, and limits of human knowledge. The term derives from the Greek language: *epistēmē* (knowledge; from *epistasthai* = know, know how to do) and *logos* (study of the nature and properties of, logic or theory). Epistemologists ask whether and to what extent knowledge is based on the existence of phenomena and/or on human perceptions. Their goal is to provide a general basis that would ensure the possibility of knowledge. A continuum of epistemological assumptions exists, ranging from the perspective that there is an objective "real" truth that humans can discover to the perspective that humans create their own meanings, resulting in the possibility of many meanings for a particular object or event. With respect to human communication theory, every theory includes assumptions about the nature of knowledge and how humans obtain knowledge. Epistemology provides background understanding about how to examine the interconnections between aspects of human communication and the best research protocol to serve as an instrument of knowledge for understanding human communication. Discussions related to processes of scholarly inquiry and theory development are inevitably grounded in epistemological issues.

History of Epistemology

The philosophical area of epistemology dates back to antiquity. During the 5th century BCE, an ongoing debate between various schools existed regarding what counts as knowledge and how we come to know what we think we know. The Sophists questioned the possibility of reliable and objective knowledge. Plato rebutted the Sophists by proposing the existence of a world of unchanging abstract forms about which it is possible to have exact and certain knowledge through reasoning. Aristotle maintained that almost all knowledge is built from experience. If people think they have a proper knowledge of something, then they know the reason or cause of the thing. This requires understanding an object within a context of explanatory propositions. Pyrrho founded a school of skeptical philosophy in the period following Aristotelian philosophy. The Skeptics maintained that they were inquirers, refusing to acknowledge claims to knowledge unless a criterion of truth could be established. The rival philosophical schools, particularly the Stoics and Epicureans, tried to produce such a criterion—something in experience that had the mark of certain truth. During the Middle Ages, philosophers blended rational methods and faith into a unified system of beliefs, restoring confidence in reason and experience.

The shift to modern philosophy is often taken to be the publication of René Descartes's *Meditations* in 1641, since it posits a radical break with the Aristotelian scholastic tradition. During Descartes's time there was a renewed interest in skepticism. There are several varieties of skepticism, including views that there can be no knowledge of other persons or other minds, no knowledge of the past, no knowledge of contingent truths, and even the stance that nothing can be known. Descartes sought a sure foundation for knowledge by employing his *method of doubt*, a form of systematic skepticism, created to ascertain what could not be doubted. Descartes's systematic skepticism went further than any previous form of skepticism in that he was willing to apply the issue of doubt to himself (the existence of the self as a thinking thing). The culmination of modern philosophy is generally marked by the critical philosophy of Kant in the late 1700s. Kant's work arose out of an assessment of the shortcomings of both empiricism and rationalism; he synthesized the constructive insights of these philosophies. From the 17th to the late 19th centuries, the main argument in epistemology was whether knowledge was acquired through reasoning (a priori knowledge) or sense perception (a posteriori knowledge). Rationalists contended that all genuine knowledge of the real world is a priori knowledge. Empiricists argued that all such knowledge is a posteriori knowledge. Other philosophers sought to reconcile these positions, aiming to preserve important features of both rationalism and empiricism. Different epistemological directions were advanced during the 19th and 20th centuries, including additional inquiry into rationalist and empiricist lines of thought, as well as the emergence of continental and analytic philosophical traditions.

Epistemologists explore and debate the nature of knowledge with a desire to provide an explanation for the nature, scope, and limits of human knowledge that would make an epistemology immune to skepticism. Epistemology has traditionally pursued two different tasks: description and justification. These tasks are not inconsistent and are often connected in the writings of epistemologists. The study of epistemology has generated many debates over these broad tasks, and varying epistemological schools, including empiricism and rationalism, approach description and justification differently.

Epistemological Issues in Communication Scholarship

Communication theorists take as their task the construction of knowledge about human communication. In generating a basis for the possibility of knowledge, epistemologists have identified various forms of knowledge. These include propositional knowledge, which asserts that something is so; nonpropositional knowledge, whereby knowledge of something is gained by acquaintance or direct

awareness; empirical propositional knowledge; nonempirical propositional knowledge; and the knowledge of how to do something. There are controversies about how these forms of knowledge are related and even whether some of these are viable forms of knowledge. Historically, the empiricist and rationalist schools of epistemology approach the description and justification of knowledge in different ways.

Epistemological Task of Description

The descriptive task aims to accurately depict features of the world, including the human mind, and to determine what kinds of cognitive content ought to count as knowledge. Epistemologists are interested in discerning whether knowledge has foundations and in what sense these foundations may exist. Empiricists objectively begin with the belief that truth or reality is material, independent of feelings, the same for everyone, and external to the human mind. According to empiricists, who identify a posteriori propositional knowledge, sense experience is the foundation of knowledge; all our knowledge must ultimately be derived from our sense experience. Through their senses, people see, hear, taste, smell, and/or touch reality. Our senses do not alter or affect objective reality. Knowledge is assumed to be discovered by humans. Since the 17th and 18th centuries, a posteriori knowledge has been widely regarded as knowledge that depends for its supporting ground on some specific sensory or perceptual experience. Empiricists hold that basic beliefs exhibit knowledge initially gained through the senses or introspection.

Rationalists, who reveal a priori propositional knowledge, claim that human intellect is the foundation of all knowledge. This view claims the quality of reasons for one's true beliefs determines whether those beliefs are converted into knowledge. For rationalists, knowledge requires direct insight obtainable through the faculty of reason. They deny foundational propositions and claim that every belief derives some of its justification from other beliefs. In that way, beliefs are mutually reinforcing. Rationalist epistemologies generally assign a greater weight to the set of basic propositions that are more difficult to dislodge. Rationalists assume there are multiple views of reality and meanings vary widely. What a person calls reality is a subjective interpretation since individuals have different experiences, values, perceptions, and life situations. For theorists who assume there are multiple legitimate realities, differences in interpretation about knowledge—and therefore human communication—are to be expected.

Fundamentally, the descriptive task of epistemologists is to seek an account of propositional knowledge, examine how we go about knowing things, and determine what counts as knowledge. Discussions of research protocol in scholarly inquiry address the specific way that scholars gather and analyze information in their attempt to generate and expand knowledge about communication phenomena. How researchers see the world, truth, and human nature influences how they seek to learn about human communication.

Epistemological Task of Justification

The justification task of epistemology aims to understand what kinds of belief can be rationally justified and how they are justified. There exists an association between research methods and research paradigms. The research methods a scholar uses can be seen as a proxy for the epistemological stance he or she adopts. The epistemological stance a communication theorist takes determines how one conducts research, interprets findings, and advances claims. Each epistemological stance holds a different ontological view of humans, most significantly regarding the extent to which human communication is determined by one's environment or one's free will. *Positivist* and *interpretivist* epistemologies reflect different views of what it means to be human and the nature of knowledge.

In the positivist epistemological tradition (empiricism), truth is justified as an objective phenomenon that can be discovered through careful observation or other scientific methods. Empiricist scholars seek to test communication theory, which appears in the form of universal or covering laws that hold true across time and space in a range of different circumstances. If human behavior is determined by biological and social forces, then we should expect to be able to predict behavior with relative certainty. Positivist epistemology holds that it is possible to explain the world because there is some type of objective truth that exists apart from our knowing of it. Theories are sufficiently general to explain a range of different observations or experiences. By combining or aggregating various research findings, scholars can weave together information about human communication. Objectivity is the quality of being uninfluenced by values, biases, personal feelings, and other subjective factors when conducting research. People may perceive things differently, but only one perception is consistent with the real world.

The interpretive epistemological tradition (rationalism) seeks to justify knowledge by articulating rules that describe patterns or regularities in human behavior within various contexts or circumstances. Interpretivist epistemologies describe patterns that occur within limited spheres of activity. A particular text may have multiple meanings for researchers (and subjects alike). Interpretivists examine how "what we know" is intimately tied up with "who we are": truth cannot exist apart from the knower of the truth. The social world is best understood from the point of view of the individuals who are directly involved in the activities that are to be studied. Some epistemologists endorse contextualism in justifying epistemic claims. These contextually basic propositions serve as starting points for inquiry and provide support for other propositions. Contextually basic propositions can vary from context to context and from social group to social group.

The epistemological tasks of description and justification are approached differently by various philosophers. Different schools of thought enhance our understanding of the nature, scope, and limits of knowledge. What theorists know about human communication is grounded in this intellectual discussion.

A scholar's epistemological assumptions influence the way he or she conducts inquiry and constructs theories. What counts as knowledge and how knowledge is obtained determines what communication scholars posit as theory. While empiricists adopt an objective approach to developing communication theory (the truth about human communication is out there to be discovered), rationalists take a subjective approach to research (how people know is directly related to how they understand and act in the social world). Epistemological ground is present in all communication theory, particularly with respect to issues such as whether knowledge exists before experience, how knowledge arises, if knowledge is changing or unchanging, if knowledge is best conceived in parts or as a whole, and to what extent knowledge can be made explicit or remains tacit. Philosophers wish to know what knowledge is and how it arises, relying on the assumption that the origin of knowledge can assist in understanding the nature of knowledge. Epistemological questions about the nature, scope, and function of knowledge are primary to the development of communication theory.

Pat Arneson

See also Axiology; Inquiry Processes; Linguistic Relativity; Metatheory; Ontology; Philosophy of Communication; Realism and the Received View; Social Construction of Reality

Further Readings

Anderson, J. A. (1996). *Communication theory: Epistemological foundations.* New York: Guilford Press.

Audi, R. (Ed.). (1999). *The Cambridge dictionary of philosophy* (2nd ed.). New York: Cambridge University Press.

Cherwitz, R. A. (Ed.). (1990). *Rhetoric and philosophy.* Hillsdale, NJ: Lawrence Erlbaum.

Littlejohn, S. W., & Foss, K. A. (2008). *Theories of human communication* (9th ed.). Belmont, CA: Wadsworth.

Wood, J. T. (1997). *Communication theories in action: An introduction.* Belmont, CA: Wadsworth.

ETHICS THEORIES

Theories about ethics attempt to answer the ancient human question, What is good? They are thereby inextricably linked to morals, values, and customs. In fact the words *moral* and *ethics* are not only cross-referenced in most English dictionaries, but the word *moral* comes from the Latin translation of the Greek word *ethics*, meaning *moral character* or *custom*. Throughout history all cultures have developed particular doctrines or philosophies of the good, many of which are classified in the West along four primary albeit overlapping lines: *virtue ethics*, which locates the good in virtuous character

and qualities; *deontological ethics*, which locates the good in adherence to duties or principles; *teleological ethics*, which locates the good in the consequences of actions and choices; and *dialogic ethics*, which locates the good in the relations between persons. During the 20th century, *postmodern ethics*, which developed largely in the West, has called these prior ethical systems into question by challenging the value of rules, procedures, systems, and fixed categories for understanding or theorizing ethics. In the field of *communication ethics*, scholars draw on all these ethical theories to address questions pertaining to issues such as truth, deception, and misrepresentation; propaganda, persuasion and argumentation; hate speech, harassment, and freedom of speech; secrecy, disclosure, and access; group decision making and institutional and corporate responsibility; ideology, hegemony, and justice; and conflict, diplomacy, and judgment, to name only a few.

Virtue Ethics

Most commonly associated with the 5th-century BCE Greek philosopher Aristotle, virtue ethics focuses on the choice, cultivation, and enactment of "virtuous" qualities, such as courage, temperance, truthfulness, and justice in both individuals and civic life. In his foundational *Nicomachean Ethics*, Aristotle describes how virtue is an expression of character in which we become temperate by doing temperate acts. In the Aristotelian sense, then, ethics is a human activity rather than a creed, principle, or goal. Most religious traditions articulate a number of overlapping virtues, many of which derive in turn from even earlier traditions and cultures. For example, the so-called *cardinal virtues* of 12th-century Roman Christianity emphasize courage, prudence, temperance, and justice; these were derived from the earlier Greek philosophies of Plato and Aristotle, which in turn derive from far earlier Egyptian wisdom literature (circa 3000 BCE). Similarly, the 5th-century BCE *paramitas* of Indian Buddhism stress generosity, patience, honesty, and compassion and are derived in part from virtues articulated in Hindu scriptures that originated around 1000 BCE. Further east, in 5th-century BCE China, both Confucianism and Taoism identified virtues such as empathy, reciprocity, and harmony for the cultivation of ethical personal and civic life. Even the 18th-century American political virtues of Jeffersonian democracy (inscribed in the Declaration of Independence as life, liberty, and the pursuit of happiness) derive in part from the Aristotelian idea of *eudaimonia*, the happiness caused by living a virtuous life. Outside religious traditions, contemporary Euro-American theorists of ethical virtue, sometimes called neo-Aristotelians, locate virtue variously, for example, in the enactment of intentions and motives (Phillipa Foot, Michael Slote); in practical action, or *phronesis* (Alisdair McIntyre); and in the civic value of emotions, especially compassion (Martha Nussbaum).

Deontological Ethics

Deontological ethics (derived from the Greek word for *duty*) is most commonly associated with the 18th-century Prussian philosopher Immanuel Kant, who constructed a theory of moral reasoning that was based not on virtues, outcomes, or emotions but on duties and obligations. In his book *Foundations for a Metaphysics of Morals*, Kant proposes that ethics is based on *a universal law* that he calls the categorical imperative. Sometimes mistakenly confused with the Golden Rule (i.e., do unto others as you would have them do unto you), the categorical imperative holds that a person should act only on the principles that she or he would want everyone else to always act on. Kant's so-called universal law is therefore *categorical* because there are absolutely no exceptions under any conditions, and it is *imperative* because it is a necessary duty to which everyone must adhere. For example, Kant argues that the ethical prohibition against lying is a categorical imperative regardless of whether a seemingly greater good, such as saving a life, could be served by lying. In the same work, Kant proposes what he calls the *second formulation* of the categorical imperative, which states that we should never treat people as means to our ends, but always as ends in and of themselves. Other deontological ethical theories include religious and monastic approaches (such as adhering to divine commands, doctrinal principles, and the fulfillment of monastic vows) and social-contract theories based on the philosophers Thomas Hobbes and Jean-Jacques Rousseau. In contemporary Euro-American contexts, deontologists, also called neo-Kantians, have developed rights-based approaches (e.g., John Rawls's theory of justice), discourse-based approaches (e.g., Jürgen Habermas's discourse ethics), and contract-based approaches (e.g., Thomas Scanlon's contractualism). Significantly for communication, both Habermas's and Rawls's theories center on processes of communication from which ethical norms and principles are derived. For example, Habermas's discourse ethics prescribes the development and acceptance of rationally grounded validity claims and nontranscendable norms that are produced in democratic argumentation, whereas Rawls's theory of justice relies on the discursive achievement of overlapping consensus and public reason. Both these approaches have been critiqued on a number of grounds from differing theoretical perspectives, including feminist, postmodernist, Marxist, communitarian, libertarian, and noncognitivist. For example, Chantal Mouffe critiques both Habermas's and Rawls's theories because they rely on idealized, conceptually impossible, and hyperrational models of deliberative democracy.

Teleological Ethics

Sometimes considered the foil of deontological ethics, teleological (from the Greek word for *goal*) ethical theories (also known as *consequentialist*) exercise moral judgments based on the outcomes and consequences of actions rather than on principles, duties, or virtues. Among the most common ethical theories are *utilitarianism* and *ethical egoism*. Utilitarianism, associated with the 18th-century British philosophies of John Stuart Mill and Jeremy Bentham, theorizes that we are ethically bound to do what is best for the most people. According to Mill, for example, actions are good when they promote the greatest happiness for the greatest number. In the contemporary Euro-American context, consequentialist theorists include Peter Singer, who extends utilitarianism to include the good of animals and other beings on the planet; Shelly Kagan, who defends consequentialism from critiques by contemporary deontological ethicists; and Amarta Sen, who applies utilitarian ethics to economics, democracy, and public health. Another form of teleological ethics—ethical egoism (which is sometimes called *rational self-interest theory*)—theorizes that all ethical actions are ultimately self-serving, even those that appear to be self-sacrificing. Some contemporary theorists argue an ethical egoist position from a psychological point of view that stresses the emotional and social benefits of ethical actions to self, whereas others argue ethical egoism from an evolutionary point of view that stresses the genetic and biological benefits to self. Still others argue ethical egoism from a rational point of view that posits that both individuals and society benefit when each individual self benefits. Teleological ethics has been critiqued on a number of grounds from a number of perspectives, most especially the deontological and virtue-based approaches. Martha Nussbaum, for example, argues that consequentialist reasoning all too easily leads to a kind of heartless cost–benefit calculation that excludes the full expanses of the ethical.

Dialogic Ethics

Rather than theorizing an ethics based in individual character, duty, outcome, or interest, *dialogic ethics* locates the ethical in the intersubjective sphere of communicative relationships between and among persons. Associated largely with the work of two 20th-century Jewish European philosophers, Martin Buber and Emmanuel Levinas, dialogic ethics posits ethics as *first philosophy* wherein the ethical relation with the other, rather than the *ontology* of the self, is understood to be foundational to human experience. To Buber, the person becomes a person by saying *Thou* and thereby entering into relation with other persons. The Thou, in Buber's understanding, is not a monadic subjectivity but a relation of intersubjectivity, or development of mutual meaning, that arises from people cohabiting communication exchanges in which understanding arises from what happens in between the subjectivity of persons. To Levinas, one's personal subjectivity can arise only through one's own responsibility to the other, who is utterly different from oneself and to whom one owes everything. Dialogic ethics thus requires a healthy respect for the irreducible alerity, or otherness, of persons with whom one has dialogue, wherein the self never mistakes its own understanding of the other for the other himself or herself. In the context of communication studies, dialogic ethics has generated a rich body of research by contemporary scholars such as Rob

Anderson, Ronald Arnett, Kenneth Cissna, Michael Hyde, and Jeffrey Murray wherein the ultimate issues in communication ethics pertain not so much to words themselves, but rather to the ethical realm in which communication is constitutive of persons, cultures, publics, and relationships. For example, to Cissna and Anderson, dialogic ethics involves an awakening of *other-awareness* that occurs in and through a moment of meeting.

Postmodern Ethics

Associated largely with late–20th-century Euro-American philosophers such as Zygmunt Bauman, Joseph Caputo, and Michel Foucault, and with feminist ethicists such as Carol Gilligan, Joan Tronto, and Nel Noddings, postmodern ethicists critique so-called *modernist* and *enlightenment* ethical philosophies such as virtue, deontological, and teleological ethics. Rather than conceptualize human beings as free, autonomous, independent, and rational agents, as do the modernist theorists, postmodernists view human beings as interrelated, interdependent, contradictory, emotional, and, occasionally at least, irrational social beings. Drawing in part on the 19th-century philosopher Friedrich Nietzsche, who crafted a brilliant challenge to traditional religion, philosophy, and morality, postmodern ethicists further reject modernist ideals of certainty, universalism, and essentialism, as well as rules, codifications, and systems. In place of ethical rules or precepts, for example, Zygmunt Bauman posits the idea of moral responsibility, in which each person must stretch out toward others in pursuit of *the good* in all situations, even, or perhaps most especially, when what is the good is most uncertain. Thus Bauman cautions against certainty, calculation, and precept, arguing that reason alone is an insufficient basis for ethical action. Similarly, feminist ethicists from a range of perspectives, such as Annette Baier's virtue-oriented ethics and Chantal Mouffe's Marxist-oriented ethics, critique deontological perspectives such as Rawls's idea of the priority of the right over the good because it categorically privileges individualistic and abstract rights over collective goods and values. From a somewhat different postmodern perspective, Michel Foucault posits ethics as caring for the self through what he calls a practice of freedom. Joseph Caputo, in contrast, argues against ethics itself and in its place posits the affirmation of the other, the singularity of each ethical situation, and the centrality of the unqualified, unconditional *gift* that requires precisely those things that are not required. The ideas of moral responsibility, care, and the gift are also central in feminist care-based postmodern ethics, which rather than focus solely on the *rights* of individuals, focuses on caring responsibilities in relationships. In her book *A Different Voice*, Carol Gilligan describes an ethic of care in which one is responsive and careful rather than careless with other people. Similarly, Noddings rejects what she calls a peculiarly rational, Western, and male conception of empathy and instead describes a process of *engrossment*, in which one does not objectively analyze or debate ethical situations.

Communication Ethics

In the field of communication, ethicists make use of all the above theories in approaching questions of ethics in interpersonal, intercultural, mediated, institutional, organizational, rhetorical, political, and public communication contexts. Clifford Christians and Michael Traber, for example, take a deontological approach in searching for ethical universals and protonorms across cultures. In contrast, Josina Makau and Ronald Arnett take a more dialogic approach in a volume on communication ethics and diversity. In contrast, Fred Casmir takes a multiperspectival approach to intercultural and international communication ethics. More recently, Michael Hyde has drawn on the dialogic ethics of Emmanuel Levinas to explore ethical rhetorical action in personal and public life, and Sharon Bracci and Clifford Christians have brought a wide range of ethical perspectives to bear on a range of communication questions in their book titled *Moral Engagement in Public Life*.

Lisbeth Lipari

See also Buddhist Communication Theory; Confucian Communication Theory; Deliberative Democratic Theories; Dialogue Theories; Empathy; Feminist Communication Theories; Hindu Communication Theory; Media Ethics Theories; Philosophy of Communication; Public Sphere

Further Readings

Aristotle. (1998). *The Nichomachean ethics* (D. Ross, Trans.). Oxford, UK: Oxford University Press.

Bauman, Z. (1993). *Postmodern ethics*. Malden, MA: Blackwell.

Buber, M. (1958). *I and thou* (R. G. Smith, Trans.). New York: Scribner.

Foucault, M. (1997). *Ethics: Subjectivity and truth* (P. Rabinow, Ed.; R. Hurley et al., Trans.). New York: New Press.

Gilligan, C. (1982). *In a different voice*. Cambridge, MA: Harvard University Press.

Habermas, J. (1990). *Moral consciousness and communicative action*. Cambridge: MIT Press.

Levinas, E. (1998). *Otherwise than being* (Alphonso Lingis, Trans.). Pittsburgh, PA: Duquesne University Press.

Noddings, N. (1984). *Caring: A feminine approach to ethics and moral education*. Berkeley: University of California Press.

Nussbaum, M. (1995). *Poetic justice: The literary imagination and public life*. Beacon Press.

Singer, P. (1995). *How are we to live?* Amherst, NY: Prometheus Books.

ETHNOGRAPHY OF COMMUNICATION

The ethnography of communication (EOC), originated by linguistic anthropologist Dell Hymes, is a field of study fundamentally concerned with the idea that culture and communication are inseparably intertwined. Within communication, the shared belief and value systems comprising culture are constructed. And within communication, people build the social structures that comprise their everyday communal way of life. Thus, whenever community members communicate, they display the verbal and nonverbal elements particular to their society while simultaneously creating (and recreating) the value systems that structure that society. By attending, then, to people's routine communication, many of the core abstract elements that characterize their worldviews or cultural life can be observed, understood, compared, contrasted, and theorized. The EOC offers both theoretical and methodological lenses in order to illuminate the particular cultures of a particular group of people.

History

The ethnography of communication was initially called the *ethnography of speaking* (EOS) by Dell Hymes in 1962. Hymes's goal for his approach to the analysis of discourse centered on the role of speech in human behavior. This work coupled two fields of study—linguistics and ethnography. With the interrelationships among language, culture, and society as a traditional anthropological concern, Hymes's proposal diverged from linguistic approaches that, until that time, studied speaking as grammars or abstract linguistic systems. Hymes's proposal also diverged from ethnographic or anthropological models that traditionally studied culture as geographic boundaries, languages, races, and/or ethnicities. Hymes sought to make speech the object of investigation and rectify the problem of taking it for granted. In 1964, Hymes renamed his perspective the *ethnography of communication* in order to more expressly account for the context-dependent uses of nonvocal (e.g., drumming and whistling) and nonverbal (e.g., gestures, silence) communication.

In 1992, Gerry Philipsen broadened the EOC by introducing speech codes theory (SCT). SCT offers a communication-based analytic framework designed for describing, explaining, and/or predicting cultural communication within the context of speech communities. As an interpretive tool, SCT seeks to answer questions about the existence of codes, their substance, the ways in which they can be discovered, and their social force on the members of cultural communities. Ultimately, the study of codes serves to describe the sets of precepts and rules by which different societies enact and interpret their ways of life. In other words, SCT helps reveal how people feel and talk about what is going on in their collective lives. It helps bring to light, for example, what identities and interpersonal relationships community members can and do construct, how community members relate to their physical (natural) and metaphysical (spiritual) environment, and how different peoples approach uses of time.

Since its inception, the EOC has resulted in hundreds of studies applied across a variety of contexts, including family, leisure, and organizational life; online communication; broadcast media; and myriad other oral and written applications. Over time, the EOC has been subject to criticisms not dealing with matters of power in social interaction. Indeed, the EOC does not advocate prejudging the incidence of particular social meanings (e.g., power and status) prior to examination of the situated interaction in question. To do so would undermine the community-based, culture-rich description the EOC calls for. Because this is a point that has too often been misunderstood, it should be underscored that the EOC can and does take power into account when it is made obvious by speech community members themselves. In such cases, ethnographers must remain open to hearing, describing, interpreting, and reporting on performances of power. For example, Philipsen's critique of a controversial speaking event involving Chicago mayor Richard Daley unveils key power-laden rules for the conduct of public discourse. Further, in a study combining the ethnography of communication and critical Whiteness theory, Patricia Covarrubias demonstrates how silence-mediated discrimination against American Indian college students is enacted in some college classrooms, thereby exposing power-laden structures.

Assumptions

The EOC operates according to particular assumptions. These assumptions reveal *what* practitioners study and *how* they study it—what, from a given perspective, counts as evidence, how evidence is interpreted, what generalizations are made about communication and communicators, and, ultimately, how those generalizations are written and presented. The EOC includes the following assumptions:

1. Communication can be described in terms of systems of rules. Community members make communication choices beyond grammar. They make choices based on what is appropriate in their sociocultural contexts. For example, blue-collar workers in Chicago, who acknowledge their speech contrasts with Standard English, deliberately use their speaking practices to garner valued in-group memberships. In fact, community members' attempts to adopt Standard English often are interpreted as symbolic moves to reject their group of origin.

2. People are users of symbols, and the particular configuration of symbols nestles the structures of sociocultural life. For example, using the Spanish pronouns *usted* (formal *you*) or *tú* (informal *you*) can help create relationships based on hierarchy or along more democratic alignments in many Latino contexts.

3. Communication is patterned. Even though an individual's personality and personal idiosyncrasies can influence communication choices, much, if not most, of human communication is structured. By and large, people's daily lives comprise many communication sequences that are repeated across contexts during the course of a routine day (e.g., what counts as polite and impolite ways for addressing others; what is the expected order of conversation in classes, at business meetings, or during doctors' appointments or religious services; and what favorite words or jargon routinely come up in conversation).

4. Communication is distinctive. What resources are available for performing communication, how communication is performed, and how communication is valued differ across sociocultural contexts. For example, the Koasati language of Louisiana provides no word for *good-bye*, thus suggesting a place to inquire about how interpersonal separations are viewed in this culture. Extending compliments between European-American communicators would most likely be considered a friendly move, whereas this might not be the case with some Chinese or Japanese communicators, whose norms about modesty would prompt them to feel uncomfortable in the same situation.

5. Communication is socially consequential, and people bear the consequences of breaches to the normative structures defined by a given society. For example, a European-American man who uses talk to resolve conflicts rather than using physical aggression could be evaluated as homosexual by some blue-collar workers in Chicago.

6. Communication is strategic, and conversants can and do artfully use verbal and nonverbal codes as cultural resources within which to achieve individual and group outcomes. Having a drink with a romantic partner every evening to talk over the day and meeting with the same group of friends for lunch regularly to blow off steam are two examples of using verbal and nonverbal codes as resources. In such situations, everyday communication rituals involve getting together with the same people and generally talking about the same topics and using the same tone, and with each shared conversation, relationships among participants become either closer or more distant. In these particular cases, episodes of communication, involving a sequence of actions, are used in culturally preferred ways to reaffirm a sense of self and a sense of relationship through talk.

7. Communication is not absolutely determined by culture or group. Because, as Hymes noted, speech communities are organizations of diversity, people are free to circumvent, challenge, and revise communicative patterns. For example, some construction workers in Veracruz, Mexico, resist adhering to their community's generally agreed on norms for using pronouns; young employees expressly use the informal *tú* with elders, a practice that in earlier decades would have been seen as very disrespectful.

The EOC as Theory and Method

The EOC's theoretical call, ultimately, is the description of a people's means of communication and the meanings these strategies have for those who use them. As a theoretical lens, the EOC seeks to generate explanations about how, in the particular case, community members use particular communication symbols (e.g., words, phrases, silences) to make sense of their experiences. Listening for these symbols enables ethnographers (and others) to isolate the sets of ideas that inform a community's worldview. Theorizing includes identifying the rules for social behavior—prescriptions (what is allowed) and proscriptions (what is not allowed)—that shape the interpersonal structures of communities.

The EOC's methodological call, ultimately, is the abstraction of an *emic* (culture specific, insider-focused) descriptive framework. This outcome is possible via the ethnographer's engagement through participation, observation, and interviews in the field within particular communities. That is, the EOC requires the researcher to join a particular group to study the group's culture. In a way of speaking, the ethnographer works "from the inside," to be better poised to investigate naturally occurring communication patterns in the course of community members' everyday activities. To isolate patterns, the ethnographer listens and watches for *who* says *what* to *whom, where, how, why,* and for *what* social objectives. By examining these patterns, the ethnographer can then extract themes and other details that will serve as evidence for articulating a coherent statement about the particular community's culture.

Speech Communities and the EOC

If, as Hymes proposed, culture should not be delineated by a geographic region, a language, an ethnicity, or a race, then what should be the unit of observation? In 1968, Hymes offered an alternative unit of observation—the speech community. He defined *speech community* as a group of people who share at least one code or system of rules for enacting and interpreting their own and others' communicative conduct.

Codes, as defined by Philipsen, are historically transmitted, socially constructed systems of symbols and meanings, premises and rules that pertain to communicative conduct. That is, the components of codes, which inextricably are woven into communication itself, are the observable expressions of beliefs of existence (what is and is not) and of value (what is good and bad). Codes comprise the inspectable infrastructure that orients a people's real time, communicatively based social behaviors.

Moreover, participants within speech communities reveal themselves to be users of *multicodality.* In other words, members of speech communities use multiple codes to conduct their daily lives. For example, construction workers in Veracruz, Mexico, routinely use two codes of communication— the code of *confianza* (code of trust, confidence, honesty, confidentiality) and the code of *respeto* (code of respect). Workers used these distinctive and contradictory paradigms to manage their interpersonal networks and, in turn, negotiate workplace cooperation.

According to Hymes, communication practices should be studied according to the following basic social units—*communicative situation, communicative event,* and *communicative act.* Additional elements such as particular words, social dramas, narratives, and even silence are available for the ethnographer to investigate.

Communicative situation is the general context of the communication. A communicative situation maintains a more or less consistent frame for observing and interpreting the particulars of communication. Examples include a class in school, a birthday party, a committee meeting, a court trial, a religious service, a dentist appointment, or a dinner with friends.

Communicative events are locally defined contexts for communication that occur, generally, within communicative situations. Communicative events constitute entry points for ethnographic analysis as they suggest unified sets of components (e.g., the same setting, the same participants, the same general topic, and the same rules for interaction). Examples include a conversation between friends during a birthday party, a call to worship during a religious service, or the opening and closing at a conference. It is during communicative events that sociocultural rules surface and can be inspected.

Communicative acts refer to the use of language to *do* or *perform* some act, to bring about some reality in the world. Examples of speech acts include commands, promises, requests, warnings, threats, compliments, apologies, suggestions, gossip, cursing, joking, and declarations of marriage. Speech acts help identify meaningful contexts for action in particular cultures. For example, cursing and swearing might be appropriate at a bar or a construction site, whereas this behavior would not be as acceptable during the delivery of a eulogy. Each context would suggest different interpersonal meanings.

Thematized terms are words that become core symbols for particular communities. Core terms or words point to concepts whose meanings are shared by community members. These terms point to places for action that are significant and relevant to the particular community members and indicate very important shared attitudes, feelings, and perspectives. For example, for the Israeli Sabra community member, the term *dugri* defines a type of communication that is immediate, blunt, and frank and expresses disagreement. The concept also is used as a cultural element to affirm a particular group identity. The particular Sabra communicators set themselves apart from other interactants because they can and do establish common ground by speaking *dugri* to each other.

Personal address involves the expressions speakers use to point to self and other in interaction. Because personal address inherently invokes relationships among communicators, this serves as uniquely rich means for accessing cultural meanings. Personal address can include a variety of options and a variety of combinations of options. Each possible configuration conveys different meanings depending on the context. For example, titles might be followed by a last name (e.g., Mr. Smith) in a boardroom or by a first name in a kindergarten classroom (Miss Jenny) to show respect. Nicknames are very prevalent in Mexican societies to indicate intimacy and friendship. Honorifics (e.g., *san*) are common in Japanese cultures to show respect (e.g., *okaasan*, or *mother*). Honorific titles are common in many societies (e.g., Dr., Your Honor, Madame President) to showcase the importance of status and authority. Occupational titles (e.g., *Arquitecto* [Architect] and *Contador* [Accountant]) are common in cultures where people set themselves apart by attaining a formal education.

Social dramas are communicative sequences in everyday life wherein the local sociocultural rules for behavior are invoked and publicly challenged. A social drama also can involve the alienation or integration from a social group of the person whose conduct is brought into question. An example of a social drama is the sex scandal involving president Bill Clinton and intern Monica Lewinsky when the president's sexual conduct was challenged by an entire nation. Another example is the controversial event involving accusations of nepotism against Chicago mayor Richard Daley.

Narratives, or stories, are sequential accounts that are told from a particular point of view. These are useful sites for hearing culture, especially when these narratives are told and retold. The fact that the stories are retold suggests that they are important and probably entail cultural significance. A narrative that is part of European-American folklore is that of Horatio Alger. Horatio Alger stories are rags-to-riches narratives that are told and retold to illustrate how impoverished persons might be able to achieve the American Dream. These stories embody American cultural values about hard work, determination, and concern for others.

Silence is the absence of oral speech. Because silence, like speech, also is subject to a community's rules for appropriate conduct, silence offers rich possibilities for gaining insight into what is going on in a particular context. Many American Indian students, for example, use silence very differently from many of their European American counterparts. For Native students, silence often is generative or productive and positive, and they use this communication resource to shape individual and group identities, connect with other community members, and promote a traditional way of life.

SPEAKING as Device for Locating Codes

In 1974, Hymes introduced an *etic* (universal, researcher-centered) descriptive framework designed to guide the uncovering, understanding, and description of communicative patterns in any culture. Culture-specific communication patterns, an *emic* (culture-specific, insider-focused) framework, could be abstracted within these categories. Under the mnemonically coded acronym *SPEAKING*, the etic framework comprises eight social units useful for describing patterns of communication and for isolating cultural themes—*scene* or *setting* (physical arena and/or psychological situation); *participants* (persons involved in the interaction and their relationships to each other); *ends* (purposes and outcome of the interaction); *key* (tone or manner in which the communication is enacted); *instrumentalities* (channels or codes of communication); *norms* of interaction and interpretation (rules for how one should behave and rules for ascertaining what the particular behavior means); and *genre* (categories or types of speech acts and events).

The framework is not intended as a mechanical checklist. Rather, it is intended to provide an initial set of questions to guide the discovery and subsequent accounting of a community's ways of life as reflected and constituted by its way of communicating. SPEAKING also serves as a useful tool for making sociocultural comparisons.

Conclusion

As a theory and a method, the EOC seeks to expose the cultural systems of meaning making—including the tensions and contradictions—that orient a people's everyday communal life. Dedicated to the production of nuanced understandings, the EOC centers inquiry squarely on communication. Moreover, the communication studied is that of the particular people producing it. A focus on locally produced communication helps reveal how interactants use verbal and nonverbal codes to achieve particular personal and social outcomes. It also helps describe how community members affirm, challenge, and/or transform their cultures by changing their ways of communicating. Finally, the EOC helps create cross-cultural understandings via comparative analyses and theories.

Patricia Olivia Covarrubias Baillet

See also Critical Ethnography; Cultural Performance Theory; Culture and Communication; Social Construction of Reality; Social Interaction Theories; Speech Act Theory; Speech Codes Theory

Further Readings

Braithwaite, C. (1990). Communicative silence: A cross-cultural study of Basso's hypothesis. In D. Carbaugh (Ed.), *Cultural communication and intercultural contact* (pp. 321–327). Hillsdale, NJ: Lawrence Erlbaum.

Carbaugh, D. (1989). Fifty terms for talk: A cross-cultural study. *International and Intercultural Communication Annual, 13,* 93–120.

Covarrubias, P. (2002). *Culture, communication, and cooperation: Interpersonal relations and pronominal address in a Mexican organization.* Boulder, CO: Rowman & Littlefield.

Covarrubias, P. (2007). (Un)biased in Western theory: Generative silence in American Indian communication. *Communication Monographs, 74*(2), 265–271.

Covarrubias, P. (2008). Masked silence sequences: Hearing discrimination in the college classroom. *Communication, Culture & Critique, 1*(3), 227–252.

Fitch, K. (1998). *Speaking relationally: Culture, communication, and interpersonal connection.* New York: Guilford Press.

Fong, M. (1998). Chinese immigrants' perceptions of semantic dimensions of direct/indirect communication in intercultural compliment interactions with North Americans. *Howard Journal of Communications, 9,* 245–262.

Hymes, D. H. (1962). The ethnography of speaking. In T. G. Gladwin & W. C. Sturtevant (Eds.), *Anthropology and human behavior* (pp. 13–53).

Washington, DC: Anthropological Society of Washington.

Hymes, D. H. (1968). Linguistic problems in defining the concept of "tribe." In J. Helm (Ed.), *Essays on the problem of tribe: Proceedings of the 1967 annual spring meeting of the American Ethnological Society* (pp. 23–48). Seattle: University of Washington Press.

Hymes, D. H. (1974). *Foundations in sociolinguistics: An ethnographic approach.* Philadelphia: University of Pennsylvania Press.

Katriel, T. (1986). *Talking straight: Dugri speech in Israeli Sabra culture.* Cambridge, UK: Cambridge University Press.

Philipsen, G. (1992). *Culturally speaking: Explorations in social communication.* Albany: State University of New York Press.

Philipsen, G. (1997). A theory of speech codes. In G. Philipsen & T. Albrecht (Eds.), *Developing communication theories.* Albany: State University of New York Press.

Philipsen, G. (2000). Permission to speak the discourse of difference: A case study. *Research on Language & Social Interaction, 33,* 213–234.

ETHNOMETHODOLOGY

Ethnomethodology is an empirical study of folk or *ethno* methods of practical action and practical reasoning that examines the cultural and linguistic competencies and practices used in everyday life, from quite mundane practices such as forming a line and buying groceries to specialized practices such as forming the social bases of scientific research. Founded by American sociologist Harold Garfinkel in the 1950s and 1960s, ethnomethodology soon inspired a variety of scholars and studies that, by the mid-1970s, had established a radically new research program, not only within American sociology but within an ever-increasing international and interdisciplinary context as well.

Influences and Impacts

Ethnomethodology draws from such diverse resources as classical sociological theory, social phenomenology, linguistic phenomenology, ordinary language philosophy, and Gestalt psychology. Influenced especially by the social phenomenology of Alfred Schutz, Garfinkel and others created a tradition of inquiry that quickly developed beyond the boundaries of phenomenology, while retaining important phenomenological interests and orientations. Schutz extended the sociology of knowledge to include the study of commonsense knowledge, and this became a foundational insight for ethnomethodology as well as for the development of social constructionism by Schutz's students Peter Berger and Thomas Luckmann. The phenomenological technique of suspending or bracketing one's natural experience in order to subject this experience to analytic study also became a crucial move in ethnomethodological studies.

The emphasis on the centrality of language use, interpretation, and communication sets ethnomethodology apart from much conventional sociology. Even in comparison with scholarship in linguistics and communication studies, where issues of language and communication are central, the ethnomethodological understanding of language and communication can still be quite distinctive. Despite its distinctiveness, ethnomethodology's emphasis on social practices and language use is at least generally consistent with broad shifts in contemporary philosophy, social science, and humanities, referred to as the *culture turn*, the *linguistic turn*, and the *practice turn*, that share an emphasis on questions of meaning, interpretation, and agency. Therefore, it is understandable that ethnomethodological insights have been taken up within such traditions as sociological theory, sociological and sociolinguistic ethnographies, various communication studies, pragmatics and discourse analysis, and other specialized subdisciplines or research programs such as social problems analysis and discursive psychology.

Focus on Practical Interaction

Ethnomethodology analyzes methods of practical action and practical reasoning, including language use, as they are observable in social interaction. Ethnomethodology typically examines specific courses of action or talk-in-interaction within specific settings, and it does so in much closer detail than is found in inductive or quantitative analysis. It understands mundane, vernacular methods of practical action and practical reasoning as foundational for social order and social science, deserving of study in their own right. By contrast, other varieties of social science are understood to rely unreflectively on these practical methods, taking them for granted and treating them as uninteresting. Ethnomethodology's focus on people's practical understandings and actions in local contexts is not a variety of individualism or subjectivism, as is sometimes claimed, but rather draws attention to the importance of shared, intersubjective methods for understanding and acting. This approach is not an alternative to the study of social structure but involves an alternative conceptualization of social structure, centered around the insight that the properties, meanings, and relevances of social structure are socially accomplished by people within social interaction.

Ethnomethodological Interests in Language and Meaning

Indexicality

Indexicality was addressed prior to ethnomethodology by scholars such as Edmund Husserl and Yehoshua Bar-Hillel and refers to the contextual or embedded nature of meaning. Ethnomethodology expanded previous scholarship on indexicality, observing that the meaning of talk and texts is irredeemably indexical, always relying for its specific sense on unstated knowledge of relevant context.

Talk as Practical Action

John Searle achieved much recognition for his treatment of speech acts, drawing on the ordinary language philosophy of Ludwig Wittgenstein and especially J. L. Austin's discussion of *performatives*—utterances, such as "I promise," that perform actions. Ethnomethodology radically generalizes this insight, emphasizing the thoroughly practical nature of language use. Thus language is understood in terms of language *use*, and language use is recognized as a primary type and medium of social interaction and social action.

Accountability

The literature on accounts, including such social actions as excuses and justifications, has become a significant topic in interpretive sociological studies of deviance. Ethnomethodology has applied a much broader interest in accounting and accountability to all social phenomena, not just those problem occasions in which excuses and justifications become relevant. A broader understanding of accountability refers to the fact that speech and actions are produced and perceived methodically and conventionally, in terms of shared and mutually intelligible categories for making sense of social interaction and communication.

Documentary Method of Interpretation and Reflexivity

Another aspect of ethnomethodology in matters of sense-making and practical reasoning is suggested by its interest in what Garfinkel called the *documentary method of interpretation*, extending a notion from Karl Mannheim's sociology of knowledge. This refers to a common type of practical inferential reasoning by which an underlying pattern is understood on the basis of certain parts, or vice versa. Certain elements come to be treated as documents of a perceived underlying pattern that both organizes and is organized by the understanding of its particular elements. Thus, for example, questions and answers are understood with reference to each other and to the context and purposes in and for which they occur. The context itself is understood with reference to the questions and answers taking place "within" it. The *hermeneutic circle* is a similar insight popularized by Hans-Georg Gadamer and others. Ethnomethodology's interest in the documentary method of interpretation is much closer to empirically available, pragmatic social action and interaction than were previous contributions in the sociology of knowledge and hermeneutic thought.

The ethnomethodological notion of *reflexivity* draws attention to the fact that descriptions partly constitute their own referents and contexts, rather than standing as independent, neutral reportage. For example, descriptions of personal schedules often perform the role of prompting or preempting invitations, actually creating and managing the schedules which are being described. The relational methods of reasoning emphasized in ethnomethodology's treatments of reflexivity and the documentary method of interpretation stand in stark contrast to traditions of research or theory that treat social phenomena as having discernible,

definitive meanings independent of each other and independent of context and independent of practices of description, as is often presupposed in causal explanation.

Programs of Research

Ethnomethodology was accompanied by the development of *conversation analysis*, founded by Harvey Sacks, whose strikingly original approach to the order of naturally occurring talk and texts was one of the forms taken by early ethnomethodology. Both the sequential analysis of conversation, associated with contemporary conversation analysis, and the analysis of talk and texts emphasizing the practical use of identity categories, as in *membership categorization analysis*, remain meaningfully rooted in ethnomethodological insights and initiatives.

On other fronts, ethnomethodological studies have progressed along a variety of lines, often related to studies of work and institutional interaction, making significant contributions, for example, to social studies of scientific knowledge, the study of computer–human interaction, the study of communication in educational settings, and the operation of rules and laws in human service agencies and legal settings. These examples merely suggest some of the clusters of ethnomethodological scholarship. Additional studies address such varied topics as improvisational jazz piano, human–animal communication, ethnic identifications in Thailand, and Tibetan philosophical discourse. Given the vast breadth and variety of members' methods of practical action and practical reasoning and their foundational importance for social interaction and social science, ethnomethodological studies will continue to inform a broad variety of scholarly inquiries and professional endeavors, even as they remain a distinctive minority interest within any particular discipline or professional field.

Tim Berard

See also Accounts and Account Giving; Conversation Analysis; Membership Categorization Analysis (MCA); Phenomenology; Pragmatics; Social Construction of Reality; Social Interaction Theories; Speech Act Theory

Further Readings

Button, G. (Ed.). (1991). *Ethnomethodology and the human sciences.* Cambridge, UK: Cambridge University Press.

Douglas, J. (Ed.). (1970). *Understanding everyday life.* Chicago: Aldine.

Drew, P., & Heritage, J. (Eds.). (1992). *Talk at work.* Cambridge, UK: Cambridge University Press.

Garfinkel, H. (1967). *Studies in ethnomethodology.* Oxford: Polity.

Garfinkel, H., & Sacks, H. (1970). On formal structures of practical actions. In J. McKinney & E. Tiryakian (Eds.), *Theoretical sociology* (pp. 338–366). New York: Appleton Century Crofts.

Heritage, J. (1978). Aspects of the flexibilities of natural language use: A reply to Phillips. *Sociology, 12,* 79–103.

Heritage, J. (1984). *Garfinkel and ethnomethodology.* Oxford, UK: Polity.

Taylor, E. (1989). Language and the study of "shared cultural knowledge." In D. Helm, W. Anderson, A. Meehan, & A. Rawls (Eds.), *The interactional order* (pp. 215–230). New York: Irvington.

EVALUATING COMMUNICATION THEORY

Scholars use several criteria to evaluate theories in order to establish their contribution to the body of knowledge and usefulness. This entry summarizes several evaluative criteria and provides a measure of the overall qualities of a good theory.

Evaluation Criteria

Theoretical Scope

Scope refers to the comprehensiveness or breadth of a theory. Although theories vary in coverage, some level of *generality* is necessary for a theory to have value. In other words, a theory must explain events beyond a single observation. One can explain an observation, but that explanation is not theoretical if it does not apply to other observations as well. In other words, a theory must cover a range of events. The more observations that a theory covers, the better the theory is judged to be.

A theory can have two types of generality. The first is the extent of a theory's coverage. If a theory addresses a wide spectrum of topics, it has value in helping us understand characteristics that span many aspects of communication. For example, a theory might explain how people create meaning in all forms of communication. Because the topic of meaning is so broad and covers such a wide spectrum of events, the theory would help us understand many things about communication in all its forms.

The second type of generality applies a narrow concept across many situations. The theory in this case would not address very many topics but would be widely applicable across many situations. For example, a theory might explain attitude change, a relatively narrow topic applicable in many kinds of communication, from interpersonal exchanges to media campaigns. Such theories have *power* because they explain something in many different kinds of situations.

Good theories can possess either of these types of generality. In applying this criterion, the critic looks at the usefulness of the theory in explaining a range of experiences. Does it have an appropriate level of generality? Is its coverage so narrow that it is not very helpful or so broad that it is meaningless? To whom is the theory's breadth most relevant? A theory that looks very narrow from one vantage point may actually turn out to be quite useful to certain scholars and practitioners who work in a relatively limited field. For example, general communication scholars may find a theory of early childhood communication development too narrow to help understand communication processes across the life span, yet early childhood specialists may find the scope of such a theory just right for the kind of work they do.

Consistency

The criterion of consistency refers generally to the coherence or fit between a theory's philosophical assumptions and substantive claims. Are the theory's concepts and explanations consistent with the theory's assumptions? For example, if a theory assumes that genetics and learning determine behavior, then it leaves little room for individual human choice. We might question such a theory's appropriateness in making claims about decision making, since deterministic premises cannot lead logically to decision-making conclusions.

Appropriateness is related to the language used in theoretical statements. For example, the term *decision making* implies weighing options and making choices, while the term *behavior* does not necessarily imply choice. On the other hand, if a theorist claims that behavior is determined by previous events, then he or she would be perfectly consistent in making behavioral predictions.

Theoretical publications are not always explicit about a theory's philosophical assumptions. Often these need to be inferred from the various statements and claims within the theory, leading to the need for internal consistency among claims and explanations. Also, we get insight into a theory's premises by the methods used to verify it. For example, case studies are often used to verify theories that rely on differences among situations, while experimental studies are often used to verify theories that make causal predictions across situations. If a critic perceives that the methods used to test the theory are inconsistent with the claims of the theory itself, he or she might fault the theory on the grounds of consistency.

Heuristic Value

A heuristic is a tool that helps set direction, solve problems, or suggest ideas. A theory can be valuable if it leads to further ideas for research and additional theory development. Theories in the social sciences are rarely ends in themselves but serve to suggest fruitful avenues for investigation and concept development. Scholars may ask the questions, Where can we go with this theory? Where does it lead us in our investigations? A theory that is helpful in this way is said to have heuristic value.

A theory has heuristic value if it suggests new ways to look at old variables, provides new hypotheses to test, points to fresh situations to investigate, or opens new fields of practice. A theory may have validity in that it seems true but does little to promote ongoing scholarship. Such a theory would fail the heuristic test.

Validity

Validity is the extent to which a theory is "true." However, truth can be measured in a variety of ways, so validity is really a great deal more than simple truth. Depending on the type of theory, validity can be assessed in three ways.

The first form of validity is the *correspondence* between the theory's claims and observations. If the theory corresponds with what people have observed in their research, it is said to be valid in this sense of the word. Indeed, one of the primary functions of research is to test the validity of theories, or, conversely, to lead to theoretical claims that are valid by establishing a correspondence between research results and theoretical claims. This first form of validity is traditional and commonly used. It is perhaps the only form of validity recognized in mainstream sciences. However, social sciences typically use theory for reasons to explain concrete reality, requiring an expansion of the criterion.

The second form of validity is *generalizability*, or scope, as defined above. A theory is valid if you can predict outcomes in new situations based on claims developed from research in known situations. Sometimes called predictive validity, this standard values theories that accurately predict what will happen in a situation that has not yet been examined. If an experiment results in outcomes expected based on the theory, this experiment adds weight to the validity of the theory. However, a theory does not have to predict a cause–effect relationship to be generalizable. A theory might explain that people use a certain type of expression in certain kinds of situations. When this is apparent in a case previously not studied, validity is at work.

Third, validity can refer to the utility or usefulness of a theory. A theory can be said to have practical validity, which means that it is valuable for some use. This is the primary form of validity applied to practical, as opposed to predictive, theories. Here the critic asks, Does this theory help us achieve an important goal? Does it highlight certain ideas that help us understand or navigate a challenging life situation? Does it identify the dimensions of situations that should be taken into account when engaging in a certain practice? Does it describe certain outcomes that might be possible and thereby help us identify our goals?

Obviously, a theory may have more than one type of validity. We already know that every theory should have some level of generalizability. In addition to this, however, the theory may display correspondence and utility. In general, the more a theory can do, the better that theory is judged to be.

Parsimony

Parsimony is logical simplicity or theoretical elegance. A theory that reaches a claim in a few simple steps is superior to one that reaches the same claim through a longer chain of logical steps. Stated differently, a theory's power is increased when it can reach its conclusions with just a few key concepts rather than many. If a theory is parsimonious, it has gotten to the bottom of things quickly: It has identified the most basic explanatory variables or mechanisms. It predicts a lot from just a little.

Like all the criteria, however, parsimony is relative. A theory should be logically simple, but not simplistic. A good theory reduces complex experiences to a manageable and understandable set of factors without losing the richness and complexity of human experience. A theory may be highly parsimonious but in the process lose much of its heuristic value. It may be parsimonious but not very generalizable. The theory may be so parsimonious that it is closed and resistant to productive change.

Openness

Although the classical ideal for a theory in science is to be final and closed—answering all questions—in many branches of the social sciences, openness is held as a higher value. Even in physics, which aims to end itself by producing a Theory of Everything, many scientists know this is unrealistic and always want openings for the next step. Thus a good theory is actually tentative and open to new extensions. A good theory acknowledges that it is incomplete.

Theories can be open in three ways. They may invite development through *intension*, or development of more detail within particular concepts; by *extension*, or development of additional concepts; and by *revolution*, meaning that there are questions the theory cannot answer, and when these are addressed, entirely new concepts come to light.

Making an Overall Judgment

Although these six criteria provide a set of measuring sticks, a good theory integrates these and emphasizes those most relevant to the goals of the theory. If a theory is successful, it will have several characteristics:

1. The theory will provide new insights. It will not belabor the obvious but lead scholars to see phenomena in ways they might not otherwise have considered. Studying a theory, or producing one, as the case may be, leads the scholar to gain new ideas.

2. The theory will be conceptually interesting. It will provide insights that are fascinating to contemplate.

3. The theory will develop over time and evolve from one set of concepts to a better, more useful set. It has a history and a literature attached to it. It continues to attract interest and new contributors.

4. It is a collaborative product. It has developed as the result of numerous contributions by various scholars. One person may be responsible for providing a key or central idea in the theory, but the theory has gotten better over the years by teams of scholars working together.

5. The theory is durable. It passes the test of time. It is not easily abandoned. Even after its heyday, the theory is still taught because its concepts are useful.

Stephen W. Littlejohn

See also Metatheory; Theory; Traditions of Communication Theory

Further Readings

Brinberg, D., & McGrath, J. E. (1985). *Validity and the research process.* Beverly Hills, CA: Sage.

Littlejohn, S. W., & Foss, K. A. (2008) *Theories of human communication* (9th ed.; pp. 26–28). Belmont, CA: Wadsworth.

Penman, R. (1992). Good theory and good practice: An argument in progress. *Communication Theory, 3,* 234–250.

Shapiro, M. A. (2002). Generalizability in communication research. *Human Communication Research, 28,* 491–500.

Shoemaker, P. J., Tankard, J. W., & Lasorsa, D. L. (2004). *How to build social science theories.* Thousand Oaks, CA: Sage.

EXISTENTIALISM

Existentialism is difficult to define. This is due, in large part, to the fact that although it was conceived as a serious philosophical doctrine, it has been frequently vulgarized to the level of some loosely related styles of writing or, worse yet, to a fad, so that the existentialist label gets applied to authors or ideas that are only remotely, if at all, connected to existentialist philosophy. More significantly, a further complication derives from the fact that, as is the case with so many philosophies, the ideas proposed by various existentialist thinkers often do not share any one cardinal point. For example, Martin Heidegger, one of the major voices of the existential philosophy, vehemently chides Jean-Paul Sartre, a giant of existentialist thinking in his own right, for misunderstanding the term *existence* and thus debasing the label *existentialism* to mean some kind of nihilistic view on life and human history. Moreover, even when existential philosophers draw on the same author as a common source of their thinking, they disagree so substantially over the interpretation of this source that the end products are hard pressed to form a coherent system of thought.

Despite all the differences among existentialist thinkers, however, there is nevertheless a core theme around which their respective works orbit, a theme that gives what is called existentialism a recognizable contour and helps gather diverse writings as parts of a distinct philosophical perspective. This theme—also known as one of the battle cries of a general philosophical revolt taking place in Europe during the early decades of the 20th century—can be stated as follows: *Existence precedes essence.* If existentialism has made any significant contribution to philosophy, this contribution can be measured by what this statement means to suggest.

The relation between existence and essence is one of the oldest problems in philosophy. To say that something exists is simply to point to the fact that "it is." Existence is therefore characterized by concreteness and particularity, in short, by a sheer givenness. The idea of "essence" is different in a significant way from that of the "givenness" that defines existence. If the existence of something has to do with the fact that "it is," the essence of that

something consists in "what it is." The essence of an object, a silver dollar, for example, is constituted by the specific characteristics that make this object, this silver dollar, one kind of object rather than another. Seen in this way, essence is something that lends itself to rational thought, to analysis, comparison, and synthesis, in ways that the sheer particularity and "thatness" of existence do not.

As the statement "existence precedes essence" suggests, existentialism prioritizes existence and conceives of essence as derivative or secondary. In contrast to rationalist thinking, which exalts existence at the expense of essence, existentialism begins by emphasizing the *fact* of existence—the undeniable fact that *there is* something rather than nothing. This emphasis is meant by existentialists to drive home two ideas that challenge what they take be a type of anemic thinking characteristic of idealist philosophers, most notably Plato and Georg Hegel. First, existence is not to be understood as a property, as the point one makes when one says that "height" is the property of a tall person; second, the priority of existence over essence must be affirmed when one makes the metaphysical distinction between *reality* and *appearance*, if only because, as Kierkegaard, following Kant, argues, no concept of a given object entails the existence of that object. Put simply, while essences are something that can be thought about, existence is a fact that has *always* and *already* taken place, and being a fait accompli, it cannot be wished away. Existence, as existentialists would say, is irreducibly *factual*; it is the very datum, the first principle, from which philosophical reflections begin and in which they should finally end.

Now, it should be noted that by *existence*, existentialists do not mean something being there in the abstract. Rather than designating a general concept arrived at by abstracting what is common to all that appears, *existence* here means—exclusively and precisely—*individual* existence or, we can say, existence grasped according to one's inalienable individuality. This emphasis on the individual follows from existentialists' insistence that existence be approached and comprehended from the first-person perspective. This perspective opens a new vista of philosophical exploration in two ways. On one hand, it constitutes the individual as a legitimate category of philosophical reflection; on the other, it calls for confronting and rethinking the individual according to the horizon of possibilities that defines his or her identity, that is, not in terms of contingent sociocultural determinations but in terms of the individual's fundamental truth as an ongoing engagement with what lies ahead of him or her. Unlike an object, a chair, which is simply and indifferently there, an individual *exists concretely*. The individual exists concretely in the sense that his or her existence is *lived* by himself or herself only—lived, that is, in the singularity of a life that is his or her own, and about which he or she cannot but be concerned in the most intimate manner.

Existentialism highlights the concept of agency as it relates to the human condition. Existence means living and acting in the world. By extension, to act is to make a choice; action is always the outcome of choice making. This is the case, not simply because we make choices all the time, but because we cannot avoid doing so; indeed, even when we refuse to make a choice, the refusal is nonetheless a choice. In this sense, choice making is always *of* the self, in that a choice is always made by the self and for the same self as well. Because one must make a choice on one's own and because the choice made is for oneself only—although the choice made might have consequence for others—one is essentially responsible for oneself and for the choices one has made. Moreover, because one is responsible for oneself as one responds to one's own calling to make a choice, one must be considered *free*. According to existentialism, in the strict sense, humans are essentially free, for no one can prevent us from making choices. Or, as existentialists phrase it aptly, we are "condemned" to freedom. In existentialism, freedom and existence collapse into each other in the figure of the individual who, willingly or not, must be held responsible for himself or herself.

Existentialism is one of the major movements in philosophy of the 20th century. Although its fundamental tenets have been challenged by subsequent developments such as structuralism and critical hermeneutics, the deep analyses of the human condition made by existentialists have continued to fascinate writers and artists working across the spectrum of the humanities. From Fyodor Dostoyevsky to Albert Camus, from Edvard Munch to Mark Rothko, the theme of human freedom and anguish in existence can be found across

literary and artistic expressions in our own time. As made clear by existentialism, the question of existence is one that comes to us all, even if we try to repress it. In existentialism, philosophy meets life in its bare truth. To understand existentialism, one must read existentialist philosophers. When we read these philosophers, we might not find any consolation for the difficulties we face in life, but we will not fail to find the truth—the all too cruel truth—of who we are and why we cannot but face a future that is solely of our own making.

Briankle G. Chang

See also Hermeneutics; Ontology; Phenomenology; Philosophy of Communication

Further Readings

Blackham, H. J. (1959). *Six existentialist thinkers.* New York: Harper & Row.

Heidegger, M. (1962). *Being and time* (J. Macquarrie & E. S. Robinson, Trans.). New York: Harper & Row.

Sartre, J.-P. (1956). *Being and nothingness* (H. Barnes, Trans.). New York: Philosophical Library.

EXPECTANCY VIOLATIONS THEORY

Expectancy violations theory (EVT) was developed by Judee K. Burgoon and several colleagues to predict and explain the impact of unexpected communication behavior. Inspired partly by Michael Burgoon's linguistic-based expectancy theory and by Robert Rosenthal's expectancy signaling work, it originated as a theory of the effects of interpersonal proxemic violations. It has subsequently been expanded to cover other forms of nonverbal and verbal communication violations.

Key Concepts

Expectations are enduring cognitions about the anticipated verbal and nonverbal communication of others. Expectations are comprised of two components, the social and the idiosyncratic. At the social level they encompass the roles, rules, norms, and practices that typify a given culture, community, or context. At the idiosyncratic level, they encompass person-specific knowledge related to another's typical communication practices. Predictions for any given individual, message, or transaction rely on a combination of generic expectancies and any individuating knowledge of how the actor's behavior deviates from those general patterns.

Expectations derive from three classes of variables: actor, relationship, and context. *Actor variables* refer to characteristics related to individuals, such as their gender, age, or country of origin. For example, women are expected to stand closer to one another than are men; people who are similar in age are expected to stand closer together than pairings of younger and older. People from "contact" cultures are expected to stand closer together than are those from "noncontact" cultures.

Relationship variables refer to characteristics jointly defined by two or more individuals, such as their status, familial relationship, or attraction. When two people are of equal status, they expect to stand closer to one another and use more mutual gaze than when there is a status difference; in the latter case, the more deferential individual may stand at a more respectful distance and avoid direct eye contact. In parent–child relationships, proximity is expected to be closer than in stranger interactions. Likewise, interactions between people who like one another are expected to be characterized by closer proximity and more eye contact than are interactions between people who dislike one another.

Context variables refer to features of the setting and the type of interaction in which communication takes place. Seated interactions have different expectations from standing ones. So do formal interactions relative to informal ones.

The combination of all these factors yields a net expectation for what communication practices are normative. Rather than being a fixed value such as a particular distance or percentage of eye gaze, expectations take the form of a range of behavior that is customary. An *expectancy violation* occurs when another's behavior falls outside this range and is sufficiently deviant to be noticed. Sometimes violations are registered consciously. Other times, the behavior may fall outside a given *limen*, or perceptual threshold, and still not be noticed at a conscious level. In these cases, whether an expectancy violation has occurred or not falls into a gray area. It may be inferred only from changes in another's behavior that it precipitates.

Expectancy violations are given a *valence* from positive to negative. The valence is partly governed by *communicator reward valence*. *Reward valence* draws from traditional rhetorical views of communicator *ethos*, in which communicators are evaluated according to character, competence, composure, sociability, and dynamism (among other dimensions of credibility), and from B. F. Skinner's models of reinforcement learning, in which the positive or negative consequences of an act affect subsequent responding. According to EVT, receivers assess (albeit usually unconsciously) the net reward value that a communicator holds for them. Reward valence is influenced by the same classes of factors that influence expectations, such as a person's gender, age, communicator style, status, and attractiveness.

Three other relevant concepts are *arousal-distraction*, *interpretation-appraisal*, and *violation valence*. These are incorporated into the predictions that are made.

Predictions

EVT predicts that violations are arousing—they elicit psychological and/or physiological activation—and distract a recipient's attention from the ostensible main topic of conversation and toward the source of the violation. Violations should cause more arousal and distraction than expectancy confirmations (i.e., conforming to the expected behavior pattern).

As sense-making organisms, humans are next predicted to engage in a two-stage interpretation and appraisal process. They attempt to assign meaning to the violation act itself. Does, for example, a personal-space violation mean that the perpetrator is being aggressive or ingratiating? They also appraise the act as desirable or undesirable. Is close proximity wanted or unwanted? In both cases, the interpretation and the appraisal may be moderated by who is committing the violation. For example, a move closer by a very attractive member of the opposite sex may be "read" as a sign of interest and may be quite welcome. The same move by a repulsive individual may be "read" as sexual harassment and may be quite unwelcome. The net result of this process, which may occur almost instantaneously, is a valencing of the violation itself as positive or negative.

The final step of the theory is predicting the effects of expectancy violations relative to nonviolations. Positive violations are predicted to produce more favorable outcomes than are positive confirmations; negative violations are predicted to produce more negative outcomes than are negative confirmations. The theory makes a strong point that the comparison of interest is not between positive and negative violations but between positive violations and positive confirmations or negative violations and negative confirmations. In other words, it makes the counterintuitive claim that violations are sometimes better than doing what is expected (when the violation is a positive one). The theory also calls attention to the prospect of violations' actually being positively valenced, unlike the common claim that violations are by definition negative.

The theory also can apply to positive confirmations of behavior, in that expectations and communicator reward valence should be influenced by the same variables as in the violation case, and the interpretation-appraisal process should still take place. However, the intensified reactions due to arousal and distraction are missing in the confirmation case.

Empirical Support

Initial tests of the theory focused on violations of conversational distance and predicted that close violations exceeding a very close threshold called the threat threshold would have negative consequences regardless of who committed them. However, the results did not support the existence of a threat threshold. The theory was then revised, and the role of violation interpretation became more prominent. Tests of arousal established that both close and far violations elicited arousal, and

tests of positive-violation and negative-violation predictions garnered support for such violations as proximity, eye gaze, immediacy, involvement, touch, and posture. The theory has been applied to persuasion, adaptation patterns in interpersonal interaction, intercultural interactions, deception, and group decision making.

Judee K. Burgoon

See also Cognitive Theories; Deception Detection; Immediacy; Interaction Adaptation Theory; Interpersonal Communication Theories; Learning and Communication; Nonverbal Communication Theories; Proxemics

Further Readings

Burgoon, J. K. (1993). Interpersonal expectations, expectancy violations, and emotional communication. *Journal of Language and Social Psychology, 12,* 30–48.

Burgoon, J. K. (1995). Cross-cultural and intercultural applications of expectancy violations theory. In R. Wiseman (Ed.), *Intercultural communication theory* (pp. 194–215). Thousand Oaks, CA: Sage.

Burgoon, J. K., & Hale, J. L. (1988). Nonverbal expectancy violations: Model elaboration and application. *Communication Monographs, 55,* 58–79.

Burgoon, J. K. & Walter, J. (1990). Nonverbal expectancies and the evaluative consequences of violations. *Human Communication Research, 17,* 232–265.

EXTENDED PARALLEL PROCESS MODEL

See Campaign Communication Theories; Persuasion and Social Influence Theories

F

FACE NEGOTIATION THEORY

The face negotiation theory, developed by Stella Ting-Toomey, explains the culture-based and situational factors that shape communicators' tendencies in approaching and managing conflicts. The meaning of *face* is generally conceptualized as how we want others to see us and treat us and how we actually treat others in association with their social self-conception expectations. In everyday interactions, individuals are constantly making conscious or unconscious choices concerning face-saving and face-honoring issues across interpersonal, workplace, and international contexts. Although face is about a claimed sense of interactional identity, *facework* is about verbal and nonverbal behaviors that protect-save self, other, or mutual face.

The researching of facework can be found in a wide range of disciplines such as anthropology, psychology, sociology, linguistics, management, international diplomacy, and human communication studies, among others. The concept of face has been used to explain linguistic politeness rituals, apology acts, embarrassment situations, requesting behaviors, and conflict interactions. The root of the face negotiation (FN) theory was influenced by Hsien Chin Hu's 1944 anthropological essay "The Chinese Concept of Face," Erving Goffman's 1955 sociological article "On Face-Work," and Penelope Brown and Stephen Levinson's 1987 linguistics monograph on "Politeness."

The foundational concepts of the FN theory first appeared in Ting-Toomey's 1985 article "Toward a Theory of Conflict and Culture." In a subsequent article in 1988, "Intercultural Conflict Styles: A Face-Negotiation Theory," the formal version of the theory became available—with five core assumptions and 12 theoretical propositions stating the relationship between individualism-collectivism and different facework interaction styles. In 1998, a second rendition of the FN theory with seven assumptions and 32 propositions was published in an essay on "Facework Competence." Based on the results of several large data sets, a third version of the FN theory appeared in 2005 in "The Matrix of Face" and contained an updated 24 FN theoretical propositions.

Core Assumptions and Face Orientations

The seven core assumptions of the FN theory are as follows: (1) people in all cultures try to maintain and negotiate face in all communication situations; (2) the concept of face is especially problematic in emotionally threatening or identity-vulnerable situations when the situated identities of the communicators are called into question; (3) the cultural value spectra of individualism-collectivism and small-large power distance shape facework concerns and styles; (4) individualism and collectivism value patterns shape members' preferences for self-oriented face concern versus other-oriented or mutual-oriented concern; (5) small and large power distance value patterns shape members' preferences for horizontal-based facework versus vertical-based facework; (6) the value dimensions, in conjunction with individual, relational, and situational factors, influence the use of particular facework behaviors in particular cultural scenes; and (7) intercultural facework competence refers to the optimal integration of knowledge, mindfulness, and communication skills in managing vulnerable identity-based conflict situations appropriately, effectively, and adaptively.

Cultural Membership and Face Concerns

Self-face concern is the protective concern for one's own identity image when one's own face is threatened in the conflict episode. *Other-face concern* is the concern for accommodating the other conflict party's identity image in the conflict situation. *Mutual-face concern* is the concern for both parties' images and the image of the relationship. Whether we choose to engage in self-face protection or mutual-face protection often depends on our ingrained cultural socialization process, individual trait tendencies, and embedded situational factors.

More specifically, for example, in a direct empirical test of the theory by John Oetzel and Ting-Toomey in 2003, the research program tested the underlying assumption of the FN theory that face is an explanatory mechanism for cultural membership's influence on conflict behavior. A questionnaire was administered to 768 participants in four national cultures: China, Germany, Japan, and the United States in their respective languages asking them to recall and describe a recent interpersonal conflict. The major results of the study are as follows: First, cultural individualism-collectivism had direct effects on conflict styles, as well as mediated effects through self-construal and face concerns. Second, self-face concern was associated positively with dominating style, and other-face concern was associated positively with avoiding and integrating styles. Third, German respondents reported the frequent use of direct-confrontative facework strategies; Japanese reported the use of different pretending and accommodating strategies and minimize the severity of the conflict situation; Chinese engaged in a variety of avoiding, accommodating, and third-party appeals' tactics;

and U.S. Americans reported the use of up-front expression of feelings and remaining calm as conflict facework tactics.

Within the pluralistic U.S. sample, multiethnic research by Ting-Toomey and her co-researchers in 2000 has also uncovered distinctive conflict interaction styles in relationship to particular ethnic identity salience issues.

Although previous research studies have focused on testing the relationship between individualism-collectivism value dimension and facework strategies, recent research effort has focused more on unpacking the small and large power distance value spectrums with particular facework practice.

Face Threatening Process Conditions

It seems that when an individual's face image is being threatened in a conflict situation, she or he would likely experience identity-based frustration, emotional vulnerability, anger, hurt, and even vengeance. The threats to face can be on a group membership level or an individual level.

In the 2005 FN theory version, the following conditions were posited concerning the valence direction of an intercultural face threatening process (FTP): First, the more important the culturally appropriate facework rule is violated, the more severe the perceived FTP. Second, the larger the cultural distance between the conflict parties, the more mistrust or misunderstanding cumulate in the FTP. Third, the more important the conflict topic or imposition of the conflict demand, as interpreted from distinctive cultural angles, the more severe the perceived FTP. Fourth, the more power the conflict initiator has over the conflict recipient, the more severe the perceived FTP by the recipient. Fifth, the more harm or hurtful the FTP produces, the more time and effort is needed to repair the FTP. Self-face concern becomes incrementally more salient if several of these conditions are present in an FTP.

For example, individuals are likely to move toward self-face saving and in-group face-saving emphasis as they perceive the escalation of the various face threatening conditions directed at them or their in-groups. Cultural assumptions, individual personality tendencies, and situational pressures frame the underlying interpretations of what count as a severe face threatening interaction episode.

Individual, Situational, and Facework Competence

Individual Personality Factors

The term *self-construal* was coined by Hazel Markus and Shinobu Kitayama in 1991 and is concerned with one's self-image as emphasizing either an independent or an interdependent self. The independent construal of self involves the view that an individual is a unique entity with an individuated repertoire of feelings, cognitions, and motivations. In comparison, the interdependent construal of self involves an emphasis on the importance of in-group-relational connectedness and intertwined interdependent fate focus. Self-construal is the individual-level equivalent of the cultural variability dimension of individualism-collectivism.

In individualistic cultural communities, there may be more situations that evoke the need for independent-based actions. In collectivistic communities, there may be more situations that demand the sensitivity for interdependent-based decisions. The manner in which individuals conceive of their self-images should have a profound influence on the expectancies of what constitute appropriate and effective responses in diverse facework situations. Both dimensions of self also exist within each individual, regardless of cultural membership identity.

For example, Oetzel and Ting-Toomey in 2003 found that independent self-construal is associated positively with self-face concern and the use of dominating-competing conflict strategies. Interdependent self-construal, on the other hand, is associated positively with other-face concern and the use of avoiding and integrating conflict tactics. It would appear that independent self-construal fosters the use of up-front and low-context demanding interaction responses, while interdependent self-construal emphasizes circumspective and high-context yielding interaction patterns.

Situational Appraisal Factors

Two other possible factors that moderate the activation of an independent versus an interdependent self are situational role appraisal and in-group–out-group distance factors. Situational role appraisal factors can include the degree of formality of the conflict setting, the interaction climate of the situation, the role relationship between the conflict participants, and the perceived goals of the facework negotiation process. To illustrate, the role-appraisal process can include an assessment of the role expectancies between the conflict parties such as professional role identities and other salient group membership and personal identity concerns. For example, Rebecca Merkin in 2006 integrated small-large power distance value dimension to the individualism-collectivism value dimension in explaining face threatening response messages and conflict styles in multiple cultures. She found that high-status individuals from large power distance cultures tend to use both direct and indirect facework strategies to deal with face threatening situations—depending on whether they were delivering positive or negative messages. Thus, an accurate assessment of the culture-based situational factors that frame facework strategy usage can be critical in promoting competent conflict management outcome.

Furthermore, many relational distance factors are important in competent facework negotiation. One of the key factors would be the intricate relationship between in-group–out-group conceptualization and facework strategy enactment. For example, according to Ting-Toomey and Jiro Takai in 2006, the broad-based in-group category in the Japanese language can be further refined into *inner-intimate in-group members* and *familiar in-group members*. Likewise, the broad-based out-group category can be further fine-tuned into *familiar out-group members* and *peripheral out-group members*. In the archetypical form, appropriate facework rituals can be suspended in the inner-intimate in-group category or the peripheral out-group category. Instead, deep heart-to-heart talks can exist in the former category, and indifferent facework tactics can permeate the latter category.

Facework Interaction Competence

The factors in the situational role and the relational distance processes have a strong impact on facework interaction competence in different cultural communities. A competent facework negotiator would need to increase his or her awareness concerning self's and other's cultural and individual facework conditioning process. An optimal degree of facework competence emphasizes the integration of *culture-sensitive knowledge, mindfulness,* and adaptive *communication skills.* Culture-sensitive knowledge is considered as the most important component that underscores the other components of facework competence. Without culture-sensitive knowledge, conflict parties cannot learn to uncover the implicit ethnocentric lenses they use to evaluate behaviors in an intercultural conflict situation. Without knowledge, negotiators cannot reframe their interpretation of a conflict situation accurately from the other's cultural frame of reference. In-depth cultural knowledge can lead to some truly "aha!" intercultural learning moments.

These aha moments coupled with mindful reflections can help an individual to develop constructive conflict skills and build competent interaction capacities. To be a mindful interpreter of intercultural conflict, individuals must develop a holistic view of the critical factors that frame the face negotiation process of a conflict situation. According to Ting-Toomey in 1999, mindfulness means attending to one's internal assumptions, cognitions, and emotions and at the same time, becoming attuned to the other's conflict assumptions, cognitions, and emotions. To be mindful of intercultural differences, individuals have to learn to see the unfamiliar behavior from a nonjudgmental, nonreactive standpoint. Mindfulness can be practiced through a deep state of listening with an uncluttered mind. To cultivate competent facework consciousness, communication skills such as mindful reframing, mutual face validation, decentering, adaptive code switching, and dialogue bridging skills are all needed to connect the culture-based knowledge with the transformative, respectful facework practice.

Stella Ting-Toomey

See also Conflict Communication Theories; Cross-Cultural Communication; Cultural Types Theories; Facework Theories; Intercultural Communication Competence; Intercultural Communication Theories

Further Readings

Oetzel, J. G., & Ting-Toomey, S. (2003). Face concerns in interpersonal conflict: A cross-cultural empirical test of the face-negotiation theory. *Communication Research, 30,* 599–624.

Ting-Toomey, S. (1988). Intercultural conflicts: A face-negotiation theory. In Y. Y. Kim & W. B. Gudykunst (Eds.), *Theories in intercultural communication* (pp. 213–235). Newbury Park, CA: Sage.

Ting-Toomey, S. (2004). Translating conflict face-negotiation theory into practice. In D. Landis, J. Bennett, & M. Bennett (Eds.), *Handbook of intercultural training* (3rd ed., pp. 217–248). Thousand Oaks, CA: Sage.

Ting-Toomey, S. (2005). The matrix of face: An updated face-negotiation theory. In W. B. Gudykunst (Ed.), *Theorizing about intercultural communication* (pp. 71–92). Thousand Oaks, CA: Sage.

Ting-Toomey, S., & Kurogi, A. (1998). Facework competence in intercultural conflict: An updated face-negotiation theory. *International Journal of Intercultural Relations, 22,* 187–225.

FACEWORK THEORIES

Physical faces are one of the primary means by which we distinguish individuals. In facework theories, however, instead of referring to one's physical face, the word *face* is a metaphorical allusion to one's desired social identity or image(s). One's metaphorical face is manifested through communication. Researchers have coined a variety of words to represent different types of facework, including: *face-honoring, face-threatening, face-saving, face-protecting, face-building, face-depreciating, face-giving, face-negotiating, face-compensating, face-restoring, face-neutral,* and *face-constituting.* Facework theories, largely grounded in Erving Goffman's writings on facework and Penelope Brown and Stephen Levinson's model of politeness, have been used to examine communication practices in multiple contexts.

Origins and Definitions of Facework

Goffman's 1955 publication, "On Face-Work: An Analysis of Ritual Elements of Social Interaction," in which he explicitly linked communication practices and facework, is often credited as the origin of facework theories about communication in the United States. Goffman referenced publications on face from Chinese and American Indian perspectives published between 1894 and 1954. In one of these publications, Hsien Chin Hu linked the word *face* to two Chinese concepts: *mien-tz* , for the kind of prestige that comes from personal success, and *lien,* for the regard bestowed upon an individual by a group based on his or her moral reputation. Through a series of illuminating contrasts, Yu-tang Lin noted that face is psychological not physiological; not washed or shaven, but granted, lost, fought for, and given as a gift; intangible, but nonetheless regulates interactions; invisible, yet shown in public; governed not by reason, but by social conventions; not purchased with money, but the most prized possession. Goffman conceptualized face as a public image (line) that is performed in front of others, an image that is consistent with approved social values and rules for social interaction.

Even though face is often treated as a psychological concept, as though the face of an individual is distinct from the face of others, it may be more accurate to conceptualize face as a sociological or interactional concept. Scholars have argued that face does not reside in the body or personality of an individual, but in interactions of communicators and the meanings assigned to those interactions. Individuals do not own fixed, unchanging faces; rather faces are coconstructed and reconstructed in social interactions. The specific rules for honoring one's own face or the face of others can vary from culture to culture, group to group, or context to context. The word *work* is appropriate in reference to face because face is dynamic and ever changing, and one has to work to create and maintain desired faces. The phrase *impression management,* as a descriptor of one type of facework, also indicates that maintaining or enhancing images requires labor; face is something communicators "manage." Unfortunately, there are also some individuals who work at threatening the face of others, as in conflicts between rivals and negative political advertisements. Still, most of the scholarship on facework has focused on its positive applications.

Politeness as One Type of Facework

Brown and Levinson developed a model of politeness grounded in Goffman's notion of face. Brown and Levinson maintained that humans possess two face-wants: the desire to have one's actions unimpeded (*negative face*) and the desire to be liked by others (*positive face*). Other scholars have described these desires as the need for autonomy and the need for approval. Tae-Seop Li and John Waite Bowers further subdivided the desire for approval into two, leading them to identify three types of face: *fellowship face,* the desire to be included; *competence face,* the desire to be respected; and *autonomy face,* the desire not to be imposed upon.

Brown and Levinson conceptualized politeness as a redress to a face threatening act (FTA). Utterances that honor one's autonomy or compensate for an imposition on autonomy (e.g., "If you are not too busy, I would really appreciate your help on party preparations") are called *negative politeness,* while utterances that expressed positive regard for the listener are called *positive politeness* (e.g., "Thank you for being such a great friend"). A single utterance can contain both negative and positive politeness (e.g., "Could I please have one of your fabulous cookies?").

Although the means for fulfilling the desires of autonomy and approval vary culturally, Brown and Levinson argued that the desires themselves are universal. Other scholars called into question whether the need for autonomy is a universal desire and demonstrated that face-needs may conflict. For example, requests were defined as inherently face threatening in that they imply a desire to impose on another, to threaten the addressee's autonomy. However, these definitional assumptions ignore other possibilities. Requests can also be signals for increasing intimacy and trust, which in turn can honor one's approval and competence face-desires.

Facework in Multiple Contexts

A review of the book in which Brown and Levinson's work first appeared was published in *Philosophy and Rhetoric* in 1980. In the early 1980s, scholars in the discipline of communication conducted research on accounts for failures, compliance-gaining, and politeness using Brown and Levinson's model. Since then, there have been many extensions and applications of facework theories to communication.

Beyond Politeness

Facework encompasses more and is more complex than politeness. Although politeness is aimed at meeting the autonomy, solidarity, and competence face-desires of others (*other-face*), facework can be threatening, as well as honoring, and it can be directed toward oneself (*self-face*), as well as others. *Mutual-face* is concerned with the face-desires of speakers and hearers and their relationship. Facework includes avoiding FTAs (e.g., criticizing, complaining, disagreeing, cursing, insulting, interrogating, stereotyping, stigmatizing, drawing attention to mistakes or limitations, challenging, demanding acquiescence, refusing a request or offer), as well as engaging in such acts. Confessions, apologies, and admissions of vulnerabilities can be simultaneous FTAs for the speakers and face-honoring or face-compensating acts for certain kinds of listeners. Celebrations of successes can be face-honoring, unless they are viewed as bragging or disrupting harmony by singling out individuals or by implying criticism of others, in which case they become face threatening. Finally, the face one tries to claim for oneself may not be the same face recognized or granted by others. Facework involves dialectical tensions in which participants balance each other's face-desires along the continuums of autonomy-inclusion and dignity-humility.

In addition, some scholars have maintained that face should not be conceptualized as belonging to an individual or as being encoded and decoded through a single utterance, but rather as something that is created interactionally. Victoria Chen describes an interconnected enactment of face for both the host and guest through her explication of the accomplishment of mien-tz and keh chee (guest spirit) at the Chinese dinner table. Her analysis also demonstrates a paradox; in order to meet the positive face-desires of both the guest and the host to be perceived as valued and competent, the host has to violate the guest's negative face (desire for autonomy) by insisting that the guest eat more. In his *Face Constituting Theory*, Robert Arundale noted that face is conjointly coconstituted in interaction. For example, an utterance such as "That's a nice dress" is understood as a compliment, as a positive face act when it is followed by "Thanks," but as a request, a negative face threat, when followed by "You can't borrow it."

Facework in Various Communication Practices

Facework is associated with a wide range of communication practices. In explorations of autonomy, researchers have used facework models to look at advice, compliance gaining, conflict, demands, instruction, negotiation, and requests. In investigations of solidarity desires, researchers have examined emotional expressiveness and responsiveness, empathic or supportive messages, relational development and decay, gratitude, invitations, listening, and offers. Competence desires are addressed in research about affirmations, appreciative inquiry, blame, compliments, criticisms, feedback, praise, and tact. In recognition of social rules regarding social status and other relational expectations, facework has included examinations of deference, demeanor, and respect. Studies that focus on accounts, apologies, denials, excuses, and explanations have included information about repairing damage to face. Facework has been associated with a wide range of emotions, including affection, anger, anxiety, contempt, embarrassment, fear, hurt, joy, pride, regret, and shame.

Some researchers have hypothesized gendered differences in facework. They reasoned that males would be more concerned with the desire for autonomy, while females would focus more on the desire for inclusion. Further, males and females were expected to vary in their attention to competence-face depending on whether a competency was linked to stereotypical notions of masculinity and femininity. The findings from research on gender and facework are mixed, with stronger differences found in beliefs about gendered behavior than in the behavior itself. One explanation for the inconsistency in the findings is that males and females sometimes occupy different social roles, which carry rights and obligations that may influence facework more than gender itself.

Communication researchers have studied facework in multiple contexts across different types of relationships, in life and in fiction. Interpersonal scholars have investigated facework in the communication of strangers, acquaintances, close friends, intimate partners, and family members. Communication that supports face-desires has been associated with greater trust, liking, satisfaction, and commitment in relationships. Facework among peers and individuals varying in organizational stature within the workplace has been the focus of several studies. In educational contexts, researchers have found that teachers and students engage in facework throughout the educational process from instruction, to feedback and evaluation, to the negotiation of grades, and that when the facework is skillful, it facilitates learning. Other investigations probed the place of facework in delivering bad news, crisis negotiations, and 911 calls. The significant role of facework in conflict resolutions has been the subject of extensive research and theoretical development by Stella Ting-Toomey and her associates in a theory called *face negotiation theory*. This theory gives considerable attention to the place of individualistic and collectivistic cultural values in facework, as well as one's view of oneself as relatively independent or interdependent.

Most of the scholarship applying facework theories to communication practices has focused on interpersonal, educational, or organizational encounters, but Kathy Domenici and Stephen W. Littlejohn illustrate the relevance of facework to community and global issues, including its central role in bringing about peaceful resolutions to conflicts between nations. Drawing upon their own work and that of others, Domenici and Littlejohn stress the importance of various aspects of facework: building face, inquiring appreciatively, looking for positive resources for change, taking risks, delaying responses, focusing on issues rather than blame or credit, and reframing problems as opportunities that lead to new ways of seeing and acting. They suggest that just as an individual's face is not a static entity, but a dynamic construction, reinforced through communication practices, so too are the faces of communities and nations. Facework can be found in all communication encounters.

Susan B. Shimanoff

See also Face Negotiation Theory; Impression Management; Interpersonal Communication Theories; Politeness Theory; Rules Theories

Further Readings

Arundale, R. B. (2006). Face as relational and interactional: A communication framework for research on face, facework, and politeness. *Journal of Politeness Research: Language, Behavior, Culture, 2,* 193–216.

Brown, P., & Levinson, S. (1978). Universals in language use: Politeness phenomena. In E. N. Goody (Ed.), *Questions and politeness: Strategies in social interaction* (pp. 56–289). London: Cambridge University Press.

Chen, V. (1990/1991). *Mien tze* at the Chinese dinner table: A study of the interactional accomplishment of face. *Research on Language and Social Interaction, 24,* 109–140.

Cupach, W. R., & Metts, S. (1994). *Facework.* Thousand Oaks, CA: Sage.

Domenici, K., & Littlejohn, S. W. (2006). *Facework: Bridging theory and practice.* Thousand Oaks, CA: Sage.

Goffman, E. (1955). On face-work: An analysis of ritual elements of social interaction. *Psychiatry: Journal for the Study of Interpersonal Processes, 18,* 213–231.

Hu, H. C. (1944). The Chinese concept of "face." *American Anthropologist, 46,* 45–64.

Lim, T. S., & Bowers, J. W. (1991). Facework: Solidarity, approbation, and tact. *Human Communication Research, 17,* 415–450.

Lin, Y. (1935). *My country and my people.* New York: The John Day Company.

Ting-Toomey, S. (Ed.). (1994). *The challenge of facework: Cross-cultural and interpersonal issues.* Albany: State University of New York Press.

Family and Marital Schemas and Types

The way people think about and act in marital and family relationships can be represented in terms of schemas and types. On the individual level, schemas determine communication behaviors in these relationships and a person's psychological and behavioral responses to these relationships. On the social level, typologies show how laypersons and scholars perceive of and evaluate relationships. Together, schemas and types play an important role in conducting and interpreting marital and family relationships.

Family and Marriage Schemas

Mental schemas are generally defined as cognitive structures representing some concept (or object)

that contain acquired knowledge of the attributes and functions of the concept. In other words, mental schemas are patterns of simultaneous activation of knowledge bits stored in long-term memory that together represent a coherent representation of the concept or object. Thus, relationship schemas in general are mental representations of relationships, and family and marital schemas specifically are mental representations of one's familial and marital relationships, respectively.

Structure of Schemas

Research specifically on relationship schemas has defined them further as interrelated pieces of declarative and procedural knowledge about relationships that reside in long-term memory. Declarative knowledge is defined as descriptive knowledge of the attributes and features of things, whereas procedural knowledge refers to a person's knowledge of if-then contingencies that often take the form of interpersonal scripts or memory organization packets, which are memories of how to do things.

The declarative and procedural knowledge contained in relationship schemas overlaps with three subsets of knowledge that, in other areas of psychology, are considered to be more or less independent: the self-, other-, and relational-schema. A self-schema contains knowledge about the self, including knowledge of one's thoughts and emotions, goals and plans for the future, and memory of past experiences. An other-schema contains knowledge about the other that mirrors knowledge of self in that it includes representations of the other's thoughts and emotions, goals and plans for the future, and past experiences. The main difference is that, depending on how well one knows the other, other-schemas are more limited than those of self. Finally, relational-schemas contain knowledge of past and future interactions with others. They include knowledge of experienced and expected interaction sequences between self and other used to interpret and to plan behavior. Although self and other schemes traditionally were thought of as independent, recent research on interpersonal cognition strongly suggests they are so highly interdependent on one another that they more likely belong to the same cognitive structure—the relationship schema.

Like many other schemas, relationship schemas consist of knowledge that exists at three levels of generality. The most general level is general social knowledge that applies to all interpersonal relationships. Examples of such knowledge include beliefs and pragmatic rules that apply to all interactions, such as the norm of reciprocity or the need to be truthful and relevant when communicating. Because it applies to all relationships, knowledge at the general social level is part of any relationship schema. At the second level of abstraction is relationship-type knowledge that includes knowledge specific to the type of relationship one has, such as romantic partner, coworker, sibling, and best friend. The knowledge stored at this level is different from that stored at the general social level in that it only applies to relationships of the specific type. It is at the relationship-type level that cultural knowledge, such as rules and norms for specific types of relationships, are stored. The most specific and least abstract level is relationship specific. Knowledge at this level applies to only the particular relationship a person has with one specific other person. Such knowledge includes memories, attributions, and experiences made within the context of that particular relationship and allow individuals to adapt their thoughts, behaviors, and interpretations to that specific relationship partner. These specific relationship beliefs, including those related to one's family, are what make each relationship unique and distinguishable from other relationships.

The knowledge contained at the relationship-specific level is different from the knowledge that exists at more general levels, and a person's complete mental representation of a relationship combines knowledge from all three levels. Thus, similarities or overlap of mental representations of relationships with different persons are the result of shared knowledge drawn from either the general social level or the relationship-type level. By contrast, differences in mental representations of relationships with different persons are due to information contained either at the relationship-type or relationship-specific level. As a rule, if knowledge at different levels of generality conflicts, the more specific knowledge takes precedent. Consequently, there must be a process that determines which information is retrieved and used in relational information processing. This could be a sequential process in which relationship-specific knowledge is accessed first, relationship-type knowledge second, and general social knowledge last. An equally plausible alternative that is more consistent with notions of parallel information processing in the brain is a recursive or iterative process that accesses knowledge at all levels of specificity simultaneously and that assigns more specific knowledge primacy over more general knowledge if there is a conflict between them. A similar process could be involved when storing relationship experiences in memory. Truly unique experiences are stored at the relationship-specific level, whereas experiences that are made with several others are stored at the relationship type or the general social level, respectively.

Content of Schemas

In regard to content, one can expect a fair degree of similarity between marriage and family relationship schemas. Obviously, relationship-specific knowledge is highly dependent on the actual persons constituting the relationships and thus varies widely between different marriages and families. Knowledge at the relationship-type level, however, which is much more dependent on culture and the norms and rules of a speech community, shows significant overlap between individuals. Furthermore, within individuals, marital, and family relationship schemas also overlap, not the least because marriage is, of course, a family relationship. Research investigating the content of marital schemas, for example, has shown that it contains beliefs related to ideology of marriage, relationship between individuals and the institution of marriage, relationship between the couple and the outside world, gender roles in marriages, communication behaviors, expression of positive and negative affect, conflict and problem-solving behaviors, the sharing of space and time, child-rearing practices, and spiritual aspects of the relationship.

Research on the content of family schemas is somewhat more limited, but it suggests similar knowledge to that of marriage schemas, such as communication norms and rules, parenting, conflict and problem solving, sharing of emotions, cohesion and adaptability, and decision making. Also, the family schema is somewhat more complex than the marriage schema because it contains knowledge at the relationship-specific level that is associated with multiple family members, whereas the marriage relationship schema only incorporates the relationship-specific knowledge associated with one other person.

Functions of Schemas

Schemas function to direct attention to specific aspects of one's environment, help interpret stimuli, guide the retrieval of information from memory, and store new information in memory. Thus, schemas play a central role in information processing and how persons understand and act in their (social) worlds. It follows that relationship schemas, such as marriage and family schemas, organize a person's knowledge of these relationships and play an important role in the cognitive processes that precede, accompany, and follow interpersonal communication in these relationships. As such, they also play an important role when scholars try to explain and predict interpersonal communication in these relationships.

Marriage and Family Types

Whereas marriage and family schemas refer to coherent mental representations of these relationships that exist as cognitive structures within individuals, marriage and family types are symbolic representations of these relationships used in lay or scholarly discourse—that is, relationship typologies are classifications of relationships imposed by outside or participant observers. If the observers are scholars, the purpose is to get a better understanding of and to theorize about relationships by grouping them based on some sort of characteristic(s), such as structural properties, composition, process, or outcome. If the observers are laypersons or participants, the purpose is also understanding, prediction, and evaluation, although in a less formalized and often implicit manner. Also, the purpose for lay-persons is application of this knowledge in their social environment and their own relationships, whereas the interest of scholarly observers is often more theoretical than practical. Despite their divergent interests and the formalized process by which scholars construct and use typologies, there is a substantial amount of overlap between scholarly and lay typologies. This is probably because both scholars and laypersons use typologies to explain the same phenomena within the same social context.

Types of Typologies

Typologies are fundamentally sense-making devices, and humans have the propensity to associate structure with function. Consequently, many typologies of marriages and families are based on structure and/or membership that imply some important differences in how these relationships function or the outcomes they produce. For marriages, examples include first and remarriages, interracial, homosexual, dual-career, long-distance, interfaith, and childless marriages. Examples for family typologies include step, blended, and patchwork families; single-parent; interracial; intergenerational; interfaith; same-sex parent; and interfaith families.

Other typologies focus on characteristics more ostensibly important to researchers, such as outcomes for couples and children. Much of early research on marriages and families, for example, was based on comparing satisfied (i.e., enduring) versus dissatisfied (i.e., divorcing) marriages and families that had well-adjusted children versus families with children that showed evidence of maladjustment, such as delinquency, criminality, or social and academic problems. The shortcoming of such typologies, however, is that they assume that either all structurally similar relationships have similar outcomes, or that all outcomes are arrived at through similar means—and empirical evidence supports neither assumption.

Recognizing these limitations, other typologies, especially those developed by communication scholars, have focused on processes and communication behaviors to distinguish marriages and families. The more successful typologies focus on communication behaviors that affect several outcomes of interest, not just on satisfaction, stability, and child adjustment. These more complex typologies also recognize that the processes that define types associated with positive outcomes in one domain (e.g., satisfaction) are not necessarily associated with positive outcomes in other domains (e.g., adjustment). Examples for such marital typologies include John Gottman's typology based on conflict styles that identifies three functional couple types (validating, volatile, and avoidant) and two dysfunctional styles (hostile and hostile-detached).

An example for family types is family communication patterns theory, developed by Mary Ann Fitzpatrick, Ascan Koerner, and their colleagues, which classifies families based on their conversation and conformity orientation as either *consensual* (high in both), *pluralistic* (high conversation, low conformity), *protective* (low conversation, high conformity), or *laissez-faire* (low in both). An increasing body of research has shown that family types differ in a number of significant outcomes, including child social and academic adjustment, resiliency, and child mental health; family satisfaction; family social support; and family violence and abuse. In addition, these families also differ predictably in how they communicate in specific domains such as conflict, problem solving and decision making, and expressions of positive and negative affect.

Ascan F. Koerner

See also Cognitive Theories; Family Communication Theories; Interpersonal Communication Theories; Relational Communication Theory; Relational Development

Further Readings

Baldwin, M. W. (1992). Relational schemas and the processing of social information. *Psychological Bulletin, 112,* 461–484.

Gottman, J. M., & Levenson, R. W. (2000). The timing of divorce: Predicting when a couple will divorce over a 14-year period. *Journal of Marriage and Family, 62,* 737–745.

Koerner, A. F. (2007). Social cognition and family communication: Family communication patterns theory. In D. Roskos-Ewoldsen & J. Monahan (Eds.) *Communication and social cognition: Theory and methods* (pp. 197–216). Mahwah, NJ: Lawrence Erlbaum.

Koerner, A. F., & Fitzpatrick, M. A. (2002). Toward a theory of family communication. *Communication Theory, 12,* 70–91.

Smith, E. R. (1998). Mental representation and memory. In D. T. Gilbert, S. T. Fiske, & G. Lindzey (Eds.), *The handbook of social psychology* (4th ed., pp. 391–445). Boston: McGraw-Hill.

Van Lear, A., Koerner, A. F., & Allen, D. (2006). Relationship typologies. In A. L. Vangelisti & D. Perlmann (Eds.), *The Cambridge handbook of personal relationships* (pp. 91–111). Cambridge, UK: Cambridge University Press.

FAMILY COMMUNICATION THEORIES

Family communication theories are coherent accounts of family communication processes and family relationships that provide explanations for phenomena of interests, which frequently are the relationships or communication behaviors themselves or their outcomes for family members. As such, family communication theories are central to any investigation of family communication processes and of outcomes that might be affected by them. Family communication theories stem from a number of different academic disciplines and are based on a wide range of methodologies, ranging from critical to scientific. As a result, there is substantial disagreement about the very nature of theory, the role theory plays in research, and the appropriate methods for studying family communication. This entry provides an overview of the theoretical approaches that are most frequently found in family communication research and introduces a few of the more influential theories in some detail.

Divergent Origins

Research on family communication is not an exclusive domain of communication scholars. Rather, academic interest in families and their communication exists in a number of academic disciplines, including child development, family social sciences psychology, and sociology. As a result, there exist many very different theories related to family communication that create very divergent accounts of family communication. Contributing to this diversity is the fact that as a discipline, communication is a relative newcomer compared to other disciplines, which have much longer histories of interest in family communication processes, their antecedents, and outcomes.

Thus, most theories of family communication originated outside the communication discipline and often share the particular assumptions and biases of the disciplines from which they originated. Even among those theories used in family communication research that originated from within the communication discipline, a majority was not developed explicitly with family communication in mind, but rather in regard to interpersonal communication more generally or in regard to specific communication processes that happen to also take place in the family context, such as self-disclosure or uncertainty reduction. As a consequence, family communication theories vary widely in the basic assumptions they make about what is important for family communication, what explains communication behaviors, and what effects communication has on other variables.

Divergent Epistemologies and Methods

The lack of coherence among family communication theories is amplified because family communication scholars employ a wide range of methods that are based on often conflicting epistemologies, from critical theory to quantitative social science. Consequently, there is significant disagreement among family communication scholars not only as to what exactly constitutes a theory of family communication, but also about the purposes and functions of theory in general and about the appropriate methods for studying family communication.

Critical Family Theory

The purpose of critical theory in general is to delineate the social processes and institutions by which individuals are oppressed and to suggest ways by which individuals can become emancipated. As such, applications of critical theory are contextually and historically specific, which necessarily limits their generalizability beyond the specific cases or time periods they address. A consequence of this lack of generalizability is that it is difficult to quantify the impact of any one application of critical theory on the field of family communication. Two recent reviews of scholarly articles in family communication, however, suggest that critical theory as an approach plays only a relatively minor role in published family communication research. Nonetheless, its impact on practical application, such as counseling or public policy, and to a lesser extent teaching, is significant.

Because of its focus on oppression and emancipation and its roots in sociology, critical family theory focuses on social practices and institutions that negatively affect families or family members, such as gender roles or how power relationships are enacted to the detriment of women, children, and minorities in social institutions such as marriage and family. When explaining family communication, critical theories usually draw parallels between family relationships and other social relationships that define societal power structures, such as the relationships between employers and laborers, how knowledge is managed in society, and ways by which governments restrict individual freedom and choice. By delineating how these larger social relationships and power structures affect family relationships, they suggest ways they can be overcome.

Social Scientific Family Theory

In contrast to critical theory, which has as its goal emancipation, the goal of social scientific approaches to the study of family communication is to discover what is important about human relationships by observing associations between variables and outcomes. Although social scientific theories are also often context specific (e.g., close relationships, marriages, or families), they assume that behavior and the underlying processes determining behavior are universal and therefore that theoretical models are generalizable, at least in principle. Because of their generalizability, social scientific studies dominate published research and textbooks in family communication.

Even among family communication scholars using social scientific approaches, however, there is substantial disagreement about the nature of the phenomena under investigation and consequently, the appropriateness of qualitative and quantitative methods, respectively. The disagreement fundamentally concerns the significance of meaning for human behavior and researchers' ability to assess meaning. For qualitative researchers, meaning is central to human behavior, is created in the interaction, and ultimately is dependent on processes specific to the participants or the interaction.

Consequently, meaning cannot be objectively assessed, and researchers must rely on some form of interpretation that is informed by the participants and/or the researchers' thorough knowledge of the participants or interaction. Furthermore, participants as well as observers of social processes can assign divergent meaning to the same processes, thus creating divergent social realities. Qualitative theories, then, function mainly as heuristic devices that enable understanding of how social processes might be understood, with no claim being made that this understanding reflects an objective reality.

Quantitative researchers, by contrast, either do not assume that meaning is as central to human behavior or they assume that the processes by which individuals assign meaning are universal (or at least sufficiently shared in a culture, for example). For them, therefore, objective observation is possible, and research should rely heavily on inferential statistics to interpret findings. The purpose of theory in quantitative social science is to model relationships between key variables to explain and predict psychological or behavioral outcomes. Theories are developed and tested by comparing their predictions to observed outcomes, which allows for falsification of a theory.

Shared Assumptions

Despite the numerous disagreements among family communication researchers about crucial aspects of human communication and relationships, there seems to be general agreement that families constitute social systems. With this view come a number of basic assumptions, most importantly that of *nonsummativity* and *interdependence*. Nonsummativity means that families are more than the sum of their parts—that is, they cannot be understood by even a complete understanding of individual family members in isolation. Rather, crucial processes and outcomes are the result of the interaction between family members, and these interactions add to the family. Similarly, interdependence in the family context means that family members influence one another and that their behavior cannot be understood without taking account of their families. It also suggests that a change in the behavior of any one family member affects all other family members as well.

Another important shared assumption among family communication scholars is that families are best defined using transactional-functional rather than structural definitions. Transactional-functional definitions use criteria based on how families interact and what they do to determine which groups of persons constitute families. Examples are definitions that include criteria such as shared household responsibilities, problem solving, and children rearing, for example. Structural definitions, in contrast, define families based on the presence of certain members, such as the definition of family as consisting of parent(s) and their biological and/or adopted child(ren). Because structural definitions exclude a large number of what obviously are families, they have fallen out of favor with most researchers. The ostensible exceptions are theories that explicitly address structural characteristics of families, such as theories of stepfamilies or of adopted families. But even here the structural characteristics are of interest because they are assumed to impact how families interact or function. Thus, the structural criterion is really a proxy for what essentially are transactional-functional characteristics.

Representative Family Communication Theories

As the preceding discussion has shown, there is significant disagreement among family communication scholars about even the most fundamental assumptions of theory and research. Consequently, it is impossible to present any one family communication theory as typical for, or representative of, the field. Nonetheless, this entry concludes with some examples of family communication theories that have reached a fair degree of sophistication and elaboration and also have had significant impact on the field. They are presented here to give the reader an idea about the range of family communication theories and not to suggest that these are necessarily the best or most important theories of family communication.

Circumplex Model of Family Functioning

One interesting theory of family communication originating from another discipline is the circumplex model of family functioning, attributable to David Olson and his colleagues. It is unique among outside theories because communication is a central concept in the theory and is defined in sophisticated terms. It is also among the broadest theories of family communication because it links family communication to family functioning in general, which it associates with a large array of child and family outcomes. The model assesses family functioning based on cohesion and adaptability of families, which exist along continua from disengaged to enmeshed and from rigid to chaotic, respectively. Moderate levels on both dimensions are associated with optimal functioning, whereas extremes on either dimension are associated with less than optimal functioning. Thus, families that are separated or engaged function better than families that are either disengaged or enmeshed, and families that are flexible or structured function better than families that are rigid or chaotic. Considering both dimensions simultaneously, families that are medium on both dimensions function best, followed by families that are medium on one dimension but extreme on the other dimension, and families that are extreme on both dimensions are the least functional.

Family communication in the circumplex model is a third, facilitating dimension. This means that family communication determines families' location along the two dimensions of cohesion and adaptability. Communication also enables families to change their cohesion and adaptability, which is particularly important for the application of the circumplex model to family therapy. Specific communication skills identified in the model that facilitate such movements include speaking skills, such as speaking for self and avoiding speaking for others; listening skills, such as active listening and empathy; and general communication skills, such as self-disclosure, clarity, continuity, tracking, and showing respect and regard for one another.

Family Communication Patterns Theory

One theory emerging from within the communication discipline that links communication behaviors in families to a similarly wide range of family and child outcomes is family communication patterns theory (FCPT) developed by Mary Anne Fitzpatrick and her colleagues. FCPT is based on the assumption that creating shared social reality is a basic function of family communication. Families create shared reality through two communication behaviors: *conversation* orientation and *conformity* orientation, which in turn affect family relationships and outcomes. Conversation orientation refers to frequent and unrestrained communication between parents and children with the purpose of codiscovering the meaning of symbols and objects that constitute the social environment. It is associated with warm and supportive relationships characterized by mutual respect and concern for one another. Conformity orientation, in contrast, refers to more restricted communication between parents and children in which the parents define social reality for the family. It is associated with more authoritarian parenting and less concern for the children's thoughts and feelings.

Theoretically orthogonal or independent, these two orientations define four family types. *Consensual* families are high on both conversation and conformity orientation. Their communication is characterized by a tension between open exploration, on the one hand, and pressure to agree and to preserve the existing hierarchy within the family, on the other hand. Families resolve this tension by parents listening to their children while simultaneously persuading them to adopt the parents' belief system. These families are well functioning and have superior outcomes for all family members.

Pluralistic families emphasize conversation orientation over conformity orientation. Their communication is characterized by open and unconstrained interactions involving all family members. Although parents are open about their values and beliefs in these families, they do not aim to control their children and accept their children's different opinions. Children of these families learn to be independent and autonomous and to communicate persuasively, and they are generally satisfied with their family relationships.

Protective families emphasize conformity over conversation orientation. Their communication is characterized by parental authority and child obedience and by little concern for conceptual matters. Parents in these families decide for their children and see little value in explaining their reasoning to them, although they clearly state rules and expect their children to follow them. Children in protective families learn to rely on rules for behaving; there is little value accorded to family discussions to figure things out, and

children tend not to trust their own decision-making abilities.

Laissez-faire families are low on both conformity and conversation orientation. Their communication is characterized by infrequent and typically uninvolving interactions. Members of laissez-faire families are emotionally divorced from one another and have little interest in the thoughts and feelings of others. Children of these families learn that there is little value in family conversations and that they have to make their own decisions. Because they do receive little behavioral guidance from their parents, they question their decision-making ability and are more susceptible to external influences from peers and media.

Family communication patterns have been associated with a number of family processes, such as conflict, confirmation and affection, family rituals, and understanding. They also have been associated with child outcomes, such as communication apprehension, conflict with romantic partners, resiliency, and children's mental and physical health.

Dialectical Theory of Family Communication

An example of an important interpersonal communication theory that has been particularly popular with family communication scholars is dialectical theory. Based on the dialectical thinking of Leslie Baxter and others, dialectical theory proposes that family communication is the result of dialectical, or opposing and inherently incompatible, goals pursued by families and family members. Unlike Hegel's dialectics, which are resolved through a synthesis of the opposing forces, relational dialectics are not permanently resolved, but the back and forth between forces permeates family communication and gives meaning to it. Although dialectical tensions can be experienced in a number of relationship domains, the most relevant ones to families are those of affiliation, predictability, and closeness; these can be experienced in intrafamilial relationships, as well as in the relationships of families with their social environment. Although dialectics are irresolvable, they are often experienced as threatening to family relationships, and families employ various strategies to manage them. Not all of these strategies are equally effective and equally functional, however. Some strategies, such as attempts to integrate opposing desires into the family and to reaffirm the centrality and interdependence of the relationship, usually lead to more positive outcomes, whereas others, such as denial or disorientation, usually lead to more negative outcomes.

Although dialectical tensions are assumed to affect all family communication, the specific dialectics experienced by each family are unique, and their effects depend to a large extent on the meaning given to them by family members. As a result, research employing dialectical theory most frequently relies on qualitative research methods.

Affective Exchange Theory

One example of a family communication theory addressing a relatively narrow phenomenon in family communication while simultaneously being grounded in and testing a metatheoretical framework is affective exchange theory (AET). AET is different from most other theories of family communication, which typically investigate how humans communicate without explicitly considering the roots of human communication, because it explicitly makes and tests the assumption that human communication is shaped by evolutionary processes. By arguing that humans' ability to experience and express affection was selected for because it created significant benefits in terms of survival and reproduction, AET connects to the large and powerful explanatory framework of human behavior that evolutionary theory provides.

Tying AET to the theory of evolution also led to very specific and unique hypotheses about family communication. For example, evolutionary theory would suggest that parental affection functions to enable one's offspring to survive and propagate. Consequently, fathers should be more affectionate with children that do propagate the father's genes—biological as opposed to stepchildren and heterosexual as opposed to bisexual or homosexual sons, for example. Both predictions were supported.

In addition, AET has been investigated mainly in the context of father–son relationships. Not only did this provide important information on an underresearched family relationship, but also demonstrated the importance of affection in nonromantic interpersonal relationships. Furthermore, by looking at how father–son communication changes in subsequent generations, research using the AET framework was also able to demonstrate

the concurrent influence of evolutionary forces and cultural forces, thereby further demonstrating that genes and culture both play important roles in the behavior of families.

Ascan F. Koerner

See also Communibiology; Critical Theory; Epistemology; Family and Marital Schemas and Types; Relational Communication Theory; Relational Dialectics; Scientific Approach; Social Construction of Reality; System Theory

Further Readings

Baxter, L. A. (2006). Relational dialectics theory: Multivocal dialogues of family communication. In D. O. Braithwaite & L. A. Baxter (Eds.), *Engaging theories in family communication: Multiple perspectives* (pp. 130–145). Thousand Oaks, CA: Sage.

Baxter, L.A., & Braithwaite, D. O. (2006). Introduction: Metatheroy and theory in family communication research. In D. O. Braithwaite & L. A. Baxter (Eds.), *Engaging theories in family communication: Multiple perspectives* (pp. 1–15). Thousand Oaks, CA: Sage.

Floyd, K. (2001). Human affection exchange I: Reproductive probability as a predictor of men's affection with their sons. *Journal of Men's Studies, 10,* 39–50.

Koerner, A. F., & Fitzpatrick, M. A. (2004). Communication in intact families. In A. Vangelisti (Ed.), *Handbook of family communication* (pp. 177–195). Mahwah, NJ: Lawrence Erlbaum.

Olson, D. H., Sprenkle, D. H., & Russell, C. S. (1979). Circumplex model of marital and family systems: Cohesion and adaptability dimensions, family types, and clinical applications. *Family Process, 18,* 3–28.

Fans, Fandom, and Fan Studies

The word *fan* has been in constant use since the 19th century, and the term *fandom* dates from the turn of the 20th century. Fan and fandom initially denoted sports-club fans and soon after, the quickly growing fanbase of science fiction. Organized fan communities existed before these groups, however; readers of Sir Arthur Conan Doyle's stories, for example, corresponded with his fictional creation and mourned Sherlock

Holmes's death. In all cases, fan implies some or all the following: a fascination, interest, and emotional investment in a particular subject; (often communal) engagement with a particular leisure activity; and an emphasis on amateur endeavors.

Fan studies is situated mainly in two areas: the social sciences and film and media studies. Psychology and sociology study the group behavior of fans as well as the passionate engagement with and possession of objects that appear uninteresting or ridiculous to others. Sports, music, and film fans are likely subjects, and the culture at large tends to accept them more readily—sports fandom, possibly because of its masculine connotations of physical exertion and competition; music and film fandom, mostly as passing teenage behavior. In fact, the more extreme edges of fandom such as football hooligans or punks tend to be seen as exceptions rather than fannish representatives. Film and media studies focuses mostly on the relation between media texts and their audiences, looking toward fans as often exemplary readers-viewers. The following will restrict itself to research and debates within fan studies that focus on television, film, and new media, with its adjacent focus on science fiction, comics, gaming, and related fields.

In media fandom, adult fans—especially of less respected and marginal cultural objects such as science fiction or television shows—often are regarded with suspicion and reproached for wasting their energies. Whereas dressing up may be acceptable for children, cosplay (i.e., costuming in media characters) is not; whereas playacting is fine on the playground and theatre stage, larping (i.e., live action role-playing games) is pathologized; whereas making up stories about one's favorite characters is a beloved tradition shared in many bedtime rituals, fan fiction is regarded less positively. Yet these examples suggest that fan behavior is an extension of behavior considered acceptable in general culture. In fact, much recent fan-studies discourse has begun to look at fannish behavior rather than fannish identity, thus suggesting that everyone may be a fan of sorts.

Especially in media studies, where the media convergence of industry and audiences encourages fannish modes of engagement, the gap is narrowing between fully immersed fans exchanging stories, analyses, and interpretations among themselves and casual viewers hitting up the bulletin board of a favorite show to discuss it after an episode airs. Media fans thus are at the center of a media convergence of text and context, producer and consumer, appropriation and ownership; they showcase ideal investment in a media product and its transmedia branding and the marketing strategies of their communities.

Media convergence also affects industry discourses around viewers and fans. Although the borders between professionals and fans always have been permeable, the past decade has celebrated the rise of the auteur fan boy in such show runners as Joss Whedon (*Buffy the Vampire Slayer*, *Angel: The Series*), Russell T. Davies (*Dr. Who*), and Ron Moore (*Battlestar Galactica*) as well as an increasing interest in fan-generated and fan-created content, such as fan-created advertisements or even episode writing contests. Fans are ever present in the contemporary media landscape, and fandom is growing both more mainstream and more difficult to define as a result. In a climate in which fannish behavior is becoming more normalized and more marketable, fan research has become a subdiscipline that interrogates the very definitions of fan, fandom, and fan studies.

History

U.S. science fiction fandom initially organized in the 1920s around Hugo Gernsback's "pulp" magazines, which published science fiction stories on cheap paper. These publications actively invited commentary from readers, which they then printed in dedicated letters sections. This focus from the text to commentary and readers and the inclusion of mailing addresses allowed fans to communicate with one another unmediated. As fans communicated with one another, they began to form clubs and organize conventions that offered ways not only to meet with one another, but also to connect with professionals. Many famous science fiction editors and writers, such as Isaac Asimov, James Blish, and Frederik Pohl, started out as members of fandom. Demographics were overwhelmingly White and male, both among professional science fiction writers and their fans.

The late 1960s saw a substantial split that would become important for fan studies, media studies, and audience research. With the rise of *Star Trek* and televisual science fiction in general, some fans—mostly women—began creating their own fanzines that focused less on criticism and scientific debates and more on creative responses. This rise of media fandom shifted fan focus away from plot and action and foregrounded characters and character interaction, often creatively expanding the fictional universes or interpolating missing scenes and backgrounds. However, what would become known as fan fiction had existed at least since readers wrote sequels to Jane Austen and *Sherlock Holmes* novels—if not since ancient retellings of Homer or John Lydgate's self-insertion into the *Canterbury Tales*. Nevertheless, media fandom was new in its organization and community focus.

Logistically, media fandom created a strong, self-aware community by using the infrastructure of science fiction fandom: conventions, APAs (Amateur Press Association, the compilation and distribution of amateur writing to all its contributing members), and fanzines (amateur publication, sold at cost to interested parties). Whereas conventions allowed fans to meet, create personal connections, and initiate new members, APAs and fanzines allowed fans to stay in contact and disseminated creative interpretations via fan fiction and fan art, often criticizing or expanding the stories provided by the media industry and illustrating their beloved characters and stories.

Throughout the 1970s and 1980s, media fandom was a small but solid community situated around various fannish sources. The Internet and rise of digital technologies afforded fans the ability to connect and communicate more easily. Fandom began to grow exponentially, its demographics shifting to include more and younger television viewers. From local bulletin boards in the 1980s through Usenet newsgroups and diverse mailing lists and archives in the 1990s to social networking sites like LiveJournal.com, fandoms have shifted, expanded, and changed to accommodate ever-changing technologies at the same time as they manipulate these interfaces to fit their demands. Meanwhile, as visual and audiovisual editing programs become more affordable and easier to use, more fans create more varied fannish artifacts. Fan works today range from poems, short stories, and multivolume novels to drawings, comics, photo manipulations, and fan vids, cartoons, and multimedia installations.

Fannish behavior is becoming more mainstream as new technologies make it easier to access media, engage with others, and create one's own content. In turn, the media industry has recognized the marketing potential of both transmedia products and user-generated content as forms of viral marketing. Meanwhile, fandoms as diverse as gaming, comics, anime, music, literature, celebrity, and sports find increasing contacts and influence one another with such fan creations as real-people fiction, which connects celebrity and fan fiction cultures or fantasy baseball, ultimately bringing narrative elements into sports fandom. The image of the extreme fan as subcultural identity is thus giving way to fannish engagement as marketable and transferable behavior that crosses interests and objects. Media fandom has grown in 40 years from a handful of women sharing their fan works to an online phenomenon that has projected fans into the limelight of media research as ideal viewers of media, early adapters and adopters of technological interfaces, and exemplary creators of user-generated content.

Research

Research into fans and fandom comes from a number of disciplines, most particularly sociology, psychology, and anthropology on the one hand, and English, communication, and media studies on the other. Whereas the former tend to look at the psychology of individuals as well as group dynamics, often with a focus on the more visible and acceptable sports fandoms, the latter tend to connect media texts to fannish communities, often working within postmodern theoretical frameworks that read culture as a text in its own right. As Kimberly Schimmel, C. Lee Harrington, and Denise Bielby note, fan studies divides theoretically along the lines of fannish objects, with more psychological interpretations of sports fans and fandoms on one side, and more cultural studies approaches to celebrity and media fans and fandoms on the other.

Most of current media fan studies can be traced to an increased research focus on audiences as well as an interest among cultural studies' scholars in subcultural communities, starting in the 1970s. The Birmingham School may be the single most influential theoretical framework for fan studies. Stuart Hall's viewer paradigm is an influential example of audience studies and reader response: He distinguished between different modes of viewing strategies in which viewers are not necessarily passive and easily manipulated, but instead can choose to agree or reject the dominant message of the text, to incorporate or resist the media text's ideology. Similarly emphasizing active engagement with cultural texts, Dick Hebdidge's work on resistant subcultures also became a desirable paradigm. As a result, fan studies of the 1980s and 1990s emphasized both the outsider status of fans and their subversive status.

The most central and influential studies connected these two interests by looking at the subcultural communities of female media fans of *Star Trek* (and other TV shows) who constituted an active audience that critiqued, interpreted, and often altered the source text of the shows of which they were fans: Henry Jenkins' *Textual Poachers* and Camille Bacon-Smith's *Enterprising Women* both closely studied these particular communities and argued for their creative and often resistant readings, thus positing fans as an exemplary audience. Rather than being passive consumers, these television viewers engaged critically and creatively; this allowed fan scholars to present a model of audience engagement that complicated earlier notions of media as simplistic ideological tools and exemplified the more complex and politically more desirable subversive viewers. Moreover, given that these studies focused primarily on creative fandom responses such as fan fiction, fan art, filk, and fan vids and that these communities were largely female, creative fan responses were often read with and against a feminist paradigm, celebrating the critical feminist take on an often misogynist media culture.

This emphasis on resistance and subversion was challenged by the next generation of scholars. Understanding fannishness as a natural aspect of human engagement, these scholars rejected the central ethos of fans as resistant and subversive viewers that had dominated the field of fan studies in the 1980s and 1990s. Nicholas Abercrombie and Brian Longhurst opposed the incorporation-resistance paradigm with a spectacle-performance paradigm. Rather than viewing fan behavior through the lens of a political or social agenda that read fan activities as subversive and thus worthy of studying, this approach to fan studies focused on engagements with media as an everyday part of

audiences' lives. In turn, Matt Hills' *Fan Cultures* and Cornel Sandvoss's *Fans* focus on the psychology of fans and fan groups and the ways fannish objects get constituted in the fans' imagination. Both studies focus on fans as individuals who might be fannish at different times and to different degrees about various things.

Considerable range characterizes contemporary fan studies: Jenkins' *Convergence Culture* focuses on the various intersections between industry and viewers-fans; Karen Hellekson and Kristina Busse's *Fan Fiction and Fan Communities in the Age of the Internet* gathers a group of academics who are all active fans to discuss specific texts and issues in the particularly active and self-aware subset of fans usually defined as media fans. Jonathan Gray, Sandvoss, and Harrington's *Fandom* stretches the definitions of fandom to study international, high culture, and antifans—issues otherwise ignored. Together they address the variety of issues that face the role of fans and the focus of fan studies in the changing environment of online engagement, industry awareness, and an ever-growing and more activist fan community.

Debates

Possibly the most central debate in fan studies at present is the relationship between fandom and audiences at large. Fannish behavior is becoming ever-more mainstream as the media industry purposefully tries to court audiences by offering transmedia entertainment, such as online games, background character information, or Webisodes, and community-building spaces, such as bulletin boards or chat rooms. After all, fans are the most loyal viewers, willing to buy tie-in products, and thus are ideal candidates for viral marketing campaigns. Jenkins's *Convergence Culture* describes how ever-more involved and active audiences are changing media culture as well as how the media industry can make use of these behavioral shifts in useful and economically successful ways.

One result of this convergence culture is a need to redefine the concept of what constitutes a fan and how we define fandom. One way to characterize the current definitional debates is around distinctions made between fannish identity and fannish behavior. For some, being a fan is defined by behavior only, whereas for others an entire ethos is attached to the term. The question is whether members of fandom are a subculture in their own right or whether they are simply consumers displaying certain actions and behaviors. On the one hand, fan studies scholars identify fans as a particular group of people; on the other, they create a spectrum of behavior in which fans are merely on an extreme end of a fandom continuum. Fans thus are either described as simply a more extreme version of viewers (thus being able to create fans) or regarded as engaging media with different intensity and investment that resembles particular forms of identity politics.

Sandvoss's *Fans*, for example, puts forth singular and personalized understanding of fans, where being a fan is primarily constituted by the individual's emotional relationship to a particular text, group, or idea. In fact, his study can easily encompass sports as well as media fans since he is most interested in the affective investment of the individual rather than the communities they create. Meanwhile, other scholars want to focus more on the real communities that get created around fannish objects, many of whom are more invested in one another and the friendships and things they have created than the affect in the fannish object. Members of fan-fiction communities, for example, often identify as media fans rather than as fans of a particular show, thus showing their higher identification with the community of other readers and writers than with other fans of a show.

Such an emphasis on community also challenges another aspect of convergence culture, namely the complicated role of fan as consumer. Traditionally, one of the central tenets of fandom has been its anticapitalist character: Often termed a gift culture of paying it forward, large sections of fandom rely on volunteer labor and a proud amateurism. As media industry begins to realize the potential of free producers, they have begun exploiting fans who happily provide free content to commercial Web sites without any reimbursement. Current debates among fans and fan academics revolve around fannish attempts to create completely alternate fannish infrastructures that honor the fannish gift economy as well as efforts to adequately reward fannish labor. In all cases, however, fans have to contend with a media industry that celebrates user-generated content as free and viral marketing yet retains the right to sue unauthorized fan productions for copyright or trademark infringements.

Other areas of debate include the question of range, both in terms of object and range of subjects. Often models developed by looking at Western fans and behaviors do not easily apply to non-Western fandoms and fans. Other current directions in research include antifans, which describes viewers who show similarly intensely negative investments in a text. Finally, the focus on popular culture has limited fan studies to look at particular fans only, often ignoring fans of highbrow subjects, such as opera, literature, or philosophy. Looking at behavior rather than objects of interest offers insight into the way fan studies has focused too narrowly on television and other popular media. Instead it might be more fruitful to look at similarities: fannish modes of behavior occur in many different venues, from history buffs and philatelists to bird watchers and knitters.

Fans have been a central force of popular culture for more than a century, often mocked or derided in turn, but more recently viewed by the industry as loyal consumers and by academia as exemplars of media engagement. The Internet has brought more and more viewers to engage with programs across multiple platforms and to become emotionally invested in different forms of entertainment. That investment and engagement results in water-cooler conversations and visits to shows' Web sites; it propels viewers to write up their thoughts in blogs and discuss their ideas on bulletin boards; it inspires people to create fiction and art and videos; it moves them to play the characters in role-playing games and to make costumes and dress up as their favorite one. And while much of this user-generated creative content is encouraged and supported by the industry, fans often move beyond expected responses, both in form and content. Fans themselves may like the validation of what they call the powers that be, but many like their independence even more. Fannish creations may not all be subversive or transformative by nature. However, fandom's affective engagement with the media text, the fan communities constituted in the process, and the very acts of creation and sharing, may together constitute a creative culture that resists media convergence models, one fan work at a time.

Kristina Busse

See also Audience Theories; Cultural Studies; Gender and Media; Media and Mass Communication Theories; New Media Theory

Further Readings

Bacon-Smith, C. (1992). *Enterprising women: Television fandom and the creation of popular myth.* Philadelphia: University of Pennsylvania Press.

Bacon-Smith, C. (2000). *Science fiction culture.* Philadelphia: University of Pennsylvania Press.

Baym, N. K. (2000). *Tune in, log on: Soaps, fandom, and online community.* Thousand Oaks, CA: Sage.

Gray, J., Sandvoss, C., & Harrington, C. L. (Eds.). (2007). *Fandom: Identities and communities in a mediated world.* New York: New York University Press.

Hellekson, K., & Busse, K. (Eds.). (2006). *Fan fiction and fan communities in the age of the Internet.* Jefferson, NC: McFarland.

Hills, M. (2002). *Fan cultures.* London: Routledge.

Jenkins, H. (1992). *Textual poachers: Television fans and participatory culture.* New York: Routledge.

Jenkins, H. (2006). *Convergence culture.* New York: New York University Press.

Sanders J. L. (Eds.). (1994). *Science fiction fandom.* Westport, CT: Greenwood Press.

Sandvoss, C. (2005). *Fans: The mirror of consumption.* Cambridge, UK: Polity Press.

Schimmel, K. S., Harrington, C. L., & Bielby, D. D. (2007). Keep your fans to yourself: The disjuncture between sport studies and pop culture studies' perspectives on fandom. *Sport in Society, 10,* 580–600.

Verba, J. M. (1996). *Boldly writing: A Trekker fan and zine history, 1967–1987* (2nd ed.). Minnetonka, MN: FTL.

FEEDBACK

See Cybernetics

FEMINIST COMMUNICATION THEORIES

Feminist communication theories place women and their experiences at the center of the study of communication and production of theory. Feminist communication theories offer explanations and speculations about the communicative strategies used to oppress women as well as those used by women to overcome that oppression. The range of feminist theories that address communication is broad, and this body of scholarship could be organized in many different ways. Covered below are the theories related to language and gender, access to the public sphere and voice within that sphere, the ways feminist communication theorists theorize about feminism and theory, and theories of masculinity and identity.

Language and Gender

Early feminist communication theories attempted to address the connections between gender, sex, and styles of communication. Such scholars as Dale Spender, Julia Penelope Wolf, Cheris Kramarae (formerly Kramer), Robin Lakoff, Hélène Cixous, and Luce Irigaray, among others, began to theorize about the ways gender constrained and influenced women's and men's communication styles and practices. These theorists argued that language is man-made—that it has been controlled by men for centuries and reflects a bias toward masculine styles of communication as well as masculine ideologies. Feminist theorists suggested that societal expectations of how women and men should behave have a powerful impact on the ways a person communicates. According to these scholars, women are prone, for example, to use more tentative language and to ask more questions in a conversation while men are prone to use more forceful language and to interrupt more. Women, too, according to Cixous, Julia Kristeva, and Irigaray, must rewrite and reclaim language so that it reflects a woman-centered ideology rather than one grounded in male perspectives and politics.

Marsha Houston and Kramarae followed these earlier theories with work that suggested that not only did a person's sex or gender influence their communication styles, but also did a person's ethnic, cultural, and economic backgrounds. Most recently, scholars such as Amy Richards and Jennifer Bumgardner suggest that feminist theorizing works to explore and explain the reasons that specific labels, such as *feminist* or *bitch,* are interpreted differently by different genders and age groups.

Feminist theorizing in this area also suggests that when individuals violate gendered expectations for communication, they exist in a double-bind state. Kathleen Hall Jamieson, for example, suggests that women in a variety of workplaces face opposing and contradictory expectations regarding communication: Women are supposed to communicate in a more masculine style, but when they do, they are deemed unfeminine and penalized. The result is a double bind for women, with penalties for choosing either option. Similarly, feminist theorists such as Elizabeth Bell and Kim Golombisky are currently exploring the gendered, raced, and classed nature of the classroom and theorizing the gendered and raced double binds in which students, as well as instructors, find themselves as they attempt to communicate with one another. Judith Butler moves theory regarding gendered expectations even further, suggesting that gender itself is a performance and that individuals both do and undo gender as they perform personhood. For Butler, theories of communication must explain the ways individuals negotiate, resist, and transcend their identities in a highly gendered society.

Feminist communication theorists also consider the impact of a person's sex or gender on their language in the realm of political oratory. Karlyn Kohrs Campbell and others address the question of whether or not women orators possess a feminine style of public speaking. This feminine style reflects the use of concrete rather than abstract reasoning, a personal and self-disclosive tone, and audience participation. Scholars theorizing about this feminine style offer explanations and theories for what may be the unique communicative choices women orators make as they communicate in the political and public realm.

Access to the Public Sphere and Voice Within That Sphere

Feminist communication theories also address the questions of who actually has access to the public sphere, has a voice in that sphere, and ways the communication discipline has constrained what is considered important public discourse. Scholarship in this area includes the identification of a rich history of women orators who have been ignored and neglected by the discipline—in effect denied access to the rhetorical tradition's view of the public sphere. This aspect of feminist communication theory is sometimes labeled *revalorist* theory and considered to be a recovery project, as it identifies and honors women's actual presence in history and celebrates the communication of these important historical figures. Feminist communication theory in this vein identifies and describes women orators who have been neglected historically and is exemplified in several anthologies of key women speakers, most notably those compiled by Patricia Scileppi Kennedy and Gloria Hartmann O'Shields and by Campbell.

This recovery project also includes the identification of women who likely influenced the rhetorical tradition centuries ago. This effort, begun by Andrea Lundsford and taken up by many other feminist communication theorists, calls attention to such women as Aspasia, Diotoma, and Christine de Pisan, who likely had a strong voice in classical and medieval times, but who have been erased and ignored as significant contributors to the communication or rhetorical tradition. Feminist communication theorists who take up this recovery effort also are exploring ways that women such as Maria Miller Stewart, Sarah Grimke, and Angelina Grimke, and more recently, Ella Baker and Anita Hill, have been driven from the public sphere. This communication theory attempts to explain the strategies used by those with power to prevent these women, and others like them, from gaining a voice in political discussions. It also seeks to understand the unique and important approaches to communication taken by these women and the ways they overcame some of the oppression they faced.

When considering access to the public sphere from a feminist organizational communication perspective, scholars such as Patrice Buzzanell and Karen Ashcraft, as well as others, work to theorize the presence of, as well as roles and constraints faced by, women in their workplaces. Feminist communication theory in this arena is focused on understanding how organizations construct particular identities for women and men, how feminist and women's organizations struggle to maintain their place in a hegemonic structure that privileges profit and power over social justice and sustainability, and how the discourses in the popular culture constrain and construct assumptions about best practices in an organization. Feminist theory in this arena also seeks to redefine what is viewed as an organization and what counts as "good work," calling attention to patriarchal definitions and practices that are antithetical to feminist principles.

Media scholars also have focused their theorizing on access. In doing so, they began to develop theories of spectatorship. In her foundational work in feminist film theory, for example, Laura Mulvey argues that Hollywood film casts all members of an audience in a particular subject position—that of the male or masculine identity. Thus, all viewers of a film, whether male or female, must adopt a male—and sexist—gaze when viewing films. Spectatorship, Mulvey theorizes, requires that women see themselves through the eyes of a sexist male person and as objects to be watched rather than as active agents in the narrative. Scholars after Mulvey suggested that the gaze may not be as disempowering to female viewers as Mulvey originally claimed and added that that view was also racist, homophobic, and classed.

In attempting to explain the lack of presence and voice in the public sphere for extremely marginalized women, many scholars began to articulate and develop a feminist postcolonial theoretical approach. Cindy Griffin suggested that the public sphere is built on essentialist principles that prevent women from being seen as legitimate communicators in that sphere. Scholars such as Gayatri Spivak, Radha Hegde, and Raka Shome, among others, explored theories of subalternity to explain women's complete lack of voice in the public sphere. These theorists suggest that under extreme conditions of oppression, the social definitions, views, and expectations of women and their voices prevent those in positions of power from even hearing their communicative attempts. As this feminist postcolonial theorizing moved into the realms of media studies, scholars explained the ways that the narratives told in popular film and television erased completely the voices of minority individuals, female and male, and replaced them with White, hegemonic, and masculine voices. As Shome suggests, minority voices are erased as White masculinity talks for all about that which is good and heroic as well as representing all that is positive in a foreign culture—doing so far better than those native to that culture.

Feminist communication theory also has attempted to understand women's lack of presence in the public sphere by studying what might be labeled nontraditional communication modes and practices. Karen Foss and Sonja Foss, for example, suggest that in order to understand women's communication and their eloquence, scholars must acknowledge women's letter writing, baking, gardening, graffiti, fashion design, and even motherhood, among other forms of expression, as rich sources and important examples of women's efforts to communicate. Mary Rose Williams suggests that women's quilting has been an avenue of political expression and resistance for women for centuries. Similarly, Williams argues that Francis Willard's refusal to abide by the social norms of her era and her insistence on riding a bicycle is a powerful example of nontraditional, yet effective, modes of communication. Additionally, theorists are exploring such venues as abortion clinics, guerilla theatre and street performances, and discourses around eating disorders and depression as ways of theorizing feminist communication outside the traditional boundaries of what important communication can be.

Finally, theory in the area of who can and is speaking addresses the question of how the communication discipline constrains and silences certain voices. In one of the first theoretical essays to take up this issue, Carole Spitzack (now Daurna) and Kathryn Carter identified several ways the discipline allowed women's communication to be included as data for study and later published a comprehensive anthology exploring ways that the masculine bias in the discipline systematically prevented women's communication from gaining legitimacy. Campbell and Kristin Vonnegut added to this conversation, theorizing specifically about the exclusion of women from public address studies, as did Sheryl Perlmutter Bowen and Nancy Wyatt, who theorized about the ways this exclusion occurred in the various branches of the discipline (organizational communication, performance studies, intercultural communication, and the like). In an essay awarded the National Communication Association's Golden Monograph award, Carol Blair, Julie Brown, and Leslie Baxter expose the constraining nature of the blind-review process for journal publication, the hostility feminist scholarship often faces in the review process, and the ways feminist voices are "disciplined." As these scholars theorize the ways that the discipline has constrained women's voices and research, they call attention to long-held beliefs and biases regarding scholarship. They expose the ways those beliefs and biases silence feminist scholarship and theory and constrain their understanding of the diversity of communication styles and practices.

Theorizing About Theory and Feminism

As feminist communication scholars began to theorize from a feminist perspective, they also sought to define theory, feminist theory, and feminism for themselves. Guided by the question, "What makes scholarship feminist?" answers and explanations addressed the nature of theorizing and scholarship, as well as the inclusive or exclusive nature of definitions of feminism. In 1985, Kramarae, Paula Treichler, and Beth Stafford published their anthology, *For Alma Mater: Feminist Scholarship in Theory and Practice,* and in 1988, the editors of the journal *Women's Studies in Communication* asked a variety of feminist scholars to offer their versions of feminism and feminist scholarship. These efforts suggest that two of the foundational pieces of feminist scholarship are a commitment to explorations of the many ways gender is constructed and communicated as well as a desire for self-reflexivity.

Early theories about what scholars mean by theory also suggest that the traditional definition of theory as an objective body of facts, which must be tested again and again over time in order to be credible, is a sexist and patriarchal notion of theory. Feminist theorists began to challenge this definition and to suggest that theory, from a feminist perspective, required neither testable fact nor objectivity, but was instead a subjective compilation of explanations that were highly contextual, bound by the ideologies of the researcher, and deeply influenced by the social milieu from which they emerged. Nancy Harding explained that each individual theorized from a particular standpoint, rather than any objective view, and called for an acknowledgment of this standpoint not only in feminist research but in all research. S. Foss and K. Foss, and Kramarae and Spender, among others, rejected the traditional view of theory as produced by an objective researcher who stood outside of and apart from the researched. They also rejected the view of theory as a linear explanation that breaks a communication event into its parts, or as a singular, finished truth. Instead, they

suggested that theory, defined from a feminist perspective, relies on researcher subjectivity, collaboration between the researcher and those who participate in the study, and seeing and honoring interconnections, process, and multiple truths.

Feminist theorists also took up the complicated task of defining feminism and how those definitions influenced communication theories and scholarship. Bonnie Dow, as well as Helene Shugart, Catherine Waggoner, and Lynn O'Brien Hallstien, for example, offered theories to explain second- and third-wave feminism and the communication practices that could be linked to or shared across each wave. Other scholars considered how a definition of feminism might influence the type of communication a scholar studied and the ways that communication might be studied. Sally Gearhart, Griffin, S. Foss, and K. Foss, for example, suggested that a patriarchal bias exists in the foundations and traditions of communication scholarship. Feminism, these scholars argue, challenges those foundations and traditions and, among other things, asks that we expand our most venerated terms, practices, and assumptions. Houston, defining feminism as necessarily including a recognition of racial and ethnic differences, also argues that a bias exists in our foundational assumptions and practices, a bias that disregards the communication styles and practices of Black women and men.

Other feminist theorists, however, challenged this call for a reconceptualization of foundational principles and practices. Celeste Condit, for example, rejects the call for reconceptualization, suggesting instead that feminism is inherently aware of gender diversity and that this awareness, rather than the revision of foundational assumptions, is enough to remedy discrimination and oppression. For Condit, feminist theory must embrace a postmodern view of gender and open itself to shifting, fragmented, context-bound identities and theories rather than challenge venerated theories and assumptions. As feminist scholars continue to explore the feminist nature of their theorizing and the unique components of that theorizing, they call attention to the underlying assumptions embedded in any body of theory. These conversations and even disagreements suggest that feminist communication theories are anything but a unified and homogenous collection of perspectives, political views, and explanations for communication.

Masculinity and Identity

Although important to feminist communication theory, explanations of the construction and deconstruction of masculinities and identities (as raced and sexualized) are just beginning receive extensive and systematic attention from feminist communication scholars. The work of Nick Trujillo, who studied baseball player Nolan Ryan, is an early example of feminist communication theory and attention to questions of masculinity. Similarly, the more recent theories of Thomas Nakayama and Robert Kriezek and Michelle Holling and Bernadette Calafell, among others, take up questions of masculinity, sexuality, ethnicity, and cultural identities. These scholars offer theories that assist in understanding how communication norms, expectations, and practices constrain individuals, locking them into prescribed subject positions and communication practices. Feminist scholars also are turning attention to and theorizing resistance and heteronormative femininity as theoretical tools that help understand lesbian identities, disabled identities, eating disorders, and sexual assault in constructive and productive ways. The goal of this body of theorizing is to call attention to unexamined assumptions and ideologies and to enrich communication theory so that it can account for a wider range of important, but previously ignored or denigrated communication phenomenon.

As each of these areas of theory suggest, feminist communication theories represent an interdisciplinary, political, and activist approach to research. Guided by a desire to understand communication as it relates to gender and sex, feminist communication theorists take up a wide range of topics and activities as they approach the study of communication. The complexity and diversity of ideas within feminist communication theory, as well as the complexity and diversity of communication phenomenon itself, suggest that this body of theory will continue to grow and add unusual and important new information to the study of communication. Similarly, as identities and constructions of femininity and masculinity respond to changing cultural and social expectations, so too will feminist communication theory.

Cindy L. Griffin

See also Chicana Feminism; Feminist Standpoint Theory; French Feminism; Genderlect Theory; Gender Schema Theory; Muted Group Theory; Postcolonial Feminism; Womanism

Further Readings

Butler, J. (1990). *Gender trouble: Feminism and the subversion of identity*. New York: Routledge.

Buzzanell, P. (Ed.). (2000). *Rethinking organizational and managerial communication from feminist perspectives*. Thousand Oaks, CA: Sage.

Campbell, K. K. (1980). Stanton's "The solitude of self": A rationale for feminism. *Quarterly Journal of Speech, 66*, 304–312.

Cixous, H. (1976). The laugh of the medusa. *Signs, 1*, 875–893.

Condit, C. M. (1997). In praise of eloquent diversity: Gender and rhetoric as public persuasion. *Women's Studies in Communication, 20*, 91–116.

Houston, M., & Kramarae, C. (1991). Speaking from silence: Methods of silencing and resistance. *Discourse and Society, 2*, 388–399.

Foss, K. A., & Foss, S. K. (1991). *Women speak: The eloquence of women's lives*. Prospect Heights, IL: Waveland.

Foss, K. A., Foss, S. K., & Griffin, C. L. (1999). *Feminist rhetorical theories*. Long Grove, IL: Waveland.

Foss, S. K., Griffin, C. L., & Foss, K. A. (1997). Transforming rhetoric through feminist reconstruction: A response to the gender diversity perspective. *Women's Studies in Communication, 20*, 117–136.

Kramer, C. (1974). Women's speech: Separate but unequal? *Quarterly Journal of Speech, 60*, 14–24.

Lakoff, R. (1975). *Language and woman's place*. New York: Harper Row.

Lundsford, A. (Ed.). (1995). *Reclaiming rhetorica: Women in the rhetorical tradition*. Pittsburgh, PA: University of Pittsburgh Press.

Mulvey, L. (1975). Visual pleasure and narrative cinema. *Screen, 16.3*, 6–18.

Olson, L. N., Coffelt, T. A., Ray, E. B., Rudd, J., Botta, R., Ray, G., et al. (2008). "I'm all for equal rights but don't call me a feminist": Identity dilemmas in young adults' discursive representations of being a feminist. *Women's Studies in Communication, 31*, 104–132.

Spender, D. (1980). *Man made language*. Boston: Routledge & Kegan Paul.

Spitzack, C., & Carter, K. (1987). Women in communication studies: A typology for revision. *Quarterly Journal of Speech, 73*, 401–423.

FEMINIST RHETORICAL CRITICISM

Feminist rhetorical criticism recognizes that the symbolic construction of women and gender is central to the study of communication. When critics select a feminist critical approach, their goal is to explore and explain that construction. Feminist rhetorical criticism is grounded in the assumption that, historically and currently, women and men often have different access to channels and positions of power. Because this differential access can affect the communication styles and strategies used by women, feminist criticism is used to understand, validate, and theorize about those communicative differences. As a critical tool or approach, feminist rhetorical criticism helps scholars explain how communication is used to constrain and/or enable women, how communication is used to resist those constraints and facilitate empowerment, and how communication is used to create nonoppressive identities and ways of being. Because feminist rhetorical criticism is an approach to the study of communication that informs every aspect of a scholar's critical process, this entry will describe the political nature of feminist rhetorical criticism and explain the methodologies, texts, and stances taken by feminist critics.

Feminist rhetorical criticism has an explicitly political agenda: The critic's goal is to advance and improve the symbolic and material positions of women. When scholars engage in feminist rhetorical criticism, they seek to understand that oppression as well as the communication used by and about women to overcome that oppression. Additionally, although feminist rhetorical criticism always begins with an explicit exploration of the position or positions of women in societies because of its overtly political goals, it also takes into account the myriad and complex identities women hold. These identities are linked to the historical, cultural, ethnic and racial, sexual, and socioeconomic realities of women's lived experiences. As such, feminist rhetorical criticism is grounded in the acknowledgment of two things related to the study of communication: Gender matters and gender does not exist in isolation; it is always present in a state of interconnection with other subject and identity positions.

Feminist rhetorical criticism can be a perspective, approach, or method that stands on its own, or it can be linked to other critical and theoretical perspectives, approaches, and methods. When used alone, the critic uses an inductive approach, asking, "How is gender symbolically constructed in this text?" or "What is the construction of gender in this text?" The critic then identifies and explains the various examples of its construction. In this inductive approach, the critic is searching for examples of how women as well as men are constructed in a text, or series of texts, and what that construction tells scholars about symbol use and women's oppression. With this inductive approach, the critic also always identifies the interconnections of race and ethnicity, economic status, and other identities and subject positions as they are linked to and influence communication. When used in combination with other critical methodologies, the critic might ask a more focused question or set of questions, such as "How does a woman's subaltern status affect her ability to communicate in this text, or texts?" or "How does a woman's token status facilitate or constrain her communicative options?" and "How does the communication strategy of appropriation function in this text?" This is the approach taken by Dana Cloud on Oprah Winfrey's biography. These more focused questions allow a critic to concentrate on a particular aspect of communication and function as guides or links to particular bodies of theory the critic finds relevant to the text under study. In this more focused approach, the critic also identifies the intersections and influences of race and ethnicity, economic status, sexuality, and the like.

Feminist rhetorical criticism also acknowledges that a wide range of texts is important to the study of women's communication. Feminist criticism in communication might be said to have begun with the work of Karlyn Kohrs Campbell, who analyzed the rhetorical practices of women speakers, thus introducing issues of gender into criticism. But because women's voices have been constrained historically, legally, socially, and economically, feminist critics came to realize that women often use unconventional and highly creative outlets for their voices. As such, a feminist rhetorical critic holds a wide definition of text and will attempt to explore the symbolic aspects of art, crafts, quilts, letter writing, testimonials, etiquette manuals, cookbooks, street or guerilla performances and protests, and other unconventional symbolic expressions.

Traditional texts, however, such as the speech, media production, interpersonal relationship, or corporate or organizational structure, also provide the critic with important examples of the use of communication to identify and resist oppression. Texts are chosen not for their familiarity, but instead for their ability to shed light on the approaches and styles of communication used by and about women. Similarly, feminist rhetorical criticism may also consider a text or texts from a single woman, a particular set or group of women, a mixture of sets or groups of women in combination with other sets or groups of women, as well as women in combination with men. With this range of options, the feminist rhetorical critic is resisting definitions of text that limit the understanding of the communication strategies and approaches used by women. Feminist rhetorical criticism allows critics to acknowledge and explore a wider range of legitimate forms of communication.

Feminist rhetorical criticism, in keeping with its political agenda, asks that the scholar or researcher identify her or his own status and subject position as researcher—that is, critics name and acknowledge the influences of their own identities on the research or study. This self-identified, self-reflexive position is important for several reasons. It assists the critic in identifying her or his own limitations and biases. It also acknowledges points of connection or difference between the critic and the individual, individuals, and political or social positions under exploration. Finally, it makes explicit the intrinsic subjectivity of all communication criticism and calls attention to the powerful influences of a critic's own experiences, worldviews, and scholarly background on the study of communication.

Cindy L. Griffin

See also Chicana Feminism; Cultural Studies; Feminist Communication Theories; Feminist Standpoint Theory; Intersectionality

Further Readings

Alexander, M. J., Albrecht, L., Day, S., & Segrest, M. (Eds.). (2003). *Sing, whisper, shout, pray! Feminist visions for a just world*. Fort Bragg, CA: EdgeWork Books.

Campbell, K. K. (1989). *Man cannot speak for her: A critical study of early feminist rhetoric* (Vol. 1). Westport, CT: Greenwood Press.

Campbell, K. K. (1973). The rhetoric of women's liberation: An oxymoron. *Quarterly Journal of Speech, 59*, 74–86.

Cloud, D. L. (1996). Hegemony or concordance? The rhetoric of tokenism in "Oprah" Winfrey's rags-to-riches biography. *Critical Studies in Mass Communication, 13*, 115–137.

Flores, L. A. (1996). Creating discursive space through a rhetoric of difference: Chicana feminists craft a homeland. *Quarterly Journal of Speech, 82*, 142–156.

Harding, S. (1991). *Whose science? Whose knowledge? Thinking from women's lives*. New York: Cornell University Press.

FEMINIST STANDPOINT THEORY

Feminist standpoint theory is a specific formulation of the broader standpoint theory. All formulations of standpoint theory contend that a standpoint arises when an individual recognizes and challenges cultural values and power relations that contribute to subordination or oppression of particular groups. For instance, a person could understand and reject racist values and power discrepancies between races, knowing that those undergird the subordination of minorities. The specific foci of feminist standpoint theory are (a) identifying cultural values and power dynamics that account for the subordination of girls and women and (b) highlighting the distinct knowledge cultivated by activities that are typically assigned to females.

Feminist standpoint theory calls attention to the knowledge that arises from conditions and experiences that are common to girls and women. This focus on experiences draws on Marxist theory's claim that the work we do—the concrete activity in which we engage—shapes what we know and how we behave. Thus, feminist standpoint theory is interested in skills and knowledge that are cultivated by typically female activities such as domestic work and caregiving. For example, feminist standpoint theorists claim that caring for others allows girls and women to develop knowledge of what others need and how to meet those needs.

Feminist standpoint theory rejects the notion that knowledge is a straightforward outcome of essential characteristics of group members (for instance, an XX chromosomal structure or having ovaries). Instead, feminist standpoint theory emphasizes social ideologies (e.g., sexism and the gender roles it authorizes) that explain why girls and women are assigned to certain activities and why those activities are less valued than activities typically assigned to boys and men. Feminist standpoint hinges on realizing that the conditions and experiences common to girls and women are not natural, but are a result from social and political forces.

For this reason, although girls' and women's circumstances and activities may shape their perspectives, they do not automatically confer a feminist standpoint. To develop a feminist standpoint, individuals must engage in an intellectual struggle to recognize, analyze, and contest broad power relations that account for the subordinate status of girls and women and the activities they are expected to pursue. For instance, many girls and women understand that assertive females are sometimes labeled *bitches*. That understanding is shaped by seeing girls and women who act assertively called bitches, but this understanding itself is not a feminist standpoint. A person who holds a feminist standpoint realizes that social expectations for females to be nice, defer to others, and not be pushy underlie derogatory treatment of assertive girls and women, including calling them bitches, whereas assertive men are admired for their confidence and leadership.

A feminist standpoint disputes privileging of men and men's interests while devaluing, marginalizing, and otherwise harming girls and women and their interests. In short, a standpoint is an intellectual achievement that reflects—and necessarily entails—political consciousness. This means, as Donna Haraway has noted, that standpoints are never innocent.

Key Claims of Feminist Standpoint Theory

Like all standpoint theories, feminist standpoint theory begins with the assumption that society is structured by power relations that generate unequal social locations; one location is occupied by members of the dominant group, and other locations are inhabited by members of subordinate groups. According to feminist standpoint theory, women's lives, in general, differ systematically and structurally from men's lives. Women and men are expected to engage in distinct activities, and the two groups are accorded different rights and opportunities. For instance, females are expected to take primary responsibility for homemaking, parenting, and kin keeping, and females are expected to defer to and please others.

Extending the foregoing premise is the second claim: The different social locations that women and men occupy cultivate distinct kinds of knowledge. Sara Ruddick, for instance, asserts that nurturing skill results not from a maternal instinct, but from the fact that girls and women, far more often than boys and men, are assigned caregiving roles and, thus, they develop competence in providing care. It is performing the role of caregiver—rather than being female—that cultivates knowledge of how to care. Also, being involved in caregiving promotes awareness of the importance and value of this activity; those who do not engage in caring for others are unlikely to develop nurturing skills or an appreciation of what is required to care well for others.

Some feminist standpoint theorists assert that knowledge from subordinated social locations is more complete than knowledge from dominant social locations. They believe that members of subordinated groups are likely to understand both their own group's perspective and the perspective of members of the dominant group, but that members of the dominant group are not as likely to understand—or have a motive to understand—the perspective of members of subordinate groups. This reasoning leads to the conclusion that members of dominant groups have less complete knowledge of the social world than members of subordinate groups. However, not all feminist standpoint theorists accept this claim. Patricia Hill Collins, for instance, expresses skepticism that some knowledge is more complete or accurate than others.

Studying subordinated locations and the knowledge they foster not only provides insight into the lives of members of subordinated groups, but also casts light on dominant group practices, especially those that create and reproduce inequality. This explains why feminist standpoint theorists claim that, while it easier for women than men to achieve a feminist standpoint, it is possible for men to do so if they engage in the intellectual struggle to recognize and reject established power relations, including male privilege.

In sum, individuals hold a standpoint when they (a) grasp the arbitrary and unfair nature of power relations that structure social life and (b) are critical of the uneven consequences of those power relations for members of different groups. A feminist standpoint grows out of encountering oppositional knowledge—through readings, attending talks and workshops, reflection, and/or participating in groups such as the consciousness-raising groups that were instrumental to the second wave of feminism in the United States. Feminist standpoint theory is inherently and unapologetically political because it aims to identify and challenge established social hierarchies and their consequences.

Julia T. Wood

See also Critical Theory; Feminist Communication Theories; Feminist Rhetorical Criticism; Marxist Theory; Power and Power Relations

Further Readings

Andersen, M., & Collins, P. H. (Eds.). (2007). *Race, class, and gender: An anthology* (6th ed.). Belmont, CA: Thomson.

Collins, P. H. (1986). Learning from the outsider within. *Social Problems, 23,* 514–532.

Haraway, D. (1988). Situated knowledges: The science question in feminism and the privilege of partial perspective. *Signs, 14,* 575–599.

Harding, S. (1991). *Whose science? Whose knowledge? Thinking from women's lives.* Ithaca, NY: Cornell University Press.

Harding, S. (Ed.). (2004). *The feminist theory standpoint reader: Intellectual and political controversies.* New York: Routledge.

Hartsock, N. (1983). The feminist standpoint: Developing the ground for a specifically feminist historical materialism. In S. Harding & M. B. Hintikka (Eds.), *Discovering reality* (pp. 283–310). Boston: Ridel.

Keller, E. (1985). *Reflections on gender and science.* New Haven, CT: Yale University Press.

Rose, H. (1983). Hand, brain and heart: Towards a feminist epistemology for the sciences. *Signs, 9,* 73–98.

Ruddick, S. (1989). *Maternal thinking: Toward a politics of peace.* Boston: Beacon.

Smith, D. (1987). *The everyday world as problematic.* Toronto, Ontario, Canada: University of Toronto Press.

Wood, J. T. (2003). From "woman's nature" to standpoint epistemology: Gilligan and the debate over essentializing in feminist scholarship. *Women's Studies in Communication, 15,* 1–24.

Wood, J. T. (2005). Feminist standpoint theory and muted group theory: Commonalities and divergences. *Women & Language, 28,* 61–64.

FIELD THEORY OF CONFLICT

Field theory of conflict is a social psychological theory of human behavior. Kurt Lewin formulated field theory to explicate the balance between nature and nurture in understanding human behavior. These ideas had enormous influence on the field of communication. Briefly, human behavior is seen as the product of interaction between internal and external states, mediated by the individual's perceptions of these states. These states consist of a matrix of forces that explain stability and change in human social systems. This entry provides a brief history of the theory's origin, explains the concepts of Lewin's field theory, examines its applications, and distinguishes it from other theories with similar names.

Lewin, associated with but not a member of the early Frankfurt School, is widely acknowledged as the father of social psychology. Most psychologists in the early 20th century ascribed either to the psychoanalytic approach led by the ideas of Sigmund Freud or to the behaviorist approach, such as John B. Watson's classical behaviorism and B. F. Skinner's radical behaviorism. Psychoanalysts explained human behavior according to internal factors, including the unconscious.

Behaviorists eschewed internal explanations for human behavior in favor of predicting behavior according to observable changes in the individual's environment. Although these two schools of thought overlapped in some ways, the commonly known nature versus nurture debate sprung from this division in the field of psychology. Lewin's field theory bridged the debate, positing that behavior is a function of both the person and his or her environment: B = f(PE).

Lewin used the term *life space* to represent environment. A person's life space is the psychological field within which he or she acts; it is influenced by and influences the person's psychological state. Each individual is seen as acting in several fields (home, school, work, church, etc.). Lewin conceptualized behavior as purposeful and goal directed and fields as consisting of various forces, understandable only in terms of the individual's perception of them. Behavior is predicted by the interaction of the individual's motivations (internal forces) and his or her perceptions of interdependent external forces in the life space, or field. *Attractive forces* pull a person toward a behavior. *Goals* exert attractive force, creating *disequilibrium* in the life space force field. By enacting behaviors that achieve the goal, the individual restores equilibrium.

For example, a student who desires good grades (goal) enacts such behavior as going to class, studying, and writing papers to restore equilibrium (achieve the goal). *Obstacles,* or threats, exert repulsive force, creating disequilibrium. By enacting behaviors that reduce the threat, the individual restores equilibrium. A student, for instance, who fears failing (threat) enacts such behavior as going to class, studying, and writing papers to restore equilibrium (eliminate the threat). Thus, the same behaviors may stem from quite different perceptions of the field.

Barriers are boundaries with variable permeability around a region in a field. Our student exerts little effort when enacting equilibrium-restoring behaviors in the geometry region of his or her life space, but works harder in the chemistry region. Obstacles can function as barriers. A simple barrier is inexplicable ("I will never understand chemistry no matter how hard I work"); an obstacle boundary is not ("I don't understand chemistry because I don't have the proper background for the course").

Intrapersonal conflict results from contradictory forces. Lewin identified three basic intrapersonal conflicts:

Approach-avoidance conflict occurs when an individual experiences forces that propel him or her toward and repel him or her from a particular behavior. For example, our student may want to pass chemistry, but is sickened by the smell of the lab or classroom. So enacting a going-to-class behavior is conflicted.

Approach-approach conflict occurs when an individual experiences two opposite, equally attractive forces. For example, our student must choose between two lab partners who are equally appealing.

Avoidance-avoidance conflict occurs when an individual experiences two opposite equally repellent forces. For example, our student must choose between taking a final examination or completing extra lab assignments, both of which he or she equally wishes to avoid.

Some scholars have added *double approach-avoidance* for situations in which oppositional goals each have their own aversive aspects. For example, our student is invited to go out for dinner with someone he or she wants to date, but does not like the chosen restaurant. On the same evening, he or she has also been invited to join a study group to help improve his or her grades, but does not get along with the others in the group.

Lewin applied field theory in the areas of social conflict, organizational change, and group dynamics. The Palo Alto group was also influenced by Lewin's ideas in their development of pragmatics. Examples of communication theory explicitly based on Lewin's field theory include Dale Hample's application of field theory to interpersonal conflict and Janet Bavelas's theory of equivocal communication. In the communication discipline, the Lewinian approach has been enormously influential. Approach-avoidance behavioral explanations, with no acknowledgement of field theory, are common in communication theory. Approach-avoidance explanations have been posited by communication scholars for such things as communicative aggression, communication apprehension, stuttering, speaker credibility, media use, media and gender, marketing, health behaviors, conflict management, and parental attachment.

Lewin's field theory should not be confused with Stephen Toulmin's field theory of argument, widely used in argumentation theory, or with Pierre Bourdieu's sociological field theory, applied in media and journalism studies. Both of these theories use similar concepts of a social field, but are not related to Lewin's theory.

Anne Maydan Nicotera

See also Argumentation Theories; Argumentativeness, Assertiveness, and Verbal Aggressiveness Theory; Conflict Communication Theories; Family Communication Theories; Frankfurt School; Gender and Media; Health Communication Theories; Palo Alto Group; Pragmatics

Further Readings

Bavelas, J. B. (1998). Theoretical and methodological principles of the equivocation project. *Journal of Language and Social Psychology, 17,* 183–199.

Bavelas, J. B., Black, A., Chovil, N., & Mullet, J. (1990). *Equivocal communication.* Newbury Park, CA: Sage.

Lewin, K. (1997). *Resolving social conflicts: Selected papers on group dynamics and field theory in social science: Selected theoretical papers.* Washington, DC: American Psychological Association. (Original works published 1948 and 1951)

Hample, D., & Dallinger, J. M. (1995). A Lewinian perspective on taking conflict personally: Revision, refinement, and validation of the instrument. *Communication Quarterly, 43,* 297–319.

FILM THEORIES

Film theory refers to the significant philosophical thought concerning film as an art form, an experience, and an ideological construct. As such, it can be distinguished from *film criticism,* which encompasses the analysis of a film or body of films, usually from an evaluative or hermeneutical (i.e., interpretative) perspective. However, the concepts of film theory often provide the premises upon which the analyses of film criticism are based. Although *aesthetics* (the branch of philosophy devoted to art) form a part of film theory, its concerns are primarily ontological and to an extent, epistemological. To put it more simply, the goal of film criticism is to determine meaning in or assign value to a specific film or cinematic corpus (e.g., the films of John Ford, musical comedies, the French New Wave); the objective of film theory is to answer the question (which serves as the title of one of the most influential works of theory), what is cinema (Qu'est-ce que le cinéma?). Not surprisingly, the proposed answers to this question have changed over time. The following will provide a historical overview of the developments in film theory from the early 20th century to the present.

Formative Theories

Contributions to the body of thought that comprises film theory predate the term itself. Practically as soon as the moving picture appeared (c. 1895), there began a discourse on its nature and purpose. The first phase of theoretical thought concerning cinema came as a response to many in the intelligentsia of the day who dismissed the moving picture (the term used in the early days of cinema to designate what we now call movie or film) as a mere recording, with no intrinsic value of its own. Any significance, they claimed, was to be found only in the subject recorded. The earliest theorists of film argued to the contrary that cinema constituted a new art form—the *Sixth Art* as it was referred to by French writers at the beginning of the 20th century. They drew analogies between film and the traditional arts, noting their shared characteristics. (The exception to this process of positive comparison was in regard to theatre: Reacting to the charge that cinema was, at best, canned theatre, the commentators were at pains to catalogue the differences between theatre and film.) Moreover, some theorists posited the idea of cinema as a synthesis of attributes found in the older art forms. For example, a painting is a visual composition, and one of the primary aspects of music is rhythm, but a film, due to movement within the frame as well as the beat of cutting from shot to shot, provides a rhythmic flow of visual images, thus synthesizing attributes of music and painting into a new aesthetic experience.

Furthermore, the early theorists disputed the notion that a movie was a mere recording, a mechanical reproduction of actuality, first of all by cataloguing all the ways a cinematic image (at that time) differed from its subject—for example, an actual event that was in color, three dimensional, and included sound was, in cinema, rendered in black and white, two dimensions, and silent. Rather than being a simple mechanical reproduction of whatever happened or was staged before the camera, the formative theorists demonstrated that the raw material was altered, manipulated, and shaped by the cinematic processes. Rudolph Arnheim, for example, pointed to the transformative potentialities of the filmmaker's choices in areas such as framing, camera angle, and lighting. But while many theorists made reference to various aspects of mise en scène (the overall creation of the visual image within the frame) and cinematography under the control of the filmmaker, the processes of editing came to predominate early theoretical thought.

Since this was the period of the silent film—before the introduction of sound technology—editing meant the juxtaposition of shots only. For many theorists at the time, editing was the sine qua non of cinema because on the one hand, it was specific to the new art form, having no analogue in the traditional arts and because editing, more than any other aspect of the filmmaker's panoply of techniques, produced signification. Although previously the French proponents of the concept of cinégraphie had adopted this position and in the United States Vachel Lindsay had predicted that cinema would become a new hieroglyphics, that is, a true picture language, it was the theorist filmmakers of the early Soviet Union in the 1920s who presented the most highly developed theory of film as founded on montage (the French word for editing that was adopted by the Russians).

Lev Kuleshov had conducted experiments, editing together footage in different ways, seeking to determine the effects on the spectator. His student, V. I. Pudovkin, proposed a theory of linkage, suggesting that meaning in a film is created cumulatively as the spectator determines the relation from shot to shot. But Sergei Eisenstein countered that the highest potential of editing lay in the collision of disparate images to generate new ideas. He noted that this approach was dialectical—the opposition of thesis and antithesis engendering synthesis—and therefore a perfect expression in cinematic form of the Marxist theoretical underpinnings of the young Union of Soviet Socialist Republics (USSR) dialectical materialism. (But elsewhere he related his concept of editing to the pictograms of the Japanese language, where, e.g., an abstract concept such as sorrow is rendered by combining the Japanese characters for heart and knife.)

Although the theorists of cinema from the period of the turn of the century through the 1930s differed in their foci, they all emphasized the transformative capabilities of the filmmaker wielding the cinematic apparatus (e.g., cameras and their lenses, editing equipment, printers) and can, therefore, be termed *formative*.

Realist Theories

In the period following World War II, theoretical concepts of cinema shifted to the opposite direction. Under the influence of the philosophical schools of phenomenology and existentialism then current, the postwar theorists asserted that cinema's definitive quality lay precisely in its unique ability to capture, by mechanical (and therefore objective) means, an image of whatever was placed before the camera's lens, or reality. (For this reason, this phase of film theory is termed *realist*.) However, this did not mean the realist theorists agreed with the notion that a movie was a mere recording; the ontological connection between a thing and its cinematic image was, they asserted, the basis of cinema's function, which they described as revelatory. In other words, as the primary realist theorists André Bazin and Siegfried Kracauer asserted, cinema did not reproduce the known world for the spectator; it revealed the unknown—or at least, the unapprehended. Although such a position has an obvious application to the documentary film, the realist theorists believed it equally relevant to narrative cinema. Realist theories of cinema, it should be noted, were congruent with a strong trend toward social realism (e.g., Italian Neorealism) in postwar cinema; realist theorists often claimed that such realist films were essentially cinematic, while, for example, German Expressionist films of the 1920s, with their stylized and frankly artificial settings and frequently fantastic subject matter, were not.

Bazin also differed with the formative theorists' position on the primacy of editing. Although he recognized that it was an undeniably important aspect of cinema, Bazin believed that films that depended on editing as their primary system of signification (as in the case of the Soviet filmmaker theorists) actually contradicted cinema's essential revelatory function. He argued that a film based on the techniques of continuity editing, in which an action is broken into its constituent parts (shots) and then reassembled, imposes meaning on that action a priori rather than allowing it to be discerned by the spectator a posteriori. Bazin favored a cinematic approach based on the long take or sequence shot (i.e., shooting an entire action or scene in one continuous shot, or take, of the camera), especially when combined with deep focus (i.e., a technique of cinematography that renders the planes of the visual field from the camera's lens to the horizon in perceptibly equal focus) since such an approach preserves the time and space of an action, rather than atomizing it. Bazin, however, never advocated that the long take approach should replace editing; he argued that filmmakers should be free to employ a range of cinematic approaches to film structure rather than being constrained to overemphasize editing.

Materialist Theories

The theories propounded in the formative and realist periods were fairly homogeneous. In contrast in the 1960s and 1970s, a plethora of theoretical approaches to cinema emerged. Despite the diversity, the various theories of this period can be seen as comprising a network or web of interconnecting and overlapping concepts based on a materialist perspective—that is, the assumption that the actions and consciousness of the human being are in great measure shaped by material (as opposed to metaphysical) forces fundamentally beyond the control of the individual. (Examples of such material forces include heredity, economics, and ideological systems.) The film theories of this period are derived from developments in the social sciences, foremost of which were the linguistic theories of Ferdinand de Saussure and the neo-Freudian theory of psychoanalysis propounded by Jacques Lacan. In most cases, these concepts from the social sciences were applied to cinema after first being applied to literature. Staunchly antiphenomenological, the theories put forward by the materialist theorists were a reaction against what was perceived as the subjectivity and impressionism of the realist theories. As a corrective, the materialist theorists sought to bring intellectual rigor and scientific systematization to the study of cinema. These theories must also be understood in their historical context: They were produced at a time of great social change (e.g., the civil rights, women's rights, and antiwar movements) as the disenfranchised and oppressed throughout the world were demanding equality and justice, as traditional ideas concerning such matters as gender and sexuality were being challenged.

Structuralism and Semiology

The first of the materialist theories to be applied to cinema, and the one that served as the methodological foundation for the others, was structuralism. Put most simply, structuralism is based on the notion that the meaning of any phenomenon lies below its surface in its underlying (or deep) structures. Structural anthropologists such as Claude Lévi-Strauss, for example, studied a given culture to ascertain the patterns and repetitions in its myths and rituals. Lévi-Strauss believed such recurrent elements form a structure of antinomies, or oppositions (e.g., life vs. death, male vs. female, the raw vs. the cooked) that are key to understanding the deep-seated values of that culture. Film theorists applied this methodology to bodies of films (genres, in particular) in order to discover what that segment of cinema reveals about the culture that produced it. For example, films of the Western genre include oppositions such as wilderness versus civilization, the East versus the West, and the individual versus society. By analyzing the deployment of such antinomies throughout the genre, structuralists sought to locate the characteristics that underlie American society.

Closely aligned to structuralism is semiology. The basic premise of semiology is that all aspects of social intercourse (e.g., manners, fashion) are articulated as signs that are read or understood in terms of shared codes. Derived from linguistics, semiology describes these sign systems in linguistic terms. The cine-semiologists, such as Christian Metz, viewed cinema as a complex of multiple codes and attempted to describe the rules (analogous to syntax or grammar in language) that govern these systems in order for any one text—film—to be understood by the spectators. The techniques of film editing, for example, form one of cinema's codes; Metz postulated the function of each of editing's signs (e.g., the cut, the dissolve, the fade) in the code of editing. If structuralism is concerned with locating the meanings below the surface of a text (or, the what), semiology is concerned with the system(s) that allow the apprehension of those meanings (or, the how).

Marxist and Feminist Theories of Film

Although Marxist and feminist film theories existed independent of one another, they were often intertwined due to certain parallels between them. Marxism challenges capitalism, and feminism challenges patriarchy, both of which were dominant ideologies in culture at the time. Marxism advocates for the end of oppression of the poor and the working class, while feminism advocates for the end of oppression of women. Either or both perspectives can and have been used as the basis for film criticism, but Marxist and feminist theories went beyond individual texts (films) to critique cinema itself. Marxist theorists note that although early cinema was artisanal in nature (i.e., crafted by individuals or small independent collectives), its development soon shifted to the industrial mode. The means of production, in other words, came under the control of capitalists. Film studios, set up in a hierarchical fashion and based on a marked division of labor, were factories for the production of movies, which were manufactured and marketed for consumption like all other commodities of a capitalist society. Not only did such a system mitigate against any personal, artistic expression, but also films made in such a fashion, Marxist theorists argued, bore the imprint of the capitalist ideology in their structure. Employing structuralist and semiological methods, Marxist theorists demonstrated that the standardized form of film that developed in the capitalist film industry—termed classical Hollywood cinema—naturalized the status quo.

Feminist theorists likewise demonstrated that the standardized construction of industrially produced films was inherently sexist. Conventional camerawork and editing construct male and female characters differently: Women are erotized, objectified, and presented as passive, while men are active, the agents of action. Moreover, the experience of a film can be perceived in sexual terms. As a primarily visual form, a film is constituted in terms of seeing. But the act of seeing is unidirectional: The camera (standing in for an imaginary viewer), and by extension the spectator in the audience, sees without being seen. The spectator of the conventional film, through the surrogacy of the camera lens, can go anywhere, see anything, but remain invisible. This confers a sense of omnipotence on the spectator, of dominance and control over the fictional events. Thus movie viewing, in conventional (industrial) cinema, is structured to naturalize the dynamic of dominance and submission upon which patriarchy is founded. Film goers may be male or female, but the gaze of conventional cinema is masculine (in the traditional sense). Because Marxist and feminist theorists viewed dominant cinema as fostering the continuation of oppressive ideologies in the deep structures of its form, they espoused alternative modes of production and alternative forms of filmic construction as the only corrective.

Current Film Theory

By the 1980s, film theory once again had begun to change direction. Although the new theories were rooted in a phenomenological perspective on cinema, they did not constitute a simple return to the realist theories of the postwar period. The new theorists rejected the basic assumptions of the materialist theorists, but implicitly acknowledged the systematic rigor that they had brought to the study of cinema. This most recent current in film theory is epitomized in the work of Gilles Deleuze. Rather than conceiving of cinema as a language system, or codes that have to be cracked in order to find its meanings hidden below its surface, Deleuze contends that film, as a complex of images and sounds, functions on a preverbal level and therefore is apprehended immediately and directly. Then, however, Deleuze set about to identify the different kinds of images that comprise cinema (e.g., the perception image, the action image, the time image), thus adopting a taxonomic approach as comprehensive in its scope as Metz's semiological project had been. Through his examination of cinematic images, Deleuze concluded that movement was the aspect central to cinema before World War II, but time is the dominant aspect of modern cinema.

Non-Western Theories

Important to recognize is that the film theories described here are the products of the West. Since Western culture in general and Western cinema (especially that of Hollywood) in particular are and have been dominant globally during the period covered, it can be assumed that these theories have been influential throughout the world. However, there are decidedly non-Western currents in the theories of cinema. For example, Chinese film theory draws upon concepts of classical Chinese aesthetics as well as the theoretical concepts imported from the West. The theories of third cinema, as another example, attempt to adapt many of the concepts of Western film theory to the revolutionary goals of emerging cinemas of the third world.

Joelle Collier

See also Asian Communication Theory; Documentary Film Theories; Feminist Communication Theories; Genre Theory; Marxist Theory; Ontology; Phenomenology; Semiotics and Semiology

Further Readings

Arnheim, R. (1957). *Film as art.* Berkeley: University of California Press.

Bazin, A. (1967). *What is cinema?* (Vol. 1). Berkeley: University of California Press.

Braudy, L., & Cohen, M. (Eds.). (2004). *Film theory and criticism: Introductory readings* (6th ed.). New York: Oxford University Press.

Deleuze, G. (1986). *Cinema 1: The movement-image.* Minneapolis: University of Minnesota Press.

Deleuze, G. (1989). *Cinema 2: The time-image.* Minneapolis: University of Minnesota Press.

Eisenstein, S. (1949). *Film form: Essays in film theory.* New York: Harcourt, Brace & World.

Houston, B., & Kinder, M. (1980). *Self and cinema: A transformalist perspective.* Pleasantville, NY: Redgrave.

Jameson, F. (1995). *The geopolitical aesthetic: Cinema and space in the world system.* Bloomington: Indiana University Press.

Kracauer, S. (1960). *Theory of film: The redemption of physical reality.* London: Oxford University Press.

Metz, C. (1974). *Film language: A semiotics of the cinema.* New York: Oxford University Press.

Mulvey, L. (1988). Visual pleasure and narrative cinema. In C. Penley (Eds.), *Feminism and film theory* (pp. 57–79). New York: Routledge.

Sobchack, V. (1992). *The address of the eye: A phenomenology of film experience.* Princeton, NJ: Princeton University Press.

FLOW AND CONTRA-FLOW

The concepts of flow and contra-flow have their origins in discourses about the free expression and flow of ideas. These were prevalent in the era after World War II, when U.S. foreign policy goals incorporated the concept of free flow of information. There was growing suspicion in developing world countries from the 1960s and 1970s that the concept so eagerly promoted by the United States, Britain, and United Nations Educational, Scientific, and Cultural Organization (UNESCO) was a form of cultural imperialism supporting the expansion of Western media and benefiting Western advertisers through the export of a Western way of life. Some critics preferred the term *free flow doctrine,* highlighting the ideological function of free flow discourse. Criticism grew less sharp in the 1990s and 2000s with the end of the Cold War, rapid development of larger developing countries such as China and India, and evidence of media vitality within many developing countries. Media export activity from developing countries to regional and global markets has been an especially noteworthy factor in mitigating criticism; Oliver Boyd-Barrett and Daya Thussu coined the term contra-flow to apply to this phenomenon (specifically, in relation to news agencies that gathered news from, about, or for the developing world). Many scholars continued using the metaphor of flow, while that of network also became popular. Attracting broader attention than flow and contra-flow, by the 1990s, were phenomena of globalization; the relationship of media to global, regional, and local identity formation; and implications for the modes and quality of expression everywhere. The discourse of globalization inspired a variety of terms to capture the complexity of transcultural media influences, such as glocalization and hybridity.

The 1950s through 1970s was a peak period for flow studies, and their predominant message was that of one-way flow from more to less powerful nations. As early as 1953, a study by the International Press Institute (*The Flow of News*) demonstrated the great influence over global news flow of the major Western countries, including heavy dependence by developed and developing world media on news supplied by Agence France

Presse (Paris), Associated Press (New York), Reuters (London), and United Press International (New York). Studies by Oliver Boyd-Barrett from 1980 through to 2008 demonstrate the continuing importance of such sources. In one of the first examples in scholarly literature of glocalization, Boyd-Barrett, in his 1980 book *The International News Agencies,* chronicled how the major agencies regionalized their news services to make them more relevant to local geopolitical regions and to head off New World Information and Communication Order (NWICO) criticism of them as agents of cultural imperialism. Jeremy Tunstall's 1977 book *The Media Are American* chronicled the global influence of U.S. media. Tunstall's main argument was that the global success of U.S. media industries was related to the size and wealth of the domestic U.S. market. U.S. media entrepreneurs were able to recoup most of their costs on their domestic market, so they enjoyed great flexibility in pricing for international markets. In a study of the flow of international television programming, Tapio Varis demonstrated strong one-way flows of popular television program exports from major Western producers to countries around the world, many of these depending on imports for high percentages of their prime-time entertainment. Many scholars, including Tunstall, examined the history of Hollywood and its unrivalled financial success as an exporter of movies and increasingly, of television series.

Flow studies were closely related to theories of dependency and of cultural and media imperialism. Dependency theories argued that hegemonic relations between imperial and colonial nations persisted beyond the achievement of formal political independence. Postcolonial countries continued to experience economic dependency on the postimperial countries for markets, investment, know-how, and advanced technology. Theories of cultural and media imperialism argued that economic dependency was rendered natural by the penetration of postcolonial societies by the cultures, languages, ways of doing business, lifestyles, and media hardware and software imported from the postimperial countries. Boyd-Barrett defined media imperialism in 1977 essentially in flow terms, specifically in terms of degrees of reciprocity of influence between the media systems of different nations, noting that this should be measured not just between developed and developing countries, but also among the developed countries themselves. This was a more restricted approach than that of Herbert Schiller who, in 1969, argued that media infrastructures and exports were essential components of postwar U.S. imperialistic hegemony, a position that characterizes some of the later work of Boyd-Barrett.

Many such concerns diminished in the 1980s to 1990s. Applications to the media of neoliberal principles, together with processes of media deregulation, privatization, commercialization, and the Internet induced exponential growth in the number of media outlets worldwide. With support from a triumphalist streak of cultural studies, sometimes associated with the work of David Morely, that celebrates the infinity of textual meanings, there appeared to be endless possibility of expression. Optimism was fueled by expansion in the number and wealth of new outlets in young democracies of the developing world. Some media began to acquire a global presence, such as CNNI or BBC World Television, to be followed in 1996 by a global station of the south, Al Jazeera. Meanwhile, policy changes in India that rationalized the financing of Bollywood movies provided these with added impetus on global markets. The production and global distribution of telenovelas, many of them made in Mexico, Argentina, and Venezuela, further contributed to the sense of a great flourishing of media product on both domestic and international markets. Some excitement survived into the 2000s, but was suppressed both by processes of industrial concentration and conglomeration and in the wake of the U.S. invasions of Afghanistan and Iraq in 2001 and 2003, respectively. These eventually prompted growing public realization that apparent diversity of outlets notwithstanding, the mainstream media in almost all countries, including the United States and Britain, were timid and often complicit in the face of serious government wrongdoing of the worst imaginable kinds (e.g., false pretexts for engagement in war; vast war profiteering; mass murder; destruction of basic infrastructure necessary to sustain civilian life; looting of national assets, such as oil reserves, at the gunpoint of an occupying army and puppet government; torture and abuse of both genuine suspects and innocents; suspension of habeus corpus).

Critical scholarship likewise survived the triumphalism of media diversity. In the United States, political economists like Robert McChesney, Herbert Schiller, and Dan Schiller kept their focus on the growing divorce between media industries and the practice and spirit of democracy. In several papers, Boyd-Barrett argued that evidence of media imperialism persisted into the new communication and information technology industries and that the world had returned to a symbiosis between imperialism and mainstream media, lambasted so forcefully by Herbert Schiller some 40 years earlier. A string of scholarly books in the 2000s by James Curran, Joseph Straubhaar, Jeremy Tunstall, and others argued in a different direction—namely that media systems tend to look very different when seen from within particular regions, nations, and even subnational territories across the world, each formed by complex, distinctive histories. Missing from some of these accounts was a systematic comparative framework. They mostly presumed that the main variable of interest is content and were uncritical of neoliberalism as a global ideology that emerged from the United States and has underpinned a global financial hegemony with U.S. interests and other strategic partners at the apex. This disseminated since the early 1980s with astonishing single-mindedness through a mixture of outright military force, manipulation of governments, guile, and propaganda. Further, many such authors are incurious about the pervasive timidity of mainstream media in the face of the increasingly desperate aggressiveness of U.S. administrations following 2001, closely tied to oil and defense interests and the relatively poor coverage everywhere of the reality of a globalized economy, even as this showed signs of implosion by 2008.

Critiquing Tunstall's 2007 work *The Media Were American*, Boyd-Barrett noted that the theory of the strongest domestic market, which Tunstall had developed in his earlier book *The Media Are American* to account for U.S. dominance, had modulated to a more dynamic account, tracing how economies of scale accrue to early market leaders and to large population countries, thus helping explain variations between nations in their respective degrees of media autonomy. Tunstall, in 2007, argued that for 200 years, media development was bound up with, directed by, and contributed to the development of the nation-state. The consequence that media were therefore deeply implicated in propagandizing the foreign policy objectives of nation-states—of particular importance in the context of all forms of imperialism—is acknowledged more boldly for the late 19th than for the early 21st century. Application by Tunstall of older theories of media imperialism, which he eschews, would have necessitated equal and systematic attention to hardware as to software, distribution as to reception, advertising as to programming, ownership as to production, technology as to patent, content as to copyright, format as to substance and—within substance—framing and argument as to mere authorship.

In a work that theorizes the range of cultural-media relationships between societies, extending beyond the flow and contra-flow dichotomy, Joseph Straubhaar's *World Television* argues that national cultures, markets, governments, and television networks still dominate the experience of television viewing worldwide. Most African and European countries continue to import principally from the United States and relatively little from each other. Latin American countries are more likely to import U.S. production ideas and genres in prime time and to import a lot of direct U.S. programming for non–prime time. Globalization, he found, was limited by the fact that relatively few people have a primarily global identity. Many people have multiple levels of identity, but most are still local, metropolitan, subnational-provincial, or national. The formation of transnational cultural-linguistic markets was as crucial as the trend toward globalization. Straubhaar acknowledged several possible modes of structural interaction between societies, including colonialism, imperialism, and dependency and argued that relations of asymmetrical interdependence were of growing importance. He identified different modes of cultural interaction between and within cultures, including penetration, one-way flows of products and influences, homogenization, interpenetration or two-way flows, hybridization, and the formation of multiple layers of culture.

The concept of globalization (denoting a process of growing integration and independency of finance and cultures among the majority of countries around the world), applied to media from the early 1990s, frequently highlights processes of cultural homogenization or McDonaldization. Others note, on the contrary, that in specific localities, globalization stimulates growing diversity, even though familiar clusters of these newly diverse cultural products and financial transactions are replicated all over the planet. Cultures are sometimes described as increasingly *glocal* or *hybrid*. The term *glocal* denotes either that locally originating enterprises or products take on some of the iconic characteristics of a global culture to make them more attractive in both domestic and transnational markets, or that multinational enterprises and their products deliberately acquire selected iconic properties of local cultures so as to seem more familiar to local consumers. The term *hybridity* has similar resonances. Although initially used in celebration of increasing diversity and flexibility of culture, darker undertones are found in succeeding literatures. These identify many ways in which products are hybridized within a continuing context of hegemony. The 2000 movie *Crouching Tiger, Hidden Dragon* was itself iconic of hybridity. A coproduction involving Chinese (mainland, Hong Kong, and Taiwan) and Western capital (Columbia Pictures and Sony), dependent on Western distribution, arguably distorts Chinese culture for the benefit of Western audiences, exploiting the previously Westernized Chinese culture of kung-fu and acquiring greater popularity in the West than in China.

Oliver Boyd-Barrett

See also Americanization of Media; Free Flow Doctrine; Hybridity; International Communication Theories; Media Sovereignty; New World Information and Communication Order (NWICO); Postcolonial Theory; Transculturation

Further Readings

Boyd-Barrett, O. (1977). Media imperialism: Towards an international framework for the analysis of media systems. In J. Curran, M. Gurevitch, & J. Woollacott (Eds.), *Mass communication and society* (pp. 116–135). London: Edward Arnold.

Boyd-Barrett, O. (1988). *The international news agencies.* London: Constable.

Boyd-Barrett, O. (2006). *Communications media, globalization and empire.* Eastleigh, UK: John Libbey.

Boyd-Barrett, O. (2008). Jeremy Tunstall's *The Media Were American,* [Book review]. *Global Media and Communication, 4,* 201–207.

Boyd-Barrett, O., & Thussu, D. (1992). *Contra-flow in global news.* London: John Libbey.

Curran, J., & Park, M.-J. (2000). *De-Westernizing media studies.* London: Routledge.

International Press Institute. (1953). *The flow of the news: A study by the International Press Institute.* Zurich: Author.

Kraidy, M. (2006). *Hybridity, or the cultural logic of globalization.* Philadelphia: Temple University Press.

McChesney, R. (2008). *The political economy of media: Emerging issues, emerging dilemmas.* New York: Monthly Review Press.

Schiller, D. (2007). *The history and theory of information as a commodity in the contemporary world.* Chicago: University of Illinois Press.

Schiller, H. (1969). *Mass communications and American empire.* New York: Augustus M. Kelley.

Straubhaar, J. D. (2007). *World television: From global to local.* Thousand Oaks, CA: Sage.

Tunstall, J. (1977). *The media are American: Anglo-American media in the world.* London: Constable.

Tunstall, J. (2007). *The media were American: U.S. mass media in decline.* Oxford, UK: Oxford University Press.

Varis, T. (1973). *International inventory of television programming: Structure and the flow of programmes between nations.* Tampere, Finland: University of Tampere.

FRAMING THEORY

Framing theory aims to identify schemes in which individuals perceive the world. The roots of framing theory are often attributed to the sociologist Erving Goffman who argued that interpretive designs constitute central elements of cultural belief systems. Goffman called these interpretive designs frames that we use in our day-to-day experience to make sense of the world. Frames help to reduce the complexity of information, but serve as a two-way process: Frames help interpret and reconstruct reality. Goffman's concept of frames has its conceptual roots in phenomenology, a philosophical approach that argues that the meaning of the world is perceived by individuals based on their lifeworld beliefs, experiences, and knowledge. Whereas traditionally, world meanings were conveyed through socialization processes, creating a collective reality within a culture or society, today so-called mediated communication delivers powerful frames of world perception that challenges and renegotiates these lifeworld experiences.

Not surprising, then, is that framing theory has become important for a variety of sectors within today's transnational media society. Knowledge about framing theory is crucial for the planning of media campaigns in advertising, public relations, and political sectors. Framing theory is, for example, utilized by spin doctors for the tailoring of a political issue in election campaigns for a specific audience. However, one of the important areas of framing theory is media research in journalism and political communication. As media maintain a fourth estate role in democratic societies, media researchers find framing theory helpful to analyze the imbalances and underlying power structures that mediate political issues. For example, the frame of a story about the environment can be quite different in conservative or liberal media outlets. However, the use of framing theory not only identifies the difference framings of one story across a number of news outlets, but allows us to detect journalistic bias. The use of stereotypical framing, frames along gender lines, or imbalances of the representation of relevant societal communities, such as ethnic minorities within a national or transnational public, are examples of different frames that might be used.

Framing theory emerged in the mass media age of the 1970s. In the United States, this was a time when media research moved away from a unidimensional media-effects model and began to address quite specific forms of media influence on audiences. Among other issues, media research began to address the powerful role of national mass media in shaping political issues within the national public. As audiences were exposed to continuous information streams, it became obvious that media not only influence audiences during election campaigns, but powerfully create world perceptions and political discourse. As Benjamin Cohen argued, although media are not especially effective at telling us what to think, they do tell us what to think about.

During the 1970s, a variety of studies began to further investigate this important distinction. Maxwell McCombs and Donald Shaw developed the agenda-setting approach that claims that there is a relation between the amount of coverage of a certain political issue and the perceived relevance of this issue among the audience's political agenda. An example for this phenomenon is the coverage of humanitarian crises in national media in the United States and the subsequent relevance of this issue among audiences (which has then, in consequence, formed foreign policy initiatives in the United States).

In addition to such an agenda-setting process, framing theory studies the different schemes in which these issues are told. Early studies in framing research identified key frames in television news: an episodic frame—definition of a particular event frame—and a thematic frame, which positions an issue in a wider context of public discourse. Others have addressed frames being used in election campaigns.

More recently, framing theory has been conceptually refined. More recent research addresses specific sets of frames, such as those around elite discourses because many news stories favor the perspective of the powerful societal stakeholders. Others have focused on slant or content frames that identify ways in which framing favors one side over the other in a dispute. Another type of framing research addresses the underlying social processes of frame building. Some theorists have repositioned framing within the terrain of other research methodologies in political communication and argue that framing consists of a macrolevel and microlevel component. Whereas the macrolevel relates to modes of presentation and overlaps with agenda setting, the microlevel relates to the way the audience uses this information as they develop attitudes toward certain issues that overlap with priming processes. Priming refers to the way media offer a prior context by which an audience will interpret subsequent information, thus creating frames of reference for audiences.

In the early 20th century, Walter Lippman, a journalist and writer, noted in his book *Public Opinion* that the world is perceived through stereotypes that serve as pictures in our heads. As the mass media age, as news stories delivered through a small number of national television channels influenced national audiences and as media transformed into a networked media world where individuals actively select information, framing theory needs to be repositioned. Lippman's notion of individual worldviews seem to determine more than ever which information channels are being used. In this sense, framing theory needs to include the individual as an actor within the framing process. More recent approaches to framing theory highlight these social constructions of frames. In these debates, frames are viewed as organizing principles that structure the social world. However, much more needs to be done to reposition this important concept of public discourse in today's networked information culture.

Ingrid Volkmer

See also Agenda-Setting Theory; Audience Theories; Broadcasting Theories; Journalism and Theories of the Press; Media and Mass Communication Theories; Media Effects Theories; Political Communication Theories; Public Opinion Theories; Social Interaction Theories; Spiral Models of Media Effects

Further Readings

Cohen, B. (1963). *The press and foreign policy.* Princeton, NJ: Princeton University Press.

Entman, R. M. (2007). Framing bias: Media in the distribution of power. *Journal of Communication, 57,* 163–173.

Goffman, E. (1974). *Frame analysis: An essay on the organization of experience.* Cambridge, MA: Harvard University Press.

Iyengar, S. (1991). *Is anyone responsible? How television frames political issues.* Chicago: University of Chicago Press.

Lippman, W. (1922). *Public opinion.* New York: Macmillan.

McCombs, M. E., & Shaw, D. L. (1972). The agenda-setting function of mass media. *Public Opinion Quarterly, 36,* 176–187.

Reese, S. (2001). Framing public life: A bridging model for media research. In S. Reese, O. Gandy, & A. Grant (Eds.), *Framing public life* (pp. 7–31). Mahwah, NJ: Lawrence Erlbaum.

Scheufele, D. A. (1999). Framing as a theory of media effects. *Journal of Communication, 49,* 103–122.

FRANKFURT SCHOOL

The Frankfurt School is a group of critical theorists who joined the Institut für Sozialforschung (Institute of Social Research) of the University of Frankfurt am Main (Germany) from 1923 to 1933. Felix Weil, an orthodox Marxist, founded the Institute in 1923 with the aim of planning, organizing, conducting, and evaluating social, historical, and cross-disciplinary research. For political reasons, the institute was relocated in Geneva, Switzerland, from 1933 to 1935, then in New York (1935–1949), and finally back in Frankfurt (from 1949 to present).

In the 1920s and 1930s the Frankfurt School theorists dealt with Marxist analyses of social and economic processes and examined the role of the individual and the group in relation to these processes. Many of the thinkers associated with the Frankfurt School directed their studies toward particular aspects of communication, seeing various links between the historical, social, and economic processes they investigated and communication—among them Max Horkheimer, Theodor Wiesengrund Adorno, Walter Benjamin, Herbert Marcuse, Leo Löwenthal, and Jürgen Habermas. The most important concepts for the field of communication theory are Horkheimer and Adorno's ideas on the culture industry and mass media and Habermas's notions of the public sphere and communicative action.

The Culture Industry and Mass Media

In *The Dialectic of Enlightenment* of 1947, Horkheimer and Adorno developed their theory on the culture industry. They coined this term to refer to the rise of mass media and other forms of communication whose production is industrialized. As a general rule, they argued, increase in technology led to an increase in the production of commodities, and this in turn enhanced the consumption of goods. As industrialization processes created leisure for millions of people, a large demand for cultural products emerged, such as film, radio, popular music, and the press. Assuming that this great number of diverse consumers has identical needs, the culture industry aims to fulfill those needs with identical goods. Therefore, through technical means of production and reproduction, organization and management, a small number of companies produce under monopoly a large number of products that seem different, but are standardized, making wide use of formulas, types, and clichés. In this way, media production can be controlled by large corporations whose targets are economical and political at the same time: earning profits by maintaining subservience to the system of consumer capitalism.

Before the advent of the culture industry, culture had a critical function in showing original alternatives to existing society. As culture became a business, cultural products such as films, broadcasts, records, or newspapers turned into stereotyped reproductions with minimal changes, having no autonomy. Occupying all their audiences' spare time and leaving little room for imagination or reflection, they foster conformity in language, gesture, and thought. Therefore, their political role has changed: They reproduce and support the existing society, providing ideological legitimation of capitalism. In this way, the culture industry manipulates consciousness, integrating individuals into the capitalist way of life. Its products become forms of social organization and control, criticism disappears, and opposition becomes ineffectual due to the elasticity and pervasiveness of the system.

Taking issue with Horkheimer and Adorno's opinion, Benjamin examined the progressive aspects of the new forms of culture. In *The Work of Art in the Age of Mechanical Reproduction*, Benjamin asserted that all new media made art products more approachable, shattering the elitist aura that had characterized works of art in an earlier era. Moreover, Benjamin claimed, film changed the perception of receivers, enabling them to process the rushing of images. So receivers can become better able to analyze and comprehend the often chaotic experience in contemporary industrialized societies, developing into more critical individuals. Benjamin, then, discerning the revolutionary potential of new mass media, proposed their refunctionalization in order to democratize and revolutionize society. He suggested that radio can produce alternative information, broadcasting democratic discussions and interventions by critical-oppositional intellectuals. In this way, Benjamin claimed, radio can be refunctioned as a progressive medium.

The theory about the culture industry was pivotal in the 1940s because it called attention to the links between mass communication, ideology, and economic and political power. Later, it came under heavy criticism. Fredric Jameson evaluated this theory as historically limited and only effective when referring to societies between 1920 and 1970. After the 1940s, he claimed, societies changed extensively, and new media developed, with important repercussions for economics and politics. For instance, in the World Wide Web, a system of documents accessible via the Internet, there are Web sites where political movements and economic concerns can bring their ideas and products to a general public and forums where registered members can hold discussions.

Deborah Cook offers an additional critique of the culture industry. She asserted that Adorno neglected to analyze the interdependence between the culture industry and other business sectors. In what concerns the specific field of film theory, Diane Waldman stated that Adorno considered films as deeply conservative in their own nature, attributing to them the aim to duplicate and reinforce reality. In her opinion, Adorno failed to recognize that films can be characterized by various styles and aesthetic conceptions, which allow films to fulfill a multiplicity of functions. This variety of characteristics not only denies the films' conservative nature as hypothesized by Adorno, but enables them to promote autonomy of thought in the audience.

The Theory of the Public Sphere

In *The Structural Transformation of the Public Sphere* (published in 1989, but written in 1961), Habermas provided historical background to Horkheimer and Adorno's analysis of the culture industry. His research began with an analysis of bourgeois society, which grew up in the late 18th century. This society, Habermas claimed, was characterized by the growth of a public sphere, where individuals and groups could express their needs and interests. In this space, whose function was similar to that of the Greek agorà, they could discuss and evaluate important contemporary issues, opposing the power of the state and of other powerful groups and helping to shape public opinion.

Since then, however, according to Habermas, the function of the public sphere in capitalism, mass democracy, and the welfare state changed: Discussions occur only between media experts, and the receivers become passive consumers of entertainment and information. He called this development refeudalization of the media, likening it to processes that are characteristic of feudal systems.

Some critics noted that Habermas idealized the bourgeois public sphere, neglecting other public spheres: Oskar Negt and Alexander Kluge pointed out the existence of a proletarian public sphere; Mary Ryan discussed a women's public sphere. More recently, Douglas Kellner claimed that Habermas neither theorized the functions of communication media within the contemporary public sphere nor recognized their use by social movements in order to educate and organize oppositional groups.

Universal Pragmatics and the Theory of Communicative Action

In his article "What Is Universal Pragmatics?" and in his two-volume work *The Theory of Communicative Action,* Habermas gave a linguistic turn to his social theory, theorizing about language and communication. Shifting from the issue of publicness to concerns of communication, he left behind historical analysis and used a more analytical approach to examine issues about communication in contemporary social life.

Building on John L. Austin's speech act theory, Ludwig Wittgenstein's concept of language games, and George H. Mead's thoughts on symbolic interaction, Habermas stated that language contains in itself norms that permit criticism of domination and promotion of democratization.

He distinguished four types of action. The first type is teleological-strategic action, which concentrates on achieving success and can be directed toward subjects-objects; it has been highly developed under capitalism. The second type is normatively regulated action; in the third type—dramaturgical action—agents constitute a public for one another before whom they can present their selves. These first three types are already existing types; the fourth one, communicative action, seems more like a suggestion to be fulfilled.

In communicative action, people exchange verbal messages with the aim of understanding each other; Habermas ignores nonverbal languages and excludes from his model other types of social actions, such as conflict or competition. Indeed, in order to perform an effective communicative action, the communication partners must be sincere, accurate, and correct and have the authority to say what they are saying. A subject who becomes an active participant in a communication must put forward four basic validity claims: uttering something understandably, giving the hearer something to understand, making himself or herself thereby understandable, and coming to an understanding with another subject.

Therefore, communicative competence is based on the ability to apply language rules in order to emit and understand utterances. Indeed, Habermas stated, there is a difference between sentences and utterances: The former are judged from a grammatical point of view; the latter are judged from a communicative point of view.

In his article "What Is Universal Pragmatics?" Habermas focused on the necessary conditions for reaching an understanding through communication. He asserted, following Noam Chomsky, that every human being has the ability to construct grammatically correct sentences and meaningful utterances. Consequently, it is the system of grammar, on the basis of which subjects think and speak, that makes communication possible. In this way, sentences become intelligible for a speech community of speakers, hearers, and bystanders.

Yet utterances are multilevel: Through them, subjects create an atmosphere of trust, establish interpersonal relations, and express intentions in addition to transmitting content. For this reason, communicative actions can realize shared understanding; therefore, the locus of rationality is no longer the single individual (as it was in the Cartesian and in the Kantian perspectives), but is the interaction between individuals. Thus, rationality takes on a communicative trait. When shared understanding is achieved, coordinated actions can be undertaken. In this way, Habermas connected his two main theories: Effective communicative actions create the premises for a rebuilding of the public sphere.

Alessandra Padula

See also Communicative Action Theory; Critical Theory; Language and Communication; Marxist Theory; Pragmatics; Public Sphere; Speech Act Theory

Further Readings

Cook, D. (1996). *The culture industry revisited: Theodor W. Adorno on mass culture.* Lanham, MD: Rowman & Littlefield.

Jameson, F. (1990). *Signatures of the visible.* New York: Routledge.

Habermas, J. (1979). What is universal pragmatics? In J. Habermas (Ed.), *Communication and the evolution of society* (pp. 1–68). London: Heinemann.

Habermas, J. (1984). *The theory of communicative action: Vol. 1. Reason and the rationalization of society.* Boston: Beacon Press.

Habermas, J. (1987). *The theory of communicative action: Vol. 2. System and lifeworld: A critique of functionalist reason.* Boston: Beacon Press.

Habermas, J. (1989). *The structural transformation of the public sphere.* Cambridge, UK: Polity Press.

Horkheimer, M., & Adorno, T. W. (2002). *Dialectic of enlightenment: Philosophical fragments.* Stanford, CA: Stanford University Press.

Negt, O., & Kluge, A. (1993). *Public sphere and experience: Toward an analysis of the bourgeois and proletarian public sphere.* Minneapolis: University of Minnesota Press.

Ryan, M. (1992). Gender and public access: Women's politics in nineteenth century America. In C. Calhoun (Ed.), *Habermas and the public sphere* (pp. 259–288). Cambridge: MIT Press.

Waldman, D. (1977). Critical theory and film: "The culture industry" revisited. *New German Critique, 12,* 39–60.

Wiggershaus, R. (1994). *The Frankfurt School: Its history, theories, and political significance* (M. Robertson, Trans.). Cambridge, UK: Polity Press.

FREE FLOW DOCTRINE

The free flow doctrine is associated with 1940s U.S. polices of international communication as promoted by William Benton, Assistant Secretary of State from 1945 to 1947. Benton was responsible for U.S. policy in the creation of United Nations Educational, Scientific, and Cultural Organization (UNESCO) and was on the Executive Board later. He lauded UNESCO's promotion of the free flow of information across national boundaries that, he claimed, would improve the plight of poorer countries. At the heart of the controversy about the free flow doctrine is the question, whose freedom to do what? Benton's proponents hailed free flow as a repudiation of the system of state-regulated media that they associated with the Soviet Union, then the world's second major superpower and Cold War nemesis of the United States. In contrast, critics called it a doctrine, a disparaging suggestion that for U.S. policy makers, it was an unquestioned article of faith that masked self-interest.

Kaarle Nordenstreng, a prominent critic, acknowledges that UNESCO's constitution does indeed promote the free flow of ideas by word and image, but that it does so in the service of mutual knowledge and understanding of peoples for the overriding purpose of contributing to peace and security. Within this framework, therefore, free flow is not an absolute good whose integrity requires that it be protected from all regulation. Nor is it merely a negative freedom, as in freedom from censorship. There are times when the conditions that underlie the possibility of expression must be regulated—in an act of positive freedom—to ensure that individuals may hold and express opinions and to receive those of others, without discrimination.

The notion of free flow resonated, for many, with purported traditions of free speech and free press in Western democracies that distinguished these from fascist and communist regimes. It extended the metaphor of flow beyond circulation of ideas within nations to traffic between nations. The idea of free expression was originally established in argument against prior state censorship, but took little account of the political economy of mass communication. The notion of a free press, for example, refers specifically to the editorial rights of newspapers and broadcast organizations. Mostly profit-driven corporations, their freedoms of expression fall far short of fulfilling Article 19 of the Universal Declaration of Human Rights, which declares that everyone has the right to freedom of opinion and expression and that this right includes the freedom to hold opinions without interference and to seek, receive, and impart information and ideas through any media and regardless of frontiers.

The presumption that news media shoulder this broader responsibility to the rights of everyone to freedom of expression would seem naïve in the light of sociological studies of the selectivity of media content and practices such as the framing of stories to highlight certain angles and obscure others. Edward Herman and Noam Chomsky identified a propaganda model in which mainstream press coverage is governed by (a) the power relations between media owners and the interests of political, business, and military elites; (b) the strategic orientation of media content to the goal of maximizing advertising revenue; (c) journalistic privileging of authoritative or official sources; (d) journalists' fear of retribution from powerful news sources; and (e) ideological convergence between media owners, practitioners, and powerful news sources.

UNESCO's original commitment to free flow came under increasing attack during the 1970s from the Soviet bloc, the Non-Aligned Movement, and critical scholars, in a multifaced campaign known as the New World Information and Communication Order or (NWICO), whose principles were outlined in UNESCO's 1980 *MacBride Report.* For many proponents of NWICO, the free flow doctrine provided ideological cover for Western media to penetrate the markets of the developing world without the likelihood—given imbalances of productive capacity between developed and developing worlds and cultural resistance of Western markets to non-Western media products—of reciprocal influence from developing to developed worlds. In this sense, free flow may be seen as an ideological enabler of neoliberalism and globalization. Western media acquired further market advantage from their early adoption of cutting-edge communication technologies such as satellite and computing. Nor was it just a matter of imbalance in media flows. There were concerns about the quality and fairness of the representations of the world provided by Western media. Western media were increasingly subject to industrial concentration and conglomeration, which undermined their credibility as agents of democracy even at home, let alone on the global stage.

Criticisms of free flow focused on inequalities of strength between different national media industries, one-way flows from more powerful to less powerful nations, and unequal accumulations of market advantages. Herbert Schiller, in his 1969 book, *Mass Communications and American Empire,* advanced a yet more critical perspective, arguing that the internationalization of Western communications was an essential component of postwar U.S. imperialistic hegemony, not dissimilar to an earlier British free trade imperialism.

Ubiquitous U.S. military presence around the noncommunist world was rendered palatable by its association with deceptive freedoms of speech, trade, and enterprise. Free speech amounted to penetration of global markets by U.S. communications industries, free trade opened up developing world markets to Western goods amid continued Western protection of key economic sectors such as agriculture, and free enterprise was distorted by global dominance of U.S. education, innovation, and business. Schiller argued in his 1973 book, *The Mind Managers,* that U.S. media serve the goals of empire by promoting the myth of individualism and personal choice, the myth of an unchanging human behavior, the myth of the absence of social conflict (serving to deny the origins of conflict in social structure), and the myth of media pluralism, which equates diversity of product with diversity of expression. The news business aids the deception through fragmentation of news content, which obscures the underlying interconnections between and the obsession for immediacy, which distracts attention from the underlying causes of events.

The free flow doctrine survived the NWICO attack and remained in evidence in various intergovernmental, UN and UNESCO programs, including the International Telecommunication Union. It resurfaced at the UN's World Summit of the Information Society in 2002 and 2005, where the focus was on inequalities of access to the Internet. Stronger media production in erstwhile developing countries, the economic rise of China and India, and contra-flows in the form of telenovelas, "Bollywood" exports, Al Jazeera, and the Korean Wave, for example, have reduced concern about dependency on first world media imports. The implication that an ideal state of free flow has been attained, however, is unconvincing to those who argue that more than mere content is at stake. Other factors, such as hardware and software patenting and copyright, program formatting, copying of business models, sources of advertising, and so on, may be equally or more important, as is the consideration that in every part of the world only a miniscule elite enjoys the opportunity of free expression, without editorial intervention, directed to large media audiences.

Oliver Boyd-Barrett

See also Americanization of Media; Flow and Contra-Flow; International Communication Theories; New World Information and Communication Order (NWICO); Uses, Gratifications, and Dependency

Further Readings

Herman, E., & Chomsky, N. (2002). *Manufacturing consent: The political economy of the mass media.* New York: Pantheon

Nordenstreng, K. (2007). Myths about press freedom. *Brazilian Journalism Research, 3,* 15–30.

Schiller, H. (1969). *Mass communications and American empire* (2nd ed.). Boulder, CO: Westview.

Schiller, H. (1973). *The mind managers.* Boston: Beacon Press.

United Nations Educational, Scientific, and Cultural Organization. (1980). *Many voices, one world: Communication and society today and tomorrow* (The MacBride Report). Paris: Author.

French Feminism

French feminism is the name for a body of philosophical, psychoanalytic, and linguistic theory that cuts across a broad array of related disciplinary interests, including rhetorical and cultural studies, queer theory, poststructuralism, and semiotics. It migrated from France to the United States in the mid-1970s and is relevant to communication studies because it provides a critical framework and set of concepts by which to understand how discourse is sexed. This entry focuses on its background, major concerns, and key critical terms.

Background

Neither distinctively French nor precisely feminist, French feminism is a neologism resulting from the reception, by U.S. American scholars, of Luce Irigaray's, Julia Kristeva's, and Hélène Cixous' work. Although identified with French feminism, none of the three are themselves French nationals: the psychoanalyst, linguistic theorist, and continental philosopher, Irigaray, is Belgian, with a name of Basque origin; the Marxist linguist, novelist, literary critic, and psychoanalyst, Kristeva, is

Bulgarian; and the novelist, dramatist, and English literature theorist, Cixous, is a German-speaking Algerian. In addition, none of them self-identify as feminist with respect to French politics.

However, as some of the most formidable contemporary intellectuals (such as Gayatri Spivak, Judith Butler, Kelly Oliver, and Elizabeth Grosz) have engaged Irigaray, Kristeva, and Cixous, moving beyond their initial insights and limits to develop new understandings of the feminine, French feminism has come to refer less to them and more to a kind of theory that most often takes the intersection between language, psychoanalysis, and philosophy as its point of departure. Although its scope has since expanded to include other French intellectuals (such as Simon de Beauvoir, Michèle Le Doeuff, Catherine Clément, Monique Wittig, and Sarah Kofman), this entry will focus only on the work of Irigaray, Kristeva, and Cixous, underscoring a few of the important similarities and differences between them.

Major Concerns

The Feminine and Subjectivity

French feminism's preoccupation has been the question of the feminine and subjectivity—that is, how can the feminine occupy a public space in which she may act beyond the prescriptions and prohibitions of masculine interests and desires? Indeed, how can the feminine know what her own interests and desires are in a culture that has systematically excluded her from the human? How can the feminine even be thought within language structures that do not recognize her?

The Discourse of Western Philosophy

Because Western philosophical discourse shapes all of Western thought, Irigaray's and Cixous' (and Le Doeuff's as well) aim has been to expose a history of the systematic exclusion of the feminine: how philosophical discourse has relegated the feminine to nature and woman to the status of mother and daughter (always as a support for the masculine) while simultaneously allying the masculine to culture and how its use of man, ostensibly standing in for both men and women, actually excludes woman from the human. Much of Irigaray's work demonstrates this ongoing exclusion and rewrites the philosophers in order to open the possibility of the feminine entering into Western thought and coming into her own subjectivity. For example, she critically revisits Plato's account of Diotima's speech and Nietzsche's reliance on the metaphor of solids that is historically allied to the masculine.

Irigaray and Cixous have found in deconstruction, or analyses that challenge and break apart traditional categories, resources for developing their notions of sexual difference. For Irigaray, sexual difference is not a biological difference between men and women, but a discursively constituted difference that organizes the symbolic order and thus, women's access to culture. Both the masculine and the feminine must be permitted their own respective symbolic orders if the feminine is to challenge the masculine's erasure of her. Irigaray's elaborate critique finds its most succinct expression in the question, "If we are to be as one, isn't it necessary for us to first be two?" For her part, Cixous turns to the experience of the overflowing feminine body as a poetic resource for the invention of a language and a discourse appropriate to the feminine. Against both Irigaray and Cixous, however, Kristeva dismisses the notion of sexual difference as something that structures the identities and relations between men and women, concerning herself instead with sexual differentiation, that is, the processes within individuals that result in sexed subjects.

The Return of Psychoanalysis

Jacque Lacan's reworking of Freud has provoked passionate debate about the general value of psychoanalysis for feminist theory. Irigaray, Kristeva, and Cixous have complicated Lacanian psychoanalysis even further by criticizing its particular exclusions of the feminine. Although Irigaray and Cixous often find themselves in theoretical agreement, they often reach profoundly different conclusions than does Kristeva. For example, whereas Irigaray and Cixous reject the very notion of the Oedipus complex (which Lacan preserves from Freud), Kristeva does not. Crucially, Kristeva has continued to insist on the value—even the necessity—of patriarchy arguing, for instance, for occidental culture as an example of one of its great accomplishments.

One of the most complex of contemporary psychoanalysis' concepts, desire is the desire of the other: simply, one desires what the other desires. The phallus signifies desire, and woman, as the phallus for the masculine, can never have the phallus: She can be the object of desire, but she can never be the desiring subject. Fundamentally, then, woman is understood by Lacan and Freud as lacking. Both Irigaray and Cixous have emphatically rejected this understanding, instead retheorizing her as a multiplicity or an excess that is figured by Irigaray as the two lips touching (the labia) and by Cixous as the body's multiple pleasures.

Within both the philosophical and psychoanalytic traditions, the mind is assigned to the masculine and the natural, procreative body to the feminine. Hence, French feminism seeks to return the feminine body to thought or, to put it differently, to find in women's embodied experience the resources for radical theoretical, political, social, and cultural change. Their emphasis on the body has had an extraordinary effect on U.S. feminist theory since the 1980s, animating a trajectory of scholarship that explores in new ways the materiality of the body.

French feminism has also, however, been the source of extended, and unsettled, controversy. Perhaps the most serious and persistent criticism leveled against French feminism is that it essentializes women, reducing them to their biology, thereby consigning them to permanent inferiority. This seems to be a consequence not only of its emphasis on the body, but especially its insistence on the maternal body, which many feminists believe plays into the hands of patriarchy by keeping its historical gendering of the sexes in place. Not intellectually committed to the Continental philosophical tradition within which French feminism has evolved, it has been generally difficult for many U.S. feminists to take seriously its claims that the body it theorizes is not the natural body, but a site of contest and social inscription.

Language, Linguistics, and Rhetoric

Traditionally, U.S. feminists have assumed that there is something like gender, a base concept for their political and theoretical work. The French language, however, has no translation for that word, and instead, French feminists have been concerned with the féminin, a word for which there is no translation in English. So while their most indispensable terms do not precisely correspond with each other, U.S. feminism's foremost concern has been with the historical analysis of patriarchy and a pragmatic material politics, while French feminism's has been the analysis of culture and language and the way in which discourse constitutes the conditions of human existence.

Both Cixous and Irigaray contend that language is sexed. They have made the strong case that Western discourse is structured by binary oppositions: man-woman, masculine-feminine, culture-nature, active-passive, reason-emotion, mind-body, light-dark, where the first term is privileged over the second. They contend that the privileged terms align with each other, producing a culture that operates to the benefit of man. From her earliest empirical research on language, Irigaray sought to demonstrate the regularity with which valued terms, such as God, are gendered masculine. For her part, with écriture féminine, Cixous introduced a writing from the body, an insurrectionary writing, that might enable women to break the grip of the resulting cultural traditions that effectively deprive women of their history and experience. (Although the phrase is often applied to the French feminists collectively, Irigaray herself does not use the term.) Hence, their concern is to make visible this binary operation and to theorize feminine resistance to it. Notably, Kristeva parts company with Cixous and Irigaray and their claim that language is masculine sexed. She believes language per se is neutral, and therefore, she has focused largely on language choices in particular situations.

Because of its specialized language and sometimes bewildering prose, some feminist critics charge French feminism with an elitist inaccessibility that makes it unusable for political action and therefore, little more than intellectual grandstanding. This criticism, however, overlooks both the intellectual traditions to which the French feminists are responding and the deliberateness of their rhetoric. They are quite aware that to interrupt a conversation elaborated over 2,500 years requires that they first gain entrance to that conversation, which can only be done through mastery of its concepts and its language, however arcane they may be. And to actually displace that conversation in such a way that something new can take place,

to make a space in which the feminine might emerge from the wreckage, requires a language so disruptive that it may initially make no sense. Without such innovation, there will be nothing to prevent men from going on speaking in the same old way. In a very real sense, then, such criticism actually makes the case for the French feminists: Western discourse has so successfully excluded women from its conversation that even many feminist scholars do not recognize its concepts, and French feminism's prose apparently succeeds in some measure in making nonsense of that discourse.

Janice M. Odom

See also Cultural Studies; Discourse Theory and Analysis; Feminist Communication Theories; Feminist Rhetorical Criticism; Postcolonial Theory; Poststructuralism; Queer Theory; Rhetorical Theory

Further Readings

Biesecker, B. A. (1992). Towards a transactional view of rhetorical and feminist theory: Rereading Hélène Cixous's The Laugh of the Medusa. *Southern Communication Journal, 57*(2), 86–96.

Mcafee, N. (2003). *Julia Kristeva.* New York: Routledge.

Oliver, K. (2000). *French feminism reader.* Lanham, MD: Rowman & Littlefield.

Sellers, S. (1996). *Helene Cixous: Authorship, autobiography and love.* Cambridge, MA: Polity Press.

Whitford, M. (1991). *Luce Irigaray: Philosophy in the feminine.* New York: Routledge.

FUNCTIONAL GROUP COMMUNICATION THEORY

The functional group communication theory is a unified and coherent set of propositions, assumptions, and claims that attempt to explain how and why communication is related to the quality of the decisions groups make. The theory has been very influential in guiding researchers' and practitioners' views about how communication affects group decision making and how communication might be structured to increase the likelihood that groups will arrive at high-quality decisions.

Origins and Influences

Dennis Gouran and Randy Hirokawa are the researchers most closely associated with the functional theory of effective group decision making. They state that the origins of the theory lie in three influences: the work of John Dewey and his work on reflective thinking, Robert Bales and his work on interaction process analysis, and Irving Janis and his work on vigilant decision making.

During the early part of the 20th century, John Dewey developed a method to describe the process that individuals should go through as they work on problem solving. In his 1910 book, *How We Think,* Dewey suggested that the process of reflective thinking involves five steps: (1) a felt difficulty, (2) its location and definition, (3) suggestion of possible solution, (4) development by reasoning of the implications and consequences of the solution, and (5) further observation and experiment leading to its acceptance or rejection.

The second influence on the development of the functional theory of effective group decision making is the work of Robert Bales. Bales and his colleagues had been working on group members' ability to deal with four functional problems: adaptation, instrumental control, expression, and integration. These are problems with which groups must deal in order to perform effectively. Adaptation and instrumental control relate to the management of task concerns (i.e., making a decision); expression and integration relate to the management of socioemotional concerns (i.e., managing relationships). Groups strive to maintain equilibrium with regard to these two concerns, and group communication is a major means of maintaining that equilibrium. For Bales, work on the task serves to disturb a group's balance in the socioemotional dimension, and group members must work to restore this balance. Group communication, then, is both a means by which deviations from equilibrium can be identified and a means by which equilibrium can be accomplished or restored. Bales developed interaction process analysis (IPA) in an effort to capture how communication functions in both the task and socioemotional domains. IPA consists of 12 categories—six related to task and six to socioemotional—into which communicative acts (utterances) may be classified.

The third influence on the development of the functional theory of effective decision making is the work of Irving Janis on vigilant decision making. Janis theorized that highly cohesive groups sometimes suffer from poor decision making because of the pressures placed on their members to reach consensus. Janis labeled this condition *groupthink.* Vigilant groups (a) survey the possible alternatives-solutions available, (b) survey the objectives to be accomplished, (c) examine the risks and benefits associated with the alternatives, (d) perform an information search, (e) process the information in an unbiased manner, (f) reappraise the alternatives in light of risks and benefits before making a final choice, and (g) work out a plan for implementing the desired choice along with contingency plans should additional risks associated with that choice become known.

In all three influences, the functional nature of communication is the focus; in other words, communication is goal oriented and serves to accomplish some purpose. In Dewey's reflective thinking method, communication is functional because when applied to group discussion, it is the means through which each of the steps of the method are accomplished, thus enabling the group to reach effective resolution of a problem. Bales's IPA denotes communication categories that function to enable a group to deal with equilibrium in task and socioemotional domains. In Janis's vigilant decision making, communication is functional because it is the means through which group members fulfill each of the characteristics of vigilance.

The Theory

The functional theory of effective group decision making rests on the assumption that decision-making effectiveness is not affected by the production of certain communicative behaviors per se, but by the extent to which these fulfill the requirements for successful task completion. These requirements, termed *functional requisites,* were spelled out by Gouran and Hirokawa in 1983. In order to make an effective decision, a group should adequately do the following:

- Understand the type of answer for which the issue under consideration calls. These answers are in response to the type of question the group is attempting to answer—fact, conjecture, value, or policy.

- Determine the characteristics of an acceptable answer. Group members develop criteria that the desired choice should satisfy.
- Marshal a realistic range of alternatives among which an acceptable answer is presumed to exist. Group members generate a broad range of possible answers/alternatives/solutions to the issue under consideration.
- Critically examine every alternative in relation to each criterion used to define an acceptable answer. This requisite assumes skill, knowledge, and a sense of objectivity on the part of group members.
- Select the alternative that best conforms to the characteristics of an acceptable answer. Group members should also compare the alternatives against each other to determine which appear to be the most desirable and appropriate.

As a group progresses on its path toward a given goal, communication may influence decision making in three ways: When communication plays a *promotive* role, it allows the group to successfully accomplish the functional requisites. When communication plays a *disruptive* role, it functions to create obstacles that hinder or prevent the group from satisfying any of the requisites for successful decision making. Finally, when communication plays a *counteractive* role, it functions to negate or neutralize a communicative act that functioned as disruptive influence. Thus, communication enables a group to resume movement along the goal path defined by the requisites of effective decision making. The theory predicts that groups that better fulfill the requisites of effective decision making will make more effective decisions.

Generally, what has been found is that groups that make better decisions also produce (a) more communicative acts fulfilling the functional requisites, (b) acts that better fulfill the functional requisites, and (c) acts that rate higher on global assessments of the extent to which they accomplished the requisites. The research, however, has been inconsistent with regard to the importance of particular requisite functions—that is, while high- and low-quality groups do differ on the requisite functions identified in the theory, the particular functions that differentiate these groups are not consistent across studies. Further, it does not appear to matter in what order the functional requisites are accomplished. Although most of these studies have been conducted in the laboratory with groups having little or no history, other investigations have used a case study approach or been conducted in the field, in a more naturalistic setting.

A Critique

The theory has been criticized on various fronts with each contributing to its evolution and present-day form. Primarily, these criticisms may be organized around three themes: assessments of group decision effectiveness, lack of attention to the broader context in which groups operate, and the static set of functional requisites specified by the theory.

The first of these criticisms—measurement and conceptualization of group effectiveness—concerns how the chief outcome variable of decision quality has been assessed in studies guided by the theory. The main method of determining decision quality has been to compare the group's decision to some preexisting standard (as in the case of intellective tasks that have a demonstrably correct answer), or to have qualified judges rate the group's decision along preestablished criteria, such as feasibility, cost, and workability. These criteria may become problematic when one considers that (a) a group(s) may be working under a different set of criteria for determining effectiveness—criteria that may have grown out of the group discussion itself, and (b) groups may, during the course of their discussion, redefine the task in a manner such that the preestablished criteria for determining a decision's quality no longer apply.

The second criticism concerns the broader context in which group members conduct their work. The functional theory of effective decision making places an emphasis on the accomplishment of the requisite functions through members' interaction in the group setting. However, in the social context in which decisions are made, group members often communicate outside of the group setting. Members take breaks and text each other, they communicate in the hallway, over the phone, at the water cooler, on the golf course, or at the organizational picnic. Some of these functions may be accomplished in group members' interactions with one another in these settings, outside of the group meeting. Yet such communication is not adequately accounted for by the functional theory, which has led to an extension of functional group theory by Cynthia Stohl and Michael Holmes, outlined in the following section.

A third criticism concerns the functional requisites themselves. Scholars have questioned whether there are some as-of-yet undiscovered requisites that may better account for decision-making effectiveness. The first argument here is that the importance of functional requisites may not be consistent across dimensions that differentiate task types. Some tasks, for example, may be more complex than others, or have more than one correct or best solution. There may be particular functional requisites that apply to particular types of tasks. The second argument is that there may be some requisite functions that are related to effective group performance that are not inherently tied to the task itself, but to establishing and maintaining the socioemotional atmosphere of the group—that is, a precondition to effectively dealing with task-related functional requisites is dealing with socio-emotional requisites related to establishing well-functioning relationships among group members. Failure to identify these socioemotional functions, then, is a weakness of the theory as originally formulated.

Evolution and Current Status

Stohl and Holmes, primarily in response to the first two criticisms identified above, have proposed an extension of the functional theory that encompasses bona fide groups—groups that are naturally occurring, interact with the broader social environment in which they are embedded, and whose members have a degree of history. They claim that most of the assumptions and methods inherent in the early conceptualizations of the functional theory have necessitated a focus on zero-history laboratory groups. To extend the reach of the theory, they suggest examining historical (understanding the past, present, and future) and institutional (understanding the group's connections to its environment) functions. Additionally, they suggest supplementary methodologies for examining the functional theory of effective decision making such as consideration of the time-ordering of messages

and obtaining information from group participants in interpreting the task and outcomes.

In response to the various criticisms of the theory and the research that has been conducted under its auspices, Gouran and Hirokawa put forth a revision in the book, *Communication and Group Decision Making*. That revision includes clarifications that explicitly spell out the propositions and assumptions that guide functional theory. The authors also include a discussion that identifies some of the factors that can interfere with successful accomplishment of the functional requisites. In this identification is an acknowledgement of the importance of the relational dimension of groups in making an effective decision. Among these factors are *affiliative* (group members are overly concerned with relationships), *cognitive* (information processing is impeded), and *egocentric* (personal motivations dominate) constraints. The scholars expand the theory by focusing on the ways in which these constraints may be managed in group discussion.

A new set of requisites, or what the authors now term the theory's propositions, are advanced. In addition to the original five requisites, which focus on the task, group members should also strive to do the following:

- Make clear their interest in arriving at the best possible decision.
- Identify the resources necessary for making such a decision.
- Recognize possible obstacles to be confronted.
- Specify the procedure to be followed in working on the task.
- Establish ground rules for interaction.
- Employ appropriate interventions for overcoming affiliative, cognitive, and egocentric constraints that interfere with successful accomplishment of fundamental task requirements.
- Review the process by which the group comes to a decision and, if indicated, reconsider judgments reached.

The functional theory has guided a great deal of research in the years since it was first introduced. Whether the theory continues to be as influential in the coming decades will depend on its utility in explaining a wide range of decision making in an increasingly diverse and technologically oriented world.

Abran J. Salazar

See also Bona Fide Group Theory; Creativity in Groups; Group Communication Theories; Groupthink; Interaction Process Analysis; Pragmatics; System Theory

Further Readings

Gouran, D. S., & Hirokawa, R. Y. (1983). The role of communication in decision-making groups: A functional perspective. In M. S. Mander (Ed.), *Communications in transition* (pp. 168–185). New York: Praeger.

Gouran, D. S., & Hirokawa, R. Y. (1996). Functional theory and communication in decision-making and problem-solving groups: An expanded view. In R. Y. Hirokawa & M. S. Poole (Eds.), *Communication and group decision making* (2nd ed., pp. 55–80). Thousand Oaks, CA: Sage.

Gouran, D. S., & Hirokawa, R. Y. (2003). Effective decision making and problem solving in groups: A functional perspective. In R. Y. Hirokawa, R. S. Cathcart, L. A. Samovar, & L. D. Henman (Eds.), *Small group communication theory and practice: An anthology* (8th ed., pp. 27–38). New York: Oxford University Press.

Gouran, D. S., Hirokawa, R. Y., Julian, K. M., & Leatham, G. B. (1993). The evolution and current status of the functional perspective on communication in decision-making and problem-solving groups. In S. A. Deetz (Ed.), *Communication yearbook 16* (pp. 573–600). Newbury Park, CA: Sage.

Hirokawa, R. Y., & Salazar, A. J. (1997). An integrated approach to communication and group decision making. In L. R. Frey & J. K. Barge (Eds.), *Managing group life: Communicating in decision-making groups* (pp. 156–181). Boston: Houghton Mifflin.

Hirokawa, R. Y., & Salazar, A. J. (1999). Task group performance and decision making performance. In L. R. Frey, D. S. Gouran, & M. S. Poole (Eds.), *The handbook of group communication theory and research* (pp. 167–191). Thousand Oaks, CA: Sage.

Paulus, P. B., Hirokawa, R. Y., Ancona, D. G., Peterson, R. S., Jehm, K. A., & Yoon, K. (2005). A look at groups from the functional perspective. In M. S. Pool & A. B. Hollingshead (Eds.), *Theories of small groups: Interdisciplinary perspectives* (pp. 21–62). Thousand Oaks: Sage.

Stohl, C., & Holmes, M. E. (1993). A functional perspective for bona fide groups. In S. A. Deetz (Ed.), *Communication yearbook 16* (pp. 601–614). Newbury Park, CA: Sage.

G

GAME THEORY

See Conflict Communication Theories; Negotiation Theory

GAY, LESBIAN, BISEXUAL, AND TRANSGENDER THEORIES

Although they are typically grouped together, these are actually three (and some might argue four) distinct sets of theories—gay and lesbian, bisexual, and transgender—with different theoretical scope, research foci, commitments to social change, and historical legacies. Within each grouping, there are diverse theories that are influenced by the historical and geopolitical circumstances leading to their development. Gay and lesbian theories, for example, meant different things to people in the 1970s than they do at the current historical moment as the focus has shifted from removing vicious stigma and mental-illness status to the battle for equal rights by lesbians and gay men in various societies in the West. Gay and lesbian theories also mean different things to people in different cultures. Theorizing same-sex relations in some Muslim societies, such as Indonesia, tends to focus on how these relations are structured by social class, age, and gender. Theorizing gay male relations in some Latin American countries, such as Mexico and Peru, tends to examine roles partners play—active and passive—in their relationship. Theorizing lesbian relations in some Asian countries, such as China and Taiwan, tends to focus on *nü tongzhi,* a discourse that indigenizes sexual politics and reclaims cultural identity as distinct from the homosexual–heterosexual binary prevalent in the West.

Given this considerable diversity in their focus across time and space, gay, lesbian, bisexual, and transgender (GLBT) theories entered the academy through different departments and programs. In the United States and western Europe, for example, lesbian theories were mostly featured in women's studies and gender studies programs. On the other hand, gay and bisexual theories were most notably examined in sociology and human sexuality studies while transgender theories were originally featured in sociology and medicine. In recent years, some GLBT theories have made their way into the curriculum of a number of programs and departments in the social sciences and humanities, including communication, in some parts of Asia, Australia and New Zealand, Europe, Latin America, and the United States. As a result, these theories are increasingly interdisciplinary and transnational. This entry provides an overview of GLBT theories by examining their conceptual foundations and common concepts.

Conceptual Foundations

One of the most important foundations of GLBT theories is the assumption that sexuality and gender are socially constructed. This suggests that concepts like homosexual and heterosexual, male, female, "third gender," "two-spirit," and transgender are historical inventions. In other words, these ideas about sexuality and gender are cultural creations that reflect the perspective of a specific culture and its history. As such, they show enormous variations. How we understand sexuality and gender differs from one culture to another (e.g., Kenyan conceptions of sexuality and gender are different from those of India, Argentina, or Australia) and from one historical period to another (e.g., the idea of sexuality in ancient Greece is considerably different from that in medieval or contemporary Greece). To say that social constructions are fluid and changing does not imply that they are trivial or inconsequential. For example, to be perceived or labeled as a transgendered person carries tremendous physical and psychological risks and dangers in many contemporary cultures in the world. Finally, *social constructionism* is generally viewed as the opposite of *essentialism*. This is because essentialism asserts that sexuality and gender are experienced as the inner core of individuals, which remains constant across cultures, geographical regions, and periods in history. Essentialists would argue that homosexuality, for example, is an essential core identity of a person regardless of whether she or he lived in ancient Japan, medieval Rome, or contemporary Canada.

Perhaps a more useful way to look at the social constructionism versus essentialism debate is to recognize that while conceptions of sexuality and gender change, these constructions exist in a cultural landscape that continues to cling to and affirm ideas of core and unchanging selves for various social and political purposes. Take, for example, the myth "homosexuals are child molesters" that extreme religious groups in the United States and England promulgate to incite moral panic in the general population so that discriminatory legislation against gays and lesbians can be passed. To claim that homosexuals are child molesters is an essentialist argument: Homosexuals are, by nature, predatory and dangerous to children, and they cannot change. On the other hand, these same religious groups also declare that homosexuals "choose" their lifestyle, and thus, legislation to protect gay and lesbian rights is unnecessary. In this instance, they are using a constructionist argument to advance the same discriminatory agenda.

As we can see in this rhetorical war, constructionism and essentialism might be more realistically understood as coexisting in ongoing and constant tension rather than completed deliberations.

Another primary conceptual foundation of GLBT theories is their general adherence to and endorsement of the "minoritizing" view. Originally coined to demonstrate the minority status of homosexuals in society, this view suggests that the homosexual–heterosexual binary, which is the foundation of Western discourses of sexuality, is of enormous importance to only a relatively small, discrete, and fairly fixed group of people (e.g., lesbians and gay men). GLBT theories extend the minoritizing view to include other sexual (e.g., bisexual women and men) and gender minorities (e.g., transgender individuals). Such a perspective is in sharp contrast with the *universalizing* view. The latter suggests that the homosexual–heterosexual binary is of tremendous importance to anyone—and everyone—in society because it exposes how sexuality is organized in a social system by showing the privileged status of heterosexuality and its ongoing dependence on homosexuality to maintain its superior status.

The minoritizing view of GLBT theories is intended to provide a positive and affirming approach to understanding the lives, experiences, and subjectivities of gay men, lesbians, bisexual people, and transgender individuals in society. Through a more complete and accurate understanding of these groups, GLBT theories strive for social change by providing ideas, arguments, information, and strategies to create a more equitable, just, and inclusive society. One of the ways in which this agenda is advanced is by naming, identifying, and exposing the oppressions that GLBT people experience daily through their interactions with others (e.g., family, friends, coworkers, acquaintances) and with social institutions (e.g., mass media, education, religion, the legal system).

To understand how GLBT people are oppressed on a daily basis, GLBT theories focus on homophobia, heterosexism, biphobia, and transphobia as the four primary sources. Homophobia generally refers to feelings of fear, dislike, distrust, disgust, hatred, and/or avoidance of individuals who are perceived to be lesbian or gay. Although various forms of panic are generally considered neither adequate nor sufficient for committing murder, *gay panic*—an individual's irrational response to an alleged homosexual advance—has been used, in the United States, as a defense strategy for gay bashers in the court of law. The degree to which this strategy has been exploited, with enormous success in some cases, indicates the strong covert and overt homophobia present in the U.S. psyche and social institutions.

More recently, *heterosexism* was introduced to refer to individual, institutional, and cultural expectations that everyone is or ought to be heterosexual. It is an ideological system that denies, disparages, denigrates, and stigmatizes any non-heterosexual experience, behavior, identity, relationship, or community. Restricting health and retirement benefits to heterosexual marriages is an example of legally sanctioned and culturally accepted heterosexism in many countries, including the United States.

Gay and lesbian theories have used homophobia and heterosexism as the context through which to understand the lives of gay men and lesbians across the globe. This has also led to the political strategy of "coming out"—the process of disclosing one's sexual orientation to others. The assumption is that disclosure leads to greater lesbian and gay visibility, which, in turn, will increase public acceptance. However, such a strategy has not been universally accepted. Some argue that the process of coming out is based on assumptions of Whiteness and other markers of privilege (e.g., social class) by pointing out that many gay people of color in the United States do not have the same advantages and resources as their White, middle-class counterparts to risk rejection and alienation from their own communities and the larger White, heterosexist society. The adoption of the "coming out of the closet" dictum in U.S. gay and lesbian liberation rhetoric has produced mixed results, pointing to the need to understand and incorporate the cultural context into such liberation movements.

Biphobia refers to feelings of fear, dislike, distrust, disgust, hatred, and/or avoidance of individuals who are perceived to be bisexual. Many contemporary cultures are *monosexual*, that is, societies that adhere to the belief that individuals can direct their sexual desire or behavior only toward members of one gender. Cultures that focus on the gender of the individual's sexual object choice (i.e., same-sex, different-sex attraction) uphold the homosexual–heterosexual binary and promote and maintain biphobia. In this scheme, individuals who identify as bisexual are treated with suspicion and mistrust. They get disciplined by being forced to conform to either homosexual or heterosexual orientations. On the other hand, in cultures such as ancient Greece, which subscribe to attraction and desire based on beauty rather than on gender of the person's sexual object choice, the concepts of bisexuality and biphobia hold very little meaning.

Given that most contemporary cultures in the West adhere to binary models of sexuality and gender (i.e., gay–straight, woman–man), bisexual theories vigorously interrogate them and attempt to propose alternate ways of thinking about sexuality. Paula Rust, for example, introduced a trinary model with three discrete categories—heterosexual, homosexual, and bisexual—to increase bisexual intelligibility, identity formation, community organizing, and political engagement. Although the model continues to be based on categorical thinking and gender of the individual's sexual object choice, it offers bisexual people social and cultural legitimacy.

Transphobia generally refers to feelings of fear, dislike, distrust, disgust, hatred, and/or avoidance of individuals who are perceived to be transgendered. Heteropatriarchal cultures—societies that uphold and sustain the dominance of men over women through institutionalized heterosexuality—are firmly rooted in the *gender binary system* (i.e., male–female). As a result, transgender individuals become unintelligible and unwanted "others," those who do not fall neatly into the rigid categories of man and woman. In these cultures, transphobia is pervasive, powerful, and violent. Social institutions in these cultures, such as the legal system, law enforcement, medicine, and the workplace, are often part of the problem, leaving transgendered people with little social and material support. This is in stark contrast with some cultures, such as some Native American groups, in which persons with gender-mixing or gender-crossing roles—the *berdache*—are treated with great respect. Indeed, many are celebrated and occupy a high status in their social hierarchy. Because the gender binary system does not seem to operate in these cultures, gender-nonconforming individuals are not denigrated or stigmatized.

Transgender theories have undergone tremendous change over the years. Early work, written by medical and sociological researchers who had a limited understanding of transgender subjectivity and experience, centered around pathologizing transsexualism and exploring treatment and gender reassignment issues. Current transgender theories, influenced by Judith Butler and Michel Foucault, have a much broader focus, ranging from the documentation and depiction of accurate and nuanced knowledge of transgender lives to the deconstruction of the category of gender and the interrogation of current gender systems. Some have examined the meanings of transgender as an umbrella category to reveal a wide range of gender presentations, performances, and expressions that intersect with race, class, sexuality, and culture. Don Kulick's work on Brazilian *travestis* is one example. These are male prostitutes who live as women—but do not identify as such—after undergoing drastic body modification procedures, including massive silicone injections to create female breasts, wider hips, and larger thighs and buttocks. The study demonstrates the complexities of gender identity as a complex mix of biological definition, social categorization, and personal identification as they interact with poverty, geography, and culture. Others, such as John Sloop's research on public representations of Brandon Teena, the John/Joan case, and Calpernia Addams, have deconstructed gender as a social category and examined how U.S. culture repeatedly attempts to reinscribe the gender binary system.

Common Concepts

As the preceding sections indicate, GLBT theories share some conceptual foundations but also diverge in their areas of interest. To pursue the work in these areas of interest—whether the focus is on how individuals experience the sexual system in their culture or how they resist gender hierarchies—GLBT theories make use of some common concepts: identity, community, identity politics, and liberation.

Although identity is used in everyday talk, it is a relatively new concept. It refers to conceptions of personhood; it is a response to the question, Who am I? Identity can be avowed (how we see ourselves) and ascribed (how others see us). GLBT theories are predicated on specific identities, or standpoints, such as marginal sexual and gender positions in society, from which their work is done. These marginal identities—gay, lesbian, bisexual, and transgender—were originally used by society and its various institutions, including medicine, psychiatry, religion, and the law, to label, denigrate, and stigmatize individuals who deviate from conventional sexual and gender norms. However, the process of classifying and pathologizing these sexual and gender deviants had an important unintended consequence. These deviants adopted such identities to question sexual and gender orthodoxies and to demand equality and social justice. In this sense, GLBT theories are "talking back" at their oppressors. But they do so from different identity positions. Using their sexual minority status, gay and lesbian theories name heterosexual privileges and question compulsory heterosexuality while bisexual theories interrogate the monosexual system based on the homosexual–heterosexual binary that writes bisexuals out of existence. Similarly, transgender theories question the "naturalness" of gender and the stability and coherence of the gender binary system. Identity is also invoked in questions of who has the right to produce knowledge about sexual and gender minorities and what forms that knowledge should take. For example, old forms of knowledge produced by nongay researchers with limited understanding of gay and lesbian experience were questioned and supplanted with "insider knowledge" produced by gay researchers themselves.

As these marginal identities were claimed by more and more sexual and gender minorities, they became the primary mechanism through which to organize and coordinate efforts to fight against oppressions based on homophobia, heterosexism, biphobia, and transphobia. To put it differently, identity has turned into the vital and powerful force that created and sustained community. Since the Stonewall riots in 1969, considered by many to be the beginning of the gay political movement in the United States, many gay and lesbian communities were formed in large metropolitan centers, such as New York, Los Angeles, and San Francisco. These communities were organized around sexual identity and envisioned by many to be safe havens from the violence and oppressions of a homophobic and heterosexist society. While such communities became a place of refuge for some (most notably, gay, middle class, White men), they also divided gay men and lesbians, Whites and people of color, middle- and upper-class individuals and working-class persons. In short, a community organized around one central identity—in this case, sexuality—cannot be sustained unless its members also learn to live with differences based on race, class, gender, and sexual practices, among others.

While gay and lesbian communities proliferated in many major cities around the world, bisexual and transgender communities encountered more challenges, and they remain fairly small. One of the challenges for bisexual communities is their lack of political visibility. Although transgenders have been fairly visible in some cities in the United States and abroad, their diversity seems to hinder community formation. For example, trans-identified women, male-to-female transsexuals, and drag queens do not necessarily have much in common with trans-identified men, female-to-male transsexuals, and drag kings. Similarly, transgender individuals whose gender presentation and politics directly challenge the gender binary system may not share affinities with transgender individuals who wish to quietly pass as members of another gender.

When sexual and gender minorities are threatened by the larger heteropatriarchal society, a powerful organizing tool to build cohesive and vocal political communities is through *identity politics*. The term refers to the practice of basing one's politics and ideologies (e.g., challenge of sexual orthodoxy, battle for gender and sexual equality, quest for social justice) on a sense of personal identity (e.g., being a lesbian, gay man, bisexual individual, or transgender person). Identity politics has been a dominant form of political organizing for sexual minorities in many countries. However, it is misleading to conceive of a global gay and lesbian community struggling for the same political goals. Indeed, gays and lesbians around the world not only assign different meanings to these labels but are also fighting for different causes, depending on the local cultural conditions and their location in the society. "Gay" and "lesbian," as sexual identities, are not comparable across cultures. In fact, the idea of a personal sexual identity is not meaningful to many. Because different cultures have their own unique

sexual and gender systems, even if they subscribe to a Western gay, lesbian, bisexual, or transgender identity, they are likely going to carry a wide-ranging set of meanings. For example, in India, the term *bisexual* is often used for individuals who are heterosexually married but either desire or actually engage in same-sex relations. To call them *closeted* gays and lesbians would be not only culturally inaccurate but also conceptually coercive, because such a move would make one set of cultural concepts, such as Western meanings of sexual identity, universal and further their use to interpret and evaluate other cultures. Identity politics also makes political mobilization across groups more difficult. If sexual identity is deployed by gays and lesbians, for example, to fight for sexual freedom, it tends to exclude others, such as labor groups and feminist organizations, from joining in and creating a stronger and more powerful coalitional presence to combat social injustices.

Finally, one of the fundamental concepts underlying the work of GLBT theories is liberation. As stated earlier, these theories take a broad political and cultural stance to claim sexual justice. Liberation, in this sense, is freedom from the social and cultural constraints that oppress and limit the life chances of sexual and gender minorities in a culture. However, there is no singular vision of a global GLBT liberation and what specific form that should take. Instead, diverse positions exist based on cultural particularities, political circumstances, historical specificities, and social exigencies. For example, in Spain, the focus of the sexual liberation movement in recent years has been to open up spaces for the diversity and plurality of gay men and lesbians to be expressed, seen, and recognized in their culture. In the United States, the most important goals of the gay and lesbian liberation movement in recent years have been same-sex marriage and the right to serve in the military. In Japan, two sets of political goals seem to exist among activists, one stressing the "normality" of gays and lesbians and the need for equal treatment under the law and another focusing on freedom of expression (including sexual) in a variety of contexts. Liberation is not only about challenging dominant forms of heterosexuality but also about reconstructing and creating new knowledge. For example, in an attempt to create more inclusiveness in a language that excludes transgender experience, Leslie Feinberg has popularized, in a limited way, non–gender-specific pronouns such as "s/he" and "hir" in English.

Gust A. Yep

See also Archeology and Genealogy; Critical Theory; Feminist Communication Theories; Identity Theories; Ideology; Queer Theory; Power and Power Relations; Privilege; Social Justice; Vernacular Discourse

Further Readings

Adam, B., Duyvendak, J. W., & Krouwel, A. (Eds.). (1999). *The global emergence of gay and lesbian politics: National imprints of a worldwide movement.* Philadelphia: Temple University Press.

Altman, D. (2001). *Global sex.* Chicago: University of Chicago Press.

Angelides, S. (2001). *A history of bisexuality.* Chicago: University of Chicago Press.

Chesebro, J. W. (Ed.). (1981). *Gayspeak: Gay male and lesbian communication.* New York: Pilgrim Press.

Drucker, P. (Ed.). (2000). *Different rainbows.* London: Gay Men's Press.

Feinberg, L. (1996). *Transgender warriors: Making history from Joan of Arc to Ru Paul.* Boston: Beacon Press.

Fone, B. (2000). *Homophobia: A history.* New York: Metropolitan Books.

Joseph, M. (2002). *Against the romance of community.* Minneapolis: University of Minnesota Press.

Kulick, D. (1998). *Travesti: Sex, gender, and culture among Brazilian transgendered prostitutes.* Chicago: University of Chicago Press.

Murray, S. O. (2000). *Homosexualities.* Chicago: University of Chicago Press.

Ringer, R. J. (Ed.). (1994). *Queer words, queer images: Communication and the construction of homosexuality.* New York: New York University Press.

Roscoe, W. (1998). *Changing ones.* New York: St. Martin's Press.

Rust, P. (1992). Who are we and where do we go from here? Conceptualizing bisexuality. In E. R. Weise (Ed.), *Closer to home: Bisexuality and feminism* (pp. 281–310). Seattle, WA: Seal Press.

Sloop, J. M. (2004). *Disciplining gender: Rhetorics of sex identity in contemporary U.S. culture.* Amherst: University of Massachusetts Press.

Stryker, S., & Whittle, S. (Eds.). (2006). *The transgender studies reader.* New York: Routledge.

Tucker, N. (Ed.). (1995). *Bisexual politics: Theories, queries, and visions.* Binghamton, NY: Harrington Park Press.

Wah-shan, C. (2000). *Tongzhi: Politics of same-sex eroticism in Chinese societies.* Binghamton, NY: Harrington Park Press.

GENDER AND BIOLOGY

Although often conflated, sex and gender are separate and distinct concepts. *Sex* refers to physiological and biological differences between men and women (e.g., male or female). *Gender* refers to one's social and psychological sex role orientation (e.g., masculine, feminine, and androgynous). Although there are several differences between men and women biologically, not all biological differences manifest themselves in communication differences. Research into differences in hormones and brain lateralization routinely explores intersections of sex, biology, and communication.

Source of Biological Differences

Scholars who have examined biology and communication have often done so from an *evolutionary perspective*. The basic idea of evolution is that species evolve and adapt in response to their environmental circumstances. For most of human history, people lived in small hunter–gatherer societies. These societies also experienced high rates of both mortality and fertility. Thus, women spent much of their lives pregnant, nursing, and caring for small children. Women were also the primary village leaders. Men, on the other hand, were primarily responsible for exploring, hunting, and gathering. Due to women's role as leaders of the group and their primary role in the development of family, communication abilities were a central issue for women, whereas they were less important for men.

Because women's success in survival and reproduction relied heavily on their ability to communicate with others in the village and care for young children, it is argued that as *natural selection* occurred, women attained greater social skills, especially nonverbal skills. Similarly, it is argued that men's survival and reproduction relied heavily on their ability to hunt, gather, and compete with other males for mating opportunities. Thus, through the process of natural selection, men attained greater strength, speed, and spatial skills. Two of the areas where biological differences could have been shaped through evolutionary processes to produce differences in communication are hormones and brain lateralization.

Hormones

One important biological difference between men and women that appears to be related to communication behavior is the type and amount of particular hormones. Sex hormones, which include androgens (male sex hormones) and estrogens (female sex hormones), are one well-known biological difference between men and women. Although both sexes produce androgens and estrogens, men produce greater amounts of androgens and women produce greater amounts of estrogens.

In women, estrogen (which includes estrone, estradiol, and other hormones) is the primary sex hormone. Estrogens play an important role in preparing the body for pregnancy and lactation. Further, low levels of estrogen and estrogen fluctuation have both been related to low mood in women. Unfortunately, there is still much that is unknown about how estrogen is related to communication behavior.

In men, testosterone is the most important sex hormone. Testosterone is essential for the continuous production of sperm. The strongest link between testosterone and communication is the link with aggressive, competitive, and dominant behavior. Interestingly, several studies have linked men's testosterone levels with both marital and parental status. Specifically, testosterone levels drop when men marry, and they drop again when men become fathers. Researchers have speculated that these decreases in testosterone lead to decreases in aggressive behavior and thus facilitate more nurturing behaviors, helpful in both marriage and parenthood.

Oxytocin is another hormone that appears to have links to communication. Oxytocin appears to have pain- and stress-reducing effects, along with several other important functions. In women who are pregnant, oxytocin initiates the delivery process by stimulating uterine contractions. It also is released when women breast-feed. Both men and women release oxytocin during sexual climax. Researchers have argued that because the body produces oxytocin at relationally significant moments and because of its positive physiological benefits, oxytocin plays a critical role in the bonding and attachment process in both romantic and parent–child relationships.

Brain Lateralization

A considerable amount of research has shown that there are differences in male and female brain specialization. When it comes to communication behavior, most individuals have a left-brain-hemisphere specialization for language and a right-brain-hemisphere specialization for nonverbal communication. In general, men have more specialized or lateralized brain functions, whereas women have more symmetrical and integrated brain functions. It has been suggested that the more integrated functioning of women's brains results in a greater coordination between verbal and nonverbal information, allowing women to be more emotionally sensitive than men are. Thus, it is argued, the fact that women are more nonverbally sensitive and adaptive than men is due in part to differences in brain lateralization.

However, differences in brain specialization are more complicated than differences between men and women, as there also appears to be variation within men and women. A large majority of the population exhibits standard dominance (SD), or a left-brain-hemisphere specialization for language and a right-brain-hemisphere specialization for nonverbal communication. Anomalous dominant (AD) individuals demonstrate reversed processing patterns (left for nonverbal, right for verbal) or a more symmetrical processing, in which neither hemisphere truly specializes in particular tasks.

Several studies found unique outcomes when brain dominance and biological sex were examined together. One study examined brain dominance as it related to communicator style. With respect to the majority of the population (SD individuals), SD women were more friendly, animated, and open than SD men were. Yet another interesting finding occurred with AD individuals. AD men reported being more friendly, animated, and open than SD men and had scores similar to those of SD women. Further, AD women reported being less friendly, animated, and open than SD women and had scores similar to SD men. In short, individuals with AD reported style preferences contrary to traditional sex roles and more in line with preferences of the opposite sex. The connections between gender and biology and communication are clearly complicated by a wide range of human differences.

Alan C. Mikkelson

See also Communibiology; Gender Role Theory; Gender Schema Theory; Identity Theories; Trait Theory

Further Readings

Andersen, P. A. (2006). The evolution of biological sex difference in communication. In D. J. Canary & K. Dindia (Eds.), *Sex differences and similarities in communication* (pp. 117–135). Mahwah, NJ: Lawrence Erlbaum.

Archer, J. (1994). Testosterone and aggression. *Journal of Offender Rehabilitation, 5,* 3–25.

Bodary, D. L., & Miller, L. D. (2000). Neurobiological substrates of communicator style. *Communication Education, 49,* 82–98.

Douma, S. L., Husband, C., O'Donnell, M. E., Barwin, B. N., & Woodend, A. K. (2005). Estrogen-related mood disorders: Reproductive life cycle factors. *Advances in Nursing Science, 28,* 364–375.

Floyd, K., Mikkelson, A. C., & Hesse, C. (2007). *The biology of human communication* (2nd ed.). Florence, KY: Thomson Learning.

Hall, J. A. (1979). Gender, gender roles, and nonverbal communication skills. In R. Rosenthal (Ed.), *Skill in nonverbal communication: Individual differences* (2nd ed., pp. 31–67). Cambridge, MA: Oelgeschlager, Gunn & Hain.

Miler, G. F. (1998). A review of sexual selection and human evolution: How mate choice shaped human nature. In C. Crawford & D. Krebs (Eds.), *Handbook of evolutionary psychology: Ideas, issue and applications* (pp. 87–130). Mahwah, NJ: Lawrence Erlbaum.

GENDER AND MEDIA

French author and philosopher Simone de Beauvoir's 1949 assertion that one is not born but rather becomes a woman marks a key moment in the development of feminist theory. It signals the introduction of a crucial distinction between sex (the biological differences between men and women) and gender (the socially constructed differences resulting from this biology)—a distinction that remains to this day a central tenet of feminist thought. Indeed, the notion that, rather than being biologically based, differences between the sexes are, by and large, culturally and socially constructed is a useful starting point to understanding feminist theory. It also starts shedding light on the role the mass media—news, magazines, movies, books, music, advertising, television programs (to name a few), and the powerful institutions that produce them—might play in the process of gender definition, as they constitute much of the fabric of the popular culture de Beauvoir is critiquing.

Feminist scholars argue that gender is predicated on a strict binary opposition between male/female that is only tenuously related to the actual biological functions or abilities of male and female physical bodies. This strict dichotomy is perpetuated through sociocultural practices. One needs only to take a stroll down the baby aisle or the toy section of a major department store to start understanding how this might work: Products targeted at children—individuals who are yet to develop clear external markers of sex (at least not ones typically exposed in public)—are unequivocally marked as intended for boys *or* girls. Biology does not offer any logical explanation as to why baby girls must wear pink pajamas or bows on their heads while their baby brothers typically won't. This color coding of infants is, in fact, an early manifestation of a process of *gendering* that individuals will experience throughout their life and that feminist scholars see as a building block of patriarchy. While what is considered appropriate clothing, attitude, or behavior within each category of gender might evolve over time, the fact that the genders remain strictly *differentiated* remains a constant. Feminist scholars argue that historically, this process of differentiation has had more dire consequences for women— kept in subordinated roles through exclusion from activities deemed appropriate only for men and that garner significant sociocultural power—than for their male counterparts.

In order to justify such exclusion, however, men and women must be constructed as *naturally* very different from each other—that is, men and women must be perceived as *biologically destined* or *naturally inclined* to perform very different roles. In other words, this process of naturalization is a hegemonic process as defined by Italian political theorist Antonio Gramsci. Gramsci theorized that dominant social groups can most effectively remain in a position of power if they can convince dominated groups that this position is justified and gain their support for an economic and sociocultural system that essentially maintains the power structure. The most effective way to gain this consent is by constructing the position of elites as natural, normal, or common sense. Scholars have pointed to the role of language, culture, and social institutions in this process of naturalization, which must be constantly renegotiated to account for contestation and protest. In the case of gender, this naturalization takes the form of two clearly separate and unequal gender categories that support a patriarchal system. The schools, the courts, the family, the church, the arts, the universities, the economic and medical systems all contribute to this construction. Louis Althusser calls these institutions "ideological state apparati." The mass media are one of them.

It is thus no coincidence that some of the most prominent figures of the second wave of the feminist movement in the United States, sparked by the 1963 publication of Betty Friedan's book *The Feminine Mystique,* were quite familiar with—and critical of—the media. Freidan herself was a freelance journalist, as was Gloria Steinem. Both vehemently criticized the media, particularly women's magazines and advertising, for their limited representations of women's roles as homemakers, mothers, or sexual objects for male enjoyment, which they felt limited women's horizons and accorded them little social status. Ever since, feminist media scholars have continued to scrutinize media representations and endeavored to better understand the role played by the media in the continued naturalization of highly dichotomized gender roles.

Early studies analyzed the content of the media to assess what kinds of images of women were created in the pages of magazines, on the television screen, or in the movie theater. In the 1970s, they found that women were virtually excluded from media representations. Overall, many more male than female characters appeared in television entertainment, and most sources, experts, and journalists in the news media were men. In 1978, Gaye Tuchman and George Gerbner called this exclusion "symbolic annihilation" and argued that it led to a trivialization of women's lives and issues. Tuchman also found that when women were represented, they appeared in a narrow range of roles limiting them to the domestic sphere and according them little social power, or they were portrayed negatively, as highly emotional, weak, or manipulative.

Research on media targeted at either a male or a female audience also clearly demonstrated how the hegemonic notion of two "naturally" very distinct gender categories was held up by the media. For instance, researchers found that cartoons designed for little boys (which, incidentally, initially constituted the vast majority of programming targeted at children) greatly differed from those intended for their female counterparts. The former were fed a diet of superheroes and quasimilitary figures, while the latter were given princesses and motherly figures with which to identify. While this market has certainly evolved in recent years, with the emergence of female action heroes (Kim Possible, the Powerpuff Girls) and cartoons intended to have greater cross-gender appeal (*Dora the Explorer, Maya & Miguel*), most children's media are still quite clearly gender segregated (Disney Princess vs. Batman). Similarly, texts targeted at an adult female audience—soap operas, tabloid newspapers, talk shows—were shown to perpetuate gender stereotypes both through their portrayal of female characters and through their conception of the female audience as interested only in stereotypically "feminine" topics. Feminist media scholars argued that such stereotyping was damaging to female consumers as it perpetuated the notion that women's roles were limited to a narrow range of activities and kept the male and female spheres carefully separated.

A number of feminist scholars, however, began to further complicate the landscape of feminist academic studies of the media, often until then dominated by White middle-class scholars coming from a mostly liberal feminist orientation. Feminists of color argued, for instance, that representations of gender in the media could not be adequately addressed without simultaneously taking race and class into account. They challenged the concept of a homogeneous female audience affected by representations of women separated from the broader context of race relations and other significant elements of women's identities. Others pointed to the role of the media in perpetuating conceptualizations of sexuality based on the assumption of heterosexuality, or to the need to pay attention to the historical conditions under which portrayals of femininity and masculinity developed in various (sub)cultural environments. In other words, these scholars brought into focus the need to pay closer attention to how different sets of oppression might intersect to influence women's experiences of various media texts. This led to a more complex understanding of mediated representations of gender more carefully located within specific contexts and to the deconstruction of the category "women" as a homogeneous group to be studied as a whole. In other words, scholars questioned the traditional and singular assumptions, meanings, and representations of women as a category.

In the 1980s, a number of scholars also started to consider representations of masculinity as equally problematic to the perpetuation of gender stereotypes, further broadening the scope of analysis. They found that male characters and media texts targeted at male consumers often perpetuated gender stereotypes in ways that were potentially damaging to both women and men, particularly in their characterizations of the latter as violent, tough, and out of touch with their emotions.

Also significant to the development of this added complexity was the work of scholars who moved away from media texts to focus on the process of media consumption and audience interpretation. In her 1984 ethnographic study of female romance novel readers, Janice Radway found that the women she interviewed did not passively accept the "patriarchal" elements of the books' narratives. Instead, they actively negotiated the often stereotypical messages about gender perpetuated in the books to draw their own interpretations and conclusions. Radway also found that the act of reading in itself was a significant element of women's engagement with media. Her informants used the act of reading as a tool to carve a space for themselves separated from their families and the daily responsibilities they engendered. Reading recommendations and discussions of various plots with other female readers also added to the pleasure of reading the books by creating a sense of community among readers. Radway concluded that while

her informants were not completely immune to patriarchal gender constructions—both in their reading of the books and in their daily lives—they were not "cultural dopes" passively consuming texts that were "bad" for them. While Radway's study focused on middle-class White women, a number of other studies similarly set out to understand how lower-class, homosexual, and/or minority women negotiated media representations.

These studies helped scholars understand the significance of examining media in relationship to women's lived experience and gave credence to the argument developed by cultural studies scholars that texts are polysemous—that audiences can create multiple meanings out of media messages, some of which were not necessarily intended by their producers. Studies of media specifically targeted at women also helped raise the status of genres previously deemed unworthy of serious academic study to that of a valuable and necessary area of inquiry.

Today, feminist media scholars are attempting to take all these factors into account in their examinations of media production, media texts, and media reception while searching for new ways to create coalitions and cooperation among various groups whose experience of gender might differ due to their diverse ethnic, racial, or sociocultural situation. Ironically, the media themselves are a crucial instrument of this feminist agenda. Ever since the days of the suffrage movement, feminists have challenged the patriarchal system in their own publications. Publications such as the suffragist newspapers *The Revolution* (1868–1869) or the *Woman's Journal* (1870–1931), as well as *Ms.* magazine, which started at the height of the second wave of the feminist movement and still is published today (the only magazine published without advertising dollars), have significantly contributed to the renegotiation of oppressive gender roles in American society.

More generally, the mainstream media have played an important, if somewhat paradoxical, role in promoting women's voices at the same time as they curtailed their representation in the broader public sphere. For instance, while early newspapers' women's pages naturalized gender dichotomies by promoting the idea that men and women have clearly distinct interests—and while their assumption that women's interests revolved around domesticity, fashion, or social gossip rather than politics or crime was far from progressive—they also provided opportunities for women to enter the journalism profession, albeit in a position that typically did not garner much respect. Similarly, women's magazines may have contributed to constructions of femininity based on a combination of domesticity and impossible-to-achieve physical attractiveness, but they have also historically provided a forum for women's artistic expression. Early women's magazines helped promote the careers of female literary talents or illustrators by showcasing their works. The *Woman's Home Companion* (1873–1957), for instance, published the works of Sarah Orne Jewett and Edna Ferber. From 1911 to 1941, its editor-in-chief was a woman, Gertrude Battles Lane. Today, women's magazines routinely employ women in their top editorial positions.

Thus, because of the media's significance as a potential tool for the promotion of oppressive gender roles predicated on a strict duality only loosely connected to the actual biological attributes of male and female bodies, the media have been the target of much feminist analysis and criticism. Feminist communication scholars also understand, however, that because of their broad sociocultural influence, the media provide a unique tool for the *deconstruction* of this dichotomy on a large scale. Cyberfeminists, for instance, have argued that the gender anonymity of the Internet and its relative disconnection from actual physical bodies provides a unique terrain on which new, more fluid definitions of gender may be constructed in the future. Ultimately, their work will contribute not only to our understanding of gender roles but also to that of American culture in general.

Fabienne Darling-Wolf

See also Critical Ethnography; Ethnography of Communication; Feminist Communication Theories; Feminist Standpoint Theory; Gender and Biology; Gender Role Theory; Gender Schema Theory; Ideology; Media and Mass Communication Theories

Further Readings

Butler, J. (1999). *Gender trouble: Feminism and the subversion of identity* (2nd ed.). New York: Routledge. (Original work published 1990)

Carter, C., & Steiner, L. (2004). *Critical readings: Media and gender*. Maidenhead, UK: Open University Press.

de Beauvoir, S. (1989). *The second sex*. New York: Vintage Books. (Original work published 1949)

De Lauretis, T. (1987). *Technologies of gender: Essays on theory, film and fiction*. Bloomington: Indiana University Press.

Friedan, B. (1983). *The feminine mystique*. New York: Dell.

Gramsci, A. (1971). *Selections from the prison notebook* (Q. Hoare & G. Nowell-Smith, Eds. & Trans.). New York: International Publishers.

Mohanty, C. T. (1991). Under western eyes: Feminist scholarship and colonial discourses. In C. Mohanty, A. Russo, & L. Torres (Eds.), *Third world women and the politics of feminism* (pp. 33–60). Bloomington: Indiana University Press.

Press, A. (1991). *Women watching television: Gender, class, and generation in the American television experience*. Philadelphia: University of Pennsylvania Press.

Radway, J. (1984). *Reading the romance: Women, patriarchy and popular literature*. Chapel Hill: University of North Carolina Press.

Rakow, L. F. (1992). *Women making meaning: New feminist directions in communication*. New York: Routledge.

Tuchman, G. (1978). The symbolic annihilation of women by the mass media. In G. Tuchman, A. Daniels, & J. Benet (Eds.), *Hearth and home: Images of women in the mass media* (pp. 3–38). New York: Oxford University Press.

GENDERLECT THEORY

Genderlect theory proposes that there are separate languages based on gender. The core of this theory explains how different sets of linguistic features used by males and females develop through the gender acculturation process and how these gender-linked language features function as identity markers for women (or men) in their social contexts. Genderlect theory (and the term *genderlect*) first appeared in the 1970s. Its development since then—although not always tied to the term itself—has been associated with a range of scholars who study how gender ideology shapes patterns in women's and men's language usage. Scholars associated with the theory include Cheris

Kramarae, Robin Lakoff, Marsha Houston, and Deborah Tannen.

Most communication scholars date genderlect theory to a 1974 article written by Cheris Kramer (later known as Kramarae) and published in the *Quarterly Journal of Speech*. In this article, Kramer considered evidence for the existence of sex-linked systems of language use. Kramer's analysis highlighted grammatical, phonological, and semantic aspects of language but also considered more general differences in the ways in which women and men use language. Her use of the term *genderlect* was intended to add to the field of sociolinguistics, which focuses on how social variables are related to language use. Sociolinguists study what are called *lects*, a term referring to social or regional varieties of speech. Within sociolinguistics, the conceptual connection is clear between the central term *dialect* and the related term *genderlect*. A *genderlect* is a set of linguistic features that characterizes the language production of a socially defined gender category (typically "woman/girl" and "man/boy"). Genderlect theory has led scholars to search for systematic linguistic correlates of women's and men's language use—mainly phonology, syntax, morphology, semantics, and suprasegmental phonemes (features related to the sound of speech, such as pitch, stress patterns, intonation).

The women's movement of the 1970s (now referred to as *second wave feminism*) shaped the emerging field of *language and sex*. A major proposition in this field was that women and men, even when they speak what is considered the same language (such as American English), actually use language in systematically different ways. Early work in genderlect theory explored how gender patterns in language use often diminish, marginalize, weaken, or even silence women's position compared to men's.

Writing at the same time as Kramer, linguist Robin Lakoff emerged as a major figure in genderlect theory. Her 1975 landmark book, *Language and Woman's Place*, which was preceded by a journal article with the same title, asserted that women experience linguistic discrimination both through the language they are taught to use and the language used to refer to them. Lakoff's central idea was that women are taught as girls to use language that is weak and characterized by triviality, compared to men, who learn throughout their lives to use more forceful and confident language. Lakoff further argued that women lack the linguistic means to convey certainty and forcefully express themselves. She outlined a set of linguistic features that comprise women's language, which sparked a spate of studies on language variants such as rising intonation at the end of sentences ("I think we should have dinner now↑" vs. "I think we should have dinner now↓"), linguistic hedging devices (*kinda, sort of, perhaps*), and syntactic tag-question forms that weaken declarative statements ("This is the best one, isn't it?" vs. "This is the best one"). By implication, the *genderlect hypothesis* (also referred to as the *sex-dialect hypothesis*) proposed that judgments about the inadequacies of women's language are triggered by the linguistic features typical of women's language-in-use. The explanation here is that certain language features lead hearers to draw conclusions about the weakness of the speaker and, thereby, diminish the speaker's value.

By the early 1980s, enough research had been conducted to warrant caution in accepting the genderlect theory as a universal, or even American-based, explanation for differences in women's and men's language production. Scholars like Kramarae moved to the concept of *style* as a more fruitful avenue for insight into the influences of gender on language and communication; style takes on dimensions of language use more in the realm of *pragmatics*, such as *interruption behaviors, top control, talk time,* and *turn taking*.

Also during the 1980s, feminist theory in general was broadening to recognize the diversity of women's experiences and behaviors. Lakoff became the flashpoint for critiques that questioned the validity of evidence supporting genderlect theory. Her evidence about women's language was faulted for its restrictedness to a homogeneous swath of middle-class, White women. Marsha (Houston) Stanback argued forcefully, not only that the features of Black women's language bore little resemblance to those Lakoff described, but also that Black women had been ignored in the study of Black English, which focused on male language. Houston's research led to more projects that explored African American women's discourse both as distinct from White women's discourse and in relation to African American male discourse. Lakoff's work has, however, been rehabilitated with emphasis on the significance of her political analysis of gendered language. Lakoff herself has written about the significance of the historical context in which she was writing her early analyses of women's language.

Another strand of genderlect theory has been developed and popularized by linguist Deborah Tannen. In 1990, she proposed in her book, *You Just Don't Understand,* that women and men fail to understand each other because they speak in different language codes and listen with different priorities. Whereas Lakoff's analysis was political in nature and stressed how women's language needs to change and become stronger in order to disrupt inequalities between the sexes, Tannen's explanation stressed that the differences needed to be revealed and understood so that communication between the sexes could be improved. Tannen engages the concept of culture to bolster her central proposition. She has likened the impact of male–female differences in language codes to the challenges of intercultural communication by introducing opposing key concepts that guide women's and men's production and interpretation of language. Women, Tannen asserts, stress *connection* and *intimacy,* and men stress *status* and *independence.* This "two languages/two cultures" approach stressed female and male differences, in contrast to Lakoff's socialization approach, which stressed male dominance.

The notion of *genderlects,* whether or not that term is used, continues to provide an illuminating spotlight on certain types of language phenomena that are marked for gender. The concept remains articulated in sociolinguistics texts, which often include summaries of research studies confirming patterns such as women's greater use of higher-status variants (for example, /-ing/ rather than /-in'/ endings, as in "going" vs. "goin'") compared to men. The kernel ideas from genderlect theory have also been applied to patterns of language use by lesbian, gay, bisexual, and transgender groups. In recent years, increasing attention has been paid to different locales and languages as these distinctively reflect and shape gender ideology.

The theory of genderlects in its pure form is rarely fully supported, but the core idea of distinction between male and female language use that emerges in many contexts provides heuristic value and helps explain some aspects of the gender ideologies that are in play across many different social situations and cultural contexts.

Fern L. Johnson

See also Gender Role Theory; Gender Schema Theory; Identity Theories; Ideology; Language and Communication

Further Readings

Bucholtz, M. (Ed.). (2004). *Language and woman's place: Text and commentaries.* New York: Oxford. (Includes full text of Lakoff's 1975 book)

Holmes, J. (1998). *Women's talk: The question of sociolinguistic universals.* In J. Coates (Ed.), *Language and gender: A reader* (pp. 461–483). Malden, MA: Blackwell.

Kramer, C. (1974). Women's speech: Separate but unequal? *Quarterly Journal of Speech, 60,* 14–24.

Leap, W., & Boellstorff, T. (Eds.). (2004). *Speaking in queer tongues: Globalization and gay language.* Urbana: University of Illinois Press.

Stanback (Houston), M. M. (1985). Language and Black woman's place: Lessons from the Black middle class. In P. Treichler, C. Kramarae, & B. Stafford (Eds.), *For alma mater: Theory and practice in feminist scholarship* (pp. 177–193). Urbana: University of Illinois Press.

Tannen, D. (1990). *You just don't understand: Women and men in conversation.* New York: William Morrow.

GENDER ROLE THEORY

Gender role theory is grounded in the supposition that individuals socially identified as males and females tend to occupy different ascribed roles within social structures and tend to be judged against divergent expectations for how they ought to behave. As a consequence, the theory predicts males and females will develop different skills and attitudes and that they will behave differently. Communication researchers have used gender role theory to explain and predict (a) the communication behaviors of females and males and (b) the evaluation of the same communication behavior, when males and females perform it. This research has led to considerable debate about whether the focus should be on gendered differences or similarities.

Margaret Mead's Early Research

Margaret Mead's 1935 book, *Sex and Temperament in Three Primitive Societies,* was particularly instrumental in challenging biological explanations for gendered differences. She identified dramatically different gender roles in the three cultures she investigated: The Arapesh required both males and females to be nurturing, cooperative, and peaceful; the Mundugumor demanded that both females and males be aggressive and violent; and the Tchambuli expected females to be dominant and impersonal, but males to be emotionally dependent and concerned with personal adornment. Mead argued that the patterns she observed clearly demonstrated that many gendered differences are not biologically determined but are socially constructed by societal preferences—preferences that could and did vary and that represented only a small fraction of the wide range of human temperaments and skills. Since Mead's investigations, many scholars have used gender roles to predict and explain the behavior of males and females.

Alice Eagly's Gender Role Theory

Alice Eagly is arguably one of the most prolific scholars using gender role theory to explicate the behavior of males and females. Among Eagly's extensive publications, her 1987 book, *Sex-Differences in Social Behaviors: A Social-Role Interpretation,* is probably cited the most often as the fullest treatment of her theoretical perspective. Eagly maintained that a community's gender roles are known to its members and that members agree and comply with and reinforce these standards. Various strategies can be used to identify gender roles in a given society, including gendered stereotypes and descriptions of the "ideal" male or female. Certain types of slang also signal such roles and associated judgments about appropriateness (e.g., *Don Juan, slut, bachelor, spinster, sissy, tomboy, stallion, chick*). Community standards for ideal behaviors for males and females are likely to be reinforced by members of the community in both subtle and not-so-subtle ways (e.g., smile/frown, conversational extensions/topic shifts, agreements/disagreements, inclusion/exclusion, praise/criticism, support/harassment,

advancement/stagnation). Gendered expectations can lead to *self-fulfilling prophecies,* with people enacting what others expect of them.

In taking a structural approach to gender differences, Eagly reasoned that because males and females are expected to fulfill divergent roles within social structures, they behave differently and are evaluated differently. More specifically, she noted that women are expected to fulfill communal roles that require one to be selfless, caring, and nurturing, while men are expected to enact agentic roles entailing independence, task orientation, and dominance. According to Eagly, these expectations lead to divisions of labor related to these roles in the workplace—with males occupying more of the high-status positions—and in the home, where women assume more of the domestic responsibilities. Further, occupying distinctive roles is likely to influence the acquisition and reinforcement of different skills and attitudes (e.g., opinions about force and compassion). Gender role theory predicts that the greater the difference in social roles performed by males and females, the greater the difference in behaviors and attitudes; conversely, the more they perform the same social roles, the more similar their behavior and attitudes. The theory predicts that gendered behavior will change when gender roles change.

Eagly observed that gender roles are more likely to influence behavior under the following conditions: (a) when other social roles do not override the salience of gender roles; (b) when situations call for behavior associated with gender role stereotypes (e.g., helping repair a car or care for children); (c) when strangers interact, since what they know about each other is limited; and (d) when an audience is present to observe and reinforce gendered expectations.

In 1987, Eagly argued that gender role theory is a better predictor of gendered patterns than are biological theories or those based on childhood socialization. She maintained that the latter theories predict consistent gender differences across situations, while research shows considerable variability among women and men, and gender role theory accounts for this variability. Later, Wendy Wood, along with Alice Eagly, embraced a *biosocial* analysis of gender differences in which they acknowledged the potential impact of physiology (e.g., body size, muscle strength, pregnancy, and lactation) on the gendering of some social roles (e.g., hunting large animals, warfare, tasks requiring strength, caring for infants). They argued that gendered differences in these social roles can contribute to patriarchal societies, leading males to reinforce gendered roles that maintain their greater power and prestige. However, Wood and Eagly also noted that social and environmental factors can and do alter who fulfills these roles and the very presence or strength of patriarchy. Eagly and her associates, as well as others, have used gendered expectations to predict differences in the communication of males and females. They have rarely linked communication to physiological differences, but they have made connections to patriarchy and to agentic and communal roles.

Gender Role Theory and Communication

Gender role theory has been used to guide research on many topics related to communication in the United States: aggression, conformity, gender stereotypes, helping, influenceability, leadership, mate selection, nonverbal communication, occupations, persuasion, social sensitivity, sociopolitical attitudes, and task and social-emotional discourse in small groups. Eagly concluded that the findings from these studies provide support for the tenets of gender role theory. Like Eagly, Deborah Tannen argued that females take a more communal perspective and males a more autonomous, independent orientation in their communication practices. Tannen considered the differences in the communication practices of males and females to be so large that she described females and males as being from different cultures, and she maintained that these differences led to misunderstandings. John Gray represented what he considered to be the vast differences with the metaphor that men are from Mars, women are from Venus.

On the other hand, Janet Hyde and many other scholars have maintained that there are far more similarities than differences between men and women. Daena Goldsmith and Patricia Fulfs analyzed the data on which Tannen's claims were made and argued that the evidence did not warrant Tannen's conclusions. Kathryn Dindia's review of research on gender and communication led her to conclude that instead of John Gray's interplanetary metaphor of difference, we should acknowledge the vast similarities with the metaphor, men are from North Dakota, women are from South Dakota.

Researchers who emphasize similarities between men and women note that even when there have been statistical differences in the mean scores of females and males studied in the United States, the vast majority of them communicate in similar ways, with only about 15% of males and females differing from one another. In addition, some scholars point to other factors (e.g., country of origin, culture, disability, ethnicity, race, sexuality, social class, status) that can interact with or that are even more influential than gender in communication. These other factors tend to be overlooked in monolithic proclamations about females and males.

An individual's identity is composed of multiple elements, so for a given individual or situation, the gendered portion of one's identity may not be the primary factor influencing one's communication. On the other hand, cultural markers make gender "visible" even when little else is known; therefore the gender identity assigned by others, especially by strangers, may play a more significant role in judgments of others than in shaping one's own behavior. When cultures, communities, or groups embrace prescriptive expectations based on gender (e.g., males should be stoic, males should lead, females should not be autocratic, females should comfort others), gender role theory predicts that these expectations will yield gendered evaluations, and some studies have provided support for such predictions.

For example, Eagly and associates found that when forced to choose a leader, groups that knew little about members other than what they could infer from what they could see (e.g., gender) were much more likely to pick men over women. But when they chose a leader after meeting more than one time, that is, after they acquired additional information, the effect size for gendered selection was significantly reduced. This finding suggests that other types of information can weaken initial gender biases in leader selection processes. However, groups may continue to demonstrate other types of gender biases. For instance, when females enacted the same autocratic style of leadership performed by males, females were evaluated more negatively. While leadership is stereotypically associated more with males, providing comfort is stereotypically associated with females, and Amanda Holmstrom and associates found that females judged other females delivering emotionally insensitive messages as less likable than males delivering the same message.

Some gender role theorists have argued that even small statistical differences in evaluations can be of practical significance. For example, Richard Martell and associates used a computer simulation to show how relatively small differences (e.g., a negative bias toward women of only 1%–5%) could have large cumulative effects on promotions. In the simulations, men and women started out in equal numbers, but after eight opportunities for promotions, only 29%–35% of the women were in the highest positions, compared with 65%–71% of the men. The cumulative outcome of this simulation mirrored the kind and size of gender discrimination that has been reported in the workplace.

Summary

Gender role theory predicts differences or similarities between males and females based on the degree of variations in ascribed roles and related evaluations. Gender role theory has generated substantial research, academic debate, and questions—processes that seem likely to continue. Since humans create, reinforce, and change social roles, including gendered ones, perhaps we should consider what is in our collective best interests as we engage in these processes.

Susan B. Shimanoff

See also Feminist Communication Theories; Feminist Standpoint Theory; Gender and Biology; Gender and Media; Genderlect Theory; Gender Schema Theory; Muted Group Theory; Rules Theories

Further Readings

Allen, M., Preiss, R. W., Gayle, B. M., & Burrell, N. (2002). *Interpersonal communication research: Advances through meta-analysis.* Mahwah, NJ: Lawrence Erlbaum.

Dindia, K., & Canary, D. J. (Eds.). (2006). *Sex differences and similarities in communication: Critical essays and empirical investigations of sex and gender in interaction* (2nd ed.). Mahwah, NJ: Lawrence Erlbaum.

Eagly, A. H. (1987). *Sex-differences in social behaviors: A social-role interpretation.* Hillsdale, NJ: Lawrence Erlbaum.

Eagly, A. H., & Carli, L. L. (2007). *Through the labyrinth: The truth about how women become leaders.* Boston: Harvard Business School Press.

Goldsmith, D. J., & Fulfs, P. A. (1999). "You just don't have the evidence": An analysis of claims and evidence in Deborah Tannen's *You just don't understand. Communication Yearbook, 22,* 1–49.

Holmstrom, A., Burleson, B. R., & Jones, S. M. (2005). Some consequences for helpers who deliver "cold comfort": Why it's worse for women than men to be inept when providing emotional support. *Sex Roles, 53,* 153–172.

Hyde, J. (2005). The gender similarities hypothesis. *American Psychologist, 60,* 581–592.

Martell, R. F., Lane, D. M., & Emrich, C. (1996). Male-female differences: A computer simulation. *American Psychologist, 51,* 157–158.

Mead, M. (1935, 2001). *Sex and temperament in three primitive societies.* New York: HarperCollins.

Tannen, D. (1990). *You just don't understand: Women and men in conversation.* New York: William Morrow.

Wood, W., & Eagly, A. H. (2002). A cross-cultural analysis of the behavior of women and men: Implications for the origins of sex differences. *Psychological Bulletin, 128,* 699–727.

GENDER SCHEMA THEORY

Gender schema theory (GST) is a cognitive theory developed to explain the role of gender in organizing meaning, both for self and for others. GST was first proposed by psychologist Sandra Lipsitz Bem in 1981. Bem's formulations built on the more general developmental process through which children learn to incorporate content-specific information into more abstract cognitive structures that are used to process and organize what the person perceives. Observing that all societies make distinctions between male and female, Bem was interested in how children learn to use the content around them related to gender both to evaluate people and situations and to assimilate new information.

Key terms for this theory are *schema* and *schema theory*. A *schema* is a network of cognitive organizations that guides how an individual perceives self, others, and situations. As such, a schema is a systematic framework for interpretive activity. In short, it is a mental representation of a broad range of attributes, traits, and behaviors that are associated with women or men in a particular culture. Once a schema is established, only minimal cues are necessary to elicit the more elaborate set of meanings associated with the schema. *Schema theory* proposes that perception and the assignment of meaning by people result from the interaction of incoming information and perceptual cues with the perceiving person's existing schema.

Several propositions guide GST, and many communication scholars have found this theory from cognitive psychology to be useful in understanding the assignment of meaning in communication transactions. The main propositions forming the core of GST revolve around the degree to which an individual has developed highly defined gender schemas. These propositions have been amply tested through research. Five propositions from Bem's work are central to GST:

1. The child learns to link certain content items to broader attributes that he or she links to "sex" and "gender" (male and female), and these linkages form the basis for "sex-typing" and cultural myths about female and male characteristics (for example, associating certain colors, postural cues, clothing, activities, etc., with female or male).

2. The child learns to use a complex network of sex-linked associations to process new information and to make sense of cues that she or he perceives, thus making perception a constructive process (for example, a preschool-aged child who has learned to identify "boys" and "girls" will have difficulty with stabilizing gender for a person with a girl's name who looks sex-indeterminate because she has short hair, a lower pitched voice than is typical for females, and does not have a visibly accentuated female body type).

3. The self-concept is made meaningful through the gender schema that a child develops such that self-monitoring and evaluation occur through application of the gender schema

(there are many daily life examples of making decisions guided by a gender schema about what to say, what to wear, how to present oneself to another person or persons in a specific situation).

4. Once formed, a gender schema is "an anticipatory structure" that works like a shorthand to assign gender meanings to self and others when relevant events or cues activate the schema (for example, seeing a woman wearing a flowered print skirt might activate a meaning structure related to her being a highly feminine woman).

5. Gender schemas are regulative for judgments of what is natural or unnatural, right or wrong, valued or nonvalued (for example, a man who stays at home to care for the children might lead to the judgment that he is weak relative to his wife).

Gender schemas function to fill out a profile of gender identity once a cue or set of cues is available from an event or person. Because cultural practices change over time, gender schemas also change. For example, the vast majority of today's children in the United States are less likely than children of the past to believe that certain occupations are restricted to men or to women. Yet, gender schemas can persist even when change has occurred. For example, even today, many people continue to fill out a male gender schema when they hear *dentist* or *airplane pilot* and a female schema when they hear *secretary* or *third-grade teacher*.

Much of the research designed to test GST has made use of the Bem Sex-Role Inventory (BSRI), which contains 60 questions used to determine the degree to which an individual's self-identity assessment is gender schematic of the broader culture in which the individual lives. Based on completing this inventory of items (words such as *assertive* and *tender*), each of which the participant rates on a 7-point scale of applicability to the self, the individual's degree of gender schematicity is calculated. Using subscales for femininity and masculinity, an individual is considered *gender schematic* if that person's profile corresponds to either the masculinity or the femininity profile. If the person's biological sex corresponds to cultural sex-typing (that is, a "male" scores clearly in the masculine area), that person is considered *sex-typed*. If biological sex and the masculinity and femininity scales are reversed, that person is considered *cross sex-typed*. An individual is *a-schematic* if her or his self-assessment is neither masculine nor feminine. Such individuals could be *androgynous* (having a balanced profile of masculine and feminine characteristics) or *undifferentiated*. Bem also argued that in U.S. culture and in many other societies, heterosexuality is a subschema of central importance to gender schema. GST predicts that sex-typed individuals have a greater likelihood of making use of the heterosexuality subschema in their interactions with others than do either androgynous or undifferentiated gender individuals.

Scores of studies have been conducted using the BSRI inventory. Based on this research, it is clear that gender schematic individuals, especially those who are sex-typed, make much greater use of gender schema and are faster in making gender-related interpretations than are gender a-schematic individuals. Past research has also found that cross sex-typed individuals are the most gender schematic of all categories—a finding of interest related to current cultural practices that demonstrate greater fluidity in the concept of gender than in the past.

GST has been useful to communication scholars because of its helpfulness in understanding differences in the ways in which boys/girls and men/women communicate and in understanding differences in responses to and evaluations of the communication of girls/boys and women/men. Some of the topics that research has probed include how gender schemas affect student evaluations of teachers, the language used in letters of recommendation, perceptions and evaluations of political candidates, and microlinguistic features such as backchannels (minimal responses to others who are talking, such as "uh-huh" and "yeah") in discourse. GST thus helps create an explanation for how gender as a mental construct shapes communication in different ways. GST can also be uncoupled from the BSRI as an assessment instrument to probe other avenues of assessment. Bem, in *The Lenses of Gender*, has herself has gone beyond the thinking behind the BSRI to suggest a more culturally oriented approach to understanding the development of gender identities.

Fern L. Johnson

See also Genderlect Theory; Gender Role Theory; Identity Theories

Further Readings

Bem, S. L. (1981). Gender schema theory: A cognitive account of sex typing. *Psychological Review, 88,* 354–364.

Bem, S. L. (1993). *The lenses of gender*. New Haven, CT: Yale University Press.

Chang, C., & Hitchon, J. C. B. (2004). When does gender count? Further insights into gender schematic processing of female candidates' political advertisements. *Sex Roles, 51,* 197–208.

Martin, C. L. (2000). Cognitive theories of gender development. In T. Eckes & H. M. Hanns (Eds.), *The developmental social psychology of gender* (pp. 91–121). Mahwah, NJ: Lawrence Erlbaum.

Trix, F., & Psenka, C. (2003). Exploring the color of glass: Letters of recommendation for female and male medical faculty. *Discourse & Society, 14,* 191–220.

GENERAL SEMANTICS

General semantics states that the transfer of culture across generations is the distinguishing feature between humans and other life forms, with symbolic communication serving as the transfer system. Intended to improve understanding among people and cultures, this tradition attempts to guide humanity toward more ethical human behavior. This entry discusses the formative history of general semantics and its relationship to communication theory.

Alfred Korzybski

General semantics is Alfred Vladislavovich Habdank Skarbek Korzybski's attempt to redirect the manner of thought individuals employ in approaching the world. Korzybski was born of Polish nobility, continuing the family occupational tradition in philosophy, engineering, and mathematics. His thinking was influenced by Georg Hegel and Immanuel Kant; by Karl Marx and Friedrich Engels' discussions of the struggle of the working class; by Charles Darwin's conclusions; by the new era of electricity led by Michael

Faraday, James Maxwell, and Nikola Tesla; and later by others, including Alfred North Whitehead, Bertrand Russell, and Albert Einstein. Initially assigned to the Second Russian Army during the World War I, Korzybski worked in intelligence and was severely injured, later serving on the Polish Commission to the League of Nations. Traveling in America for the U.S. government, he lectured on the importance of Liberty Bonds and of increased production.

Particularly influenced by World War I, Korzybski sought to end the suffering brought about by humans' inhumanity, which contrasted greatly with recent rapid advances in science. He questioned how humans could cooperate so well in the advancement of science, yet fail so badly in international politics and culture. While culture could be transmitted through symbolic communication, animal territoriality remained, and for much of humanity, the advances of science were lost in the insanity of wars. Rejecting religious and philosophical approaches to the problem as metaphysical speculation, Korzybski sought to apply the methods of physics and mathematics to the problems of human interaction for the benefit of humanity. Based on his attempts to apply mathematical methods in psychoanalysis, he studied psychiatry for 2 years at St. Elizabeth's Hospital in Washington under William Alanson White. This work included reading case histories, interviewing patients, attending meetings of the staff and Washington meetings of professional psychiatric societies, and holding occasional discussions of his work with Harry Stack Sullivan.

Following this work and except for his own Institute of General Semantics and the International Society for General Semantics, which merged with the Institute in 2003, Korzybski had no official connection with a formal organization. This may have affected the credibility accorded to his work. Bronislaw Malinowski and Roscoe Pound, among others, were honorary trustees of the Institute. The writings of Samuel Ichiye Hayakawa helped to popularize general semantics. Korzybski taught many seminars and lectured at universities, several offering courses in the subject. He usually incorporated diagrams into his lectures and was visual in his own thinking. Korzybski became a naturalized citizen of the United States in 1940. Richard Bandler and John Grinder's *Frogs Into Princes:* *Neuro Linguistic Programming*, Albert Ellis's *Rational Emotive Behavior Therapy*, and Aaron Beck's *Cognitive Therapy and the Emotional Disorders* were each directly influenced by Korzybski's work.

Origins

Searching for the characteristic qualities that make people human, Korzybski considered the qualities of plants and animals. Plants appear dependent on chemical interactions with the soil and light. Animals' major advance was in their ability to move. He recognized the human advance over animals in the transmission of culture between generations so that the same lessons did not need continual relearning for survival. Similar ideas are found in the later analyses of Carl Sagan, progressing from evolutionary information stored in DNA, through brain and cognitive storage, and culminating in the storage of cultural survival information in libraries and hard drives. Korzybski labeled the characteristic qualities of plants *chemistry binding* and used *space binding* for animals. He labeled the characteristic quality distinguishing humans *time binding*.

Observations of human behavior suggested to Korzybski that people did not evaluate clearly the events of the world and their causes. Most thought occurs through the words of a language, and Korzybski reasoned that inaccuracies in language should then affect accuracy of thought. The solution to humanity's problems might then lie in the study of how people assign meaning to words. People conceived of these words as having fixed meanings. This resulted, he believed, from the common interpretation of Aristotle's concept of definition as the search for the *essence* of a concept, a predetermined meaning. Korzybski defined humans in terms of their actions rather than in terms of what they *are*, as the latter would presume a preexisting essence.

The realities of life are distinct and constantly changing. They are separate from the meanings assigned to words. When people hear a word, their own beliefs about its essence may not correspond to its intended usage. Rather than seeking the thrust and nuances of the intended meaning, people tend to assign meaning to an utterance based on fixed essences without evaluating background, situation, and intended meaning. People confuse the steps of the processes in converting from observation to thought to speech and back, speaking before observing and treating speech as though it were fact. Thus, the power of words in communication is reduced and the accuracy of expressions suffers, forming the basis for much of the miscommunication in the world. This is similar to Edwin Howard Armstrong's bitter comment after the U.S. Supreme Court initially nullified his patents on the regenerative circuit: Lawyers substitute words for reality and then argue about the words.

Korzybski also rejected the use of syllogisms and syllogistic logic due to their two-valued nature, believing them incapable of capturing the complexity of life. In an unfortunate selection of terms, Korzybski referred to the search for essence and use of syllogistic logic as *Aristotelian,* which it was, but then labeled his own conception as *non-Aristotelian:* His system was an alternative to Aristotle. To some, this implied that he saw his own status as equal to that of Aristotle. While Korzybski believed Aristotle would oppose the use of *essence* as it is commonly applied, attributing the error to Aristotle's interpreters, the implication was still there.

Korzybski believed his system of analysis was applicable to all people, people whose faulty thinking was a major source of the world's problems. Rather than curing pathology, as in psychotherapy, he focused on increasing each individual's ability to evaluate the world clearly as it affected the person. He called this *general semantics,* a form of mental discipline enabling its users to circumvent traps in the use of language and in common sense, and thus to think clearly.

Central Purpose

The central purpose of general semantics is often stated as making people consciously aware of the evaluation process they use when *abstracting* from words or other information. Abstracting is the general semantics term for meaning assignment— selecting some aspects of the information and ignoring others. This is similar to distinguishing between the map, or words, and the territory, the reality behind the words. Perfunctory understanding of the map–territory distinction was not deemed sufficient. Full human sanity was seen as

possible only if deliberate conscious abstracting became a natural reflex, delaying reactions until thought was more complete rather than engaging in immediate, unthinking, knee-jerk reactions. General semantics techniques would thus serve as a defense against the manipulative propaganda of advertising, politics, and religion and against the self-deception that routinely creates semantic distortions during evaluation that lead to the world's problems.

Fundamental Concepts of General Semantics

General semantics proposes many concepts required for evaluation. A few of those Korzybski thought most important for human survival are outlined below.

Time Binding

Time binding is the human ability to communicate symbolically, thus passing on culture to the next generation. Furthermore, this cultural transfer occurs at a rate that accelerates exponentially with the passage of time. While animals teach some behaviors to their young, there is no acceleration in the transfer rate. Each generation of animals is similar in its behavior. Yet human societies have evolved rapidly from hunter–gatherer status. Time binding provides the basis for an ethical standard for evaluating human behavior: Does a given behavior advance human progress as we know it at the time? Understanding that human culture is time bound serves to counter notions of eugenics that successful people are *self-made,* emphasizing the debt we owe to others and creating a clearer understanding of our own limitations.

Extension, Not Intension

This concept refers to seeking relations between observations in the search for knowledge, rather than searching for presumed set properties of the observed.

Scientific Approach

This concept involves continued testing of all assumptions and beliefs, gathering as much data as possible, revising assumptions and beliefs as needed, and holding conclusions and judgments only tentatively until more data become available.

Process-Oriented Universe

The universe is a process with everything in constant flux and change, sometimes microscopic in nature and sometimes involving macro change. People need to be aware of constant change, especially when it appears none has occurred.

Conditionality and Delayed Reaction

These concepts involve replacing an automatic conditioned response with a delayed, controlled, deliberate response.

Identification

Identification involves awareness of the abstracting process. Individuals tend to confuse orders of abstraction, conflating reactions about an event such as descriptions and judgments with the event itself. This conflation ignores the role of neurons in the construction of experience. Grass is not green. Rather, our neurons interpret a particular frequency of electromagnetic radiation as green. "Grass appears green to me" may be more accurate.

Dating and Indexing

Categories are dangerous. Assigning dates to each observation reminds people that nothing is ever the same, change is continual, and no word, person, place, event, or thing has exactly the same meaning a second time or in another place.

Criticisms

Korzybski substantially overclaims the potential influence of general semantics as a possible cure-all for the ills of humanity, especially with respect to its neurological basis. While many tenets of the theory now form the basis of major approaches to the study of communication and other social sciences, his excessive claims and the label choice of *non-Aristotelian* were improvident and unnecessary. The most influential though relatively brief critique of general semantics was first published in 1952 by Martin Gardner, ridiculing Korzybski in referring to him as the Count. Stating that general semantics may or may not have scientific merit,

Gardner makes many points on neurology; on clear overstatement; on the verbose, obtuse writing style; on Korzybski as incorporating the views of others; and on the hodgepodge feeling of the academic areas pieced together in his book *Science and Sanity* that are on target. Yet syntheses of others' work are the basis for most new ventures, and the ability to write clearly has seldom been the hallmark of philosophers. Some critical comments by Gardner, such as those on Korzybski's limited formal education and his late decision to adopt the term *semantics,* are irrelevant to his point.

Gardner argues, correctly, that the two-valued logic of Aristotle can account for even the most complex systems. This is clearly true since computers and computer languages depend on the two-valued property of magnets, north and south, to store the most complex thoughts and data sets. Yet the ability to reduce the representation of thoughts to a two-valued system is quite different from creating those thoughts within a two-valued system. Korzybski is not discussing computer storage or modeling but human reactions to language and perceptions of reality, a context in which two-valued logic has not distinguished itself as a heuristic system. Gardner overclaims the impact of his arguments on the utility of general semantics and ignores the similarities of Korzybski's arguments to the basis of his own. Particularly, Gardner's work, but not his critique, implies the acceptance of Korzybski's *scientific approach* and *delayed reaction* and Korzybski's rejection of *essence*, since the latter implies the existence of a predeterminer. Gardner's points on Korzybski's overstatement, verbosity, incorporation of others' work, and assessment of neurology, while credible, do not deal with arguments that diminish the importance of the fundamental issues concerning perceptions of the world articulated by general semantics.

Thomas M. Steinfatt

See also Argumentation Theories; Cognitive Theories; Language and Communication; Rhetorical Theory; Semiotics and Semiology

Further Readings

Bandler, R., & Grinder, J. (1979). *Frogs into princes: Neuro linguistic programming.* Moab, UT: Real People Press.

Beck, A. T. (1976). *Cognitive therapy and the emotional disorders.* New York: International Universities Press.

Gardner, M. (1952). *In the name of science.* New York: Putnam.

Hayakawa, S. I. (1949). *Language in thought and action.* New York: Harcourt Brace.

Korzybski, A. (1941). *Science and sanity.* New York: Science Press.

Postman, N. (1976). *Crazy talk, stupid talk.* New York: Delacorte Press.

Rapoport, A. (1953). *Operational philosophy: Integrating knowledge and action.* New York: Harper & Row.

Weinberg, H. L. (1959). *Levels of knowing and existence.* New York: Harper & Row.

GENRE THEORY

Genre theory refers to a diverse set of approaches or methods for identifying patterns in, and expectations for, a variety of communicative phenomena. In the broadest sense, a *genre* refers to a recurrent language-based category that guides or constrains communication. In contemporary culture, the concept of genre is most often used to describe types of film (e.g., action, drama, romantic comedy), literature and poetry (e.g., gothic, epic, mask lyric), and music (e.g., dance, hip-hop, alternative rock). In scholarship, genre theory originates in ancient Greek advice about public speaking. Today, however, genre is studied in three broader contexts: rhetoric and oratory, literature and poetry, and media studies.

Ancient Origins of Genre Theory

Genre theory is derived from ancient Greek advice on public speaking in the 4th and 5th centuries BCE. Aristotle is often credited with standardizing and organizing the study of genre. He held that there are three basic speech genres: *deliberative,* or political speaking; *forensic,* or legal speaking; and *epideictic,* or speaking at celebrations, funerals, and other meetings in which a community is honored. Aristotle observed that over time, each genre of speaking developed a series of expectations that constrained what a given speaker could say. For example, at a funeral, audiences expect to hear a speaker praise the life of the deceased. If a speaker insulted the deceased at a funeral, the speaker would violate a generic norm and risk upsetting those in attendance. Aristotle argued that good speakers may creatively challenge expectations but ultimately must work within them to satisfy audiences.

Genre in Rhetoric and Oratory

In the contemporary world, genre is of special interest to scholars who study public speaking and writing, especially that of politicians and public officials. For example, rhetorical scholars in the United States have been interested in studying the generic norms of presidential inaugural addresses. Campbell and Jamieson have argued that when a new president takes office, he or she delivers an inaugural speech that is constrained by five expectations: (1) an attempt to unify the audience as a people; (2) a restatement of commonly shared values; (3) a list of the principles that will guide the new administration; (4) a recognition of the powers and limits of the office of the presidency; and (5) a recognition of the present moment in a mood of contemplation, not immediate action. A presidential speaker may meet these expectations in novel and creative ways; however, all five must be addressed, or the president will likely be criticized.

In addition to political speeches, communication scholars study genres in written forms of communication in a variety of contexts. For example, in the context of business communication, scholars have studied how genre enables and constrains a variety of writing strategies in the workplace. Public relations briefs, memos, and news releases intended for the mass media tend to follow predictable, generic patterns.

Although genres tend to be associated with forms of discourse (speech or writing), generic patterns are not limited to discourse. Scholars studying interpersonal communication have noted behavioral patterns that function generically; for example, some scholars have argued groups working on a common goal sometimes develop a story or *fantasy theme* about their relationship to each other and the goal. Other scholars have found that individuals develop certain *attachment styles* in their interpersonal relationships. Yet other scholars study the nondiscursive features of artifacts—buildings, memorials, photographs, game shows—to understand how the generic characteristics function to meet certain rhetorical objectives.

Genre in Literature and Poetry

In the area of literary studies, genre theory has stayed within traditional boundaries, unlike what has happened in communication studies, in which generic investigations are diverse. Literary scholars tend to associate genre with five categories of composition: comedy, epic, novel, short story, and tragedy. Poetry scholars have an ever-expanding list of genres and generic conventions that extend categorization far beyond the three Aristotle identified in his theory of poetics: the lyric, the narrative, and the dramatic.

Genre in Media

Perhaps the most widely recognized and understood form of genre today is associated with music and film, and this is because genre has become an important component of marketing. Prior to the 20th century, only music was categorized by genre (e.g., baroque, romantic, folk); however, with the advent of technological reproduction, music and film have become commodities. Consequently, film and music genres have evolved to help audiences identify artists and filmmakers that appeal to their tastes. Media companies use generic labels to help promote and sell film and music to particular niche markets. For example, hip-hop, a music genre that tends to feature a vocalist rapping over a series of sampled beats, is primarily marketed to White male teenagers, while the romantic comedy genre of film is primarily marketed to young women. Each niche audience knows what to expect when watching or listening to a film or song associated with a generic category.

Controversies

In all contexts of study, genre theory has been criticized as too rigid and formulaic to be useful. In rhetorical studies, genre theory has been criticized for creating taxonomies (classification systems) that overlook the peculiar and distinctive features of a speech or text. In literary studies it has been argued that, if examined closely enough, any composition will defy its generic categorization.

Filmmakers and musicians have criticized genres for creating false expectations and encouraging thoughtless judgments about their work. Defenders of genre theory have responded that such criticisms misunderstand genres as inherent to the speech, text, composition, film, or music. Genres, they argue, are actually psychological or mental in character and are found in the imaginations and expectations of audiences.

Joshua Gunn

See also Discourse Theory and Analysis; Media and Mass Communication Theories; Political Communication Theories; Popular Culture Theories; Rhetorical Theory; Symbolic Convergence Theory

Further Readings

Altman, R. (1999). *Film/genre*. London: British Film Institute.

Aristotle. (2006). *On rhetoric: A theory of civic discourse* (G. A. Kennedy, Trans.). New York: Oxford University Press.

Campbell, K. K., & Jamieson, K. H. (Eds.). (1978). *Form and genre: Shaping rhetorical action*. Falls Church, VA: Speech Communication Association.

Campbell, K. K., & Jamieson, K. H. (2008). *Presidents creating the presidency: Deeds done in words*. Chicago: University of Chicago Press.

Rosemarin, A. (1985). *The power of genre*. Minneapolis: University of Minnesota Press.

GLOBALIZATION THEORIES

Globalization is often associated with either neoliberalism or a new political world order. These processes, which reveal a new connectedness of worldwide conflicts and crises, including concerns for a sustainable environment, for human rights, and the protection of cultural traditions, have led to new research fields on one hand and academic debates about theories of globalization on the other. These theories are important as they help to reposition conventional concepts of political and social organizations, such as nations and communities, within a globalized sphere.

Media and communication technologies play an important role in the "mediation" of these processes and are sometimes even viewed as key drivers of globalization. Since the mid-1990s, media and communication studies have increasingly addressed the phenomenon of globalization; theories of globalization, however, originated in other disciplines, such as sociology.

Globalization as a Sociological Construction

Two globalization concepts—or what we might call *paradigms*—had already been established in sociology by the late 1990s, when communication studies had just begun to debate these new, complex phenomena. The first approach represents the critical paradigm of the skeptics, who question the concept of globalization itself and consider globalization as an outcome of neoliberalism. Skeptics consider globalization primarily as a "Western project." These approaches strongly believe in the centrality of the modern nation-state and primarily address the implications of globalization for the nation-state. Ulrich Beck is one of the key proponents of this paradigm and was the first theorist who identified the implication of globalized "risks" for nation-states in the late 1980s. Beck argued that these new forms of globalized risks transform the nation-state because they can be solved only through new forms of international cooperation, that is, cooperation between nations, decreasing the political power of the nation per se. Other globalization skeptics, such as Anthony Giddens, argue that globalization is characterized by new forms of distanciation of time and place, a complex but powerful process that intensifies "world relations" as local happenings are influenced by things that occur in some other place, or vice versa. This new notion of "place" of a nation, along with the availability of an enlarged communication space, challenges, according to Giddens, traditional social and political structures of nations. These in turn lead to complex forms of national *disembedding* of individuals from cultural traditions and the "lifting out" of social structures. Another famous skeptic is Jürgen Habermas; his most recent primary work addresses the processes of denationalization and normative public reasoning through the emergence of new spheres of supranational legitimacy.

The second group of globalization theories, following David Held and Anthony McGrew's model,

can be described as a "globalist" or "transformationalist" paradigm that claims a somewhat pragmatic view. Proponents of this paradigm analyze the transformation of modern social, economic, political, and cultural structures from globalization through new forms of globalized "difference." A major theorist of this transformational paradigm is Roland Robertson, whose work has greatly influenced today's conceptualization of globalization. Robertson was the first sociologist who identified globalization as a differentiated transnational process with more than national implications. His work is less concerned with globalization as an influential factor on Western nations or modernity than with the profound transformation of local cultures worldwide. It is this interesting dialectic between the global and the local for which Robertson coined the term *glocal*, highlighting globalization*s*—the differentiated local perceptions of globalizing processes. Robertson's notion of globalization as "globalization of difference" relates not only to the identification of diverse globalizing implications on local cultures but also to a variety of globalizing "spheres," including individuals, societies, and worldwide systems of societies. This differentiated notion of globalization has influenced discussions of a new relationship of not only global and local cultures but also new forms of globalized local phenomena, such as diasporic cultures—those spread out across various parts of the globe.

One of the most important theoretical frameworks in this area, which can also be considered a transformationalist paradigm, is *cultural hybridity*, a process of reconceptualizing the "location of culture" within a globalized framework. This theory has led to new differentiated approaches to world terminologies such as *North, South, developing*, and *developed* within a new complex set of supranational and subnational cultures. It should also be noted that most recent globalization debates in sociology address new forms of global consciousness such as that of a *cosmopolitan vision*, a term coined by Beck to describe a contemporary sense of *boundarylessness* combined with a sense of reflexivity and ambivalence about the various cultural differentiations and contradictions, as well as their possibilities.

Paradigms of globalization, even in sociology, assume that media are drivers of globalization processes. Theorists of globalization in sociology, however, do not specifically study the role of media within a transnational communication culture.

Constructions of Mediated Globalization

These highly specified debates have only recently begun to influence the theoretical discussion of globalization in media and communication studies, which is surprising given the long history of transborder communication. Transborder communication has existed since ancient times, when trade routes in various parts of the world served also as "communication" routes for the delivery of oral "news" for centuries. Examples are the Silk Road, stretching from China to Egypt, and the Hanseatic League in Europe, an alliance of cities in northern Europe that formed a trade monopoly during the period of the late Middle Ages. To assume that globalization is a phenomenon of the 20th century is in this sense quite misleading. Furthermore, the invention of the printing press— first in Asia in the 14th and in Europe in the 15th centuries—and the subsequent transborder "flow" of books (so-called newsbooks and news pamphlets) shaped a quite sophisticated culture of transborder communication. Printed news in those days consisted of reports of wars, sensationalism, crime, and royals that arrived sometimes years after the events occurred. However, these early forms of transborder flows, made possible through the printing press, are rarely mentioned in debates about globalization.

The first forms of transborder broadcasting emerged after about 1920 with shortwave radio stations, such as *Voice of Russia,* founded in 1922; *BBC World Service,* founded in 1932; and *Voice of America,* founded in 1953. These and many other national shortwave stations targeted clearly defined audiences in a variety of countries and can be considered a first form of international communication, in the true sense of communication between nations. Beyond these first forms of transborder delivery, national broadcast signals—intentionally or unintentionally—crossed national borders into neighboring countries, such as from the United States to Canada and Mexico.

However, the first theory of what we might call "international communication" was developed in the late 1950s. This approach aimed to utilize communication for the modernization of developing countries. This concept is based on a typically Western model of modernity in which media are traditionally viewed as platforms for public communication, that is, for public deliberation within a functioning democracy. Daniel Lerner, who taught at MIT from 1953 onward, coined the term *development communication* to describe this first "modern" approach to the strategic use of media as drivers of the transformation of "traditional" societies, meaning developing countries. Lerner's 1958 work on *The Passing of Traditional Society* was, in fact, the first international comparative study on these "mediated" modernization processes in various Middle East countries, such as Turkey, Lebanon, Egypt, and Syria.

Throughout the 1960s, new complex geopolitical structures emerged that refined international relations in a new sense of political, cultural, and social "connectedness"—not, however, in the sense of a global connectedness but connectedness within the sphere of the West, led by the United States, and within the sphere of the "East," led by the Soviet Union. Each of these superpowers created its own transnational media sphere and attempted to link countries within its sphere of influence politically, culturally, and economically. In the West in particular, international trade—including trading film and television shows—became a crucial component of post–World War II Western economies. The "free flow doctrine," which dominated the Western world of those days, was promoted by the United States after the end of World War II as an unregulated transnational trade doctrine that enabled the unregulated sale of U.S. media products on an international scale. As television became a household medium among emerging middle classes—not only in the United States, but also in other Western industrialized countries (such as Japan)—the already well-established and technologically advanced television production industry in the United States was ideally positioned to sell its programs to these new transnational television cultures where newly formed national television stations were in need of attractive audiovisual formats of entertainment programs. In addition, the early satellite age of the 1960s, with the first satellites provided by the *Intelsat* consortium being positioned above the Atlantic Ocean, created the technological infrastructure for this new form of internationalization. Television shows, news, and a small number of live events could be easily delivered across continents. However, given the tremendously expensive satellite dishes at this time, these were not directly delivered to households (as is the case today) but to national broadcasters. One of the early moments of transcontinental collective "mediated" world experience was the moon landing of Apollo 11 in 1969, which was delivered live by satellite to a great variety of countries. This televised experience inspired Marshall McLuhan's theory of the world as a *global village,* which envisions the shrinking of the world due to an "electronic connectedness."

The internationalization of Western (mainly U.S.) media was soon criticized as a way of homogenizing the world through American values, identities, and lifestyles. Herbert Schiller defined these powerful influences as "media imperialism." The delivery of Western media, in particular television programs and films, created international economic structures around "centers" and "peripheries" and—in consequence—reproduced old imperial models in an international media world where Western transnational corporations delivered mainstream products to "passive" audiences, thus creating various dependencies from an emerging Western media empire. A quite profound critique of such a dominance, which is also described as *cultural imperialism,* was drafted by a United Nations Educational, Scientific, and Cultural Organization commission chaired by Sean MacBride—a first approach to conceptualize policy frameworks of globalization. The internationally published report of this commission in 1980, famously called the *MacBride Report,* suggests a number of policies, such as the elimination of imbalances and inequalities of media trade from the North (i.e., the northern hemisphere of mainly developed countries) to the South (i.e., the Southern hemisphere of mainly developing countries). Furthermore, the report argues that communication is an individual and collective right required of nations and communities. This important conviction had strong ideological connotations in the late Cold War climate. Western governments (such as the United States and the United Kingdom) considered the idea of such an unrestricted universal right as politically provocative because this idea was taken to legitimize censorship by authoritarian governments in

the developing world. In today's view, the severe criticism of the MacBride report among Western nations can be seen as an overreaction; however, in the Cold War period of internationalization, these concerns seemed to be justified. Important to note is that the *MacBride Report* was one of the last debates in which transborder flows were linked to Cold War political ideologies.

With the emergence of a second phase of satellite communication throughout the 1980s and 1990s, when advanced technologies enabled an increase of satellite platforms and, in consequence, a decrease of leasing costs, a great number of new radio and television formats were developed that combined global delivery and local programs for a variety of world regions. So-called satellite television channels, such as Cable News Network (CNN) and Music Television, began to deliver their programs globally and locally. "Around the World in Thirty Minutes" was CNN's famous promotional slogan: Indeed, "breaking news" delivered worldwide was followed by a "local" analysis through regional (or even national) CNN outlets directly to households. These new forms of not so much transborder flows or internationalization (in the original sense, between nations, as in earlier decades) as now supranational and subnational program delivery became quite difficult to conceptualize within media and communication studies. As the old paradigms of "mass" communication and traditional forms of media imperialism began slowly to diminish, the conceptual debate in media and communication studies began to shift. In particular, cultural studies began to reconceptualize audiences in a new transnational sphere. Studies of diaspora—ethnic minority communities—as well as new transnational audience cultures and journalism helped to conceptualize at least the contours of a paradigmatic change within the field of media and communication. One of the key theorists of these new forms of disjunctures is Arjun Appadurai, who defined a number of transnational cultural "landscapes": *ethnoscapes,* the globalizing sphere of migrants and refugees, but also *mediascapes,* or the culture of "imagined" lives, delivered through transnational media. These studies also revealed that former approaches, such as media imperialism, required some refinement as new forms of communication emerged in a transnational context, reshifting the former center–periphery model.

In addition, international communication as an early form of globalization, that is, communicating between nations, was increasingly replaced by supranational and subnational communication spheres. Advanced satellite technology and the Internet allowed for the possibility of reaching and connecting individuals directly within nations. These advanced communication technologies, in particular satellite communication and the Internet, have created a transnational media infrastructure that requires new conceptual approaches in order to understand new forms of public participation and media cultures.

Manuel Castells is the first theorist who combines technological developments and the paradigm of globalization. His 1996 theory of *global network society* has shifted the globalization paradigm to a new level, and new technologies such as the Internet are transforming nations, identities, and political power. Castells argues that the social organization of a global society is being organized as "networks" operating through a "space of flows," creating communication hubs in a "timeless time," resulting in constant, 24/7 communication. Castells's network society theory constitutes a first social theory of the global communication sphere. In this sense his work is linked to globalization theories, such as that of Anthony Giddens, that have claimed that globalization creates "disembedding" processes due to new communication spaces. The network society approach reveals new forms of reembedding within today's global communication space.

Ingrid Volkmer

See also Diaspora; Free Flow Doctrine; International Communication Theories; International Development Theories; Media Sovereignty; Network Society; Structuration Theory

Further Readings

Appadurai, A. (1990). Disjuncture and difference in the global cultural economy. In M. Featherstone (Ed.), *Global culture: Nationalism, globalization and modernity* (pp. 295–319). London: Sage.

Beck, U. (1992). *Risk Society: Towards a new modernity* (M. Ritter, Trans.). London: Sage.

Beck, U. (2006). *Cosmopolitan vision*. Cambridge, UK: Polity Press.

Bhaba, H. (1994). *The location of culture*. London: Routledge.

Boyd-Barrett, O. (1977). Media imperialism: Towards an international framework for the analysis of media systems. In J. Curran, M. Gurevitsch, & J. Wollacott (Eds.), *Mass communication and society* (pp. 116–135). London: Edward Arnold.

Castells, M. (1996). *The rise of the network society* (3 Vols.). Oxford, UK: Blackwell.

Galtung, J. (1971). A structural theory of imperialism. *Journal of Peace Research, 8*, 81–117.

Giddens, A. (1990). *The consequences of modernity*. Stanford, CA: Stanford University Press.

Habermas, J. (2001). *The inclusion of the other*. Cambridge: MIT Press.

Held, D., & McGrew, A. (2006). The great globalization debate. In D. Held & A. McGrew (Eds.), *The global transformations reader* (pp. 1–50). Cambridge, UK: Polity Press.

Lerner, D. (1958). *The passing of traditional society: Modernizing the Middle East*. New York: Free Press.

MacBride, S. (1980). *Many voices, one world: Communication and society, today and tomorrow: Towards a new more just and more efficient world information and communication order*. London: Kogan Page.

McLuhan, M., & Powers, B. R. (1992). *The global village: Transformations in world life and media in the 21st century*. Oxford, UK: Oxford University Press.

Robertson, R. (1992). *Globalization: Social theory and global culture*. London: Sage.

Schiller, H. I. (1976). *Communication and cultural domination*. New York: International Arts and Sciences Press.

GROUNDED THEORY

Grounded theory (GT) is a qualitative research methodology commonly employed by scholars to analyze communication processes and content, often for the development of *interpretive* theories. As a methodology, GT is more than a method or set of methods for collecting or analyzing data. Instead, GT is an approach to social research that specifies an emergent rather than predetermined research design through an atypical sequence of activities for building and developing theory; it is an approach that arguably runs counter to traditional notions of scientific method as developed initially in what is referred to as the natural sciences. Distinguishing characteristics of GT include delay of the literature review, simultaneous collection and analysis of data, *emic* construction of analytic codes and categories from data (vs. *etic* or a priori application of previous theory), development of *midrange theories* (vs. universal laws) to explain communication behavior and processes, the composition of theoretical memos to define analytic categories, and sampling procedures inspired more by a concern for theory construction than for representativeness.

Traditional social science methodology proceeds predictably in discrete stages that are predetermined: the development of hypotheses from a single theoretical perspective, data collection, data analysis, and interpretation of results. GT does not. Instead, research employing GT is highly emergent, allowing for the possibility that research questions, access to participants, and even definitions of core constructs may change over the course of a study. For example, in most variable-analytic research methodologies, one does not begin analyzing data until all are collected. Alternatively, GT methodology suggests an iterative process in which data are analyzed during an evolving data collection process. Tentative hypotheses are developed, tested, and refined in a manner that is *abductive*—both inductive and deductive.

The purpose of abduction in GT is to develop *tentative theoretical propositions* (sometimes called exploratory hypotheses) that can be explicated through deduction and validated through induction. In other words, theory development involves two overlapping logics. Inductive logic must be used to identify its observable qualities and components of phenomena and speculate about the ways in which they may be related. At the same time, deductive logic must be employed to evaluate explanations of why the phenomenon proceeds in the manner that induction revealed. Therefore, sampling, analyzing data, and interpreting findings are interdependent activities that together comprise a cycle of inquiry.

Origins

Outside of variable-analytic content analysis, GT is among the most common methodological approaches taken to qualitative research in the communication studies discipline. GT was created by sociologists Bernie Glaser and Anselm Strauss, who began formalizing the methodology while conducting field studies through the University of California–San Francisco Medical School about the relationships between expectations of death and interaction with people who were dying. Strauss, who had been a student of symbolic interactionist Herbert Blumer, recruited Glaser, a student of Paul Lazarsfeld and Robert K. Merton, to assist with the project. Their work yielded not only a topical book (*Awareness of Dying*) but eventually a methodological treatise (*The Development of Grounded Theory*). GT became one of the first qualitative research methodologies to find some acceptance among U.S. social scientists.

Relationship to Traditional Modes of Inquiry

The potential of GT research to inform, extend, corroborate, or challenge extant theory is likely a primary explanation for its acceptance within mainstream social science generally and communication studies specifically. GT studies typically do not meet many of the validity criteria pursued in variable-analytic social science. However, a primary function of GT, particularly as it is interpreted in communication studies, is to produce conceptual definitions and hypotheses with sufficient heuristic value that they may be tested through traditional methodologies more likely to meet those criteria. For example, researchers may rely on the tenets of GT methodology to develop a traditional survey instrument that operationalizes a communication phenomenon. They can generate data by conducting various forms of observation and interviewing relevant to the theory in question.

GT methodology is primarily used to ground concepts, constructs, and the hypothesized relationships among them in data derived naturalistically from the context for which an application of theory is intended. Research designs that include conceptualizations, operationalizations, and hypotheses without this grounding are less likely to be internally valid. Internal validity concerns a range of criteria most social scientists try to apply in evaluating whether a phenomenon is measured or described as intended. Thus, GT is one among many useful tools not only for generating new theoretical propositions but also for confirming, revising, or adding detail to those that have already gained some acceptance.

Constant Comparative Analysis

GT is also bolstered by the formality of its data analysis protocol, which is relatively technical and systematic yet straightforward. Constant comparative analysis calls for the analyst to begin coding a portion of collected data line by line (open coding), identifying topics, characteristics, or themes suggested by the text. Where possible, code labels and tentative code definitions should mirror the language used by the research participants (*in vivo coding*). Next comes *focused*, or hierarchical, coding in which the codes appearing most continuously or commonly during open coding become categories, which ascribes them more significance than a code. Categories are defined through *theoretical memos* that describe properties of the phenomenon; tentative conclusions about its consequences; the circumstances in which it emerges, endures, and changes; and how it relates to other phenomena. Focused coding also requires that the analyst account for variations within a category by constructing subcategories and theoretical memos that describe distinctions between them. Importantly, because researchers are still collecting data as they analyze it, the coding system or framework is continuously refined on the basis of new or conflicting cases and insights until the final stages of the research project.

Theoretical Sensitivity

The capacity of GT to incorporate contextual factors into theorizing can be considered a final explanation for the success of GT. The point of GT is to develop more theoretical propositions than from previous research by using data derived from observations of the context in which phenomena operate. Thus, GT is intended to privilege the perspective scene of the social actor over prevailing theoretical assumptions or scholars' respective points of view.

Confusion and Conflict

In spite of its popularity, GT is an often disputed and confused—if not misused—term. Although some of this can be blamed on careless application of basic GT principles, much of what remains is explained by a core contradiction that has never been resolved.

Conflation of Methodology and Method

In research reports, GT is often equated with the "constant comparative method" of qualitative data analysis, which is an important but still partial element of the larger approach Glaser and Strauss originally proposed. Thus, some studies claiming to take a GT approach could more accurately be described as employing the constant comparative method in data analysis because GT was not applied to other elements of the research design. For example, many studies espousing a GT approach employ the constant comparative method of data analysis because, while espousing a GT approach, they ignore other key tenets of GT such as emergent research design or simultaneous data collection and analysis.

Latent Contradiction in Early Grounded Theory

Furthermore, as proponents have developed protocols, guides, and other reference material that detail and clarify the methodology, conflicts have formed regarding how GT is executed analytically. Glaser has argued that the more recent work contradicts the original formulation outlined in *The Development of Grounded Theory*. Others have argued that Glaser and Strauss's original work glossed over mutually exclusive understandings of the relationship between data and theory. In either case, most of the disagreement seems to result from two competing needs: (1) the extent to which constructs and theoretical propositions can be identified through constant comparative analysis in a truly emic manner (*emergence*) without the influence of preexisting theories and concepts and (2) the extent to which analysis of data should strategically relate to or rely on terminology and constructs of the theories researchers are attempting to revise or extend (*theoretical sensitivity*).

GT specialists generally deal with this tension in one of two ways. Strauss and Corbin and colleagues, whose work since Strauss's death is often seen as a continuation of a "Straussian" view of GT, suggest that analysts rely on a general action model of behavior based on symbolic interactionism and pragmatist social theory that emphasizes intentions, strategies, goals, and processes that comprise human action and interaction. Alternatively, Glaser and colleagues call for relatively pure *substantive* codes that are emic, serving the goal of emergence, and *theoretical* codes that rely on basic sociological concepts that can be used to make fundamental claims about how the social world is ordered. These include terms like conditions, causes, contexts, and consequences, which Glaser and colleagues have mapped to a complex array of *coding families*.

Views of Grounded Theory in Communication Research

Straussian approaches to GT have found more favor in communication studies than have those suggested by Glaser and colleagues. Given the historical influence of pragmatism and symbolic interactionism on the fields of interpersonal, group, and organizational communication, the favor found with Strauss is not terribly surprising. However, it can be argued that this approach to GT privileges micro phenomena to the exclusion of macro forces. Some communication methodologists who specialize in qualitative fieldwork argue that the tension between emergence and theoretical sensitivity is best resolved through greater *self-reflexivity*. They suggest that researchers account for the unavoidable influence of subjectivity in their analyses by actively highlighting their own predispositions, standpoints, and personal experiences. By revealing these subjectivities somewhat openly in their work, they hope to empower readers with added insight for evaluating the validity of their claims.

Cliff Scott

See also Culture and Communication; Empiricism; Epistemology; Ethnography of Communication; Inquiry Processes; Interpretive Theory; Pragmatics; Scientific Approach; Symbolic Interactionism

Further Readings

Glaser, B. (1978). *Emergence vs. forcing: Basics of grounded theory analysis*. Mill Valley, CA: Sociology Press.

Glaser, B., & Strauss, A. L. (1967). *The discovery of grounded theory: An inquiry into the conceptual foundations of science*. Chicago: Aldine.

Goodall, H. L. (2000). *Writing the new ethnography*. Walnut Creek, CA: Alta Mira.

Kelle, U. (2005). "Emergence" vs. "forcing" of empirical data? A crucial problem of grounded theory reconsidered. *Forum: Qualitative Research*, 6(2), A27.

Lindlof, T. R., & Taylor, B. C. (2002). *Qualitative communication research methods*. Thousand Oaks, CA: Sage.

Strauss, A. L. (1987). *Qualitative analysis for social scientists*. Cambridge, UK: Cambridge University Press.

Strauss, A. L., & Corbin, J. (1990). *Basics of qualitative research: Grounded theory procedures and techniques*. Newbury Park, CA: Sage.

GROUP AND ORGANIZATIONAL STRUCTURATION THEORY

The theory of structuration, developed by Anthony Giddens, has been applied extensively in the study of group and organizational communication. Its central concepts—the distinction between system and structure, the duality of structure, the reflexive model of agency, the role of social institutions in human action, the three modalities of structure, the dialectic of control, and time–space distanciation—have been appropriated by numerous communication scholars. Structuration theory takes a processual view of the social world and features communication as one of the primary modes of being. It bridges conceptual divides between action and structure, stability and change, and macro- and microlevels of analysis. It offers a nondeterministic account of the social world but allows for regularities and the scaffolding of norms, power, and institutions to influence communication and its impacts. It also provides the foundation for a critical stance.

Structurational Theory in Group Research

Most theoretical applications of structuration in group research have focused on aspects of group decision making. From a structurational perspective, group decision making is the production and reproduction of positions regarding group action, directed toward the convergence of members on a final choice. This occurs through the structuration of three elements of interaction—expression of preferences, argumentation, and tactics employed to garner assent.

Influences on structuration processes in groups include (a) immediate interaction in which interpretive schemes, norms, and power resources are invoked and reproduced through group communication patterns, decision rules, and the influence of members over one another; (b) features of the group's external system, including tasks and environment; and (c) structural dynamics, including the mediation of the elements of immediate interaction by other structures (e.g., when an economic "lens" is imposed on the discussion) and contradictions among structural features (e.g., the tension between pressure to act and the desire to make a reflective, rational decision). These factors, and member knowledge of them, also limit group and member agency, or freedom of action.

Groups acquire coherence through being structured and, as self-organizing systems, can channel the agency of their members into common projects. The members of groups are themselves formed and reformed through structuration. So rather than being prior to the group, members are positioned within the group through actions and discourse creating and sustaining various roles and arguments. Hence, groups may be the primary unit of analysis rather than individuals. Three theoretical tributaries flow from this basic framework—decision development, group argument, and use of information technology.

Decision Development

The structurational theory of decision development attempts to explain why groups follow varied paths as they make decisions, rather than the single rational sequence of events emphasized in prior research. The theory posits that the influence of factors such as the group's task and decision-making norms on decision development is mediated by structuring processes in group interaction. How a group represents its tasks, in other words, serves as an implicit model of prerequisites for what a good decision is and how the group should organize the process by which it makes decisions.

These representations influence the phases and sequence of the group's interaction. For instance, a group may conclude that it already understands the problem and so the next steps are identifying a suitable solution and planning its implementation (a solution-oriented decision path). Task representations are the modalities through which the group's decision process is structured.

The group generates a sequence of decision phases by developing foci—internally unified episodes of discussion focused on a single topic or concern. These foci articulate the content of the discussion, and a phase may contain a single focus or several linked foci—for example, all being related to problem analysis. A central problem is maintaining coherency of discussion within and between foci to avoid disjointed talk that does not build toward a decision. Members manage coherence through moves including (a) moves that tie together the talk so that discussion is coherent from one sentence to the next (e.g., the next sentence refers to the topic of the previous one); (b) alignment moves, designed to avoid or remedy misunderstandings (e.g., a disclaimer that the speaker is just trying out an idea); and (c) structuring moves, which rebuild interrupted coherence (e.g., a procedural message that the last utterance is irrelevant).

The group, then, is acting on at least two levels as it makes decisions: working out the substance of the decision and structuring the way it represents its task, which recursively structures the decision process. When members agree on a task representation, the group's decision path is likely to unfold as it specifies, with complications introduced mainly by task-related issues such as accuracy about actual task requirements. When, however, there is disagreement on task representation and/or the logic of the decision, the group is trying to sort through these while working on its decision, and the resulting decision path is much more complex.

Group Argument

A second tributary is represented by the structurational theory of group argument, which focuses on constituents and combinations of expressed arguments. The theory conceptualizes argument as both structure—the rules and resources individuals draw on to produce argument—and system, the observable interactive practices in which structure is implicated. The view of argument as emergent structure allows for development of norms and commonplaces, or typical lines, of argument that may differ from best practices. As a system, argument is construed as a pattern of reason giving, agreement and disagreement, and seeking of resolutions in communicative practice.

The theory proposes that argument structures interaction through three mechanisms. At the microlevel, members use logical and cultural norms and recipes. Second, members may generate broader, idiosyncratic argument webs by chaining arguments together, engaging in collaborative argumentation with other members, and generating multiple levels of argument. Finally, members invoke macrosocial norms, interpretive schemes, and various resources (status in the group, expertise, formal authority) to influence other members.

Information Technology

The third tributary is represented by adaptive structuration theory (AST), developed to explain the use of information technologies in task-oriented groups. It has been applied most to study groups using computerized group support systems but has also stimulated research on larger systems.

AST proposes that information technology (and all technologies or procedures) have a two-layered structure consisting of their *spirit*—the general values, goals, and attitudes the technology promotes (such as democratic decision making)—and specific *structural features* built into the system (such as anonymous input of ideas or a voting procedure). A structural feature is a specific rule or resource that operates in a group, whereas spirit is the principle of coherence that holds a set of rules and resources together. Usually the features of an information technology, such as a group support system, are designed to promote its spirit, barring disconnects between conception and system development.

AST focuses on appropriation, the ways in which groups take structural features and employ them in interaction. For example, members of a group may use a group voting system to promote democratic deliberation, or some members may use voting results to pressure members of the minority to accept the "will" of the group. Groups appropriate information technologies in diverse ways, influencing the resulting group structures-in-use, process, and outcomes. AST posits that appropriations of information technologies will be most effective if they are (a) consistent with the spirit of the technology; (b) linked instrumentally with task execution and building the group; (c) based on positive attitudes of comfort, respect, and challenge toward the technology; and (d) consensual.

Structurational Theories of Organizational Communication

Structuration theory has been applied to the study of organization constitution and structure, to organizational climate and culture, to the generation and maintenance of communication networks, and to organizational identity.

Structuration and the Constitution of Organizations

Scholars increasingly view communication as a basic social process with powers to constitute social reality, so the communicative constitution of organizations has emerged as a focus of inquiry. As a result of structurational emphases on time–space distance and on multiplicity of structurating processes, one structuration-based theory argues for four distinct flows of constitutive communication. Each "flow" is a web of interaction across time and space, distinguished by the distinct impact it has on the organization.

The first flow, *membership negotiation,* produces and reproduces the way in which individual members relate to the organization. A product manager negotiates his or her staff, product responsibilities, responsibilities vis-à-vis other organizations, and career ladder, and the sum of all members' negotiations helps create the organization. A second flow is the *institutional positioning* of the organization vis-à-vis the local and global ecology of regulators, suppliers, competitors, and customers. This flow can involve coordinated *image presentation* by members to outsiders and *environmental exploration* to find complementary outsiders and build relationships with them.

The third flow is spontaneous *activity coordination* among members and others in organizationally relevant contexts. As in groups, members build and rework task representations and exchange signals about how to behave in sync. The last flow, *reflexive self-structuring*, creates abstract documents and demands that establish the organization and tie the other communication flows together as an official system. Research on organizational and even national policies has revealed the mercurial stream of interpretation and wrangling that accompanies attempts to steer or constrain broad domains of member activity.

One outcome of reflexive self-structuring is documents making up an organization's formal structure. A related line of structurational inquiry at the organizational level addresses a paradox of formal organizational structure: On one hand, formal structuring creates efficiency and coordination; on the other hand, formal structure inexorably becomes oppressive or maladapted and is ignored or manipulated.

The theory takes off from two main themes in the literature on organizational structure: (1) Formal structure substitutes for and preempts other communication. Once the organizational structure is set, its authority does away with the need to communicate to figure out what to do. (2) Formal structures are an authoritative metacommunication system—or communication about how communication is supposed to occur—for the organization that makes members aware of the authority structure and ways to manipulate it. The structurational concept of *distanciation* can be used to explain these attributes of formal structure. Distanciation means that people's decisions and actions are distanced, or separated, from their consequences in other times and places so that, for example, in some sites of the organization (the board room, the executive suite), formal structure is a tool for influence by powerful actors, while in others it is the focus of work (e.g., human resources departments) or just a contextual constraint (e.g., in production lines).

An element of formal structure that illustrates this pattern particularly well is the vertical hierarchy. This is often conceived of as a chain of command or chain of communication, yet research has repeatedly found that almost no communication flows for any distance through it. Instead, the chain of command is produced and reproduced on three different levels. At the top is the *executive* level, where many chains of command intersect, potentially overwhelming top managers. To enable the executives to cope, formal mechanisms substitute for direct involvement with lower levels. Below the executive level is the *managerial* level, where managers have the responsibility for structuring and communicating with their units. These managers are distanced from their subordinate units in two respects: They view the organization differently from the way unit members do, and their downward communication is limited by a heavy cross-unit workload. At the lowest, *technical* level, the formal structure is taken as a given, but supervisors and workers often feel misunderstood and resist the programs of the managers. Within each level is a highly interconnected communication network, considerable consensus about important problems, and strategic posturing using or aimed to influence the other levels. However, there are often communication and perspective gaps between levels. The production and reproduction of the hierarchy maintains these variations in the character of a hierarchical structure across the three distanciated levels.

Structuration of Organizational Climate

Structuration theory has also been applied in the study of organizational climate. In traditional organizational research, *climate* is defined as a general property of the organization ("This company is supportive") measured using standardized questionnaires to find patterns of agreement. Instead, a structurational approach regards climate as an array of rules and resources present at a deep level underlying organizational interactions. On this view, company "supportiveness" is an intersubjective belief that is contextualized differently by different people—some see it as present throughout the organization, others see it as applying only for a select group of employees, while still others see it as a myth preached by the powerful.

An underlying core climate level includes basic constructs and kernel climate tenets ("This company is supportive"), variably interpreted to generate particularized climates. These particular climates then influence organizational outcomes such as commitment, satisfaction, and performance, which may differ across the groups. Similar or differing orientations toward climate (co-orientation) constitute an important intermediate aspect of the structuration process. Thus, climate communication can yield disagreements, misunderstandings of others' views, and even different degrees of realization that there is understanding or misunderstanding. Only if there is agreement, understanding, and realization is a climate truly shared and most impactful.

Three classes of elements shape the structuration of climate: (1) structural properties of organizations, such as centralization, formalization, and size; (2) various communication apparatuses, including newsletters, training programs, key managers, and workgroups; and (3) member characteristics, particularly their knowledge about the organization and its climate. These influence the generation and diffusion of climate themes in organizations. Spatial distanciation can also affect the emergence of particular climates in different parts of the organization, especially if there are spatial or symbolic barriers between units or subdivisions of the organization.

Structuration of Organizational Communication Networks

Self-reported perceptions of who is connected to whom in a network often differ from actual observations of who interacted with whom. This frustrating finding can be explained by the structurational theory of communication networks. The observable communication behavior is the communication *system*, while the network is more basically an abstract rule/resource *structure* employed by actors in the generation of the system. Self-reported network perceptions are based on the structure plus individually biased observations of behavior. Hence, observable networks and the structures that generate these are two different but interrelated orders of phenomena.

Three modalities—enactment, activation, and reticulation—underlie the structuration of networks. *Reticulation* encompasses varied member understandings of who may talk to whom and which are the most useful or valuable links. These enable communication activity, which in turn reproduces the network structure. This process is mediated by *activation,* an individual response tendency based on common systems of activity, or *foci,* in the organization. Structural foci give rise to the observable system of coparticipation in activities, which in turn reproduce the foci. Both reticulation and activation are mediated by *enactment,* the process of making sense of and actually responding to significant events.

The three modalities are discussed as though they occur independently and mutually influence one another, but in reality, they are simultaneously involved in each case of observable communication in an organization.

Structuration of Identity in Organizations

Identity and identification in organizations have been a central concern of organizational communication scholarship. In the structurational model of organizational identification, *identity* is viewed not as the more or less fixed core of an individual, but as a set of rules and resources that function as an anchor for who one is; *identification* is interaction or other behaviors illustrating one's attachment. In this model, identification is system and identity is structure. There is a duality of identity and identification in which identity figures both in the process of forming and maintaining attachment to the organization and as the product of this process.

For instance, when an employee is home with his children, he might draw on rules and resources including accumulated knowledge about his children and norms about appropriate parenting and the importance of family time together. A very different set of structural features might be invoked when the same person is at work. Cueing of identities that fit a particular situation is also influenced by institutions—organizations to which an individual belongs—and the nature of the family's situation, such as neighbors and local customs.

Time–space distanciation helps to create separate subidentities or identity "regions." Regional identities develop because people enact subidentities fairly consistently in the various activities in which they engage. For instance, fatherhood is enacted mainly in the home, while employee roles correspond to the workplace. Four "regions" are particularly important in organizational identity: group, organization, personal life, and occupation.

This model can account for multiple identities and identifications common in organizational life and for changes in identities over time and across situations. It allows both for external influences shaping subidentities and for agency to construct, differentiate, and qualify identification within organizations.

Critiques and Debates

A common criticism of applications of structuration theory is that Anthony Giddens accords too much freedom to agency and underestimates the constraints imposed by material resources, ideology, or power processes in organizations. In response, defenders argue that the theory and its communicative applications acknowledge the role of institutional and material phenomena as vital in explanations of society and communication. The theory attempts to cover the whole continuum from micro-interaction to macro-institutions, thereby according influence to both agents and structural tendencies.

Another argument against group and organizational theories of structuration is that they take existing constructs, such as climate or organizational structure, and attempt to reframe or rework them in structurational terms. Instead, the argument goes, it would be better to take structuration theory as a basic ontology for communication research and develop novel constructs or analyses of communication guided by structuration theory. One response to these criticisms is to note that theorists can do both: generate new ideas or reframe and reinvigorate old ones.

A third critique is that group and organizational structuration theories underemphasize the role of power in organizations. In response, it can be argued that domination is without question an important phenomenon but that it is not the only process that figures in organizations.

Marshall Scott Poole and Robert D. McPhee

See also Argumentation Theories; Constitutive View of Communication; Critical Organizational Communication; Group Communication Theories; Identity Theories; Institutional Theories of Organizational Communication; Organizational Communication Theories; Structuration Theory

Further Readings

Banks, S. P., & Riley, P. (1993). Structuration theory as an ontology for communication research. In S. Deetz (Ed.), *Communication yearbook 16* (pp. 167–196). Newbury Park, CA: Sage.

DeSanctis, G., Poole, M. S., Zigurs, I., & Associates. (2008). The Minnesota GDSS Research Project: Group support systems, group processes, and group outcomes. *Journal of the Association of Information Systems, 9,* 551–608.

Giddens, A. (1984). *The constitution of society: Outline of the theory of structuration.* Berkeley: University of California Press.

Giddens, A. (1987). *Social theory and modern sociology.* Stanford, CA: Stanford University Press, 1987.

McPhee, R. D., & Poole, M. S. (2000). Communication and organizational structure. In F. Jablin & L. Putnam (Eds.), *Handbook of organizational communication* (pp. 503–543). Thousand Oaks, CA: Sage.

Poole, M. S., & McPhee, R. D. (2005). Structuration theory. In S. May & D. Mumby (Eds.), *Engaging organizational communication theory and research* (pp. 171–195). Norwood, NJ: Ablex.

Poole, M. S., Seibold, D. R., & McPhee, R. D. (1985). Group decision-making as a structurational process. *Quarterly Journal of Speech, 71,* 74–102.

GROUP COMMUNICATION THEORIES

When we meet together, face to face or online, in small- or medium-sized assemblies, associations, bands, clubs, cliques, and the like, we engage in group communication. As members of groups, we permit a part of our identity and goals to exist as part of a small collective, and the convergence of these parts of our individual lives gives the group a coherent meaning, boundary, purpose, structure, and norms. Group communication theory examines the formation, dynamics, and dissolution of such small groups, and it examines the mutual influence that occurs between the individual and the group.

General Features

From its inception, theories of group communication have aimed to develop practical knowledge about group behavior that can aid us as group participants and facilitators. This applied emphasis has steered group theory and research toward common and purposeful group settings, particularly decision-making entities (e.g., juries and councils) and task-oriented bodies (e.g., athletic and work teams). The development of theory in a university setting with limited research funding has also led to an emphasis on student groups with limited shared history and straightforward assignments. Though recent research has moved in wider directions, these constraints meant that group theories had relatively little to say about principally social/emotional groups (more commonly studied in social work and psychotherapy) and long-lived clans, collectives, and organizational groups (regularly studied in sociology, anthropology, and industrial-organizational psychology).

Epistemological and methodological traditions have also shaped group communication theory. Group communication scholars have principally developed theory within an empiricist approach to knowledge. That is, group communication theorists have sought to develop general propositions about group behavior, or at least context-dependent statements about how and why groups behave the way they do. By contrast, relatively few group communication theories have concerned themselves principally with the interpretation of action (i.e., the hermeneutic investigation of the subjective experience and meaning of group life). Even rarer are critical theories of group behavior, which provide philosophical advances in our understandings of moral/ethical questions, such as modes of domination and exploitation within groups. Significant exceptions to these tendencies exist in modern approaches, particularly the more recent move toward studying *bona fide* groups, discussed below, and feminist critiques of group theory and practice.

Methodologically, group communication scholars have confronted formidable obstacles that have alternately spurred innovation and stunted the growth of group research. From the outset, group communication scholars had to decide what constituted *group* behavior; after all, a group does not have its own brain, which contains the motivations, memories, mores, and meanings that shape behavior. To rectify this problem, group researchers have pioneered means of aggregating individual-level data, such as questionnaires, to identify group-level attributes. Within-and-between statistical analysis helps theorists distinguish between within-group variance (i.e., members' divergent levels of satisfaction with a group decision) and between-group differences (i.e., between wholly satisfied and unsatisfied groups). Group theorists

have also foregrounded the concept of the *decision rule* (e.g., consensus vs. majority rule), a means whereby a group itself (and researchers) can determine the aggregate will of a group's members.

The methodological demands of group theory have also spurred the creation of intensive behavioral observation and coding systems. One of the most famous and widely used systems is the interaction process analysis tool created by Robert Bales in 1950 (refined as Systematic Multiple Level Observation of Groups in 1970); this tool permitted efficient categorization of each individual statement made by the members of a group. Subsequent advances made possible not only the classification of individual actions but also the recognition of patterns of communication behavior over the course of a group's life span. This allowed theorists to model how one member's statement might influence the next utterance, ultimately producing complex sequences and chains that shape the character of the group and its outcomes.

Early Developments

Among the earliest instances of group communication theory was the work of group discussion scholars in the early 20th century. The field of speech communication had experienced a shift from a focus on individual eloquence through oratory to a more balanced emphasis on a range of rhetorical skills, including the ability to lead and participate effectively in group discussions. Perhaps as an echo of the progressive era that preceded it, this period emphasized a collaborative, participatory view of democratic citizenship in which individuals could aspire to play an active role in the affairs of the day by studying and learning together in groups and arriving at their own informed, reasoned judgments. In the modern day, deliberative democracy theorists have revitalized the moral-philosophical thread in this work, but group communication theorists principally carried forward the interest in the mechanics and outcomes of effective discussion.

Social psychologist Kurt Lewin shared this interest in the efficacy of group discussion and developed a wide range of original concepts and theories, as well as the National Training Laboratory, which continues to shape group practice to the present day. In the 1930s, Lewin and his colleagues compared the consequences of three different group leadership styles—autocratic, democratic, and *laissez faire*—on children's groups. The core finding was that a participatory, encouraging, and egalitarian leadership style yielded the best student decisions and behavior, and this single finding grounded an optimistic approach to theory and practice that valorized democratic practices (e.g., using majority rule or consensus) and assumed that such democratic behaviors generally characterized any high-functioning group.

A separate study Lewin conducted for the National Research Council during World War II showed another direction that small-group research would take. To aid the war effort, Lewin showed that homemakers would more readily accept the idea of cooking with sweetbreads (organ meat) after participating in a group discussion than after listening to a lecture on the subject. Though Lewin viewed these findings as a useful insight consistent with democratic discussion principles, it foreshadowed a growing concern about the potential damage group pressure could wreak on otherwise independent-thinking individuals.

In the 1950s, Solomon Asch devised an experimental paradigm that showed the extent of precisely this danger. Like many of his contemporaries in social psychology, such as Stanley Milgram and Theodor Adorno, Asch hoped to understand the processes that could lead people to embrace fascist ideology or authoritarian rule, as had occurred in the Axis powers during World War II. Asch had individuals look at a card featuring three lines and asked them to identify which line was longest. In his experiment, the group members each answered in turn, with all but the last individual being *confederates,* trained actors whom the other subject(s) mistakenly thought to be fellow participants. Each confederate would give the same wrong answer, and if the final member also gave the wrong answer, Asch took this as evidence of conforming to an (incorrect) group judgment. As Asch had theorized, some people did, indeed, conform, but the majority of study participants did *not;* moreover, Asch found that if a single confederate gave the correct answer, that act typically would embolden the last group member to give the correct answer instead of conforming.

The legacy of Asch's research, however, was an enduring concern about the prevalence of group conformity and misperception. Reinforcing that anxiety, among the lay public as well as scholars, in the late 1970s Irving Janis blended social-psychological theory with archival historical research to discover that many U.S. foreign policy blunders traced back to *groupthink.* Groups falling victim to this malady reached a premature decision as a result of their insularity, rigid thinking, biased leadership, and conformity pressure. The key factor for Janis was high cohesion—the mutual attraction and bonding that can occur in groups. Subsequent researchers clarified that cohesion, per se, does not limit a group's productivity, but many investigations confirmed that cohesive groups could fall into groupthink if they also featured a constellation of other structural defects.

Much of the work that followed the path blazed by Lewin, Asch, and Janis kept sight of the fact that groups can yield widely varying outcomes depending on their procedures, as originally suggested by the group discussion pioneers who preceded them. By the 1970s and continuing to the present day, studies investigate the efficacy of a wide range of group practices, such as different ways of polling members, voting, taking speaking turns, or structuring a discussion. Practices such as devil's advocacy (being responsible for articulating a dissenting point of view), round robins (taking turns one by one around a group), and trained facilitation (keeping groups on task, monitoring a group's social/emotional behavior) have become commonplace in the contemporary practice of small groups in everyday life as a result of these studies.

Modern Communication Theories

In spite of the fruits of these and other social-psychological theories, the volume and visibility of small-group research declined in the fields of psychology and sociology during the 1970s and 1980s, leaving a widening vacuum. Filling this vacuum were small-group theories originated within the field of communication. Interdisciplinary studies of small groups had failed to study carefully certain aspects of group interaction, and group communication theorists developed original theoretical frameworks and study designs that complemented the existing body of social-psychological theories.

Ernest Bormann's *symbolic convergence theory* brought insights from rhetorical scholarship to bear on the study of group behavior. Bormann found that groups invariably gravitated toward a shared set of self-descriptions and self-understandings—what he called a symbolic convergence. Careful examination of discussions revealed that groups came together through a kind of dramatic negotiation. When a member used a rhetorical device, such as a word play or a metaphor, it could shape the group's symbolic reality if one or more of the other group members picked up on, amplified, and reinforced it. Once a symbolic identity emerged, it could shape the group's trajectory, such as when a group takes on an achievement-oriented identity that pushes its members to bring more energy and effort to its tasks (or a playful group runs the opposite course).

Dennis Gouran and Randy Hirokawa also advanced the group literature by developing a functional theory of group decision making. Drawing on earlier writings by the American philosopher John Dewey, Gouran and Hirokawa theorized that the same steps taken in rational thinking would be critical for arriving at effective group decisions. In their view, the *function* of task-oriented communication is to lead group members through these necessary analytic stages—from defining the problem to arriving at a final judgment. Among the many findings their research yielded were that groups too often fail to explicitly consider which evaluative criteria should be used to judge alternatives. Also, the most effective decision-making groups typically devote considerable effort to weighing the potential negative consequences of potential decisions, a sober exercise that contrasts with the wishful thinking and avoidance of dissent characteristic of dysfunctional groups. Gouran and Hirokawa also linked their theory to others by identifying the various individual and contextual constraints on decision making that cause groups to fail to engage in rigorous discussion.

Marshall Scott Poole and his many collaborators introduced another set of influential ideas. Poole's initial research dispelled the commonly held belief that groups routinely developed through a series of stages, such as Bruce Tuckman's poetic sequence of *forming, storming, norming, performing,* and *adjourning.* Some groups do mature in this way, but many others follow different courses as they develop over time.

Not coincidentally, Poole's attention turned to structuration theory, a *grand theory* (i.e., an overarching set of theoretical concepts and models) developed by British sociologist Anthony Giddens in the late 1970s. Poole, along with Robert McPhee and David Seibold, suggested that group researchers view groups in structurational terms: In choosing what to say or do, each group member draws on his or her own understanding of how society operates—the *structures* of meaning, norms, and power perceived to exist. When deploying these structures in interaction, group members are often reproducing existing social structures or, other times, challenging and potentially altering them. Small groups, in this view, play a uniquely important role in society as one of the most tangible contexts in which individuals can apprehend societal-level structures (i.e., speaking norms, patterns of authority, linguistic conventions) and either sustain or subvert them. This fluidity inherent in structuration theory provided an account of group behavior that could explain both regularized patterns and deviations, such as the ones Poole had earlier uncovered.

Poole also advanced group communication theory by narrowing the scope and meaning of this approach to create an adaptive structuration theory. This theory explained how groups adapt to new technologies, particularly the group decision-support software systems that Poole himself helped develop. This particular research program also presented group communication scholars with a new model of research that combined systematic experimentation, licensed software innovations, and major grant funding from the National Science Foundation—a synergy that could support intensive, sustained inquiry and rich theory development.

As group communication scholars developed and refined these theories, they came to define a new approach to studying small groups—one focused on the content of group discussion, not merely the structural features of the group or the personalities of individual members. Contemporary small-group research continues along this same trajectory, with the most ambitious work using detailed direct observations, videotapes, and transcripts to understand the complex structure of discourse that leads to group decisions, role structures, cohesion, and other group outcomes.

Future Trajectories

The most striking trend in small-group research, however, traces back to the aforementioned *bona fide* group perspective. Developed by communication scholars Linda Putnam and Cynthia Stohl, this is not so much a set of theoretical propositions as it is a governing set of assumptions and methodological commitments. In this view, the bulk of real groups have long histories embedded in richly textured natural settings; groups and their members have multiple interdependencies with other groups that shape their behavior. To understand a laboratory group is to understand an exceptional kind of *zero-history* group—an assemblage of strangers who tackle a single task and then dissolve. Although such groups do play important roles in society, such as in the case of the American jury, strong group theories need to look at groups in their natural settings.

Adopting this orientation leads group researchers to adopt an intensive case study approach to see the full complexity of a single group, rather than measuring some of the surface features of a sample of groups. This naturalistic approach often involves participant observation, ethnographic interviewing, and archival research, along with traditional transcription and survey research methods. From this multimethod mountain of data, one often aims to develop a *grounded* theory, one built from the details in the "ground" (i.e., raw data) up to the level of more general theoretical statement.

The clearest evidence of the ascendance of this approach is the proliferation of widely varied case studies that populate the group communication field's edited volumes, journals, and conferences. Original studies now exist on a much wider range of small groups, including such diverse group forms as musical troupes, covens, Bible-study groups, support groups, and criminal gangs. Intensive group case studies predated the *bona fide* movement, such as the aforementioned studies by Janis and Helen Schwartzman's landmark book *The Meeting*. This approach, however, has become common—perhaps even the norm—in small-group research, particularly within the field of communication.

The other movement reshaping group communication theory is the emergence of a coherent field that encompasses but reaches far beyond the communication discipline. The Interdisciplinary Network for Group Research (INGRoup), which first met in 2006, has fostered the cross-pollination of concepts, theories, and methods among group researchers who come from different academic traditions. If successful, INGRoup and other interdisciplinary initiatives simultaneously will enrich group communication theory and widen its influence.

It may also be possible to forecast the topical direction of small-group researchers, thanks to a recent survey of this field's leading theorists. The highest research priorities for these scholars included many traditional topics—leadership, status/power, decision making, social identity, and conflict in and between groups—but interest has grown in the understudied subjects of creativity, diversity, and technology in groups. Researchers also intend to pay greater attention to cross-cultural variations in group behavior and the relationships between groups and their larger organizational and social contexts.

In the end, theoretical advances in each of these areas will likely continue to serve the same aim initially proposed by group discussion pioneers—effectively participating in and facilitating the many groups that populate our lives. Given the ubiquity of group discussion, the public creation and distribution of this knowledge not only meets our practical needs but also could help us better secure a social and political commitment to democratic group process.

John Gastil

See also Bona Fide Group Theory; Deliberative Democratic Theories; Functional Group Communication Theory; Group and Organizational Structuration Theory; Groupthink; Structuration Theory; Symbolic Convergence Theory

Further Readings

Bormann, E. G. (1980). The paradox and promise of small group communication revisited. *Central States Speech Journal, 31,* 214–224.

Frey, L. R. (Ed.). (2003). *Group communication in context: Studies of bona fide groups.* Mahwah, NJ: Lawrence Erlbaum.

Frey, L. R., Gouran, D. S., & Poole, M. S. (Eds.). (1999). *The handbook of group communication theory and research.* Thousand Oaks, CA: Sage.

Gastil, J. (2009). *The group in society.* Thousand Oaks, CA: Sage.

Hare, A. P. (1976). *Handbook of small group research* (2nd ed.). New York: Free Press.

Levine, J. M., & Moreland, R. L. (1990). Progress in small group research. *Annual Review of Psychology, 41,* 585–634.

Poole, M. S., & Hollingshead, A. B. (Eds.). (2005). *Theories of small groups: Interdisciplinary perspectives.* Thousand Oaks, CA: Sage.

Wheelan, S. A. (Ed.). (2005). *The handbook of group research and practice.* Thousand Oaks, CA: Sage.

Wittenbaum, G. M., Keyton, J., & Weingart, L. R. (2006). A new era for group research: The formation of INGRoup. *Small Group Research, 37,* 575–581.

GROUPTHINK

Irving Janis used the term *groupthink* to refer to a condition in which highly cohesive groups strive to reach unanimity in their decision making at the expense of adequately examining alternative solutions. Such groups desire to maintain a cohesive atmosphere in the group to the extent that members are not to "rock the boat" or "stir the waters." The condition ultimately leads to a deterioration in decision processes that usually results in poor decisions. The groupthink hypothesis is intimately tied to how group members communicate with one another. This entry explores groupthink, identifying its antecedent conditions, corresponding symptoms, effect on decision processes and decisions, and ways the phenomenon might be prevented.

Although Irving Janis did not coin the term, his conceptualization of groupthink has had the most significant and lasting impact on those wishing to learn more about group and organizational functioning. It all started with the Bay of Pigs fiasco. In April 1961, a rebel force backed by the U.S. government made a landing at the Bay of Pigs,

Cuba, in an effort to topple the newly established government of Fidel Castro. President John F. Kennedy and some of his most trusted advisers made decisions to cancel plans for additional rounds of bombings of Cuban airfields, changed the original and better landing site of the invasion force, and failed to provide air support for the rebels. The decisions doomed any hopes of the success of the invasion. A substantial number of the rebel force were killed in battle or captured and executed.

Irving Janis later claimed the Bay of Pigs disaster was one of the biggest fiascoes ever perpetrated by a government. He was bothered with the question of how groups of learned people could collectively make such bad decisions. He suggested this topic to his daughter, who was writing a term paper. Examining her research, Janis's curiosity was piqued, and he subsequently formulated the essential features of what would come to be known as the *groupthink hypothesis*.

There are certain characteristics that lay the foundation for groupthink. Among these antecedents are group cohesiveness, structural faults, and a provocative situational context. *Cohesiveness* refers to a state of mutual liking and attraction among group members; group members are amiable and united and have a desire to maintain positive relationships, and a feeling of esprit de corps is present. *Structural faults* may include the group's insulation from external sources of information and counsel, lack of an established tradition of impartiality on the part of the leader, lack of norms for decision-making procedures, and homogeneity of group members with regard to social background and ideology. *Provocative situational contexts* are the kinds that impose high levels of stress on group members. These stresses may be due to a previous or recent record of failure, perceptions that the task may be too difficult, or the belief that there is no morally correct alternative available.

Of the three antecedents, cohesiveness is believed to be primary and, when paired with one of the other two antecedents, results in a greater likelihood that the group will suffer from groupthink. When cohesion is moderate to high, and one of the other antecedents is present, group members are likely to have a concurrence-seeking tendency when making decisions. This tendency in turn is likely to manifest itself in the eight symptoms of groupthink outlined by Janis:

1. *Illusion of invulnerability:* Members are highly optimistic and willing to take extreme risks.

2. *Collective efforts to rationalize:* Members cast doubt on the validity of information that brings into question assumptions made.

3. *Illusion of morality:* The moral consequences of a decision go unexplored because group members do not question the morality of the group.

4. *Excessive stereotyping:* The group views rivals as too evil to warrant serious negotiation with them, or too weak or stupid in efforts to defeat the group.

5. *Pressure to conform:* Pressure is brought to bear against those members who disagree with the group, often through claims that such disagreements are indicative of disloyalty.

6. *Self-censorship:* Members do not voice dissenting or contrary views to the group consensus.

7. *Illusion of unanimity:* There is a false perception that members have achieved a consensus; silence is consent.

8. *Self-appointed mindguards:* Some members take on the role of guarding the group from information that might call into question the effectiveness and morality of decisions made.

If these symptoms are present, the group fails to use *vigilance* in its decision-making process. When groups engage in *vigilant decision making,* they adequately (a) survey the possible alternatives/ solutions available; (b) survey the objectives to be accomplished; (c) examine the risks and benefits associated with the alternatives; (d) perform an information search; (e) process the information in an unbiased manner; (f) reappraise the alternatives in light of risks and benefits before making a final choice; and (g) work out a plan for implementing the desired choice, along with contingency plans should additional risks associated with that choice become known.

When vigilance is not present, the likelihood of making bad decisions increases and ultimately may result in a decision-making fiasco. Given the negative consequences of groupthink, there are several steps a group should take in an effort to prevent it. The group leader should establish an atmosphere of open inquiry and impartiality and should withhold stating preferred courses of action at the outset. The leader should also encourage members to air objections and doubts; one or more members should play the role of *devil's advocate,* taking and voicing informed positions contrary to the prevailing position. Several subgroups working on the same problem should be formed, coming together at a future time to iron out differences. Finally, individuals from outside the group should be brought into group meetings to observe and challenge prevailing views, especially those of powerful group members.

The research that has investigated the groupthink phenomenon has at times yielded equivocal results. Primarily, the importance of cohesiveness in the groupthink model has been questioned. As a consequence, some have called for a reformulation of the original model to include other variables that might help to better explain the tendency toward ineffective group decision making. Among these calls has been a need to focus on, for example, the concept of collective efficacy (the belief of group members about their ability to effectively accomplish the group's task) and the role of motivations in decision making.

The groupthink hypothesis has spurred much research, and the phenomenon has been put forward as a reason for faulty decision making in many historical contexts: the Bay of Pigs, Pearl Harbor, Viet Nam, the Watergate break-in, and the space shuttle *Challenger* explosion. The research and analyses concerning the groupthink hypothesis have also had a tremendous impact on policymaking in organizational and community settings. In the communication discipline, Janis and his colleagues' work on groupthink has directly influenced the development of the functional perspective of effective decision making and the vigilant interaction theory. The hypothesis has retained its appeal in the years since it was first put forward, as evidenced by the number of scholarly references to it, the research it has spurred, and the changes it has instigated in the workplace.

Abran J. Salazar

See also Bona Fide Group Theory; Creativity in Groups; Functional Group Communication Theory; Group Communication Theories

Further Readings

Janis, I. L. (1972). *Victims of groupthink: A psychological study of foreign-policy decisions and fiascoes.* Boston: Houghton-Mifflin.

Janis, I. L. (1982). *Groupthink: Psychological studies of policy decisions and fiascoes.* Boston: Houghton-Mifflin.

Janis, I. L., & Mann, L. (1977). *Decision making: A psychological analysis of conflict, choice, and commitment.* New York: Free Press.

Raven, B. (1998). Groupthink, Bay of Pigs, and Watergate reconsidered. *Organizational Behavior and Human Decision Processes, 73,* 352–361.

Whyte, G. (1998). Recasting Janis's groupthink model: The key role of collective efficacy in decision fiascoes. *Organizational Behavior and Human Decision Processes, 73,* 185–209.

H

HAPTICS

See Nonverbal Communication Theories

HAWAIIAN *HOʻOPONOPONO* THEORY

Hoʻoponopono, or setting to right, is a method of interpersonal conflict resolution practiced in the traditional Native Hawaiian culture. As a highly collectivistic society, the Native Hawaiian community generally perceives interpersonal conflict as negative and to be avoided or ignored whenever possible. However, when interpersonal conflict between members of the community creates much distress for any of the parties involved or the community at large, hoʻoponopono is likely to be performed. Essentially, then, the overall goal of hoʻoponopono is not only to resolve interpersonal conflicts but also to restore a sense of togetherness and harmony among all members of the community.

A third party, normally a respected elder of the community, serves as the facilitator. This elder is responsible for monitoring and controlling both the verbal and the nonverbal behaviors of the disputants as he or she guides them through an opening, discussion, resolution, and closing phase. In the opening phase, the facilitator typically says a prayer to bless the conflicting parties. He or she then encourages the disputants to conduct themselves in a sincere and truthful manner and may remind them about how the whole community has been affected by their discord. The elder then outlines the alleged problem and describes how hoʻoponopono will proceed.

During the second phase, the discussion, the facilitator attempts to identify the source(s) of the problem. This phase is normally the most time-consuming because family members and others who have been affected by the conflict may share their views at this juncture. As can be expected, this process of uncovering the cause(s) of the conflict can also be extremely emotional. Therefore, the elder must be able to steer all participants away from blaming and recrimination. Should tempers flare at this point, the leader would call for a period of silence to bring emotions under control. He or she would then remind participants of the purpose of hoʻoponopono and emphasize self-scrutiny over finding fault with others.

In the third phase, resolution, parties express sincere apologies and ask for forgiveness. It is important that forgiveness is granted, for this symbolizes a release from the ties of conflict and discord that linked the disputants. If forgiveness is not given, hoʻoponopono is not complete.

When the facilitator feels that all issues of conflict have been resolved between disputants, he or she moves the participants to the closing phase. In this phase, the hoʻoponopono leader reaffirms a sense of harmony among all community members and reminds all those who have been affected that the conflict should never surface again. This sense of harmony is readily evidenced by the mutual preparation and partaking of a celebratory meal.

Essentially, ho'oponopono is a method of conflict resolution designed to maintain harmony among members of the traditional Native Hawaiian community. Further, as with collectivistic societies, it emphasizes the importance of face-giving rather than the face-saving concern of individualists.

It is believed that the practice of ho'oponopono predates the arrival of British explorer James Cook in 1778. However, as Western influence dramatically altered the social and cultural systems that flourished during the precontact years, the use of ho'oponopono sharply declined. It was not until the early 1970s, when a highly respected elder of the Native Hawaiian community, Mary Kawena Pukui, who described in some detail her understanding of ho'oponopono, that the practice experienced a renaissance. Today, ho'oponopono is used to resolve interpersonal conflicts in business and professional organizations and with people of non-Hawaiian ancestry.

Steven Y. Miura

See also Conflict Communication Theories; Culture and Communication

Further Readings

Chun, M. N. (1995). *Making peace: Ho'oponopono then and now.* Honolulu, HI: Queen Lili'uokalani Trust.

Miura, S. Y. (2000). The mediation of conflict in the traditional Hawaiian family: A collectivistic approach. *Qualitative Research Reports in Communication, 1,* 19–25.

Pukui, M. K., Haertig, E. W., & Lee, C. A. (1972). *Nana ike kumu: Vol. 1.* Honolulu, HI: Hui Hanai.

Shook, E. V. (1985). *Ho'oponopono: Contemporary uses of a Hawaiian problem- solving process.* Honolulu, HI: East-West Center.

HEALTH COMMUNICATION THEORIES

Health communication is a relatively young, vibrant, and interdisciplinary applied subfield of communication studies that examines the powerful roles performed by human and mediated communication in the delivery of health care and the promotion of individual and public health. Health communication is a very broad and complex field of study that draws from the research and theory of just about every other area of communication research, including intrapersonal communication, interpersonal communication, group communication, organizational communication, media studies, public relations, intercultural communication, rhetorical studies, and new information technologies. Not surprisingly, health communication scholars apply a wide range of different theories, models, and research methods from these different areas of communication inquiry to examine health communication phenomena. They also adopt theories and methods that derive from many other related disciplines, such as psychology, sociology, anthropology, public health, medicine, nursing, health education, epidemiology, and social work. There are a growing number of dedicated health communication theories that guide current health communication research and applications that will be reviewed here.

Health communication research investigates the ways health care providers, consumers, and many relevant others (such as health care administrators, health care suppliers, health system regulators, insurance company representatives, family members, legislators, and researchers) use communication, both in person and through mediated channels, to coordinate the efforts of many different people in promoting health and delivering health care. Health communication scholars also examine the many different ways communication strategies can be used to disseminate relevant health information to key audiences. This is particularly evident in the development, implementation, and evaluation of strategically designed persuasive communication campaigns for health education and promotion. Health communication scholars study the important ways that communication can be used to alert key publics about relevant and dangerous health risks and coordinate prevention and response to public health emergencies. Health communication scholars also examine the many different ways news, entertainment, and social media channels, including new computerized information technologies (e-health), influence health care and health promotion. Health communication inquiry will be examined here from four different interrelated perspectives: (1) health communication and the delivery of health care, (2) health communication and the promotion of health, (3) health and risk communication, and (4) health communication and new information technologies (e-health).

Delivery of Health Care

Scholars who study the ways communication influences the delivery of health care are part of the larger interdisciplinary *health services research* tradition. These scholars often examine the interpersonal interactions between health care consumers and providers, evaluating both the *verbal* and the *nonverbal messages* exchanged during patient appointments, diagnostic interviews, checkups, and examinations. A number of theories guide this examination of *message exchange patterns* between health care consumers and providers, often with the use of *interaction and conversation analysis* research techniques. A large number of interpersonal communication theories have been used to guide the consumer–provider interaction health communication research tradition, including *social penetration theory* (examining the development of relational closeness through self-disclosure), *uncertainty reduction theory* (examining how interpersonal exchanges are used to gain knowledge and understanding), *social exchange theory* (examining the negotiated costs and benefits of relational exchanges for participants), *communication accommodation theory* (examining the ways personal and social identities are negotiated in interactions), and *expectancy violations theory* (examining the ways unexpected behaviors that break social norms can influence participant beliefs and behaviors).

There are also a number of dedicated health communication theories and models that have been developed to guide consumer–provider communication research. These dedicated health communication theoretical perspectives include the *transformation model of communication and health outcomes* (which predicts how antecedent participant and situational conditions combine with consumer–provider communication processes to achieve cognitive, behavioral, and physiological health outcomes, the *relational model of health communication competence* (which posits the influences of health care participants' level of communication competence on achieving desired health outcomes), the *cognitive–affective model of relational expectations in the provider–patient context* (which describes the ways participants' expectations for content and relational information influence health care interactions), the *cancer advocacy and liaison model* (which describes how communication can be used to empower patients to take control of their health care), and the *health care partnership model of doctor–patient communication* (which describes how patient advocates with doctors and patients can influence the outcomes of health care exchanges).

Communication variables and outcomes that are often examined from the consumer–provider interaction research tradition include *relational dominance* between health care providers and consumers. For example, verbal messages are often examined to determine dominance by examining who does most of the talking, who introduces new topics, who controls the conversation, and who asks most of the questions during consumer–provider encounters. Nonverbal messages that are examined to assess conversational dominance include the use of different *paralinguistic cues* (such as speaking volume and tone), *proxemic cues* (such as physical distance established between interactants, their postures, and the extent to which the interactants face one another), as well as examination of eye contact and the use of gestures during conversations. A large body of research has established that health care providers typically dominate conversations with consumers, establishing an imbalance in *relational power* in health care communication. Another conversational outcome examined in consumer–provider research is *message congruence* (the extent to which responses to comments match the topics and requests made in those comments). Research has shown that too often in health care situations, consumers and providers do not directly answer the questions asked of them or respond congruently to topics raised during conversations. Sometimes health care participants have different agendas for the conversation, may not be ready to disclose personal information that is requested, or have difficulty understanding comments or effectively articulating responses. Incongruencies in conversation often lead to misunderstandings between health care providers and consumers and can limit the participants' satisfaction with communication encounters. They can also lead to mistakes with diagnoses and poor adherence to therapeutic recommendations. Another communication outcome that is often studied is the expression of *empathy* between communicators (do the messages that are exchanged demonstrate concern and compassion for the relational partners?). Research has shown that the expression of empathy is a key factor in establishing trust, rapport, and cooperation in health care encounters, but unfortunately there are many instances in the delivery of health care in which empathy is not expressed particularly well.

A related area of research within the health care delivery approach to health communication examines the provision and influences of *social support* through interpersonal, group, and organizational communication to help individuals cope with difficult situations and events. Much of the social support research derives from *social network theory*, which describes the patterns and influences of interactions between communicators within social systems. People facing major health challenges often need social support to help them maintain socioemotional balance and build strength to confront health problems. Sensitive, caring, and empathic interpersonal communication has been shown to be the primary channel for providing social support, yet too often individuals who are confronting serious health challenges do not have access to sufficient social support. *Social penetration theory* has been used to examine the development of relational closeness and social support between participants within the health care system, as well as how closeness progresses and how self-disclosure enables movement from a superficial to an intimate relationship.

Still other research conducted within the health care delivery tradition examines *interprofessional* and *team communication* among interdependent health care providers and consumers within health care delivery systems, such as hospitals and clinics. This research illustrates the tremendous need for information sharing, conflict management, and coordination among interdependent members of health care teams, as well as the many impediments to achieving cooperation in the delivery of health care within complex and bureaucratic modern health care systems. Much of the team

communication research has been grounded in different *role theories*, *leadership theories*, and *decision-making theories*.

Promotion of Health

Scholars who study the ways communication influences the adoption of recommended health behaviors for prevention, early detection, and treatment of health problems are part of the *health promotion* tradition of health communication research. These scholars examine both the persuasive strategies that are used for developing and implementing *health communication campaigns* and the many ways that relevant health information is disseminated to key publics through a variety of communication channels.

There are a number of theories of mass communication that have been used to guide health promotion research. Some of the mass communication theories that have been adopted in health communication include *cultivation theory* (which describes how audiences learn about the world and model behavior from media portrayals of people and events), *uses and gratification theory* (which describes how people use media to achieve various goals), *agenda-setting theory* (which describes the ways media influence audiences' prioritization of important topics and social issues), the *two-step flow model* (which describes how human agency, such as *opinion leadership*, combines with the media to influence audiences), and the related *diffusion of innovations theory* (which describes how new ideas and activities are communicated and adopted in society). The *knowledge gap hypothesis* describes the differential acquisition of health information by different groups in society.

There are also a wide range of persuasion theories that are commonly used to direct health communication inquiry. These theories include the *theory of reasoned action* (sometimes referred to as the *behavioral intentions model*, which predicts behavior change by examining attitudes, beliefs, and behavioral intentions), *social learning theory* (which posits how behaviors can be learned through reinforcement, punishment, and observation), and the related *social cognitive theory* (which describes how people learn new behaviors by observing and modeling relevant others to develop *self-efficacy* or confidence in their abilities to enact new behaviors). Models of *edutainment* (the use of entertainment media to communicate engaging health information to diverse audiences) have developed from social cognitive theory, *message framing theory* (which describes the different ways messages that emphasize positive outcomes and negative outcomes affect audiences), and *information processing theory* (which illustrates how attention, comprehension, and acceptance of messages influence persuasion). There are also numerous theories of *attitude change, source credibility, social influence,* and *message exposure* that are used to guide health communication research, including *cognitive dissonance theory* (which describes the motivation to reduce cognitive imbalance or dissonance by changing or rationalizing attitudes, beliefs, and behaviors), the *elaboration likelihood model* (which describes both central and peripheral routes for analyzing, forming, and changing attitudes), *social judgment theory* (which describes how personal involvement, the structure of messages, and the sources of messages influence attitude change), *balance theory* (which describes how the drive for personal consistency influences responses to messages and social influence attempts), *protection motivation theory* (which describes the adoption of adaptive behaviors in response to threats), and the related *extended parallel process model* (which specifies how to channel fears into productive, adaptive actions).

There are several models that have been used to direct strategic design and implementation of health promotion campaigns. For example, the *social marketing model* (which illustrates how the traditional marketing mix for utilizing and blending product, price, place, and promotion can be used to guide the development of health promotion campaign messages and delivery strategies. Similarly *the transtheoretical model,* which is sometimes referred to as the *stages of change model* (which describes audience members' relative readiness to adopt recommended changes as one of five *stages of readiness:* precontemplation, contemplation, preparation, action, or maintenance), is often used to analyze the readiness of target audiences and to guide message development for health promotion campaigns. The *precede–proceed model* (which explains how predisposing, enabling, and reinforcing factors contribute to adopting recommended

behavior changes) is also often used to help plan health promotion campaigns. Similarly, the *health belief model* (which explains how beliefs about perceived threats and net benefits—perceived susceptibility, perceived severity, perceived benefits, and perceived barriers—influence adoption of health recommendations) is often used to guide health promotion campaigns. The recently proposed *people and places model* presents an *ecological framework* for guiding health communication interventions by explaining and predicting how the health of populations can be influenced by communication according to the unique attributes of audience members, the attributes of the environments where people live and work, and the important interactions between people and places.

Health and Risk Communication

Health and risk communication research examines the significant communication demands involved in identifying serious health risks such as potential epidemics (such as the spread of infectious diseases; natural disasters; bioterrorism; public exposure to poisons; or contamination of food, air, or water), preparing at-risk publics to confront imminent health risks, and coordinating responses when these serious health crises occur. The advent of dramatic health-threatening public emergencies (such as the exposure to anthrax through the mail, spread of the avian flu and the West Nile virus, as well as the health-related repercussions from Hurricane Katrina and the terrorist attacks on the World Trade Center) have sensitized health communication scholars to the need to study risk and emergency communication in response to dangerous health crises. The U.S. Centers for Disease Control and Prevention, in particular, has become a leader in risk communication, developing extensive health and risk communication programs to help the nation respond effectively to health crises.

Several theories have been used to guide health and risk communication efforts. For example, the *risk perception model* describes the many interrelated factors (including voluntariness, controllability, familiarity, equity, benefits, understanding, uncertainty, dread, trust, reversibility, personal stake, ethics, origin of the risk, victim identity, and catastrophic potential) that influence how different audiences perceive and are likely to react to health risks. The *mental noise model* examines how different publics process information under stress about health risks and how their interpretations influence their responses to risk communication. The *negative dominance model* describes the ways audiences process both negative and positive information when confronting health risks. The *trust determination theory* examines communication strategies (such as the use of caring and empathy, competence and expertise, honesty and openness, and dedication and commitment) risk managers can use to establish trust when communicating with different audiences about health risks. The *CAUSE model* has been used to guide risk communication efforts by encouraging risk communicators to earn the confidence of respected journalists, create awareness of health issues, increase public understanding, enhance public satisfaction with news coverage, and motivate enactment of risk management behaviors. The *strategic bio-defense communication model* describes a three-stage strategy risk managers can use to promote risk prevention, preparation for risks, and responses to biological threat crises. Recently *Weick's model of organizing*, which describes the systemic role of information and communication for social organizing and has seen long use by communication scholars, has been proposed as a theoretical perspective for guiding health risk communication research and intervention.

New Information Technologies (E-Health)

E-health is a relatively new area of health communication inquiry that examines the ways that computers and other digital information technologies can be used to enhance the delivery of health care and the promotion of public health. The rapid diffusion of the Internet and other relevant information technologies (such as electronic health records, *health information portals*, *tailored behavior change programs*, interactive health education systems, *telehealth* information and monitoring applications, *online support groups*, tobacco cessation *quitlines*, and even *virtual reality* training programs) has revolutionized the modern health care system and promises many additional changes and innovations in health communication. Research suggests that the vast majority of Americans are now using the Internet as a primary source of health information. Yet, there are concerns about the accuracy of the information provided and the computer literacy of consumers to interpret the information they may access. In fact, there are major concerns about issues of information overload, misinformation, equal access to health information, lack of information privacy, and the predatory use of health information technologies to swindle health consumers.

A number of well-accepted communication theories and models, as well as new theoretical perspectives, have been used to guide e-health research. Several well-established communication theories have been applied to the study of e-health, including use of the *diffusion of innovations theory* to track adoption of new information technologies by health care providers and consumers. *Organizational culture theory* has been used to examine the ways the modern health care system has changed to embrace the use of information technologies for patient care, education, and support. Adoption of new information technologies in health care has been compared to the diffusion of other communication media, such as the television, the radio, and the cell phone. The *digital divide model* developed as a description of unequal access to and diffusion of new information technologies, as well as to describe the impact of this information inequality on access to health information. *Media complementarity theory* and *attribution theory* have been used to explain nonpurposive media usage in the health information acquisition process. The *comprehensive model of information seeking* has been used to model consumers' search of online health information.

Similarly, research on the provision of social support online has been compared to earlier research on *social support networks*. For example, *social penetration theory* has been used to examine how online relationships are developed in online support groups and in the delivery of telehealth. *Social network theory* has been used to guide analysis of patient-centered social networks and communities of care online. The *online support group participation model* explains why some consumers use online support groups and others do not. *Social information processing theory* describes how online support group participants portray themselves in favorable ways to foster future interactions.

E-health inquiry has also borrowed from research on interpersonal communication. For example, *uncertainty reduction theory* has been used to guide examination of the ways e-mail is used between doctors and patients to provide relevant information concerning health care diagnosis and treatment. *Social cognitive theory* has been used to examine satisfaction with the use of e-health services. Theories of relational development have also been used to model the development of online health relationships.

Several dedicated e-health theories and models have been developed in recent years, often building on other health communication theoretical frameworks. For example, the *e-health behavior management model* combines the *transtheoretical model*, the *theory of planned behavior*, and several theories of persuasive communication to describe the ways consumers negotiate the Internet to gather relevant health information. The World Health Organization introduced the *5-C Model for eHealth* to model the development of e-health systems in developing countries. The five Cs include context, content, connectivity, capacity, and community development. As the e-health communication research area grows and matures, there will certainly be additional new theories and models developed to describe the intricacies of interactive online health information systems.

Gary L. Kreps

See also Accommodation Theory; Agenda-Setting Theory; Attitude Theory; Campaign Communication Theories; Cognitive Dissonance Theory; Cognitive Theories; Conversation Analysis; Corporate Campaign Theories; Diffusion of Innovations; Digital Divide; Elaboration Likelihood Theory; Empathy; Expectancy Violations Theory; Framing Theory; Group Communication Theories; Interpersonal Communication Theories; Language and Communication; Nonverbal Communication Theories; Organizational Communication Theories; Organizational Culture; Organizing, Process of; Persuasion and Social Influence Theories; Power, Interpersonal; Reasoned Action Theory; Relational Communication Theory; Social Exchange Theory; Social Judgment Theory; Social Penetration Theory; Social Support; Uncertainty Reduction Theory; Uses, Gratifications, and Dependency

Further Readings

Covello, V. T., Peters, R. G., Wojtecki, J. G., & Hyde, R. C. (2001). Risk communication, the West Nile virus epidemic, and bioterrorism: Responding to the communication challenges caused by the intentional or unintentional release of a pathogen in an urban setting. *Journal of Urban Health: Bulletin of the New York Academy of Medicine, 78*, 382–391.

Jackson, L. D., & Duffy, B. K. (Eds.). (1998). *Health communication research: A guide to developments and direction*. Westport, CT: Greenwood Press.

Kreps, G. L., O'Hair, D., & Clowers, M. (1994). The influences of human communication on health outcomes. *American Behavioral Scientist, 38*, 248–256.

Kreps, G. L., Query, J. L., & Bonaguro, E. W. (2007). The interdisciplinary study of health communication and its relationship to communication science. In L. Lederman (Ed.), *Beyond these walls: Readings in health communication* (pp. 2–13). London: Oxford University Press.

Lederman, L. (Ed.). (2007). *Beyond these walls: Readings in health communication*. London: Oxford University Press.

Thompson, T., Parrott, R., Miller, K., & Dorsey, A. (Eds.). (2003). *The handbook of health communication*. Hillsdale, NJ: Lawrence Erlbaum.

Wright, K. B., Sparks, L. S., & O'Hair, H. D. (2008). *Health communication in the 21st century*. Malden, MA: Blackwell.

HERMENEUTICS

Hermeneutics appears now to be something more than a passing fashion of continental theory. Like rhetoric, hermeneutics has a great and venerable provenance and a genuinely interdisciplinary breadth. But unlike rhetoric, its definition is contested and its standing controversial. It is considered a generic designation for interpretive criticism, a humanist philosophy that challenges the primacy of scientific method. It is an ontology of linguistic being, or a philosophy in which human experience becomes defined in language use. As such, hermeneutics is also a corollary to the idea of rhetorical agency, the idea that communicators act with intention. In its contemporary guise, it gained international notoriety in the 1960s after the publication of Hans-Georg Gadamer's *Truth and Method* and has continued to propagate in disciplines as various as theology, architecture, organizational communication, and physics. Although remaining strongly associated with Gadamer, a longtime student of philosopher Martin Heidegger, it has been further shaped and extended by such intellectual luminaries as Paul Ricoeur and Jürgen Habermas.

History of the Term

Long before the term *hermeneutics* was widely used, interpretive practices developed rules and conventions in various ancient school traditions of orality and literacy. Among the earliest and most significant are the extraordinary exegetical traditions of Hebrew scriptures. The Gemara, for instance, was a transcription of interpretive dialogues between rabbi and congregation over the meaning of the Mishnah (itself an interpretation of scripture), and these exegetical exercises became in turn a part of scriptural law. Canons of interpretive practice were embedded in Roman rhetorical teaching from Cicero and Quintilian to the Church Fathers, most famously in Augustine's *De Doctrina Christiana*. It was in this rhetorical environment that the principle of the *hermeneutic circle* gained prominence—the idea that textual meaning has a mutually reciprocal relation to its context. Initially this meant that one could understand a textual passage by relating it to the context of the larger work. Later this relation would be expanded to a work and the life of the author and then to any textual expression and its cultural–historical context.

Hermeneutics per se gained an independent disciplinary standing after the Protestant Reformation. The issue of interpretative method as a special study came to the fore with the rise of a culture of vernacular reading; the requirement for biblical exegesis, or interpretation, in Protestantism; the expanding interest in classical texts with the concomitant development of philology, or the study of human speech, literature, and language as a field that sheds light on cultural history; and a burgeoning jurisprudential interest in legal codes. These various disciplinary initiatives were carried on by many scholars. Philip Melanchthon was both a humanist and an aid to Luther's Reformation; he modified the Renaissance rhetoric curriculum to teach his Protestant students how to read as well as speak (*bene dicendi, bene scribendi*). Martin Luther himself was a significant influence in hermeneutics, establishing the scriptural text as the authoritative key for interpretative practice (*sola scriptura*). Matthias Flacius, a follower of Luther, attempted to develop comprehensive linguistic and grammatical principles for deciphering obscure passages of scripture. The theologian Johann Dannhauer early on suggested the universality of hermeneutic understanding, anticipating both Romantic and 20th-century hermeneutics. The theologian and historian Johann Chladenius developed hermeneutics as a humanist alternative to Cartesian epistemology and famously transformed the rhetorical concept of *scopus* (point of view) into a powerful hermeneutic tool of psychological perception. These are only a few of the many Protestant scholars who contributed to the development of early hermeneutics. It should be noted that this early tradition was in the main a German phenomenon, and remained so through Heidegger.

It is difficult to locate precisely where hermeneutics migrated from a specialized interpretive method for particular fields of study into a broadly applied philosophical perspective, because elements of its universal tendency were present almost from the beginning of hermeneutics. Chladenius, in 1742, already spoke in general terms of hermeneutics as a science comprehending all writing and speaking. Georg Friedrich Meier extended hermeneutics beyond the interpretation of texts to a semiotic theory encompassing all signs. The philologist Friedrich Ast lectured on principles of interpretive practice (including the circularity of the relation of text and cultural context) that sketch out a general hermeneutics.

But the movement toward making hermeneutics universal in interpreting all matters culminates with Friedrich Schleiermacher; he combined a devotion to Protestant theology with a close involvement in the early Romantic movement and proposed a systematic universal hermeneutics as the art of understanding coordinate to the art of speaking (rhetoric). Schleiermacher developed hermeneutics as a technique of transposition, of placing oneself in the whole context out of which a text emerges in order to understand it accurately and fully. He saw the subject of hermeneutics to be essentially the problem of *communication*, that is, how one person can understand the meaning of another across the barriers of speech, culture, history, and textuality. His psychological focus shifted hermeneutics from the understanding of a text to the understanding of understanding itself. This conceptual change in the function of hermeneutics would make possible its later appropriation for, respectively, a fundamental ontology and a humanist philosophy.

At this stage another development in German intellectual culture had a profound impact on hermeneutics: the movement known as German historicism. The linguist Wilhelm von Humboldt had prepared the way for this movement by moving away from what we now call the instrumentalist view of language and adopting the view that culture resides within language, and meaning arises in discursive interaction. Humboldt also shifted the emphasis of the circle of interpretation from the interior life of the individual mind to the spirit of the age.

Hermeneutics thereafter exchanged a primarily psychological orientation for a cultural one. With the rise of the historicist school, hermeneutics became the methodological basis for distinguishing the human studies (*Geisteswissenschaften*) from the natural sciences. August Böckh, Gustav Droysen, and Leopold von Ranke were among the leaders of this movement. Further radicalizing Humboldt's cultural perspective on language, they shifted the agency of human development further from the will of the individual to the active determination of history and culture by the spirit of the age.

The next great hermeneutic impetus came from Wilhelm Dilthey, who still hearkened back to strands in German Romanticism; he mediated the historicist and psychological perspectives by melding the biographical and sociohistorical into an interconnected system. He continued the effort to put the human studies onto a sound scientific footing and immortalized the distinction between explanation and understanding as the modalities, respectively, of the natural and human sciences. He appropriated Schleiermacher's hermeneutics as a methodology of the human sciences, treating the outward signs of expression and culture as a key to the inner life of the human being. His massive system was never completed, but his work has served as an impetus for hermeneutics that is still being felt today.

Following close on him in the next generation, Edmund Husserl, the father of phenomenology, did not extend the hermeneutic tradition directly, but his theory of intentional consciousness would be an important impetus for hermeneutics—a link between the effort to ground the human studies in nonobjectivist methods and Heidegger's effort to dissolve the subject–object dichotomy with a hermeneutics of being-in-the-world. Husserl epitomized his rigorous descriptions of the organic link between consciousness and "worldhood" by coining a famous term, the *lifeworld*, which became a resonant descriptor for the existential ground of hermeneutics.

Martin Heidegger was an inheritor of all these lines of thinking—the textual-interpretive, historicist, subjectivist orientation of the human sciences, the Hegelian ideal of objective spirit—all of which he brought to bear in a revolutionary effort to move beyond the transcendental subject–object dualism of the Western tradition. He did this in part by historicizing Husserl's idea of the lifeworld. The organic relation of inextricably embodied consciousness now also traverses the dimensions of culture and time. In the early 1920s, Heidegger briefly appropriated the term *hermeneutics* to signify that human life itself is an interpretive movement between the hidden cultural-historical currents that carry us along and our existential orientation to an indeterminate future. The circular movement between the whole expanse of our life and the present, as it disappears into both the abysm of memory and the contingent future, is analogous to the complex process of finding meaning in a text.

This explosion of the interpretive metaphor to the level of ontology, or being, was a major impetus behind the linguistic turn that dominated 20th-century cultural studies and continental philosophy. For the German successors of Johann Gottfried Herder and Humboldt, it was not difficult to link factual being-in-the-world to a linguistic paradigm. In the latter half of the 20th century, Gadamer carried on Heidegger's legacy by focusing on how a hermeneutic perspective transforms the premises underlying knowledge production in the human sciences. Gadamer's allegiance to the classical tradition of the humanities, including what he referred to as rhetoric's "broad" and "ancient" meaning, was the basis for his development of an alternative to the model of empirical science and technology that he felt dominated not only the learning culture but contemporary life. Gadamer himself defined *hermeneutics* variously—as a practical philosophy, a theory of understanding, a theory of speech as the basis of human interchange—and probably quite intentionally cultivated a certain ambiguity around his theme. Nevertheless, it is clear that Gadamer sees hermeneutics as a bid to undermine a knowledge paradigm underwritten by positivist assumptions and return to its rightful preeminence a humanist standard of judgment and practice that guides the progress of science rather than the reverse. At the root of this proposal is a shift from monologic instrumentalism to understanding through dialogue. Rejecting the model of an inner mental agency of pure reason, hermeneutics locates deliberative judgment in the social process inherent in our speaking with one another.

This thrust has been challenged by more orthodox sociological perspectives. The Italian juridical scholar Emilio Betti, the philosopher Karl-Otto Apel, the sociologist Jürgen Habermas, the American literary critic E. D. Hirsch, and others have attempted to refashion hermeneutics into a more objectivist methodological procedure, but Heidegger and Gadamer cast a long shadow, and their influence remains dominant. Ricoeur attempted to mediate these opposing efforts dialectically, showing how the interplay of these two sets of ideas yields value.

Hermeneutics in Communication Studies

This history of hermeneutics as a once-marginal "special discipline" turned major philosophical perspective has not left communication studies in the United States unaffected. Hermeneutics rode quietly into the discipline on the tail of continental theory over the past several decades, but it remains intact and in dialogue with communication while many of the more fashionable imports have lost their currency. Despite Gadamer's overriding determination to prevent hermeneutics from being assimilated as a method, a number of communication scholars have attempted to systematize hermeneutics methodologically. This manner of appropriation is not universal. Both interpersonal and intercultural communication have been less methodological, using hermeneutics more as a perspective than as a method.

The relation of hermeneutics to rhetoric studies eclipses all this. In 1994, Jeffery Bineham suggested that rhetoric should turn from epistemology, or knowledge claims, to the more interpretation-based position of hermeneutics. In so doing, he essentially reversed Klaus Dockhorn's famous 1966 effort to reveal the deep rhetorical origins of Gadamer's *Truth and Method* of 1980. Both statements become ironic in the light of history. Since its inception as a disciplinary practice, from Cicero to Augustine, from Melanchthon to Schleiermacher, hermeneutics has been intimately tied to, even housed in, rhetoric and its teaching traditions. In its early modern history, hermeneutics separated from rhetoric, its mother discipline, to become a satellite field allied with philology, theology, and legal studies, but up until late in the 19th century, the ground of hermeneutics was reflexively understood to be the school tradition of rhetoric. Academic rhetoric is still discovering that organic relationship.

To be sure, there have been significant inroads toward a recovery. Michael Hyde and Craig Smith were among the first to bring a Heideggerian frame of reference to academic rhetoric in order to harvest its onto-epistemic (being-knowledge) potential. Steven Mailloux in literary studies has developed a concept he calls *rhetorical hermeneutics*, which is primarily a reflective examination of how critics interpret the tropes, or nonliteral expressions, of a culture. Michael Leff inverted Mailloux's phrase and offered a *hermeneutical rhetoric*, pointing to the fact that the rhetor has always acted as an interpreter of texts for a public. Mailloux's and Leff's appropriations tend toward field-specific applications, which is to say, respectively, literary criticism and public address. Dilip Gaonkar's attribution of a hermeneutic function to rhetoric broadens the field of hermeneutics, attributing a new theorizing impulse to a wide swath of academic rhetorical education. Rhetoricians, in Gaonkar's view, no longer educate students in the art of public speaking, but become cultural critics who deploy rhetorical concepts in the analysis of culture. Hermeneutics in this sense designates a critical–interpretive activity performed by humanist scholars. A strong indicator of increased interest in the rapprochement between rhetoric and hermeneutics is represented by the publication of the interdisciplinary volume entitled *Rhetoric and*

Hermeneutics in Our Time. But perhaps the most intriguing sign of a new alliance is Daniel Gross and Ansgar Kemmann's 2005 book, *Heidegger and Rhetoric*, a collection of essays by rhetoricians and philosophers that uncovers Heidegger's early and largely unknown debt to Aristotelian rhetoric.

Despite these incipient links, mainstream rhetoric studies has been cautious of a too close alliance with hermeneutics. This hesitation is a function of disparate disciplinary histories and of genuine concern for the ambitions of hermeneutics to become a universal framework, as Gaonkar's important essay warns. Cultural and critical studies perspectives, in addition, look on Gadamerian hermeneutics with suspicion as a nod to traditionalism. In addition, the extreme diversity of understandings of both rhetoric and hermeneutics multiplies the difficulties of finding a workable relation between them.

Yet it is important to note that Gadamer himself, with repeated urgency toward the end of his life, called for a revitalization of a humanist rhetoric, which he tied to hermeneutics through the concept of phronesis and dialogic practice. Gadamer courted rhetoric through his long career as a paradigmatic counterthrust to the hyper-rationalism of the method-driven sciences, but in his last years this appeal became more and more insistent.

What Hermeneutics Offers Communication

Hermeneutics provides a rich and focused challenge to the methodological presuppositions of the social sciences, so students of communication who wish to interrogate the tools of their trade could hardly find a richer source for this topic. The question of methodology was at the root of Gadamer's writing, and the debate between humanist and methodological perspectives animated many of the great writings in hermeneutics.

In addition, hermeneutics, as much as any perspective, moves communication from its instrumental identity to its ontological (i.e., constitutive) function. In attempting to break down the subject–object paradigm by relocating and dispersing agency across audience, issue, and situation and relocating speaker or writer from the center to the margins, it supports the general move toward dialogic models of communication. Listening studies will find much material in hermeneutics, which insists that word, world, and other must speak to us first.

At the heart of hermeneutics is a novel view of the structure of discursive understanding, which it takes to be circular rather than linear. Analytic logic moves one step at a time toward a conclusion and attempts to exclude presuppositions or predeterminations. Hermeneutics not only affirms the impoverishment of this kind of thinking, but it makes predispositions and predeterminations constitutive and central to the communication process itself.

Hermeneutics teases out the implicit philosophical implications of rhetorical practice and engages rhetoric on the complex and controversial interaction between theory and practice. The enduring strength of rhetoric's focus on the particular and the pragmatic is the premise of the hermeneutic approach toward theory.

Philosophical hermeneutics is one of the preeminent traditions offering defensible alternatives to the philosophies of the subject. The particular inflection of its polemic is particularly congenial to communication studies, since its emphasis is on communality through dialogue as the counterweight to the Western tradition of the soul thrust back on itself.

Future Directions

The future of hermeneutics in communication studies will depend on answers to a series of unresolved questions about its disciplinary appropriation: Is hermeneutics to be treated primarily as a paradigm, a perspective, a corollary to rhetoric (as listening to speaking), a critical approach, a method of analysis? Does it work its way into the texture of rhetorical thought, for instance, and simply die of its own success? Does it develop its own disciplinary niche in ways analogous to, for instance, the theory of Kenneth Burke or critical rhetoric? Or does it stand in its own disciplinary orbit in cooperative tension with rhetoric, as, for instance, cultural studies? If it is to be useful in the wider area of communication studies, particularly as it impinges on the social sciences, then it will have to resolve hermeneutics' relation to methodology. Most critically, the discipline of communication must revisit the philosophical impulse to transform a general hermeneutics from a systematic canon of textual exegesis into a theory of knowledge. It was that historical turn in the road that eventually led hermeneutics, as its own self-standing theoretical perspective, to fuse epistemology and ontology against the dualism of positivist science. Gadamerian hermeneutics can be read as an argument for the return of communication to its preeminent status as the foundation of the humanities and general education, not simply as training in speaking and writing skills, but as the underlying framework for the liberal arts.

John Arthos

See also Critical Discourse Analysis; Discourse Theory and Analysis; Existentialism; Interpretive Theory; Language and Communication; Phenomenology; Rhetorical Theory

Further Readings

Deetz, S. (1978). Conceptualizing human understanding: Gadamer's hermeneutics and American communication research. *Communication Quarterly, 26,* 12–23.

Dilthey, W. (1996). *Hermeneutics and the study of history* (R. A. Makkreel & F. Rodi, Eds.). Princeton, NJ: Princeton University Press.

Dockhorn, K. (1980). Hans-Georg Gadamer's truth and method. *Philosophy and Rhetoric, 13,* 160–180.

Eden, K. (1997). *Hermeneutics and the rhetorical tradition.* New Haven, CT: Yale University Press.

Gadamer, H.-G. (1981). *Reason in the age of science* (F. G. Lawrence, Trans.). Cambridge: MIT Press.

Gadamer, H.-G. (1993). *Truth and method* (2nd ed., J. Weinsheimer & D. G. Marshall, Eds.). New York: Continuum Press.

Gadamer, H.-G. (1998). *Praise of theory* (C. Dawson, Trans.). New Haven, CT: Yale University Press.

Gross, D. M., & Kemmann, A. (Eds.). (2005). *Heidegger and rhetoric.* Albany: State University of New York Press.

Heidegger, M. (1971). *On the way to language* (P. D. Hertz, Trans.). New York: Harper & Row.

Humboldt, W. (1999). *On language* (M. Losonsky, Ed.). Cambridge, UK: Cambridge University Press.

Hyde, M. J., & Smith, C. R. (1979). A seen but unobserved relationship: Hermeneutics and rhetoric. *Quarterly Journal of Speech, 65,* 347–363.

Jost, W., & Hyde, M. J. (Eds.). (1997). *Rhetoric and hermeneutics in our time: A reader.* New Haven, CT: Yale University Press.

Ricoeur, P. (1981). *Hermeneutics and the human sciences* (J. B. Thompson, Trans.). Cambridge, UK: Cambridge University Press.

Schleiermacher, F. (1998). *Hermeneutics and criticism and other writings* (A. Bowie, Trans.). New York: Cambridge University Press.

Warnick, B. (1987). A Ricoeurian approach to rhetorical criticism. *Western Journal of Speech Communication, 51,* 227–244.

HEURISTIC-SYSTEMATIC MODEL

Shelly Chaiken's heuristic-systematic model (HSM) is a "dual process" theory that identifies *two* coexistent, but qualitatively dissimilar, means by which receivers of persuasive messages process information. It applies to those contexts in which receivers aim to assess the validity of a point of view, to determine the truth of the persuasive message, or to connect attitudes with relevant facts. This model posits that there are two cognitive paths—systematic and heuristic processing—that can be used by persuasive message recipients in this quest. The HSM is one dominant theoretical perspective in investigating persuasion and attitude change. This entry defines the two process modes and their determinants.

Message Processing Modes

Systematic processing involves methodological, critical, and thorough processing of messages in which receivers scrutinize message-relevant content in relation to other information concerning the object or issue addressed. Here receivers carefully ascertain or evaluate the validity of the position advocated in a message. In persuasion of this type, recipients' comprehension and careful cognitive examination may mediate the message's influence.

Heuristic processing, in contrast, occurs when receivers attend only to a subset of available information, exert limited cognitive effort, and employ relatively simple decision rules called *schemata* or *cognitive heuristics* most probably learned from experiences and observations in life. They use such heuristics in this mode to judge the validity of messages and arrive at attitude judgments. Chaiken offers three sets of heuristic cues that lead receivers to utilize certain heuristics. These are communicator cues, context cues, and message cues.

With regard to *communicator cues*, persons may consider statements by experts as more veracious than statements by nonexperts, leading to the use of the expert heuristic, "statements by experts can be trusted." Similarly, people may retrieve and employ a liking-agreement heuristic such as "people agree with people they like" or "people I like usually have correct opinions on issues."

Contextual cues in the message or situation may also affect attitude change. For example, overhearing an audience member's approval of a message may prompt receivers to utilize the consensus heuristic of, "if other people think the message is correct, then it is probably valid." *Message cues* also have their heuristic processing implications. According to Chaiken and associates, people may have experienced situations in which strong, convincing messages characteristically contain extra arguments, longer and more comprehensive arguments, statistically grounded arguments, or arguments from highly credible sources. In this case, "length implies strength," "more arguments are better arguments," and "arguments based on expert opinions are valid" may be the derived rules employed in the presence of such message cues. The HSM suggests that message receivers may use such premises to ascertain the veridicality, or truth, of a persuasive message rather than carefully examining the quality of the arguments. In such cases, people agree more with messages containing numerous (vs. few) arguments, with messages that are of considerable length (vs. shorter), or with statistically laden messages or messages attributed to expert sources.

The use of systematic or heuristic modes will have implications for the persuasion that occurs. Attitudes formed or changed solely on heuristic processing will likely be less stable, less resistant to messages of a counterattitudinal nature, and less predicative of subsequent behavior than attitudes fashioned via systematic processing.

Determinants of Message Processing Mode

The heuristic-systematic model identifies the factors that must be present for either processing mode to operate. For instance, systematic processing requires motivation (e.g., issue involvement or response involvement) and the ability of the receiver to engage in effortful cognitive processing. When processing systematically, an individual must have knowledge of the topic and be free from the constraints of time. Thus, comprehensive processing of a message, requiring attention to message and topic details, is likely to affect the nature of persuasion that occurs.

Heuristic processing depends on the existence of heuristic cues in the persuasive environment. Humans are assumed to be "economy-minded souls" who seek to accomplish the tasks and goals in the most efficient means available. HSM's *least effort* principle states that people in general prefer the heuristic mode, involving considerably less effort, to the more effortful systematic processing.

People will follow the *sufficiency* principle, or the idea that resourceful information processors must find the balance between satisfying their motivational concerns and reducing the effort they must put forth. That is, people will put forth the level of effort that meets a "sufficient" degree of assurance that they have satisfactorily attained their message processing goals.

Systematic and heuristic processing are considered parallel modes of information processing. For this reason, both modes can operate simultaneously when the persuasive context is favorable. When operating both modes simultaneously, message receivers are engaging in what HSM considers *concurrent processing*. Here, each form contributes statistically as both independent (i.e., additive) and interdependent (i.e., interactive) variables related to message and attitude judgment. A receiver might evaluate a message containing several strong arguments attributed to a credible source by using both forms of processing. For example, if motivated and able, the receiver might use systematic processing to evaluate the strong arguments and, independently, use heuristic processing to judge the source of these arguments. Or a receiver might use both processing modes interdependently, if the credibility of the message source affected the perceptions of argument quality.

Bryan B. Whaley

See also Attitude Theory; Cognitive Theories; Elaboration Likelihood Theory; Inoculation Theory; Persuasion and Social Influence Theories

Further Readings

Chaiken, S. (1987). The heuristic model of persuasion. In M. P. Zanna, J. M. Olson, & C. P. Herman (Eds.), *Social influence: The Ontario symposium: Vol. 5* (pp. 3–39). Hillsdale, NJ: Lawrence Erlbaum.

Chen, S., & Chaiken, S. (1999). The heuristic-systematic model in its broader context. In S. Chaiken & Y. Trope (Eds.), *Dual-processing theories in social psychology* (pp. 73–96). New York: Guilford.

Todorov, A., Chaiken, S., & Henderson, M. (2002). The heuristic-systematic model of social information processing. In J. P. Dillard & M. Pfau (Eds.), *The persuasion handbook: Developments in theory and practice* (pp. 195–211). Thousand Oaks, CA: Sage.

HIERARCHY OF EFFECTS MODELS

See Advertising Theories

HINDU COMMUNICATION THEORY

Hindu communication theory, or the account of the methods and purposes involved in the use of language, concerns a diverse grouping of religious/philosophical traditions on the Indian subcontinent. In some cases, sources in the Hindu tradition explicitly theorized about communication (such as Bharata on *rasa* theory and Bhartrhari on speech). In most cases, however, accounts of language and its use were bound up with other concerns. This entry will largely concentrate on the implicit theory of communication in Hindu tradition. The purposes/ends and methods/means of communication will be examined.

Hindu tradition begins with an important group of texts called the *Vedas*. The earliest of these texts dates from around 2000 BCE. The *Vedas* were learned and transmitted among priestly castes (classes) by the oral means of chanting. These texts are classified as *śruti*, a term that literally means "perceived through hearing." There are no known actual authors of these texts; instead, they are likely a collection of verses inspired by tribal experience and are remembered as useful as parts of vedic rituals. Whereas the *Vedas* tend to focus on ritual means of edifying the gods and in gaining worldly goals, another group of texts began to become prominent between 1000 BCE and 400 BCE—the *Upaniṣads*. These texts contain the core of what would become modern Hinduism—the commitment to reality being undivided at its most basic level and to a general renunciation of worldly goods. After the time of the Buddha (circa 563–483 BCE), a prominent critic of vedic concerns, what could be identified as modern Hinduism began to develop the upaniṣadic themes in a variety of ways. These include the six orthodox schools (*darśana*) of Indian philosophy that flourished in India after the time of the Buddha.

One significant aspect of Hinduism presupposed by most schools of Hindu thought is the idea of liberation (*mokśa*). This end is important to communication, as the way that a person understands language (such as *śruti* or philosophical texts) will impact that person's chances for liberation. From what is a person to become free? In most schools of Hindu thought, the sources of suffering are the cycles of change evident in this world. Often the problem relates to how one orients to desire and its changing objects and to the "self" that supposedly gains from attaining the objects of one's desires (success, goods, etc.). Thus, Hindu traditions tend to emphasize the desirability of relieving the burden of harmful orientations to the world; indeed, this liberation is often talked about as becoming enlightened about the true nature of one's self and the world. Instead of the normal everyday notion of self (the empirical body one appears to have), the *Upaniṣads* argue that a person's true self (*Atman*) is really the Self of all beings and objects (*Brahman*). One's self is the Self of all things, undivided and nonindividuated.

Hindu views of communication have an interesting relationship to this underlying *monism* (the view that reality is without divisions or parts). On one hand, language is extolled as a way to achieve such knowledge. Instead of merely transmitting knowledge, the Hindu tradition tends to see the hearing and understanding of language as a realization of some state of affairs. Thus, if one has an enlightened teacher (*guru*), one can attain the state of liberation by attending to that teacher's utterances and commands. In such accounts as that offered by the rasa theory, attending to poetic or dramatic uses of language can instill certain moods of renunciation or detachment (i.e., that of realizing that one's empirical, divided self is not really "who" one is). In this view, then, language holds the power to remove ignorance and illusion about the world. On the other hand, Hindu communication theory seems pessimistic about the ability of language to "grasp" ultimate reality (Brahman), since that reality is undivided and utterly whole. Language excels at categorizing and dividing, whereas reality is the undivided substratum to all change and division we appear to witness in life.

These two themes can be unified in another concern of Hinduism—the activity of the receiver in interpreting language. Some language use can encourage enlightened states of mind, whereas others can lead one to focus more on the empirical self and on the objects of one's desires. The purpose of good communication, on the Hindu account, would be to maximize enlightening uses of language that help free individuals from the illusion that individuation (the separation of different selves) is real. Instead, by focusing on how words are understood, speakers can use language in a way that has a better chance of enlightening listeners. This seems to be the point of Bhartrhari's 6th- or 7th-century analysis of spoken language in his book, *Vakyapadiya*, as well as the assumed purpose behind Śankara's analysis of vedic scripture in his *Advaita Vedānta* school of philosophy, which most likely appeared in the 8th century.

The methods or means of using language to enlighten are often different from those employed in Western traditions. Dialogue between a teacher and a student is often used, as well as the method of composing aphoristic *sutras* (literally, thread). In the latter method, short and memorable phrases are used to continue a tradition of scholarship and learning. After the sutras are composed, subsequent teachers write commentaries elucidating the meaning of these cryptic and ambiguous phrases, and these commentaries are then transmitted to and analyzed by students. A respect for the power of language and the extralinguistic nature of enlightenment is evidenced by this practice—words and commentary are used to get at knowledge beyond any mere set of words.

Another common communicative means employed in Hindu tradition is narrative. Narratives used range from short examples (such as the common example of mistaking a rope for a snake) to complex stories with plot and characters (such as the *Bhagavad Gita*). Such a method is useful as it can combine various values and propositions in an attempt to get a reader or hearer to move beyond assumed illusions into a more enlightened state.

Scott R. Stroud

See also Asian Communication Theory; Indian *Rasa* Theory

Further Readings

Dissanayake, W. (1987). The guiding image in Indian culture and its implications for communication. In D. L. Kincaid (Ed.), *Communication theory: Eastern and Western perspectives* (pp. 151–160). New York: Academic Press.

Dissanayake, W. (1988). Foundations of Indian verbal communication and phenomenology. In W. Dissanayake (Ed.), *Communication theory: The Asian perspective* (pp. 39–55). Singapore: Asian Mass Communication Research and Information Centre.

Kennedy, G. A. (1998). *Comparative rhetoric: An historical and cross-cultural introduction.* New York: Oxford University Press.

Oliver, R. T. (1971). *Communication and culture in ancient India and China.* Syracuse, NY: Syracuse University Press.

Saral, T. B. (1983). Hindu philosophy of communication. *Communication, 8,* 47–58.

Stroud, S. R. (2004). Narrative as argument in Indian philosophy: The *Astravaka Gita* as multivalent narrative. *Philosophy and Rhetoric, 37,* 42–71.

HUMANISTIC PERSPECTIVE

The humanistic perspective, often called the *third force* in psychology because it was developed after behaviorism and psychoanalysis, took form in the middle of the 20th century and expanded greatly in the 1970s and 1980s. This perspective arose in reaction to the deterministic and pessimistic view espoused by both behaviorism and psychoanalysis. According to the humanistic perspective, to understand a person's motives and behaviors, you must view the person as a whole, and you must focus on the subjective experience of the individual. The focus must be on the individual, and it is assumed that a person's behavior is connected to his or her inner feelings and self-image. Humanistic psychology rejects behaviorism and psychoanalysis because they are too deterministic and too often see unconscious, instinctive forces as determining human thought and behavior. The humanistic approach was a radical change in then current psychological thought because, unlike behaviorism and psychoanalysis, one of the assumptions behind the humanistic approach is that human beings have free will and personal agency. The humanistic perspective sees behavior as not determined by the subconscious mind.

Humanistic psychology approaches the study of human behavior from a more phenomenological approach than either behaviorism or psychoanalysis. There are five main ideas that are often used to summarize the humanistic perspective. First, human beings cannot be reduced to components. Second, human beings must be understood in a uniquely human context. Third, human consciousness includes self-awareness and a concept of oneself in the context of other people. Fourth, human beings have and make personal choices. And fifth, human beings are intentional beings who seek meaning and value in their lives.

Assumptions Behind Humanistic Psychology

Beyond humans' having free will and personal agency, there are many other assumptions behind the humanistic approach absent from behaviorism and psychoanalysis. Humanism sees people as having an innate drive to achieve their maximum potential. In other words, people are basically good, and humans continuously strive to make themselves and the world a better place. The humanistic approach emphasizes the worth of the individual and the centrality of human values. Personal growth and fulfillment are the basic human motives. We strive to make our lives better, and this is the guiding force behind our behavior. This is inherent in being a human being.

Another assumption of the humanistic perspective involves the locus of study when examining the individual. The humanistic psychologists argued that objective reality is less important than a person's subjective perception and subjective understanding of the world. Each individual is unique, and what matters is each person's subjective view

and not objective reality. Reality is defined by the individual's perspective.

Studying Human Behavior

Because the humanistic perspective focuses on the subjective experience of the individual, studying communication or psychology from the humanistic perspective requires the study of the individual case rather than the average performance of a group. Typically, then, qualitative research is employed when studying behavior from the humanistic perspective. It is important for the humanist to study at the individual level, so techniques such as diary accounts, open-ended questionnaires, and unstructured interviews are often used to gather data and find out, in depth, how people think and feel. Another major difference between the humanist perspective and behaviorism and psychoanalysis is the use of animals as study subjects. Humanists who work in psychology would never study animals in an attempt to determine the causes of human behavior because humans are conscious beings capable of thought, reason, and language. Therefore, research on animals is of little value because it can tell you little about human thoughts and motivation.

Major Researchers

Perhaps the most well-known researcher to use the humanistic approach is Abraham Maslow. Maslow felt that individuals have certain needs that must be met in a specific, hierarchical fashion. These are (in order from lowest to highest) basic needs, safety needs, love and belonging needs, achievement needs, and ultimately *self-actualization*. All lower needs must be satisfied before a person can fulfill a higher need. For example, all basic needs must be satisfied before safety needs or achievement needs can be satisfied. People move from the lowest level of needs up to the highest as they go through life and gain wisdom and knowledge about how to handle different situations. That humans are motivated by unsatisfied needs is what guides human behavior. Because each individual's motivations are different, the individual must be the unit of analysis, and the results cannot be generalized to others or to a larger population.

Carl Rogers was another researcher who came from the humanistic perspective. He believed that all people have the tendency toward growth and a strong need to maintain and enhance life. Existence itself, according to Rogers, has the main goal of satisfying these needs. Becoming self-actualized is the primary goal of human existence and guides much of our behavior. According to Rogers, we all have a real self (how we see our characteristics, traits, and abilities) and an ideal self (perceptions of what we would like to be). The ideal self comes from the influences we have had in our lives, including our friends and parents. It is the ideal self which we strive to become, which would lead to self-actualization. On the way to becoming self-actualized, Rogers claims, we engage in a process called *organismic value processing*. Experiences we perceive as enhancing our lives are valued as good and therefore sought after. Experiences perceived as not enhancing are seen as bad and are avoided. Rogers saw the self-actualized person as open to experiencing his or her feelings and not threatened by those feelings, regardless of what they are. Rogers considered a self-actualized person "fully functioning."

Rogers felt the main determinant of whether we become self-actualized is our childhood experiences. These experiences guide the development of our ideal self. He felt that it is crucial for children to receive positive reinforcement and affection and approval from the important people in their lives. This was particularly important from their parents. He thought that it is important for us to receive unconditional positive regard and acceptance with no strings attached. However, he noted, acceptance often does come with strings attached. Children are told that to be loved and to receive approval, they must be quiet and well behaved and meet other socially constructed ideas of "the good child." These things are incorporated as conditions of worth. If the conditions are few and reasonable, then the child will be fine. But if the conditions of worth are severely limiting, self-actualization will be severely impeded.

Strengths and Weaknesses

Many of the strengths and weaknesses of the humanistic perspective are inherently linked. One strength of the humanistic perspective is its focus on phenomenology and the whole person rather than on the unconscious mind and observable behavior. Both behaviorism and psychoanalysis see the unconscious mind as controlling thoughts and behaviors. The humanistic perspective sees humans as having free will and as in control of their own lives. However, some theorists feel this is an ethnocentric point of view and that while it might be a reality for middle-class Westerners, it is not necessarily true for less-developed parts of the world. Additionally, some feel that the disregard of the humanistic perspective for the unconscious mind is a weakness.

Another advantage of the humanistic perspective comes from the way that it is studied: through qualitative data analysis. While this allows the researcher or clinician to thoroughly understand the subject being studied, it makes it difficult to generalize to others or to larger populations. Additionally, it is more time-consuming and difficult to interpret than quantitative data analysis.

One weakness of the humanistic perspective is that some of its concepts are difficult to measure. For example, how would one measure self-actualization? The theory itself does not lend itself to empirical verification because many of the tenets of the theory are vague and untestable. For example, Maslow described self-actualized people as open, spontaneous, loving, and self-accepting. Some argue that these are value judgments and do not constitute a scientific definition. Additionally, the humanistic perspective assumes that we are all capable of achieving self-actualization. This may not be true as differences in intelligence, education, and personality may be mitigating circumstances. Additionally, critics often argue that the humanistic view of personality paints too "rosy" a picture. It fails to recognize the human capacity for evil and that, for some, doing good for humankind is not a motivating behavior. The humanistic perspective ignores the more negative aspects of human nature.

Kevin J. Pearce

See also Agency; Epistemology; Interpretive Theory; Ontology; Rogerian Dialogue Theory

Further Readings

Bugental, J. F. T. (1964). The third force in psychology. *Journal of Humanistic Psychology, 4,* 19–25.

Diaz-Laplante, J. (2007). Humanistic psychology and social transformation: Building the path toward a livable today and a just tomorrow. *Journal of Humanistic Psychology, 47,* 54–72.

Giorgi, A. (2005). Remaining challenges for humanistic psychology. *Journal of Humanistic Psychology, 45,* 204–216.

Höijer, B. (2008). Ontological assumptions and generalizations in qualitative (audience) research. *European Journal of Communication, 23,* 275–294.

Joy, M. (2005). Humanistic psychology and animal rights: Reconsidering the boundaries of the humanistic ethic. *Journal of Humanistic Psychology, 45,* 106–130.

Maslow, A. H. (1968). *Toward a psychology of being.* Princeton, NJ: Van Nostrand Reinhold.

Rogers, C. (1961). *On becoming a person: A therapist's view of psychotherapy.* Boston: Houghton/Mifflin.

Rogers, C. (1995). *A way of being.* Wilmington, MA: Mariner Books.

Sillars, A. L. (1974). Expressions and control in human interaction: Perspectives on humanistic psychology. *Western Speech, 38,* 269–277.

HUMOROUS COMMUNICATION THEORY

Humor is fundamentally a communicative activity. Humor is an intended or unintended message that is considered funny or evokes laughter. As a result, humor is a communicative process that is subject to the interpretation of the receiver. Shakespeare noted in act 5, scene 2, of *Love's Labour's Lost* that "a jest's prosperity lies in the ear of him that hears it, never in the tongue of him that makes it." Put another way, a comedian knows a joke works if the audience laughs. Even though humor is recognized as a communicative process, there is not a communication-based theory of humor that can fully explain what humor is (or is not) or encapsulate the diverse role humor has within our social lives. Humor, like power, love, and communication itself, is far too ubiquitous and meaningful in our lives to fit neatly into one theory or framework. To add complexity to an already complex subject, one also has to consider the *duality* of humor—that when humor is assumed to have one function or meaning, it always simultaneously supports (on some level) the opposite. This duality is also termed the *paradox of humor* or *double*

edge of humor. In other words, humor is a juxtaposition of layers of meaning; this is what gives humor its edge, what makes something funny. Because of the complexity and significance of humor, there is a vast body of literature that examines humor from a philosophical, psychological, sociological, and communicative perspective that can be used to reveal both why we use humor and the role that humor has within social interactions and organizations.

Why We Use and Laugh at Humor

There are three broad and competing theories of why we use humor: to express *superiority*, to *relieve tension*, and to make sense of *incongruity*. Though each of these conceptions does not provide a universal understanding of humor, taken together they can form a scheme to help us fully appreciate the complexity of our motivations for using humor. From a communication perspective, scholars should also consider not just the motivations of the humorist but why the audience corroborates a symbol or message as humorous with its laughter.

The origins of the *superiority theory of humor* trace back to Aristotle, but in recent literature the theory is usually attributed to the writings of Thomas Hobbes. Hobbes believed that all human action arises out of the desire for self-preservation. The passion of laughter is then the expression of sudden glory that humor brings as another is ridiculed. Superiority humor is usually associated with laughing at others' perceived inadequacies, in effect making a caricature of the target that centers on a scorned quality. Kenneth Burke's *burlesque frame* describes how humor exaggerates the absurdity and neglects the humanity of a situation. For example, Sen. John Kerry never recovered from his caricature as a flip flopper in the 2004 U.S. presidential election campaign.

Superiority can be ugly and can reflect the brutish side of the joke teller and the corresponding coarse qualities of the laughing audience. For this reason a joke that *ridicules* requires strong *audience analysis* and can be used effectively to reinforce *social bonds*. If ridicule is used unsuccessfully, the opposite is true. Consider if a person of perceived privilege (or hierarchical authority) makes fun of a person or group with less perceived power: He or she runs the risk of being interpreted not as a humorist but as a bully. Don Imus's racist caricature of the Rutgers women's basketball team in 2007 is an example. Curiously, humor as *self-derision* can be considered superiority at its base. When a joke teller is laughed at, it demonstrates the duality of humor. The humorist is also recognized for his or her honesty and self-confidence.

The *relief theory of humor* explains how a joke or laughter can be used to reduce tension or stress. Herbert Spencer, the father of social Darwinism, is credited with providing the first reference to relief humor when he suggested that laughter was a result of the physical energy that is built up to deal with disagreeable feelings. Spencer's work has had considerable influence on the conception of humor as a relief of tension, but the primary text of relief theory used in modern analysis is Freud's *Jokes and Their Relation to the Unconscious*. According to Freud, relief humor has two properties. First, it has a healing quality, allowing built-up tension and energy to be released. Second, humor is an act of *disguised aggression* and *sanctioned resistance*. This second property of Freud's relief theory will be examined further below because of its influence on humor research within organizations. A scholar who has had very little influence on humor theory and research outside of rhetorical studies of communication is Burke, who wrote about the *comic frame*. Burke's lack of influence in this area is both unfortunate and ironic because he argues that the comic frame provides relief from human folly and tragedy. This humorous framing of misfortune is necessary for humans to respond to life in a moral way and work toward a peaceful coexistence.

The *incongruity theory of humor* argues that something can be found to be funny if it is irrational, paradoxical, illogical, incoherent, fallacious, and/or inappropriate. Henri Bergson and later Mary Douglas saw humor as a result of juxtaposing two unlike things. Laughter comes from the recognition that something is inconsistent with the expected rational nature of the perceived environment. Jokes, as a rhetorical form, capitalize on the incongruous nature of humor because their very structure is designed to build cognitive tension (a horse walks into a bar) and then smack you with a *punch line* that relieves this tension in an unexpected way (barman says "why the long face?"). The conception of humor as incongruity does not exclude the superiority or relief motivations of humor but suggests that humor is based on intellectual activity rather than a drive to feel superior or to relieve tensions. This cognitively based activity is successful when it elicits laughter, which is a physical response. A good laugh is actually a loss of bodily control. It is this paradox of mind and body that attracted philosophers to take humor quite seriously.

Incongruity as humor is found not only in violation of the expected, but also in the realization that what is taken as normal, appropriate, logical, and rational in the everyday can be revealed to be absurd. For example, consider the popular show *Seinfeld*, which often based its humor in questioning the presumed rationale behind everyday social activities such as standing in line. Incongruity humor defamiliarizes the familiar, therefore presenting an opportunity for change by revealing that what is expected is not necessary. Using humor in this way also provides comic relief that soothes tensions that if left free may push individuals to actually challenge the status quo.

Humor Within Social Interactions and Organizations

Humor serves a large variety of functions in social interactions. Beyond simply entertaining and demonstrating a sense of humor, 21 additional and separate interpersonal functions of humor are derived from literature in a meta-analysis by Elizabeth Graham, Michael Papa, and Gordon Brooks. These functions of humor can be categorized by the motivational basis behind the three humor theories: *superiority humor* (to transmit verbally aggressive messages, demean others, control others, defend the ego against possible attack, put others in place), *relief humor* (to disarm potentially aggressive others, decrease aggression, minimize anxiety, disclose difficult information, allow others to cope with difficult situations), and *incongruity humor* (to allow insight into another's state of mind, adjust to a new role, ease tensions around new information and situations, express feelings, avoid revealing information). To document and expand on many of these asserted functions of humor, there is a growing body of work that first came out of the Victoria University of Wellington Language in the Workplace project. These researchers analyzed spontaneous conversations of friendship and workplace groups that have been recorded over long periods. This research, discussed by Holmes and Marra, reveals the multifunctional role of humor in social interactions, as well as the differences and similarities in the use of humor by men and women, management and subordinates, and people of different ethnic origins.

Organizational scholars have long recognized humor as an essential and pervasive part of workplace culture and practices. The goal of organizational studies, especially recent studies from a communication perspective, is less focused on revealing the motivations for humor's use and more concerned with the role everyday humor has within the dynamic process of organizing. As a result, organizational researchers have examined humor's role as the basis for *workgroup cohesiveness*, *identification*, and *sensemaking* and its impact on *managerial control* and *organizational effectiveness*.

Laughing at work implies both a shared meaning and a shared bond between members as they negotiate their roles within the organization. It is widely contended that many of the workplace jokes either take the form of inside jokes or take on specialized meaning for those who tell jokes and laugh at the humor. Everyday humor at work therefore (re)produces the specialized language, stock knowledge, sensemaking processes, and shared experiences that form the basis for inclusion or bonding within a group while simultaneously keeping the outsider at a distance. The inclusion and exclusion role of humor at work engenders *in-group cohesion* and *out-group conflict*. The tighter the in-group cohesion, especially within the context of work that is demanding and/or demeaning, the more prominent role humor has in retaining and selecting self-affirmed meanings and constructing identity.

Humor is never power neutral, and exploring humor's role within the dynamics of organizational power is a pervasive and well-documented area of research in organizational studies. Humor's role in negotiating power at work can be grouped into four categories: humor as managerial control, humor as social control, humor as sanctioned resistance, and humor as subversive resistance.

The first category, humor as *managerial control*, is seen when a person with hierarchical status uses humor to gain compliance without emphasis on the power differentials. Humor can be used as a rhetorical strategy to mask the sting of authority, also called "doing power politely" in humor research. This use of polite humor (or disguised authority) by managers is a cornerstone of a broader emphasis on functional humor research: how humor as a discursive strategy ensures organizational effectiveness and successful business culture. Humor, beyond providing entertainment at work, is said to increase workplace collegiality, organizational identification, worker compliance, group problem solving, and the acceptance of change.

The second category, humor as *social control*, argues that humor is the basis of in-group cohesion within a work culture. Humor as social control is also recognized as a powerful means by which members enforce conformity in the workplace. *Barbed humor*, *jocular abuse*, *shaming*, and/or *teasing* are all forms of humor that is directed at someone. Teasing humor is often used in workgroups between peers to socialize new members because it encourages the target to play along or accept the "joke." Teasing is an ambiguous form of *social control* and a significant element of *peer management* (or *concertive control*) as subordinates use humor to discipline each other and enforce social norms.

The third category, *humor as sanctioned resistance*, emphasizes how subordinates and group members can also use humor to criticize or ridicule a higher member or an organizational rule or norm without causing change. *Humor as sanctioned resistance* is a well-established and still vibrant area of study. However, these organizational case studies have traditionally supported the relief theory frame that states that the organizational impact of resistance humor is only temporary. Resistance humor is allowed/tolerated in organizations as *sanctioned disrespect* that reduces the physical and psychological stress of the workers without significantly challenging the basis of power and authority itself. Resistance humor is generally viewed as a *safety valve*, a means of blowing off steam, to deal with incongruity or the stress of organizational life.

The last category, *subversive resistance humor*, or humor that functions as actual resistance—challenging authority and creating change—is an emerging yet still undeveloped area of research, due possibly to the overemphasis (or reality) of humor as temporary relief, not as a transformative force. David Collinson, in *Managing Humor*, and other researchers have begun to warn against the growing trend of management's attempts to use humor to make the workplace fun and productive. These researchers argue humor is not a thing that can be turned on and off, that formalizing humor actually suppresses it, and that incorporating humor as a basis for organizational control is unethical. They also remind management, and the functional scholars of humor, of the duality and unpredictable nature of humor. Managers who attempt to use humor strategically are at best unlikely to succeed and risk backlash. Humor can be a subversive act, but the grounds for recognizing humor as a critical practice in organizations have not been fully developed.

Owen Hanley Lynch

See also Group Communication Theories; Identification; Interpersonal Communication Theories; Organizational Communication Theories; Organizational Control Theory

Further Readings

Burke, K. (1988). *On symbols and society.* Chicago: University of Chicago Press.

Collinson, D. (2002). Managing humor. *Journal of Management Studies, 39,* 269–288.

Critchley, S. (2002). *On humor.* London: Routledge.

Graham, E., Papa, M., & Brooks, G. (1992). Functions of humor in conversation: Conceptualization and measurement. *Western Journal of Communication, 56,* 161–183.

Holmes, J., & Marra, M. (2006). Humor and leadership style. *Humor: International Journal of Humor Research, 19*(2), 119–138.

Lynch, O. (2002). Humorous communication: Finding a place for humor in communication research. *Communication Theory, 12,* 423–446.

Tracy, S., Karen, M., & Clifton, S. (2006). Cracking jokes and crafting selves: Sensemaking and identity management among human service workers. *Communication Monographs, 73,* 283–308.

HYBRIDITY

Hybridity has become a favorite buzzword in academic circles and in popular reflections on processes of globalization—typically presented in the American media as emanating from the United States—on various parts of the world. Celebratory accounts of transcultural fusion as U.S. businesses spread their fares around the globe have come to dominate this popular discourse. While the term's definition has remained vexingly vague and its meaning varies greatly depending on the context of its use, as generally conceptualized by communication scholars, *hybridity* relates to processes of racial, linguistic, or cultural mixing that are understood to result in something different from the sum of their discrete parts.

From a historical perspective, the modern notion of hybridity started to take shape in the 18th century, as European imperialist nations had to come to terms with the possible consequences of racial mixing with members of colonized nations. The deep racist anxieties of European colonial powers were manifest in the perception of hybridization as a dangerous process resulting in the contamination of superior (White) races. In this context, racial mixing and its resulting hybridity were to be avoided in order to protect not only the racial purity of colonial powers but also their cultural identity as imperialist aggression spread their influence beyond national borders.

The meaning of hybridity further evolved, however, in the aftermath of postimperialist liberation movements. Reclaimed by newly independent nations needing to come to terms with the racial and cultural legacies of their colonial past, hybridity—and its more culturally specific manifestations in the concepts of *mestizaje* or *creolization*, which developed to incorporate the heterogeneous elements of various Latin American cultures into new national identities—took on more positive connotations. Used as a tool for nation building and cultural-identity formation in an effort to revalorize and ultimately embrace the complex consequences of historically imposed transcultural and racial mixing, hybridity was conceptualized as a set of unique and generally positive cultural processes.

More recently, postcolonial scholars have similarly celebrated hybridity as a source of cultural renewal and resistance against imperialist forces and cultural domination. Focusing on the demographic and ideological movements between Europe, Africa, and the Americas in his book *The Black Atlantic*, British sociologist Paul Gilroy challenges conceptualizations of transcultural exchange that are based on dichotomized perceptions of race and culture that falsely reduce these to some kind of "essence"; he argues for a more complex understanding of intercultural exchange, paying closer attention to the dynamic nature of processes of hybridization. Exploring hybridity in the context of the postcolonial novel, postcolonial theorist Homi Bhabha emphasizes its potential as a subversive practice used to challenge and reappropriate dominant colonial discourse and create new forms of subaltern agency. Argentinean-Mexican scholar Néstor García-Canclini focuses on border towns between Mexico and the United States to explore hybrid cultural forms such as graffiti and comics as examples of cultural resistance to dominant interpretations of modernity. He sees the notion of hybridity as a useful analytical tool for the investigation of the complex tension between externally imposed definitions of modernity and local traditions in places where the former have rarely replaced the latter in a straightforward manner.

This approach has helped complicate communication scholars' understanding of mediated transnational exchange by challenging interpretations of transnational cultural flows as one-way processes of homogenizing "cultural imperialism" imposed by powerful Western nations on the rest of the world. It has also encouraged communication scholars to pay attention to the reception and interpretation of "foreign" media in various local environments, as well as their global production and distribution.

As a theoretical concept, hybridity has also proven useful to feminist scholars intent on deconstructing the essentializing categories of gender, race, class, culture, ethnicity, and sexual orientation, which they see as problematically naturalized in (White/male/middle-class/Western/heterosexual) dominant media discourse. By treating the clearly dichotomized character of these categories as a problem, hybridity brings to light their socioculturally constructed nature and consequently challenges the patriarchal naturalization of difference into subordination. Hybridity also provides a useful theoretical space through which to explore the interlocking nature of various sets of oppression and the complexity of identity formation and representation. Feminist scholars recognize this effort as a crucial step toward developing a useful understanding of gender dynamics and power relationships in an increasingly global environment.

The concept of hybridity is not, however, without critiques or dangers. The vagueness of its definition, its polysemic (having multiple meanings) nature, and its early origins in colonial discourse have led some scholars to question whether the term should even be employed. Others argue that the concept is not particularly useful since cultural exchange has been going on for centuries, and all cultures are thus necessarily hybrid. Still others are concerned that hybridity may be used to gloss over remaining power relations among different actors on the global geopolitical scene by constructing a version of transnational influence based on a cheery pluralism that ultimately celebrates American-style capitalism and excuses its abuses. Much of the popular discourse on globalization in the U.S. media illustrates this tendency. By pointing out the increasingly hybrid nature of a global capitalist culture fueled by other nations' desire for American-style products with a local twist—green-tea frappuccinos come to mind—this scenario of hybridity suggests that processes of globalization are not only necessary but fair and justified since, after all, we all are influencing each other. Communication scholar Marwan Kraidy calls this strategic rhetoric "corporate transculturalism" and warns against its excesses.

In response, communication scholars have advocated a more critical approach to hybridity that considers how global influences are locally constituted and negotiated in relationships of unequal power—what García-Canclini calls "oblique powers"—in culturally, socially, and historically specific contexts. While sharing the broad concerns of theories of cultural imperialism about power and cultural influence, this approach proposes to explore transcultural exchange empirically in order to tease out the multiple ways in which global power and local resistance may be mutually constitutive. By recognizing the power of globally produced and distributed commodified cultural forms while remaining sensitive to local agency, this critical form of hybridity offers the potential to bridge the gap between pessimistic analyses of global economy and celebratory accounts of local resistance.

Fabienne Darling-Wolf

See also Culture and Communication; Feminist Communication Theories; Postcolonial Feminism; Postcolonial Theory; Transculturation

Further Readings

Bhabba, H. (1994). *The location of culture.* New York: Routledge.

Butler, J. (1999). *Gender trouble: Feminism and the subversion of identity.* New York: Routledge.

García-Canclini, N. (1995). *Hybrid cultures: Strategies for entering and leaving modernity.* Minneapolis: University of Minnesota Press.

Giddens, A. (1999). *Modernity and self-identity: Self and society in the late modern age.* Cambridge, UK: Polity.

Gilroy, P. (1993). *The black Atlantic: Modernity and double consciousness.* Cambridge, MA: Harvard University Press.

Kraidy, M. (2005). *Hybridity: Or the cultural logic of globalization.* Philadelphia: Temple University Press.

Kraidy, M. M. (2002). Hybridity in cultural globalization. *Communication Theory, 12,* 316–339.

Spivak, G. C. (1988). *In other worlds: Essays in cultural politics.* New York: Routledge.

I

I AND THOU

I and Thou is the most durable and important conceptual contribution of the 20th-century philosopher of dialogue, Martin Buber, and the title of his most famous book. As often happens with such terms, it became so well known and seemingly accessible that it developed its own reputation as a pop-culture slogan. Self-help gurus and critics alike have used it in ways that surely would have surprised Buber and other Continental philosophers, such as Gabriel Marcel and Hans-Georg Gadamer, who developed similar concepts and applied them in sophisticated ways.

Although it can be mischaracterized and even parodied, I and Thou is not a simplistic exhortation to love your neighbor, to avoid confrontation or conflict, or to be your most honest and genuine self. It is neither an uncritical celebration of subjectivity nor an attack on rationality. Buber was not advocating mystical experience or a near-religious obligation to sustain intimate relationships with people who should be treated as solemn "Thous." He was creating nothing less than an ontology of, or way of characterizing, communication that could ground the human sciences: "All real living is meeting," he wrote in *I and Thou,* in a line that captures its theme. At the center of this ontology was neither the individual self, as *I,* nor others with whom the individual interacts. Buber focused instead on relationships and relational attitudes—the often forgotten realm of the "between." This entry briefly discusses Buber's biography, describes

the basic I-Thou concept, and explores several relevant implications for communication theory.

Biography and Background

Martin Buber was influential on the world's intellectual stage for more than 6 decades and participated in many of the 20th century's major philosophical, theological, literary, and political controversies. Fluent in nine languages, he had a multifaceted career that involved many roles, including journalist, editor, sociologist, theologian, novelist, translator, political activist, educator, and, although he was at times reluctant to embrace the term, philosopher. He knew and corresponded with many of the century's celebrated intellectuals and was himself intellectually versatile enough to be nominated for Nobel Prizes in both literature and peace.

First published in German in 1923, *I and Thou* has been widely translated internationally, but two important English translations exist in an uneasy relationship to each other. The first, by Ronald Gregor Smith, appeared in English in 1937 and has been available in a second revised edition (with a new postscript by Buber) since 1958. The more recent is Walter Kaufmann's 1970 translation, which he claimed made the book clearer and corrected conceptual errors from the previous version. Some scholars prefer Kaufmann's work, which kept the earlier title but in the text revised its central concept to the more familiar, if prosaic, *I-You.* Others, including Maurice Friedman, Buber's most famous biographer and scholarly commentator, believe Smith's version to be more accurate and to have more engagingly captured the poetic meaning Buber had in mind. Kenneth Paul Kramer quotes from both translations side by side in his readable explication of *I and Thou*.

I-Thou and I-It

Buber's *I-Thou* and *I-It* are what he called "primary words" for understanding human relationships. I-Thou refers to the relational attitude or orientation of regarding the other in his or her concrete uniqueness, as someone capable of full responsiveness to one's own speech. An I-It attitude, on the other hand, primarily regards the other as an object to be dealt with, affected, changed, measured, endured, or understood in role. The hyphenated paired words are "primary" for Buber because the *I* moves into different forms of being as a result of its relation with elements outside itself. It is impossible, thus, to understand the *I* apart from its relations, or from the manner in which it is expressed. Although the I-It can be spoken—enacted—with less than one's full presence or being because it refers to the world of things, the I-Thou involves the person's whole being in its address to a mutualized, and mutualizing, person. Buber believed the potential of a dialogic I-Thou attitude distinguished the action of *persons* from mere *individuals* whose inclination is persistently toward the world of It—the conceptualization, manipulation, and accumulation of things. There is nothing necessarily wrong or deficient about the It or the I-It attitude. Both the I-Thou and I-It are essential to what Buber called the *twofold I* and to human life. In fact, Buber indicated realistically that each I-Thou relation, because it so thoroughly involves "whole being" dialogic speech, is by nature transitory and must return to the world of I-It. Treating reality in objectifying ways is not immoral or unethical but normal, natural, and even necessary; defining reality as if it is essentially objectification (measurement, strategy, disseminating facts and opinions to passive audiences) misses the interhuman potential of our existence. Buber was not worried about the existence of the world of I-It; he was worried about the tendency of his era (as surely he would have been of ours) to elevate the It to supreme status.

Buber for Communication Theorists

In the 4 decades following the publication of *I and Thou*, Buber extended his ideas about dialogue expressed there. Six implications for communication theorists of *I and Thou* and Buber's subsequent writing on dialogue are discussed below.

Listening and Turning

Speech and the between are intricately woven in how humans co-construct a meaningful world. The element of spokenness, or enactment through communication, in fact, was Buber's entrée to understanding what makes us human, and it is in the occasions of speaking that readers most clearly glimpse his concerns. His analogy of embodiment, *turning*, set the stage for his distinction between monologic performance—to which creative response is neither expected nor required—and dialogic "genuine spokenness," which demands a responsive listening presence. Listening is a relational, not a psychological, phenomenon. We turn toward others when we expect meaningfulness. If we are interested merely in hearing or accumulating messages, any posture will do; monologue is fine. The problem of monologue is not that someone fails to hear a message but that he or she does not listen as a potential interlocutor. The difference, Buber thought, has enormous implications for what it means to be a person, and a person in relation to others, which he called "philosophical anthropology." Monologue works well for some purposes, such as announcing cast changes before a theater production, but is ill-suited for deliberative bodies, citizen mobilization, or family problem solving. Thus, the baseline implication of Buber's thought for communication studies is how it recommends a philosophy of *turning toward and listening* as a guiding center for personal discipline. As communication researchers study voice and persons' availability for relational difference and surprise in personal, organizational, cultural, or political relationships, they discover a focus for their theoretical concerns.

Mutual Definition and Polar Reality

For Buber, causality, traditionally defined, is an outgrowth of the world of It. In the "world of relation," I and Thou freely confront one another with plural, mutual, and interdependent consequences that cannot be traced to one-way causes. Each side in effect helps to define the other(s)—an interdefinition—that brings things into existence without causing. Thus, human categories are not static, dualistic, or mutually exclusive, despite Buber's tendency to describe polar opposites in dialectical or transactional terms. Although skeptical readers have suggested that he encouraged exclusivist either–or dichotomies ("you're either dialogic or you're not"; "'I-Thou' communication must replace the 'I-It'"), he forcefully denied this interpretation. Instead, he described an approach in which two contrary principles could be held simultaneously, in tension with each other, each influencing the other while being influenced by it.

For example, when Buber wrote about dialogue and monologue, he was not describing a relation of one *versus* the other, as if one is always right and the other wrong: he saw them as polar possibilities, each influencing the other, both as constant choices in human existence and both valuable, although in different ways, to human beings. They exist in tension with, not separation from, each other. Buber saw no inconsistency between standing one's ground in an argument and being radically available for, even vulnerable to, another person's assertions. Each defined the other. Being persuaded means little if your position was not strongly held in the first place. Another example of this necessary tension of polarities can be seen in Buber's treatment of the relationship between *distance* and *relation*. Although it would be easy to think he would favor relation over distance (the too-easy assumption that communication, a "good thing," bridges distance, a "bad thing"), Buber showed how genuine communication relies as much on difference and gaps between persons as on the friendly sounding goal of interpersonal closeness or bonding.

Narrow Ridge

Buber was suspicious of what he called the *psychologizing* of human experience—the tendency, even among scholars, to believe that genuine reality is based on inner phenomena such as the "self," which govern perception, thought, and emotion. Yet Buber was equally suspicious of the collective social tendencies he saw around him, and how they impeded the uniqueness of individuals. How to resolve the dilemma? Again: Keep the tension. Between these twin threats—immersion in the self or in the collective—dialogically conscious persons must walk as if on a narrow ridge, equally aware of the challenges on either side. In this engaging metaphor, humans need not reconcile oppositions into an artificial unity; rather, the human task is to seek contact with them both by walking the ridge between. Maurice Friedman considered this concept so important that he put it in the foreground with the title of his one-volume biography of Buber.

Concreteness and the Particular

I and Thou, or dialogic thinking, as Buber developed it, is a curious blend of the intensely particular and the poetically abstract. It is not systematic enough in elaborating intellectual principles to qualify as philosophy for some academic philosophers, but it offers a philosophical perspective with a particularly *applied* tone. Buber invited readers and listeners to use his examples to flesh out their own. This may explain the lasting appeal of *I and Thou*, despite its challenging syntax and sometimes obscure language: While it might appear to float above acts of everyday organizational and political life, it also enfolds such contexts, inviting readers' own recognition.

Buber's focus on difference and particularity suggests cultural implications as well. By insisting that real meeting is uniquely immediate, that persons must encounter the other with as few prior conceptions as possible, his nonprescriptive ethic of dialogue applies especially well to intercultural relations. Knowledge about others' situations and practices can help people respond to unfamiliar cultural encounters. But knowledge is not enough. The other is not simply a representative of a culture or group, and a preoccupation with knowledge about group characteristics can lead communicators to miss the uniqueness of the very person(s) before them. Similarly, too much conscious reliance on one's own cultural or group affiliations can mean the difference between being (and being perceived as) a genuine "person," on one hand, and a self-absorbed "individual," on the other. The former can speak and listen in the moment, while the latter becomes caught in the web of "my"—*my* characteristics, *my* race or ethnicity, *my* habits, *my* way of doing things.

Surprise

One of the traditional problems of conceptualizing communication often lurks just below the discursive surface of everyday life: What is communication for? Is it to be understood in terms of fidelity to intention? To express clearly what we already believe and feel? To persuade others of the validity and appropriateness of our beliefs? To hear what another is saying? Or, as Buber and other dialogue theorists would have it, is it also to generate creativity out of a conversational meeting with otherness and difference? In dialogue, in other words, surprise is a key criterion.

Communication scholars have often studied occasions of persuasion or influence, arising from speakers' entrenched positions, commitments, or certainties; they have been relatively less interested in exploring occasions of genuine surprise in which communicators find themselves taken to places and ideas they never expected they would go. Thus, the newfound interest in dialogue theories is encouraging. Ironically, perhaps, given that some have celebrated the Socratic method as a model for dialogue, Buber believed that it was not motivated by an appreciation of dialogical surprise; Socrates' questions were like "moves" in a game designed to reveal the deficiency of the learner's position. For Buber, the questioner's or teacher's more dialogic impulse would be to ask *real* questions—those that explore what is not already known. In Buber's philosophy of I and Thou, teachers can be changed by their students, just as students are changed by their teachers. Despite his admiration for Socrates the man, Buber considered his dialectical method, however skillful, as a monologic event of one participant, set in the participant's own beliefs, applying a technique to persuade another. The student was surprised, of course, but only by recognizing his own deficiency and the answers the teacher had already decided were necessary. Socrates, of course, seemed not to be surprised at all. Neither became a genuine Thou for the other.

Inclusion

Dialogic meetings are characterized in part by *inclusion*, the willingness of partners to attempt to imagine what others' reality might be, how the world looks and sounds "over there," without relinquishing one's own personal ground. At various times in his career, Buber invoked similar concepts, such as *imagining the real* or *making present,* to indicate communicators' responsibilities to each other as well as to standing their own ground. Inclusion could be distinguished from *empathy,* he thought, because empathizing encouraged persons to forgo their own side in order to see the other. This distinction became an issue in the famous 1957 public dialogue between Buber and the American psychologist Carl Rogers.

Presence as Confirmation

Not surprisingly, Buber's *I and Thou* has become known in communication studies as an evocation of the power of dialogue. Yet, contrary to a popular misconception, Buber's dialogue is not an extended state of being to be desired; it appears to spark only in transitory moments of meeting. It is not a transcendence of everyday mundane reality but an immersion in its concrete detail. Dialogue is associated with an intense presence in the immediate situation that cannot be sustained for long. It is not the skill of knowing exactly what the other is thinking, or of predicting the future, but the willingness—even between opponents—to include the other in one's own experience, listening for responses. Buber asks whether communicators could persistently be open to such moments. This openness is what counts as confirmation. Through it, we become human.

Rob Anderson and Kenneth N. Cissna

See also Dialogue Theories; Interpersonal
    Communication Theories; Ontology; Relational
    Communication Theory; Rogerian Dialogue Theory

Further Readings

Arnett, R. C. (1986). *Communication and community: Implications of Martin Buber's dialogue.* Carbondale: Southern Illinois University Press.

Buber, M. (1958). *I and thou* (2nd ed.; R. G. Smith, Trans.). New York: Charles Scribner's Sons. (Original work published 1923)

Buber, M. (1965). *Between man and man* (R. G. Smith, Trans.). New York: Macmillan. (Original work published 1947)

Buber, M. (1965). *The knowledge of man: A philosophy of the interhuman* (M. Friedman, Ed. and Intro.;

M. Friedman & R. G. Smith, Trans.). New York: Harper & Row.

Buber, M. (1970). *I and thou* (W. Kaufmann, Trans.). New York: Charles Scribner's Sons. (Original work published 1923)

Cissna, K. N., & Anderson, R. (2002). *Moments of meeting: Buber, Rogers, and the potential for public dialogue.* Albany: State University of New York Press.

Friedman, M. (1991). *Encounter on the narrow ridge: A life of Martin Buber.* New York: Paragon.

Friedman, M. (2002). *Martin Buber: The life of dialogue* (4th ed.). London: Routledge.

Kramer, K. P., with Gawlick, M. (2003). *Martin Buber's I and Thou: Practicing living dialogue.* New York: Paulist Press.

Schilpp, P. A., & Friedman, M. (Eds.). (1967). *The philosophy of Martin Buber.* La Salle, IL: Open Court.

Shapira, A. (1999). *Hope for our time: Key trends in the thought of Martin Buber* (J. M. Green, Trans.). Albany: State University of New York Press.

Stewart, J. (1985). Martin Buber's central insight: Implications for his philosophy of dialogue. In M. Dascal (Ed.), *Dialogue: An interdisciplinary approach* (pp. 321–335). Amsterdam: John Benjamins.

IDENTIFICATION

Identification is a key term in contemporary rhetorical theory that describes the fundamental process of using symbols to overcome inherent divisions among human beings. It is important in understanding the increasing complexity of the process of social influence as nonlinear, sometimes unintentional, and potentially nonverbal. This entry will examine the transition from the old rhetoric to the new rhetoric, the concepts of identification and consubstantiality, and the three strategies of identification.

The key term for traditional Western rhetorical theory or *old rhetoric* prior to the 20th century was *persuasion*, a concept that stressed the deliberate design of messages by rhetors as they attempted to convince audiences. Among the old rhetorics is Aristotle's definition of the available means of persuasion, as well as the medieval emphasis on the credibility of religious texts, the epistemology of the 18th century, and the *elocution movement* of the early 19th century. The common denominator among the old rhetorics was the emphasis on deliberate design of influence.

Identification, according to Kenneth Burke, its primary contributor, is a term that is associated with contemporary rhetoric because it acknowledges the complexity of interactions that may not have a single, identifiable rhetor directing a message to a specific, known audience. For contemporary theorists, identification allows for unconscious or unplanned meaning to influence many people in multiple ways. Unlike traditional rhetoric, this removes the deliberative intention and planning from the equation. So, if the interests of A are joined to those of B, they have identified with each other even though A and B are not identical. To the extent that A and B identify with each other, they have become *consubstantial.* For Burke, consubstantiality is a way of acting together, of sharing sensations, ideas, attitudes, and approaches to life. It allows human beings to overcome, although temporarily, their inherent biological division and the separation created by social hierarchies. And it is through consubstantiality that identification is achieved.

The impact of this change expands the scope of rhetoric from the deliberate planning and execution of persuasive strategies to the nondeliberate identification among people through *consubstantiation.* This expansion of the scope of rhetoric suggests that wherever there is meaning, there is also persuasion, and wherever there is persuasion, there is rhetoric. Rhetoric, for Burke, includes any and all the resources that function to induce attitude or action and to promote social cohesion. Although the preeminent tool of rhetoric is language, images and other nonverbal forms can also convey meaning. And since we can simultaneously be both sender and receiver of messages, as when we talk to ourselves or write in a diary, there is also the possibility of a *rhetoric of the self.*

For the new rhetoric, persuasion occurs to the extent that a communicator uses words, gestures, images, attitudes, and ideas that mesh with those of the receiver. Such choices are called *strategies.* Among potential strategies, at least three deserve special attention: strategies of naming, strategies of form, and strategies of spiritualization. Note that these strategies begin with more concrete uses of language, move to larger forms, and finally transcend both language and form to create a cluster of values.

Strategies of naming exploit the rhetorical nature of language that posits language is never neutral. By choosing a term or cluster of terms to describe a situation or thing, we name it. Along with the name, we have applied the values that are inherent in the name we have chosen. Thus, a person might be called "savage" or "civilized," implying a value judgment and specifying the appropriate response toward the person. Names also suggest our orientation toward the situation or thing, establishing a preferred point of view or position in relationship to the named thing. Even seemingly neutral names convey an orientation and place those using the names in some relationship to the thing that is named. Some scholars have called names associated with a constellation of explicit positive or negative values—such as *freedom* or *communism*—*god and devil terms* or *ultimate terms*.

Strategies of form arouse and fulfill desires among listeners through the structure of the form of the expression. Messages have form to the extent that one part leads receivers to anticipate and be gratified by the part that follows. Thus, we are satisfied when villains in a film receive their due, when sonnets rhyme, and when presidents use formal language on state occasions. There are five potential forms, according to Burke: syllogistic or progressive form, qualitative progression, repetitive form, conventional form, and minor or incidental forms.

Syllogistic or progressive form allows that if A then B, if B then C, if C then D, and so on. In contemporary Western culture, if two people fall in love, they will marry, raise a family, and grow old together. *Qualitative progression* links qualities together. If a person is kind to his or her mother, that person will probably be kind to others. *Repetitive form* occurs when there is restatement with new details, such as when a character whose nature is flighty wears a feathered hat and frilly collar. *Conventional form* recognizes the appeal inherent in forms that have been learned. For example, national holiday celebrations such as the Fourth of July or Cinco de Mayo are marked by similar foods and events every year. *Minor or incidental forms* are usually imbedded in other forms, such as when a metaphor, paradox, disclosure, or reversal occurs in a written text or when montage, freeze frame, slow motion, or rack focus is used in a film.

Strategies of spiritualization occur when symbolic actions are tied to ideals in a way that resembles secular prayer. Such ideals transcend individual concerns to unite groups in their common struggle toward perfection. Thus, the sacrifice of something held dear for a larger good, the regeneration of the past in light of a better future, and the overcoming of sin for eventual salvation are all strategies of spiritualization. Thus, the community that glorifies a war hero, parents who sacrifice for the education of their children, and ceremonies that cleanse participants of their transgressions are all utilizing the strategy of spiritualization.

Kathleen M. German

See also Persuasion and Social Influence Theories; Rhetorical Theory; Symbolic Interactionism; Values Studies: History and Concepts

Further Readings

Burke, K. D. (1931). *Counter-statement.* New York: Harcourt, Brace.

Edelman, M. (1964). *The symbolic uses of politics.* Chicago: University of Chicago Press.

Weaver, R. M. (1953). Ultimate terms in contemporary rhetoric. In R. M. Weaver (Ed.), *The ethics of rhetoric* (pp. 211–232). Chicago: Henry Regnery.

IDENTITY MANAGEMENT THEORY

See Identity Theories

IDENTITY NEGOTIATION THEORY

See Identity Theories

IDENTITY THEORIES

Identity is defined as the cultural, societal, relational, and individual images of self-conception, and this composite identity has group membership, interpersonal, and individual self-reflective implications. Identity is a colorful kaleidoscope with both stable and dynamic characteristics. The study of identity and communication issues is a challenging and yet rewarding enterprise. By understanding how individuals define themselves and how others define them on multiple grounds, persons can communicate with culturally different others with more interpersonal sensitivity and understanding.

Two macro theories of identity that guide the development of this review are Young Yun Kim's 1986 *contextual theory of interethnic communication,* with a recent update version in 2005, and Henri Tajfel and John C. Turner's 1986 *social identity theory of intergroup relations.* Young Yun Kim conceptualized *cultural identity* as both a sociological (or demographic) classification and an individual psychological attribute with a particular group. She uncovered five themes that are relevant to the study of contemporary cultural identity issues from the critical theory perspective to the social science perspective. These include intrapersonal processes, intercultural communication competence, adaptation to a new culture, cultural identity in intercultural contexts, and power inequalities in intercultural settings. While critical theorists emphasize the dominant societal structure that slots co-cultural members along a pecking-order ladder, social science theorists emphasize the power of interindividual identity negotiation process in reframing group membership and personal identity issues.

Henri Tajfel conceptualized an individual's identity as comprised of both social identity and personal identity dimensions on the psychological level. *Social identities* can include cultural or ethnic membership identity, gender identity, sexual orientation identity, social class identity, or social role identity, to name a few. *Personal identities,* on the other hand, can include any unique attributes that we associate with our individuated self in comparison with those of others. Both social identity and personal identity dimensions influence our everyday behaviors in a generalized and particularized manner.

Identity Theories: Conceptual Approaches

This section is organized in two sections: identity theories that focus on the interindividual level of analysis and identity theories that focus on the interface of dominant societal practice and individual identity resistance practice. The two camps share a permeable boundary rather than a rigid one: Some key concepts can be located on the borders of both sites.

Interindividual Interactional Approaches

According to Stella Ting-Toomey's *identity negotiation (IN) theory,* developed in 1986 and updated in 2005, human beings in all cultures desire identity respect in the communication process. However, what constitutes the proper way to show identity respect and consideration varies from one culture to the next. The IN perspective emphasizes particular identity domains in influencing individuals' everyday interactions. *Cultural identity salience* is defined as the emotional significance that members attach to their sense of belonging or affiliation with the larger national culture. *Ethnic identity salience* is defined as the subjective allegiance and loyalty to a group—large or small, socially dominant or subordinate—with which one has ancestral links.

The IN theory assumes that human beings in all cultures desire both positive group-based and positive person-based identities in any type of communicative situation. How individuals can enhance identity understanding, respect, and mutual affirmative valuation of the other is the essential concern of this approach. To illustrate, two of the IN theoretical assumptions are posited as follows: (1) The core dynamics of people's group membership identities (e.g., cultural and ethnic memberships) and personal identities (e.g., unique attributes) are formed via symbolic communication with others, and (2) individuals in all cultures or ethnic groups have the basic motivation needs for identity security, inclusion, predictability, connection, and continuity. However, too much emotional security will lead to tight ethnocentrism (i.e., thinking of your own cultural community as the center of the universe), and too much emotional insecurity (or vulnerability) will lead to fear of out-groups or strangers. Identity-support strategies, such as mindful listening and dialogue, and confirmation and empathic inclusion behaviors are some productive moves that can promote quality intergroup relationships.

Closely aligned with the IN theory is Tadasu Todd Imahori and William Cupach's *identity management theory,* developed in 1993 and updated in 2005. The theory emphasized the importance of facework support in developing quality intercultural relationships. Identity management theory suggests that individuals manage their identities differently at different junctures of their relationships. It also proposed three interdependent phases of an intercultural relationship development process: trial, enmeshment, and renegotiation. The trial phase refers to the trial-and-error experimentation stage of finding the balance point of how to negotiate cultural identity differences via appropriate facework balancing acts. The enmeshment phase refers to the stage of moving beyond cultural identity emphasis to a focus on building a common relational culture via symbolic convergence (e.g., use of nicknames) and relational expectancy coordination. The renegotiation phase refers to the reincorporation of the cultural identity negotiation process due to the secure base of the relational identity culture.

Ronald Jackson's *cultural contracts (CC) theory,* developed in 1999 and updated in 2005, conceptualized the term *negotiation of cultural identity* as a contractual process in which individuals consider the potential gain or loss of their interpretations of their own cultural worldviews or identity options. The basic premise of the theory asserts that the coordination of intercultural relationships is initiated after an initial negotiation with one's self concerning which worldview to "buy in" or contract.

A *cultural contract* refers to the patterns of norms, rules, and interaction that guide everyday behavior. There are three contract types: ready-to-sign contracts (nonnegotiable contracts with assimilation expectation), quasi-completed contracts (room for partial negotiation of identities and relational coordination), and cocreated contracts (room for mutual identity negotiation and valuation). If cultural contracts are breached, there are relational penalties associated with the "rule" violation. Two points from the theory illustrate its assumptions: (1) Communicators' personal histories and antecedent interactions influence the degree to which they are open to entering identity negotiations with others and (2) a contract will be completed or "tendered" if there is a strong desire or perceived need for it, even if it is forcibly signed for the sake of survival. Jackson's CC theory starts to bridge the macrolevel societal lens with the individual's stance on self-identity preservation work. In addition, Michael Hecht's *layered communication theory of identity,* with its developmental root in 1993 and updated in 2005, echoed the importance of communication as the locus of performance for all identity layers.

Macrosocietal Critical-Interpretive Approaches

Mary Jane Collier's *cultural identity (CI) theory* was developed in 1988, with the latest version appearing in 2005. She conceptualized *cultural identifications* as shared locations and orientations evidenced in a variety of communication forms, including discourse in public texts, mediated forms, artistic expressions, commodities and products, and individual accounts about group conduct. Working from a combined interpretive and critical perspective, she fine-tuned her CI theory with seven theoretical assumptions. Two of the assumptions are that (1) cultural identities are formed through processes of avowal (self-views) and ascription (views communicated by peers) and (2) the intensity with which particular cultural identities are avowed and ascribed differs depending on situation, context, topic, and relationship. She also incorporated critical perspective into the CI interpretive theory with the broader goal of uncovering social injustice and power inequality issues in the larger hierarchical structure of a society. Judith Martin, Thomas Nakayama, and Robert Krizek in 1996 and 2002 also worked from a critical theory lens in addressing the *privilege of Whiteness* issue and viewed the study of cultural identity as a contested zone of identity meaning construction. For them, communication is a way of contesting and resisting a dominant culture's encroachment.

Mark Orbe in 1998 and together with Regina Spellers in 2005 strengthened the base of the *cocultural theory* with the goal of understanding the various interactional ways in which marginalized or co-cultural members negotiate their everyday identities. Two core assumptions guide this critical theory: (1) A hierarchical structure exists in each society that gives privilege to certain groups of people. In the United States, these groups include men, European Americans, heterosexuals, and so forth. (2) Dominant group members, on the basis of varying levels of privilege, occupy positions of power that they then use to create communication systems that reinforce their own fields of experience. Co-cultural group members, however, can strategically adopt certain communication behaviors to navigate the oppressive dominant structures. The communication strategies include the interaction between three communication approaches (nonassertive, assertive, and aggressive strategies) and three preferred interaction outcomes (assimilation, accommodation, and separation).

The major differences between the critical and interindividual interactional camps are as follows: First, for the critical theorists, the bargaining table is an unequal playing field, and the bargaining chips are loaded toward the power holders of the dominant group. For the interindividual identity theorists, the starting point of identity negotiation is the persuasive communication process of identity support or assertion. Second, from the critical theorists' lens, the voices of co-cultural group members or minority group members are often muted or suppressed. From the interindividual theorists' standpoint, it is possible to create collaborative partnership via authentic dialogue or mutual identity valuation work. Third, from the critical theorists' lens, identity negotiation often entails internal and external struggles, and co-cultural group members are often placed in the "victim" or "marginalized" roles while dominant group members are positioned in the "oppressor" roles. From the psychological, interindividual theorists' viewfinder, the dynamic use of verbal and nonverbal messages can transform an individual's identity entrapment and encapsulation. Finally, from the critical theorists' camp, institutional oppressive power creates the condition of identity resistance and intergroup separation. From the interindividual theorists' camp, identity struggles can ultimately lead to a committed, multicultural identity with strong ties to other co-cultural and dominant members' vulnerable selves. Overall, while critical theorists emphasize the struggles of domestic co-cultural groups and their struggles to get their "voices" heard, the interindividual identity theorists emphasize the struggles of new arrivals or immigrants and their aspirations of "making it" in their adopted homeland.

Conclusions

Young Yun Kim's *integrated communication* theory on the cross-cultural adaptation process is one of the rare theories that connects the macrolevel factors such as the institutional patterns of the host environment to the microlevel factors such as the background and psychological characteristics of the immigrants. The theory can be traced to 1979, with a last update in 2005. Drawing from open-systems principles, the integrated communication theory emphasizes the inevitable adaptive change process of immigrants and their identity strain and stretch process. This stress–adaptation–growth spiraling process is played out within a macro-structural model of environmental factors such as host receptivity to cultural strangers and host conformity pressures. Mass communication activities, interpersonal interaction activities, and personality traits such as openness, strength, and positivity also help to motivate cultural strangers to take on the challenges of identity stretch and growth.

Cultural strangers achieve increasing levels of functional fitness and positive psychological health by embracing change and engaging in various self-adjustments. It is the individual resilient spirit that, in the end, can transform a static identity into an all-encompassing, multicultural identity field. Communication plays a pivotal role in either reinforcing the identity status quo or challenging self-views and other-views of the dynamic, multi-faceted self.

Stella Ting-Toomey

See also Co-Cultural Theory; Communication Theory of Identity; Contextual Theory of Interethnic Communication; Critical Race Theory; Cross-Cultural Adaptation Theory; Cultural Contracts Theory; Cultural Identity Theory; Face Negotiation Theory; Social Identity Theory; Whiteness Theory

Further Readings

Collier, M. J. (2005). Theorizing cultural identifications. In W. B. Gudykunst (Ed.), *Theorizing about intercultural communication* (pp. 235–256). Thousand Oaks, CA: Sage.

Imahori, T. T., & Cupach, W. (2005). Identity management theory. In W. B. Gudykunst (Ed.), *Theorizing about intercultural communication* (pp. 195–210). Thousand Oaks, CA: Sage.

Jackson, R. L. (2002). Cultural contracts theory. *Communication Quarterly, 50*(3–4), 359–367.

Kim, Y. Y. (2005). A contextual theory of intercultural communication. In W. B. Gudykunst (Ed.), *Theorizing about intercultural communication* (pp. 323–349). Thousand Oaks, CA: Sage.

Orbe, M. P., & Spellers, R. E. (2005). From the margins to the center. In W. B. Gudykunst (Ed.), *Theorizing about intercultural communication* (pp. 173–191). Thousand Oaks, CA: Sage.

Ting-Toomey, S. (2005). Identity negotiation theory. In W. B. Gudykunst (Ed.), *Theorizing about intercultural communication* (pp. 211–234). Thousand Oaks, CA: Sage.

IDEOLOGICAL RHETORIC

While there are multiple ways to define *ideology*, for our purposes the most general will suffice—an ideology is a belief/value system that functions to maintain or challenge the existing order. This implies a relationship to power as a central feature of an ideological orientation to the world but does not restrict ideology to the early Marxist sense as "false consciousness." Ideology may be theorized as distinct from rhetoric in that its expression is merely a by-product of its attitudinal perspective. The preference taken in this discussion is the opposite: An ideology exists in and through the symbol system that gives it meaning. An ideology is a rhetorical construct. As such, it lives or dies by virtue of the resonance its expression has in the lived experience of those who declare allegiance to the orientation it takes toward the world. An ideology, thus, is not a fixed but rather relatively fluid system whose principles may appear permanent but are in fact subject to change.

As noted above, an ideology is keyed to relations of power. What this means, in a postmodern context, is that changes in ideology manifest themselves as changes in power relations between social actors. The critique of power is inescapably a response to the shortcomings of a particular ideological orientation. Power, in this context, is not totally a repressive instrument of social control, though that is a dimension that an ideological critique will focus on in challenging the outcome or consequence of a specific relationship. From another perspective, power may also be seen in productive terms—what relationships allow to be created through the use of power in positioning people to engage in positive change. In this context, an ideological critique will focus on how power can be used in fashioning relationships that have the potential to demarginalize a group or to otherwise enable its members to gain control of their own lives in ways a prior power relationship did not.

From this perspective, *ideological rhetoric* is that discourse (which includes visual as well as textual artifacts) that reflects, establishes, or challenges existing power relations between and among people. It is a rhetoric that, in Burkean terms, pronounces how people should behave toward one another. The discourse of skinheads (as repelling as that may be personally) is just as ideological as that of progressive politicians seeking to redress the marginalization of a people. Moreover, both discourses contain a clear sense of what the power relationship is seen to be or is proposed to be in a given context.

In the context of the 2008 presidential election, race relations were never far from the surface in the discourse during the campaign. Once it concluded, those who see the election of a "Black man" as president as anathemic to their vision of America have begun voicing their displeasure in vitriolic terms. Conversely, those who see in the same event hopefulness for a better future voice their pleasure in positive language. Both reflect different (and perhaps incommensurable) ideological positions in that either vision, in the language of the other, is a "false consciousness" of the real social relation. From a visual perspective, Gustave Courbet's *The Stonebreakers* and Picasso's *Guernica* function as representational icons of a specific ideological formation. The one, in the mid-1800s, can be seen as a socialist orientation toward privation, while the other is a response to war. The point, with these examples, is to suggest that an ideology is not something external to the discourse that gives it life. It is not "out there" to be pointed to as if it were a fixed entity apart from ourselves. Rather, to critique each vantage point, or to see in a painting a vision of privation or a reaction to war, is to react to the symbolic reality each manifests at a given point in time. If one is unaware, for example, of *The Stonebreakers'* or

Guernica's history, the interpretive reaction may be far different.

With this broad gloss on "ideological rhetoric" as a starting point, it is important to note the historical development of this perspective. From the early part of the 20th century through the 1950s and into the 1960s, critical approaches to discursive events were seen in more objective terms—the role of the critic was to stand at a distance, in both time and space, from the artifact and critically assess the impact a text might have on others. Criticism, from this perspective, was not about the critic. That orientation began to change with the publication, in the early 1970s, of Phillip Wander and Steven Jenkins's "Rhetoric, Society, and the Critical Response." This was followed by Michael McGee's work on "ideographs" and McGee and Wander's trenchant critique of the kind of criticism that neither acknowledged nor interrogated the relationship between rhetoric and ideology. The "proper role" of the critic was reformulated during this period between the early 1970s and late 1980s. This transformation proved a fertile ground for the development of more politicized orientations toward critical reflection. At the same time, a view of what could or should be considered "rhetorical" was also undergoing alteration. The resulting expansion of rhetoric's "province" meant that discourse or "oral/written text" was not the only purview of the critics. Today, these developments are represented in the growth of "critical-cultural" and visual approaches to the study of symbolic events.

A caveat is important: The transformation of the role of the critic, in what has been styled an *ideological turn,* is not to be seen as the better way to conduct critical inquiry. Whatever form criticism takes, it always is subject to the question being investigated. Thus, a close reading of what a text says can be the best way to answer some questions, but not others. Likewise, an avowedly ideological perspective can also be the best way to answer other questions—especially those involving an interrogation of how symbols construct, maintain, or challenge existing power relations.

Raymie E. McKerrow

See also Critical Rhetoric; Critical Theory; Ideology; Rhetorical Theory

Further Readings

Eagleton, T. (2007). *Ideology: An introduction* (2nd ed.). London: Verso.

McGee, M. C. (1980). The "ideograph": A link between rhetoric and ideology. *Quarterly Journal of Speech, 66,* 1–16.

McKerrow, R. E. (1983). Marxism and the rhetorical conception of ideology. *Quarterly Journal of Speech, 69,* 192–205.

Wander, P. (1984). The third persona: An ideological turn in rhetorical theory. *Central States Speech Journal, 35,* 197–216.

Wander, P., & Jenkins, S. (1972). Rhetoric, society and the critical response. *Quarterly Journal of Speech, 58,* 441–450.

IDEOLOGY

An ideology is a concept that refers to the collective beliefs, attitudes, and values of a given group of people, from social cliques and small communities to an audience or an entire nation. Although ideologies can be positive, most scholars who study or critique them focus on those that cause harm or suffering. For example, in Western societies the ideology of individualism is believed to be positive, while the ideology that promotes the idea that men are superior to women, sexism, is believed to be negative. Consequently, sexism is studied and critiqued more heavily than individualism, although both ideologies are operative in the United States. In this respect, there is a rather long history of studying subordinate ideologies in communication studies, such as sexism and racism. Recently, however, there has been a growing interest in studying dominant ideologies such as Whiteness (that about identity which goes unmarked and unnoticed) and masculinity.

In general, it is believed that ideologies work largely unconsciously and tend to promote the status quo, usually by supporting those individuals who are in power. Although the concept derives from the materialist theories of Karl Marx, the use of ideology is not limited to materialist contexts. Today, the notion of ideology is widely assumed and referenced in a variety of communicative contexts.

Marxist Origins

Now commonly assumed in communication scholarship, Marx's main philosophical argument is that the way the world is materially arranged determines how we think about it. Until the articulation of this philosophy, it was widely assumed that society as we know it is the product of human ingenuity: A group of individuals got together and dreamed up the way society should look and function and then went about making society in conformity with that dream. If this were truly the case, suggested Marx, then why hasn't utopian thinking brought about a better world? When Marx was working out his philosophy in the mid- to late 19th century, he witnessed an increasingly prosperous class of people (capitalists) exploiting poorer people for profit. Factories were inhumane, and people—sometimes even children—worked long hours for a meager wage. Despite the increasing successes and growing wealth of the individuals who owned the factories, their workers were getting poorer, even dying. Observing how willingly the working class accepted their poor conditions, Marx concluded something was wrong; thought had become "inverted" or turned upside down from what it should be. *Ideology* was the concept that Marx developed to help explain how this inverted thought came about.

Although it is true that one must imagine and then create a blueprint for a building before it is built, Marx argued that the ideas behind the blueprint were actually influenced by material conditions including (a) what resources were available for building, (b) who owned the resources for building, (c) what class of individuals was ruling society, and so on. Marx argued, in other words, that the building imagined by an architect and then subsequently built would reflect the way the world was materially arranged at the time, ultimately serving the interests of those in power (e.g., those who owned the resources and means for making things).

Analogously, Marx argued that state governments tend to support the material and political interests of a dominant group of people (the "ruling class"). For example, it is often taught in American schools that the founding fathers of the United States of America gathered together at the Philadelphia Convention in 1787 and invented the current government system, which is designed to serve "the people." A Marxist perspective, however, would emphasize that the government structure created at this convention only reinforced and stabilized the status quo: To this day, the government created by the founding fathers continues to support the most empowered in American society, who are wealthy White men. In sum, Marx reversed the way we think about thinking: it is not that we dream up a better world and then create it; rather, it is that the material, concrete world preexists us, and that whatever we create will conform to the constraints of this preexisting, material world. This view is known as *materialism*.

What, then, continues to maintain the existing material arrangement of society? Why do governments continue to support those in power? Even though technology is constantly changing our material and communicative interactions, why does it seem the same group of people always continues to benefit? In other words, despite obvious, dynamic change, why do political and state structures seem to stay the same? Marx's answer is *ideology*. For him, ideology was fundamentally an inversion of the materialist view. If materialism is the idea that the concrete arrangement of the world influences how we think about it, then ideology is the inverse notion that thought distorts people's views of material reality. For Marx, then, ideology referred to something negative. Fundamentally, ideology is a kind of consciousness that makes one incapable of seeing the fundamental contradictions of material reality that might lead to radical change. An individual under the sway of ideology, for example, believes that social class (e.g., rich and poor) is a natural arrangement and not the product of oppression and force. Because ideology is so powerful, argued Marx, only a violent, material disruption could change how we think about the world: revolution.

Positive and Neutral Ideology After Marx

After Marx's death in 1883, the concept of ideology expanded to include new meanings, some of which were positive. Vladimir Lenin was most influential in shifting the negative connotation of ideology toward a more neutral connotation. If Marxism mounted a critique of the status quo and its commonly held beliefs, attitudes, and values as an inversion of material conditions, then such a critique must be coming from an alternative position with its own beliefs, attitudes, and values. In other words, Marxism is itself an ideology. Consequently, Lenin argued that ideology must be understood as the political consciousness of a given group of people, most especially that of an economic and social class. After Lenin, the concept of ideology became "neutral" when it was understood that the working class, which Marxism champions, was ideologically opposed to the capitalist ideology of those in power, the wealthy ruling class.

After Lenin, the most influential thinker of ideology was Antonio Gramsci, who further expanded the concept to denote a set of representations or mental images of reality that is gleaned from a given culture's legal and economic systems, as well as art and other forms of community expression. For Gramsci, this concept of the world also included codes for social behavior and action. Consequently, if a given group's ideology was pervasive, then that ideology had *hegemony,* or a tacit, largely unconscious control over social behaviors, forms of art, economics, and the law. If a group's ideology has hegemony, then that group's beliefs, attitudes, and values seem natural and like common sense. Like Lenin, Gramsci believed ideology was neutral and governed the political consciousness of a given group. Whereas Lenin argued that a group's ideology only achieves hegemony over others through contest and struggle, Gramsci believed that hegemony is increasingly achieved without direct force or coercion and often with the unwitting help of intellectuals. According to Gramsci, two forces—the State and leadership within civil society—were responsible for perpetuating dominant ideologies. In this way, Gramsci challenged the classical Marxist view that the dominant ideology of a given society was a direct reflection of ruling class mentality. Ideological hegemony was achieved through struggle and in concert with multiple agencies and could not be reduced to a narrow reflection of basic, economic arrangements.

Althusser and Ideology

Perhaps the most recent and influential thinker on ideology today is Louis Althusser, a French Marxist thinker who Jorge Larrain has argued sought to reconcile the negative and neutral understandings of ideology. Although Althusser would agree with Gramsci that ideology is struggled over, he expanded the concept further by adding a psychological dimension: Ideology concerns the imagined relationship that individuals harbor about their real, material conditions. In other words, ideology concerns how a given person thinks about his or her relationship to the "real world." Althusser argues that we have to understand ideology as a kind of necessary illusion, which we borrow from the world outside to make sense of our identity and purpose in life. No one of us, suggests Althusser, has direct access to the real, material world; our relationship to the world is filtered through and by representations (at the very least, by language itself). Ideology is the main source of those representations. Consequently, some of us grow up and reckon with our real conditions of existence as Chinese citizens, while others of us contend with material reality as evangelical Baptists from the southern United States. In this respect, for Althusser ideology is unavoidable and necessary because it is the very basis of identity itself.

Althusser's contribution to the concept of ideology cannot be underestimated, for it is the basis for a relatively recent theoretical movement, *post-Marxism,* that has had a strong impact on communication theory. For Althusser, one needs to incorporate an ideology to become a self-conscious person. If I am a Marxist, for example, then I know material conditions directly influence what is thinkable, that my purpose in life is to uphold the ideology of the working class, and so on. If I am a Christian, then I know material reality is but an illusion of a greater, spiritual reality, that Jesus will return to earth again, and so on. In either case, ideology gives me a sense of who I am and what my relationship to the "real world" is about. Absent ideology, I cannot "know" who I am. Hence, every communicative encounter with another person is in some sense an ideological negotiation.

Another important element of Althusser's understanding of ideology is that it is diffuse and dynamic. For an individual to assume a set of beliefs, attitudes, and values about, say, the importance of capitalism, he or she must be confronted by them in multiple venues. A given ideology is not promoted by one person or even a class of persons, but rather by multiple agencies working simultaneously and in concert: the mass media, the educational system, economic and legal structures, the family, and so on. For example, let us use the ideology of individualism, which consists of the belief, attitude, and value that every person is unique and should take personal responsibility for his or her destiny.

One is not born to value individuality but learns it through multiple agencies over a long time. As a youngster one is told about one's unique and special character by one's parents; the family teaches individualism. At the church, synagogue, or mosque, one is taught that Deity has a unique plan for one's life; religion teaches individualism. On television, talk show hosts tout the virtues of individual achievement and personal responsibility; the media teaches individualism. At school, one is given one's own desk, told to bring one's own materials to class, and is cautioned that one should keep one's eyes on one's own paper because one's grade is determined by singular, individual effort; school teaches individualism. In this way, different agencies—the family, the media, the education system—work to instill and reinforce the ideology of individualism. Borrowing a concept from psychoanalysis, Althusser terms the way in which multiple sources perpetuate a given ideology *overdetermination*.

The Concept of Ideology Today

Since Althusser's attempt at compromise, the concept of ideology has been freed of its Marxist origins. Absent the materialist tie, the concept of ideology differs from one context to the next. In the popular media, ideology is frequently used as a synonym for one's political orientation. In academic work, however, the concept of ideology is associated with scholars who critique culture (e.g., the mass media). Generally, it remains the case that those who study ideology are interested, as Terry Eagleton has noted, in how people become invested in their own unhappiness. Although some ideologies—for example, the Christian ideology of loving one's enemy—can promote good things, in general scholars are interested in the ways in which ideology can harm and oppress people and often without their noticing it.

Owing to the psychological turn of Althusser and the more popular work of mass movement

scholars such as Eric Hoffer, however, in the last half-century, ideology has taken on the connotations of political brainwashing. Unwilling to believe that individuals are "dupes" of ideology, many scholars abandoned the concept. Coupled with what is sometimes termed the *poststructural turn* in theoretical debates of the late 20th century, this negative connotation has also led some scholars to call for abandoning the concept because it is self-defeating. In a charge that recalls Lenin's reworking of Marx's negative conception, some critics argue that ideology critique presumes a privileged vantage external to ideology for the critique to be possible. Such a presumption is, in fact, ideological itself, and consequently, any claim to discern hidden or obscured contradictions is itself an ideological ruse. Instead, critics of ideology have argued for abandoning the concept in favor of Michel Foucault's conception of *discourse* or *power/knowledge*. Contemporary defenders of ideology and ideological critique frequently counter by returning to Lenin's or Gramsci's more complicated notions of ideology as reflecting a deeper, material contradiction or antagonism or by arguing that the abandonment of ideology critique is motivated by an investment in the status quo.

More recently, Slavoj Žižek has defended the utility of ideology for scholarship by offering a Leninist rereading of the concept. He suggests that an ideology can be known only in contrast to a competing ideology. Insofar as ideology denotes the collective beliefs, attitudes, and values of a given group of people, one cannot become conscious of another set of beliefs, values, and attitudes unless there is a conflict between the sets. Consequently, ideology critique is not self-defeating, but rather self-interested.

Ideology in Communication Studies

In the field of communication studies, two contexts in which ideology is frequently studied include rhetoric and organizational communication. For rhetorical scholars, *ideological criticism* is a form of scholarship in which *texts* are closely scrutinized in order to uncover the hidden beliefs, attitudes, and values promoted by and/or influencing them. One popular method among rhetoricians for studying ideology across different texts is known as *ideographic criticism.* This method traces a singular term, or an *ideograph,* across multiple texts, which is itself symptomatic of a much larger, external set of beliefs, attitudes, and values. Another approach to the study of ideology has been the *critique of concord,* which Celeste Condit argues derives from Gramsci's understanding of hegemony. Condit argues a critique of concord consists of examining the rhetoric of multiple contesting groups over a political or ideological issue. Dana Cloud has critiqued the idea of "hegemony as concordance" as "idealist" for ignoring the class-based and economic struggles at the center of Gramsci's theory of ideology. As a final example, *symbolic convergence theory* straddles both social scientific and rhetorical approaches to communication by tracking ideology in terms of *fantasy themes* or *visions* that are created and exchanged among small groups of people working toward a common goal.

In organizational communication studies, ideology has been studied to show how one ideology becomes dominant or hegemonic, influencing organizational cultures. In this respect, the work of Dennis K. Mumby on hegemony as a dialectical force among organizations has been instrumental.

Joshua Gunn

See also Critical Organizational Communication; Critical Rhetoric; Ideological Rhetoric; Marxist Theory; Materiality of Discourse; Rhetorical Theory; Symbolic Convergence Theory

Further Readings

Althusser, L. (1971). *Lenin and philosophy and other essays* (G. Brewster, Trans.). New York: Oxford University Press.

Bormann, E. G. (2001). *The force of fantasy: Restoring the American dream* (2nd ed.). Carbondale: Southern Illinois University Press.

Cloud, D. L. (1996). Hegemony or concordance? The rhetoric of tokenism in Oprah Winfrey's rags-to-riches biography. *Critical Studies in Mass Communication, 13,* 115–137.

Condit, C. (1994). Hegemony in a mass-mediated society: Concordance about reproductive technologies. *Critical Studies in Mass Communication, 11,* 205–230.

Eagleton, T. (1991). *Ideology: An introduction.* New York: Verso.

Gramsci, A. (1971). *Selections from the prison notebooks* (Q. Hoare & G. N. Smith, Trans. & Eds.). New York: International Publishers.

Gunn, J., & Treat, S. (2005). Zombie trouble: A propaedeutic on ideological subjectification and the unconscious. *Quarterly Journal of Speech, 91,* 144–174.

Hoffer, E. (1951). *The true believer: Thoughts on the nature of mass movements.* New York: Harper & Row.

Larrain, J. (1979). *The concept of ideology.* Athens: University of Georgia Press.

Larrain, J. (1983). *Marxism and ideology.* London: Macmillan.

McGee, M. C. (1980). "The ideograph": A link between rhetoric and ideology. *Quarterly Journal of Speech, 66,* 1–16.

Mumby, D. K. (1988). *Communication and power in organizations: Discourse, ideology, domination.* Norwood, NJ: Ablex.

Mumby, D. K. (1997). The problem of hegemony: Rereading Gramsci for organizational communication studies. *Western Journal of Communication, 61,* 343–375.

Sholle, D. J. (1998). Critical studies: From the theory of ideology to power/knowledge. *Critical Studies in Mass Communication, 5,* 16–41.

Wander, P. (1983). The ideological turn in modern criticism. *Central States Speech Journal, 34,* 1–18.

Žižek, S. (1995). Introduction. In S. Žižek (Ed.), *Mapping ideology* (pp. 1–33). New York: Verso.

IMMEDIACY

Immediacy behaviors are actions that simultaneously communicate warmth, involvement, psychological closeness, availability for communication, and positive affect. Immediacy is the primary way humans signal interpersonal closeness, willingness to communicate, and positive feelings for other people. Immediacy behaviors are both verbal and nonverbal but typically occur in a cluster or group of consistent behaviors that provide fundamental connections between human beings.

Verbal immediacy behaviors include both styles of communication that signal warmth and connection and linguistic messages that explicitly communicate immediacy. Stylistically, verbal immediacy behaviors include plural pronouns such as *we* and *us* that promote connection and relational closeness rather than individual pronouns such as *you* and *I* that express independence and separation. Similarly, informal forms of address, such as using first names or nicknames as opposed to formal names or titles, are a powerful, unobtrusive immediacy behavior. Open communication and increased self-disclosure are often classified as immediacy behaviors.

Verbal immediacy can be communicated explicitly through positive references to another person or to one's relationship. Compliments regarding another's personality, accomplishments, or appearance increase interpersonal immediacy. Likewise, positive, explicit relational comments such as saying "I love you" or saying how much one values a relationship are powerful, explicit indicants of immediacy.

Nonverbal behaviors communicate even more powerful messages of immediacy than verbal behaviors according to most theorists and researchers. Nonverbal immediacy is communicated as a consistent multichanneled message consisting of an entire set of interrelated nonverbal behaviors such as interpersonal touch, eye contact, closer distances, smiling, and positive vocal tones. Nonverbal immediacy is typically expressed spontaneously and mindlessly as a message of involvement with and affect for another person. Encoders are rarely aware of the many components of an immediacy display due to immediacy's spontaneous, mindless, multichanneled quality. Similarly, receivers typically perceive a message of warmth, interpersonal closeness, and involvement without being aware of all the components of multichanneled display. Communication theorists and researchers have analyzed the components of nonverbal immediacy, but typically immediacy is sent and received with little awareness of the components comprising an immediacy display.

In most relationships and interactions, immediacy is received positively by interactants according to Peter Andersen's direct effects model and Judee Burgoon's social meaning model. However, in some cases, immediacy displays are perceived as inappropriate or excessive, resulting in negative reaction, compensations, and relational deterioration. Tests of Andersen's cognitive valence theory suggest that the most common reason for perceptions of excessive immediacy is relational inappropriateness; some immediacy displays are inappropriate in professional or nonintimate relationships. The theory has shown that perceptions of excessive or inappropriate immediacy can also result from cultural differences, lack of attraction for the person initiating immediacy, personality of the recipient, the physical or psychological state of the recipient, or the situation.

Tactile behaviors are conceivably the most immediate actions because touch is inherently involving and reduces physical and psychological distance between communicators. Tactile or haptic immediacy includes warm handshakes, handholding, pats, hugs, and other touch that is relationally appropriate.

Similarly, immediacy can be conveyed proxemically through decreased interpersonal space and distance. In North America and northern Europe, the most immediate distance is less than 1.5 feet, a distance called the intimate space zone. Larger distances are progressively less immediate, signaling unavailability, less positive affect, and greater psychological distance. Face-to-face positions are most immediate, side-to-side less immediate, and back-to-back least immediate. Similarly, communicating on the same visual plane rather than towering over someone is more immediate.

Eye contact and other oculesic displays constitute primary immediacy behaviors. Eye contact characterizes most interpersonal interaction and signals availability and invites communication. In public settings such as elevators or trains, passengers assiduously shun eye contact to avoid interaction.

Kinesic behavior, commonly called body language, constitutes meaningful movements that can communicate immediacy. Positive facial expressions, particularly smiles, are primary immediacy cues, as are facial animation, enthusiasm, and warm expressions. Negative expressions including emotional displays of fear, anger, and dominance are nonimmediate. Head nods, particularly when used as listener responses, establish rapport and immediacy between communicators. Bodily relaxation and an absence of tension, particularly relaxed arms and legs, are immediacy cues; tense, nervous people do not communicate positive affect, warmth, or approachability. Increased gestures produce greater rapport, enthusiasm, and immediacy. Matching and mirroring an interactant's bodily movements are associated with perceptions of immediacy. Similarly, people who deploy synchronous kinesic behaviors, such as dancers in step with one another, produce perceptions of connection and immediacy. Finally, open body positions signal warmth, approachability, and readiness for interaction. Body barriers such as folded arms, facial covering, or hiding behind objects signal defensive avoidance and low immediacy.

Immediacy is also communicated vocally; warm tones of voice, an enthusiastic speaking style, and vocalized listener responses are associated with greater immediacy. Likewise, in the chronemic channel, the use of time can increase immediacy. Interruptions, late arrivals, and acting preoccupied or hurried are not indications of immediacy. One of the most powerful immediacy cues is spending time with a relational partner.

In sum, across a number of relational contexts including romances, close friendships, and new acquaintances, greater immediacy seems to be predictive of more relational closeness. Similarly, greater immediacy is beneficial in organizational contexts, especially instructional contexts, where greater teacher immediacy has been consistently associated with positive relational outcomes, particularly increased affect for learning, the classroom, and the teacher.

Peter A. Andersen

See also Emotion and Communication; Expectancy Violations Theory; Kinesics; Language and Communication; Nonverbal Communication Theories; Proxemics

Further Readings

Andersen, P. A. (1998). The cognitive valence theory of intimate communication. In M. T. Palmer & G. A. Barnett (Eds.), *Progress in communication sciences: Vol. XIV. Mutual influence in interpersonal communication: Theory and research in cognition, affect, and behavior* (pp. 39–72). Stamford, CT: Ablex.

Andersen, P. A. (2008). *Nonverbal communication: Forms and functions* (2nd ed.). Long Grove, IL: Waveland.

Andersen, P. A., & Andersen, J. F. (2005). The measurement of nonverbal immediacy. In V. Manusov (Ed.), *The sourcebook of nonverbal measures: Going beyond words* (pp. 113–126). Mahwah, NJ: Lawrence Erlbaum.

Jones, S. M., & Guerrero, L. K. (2001). The effects of nonverbal immediacy and verbal person centeredness on the emotional support process. *Human Communication Research, 27,* 567–596.

Mehrabian, A. (1971). *Silent messages.* Belmont, CA: Wadsworth.

Weiner, M., & Mehrabian, A. (1968). *Language within language: Immediacy, a channel in verbal communication.* New York: Appleton-Century-Crofts.

IMPRESSION FORMATION

An *impression* is our image of another person, consisting of the beliefs that we have of that person's characteristics. These characteristics include descriptors for the person's personality (warm, curious), roles (mother, lawyer), physical attributes (red-headed, tall), and normal behaviors (smiles a lot, talks loudly). *Impression formation* is the psychological process by which impressions are developed. Despite its psychological nature, communication scholars are interested in the impression formation process because it occurs through communication.

This entry focuses on the psychological approach to this topic. Readers should also consider entries that describe impression formation as a strictly communicative process (e.g., uncertainty reduction theory), that concentrate on communicative skill differences (e.g., constructivism), and that consider intentional impression management strategies (e.g., facework) for a full understanding of this topic.

The study of impression formation was inspired by the work of the German Gestalt psychology movement of the 1920s and 1930s. Gestalt psychologists believed that people actively strive to understand the world around them, in contrast with the mostly American learning theorists of that time who conceived of people as responding passively to their environment. The Gestaltists also differed from learning theorists in their interest in human cognitive processes, which probably led impression-formation theorists to ignore emotional factors in favor of the cognitive. One consequence of the Gestaltist legacy is the metaphor of the observer forming an impression as a *naive scientist*. This metaphor implies that, just like scientists, we form an impression of a person because we are trying to understand that person, and the formed impression functions as a scientific theory does for a scientist. Scientific theory attempts to describe, explain, and allow for predicting and controlling real-world events. Analogously, an impression provides both a description of a person's behaviors and appearance and an explanation for behaviors and appearance in terms of the person's personality and roles, and it enables one both to predict the behaviors and appearance of the other person in future circumstances and to try to control when and how to interact with that person. The work of two Gestaltists who moved to the United States to escape the Nazi government, Solomon Asch and Fritz Heider, was reflective of the naive-scientist metaphor and helped define the issues with which impression formation theories have grappled.

During an initial interaction between two people, the cognitive process by which an *observer* (hereafter known as Ann) forms an impression of a second, *target* person (Bob) can be modeled as a four-stage process. First, Ann observes Bob's behavior. Second, Ann attributes a cause to that behavior. Third, if Ann interprets that cause as associated with a permanent characteristic of Bob, Ann forms an impression of Bob. Fourth, Ann uses the impression to establish an evaluation of Bob. The following four sections consider each of these stages in turn.

Behavioral Observation

The first stage in impression formation is the observation of behavior. Although the potential exists for anything that people do to influence our impressions of them, behaviors that are unusual, surprising, or viewed negatively are more likely to gain our focus and to influence the impression formation process. Given such focus, there are two substages to behavioral observation: *unitizing* and *labeling*. Beginning with the first, behavior occurs in a nonstop stream, so we must divide this stream into manageable units. The size of the unit depends on several factors. One such factor is our knowledge about the observed activity; a novice typist typing the word *angry* would be likely to divide his

or her own behavior into typing an *a*, then typing an *n*, and so on, whereas experienced typists would think in terms of the entire word as one unit. A second factor is our goal; research has revealed that observers intending to form an impression of a person tend to divide the person's behavior into larger units than if they are trying to remember that person's actions. Given the same knowledge and goals, people watching the same activity tend to divide it into similarly sized units.

After we unitize, we establish a label for the unit. Our language often gives us alternative ways of describing the same behavior. For instance, what could be described in neutral terms (moves quickly toward me) might be viewed positively (runs excitedly toward me) or negatively (attacks me). The situation we are in (meeting a loved one at an airport vs. walking through a dangerous part of town) or our current mood will impact on the type of label we provide. The result of the labeling process is significant because its original positivity or negativity may color the subsequent stages in impression formation.

Causal Attribution

During the second stage of impression formation, we establish a cause for the observed behavior, specifically, whether responsibility for the behavior rests in the person who performed it or the situation which the person was in. In short, if Ann sees Bob insult Chris, Ann uses the information at her disposal to decide whether this action is indicative of something inherent about Bob (he characteristically acts this way) or circumstance (e.g., he is just in a bad mood today). If circumstance appears to be the better explanation, she will conclude that the behavior tells us nothing about Bob, ending the impression-formation process at that point. If, instead, something inherent to Bob seems a more likely cause, then Ann begins to form the basis for her impression by assigning a personality characteristic that is implied by the behavior (mean to others). The more that a given behavior is typical of the situation in which we see it occur, the more likely we see it as caused by that situation and not indicative of the person who performed it. As a consequence, behaviors that are unusual tend to induce causal responsibility judgments to the person. Note that these are the types of behaviors that are more likely to have been noticed in the first place.

Impression Formation

When the observer has concluded that the target's character is responsible for the observed behavior, the result of the attribution process is the assignment of a personality characteristic to the target (in our case, Bob is mean). The subsequent impression-formation process consists of the assignment to the target of additional attributes believed to be associated with that originally attributed. If Bob is the type of person who insults others, Ann concludes that he would also break promises he makes to others and refuse to grant people's requests for help. If Bob is mean, then he is also untrustworthy and selfish.

Additional attributes are often evaluated similarly to the original ones. Since research in the 1920s, we have known that once an individual has attributed a behavior to a personality characteristic, he or she will tend to assign other evaluatively similar characteristics to that person. The term *halo effect*, in which both the originally attributed and later assigned characteristics are positive, dates back to 1920. This finding was extended as well in 1922 to the corresponding *horns effect* with negative attributes. By the 1930s, research showed that a similar effect occurs in evaluating behavior. Beginning in the mid-1950s, there has been an ever-increasing body of evidence implying that impressions are organized within a three-dimensional structure consisting of degree of positivity versus negativity, degree of power, and degree of activity or intensity.

The basis for impression formation can often be found in what has alternatively been referred to as *implicit personality theories* or *prototypes:* our beliefs about the characteristics of types of people. Research during the 1950s and 1960s indicated shared beliefs about the attributes of occupations such as police officers, librarians, and lawyers. More recent work has established analogous conceptions for more general categories such as the good communicator or good leader. When actions performed by a person lead to the judgment of, for example, a good leader, the relevant prototype serves as a mold from which an impression of the person's leadership-relevant characteristics is formed.

Target Evaluation

The final stage of the impression-formation process is the evaluation of the target. In general, that overall evaluation is the result of the evaluation of the specific attributes in the impression. If the attributes in the impression are consistently either positive or negative, the evaluation will be so as well. Attempts to model the evaluation process resulted in theoretical controversy during the 1960s and 1970s. Imagine that after forming an extremely positive impression, a judge notices an only modestly positive behavior. Some theorists argued for an *additive* process in which, since the additional information is positive, the overall impression becomes even more favorable, whereas others argued for an *averaging* process in which, since the new information is less positive than the old, the overall impression becomes less favorable. Research findings have tended to favor an averaging model weighted by the perceived importance of the characteristics. Solomon Asch preferred a model in which the actual interpretation of the additional characteristics can be influenced by those previously attributed. This can account for the circumstance in which specific combinations of characteristics bring relevant stereotypes to mind. Although *blonde* standing alone is at least neutral if not positive, linking it with *dumb* calls up a particularly negative image. In general, however, a mixture of positive and negative characteristics results in a neutral impression.

Mediated-Impression Formation

The study of mediated-impression formation began in the 1970s with the examination of the process via telephone and closed-circuit television and progressed to interaction via computer in the late 1980s. Early findings implied that impressions formed through mediated channels tended to neutrality, due to the absence of nonverbal cues that are critical for the process in face-to-face contexts, and these findings informed proposals such as media richness theory that implied an inability to form rich impressions through mediated interaction. However, since the early 1990s, research by Joseph Walther in particular demonstrates that in computer-mediated interaction, people compensate for the absence of nonverbal behaviors with other relationally relevant cues, allowing the impression formation process to take place as it does face-to-face although at a distinctly slower rate.

Conclusion

Although laid out here as occurring in sequence, the four stages of impression formation actually occur simultaneously. We begin forming impressions and making preliminary evaluations of others soon after meeting them, and although these first impressions color subsequent judgments, continued observation of behavior may change our impressions over time. In particular, first impressions are prone to be unrealistically consistent—either all positive or all negative—but they become more nuanced with continued opportunities to observe.

There are times when the cognitive processes described here are short-circuited by evaluations based on physical appearance and nonverbal behavior. Such *snap judgments,* as these are called, consist of evaluations resulting directly from emotional responses to direct observations of targets.

Charles Pavitt

See also Attribution Theory; Cognitive Theories; Constructivism; Facework Theories; Impression Management; Media Richness Theory; Nonverbal Communication Theories; Social Information Processing Theory; Uncertainty Management Theories; Uncertainty Reduction Theory

Further Readings

Bruner, J. S., & Tagiuri, R. (1954). The perception of people. In G. Lindzey (Ed.), *Handbook of social psychology* (pp. 634–654). Reading, MA: Addison-Wesley.

Fiske, S. T., & Taylor, S. E. (1984). *Social cognition.* Reading, MA: Addison-Wesley.

Newtson, D., & Engquist, G. (1976). The perceptual organization of ongoing behavior. *Journal of Experimental Social Psychology, 12,* 436–450.

Pavitt, C. (1989). Accounting for the process of communicative competence evaluation: A comparison of predictive models. *Communication Research, 16,* 405–433.

Schneider, D. J., Hastorf, A. H., & Ellsworth, P. C. (1979). *Person perception* (2nd ed). Reading, MA: Addison-Wesley.

Wyer, R. S., Jr. (1974). *Cognitive organization and change: An information processing approach.* Potomac, MD: Lawrence Erlbaum.

IMPRESSION MANAGEMENT

Impression management is not a clearly focused theory but a construct representing the presentation and maintenance of social identity during interaction. When scholars speak about managing an *impression,* they are not suggesting an artificial or manipulative agenda. They are simply referring to the image that a person displays during interaction. Some scholars use the term *social* or *public self* to distinguish social identity from the private self. As individuals, we are constituted of countless idiosyncrasies—habits, mannerisms, beliefs, attitudes, values, abilities, needs, interests, family history, and so forth. When interacting with others, we cannot display all aspects of our private self. We therefore select characteristics from our psychological and behavioral matrix that we believe will present the person (the self) we should be during that occasion. We might be aware that we do this only when our identity is important, such as preparing for a job interview, or when we have lost our composure during an embarrassing experience. However, we actually display a social self during all our interactions—during a conversation with friends, when conducting a meeting at work, as a student in the classroom, and even on a first date. Indeed, although cultural norms for what is appropriate may differ, individuals within all cultures present and manage the impression they believe to be appropriate for a particular context.

Few concepts are more fundamental to our understanding of communication than impression management. If individuals did construct a public self constrained by interaction norms, coherent communication would not be possible. Individuals would simply say whatever was on their mind, would enter and leave the conversation at will, and respond (or not respond) randomly to the comments of others. In short, without recognizing and adhering to norms of appropriate communication conduct, the co-construction of meaning would not be possible. The purpose of this entry is to provide the historical background for the concept of impression management and then to integrate the several related theories into a model of impression management goals and strategies.

Historical Background

Remarkably, although impression management is currently considered one of the essential features of communication, it is actually a relatively recent area of interest among communication scholars. Its origin lies in several theories formulated in the 1960s, 1970s, and 1980s by scholars in other areas of the social sciences.

Self-Presentation

The terms *self-presentation* and *strategic self-presentation* were used by Edward Jones and his colleagues to describe their conceptualization of impression management. Scholars in this tradition were psychologists and social psychologists interested in the link between patterns of behavioral displays in public and the psychological motivations behind these displays. The theory of self-presentation is predicated on the assumption that a person's presenting a coherent set of behaviors during interaction will lead others to make certain types of attributions about the person.

These behaviors and associated attributions have been summarized into a typology of five types of attributions, a characteristic strategy that should elicit each attribution, and various tactics to implement that strategy: (1) A person who wants to be perceived as likable or friendly will use the strategy of *ingratiation* and such tactics as displaying positive emotions during interactions, doing favors, giving compliments, and perhaps using self-deprecating humor. (2) A person who wants to be perceived as competent will use the strategy of *self-promotion* and such tactics as telling others about his or her achievements, good deeds, or accomplishments or by displaying plaques and awards for others to see. (3) A person who wants to be perceived as worthy will use the strategy of *exemplification* and such tactics as quietly demonstrating his or her abilities, competence, integrity, or values rather than stating them directly to others.

(4) A person who wants to be perceived as helpless will use the strategy of *supplication* (also called *self-handicapping*) and the tactics of appearing weak or sad to elicit nurturing behavior from others or of claiming lack of knowledge or experience to avoid responsibility for a task. (5) A person who wants to be perceived as powerful or in control will use the strategy of *intimidation* and the tactics of displaying anger or demonstrating the willingness to punish or cause harm to others.

Contemporary researchers have drawn on the theory of strategic self-presentation to examine communication practices in the workplace and the classroom, such as supervisors' and teachers' use of intimidation strategies. Emotion scholars have examined the manipulation of emotion displays such as simulating or intensifying positive or negative emotions to be perceived as likable or powerful. Scholars interested in gender have examined the differential effects of supplication strategies when used by women compared with their use by men in the workplace and in personal relationships. Finally, scholars interested in individual differences in impression motivations or strategies have explored the influence of personality traits such as self-monitoring, need for approval, public self-consciousness, shyness, communication apprehension, and extraversion. Taken together, this research supports the fundamental premise that impressions are strategically managed to elicit certain types of goal-directed attributions suitable for certain contexts. This research also, however, reminds us that if not very carefully managed, behaviors designed to elicit desired attributions can be misperceived, such as when self-promotion strategies elicit, not judgments of competence, but judgments of arrogance, conceit, or self-importance.

Situated Social Identity

The term *situated social identity* originated in sociology with the essays of Erving Goffman. Although he was developing his theory at the same time the social psychologists were developing the theory of strategic self-presentation, he was not concerned with psychological motivations for public displays of behavior. He simply stated that the organizing principle of all social interaction is the coordinated management of social identity, or *face*. Goffman used the metaphor of a play to explain this view of impression management. He argued that when people engage in interaction, they construct and maintain face in much the same way that actors perform their scenes on stage. That is, people prepare for performance in the "back-stage," deliver their lines in the front stage, manipulate their props, and dress according to their role. Other interactants serve as the audience and presumably support the role being performed. Although this metaphor is most obvious in scripted roles such as doctors, nurses, restaurant servers, and teachers, ordinary conversations are performed in much the same way. We prepare public performances in the backstage of our home or apartment; we "costume" ourselves appropriately (sweats for home, jeans for class, slacks or skirts for work) and grab our props on the way out (glasses, wallet/purse, cell phone, and book bag). We deliver our lines when greeting others, when giving emotional support to friends who are distressed, and we laugh at jokes told by others, even when not very funny, to support their face.

Of course performances do not unfold automatically, nor do they always unfold smoothly. Constructing and maintaining face is accomplished through the various strategies known as facework. Facework strategies that prepare for a possible loss of our own face or the face of others are called avoidant or *preventive facework*. For example, we sometimes don't speak up during a conversation or in a meeting to avoid saying something that will discredit us and thereby damage our face. If we do speak, we preface our comments with disclaimers such as "I may be wrong but. . . ." We also try to prevent face loss to other people. We would not likely turn to a person who is trying to make a point during a discussion and say bluntly, "You are very stupid and your idea is dumb." If we have to call a person's face into question, we usually soften the threat by confirming aspects of his or her competence first, for example, "I know that you tried very hard, but. . . ."

Facework strategies that help repair a scene and restore face after it is lost are called *corrective facework*. For example, when we lose face and experience embarrassment, we apologize and try to correct our poor performance (e.g., apologize for spilling our coffee and quickly clean it up). If our face loss is more serious, such as arriving late for an important meeting, we also offer an explanation or account (e.g., "I'm sorry I'm late; I got stuck in traffic"). If another person loses face, we let it pass unnoticed, we accept their account or apology, or we otherwise support their corrective facework efforts. In other words, whether as performer or audience, participants can only continue the scene (i.e., the interaction) when face is maintained or restored.

Several decades after Goffman's initial formulation of face theory, two sociolinguists, Penelope Brown and Stephen Levinson, extended Goffman's notions of face and preventive facework in their formulation of *politeness theory*. According to politeness theory, people have two fundamental human needs: autonomy and validation. These are labeled *negative face* (the desire for autonomy and freedom from imposition) and *positive face* (the desire to be valued and included). Threats to negative and positive face are inherent in interaction. When we ask a favor, make a request, borrow change, or even force a person to answer the phone when we call, we threaten negative face. When we disagree with someone's opinion, criticize their behavior, suggest that we don't like their work or their appearance, we threaten positive face. In order to soften these *face threatening acts*, we use politeness. For example, to soften a threat to negative face such as asking for a ride, we might minimize the imposition by saying that we can be available any time that is convenient, or we might offer to do a favor in return (threatening our own negative face). To soften a threat to positive face such as in the classic dilemma, "does this make me look fat?" we might avoid the threat entirely by saying, "oh, no, you look great," or we might use positive politeness by saying that another outfit is more flattering.

Impression Management Model

The several theories of impression management that have emerged over the past 50 years differ somewhat in their focus and terminology. However, they can be integrated within a hierarchical model of the impression management process. Although specific interactional goals are fluid and emergent, four broad metagoals represent increasingly complex and challenging demands on speakers' impression management competence. At each level, more conscious effort must be directed toward interpreting the situation and enacting appropriate behaviors.

The first metagoal is simply *demonstrating social competence*. When we meet this metagoal, we conduct interactions so smoothly that social identities are formed and sustained without much conscious effort. They are in the background, and the content of the interaction is in the foreground. Interactants interpret situational cues such as status, relational definitions, and episode parameters appropriately and act in accord with these cues. They are willing and able to follow the communication norms, rules, and expectations for the episode(s) and the context. Interactants are mutually competent in displaying deference toward face that characterizes routine interactions.

On occasion, it is necessary to more consciously construct an identity. When giving a public presentation, for example, we are keenly aware that we want to be perceived as prepared, knowledgeable, and poised. When meeting new people or at a social event, we want to be perceived as pleasant, charming, funny, attractive, and so forth. If a pay raise at work is based on the supervisor's evaluation of our competence, we will attempt to construct an impression of being hardworking, productive, conscientious, and loyal. Thus, a second and somewhat more challenging metagoal is *impression construction*. We draw on the skills of interpreting the situation and then enacting the impression management strategies that we assume will create the most suitable impression. Of course the key to continued smooth interaction in these circumstances is the ability to monitor the impression that is created but have enough cognitive resources to also demonstrate basic social competence.

The third and fourth metagoals arise from the fundamental defining feature of social identities. Whether we call them face, face needs, self-presentations, or impressions, they are necessarily and always intangible—they exist only in their performance. The pervasive norm of reciprocity encourages people to be mutually responsive to each other's identity performances—if I support your identity performance, you will return the favor to me, and our interaction will be uneventful. In reality, no performance is perfect, and threats to identity are inevitable. Thus, the third metagoal is called *protecting impression integrity*. Interactants must be attentive to potential threats to a situated identity and must be capable of avoiding or minimizing these threats (both to self and to others).

Skillful use of preventive facework and elaborated politeness strategies can facilitate this need.

When efforts to prevent face loss are not successful, interactants work toward achieving the fourth and most challenging metagoal, *restoring impression integrity*. In order to do this, it is necessary to bracket, or single out, the ongoing interaction in order to reestablish the legitimacy or viability of social identity that has been lost. Restoration strategies might focus on restoring moral character, denying negative intent, or accounting for untoward or inappropriate actions. The offending person might offer a fully developed apology that expresses remorse, an excuse that denies intent or responsibility, or a justification that accepts responsibility but offers extenuating circumstances. Alternatively, if another interactant needs to restore impression integrity, a competent action would be to support his or her restoration attempts.

In sum, impression management is sometimes routine and sometimes strategic, sometimes successful and sometimes not. It is always, however, a fundamental and defining aspect of social interaction.

Sandra Metts

See also Accounts and Account Giving; Facework Theories; Politeness Theory; Social Interaction Theories

Further Readings

Brown, P., & Levinson, S. C. (1987). *Politeness: Some universals in language usage.* Cambridge, UK: Cambridge University Press.

Cupach, W. R., & Metts, S. (1994). *Facework.* Thousand Oaks, CA: Sage.

Domenici, K., & Littlejohn, S. W. (2006). *Facework: Bridging theory and practice.* Thousand Oaks, CA: Sage.

Goffman, E. (1959). *The presentation of self in everyday life.* New York: Doubleday.

Jones, E. E., & Pittman, T. S. (1982). Toward a general theory of strategic self-presentation. In J. Suls (Ed.), *Psychological perspectives on the self* (pp. 231–263). Hillsdale, NJ: Lawrence Erlbaum.

Metts, S., & Grohskopf, E. (2003). Impression management: Goals, strategies, and skills. In J. Greene & B. R. Burleson (Eds.), *Handbook of communication skills* (pp. 357–399). Orlando, FL: Academic Press.

INDIAN *RASA* THEORY

Speculation in classical India concerning the effects of art and language arguably began in a fully developed form with Bharata's *Nātyaśāstra* (composition dates range from 100 BCE to 400 CE). A vital concept in explaining the impact of the dramatic (and later, poetic) arts was the notion of *rasa*. Later writers, such as Abhinavagupta in his commentary (c. 1100 CE) on the *Nātyaśāstra*, expand the range of rasa and aesthetic psychology, making it a more useful theory to explain the aesthetic experiences of certain audiences. The concept of rasa will be detailed here, as well as its connection to issues in communication.

Rasa literally means *taste*—both in the sense of *a* taste and the ability *to* taste some object. Thus, rasa refers to both an experience and an ability. The rasa theory holds that artworks operate by suggesting or exemplifying one of several universal moods or emotions (rasas) in an attending audience. Rasa theory holds that ordinary emotions (*bhāvas*) typically involve a specific agent reacting to a specific situation. These emotions exist primarily as latent impressions (*samskāras*) due to the person's past experience. Our everyday experience of emotion, then, is thoroughly idiosyncratic and centered on an individualized notion of self (*one's own* self, in other words). These changing and everyday emotions are known as fleeting or temporary emotions (*vyabhīcārībhāvas*).

Contrary to these particularized ways of responding to one's exact situation and needs or desires are permanent emotions (*sthāyībhāvas*), which then attain the status of rasa. The former (*sthāyībhāvas*) are the moods that one experiences, and the latter (the rasas) are the moods used in response to some situation or object experienced by some auditor. Eight of these permanent *bhāvas* (*sthāyībhāvas*) are identified by Bharata: pleasure (*rati*), humor (*hāsa*), sorrow (*śôka*), anger (*krodha*), courage (*utsāha*), fear (*bhaya*), disgust (*jugupsā*), and wonder (*vismaya*). These are said to be caused by a subject's reaction to some specific situation containing various causes (*kārana*) and to lead to certain effects (*kārya*) in terms of the bodily reactions of a subject (facial expressions, bodily gestures, etc.).

These signs of emotions are then incorporated into the writing and staging of dramatic artworks.

A sympathetic auditor attends to the artwork and experiences certain emotions. Due to the removal of his or her interests from the aesthetic situation, the audience member does not feel *real* fear, since there is no actual threat to his or her life. This detachment in the aesthetic situation is vital to producing the experience of rasa, universal experiences or moods that transcend everyday, particularized reactions of actual individuals. Bharata lists eight such rasas: the erotic (*śrngāra*), the comic (*hāsya*), the compassionate (*karuna*), the furious (*raudra*), the heroic (*vīra*), the terrible (*bhayā naka*), the odious (*bībhatsa*), and the marvelous (*adbhuta*). Abhinavagupta, in his commentary on Bharata's categories, adds a ninth rasa—the peaceful (*śānta*).

The important factor about all these states (rasas) is that they all occur in the detached and disinterested state engendered by attending to a work of art such as a play. These qualities hit a high point in the culminating *śānta* rasa. For example, in regard to anger (*raudra* rasa), one is not focused on anger toward those threatening one's interests; one feels or experiences the anger of that fictional character. Thus, classical Indian drama tended to ignore modern artistic demands such as the use of realistic and complex characters, naturalism in setting, and realism in plot. Instead, the play was seen as a highly artificial and contrived way to create these rasas in auditors who usually experience emotions (*bhāvas*) as they relate to themselves and their projects. The qualified auditor, one with a "similar heart" (*sahridaya*), is also a vital part to the experiencing of rasas. If the auditor is not prepared for the artwork, or if he or she is focused too much on issues centering on himself or herself, the details of the play will not interact with him or her to form the universal emotion (the rasa). Some classical commentators such as Bhattanayak (10th century CE) discuss the communicative potential of Bharata's rasa theory as *Sadharanikaran* (literarily, "simplification") and emphasize the simplification of the I–other relationship through one's relatively impersonal sharing of the mood or emotion of some portrayed character. Thus, the parallel experience of rasa is not only precipitated by a sympathetic heart (*sahridaya*); it also encourages states of convergence between an agent and other individuals (even fictional ones). This point of decreasing the distance between self and others made rasa theory particularly valuable to Indian approaches to morality.

Rasa theory, especially as discussed by Abhinavagupta, was particularly important because it offered a chance for moral cultivation of the audience. *Moral cultivation* here implies a general improvement in how one relates to his or her self (*Atman*) and emotions. Abhinavagupta was influenced by the monistic strain of thought of *Vedanta*, a traditional school of thought (*darśan*) of classical India. Thus a major concern was in identifying ways to reduce one's belief in one's self being truly separate from other selves and from the objects of one's desires. Instead, the monistic view of *Vedanta* sees one's self (*Atman*) as not identical with one's physical body (or even an individuated soul). Instead, *Vedanta* follows the ancient Indian texts, the *Upaniśads*, and identifies one's self (*Atman*) with the ground of all that appears to be real (*Brahman*). In a real sense, one *is* all things. Thus, rasas are important as aesthetic instances of detachment and disinterestedness, states that are often hard to instantiate when one thinks that one's body and desires are truly the most important parts of the world in which one acts. All the rasas represent nonordinary (*alaukika*), non–individually based emotions. In this rarified or universal form they transcend individual experience and history and stand as a sort of aesthetic experience any auditor can have, as long as the artist has taken care in designing the artwork and as long as the auditor is open to a detached experience of the play qua art object. In a real sense, rasas constitute an experience of self as *Atman*— namely as separated from one's ego-driven desires and individuality.

Rasa theory holds at least three important points for the study of communication. First, the account given by Bharata and Abhinavagupta highly values the audience. Art objects work only insofar as they have a certain sort of interaction with a specific, actual audience. This theme is not far from Aristotelian and modern notions of communication being audience centered and effect driven. The auditor is said to play an important role in the actualizing of rasas. This includes being prepared or open in a certain way, as well as approaching the art object as an art object.

While this may lead one to see some notion of *identification* going on behind the rasa, such identification is tempered by the second point rasa theory makes about communication. Artistic communication in rasa theory occurs only when the auditor is detached and disinterested in the action occurring in the drama. Thus, an auditor does not identify with a character on stage in regard to his or her specific ego needs, but instead experiences the general state of emotion evoked by observing that character. The main identity in such experience is in the mood that is experienced by both the character and the auditor. Rasa theory tends to use the evocation of experience in an audience in a communicative, albeit non-identification-based, fashion.

The third interesting point rasa theory makes concerning communication is that the detached communication that occurs in aesthetic contexts cannot be experienced in everyday communication. Classical rasa theory (that discussed here) was very emphatic about this—interested and individualized experience leads only to the temporary or transient *bhāvas,* not to the experience of a transcendental emotion (i.e., the rasa). Additional theorizing would be needed to extend the detachment and disinterestedness characteristic of the experience of dramatic plays to the interested and attached action of normal life. Thus, aesthetic communication differs from everyday communication from the perspective of rasa theory.

Scott R. Stroud

See also Asian Communication Theory; Emotion and Communication; Hindu Communication Theory

Further Readings

De, S. K. (1963). *Sanskrit poetics as a study of aesthetic.* Berkeley: University of California Press.

Deutsch, E. (1975). *Studies in comparative aesthetics.* Honolulu: University of Hawai'i Press.

Gerow, E. (1997). Indian aesthetics: A philosophical survey. In E. Deutsch & R. Bontekoe (Eds.), *A companion to world philosophies* (pp. 304–323). Oxford, UK: Blackwell.

Kirkwood, W. (1990). Shiva's dance at sundown: Implications of Indian aesthetics for poetics and rhetoric. *Text and Performance Quarterly, 10,* 93–110.

Patnaik, P. (2004). *Rasa in aesthetics.* New Delhi: D. K. Printworld.

Tewari, I. P. (1992). Indian theory of communication. *Communicator: Journal of the Indian Institute of Mass Communication, 27,* 35–38.

Yadava, J. S. (1987). The tenets of *sadharanikaran.* In D. L. Kincaid (Ed.), *Communication theory: Eastern and Western perspectives* (pp. 161–171). San Diego, CA: Academic Press.

INFORMATION PROCESSING

See Cognitive Theories

INFORMATION THEORY

Information theory is the quantitative study of signal transmission. Primarily applicable to information technology and communications engineering, in human communication theory, it serves primarily as a metaphor for linear transmission between human senders and receivers. Although information theory has historical significance, contemporary theories of human communication rarely refer to it directly. Originating in physics, engineering, and mathematics, the theory addresses uncertainty in code systems, message redundancy, noise, channel capacity, and feedback. This entry defines basic concepts from the field, applies these to language and human communication, and summarizes insights about information transmission.

Information is a measure of uncertainty in a system of signals. In a counterintuitive way, information theory states that the higher the information in a system, the greater the uncertainty. This is because more information entails a larger number of states, which decreases clarity. The concept of *entropy* is the starting place for understanding this seemingly contradictory idea.

Entropy, taken from thermodynamics in physics, is the randomness or lack of predictability within a system. Highly entropic situations have little organization, reduced predictability, and therefore great uncertainty. In low-entropy systems, there is more organization, greater predictability, and therefore less uncertainty. Two dice have more entropy than one die, and a die has more entropy than a coin flip. In thermodynamics, as atoms heat up, they "go crazy" and move all over the place in a frantic, entropic system. As they cool off, they slow down, assume a more organized order, and are more predictable. When entropy is high, there is more information; when it is low, there is less.

To grasp this correlation, think of making predictions based on a set of signs. If you worked in a chaotic organization in which so much is going on that you can never tell from one moment to the next what is going to happen, you would be experiencing "too much" information to process and predict outcomes. If the organization is simpler, with fewer variables to keep track of, prediction is easier because the information level would be lower. This is like cracking a code: Complex codes have more information and are harder than simple ones to decipher. A completely predictable situation is said to have *negentropy.* An example of negentropy is that every time you tap a certain place on your knee, your leg jerks. This is a completely predictable situation.

Another way to understand the concept of information is to think of the number of choices you could make in predicting an outcome: the more choices, the lower the predictability, and the greater the information inherent in the system. A complex system has many possible outcomes, choices, or alternatives, while a simple system has fewer. This is why there is more information in throwing a die than in tossing a coin. In the former, you have a 17% chance of being right; in the latter, a 50% chance.

The inverse of information is *redundancy,* which is a measure of predictability in the system. Like information, redundancy is a quantitative measure—the ratio of the entropy to the maximum amount possible in the system. Entropy is maximized when all alternatives are equally possible, as would be the case with a six-sided die. When a die is thrown, all sides have about a 17% chance of landing up. If the die is fixed and has two sides with one dot, there would be about a 35% chance of predicting this outcome, which is a measure of redundancy in the system. With the fake die, there would be more redundancy than with a fair one.

Language is an entropic code system because it consists of a sequence of signals (sounds in oral language, letters in written language, binary digits in information technology). In writing, for example, one letter follows another in a sequence. If the letters appeared completely randomly, there would be 100% relative entropy—the highest possible information. Reading would be very difficult because the reader never could anticipate anything based on what had already been read. In actuality, however, language always has a lot of redundancy built in. In English, for example, the letter *q* is almost always followed by *u*. The article *a* is always followed by a noun or an adjective, and by the time a reader gets to the middle of a sentence, he or she can predict fairly well how the sentence will end. This kind of redundancy gives the language organization and patterning.

If language were 100% redundant, there would be no flexibility in how it could be used. Once the first letter was written, everything would follow automatically with complete predictability. It is clear, then, that language and other codes (including computer codes) should have some entropy and some redundancy. English, for example, has an average of about 50% relative entropy. Linguists and code breakers first look for the redundancy in the code to begin to decipher it.

Information and redundancy are very useful in designing transmission systems. Information theory does not address the meaning of a message, but it does provide equations that help engineers figure out how to get signals efficiently from one place to another. The basic model of information transmission appeared in 1949 in the classic text *The Mathematical Theory of Communication,* by Claude Shannon and Warren Weaver. This simple model depicts a communication process of eight parts: (1) source, (2) message, (3) transmitter, (4) signal, (5) channel, (6) receiver, (7) destination, and (8) noise. The source sends a set of signals from a transmitter through a channel to a destination through a receiver. Noise is interference that can disrupt this process. The goal is for the message to get to the destination efficiently and accurately: The signal should arrive with sufficient fidelity to be deciphered.

In live human interaction, one person (the source) sends a set of oral signals (sounds) through the airwaves (channel) to the second person (destination) via that person's ears (receiver). If there is a lot of physical noise, this oral message may not get through. In terms of electronic communication, a message may go through several links of signals and channels before reaching a final destination. Noise can occur anywhere in this complex transmission system, which is why the signal must have a certain amount of redundancy, which, indeed, does counteract noise. Further, the channel must have a certain capacity to carry the signal efficiently. *Channel capacity* is technically defined as the maximum amount of information that can be sent over a channel in a particular amount of time. The increasing demands on broadband systems to carry large amounts of information through the Internet suggest the importance of channel capacity. Transmission is considered efficient if the amount of information does not exceed channel capacity and there is enough redundancy in the signal to counteract the noise the signal may encounter in route.

Stephen W. Littlejohn

See also Cybernetics; System Theory

Further Readings

Broadhurst, A. R., & Darnell, D. K. (1965). An introduction to cybernetics and information theory. *Quarterly Journal of Speech, 51,* 442–453.

Krippendorff, K. (1975). Information theory. In G. Hanneman & W. McEwen (Eds.), *Communication and behavior* (pp. 351–389). Reading, MA: Addison-Wesley.

Shannon, C., & Weaver, W. (1949). *The mathematical theory of communication.* Urbana: University of Illinois Press.

INFORMATIZATION

Informatization, first coined in Japan in the late 1960s as *johoka,* is now used with at least the following three meanings: (1) intentional policies or strategies using information technologies to promote socioeconomic development; (2) the penetration of modern information and communication technologies into government, industry, and the home, in the broadest sense; and (3) the development of communication technologies, the increase of information flows, and the diffusion of mass media and education among the general public.

Informatization Policies

In the late 1950s and early 1960s, futurology was popular, especially in the United States and Japan, and many social scientists and engineers attempted to predict the future based on some scientific or pseudoscientific methods. The important outcome of this intellectual fad was the birth of many new future-oriented concepts rather than futurology itself. Daniel Bell's "post-industrial society," Alvin Toffler's "third wave," Fritz Machlup's "knowledge economy," Tadao Umesao's "information industries," and Yoneji Masuda's "information society" are good examples.

If the information society is the society of the future and the information industry is the industry of the future, it would behoove us to promote *informatization*. Based on this idea, the Industrial Structure Council of the Japanese Ministry of International Trade and Industry started informatization policies in 1965 as the Industrial Structure Reform Policy. The Japanese government not only provided measures to help computer and telecommunication industries but also conducted many social experiments using new information and communication machines such as videotext, high-speed facsimile, and TV telephone.

These attempts had a significant impact on neighboring countries such as South Korea, Taiwan, Hong Kong, and Singapore. As the effects of informatization policies in these countries became obvious in the 1990s, similar policies were also adopted in Malaysia, Thailand, mainland China, and India.

In contrast, the Latin American and Eastern European countries, whose industrial levels were about the same as the East Asian countries mentioned above, were under the strong influence of neo-Marxist "dependency" theories; as a result, the idea of informatization was rejected for being too ideological. It was seen as a plot to accelerate efficiency, control labor, and maximize profits for the ruling classes. No matter which class informatization benefits, it seems that, just as industrialization in the 19th century caused industrial gaps, the acceptance or rejection of informatization in the 20th century causes a "digital gap" among different areas of the world.

What Caused Informatization?

There are contrasting views regarding the nature of technology. One is that new technologies emerge almost accidentally, as in the case of a genius's intuition. The other is that new technologies "are developed," reflecting the needs of the time. Actually, both of these views are true. It is well known that electromagnetism, which made the telegraph possible, was discovered accidentally when a magnetic coil dropped from Hans Christian Oersted's desk near a compass on the floor. As developed by Samuel Morse, however, this technology solved many serious problems of long distance international trade such as that between Europe and East Asia. In other words, this kind of technology was urgently needed by international traders of that time.

As another example, the idea of electronic digital computers (ENIAC) was born during World War II, and its purpose was to calculate trajectories and raise the hit rate of cannons. After the war, computers were first used in data processing in large organizations. This was followed by the penetration of computers into a variety of areas that the original developers had never imagined. When the transistor was invented at Bell Laboratories in the United States, the inventors had no idea how it could be used because it was very large and expensive. It was the Japanese Sony engineers who gave them an answer by making it smaller and inexpensive.

As these examples indicate, basic technologies that promoted informatization were not born out of carefully laid plans. These technologies, however, were refined and applied to many areas where they were potentially needed. But why informatization now? Abraham Maslow's "hierarchy of human needs" and Ronald Inglehart's "post-industrial values" are often referred to as having a possible answer to this question. According to these theories, human interests and concerns shift from basic needs such as food and security, once those needs are met, to "higher needs," including those of entertainment, news, information, and knowledge.

James Beniger offered an answer to the same question from a different perspective. According to Beniger, technologies are roughly divided into two categories: (1) technology to accelerate speed and enhance efficiency and (2) technology to control machines. Computers and information technologies belong to the second category, and they were needed to control the former type of technologies that had developed to a dangerous level.

A Driving Force of Social Change

Informatization, in its broadest definition, refers to the development of, increase in, and diffusion of information throughout society. Informatization processes cannot help but impact society in a variety of ways, and scholars of informatization study the effects of informatization processes on social change. Many historical changes—from the decline of religion to the rise of nationalism, capitalism, and rationalism—have been linked to informatization. The degree to which newspapers promoted democracy and the mechanisms by which the diffusion of popular novels, television, and the telephone promoted individualism are some of the phenomena studied by scholars, across disciplines, who research informatization processes.

The study of informatization also involves potentially negative social impacts. Some modern information and telecommunication technologies, including the Internet, rental videos, on-demand TV services, and the mobile telephone, have been accused of splitting up the family, creating "excessive individualism," and causing increases in divorce, crime, and mental illness. Whether the Internet promotes or hinders democracy is an important subject of informatization research.

Youichi Ito

See also Asian Communication Theory; New Media Theory

Further Readings

Beniger, J. R. (1986). *The control revolution.* Cambridge, MA: Harvard University Press.

Duff, A. S. (2000). *Information society studies.* London: Routledge.

Freeman, C. (1987). The case for technological determinism. In R. Finnegan, G. Salaman, & K. Thompson (Eds.), *Information technology* (pp. 5–18). Sevenoaks, UK: Hodder & Stoughton.

Ito, Y. (1991). Birth of *joho shakai* and *johoka* concepts in Japan and their diffusion outside Japan. *Keio Communication Review, 13,* 3–12.

Ito, Y. (1991). *Johoka* as a driving force of social change. *Keio Communication Review, 12,* 33–58.

Masuda, Y. (1981). *The information society.* Washington, DC: World Future Society.

Slack, J. D., & Fejes, F. (Eds.). (1987). *The ideology of the information age.* Norwood, NJ: Ablex.

Webster, F. (2002). The information society revised. In L. Lievrouw & S. Livingstone (Eds.), *Handbook of new media* (pp. 22–33). Thousand Oaks, CA: Sage.

INOCULATION THEORY

Persuasion research in the 1950s found that providing two sides of an issue seemed to create greater resistance to later arguments. To explain this phenomenon, William McGuire and his colleagues a decade later began to explore ways in which messages might inoculate recipients against belief attacks. By 1964, he proposed the original inoculation theory. This theory says that persuasive message recipients become resistant to attitudinal attacks in the same way that bodies become immunized from viral attacks. A weak dose of the virus activates the immune system. Likewise, challenges to attitudes, beliefs, and behaviors make them more resistant to change if the exposure to counterviews is given in weakened, small doses. The theory is relevant because unchallenged beliefs can be swayed if the holder is not used to defending them. A weak dose of a counterargument will cause the belief to become more resistant. In the medical venue, the approach has been more effective than the supportive treatment in producing resistance. In the persuasive venue, presenting arguments supporting beliefs is less effective than exposing the receiver to a weak attack on the belief.

In his first experiments, McGuire selected cultural truisms, or beliefs rarely challenged, such as brushing teeth. When considering expanding the boundaries of inoculation theory, he reasoned that because people tend to avoid arguments that oppose their views on controversial issues, almost all beliefs are protected from counterattack. John B. Pryor and Thomas M. Steinfatt offered an opposing view for extending inoculation's boundaries beyond cultural truisms in observing that almost no beliefs are completely protected. If one rarely exposed one's beliefs to threats, those beliefs could be changed if attacked by a particular virus, as it were. Pryor and Steinfatt's rationale propelled the investigation of inoculation into controversial topics.

McGuire found that a passive reception of a message (requiring participants to read a section in which counterarguments were mentioned and rebuked) had a greater effect in making attitudes resistant to persuasion than did active reception (a writing assignment in which subjects explained their responses to the counterarguments). Participants in the reading conditions had more independent action in their immunizing treatments; that is, they had to work harder in the reading treatment than in the writing treatment and generate their own independent arguments in support of the original beliefs.

Subsequent research has shown that active, passive, and mixed refutational conditions can be effective in inoculation, but their effects are not necessarily the same and depend on other variables. Exposing a person to weakened, defense-stimulating forms of argument seems to be more effective in inoculation than exposing an individual to arguments supporting the individual's belief. This happens because threat provides an explicit forewarning of a challenge, enabling the recipient to prepare counterarguments. People prefer, however, to inoculate the beliefs of others by using bolstering strategies, even though these have been shown to be less effective than counterarguing strategies.

Inoculation is often used in courtrooms. An attorney says, "You're going to hear the prosecution call Mrs. Smith mean, evil, a terrible mother, and a poor member of society, but this is not true, as I will show you over the next couple of weeks." When the prosecutor stands up and states anything close to what the defense attorney has claimed he will, the jury is prepared, thinking he is acting exactly the way the defense said he would. This gives the jurors a way to ignore or even discount the prosecutor's arguments.

In the 1990s, long-distance phone service companies were hypercompetitive, trying to keep customers by inoculating them. An AT&T ad began by stressing that other companies are going to try to steal you from AT&T. An AT&T customer gets a call from "another phone company" boasting how much better its plan is over that of AT&T.

The customer is adamant about not being impressed.

Inoculation is used in political advertisements as well. Candidate A's ad might begin by saying that Candidate B is attacking him, then citing three or four things that candidate B is asserting against Candidate A, all presented in such a way as to activate the viewer's defense mechanisms for Candidate A.

The communicator with the goal to make attitudes, beliefs, and behaviors resistant to change should first warn the audience of a prevalent counterargument toward the attitude. The warning serves to activate the defense component. When individuals' beliefs are threatened, they immediately begin to generate defenses. Without this, optimal resistance will not be achieved. The next step is to make a weak attack. The communicator must remember that too strong a dose would overwhelm the audience member's immune system, as it were. The final step in the inoculation process is to encourage passive defense by generating a defensive response. The recipient's belief becomes strong only by doing the defensive work. In theory, when the message recipient listens to the weak attack, he or she will think of refutations for the attack. Like antibodies against a disease, the refutations form the foundation for attacking stronger arguments in the future.

Joshua A. Compton and Michael W. Pfau have pointed out that inoculation research proliferated in the 21st century. The role of threat, counterarguments in tandem with other theoretical concepts, involvement (the salience of an attitude to a subject), and the role of time in resistance are being explored. Research findings are leading to a keener awareness of how inoculation operates and to practical uses in public relations, marketing, and other realms.

Don Rodney Vaughan

See also Attitude Theory; Learning and Communication; Persuasion and Social Influence Theories

Further Readings

Compton, J. A., & Pfau, M. W. (2005). Inoculation theory of resistance to influence at maturity: Recent progress in theory development and application and suggestions for future research. In P. J. Kalbfleisch

(Ed.), *Communication yearbook 29* (pp. 97–145). Mahwah, NJ: Lawrence Erlbaum.

McGuire, W. J. (1964). Inducing resistance to persuasion: Some contemporary approaches. In L. Berkowitz (Ed.), *Advances in experimental social psychology.* New York: Academic Press.

McGuire, W. J., & Papageorgis, W. (1961). The relative efficacy of various types of prior belief-defense in producing immunity against persuasion. *Journal of Abnormal and Social Psychology, 62,* 327–337.

INQUIRY PROCESSES

Inquiry is a process of developing knowledge through research and theory building. A theory results from an ongoing process involving research and the refinement of theory. The general process of inquiry, branches of inquiry, the research and publication work that scholars undertake, communities of scholarship, and the process of theory development all contribute to an understanding of the nature of inquiry.

Nature of Inquiry

When scholars attempt to answer questions in a systematic way, they are engaged in inquiry. Many variations of inquiry exist, but all follow three sets of related activities—asking questions, making observations, and forming theories.

At base, all inquiry begins with interesting *questions.* What do we want to find out? *Questions of definition* seek clarification on concepts that delineate one thing from another—what something is and what it is not. *Questions of fact* ask about properties, connections, and characteristics. These questions form the basis for observations of how things appear in our experience. *Questions of value* look at the beauty, utility, or ethics of a set of ideas, experiences, or practices.

Questions determine what kind of *observations* to undertake, and there are many variations of observation. Some researchers look at behavior, some at self-reported feelings and thoughts, and some at records and discourse. Researchers may conduct observations firsthand, by doing experiments, by using instruments, by talking to people, or by careful reading and analysis.

The third part of inquiry is forming answers to questions, which is really the process of *theorizing.* Scholars carefully analyze their observations, interpret what they mean, and describe or explain what they saw in answer to their questions. Once patterns become apparent across situations, tentative theories can be created.

The three parts of inquiry—questions, observations, and theories—are intimately tied to one another in a circular way. Questions guide observations, observations form the basis of theories, theories help structure observations, and theories and observations suggest new questions.

Science, Humanities, Social Science

Three branches of scholarship primarily contribute to communication theory. These are science, humanities, and social science. *Science* is that branch of knowledge that relies mostly on objectivity, standardization, and quantification. Scientific research must be replicable, meaning that all observers using the same methods should come up with the same results. Scientists assume the world has a potentially observable structure and rely on methods of discovering this structure. Science is therefore mostly interested in nature.

Humanities is the branch of knowledge associated with subjectivity, or individual interpretation. Events may be understood in a number of ways, and scholars try to establish interpretations that make sense or are useful in answering certain kinds of questions. While science concentrates on what is "out there" in the world, humanities emphasizes what is "in here" within the interpreter. The humanities also are associated with human experience and human products such as literature, history, and philosophy, in which art, experience, and values are at stake.

Although often considered science, in reality the *social sciences* blend aspects of science and humanities. Because human social life is the object of social science, both objectivity and subjectivity are included. Social scientists who believe that social behavior can be observed objectively emphasize the scientific aspects of this branch; those who believe that individual subjective response is key emphasize humanistic methods. In fact, much of social science combines both—objective observation of patterns, followed by subjective interpretation of these patterns.

Some scholars study natural, biological, and behavioral aspects of communication, and they use scientific methods to do so. These researchers would feel quite comfortable characterizing themselves as "scientists." Other researchers are more interested in discourse and media and look at these much as literature scholars or art critics analyze written artifacts. This group would feel quite comfortable in the world of humanities. Recognizing that the discipline of communication benefits from a mélange of approaches, most scholars in the field are most comfortable referring to communication as a social science.

Research and Publication

Inquiry follows a standard path across academic disciplines. Beginning from a point of curiosity, the scholar pursues inquiry into something significant in his or her own life, something previously studied in the literature, a topic of conversation within a group of scholars, or questions raised by students. Since most scholars have advanced degrees, they may begin a line of work with the dissertation or other work started in graduate school. Once established, a professional scholar must continue a research program in order to get pay raises, tenure, and promotion. As well, grant money, travel funds, and recognitions and awards are incentives for ongoing inquiry.

Inquiry is never a solitary process but relies heavily on interaction within the scholarly community. Often professors work on ideas with students in the classroom or with graduate students interested in similar subject matters. Scholars frequently refine their ideas in convention papers presented to groups of colleagues at meetings and later submitted for publication, usually in academic journals. Peer reviewers provide additional input that can help refine questions, observations, and theories. Indeed, the peer-review process is vital to the advancement of inquiry in all fields. Often papers are critiqued publicly by convention panel respondents and later by journal commentators who read and critique the manuscript for possible publication.

In the world of research and theory, two forms of publication are valued most—the journal article and the scholarly book. A journal article can appear in any of a number of peer-reviewed national and regional journals. Many journals publish articles relevant to communication inquiry, including the prestigious *Communication Theory*, published by the International Communication Association. Within the long list of highly regarded journals are, for example, *Human Communication Research*, *Critical Studies in Media Communication*, and *Communication Monographs*. Since only the best articles are published in journals of this stature, these outlets showcase leading research and theory at any given moment in the field. Scholars subscribe to paper or online versions of the journals most relevant to their own work and rely on these to provide information about the latest advancements in their areas of interest.

No substitute for rigorous peer review exists. The evaluation of inquiry is subjective, and consensus is still the primary gauge of quality in a field of study. Scholars do disagree about whether a particular line of research and theory building is worthy, so, at least in the social sciences, the establishment of universal consensus is impossible. It is possible and appropriate, however, to ask whether a line of work has credibility within a particular community of scholars. Lines of inquiry and resulting theories judged generally interesting, useful, or valid over time become the standards for scholars engaged in those areas of work.

Much scholarly work is published in larger monograph form, usually in academic books published by university and academic presses. Indeed, many important theories of communication have come out in this form. Another common and helpful kind of book consists of edited volumes of several chapters related to a topic. The book editor invites various well-known scholars to write chapters on their own work, and these summaries can be helpful for students and researchers to get a sense of the state of the art in regard to the subjects covered by the book.

Communities of Scholarship

Although the processes outlined in the previous sections are nearly universal, they belie the complexity and variation of work within a field like communication. The details of inquiry vary significantly from one group of scholars to another. In this section, three lines of difference that distinguish among traditions of inquiry in communication are examined.

Differences of Focus

The first line of difference deals with objects on which the researcher–theorist chooses to focus. Typically, there are three—individuals, social relations, and texts. A scholar's focus determines in large measure what he or she observes, and this is primarily determined by the kinds of things the scholar finds most fascinating.

Some are intrigued by *individual human behavior* and focus on the individual communicator. These scholars are curious about why people behave as they do; how people think; and how thoughts, feelings, and emotions relate to actions. This kind of inquiry consists largely of research based on observation and measurement of behavior. Individually oriented communication scholars spend a lot of time classifying behavior into types and establishing causal links between various antecedents and behavioral outcomes. Trait theories that provide typologies of individual behavior provide a good example of this kind of work.

Some scholars are more interested in *interpersonal patterns of interaction* and relationships among individuals. Here the focus is on connections between individuals, not so much on individual behavior itself. Such work often observes dyads, groups, organizations, and communities. These scholars notice different types of relationships, observe patterns of mutual behavior, and look for system connections. Indeed, a body of work in relational theories illustrates this focus.

A third focus in communication inquiry is *text* or *discourse*. Although nonverbal forms can be a kind of text, this focus usually consists of language and messages. Such scholars look at what people say and how messages are used in practical situations. Many theories of communication result from this focus. One example is conversation analysis, which explains how people organize their talk through a series of turns.

Differences of Method

Inquiry also differs in terms of how observations are made. For some, observation is a matter of objective measurement, and for others it is subjective interpretation. This difference reflects the distinction made earlier in this entry between science and humanities. This is a difference in how scholars work and what counts as data in their research. Should data be quantitative and objective, or should it be a qualitative reading or judgment of a situation or text? Does the scholar rely on an instrument that detects some quality, or is the scholar himself or herself the instrument? All researchers acknowledge that some interpretation is necessary, but they disagree on how primary the interpretation is to the inquiry process. Interviews are often used as a source of data in communication research. Here the researcher asks subjects questions about their experience and then interprets their qualitative (not quantitative) responses.

For example, much inquiry into interpersonal communication relies on experiments in which test conditions are set up in a laboratory and outcome measurements taken to identify causal patterns in various interpersonal situations. On the other hand, much media research relies on careful examination and interpretation of the media environment.

Differences of Value

Inquiry divides along a third line as well—the degree to which scholars express their values in their work. Two general schools capture this fracture point. The first is a generally *descriptive* approach, in which the scholar aims to describe and explain what is observed without evaluative comment; the second is *critical* in stating what is good and/or bad about what is observed. The descriptive approach sees itself as neutral in observation, while the critical approach projects an expressly political perspective. Most academics today would not claim that some work is objectively neutral and other work is value-laden, but instead acknowledge that not all scholars acknowledge their values explicitly. Notice the difference, for example, between ethnography, which aims to describe cultural patterns, and critical ethnography, which aims to cast light on the oppressive structures within certain cultural patterns.

Inquiry Over Time

Inquiry is a process, meaning that it is dynamic. Scholars do not just conduct one inquiry or single study to discover the truth of a matter and then move to a new subject. Instead, they continually evolve their work through ongoing inquiry that refines questions, observations, and theoretical statements. You can see this clearly in the research/theory literature in any aspect of the field. Ideas change, which leads to fresh research and new ways of thinking about the subject. Thus, knowledge within a topical area grows and changes through ongoing inquiry. This change occurs in several ways.

The first is *incremental growth*. Here knowledge is added piece by piece. Over time, more questions are asked, more observations are made, and theories expand in number, each helping to explain a different aspect of the process. These theories are not really competitive, but each offers a different bit that adds to how we can understand a topic. In incremental growth, knowledge expands piece by piece. Attitude theory is a good example of incremental growth. From the 1940s through the 1970s, understandings of attitude and attitude change grew incrementally as scholars understood more and more about attitudes.

The second way in which the knowledge base changes is through *developmental growth*. Here individual theories become increasingly refined and exacting. They improve over time in their power, validity, and utility. A theory that began as a simple idea expands and grows to explain more variables and provide a more complete picture of the topic. The theory of the coordinated management of meaning is a good example. Beginning with a relatively small set of concepts, the theory has developed over the years to include a wide variety of ideas that expand the theory's usefulness for explaining many communication phenomena.

The third means of change is *canonical development*. The canon consists of the predominant lines of work and resulting theories at a given time. The canon, or set of theories in vogue, expresses the state of knowledge during this period in the history of the field. But the canon changes as new theories are admitted and old ones decline. Thus knowledge changes as the canon changes. Media effects studies offer a perfect example of canonical development. Once restricted to theories of how media affect audiences, the canon has shifted a number of times over the years to (a) how audiences use and affect media, (b) how media create communities, and (c) how media become personal and social tools.

Of course, knowledge typically changes in all three ways simultaneously. These three processes taken together characterize the normal course of

events, but sometimes a new discovery upsets this normal course of change by shifting the entire perspective on how we view the subject matter. This is change by *revolution*. After a period of stability in which knowledge grew incrementally, developmentally, and canonically, this entire course of events is called into question, perhaps by a new line of inquiry, that requires a complete transformation in thinking. This happened in critical theory. During much of the 20th century, critical theory was based on Marxist ideas, which posited preexisting oppressive social structures tied intimately to class and economics. However, toward the end of the century, cultural studies began to look more closely at how oppressive structures change and evolve in a dynamic power struggle among communities, which transformed the nature of social critique.

Stephen W. Littlejohn

See also Metatheory; Theory; Traditions of Communication Theory

Further Readings

Kuhn, T. S. (1970). *The structure of scientific revolutions.* Chicago: University of Chicago Press.

Littlejohn, S. W. (2007). The nature and evaluation of theory. In B. B. Whaley & W. Sampter (Eds.), *Explaining communication: Contemporary theories and exemplars* (pp. 1–14). Mahwah, NJ: Lawrence Erlbaum.

Littlejohn, S. W., & Foss, K. A. (2008). *Theories of human communication* (9th ed.; especially pp. 7–10). Belmont, CA: Wadsworth.

Miller, G. R., & Nicholson, H. (1976). *Communication inquiry.* Reading, MA: Addison Wesley.

Snow, C. P. (1964). *The two cultures and a second look.* Cambridge, UK: Cambridge University Press.

Institutional Theories of Organizational Communication

Institutions are socially constructed frameworks composed of conventions that prescribe behavior, cognition, and communication in given contexts.

Institutions are maintained or changed by people who act and interact with each other. Examples of institutions include long-established organizations such as universities or hospitals but also include widespread practices such as marriage or voting and ways of working and interacting, such as markets, governments, and the professions. Institutions are important to organizations because they become taken for granted, transcend and penetrate particular organizations, and are constituted by normative systems and cognitive understandings that give enduring meaning to social exchange, thus enabling a self-reproducing social order. Thus, institutions may be thought of as the foundations of organizations. This entry explores the history of the institutional approach to organizational communication, the communicative nature of institutions, and the key concepts used in institutional theory and analysis. The process of institutionalization is also discussed.

History of the Institutional Approach

The institutional school of thought has its roots in the work of the 19th-century German sociologist Max Weber, who compared and contrasted historical modes of organization in China, Rome, and Germany. Weber defined institutions as involuntary membership associations, such as the church or the state, to which individuals were permanently attached by virtue of their birth.

The thread of the institutional school was picked up in the 1940s by Philip Selznick, whose studies of leadership and administration in the Tennessee Valley Authority and local communities showed how organized efforts were constrained by local, stronger forces. *Co-optation* is the term Selznick used to describe how local community institutions found ways to express themselves in spite of the power and resources of the federal government. In the 1950s, Peter Berger picked up the concept in his work outlining how social change had eroded traditional institutions and left the modern person with a seemingly rudderless existence. Berger drew on the work of the German philosopher Arnold Gehlen, who viewed institutions as a human extension of *instincts* and was concerned with *deinstitutionalization* and the consequent drift of modern people away from tradition.

The institutional school of organizational sociology arose in the late 1970s, led by John Meyer and Brian Rowan's observation that much of an organization's structure was a symbolic reflection of external forces such as markets and laws governing hiring practices. They coined the term *rational myth* to describe an untested shared belief about the rational functioning of organizations. Paul DiMaggio and Walter Powell supplemented this perspective on organizations with their observation that organizations were constrained by the fieldwide forces of *coercive, mimetic,* and *normative isomorphism.* These are structural parallels (isomorphism) based on force (coercion), imitation (mimetic), and rules and conventions (norms), which resulted in recognizable similarities in fields of organizations. DiMaggio and Powell offered a hook for communication scholars in their recognition of the role of increasing information requirements as a force shaping organizations. Ultimately, the institutional approach to organizational communication emphasizes the role of messages external to organizations as impinging on the intentions and behaviors of actors within organizations.

Distinctiveness of the Institutional Approach

An institutional approach to organizational communication emphasizes several aspects in contrast to micro, intraorganizational approaches. First, an institutional approach directs attention to formal communication, defined as the media of written codes. These include laws at district, regional, local, state, federal, and international levels of jurisdiction. Formal codes also include lawlike policies enacted by nongovernmental associations that establish procedures and unquestioned practices. Although not enforceable as government policies, the codes of professional and business associations have weight that can sometimes be the basis of governmental policies. Formal media also include contracts that stipulate the activities of parties that include corporate entities and their members. Such contracts may be explicit agreements between legal entities, such as those that stipulate products or services to be provided to or delivered according to certain terms and in exchange for certain considerations. The contracts may also stipulate how individuals shall perform services. In both cases it is the legal codes that give organizations their lives well independent of their members. Rule-guided behavior may be taken for granted and may not be available as explicit messages or even as social objects that managers can isolate.

An institutional approach also requires attention to the boundaries of organizations. One reason that interest in organizational identity and identification runs so high in the early 21st century is that individuals move quite freely across organizational boundaries. Thus, their attachment to organizations is problematic. An institutional view observes that specific organizations' boundaries may well be defined better by external (macro) rather than internal (micro) forces. Nominally boundaries are defined by membership, activity, and space. However, the activities of many organizations, especially service and knowledge-based organizations, appear to be losing their distinctiveness. Moreover, with the digital revolution, space is hardly a boundary for many organizations. Thus, industry-wide norms and regulations may be better clues to what bounds particular organizations and the careers of their members.

An institutional perspective on organizations also directs attention to new levels of analysis. In addition to the traditional individual, group, and organizational levels of analysis, the institutional perspective identifies industry, sector, region, and national levels. The institutional perspective observes many commonalities among organizations within sectors. In addition to aggregated levels of organization such as the aforementioned, the institutional point of view identifies professions, trade associations, unions, and accrediting agencies as having influence across whole sectors of organizations. The institutional perspective therefore sees opportunities to identify patterns and trends across organizations that would be unapparent when studied on an organization-by-organization basis.

In addition, an institutional perspective offers an opportunity to understand the role of history, change, and time in the life of organizations. Many studies of organizations are based on observations of a very short duration in the lives of organizations. Responses to single surveys or observations of events over the period of as long as a year still remain a very short period in terms of the duration of institutions. The institutional view emphasizes the role that slow change plays in the lives of organizations and

their members. Even the interpretation of time within organizations, though realized in the interaction of individuals, would find replication in other similar organizations.

An institutional approach may seem to be one that would neglect or lack focus for individual behavior. But by contrast, such a view also offers a greater understanding of agency. By observing behavior in multiple organizations, one gains a new view of individual behavior, its patterns, causes, and consequences. If persons in apparently separate organizational locations are simultaneously communicating in similar ways, for similar purposes, we may find common causes for that behavior. On the other hand, if individuals behave differently across similar organizations, we can isolate the circumstances that make agency and creativity unique. Thus, the focus of the institutional lens is organizational but not on individual organizations.

Finally, an institutional view offers an opportunity to study the way cultures external to organizations are manifest within organizations. While the vast majority of communication studies are based in North America, few control for the effects of culture external to the organization. Although valid arguments can be made for the creation of culture in the very micro processes of organizational life, we know also that beliefs have lives of their own well beyond an organization, and that these also have an influence on what happens within an organization.

One critique of an institutional view is that it cannot be distinguished from a *cultural* approach, also emphasizing commonly held beliefs and values. But the institutional lens recognizes and attends to a particular type of constellation of values and beliefs—those that contribute to the creation of cultural schemes defining means–ends relationships and standardizing systems of control over activities and people. Thus we might say that the institutional approach is consistent with a cultural approach but in particular is focused on rational beliefs and rules about means and ends.

Key Concepts in the Institutional Approach

The implication of this emphasis on rational rules for organizational communication scholarship is that it identifies a particular kind of message. The relationship of any particular organization to institutions in its environment has been described as a particular type of *message flow*. Organizations are characterized by interactive flows of messages that allow them to manage their members, to structure themselves, and to coordinate their activities. The process of managing an organization's relationship with its external environment of other organizations, regulators, competitors, customers, and diffuse media may be thought of as *institutional positioning* via the use of *institutional rhetoric*, or messages that offer specific interpretations of social issues of importance to the organization's survival and success. Examples of institutional rhetoric include corporate statements of social responsibility, policies on the environment, or other broad, often indirect marketing campaigns aimed at diffuse audiences.

The institutional view results in several propositions that may guide organizational communication research. First, communication processes like the message flows mentioned above sustain institutions. That is, organizational practices reinforce institutions. Second, communication aligns organizations with institutions. Organizations can choose to align themselves with certain institutions via media relations, hiring practices, or employment polices. Third, institutions operate in organizing through formal communication. Fourth, the success of boundary-spanning communication between organizations depends in part on the presence of shared institutions, such as trade associations, markets, or professions. Fifth, institutional hierarchy, that is, the pattern of values and priorities in a particular organizational field, is manifested in the organizing behaviors of managers and participants in particular organizations.

Institutionalization

Communication scholars have also developed contributions to understanding how institutions arise. The prevailing view is that institutions arise through a recursive process very similar to *structuration*, which is the accumulation of past practices and previous understandings that set conditions for future action. Thus one way of thinking about institutional creation is as *sedimented* social habits. Once formed, the habits guide future social action without the conscious intent of actors.

A more detailed view involves a four-stage process model of institutionalization. *Encoding* involves individuals' internalizing rules and interpretations of behavior appropriate for particular settings, which can occur through simple socialization but might also involve learning formal rules or customary work procedures. The second moment involves *enacting* the coded script for behavior. Importantly, the actors may or may not be conscious of the reasoning behind the action, for they may be simply following a customary way of doing business. In the third moment in institutionalization, scripts may be *revised* or *replicated* as individuals reenact previously learned routines or resist a routine and revise action. Without considerable external support or pressure, revision is typically less likely than replication. The fourth and final moment of institutionalization involves *objectification* and *externalization* of the patterned behaviors and interactions produced, wherein particular actions are disassociated from particular historical circumstances. The patterned behaviors, or what we refer to as institutions, acquire a normative, unchanging quality, and their relationship to the interests of specific actors becomes obscured. In this way, institutions become an important but hidden context for organizational communication.

John C. Lammers

See also Actor–Network Theory; Community of Practice; Corporate Colonization Theory; Critical Theory; Group and Organizational Structuration Theory; Organizational Communication Theories; Structuration Theory; System Theory

Further Readings

Barley, S., & Tolbert, P. (1997). Institutionalization and structuration: Studying the links between action and institution. *Organization Studies, 18,* 93–117.

Deetz, S. (1992). *Democracy in an age of corporate colonization: Developments in communication and the politics of everyday life.* Albany: State University of New York Press.

Greenwood, R., Oliver, C., Sahlin, K., & Suddaby, R. (Eds.). (2008). *The Sage handbook of organizational institutionalism.* Thousand Oaks, CA: Sage.

Lammers, J. C., & Barbour, J. B. (2006). An institutional theory of organizational communication. *Communication Theory, 16,* 356–377.

McPhee, R. D., & Zaug, P. (2000). The communicative constitution of organizations: A framework for explanation. *Electronic Journal of Communication, 10.* Retrieved July 30, 2008, from http://shadow.cios .org:7979/journals/EJC/010/1/01017.html#Figure

Scott, W. R. (2001). *Institutions and organizations* (2nd ed.). Thousand Oaks, CA: Sage.

Taylor, J. R., & Van Every, E. J. (2000). *The emergent organization: Communication as its site and surface.* Mahwah, NJ: Lawrence Erlbaum.

INTEGRATED THREAT THEORY

See Conflict Communication Theories

INTERACTION ADAPTATION THEORY

Interaction adaptation theory (IAT) was developed by Judee Burgoon, Lesa Stern, and Leesa Dillman. Interested in the ways in which people adapt to one another in dyads, the research team, led by Burgoon, realized that many of the theories in this area did not attend to a broad array of communication behaviors and functions, and the theories often undervalued the effect of one person's behavior on another person during everyday encounters. To address these concerns, Burgoon, Stern, and Dillman developed IAT and formally introduced their theory in 1995. IAT built on previous theoretical work on interpersonal adaptation and dyadic interaction processes, particularly expanding Burgoon's expectancy violations theory, and provided a more comprehensive explanation of interpersonal adaptation by incorporating a stronger emphasis on biological and sociological influences. IAT is predicated on nine guiding principles and five fundamental concepts.

Guiding Principles

The first principle of IAT is that people are innately predisposed to adapt and adjust their interaction patterns to each other. For example, if one person turns slightly toward the other person, the second individual may turn slightly away in response. This inclination to adjust one's behavior fulfills a variety of purposes, including survival, communication, and coordination needs. The second principle of IAT is that people biologically move toward synchronicity with each other. In other words, there is biological pressure for interaction behaviors to mesh together and match each other at particular moments in time, as happens, for example, when parent and infant sounds and movements become coordinated with each other. The only exception to this principle is when physical safety or comfort is in question. The third principle of IAT is that one's needs for closeness (need to approach and be approached) and avoidance (or separation) are cyclical and dialectical rather than uniformly fixed. When approach needs are met, then the pull of avoidance needs becomes stronger and vice versa. You might see this principle in action when, for example, two people stand close together at a crowded party, but as soon as there is a little more room in the area, they step or lean away from each other.

The fourth principle of IAT is that in a social situation, people tend to reciprocate and match each other's behaviors. This is especially true in socially polite, normative, and routine communicative interactions and less true when communicators have a structural relationship such as mutual role expectations. Smiling is a good example. Two strangers meeting at a party will probably exchange smiles, but you might not see the same behavior in a routine task interaction at the workplace. The fifth principle of IAT is that when communicating with each other, people exhibit both reciprocal and compensatory behaviors. To build rapport, an employee might exhibit reciprocity, through behaviors that function similarly, such as laughing and showing pleasant facial expressions whenever the boss does the same. A librarian might show compensatory behaviors that function in opposing ways, such as lowering one's voice when a patron is talking loudly. The sixth principle of IAT is that, although people have biological and sociological pressures to adapt to one another, the degree of strategic adaptation will vary depending on several factors, such as the consistency of an individual's behavior, an individual's awareness of himself or herself and of the other person, the ability to adjust behavior in response to others, and cultural differences.

The seventh principle of IAT is that there are limits to the prevailing interaction patterns. That is, biological, psychological, and social needs combine to limit how much individuals will tend to adapt. Outside these parameters, nonaccommodation and compensation are likely to occur. For example, individuals with a low need for social interaction with others may adapt less than individuals with a high need for interaction. The eighth principle of IAT is that there are many factors outside and inside the dyad that can moderate the pattern of adaptation in an interaction, such as nature of the relationship, location of the interaction, physical attractiveness, age, and gender. The ninth principle of IAT is that communicative functions of behaviors are crucial for understanding interpersonal adaptation rather than individual behaviors isolated from their functions. A clear example of this is that behaving dominantly can be done in a variety of ways (e.g., scowling, pointing a finger, placing the arms akimbo, and yelling). Given that communicative functions can be fulfilled with multiple behaviors, examining adaptation by comparing only a single behavior may lead to inaccurate conclusions.

Fundamental Concepts

In any interaction, there are three classes of interrelated factors that are taken into account by individuals in their interpersonal adaptation behavior. *Required factors* are those that are biological in origin and pertain to basic human survival and safety needs. For example, if one person swings a fist at another person, the second individual would probably turn and move away to protect more vulnerable parts of his or her body. *Expected factors* are those that are sociological in origin, stemming from social norms, cultural norms, communicative goals, and general knowledge of an interaction partner's behavior. For example, when one person greets another, the other person is obligated to respond similarly. This is a cultural norm. *Desired factors* are individualized and idiosyncratic to a person's specific preferences and goals. Close friends, for instance, may have a specialized greeting ritual that involves punching each other on the arm. These three sets of factors—required, expected, and desired—are the first three fundamental concepts of the theory. The fourth relates to interactional position.

The *interactional position* represents the likely interaction behavior of an individual or the likely projected interaction behavior of another person based on the hierarchical combination of the required (needed), expected (anticipated), and desired (preferred) classes of factors. That is, what is required is more heavily weighted in importance than what is expected and desired; what is expected is more heavily weighted in importance than what is desired. In the case of greeting another person, an interactional position may be the pooled assessment of the need to show no ill intentions (required factors); sociocultural expectations for enacting a greeting, as in shaking hands, kissing, or bowing toward each other (expected factors); and the unique greeting preferences of the individuals, such as mock fighting or a fraternity handshake (desired factors). If safety is in question, then the interactional position will likely be based on behaviors that show no harm, rather than expected and desired factors. When safety is not an issue, then expected and desired factors play a more significant role, respectively. For instance, if a person from Japan greets an American, the Japanese person may extend his or her hand instead of bowing (expected taking precedence over desired factors). If these people from Japan and the United States are old friends from school, then they may prefer their unique college greeting by hugging each other, slapping each other on the back twice, and doing three fist bumps (emphasizing desired factors when required and expected factors are not pressing).

The fifth basic concept, *actual behavior,* is a person's behavior in an interaction. Both interactional position and actual behavior lie on a continuum from positively valenced, meaning liked, to negatively valenced, or unliked. According to IAT, dyadic interaction patterns are determined by comparing each person's interactional position with the partner's actual behavior. When there is no discrepancy between the interactional position and actual behavior, they are congruent, and the interaction patterns of matching and reciprocity will be evident in the communicative encounter. For instance, suppose a husband and wife are having a disagreement; if the interactional position is to be moderately involved in the discussion by the husband, and the husband's actual behavior exhibits this moderate involvement, then according to

IAT, the wife will reciprocate with comparable involvement behaviors. Similarly, when there is a slight discrepancy between the interactional position and actual behavior, this discrepancy will likely go unnoticed and will result in the same pattern as when there was no discrepancy.

When there is a large enough discrepancy between the interactional position and a partner's actual behavior, people will adapt toward whichever is more positively valenced, the interactional position or the partner's actual behavior. If the actual behavior is more positively valenced than the interactional position, then convergence, matching, and reciprocity are the predicted interaction patterns. Continuing with the disagreeing-couple example, if the interactional position is moderate conversational involvement by the husband, and the husband actually behaves in a more highly involved manner (which is welcomed), then the wife will respond with more conversational involvement too. If the interactional position is more positively valenced than the actual behavior, then divergence, compensation, and maintenance are the predicted interaction patterns. If the interactional position is a moderate level of involvement by the husband, and the husband's actual behavior is highly involved (but it is unwelcome and disliked), then IAT predicts that the wife will maintain her own level of involvement or will show reduced involvement behaviors in the interaction.

Amy Ebesu Hubbard

See also Accommodation Theory; Cross-Cultural Adaptation Theory; Expectancy Violations Theory; Immediacy; Nonverbal Communication Theories

Further Readings

Burgoon, J. K., & Ebesu Hubbard, A. S. (2005). Cross-cultural and intercultural applications of expectancy violations theory and interaction adaptation theory. In W. B. Gudykunst (Ed.), *Theorizing about intercultural communication* (pp. 149–171). Thousand Oaks, CA: Sage.

Burgoon, J. K., Stern, L. A., & Dillman, L. (1995). *Interpersonal adaptation: Dyadic interaction patterns.* New York: Cambridge University Press.

Floyd, K., & Burgoon, J. K. (1999). Reacting to nonverbal expressions of liking: A test of interaction adaptation theory. *Communication Monographs, 66,* 219–239.

White, C. H., & Burgoon, J. K. (2001). Adaptation and communicative design: Patterns of interaction in truthful and deceptive conversations. *Human Communication Research, 27,* 9–37.

INTERACTION INVOLVEMENT

Interaction involvement is defined as the extent to which an individual participates in a social environment. This entails the individual's being aware of his or her own thoughts/feelings about messages from others, as well as attending to the likely meanings other people intend for their messages. It also means responding to those messages in an effective, appropriate manner. As such, interaction involvement is a fundamental element of competent interpersonal communication. This entry describes the components of interaction involvement and how these relate to interpersonal communication.

The concept of interaction involvement is grounded in the early work of Erving Goffman. Among other important ideas, Goffman observed that interpersonal society is governed by the meanings and interpretations people attribute to social acts, the pattern of verbal and nonverbal behavior that expresses one's view of the situation and evaluation of the participants, including self. Such a view of communication underscores the realities of interpersonal society as extremely fragile, whereby the slightest untoward act can potentially tear a delicately woven social fabric and significantly affect how one sees the relationships among participants and the reality of what is going on at a particular moment. Thus, the collective sense of social reality based on interaction is sustained by each person's assumed responsibility for regulating the flow of communicative events.

Consistent with most contemporary views of interpersonal communication competence, the central idea of interaction involvement is individuals' ability to regulate the flow of communicative events. Based on Goffman, interaction involvement consists of three related components, attentiveness, perceptiveness, and responsiveness.

Attentiveness is the most basic component of interaction involvement. It is concerned with an individual's attention to visual and auditory sources of information in the immediate social environment. For example, attentiveness includes listening carefully to what others say, taking note of what appear to be significant nonverbal cues, and keeping focused on the social events as they evolve. Goffman notes several ways in which individuals may become inattentive during social interaction. For example, one of the most common ways is to become preoccupied with something unrelated to the present conversation; another is to overly focus on some aspect of the conversation to the point that other important matters are missed or only partially processed.

Attentiveness to the flow of communicative events is a necessary, but not sufficient, condition for adequate monitoring of the expressive order. One must also demonstrate *perceptiveness,* in other words, awareness of the meanings/interpretations others have placed on one's behavior and what meanings/interpretations one should perhaps place on their behavior. Basically, perceptiveness is one's ability to determine and integrate meanings associated with self and other(s) and generally understand what is going on in a particular social encounter. Examples of perceptiveness include suspecting that a person is lying, understanding what another's emotional needs are, and realizing that one has behaved inappropriately or at least may have been seen as such by others.

The first two components of interaction involvement—attentiveness and perceptiveness—reside in the cognitive/affective domain. The third component, *responsiveness,* lies in the behavioral domain. It is concerned with an individual's ability to adapt to the immediate social environment by knowing what to say and when to say it. As such, responsiveness is important to Goffman's notion of social acts, the pattern of verbal and nonverbal behavior that constitutes the expressive order.

The research on interaction involvement has generally taken two paths. One set of studies has examined various cognitive/affective aspects of people who are high and low in interaction involvement, while another set of studies has examined the verbal and nonverbal behavior of communicators who vary in their interaction involvement. Among other things, it has been reported that high-involved people, in comparison with low-involved individuals, have higher self-esteem, are more emotionally stable, generally experience more positive and less negative moods, and have higher self-reported communication competence. The second line of research has revealed several observable differences between high- and low-involved individuals. One study found that high-involved communicators are better able to obtain sensitive information from another with minimal face loss (e.g., embarrassment). Another study showed that high-involved people use more immediate language, speak with greater certainty, and use more relational pronoun references in their interpersonal communication than their low-involved counterparts do. Other studies reveal that low-involved communicators often respond to their conversation partner's utterances at a surface text level, which implies that their responses are less complex, less elaborate, and less likely to extend the topic of conversation in meaningful ways.

It is important to note that the research on interaction involvement has been based on a self-report trait scale. While most of the research hypotheses have been supported about interaction involvement, defining it in a traitlike fashion has restricted understanding of how involvement influences communication in an ongoing, dynamic manner. For example, the trait approach emphasizes how people who are characteristically high or low in interaction involvement tend to behave, but it is not particularly informative about individuals who are less extreme or how or why individuals' interaction involvement varies over the course of a given conversation. Such online monitoring of individuals' interaction involvement poses a major methodological challenge that is not likely to be solved in the near future.

Donald J. Cegala

See also Face Negotiation Theory; Facework Theories; Impression Management; Politeness Theory; Social Interaction Theories; Trait Theory

Further Readings

Cegala, D. J. (1989). A study of selected linguistic components of involvement in interaction. *Western Journal of Speech Communication, 53,* 311–326.

Cegala, D. J., Savage, G. T., Brunner, C. C., & Conrad, A. B. (1982). An elaboration of the meaning of interaction involvement: Toward the development of a theoretical concept. *Communication Monographs, 49,* 229–248.

Goffman, E. (1967). *Interaction ritual: Essays in face-to-face behavior.* Chicago: Aldine.

Villaume, W. A., & Cegala, D. J. (1988). Interaction involvement and discourse strategies: The patterned use of cohesive devices in conversation. *Communication Monographs, 55,* 22–40.

INTERACTION PROCESS ANALYSIS

Robert F. Bales was among the first to investigate communication processes in small decision-making groups. He developed the interaction process analysis (IPA), a tool for coding contributions to discussion. The IPA is a category-based system, and as is often the case with such systems, the distinctions among the categories reflect assumptions regarding characteristics of discussion; it is a deductive taxonomy. Bales assumed that contributions to discussion were purposeful in the sense that they advanced the group toward a desired or optimal outcome and that the purposes or functions of the contributions influence what is said and to whom. Having first appeared in 1950 in his book *Interaction Process Analysis: A Method for the Study of Small Groups,* the IPA, including its theoretical underpinnings, has been reframed and revised through the years, most notably by Bales himself. A consistent feature of the IPA is a systems approach, with *equilibrium* a key concept; group members endeavor to maintain a balance between focusing on the task and interpersonal relationships within the group. The IPA reflects this assumption, most notably in framing contributions to discussion as either task or socioemotional (i.e., relational) in nature.

Features of Group Discussion

Groups as Systems

Bales's model of group interaction is based on the system metaphor. The elements of a system, in this case the group members, are interdependent; each member's actions affect and are affected by those of other members. For example, the extent to which a given member participates during discussion is directly related to the participation of the other members. Systems have an optimal operating state, and members are compelled to behave in ways that maintain that state. Systems, however, do not operate in a vacuum; environmental pressures (e.g., a new task, new members, changes in political structure) influence the working atmosphere of the group. When such changes occur, members work to return the group to its optimal state (or, perhaps, evaluate and accept the new state when it is advantageous to do so).

Functions of Group Discussion

People join (or are assigned to work in) groups because of the assumption that the outputs of groups are superior to those of individuals. Yet group work often involves disagreement, give-and-take, and compromise, which often leaves some members unhappy with or dispirited about the process and its outcomes. For example, a member's suggestion might be disregarded in favor of one proposed by another member. The disaffected member may become reticent to contribute further or may behave passive-aggressively, neither of which is desirable because of its potential negative effect on outcomes. It is in the group's interest to prevent such situations from occurring.

There will be times when task concerns dominate discussion and other times when relational issues will, but overemphasizing one means that important issues related to the other go unaddressed. Bales argued that groups need to balance their focus on task and socioemotional concerns in order to succeed. Bales (with Fred L. Strodtbeck) opined that discussion is characterized by phases—periods when groups naturally focus on task or relational problems. In his initial treatment, Bales (and Strodtbeck) argued that groups, at various times, focus on *orientation, evaluation,* and *control.* Orientation is the development of familiarity with a problem (or the reduction of uncertainty about it), evaluation the assessment of possible solutions, and control the exertion of pressure on members to adopt a particular position advocated by others. These task-based phases are complemented by relationship-based phases: *solidarity, tension reduction,* and *group identification.*

Successful groups tend to display these cycles, whereas unsuccessful groups do not.

Leadership

Most groups have leaders, some of whom are designated by the organization or institution (e.g., a jury foreperson) and others who emerge in initially leaderless groups (and in some cases, leaders emerge in groups with a designated leader). In either case, leaders in successful groups encourage groups to focus on task or relational concerns when appropriate. It is not always the case, however, that one leader can successfully focus the group task or relationship issues. Research has also documented cases in which two types of leaders emerge, one whose focus is on task issues (and is often the most frequent participator) and another who emphasizes relational concerns (typically not the most frequent participator). Groups tend to be successful if both types of leaders emerge and are less so if only one type of leader influences discussion.

The Interaction Process Analysis Categories

The IPA consists of 12 categories, with 6 that index task comments and 6 that deal with relational comments. The 6 task categories are *gives opinion, gives orientation/information, gives suggestion, asks for opinion, asks for orientation/information,* and *asks for suggestions.* (Presumably, one could ask for suggestions or opinions about how to handle relationships in the group, but such comments would not be coded as task-based contributions.) The 6 that reflect socioemotional concerns are *shows solidarity/seems friendly, dramatizes/releases tension, shows agreement, shows disagreement, shows tension,* and *shows antagonism/seems unfriendly.* Clearly, the latter three types are negatively valenced (i.e., they worsen relationships) whereas the first three are positive. Successful groups tend to emphasize the more positive relationship messages and balance those with task-related comments.

Bales's work provided a model for examining the character of discourse, as well as a basis for understanding which contributions are likely to be made and when during discussion. Not all his predictions and assumptions were supported (e.g., a predictable cycle of group phases), but perhaps his greatest contribution was to show how and why communication matters during small-group decision making. His work still permeates communication research, most notably in the variations on the functional approach to groups.

Joseph A. Bonito

See also Cybernetics; Group Communication Theories; System Theory

Further Readings

Bales, R. F. (1970). *Personality and interpersonal behavior.* New York: Holt, Rinehart, & Winston.

Bales, R. F. (1999). *Social interaction systems: Theory and measurement.* New Brunswick, NJ: Transaction.

Bales, R. F., Cohen, S. P., & Williamson, S. A. (1979). *SYMLOG: A system for the multiple level observation of groups.* New York: Free Press.

Bales, R. F., & Strodtbeck, F. L. (1951). Phases in group problem-solving. *Journal of Abnormal Social Psychology, 46,* 485–495.

Hewes, D. E. (1996). Small group communication may not influence decision making: An amplification of socio-egocentric theory. In R. Y. Hirokawa & M. S. Poole (Eds.), *Communication and group decision making* (2nd ed., pp. 179–212). Thousand Oaks, CA: Sage.

Hirokawa, R. Y. (1980). A comparative analysis of communication patterns within effective and ineffective decision-making groups. *Communication Monographs, 47,* 312–321.

INTERCULTURAL COMMUNICATION COMPETENCE

The study of intercultural communication competence is an extension of communication competence with a specific application to culture. The complexity of culture makes the study of communication competence more dynamic. The globalization of human society due to the rapid development of communication and transportation technology also makes the study of intercultural communication competence more critical and significant in promoting productive and successful communication among people from different cultural, racial, and religious backgrounds.

The three models developed by Guo-Ming Chen and his colleagues in 1987, 1996, and 2005 illustrate the content, scope, and history of the study of intercultural communication competence.

Progression of Theories

Initial Work: 1987

In 1987, based on a comprehensive literature review from a variety of disciplines, Chen defined communication competence as the individual's ability to execute certain actions in order to elicit a desired response in a specific environment. When the concept is applied to the intercultural context, culture itself should be emphasized. The model of intercultural communication competence generated from the literature was comprised of four dimensions, and each dimension contains four components. The first dimension, *personal attributes,* includes self-disclosure (the ability to self-disclose or be open to others), self-awareness (the ability to monitor or be aware of oneself), self-concept (the ability to develop a positive self-concept), and social relaxation (the ability to be relaxed in social interaction). The second dimension, *communication skills,* includes message skills (the ability to send and receive messages), social skills (the ability to demonstrate social skills), flexibility (the ability to demonstrate behavioral flexibility), and interaction management (the ability to manage interactions). The third dimension, *psychological adaptation,* includes frustration (the ability to deal with frustration), stress (the ability to deal with stress), alienation (the ability to deal with social alienation), and ambiguity (the ability to deal with ambiguous situations). The last dimension, *cultural awareness,* includes social values (the ability to understand social values), social customs (the ability to understand social customs), social norms (the ability to understand social norms), and social systems (the ability to understand social systems).

Continued Work: 1996

In 1996, Chen and William J. Starosta reexamined the four dimensions of the intercultural communication competence model and suggested that the concept could be studied from the three aspects of human ability: cognitive, affective, and behavioral.

The *cognitive* aspect of intercultural communication competence is represented by intercultural awareness, which refers to the ability to understand cultural conventions that affect how people interact with each other. In other words, intercultural awareness is a process of attitudinally internalizing insights about the predominant values, attitudes, and beliefs of a group of people. As the ability to draw an accurate *cultural map,* to sort out the *cultural theme,* or to understand *cultural grammars,* intercultural awareness proceeds from the level of knowing superficial cultural traits to the level of knowing significant and subtle cultural traits that contrast markedly with our own to the level of how another culture feels from the insider's perspective. Moreover, intercultural awareness can be studied from culture-specific and culture-general approaches. The former approach aims to impart information about cultural guidelines in order to interact effectively and appropriately with people from a specific culture; the latter aims to understand the universal influence of culture on human behaviors through different learning methods. Cultural games, such as "baFa baFa," through which people can come to know the possible variations in and general influence of culture, is one kind of learning method available.

The *affective* aspect of intercultural communication competence is demonstrated by intercultural sensitivity. It is the ability to understand, respect, and appreciate cultural differences in an intercultural interaction. Intercultural sensitivity is demonstrated by six elements, including self-esteem, self-monitoring, open-mindedness, empathy, interaction involvement, and suspending judgment. A valid measuring instrument of intercultural sensitivity based on these elements was developed by Chen and Starosta in 2000.

The *behavioral* aspect of intercultural communication competence is displayed by intercultural effectiveness, which refers to the cultivation of communication skills in order to accomplish specific goals, such as getting relevant information about these goals, accurately predicting the responses of one's counterpart, and assessing the potential communication results. It also refers to the ability to recognize communication rules, meet the contextual requirements of those rules, and recognize the rules in different contexts. The necessary behavioral skills for reaching intercultural effectiveness include language ability, behavioral flexibility, interaction management, identity maintenance, and relationship cultivation.

Latest Work: 2005

In order to take into account the impact of global trends on society, Chen extended the study of intercultural communication competence in 2005 to the global perspective. Chen argued that successful global citizens must foster the ability to negotiate their status in and among local, national, and global communities. In other words, on the global level, communication competence requires people to cultivate the ability to acknowledge, respect, tolerate, and integrate cultural differences in order to become enlightened global citizens. Thus, globally competent individuals need not only to recognize the necessity of developing a mind-set and skills to manage environmental trends, but also to acquire new modes of thinking, organization, and behavior by seeing through the eyes, minds, and hearts of people from different cultures. Global communication competence thus enables people to build mutual understanding and a sense of multiple identities that lead to unlocking human potential in an effort to develop a peaceful and productive society.

The four dimensions of global communication competence include (1) having a global mind-set, (2) unfolding the self, (3) mapping the culture, and (4) aligning the interaction. *Global mind-set* is the first dimension and foundation of global communication competence. It enables people to envision the global trends and change of human society and to execute communication skills appropriately and effectively to live a productive life. By broadening and expanding our thinking through the elimination of filters we possess about different cultures, a global mind-set helps to decrease ethnocentrism and parochialism.

Individuals with a global mind-set, then, are equipped with five characteristics. First, they are sensitive toward cultural diversity; they are open-minded toward cultural variety; they are knowledgeable in terms of local and global events; they are critical and holistic thinkers; and they are conceptually and behaviorally flexible. More specifically, a global mind-set impels individuals to broaden their perspectives, respect diversity, reconcile conflict, regulate change, and orient to the globalizing process.

Unfolding the self—the second dimension of global competence—refers to the ability to expand personal identity attributes while at the same time taking into account broader intercultural, interethnic, and interreligious concerns. In other words, globalization represents the pushing and pulling and adjusting and readjusting between the two forces of personalizing and globalizing. Only through the fostering of self-identity can people avoid being lost in the process of globalization and in turn establish an integrative future of human society. Successfully unfolding the self thus requires at least five aspects of personal effort, including purifying the self, learning continuously, cultivating sensitivity, developing creativity, and fostering empathy.

Mapping the culture—the third dimension of global competence—requires the cognitive ability to acquire cultural knowledge, or to "map" a culture, if you will. The mutual awareness of one's own and other cultures is the basis for tolerating, respecting, negotiating, and integrating cultural differences as well as reducing ambiguity and uncertainty in the process of intercultural communication. The development of cultural awareness usually undergoes four stages. The first stage is the bewilderment of differences, in which cultural differences are considered bizarre based on the knowledge of the superficial traits of the culture involved in the interaction. The second stage is frustration about the differences, in which internal conflicts and frustrations are provoked due to the awareness of the contrasting differences between the deeper cultural traits of the two cultures. The third stage is the cognitive analysis of cultural differences on a rational and intellectual basis, which leads to the gradual belief in the differences. The last stage is the empathic immersion, in which interactants can examine cultural differences from their counterparts' perspective and begin to appreciate and accept the differences without a feeling of distress.

Aligning the interaction—the last dimension of global competence—demands a set of behavioral skills to assist in adjusting to the new patterns of global interaction embedded in the complexity and multiplicity of meanings. The ability to align interaction effectively is thus the sine qua non necessary for global citizens to accomplish their jobs and attain communication goals in intercultural communication. Similar to the dimension of communication skills in the first model, crucial elements for aligning interaction in intercultural communication consist of language ability, behavioral flexibility, interaction management, identity maintenance, and the ability to manage change.

Training Applications

The application to training programs reflects the practical aspect of the study of intercultural communication competence. Intercultural training aims to help people interact effectively with others from different cultural backgrounds, including living and working in a new cultural environment. Through specific training techniques such as role-playing, case studies, critical incidents, and cultural simulations, trainees are equipped with the abilities of intercultural awareness, intercultural sensitivity, and intercultural effectiveness. The theoretical pursuit and the practical need for training reflect the continuous demand of the study of intercultural communication competence in an increasingly global human society.

Guo-Ming Chen

See also Competence Theories; Culture and
　Communication; Intercultural Communication
　Theories

Further Readings

Chen. G.-M. (2005). A model of global communication competence. *China Media Research, 1,* 3–11.

Chen, G.-M. (2007). A review of the concept of intercultural effectiveness. In M. Hinner (Ed.), *The influence of culture in the world of business* (pp. 95–116). Hamburg, Germany: Peter Lang.

Chen, G.-M., & Starosta, W. J. (1996). Intercultural communication competence: A synthesis. *Communication yearbook 19,* 353–383.

Martin, J. N. (Ed.). (1989). Intercultural communication competence [Special issue]. *International Journal of Intercultural Relations, 13*(3).

Wiseman, R. L., & Koester, J. (Eds.). (1993). *Intercultural communication competence.* Newbury Park, CA: Sage.

INTERCULTURAL COMMUNICATION THEORIES

Intercultural communication refers to the process of interaction between people from different cultures. More specifically, Karlfried Knapp defines it as the interpersonal interaction between members of groups that differ from each other in respect to the knowledge shared by their members and their linguistic forms of symbolic behavior. As such, intercultural communication is affected by how people from different countries and cultures behave, communicate, and perceive the world around them. Culture affects communication in subtle and profound ways. Our cultural perceptions and experiences help determine how the world looks and how we interact in that world. Today the world has grown so small that we all depend on each other. As more immigrants move from one culture to another, the issue of cultural adaptation takes on added significance. Globalization is changing the way individuals define themselves on the basis of economics, religion, culture, customs, language, and ethnic identity.

In addition to the field of communication, the study of intercultural communication includes fields such as anthropology, cultural studies, and psychology. The main theories for intercultural communication are based on the work especially of Edward T. Hall, Richard D. Lewis, Geert Hofstede, and Fons Trompenaars. Clifford Geertz was also a contributor to this field. Intercultural theories have been applied to a variety of different communication settings, including general business and management (Fons Trompenaars and Charles Hampden-Turner) and marketing (Marieke de Mooij, Stephan Dahl). There have also been several successful studies that concentrate on the practical applications of these theories in cross-cultural situations.

Intercultural communication existed since the very beginning of history. Human groups embarked on long-distance travels almost as soon as *Homo sapiens* emerged as a species. Later humans had spread to almost all the earth's habitable regions. By analyzing the characteristics and distribution of language families, blood types, and material remains, scholars have been able to trace the prehistoric movements of some peoples with remarkable precision. Although surviving evidence does not permit insights into the experiences of migrating peoples, their travels certainly led them into cross-cultural encounters even in prehistoric times. Widely spread tools, weapons, and deities in particular suggest communications across long distances by prehistoric peoples.

The influence of culture on communication is so strong that anthropologist Edward Hall virtually equated culture with communication. Differences in cultural values and perceptions can be a quiet, invisible source of great misunderstanding between people from different regions. Actually, the problem begins when our cultural verbal and nonverbal meanings are attached to the people of other cultures.

The theoretical literature on intercultural communication is large and growing, as shown by the number of entries in this encyclopedia related to this topic. This entry summarizes four prevalent themes—cultural difference, face-to-face negotiation, uncertainty and anxiety, and accommodation.

Cultural Difference

In the field of intercultural research, much work has been done on cultural differences and cultural types. One of the most significant studies of this nature was conducted by Geert Hofstede. The research identified four dimensions on which the cultures of various nations and regions differ: (1) *individualism–collectivism*; (2) *power distance*; (3) *uncertainty avoidance*; and (4) *masculinity-femininity*. Hofstede and his colleagues provided theoretical and empirical evidence that the value orientations of individualism and collectivism are pervasive in a wide range of cultures. The value orientation approach has been researched for more than 40 years in multiple academic disciplines. Primarily, *individualism* refers to the broad value tendencies of people in a culture to emphasize individual identity over group identity, individual rights over group obligations, and individual achievements over group concerns. In contrast, *collectivism* refers to the broad value tendencies of people in a culture to emphasize group identity over the individual identity, group obligations over individual rights, and in-group-oriented concerns over individual wants and desire. The degree of

individualism or collectivism of a culture has a great impact on communication behaviors.

Power distance is the degree to which less-powerful members will tolerate unequal distribution of power. Cultures vary from emphasizing low to high degrees of power distance. Low and high power distance tendencies exist in all the cultures, but one tends to predominate. Cultures in which low power distance tends to predominate include Austria, Canada, Denmark, Germany, New Zealand, and the United States. Cultures in which high power distance tends to predominate include Egypt, Ethiopia, Ghana, India, Saudi Arabia, and Venezuela. In India, for example, hierarchies are very steep. Employees at the lower level may not have easy access to the top managers. Distance is deliberately kept between levels. Power distance is quite high. "Sir" or "Madam" is frequently used by younger employees when addressing their seniors.

Further, William Gudykunst argues that egalitarianism mediates the influence of cultural power distance on communication behavior. Egalitarianism involves treating other people as equals. Low levels of egalitarianism at the individual level would be equated with high power distance at the cultural level, and high levels of egalitarianism at the individual level would be equated with low power distance at the cultural level.

Uncertainty avoidance is the tendency to arrange things in a way that minimizes unforeseen consequences; tolerance of uncertainty results in behavior that is less concerned with unforeseen consequences. Members of high uncertainty avoidance cultures resist change more, have higher levels of anxiety, have higher levels of intolerance for ambiguity, worry about the future more, see loyalty to their employer as more of a virtue, have a lower motivation for achievement, and take fewer risks. Different degrees of uncertainty avoidance exist in every culture, but one tends to predominate. Members of low uncertainty avoidance cultures appear to engage in more vocalization of anger toward out-group members and to control their anger toward out-group members less than do members of high uncertainty avoidance cultures.

Masculinity, according to Hofstede, is a way to characterize cultures that value assertiveness, competitiveness, and material success, whereas *femininity* characterizes cultural preferences for collaboration, nurturing, and harmony. High masculinity involves a high value placed on things, power, and assertiveness, whereas systems in which people, quality of life, and nurturance prevail are low on masculinity or high on femininity. All these dimensions have a great impact on the communication behavior of individuals. Psychological sex roles mediate the influence of cultural masculinity–femininity on communication behavior. Independent of biological sex, *feminine* individuals tend to prefer a sharing, expressive communication style, whereas *masculine* individuals are more likely to prefer a dominating, assertive communication style.

A second influential typology is that of Edward T. Hall, who observed two types of cultures, namely, *high-* and *low-context* cultures. The communication behavior of an individual is very much linked to the type of his or her culture. A high-context communication or message is one in which the most important information is embedded in the situation or internal to the person and is not directly included in the verbal message. A low-context communication or message, in contrast, is one in which the primary meaning is directly expressed in the verbal message.

Hall classified certain countries of Europe, North America, Australia, and New Zealand as low-context culture, whereas countries in Africa, Asia, and other non-Western areas of the world are high-context cultures. In general it has been found that members of low-context cultures tend to communicate directly, while members of high-context cultures tend to use indirect messages. People from high-context cultures are less verbal, hence more inclined to communicate nonverbally, while people from low-context cultures value verbal expressions and are more communicative. As an example of high-context communication, people in India are very context sensitive. In Indian culture, one needs to learn about the expectations regarding food and hospitality—when, where, what, and how food is prepared, presented, and eaten—and should expect to socialize and establish a relationship before one starts doing business. In many formal and informal business meetings or discussions, the context serves as a basis for expressing views and opinions. Many times, people avoid saying no or criticizing others to their face due to strong cultural norms. Indirect communication is very common, and sometimes people understand each other without uttering a word. Indian culture is very complex in nature, as

people speak different languages and have different food habits, clothes, and styles of living. In the Indian family, context has a great significance. A wife can easily decode the subtle contexts of her husband's communication. In a joint family, too, members adjust their communication patterns, promoting a congenial atmosphere in the family.

Face Negotiation

Closely related to the question of context is *face*. Most of us have the experience of blushing, feeling embarrassed, feeling awkward, feeling shame, or feeling enthusiastic. Many of these feelings are face-related issues. When our social dignity is attacked or teased, we feel the need to restore or save face. When we are being complimented or given credit in front of others for a job well done, we feel that our self-esteem is high. Losing face and saving face are some of the key concepts under this "face negotiation" umbrella. Face negotiation theory emphasizes the influence of culture on facework, and facework theory focuses on the influence of the interpersonal relationship on face.

Members of collectivistic, high-context cultures have concerns for mutual face and inclusion that lead them to manage conflict with another person by avoiding, obliging, or compromising. Because of concerns for self-face and autonomy, people from individualistic, low-context cultures manage conflict by dominating or problem solving. Whenever two people meet for the first time, there is uncertainty accompanied by feelings of uneasiness known as anxiety. These feelings are heightened whenever there is an intercultural encounter between two individuals.

Using a cultural variability approach to the study of face and facework, Stella Ting-Toomey and her colleagues propose a theoretical model—face negotiation theory. According to Ting-Toomey, face is conceptualized as an individual's claimed sense of positive image in a relational and network context. Ting-Toomey's face negotiation theory assumes that (a) people in all cultures try to maintain and negotiate face in all communication situations; (b) the concept of face is especially problematic in situations of uncertainty (such as request, embarrassment, or conflict) when the situated identities of the communicators are called into question; (c) the cultural variability dimension of individualism–collectivism influences members' selection of one set of facework strategies over others (such as autonomy face vs. approval face, and self-oriented face-saving vs. other-oriented face-saving); and (d) individualism–collectivism in conjunction with other individual, relational, and situational variables influences the use of various facework strategies in intergroup and interpersonal encounters. Thus, Ting-Toomey's face negotiation theory emphasizes sociocultural appropriateness in the enactment of facework strategies.

Uncertainty and Anxiety

Uncertainty reduction theory has had significant influence in the field of communication. This theory was initially proposed by Charles Berger and Richard Calabrese as a first effort to model the process of interaction during the initial stage of relational development. Uncertainty reduction theory suggests that when strangers meet, their primary focus is on reducing their levels of uncertainty in the situation. Their levels of uncertainty are located in both behavioral and cognitive realms. That is, they may be unsure of how to behave (or how the other person will behave), and they may also be unsure what they think of the other and what the other person thinks of them. Further, people's uncertainty occurs at both an individual and a relational level. People are highly motivated to use communication to reduce their uncertainty, according to this theory.

Berger attempted to explain why we want more certainty in an initial interaction and lays out situations in which the need to reduce anxiety is required. He considered three factors that influence the need to reduce uncertainty. The first of these is incentives. This factor suggests that we will be more likely to want to reduce uncertainty about an individual if we perceive that the individual can be helpful or rewarding to us in some way. The second factor is deviation—if people act in ways that are unexpected or that violate rules and norms of interactions. Finally, Berger proposes that need to reduce uncertainty will be enhanced by the prospect of future interaction. That is, if we know we will be talking with someone in the future (regardless of whether we want to—that is an issue of incentive), we will want to reduce uncertainty about that individual. However, if we know we

will never speak to someone again, there is little motivation to learn more about the individual.

Applying this idea to intercultural communication, William Gudykunst suggests that effective intergroup/interpersonal communication is a function of the amount of anxiety and uncertainty individuals experience when communicating with others. *Anxiety* refers to the feeling of discomfort or awkwardness when two strangers (from different cultures or the same culture) try to relate to each other. *Uncertainty* means the perceived unpredictability of the various intergroup/interpersonal situations. The concept of *management* refers to the importance of cultivating awareness or "mindfulness" in dealing with unfamiliar values and interaction scripts.

Gudykunst and his associates have been testing and refining the theories based on uncertainty and anxiety. They uncovered that greater anxiety is experienced in intergroup (i.e., interethnic and intercultural) encounters than in intrapersonal encounters. Anxiety is associated positively with the degree to which social identities (i.e., group membership identities) are activated in the interaction and the amount of uncertainty experienced. In addition, they found that there is greater uncertainty in intergroup encounters than in intragroup encounters. Uncertainty is associated negatively with positive expectations, communication satisfaction, and quality of communication. They have also observed that both anxiety and uncertainty decrease over time in intergroup encounters. However, the decrease does not fit a linear pattern (i.e., the pattern fluctuates across time). Finally, the ways that individuals gather information to reduce uncertainty differ in individualistic and collectivistic cultures. Members of individualistic cultures (e.g., the United States) seek out person-based information to reduce uncertainty about strangers while members of collectivistic cultures (e.g., Japan) seek out group-based information to reduce uncertainty. In sum, Gudykunst claims that anxiety and uncertainty exist in all cultures, but how people define these two terms varies from culture to culture.

Accommodation Processes

Communication accommodation theory, originally proposed by Howard Giles and his colleagues, emphasizes the importance of understanding speech convergence and speech divergence to increase or decrease communicative distance among members of different groups. The theory focuses on explaining the motivations, strategies, and contexts whereby group members (e.g., from different cultures, ethnic groups, or age groups) use different communication strategies to converge with or diverge from their patterns linguistically.

According to Giles and associates, speakers move through their linguistic repertoire so as to converge or diverge linguistically, based on three motivations: to gain approval from their discourse partners vis-à-vis linguistic similarity, to show distinctiveness and thus accentuate their own group membership, and to achieve clearer and smoother communication.

The most recent version of communication accommodation theory incorporates the cultural variability dimension of individualism and collectivism in its theoretical propositions. Cindy Gallois and her associates found that nonaccommodating students and faculty members were rated less favorably than accommodating ones. They further found that the multiple roles (students vs. faculty member, gender, and ethnicity) of the speakers and the judges all exerted influences on perceived interaction accommodation.

Thus, accommodation processes examine the perceived motivation and role dimensions of the intergroup speakers and how these dimensions affect interaction convergence/divergence issues. In addition, the theory probes how the interaction convergence/divergence process fosters the evaluative reactions by observers. It moves beyond survey data and actually taps into how members from different cultural or linguistic groups communicate with one another on verbal or nonverbal interactional levels.

Vijai N. Giri

See also Co-Cultural Theory; Contextual Theory of Interethnic Communication; Conversational Constraints Theory; Cross-Cultural Adaptation Theory; Cultural Contracts Theory; Cultural Performance Theory; Cultural Theories of Health Communication; Cultural Types Theories; Culture and Communication; Effective Intercultural Workgroup Communication Theory; Face Negotiation Theory; Intercultural Communication Competence

Further Readings

Burgoon, J. K. (1995). Cross-cultural and intercultural applications of expectancy violations theory. In R. Wiseman (Ed.), *Intercultural communication theory* (pp. 194–214). Thousand Oaks, CA: Sage.

Calloway-Thomas, C., Cooper, P. J., & Blake, C. (1999). *Intercultural communication: Roots and routes.* Boston: Allyn & Bacon.

Gallois, C., Giles, H., Jones, E., Cargile, A., & Ota, H. (1995). Accommodating intercultural encounters: Elaborations and extensions. In R. Wiseman (Ed.), *Intercultural communication theory* (pp. 115–147). Thousand Oaks, CA: Sage.

Griffin, E. (2000). *A first look at communication theory.* Boston: McGraw-Hill.

Gudykunst, W. B. (1985). A model of uncertainty reduction in intercultural encounters. *Journal of Language and Social Psychology, 4,* 79–97.

Gudykunst, W. B. (1995). Anxiety/uncertainty management (AUM) theory: Current status. In R. Wiseman (Ed.), *Intercultural communication theory* (pp. 8–58). Thousand Oaks, CA: Sage.

Gudykunst, W. B., & Matsumoto, Y. (1996). Cross-cultural variability of communication in personal relationships. In W. B. Gudykunst, S. Ting-Toomey, & T. Nishida (Eds.), *Communication in personal relationships across cultures* (pp. 19–51). Thousand Oaks, CA: Sage.

Gudykunst, W. B., & Ting-Toomey, S. (1988). *Culture and interpersonal communication.* Newbury Park, CA: Sage.

Hall, E. T. (1976). *Beyond cultures.* Garden City, NY: Anchor Press/Doubleday.

Hall, E. T., & Hall, M. R. (1990). *Understanding cultural differences: Germans, French and Americans.* Yarmouth, ME: Intercultural Press.

Hofstede, G. (1991). *Cultures and organizations: Software of the mind.* London: McGraw-Hill.

Samovar, L. A., Porter, R. E., & Stefani, L. A. (1998). *Communication between cultures.* Belmont, CA: Wadsworth.

Ting-Toomey, S. (1985). Toward a theory of conflict and culture. In W. B. Gudykunst, L. P. Stewart, & S. Ting-Toomey (Eds.), *Communication, culture & organizational processes* (pp. 71–86). Beverly Hills, CA: Sage.

Ting-Toomey, S. (Ed.). (1994). *The challenge of facework: Cross-cultural and interpersonal issues.* Albany: State University of New York Press.

Ting-Toomey, S., & Chung, L. (1996). Cross-cultural interpersonal communication: Theoretical trends and research directions. In W. B. Gudykunst, S. Ting-Toomey, & T. Nishida (Eds.), *Communication in personal relationships across cultures* (pp. 237–258). Thousand Oaks, CA: Sage.

Triandis, H. C. (1995). *Individualism and collectivism*. Boulder, CO: Westview.

Trompenaars, F. (1995). *Riding the waves of culture*. London: Nicholas Brealey.

International Communication Theories

International communication is the name given to a field of inquiry that includes the study of various forms of interaction globally, including global communication via mass media, cross-cultural communication, and telecommunications policy. Therefore, by its very nature, international communication is an interdisciplinary field of study, utilizing concepts, research methods, and data from areas as diverse as political science, sociology, economics, literature, and history. The field has two broad dimensions: (1) policy studies and (2) cultural studies. Policy studies refers to the analysis of how the actions of governance entities (such as governments and intergovernmental organizations) influence the nature of international communication. The cultural studies approach to international communication examines the relationship between culture and international communication. However, finding a definition of international communication on which there has been wide agreement among academic journals and scholarly associations—the entities that usually have the most power in defining fields and disciplines—has been elusive. Indeed, the *Journal of International Communication* acknowledged in 2008 that what it considers international communication often goes by different names and that a number of academic fields study "global communication."

This entry defines theories of international communication as macro hypotheses about how best to understand global communicative relationships. This approach includes, for example, theories of internationalism and cultural imperialism, but it would not include theories of regional media systems or models of press freedom.

All paradigms in international communication place varying degrees of emphasis on three elements: (1) actors, (2) technology, and (3) modes of production.

Elements

Theory making in international communication borrows heavily from academic disciplines outside communication. The paradigms that place greatest emphasis on actors must rely on the field of international relations for their basic ideas about what exactly constitute *the international*—the actors whose relationships are being theorized. It is on "natural" science fields, such as engineering and computer science, that technologically deterministic paradigms in international communication have relied for their assumptions about the past, present, and future. Similarly, economics and the study of political economy have had a profound impact on how scholars have theorized the configuration of international communication.

Actors

Embedded in the very term *international communication* is the assumption that the nation-state is the primary actor in global interactions. This is derived from the fact that the Westphalia states system (nation-state sovereignty) is the basis of the contemporary international political order. This system assumes that states are the primary actors and that the principle of state sovereignty is sacrosanct. The international is, therefore, an arena dominated by states that are the primary sources of agency. Less rigorous theories of international communication are built on this assumption. Therefore, theories of international communication in these paradigms are essentially theories of how states interact with each other. Even when the principle of state sovereignty and agency is complicated by the presence of significant transnational players, such as transnational corporations, these players are still assumed to be appendages of the states that are the only actors with the legitimacy to create the domestic and international laws that control the behavior of these other actors. Postmodern approaches to international communication have had a more thorough engagement with this question of what exactly constitutes the international, and they have been less eager to use the state as the starting point for theory building in international communication.

Technology

The revolution in communication technology of the late 19th and the 20th centuries is the single most powerful factor that accounts for there even being an area of research that we can call international communication. The quest to understand the impact of new communication technologies on international relations has been one of the most powerful motivations for theorists. Advances in new international communication technologies have tended to increase the velocity of information and enhance the ability to communicate over time and space. The telegraph and the Internet are just two technologies whose inventions have been at first startling to scholars who have then tried to theorize their meaning for the nature of the international system. The trend has been to think of new telecommunication technologies in utilitarian, strategic terms—tools for the diffusion of specific kinds of ideas and to give the technologically advanced more advantages.

Modes of Production

The economic systems that produce goods and services, provide employment, configure trading relationships, and produce patterns of wealth creation and investment have been the third major element in international communication theory building. Theorists have tended to see modes of production as constitutive of patterns of international communication. This has especially been the case with the Marxist paradigm that was so popular in the early history of the field, but it has been attractive even in later years with the rise of transnational neoliberalism. Theorists have tended to see international communication as reflecting these economic relationships, for example, the tendency of news flows to mirror patterns of global trade.

Five Paradigms

International communication theories can be sorted into five paradigms: theories of internationalism, the Marxist paradigm of international communication, theories of representation, reception theories, and theories of identity.

Theories of Internationalism

The internationalist paradigm is the most accessible and attractive of the five. It is a technologically deterministic paradigm that asserts that the more interconnected the international system becomes via the new technologies, the more democratic and peaceful the world will be. Internationalism is based on a number of key assumptions. These include the view that human beings share a number of core values that can be found throughout the world, regardless of culture and geography; the assumption that there is such an entity as an international society; the idea that increased opportunities to communicate awaken these values in people if they are dormant; the belief that public opinion is always in favor of peace; and the idea that instrumentalist international communication projects can be devised to propagate the ethics needed for a peaceful world. Although the continued improvements in telecommunication have not been accompanied by declines in transnational bellicosity, theories of internationalism still persist in various permutations. This is because the internationalist paradigm contains much variation. For example, theories of internationalism popular early in the 20th century incorporated pseudoscientific assumptions about racial difference that were discredited in the second half of the century. Internationalist theories do not necessarily begin from the position that all human beings, or their various political formations, are equal. Hence the various development communication projects sponsored by the United Nations system in the years after World War II were based on theories of how communication technologies would modernize backward societies and diffuse ideas from advanced peoples. Although such blatant prejudice was not so popular by the end of the century, the theories about how the Internet would transform international society shared the core assumptions of the internationalist paradigm. It is for this reason that we can, for example, group the ideas of Bill Gates with those of diffusion theorist Daniel Lerner, who wrote 50 years earlier—and who is also the paradigmatic bedfellow of Norman Angell, who wrote 50 years before Lerner and was among the first international communication theorists.

Perhaps the most influential of theorists in this tradition was the Canadian Harold Innis, whose theorization of time-biased and space-biased media had a profound influence on his protégé Marshall McLuhan, who developed the idea of hot and cold media according to a similar schema. Innis theorized communication technologies as being central to the formation and character of political empires. Time-biased media were those that could store information over long periods of time but were difficult to transport over long distances (such as stone tablets and parchment). Space-biased media (such as paper and papyrus) were more transportable but could not store information for long periods of time. According to the theory, empires could hope to survive only if they were based on a fine balance between time-biased and space-biased media. That is because the different types of media provoked two distinct types of political organization. Time-biased media encouraged centralized authority and hierarchy. Space-biased media favored decentralization.

Marxist Paradigm

The central proposition of Marxist theories of international communication is that the way the international system communicates is a function of the modes of economic production. In the 1960s and 1970s, the popular theories of international communication were mainly inspired by dependency theory, which theorized that there was a structure to international communication that reflected the power imbalance between "core" and "periphery" states. The whole world was envisioned as a site of global class struggle. International mass communication was dominated by transnational capitalist interests, especially corporations. Theorists such as Herbert Schiller, Armand Mattelart, and Cees Hamelink began their analyses by pointing to how the capitalist system of production grew. Imperialism was the expression of mature capitalism, and just as imperialistic relationships characterized the international division of labor, they also molded international trade and international communication.

Herbert Schiller's writings were for many years most representative of this approach. Over several books, he set out a theory of cultural imperialism based on classic Marxist propositions. Schiller's approach was decidedly one sided in placing the blame for the imbalance in global communication squarely on the shoulders of the mature capitalist economy of the United States. The state is conceived as an extension of the capitalist project. It allows new technologies to be exploited for surplus value instead of the wider social good. The massive audiovisual industry is able to take advantage of economies of scale to saturate foreign markets. The military–industrial complex further facilitates this dominance by taking control of international intergovernmental organizations that regulate communication technologies and by sponsoring international propaganda. But, ironically, the theory arrives at the conclusion that this very state is the entity that should use its power to regulate communication industries for the social good, not in the interest of a minority of capitalists. This was a proposition that found its way into actual attempts at international policymaking in the early 1980s, following the release of the United Nations Educational, Scientific, and Cultural Organization's report on international communication problems. The Marxist critique asserts the primacy of the state and wants to give it more control, not less.

The internationalist and Marxist paradigms are grand theories of international communication because they seek to describe and provide normative rules for understanding the entire international communication system. In contrast, the other three paradigms seek to provide clues to understanding international communication via specific points of intervention into the communicative process.

Theories of Representation

Theories of representation are interpretive schemes that provide tools for understanding tendencies in international communication, especially unequal international communication relationships. Some of the assumptions on which they are based include the following views: Popular culture (such as print fiction, movies, television shows, comic strips, etc.) should be taken seriously for its value in providing insights into international political relationships; techniques from linguistics and literature studies can be deployed to read international media as texts; meanings are not fixed, so there is a constant struggle to maintain dominant ideologies; and discursive tendencies in popular media often mirror international political agendas.

Therefore, theories of representation share similar preoccupations with Marxism, but whereas the Marxist paradigm is focused on the behavior of political actors, representation theorists are most concerned with what tendencies in media texts mean for international relationships. It is for this reason that Edward Said's thesis of *orientalism* is based on the same assumptions as Ruth Mayer's notion of artificial Africas.

Theories of Reception

Marxist, structuralist critiques of the international communication system inspired the call at the United Nations for a New World Information and Communication Order in the 1970s and 1980s, but these intellectual debates provoked theory building that sought explanations for international communication imbalances in places other than modes of production. Theories of reception argue that international media flows are unequal due to reasons inside their texts, not because of cultural imperialism. Therefore, they share with the representation paradigm the preoccupation with the analysis of texts.

A good illustration of one such reception theory is Scott Robert Olson's narrative transparency model, which sought to explain the phenomenal popularity of American audiovisual productions around the world. The theory asserts that U.S. movies and television shows are transparent texts because they can be easily decoded by people from different cultures. The transparent text deploys mythotypes that are present in systems of myths around the world, and these mythotypes include such emotions as purpose, awe, participation, and wonder. American producers are good at including these in their narratives, and so their works achieve popularity around the world. The theory conceives of transparent texts as apolitical, eschewing essentialist identity politics and producing an anarchic international cultural sphere. This rejects the position of the Marxist or representation paradigm that either the material structure of transnational communication systems or their texts are ideologically loaded.

Theories of Identity

The identity paradigm is the most steeped in the postmodern intellectual tradition. One of postmodernism's key breaks with modernism is its willingness to assume that the main contours of human identity formation are not along lines of class but according to other markers of identity. These are often called new social movements, and they include identity configurations around gender, race, ethnicity, disability status, and sexual orientation. The identity paradigm represents a considerable change in how the fundamental nature of international communication is conceptualized because it does not necessarily assume the primacy of nation-states. In this paradigm the emphasis is on the element of actors. These actors are given agency that can undermine and surpass the power of states. This paradigm confronts a problem that often plagues all attempts to theorize the international—the tendency of theorists not to be able to provide an ecology of interests. For example, state-centric theories have traditionally assumed that states in the international system act relatively autonomously based on rational conceptions of self-interest. But there is no explanation of the process through which actors devise their understanding of their interests. Technological determinism pays too little attention to the mix of factors that determine how human beings eventually adopt and use new technologies.

Most illustrative of this innovation in conceptualizations of international communication is Manuel Castells's trilogy of texts, published on the eve of the new millennium, which set out a theory of the interaction between communication networks and the politics of identity. The theory is based on the fundamental premise that the search for identity is the fundamental source of social meaning. This yearning determines how individuals use communication technologies. These tools by themselves do not determine the nature of international communication, but rather the interaction between technologies and how people construct subjectivities and the interests that devolve from these understandings of identity. The networked state does not have the autonomy and sovereignty it once had because it is interconnected with other nodes of power that partake in policymaking and are influenced by the behavior of the very same networked state. Neither are transnational corporations as powerful as they once were because they are more vulnerable to the subjectivities of capital markets and other networks. The era of networks means that people interact in networks as individuals instead of through communities. This means that there will always be clashes between individualism and communalism.

The clear trend in international communication theory has been a move away from the social sciences to the humanities. The early internationalist and Marxist theories were based on positivist approaches to the perceived realities of the international social environment. They could be supported and tested with empirical research. These were approaches that did not interrogate very carefully assumed identities and saw international communication as an arena of rational choice. The increased scholarly attention to international communication has found these assumptions from social science to be inadequate for theorizing the texture of international communicative relationships. This has meant that critical interpretive methods and theories have become more popular in the field. They make sense of the seemingly irrational. This trend also originated in the increasing popularity of postmodernist tendencies in both the social sciences and the humanities. This will mean that there will be increasingly fewer attempts to produce grand theory and more attempts to interrogate carefully the individual elements of theory building.

Mark DaCosta Alleyne

See also Cultural Studies; Culture and Communication; Diffusion of Innovations; Film Theories; Flow and Contra-Flow; Free Flow Doctrine; Globalization Theories; Identity Theories; Intercultural Communication Theories; Marxist Theory; Media Sovereignty; Medium Theory; Neocolonialism; New World Information and Communication Order (NWICO); Postcolonial Theory

Further Readings

Alleyne, M. D. (1995). *International power and international communication*. New York: St. Martin's Press.

Angell, N. (1914). *The great illusion: A study of the relation of military power to national advantage.* London: W. Heinemann.

Castells, M. (2000). *End of millennium* (2nd ed.). Malden, MA: Blackwell.

Castells, M. (2000). *The rise of the network society* (2nd ed.). Malden, MA: Blackwell.

Castells, M. (2004). *The power of identity* (2nd ed.). Malden, MA: Blackwell.

Cherry, C. (1978). *World communication: Threat or promise: A socio-technical approach.* New York: Wiley.

Gates, B., Myhrvold, N., & Rinearson, P. (1996). *The road ahead.* New York: Penguin Books.

Mayer, R. (2002). *Artificial Africas: Colonial images in the times of globalization.* Hanover, NH: University Press of New England.

Olson, S. R. (1999). *Hollywood planet: Global media and the competitive advantage of narrative transparency.* Mahwah, NJ: Lawrence Erlbaum.

Said, E. W. (1979). *Orientalism.* New York: Vintage Books.

Schiller, H. I. (1992). *Mass communications and American empire* (2nd ed., updated). Boulder, CO: Westview.

INTERNATIONAL DEVELOPMENT THEORIES

International development theories refer to the practice of systematically applying the processes, strategies, and principles of communication to bring about positive social change. Development has been a major theme in communication literature since the 1950s. Many theories emerged in this context. Earlier development discourse focused on how the third world could become more like the first world in terms of social, economic, political, and even cultural frameworks. The concept of development was defined essentially by the first world powers to suit their so-called progressive sensibilities. These sensibilities directed attention toward rebuilding the third world sectors with first world assumptions of development. The obvious markers of development were levels of literacy, extent of industrialization, attention to medical interventions, and a working democratic system of governance. All these ideals were imposed on the third world by the first world through the rhetoric of development. There was only one way of defining development, and it was the first world's prerogative to do so.

Over time, various definitions of development communication have surfaced that provide a deeper understanding of this phenomenon. Recent dialogue on development communication emphasizes that the objective of any communication for development has to do with privileging the voices of those for whom the process of development is critical. Hence the goal of development communication is to improve the socioeconomic existence of the people in the developing world within a framework of social justice in which their voices can be recognized and respected. In doing so, development communication will serve the people by providing them with decentered control of their communication systems, leading to effective social change.

This entry will first offer a brief history of development by discussing modernization theory and dependency theory. The second section will discuss the role of communication and participation in development theories. Finally, development will be described in colonial and postcolonial contexts.

History of Development

The 1950s provided a significant historical moment to this field as different theoretical and philosophical approaches intersected to articulate development communication studies. This intersection resulted in not only a critical dialogue but also a complex one as no single approach could offer a replacement for the earlier one but added more layers of intellectual dynamism to the discourse of development communication. This section will identify the two main approaches to development studies and provide a brief survey of their application in communication.

The first dominant approach to development communication is *modernization theory,* which evolved in three phases. The first phase emerged in the 1950s and 1960s, and this phase claimed that mass media can be used effectively to diffuse social and technical innovations. It further identified the strengths of mass media to teach messages of modernity to an unskilled audience. This vision of modernity would propose a modern lifestyle over a traditional one. The second phase of modernization can be traced to the 1970s, when the dialogue on development took a progressive turn as it criticized the influence of modern-Western society on the rest of the developing world. The last phase of modernization discourse gained momentum in the 1990s as it strategically took the middle path of

not being against or in support of Western notions of modernization processes. Instead it pointed out the defects of universalizing ideas of modernization across different communities and described the paradoxes of development in striving for modernization as defined by the Western political powers.

Modernization theory received heavy criticism from *dependency theory,* which rapidly gained popularity and became the next paradigm to approach development across the world. According to dependency theory, problems of the third world reflected development problems that were caused by Western capitalization of the world, thus creating pockets of unequal resources for the people. Dependency theorists believed that third world countries were underdeveloped, not due to lack of information, but because of socioeconomic determinants that always positioned them weaker to their first world competitors. Conditions of underdevelopment existed due to a symbiotic relationship with development. In order to address this dialectical relationship between development and underdevelopment, the third world would need to reassess its political, economic, and social conditions and reconstitute its sense of autonomy from the first world order. This would entail a major reconfiguration of media structures that traditionally have been monopolized by the first world to serve its own economic and political gains in these countries.

During the 1970s and 1980s, the United Nations Educational, Scientific, and Cultural Organization (UNESCO) sponsored several conventions for developing countries to reclaim control of their media from foreign capitalists who simply wanted to create economies of self-interest. During these forums, representatives from third world countries proposed control of their own media and defined the need to form their own communication polices. While there is a need for third world countries to claim their rights in regard to their communication systems, it becomes critical to question the colonial context in which most development discourse has taken place. The next section will decolonize the Western-centered approach toward development and situate it in postcolonial sensibilities.

Postcolonialism and Development

While the possibility of producing a decolonized, postcolonial knowledge in development studies became a subject of considerable debate in the 1990s, there has been little dialogue between postcolonialism and development. However, the need for development studies that are postcolonial in theory and practice is now increasingly acknowledged. This means recognizing the significance of language and representation and the power of development discourse and its material effects on the lives of people subject to development policies. It also means acknowledging the already postcolonial world of development in which contemporary reworkings of theory and practice, such as grassroots and participatory development, indigenous knowledges, and global resistance movements, inform postcolonial theory.

Early approaches saw development as a linear process based on the belief that central control of media can lead to mass social transformation. In this macroapproach to development, often audience reception and effectiveness of message were neglected as part of the communication process. Little effort was made to understand whether the audience understood the message and whether the message led to any social change.

In the 1970s and 1980s, development was understood not only as a function of political economies of the first world but also as a viable process of colonialism. As a component of colonial discourse, development literature started to recognize diversity as a critical factor in dialogue for change. Development communication supported diversity of cultures, classes, communication, and ideologies while defining common development goals and initiatives. This changed the vernacular of development theories and made them more inclusive.

There is an increasing involvement of local communities in defining their needs and creating their own developmental models for change. Several agencies of change started to work with local governments at the grassroots level to develop communications projects that were collaborative and dynamic in nature. The United Nations provided aid to nonprofit organizations and to government organizations to manage development projects using indigenous knowledge and expertise. Agencies such as the United States Agency for International Development, UNESCO, the United Nations Development Program, and many others provide assistance to developing countries to develop new models for building infrastructures leading to self-reliance.

Communication and Development

Communication for development is the strategic application of communication technologies and processes to promote social change. When communication is a full partner in the development process and is executed intelligently, the process of development becomes more sustainable. Two main schools of thought have been identified for thinking about communication for development. The first is aligned with the dominant paradigm, which views social problems as stemming from a lack of information. The second, which takes a more participatory approach, sees problems as resulting from structural power inequality.

People who favor the dominant paradigm tend to believe that problems in developing countries are the result of traditional values and a general lack of information about how to modernize. Communication in this sense is generally seen as a one-way, top-down, linear process and is used to affect behavior change by altering knowledge, attitudes, and practices. The mass media then play a role by informing the population about projects, illustrating the advantage of these projects, and recommending that they be supported.

On the other end of the continuum is the participatory approach, which seeks to work with community members and empower them to have more control over issues that affect them, instead of imposing an intervention on them. The participatory approach is based on the idea that communication for development needs to be a two-way process in which information is exchanged and not forced on anyone. However, development scholars and practitioners are recognizing more and more that most initiatives cannot be classified as purely top-down or purely participatory. Instead, a theory of convergence seems to be emerging that acknowledges the fact that there are elements of both in the majority of development projects.

Another important factor that is recognized as important to communication for development is the role of interpersonal communication. Research has shown that development project outcomes depend hugely on interpersonal dialogues inspired by multimedia intervention. Regardless of the approach or method used in an initiative, cultural sensitivity is critical to any message. A development project can be more successful by working within local contexts and cultures. Hence, a cultural perspective has become central to the debate on communication for development. Consequently, development work has moved away from a traditional approach that emphasized economic and materialistic criteria to a more multiple appreciation of holistic and complex perspectives.

Participation and Development

Recent years have witnessed a phenomenal upsurge in commitment to participatory processes in development. A widely shared view in the development community is that without commitment, creativity, energy, and involvement of the people, the pace of development will not accelerate. This is the constant tension between the two positions that communities can be built or that communities build themselves.

Community participation and organizing are being encouraged all over the world. It is the top agenda of every developed and developing nation. This, however, does not protect it from resistance. Community participation ought to be considered as a political tool to bring people together so that they may lobby the state for services. For an oppressed community, participation can also be expressed in more radical terms as a prerequisite to liberation.

The language of community participation has tended to obscure the fact that there is always an *us* and a *them*. The borderline between the two groups is not fixed. In some circumstances *us* means the governments of the handful of wealthy industrial nations and *them* is everybody else. But in other circumstances, *us* may include local field workers who are drawn from, and live in, the villages that are the target of aid. Similarly, *them* sometimes refers solely to government ministries; at other times, the term encompasses householders and sometimes more specific groups such as the lower castes in a particular village.

What makes development both an interesting and an immensely difficult field is that all facets of life are involved—economy, politics, technology, and culture. Nongovernmental organizations (NGOs) are usually portrayed as latter-day missionaries

doing good among the poor. In reality, NGOs are established either to promote political or religious views or out of frustration of the government to meet the demands of the oppressed people. Most NGOs are not multidisciplinary and cannot cohesively analyze a situation as the team is fragmented and has little training to sustain group understanding of an issue.

There are, however, several obstacles to participation that could lead to community building from within the community. These obstacles typically do not discourage the development professionals from going into local communities and finding innovative ways to organize the disempowered into sustainable groups and helping them to be self-reliant. Robert Chambers is a follower of Paulo Freire and is inspired by the Freirian theme that poor and exploited people can and should be enabled to analyze their own realities. In the quest to empower the oppressed, Chambers's Participatory Rural Appraisal is widely used to encompass approaches and methods that have, in various ways, combined action, reflection, participation, and research in an approach in which outsiders and insiders carry equal responsibility to work together and make the interaction successful. The local people realize their potential, and the outsiders simply facilitate their discovery of themselves. The organizing takes place in an empowering way and also in a sustainable way so that when the outsider exits from the community, the community can continue on its own as it has achieved the variable of self-reliance above all other attributes.

While participation is integral to the discussion of development, it needs to be understood in nondemocratic conditions where choices are imposed and enforced. In nondemocratic societies, participation can be coercive and manipulative. It is imperative to contextualize the dialogue on participation from non-Western standpoints as often ideas of participation are borrowed from a first world understanding of the third world. This colonized framework of participation is counterproductive to the process of development.

Gender and Development

Finally, there is the gender and development (GAD), or empowerment, approach, which argues that development initiatives should come from women themselves, leading to their empowerment. This approach sees the subordination of women as the result of, not only gender relations, but the effects of colonialism and neocolonialism as well, thus challenging the entire field of development and making it unpopular with governments and agencies. The research on GAD focuses on five main points: it focuses on gender relations, not just women; it sees women as active agents who do not necessarily understand the structural inequalities that lead to their subordination; it takes a holistic approach instead of dealing with just the reproductive or productive roles of women; it takes into consideration aspects of welfare, antipoverty, and equity approaches to evaluate whether minor reform or radical change is needed; and it places less importance on economics and more focus on self-organization, especially at the local level.

In development discourse, the issue of gender is prominent. In the development literature of earlier decades, women were largely ignored, either on the assumption that gender distinctions were irrelevant or on the categorization of women as dependents in male-headed households. The surge of interest in gender and development is attributed primarily to the vigorous efforts of feminist scholars. With the exit of women from the household into the industrial labor force—and hence beyond their traditional confinement to subsistence and petty trade activities—the rupture of traditional family structures and established gender relations has become a prime topic for research.

There has always been a contingent concern with gender relations in development, and this has encouraged development practitioners to redefine development and how gender can situate itself in the center of this conversation.

Paradox of Development: An Indian Case Study

Contemporary India has become a country with disparate pockets of growth and underdevelopment. India is an example of a developing country where many areas are unaffected by the process of development and the beneficiaries of development are few. This paradox of development is reflected in India's technological advancement as it is one of the leaders in technically skilled labor. India is on the world map for computer technology and

software development. While these numbers are staggering and indicate technological progression, India continues to live under dire conditions of poverty.

While the road to development is difficult and long, the forces of industrialization offer a promising future for development and progress. This case study of India illustrates that development is not linear and simple. There is no single equation that can be applied to every development scenario. The process of development needs to emerge from the ground up and include the voices of people who thrive in it. Communication strategies for change should be sensitive to the needs of the local communities, and local media strategies should be engaged to achieve development goals.

Saumya Pant

See also Digital Divide; Flow and Contra-Flow; Globalization Theories; Informatization; International Communication Theories; Neocolonialism; New World Information and Communication Order (NWICO); Postcolonial Feminism; Postcolonial Theory

Further Readings

Chambers, R. (1997). *Whose reality counts: Putting the first last*. London: Intermediate Technology Publications.

Cornwall, A. (2003). Whose voices? Whose choices? Reflections on gender and participatory development. *World Development, 31*, 1325–1342.

Freire, P. (1970). *Pedagogy of the oppressed*. New York: Continuum.

Harter, L. M., Sharma, D., Pant, S., Sharma, Y., & Singhal, A. (2007). Catalyzing social reform through participatory folk performances in rural India. In L. Frey & K. Carragee (Eds.), *Communication and social activism* (pp. 269–298). Cresskill, NJ: Hampton Press.

Morris, N. (2003). A comparative analysis of the diffusion and participatory models in development communication. *Communication Theory, 13*, 225–248.

Moser, C. O. N. (1993). Third world policy approaches to women in development. In *Gender planning and development: Theory, practice and training* (pp. 55–79). New York: Routledge.

Mumby, D. K. (2000). Communication, organization, and the public sphere. In P. M. Buzzanell (Ed.), *Rethinking organizational and managerial* communication from feminist perspectives (pp. 3–23). Thousand Oaks, CA: Sage.

Pant, S. (2007). Enacting empowerment in private and public spaces: The role of Taru in facilitating social change among young village women in India. Unpublished doctoral dissertation, Ohio University, Athens, OH.

Papa, M. J., Singhal, A., Law, S., Sood, S., Rogers, E. M., Shefner-Rogers, C., et al. (2000). Entertainment-education and social change: An analysis of parasocial interaction, social learning, collective efficacy, and paradoxical communication. Journal of Communication, 50(4), 31–55.

Servaes, J. (2002). Communication for development: One world, multiple cultures. Cresskill, NJ: Hampton Press.

Wilkins, K. G. (2000). Accounting for power in development communications. In K. G. Wilkins (Ed.), Redeveloping communication for social change (pp. 197–209). New York: Rowman & Littlefield.

Zimmerman, M. A. Taking aim on empowerment research: On the distinction between individual and psychological conceptions. American Journal of Community Psychology, 18, 169–177.

INTERPERSONAL COMMUNICATION THEORIES

Interpersonal communication (IPC) is one of the most popular teaching subjects and research areas in communication studies. At its most basic, IPC examines how people in relationships talk to one another, why they select the messages they select, and the effect the messages have on the relationship and the individuals. This entry will first offer a brief history of the development of the IPC field. The second section is a description of the criteria used to identify communication as interpersonal. Finally, four categories of IPC theories are reviewed, and specific theories of IPC are described.

IPC is important to study for a number of reasons. First, people create meaning through communication—we learn who we are through communication with others and, more importantly, our communication with others influences how we think about and feel about ourselves. Second, IPC is important for practical reasons—we need to be able to talk to people in order to get things done and make positive impressions. Third, IPC is important to us physically—people who have good interpersonal relationships are physically and mentally healthier. Fourth, humans are social animals, and IPC helps us fulfill our social needs—understanding the IPC process will provide insight into how relationships can be more successful and satisfying. Finally, IPC research is important because how people think they communicate in relationships and how they actually communicate in relationships are very different.

Brief History

The academic study of communication is both very old, tracing its roots back to the ancient Greek philosophers, and relatively new, with most universities recognizing communication as a separate department only within the past 40 years. The study of communication as a separate discipline was strongly influenced by researchers in psychology, sociology, anthropology, English and rhetoric, and linguistics. Much of the early work by researchers interested in communication focused on mass communication issues and attitude changes. This focus on persuasion issues eventually began to wane, and researchers started to examine other areas of research. In the late 1950s and early 1960s, a social scientific approach to the study of human communication emerged as communication researchers began to investigate the interactional patterns of personal relationships.

Given the diverse influences on the development of the communication field, not surprising is that the first books written about IPC were not written by communication scholars. In the 1950s, Ray Birdwhistell and Edward T. Hall, both anthropologists, published books on the interpersonal nature of nonverbal communication. In 1958, psychologist Fritz Heider's book, The Psychology of Interpersonal Relations, examined attribution theory in close relationships. In the late 1950s and early 1960s, Erving Goffman, a sociologist, published books about how communication can be used to affect perceptions and manage interactions. His book, The Presentation of Self in Everyday Life, examined how people create roles for themselves and use communication to shape impressions. The ideas in these books, combined with the social upheaval of the 1960s, had an effect on Paul Watzlawick, Janet Beavin, and Don Jackson, who, as researchers at the Mental Research Institute in Palo Alto, California, were also influenced by Gregory Bateson's interests in systems theories and his research program on understanding human nature and the role of communication in mental illness. Watzlawick, Beavin, and Jackson, in their 1967 book *The Pragmatics of Human Communication,* noted that relationships are systems within which people develop and adapt their interaction patterns. This book, now a classic of communication study, helped establish the study of communication in relationships as an important discipline.

In the 1970s, research and theories of IPC largely focused on attraction, with questions such as, Can we predict attraction? Can we explain why two people find each other so appealing? and What messages are more successful at gaining compliance? In the early 1980s there were some major shifts in the research emphasis. Researchers moved from simple questions of who is attracted to whom and began to focus on analyzing long-term relationships. Research investigated an increased breadth of relational topics, and a number of new theoretical perspectives emerged.

Although interpersonal research started out focused on the relationship between communication and social influence processes, this area is now so broadly defined that researchers generally study a specific area of IPC, such as why people communicate the way they do; how people produce or process messages; or how relationships are initiated, maintained, and dissolved through communication. In fact, IPC is a popular area of communication research and is the focus of approximately 40% of the publications in *Human Communication Research,* one of the top journals in the communication field.

What Is Interpersonal Communication?

Researchers agree that IPC is communication that occurs between people in relationships. To narrow down this broad definition, researchers have proposed a variety of criteria. Instead of categorizing communication as either interpersonal or not interpersonal, these criteria can be used to decide the degree to which the communication is interpersonal.

Criteria for Interpersonal Communication

Numerical—How many people are involved in the interaction? Two people is the classic number for IPC, but, depending on the situation and topic, three or four, perhaps even five people talking to each other may be interpersonal. One thing to consider is how groups larger than four or five often split into smaller sizes for conversation. So, when there are too many people to maintain one conversation in which everyone can participate, the size is too large to be classified interpersonal.

Channel—What medium is used for the communication? Most IPC needs some element of the interaction in the here and now. Face-to-face communication is the most immediate, but there are other channels, such as the telephone and e-mail, that allow partners to communicate in the moment.

Feedback—Is there any opportunity for feedback, adaptation, and responsiveness? The ability to adapt and respond to the other person enhances the communication and makes it more interpersonal.

Privacy—Is the interaction in public or private? Interactions that happen in front of many other people, or those that lots of other people are a part of, tend to be less intimate and have more superficial communication.

Goal—Are the participants focused on completing a specific task, or are they more focused on identity and relationship issues? Those situations in which people are concerned about their own and the other's identity, as well as the relationship, are more interpersonal.

Relationship type and stage—Do the communicators have a recognized and established relationship? If the people in the relationship are interchangeable (e.g., customer and clerk), the communication is less interpersonal.

Knowledge—How much do the communicators know about each other and how the other person will react? Do the communicators have expectations for each other's behavior? The more we know about the other person and the better able we are to predict that person's reactions, the more interpersonal the communication.

Mutual influence—Do one person's actions influence the other's subsequent actions? The more there is mutual influence, the more the communication is interpersonal.

Examining these criteria reveals that though there are some situations that can be easily classified as highly interpersonal, others may be clearly not interpersonal. However, many interactions are "fuzzy"—they meet some of the criteria but not all the criteria. Instead of categorizing communication as either IPC or not IPC, researchers usually consider the degree to which the interaction is interpersonal.

Theories of Interpersonal Communication

Though there are a number of IPC theories that provide different lenses through which to view communication in relationships, these theories fall into four categories: theories about meaning in relationships, theories about motives in relationships, theories about messages in relationships, and theories about movement in relationships.

Theories About Meaning in Relationships

Humans have created and live in a world of signs and symbols. The very relationships people need in their lives are developed and sustained though their use of symbols. The success of both personal relationships and superficial encounters requires that people negotiate the complex world of meaning and interpretation.

Constructivism is a theoretical framework that attempts to explain why people communicate the way they do and why some communicators are more successful than others. In the early 1980s, Jesse Delia and colleagues, building on psychological theories of *personal constructs,* argued that people's communicative choices are influenced by their situational *schemas,* or mental maps, of how they should act in a given situation. People with highly developed or complex maps of a situation and other people tend to have a better understanding of others' perspectives and goals. Those people with complex maps are called *cognitively complex.* They tend to attach more meaning to situations and others' actions, which enables them to be more person centered in their communication and

to develop messages that are more likely to achieve their goals.

Coordinated management of meaning theorizes that communication is a process through which people make sense of their world and produce a social reality. Barnett Pearce and Vernon Cronen, who first proposed this theory in the late 1970s, argued that communication is central to being human and that people create their own conversational reality. Creating meaning in interaction is achieved by applying rules based on the content of the communication, the actions being performed, the situation, the relationship between the communicators, the individuals' backgrounds, and the cultural patterns. According to Pearce and Cronen, the goal of communication is not necessarily for people to reach agreement but, instead, for the communicators to reach a level of coordination.

Symbolic interactionism is a foundational sociological perspective that was influenced by many theorists, notably George Herbert Mead and Herbert Blumer. Though originally a sociological theory, symbolic interactionism is important in communication research. The title of Mead's book, *Mind, Self, and Society,* published in 1934, provides a glimpse of the theory. In brief, symbolic interactionism describes how people use language to construct meaning; how they create and present themselves; and how, working with others, they use symbols to create society. In the late 1960s, Herbert Blumer set out three basic premises of the perspective: (1) People's behavior is influenced by the meanings they have about people and events; (2) interactions, specifically conversations, are important for developing and conveying meaning; and (3) a person's meanings about events and others can change over time. The basis of this theory is that people behave based on the meanings they attach to situations.

Theories About Motives in Relationships

People have reasons for the way they behave. Operating off assumptions about others, interpretations of situations, and the desire to fulfill their own needs, people make choices about their communication.

Attribution theory provides a framework for understanding how individuals interpret their own and others' behavior. According to attribution theorists such as Fritz Heider, people are motivated to make sense of behavior and explain patterns. People develop personal explanations about others' motives and meaning, which, in turn, influence the person's actions toward others. After observing behavior and determining whether the action was deliberate, people tend to categorize the behavior as caused by the person (internally motivated) or caused by the situation (externally motivated).

Fundamental interpersonal relationship orientation theory, introduced by William Schutz in 1958, argues that people are motivated to satisfy three needs: inclusion, control, and affection. People begin relationships to meet these needs. Inclusion is the need people feel to belong and be included. Control refers to people's desire to shape their interactions. Affection is the need to be liked and maintain relationships. These motives can be used to explain people's communication behaviors.

Uncertainty reduction theory assumes that people want stable and predictable interactions, which lead people to reduce their uncertainty about others and events. Uncertainty stems from the number of different things that might occur in a situation. Charles Berger and Richard Calabrese's theory provides insight into how uncertainty motivates communication behaviors, specifically information seeking, reciprocity, verbal intimacy, nonverbal expressiveness, and the amount of information shared. Additionally, uncertainty reduction theory makes predications about liking and perceived similarity.

Theories About Messages in Relationships

People have a variety of communication choices. A single communication goal can be achieved through many different messages, and a single message can meet many different goals. Theories about messages in relationships attempt to explain why people say what they do during interaction and how they process messages.

Action assembly theory attempts to explain where our thoughts come from and how we translate those thoughts into verbal and nonverbal communication. John Greene, who first published this theory in 1984, proposes that people organize and store knowledge about what things mean and how to do things, and then use that knowledge in action. When people encounter similar situations, they recall, or assemble, these memories and plan a course of action.

Communication accommodation theory is interested in how and why people modify or change their communication behavior in different situations. This theory, developed by Howard Giles and colleagues in the 1960s and 1970s, explains the ways in which people influence and are influenced by each other while they are communicating. Communication accommodation theory proposes that when communicating, people seek to reduce or increase the differences between themselves and the other. They do this either by converging, communicating more like the other, or diverging, to exaggerate their communicative differences.

Expectancy violation theory was proposed in the 1970s by Judee Burgoon and colleagues. This theory argues that interpretations of a message are not simply about what is said or even how it is said. Instead, interpretation is determined by the situation, the other's reward value (i.e., the positive and negative characteristics of the person), and how the message meets or violates one's expectations. When what you expect to happen in an interaction does not happen, you frequently note the occurrence and pay more attention to the event. Though violations result when someone breaks a verbal or nonverbal rule, such as standing too close or saying inappropriate things, violations are not necessarily negative. The violation may be perceived as positive, either because the action was welcome or because the actor has positive reward value.

Politeness theory, published in the 1980s by Penelope Brown and Stephen Levinson, argues that people will use different messages depending on their perception of the situation and the listener. Politeness is the way through which people attempt to lessen the potential threat in certain messages. This theory was strongly influenced by Erving Goffman's notion of *face*, which is the positive social identity we claim for ourselves. Face is about the way you see yourself and want other people to see you. Politeness theory proposed that face is a multidimensional concept that includes positive face, or one's desire to be liked, respected, and included, and negative face, one's desire to be independent, autonomous, and unconstrained by others. The theory focuses on how people construct messages that address one or both aspects of face and the factors that influence message production.

Speech act theory is about how people accomplish things with words. Developed during the 1960s by John Austin and refined in the 1970s by John Searle, this theory explains how people use language as action. In other words, how can we talk things into being? Though one of the primary goals of speech act theory was to categorize speech acts, this theory also explains how speakers rely on conventional assumptions about speech to make sense of interactions.

Theories About Movement in Relationships

Relationships are always evolving. As people talk to each other and develop shared meanings, relationships are established, maintained, and sometimes even dissolved. Theories about movement in relationships describe how communication functions to move relationships along different trajectories.

Relational dialectics theory presents relationship change as the result of individuals' navigating and negotiating their internal, contradictory desires. Relational dialectics theory, presented by Leslie Baxter and her colleagues, is rooted in the historical dialectic perspective of opposing but connected forces. People in relationships often want two different things at the same time. In relationships, the three common dialectics, or simultaneous desires, are integration–separation (desire to be close and separate), stability–change (desire for predictability and spontaneity), and expression–privacy (the desire to be open and private).

Social exchange theory offers the perspective that relationships are commodities and attributes movement in relationships to people's desire to maximize their rewards while minimizing their costs. As relational partners become too costly, either through time or energy, people begin to minimize interactions. However, we maximize interactions with people perceived as rewarding. This theory, by John Thibaut and Harold Kelley, explains that perceptions of cost and rewards are not fixed but determined by one's level of comparison.

Social penetration theory, by Irving Altman and Dalmas Taylor, describes how self-disclosure moves relationships from superficial to intimate. This was one of the first theories about how changes in communication patterns can effect changes in relationships. The theory, first published in the early 1970s, is often called "the onion model" because it portrays people as having multiple layers centered on a core. At the core are a person's deeply held beliefs, values, thoughts, and feelings. This core can be conceptualized as the "true" self that is private and protected. People's layers have both depth and breadth, so there are different topics that we can know about a person (breadth), as well as lots of detail about each topic (depth). As people get to know each other, they self-disclose and "shed" layers, which moves the relationship deeper. Relationships develop as people move from the superficial layers closer to the core layers.

The relationship development model depicts relationship movement as a series of stages through which couples may move. In the 1980s, Mark Knapp presented a 10-stage model of relationships coming together and coming apart. Each stage is characterized by different communication patterns. Though movement through these stages is generally sequential and systematic, people may skip stages, stay in a stage, or repeat stages.

Summary

Theories about IPC have been developed to explain how people attach meaning to events, why they act the way they do, how they make decisions about messages, and the effect that communication has on relationships. Though this entry presents these theories in separate categories about meaning, motives, messages, and movement, most of the theories can be used to understand the communication processes in other categories.

Virginia M. McDermott

See also Accommodation Theory; Action Assembly Theory; Attribution Theory; Constructivism; Coordinated Management of Meaning; Expectancy Violations Theory; Politeness Theory; Relational Development; Social Exchange Theory; Social Interaction Theories; Social Penetration Theory; Speech Act Theory; Symbolic Interactionism; Uncertainty Reduction Theory

Further Readings

Baxter, L. A., & Braithwaite, D. O. (Eds.). (2008). *Engaging theories in interpersonal communication.* Thousand Oaks, CA: Sage.

Cappella, J. (1987). Interpersonal communication: Definitions and fundamental questions. In C. Berger & S. Chaffee (Eds.), *Handbook of communication science* (pp. 184–238). Newbury Park, CA: Sage.

Fitch, K. (1994). Culture, ideology and interpersonal communication research. In S. Deetz (Ed.), *Communication yearbook 17* (pp. 104–135). Thousand Oaks, CA: Sage.

Knapp, M. L., & Daly, J. A. (2002). *Handbook of interpersonal communication*. Thousand Oaks, CA: Sage.

Parks, M. R. (1982). Ideology in interpersonal communication: Off the couch and into the world. In M. Burgoon (Ed.), *Communication yearbook 5* (pp. 79–107). New Brunswick, NJ: Transaction Books.

Stamp, G. (1999). A qualitatively constructed interpersonal communication model: A grounded theory analysis. *Human Communication Research, 25,* 531–547.

Interpersonal Deception Theory

Deception refers to behavior intentionally enacted to mislead another. Interpersonal deception theory (IDT) is one contemporary communication theory intended to predict and explain deception in the context of interpersonal interactions. IDT was developed by David Buller and Judee K. Burgoon to offer an alternative perspective to prevailing psychological perspectives on deception. Growing out of several decades of research into credibility and interpersonal communication, it is an interrelated set of assumptions and propositions, or testable statements, drawing on principles of interpersonal communication to predict and explain deception in interpersonal interactions. Its scope is thus deception *during* communication, which can include face-to-face, public, computer-mediated, or virtual communication. To date, over 20 experiments have been conducted testing various aspects of IDT. Many, but not all, have received support.

IDT is not meant to focus on a single cause but instead to provide a comprehensive depiction of the communication-relevant factors in deception message production and deception detection. This entry summarizes the assumptions of IDT and some of the key propositions of the theory that illustrate its claims.

Assumptions of Interpersonal Deception Theory

Assumptions are the "givens" in a theory that underpin it but are not tested. IDT enumerates several assumptions about the nature of interpersonal communication and the nature of deception. It assumes, first, that interpersonal interactions place all parties in the simultaneous role of sender and receiver. As senders they must mentally create messages, encode those messages into verbal and nonverbal signals, observe other communicators' feedback and reactions as they speak, and adapt their ongoing communication to those reactions. As listeners, they must recognize and interpret another's messages, manage their outward demeanor, send feedback, and formulate their own upcoming turn at talk. There are several implications of this general depiction of the process of interpersonal communication. One is that it *is* a process, a continually changing stream of verbal and nonverbal signals that cannot be captured by a single snapshot. Another is that both sender and receiver are active, not passive, goal-oriented participants who anticipate, plan, and adapt as the interaction unfolds. Yet another is that sender and receiver perform several different communication functions at once, including generating and processing verbal messages, presenting self favorably, regulating turn taking, and managing emotional displays, among others. Yet another implication is that sender and receiver are interdependent. Each person's actions influence the other and cannot be understood without taking account of what the other is doing.

A central assumption regarding deception is that sizing up the credibility of other communicators is an inherent part of all interactions. Even though it typically occurs at a subconscious level, gauging another's truthfulness is an implicit part of all human encounters.

Another key assumption is that deception entails three classes of strategic, or deliberate, activity—information, behavior, and image management. *Strategic* actions are motivated and deliberate, whether for self-benefit (such as bilking someone of their savings) or for the benefit of another person (such as saving someone from embarrassment). However, Buller and Burgoon subscribe to the view that deception, as with other planned and overlearned behavior, can be strategic without being highly conscious. *Information management* refers to efforts to control the verbal contents of a message. *Behavior management* refers to efforts to control accompanying nonverbal behaviors to suppress any telltale signs of deceit and to appear "normal." *Image management* refers to more general efforts to maintain credibility and to protect one's face if caught. Handled skillfully, these three classes of strategic activity should work together to create an overall believable *communication performance*. At the same time, other *nonstrategic,* or unintentional, behaviors—such as signs of nervousness, fear, or excessive behavioral control—may also occur, producing unnatural behavior, damaging performances, and undermining credibility.

A related assumption is that deception is more cognitively demanding than truth telling. It poses more difficulty for senders to create a deceptive than a truthful version of reality because the sender must not only mentally create the truthful rendition but must also concoct the deceptive one and mentally edit its presentation so that it is plausible and consistent with prior statements.

The relevance of these various assumptions is that, in contrast to perspectives that focus primarily or exclusively on involuntary and unintentional manifestations of deceit, deception should be viewed as intentional, goal-directed activity and as a social phenomenon (i.e., something that happens between people), not just a psychological one (i.e., something that happens within people). Additionally, its assumptions draw attention to the dynamic nature of deception displays and deception detection, as well as to the influence of receiver thoughts and behavior on sender displays. For example, receiver suspicion should influence sender thoughts, feelings, verbalizations, and nonverbal displays, which in turn should affect the receiver's subsequent level of suspicion and own verbal and nonverbal behavior.

Testable Propositions

The heart of IDT is its series of 18 interconnected and testable propositions that together are meant to provide a more accurate depiction of how interpersonal deception is enacted and with what effects. Here are a few of the most central of these propositions related to context, relationship, interactivity, bias and suspicion, and accuracy.

Context and Relationship

Two central propositions are that (1) *deceiver and receiver thoughts, feelings, and behaviors vary systematically with (a) access to nonverbal cues and (b) conversational demands;* and (2) *deceiver and receiver thoughts, feelings, and behaviors vary systematically with (c) relational familiarity and (d) relational valence (positive to negative).* These propositions identify the communication context and the nature of the relationship as key influences on cognition, affect, and behavior during deception. Contexts such as face-to-face interaction and videoconferencing that give communicators access to the full complexion of one another's nonverbal cues should produce different thoughts, behavioral displays, interpretations, and detection accuracy than ones such as e-mail or phone conversations that have fewer nonverbal channels available. The type of interaction, such as a task-oriented versus a social one, should also influence how deception is enacted and detected. For instance, a business negotiation may invoke more perceptions of ulterior motives and possible deception than a chat about sports. The relationship between communicators— friendly or adversarial, family versus strangers— should also make a difference. These initial IDT propositions do not state the specific direction of these relationships. Instead, they must be combined with other propositions and with the assumptions to generate specific hypotheses.

Interactivity

One variable that can make a difference is the degree of interaction in the exchange. The proposition that *the more interactive the communication context, the more that deceivers increase strategic activity and reduce nonstrategic activity over time* draws on the factor of nonverbal-cues access and assumptions about interaction dynamics, strategic activity, and the cognitive demands of deceptive message production. Interactive communication contexts typically include more nonverbal channels through which communicators are interdependent and will therefore motivate senders to exert more control over their verbal and nonverbal behavior so as to evade detection. Conversely, less interactive contexts, such as e-mail exchanges, will place fewer demands on senders to manage so many different facets of behavior in real time and thus may entail less motivation to manage information, behavior, and image.

Other propositions similarly predict what cognitions, emotions, and behaviors will be observed under what conditions and how accurately receivers will detect deception. Several of these propositions relate to bias, suspicion, and detection accuracy.

Bias and Suspicion

Suspicion and truth bias are expected to influence receiver judgments. For example, one proposition states that receivers will manifest their suspicions through strategic and nonstrategic behavior. They may choose a questioning style that either makes their suspicions evident or attempts to minimize any signs of skepticism. At the same time, some of their incredulity may "leak out" unintentionally in their demeanor, tipping off the sender to the presence of suspicion.

Accuracy of Judgment

Another proposition specifies what leads to inaccurate or accurate judgment: *Receivers are less accurate in detecting deception when (a) receivers hold truth biases, (b) contexts are interactive, and (c) senders are skilled encoders; they are more accurate when (d) they are familiar with the deceiver, (e) they are skilled decoders, and (f) senders deviate from expected patterns.* Put differently, if receivers are truth biased, that is, judging most senders as truthful, they will fail to detect deception (although they will be seen as accurate when judging truth because they judge most people as honest and straightforward). Interactive contexts are posited to lead to inaccuracy because senders will take better advantage of them than will receivers. Receivers will also be less accurate detecting the deception of senders who are skillful communicators than of those who are not. Factors that

should give receivers more of an edge are having familiarity with the sender's behavioral patterns (as would be possible with exposure to baseline truthful verbal and nonverbal behavior), familiarity with other information about the sender (as would be possible when doing background checks or reading a resume), or relational familiarity (as when sender and receiver are from the same family or are close friends). Relational familiarity, however, also triggers more truth bias, so this last form of familiarity is thought to be less of a force for accuracy than the others. Receiver communication skills are posited to aid accuracy, just as they aid sender performance, but the empirical evidence has yet to confirm that receivers who are generally skillful at decoding others' communication are skillful at decoding deception. Finally, receivers should be more accurate to the extent that sender verbal and nonverbal behavior is abnormal and violates expectations; if senders maintain a normal-appearing demeanor, receivers will not be as successful in detecting deceit.

Judee K. Burgoon

See also Expectancy Violations Theory; Interpersonal Communication Theories; Nonverbal Communication Theories

Further Readings

Buller, D. B., & Burgoon, J. K. (1996). Interpersonal deception theory. *Communication Theory, 6,* 203–243.

Burgoon, J. K., Blair, J. P., & Strom, R. (in press). Cognitive biases, modalities and deception detection. *Human Communication Research.*

Burgoon, J. K., & Buller, D. B. (2008). Interpersonal deception theory. In L. A. Baxter & D. O. Braithwaite (Eds.), *Engaging theories in interpersonal communication: Multiple perspectives* (pp. 227–239). Thousand Oaks, CA: Sage.

Burgoon, J. K., Buller, D. B., Dillman, L., & Walther, J. (1995). Interpersonal deception: IV. Effects of suspicion on perceived communication and nonverbal behavior dynamics. *Human Communication Research, 22,* 163–196.

Burgoon, J. K., Buller, D. B., Ebesu, A., & Rockwell, P. (1994). Interpersonal deception: V. Accuracy in deception detection. *Communication Monographs, 61,* 303–325.

INTERPERSONAL POWER

See Power, Interpersonal

INTERPRETIVE COMMUNITIES THEORY

The theory of interpretive communities attempts to explicate the social processes involved in interpreting cultural texts. In the communication discipline, it has been applied most often in media studies, particularly the semiotic domain of audience experience. According to the theory, the meanings ascribed to cultural texts are neither wholly subjective nor a property of material objects; rather, such texts as television programs, romance novels, and Web content become meaningful only through the interpretive strategies practiced by the memberships of communities. The *community* of the term often references a shared consciousness of core beliefs, ideals, or identity in a broad population of people. In this sense, the term is, like Benedict Anderson's concept of *imagined community,* a useful heuristic for exploring the social dimensions of interpretation. However, *community* is also sometimes used to characterize the situated sense-making practices of fan groups, subcultures, and other types of social collectivity. The question of whether the interpretive community is a metaphorical construct or an empirical description remains a source of debate in media and communication studies.

Development of Interpretive Community Theory

Interpretive community theory is of fairly recent origin, although its epistemological roots extend back more than 100 years. The basic idea of the interpretive community is foreshadowed in the work of the American pragmatist and semiotician Charles Sanders Pierce, who argued that public knowledge arises out of the discursive practices of communities of inquiry. The hermeneutics of Wilhelm Dilthey, Paul Ricoeur, and Hans-Georg Gadamer contributed a method for studying the active, contextualized nature of textual interpretation, while the work of the linguistic theorists Valentin Volosinov and Mikhail Bakhtin stressed the polysemic (characterized by many meanings) and dialogic nature of language in social usage. Meanwhile, several strains of the constructivist movement during the mid-20th century—among them social phenomenology, symbolic interactionism, and ethnomethodology—forwarded the view that reality is a social construction that takes variable forms and is created through processes of face-to-face interaction. Toward the end of the century, belief in the stability of texts and historical metanarratives was questioned by poststructuralist philosophers who argued that knowledge is created through the contingencies of power and discourse. Similarly, in literary studies, the deconstructionist and reader-response (or reception) camps promoted the role of the reader-as-subject in bringing textual meanings to life. These latter developments set the stage for the literary theorist Stanley Fish to coin the term *interpretive community.*

In his volume of essays *Is There a Text in This Class?* Fish proposed that a text is meaningless—mere ink marks on paper—without readers to engage it. Other reader-response theorists said much the same thing, but most of them located the mechanisms for meaning making in psychological explanations. Stanley Fish's formulation was set apart by its emphasis on the social world of readers. He argued that the interpretive strategies that a reader deploys in the act of reading—indeed, the strategies for deciding what counts as a text of a certain kind—existed long before the reader encountered the text. Furthermore, these strategies are not the property of an individual but of a social community of readers. Through networks of discourse, new members are socialized into the cultural presuppositions for reading and evaluating texts, as well as the specific rules for how to read a text competently. Importantly, members also learn the rules for debating the value of an interpretation; such debates can be fruitful for signaling the core values of a community, clarifying the range of coherent readings, or indicating new ways of reading. However, any serious disagreements that emerge about what a text means—or about what constitutes a text—can be evidence of different interpretive communities. Therefore, what we conventionally think of as the act of reading a work of literature is actually an act of "writing" it—creating and shaping its contours of meaning—and the strategies that enable these achievements are produced by the social entity called an interpretive community. A textual reading is judged right or wrong, worthy or unworthy, by the standards of this community. Other communities may have very different aesthetic or ideological commitments and thus abide by different standards for interpreting the same work.

Interpretive Community Research in Media Studies

The prototype community that Fish had in mind was literary critics, whose business it is to sharpen and refine their evaluations of a body of texts (usually works of literary art) and communicate those evaluations to other experts. This type of community is marked by an extensive period of formal training; moreover, the discursive activity of its membership can be widely dispersed in time and space. Yet it became apparent by the early 1980s that the concept could apply to more mundane settings. Spurred by new developments in British cultural studies, particularly Stuart Hall's encoding/decoding model and David Morley's pioneering *Nationwide* audience study, the field of media studies was undergoing a major paradigm change. The locus of meaning in the mass-communication process rapidly shifted away from the text alone and toward the text–audience relationship. Yet even as early qualitative audience studies registered patterns of text decoding, the underlying mechanisms remained unclear. The concept of interpretive community entered the lexicon of media scholarship with the 1984 publication of Janice Radway's *Reading the Romance*. Studying a group of women readers of romance novels who frequented a bookstore, Radway found that the women had very clear, and mostly coherent, understandings of how romance stories are told. They seemed to be united in their evaluations of "good" and "bad" romances, the attributes of male and female protagonists, and other features of the genre. Importantly, Radway also inquired in the focus group interviews about the social background of romance reading, including the women's negotiation of the novels in the context of family roles and responsibilities.

While *Reading the Romance* represented a breakthrough study in many respects, its adaptation of Fish's interpretive community concept to everyday media reception was one of the most notable. Mass-communication theorists followed up on Radway's study with efforts to flesh out the then-embryonic concept into a theoretic form. Klaus Bruhn Jensen, for example, conceptualized the interpretive community as an intersection of prior cultural traditions and newer media competencies. Thomas R. Lindlof proposed that interpretive communities may be identified in three ways: their consumption of specific genres, the commonalities of their media interpretations, and their performance of social actions of media use. The morphology of interpretive communities also came under scrutiny: Jensen hypothesized that interpretive communities crisscross each other in the cultural arena; Lindlof suggested that not all "communities" map neatly onto a social group but rather function as an informal social tie that lasts only for as long as the relationship endures.

Following Radway, many of the media studies of interpretive communities share an interest in popular genres and the competencies and pleasures that characterize audience reception of genre texts. Among the genre-based communities that have been studied thus far are those for science fiction, soap operas, talk shows, self-help books, and oppositional political texts. Genres have served as a focus of investigation and conceptual development for several reasons. First, media content is often designed, produced, and marketed to the public by means of genre classifications. Thus, the genre system represents an implicit contract between the media industries and the normative codes of readers (and viewers). Second, genres always exhibit some variance in the meanings of their signifiers, both synchronically and diachronically; consequently, the researcher can track the variations in audience decodings as the genre itself undergoes change. Third, from a practical standpoint, it is thought to be easier to find an interpretive community if one can make a case that a genre has a highly devoted following. By the same token, however, genres are problematic because not all consumers of a genre can be safely regarded as members of an interpretive community, and not all interpretive communities subsist on genres. In this regard, there has been, in recent years, an expansion in the types of mediated communities under active study. The explosive growth of the Internet has led legions of scholars to study the communicative action of *virtual communities* that organize their users along the lines of an ideology, lifestyle, or another common interest. The study of *brand communities*—people who align their interpretations of a branded product with others of similarly intense affinity—has developed rapidly in the field of consumer research. Also in media studies, the concept of interpretive community has been applied to the cultural identity and collective memories of journalists and other professional communicators.

Methodological Issues

Methodologically, audience studies have largely relied on qualitative interviews to elicit discourse about the content uses, strategies, and textual discriminations of an interpretive community. The devoted users of a genre are typically recruited for these interview studies because, as mentioned earlier, many interpretive communities are defined by their affiliation with genre texts. Focus group interviews, in particular, are often used for tapping into the group context of audience interpretation, although relatively few focus group studies consider strings of dialogue as their units of analysis. Ethnography is probably most suitable for studying how interpretation and behavior are actually joined in natural settings; one example of ethnographic investigation of interpretive communities is Roger Aden, Rita Rahoi, and Christina Beck's study of visitors to the *Field of Dreams* site in Iowa. Ethnography is rarely employed in interpretive community studies, due in part to the greater demands of logistics, time, and social participation. Documentary evidence and hermeneutic methods have also been employed in studies of media production cultures and historical moments of audience reception.

Criticisms

Criticisms of the interpretive communities theory have centered on three issues: the meaning and validity of community, its ideological blind spot, and the underspecification of theoretical components. The first critique has to do with the meaning of the *community* referent. Many studies have marshaled considerable evidence that interpretive communities either closely resemble aspects of geographically bounded communities or that they operate as part of the normal semiotic functions of real communities. Yet some also claim that people do not so much belong to mediated communities as they learn "interpretive repertoires" for use on media texts in specific situations. For these critics, the community metaphor should not be applied too literally. Second, it is often alleged that the concept's seeming emphasis on audience autonomy ignores the power of media texts (and the institutions that produce them) in determining meanings. This ideological blind spot, some believe, can be redressed only by taking account of the audience's susceptibility to hegemonic common sense as well as media manipulation, misdirection, and cooptation. Finally, the theory of interpretive communities has been amply criticized for lacking the specificity required of a theoretical account. There is little disagreement, even among its adherents, that rigorous theorizing of interpretive communities has been piecemeal at best. Achieving progress in such areas as specifying the boundary conditions for interpretive communities, verifying and describing the types of interpretive communities that exist, and modeling their evolutionary paths would help establish a firmer foundation for theory and empirical research.

Thomas R. Lindlof

See also Audience Theories; Community; Cultural Studies; Ethnography of Communication; Hermeneutics; Interpretive Theory; Media and Mass Communication Theories; Semiotics and Semiology

Further Readings

Aden, R. C., Rahoi, R. L., & Beck, C. S. (1995). "Dreams are born on places like this": The process of interpretive community formation at the Field of Dreams site. *Communication Quarterly, 43,* 368–380.

Anderson, B. (1983). *Imagined communities.* New York: Verso.

Berkowitz, D., & TerKeurst, J. V. (1999). Community as interpretive community: Rethinking the journalist-source relationship. *Journal of Communication, 49,* 125–136.

Bloustien, G. (2007). "Wigging people out": Youth music practice and mediated communities. *Journal of*

Community & Applied Social Psychology, 17, 446–462.

Carragee, K. M. (1990). Interpretive media study and interpretive social science. *Critical Studies in Mass Communication, 7,* 81–96.

Fish, S. (1980). *Is there a text in this class?* Cambridge, MA: Harvard University Press.

Jensen, K. B. (1987). Qualitative audience research: Toward an integrative approach to reception. *Critical Studies in Mass Communication, 4,* 21–36.

Jensen, K. B. (1991). When is meaning? Communication theory, pragmatism, and mass media reception. In J. A. Anderson (Ed.), *Communication yearbook 14* (pp. 3–32). Newbury Park, CA: Sage.

Jensen, K. B. (2002). Media reception: Qualitative traditions. In K. B. Jensen (Ed.), *A handbook of media and communication research: Qualitative and quantitative methodologies* (pp. 156–170). London: Routledge.

Lindlof, T. R. (1988). Media audiences as interpretive communities. In J. A. Anderson (Ed.), *Communication yearbook 11* (pp. 81–108). Beverly Hills, CA: Sage.

Lindlof, T. R. (2002). Interpretive community: An approach to media and religion. *Journal of Media and Religion, 1,* 61–74.

Mayer, V. (2003). Living telenovelas/telenovelizing life: Mexican American girls' identities and transnational telenovelas. *Journal of Communication, 53,* 479–495.

Morley, D. (1980). *The Nationwide audience: Structure and decoding.* London: British Film Institute.

Muniz, A. M., Jr., & O'Guinn, T. C. (2001). Brand community. *Journal of Consumer Research, 27,* 412–432.

Radway, J. (1984). *Reading the romance.* Chapel Hill: University of North Carolina Press.

Rauch, J. (2007). Activists as interpretive communities: Rituals of consumption and interaction in an alternative media audience. *Media, Culture & Society, 29,* 994–1013.

Zelizer, B. (1993). Journalists as interpretive communities. *Critical Studies in Mass Communication, 10,* 219–237.

INTERPRETIVE THEORY

The expression *interpretive theory* refers to a relatively large umbrella category that includes analytical perspectives and theories spanning the fields of communication, sociology, anthropology, education, cultural studies, political science, history, and the humanities writ large. Interpretive theories, sometimes referred to as interpretivism or philosophical interpretivism, are orientations to social reality based on the goal of understanding. Thus, we can define interpretive theories as *ontological* and *epistemological* tools used in research concerned with understanding how individuals and groups create meaning in their everyday practices, communication, and lived experiences.

Loosely speaking, interpretivists are (a) scholars who are interested in the ways communities, cultures, or individuals create meaning from their own actions, rituals, interactions, and experiences; (b) scholars who wish to interpret local meanings by locating them into a broader historical, geographical, political, linguistic, ideological, economic, and cultural milieu; (c) researchers who look at the meanings of texts and the codes and rules on which they rely to convey meaning; and (d) theory- and philosophy-oriented scholars who explore ideas of meaning and interpretation in and of themselves.

To comprehend the quintessential characteristics of interpretivism and better appreciate its uniqueness and usefulness, it is useful to begin by looking at its philosophical origins and then juxtaposing interpretivist theories with interpretivism's most notable counterpart: the perspective of positivism. Subsequently, this entry explores interpretivism as it relates to social scientific communication research by examining its common ontological and epistemological characteristics.

Philosophical Background

The historical foundations of interpretivism can be traced back to the late 19th and early 20th centuries and mainly to two geographical sites: continental Europe and the United States. Philosophers commonly associated with the growth of interpretivist influence in Europe include Georg Simmel, Max Weber, Hans-Georg Gadamer, Edmund Husserl, Friedrich Schleiermacher, Friedrich Nietzsche, Martin Heidegger, Ludwig Wittgenstein, and Wilhelm Dilthey. These philosophers are also known contributors to the development of perspectives known as hermeneutics and phenomenology. The list of American scholars and intellectuals includes William James, Charles Sanders Peirce,

John Dewey, George Herbert Mead, and Charles Cooley. These American scholars are also universally recognized to be the founding fathers of the philosophy of pragmatism. Despite the geographical, political, and philosophical distance between these two European and North American schools of thought, their intellectual origins—those of interpretivism—are generally found to be remarkably similar in both Europe and North America insofar as they constituted a strong challenge and rejection of the then absolutely dominant ontology and epistemology of positivism. But before we examine interpretivism against positivism, let us briefly outline the main principles of hermeneutics and phenomenology. The main principles of pragmatism will be the subject of exploration in a later section.

Phenomenology

Phenomenology is the philosophical tradition that seeks to understand the world through directly experienced phenomena. By reflecting on such experiences, one can derive an understanding and an appreciation of the multiple, contingent, and diverse meanings of the lifeworld, rather than merely metaphysical conjecture. It follows that phenomenology does not seek to gather up and reflect on knowledge that is speculative in nature, but rather knowledge that is already present in the social world in which we live—that of immediate experience. Therefore, in social sciences such as communication studies, phenomenological theorizing and research studies seek *empirical* data gathered by using various methods in order to understand concrete social phenomena.

The philosophical tradition of phenomenology has emerged through various movements of thought that have spanned two centuries and through the contributions of key American and European thinkers who have progressively made a complex philosophy more and more useful for the practical inquiry needs of social scientists. The notion of studying phenomena rather than essences alone first appeared in the philosophical thought of Immanuel Kant, who asserted that the study of phenomena should derive from the investigation of actual objects of real or illusory experiences. This, he felt, was an activity distinguishably different from the investigation of *noumena,* or the unknowable.

Later, in a critical development of phenomenological thought, Georg Hegel asserted that the science of phenomena was the study of the mind's own knowledge and consciousness.

However, not until the work of German philosopher Edmund Husserl (by many considered the true founding father of phenomenology) did the term *phenomenology* became a distinct tradition within continental philosophy. Husserl's approach—known as *transcendental phenomenology*—has influenced many other thinkers in the phenomenological tradition. Husserlian phenomenology aims at developing a pure, rigorous science that seeks to capture "knowledge of essences" by bracketing all conditions that may make one's consciousness of something partial. Later thinkers such as Martin Heidegger, Maurice Merleau-Ponty, and Jean-Paul Sartre moved away from Husserl's purely cognitive approach to phenomenology that—in their mind—reduced empirical knowledge to a pure realist and ahistorical essence.

In contrast to his teacher Husserl, Heidegger believed that each person can have remarkably different experiences in his or her lifeworld; therefore, bracketing and reducing phenomena to a pure objective essence is impossible and undesirable. Heidegger's rejection of Husserl's phenomenology created a new movement known today as *existential phenomenology* and also laid the foundations of interpretivism. Existential phenomenology is also closer than Husserlian phenomenology to interpretive theory because it is strongly related to and influenced by another continental philosophical tradition, called hermeneutics.

Hermeneutics

Hermeneutics is the philosophy of interpretation and understanding. It examines how experience, language, and dialogue contribute to the process of interpretation. Hermeneutics began as a study of interpreting ancient religious manuscripts but eventually incorporated (through the thought of scholars such as Friedrich Schleiermacher and Hans-Georg Gadamer) the agendas of other academic traditions: Hermeneutics began to look at interpretation not only as a process of uncovering the meanings of texts, but also as a process for understanding everyday experiences and the meanings of the social world. A hermeneutic approach to the social world pays attentions to how individuals spin webs of significance—to paraphrase anthropologist Clifford Geertz—and thus create different meanings for their experiences through their own interpretive lenses and frames.

The central idea of a hermeneutic approach to reality is that of the hermeneutic circle. The *hermeneutic circle* can be explained as a dialectical process of meaning making that takes into account the meanings of an object against a context and the meanings of a context on the basis of a set of present objects. This rather convoluted idea is always best explained through a simple example. Imagine you suddenly hear a whistle. Startled by it, you immediately and quickly try to come up with possible interpretations of its meaning. Hence, you probably turn around to see where it may have come from. If you're walking nearby a soccer pitch, you may determine that the whistle was directed to soccer players by the referee, and thus you assign to the whistle the meaning of *foul*. If you are standing at an intersection and a traffic officer is standing nearby, you may instead find that the whistle was directed at a jaywalker and was meant to attract the jaywalker's attention in order to reprimand him or her. Or perhaps you may feel that the whistle was directed at you; after all, you did just get a fashionable new makeover! Regardless of what it may be, we generally interpret the meaning of an object—such as a whistle—on the basis of the context in which it is encountered. In addition, we use a multitude of social objects—such as a police or referee uniform—to grasp what makes up a social context. Interpretivist theories always utilize the hermeneutic approach and always utilize the phenomenological approach of understanding realities on the basis of people's consciousness of them.

Interpretivism Versus Positivism

A theory—according to the classical logical positivist model—should serve the purpose of explaining relations of cause and effect. In doing so, it should allow for the prediction of future phenomena and possibly allow the scientist a great degree of control over reality. The building of theory should occur by measuring variables and relations among variables, testing hypotheses that explain causal or correlational relations, and building lawlike statements that accumulate in the shape of a formal, universally valid, objective system of propositions. Theory should constantly be subject to extension and improvement through confirmation of the *validity* of its precepts and testing of new hypotheses by way of valid and reliable research such as experiments.

The classical positivist perspective on theory outlined above is most typically associated with the natural sciences. But, interpretivists argue, natural scientists have a radically different research subject than social scientists have. Whereas a rock, for example, has no known capacity to react to the scientist's investigation, a human being does. Indeed a human being is not only reactive, but is so in relatively unpredictable ways due to the human's capacity for meaningful, reflective, intentional action. The natural sciences—or *Naturwissenschaften*, as German interpretivists notably referred to them—are therefore dramatically different from scientific investigations into the human *Geist*, or spirit. The *Geisteswissenschaften*, or social sciences, should therefore adopt an entirely different ontology and epistemology—the early interpretivists argued.

So, what should theory attempt to accomplish within a renewed social scientific project that no longer attempts to model itself after the natural sciences? First and foremost it should attempt to explain *meaning*: the meaning of human action, experience, communication, and how meaning informs people's everyday life, the things they do, what they experience, and the ways in which they relate to other people. Rather than explaining causal relations among variables, it should attempt to comprehend the meanings people give to social things. Thus, rather than focusing on prediction, control, and explanation, an interpretivist perspective focuses on *Verstehen*, that is, understanding. Because of the great diversity of ways in which people assign meanings to things, interpretive theories reject the pretension of building universalist models that are valid across time and space. People's activities are thus contingent, rather than universal.

Moreover, instead of basing their theoretical models on fundamental principles and assumptions that are the unchallengeable basis for further knowledge and inquiry, interpretivists give primacy to insights inductively gathered from observation and experience, even when those insights contradict existing assumptions. Interpretivism is therefore antifoundationalist. Interpretive theories are also built around the idea of emergence—that things are never the same as they are constantly subject to renegotiation, novelty, and unexpected outcomes. Their theorizing, therefore, does not aim for a formalist—that is, a rigorous system of clear rules—approach to reality, but instead for one that is itself emergent and fluid. Interpretivists also generally shy away from experimental or similar kinds of research that create conditions not generally encountered within the contexts of everyday life. Even survey questionnaires—with their characteristically closely structured system of answers and scales—are generally eschewed by interpretivist researchers, who prefer instead to directly immerse themselves in "natural" social situations they wish to understand (most notably through methods such as unstructured interviewing and ethnography).

Finally, interpretive theories take into account the great multiplicity of perspectives that inform meaning and thus reject the very possibility that knowledge be built by dispossessing oneself of values, by relegating the possibility of alternative interpretations to an unlikely accident, and by embracing a form of inquiry that places the researcher/theorist outside and above the reality he or she wishes to comprehend. Rather than objectivist, bias-free, and etic (focusing on external categories and structures), interpretivist theorists embrace a multiplicity of perspectives and possible interpretations, take into account the researcher's own values, and aim at a form of inquiry that works from the inside. All the characteristics of interpretivism discussed above are outlined in Table 1 and juxtaposed against the characteristics of classical logical positivism.

Interpretivism: Theory or Perspective?

Interpretive theory building is so remarkably different from its positivist counterpart (at least in the mind of most interpretivists) that it might even be considered a misnomer to utilize the word *theory* to refer to the analytical practices of interpretivists. This is certainly the case among some empirical researchers, who prefer the label *perspectives*—rather than *theories*—for the sets of analytical tools that allow their generalizations and interpretations. The expression *perspective,* as opposed to *theory,* emphasizes the fact that in the end an interpretation is but an angle, a position, and ultimately a possibility that is easily contradicted by the endless availability of alternative interpretations. In light of this, interpretive perspectives are nothing but toolboxes full of concepts that sensitize inquiry to take a particular shape, emphasis, or direction. While debates over whether interpretivism is a theory or a perspective, a clearly identifiable philosophical

Table I   Classical Logical Positivism and Interpretivism Compared

Classical Logical Positivism	Interpretivism
Focused on explanation	Focused on understanding
Universalist	Contingent
Foundationalist	Antifoundationalist
Formalist	Emergent
Experimental	Naturalistic
Objectivist	Multiperspectival
Bias-free	Reflexive on own standpoint
Etic	Emic

Source: Author.

tradition versus a mere common posture toward inquiry, abound, what matters in the end is that interpretivists share an extremely practical approach to realities that is characterized by empathic identification, intentionality, reflexivity, and nominality—the subjects of the next section.

Common Characteristics of Interpretive Theories

Interpretive theories abound. There are ethnomethodologists and social phenomenologists; there are objective and philosophical hermeneuticians; there are social semioticians and students of pragmatics; there are classical, contemporary, and critical pragmatists; there are postmodernists and social constructionists; there are symbolic interactionists of the structural and processual variety, and so forth. But regardless of these differences, it is fair to say that all interpretivists agree that their perspectives (or theories!) hinge on empathic identification, intentionality, reflexivity, and nominality. These four characteristics epitomize the pragmatist tradition mentioned earlier, but also the phenomenological and hermeneutic traditions.

By *empathic identification* interpretivists mean that in order to understand the meanings of all social action and communication, one must take the role of the people one wishes to understand. Take, for example, a wink—a famous example of this argument. Imagine one wished to understand the meaning of a particular wink as expressed at a particular point in time and space. Could a wink symbolize flirting? Or that perhaps two people are in cahoots? Or could it simply be a meaningless nervous tic? To find meaning in a wink—or in any kind of action and communication—requires reaching into the subjective consciousness of the actor. In other words, to understand meaning requires investigating what one intends by it and the response it generates—a central pragmatist tenet. Empathic identification is thus a way of getting into a communicating actor's mind, body, and soul; it is a way of experiencing the world from that actor's perspective and a way of taking his or her role. By putting himself or herself into the shoes of those he or she wishes to understand, an interpretivist can uncover motives, thoughts, ideals, desires, goals, and circumstances.

Second, interpretive theories are phenomenological and pragmatic with respect to people's intentions for action. Phenomenologists and pragmatists argue that the social world is constituted through actions and experiences. In other words, there would not be any kind of social world were it not for people's shared experiences, shared meanings, interpersonal communication, and collective action. According to this view, people are not the victims of their circumstances; while their power may differ on the basis of the situation, individual capacities, social norms, and social roles, people do have some degree of agency in shaping their social existence. Their agency or capacity for action is a direct manifestation of their *intentionality*. Intentionality is human will: the will to direct action toward an object in a way that therefore becomes meaningful to the actor.

Third, interpretive theories emphasize the importance of reflexivity. They do so in the context of their own research, as we have seen earlier, but they also do so in positing a view of humanity that is based on the reflective power of human beings. Reflexivity—or *reflectivity,* as it is sometimes spelled—refers to the human ability to imagine oneself from perspectives other than one's own. Thus, for example, a person may imagine himself or herself from the perspective of a neighbor, but also from the perspective of another culture, a different social group, or a different historical perspective. Reflexivity is a key condition for formation of a sense of self and identity, as well as for the formation of society and culture. Viewing people as reflexive beings encourages interpretivists to focus on how they construct and reproduce their social realities and how those social realities are thus continuously subject to reevaluation and reinterpretation.

Finally, interpretivists share an approach to reality that is nominal. By this, it is simply meant that human beings make their own lives meaningful by way of assigning symbols, names, categories, and rules to social objects and by way of respecting the very "game" they have created. Thus, no matter how strange it may seem that things are a certain way, those things remain consistently meaningful across situations. For example, think of how strange an infield fly rule may seem to someone who does not understand the game of baseball. And yet, think of how real and "set in stone" that rule is to baseball players and fans. It is indeed so real in its consequences that it evokes emotions, actions, states of mind, and consequences that are virtually unchallengeable and yet so obviously dependent on a rather fragile agreement (after all, the rule could be changed by a ruling commissioner with a single stroke of a pen!).

Together, the four characteristics discussed above point to how interpretivists share a common pragmatist, phenomenological, and hermeneutic heritage and a common approach to social reality. Their approach views human interaction as meaningful and real in its consequences, views people's ideas and lifeways as worthy of respect, and—in their emphasis on human diversity—reveals how a common and intersubjectively shared understanding (however nuanced) may be achieved.

April Vannini

See also Ethnomethodology; Hermeneutics; Phenomenology; Philosophy of Communication; Postpositivism; Pragmatics; Theory

Further Readings

Creswell, J. (2007). Philosophical, paradigm, and interpretive frameworks. In J. W. Creswell (Ed.), *Qualitative inquiry and research design: Choosing among five approaches* (2nd ed., pp. 15–33). Thousand Oaks, CA: Sage.

Denzin, N. K. (1994). The art and politics of interpretation. In N. K. Denzin & Y. S. Lincoln (Eds.), *Handbook of qualitative research* (pp. 500–515). Thousand Oaks, CA: Sage.

Geertz, C. (1973). *Interpretation of cultures: Selected essays.* New York: Basic Books.

Kincheloe, J. L., & McLaren, P. (2003). Rethinking critical theory and qualitative research. In N. K. Denzin & Y. S. Lincoln (Eds.), *The landscape of qualitative research: Theories and issues* (3rd ed., pp. 433–488). Thousand Oaks, CA: Sage.

Littlejohn, S. W. (1989). Interpretive and critical theories. In S. Littlejohn, *Theories of human communication* (3rd ed., pp. 134–149). Belmont, CA: Wadsworth.

INTERRACIAL COMMUNICATION

Interracial communication is a genre of communication study that embraces the interactions between people representing different historical races. As such it encompasses the encounters between people in a practical sense—the ordinary engagement of human beings from various racial, cultural, linguistic, and ethnic backgrounds with each other in the quite human activity of social interaction. It also entails the researching of the phenomenon of racial engagement, seeking to determine the problems and prospects of such discursive engagement with people of different racial backgrounds.

One might say that interracial communication is a variety of communication inasmuch as mass communication, interpersonal communication, intercultural communication, cyber communication, and institutional communication are all parts of the same overarching field. What distinguishes each of these discrete subdisciplines from the other represents the defining coin of that particular area. For example, in the case of interracial communication, the defining coin is racial biography itself. This does not mean that race is the only factor that enters the picture in an interpersonal interaction situation; it simply means that a major—perhaps the major—factor involved in a communication experience that is defined as *interracial* is race itself.

While almost all scientists agree that there is no singular racial worldview and that race itself as a concept has been hierarchically constructed by ruling classes for control and power, it remains a salient, although waning, idea in contemporary society. The old notion of discrete biotic entities was never based on objective variations in language, culture, or social groupings. Rather the race idea eclipsed language and culture and included superficial assessments and judgments based on phenotypes and behaviors. Interracial communication has sought to provide a canvas for themes, issues, and ideas in spite of the lingering presence of antiquated ideas of race. In the United States of America, race has played a fundamental role in shaping policy, behavior, and attitudes despite the lack of science to support race as a valid concept.

In voting for the Democratic presidential candidates during the 2008 presidential primary contests, nearly one in every five individuals who voted in the Appalachian region of the United States claimed that their vote was based on the race of the candidate. Thus, race remains socially and politically salient in some communities although its biological basis has been in doubt scientifically since the latter part of the 20th century. The election of Barack Obama as President of the United States fueled a new discourse on race because he was biologically Black and White, according to the science of his origin, but defined socially in the United States as African American.

The practice of interracial communication emerged before the study of interracial communication in the same way that humans began to speak much earlier than anyone thought about examining the meaning of human speech. When we consider the fact that interracial communication, as a variety of the field of communication, emerged as a legitimate division of study only in the 1970s and 1980s, we are confronted with the youthfulness of this area of study.

Most of the work done in communication prior to the 1970s could be classified as either work in rhetorical communication or cybernetics, and neither of these fields imagined interracial work. One could look to the cross-cultural work done by the anthropologists and some of the early research on African and Asian cultures advanced by Edward Hall, Margaret Mead, and others.

In 1970, Andrea Rich and Arthur L. Smith (later Molefi Kete Asante) wrote an article for the *Speech Teacher*, the forerunner of the *Communication Teacher*, entitled "An Approach to Teaching Interracial Communication," which became the initial intellectual discussion of interracial communication in the field. This publication was the first modern introduction to the field of interracial communication. During the next 3 years, Rich and Smith prepared major works on interracial communication. The publication of two books in the 1970s, Arthur L. Smith's *Transracial Communication* in 1973 and Andrea Rich's *Interracial Communication* in 1974, laid the foundation for the study of how people communicate across racial groupings. In fact, Smith and Rich had been students of Charles Lomas and Paul Rosenthal, two speech professors at the University of California, Los Angeles, who had explored the multidimensional nature of the communication field.

Dennis Ogawa, also a member of that early team, explored Japanese American communication styles and behaviors in an effort to enrich the discourse about race in communication. Indeed,

although Ogawa had been a student of communication, he titled his 1971 book *From Jap to Japanese: The Evolution of Japanese-American Stereotypes*. A few years later he would write the seminal essay on the studies of Japanese Americans in film and become known as the father of Japanese American film studies. While not strictly on interracial communication, Ogawa's works must be seen as contributing to the new discourse on race in America. However, this school of thought—essentially dedicated to resolving issues related to race relations given the realities of the 1960s and the civil rights struggle—soon gave way to more robust theories around issues of culture and regionalism. Thus, the initial thrust for race analysis in communication did not bring the dynamism that was predicted in the earlier works.

In 1975 Diana Corley wrote "An Interracial Communication Course for Community Colleges," published in *Speech Teacher*, which expanded the ideas found in the earlier foundation works of Rich and Smith. However, neither the work by the earlier scholars nor Corley's work resonated with the editors of the top journal in the field of communication. For example, only a book review in the *Quarterly Journal of Speech* in 1976 indicated that there was any interest in this area of research. Robert Oliver's review in *QJS* in February 1976 suggested that the field might find some value in the synthesis made by Andrea Rich. This review was preceded by Jerry Burk's review in *Speech Teacher* the year before.

There was more than a 20-year hiatus between the time Dennis Ogawa published his piece on "Identity, Dissonance, and Bilingualism: Communication Problems of Asian American Assimilation" in the *Association of Communication Administration Bulletin* in 1976 and Richard Buttny's "Discursive Construction of Racial Boundaries and Self Segregation on Campus" in the *Journal of Language and Social Psychology* in 1999. One could reasonably say that culture trumped race as a factor for research and study during the 1980s and early 1990s. There were several articles written by Michael Hecht and Sidney Ribeau in the late 1980s dealing with interethnic communication. However, the field of communication itself did not admirably step back into the discourse on interracial communication until works by Debian Marty, Tina Harris, Marsha Houston, Leda Cooks, Mo Bahk, Fred

Jandt, and Aaron Cargile started to appear in 1999 and then into the 2000s.

Much of the work on racial codes in communication, styles of racist language, and racial concealment in communication has been left to scholars in social work, psychology, and anthropology. Wade Nobles, Na'im Akbar, Linda James Myers, and Charles White have examined the role of African American language as it relates to communication across racial lines in the field of psychology. While a few of the scholars of communication ventured into the area of human interaction between different races, the overwhelming influence of Asian cultural communication scholarship superseded the discourse on race in communication. It appeared that many researchers were eager to move away from the distress and agony of researching an area of human communication that was too close for comfort in order to seek more distant analyses of communication involving regions of possible commercial or capital interest, such as China, Japan, and Vietnam. Racial discourse was probably seen as fraught with too many domestic social problems and volatile political factors for adequate understanding.

Nevertheless there are a few scholars, such as Mark P. Orbe and Tina M. Harris, who have continued the discourse on race in America. In their book, *Interracial Communication: Theory Into Practice*, they have demonstrated that the field is as important as ever. First published in 2002, the authors' new edition was published in 2007 with a new publisher and new ideas. Their attention to issues of diversity management, media framing of race, and self-reflective experiences is extraordinary as a creative response to the contemporary society. In their writings, they have expanded the arena for interracial communication and demonstrated practical approaches to claiming territory.

One problem that remains in the field is how to deal with the question of dominance and inequality. Here the interracial communicationists can learn from some of the material on centricity found in the works of Ama Mazama, Yoshitaka Miike, and Ronald Jackson. Without an assertion of agency and an equal acceptance of another person's agency, one cannot reasonably speak of effective interracial communication; one speaks only of domination and terror in that case. What emerges in the work of these scholars and others is that the principal concern with effectiveness, that is, the appreciation and acceptance of communication, may miss the point of power relations. In other words, how individuals relate to each other on the basis of power, hierarchy, control, and societal position might have more salience than race itself. Here we are at the most complicated juncture in interracial communication because scholars must constantly delve into the question of effectiveness, knowing that the political, social, and symbolic power of the society plays a profound role in how we interpret what occurs between individuals.

Among the issues that remain to be examined in the field of interracial communication are issues dealing with the communicating of prejudice, the use of racist signs and symbols in conversation, domestic political language and racial terror, and the elements of authentic and centered communication in which all communicators have agency. There has been a lag in comprehensive analyses of interracial communication, and there remains a significant need for further research in the area of race and communication. One could conceivably undertake a study of communication between people in the age of race as a nonessentialist element in human society. Such a study would reveal further complexities of race in a heterogeneous, pluralist, and multiethnic society.

Molefi Kete Asante

See also Afrocentricity; Co-Cultural Theory; Contextual Theory of Interethnic Communication; Critical Race Theory; Cross-Cultural Adaptation Theory; Cultural Contracts Theory; Culture and Communication; Face Negotiation Theory; Intercultural Communication Competence; Intercultural Communication Theories; Intersectionality; Privilege; Racial Formation Theory; Transculturation; Whiteness Theory

Further Readings

Hecht, M. L. (Ed.). (1998). *Communicating prejudice.* Thousand Oaks, CA: Sage.

Orbe, M., & Harris, T. (2007). *Interracial communication: Theory into practice.* Thousand Oaks, CA: Sage.

Rich, A. (1974). *Interracial communication.* New York: Harper & Row.

Smith, A. L. (1973). *Transracial communication.* Englewood Cliffs, NJ: Prentice Hall.

INTERSECTIONALITY

Intersectionality is the notion that one social category cannot be understood in isolation from another social category. It grew out of criticism that antiracist and feminist movements in the 1960s and 1970s homogenized categories of race and gender. While antiracist and feminist discourses were criticized for either ignoring or simply adding social categories together (race + gender + class + sexuality), intersectional scholars called for an approach that recognized that differences coincide simultaneously, multiplying social categories rather than adding them (race × gender × class × sexuality).

North American law professor Kimberlé Crenshaw was first to coin the term *intersectionality*. Joined by Black feminists, she pointed to the ways in which race and class intersect with gender as a type of crossroads or intersection where different types of dominations meet. This challenge was also made explicit in the titles of several books written throughout the 1980s and 1990s, such as *All the Women Are White, All the Blacks Are Men, But Some of Us Are Brave*, edited by Gloria T. Hull, Patricia B. Scott, and Barbara Smith, as well as *Ain't I a Woman? Black Women and Feminism*, written by Black feminist author bell hooks.

Intersectional theorists tend to view category formation as a social and cultural construction, and they challenge essentialist notions of identity. Social categories are not seen as merely discursive entities, however, but rather as entities that are constituted in communication and have real social consequences. Intersectional theorists are skeptical of work that seeks to deconstruct difference; instead, they choose to demonstrate how power is clustered and frequently interwoven around particular social categories such as gender, race, sexuality, and class.

Crenshaw's work on intersectionality has laid the groundwork for intersectional analyses. She has explored the notion that racism and sexism intersect in "structural," "political," and "representational" intersections. In her analysis of violence against women of color, for instance, she illustrates how women of color frequently have limited access to housing, education, employment, and wealth. Shelter policies tend to locate women's experiences solely in light of an ideology of male domination and ignore the racial, socioeconomic, or legal realities of women of color as well as immigrant women. Consequently, women of color and immigrant women face a structural barrier when they turn to shelters for help in cases of violence, such as a lack of assistance related to employment, translations, or legal matters. Politically, women of color and immigrant women are simultaneously located within two conflicting political agendas. While feminist politics fails to successfully interrogate race, antiracist discourses perpetuate sexist thinking. As a result, the experiences of women of color and immigrant women are politically unaccounted for.

Crenshaw has widely applied her intersectional approach to other cases as well. Her work on representational intersectionality explores how sexist as well as racist stereotypes underlie the representation of Black women in musical lyrics. In her analysis of the controversy surrounding 2 Live Crew's lyrics, for instance, Crenshaw shows how the accusations made against 2 Live Crew, which appeared under the disguises of antisexism, vividly supported a racist ideology in the representation of an uncontrollable Black male sexuality. Yet, if antisexist rhetoric serves to perpetuate a racist ideology, so does antiracist rhetoric perpetuate a sexist ideology. The argument that any critique of 2 Live Crew is racist because the lyrics represent a unique Black mode of communication disguises misogyny as just a matter of culture. Other intersectional scholars, such as Patricia Hill Collins, have demonstrated an intersectional approach in their analyses as well. Collins argues, for instance that the politically popular concept of "family values" supports a particular (White, middle-class, heterosexual) way of thinking about race, gender, and nation.

Intersectionality operates at the methodological level of analysis as well. Focus rests with a limited number of intersections, in select contexts, such as Malaysian migrant women domestic workers in Singapore households or the communication that takes place between European American midwives and immigrant women from Mexico in California. Intersectional scholars call for a reflexive approach to research methodology. This entails critically interrogating, for instance, which research participants to include, as well as the researcher's own position as a particularly gendered, raced, classed individual.

Scholars working within the field of postcolonial theory, critical Whiteness studies, queer theory, and critical studies of masculinity also critically interrogate intersections related to nationality, race, sexuality, and masculinity. In postcolonial theory and critical Whiteness studies, the intersectional focus rests with postcolonial power relationships and Whiteness as an unmarked category. The goal here is to make the unmarked category marked. In contrast, queer scholars critically interrogate intersections between sexuality and gender to show how heterosexuality serves as a regulatory frame through which gender is understood. Australian masculinity researcher Robert W. (now Raewyn) Connell has added an intersectional approach to the study of masculinity. According to Connell, "hegemonic masculinity" works to secure the dominant position of (some) men over women and (some) other men. Blending queer and masculinity research, North American scholar Judith Halberstam similarly interrogates intersections between masculinity and gender in her work on *female* masculinity. Jointly, these scholars theorize particular lines of difference.

While intersectional analyses have come to occupy an important theoretical and methodological space, one reoccurring question is which intersection(s) to analyze? Some scholars pinpoint many lines of difference, yet others are skeptical as to the political consequences of these. Feminist scholars might question whether gender as a category, for instance, is in danger of getting overlooked in favor of other categories, such as sexuality or race. An inability to speak on behalf of women as a group may, they note, serve the perpetuation of patriarchal ideology. Others point to the notion of strategic alliances as an alternative framework. Individuals make temporary (strategic) alliances for particular purposes, and thus, an intersectional approach that recognizes strategic alliances opens up a space for collective agency, which, because it is temporary, avoids viewing social categories as either closed or static.

Intersectional perspectives have gained in popularity throughout the communication discipline because they offer a more nuanced understanding of the interplay of social categories and communication. Such perspectives have been applied to a range of communication studies, from understanding multicultural issues to political rhetoric to considerations of gender mainstreaming.

Charlotte Kroløkke

See also Critical Race Theory; Feminist Communication Theories; Identity Theories; Postcolonial Theory; Queer Theory; Whiteness Theory

Further Readings

Collins, P. H. (1998). It's all in the family: Intersections of gender, race, and nation. *Hypatia, 13,* 62–82.

Crenshaw, K. (1989). Demarginalizing the intersection of race and sex: A Black feminist critique of antidiscrimination doctrine, feminist theory and antiracist politics. *University of Chicago Legal Forum,* 138–167.

Crenshaw, K. (1991). Mapping the margins: Intersectionality, identity politics, and violence against women of color. *Stanford Law Review, 43,* 1241–1299.

Halberstam, J. (2002). The good, the bad, and the ugly: Men, women, and masculinity. In J. K. Gardiner (Ed.), *Masculinity studies and feminist theory: New directions* (pp. 344–368). New York: Columbia University Press.

hooks, b. (1981). *Ain't I a woman.* Boston: South End Press.

Hull, G. T., Scott, P. B., & Smith, B. (Eds.). (1982). *All the women are White, all the Blacks are men, but some of us are brave.* New York: Feminist Press.

Yuval-Davis, N. (2006). Intersectionality and feminist politics. *European Journal of Women's Studies, 13,* 193–209.

INTRAPERSONAL COMMUNICATION THEORIES

The fact that humans talk to themselves, especially in difficult circumstances, has been observed by scholars since the Middle Ages. Writings on self-communication have been documented in virtually every epoch of human history since that time. However, in the 20th century, psychologists such as Jean Piaget and L. S. Vygotsky have paid close attention to this mode of communication as they formulated their respective theories of human development. Vygotsky in particular assigned intrapersonal communication (IC) special status within his developmental theory, and this perspective forms the basis of the following discussion.

According to Piaget, whose theory of human development is grounded in biological mechanisms, at around the age of 3, children begin to display what he called *egocentric speech*—speech directed at no one other than themselves—as they engage in various kinds of play activities. Piaget referred to IC as egocentric because he believed that children at this age are heavily focused on themselves as individuals and have not yet developed into social beings. As they become less egocentric and more social, this form of speech dies away, leaving social speech as the primary form of human communicative activity.

Vygotsky, on the other hand, adopted a social orientation to human thought, arguing that mental activity is derived from social, or interpersonal, interaction between children and other members of their sociocultural community. He reasoned that egocentric speech does not emerge from egocentric thinking in children but represents instead a stage in the transition from social to inner speech (i.e., speech no longer social in function that is also shed of its linguistic form, leaving a residue of pure meaning), which serves to complete the thinking process. Thus, egocentric speech is simultaneously quasi-social and quasi-psychological speech; while it may appear to be social in form, it gradually takes on psychological functions. Early in life, children frequently engage in activities more or less spontaneously, without the benefit of planning. Hence, they create drawings and, after the fact, decide what they depict. As children mature, however, they begin to use speech to plan what it is they will draw before realizing the plan in a concrete drawing. When this occurs, speech becomes fully psychological. The planning process may be carried out, in part at least, in vocalized language, or it may remain hidden from observation as inner speech.

Vygotsky proposed and tested a number of predictions to determine the adequacy of his theoretical claim regarding the development and fate of egocentric speech. He predicted that if egocentric speech is in fact social speech on the way to becoming psychological speech, it should reflect traits of social speech. Thus, in contradistinction to Piaget, he argued that if, in the early stages of development,

children perceive a circumstance as nonsocial, there should be a decline in the quantity of egocentric speech they produce. In a series of experiments in which children were placed in circumstances in which they were isolated, surrounded by loud noises, or placed in the presence of other children who did not speak their language, the incidence of egocentric speech declined when compared with other clearly social situations. He also predicted that over time egocentric speech would become less audible and understandable to others and that it would lose its linguistic structure—typical of fully social speech—and would therefore consist of linguistic fragments such as short phrases, single words, or even parts of words. Eventually, egocentric speech would become fully internalized as its linguistic form continued to fall away, resulting in inner speech—the psychological speech humans use to complete the thinking process.

Functions of Intrapersonal Communication

IC carries two fundamental psychological functions: the *internalization* of culturally organized ways of thinking and the *regulation* of one's own mental activity. Clearly, these functions are related. In ontogenetic, or individual, development, IC is the conduit through which social communicative activity is integrated into psychological processing. In social interaction, children regulate and are regulated by others primarily through the use of language. The language used during interpersonal interactions is eventually taken over by the individual and (re)deployed for intrapersonal (i.e., mental) activity. Thus, a parent interacting with a child as they jointly solve a picture puzzle might say to the child as he or she reaches for an incorrect piece, "Wait, think." The intent of the utterance is to inform the child that his or her original plan of action was incorrect and to advise him or her to reconsider the selection. The utterance is far from fully syntactic, containing only two words, but because the interlocutors share the same discursive information on what is happening, it is effective. Importantly, while the utterance is social, it also has a psychological function aimed not only at inhibiting the child's physical movement of inserting the incorrect piece but also at exhorting the child to reprocess his or her mentally organized plan of action. Should the initial utterance fail to elicit the appropriate behavior from the child, the parent might resort to a more explicit utterance, such as "No, the red one." This utterance, as with the first, makes little sense outside the discursive space of the interactants. On the face of it, *the red one* can refer to a wide array of entities, but in the puzzle situation, it should be quite easily and appropriately interpreted by the child.

One way of looking at the transformation from social, interpersonal communication to psychological IC is as a shift in dialogic roles. Social interaction occurs between an "I" and a "you," as for example between the parent and the child in the puzzle activity described above. IC, on the other hand, takes place between an "I" and a "me," where the "me" replaces the "you" of social dialogue but fulfills the same function—the function of accepting, modifying, rejecting, and so forth—decisions made by the "I." Expanding on the above example, the child, when eventually attempting to complete the puzzle alone, might well appropriate the language used by the parent during their social interaction and say to himself or herself, "Wait, no, the red one." Through the utterance the child instructs himself or herself (i.e., "I") to abandon the current plan and deploy a different one, just as the parent had instructed the child to follow a similar procedure.

Interpersonal communication between individuals who share a great deal of background knowledge on a particular topic or who interact in a highly contextualized space is not likely to be linguistically explicit. The parent and the child in the puzzle example understand what they are doing. Therefore when the parent says "Wait, think" or "no, the red one," the child recognizes what the parent is talking about despite the absence of a fully syntactic utterance. Similarly, if two strangers are standing together and looking at the same painting in an art museum and one says, "It's beautiful," it is quite likely that the other will have little difficulty understanding that the "it" refers to the painting. Interlocutors are able to integrate into their communicative behavior the circumstances in which they find themselves and therefore avoid the production of fully explicit utterances. Indeed, in the museum example, the utterance could easily have been reduced to a single word *beautiful* with little loss of comprehension. On the

other hand, had the same individuals encountered each other in a café where the context does not as readily lend itself to being integrated into a discussion of art, it would be necessary to rely on more explicit language in order to express the same sentiment. Thus, the speaker might produce an utterance such as "Renoir's 'The Country Dance' is beautiful."

IC, because it is derived from interpersonal communication, is subject to the same constraints that operate in social interaction. If interlocutors take account of shared information when communicating with each other, it would be expected that in IC this same process would be at work only more so, given that the "I" and "me" of IC clearly share a lot more than the "I" and "you" of social communication. Thus, we would expect IC to be even more reduced than social speech. Indeed, a child—or an adult, for that matter—assembling a picture puzzle might say only "red" to tell himself or herself that the next piece to be inserted is the red one. It would be quite odd for the individual to produce a maximally explicit utterance, such as "Next, I need to pick up the red piece and insert it into the puzzle at this location." All the information regarding the fact that a piece must be picked up and placed in a particular location is assumed background knowledge. The fact that it is the red piece that is the relevant one, however, must be kept in focus by the speaker, and it is for this reason that it is the optimal candidate for verbalization. As the difficulty of an activity increases (and this is usually relative to the individual), the likelihood that IC will be externalized, in part, at least, increases. In this way it betrays its origins in social speech. Interestingly, in social settings, because adults, unlike young children, are able to distinguish themselves from others, they do not normally engage in "out loud" IC, and if they do, it is perceived as marked behavior, often drawing the attention of those in the vicinity.

Adults can and do make use of written forms of IC as, for instance, when we take notes in school or when we produce jottings in the margins of texts as we read, or even when we produce shopping lists. All these are instances of IC and not only may serve memory, as in the case of shopping lists, but may also function to work out problems, as when reading a difficult academic text or when listening to a teacher explaining how to solve a math problem. Finally, adults often use IC in order to internalize new knowledge, as for example when we undertake to learn a new language. The research shows that adults in such circumstances rely on IC to work out ways of saying things in the new language, or to help them remember vocabulary. In essence, IC is an exceptionally powerful and pervasive tool for thinking.

IC can also occur in modalities other than language. For example, musicians, painters, and choreographers often work out compositions, paintings, and dance routines, respectively, in very sketchy patternings intended for no one other than their creator. People use gestures as well as a means of complementing the verbal component of their IC. Gestures are especially powerful tools for thinking because they depict in a holistic way meanings that speakers frequently have difficulties externalizing through purely verbal expression.

Multiple Intrapersonal Communication Systems

An interesting issue regarding IC is whether people who speak more than one language use more than one form of IC—one that corresponds to each of their languages—or whether they have only one version of IC that corresponds to their dominant interpersonal language. In German, for example, the expression *so* is frequently used to indicate that a particular activity has been completed and that another is about to begin. It is roughly the equivalent of English *OK* or *all right* or *done*. German speakers use *so* not only in social communication but also in IC. At issue is whether people who learn German as a second language, especially in adult life, use this particle appropriately when engaged in IC, or do they continue to rely on their native language patterns to regulate their mental and even physical activity? Although only a small amount of research has been conducted on this matter, it has shown that adults have a difficult time deploying IC in their second language and either are unable to resolve the problem they are dealing with or have to switch to IC in their native language.

James P. Lantolf

See also Cognitive Theories; Communication and Language Acquisition and Development; Language and Communication; Social Interaction Theories; Symbolic Interactionism; Visual Communication Theories

Further Readings

Centeno-Cortés, B., & Jiménez-Jiménez, A. F. (2004). Problem-solving tasks in a foreign language: The importance of the L1 in private verbal thinking. *International Journal of Applied Linguistics, 14*, 7–35.

Diaz, R. M., & Berk, L. E. (Eds.). (1992). *Private speech: From social interaction to self-regulation.* Hillsdale, NJ: Lawrence Erlbaum.

Frawley, W. (1997). *Vygotsky and cognitive science: Language and the unification of the social and computational mind.* Cambridge, MA: Harvard University Press.

John-Steiner, V. (1997). *Notebooks of the mind: Explorations of thinking* (rev. ed.). Oxford, UK: Oxford University Press.

McNeill, D. (2005). *Gesture and thought.* Chicago: University of Chicago Press.

Ohta, A. S. (2001). *Second language acquisition processes in the classroom: Learning Japanese.* Mahwah, NJ: Lawrence Erlbaum.

Vocate, D. R. (Ed.). (1994). *Intrapersonal communication: Different voices, different minds.* Hillsdale, NJ: Lawrence Erlbaum.

Vygotsky, L. S. (1986). *Thinking and speech.* Cambridge: MIT Press.

INVITATIONAL RHETORIC

Invitational rhetoric, developed by Sonja K. Foss and Cindy L. Griffin in 1995, is an alternative to the traditional conception of rhetoric as persuasion. Invitational rhetoric is defined as an invitation to understanding as a means to create a relationship rooted in equality, immanent value, and self-determination. It constitutes an invitation to the audience to enter the rhetor's world and to see it as the rhetor does. Thus, it is a form of communication designed to generate understanding among individuals with different perspectives.

Invitational rhetoric challenges the traditional definition of rhetoric as persuasion, the conscious intent to change others. A key assumption on which invitational rhetoric is based is that the effort to change others constitutes an attempt to gain control or power over them and is a devaluation of their lifeworlds; traditional rhetoric thus is seen as reflecting the values of competition and domination. In contrast, invitational rhetoric is rooted in the feminist principles of equality, immanent value, and self-determination. *Equality* is a commitment to replace the dominance and elitism that characterize most human relationships with intimacy, mutuality, and camaraderie. Invitational rhetors eschew a hierarchical ranking of individuals according to external criteria and instead recognize the *immanent value* of all living beings. They see every being as a unique and necessary part of the pattern of the universe and thus as valuable. Concomitant with a recognition of immanent value is a rejection of efforts to change the unique perspective that each individual holds. *Self-determination,* then, allows individuals to make their own decisions about how they wish to live their lives and accords respect to others' capacity and right to constitute their worlds as they choose.

Invitational rhetoric assumes two primary rhetorical forms: (1) offering perspectives and (2) creating external conditions that allow and encourage others to present their perspectives. In offering perspectives, rhetors tell what they currently know or understand. They present their vision of the world and show how it looks and works for them. This vision represents an initial, tentative commitment to that perspective—always one subject to revision as a result of the rhetor's interaction with the audience.

The second rhetorical act involved in invitational rhetoric is the creation of external conditions. If invitational rhetoric is to result in a mutual understanding of perspectives, it must involve not only the offering of the rhetor's perspective but the creation of an atmosphere in which audience members are willing to share their perspectives with the rhetor. To facilitate such an environment, an invitational rhetor seeks to create particular external conditions in the interaction between rhetors and audience members. These external conditions are states or prerequisites that are required if the possibility of mutual understanding is to exist.

The three external conditions the invitational rhetor seeks to create in an interaction are safety, value, and freedom. *Safety* involves the creation of a feeling of security and freedom from danger for the audience. Rhetoric contributes to a feeling of safety when it conveys to audience members that the ideas and feelings they share with the rhetor will be received with respect and care. The condition of *value* is acknowledgment by the rhetor that audience members have intrinsic or immanent worth. It is created when rhetors approach audience members as unique individuals and avoid distancing, paternalistic, and depersonalizing attitudes. Value is also fostered when the rhetor listens carefully to the perspectives of others and tries to think from those perspectives.

The third external condition, *freedom,* or the power to choose or decide, is enacted in various ways in invitational rhetoric. Freedom is demonstrated when rhetors do not place restrictions on an interaction—when participants can bring any and all matters to the interaction for consideration. Invitational rhetors also do not privilege their ideas over those of the audience and provide opportunities for others to develop and choose options from alternatives that they themselves have created. Freedom is created as well when the audience's lack of acceptance of or adherence to the perspective articulated by the rhetor truly makes no difference to the rhetor. Either outcome—acceptance or rejection of the perspective offered by the rhetor—is seen as perfectly acceptable by the invitational rhetor, who is not disappointed or angry if audience members choose not to adopt that perspective.

Change may be an outcome of invitational rhetoric, but change is not its objective. When change occurs through the process of invitational rhetoric, it may occur in the audience or the rhetor or both. All communicators in the interaction may change as a result of new insights they gain in the exchange of ideas and perspectives.

Invitational rhetoric is not an ideal for which rhetors should strive or a type of rhetoric that should or can be used in all situations. Invitational rhetoric is one of many useful and legitimate rhetorics, including persuasion, that are available to rhetors. It is a model of rhetoric that enables rhetors to recognize situations in which they seek not to persuade others but simply to create an environment that facilitates understanding, accords value and respect to others' perspectives, and contributes to the development of relationships of equality.

Sonja K. Foss

See also Empathy; Feminist Rhetorical Criticism; I and Thou; Persuasion and Social Influence Theories; Rhetorical Theory

Further Readings

Foss, S. K., & Foss, K. A. (2003). *Inviting transformation: Presentational speaking for a changing world* (2nd ed.). Long Grove, IL: Waveland.

Foss, S. K., & Griffin, C. L. (1995). Beyond persuasion: A proposal for an invitational rhetoric. *Communication Monographs, 62,* 2–18.

Gearhart, S. M. (1979). The womanization of rhetoric. *Women's Studies International Quarterly, 2,* 195–201.

ISSUES LIFE-CYCLE THEORY

See Corporate Campaign Theories